Managing Occupational Health and Safety
A Multidisciplinary Approach

Third Edition

MICHAEL QUINLAN, PHILIP BOHLE and FELICITY LAMM

palgrave
macmillan

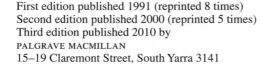

First edition published 1991 (reprinted 8 times)
Second edition published 2000 (reprinted 5 times)
Third edition published 2010 by
PALGRAVE MACMILLAN
15–19 Claremont Street, South Yarra 3141

Visit our website at www.macmillan.com.au

Associated companies and representatives
throughout the world.

National Library of Australia
cataloguing in publication data

Author: Quinlan, Michael, 1951–
Title: Managing occupational health and safety / Michael Quinlan,
           Philip Bohle, Felicity Lamm
Edition: 3rd ed.
ISBN: 978 1 4202 5607 9
Notes: Includes index. Bibliography.
Subjects: Industrial safety—Australia.
           Industrial hygiene—Australia.
           Occupational health—Australia.
Other authors/contributors: Bohle, Philip.
                       Lamm, Felicity.

Publisher: Elizabeth Vella
Project editor: Kirstie Innes-Will
Editor: David Fryer
Cover designer: Dimitrios Frangoulis
Text designer: Patrick Cannon
Permissions clearance: Sarah Johnson
Typeset in 10.5pt Bembo by Cannon Typesetting
Cover image: Getty Images / Terje Kveen
Indexer: Karen Gillan

Printed in Malaysia

Internet addresses
At the time of printing, the internet addresses appearing in this book were correct.
Owing to the dynamic nature of the internet, however, we cannot guarantee that all
these addresses will remain correct.

Contents

List of tables and figures

List of abbreviations

ACC	Accident Compensation Corporation (New Zealand)
ACCI	Australian Chamber of Commerce and Industry
ACGIH	American Conference of Government Industrial Hygienists
ACT	Australian Capital Territory
ACTU	Australian Council of Trade Unions
AIG	Australian Industry Group
AIHA	American Industrial Hygiene Association
AIRC	Australian Industrial Relations Commission
AS	Australian Standard
BBS	behaviour-based safety
CBA	cost–benefit analysis
CFMEU	Construction, Forestry, Mining and Energy Union
CHD	coronary heart disease
CSDH	Commission for the Social Determinants of Health (WHO)
DCS	demand-control-support model (Karasek)
EAP	employee assistance program
EFILWC	European Foundation for the Improvement of Living and Working Conditions
ERI	effort-reward imbalance model (Siegrist)
ESA	Ergonomics Society of Australia
ESR	Employee Safety Represrentative
EU	European Union
FIFO	fly-in, fly-out
FTE	full-time employee
GHS	globally harmonised system of classifying and labelling chemicals
HFE	human factors and ergonomics
HRM	human resource management
HSR	Health and Safety Representative
IARC	International Agency for Research on Cancer
ILO	International Labour Organization
JIT	just in time
JSA	job safety analysis
KPI	key performance indicators
LTIFR	lost time injury frequency rate
MCS	multiple chemical sensitivity
MSD	musculoskeletal disorder
MSDS	material safety data sheet

NICNAS	National Industrial Chemicals Notification and Assessment Scheme
NIOSH	National Institute of Occupational Safety and Health
NORA	National Occupational Research Agenda
NSW	New South Wales
NSWIRC	New South Wales Industrial Relations Commission
NT	Northern Territory
NZ	New Zealand
OHS	occupational health and safety
OHSM	occupational health and safety management
OHSMS	occupational health and safety management system
OOI	occupational overuse injury
OOS	occupational overuse syndrome
PDR	economic pressure, disorganisation and regulatory failure model
PEL	permissible exposure limit
PPE	personal protective equipment
PTSD	post-traumatic stress disorder
ppm	parts per million
Qld	Queensland
RSI	repetitive strain injury
RTW	return-to-work
SA	South Australia
SCR	safety case regime
SIA	Safety Institute of Australia
SMR	standard mobility rate
SWP	safe working procedure
Tas.	Tasmania
TLV	threshold limit value
UK	United Kingdom
US	United States
Vic.	Victoria
VPP	Voluntary Performance Program
WA	Western Australia
WHO	World Health Organization
WHP	workplace health promotion
WHSO	Workplace Health and Safety Officer
WPI	whole person impairment

Preface

THE third edition of this book represents a substantial revision of the second edition—which itself entailed a major rewriting of the first edition. All chapters have undergone major revisions, two chapters have been dropped and two others have been replaced (the chapter on RSI with a broader chapter on musculoskeletal injury and the shiftwork chapter with one on working hours more generally). Changes to several chapters are particularly notable. The chapter on OHS regulation takes account of recent Australian developments in national harmonisation and contemporary international policy debates, for example on the regulation of hazardous substances and supply chains. It also presents the findings of recent detailed research on the activities of OHS inspectorates. The chapter on workers' compensation and rehabilitation includes more material on rehabilitation, return to work and injury impacts drawn from the health sciences. The chapter on working hours now extends beyond shiftwork to examine long and irregular hours, the growing evidence on disease effects and risks to older workers. The chapter on management has been expanded and includes a discussion of high-hazard workplaces, complementing a discussion of this issue in the regulation chapter.

The book incorporates the results of recent research across many fields (from health and medicine to psychology and regulation) including some of our own hitherto unpublished research on health, regulation and management. We have sought to address limitations in the second edition, making improvements kindly suggested by readers. For example, chapter 2 and later chapters include a better balance of disciplinary contributions to OHS, notably those of the health sciences (such as occupational therapy, physiotherapy and rehabilitation) and occupational health nursing. At the same time, the specialist technical chapter and the chapter on New Zealand have been removed with much of the New Zealand information being relocated to other chapters, to better reflect the closer economic ties between Australia and New Zealand. In any case, the OHS problems and remedies being addressed in this book are essentially global and the book draws heavily on international research and commentary.

The book maintains a fundamental philosophy that OHS can only be successfully understood from a multidisciplinary perspective and that only by understanding why OHS problems arise can we hope to develop and implement effective remedies. The book tries to explain the insights and approach to OHS of particular fields and disciplines as well as their respective strengths and limitations. We have tried to take a nuanced approach, identifying differences of opinion and approach as well as trends within particular fields and disciplines. Undoubtedly, some will disagree with the balance and nature of our coverage, including the attention devoted to particular disciplines. In our efforts to improve the book comments are always welcome and valued. Notwithstanding any limitations, the explicit attempt to reconcile different disciplinary contributions remains unusual, and possibly unique. Further, we believe the evidence increasingly supports our case for a multidisciplinary and more holistic understanding of OHS. Indeed, since the first edition there has been a clear trend towards a more multidisciplinary approach to research, policy and practice.

Fundamentally, work is a social process and creating work that is meaningful, productive and healthy requires the active engagement of government (and its agencies), healthcare and other professionals, researchers and educators, managers, employers and industry associations, unions and workers. As in the past, the book aims both to assist students to learn about OHS and to serve as a reference source for OHS professionals and practitioners.

This edition also marks the addition of a new author, Felicity Lamm, for whose input we are truly grateful. Felicity brings to the book her extensive knowledge of New Zealand and OHS more generally.

Finally, we would like to thank the many OHS professionals, academics, managers, workers and their families, government agency officers (including inspectors) and union officials who have helped expand our knowledge of OHS. Individual thanks will do grave injustices to those we don't name but nonetheless we would like to thank Michael Belzer, Joan Benach, Yossi Berger, Liz Bluff, Cath Duane, Andrew Ferguson, Simon Folkard, Kaj Frick, Wendy Lark, Nick Glozier, Neil Gunningham, Steve Hyam, Phil James, Richard Johnstone, Kevin Jones, Mike Kaine, Jim Leigh, Tony LaMontagne, Wayne Lewchuk, Katherine Lippel, Nina Lynne, Martin Mackey, Scott Marriset, Lynda Mathews, Maria McNamara, Peter Moylan, Carles Muntaner, Kate Murphy, George Nossar, Igor Nossar, Rory O'Neil, Anne Pisarski, Claudia Pitts, Olivia Rawlings-Way, Vilma Santana, Toni Schofield, Peter Schweder, Andrea Shaw, Tony Sheldon, Rosie Sokas, Phil Taylor, Don Tepas, Eric Tucker, Elsa Underhill, Laurent Vogel, David Walters, Hal Willaby, Ann Williamson and Charles Woolfson.

We would like to extend out gratitude to Nadine McDonnell whose work and expertise, particularly on workers' compensation matters, was invaluable. Thanks to Rob Guthrie for providing expert comments on the workers' compensation chapter at short notice. We would also like to thank Karen Lo for her contribution. Finally, a special thanks to Elizabeth Vella, Kirstie Innes-Will and the publication team at Palgrave Macmillan.

A special thanks to our families who are forever patient while we pursue our interests.

The first two editions covered a span of almost 20 years. We hope the third edition will make some contribution to OHS education and practice in the second decade of the twenty-first century.

Michael Quinlan[1,2], Philip Bohle[2] and Felicity Lamm[3]

1   School of Organisation and Management, The University of New South Wales
2   Work and Health Research Team, Faculty of Health Sciences, The University of Sydney
3   Department of Management and Employment Relations, Auckland University of Technology

Acknowledgments

The publishers and authors are grateful to the following for permission to reproduce copyright material:

Data copyright © *Work-Related Injuries*, ABS Catalogue No. 6324, Canberra, 2005–06, page 18. Australian Bureau of Statistics, **49**; Table from 'Comparison of workers' compensation arrangements in Australia and New Zealand', 2007. Australian Government, copyright © Commonwealth of Australia, reproduced by permission, **406**; Table from 'Comparison of workers' compensation arrangements in Australia and New Zealand', 2009. Australian Government, copyright © Commonwealth of Australia, reproduced by permission, **410, 414, 418, 424, 434** (both), **440**; Table from 'Comparative performance monitoring report', *Comparison of occupational health and safety and workers compensation schemes in Australia and New Zealand*, 9th Edition. Workplace Relations Ministers Council 2008 copyright © Commonwealth of Australia, reproduced by permission, **51**; Graph from 'Comparative performance monitoring report', *Comparison of occupational health and safety and workers compensation schemes in Australia and New Zealand*, 10th Edition. Workplace Relations Ministers Council 2008 copyright © Commonwealth of Australia, reproduced by permission, **453**; Table from 'Towards an evaluation of accident investigation methods in terms of their alignment with accident causation models', by P Katsakiori and G Sakellaropoulos (2009), *Safety Science* 47(7): 1007–15, with permission from Elsevier, **168–9**; Map from 'When workplace safety depends on behaviour change: Topics for behavioural safety research' by O Wirth, and S O Sigurdsson, (2008), *Journal of Safety Research*, 39(6), with permission from Elsevier, **545**; Table copyright © R Johnstone and M Quinlan (2008) from 'The shift to process standards in OHS in Australia', **364, 366, 367, 368, 369, 370** (both); Extract from 'History of occupational disease recognition and control' by Dr Jim Leigh, 2007, *Journal of Occupational Health and Safety – Australia and New Zealand* 23(6), **273**; Table copyright © Claire Mayhew and Michael Quinlan, **59**; Table copyright © Department of Labour, New Zealand Government, **142**; Data from 'Household labour force survey and income survey', copyright © Statistics New Zealand, **36, 39** (both), **42**; Table copyright © 'Theories of work-related musculoskeletal disorders: Implications for ergonomic interventions', by B T Karsh, (2006). *Theoretical Issues in Ergonomic Science,* 7(1), 71–88, reprinted by permission of

Taylor & Francis Group, <www.informaworld.com>, **195**; Diagram copyright © James T Reason from 'Achieving a safe culture: theory and practice'. *Work and Stress*, 12 by James T Reason, reprinted by permission of the publisher Taylor & Francis Group, <www.informaworld.com>, **156**; Extract copyright © Cullen 1990: Ch 21:84 cited in Woolfson et al 1997, *Deregulation: The Politics of Health and Safety*, Computer Publishing Unit of the University of Glasgow, **580**.

Work and health: an overview

Introduction

THE introduction to the first two editions of this book began with a brief description of a number of catastrophic incidents of workplace death, some in the past (such as the Triangle Shirtwaist factory fire in New York in 1911) and some more recent (such as a strikingly similar fire at the Kader International factory in Bangkok in 1993). Both incidents claimed the lives of well over 100 young women. We used these incidents to highlight the fact that serious failings with regard to workplace health and safety remain a global issue, notwithstanding the progress that has been made over the past century. Even in developed countries death or serious injury at work is not exceptional, especially in industries like construction, road transport and mining.

At the same time, parallels between developed countries a century ago and developing countries today demonstrate that the development of regulatory regimes that are enforced, community and worker mobilisations, better management practices and improvements in healthcare/social security infrastructure do matter. Poor OHS didn't disappear simply as countries became wealthy, as technology changed production systems, as scientific and medical evidence was collected, or as key decision-makers became more 'enlightened'. If this had been the case there would be no significant differences in the level of work-related illness among wealthy countries using similar technologies. As noted in the second edition, developed countries can also export work-related hazards to poor countries by, for example, using them as a venue for battery recycling and ship-breaking, by offshoring manufacturing activities and through the use of elaborate supply chains or networks of subcontracting (the worst instances of which result in children making goods in sweatshop conditions—see EMCONET, 2007). Further, goods imported into or exported from developed societies are often carried on ill-maintained 'flag of convenience' ships registered in countries where regulatory standards are effectively non-existent. The ships are crewed by seamen from Third World countries such as the Philippines, whose employment is characterised by low rates of pay and poor and hazardous working conditions (including dictatorial management).

This means any presumption that OHS will gradually improve in both developed and developing countries is naive. Further, just as the nature of work undergoes change within both developed and developing countries, so do the health hazards associated with work. There are emerging or new challenges to OHS that will require new or revised responses. As this book will try to show, a broadly-based social commitment to OHS with the involvement of government, industry/managers, unions, professions, workers and community groups is essential if longstanding sources of illness as well as new challenges are to be tackled.

Returning to our original observation, it would be a simple matter to provide new examples to parallel those (such as the Kader fire) of earlier editions. Since 2000 there have been major mine disasters in Russia, the Ukraine, China, Turkey and the US. Similarly, even a brief scan of news reports in 2008 reveals a string of serious incidents on construction sites, including the collapse of a crane in New York and two workers plummeting to their death from a 26-storey apartment tower on the Gold Coast in south-east Queensland, Australia. Apart from construction other industries where the risks of serious injury or disease remain high include farming, fishing, forestry work, mining and road transport. Long-haul truck driving remains one of the most dangerous occupations in both the US and Australia (Quinlan, Johnstone and Mayhew, 2006) but the death of these workers is so 'routine' that it barely rates a mention in the media.

As some of these examples illustrate, it would be quite wrong to believe that flagrant disregard for OHS no longer occurs within developed countries like Australia, the US or Canada. In some industries and activities OHS standards remain abysmally low in practice, and breaches of the most basic legislative requirements are common. In the Australian clothing industry, for example, home-based and 'garage' factory workers—overwhelmingly female—typically receive low wages (as little as 80 cents per garment), work exceedingly long hours and have little or no OHS protection. Research indicates home-based workers experience three times the number of injuries as those doing the same work in factories (Mayhew and Quinlan, 1999) These problems are made more acute by the fact that in Australia, as in Canada and the US, many clothing workers (especially homeworkers) are recently arrived immigrants, including illegal immigrants, not to mention child labour. Long hours and risks of assault are common among taxi drivers. In several of the industries just mentioned there appears to be a connection between economic pressures, pervasive self-employment or subcontracting arrangements, and hazardous practices, including the flouting of safety laws (Quinlan and Bohle, 2008).

Further, even if developed countries have managed to control or export exposure to some hazardous substances, occupational diseases continue to exact a heavy but more insidious toll. Public recognition is limited to a small number of hazardous substances and not necessarily those that constitute the greatest risk. In some cases it takes years for the health effects to become manifest and even longer for regulatory agencies to respond, a prime example being asbestos where the toll is yet to peak even in countries like Australia, which banned its use some years ago. Asbestos also illustrates the capacity of some work-related hazards to extend to the families of workers and the wider community (McCullock and Tweedale, 2008). Nor can we presume that other insidious risks to health like long or irregular working hours have been addressed. In Japan, where long hours remained the norm in the late 1970s, concerns at the health effects of this translated into the term Karoshi (sudden death by overwork). Although it was initially treated with scepticism, by 2000 the Japanese Ministry of Labour had accepted it as a major problem with over six million Japanese working over 60 hours per week and around 300 instances of brain and heart disease being recorded between 2002 and 2005 (Iwasaki et al., 2006). From 2001 onwards the ministry responded by setting standards for overtime, launching a prevention program and enacting medical-guidance legislation in 2005. In Europe, North America and Australasia the decline in standard (full-time) working hours during the twentieth century had largely stalled by the 1990s and, indeed, long hours (i.e. over 50 hours per week) were becoming the norm for a substantial group (around 20 to 30% of the workforce) in many countries (Quinlan, 1998). As we will show later, recent legislative developments have not always enhanced OHS standards and even apparent improvements have not always had a significant effect due to a lack of effective implementation.

In sum, even in the most industrially advanced societies OHS is a significant and resilient problem. It is a problem that needs to be examined and understood in both a national and international context. Thus far we have only pointed to the most publicly visible dimensions of the problem. In the past it was the visibility and public outrage associated with mass death which drove governments to initiate inquiries, introduce new legislation and strengthen enforcement activities. Visibility remains a significant influence today. While OHS receives more public recognition than it did 30 years ago, the overall incidence of occupationally related mortality and morbidity is (unlike the road toll) neither accurately recorded nor the subject of ongoing debate and political action. It is accorded less media and political attention than environmental hazards and climate change (with which it overlaps), violent crimes, public hospitals and a host of other health-related matters.

The lower ranking of OHS cannot be explained in terms of the scope of the problem as the toll from occupational injury and disease exceeds virtually all the other issues just mentioned. The same also applies to most wars. More Americans died at work during the period of the Vietnam War than were killed in that conflict (as was the case with Australians even during their peak period of involvement). An attempt to measure the global burden of death due to occupational injury estimated there were over 300 000 deaths annually and another 113 000 work-related fatalities were probably missed 'due to under-reporting alone' (Concha-Barrientos et al., 2005). Further, as will be demonstrated later in this chapter these estimates do not include the far larger number of workers who die as a result of exposure to hazardous substances. However much the work-related death fails to evince the public attention of other health-related issues, this toll represents an incomplete picture of the scope of occupational injury and disease.

We might, like others, conceive of the incidence of occupational illness in Australia in terms of a pyramid of severity. At the tip there are fatalities, below that a larger number of permanent incapacities of various types, below this an even larger number of temporary incapacities requiring time off work, and below this an even greater number of essentially minor illnesses. At the very bottom can be included a greater number of potentially hazardous incidents which have not resulted in injury or illness (see Bird, cited in CCH, 1987: 6). This approach has the advantage of placing fatalities within the context of the broader problem of which they form a part. It could even be used to place incidents of mass death like those described above into a broader spectrum of illness probability. Available statistics on occupational illness endorse such a pyramid. Available data for Australia indicates that annually occupational illness and injury results in almost double the fatalities and far more non-fatal incapacities than those arising from traffic incidents. (In 2008, 1464 Australians were killed in road incidents and both absolute toll and incidence per 100 000 head of population has declined significantly over the past 30 years. Department of Infrastructure, Transport, Regional Development and Local Government, 2009: 1-2) As shown below, official statistics underestimate the extent of occupational illness. Thus, the precise dimensions of the pyramid, if it is a pyramid, are unknown. Moreover, conceiving of occupational illness in terms of a pyramid of risk probability and severity is flawed because it tends to deflect attention away from the incremental and cumulative character of many occupational health problems. Some hazards entail such a high risk probability it would be misleading to conceive of them in terms of a pyramid of risk.

How then do we grasp the dimensions of the OHS problem? There is no simple answer to this question given the flaws in knowledge already alluded to. However, we can consider what we do know about particular dimensions of the problem, including the array of hazards, the extent of illness, the impact of illness and trends, if any, in the scope of the problem. These dimensions will form the subject for the remainder of the chapter.

The array of health and safety hazards at work

Taken as a whole, work activity entails potential exposure to a wide array of hazards. Some hazards, like dust, heat and rockfalls in mines, have been around for many years, while others, like those associated with radioactive substances, are comparatively new. New technologies may eliminate or mitigate some hazards but also introduce or contribute to new hazards. Sometimes the effects may be simultaneous. For example, mobile phones may assist those working in isolation (or provide another source alerting danger) but use of phones (or worse, texting messages) while operating mobile equipment is hazardous. In October 2008, the driver of a Los Angeles Metrolink commuter train that crashed into a freight train, killing 25 people, is believed to have been texting shortly before the incident (*Human Resource Executive* Online, 9 October 2008). Some hazards, such as the risk of suffering a laceration in a job requiring the use of knives or falls on a construction site, are reasonably apparent. Other hazards, like toxic poisoning, are often insidious. This section is concerned to briefly identify the range of health hazards found at work.

It is important to recognise that current understandings about the scope of occupation-related health problems depend on, among other things, the definition of health that is employed, the existing state of medical knowledge and social processes affecting recognition. There are important value judgments and debates here that will be taken up in later chapters. At this point we will simply provide a broad definition of health and then briefly outline the array of hazards at work which are known or are the subject of current debate.

At a joint meeting held between the World Health Organization (WHO) and the International Labour Organization (ILO) in 1950, health was defined to be a state of complete physical, mental and social wellbeing and not merely the absence of disease and deformity (cited in NHMRC, 1973: 1). Despite this longstanding formal definition, dominant understandings of what constitutes health on the one hand, and injury and illness on the other, have been a good deal narrower. Most workers are presumed to be healthy unless they are recognised as suffering a clearly diagnosed physiological disorder which existing medical knowledge has unambiguously linked to their employment.

NIOSH (2004: xxi) has defined occupational injury as 'any injury such as a cut, fracture, sprain, amputation etc. that results from a work-related event or from a single instantaneous exposure in the work environment'. NIOSH (2004: xxi) defines occupational illness as 'any abnormal condition or disorder (other than one resulting from an occupational injury) caused by exposure to factors associated with employment. Occupational illness includes acute and chronic illness and diseases that may be caused by inhalation, absorption, ingestion or direct contact'. In our view occupational illness includes mental illness and distress associated with work. In this book, the broad categories of occupational injury and occupational illness will be used.

Our knowledge of occupationally related illness is piecemeal and often based on partial understandings of causal links. It is not simply a matter of identifying the various physical, chemical, organisational and other aspects of the workplace and work processes that have adverse effects on worker health. These aspects interact in often complex ways. The simultaneous exposure of workers to excessive heat and noise, to two or more hazardous substances (say lead and diesel fumes), or to excessive hours of work and supervisory pressure or sexual harassment will have health outcomes which cannot be deduced by simply adding those associated with exposures to each hazard individually. Further, physical, chemical and organisational hazards can and do interact. Indeed, it is relatively easy to conceive of a workplace, such as a lead/zinc mine or foundry, where all those factors just mentioned could be found. Adding to this complexity, even within the same industry no two workplaces are identical and within any given workplace not all workers will be exposed to an identical array of hazards.

Recognising these interactions does not represent a new observation. Three hundred years ago Rammazzini's pioneering work on occupational medicine took a holistic approach of examining the array of overlapping social (including living conditions), psychological, physical and chemical hazards confronting each occupation he considered. However, since then the pursuit of single disciplinary interpretations has led much of literature on OHS hazards to ignore, downplay or interpret these interactions in a highly constrained framework (Quinlan, 1997). Examining these interactions is critical to a more holistic approach to OHS—a central aim of this book. Nevertheless, to appreciate the array of different factors that may affect health at work it is useful to use a number of recognisable categories, mentioning some interactions in passing. Finally, it should also be acknowledged that our understanding of workplace hazards is predicated to some degree on human physiology and the anthropometric characteristics of particular populations as well as the unique characteristics of each individual (for an examination of physical load see Hagg et al., 2009: 132–89). It is beyond the scope of this book to explore these aspects but particular disciplines like ergonomics, hygiene and psychology examined in later chapters draw on this knowledge base.

Physical hazards

A wide range of physical phenomena can be associated with injury and illness in the workplace. These include sound/noise, vibration, excessive heat and cold (as well as exposure to rapid changes in temperature), electrophysical agents and pressure. It needs to be stressed that these subcategories are not, in practice, mutually exclusive. Illness and injury can result from a combination of exposures. Referring to a series of disorders associated with repeated trauma (such as carpal tunnel syndrome, tendonitis, tenosynovitis and bursitis), the National Institute of Occupational Safety and Health (NIOSH, 2004: 73) noted that the conditions arose from repeated motion, vibration or pressure. As a later chapter on injury will indicate, ergonomic and psychosocial characteristics of the workplace (including workloads) are also relevant to understanding the origins of at least some strain-related disorders. As recognised by the European Agency for Safety and Health at Work (2005: 8), lack of physical activity also constitutes an emerging physical hazard, as work systems encouraging long sedentary periods, often at the same time (in the case of IT workers, for instance) as intense activity of the arms and upper body, are conducive to musculoskeletal disorders (MSD). This highlights the interaction between complex technologies, work processes and workers.

Recognising these interactions, it is still valuable to identify different types of physical hazards.

Sound and noise

Hearing damage associated with noise (undesirable sounds) is a very widespread occupational hazard and a common source of disability within working populations (Bohgard et al., 2009: 221). Industries traditionally associated with exposure to high levels of noise include agriculture, mining, oil and gas extraction, building and construction, metal manufacturing, transport (road, rail and air) and automotive services (NIOSH, 1996a: 19–20). Relatively high and sustained noise levels can also be found in shopping centres, large childcare centres/nurseries and hospitality (like pubs) or entertainment venues (race courses, concert halls, casinos and the like). A survey undertaken by Statistics Sweden (cited in Bohgard et al., 2009: 222) found half or more of workers in the industries/jobs just mentioned indicated noise levels made it hard to conduct a normal conversation at least a quarter of the time at work.

Noise level refers to the strength of sound measured in terms of decibels (dBA) with limits usually being set according to exposure time. However, as Bohgard et al. (2009: 220) point out, noise level is only one aspect of whether sound is undesirable and has adverse health effects. Whether sound is undesirable is influenced by time, duration, whether or not sound carries meaningful information, predictability and frequency, and the context of the work being undertaken (Bohgard et al., 2009: 220). Thus, for example, the unpredictability of 'screech' may exacerbate its effects on call centre workers. Even background conversation or minor equipment noise may be disruptive to workers engaged in activities requiring elaborate and concentrated thought processes (an often overlooked aspect of open-plan offices). In short, undesirable sound is an issue for a far wider array of work venues and tasks than is often considered.

Exposure to excessive noise can lead to a temporary or permanent (partial or total) loss of hearing (the loss may be restricted to certain frequency bands or complete deafness) or ringing in the ears (tinnitus), and cases of acute exposure may result in acoustic trauma, analogous to 'shell shock' (Mathews, 1993: 110–11; Bohgard et al., 2009: 228–30). Noise is an insidious hazard because in many instances the onset of hearing loss will occur gradually and subtle adjustments in work and home behaviour (turning up the sound level of the television, for instance) can delay recognition. Further, in some occupations hearing loss is so prevalent that it is treated as normal for the job.

In general, legislative protection from work-induced hearing impairment is confined to noise levels rather than the broader concept of undesirable noise. Even the adequacy of threshold levels of protection for noise-induced hearing damage has been the subject of ongoing conjecture. In Australia, the US and a number of other countries OHS legislation imposes a maximum periodised exposure limit of 85 dBA over an 8-hour period and a maximum absolute exposure limit of 115 dBA. Where employees regularly work longer than eight hours the effect of cumulative exposure means limits should be recalibrated to a level below 85 dBA (less than 83 dBA according to NIOSH, 1996a: 15). Often it appears such adjustments are not undertaken (or enforced) despite the growing use of 12-hour shifts in Australia and other industrialised countries. Further, evidence that even where workers only perform eight-hour shifts extended exposure will still result in hearing impairment for a significant minority of workers at the 85 dBA limit led NIOSH (1996a: 1–2) to recommend a lower limit of 82 dBA (a substantial reduction). While arguably covered under general duties (see chapter 7) the existing legislative framework in Australia and New Zealand fails to provide sufficient incentive for changes in workplace planning/design, tool technology and work processes that could significantly reduce exposure to undesirable sound—examples of which have been known for many years (see Bohgard et al., 2009: 240–56).

In addition to hearing impairment undesirable sound may affect OHS in a number of ways. First, noise may disrupt communication in the workplace and thereby pose a safety risk if workers are unable to hear a shouted warning or other sounds indicating an impending danger. This risk can be exacerbated if workers have already suffered hearing loss or are wearing ill-fitting or poorly designed hearing protection that can itself have adverse health effects such as discomfort and the risk of infection in warm and humid climates. These limitations highlight the importance of primary interventions according to the hierarchy of control whereby attention should focus on reducing noise levels/workplace exposures through engineering interventions and with personal protective equipment (PPE) as a last resort/temporary measure (NIOSH 1996a: 100). The former approach may also be used to address a number of hazards simultaneously (e.g. guarding or more fundamental re-engineering to reduce exposure to noise, dust/ fumes and dangerous pieces of moving machinery). Second, exposure to noise can lead to physiological stress (Bohgard et al., 2009: 231) with both immediate/short-term responses (including fatigue) and long-term effects of prolonged exposure (including high blood pressure and poor circulation). Third, exposure to noise can be disruptive and psychologically stressful, and can affect behaviour in other ways (NIOSH, 1996a: 18; Bohgard et al., 2009: 232–3). Fourth, infrasound (common in vehicles and power plants) and ultrasound (emitted by plastic welding and cleaning machinery) may have health effects, though there has been little research on this (Bohgard et al., 2009: 233–4). Fifth and finally there is the possibility of synergistic effects resulting from simultaneous exposure to noise and other hazards. For example, it has been suggested that some chemicals, including solvents such as toluene and xylene as well as drug medications (including aspirin), can exacerbate tinnitus or hearing deficit.

The complex and interactive effects on health of the mechanisms just described require further investigation but there is enough evidence in relation to most to indicate they warrant serious attention.

Vibration

Vibration exposure refers to rapid mechanical oscillations transferred to the worker through a mechanical device they are operating or in other ways in contact with (Bohgard et al., 2009: 257). Examples of vibration sources include pneumatic drills, motorised hand tools (like chainsaws) and heavy equipment (trains, trucks, mobile cranes, excavators, mechanical harvesters and the like). Though by no means as prevalent as exposure to undesirable sound, vibration exposure has been spread by increased use of machinery (such as chainsaws) historically to a widening range of occupational groups (Mathews, 1993: 139–40). Industries where exposure to vibration is most common include agriculture, transport, construction and manufacturing.

Vibration exposure may affect specific parts of the body (most commonly hand–arm contact from tools or machinery) or the whole body (as in cases of riding on vibrating equipment such as a truck, tractor or excavator). Exposure, especially prolonged exposure, to vibration can have an array of short-term and longer-term health effects. Short-term effects include loss of muscle strength and pain (though both may become permanent), blurred vision, nausea and giddiness. Longer-term effects include injuries to the neck, back or lower extremities in the case of whole-body vibration, or in the case of hand–arm vibration, carpal tunnel syndrome or permanent damage to the tissue and blood vessels (constricting blood flow), in fingers in particular, known as Raynaud's syndrome/disease or white finger (Mathews, 1993: 137–8 and Bohgard et al., 2009: 259–60). Like hearing loss, there is no cure for white finger.

Personal protective equipment cannot address vibration hazards. Engineering controls and ergonomic interventions that redesign machinery and work processes (such as better cab and wheel suspension and improved seating in the case of heavy vehicles, the use of vibration isolators, or the redesign of pneumatic tools and chainsaws) and work reorganisation (including task rotation) to restrict exposure constitute the only effective solutions. In Australia, New Zealand and many other countries little legislation directly addresses vibration as a workplace hazard (although there are exceptions such as Sweden; see Bohgard et al., 2009: 262). Inspectorates in Australia and elsewhere have produced guidance material (on exposure and controls), as have bodies like Standards Australia (AS 2670–1983) and the International Standards Organisation (ISO) (Mathews, 1993: 142–4; Bohgard et al., 2009: 263–5).

Heat, cold and thermal comfort

Workers from a wide range of occupations encounter temperature extremes on either a periodic or regular basis as part of their tasks. For example, those working in iron and steelworks, mines and smelters, kitchens/restaurants/bakeries, laundries, plastics or glass factories, boiler rooms, canneries, or brick and ceramic operations all face hot or hot and humid environments (NIOSH, *Working in Hot Environments*, 1992). Construction and farmworkers can encounter extremes of heat and cold. Those repairing electricity grids or telephone cables in alpine areas of Australia and New Zealand, or workers more generally in the Northern European, Asian or American winter, may have to work in sub-zero temperatures. Beyond the threats posed by temperature extremes there is a growing recognition that thermal discomfort (due to heat, humidity or poorly installed air conditioning) can affect workers' overall stress and wellbeing in a far broader range of workplaces (European Agency for Safety and Health at Work, 2005: 8).

Exposure to extremes of heat or cold may occur in a number of ways. First, the worker may come into direct contact with an object that is either so hot or so cold as to cause injury. Examples of this include burns resulting from contact with hot or molten metal and plastics, steam, water and other substances. Contact with extremely cold substances such as dry ice or liquified gases can be equally hazardous. Second, exposure to heat or cold may also occur through the general or immediate working environment. Many industrial processes and pieces of machinery generate considerable heat that can affect those working nearby. Other workers employed in industries using refrigeration may be subject to intense cold.

Exposure to heat or cold can be exacerbated by seasonal climatic conditions, as in the case of furnace workers employed at the height of summer. Often factories are not air-conditioned (although the office area will be) or have not been effectively designed to minimise heat (including the isolation of hot work processes and use of vegetated barriers or other devices to block radiant heat or hot winds) and maximise ventilation. Even where workers are not subject to artificial sources of heat and cold, the general nature of their work may entail exposure to potentially hazardous climatic conditions. A degree of acclimatisation—physiological adjustment following repeated exposure—can occur in relation to those working in hot working environments but this dissipates if there is a period of absence to exposure (Bohgard et al., 2009: 207). There is less evidence that similar adjustments can occur in relation to cold (Mathews, 1993: 159).

Some workers, such as farmworkers, seamen/fishermen, construction workers and electricity/telephone lineworkers, can confront both climatic extremes. Exposure to rapid changes in temperature and humidity, as in the case of storemen or food processers continuously entering and leaving refrigerated storerooms in an otherwise hot work environment, can also adversely affect health.

The debilitating effects of extremes of heat or cold are influenced by the amount and type of clothing worn (in terms of insulation and water vapour resistance) as well as the nature of the work tasks in terms of demands for physical effort, manual dexterity, location (such as working at height, on a cherry-picker, etc.) and mental concentration (Bohgard et al., 2009: 195–216). Body heat balance is determined by the interaction between the body's energy production (power production) and the process of heat exchange with the environment (Bohgard et al., 2009: 197). Holding other things equal, the more strenuous the task the shorter the period of time before heat will have debilitating effects. On the other hand, lack of activity (so long as movement is not impaired) and windchill factors may exacerbate exposure to cold. The comfort climate also needs to be assessed in relation to indoor workplaces not just outdoor workplaces (Bohgard et al., 2009: 216).

Exposure to excessive heat or cold can have a number of health effects (Mathews, 1993: 157–73; Bohgard et al., 2009: 206). One effect of heat exposure is thermal stress—skin temperature and the heart rate rises, prolonged sweating leads to the loss of fluids and salts (which can lead to muscle pain and cramps and impair stomach and intestine functions) and 'hostility can rapidly change to tiredness and symptoms of exhaustion' (Bohgard et al., 2009: 206). Thermal stress is influenced not only by air temperature but also by relative humidity, air movement and the radiant temperature of the surroundings. Radiant heat may interfere with reproduction by lowering semen quality as has been found in the case of welders (see Bonde, 1992: 5–10). Exposure to super-heated air, as in the case of a fireman or kiln worker, may cause lung damage while contact with steam caused by water contacting hot surfaces may cause serious burns. Excessive heat may have a number of short- and long-term effects on health including:

- reducing the ability to concentrate and the stress and risks of injury associated with this
- aggravating the effect of other hazards such as noise or toxic substances
- aggravating existing medical conditions for workers such as heart or blood pressure problems

- lung damage or burns arising from contact with heated air or steam
- heat illness such as heat cramps, heat exhaustion and heat stroke
- heat rash, chronic heat fatigue and reproductive disorders (Mathews, 1993: 160; Bohgard et al., 2009: 206).

Adverse effects of cold on health also include short- and long-term effects such as:

- numbing the senses and slowing reaction times, thereby increasing the risk of injury (such as slips, falls, strains/sprains, cuts and abrasions)
- inducing erratic behaviour, muscular weakness and cramps
- hypothermia
- frostbite
- arthritis, rheumatism, chest and heart problems (Mathews, 1993: 162–3; Bohgard et al., 2009: 210–15).

In Australia and many other countries, while inspectorates and other bodies (such as Standards Australia and the American Conference of Government Industrial Hygienists) have produced guidance material/advisory standards (for example, with regard to heat stress or indoor work) there are few legal requirements in relation to exposure to the extremes of heat and cold, except in the most extreme circumstances (Mathews, 1993: 167). Such controls or guidance materials as exist are often limited. For example, reference to the provision of water, break periods and stopping work when temperature reaches a specific level do not address the multiple elements that influence heat exposure. More comprehensive approaches have been recommended (see Gavhed and Holmer, 2006, cited in Bohgard et al., 2009: 211) that address body heat balance (including convection, radiation and evaporation), work organisation (including limiting exposure time, changing task mix and flexibility, rest breaks, climate-controlled rest areas and monitoring), PPE (reflective or insulated clothing, multilayer clothing and extremities protection) and other protective measures (like fluid intake, acclimatisation procedures, symptoms information and reporting mechanisms). In practice, as with other physical hazards, remedies too often focus on PPE and administrative controls rather than eliminating or minimising exposure through more fundamental engineering/ workplace design or work reorganisation interventions. For example, at one major industrial site in the north of Western Australia we observed welders and others doing erection work at a port facility in high temperatures and full exposure to radiant heat from the sun when the erection of even a simple demountable set of shades would have made a substantial difference.

Lighting, electrophysical agents and other sources of radiation

Eyesight is a critical sense in perceiving and responding to work and workplaces and so the lighting environment (the lighting conditions of the workplace including light sources and their properties) and visual ergonomics (the needs of individual workers in different work activities or circumstances) can have significant bearing on OHS (Bohgard et al., 2009: 269). Lighting, the availability of natural or preferred lighting sources and the capacity to adjust lighting to changing circumstances (such as shading direct sunlight or glare in outdoor work or when operating screen-based equipment) can have an array of effects on OHS. Poor lighting can, for example, lead to headaches and eyestrain while excessive exposure to sunlight can lead to premature eyesight degeneration or retinal damage. Poor matching between lighting and activity (including mobile equipment like trucks and the roads they operate on) can affect mental health and wellbeing or expose workers to an increased risk of injury (through collision with objects, slips/trips or inhibiting the capacity to avoid dangerous circumstances, judge distance and the like). Designing work and workplaces to eliminate or minimise these problems requires attention to light sources and fittings, the level and distribution of luminance, the specific requirements of the task and the needs of workers with existing visual impairments (Bohgard et al., 2009: 284–92).

Other aspects of the work context need to be considered, including demographics and work organisation. For example, an ageing of the population in many countries means that greater attention needs to be given to age-related eyesight degeneration in work design (Bohgard et al., 2009: 277–8). It should also be recognised, for example, that most long-haul trucking and a considerable amount of short-haul trucking is carried out at night and in Australia (if not elsewhere) this workforce is also ageing. Deficiencies in lighting may also assume more critical consequences in work situations (such as a factory complex) where there are poor traffic management systems (including physical separation of workers from vehicles and mobile machinery). Even in circumstances where PPE is required at least in a residual or emergency role (as in personal lights for underground mine and construction workers), this is not an alternative to better work environment lighting (and in coal mines further emergency interventions are required such as touch-based cone-lines to assist exits when dust obscures vision). The foregoing observations highlight the need for a holistic and integrated approach to OHS-related lighting.

Electrophysical agents, also labelled as electromagnetic radiation, incorporate a range of sources of radiant energy emissions including microwaves and ultraviolet radiation such as lasers, ultrasound and X-rays. As with a number of other physical hazards, use of equipment and work processes incorporating electrophysical agents is growing. Health hazards can extend not only to workers using this equipment but also to those working in close or prolonged proximity to sources of electromagnetic radiation. Workers exposed to such agents are to be found in office and clerical occupations, printing, construction, manufacturing, telecommunications and healthcare (the latter via X-ray machines and the increased use of magnetic resonance equipment). A report on emerging physical hazards undertaken by the European Agency for Safety and Health at Work (2005: 9) noted strong agreement that ultraviolet radiation (UVR) was an emerging risk. The report noted that as UVR was cumulative 'the more workers are exposed the more UVR-sensitive they are'. As with chemicals and other hazardous substances, knowledge about the extent of exposure to harmful doses of radiation across a range of industries and workplaces is fragmentary and inadequate.

In addition to electromagnetic radiation there is particle radiation (Bohgard et al., 2009: 293). Radiation is divided into ionising and non-ionising radiation as these entail different mechanisms affecting human health. High levels of exposure to non–ionising radiation (electromagnetic radiation with a wavelength equal to or higher than UV radiation), including optical radiation and microwaves, can lead to skin and eye damage and harmful increases in body temperature and blood pressure. In some circumstances the presence of chemicals like trichloroethylene can result in synergistic effects (Bohgard et al., 2009: 294–5). The health effects of low–intensity and frequency magnetic fields are not established although there have been reports of health problems among workers using CRT monitors (including risks to pregnant women) and an increased risk of child leukaemia and brain tumours from proximity to powerlines (Bohgard et al., 2009: 293, 295). Periodic concerns that prolonged use of mobile phones could lead to brain tumours or other forms of cancer have not been confirmed by research. For its part, ionising radiation (such as that emitted by X–ray equipment where charged particles are accelerated) ionises atoms in human cells (Bohgard et al., 2009: 297–8). Exposure to ionising radiation can result in serious cell damage affecting tissue and key organs, including fatal forms of cancer (International Agency for Research on Cancer, 2007: 49).

Although ionising radiation can have catastrophic consequences, potential exposure to this hazard is relatively restricted in comparison to non–ionising radiation, with exposed groups including health and veterinary workers, those in the nuclear industry and researchers (International Agency for Research on Cancer, 2007: 49). Even in countries with strong regulatory regimes, like Sweden, regulations only exist for high–frequency electromagnetic fields, leaving other electromagnetic hazards unaddressed. The ongoing introduction of new work processes and equipment incorporating electrophysical agents (such as lasers on construction sites and electromagnetic plastic heat–sealing machines) raises significant issues about worker and regulator awareness, inadequately researched OHS properties and hazards arising from improper operation or maintenance. Enough incidents have occurred to suggest these concerns require more attention (Dalton, 1991: 67–8). The growing use of irradiation to preserve/inhibit bacteria in food products has also raised concerns both from an OHS and a consumer/ environmental perspective but again research is lacking. In Australia and New Zealand there is legislation governing the transport, storage and use of radioactive substances. However, there is little direct regulation of workplace exposures although, as is the case in the US, some guidance material has been produced. As with a number of bacteriological, viral and temperature–related hazards, climate change will extend exposure to the sun's radiant energy and present other challenges to healthy working environments (Costello et al., 2009). A strong public health campaign directed at preventing skin cancer in Australia has had spillover effects on OHS but more needs to be done.

Pressure

In certain situations workers may be subject to abnormally high levels of pressure and with it a number of associated health hazards. An example is the pressure–related health problems experienced by divers, which include the bends and bone damage or necrosis

(Phoon, 1988: 135–42). The bends were responsible for the death of hundreds of divers in the Queensland and Western Australian pearling industry in the late nineteenth and early twentieth century. The advent of recompression chambers saved many potential victims but decompression illness remains a problem (Richardson, 1995). Bone necrosis remains a problem for long-term abalone divers as well as divers employed in maintaining oil rigs, those servicing the tourist industry and other pursuits. These health problems among divers are exacerbated by a combination of inadequate training, inadequate regulation and the fact that many divers work in isolation and are subject to the competitive pressures of self-employment or incentive-based rewards (in the case of abalone divers) which encourage hazardous work practices. In recent years a number of state governments have strengthened regulations in relation to diving but interstate inconsistencies remain a problem (Kristovskis, 1995).

Chemical hazards

Exposure to harmful chemicals is one of the most widespread but least well documented occupational health hazards. Most jobs will involve some level of exposure to chemicals although the level, type and variety of exposures will vary markedly (Bohgard and Albin, 2009: 330). Chemical hazards are not new (see, for example, eighteenth-century tanning and dyeing processes). Nevertheless, the proliferation of potentially hazardous chemicals far outstrips the potential to either investigate their health effects or fully regulate their usage (see chapters 5 and 7). Even by the early 1990s there were estimated to be more than seven million known chemical substances with about 25 000 new chemicals being developed each year (ILO, 1991). More than a decade earlier the Assistant Surgeon General of the United States estimated that there were about half a million chemicals being produced and used by industry with an additional 500 new chemicals finding their way into the workplace each year (cited in Ashford, 1976: 88). Neither the number of those chemicals whose use would constitute a health risk nor the precise nature of such hazards is known.

In Australia knowledge concerning the manufacture and use of chemicals is limited. In 1999 there were 38 500 single substances included in the Australia Inventory of Chemical Substances (AICS) and therefore presumably in use to varying degrees. However, these single substances are then mixed or blended into a series of products that are made, used, stored or handled. Following the European approach the figure on single substances can then be multiplied by a factor of 10, suggesting that over 350 000 products are in circulation here. The size, complexity and rapid innovation within the chemical industry has outstripped resources for notification, assessment and regulation in Australia and many if not all other countries, especially in the absence of stringent licensing requirements like those which apply to food additives.

Chemicals can harm health in five different ways (Mathews, 1993: 187–8), namely:

- being poisonous or toxic—the effects may be either acute (leading to rapid collapse or asphyxiation) or chronic (such as the long-term development of cancer or other diseases)

- being corrosive and burning the skin, eyes, lungs or other body tissues
- acting as an irritant of the skin (which may lead to a form of dermatitis) or of the respiratory system (including bronchitis)
- acting as a sensitiser which can lead to long-term skin, lung or allergic complaints, including dermatitis and asthma
- through their explosiveness properties or flammability (leading to burns or asphyxiation).

Precise information regarding the chemicals used by particular industries and work-places, and the resulting hazard exposures, is sparse. It is only comparatively recently that the chemicals used by hairdressers were the subject of some scrutiny and for many years the chemicals used in agriculture received little attention despite the clearly poisonous nature of pesticides and herbicides. In the US, NIOSH (2004: 139) has reported that agricultural workers have a markedly higher risk of acute poisoning than other workers. More widespread illnesses associated with chemical exposure are work-related skin and respiratory diseases, especially dermatitis and occupational asthma (NIOSH, 2004: 143, 181). NIOSH (2004: 143) identified agents most frequently associated with work-related asthma as 'miscellaneous chemicals, cleaning materials and mineral and inorganic dust'. However, since many chemical exposures are not unique to work, let alone a specific workplace, it is frequently difficult to isolate or attribute the extent to which a disease such as asthma is the result of a work-related chemical exposure.

Moreover, the introduction of new chemicals and turnover in the use of existing chemicals means that new hazards are being revealed on an ongoing basis but this is not necessarily reducing the overall number of chemicals which pose currently undetected health risks. For example, in the US, NIOSH (2003) issued an alert for preventing lung disease in workers making flavourings while the Centers for Disease Control (2008) identified neurological illness associated with workplace exposure to 1-bromopropane— a solvent used to substitute for ozone-depleting chlorofluorocarbons.

The health-damaging properties of chemicals may operate independently or in combination, as in the case of a chemical fire where workers or firemen may risk suffocation/heat exhaustion/burning and inhaling toxic fumes. Like other hazardous substances (see below) chemicals can be absorbed by the body through three different mechanisms (Bohgard and Albin, 2009: 311–21), namely absorption through the skin (including open wounds), absorption through the airways and absorption through the intestinal tract (including being consumed accidently from a residue on hands or food surfaces). The absorption mechanism, along with the form the substance takes and the amount absorbed, can influence health consequences in relation to the chemical substance (for a recent discussion see Bohgard and Albin, 2009: 311–21).

Exposure to specific chemicals may have multiple health effects. For example diisocyanates such as toluene (used in the manufacture of foams, fibres, paints, varnishes and elastomers) act as powerful irritants on the mucous membranes of the eyes and respiratory and digestive tracts, are sensitisers (leading to hypersensitivity pneumonitis) and are carcinogenic. In 1996 NIOSH (1996c) issued an alert that workers sensitised by past exposure to diisocyanates were at risk of suffering a severe even fatal asthma attack if they were exposed again—even at concentrations below the NIOSH Recommended Exposure Limit. Reference can also be made to less extreme cases, including ones where PPE (such as the increased use of latex gloves to combat HIV exposure among healthcare workers) have themselves become a source of discomfort, sensitisation and allergic reactions (Hunt, et al., 1996: 765–70).

Simultaneous exposure to a number of chemicals, some of which may be relatively harmless in isolation, can have cumulative or combination-specific health effects. From the early 1980s there was growing concern in the US, Australia and other countries about increased cancer risks among coke oven workers. The International Agency for Research into Cancer (IARC) identified well over a dozen potentially carcinogenic substances (including the metals arsenic, cadmium, chromium and nickel) in coke oven emissions. The term additive effect is used where the combined effect of a multiple exposure is equal to the sum of effects associated with each individual exposure (i.e. $2+2=4$). The term synergism or synergistic effect is used to describe the situation whereby the combined effect of a multiple exposure is greater than simply summing the effects of individual exposures (i.e. $2+2>4$). The Canadian Centre for Occupational Health and Safety cites a number of examples of synergistic effects related to workplace exposures including the higher incidence of lung cancer among asbestos workers who smoke and increased liver damage among workers exposed to both carbon tetrachloride and ethanol (both which cause liver damage). The term potentiation is used to describe circumstances whereby the combination of a substance not normally considered toxic with another chemical makes the latter far more toxic (i.e. $0+2>2$). A final relevant term is antagonism or antagonistic effect which describes a circumstance whereby the combined effects of two or more chemicals is less than the addition of their individual effects (i.e. $2+2<4$). For example, alcohol consumption has been found to inhibit mercury oxidation.

One implication of synergistic effects is that serious health effects may occur at lower levels of exposure to particular substances—levels that might be thought not to constitute a significant risk. These effects, especially where they involve long-term low-level exposures, can be difficult to identify with any certainty. In addition, the adverse health effects of chemicals can be exacerbated by or interact with other hazards including physical hazards (heat, ventilation, radiation) and organisational hazards (excessive workload, supervisory pressure, poor communication, isolation, etc.). For example, higher temperatures may increase the level of noxious fumes discharging from machines, such as those associated with solvents used in photocopiers. While most workplace exposure to hazardous chemicals is involuntary, in some instances workers, like long-distance truck drivers and transit operators, will turn to potentially hazardous drugs (including pain relievers or stimulants) in an effort to combat stress or fatigue or to cope with burnout and job-related stress (Chen and Cunradi, 2008). More generally, exposure to chemicals and other hazardous substances in factories, vehicles and offices can be seen to arise from poor design decisions and inadequate maintenance. Indeed, the lack of consideration of OHS in workplace design (very few architecture or built environment students receive instruction in OHS) has been linked to 'sick building' syndrome.

As with multiple chemical exposures, the simultaneous exposure to both a chemical and a physical hazard may have synergistic effects. This includes simultaneous exposures which are by no means rare, such as exposure to organic solvents (like toluene, xylene and trichloroethylene) and noise (Morata et al., 1994: 359–65). Further, researchers have noted that workers exposed to organic solvents over long periods often report symptoms of fatigue as well as memory and concentration problems—symptoms which could have a range of OHS consequences in the workplace. There is also evidence linking such exposure to sleep apnoea (Edling et al., 1993: 276–9). The combination of hazardous chemicals and disorganisation at the workplace can have disastrous consequences. On 29 November 1986 an explosion at the ICI chemical plant in the Sydney suburb of Rhodes killed five men (all contractors) following what the coroner later described as a complete breakdown in communication which led to an oxy-acetylene torch being used within three metres of a tank containing a volatile liquid (*Sydney Morning Herald*, 16 May 1987).

The regulatory context is also important. It was only with the development of more stringent environmental legislation in the 1990s that special protocols have been introduced to protect firefighters and other emergency workers from the risks of being exposed to 'chemical cocktails' after being called in to deal with a spill or fire. The complex intertwining of chemical risks with organisational and regulatory considerations is well illustrated by the case of smoking in the workplace. During the 1990s in Australia and other countries like Sweden, governments and large employers took decisive action to ban smoking in the workplace and public buildings as well as on air, public road and rail transport. The apparent stimulus for this was mounting evidence on the adverse health effects of passive smoking and some well-publicised cases where workers exposed to passive smoke successfully sued their employer. Yet when measured against far less decisive efforts in relation to hazardous chemicals at work a set of less-obvious influences emerge. Unlike other sources of chemical exposure at work, smoking results from individual worker behaviour and is therefore not directly connected to production or service provision. It also helps to explain why industries like hospitality/tourism opposed government regulation. This being said, it can still be noted that the fact that countries like Australia and Sweden are more willing to regulate on this issue than other countries (not only poor countries but also the US) reflects differences in the role of the state and collective social protection. Notwithstanding such differences the failure to regulate hazardous chemicals used at work, including lengthy delays between the accumulation of evidence and the introduction of new regulatory standards, is a global problem. Even when regulatory exposure standards are introduced it is not uncommon for these to be significantly tightened as more evidence emerges on negative health effects. We will return to this issue in chapter 7.

The health effects of chemical exposure can extend beyond workers to their families. Some chemicals have profound effects on the reproductive system. For example, research has identified changes in reproductive hormone levels among chemical workers exposed to dioxin (Egeland et al., 1995). Research has indicated an increased risk of spontaneous abortion in workers exposed to toluene (Ng et al., 1992: 804–8).

Teratogenic and mutagenic properties have also been demonstrated in relation to chemicals such as benzene. From a public health and regulatory perspective another complicating factor is that chemical exposures may result from a range of different sources. For example, benzene—a known carcinogen—is widely used as an industrial solvent in the chemical and drug industries as well as an additive in petrol. Hazardous chemicals not only originate from sources inside and outside the workplace but may also be carried into or out of the workplace via the air (dust, fumes and particulates), water supply or discharge, via inadequate waste disposal and as residues in plants and animals (including humans). In some cases the impact occurs as a result of a catastrophic incident, such as the leaking of methyl isocyanate at Union Carbide's Bhopal plant in 1984 where the cumulative death toll now exceeds 10 000 persons (*New York Times*, 15 January 1997). More often, profound but insidious effects of workplace emissions on community health are revealed by epidemiological studies or by chance incidents, as in the late 1980s when the closure of the steel mill at Provo Utah due to a strike was associated with an over 60% drop in the number of children being hospitalised for lung complaints (*New York Times*, 21 January 1997).

Overall, far less is known about the extent of health problems due to chemical exposure than is the case with occupational injuries (or at least those caused by strains, sprains, slips, falls, hitting or being hit by objects, lacerations or contact with moving machinery). While a significant proportion of workplace injuries result in workers' compensation claims—a prime source of official OHS statistics in many countries—the overwhelming majority of diseases due to chemical exposure at work do not result in a workers' compensation claim. The complexity of multiple exposures (and multiple exposure sources), the problem of measuring the effects of low-dosage exposures and the long gestation period before some diseases manifest themselves (by which time workers may have changed their occupation) make it difficult to identify the number of workers whose health has been affected by exposure to chemicals.

There are few studies that try to track chemical exposures in an array of work-places. One such study undertaken in Denmark identified 13 000 different chemical products, including 36 substances with chronic toxic effects (7 were carcinogens, 17 were reproductive toxicants, 12 were allergens and 18 were neurotoxins) to which a large number of workers were exposed. Those industries found to have the highest number of exposure events were fabricated metal manufacturing, personal services, cleaning and hairdressing (Brandorff et al., 1995: 454–63). Animal-based research into the carcinogenic properties of particular chemicals is an expensive, slow and not always conclusive process. At best, it provides evidence on a small number of chemicals among a much greater pool of potentially hazardous candidates. A number of chemicals identified as carcinogens, such as sulphuric acid, vinyl chloride and formaldehyde, continued to be in widespread industrial use for many years if not up to the present, highlighting the limitations of reactive regulation (see chapter 7).

Nevertheless, there is sufficient evidence to indicate that exposure to chemicals represents a significant workplace hazard. In Australia, Winder and Lewis (cited in Industry Commission, Vol. II, 1995: 25) estimated that about 1230 cancer deaths each year are the result of occupational exposure to chemicals. Serious cancers induced by chemical exposure represent only the tip of the iceberg of health effects associated with chemicals in the workplace. Potentially harmful chemicals are present in virtually every workplace, including air-conditioned offices where they can be found in cleaning fluids, the inks and solvents used in photocopiers, and correcting fluids/liquid paper to name but a few locations. Much research remains to be done with regard to the range of chemicals to which workers in particular industries or occupations are exposed.

Other hazardous substances

Aside from chemicals there are a range of other hazardous substances, including some minerals (such as cadmium, chromium, lead, manganese, beryllium, phosphorus, arsenic and mercury); mineral fibres (most notably asbestos but also artificial mineral fibres); coal, oil and petroleum; organic and inorganic dusts and other airborne pollutants; and biologically infectious agents (such as Q fever, brucellosis, hepatitis, HIV, SARS and various flu strains). Exposure to these substances varies widely across industry and time. For example, animal pathogens such as Q fever and brucellosis are a concern for abattoir workers and others in the livestock industry while exposure to blood-borne infections (via percutaneous injuries, contact with mucous, and broken skin or bites) is a serious hazard for healthcare workers. In 2004 the National Institute for Occupational Safety and Health (NIOSH, 2004: 41) in the US estimated that there were up to 800000 percutaneous injuries (injuries through the skin with contaminated sharps such as needles and scalpels) annually to healthcare workers (with average risk of infection being 0.3% for HIV and 6 to 30% for hepatitis B). At the other extreme, pandemic strains of flu may affect large numbers of workers across a range of industries. In this context work becomes hazardous because the congregation of persons in workplaces can facilitate infection and transmission of the disease to wider sections of the community.

As is the case with chemicals, our knowledge of exposure to other hazardous substances in particular industries and workplaces is limited and often lags behind changes in workplaces and production processes. As with chemicals, identifying the extent to which diseases are the result of work-related exposures to hazardous substances is often difficult, except where the work exposure overwhelms all other possibilities. Asbestos is the leading cause of malignant mesothelioma, which currently causes the death of more Australians through work-related exposures than any other occupational disease and is also a major source of work-related disease fatalities in the US and other countries (NIOSH, 2004: 149). A recent epidemiological study (dos Santos Antao et al., 2009: 335–8) found a clear association between asbestos consumption in the US and deaths from asbestosis. Given the long gestation period before the onset of disease the study found that while asbestos consumption had declined rapidly after 1973, asbestosis-related deaths would average around 1290 a year until 2027 and a rapid decline in deaths could not be expected within 10 to 15 years (dos Santos Antao et al., 2009: 335). However, such unambiguous and well-documented connections (in terms of the

Australian mesothelioma register and the like) are exceptional. In poor or developing countries like India recognition/action is lacking even with regard to well-known hazards like asbestos (EMCONET, 2007; Allen and Kazan-Allen, 2008). Even in rich and developed countries it is very likely that an unknown number of diseases associated with work-related exposure to hazardous substances go unrecorded.

As with chemicals, technological innovations can introduce new and potentially hazardous substances. Perhaps the best known recent examples are nanotechnology—engineering at an atomic or molecular scale to produce new materials and production processes—and the genetic modification of plants and animals. As with chemicals (and nanotechnology may result in new chemicals), the introduction of products, materials, plants, animals and processes occurs without stringent vetting (or adoption of the precautionary principle) with regard to their health effects, either in terms of workers or the broader communities. Very little research has been undertaken with regard to their health effects (both short- and long-term, latency periods and the like) although it has been estimated that two million workers will be exposed to nanotechnology in the next 15 years (Schulte et al., 2008, cited in Albin et al., 2009: 3). Nor has there been an assessment of the adequacy of current laws and regulations, although nano-technology is beginning to attract the attention of OHS professionals and regulators (Goldsmith, 2007).

Changes in technology can also affect exposure to harmful biological agents. An obvious example is legionnaires disease, a potentially lethal bacteria found in poorly maintained air conditioning units, first identified in the late 1970s (after an outbreak killed 22 people and hospitalised 130 others attending an American Legion convention in Philadelphia). Retrospective analysis later revealed there had been misdiagnosed outbreaks since the 1940s when air conditioning was first introduced (McDade et al., 1979: 659–61). Bacteria and viruses are also evolving or being redistributed due to changes in climate, population movements, travel vectors and the like. This process can be seen in the emergence of HIV and of different forms of hepatitis, each posing distinct occupational as well as public health hazards (Stevens and Coyle, 2000). In Australia, climatic change may shift the areas of exposure to Ross River fever and dengue fever further south. Recent developments in relation to the potentially fatal hendra virus indicate the scope for a new threat to emerge as the disease shifted from native animals to domesticated animals (in this case horses) and from there to occupational groups in contact with the latter, such as horse trainers and veterinary surgeons (*CCH OHS Alert*, 14 July 2008).

At the same time, there is longstanding awareness of specific hazardous substances, some stretching back into ancient times as in the case of lead (used among things as a protective cover on the bottom of ships). An early instance of occupational poisoning arose from the use of mercury compounds to convert animal fur to felt for hats and gave rise to the phrase 'mad as a hatter' (Waldron, 1990: 18, 21). Inorganic and organic mercury compounds are still used in a wide range of industrial processes despite the well-documented health effects including acute and chronic poisoning, neurological effects and erethism (Waldron, 1990: 18–23). Some occupation-related infectious diseases are also longstanding such as anthrax in workers exposed to diseased sheep.

As with chemicals, these hazardous substances are found in the workplace in a number of different forms (dusts, fumes, mists, gases, fluids and solid matter) and worker exposure may occur in a number of different ways including inhalation, ingestion and contact with the skin. The predominant methods of exposure for any particular substance will depend on the physical properties of the substance and the specific characteristics of work process and working environment. For example, for workers involved in manufacturing, welding and tanning operations using chromium, exposure will largely occur via airborne fumes, dusts and mists.

Again, as with chemicals, these substances can harm health through a variety of mechanisms acting in isolation or simultaneously. These mechanisms include toxicity, corrosive properties, the capacity to act as irritants or sensitisers, and flammability or explosive characteristics. For example, quite apart from its volatility, long-term exposure to respirable coal dust is associated with a series of diseases including pneumoconiosis, progressive massive fibrosis and chronic obstructive pulmonary disease.

Examples of toxic minerals include arsenic, cadmium, mercury and lead. Exposure to these substances may result in either acute or chronic poisoning. Acute cadmium poisoning can lead to severe nausea and continuous vomiting, diarrhoea, shock and collapse, while chronic poisoning may be associated with fatigue, weight loss, pain, nausea and mild hypochromic anaemia (Waldron, 1990: 24). Health effects will also be influenced by whether exposure to an organic or inorganic form of the material occurs. Symptoms of inorganic lead poisoning include abdominal pain, constipation, vomiting, asthenia, psychological symptoms and diarrhoea, while symptoms of organic poisoning include disturbed sleep, nausea, anorexia, vomiting, vertigo and headaches, muscular weakness, weight loss, tremors, diarrhoea, abdominal pain and hyperexcitability (Waldron, 1990: 15).

Stone/silica, coal, mineral, and organic dusts (such as wheat and soya bean dust encountered by silo workers, pollens and fungal spores) may act as irritants, affecting the skin or the respiratory system and causing a range of health problems including dermatitis, skin ulceration, bronchitis, emphysema, allergic alveolitis, occupational asthma and various types of cancer (Bardana, 2008). Overall, dust composed of inorganic or organic material represents a major occupational health hazard. Crystalline silica is the second most common mineral in the earth's crust and those workers at risk of contracting silicosis and other lung diseases from fine airborne particles of silica include construction workers, miners, sandblasters and foundry workers. Prior to the 1920s (and the introduction of stringent regulatory controls and changed work practices including the use of wet drills) silicosis was responsible for a high incidence of death and disablement among miners, including thousands of coal and metalliferous miners in Australia. In the early 1930s at least 500 (and perhaps as many as 1500) mainly black construction workers died of acute silicosis while engaged in tunnelling through almost pure silica at the Gauley Bridge hydroelectric project in West Virginia—perhaps the worst single occupational health disaster in US history. The company responsible (a subsidiary of Union Carbide) disregarded approved prevention methods and workers complaining of ill health were misled by company officials and doctors (see Rosner and Markowitz, 1991: 96–8). Despite improved work practices, protection devices and more stringent legislation, silica remains a major occupational health risk. In 1996 the IARC reclassified crystalline silica, moving it from the probable carcinogen group (2A) to the known human carcinogen group (1) on the basis of a large number of epidemiological studies. More recently, a report by the US Centers for Disease Control (2008: 771–5) noted that while there had been a decline in the number of silicosis-related deaths between 1968 and 2005 an increased proportion of deaths among younger adults pointed to the need for targeted prevention programs.

The health effects of dust exposure depend on the physical and chemical properties of the dust, particle size and shape, the amount of airborne dust and the length of exposure. In many working situations a number of hazardous materials will be present, such as the combination of silica dust and the carcinogen radon present in uranium mines (Waldron, 1990: 139 and Roscoe et al., 1995: 535–40). In Australia, Canada and other countries with significant timber/timber product industries a large number of workers are exposed to wood dusts containing chemicals and micro-organisms which are potentially antigenic, irritant and carcinogenic (*Worksafe Research Update*, April 1996). Grain dusts also represent a major risk factor in Australia and Canada. Coal, oil, natural gas and petroleum are all flammable and potentially explosive. The mining of coal results in the release of methane and coal dust, both of which are highly volatile, as well as dangerous levels of hydrogen in some mining regions (as in the central Queensland coalfields). Under certain conditions coal may spontaneously combust. The methane released from other organic material including animal waste and garbage can also pose a risk of fire and explosion.

As already noted, contact with certain living organisms may also present an occupational health risk. Some workers face a direct threat from animal contact including dog attacks on delivery workers, shark attacks on commercial divers, lacerations from fish spikes among fishermen and the poisonous bites of snakes and other animals on rural workers. In far more instances the risk is related to bacterial, fungal or viral biological agents. The temperature and humidity of the working environment, as well as practices in relation to cleaning and changing rooms, will influence the risk posed by fungal agents such as tinea, which are a major source of discomfort if not a life-threatening illness. Sources of contact with bacterial or viral agents include diseased animals, meat and vegetable matter, waste materials or the atmosphere of the workplace as in the case of legionnaires disease. Infectious diseases may be transmitted to workers from animals they are working with, as in the case of vets and abattoir workers contracting brucellosis or Q fever and occupational psittacosis among those working with birds. In addition to those working with animals, occupational disease can also be associated with the presence of animals (such as insects, rodents, birds, bats or other mammals) in or near the workplace. Those handling waste material including garbage and sewage risk both low-level infections and more serious diseases such as hepatitis (De Serres, 1995: 505–7).

Contact with other humans can also pose infection risks, including contact with body fluids among medical and mortuary workers and the risks of infection encountered by childcare workers.

In Australia, the US and other advanced industrial countries governments have moved relatively promptly to address hepatitis and HIV by issuing policies and workplace procedures (Stevens and Coyle, 2000). This is in marked contrast to some chemicals and other hazardous substances to which a far larger number of workers are exposed. In part the more rapid response to HIV was spurred by the potentially catastrophic consequences of AIDS, especially in the context of emerging evidence on high-risk work practices and the prevalence of needle-stick injuries in the healthcare industry, the resilience of the virus in deceased bodies, and the additional hazards posed in emergency situations, needle exchange/drug control centres and prisons. However, variations in the speed and level of government response to different infectious diseases are apparent. These differences are not simply the product of objective assessments of evidence as to relative levels of risk. They also reflect the degree of public attention given to the particular disease and the social, industrial and political influence of particular lobby groups representing workers (compare doctors to mortuary workers) or other interested parties (compare those at risk to AIDS with those at risk to hepatitis). The role of interest groups has led to significantly different outcomes in terms of balancing concerns for individual rights with specific occupational health risks and more general public health considerations.

Like chemicals, specific substances may entail multiple hazards. Exposure to asbestos fibres can result not only in scarring of the lung tissue and associated effects on the heart but also various types of cancer including mesothelioma (a cancer of the sac lining the chest). The presence of coal dust may entail not only a risk of silicosis for workers but can be highly flammable—even in the absence of methane—and any resulting fire may also produce toxic gases (Bunch, 1981: 1–7). Health problems associated with petroleum include those related to the lead content of some petroleum products, its corrosive effects and evidence indicating it is carcinogenic. In addition, as just implied, these hazards may act in combination with other hazards including those mentioned already and others we will discuss below. For instance, mechanisation has increased the array of combustible materials found in coal mines and created new problems in terms of ventilation and noise control.

Like chemical hazards, some of the hazards we are concerned with here may be both insidious and capable of affecting the health of non-workers who visit or reside near the workplace, or use its products. Examples include the mercury poisoning at Minamata in Japan in the 1950s and 1960s, legionnaires disease and a 1996 outbreak of Q fever in the rural town of Rollshausen in the state of Hessen, Germany. In the case of specific infectious agents such as HIV, complex two-way patterns of transmission can occur between workers and other persons (as in a recent case in France where a surgeon who acquired HIV occupationally subsequently transmitted it to a patient during an operation). The history of lead mining/smelting at Port Pirie in South Australia and at Mount Isa in Queensland illustrates the effects of a specific hazard upon an entire community and the belated and inadequate regulatory responses where medical evidence and health considerations were compromised by industry-complicit government (Gillespie, 1990).

Asbestos also illustrates the complex interplay of medical, legal and sociopolitical factors which shape responses to an occupational hazard (see Castleman, 1990; McCulloch and Tweedale, 2008). Asbestos also illustrates the profound health consequences of belated regulatory intervention. As with some hazardous chemicals discussed earlier there was by no means a close connection between knowledge of the health effects of asbestos and the introduction of regulatory controls. Reference to the health hazards associated with exposure to asbestos can be traced back over 2000 years. Canadian insurance companies refused to provide cover for asbestos workers as early as 1904. From the 1930s medical evidence based on case histories began to firmly establish the health risks associated with asbestos, a process aided by Doll's (1955: 81–6) study of lung cancer mortality among asbestos workers. Yet in the same period, as evidence as to its hazardous properties mounted so did asbestos production and usage (as a fire retardant material in shipbuilding, construction, vehicle brake pads and a wide range of other products). In Australia asbestos tailings were dumped on what later became housing developments, used in gardens and as road fill in asbestos mine communities like Wittenoom and Barulgil. Regulatory controls were not introduced until the 1970s. Even then exposure standards lagged behind those recommended internationally, and major companies using asbestos sought to minimise the risks (by devices such as debating safe exposure limits, highlighting that many asbestos workers were at risk from smoking and pointing to the differential risk associated with particular types of asbestos). By 1990 research had firmly linked white asbestos—supposedly the safest type—to mesothelioma and it was internationally recognised that there was no safe level of exposure. This led to a progressive banning of its production and use, though not in Canada and a number of developing countries.

The belated response in terms of compensating victims meant that the toll only began to gain much official recognition in Australia from the late 1970s. While asbestos usage peaked in the mid-1970s the long gestation period (up to 40 years) of some diseases associated with asbestos (notably mesothelioma) meant that the annual death toll kept rising and the annual mesothelioma death toll did not peak until 2004 (at 545 deaths). The Australian National Mesothelioma Register operated since 1980 revealed that mesothelioma alone accounted for about 16% of deaths due to workplace exposures to hazardous substances and that the annual age-standardised death rate remained relatively stable, ranging between 2.1 and 2.7 (being 2.3 in 2006 when 486 deaths were reported; Safework Australia, 2009: 3). These calculations do not include asbestosis or other types of cancer associated with exposure to asbestos, including some which specifically affect women such as ovarian cancer (Acheson et al., 1982: 344–8).

In France the number of 'recognised' cases of asbestos-related occupational diseases rose rapidly from the early 1970s onwards. By 1996 it was estimated that the annual death toll from asbestos-related cancers had reached 1950 (750 deaths being due to mesothelioma and 1200 due to lung cancer; see Zerbib, 1996: 3–4).

Much remains to be learnt about the extent of the exposure to hazardous substances in the workplace. As in the case of occupationally induced cancer already discussed, we have limited information on a whole range of health effects and the workers/workplaces most at risk of exposure. On occasion, particular surveillance programs are initiated, such as the surveillance of work-related occupational respiratory disease (SWORD) project in the UK where specialists in occupational and respiratory medicine have been encouraged to report new cases of occupational respiratory disease. The project identified almost 9000 new cases of occupational respiratory disease between 1989 and 1992, about half of which were of long latency (Meredith and McDonald, 1994: 183–9). However, despite a number of efforts examined below there is nothing approaching systematic and comprehensive surveillance of workplace exposures to hazardous substances. As with chemicals, the proliferation of new hazardous substances in the workplace appears to outstrip both research on their health effects and the introduction of new regulatory controls.

Work organisation and the psychosocial work environment

Over the past 20 years there has been a growing recognition that the way work is organised, or what is often referred to as the psychosocial work environment, affects the health and wellbeing of workers. Health and safety problems arise not only from physical, chemical and other features of the working environment already mentioned. The workplace—whether it be a truck, a factory, an office or whatever—and the work process—whether it be moving cargo with a truck, producing goods in a factory, providing information services from an office or whatever—entail a complex set of socially constructed or arranged physical features and physical, chemical, social and individual interactions. The presence of a particular chemical or machine in the workplace and the associated risk is mediated by an often long and complex web of human decisions—decisions by factory and equipment designers, manufacturers, employers, managers, regulators and a host of others. Even if all hazardous substances and dangerous physical agents could be removed from the workplace this would not eliminate OHS hazards. The way the workplace is organised can be a significant source of OHS problems.

Work and organisational psychologists were among the first to recognise a significant and complex relationship between the working environment and the health and wellbeing of workers, coining the term psychosocial work environment, which has been widely adopted (Thylefors, 2009: 21–3). At the same time, the development needs to be seen in the context of legislative developments and the input of other researchers (such as sociologists and disaster researchers) that gave greater recognition to organisational sources of health and safety hazards. When the first edition of our book was published (1991) the inclusion of a section on work organisation was by no means the norm for an OHS book and we only had a limited range of sources to draw on. Now there is extensive research dealing with this area and a growing—if still limited and sometimes disputed—recognition of its importance among government agencies, employers, unions and OHS professionals. To some extent this trend represents a response to changes in work organisation over the past 20 years, including the development of more intensive work systems—some of which are discussed below. However, we would argue both that the organisation of work (including production and labour management regimes) has undergone significant changes in the past (Johansson and Abrahamsson, 2009) and that it was always important in terms of OHS. The problem was a failure to investigate or acknowledge these aspects until comparatively recently. Thus, while scientific management (coined by Frederick Taylor) and Fordism were developed in the early twentieth century, their effects on OHS have only been the subject of systematic research comparatively recently. Similarly, while recent research increasingly recognises that social processes (inside and outside the workplace) linked to gender, age and ethnicity/foreign worker status can affect OHS outcomes, these demographic features of the workforce, and the distinctive social processes or vulnerabilities associated with them, are not new.

Organisational and workforce characteristics that can affect OHS include:

- organisation size, resources, stability/employment security and economic characteristics of the industry or general business cycles
- organisation induction, training and promotion systems, leave provisions, childcare facilities and sexual harassment programs
- management commitment to OHS, structures, supervisory and discipline systems
- the arrangement of work processes and task structures including the interface between workers and machinery and changes in technology
- payment, reward and incentive systems
- hours of work and shift arrangements
- staffing levels, workload and production or service delivery pressures
- workforce age, gender, ethnicity, experience, language skills, literacy and training
- union involvement and role
- the use of outsourcing/subcontracting
- the regulatory regimes dealing with employment and OHS and their implementation
- healthcare infrastructure and policies.

In practice these characteristics do not operate independently of physical, ergonomic or chemical aspects of the workplace. For example, staffing levels/workloads or the use of subcontractors/agency workers can affect the extent and distribution of manual handling tasks, exposure to hazardous substances (including who is exposed) and compliance with employer rules or other controls relating to exposure to temperature extremes or undesirable sound. Similarly, downsizing has been linked to psychotropic drug use (Kivimaki et al., 2007). It is worth noting in passing that recent research on the OHS effects of work reorganisation may be both informed by and provide a context for earlier research on the increased injury risk of workers new to the job and linking trends in OHS outcomes to business/production cycles (Fabiano et al., 1995).

As with chemicals and physical hazards, work organisation can have multiple health effects that may only be identified by sustained and focused research. For example, shiftwork (including overtime and extended shifts) is one of the most heavily investigated aspects of work organisation and has been linked to an array of health problems (Caruso et al., 2004; Albertsen et al., 2007). Yet it is only comparatively recently that the International Agency for Research on Cancer labelled shiftwork involving circadian disruption as a probable (2A) carcinogen to humans (Straif et al., 2007). The organisation of work—including excessive or irregular hours—can also impact on the health and wellbeing of those outside the workplace, especially family members (see, for example, Miller and Han, 2008 and chapter 6).

There is also a need to recognise power, conflict and informal groups, rules and interactions within organisations and the wider society that shape work (Thylefors, 2009). In this regard systematic global differences need to be recognised such as the particular health effects of unemployment, informal work (i.e. work not subject to regulatory controls), child labour and the poor living conditions/urban settings found in many poor countries (Barten et al., 2008; Giatti et al., 2008; Benach and Muntaner, 2009). Further, there are elaborate models of how organisational factors affect worker health, including imbalances in demand and control or effort and reward at work developed by Robert Karasek and Johannes Siegrist respectively (see chapter 5). Chapters 2 to 6 examine in more detail how the link between work organisation and occupational illness and injury has been investigated by ergonomists, epidemiologists, psychologists, sociologists and others. Their findings have yielded important though often partial insights.

Without pre-empting what is to follow in later chapters, it is important to demonstrate how fundamental work organisation is to a meaningful understanding of OHS as well as how the level of analysis or perspective adopted can shape this understanding. A good illustration of this point is body-stressing injuries—sprains and strains—a very significant workplace hazard (commonly the biggest single cause of injury in a workplace) that has not be discussed so far. Body stressing arises from a complex array of factors at work but important contributing factors include workplace and equipment design and layout, the organisation of tasks and production/service delivery flows, staffing and effort levels—all factors involving a significant element of human decision making. The dominant discipline to have addressed this area has been ergonomics. Ergonomics is primarily concerned with the physiological loads associated with particular tasks, including the relationship of workers to tools, machinery or equipment, although account is also taken of psychological factors (such as error rates) and comfort. For example, in assessing the risk of injury or disease from manual handling tasks, ergonomists will give attention to immediate load, the cumulative load, frequency and 'creep' factors. Immediate load consists of the weight of the object to be lifted (and was the only basis for much early legislative intervention). Cumulative load involves a consideration of where an object is placed before lifting, where it is going to be lifted to, how frequently objects are lifted and the static load placed on the body while maintaining posture. Lifting objects held at a distance or by bending or twisting entails an additional risk of sustaining an injury. With regard to frequency of load it has been found that a worker who is regularly moving is less at risk than is a stationary worker (providing the weight is within acceptable limits). Maintained postures can be hazardous as in the case of data entry workers whose risk of contracting RSI is exacerbated by the fact that their arms are stationary. Creep factors recognise that although the body-bearing load is important, incremental increases in added load can have exponential effects on back damage. No pain or other indication of damage to the spine may appear until after age 35, yet the damage may be permanent. Further, vibration—a hazard discussed earlier—exacerbates degeneration markedly.

If jobs require risk-taking movements, ergonomists have argued that workers should be protected in every way possible based on a close examination of all their job tasks. For example, ambulance officers are at risk of back injury because of the frequency and cumulative loads involved when people are being rescued after vehicle collisions. Typical preventative measures include improved seating in ambulances, ensuring officers get out of their vehicles at least every hour and ensuring all benches are at the correct height. The 'correct' height, of course, varies according to the size of the worker. While the ergonomic approach has value it represents only a partial understanding of the problem. In practice, the ergonomic approach to manual handling operates within covert organisational constraints relating to job structure, performance levels and authority. For ambulance workers (like nurses and other healthcare workers) staffing levels and management efforts to reduce costs/intensify work often influence work practices (for example, requiring ambulances to remain near areas of known demand rather than returning to base where workers can rest). In a similar vein, the work context and exposure to manual handling and other hazards can differ significantly for a nurse working in a large hospital or a nursing home or in a homecare setting. Though in the same industry, these workplaces often differ substantially in terms of management, resourcing and work practices; whether the nurse concerned is a union member and able to raise/resolve problems; and the degree of regulatory oversight. In contrast to ergonomists, psychologists and sociologists do take more explicit account of organisational factors. But as demonstrated in later chapters the organisational factors considered by psychologists are still typically confined and tend to ignore a number just mentioned (such as staffing levels). Sociologists do pick up wider organisational and social influences but the number contributing to the field of OHS remains relatively small. In sum, while ergonomics has made a significant contribution to dealing with body-stressing injuries it represents a partial perspective that entails a narrow and inadequate consideration of work organisation.

The passing references just made to work intensification, unions and regulation raise another salient point. Earlier parts of this chapter have referred to changes in hazard exposure over times such as the proliferation of chemicals used by industry. It is equally important to acknowledge significant changes to the organisation of work over time. A number of critical shifts involved a close interplay with new technologies. For example, the rise of a professional management class, the 'scientific management' concept of engineer Frederick Taylor and its extension to assembly-line based 'Fordism' by Henry Ford, harnessed wage labour and mechanisation to secure mass production. These principles then extended to the growing service sector (major fast food chains are commonly exemplars of 'Fordism'). Scientific management and Fordism both entailed a particular approach to labour management including new means of work intensification that had, among other things, consequences for OHS. Similarly, the more recent IT revolution has facilitated new forms of production and work organisation (for example, enhanced communication has facilitated the growth of complex logistics and elaborate subcontracting-based supply chains). At the same time, methods of intensifying work such as 'lean production' and business process re-engineering are being introduced, discarded, revised and revived under new labels on an ongoing basis.

It is beyond the scope of this book to discuss these changes or their consequences for OHS in detail (for an examination of production system changes and technology/ work interfaces from an OHS perspective, see Johansson et al., 2009; Osvlander and Ulfvengrenl, 2009). However, it is critical to recognise their significance for OHS. For example, within industrialised countries the advances in mechanisation/automation and labour-saving forms of manufacturing, offshoring to developing countries, and the growth of service industries has substantially altered the industry workforce mix and exposure to work-related hazards over the past 50 years (albeit the effects do not amount to a simple reduction in hazard exposure; see Ostry et al., 2000a & b). Berggren (1993) labelled lean production as 'management by stress', linking it to an increase in manual handling injuries. Wright and Lund (1998: 6) found the introduction of engineered standards in the grocery warehousing industry in Australia and the US lifted work rates (by 30% or more) to levels that significantly increased the risk of manual handling injuries and which two NIOSH studies found were unsustainable. The growth of performance payment systems has also been linked to health problems (Yeh et al., 2009). Whether they are seen as an extension of Taylorism or something new these work methods increased demands on workers but did not provide them with the level of autonomy necessary to safeguard their safety.

Further, new technologies (like mobile phones and electronic forms of worker/ performance monitoring) can introduce new hazards and increasingly complex tech- nologies and work systems can also pose serious challenges to OHS. History shows that even safety-based technologies or innovations do not always lead to an unambiguous improvement in OHS. The introduction of the Davy Safety Lamp into British coal mines in the nineteenth century actually led to the death of more miners because it enabled the opening up of areas hitherto considered too dangerous to work with naked flame lights (Albury and Schwartz, 1983: 362–4). Other examples of complex technology/work interfaces such as managing high-hazard workplaces are examined later in the book.

Finally, consideration of work organisation cannot be disembodied from the societal context, including the influence of institutions such as unions and regulation as well as cyclic shifts in the level of economic activity and employment. Historically, the combination of union campaigns, allied social movements (like anti-sweating leagues) and regulation wrought changes to work arrangements with significant implications for OHS, including the abolition of child labour; minimum wages and hours laws; pension/ social security/unemployment benefits and workers' compensation; and OHS laws (see chapters 7 and 9). As noted in the introduction to this chapter the importance of this context is demonstrated when comparisons are made between developed countries today and a century ago or between developed and developing countries today. In both cases limited and poorly enforced regulation/social protection and limited union presence was/is associated with the exploitation of child or bonded labour, excessive hours of work and inadequate diet, which have in turn a critical impact on worker health and wellbeing (EMCONET, 2007).

Within particular societies we may identify other features which impact on OHS, including patriarchy and the level of gender or minority group discrimination (based on race, caste or ethnicity). Another differentiating feature of particular countries may relate to the role occupied by the state and political regimes (affecting accountability, the use of coercion and levels of corruption), the power of specific interest groups and dominant social values. For example, it is hardly surprising that in a gun-ridden society such as the US homicide has become a major source of death in the workplace. At the same time, in some poor countries the simple act of raising an issue like OHS in the workplace or representing workers through a union is hazardous, regularly resulting in the beating, disappearance or murder of activists. Finally, both country-specific and global shifts in the level of economic activity can alter working conditions in ways that can affect OHS. For example, major downturns increase unemployment, job insecurity and the number of vulnerable jobs as well as influencing the willingness or capacity of workers, unions, employers and regulators to report or address OHS problems. The Great Depression of the 1930s brought with it a serious period of setback for OHS and a recent ILO (2009) report identified disturbing trends in work quality following the onset of a global recession in 2007.

A related set of work-related hazards that has assumed growing importance in recent years and illustrates both the role of psychosocial factors and the complex social interactions just discussed is occupational violence, bullying and harassment. (Similar points could be made with regard to the broader notion of work-related stress but this is examined in chapter 5.) Adopting a broad definition that encompasses abuse and harassment as well as physical assault, occupational violence could be used as a rubric term to incorporate the terms just described. It is an extremely complex phenomenon involving a wide range of causal factors and taking a number of distinct forms (including robbery, domestic/family violence transposed to the workplace, customer/client-initiated violence and violence among workers or with managers). While there is no universally accepted definition, most researchers view occupational violence as an array of behaviour at work including verbal abuse, threats, physical violence, sexual harassment, 'activities that create an environment of fear', stalking, bullying or behaviour that leads to stress or avoidance behaviour by the victim.

What all entail is a level of threatening or demeaning behaviour directed towards an individual or group by other individuals or groups at work and, in many (though not all) instances, involves a pattern of activity (rather than isolated acts) that can escalate over time. It can involve unwelcome physical interaction (shouting in one's face and touching), actual physical assault, threatened or implied physical violence as well as a range of emotional assaults on a worker's wellbeing (including the use of anger, threats, abuse, ridicule, being sent unwelcome emails/attachments, social exclusion and 'practical jokes'). It should be noted that only a fraction of this activity or its impacts on the health, safety and wellbeing of workers will find its way into workers' compensation data or official OHS statistics even though a growing body of research indicates occupational violence is a widespread phenomenon found in many different industries and with serious health consequences (Mayhew et al. 2004; Rospenda et al., 2005, 2009; Shannon et al., 2007; Nielsen et al., 2009). The perpetrators may be fellow workers, supervisors/managers, customers/clients, criminals or members of the public.

As just implied, occupational violence can take on a diverse array of forms and available research indicates its origins and incidence are also shaped by an equally diverse array of factors. In some cases there is a direct link between the type of violence and the type of work undertaken and even its geographic location. For example, robbery-related violence is targeted towards retail and other establishments handling money (targets have shifted in response to improved security by banks and other financial institutions) and can be worst in deprived urban areas (especially those where drug use is high). There is also evidence that particular types of work arrangements and changes to work organisation can affect the incidence of violence. For example, a number of studies have identified a link between downsizing/inadequate staffing, employment status and lean management regimes (including the use of JIT that increases pressures on transport workers) and bullying behaviour by supervisors or aggressive behaviour on the part of customers, patients or clients (Snyder, 1994; Mayhew and Quinlan, 2000, 2002; LaMontagne et al., 2009). These may combine with other factors, such as ethnicity and gender, as in the case of home-based female garment workers whose vulnerability to aggressive behaviour from 'middlemen' results from supply-chain pressures, their isolation (at home), their gender (middlemen who give out work to them are predominantly male) and their status as recently arrived immigrants (Mayhew and Quinlan, 1999).

Gender is also an important influence, in terms of occupation (and exposure to higher-risk activities), in terms of responses to aggressive behaviour, and—most significantly—in terms of vulnerability/targeting. Unwanted sexual advances and harassment are overwhelmingly directed at women, who also appear over-represented in more generalised bullying, harassment and intimidation—a reflection of broader gender relationships in society and ongoing patriarchy within the workplace (Rospenda et al., 1998; Richman et al., 1999; LaMontagne et al., 2009). As with other hazards, bullying and harassment can interact with other hazards and can also have cascading health effects by affecting behavioural change. For example, a US study by Rospenda et al. (2005) found sexual harassment and generalised workplace harassment were associated with an increased odds ratio of illness, injury and assault. Further, harassment and abuse can lead not only to psychological distress but also to increased alcohol consumption.

It is likely differences (and trends over time) in the extent of patriarchy and social power, the structure of and changes to work arrangements together with the level of gun ownership (already discussed), societal violence and the regulatory response within particular societies will influence the pattern and incidence of harassment, intimidation and other forms of occupational violence. However, much more comparative research is required in this regard (for a comparative Norwegian study, see Nielsen et al., 2009).

The foregoing discussion has only briefly addressed the multitude of ways in which the organisation of work can interact with OHS. The key point to be made is that organisational factors constitute a significant source of OHS problems, both in isolation and as they interact with other hazards. Work organisation and its interaction with institutional and regulatory apparatuses will be examined in more detail in later chapters.

Changes to labour markets, work organisation and workforce demographics

As already indicated the array of workplace hazards and those exposed to them have undergone significant changes over time. A number of especially significant changes have occurred since the 1970s, affecting not only Australia and New Zealand but most other countries. As we will endeavour to show, recognition of changing workforce characteristics is critical to understanding OHS problems. The discussion here also sets a context for issues and ideas examined in later chapters. A number of major changes and evidence pertaining to them will be addressed in turn.

Changes to industry mix and work organisation

As in other developed countries, over the past 50 years changing patterns of employment have altered where most Australians and New Zealanders work. In general terms, the proportion of the Australian workforce employed in industries/sectors like mining, manufacturing, agriculture and rural activities has declined while there has been a corresponding growth in the service sector such as accommodation and food services, education and training, healthcare and finance, insurance and administration. The survey undertaken for Australia@Work in 2007 as well as Australian Bureau of Statistics data (van Wanrooy et al., 2007: 24) indicated that the five sectors of manufacturing, retailing, education/training, construction and healthcare each employed about 9 to 10% of the workforce while the combination of mining and agriculture, forestry and fishing accounted for less than 5% of the employed workforce. Changes to business and employment practices have wrought significant changes to work organisation over the past 30 years that evidence suggests can entail serious challenges to OHS. While these changes often originated in business strategies (such as lean production, outsourcing/offshoring and business process re-engineering), they were both facilitated and translated into the public sector through changes to industrial relations/social security legislation and governments pursuing analogous measures (such as new public sector management) under the broader influence of neo-liberal policies.

Among the most significant changes affecting work organisation were:
- Often-repeated rounds of restructuring/downsizing by large private and public sector employers (with consequent effects on work intensity via changes to staffing

levels/workloads, multi-tasking and the like). Downsizing has also been associated with increased hours/presenteeism and unpaid overtime.

- A decline in the proportion of the employed workforce in full-time permanent employment (especially for males) and associated increases in part-time, temporary, fixed-term and leased (agency) work.
- Outsourcing entailing elaborate national/international supply chains and growing use of (multi-tiered) subcontractors and agency workers. Outsourcing in the public sector usually results in privatisation (although privatisation may occur independently of this).
- Increased use of outsourcing/subcontracting and franchising (essentially a structured form of internal subcontracting) has led to growth of self-employment, microbusinesses and small business employers.
- Subcontracting/franchising as well as use of IT has facilitated the growth (sometimes re-emergence) of home-based work, remote, transient (e.g. short-term call centres) and telework.
- Increases in multiple job-holding (often associated with part-time and temporary work. See Louie et al., 2006).

Some of these changes are cyclical while others represent long-term structural shifts. Nevertheless, even temporary changes can impact on OHS for years to come. These changes also interact in complex ways. A number of examples illustrate this.

First, there is now an extensive body of research (Quinlan et al., 2001; Quinlan and Bohle, 2009) linking downsizing/restructuring and job insecurity to adverse health outcomes for those that keep their jobs (not to mention those that lose jobs or are left in intermittent employment). Adverse outcomes include deteriorations to physiological and psychological wellbeing, poorer work–life balance and problems of occupational violence/bullying. In a quality-filtered review of over 100 studies of job insecurity and downsizing more than 80% found OHS had been adversely affected (Quinlan and Bohle, 2009). The underlying causes of these changes require further research but include the stress arising from job insecurity, presenteeism pressures, increased workload and disorganisation due to reduced staffing levels/cost-cutting, and changes to organisational climate/management behaviour. Very few organisations undertaking restructuring have anticipated or sought to address these issues and the response of regulators has been largely limited to addressing some symptoms, most notably violence and bullying behaviour (Quinlan, 2007). There is less research into the OHS effects of privatisation (Egan et al., 2007; Ferrie et al., 2007).

Second, like many other industrialised countries, the decline in full-time permanent work and growing job insecurity in Australia and New Zealand has paralleled a significant growth in part-time and casual employment as well as short-term employment contracts over the last 25 years. The survey undertaken for Australia@Work in 2007 (van Wanrooy et al., 2007: 20) indicated that 61.1% of employees were permanent, 18.8% were casually employed and 5.2% worked under fixed-term contracts. This is broadly comparable with Australian Bureau of Statistics data and other large surveys (Louie et al., 2006). Again, reviews of international studies suggest temporary employment is associated with a number of adverse OHS outcomes including higher injury rates, although the findings are not quite as conclusive with regard to downsizing/job insecurity and outsourcing/home-based work (Quinlan et al., 2001; Virtanen et al., 2005; Benavides et al., 2006).

Third, increased use of outsourcing is a feature of most countries and elaborate subcontracting networks to secure goods and services, commonly called supply chains, operate at both the national and international level. The survey undertaken for Australia@Work in 2007 (van Wanrooy et al., 2007: 20) indicated that 14.9% of the employed workforce in Australia were self-employed (the remaining 85.1% were employees) and of this group 8.9% were contractors/subcontractors and 2.6% (or 248 771 persons) were dependent contractors. There is now substantial international evidence that subcontracting and related arrangements (such as home-based work) have significant adverse effects on OHS (Quinlan and Bohle 2008). Reasons for this include competitive pressures on subcontractors (resulting in corner-cutting, work intensification and excessive hours), disorganisation (more attenuated control systems in the workplace, under-resourced operators, having strangers on site, etc.) and undermining regulatory controls (Mayhew and Quinlan, 1997, 1999, 2006; Johnstone et al., 2001). Outsourcing of maintenance or other services has raised concerns over public health and safety in some industries such as food production/services and transport. For example, investigations by US regulators following the crash of the ValuJet airliner into the Florida Everglades in 1996 found that there had been a series of maintenance lapses within the company prior to the incident and that the company was unable to control its outside maintenance contractors (Johnstone et al., 2001). Finally, it should be noted that while small business is often studied in isolation, many small businesses are actually dependent subcontractors. Reviews of research on OHS outcomes (Salamen et al., 1993; Quinlan et al., 2001) generally indicate that small businesses (not synonymous with small workplaces which may belong to a large business) experience worse OHS outcomes. This is usually attributed to a combination of logistical constraints, poor OHS organisation and ignorance. Other relevant considerations include industry concentration, type of injury and offsetting reporting effects (Fabiano et al., 2004). How much the effects are also associated with the subcontracting issues is seldom explored (for an exception see Mayhew and Quinlan, 2006).

Fourth, the slow decline in average working hours has stalled or gone into reverse in recent years, especially if unpaid overtime is taken into account. Around 15 to 20% of the working populations of many advanced countries now perform shiftwork or night work and this figure has been growing since the 1970s. In a number of industries eight-hour shifts have been increasingly replaced with 12-hour shifts (have TLVs been recalibrated?). The changes mean that fatigue is re-emerging as a major OHS issue. Further, the growth of shiftwork in the context of an ageing workforce means that the adverse health effects will multiply for both individuals and the community at large (Dawson, 1996).

Fifth and finally, in many though by no means all countries there has been a shift in the locus of industrial relations towards the enterprise or workplace level as well as a decline in union density and collective bargaining/negotiation. This shift provides a context where non-unionised/weakly organised workers are less able to retain their working conditions; where the OHS and family implications of changes to payment systems, hours and production pressures are seldom considered; and where OHS risks are more likely to be individualised (Heiler, 1996, Quinlan, 1993). In both Australia and New Zealand from the 1980s there was a move away from collectivist industrial relations, as well as the role of arbitration tribunals (especially in New Zealand workers), that research indicates has had significant implications for OHS (Anderson and Quinlan, 2008; Quinlan and Johnstone, 2009). The federal Labor government's Fair Work legislation amending 'WorkChoices' laws enacted by a neo-liberal federal government has only partly addressed these issues (see chapter 9).

The changes just identified cannot be viewed in isolation. The more frequent job changes associated with downsizing and the increased use of temporary employment as well as the short-cycle tasks associated with greater use of contractors have profound implications for surveillance of exposure to hazardous substances and therefore detecting work-related disease (Thebaud Mony, 1999; Quinlan, 2005).

Changes to the population and workforce

In addition to changes in work organisation, changes to the workforce also have implications for OHS. Over the past 30 years the workforce of Australia, New Zealand and other industrialised countries has undergone a number of significant changes. Changes in general health and lifestyle can both be affected by and interact with occupational health, with an obvious example being rising levels of obesity in Australia, the US and a number of other developed countries. Reviewing this issue, Schulte et al. (2007, 2008) note that evidence suggests a complex set of interactions. Obesity may contribute to work-related injuries (such as vibration-induced injury and musculoskeletal disorders) and diseases (asthma and cardiovascular disease) but it also appears that particular work environments and work arrangements (such as long hours) contribute to obesity.

Some of the issues related to workforce and workplace change will be explored further in the chapters on work-related injury and health and disease. At this point attention will focus on three notable changes to have occurred in the last 20 years, namely increased female participation in the workforce, an ageing of the population and workforce, and increased ethnic diversity in the workforce. Each of these changes will be dealt with briefly and in turn.

Gender and increased female participation in the workforce

Evidence indicates important gender-based differences in OHS outcomes although the OHS experiences of women remain under-researched. For example, Artazcoz et al. (2007) argue classic occupational epidemiology has paid limited attention to gender issues, identifying gaps in knowledge of work-related gender inequalities in health and making recommendations as to how these might be addressed. Since World War II the level of female participation in the workforce has grown substantially in most developed countries (see table 1.1) and while women remain concentrated in a number of jobs and industries this change has also seen women moving into jobs that are traditionally male preserves (such as transport, security, police and the emergency services).

Table 1.1 New Zealand: labour market outcomes by gender and ethnicity, December 2001–06, per cent

	Female % 2001	Female % 2006	2001–06 Female change	Male % 2001	Male % 2006	2001–06 Male change
European						
Labour force participation rate	60.4	62.8	2.4	75.3	76.7	1.4
Unemployment rate	3.9	2.9	–1.0	3.9	2.6	–1.3
Maori						
Labour force participation rate	55.6	60.4	4.8	73.7	74.8	1.1
Unemployment rate	12.7	8.7	–4.0	11.9	7.3	–4.3
Pacific Peoples						
Labour force participation rate	51.3	55.2	3.9	71.2	69.7	–1.4
Unemployment rate	8.1	6.5	–1.6	10.8	6.3	–4.5
Other*						
Labour force participation rate	48.5	56.6	5.1	64.3	71.5	7.2
Unemployment rate	8.3	6.8	–1.6	9.1	5.8	–3.1

Source: Household Labour Force Survey and Income Survey, © Statistics New Zealand.

* The 'Other' ethnic group includes people who do not identify as European, Maori or Pacific Peoples.

In relation to OHS, the injuries sustained by men and women vary in both cause and mechanism. Injury rates largely reflect gendered patterns of employment across industries, occupations, employment conditions, and patterns of work, although biological and psychosocial differences may also contribute to this. For example, in the US male workers accounted for 58.7% of hours worked but 66.1% of occupational injuries and illnesses (NIOSH, 2004: 25). Hazardous industries such as agriculture and forestry, and mining and construction, and hazardous occupations (in terms of severe injuries) such as truck drivers, plumbers and construction workers are male dominated (NIOSH, 2004: 27). This helps to explain why women are far less likely to experience a fatal injury at work. Male workers were three times more likely to die as a result of contact with objects and equipment and more than twice as likely to die from exposure to harmful environments. On the other hand, women's predominance in health and retail service sector jobs helps to explain why they were far more likely to die as a result of an assault or violent act (accounting for one-third of all fatal work injuries to women in 2004; NIOSH, 2004: 51; Hoskins, 2005: 31–7).

Gender differences with regard to OHS require further detailed research. Research into downsizing/job insecurity has identified a number of gender differences (Ferrie et al., 1998b; Cheng et al., 2005) that appear to reflect, in part, different non-paid work roles (notably those in the family) and similar gender differences have also been noted in post-injury responses (Quinlan, 1996). The implications of women's concentration in particular types of work that are growing such as temporary work, remote/telework and home-based work also need to be recognised. For example, several studies have pointed to a higher incidence of sexual harassment or occupational violence among home-based workers (Mayhew and Quinlan, 1999; Barling et al., 2000) and there appear to be some parallels with the female-dominated and expanding homecare industry (Quinlan and Bohle, 2008). A recent survey of 1100 Victorian workers found that unwanted sexual advances were strongly associated with three types of work arrangement (full-time casual/temporary workers, fixed-term contract workers and self-employed workers (Lamontagne et al., 2009). Moving more workers into the home (for part or all of their working activities), into remote/temporary locations (such as short-term call centres) or into homecare settings has implications for injury and disease surveillance because such activities are often not incorporated into labour-force statistics or existing surveillance activities. More generally, the question as to whether precarious employment has different implications for women and men needs to be considered (Menendez et al., 2007). In short, the combination of shifting gender-based patterns of employment and other gender-related effects with changing patterns of work requires further investigation.

Further research is also needed into the relationship between gender and reporting injury and illness in the workplace. The large discrepancy in the reported rates of workplace disease and injury between men and women may be related to women being less inclined to report workplace-caused illnesses. In many female-dominated occupations, particularly those that are low-wage and low-skilled, women have weaker bargaining positions, are less unionised and have more precarious forms of employment. Fear of loss of employment, or a downgrade in hours is a very real barrier to reporting OHS concerns or injury. While empirically quantifying under-reporting is fraught with methodological difficulties, anecdotal evidence suggests the need for specific gender-based research in relation to OHS risks and reporting.

From a policy perspective it should be noted that there is an often complex and even potentially inconsistent relationship between laws regulating OHS, gender discrimination and sexual harassment (for an illustrative case involving lead exposure see Quinlan, 1996). A clear set of policies is needed to resolve any potential problems (Johnstone and Jones, 2006).

Increased female participation in the workforce has raised critical questions about work–life balance as working women try to fulfil both work and family commitments, including child-rearing and (for the baby boomer generation) also caring for ageing parents (a little-discussed but critical aspect of the ageing population). While it is often presumed that flexible work is family-friendly there has been little systematic research into the relationship between age, commitments outside work and the less regulated working hours of some types of flexible work. Australian employers have increasingly adopted extended work shifts and longer weekly working hours (ACIRRT, 1999). However, there is substantial evidence that long hours have negative effects on OHS, including injury rates and long-term health and wellbeing (Harrington, 1994; Smith et al., 1998; Dembe et al., 2005). Despite evidence that flexible work can involve very long hours (Bohle et al., 2004), there has been little research on the OHS effects of extended hours in flexible work. Interestingly, an Australian study found working time was not linked to injury for full-time workers but longer hours led to greater injury for part-time workers.

Work scheduling can produce significant work–life conflict and pervasive negative effects on health, family functioning, work-related attitudes and job performance (Frone, Yardley and Markel, 1997; Krausz, Sagie and Biderman, 2000). Limited evidence suggests, somewhat counter-intuitively, that casual and part-time work can increase work–life conflict and produce negative OHS effects (Bohle et al., 2004). A European study of public sector employees highlighted problems regarding inconvenient shift arrangements in flexible work. Other evidence indicates flexible work may involve longer working days, longer working weeks, more weekend work, less regular working hours and less access to flexitime (Quinlan, 1999).

Changes to youth employment and the ageing population and workforce

As in many other countries the population and workforce in Australia and New Zealand has been ageing due to sustained low fertility (and passing of the baby boomer generation) and increased life expectancy. The median age of the Australian population has increased by 5.8 years over the past two decades (ABS 3201.0, 2006: 2). It has been recognised that workforce ageing has significant implications for labour supply, labour under-utilisation, productivity and health (Wegman and McGee, 2004; Productivity Commission, 2005). For example, chronic injuries and disease among older persons inhibits workforce participation and may also make those who are working more susceptible to further injury (Schofield et al., 2008). Age also affects work ability, capacity to secure jobs following retrenchment and capacity to adapt to economic slowdowns (Sluiter, 2006; Brown, 2009).

Age-related differences in OHS outcomes have long been recognised with regard to male workers, with older workers experiencing more severe injuries and taking longer to recover (Rogers and Wiatrowski, 2005). Data for the year 2006 in New Zealand indicates that older men (aged 65 and older) and younger men (aged 15 to 24) have the highest incidence of work-related injuries (figure 1.1). The incidence of injury among women is fairly consistent across different age groups although the incidence for women aged 65 and over is higher than for other age groups. The reasons for these associations are complex and need to be treated with caution. In part, OHS outcomes for young workers are a reflection of their concentration in particular industries and occupations, as well as shorter tenure and part-time jobs (McCloskey, 2008; Windau and Meyer, 2005). Differences in labour force participation rates (that may mask a healthy worker effect) also need to be acknowledged (see figure 1.2 in relation to New Zealand). Other influences include age-based differences in the level of self-employment (where OHS reporting is often inferior) and socioeconomic status (Sacker et al., 2008). Further, changes in the labour market and work arrangements can also affect age-based relationships between work and health.

Figure 1.1   New Zealand: injuries claims per 1000 FTEs by sex and age, 2006

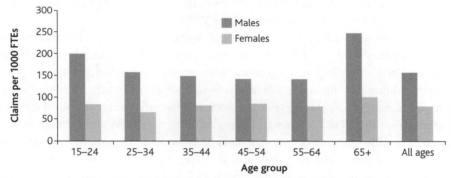

Source: Data © Statistics New Zealand, *Work Related Injury Claims*, October 2006, New Zealand Department of Labour, 2.

Figure 1.2   New Zealand: participation in the workforce by age, 2001–06

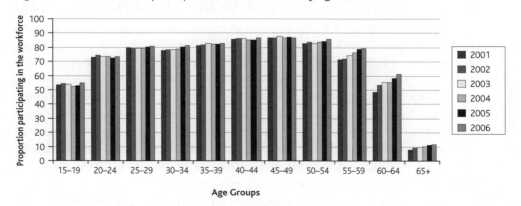

Source: Data © Statistics New Zealand, *Labour Force Participation of New Zealanders Aged 65 and over*, 1986–2006, 2009, 6.

Recent research (Louie et al., 2006; ABS 4905.0.55.001, 2004: 7–8) indicates older workers are increasingly working on a part-time or temporary basis and are more likely to be self-employed. Younger workers (below 25 years of age) still hold the majority of temporary and part-time jobs (in 2004 males under 25 accounted for 62% of men employed less than eight hours a week) and are becoming more concentrated in these jobs over time. However, older workers (especially males over 55 years of age who accounted for 22% of those employed less than eight hours per week) are also increasingly taking up part-time and temporary work—often in different occupations to younger workers—after retrenchment or in the transition to retirement (ABS 6105.0, 2005: 12–19).

Flexible work has been promoted as a desirable choice for older workers but, while it does offer opportunities for workforce re-entry, limited research indicates it also has marked disadvantages for older workers (Platman 2003, 2004). In some industries and occupations, such as hospitality and retailing, there is age segmentation between flexible workers and workers in continuing employment (Breslin and Smith, 2006). Insecurity can impact on the emotional and physical wellbeing of older workers in complex ways (Clarke et al., 2007) and attempts to examine policy options have had to rely on fragmentary evidence (Wegman and McGee, 2004: 56–72).

There is extensive OHS research on young workers. A review of 108 studies found younger workers were generally at greater risk of work-related injury but their injuries were less likely to be fatal than those of older workers (Salminen, 2004). Reviews of research indicate that the injury and disease risks (such as respiratory and skin disorders, drug and alcohol abuse) among younger workers reflect the occupations and industries they are concentrated in (such as agriculture, retailing, hospitality and entertainment)—at least in developed countries—and that many are undergoing training/apprenticeship or have limited job tenure (see Breslin et al., 2005, 2006). However, less attention has been given to the disorganisation associated with job churning (as young workers move through a succession of jobs) and undermined induction/training, supervision/OHS management and regulatory regimes (for exceptions see Mayhew and Quinlan, 2002 and Lipscomb et al., 2007). Serious injuries to younger workers have been addressed by various initiatives (special guidance material, information hotlines and 'high priority' enforcement) by government agencies in Australia and elsewhere. Further, while evidence suggests extensive paid employment is undertaken by very young workers including children (New South Wales Commission for Children and Young People, 2005), there has been little research into OHS among these workers in Australia, although the subject is attracting attention in other developed countries, like the US.

Less research and policy attention has been devoted to older workers. Increasing age has been linked to various specific injury risks, hazard exposures and occupational violence (Chau et al., 2004; McCall and Horwitz, 2004). Older workers with poor health are less likely to find new work following retrenchment and occupational ill health or injury is the most common reason for retirement before age 60 (NOHSC, 2005; Pransky et al., 2005; Rogers and Wiatrowski, 2005). Psychosocial factors, such as poor job control have been linked to earlier retirement and dementia among older workers (Elovainio et al., 2005; Pransky et al., 2005; Seidler et al., 2004). These findings have prompted a growing recognition among policymakers that better understanding of the relationship between age, work and health is critical to the retention of older workers (Griffiths, 2000).

Despite this, there has been little investigation of the interactive effects of age and different forms of flexible work on OHS. There is a growing recognition that an ageing workforce has profound implications for health, especially when changes in work processes such as work intensification and the failure to modify work performance and design to take account of age are considered (for a review see Griffiths, 2007). Even within the same job tacit differences in role and experience may mean that older workers experience greater emotional and mental demands (Sluiter and Frings-Dresen, 2007). A British study (Bartley et al., 2004) found secure employment and favourable employment conditions reduced the risk of healthy workers developing limiting injuries and also improved recovery from injury. Studies of downsizing, job insecurity and involuntary job loss have identified adverse health effects for both those losing their jobs and survivors, with older workers especially at risk (Moore et al., 2004; Gallo et al., 2004; Cheng et al., 2005). A US study of involuntary job loss highlighted the need to shape health and employment policies and services to meet the needs of older workers (Gallo et al., 2004). In a long-term study in the Finnish local government sector, Vahtera et al. (2005) found that workers who survived downsizing, especially older workers, had an increased risk of transferring to a permanent disability pension. Inexperience and shorter job tenure have been found to be significant OHS risk factors for younger workers (McCall and Horwitz, 2004), but the growth of flexible work has increased short job-tenure among older workers. Indeed, a recent study found that short job-tenure was a risk factor for all workers but the risk was highest for older workers (Breslin and Smith, 2006). Other studies point to health problems of older workers who find themselves in intermittent employment (Malefant et al., 2007, Clarke et al., 2007). Older workers holding insecure or temporary jobs may experience immediate financial stress due to family and other commitments (Aronsson et al., 2005) and will find it difficult to plan/budget for their retirement. Poorer health and discriminatory attitudes are liable to inhibit prospects of older workers obtaining work in a labour market more dominated by short-term engagements.

The growth of foreign-born workers and ethnic diversification of the workforce

As with age, it is possible to identify differences in OHS outcomes among various ethnic groups but this data needs to be qualified and treated with caution because of the concentration of foreign-born or minority workers in particular jobs and industries. With regard to New Zealand, recent statistics indicate that non-Europeans have a higher incidence rate of injury than Europeans (table 1.2). Among non-European groups, Maori workers have the highest rate of injury—27 per 1000 FTE or almost double the labour market average of 17 per 1000 FTE (Bohle et al., 2009). In the UK and North America there is evidence of higher rates of death and serious injury among immigrant workers, especially Latino workers in the case of the US (Centers for Disease Control, 2008a; Irwin Mitchell and the Centre for Corporate Accountability, 2009).

Table 1.2   Incidence rate: number of claims by ethnic group per 1000 FTEs, 2002–06

	2002	2003	2004	2005	2006
European	133	130	125	121	114
Maori	182	181	191	185	165
Pacific Peoples	135	151	153	160	149
Asian and other	109	111	115	116	133

Source: Data © Statistics New Zealand (2007).

Ethnicity can interact with OHS in complex ways. In societies subject to European settlement/invasion indigenous workers may be concentrated in particular jobs or experience specific vulnerability. Foreign-born workers are themselves a diverse group and an increasingly important component of the labour market in many developed countries (and some developing countries). They include permanent migrants from a range of backgrounds (or Australians and New Zealanders able to move between the two countries on a permanent or temporary basis), refugees (or those who have arrived and applied for refugee status), illegal or undocumented workers (including those overstaying a visitor visa) and a range of temporary resident foreign workers.

Both the latter two groups appear to be growing in most developed countries. Foreign temporary residents are an increasingly important component of the workforce of developed countries in Western Europe, North America, Australia, New Zealand and elsewhere. In English-speaking countries like Australia, the US, Canada, the UK and New Zealand temporary foreign workers include backpacker tourists (whether or not they have work permits), foreign students undertaking a program of study (some of whom subsequently apply for residence), and temporary or guest workers (including foreign-born workers on short-term contracts, Islanders able to work in New Zealand, and guest workers such as those on the s457 visa scheme in Australia). The groups just identified often tend to concentrate in different segments of the labour market (although there is considerable overlap with regard to those possessing little vocational training or skill) and illegal immigrants and temporary guest workers may not possess the same legal entitlements under employment laws or be able to access as easily those rights they do possess. Elaborate networks of 'middlemen', labour gangers, migration agents and ethnic businesses specialising in the exploitation of fellow countrymen may construct a reality very different from the formal rights and entitlements these workers may appear to possess (Jones et al., 2006).

The introduction of immigrant or guest workers can pose additional though usually manageable (through screening) public health risks where there are higher incidences of particular diseases within particular populations, including communicable diseases that have been all but eradicated in host societies (like tuberculosis) or have lower incidence rates, such as AIDS. The process can also work the other way, with diseases being transmitted back to the sending society (Mtika, 2007).

As with gender, there are complex interplays between ethnicity and precarious employment. Unfortunately, like studies of gender and age much research on immigrant/foreign workers and those from ethnic subgroups (such as indigenous, Maori or Aboriginal workers) do not consider the effects of employment status in sufficient detail. There are some notable exceptions where researchers have tried to examine all three aspects in terms of better understanding OHS, including Siefert and Messing's (2006) study of female and predominantly immigrant hotel cleaners in Quebec. Lipscomb et al.'s (2008) and Marin et al.'s (2009) studies of predominantly African-American and Latino female poultry workers in the US also point to the compounding effects of (often undocumented) immigrant status and precarious employment, with the latter identifying an association between abusive supervision and injuries. Analysis of labour market vulnerability also informs the study by Berdahl and McQuillan (2008) while Woolfson and Likic-Brboric (2008) argue that hyper-precarity of migrant workers results in an unequal burden of 'toxic' risk.

In a number countries there are known to be concentrations of immigrant workers in contingent work arrangements or industries where such practices are widespread (such as construction work in the US and parts of Europe) but broader statistics on employment by ethnicity are lacking and, as already noted, many studies ignore this connection. For example, a number of studies have examined injury rates, including fatalities, among immigrant minority workers in industries like construction for men (see, for example, Dong and Platner, 2004) or light manufacturing/food processing for women (see, for example, Quandt et al., 2006). A number of studies identify particular problem areas that may be linked to both contingent work and the vulnerability of particular immigrant or minority groups within an industry. For example, a study of health and safety training among young Latino construction workers in the US (O'Connor et al., 2005) found that while a number performed hazardous tasks training was inadequate, especially for those with a low level of English communication skills. At the same time, the role of poor language skills should not be exaggerated to the exclusion of other factors such as poor training, induction and supervision or disorganised high-pressure work settings with limited union input and widespread regulatory noncompliance (Bohle and Quinlan, 2000). Some population-based studies have also found foreign-born workers at greater risk of injury (see, for example, Ahonen and Benavides, 2006) but these studies, while not without value, provide even fewer insights into causal factors.

Migrant or ethnic minority group status may exacerbate the vulnerability of workers already in vulnerable jobs with little if any union representation and where noncompliance with OHS and workers' compensation regulations is common if not the norm. However, there may also be a need to identify particular subgroups as especially vulnerable to exploitation and unable/unwilling to report safety problems or to access their rights and entitlements, including illegal immigrants, foreign-born temporary residents working contrary to their visa (because it prohibits paid work altogether or limits the hours or occupation where engagements can occur) or guest workers who require ongoing employer sponsorship to remain in the country. There is evidence that these workers do encounter particular difficulties (Guthrie and Quinlan, 2005; Toh, 2007). The growing use of guest workers has attracted particular controversy in Australia following a number of serious incidents and because these workers are not guaranteed the same wages and employment conditions of other workers doing the same job, rely on employer sponsorship (inhibiting their capacity to complain) and have been used by some employers to circumvent unions. The large number of illegal immigrants in the US has posed particular problems and, indeed, led to conflicts between OHS authorities and Immigration agents, and raised questions as to their access to workers' compensation if injured. In Europe and North America a number of community-based initiatives have sought to better protect these workers (see, for example, Cho et al., 2007).

The foregoing discussion is not exhaustive. Changes to the ethnic composition of populations can also affect average size (height) and body shape that in turn will require adjustments to the anthropometric principles used to design machinery and work-related equipment or at least require more flexibility/adjustability in this regard. Again, given the concentration of particular ethnic groups in some jobs there will be specific as well as more general effects.

Extent of occupational injury, disease and ill health

The last section examined the array of hazards confronting workers as well as changes to the workforce that encounters those hazards. While it is convenient to disentangle different types of OHS hazards, in any given work setting hazards interact in complex ways. For example, the onset of disease may result from a combination of multiple exposures to a range of chemicals while working in extreme temperatures. Similarly, the health of a truck driver may suffer as a result of a combination of prolonged exertion, long hours/cumulative sleep-deprivation (and drugs used to combat this), noise, vibration, poor diet and stress.

In this section, we will examine evidence on the extent of occupational injury and disease in Australia and New Zealand, comparing it with the data pertaining to other countries. At the outset, it should be noted that while OHS statistics may include volunteer workers and family helpers this figure is likely to be an understatement due to poor reporting. Further, as several examples already given indicate, work-related incidents can include non-workers (such as children riding in trucks or sitting on tractors, or passengers/commuters in a car, bus or train) and the same applies to some work-related exposures to hazardous substances (such as family members exposed to asbestos). In short, even the most accurate and comprehensive OHS statistics would still understate the health effects of work on the community.

At the outset it needs to be acknowledged that the precise extent of occupational injury and disease is unknown even within countries with relatively comprehensive workers' compensation systems and diligent and well-funded statistical bureaus. In Australia official statistics indicate that the number of serious injuries and diseases associated with work is greater than those resulting from road traffic incidents and violent crimes combined (note all three categories overlap). There are also good reasons to believe that the gap is even wider than available statistics suggest because the statistics on deaths and serious injuries resulting from road transport incidents and crimes of violence are relatively more accurate than OHS statistics. As indicated in the last section, workers may be exposed to a multiplicity of potentially harmful substances in the course of their working careers and, as we will see in a later chapter, for this and other reasons the attribution of disease to a particular exposure is often problematic. In some cases particular hazards will only be identified when a cluster of critical cases is identified—and the identification itself may be serendipitous. Even then detection may prove difficult and some clusters will simply represent essentially random coincidence. The diagnosis of women with breast cancer who had worked at the ABC's Toowong Studios in Brisbane highlights these difficulties. The original cluster of 12 cases was first reported in July 2006 and by February 2008 five more cases had been identified. While this was well beyond the norm (based on incidence in the broader community), by July 2008 a study undertaken by cancer expert Professor Bruce Armstrong was still unable to identify the workplace factors (if any) responsible (*Thomson Occupational Health News*, 780, 7 May 2008: 1).

These problems are not confined to Australia and New Zealand. Indeed, there is a growing international recognition that there are serious under-reporting problems with regard to official OHS statistics. Aside from outright gaps in reporting, there is evidence that significant under-reporting can occur even where employers are required to report injury by law, especially where monitoring of reporting is less than comprehensive (for evidence relating to the US, see Rosenman et al., 2006 and Miller, 2008). One US study (Probst et al., 2008) found a significant discrepancy between OSHA recordable injury rates and those based on insurance medical claim data, with companies with a poor safety climate having the highest rates of under-reporting. There is evidence that even changes to record keeping rules and conventions can have significant effects on 'apparent' trends at aggregate or industry level (Friedman and Forst, 2007; Welch et al., 2007). Studies undertaken in other countries such as Korea (Won et al., 2007) have identified similarly conspicuous errors in official statistics.

Given this, trends in official data suggesting an overall improvement in OHS performance need to be treated with caution, especially in the context of mounting evidence that changes to work organisation and the growth of precarious employment are having adverse effects on health (Azaroff et al., 2004). Ideally, multiple datasets (Boufous and Williamson, 2002; Mustard et al., 2003) and enhanced surveillance systems should be used to confirm trends. The remainder of this section will examine the various sources of OHS statistics and their strengths and limitations.

Workers' compensation claims–based data

In Australia and many other countries the primary source of statistics on work-related injury and disease are claims made under the workers' compensation system. There are significant limitations with using workers' compensation claims to derive injury and disease statistics. As demonstrated below, the majority of the economic (let alone human and social) costs of work-related injury and disease are not included in workers' compensation claims data used for OHS performance monitoring in Australia. Further, in addition to serious inconsistencies in the recording of workers' compensation claims, many work-related injuries and diseases do not result in a workers' compensation claim (due to deficiencies in surveillance of occupational disease and work-related mental health problems) and changes to work arrangements (such as the growth of 'self-employment' and other contingent work arrangements) have almost certainly exacerbated this under-reporting. In more detail the following limitations can be identified:

- First, for various reasons, including claim-recording conventions, the conversion of claims data into accurate annual injury and disease statistics can be problematic (Skegg, 1991; Leggat, 1998). There are minimum requirements for making claims in terms of lost time and particular recording conventions in relation to the year in which a claim is counted and how longstanding injuries and diseases are addressed. This means that many minor injuries and diseases requiring only medical treatment or a short absence from work are excluded. In Australia, the separate federal, state and territory workers' compensation schemes have exacerbated these problems. For example, since the minimum period of absence from work varied widely between the state and territory systems prior to 1993–94, NOHSC could only construct national work-related injury and disease figures by adopting a lowest-common-denominator approach of counting only those that resulted in at least five working days lost. Even this compromise was undermined in 1993–94 when Victoria amended its workers' compensation legislation to set a minimum of 10 working days lost for claims (improving its OHS performance at the stroke of a pen). In short, a substantial number of injury and disease claims recorded by some jurisdictions are not included in national statistics. There are also variations in how particular injuries or diseases are recorded, with some complaints being recorded as an injury in one state and as disease in another (see, for example, a number which fall under the appellation of RSI). Recording conventions can also introduce industry-specific sources of distortion. For example, the growing use of contractors and agency workers/labour hire has affected injury statistics in industries like mining, construction and manufacturing because these workers are included in a different industry/sector category for workers' compensation (Quinlan, 2004c). This problem has been identified in Sweden and other countries (Blank et al., 1995: 23).
- Second, workers' compensation systems in virtually all countries seriously understate the extent of occupational disease (Dement and Lipscomb, 1999). When introduced around a century ago workers' compensation regimes focused on injuries. Although scope for compensating work-related disease has been progressively widened systems still only address a small fraction of known or suspected occupational diseases (Industry Commission, 1995; Kerr et al., 1996; Goldsmith, 1998: 389–90; Mayhew and Peterson, 2005). This includes serious cases resulting in death. For example, while workers' compensation data for Australia suggests that more fatalities arise from traumatic injuries than disease Kerr et al.'s (1996) study found almost five times

more workers die of occupational disease than are killed by injuries. This finding is consistent with evidence relating to other countries like the US—indeed the actual gap may be greater (Leigh and Robbins, 2004). In 2008 the Australian Safety and Compensation Council (2008a) released a report on occupation disease indicators. However, with several exceptions—notably additional use of the National Notifiable Disease Surveillance System, National Hospital Morbidity Database and National Cancer Statistics Clearing House with regard to infectious disease, respiratory disease and cancer respectively—information was overwhelmingly drawn from the National Data Set (i.e. based on workers' compensation claims data). The value of the overall incidence and trend data in these 'disease indicators' is debatable to say the least.

- Third, observations about under-reporting analogous to that just made with regard to disease can be made with regard to adverse effects of work on mental health and wellbeing, including work-related stress (Mayhew and Peterson, 2005; Cox and Lippel, 2008). For example, a study based on Victorian data by Keegel et al. (2009: 17) found that workers in lower socioeconomic positions highly exposed to job strain were under-represented in claims statistics, indicating that workers' compensation statistics 'substantially under-estimate job stress for these groups'. A Canadian study (Cox and Lippel, 2008) also identified chronic work-related stress as a major exclusion within workers' compensation coverage.

- Fourth, in many countries there are significant omissions in the formal coverage of the workers' compensation system. A major exclusion is volunteer workers who constitute a significant part of the workforce in the not-for-profit sector such as churches, charities and community groups. While data on OHS among volunteer workers is rare the problems have been sufficient to attract increased attention by OHS inspectorates (Quinlan, 2002). Also revealing is a report of deaths of firefighters in the US in 2007 (C^2 Technologies, 2008) that of the 118 who died while on duty more than half (68) were volunteers. Another significant exclusion is self-employed workers and workers in micro-small businesses (including family helpers). A significant number of self-employed workers are found in hazardous industries like construction, road transport, fishing/forestry and rural/agriculture (Fosbroke et al., 1997: 461). In some countries coverage applies to specified categories of self-employed workers but not all. Further, in Australia there is no consistent approach in this regard. This, together with inconsistent definitions of 'employee' and 'self-employed worker' under different bodies of legislation (industrial relations, taxation, OHS and workers' compensation) results in considerable confusion and an even lower level of coverage in practice (Quinlan and Mayhew, 1999; Quinlan, 2004). Complexities and ambiguity if not outright exclusion from coverage also arise with regard to teleworkers, home-based workers and domestic workers—categories where women are often over-represented (Bernstein et al., 2001; Montreuil and Lippel, 2003; Cox and Lippel, 2008). In some jurisdictions (such as several provinces in Canada; Cox and Lippel, 2008: 12–13) small businesses are excluded from workers' compensation coverage. Another significant exclusion occurs with regard to the many children or young adolescents who work (New South Wales Commission for Children and Young People, 2005).

■ Fifth, formal exclusions in coverage are exacerbated by groups of workers who fail to make use of their nominal entitlements to workers' compensation. As a result of ignorance, economic pressures to keep working or fear of losing future work some injured workers are reluctant to make workers' compensation claims. Vulnerable groups include self-employed workers (where covered), home-based workers, children and foreign workers (especially those working illegally), women, young workers, remotely located unskilled and itinerant workers and those in precarious jobs such as casual, part-time, home-based or labour-hire agency workers (Committee on the Health and Safety Implications of Child Labour and others, 1998: 179; Boufous and Williamson, 2002; Quinlan and Mayhew, 1999; Quinlan, 2004; Guthrie and Quinlan, 2005; Toh and Quinlan, 2009). The increased use of rigorous claims management/ experience rating as well as the growth of precarious employment (including foreign workers) since the 1980s has exacerbated these problems (Hopkins, 1994a & b; Hyatt and Kralj, 1995: 95–106; Quinlan, 1999, 2004; Quinlan and Mayhew, 1999). The policy implications of this should not be understated. For example, in one jurisdiction (New South Wales) a purported improvement in OHS performance in the building industry was actually a statistical artefact caused by changes in the level of evasion of compensation cover among contractors (Hopkins, 1994a: 81).

■ Sixth and finally, conventions and conflicts in the granting of workers' compensation, as well as the administrative and evidentiary requirements for lodging claims can also affect injury and disease statistics (Cox and Lippel, 2008). For example, delays in the recognition of particular diseases or injuries as work related can result in an initial understatement followed by a bulge of claims after recognition (as occurred with asbestos). Administrative conventions in relation to recognition also affect reporting. For example, prompt recognition of a particular disease is often linked to a list of prescribed occupations. This approach has led to cases where a claim for brucellosis by an abattoir worker will be accepted but a claim for the same disease by a veterinary lab worker in a government rural industry agency will not. Another complicating factor is a time limit for lodging claims contained in many compensation systems. The cost implications of recognising a new set of illnesses has tended to make compensation bodies conservative, especially where medical evidence is inconclusive, where the causes are complex or where the illness results from a combination of work and non-work activity. Work-related stress provides an example where the granting of compensation is restricted to occupations and 'events' in ways that do not reflect knowledge about the incidence of the problem across the workforce. Finally, where there is an option for the worker to make a claim for their injury under the common law system existing in most English-speaking countries then a workers' compensation claim may never be lodged or its pursuit cancelled.

The overall extent of under-reporting of injury and disease by workers' compensation data is unknown but evidence indicates it is substantial. In 2005 a report to the Association of Workers' Compensation Boards of Canada indicated that on average 20% of workers were formally excluded from coverage under workers' compensation legislation—a figure that does not include eligible workers who did not apply for compensation (cited

Table 1.3   Persons who experienced a work-related injury or illness[a] by whether they received workers' compensation, 2005–06

	Received workers' compensation		Did not receive workers' compensation	
	'000	%	'000	%
Status in employment of job where most recent work-related injury or illness occurred				
Employee	214.0	34.2	411.9	65.8
Employer/own-account worker	1.8**	2.8**	61.9	97.2
Full-time or part-time status of job where most recent work-related injury or illness occurred				
Full-time	175.4	34.4	334.6	65.6
Part-time	40.4	22.5	139.1	77.5
Occupation of job where most recent work-related injury or illness occurred				
Managers and administrators	6.8*	13.4	43.9	86.6
Professionals	19.1	22.1	67.0	77.9
Associate professionals	19.3	27.6	50.5	72.4
Tradespersons and related workers	50.7	38.1	82.2	61.9
Advanced clerical and service workers	3.1*	24.6*	9.5*	75.4*
Intermediate clerical, sales & service workers	29.6	31.1	65.7	68.9
Intermediate production & transport workers	39.3	44.7	48.6	55.3
Elementary clerical, sales and service workers	16.5	25.9	47.2	74.1
Labourers and related workers	31.5	34.7	59.2	65.3
Industry of job where most recent work-related injury or illness occurred				
Agriculture, forestry and fishing	5.8*	13.9*	35.7	86.1
Mining	5.5*	47.6*	6.0*	52.4*
Manufacturing	32.9	34.7	62.0	65.3
Electricity, gas and water supply	0.8**	16.8**	4.1*	83.2*
Construction	26.0	34.3	49.7	65.7
Wholesale trade	5.8*	26.6*	16.0	73.4
Retail trade	29.5	27.0	79.7	73.0
Accommodation, cafes and restaurants	10.3*	30.1*	23.9	69.9
Transport and storage	20.0	51.3	19.0	48.7
Communication services	2.5**	32.0**	5.3*	68.0*
Finance and insurance	2.7*	37.8*	4.4*	62.2*
Property and business services	10.2*	23.5*	33.1	76.5
Government administration & defence	14.0	39.9	21.1	60.1
Education	10.8*	29.9*	25.5	70.1
Health and community services	23.3	29.3	56.3	70.7
Cultural and recreational services	4.2*	23.7*	13.5	76.3
Personal and other services	10.9*	37.2*	18.4	62.8
Total	215.8	31.3	473.7	68.7

Source: Australian Bureau of Statistics (2009), *Work-Related Injuries 2005–06*, ABS Catalogue No.6324, Canberra: 18.

[a]   Refers to the most recent work-related injury or illness
*   estimate has a relative standard error of between 25% and 50% and should be used with caution
**   estimate has a relative standard error greater than 50% and is considered too unreliable for general use—nil or rounded to zero (including null cells)

in Cox and Lippel, 2008: 11). In Australia there is evidence indicative of the proportion of injuries and illness that do not translate into a workers' compensation claim. An Australian Bureau of Statistics (ABS, 2009) survey of workers who experienced work-related injuries and illnesses in 2005–06 indicated that of these only 31.3% received workers' compensation (table 1.3). Table 1.3 also indicates significant variations in those applying for and receiving workers' compensation by occupation, industry and employment status. As might be expected, industries non-receipt of compensation was higher in industries characterised by high levels of self-employment and small business such as agriculture, forestry and fishing. But the results are complex. For example, while self-employment might seem to explain the low rate of compensated injury or illness among managers it is less clear why this should be the case (to an even greater extent) for labourers and related workers where a lower rate of self-employment might be expected. This might partly reflect simply the higher incidence of injury among labourers, some of which result in compensation claims and some of which do not.

When asked in the survey (ABS, 2009: 21) why they had not applied for workers' compensation (this wouldn't include those who applied but were rejected) just under half (48.6%) of those reporting an injury or illness indicated it was because they considered the injury minor or not requiring compensation. Of the others, 7.3% indicated they were not covered by or were unaware of compensation, 9% believed they were not eligible, 6.7% felt a claim might impact negatively on their employment, 7.1% indicated a claim would require too much paperwork/effort and 15.7% gave another (unspecified) reason.

With regard to employment status the survey found that, in comparison to full-time employees, both part-time employees and own-account workers were less likely to apply for workers' compensation. This finding matched an earlier 2001 ABS survey that also indicated that those part-time and own-account workers who did make claims were more likely to have their claims rejected. The ABS surveys have not published data distinguishing claims behaviour among permanent and non-permanent/temporary workers. However, analysis of unpublished data from the earlier 2001 ABS survey carried out by the National Occupational Health and Safety Commission (2002) found casual/temporary workers were less likely than permanent workers to claim workers' compensation.

In sum, workers' compensation claims provide the most comprehensive single dataset on occupational illness in Australia and many other countries. This data is of value to government, employers and others. Nonetheless, it is essential to recognise that workers' compensation data significantly understates the level of occupational injury and disease. Nor can it be presumed that under-reporting is roughly equal across different industries and occupations. Thus, workers' compensation data must be treated cautiously and its use for particular tasks must be informed by recognition of its limitations (including the different recording conventions used by different jurisdictions in Australia). Unfortunately, even where these limitations are acknowledged, indiscriminate or 'default' use of the data is common both within government and industry.

In recent years the Workplace Relations Ministers' Council (representing state, federal and territory ministers) has published annual reports on OHS and workers' compensation data for Australia and New Zealand. To achieve uniformity in the context of different practices among state jurisdictions a number of compromises have had to be adopted with regard to the compilation of Australia-wide data (in New Zealand the single jurisdiction and national Accident Compensation Scheme obviates this problem). This means absolute figures for Australia must be viewed as an understatement and it is more meaningful to examine incidence and frequency rates. While this caveat applies even to work-related fatalities it is still worth briefly examining the available data. As can be seen from table 1.4 the five-year average of work-related fatal injuries was 264 in Australia and 96 in New Zealand. Table 1.4 suggests well over 50% of the deaths in both countries arose from injuries or musculoskeletal disorders but again it needs to be stressed that these figures represent a significant underestimate of the number of workers who die as a result of occupational disease (Mayhew and Peterson, 2005).

Table 1.4   Compensated work-related fatalities in Australia and New Zealand, 2002–03 to 2006–07

	Australia	New Zealand
Injury and musculoskeletal disorders		
2002–03	197	59
2003–04	169	55
2004–05	168	61
2005–06	186	60
2006–07	177	56
Five-year average	175	58
Mesothelioma and asbestosis		
2002–03	49	32
2003–04	44	27
2004–05	53	45
2005–06	34	44
2006–07	33	35
Five-year average	43	37
Other diseases		
2002–03	56	0
2003–04	58	0
2004–05	34	1
2005–06	34	1
2006–07	26	3
Five-year average	42	2
Total		
2002–03	302	91
2003–04	271	82
2004–05	255	107
2005–06	254	105
2006–07	236	94
Five-year average	264	96

Source: Workplace Relations Ministers' Council (2008): 10.

Data published in the Workplace Relations Ministers' Council (2008) annual report also provides a comparison of the incidence of work-related fatalities in Australia and New Zealand with a number of European countries (Denmark, Finland, Norway, Sweden, Switzerland and the UK). This data (for the years 1999–2006) suggests the incidence of work-related fatalities in New Zealand is by far the worst (at over three deaths per 100 000 employees compared to fewer than two deaths per 100 000 employees among European countries except Finland which has risen to above two). In Australia the incidence of work-related fatality dropped from near three to about two deaths per 100 000 employees in the same period (still worse than most comparators). Again, it needs to be stressed that this trend data needs to be treated with extreme caution. Countries with more accurate data recording may actually appear worse in comparison to countries where fewer fatalities find their way into official statistics (the same points apply to non-fatal injuries and diseases).

The Workplace Relations Ministers' Council (2008) report also includes data on the incidence and frequency rate of serious occupational injuries and disease (table 1.5). Frequency data can be especially useful because it takes account of exposure (in terms of hours worked). Incidence data can be highly misleading where there are significant differences in hours worked (say between a full-time and part-time or seasonal workers).

Unlike earlier NOHSC and state workers' compensation authority annual reports, the annual report of the Workplace Relations Ministers' Council does not contain detailed breakdowns of injury and disease by industry, occupation, type of injury, age and gender. Reports prepared for the Australian Safety Compensation Council (2008c), which succeeded NOHSC (but has now been replaced in turn by Safework Australia), did include this data. The Workplace Relations Ministers' Council (2008: 12) report does include the number of injuries/diseases by mechanism, which indicates that body stressing is by far the most prevalent followed by falls, trips and slips, and being hit by moving object. It also includes (2008: 13) incidence rates by business size, a summarised version of which can be found in table 1.6. The latter data needs to be treated with caution as research in the US (Morse et al., 2004) and elsewhere has identified a 'reporting-effect' resulting in an understatement of injury in smaller operations.

As in other countries, workers' compensation data or reported injury and illness data has generally revealed a consistent ranking of the incidence of injury and disease by industry and occupation over time. For example, Australian data for 2005–06 (Australian Safety and Compensation Council, 2008c: 9) indicates that the industries with the highest incidence of serious injury were manufacturing; transport and storage; agriculture, forestry and fishing; and construction (with mining next but some way further back). For the US (Bureau of Labor Statistics, 2006: 3), the ranking of serious injury incidence by industry for the year 2005 is headed by transportation and storage followed by manufacturing; construction; agriculture, forestry and fishing/hunting; healthcare; and mining.

This pattern has also been confirmed by more focused and detailed studies, using disaggregated data. For example, a study by James (1989) found high-incidence industries were (in order) meat, fabricated metal, transport equipment manufacturing,

Table 1.5 Incidence and frequency rates of serious* occupational injuries and disease in Australia and New Zealand, 2002–03 to 2006–07

	Incidence of serious injury & disease claims		Frequency of serious injury & disease claims		Incidence of long-term (12 weeks or over) injury & disease claims		Frequency of long-term (12 weeks or over) injury & disease claims	
	Australia	New Zealand	Australia	New Zealand	Australia	New Zealand	Australia	New Zealand
2002–03	16.9	14.1	10.1	7.7	4.4	2.6	2.6	1.4
2003–04	16.7	14.9	10.1	8.2	4.2	2.8	2.6	1.6
2004–05	16.2	15.4	9.7	8.6	4.0	2.9	2.4	1.6
2005–06	15.3	15.8	9.3	8.9	3.6	3.2	2.2	1.8
2006–07	14.2	15.7	8.8	8.9	3.2	3.1	2.0	1.8

Source: Workplace Relations Ministers' Council (2008): 6–7.

* All workers' compensation claims involving temporary incapacity of one or more weeks plus all fatality and permanent incapacity claims.

Note: Incidence calculated as number of injuries per thousand employees and frequency calculated as number of injuries per million hours worked.

Table 1.6 Size of business incidence rates (claims per 1000 employees) of serious workers' compensation claims in Australia* and New Zealand, 2002–03 and 2006–07

	1–4 employees	5–19 employees	20–99 employees	100 or more employees
2002–03				
Australia	14.9	11.2	15.6	15.1
New Zealand	12.1	12.8	16.4	14.7
2006–07				
Australia	13.1	10.1	14.2	12.2
New Zealand	21.7	13.5	15.1	15.4

Source: Workplace Relations Ministers' Council (2008): 13.

* Based on incomplete set of jurisdictions

other machinery manufacturing, furniture manufacturing, construction, non-metallic manufacturing and mining. In terms of occupational categories, James identified the high-incidence jobs as labourers, food and beverage process workers, packers and labellers, metal tradesmen and process workers, and miners. In both cases, reference to severity altered the rankings somewhat. In terms of gender, James (1989) found that the average incidence rate of injury and disease among males exceeded those of females for all industries and all but two occupations (packers and labellers, and professional and managerial workers). James identified a stratified pattern whereby higher status jobs have low injury incidence rates and low status jobs have generally high incidence rates. Overall, the patterns of incidence by gender, occupation and industry groups are sufficiently consistent over time that a 'normal' incidence rate can be identified. In short, work-related injuries and illness constitute statistical probabilities. This observation undermines attempts to portray work injuries as essentially unexpected or aberrant events. It also has implications for 'accident-proneness' and other victim-blaming explanations of occupational illness.

Censuses, surveys and other datasets

Aside from workers' compensation statistics, there are other sources of occupational illness statistics. These include fatality and serious injury censuses; legislative reporting requirements, inspectorate data and the records kept by government agencies (including specialist bodies such as state and federal transport authorities); hospital admissions data; coronial records and inquests; workforce surveys; and epidemiological studies/registers. Large employers may also keep detailed records but these are seldom available for public scrutiny or analysis.

In Australia the Australian Bureau of Statistics carries out periodic surveys (about every five years or so) to estimate work-related injuries. The latest survey (Australian Bureau of Statistics, 2006; Linacre, 2007) found that for 10.8 million Australians employed at some point during the year to June 2006, 690 000 or 6.4% reported experiencing at least one work-related injury or illness. Men experienced a higher injury rate (74 per thousand) than women (51 per thousand). The survey found younger workers also experienced higher injury rates (especially young men aged 20–24 years who reported 98 injuries per thousand workers). In the US there are six national data collection or surveillance systems on occupational injuries and diseases (Murphy et al., 1996). Over a number of years Sweden conducted a long-running extensive survey of living conditions covering employed and self-employed workers. Detailed analysis of inspectoral activity provides another source. (Since 1978, German labour inspectors have used a questionnaire to collect information on age, occupation and firm size with regard to workplace fatalities.)

Judicious use of alternative sources may offset some limitations in compensation statistics. For example, hospital admissions data can augment gaps in injury reporting, especially with regard to self-employed workers, volunteers and young workers (Boufous and Williamson, 2002). Nonetheless, many alternative datasets also suffer from limitations. For example, in Australia (Mayhew and Wyatt, 1995) and the US if not elsewhere there is evidence of widespread noncompliance with legislative requirements to report serious injuries to OHS agencies, particularly but by no means exclusively among smaller firms. A study by Boden (1995: 199) found that US employers who denied workers' compensation claims were also unlikely to report injuries to the Bureau of Labor Statistics. Further, most official datasets of which we are aware suffer from a more general conceptual limitation. They either ignore employment status altogether, or provide only a few categories. The self-employed/employee breakdown used in US and Australian fatality censuses is useful. However, it needs to be remembered that all datasets are based, implicitly or explicitly, on a legal definition of what constitutes a worker and what constitutes a standard employment relationship (including presumptions about the age at which persons commence work). There is lack of consistency in the definitions used in different datasets even in the same country. In some instances the definition is specified in legislation (as in many workers' compensation statutes). For other official datasets a more generic definition is used, namely the standardised definition adopted by the agency responsible for labour statistics (the US Bureau of Labour Statistics, the Australian Bureau of Statistics and the equivalents in other countries). Finally, agencies continue to rely on definitional categories that presume full-time permanent employment as the norm and take no account of the significant growth in part-time, temporary, leased labour and other forms of precarious employment that has occurred in Australia and many other countries over the past 15 years.

Thus, while different datasets may help to fill some gaps, omissions in relation to particular hazards, employment sectors and groups of workers remain, including children/young workers and foreign workers—especially those working contrary to legislation (Committee on the Health and Safety Implications of Child Labour and others, 1998: 217–8; Boufous and Williamson, 2002).

The issue is not simply the availability of information but what bodies of information are liable to be used. Although strategic use is made of other data sources, in many if not most countries workers' compensation/insurance data remains the dominant source for employers, government agencies and others. Indeed, in many countries it is becoming more important as a result of the shift to neo-liberal policies that promote an economic incentive-based approach to OHS (for proposals to use such approaches in the EU and elsewhere see Bailey et al., 1995 and Industry Commission, 1995). The policy trend is associated with the growing use of risk management/loss control and cost–benefit analysis to drive OHS policies at both organisational and government level. These devices are usually underpinned by the most readily available measures of incidence and costs, namely workers' compensation claims data (Hopkins, 1994a).

Overall, other datasets or surveillance systems only partly offset omissions from workers' compensation claims data. Nevertheless, they can be used to fill some significant gaps and provide valuable insights into the extent of occupational illness. One useful data source is censuses of occupational fatalities due to trauma undertaken in the US, Australia and a number of other countries. These censuses (in Australia based on the National Data Set with additions drawn from the Notified Fatalities Collection and the National Coronial Information System) include many fatalities not found in workers' compensation data. The report for 2004–05 (Australian Safety and Compensation Council, 2008b: 1) identified 405 work-related deaths (or 2.5 per 100 000 employed persons)—still seen to be an understatement—with vehicle accidents being the most common cause of death, followed by falls from heights and being hit by objects. In the US a census is conducted annually by the federal Bureau of Labor Statistics. In 2007 this indicated that 5488 US workers died of occupational injuries, compared to an estimated 49 000 deaths each year attributable to work-related disease (Bureau of Labor Statistics, 2008; Steenland, K et al., 2003).

With regard to fatal work injuries, especially dangerous occupations included truck drivers, forestry workers, farmers and fishermen, construction workers, fabricators and labourers. A ranking of dangerous industries and occupations in Australia is roughly comparable to the US census and is headed by forestry, fishing, mining, transport, agriculture (farming) and construction. The occupational breakdown is less detailed than that available in the US census but again there appears to be considerable agreement in terms of ranking the most hazardous jobs. The same applies to agency of death (Australian Safety and Compensation Council, 2008b: 11) which is headed by vehicle incidents (46%) followed by falls from height (12%), being hit by falling objects (10%) and being hit by moving objects (10.3%). One distinction between US and Australian data is in relation to occupational homicide which past censuses indicate has been a more conspicuous source of workplace fatalities, especially among women, in the former (Bureau of Labor Statistics, 1998: 3; NOHSC, 1998: 53). This is probably just a reflection of broader societal differences in the incidence of homicide between the two countries.

Fatality censuses are valuable, indeed essential, to policymakers, OHS professionals and others. However, they are restricted to cases where death arose from trauma or acute poisoning/exposures to hazardous substances. They are do not assist us to assess the extent of death, let alone serious illness, that results from long-term and often insidious exposure to harmful substances such as chemical and biological agents—areas where workers' compensation data is very deficient. As will be discussed in the next chapter, many medical practitioners have little training in occupational medicine. This and other features of the healthcare system are not well attuned to identifying work-related health problems (in relation to death certificates, hospital admissions data and research to name but the most obvious). Undoubtedly a large number go undetected.

One way of bridging this gap, especially in relation to disease, is epidemiological studies and registers. An example of this is the Australian Mesothelioma Register initiated in 1980 (then maintained by the Epidemiology Unit of NOHSC during its existence) referred to earlier. The register is based on a notification system and questionnaire that utilises a network of physicians, pathologists, surgeons, medical administrators, state and territory departments, cancer registries, compensation agencies and other sources (Leigh at al., 1998: 2). Mesothelioma is an invariably fatal cancer associated with exposure to asbestos. In the post-1945 period Australia was a leading producer (with mines at Baryulgil, Barraba, and Wittenoom), importer and consumer of asbestos products, with consumption peaking at 70 000 tonnes in 1975 (Leigh et al., 1998: 1). Asbestos was widely used in building products, brake linings and as a fire retardant in public buildings, trains and ships as well as power stations and other electrical installations. The register was established in an effort to measure the most unambiguous health outcome of asbestos exposure. Not surprisingly, the register has recorded the highest number of cases among those directly exposed to a significant level of asbestos, including miners (and mine communities), asbestos product workers, building and building maintenance workers, ship and railway workers and naval personnel (Leigh et al., 1998: 23–6). The register showed a steady increase in the number of reported cases from 156 in 1982 to 645 new cases in 2003 before recording a decline (597 cases were diagnosed in 2005; Safework Australia, 2009: 3).

Epidemiological studies and registers such as the Australia Mesothelioma Register provide a more accurate measure of the level of occupational disease than can be found in workers' compensation statistics and in so doing highlight the scope of a problem too often neglected by policymakers and others. They can also capture overlapping health risks to the family and other members of the community from occupational hazards that find their way into the immediate environment (again, something excluded from workers' compensation). However, epidemiological studies are expensive to maintain and, like the Mesothelioma Register, restricted in scope (although they provide a basis for broader generalisations about the incidence of disease). The knowledge gap is substantial even in relation to what seem to be significant categories of work-related disease. For example, a national workshop on occupational asthma sponsored by the Australian Institute of Health and Welfare (2008) identified information needs in relation to prevalence, incidence, at risk populations, risk factors, economic burden, and prevention strategies. Data deficiencies identified included the absence of a national surveillance system, validated exposure data and the extent of under-diagnosis. In a report to the Australian and New Zealand government, Tim Driscoll (2006: xv) identified an absence of 'proper exposure surveillance systems at national, jurisdictional or regional level', evaluated existing workplace exposure surveillance systems and pointed to the need to devote considerable resources to resolving this gap.

This problem is not confined to Australia and New Zealand nor is it confined to occupational disease. An international review (Dollard et al., 2007) found that there was an absence of national surveillance systems with regard to psychosocial risk factors. Dollard et al. (2007: 1) argued the development of national systems—and international coordination in this regard—should be a priority for OHS research and policy, with a focus on emotional labour; bullying, harassment and violence; exposure to acute stressors; workplace change; and organisational justice. Other reviews of the significance of psychosocial work environment factors have reached similar conclusions (Kelloway et al., 2008; Bambra et al., 2009). In New Zealand the National Occupational Safety and Health Advisory Committee commissioned a number of surveillance reports, including one on the effect of changes to work and population (Driscoll et al., 2004, 2005; Bohle et al., 2008). However, as at September 2009 neither country had taken steps to address these gaps or develop a national surveillance system. The failure of governments to provide systematic support for epidemiological research and surveillance systems means that this source of OHS information fills only a few of the gaps in our knowledge of the extent of occupational illness already alluded to.

Epidemiological research (and a more effectively pooling of the resulting information internationally) is clearly vital to filling major gaps in our knowledge of the incidence and severity of occupational illness in industrialised countries such as Australia. However, it cannot be presumed that conventional medico-legal definitions of occupational injury and disease are unproblematic or indeed sufficient to obtain a complete measure of the impact of work on a community's health and wellbeing. As later chapters will show, understandings of what constitutes occupational injury and disease require continuous reassessment in the light of new knowledge, and some areas like strain-related injuries and work-related stress are always liable to be subject to considerable debate. Further, in some instances at least, in order to understand and manage OHS it is important to examine a range of workplace behaviour and experiences, not simply those indicators that are most readily measured through compensation claims, coronial records, hospital admissions or designated injury or disease outcomes.

Available data provides limited information about the effect of work processes or the working environment—and changes to this—on occupational health, especially changes in the psychosocial working environment. While research (for example, studies of downsizing and job insecurity) has provided useful insights there is little generalisable data on the incidence of work stress-related illness and the like. A good illustration is occupational violence and the use of self-report surveys to measure this. As already indicated, occupational violence encompasses a wide array of health-harming practices but of these only serious physical assaults (including fatalities) and a few stress claims are liable to find their way into the major OHS datasets discussed above. For example, physical assaults are incorporated in NIOSH's *Annual Survey of Occupational Injuries and Illnesses*.

Wide-ranging and representative surveys of psychosocial factors at work are exceptional. Since the early 1990s the European Union has been undertaking a survey of a sample of workers in its member countries about every five years. This survey does attempt to measure changes in psychosocial working conditions and presents a model that, in our view, should be adopted by Australia, New Zealand and other countries. The 1996 survey (European Foundation for the Improvement of Living and Working Conditions, 1998) found that 9% of workers claimed to have been subjected to intimidation at work. If representative, the survey indicates that three million EU workers have been subject to sexual harassment, six million to physical violence and 12 million to psychological violence. No similar survey has been undertaken in Australia, although a survey of work-related health among 1100 workers was undertaken in Victoria (LaMontagne et al., 2006). Though not representative, a series of surveys (1993–98) of work-related violence involving over 1400 workers in 13 different occupations, including factory workers, young casual fast-food workers and small business owner/managers provides some insights (Mayhew and Quinlan, 2000). The findings suggest low-level occupational violence is widespread and endemic in some occupations (table 1.7). Threats and physical assault are common among clothing outworkers, child-care employees, hospitality workers and self-employed building workers and truck and taxi drivers. The type of violence (robbery, co-worker/manager or customer/client) varied significantly among different occupations. There were also important gender differences. Female workers across virtually all occupations generally reported more abuse but fewer threats or physical assaults, reflecting in part both job task differences and gendered norms of behaviour (Mayhew and Quinlan, 2000).

The foregoing discussion has only briefly canvassed tools for measuring the extent of OHS problems. By discussing various sources we have sought to provide some insights into the extent of occupational ill health. We have also identified limitations in these sources, especially official data. The limitations in workers' compensation–based data should give serious cause for concern given their widespread use by government policymakers and agencies, employers and others in countries like Australia. The overall

Table 1.7 Occupational violence incidents experienced by 1438 workers in 13 occupational groups (% of each sample)

Study title	Year done	Total no. interviewed	Abuse	Threats	Physical assault	hold-up/ snatch & grab
Young casual	1998	304	48.4	7.6	1.0	2.3
Clothing mfg	1997–98	200				
Factory-based			4.0	1.0	1.0	
Outworkers			49.0	23.0	7.0	
Interventions	1997	331				
Contractors			8.0	2.7	2.7	
Cabinetmakers			13.3	6.7	1.3	
Demolishers			35.7	7.1	7.1	
Barriers	1996–97	248				
Garage			9.7	4.2	-	
Café			45.7	15.7	1.4	
Newsagent			62.9	11.4	1.4	
Printing			37.1	2.9	2.9	
Outsourcing	1995	255				
Childcare			50.0 (15.0)	13.0 (2.5)	11.0 (-)	
Hospitality			57.0 (53.0)	46.0 (30.0)	11.0 (7.0)	
Transport			47.0 (13.0)	6.0 (13.0)	- (13.0)	
Building			15.0 (56.0)	- (17.0)	- (-)	
Taxi drivers	1993	100	81.0	17.0	10.0	

Source: Mayhew and Quinlan (2000).

Figures in brackets for outsourcing study refer to subcontract workers while figures not in brackets are for employees.

effect of these limitations is to seriously understate the level of occupational ill health in the community. This applies to all countries although evidence is relatively better for some countries and regions than others. Further, for reasons that should now be clear it is extremely difficult to make more than crude comparisons between the aggregate OHS performance of various countries. There are ways of meeting some of the gaps identified. In terms of psychosocial working conditions the periodic surveys undertaken by the European Union indicate that large and representative surveys can fill gaps, identify trends and provide a useful basis for policy making at national and international level. Similar initiatives are warranted in Australia, New Zealand and other countries along with more systematic assessment of the incidence of work-related disease.

Leaving aside debate about sources and ways of improving them, three critical points need to be made. First, measuring the extent and trends of OHS problems requires the use of a number of sources. Second, evidence from the combination of measures currently available indicates occupational illness is extensive in Australia, New Zealand and other countries. Third, this evidence suggests mixed trends with regard to OHS indices and does not allow us to conclude there is an overall improvement or deterioration in the level of occupational health. Statistics and measures of occupational illness provide no direct indication of its economic and social impact or the suffering and harm it inflicts on workers and their families. It is to this issue that attention will now briefly turn.

Assessing the impact of occupational injury and illness

In order to appreciate the scope and nature of the OHS problem it is necessary to consider its human, social and economic costs. Although the economic, social and psychological costs are interrelated, economic costs have been separated out for reasons of simplicity and to tease out limits with prevailing perceptions about costs. Indeed, the first point to be noted is the predilection to view the impact of injury only in terms of quantifiable costs, the responsibility for which can easily be allocated. As will be demonstrated, this is too narrow.

Economic costs

Occupational illness imposes very substantial economic costs on Australia, New Zealand and other countries (for an early effort to measure costs in New Zealand see Berkowitz, 1979). In 1989 the National Occupational Health and Safety Commission (NOHSC) estimated the annual total cost for Australia at around $10 billion, or between 3 and 6% of gross national product. Within five years a more detailed investigation by the Industry Commission (1995, Vol. II: 106) placed the figure between $18.9 billion and $20 billion. Six years later a revised estimate for the year 2001—the latest available—by NOHSC (2004: 2) placed the economic costs of occupational injury and disease in Australia in the year 2000–01 at $34.3 billion or 5% of GDP. While they usually occupy most prominence in terms of policy debates, workers' compensation claims costs make up only a fraction of these costs. Indeed, most of the costs are indirect, and thereby hidden, and are borne largely by injured workers, their families and the community rather than employers. Changes in the labour market, including the growth of self-employment, are moving the cost burden further away from employers and onto workers, their families and the community (Quinlan and Mayhew, 1999; Quinlan, 2004; Rosenman et al., 2006).

Hidden costs include the burden of long-term or permanently disabled workers and their dependents having to seek relief from the federal social security system. To this can be added the loss of working years associated with premature retirement or death and the reduced productivity of permanently disabled workers who return to work. Death and severe injury can have significant long-term effects on dependents through the impact of long-term trauma, disruption to families, and the effect of altered financial circumstances on the health, education and career options of children. To this may be added an economic estimate—however inadequate—of the pain and suffering experienced by workers, their families and loved ones. As NOHSC (2004: 2–3) observed, if estimates of the hidden costs just mentioned are included the total cost of occupational injury and disease to the Australian community more than doubles to $82.8 billion in 2001. As this estimate was almost a decade old in 2010, the current figure is undoubtedly substantially higher. While these estimates will always be open to some debate similar exercises in Europe and the US (see Schulte, 2005) reinforce the point that occupational injury and disease impose a significant burden on the community.

In practice, these costs are distributed among employers, workers and the community. In public health policy terms, the distribution of the costs associated with occupational illness are at least as important as aggregate costs. For example, the cost burden on workers diminishes family income and in so doing may affect the health, education and life chances of an injured worker's children. These can have cascading effects on the community. The 1995 Industry Commission (Vol. II: 105) report observed that the more severe the injury the greater proportion of the costs borne by the community. Changes to the labour market in recent decades, such as the growth of self-employment and other flexible work arrangements have affected workers' compensation coverage in ways that have shifted cost burdens away from employers and onto the community (Quinlan, 2004). Hence, the relationship between workers' compensation entitlements, access to public healthcare and social security needs to be carefully monitored. Further, the fact that employers only bear a fraction of the economic burden of occupational illness has implications for cost-pressure policies for improving OHS. A regulatory strategy that tries to shape employer behaviour by focusing on the direct costs may simply result in a cost-shedding response by employers rather than a real effort to minimise disease and injury incidence.

At this point, it is useful to identify the different array of direct and indirect costs borne by employers, workers and the community.

Employers

- loss of productivity
- consequential overtime and relief staffing

- legal penalties
- investigation of incidents and claims
- rehabilitation and retraining costs for injured workers
- damage to tools, machines, plant and equipment (including replacement costs)
- disruption to production/service delivery processes
- employee turnover training costs
- loss of institutional memory
- undermining of employee morale
- loss of goodwill and corporate image

Workers

- medical and rehabilitation costs
- loss of income
- loss of future earnings
- travel to doctors, other professionals and government agencies
- expenditures consequent on revised lifestyle
- loss of leisure opportunities and a general decline in the quality of life for the workers and their families
- family disruption and additional load on other family members caring for disabled workers
- loss of self-esteem and morale
- reduced social interaction and social status
- less tangible costs including the impact that illness may have on the morale, motivation, job satisfaction and loyalty of those workers who witness injuries/illnesses or their ramifications. While difficult if not impossible to measure such intangibles may have a profound effect on productivity in an aggregate sense.

Community

- health and medical costs borne through general healthcare apparatus
- social welfare payments to the seriously injured or their dependents
- loss of human capital
- premature retirement from the workforce due to chronic injury
- inspection and investigation
- rehabilitation
- community service costs, including those provided informally or on a voluntary basis
- travel and other concessions to the permanently incapacitated and their dependents
- costs to unions dealing with occupational injury and illness
- cost of OHS promotion, research, standard setting and education

(adapted from Industry Commission, 1995, Vol. II; see also Chapman Walsh, 1991)

Several additional points need to be made about the measurement of costs. Many indirect costs are difficult to measure. The precise impact of some indirect costs will vary from workplace to workplace and from industry to industry due to a wide array of factors. These include the ease with which incapacitated labour may be replaced and the predictability of a specific injury or illness within a particular workplace/industry/ occupation to name just two. This means that a simple combination of injury and illness frequency and severity would not represent an adequate indication of the comparative cost of illness within a particular establishment. Relying on those costs that are easiest to calculate could have unforeseen adverse consequences. If a firm concentrates on reducing workers' compensation costs through a claims management system it may not address significant but other costs associated with injury, including loss of worker morale, job satisfaction and loyalty, or potential benefits such as the scope to improve long-term productivity. While difficult if not impossible to measure, such intangibles may have a profound effect on productivity. At the national level, disparities in cost measurement may critically affect the development of standards or regulatory strategies, particularly where these strategies are driven by private insurers/healthcare providers or workers' compensation data, as is increasingly the case in a number of countries.

Costs need to be assessed in relation to benefits. By this we do not mean the attempt by some neo-liberal economists to place a market price on safety where the cost of safety interventions is measured against the retention of jobs (for a critique of economic rationalist perspectives on OHS see Dorman, 1996). This is both an empirically flawed and unethical form of so-called rationality. What we would point out is that, overall, far more attention has focused on measuring the costs of occupational injury and disease than in trying to calculate benefits associated with improvements in OHS. The direct costs of regulatory compliance are easier to calculate, fit with the confined notion of meaningful costs used by the accounting and finance professions, or are (like lost jobs) part of the dominant discourse of neo-classical economists and policymakers. On the other hand, benefits represent a long-term stream of more diffuse gains (i.e. general community benefits as opposed to those applying to a more directly concerned industry lobby group). As Ashford and Caldart (1996: 249–53) observe, public policy benefits and public policy costs are both difficult to calculate. However, the issue is not simply one of difficulty but of the willingness of business economists and even governments to ignore this and other flaws in their methodology that disguise significant adverse distributional consequences. Ashford and Caldart (1996: 254) argue that cost–benefit analysis is not ethically neutral but value laden because it relies on observed market values that reflect the existing distribution of wealth, and misconstrues policy effects that are not intrinsically economic (including intergenerational effects on health). It portrays decisions about workplace safety as voluntary transactions (for example, workers accepting greater risk in return for higher remuneration), ignoring that decisions are embedded in social contexts that shape access to knowledge, the ability to respond and the responses that are available.

In its report the Australian Industry Commission (1995, Vol. II) noted a series of studies indicating an association between superior productivity performance and higher levels of OHS but far more needs to be done in this area. While some regulatory agencies have tried to establish a strategy based around 'best practice' and OHS is 'good for business' the arguments tend to be over-generalised and ignore regulatory and market constraints. It is likely that, at the firm and even industry level (see Frick, 1995, 1996), the weighing of the benefits of improving OHS against the costs of such injury can be best seen as contingent and influenced by factors such as the level of the domestic and international regulatory playing field. Nor can it be assumed that employers make careful calculations in relation to the OHS implications of their decisions. Indeed, without regulatory intervention and assistance few employers would undertake such tasks or be able to introduced appropriate control systems. In sum, costs and benefits need to be simultaneously considered but not in a narrowly conceived cost–benefit format where this entails a significant number of unrecognised distortions.

The final and perhaps most intriguing point to be made in connection with the economic costs of occupational illness is its limited impact, comparatively speaking, on public debate and policy making. The act of working injures and maims far more persons than travelling by car and crimes of violence combined. Over the postwar period it has also accounted for well over three times the working days lost through strikes (and the gap has considerably widened in the last decade). Yet, for all this, occupational illness occupies far less media and political attention in Australia (and in many other countries for that matter) than any one of the other three issues just mentioned. The reasons why economic costs have not translated into political action and public debate are too complex to discuss here, although at various points in the book we will indicate some reasons why the OHS debate has not commanded the level of attention its economic dimensions might seem to warrant.

Social and psychological costs

In many discussions of the costs of occupational illness mention of the social and psychological or human costs constitutes little more than lip service. Indeed there has been limited exploration of these aspects of OHS (for an exception see McCulloch, 1986). Yet, as the submissions given by grieving parents, spouses and children to a number of government inquiries (see evidence of Fran Kavanagh to Legislative Council Standing Committee on Law and Justice, 1998; and evidence of families in Nile, F., 2004) and court cases testify, the social and human toll of occupational injury and disease is profound and must be borne in mind when considering OHS. It is absolutely essential that the wellbeing of workers and their families be at the forefront of any consideration of OHS and that the highest levels of protection be pursued, notwithstanding the alleged inconvenience this may cause to others who seldom if ever personally experience these costs.

In our view the failure to consider the social and psychological costs of injury and illness on workers, their families, friends and colleagues is not consistent with the effective management of OHS. The economic, social and psychological costs are inextricably intertwined in complex ways that need to be identified and understood if they are to be addressed. We will pursue these links in later chapters. At this point it is worth identifying a few of the physical, psychological and other burdens that occupational injury and disease imposes on workers, their friends and family.

- physical pain and suffering
- emotional strain and suffering associated with the injury/disease, medical treatment, pursuing compensation and damages claims
- disruption to career development/potential and unwanted job changes
- disruption to outside work activities, including recreation, education and personal development
- temporary or permanent disruption to work and the social meanings this imparts in terms of identity, self-esteem and ordering of life
- disruption to social roles, personal relationships and family routines and responsibilities (task displacement, such as the inability to do conventional domestic chores, can be very disruptive especially for males who are more inflexible in this regard)
- the burden of family members and partners (especially women) in dealing with anguish and helping injured workers adjust to their injuries or disease, dealing with medical and rehabilitation practitioners, compensation agencies, courts and others
- the traumatic effect of death or serious injury on workmates, close friends and relatives.

This list is by no means comprehensive and hardly does justice to the suffering involved. A number of these impacts are difficult if not impossible to measure. In some cases, we should not try to. How do you measure the anguish of a woman who learnt she had lost her husband and two young sons in the Bulli Mine disaster of 1887? However, her anguished cry 'Oh my boys, my beautiful, beautiful boys' captures something real and important (Dingsdag, 1993). Her anguish is not something of only historical interest. It is something shared by others who have lost someone precious to them in a workplace fatality, such as the family of Larry Knight who was killed in a rockfall at the Beaconsfield goldmine in 2006.

In some instances, such as disasters in single-industry towns, workplace hazards can have profound long-term effects. For example, it can be argued that the series of mine disasters affecting the town of Moura in central Queensland over a 20-year period have left long-term scars on the entire community. Most working in the mines will have known some of those who died and a not insubstantial number of families will be missing a son, father, cousin or uncle. Situations where community-wide effects are apparent are atypical but this does not mean the more typical incidents leave no traces on larger communities. As we will illustrate in chapter 10, serious health risks in the workplace can certainly affect the relationship of workers and managers and there can be little doubt that this flows on to the broader community. Chapman Walsh (1991: 218) has indicated that illness and disability may affect work ethics and community confidence. These aspects have been seldom researched and there are some obvious disjunctions. Most notably, while Australian and overseas surveys indicate that industrialised communities see workplace death as extremely serious (ranking immediately below things such as child murder) this has not translated into a similar prioritising of government policies.

Many of the impacts just mentioned are seldom addressed in more than passing by the official discourse on occupational illness. Some go unreported altogether while others only rarely break the surface of public recognition. The introduction of victim impact statements in court proceedings in Victoria has provided opportunities for hitherto unheard voices, such as a 12-year-old boy telling the court about the changing relationship with his father (killed due to the negligence of two contractors who failed to supply and erect proper scaffolding) in the period immediately before his death. The boy mentioned the joint sport and recreation activities he had begun to enjoy. These shared experiences, and the emotional bonding embedded in them, cannot easily be replaced. We are talking about more than emotional distress and suffering here although we make no apology for raising this aspect because it is important. Knowledge of OHS requires an ethical base and understanding the human dimensions of the problem (not simply its economic costs) is critical to this. At the same time, the case just cited illustrates how a failure to provide a safe workplace can impact on social relationships in a profound and far-reaching fashion.

It is necessary to make these points because the human dimension is frequently obscured by the largely technocratic and fragmented way in which OHS is often conceived and addressed. The treatment of occupational illness has been compartmentalised into a series of discrete processes (medical diagnosis and treatment, payment of compensation, rehabilitation and return to work, etc.) provided by a number of distinct agencies, organisations and professions, each with its own responsibilities and interests. The resulting operations do not always serve to minimise the social and psychological impact of injury on workers and their families. For instance, delays in compensation payments—a common occurrence—exacerbate the emotional trauma associated with injury for a worker and their family. This may disrupt recovery and rehabilitation, not to mention affecting family relationships and even attitudes to reporting illness in the future. Disputes about medical diagnosis and treatment or litigation may have similar effects. The psychological impact of illness may continue long after an apparently successful recovery and return to the workforce. While the long-term emotional effects of major disasters have been recognised, even seemingly minor injuries or hazardous incidents may have profound effects. The overall impact of an injury is not necessarily commensurate with its severity in terms of direct physiological effects. Injury impacts will be influenced by job and labour market characteristics, the nature of informal family and community support networks, and a range of other factors (James, 1989). These issues will be taken up in the chapter devoted to workers' compensation and rehabilitation. At this point it is enough to say that the social and psychological costs of occupational injury and illness are at least as important as the economic costs in terms of assessing the OHS problem.

Conclusion

The aim of this chapter is to provide an overview of how work affects health. We are concerned to show that work entails exposure to a wide array of hazards, that exposure to these hazards is widespread (and seriously understated by official statistics) and imposes significant social, economic and human costs on the community (whether that be a rich or poor country). Therefore, the effects of work on health are an important consideration for governments, employers, unions, a range of professions (including healthcare workers, workplace designers, researchers and lawyers), all workers and the community in general.

As well as identifying and briefly discussing a wide array of work-related hazards it was shown that exposure to hazards changes over time—and not always in a positive direction. Indeed, improvements need to be carefully balanced against the introduction of new hazards or other negative changes. Further, hazards cannot be treated in isolation because multiple exposures are common and hazards also interact in complex ways. As we have begun to show, particular disciplines that have addressed OHS provide partial insights—a point taken up in more detail in later chapters. If OHS is to be better understood and addressed in ways that secure a significant overall improvement over time, a more holistic multidisciplinary approach is needed. Succeeding chapters will provide a more detailed examination of OHS; the perspective and role of particular disciplines/professions; how government, management and workers/unions address OHS; and how knowledge of and interventions with regard to OHS can be reshaped to create a healthier and more rewarding working environment.

QUESTIONS FOR DISCUSSION

1   Identify and discuss the array of hazards in a workplace or industry that you have been employed by or visited.
2   What are the advantages and disadvantages of separating physical, chemical and organisational hazards when examining OHS?
3   Is the pattern of occupational risks changing over time? If so, why are such changes occurring?
4   What are the major limitations of official statistics data on occupational illness?
5   Looking ahead to the next decade, anticipate what the new occupational hazards facing workers might be.

FURTHER READING

Australian Safety and Compensation Council (2008), *Compendium of Workers' Compensation Statistics Australia 2005–06*, Australian Government, Canberra.
Benach, J. and Muntaner, C. with Solar, O., Santana, V. and Quinlan, M. (2009), *Employment, Work and Health Inequalities: A Global Perspective*, World Health Organization, Geneva.

Bohgard, L. et al. (eds) (2009), *Work and Technology on Human Terms*, Prevent, Stockholm.

Concha-Barrientos, M., Nelson, D., Fingerhut, M., Driscoll, T. and Leigh, J. (2005), 'The global burden due to occupational injury', *American Journal of Industrial Medicine*, **48**: 470–81.

Cox, R. and Lippel, K. (2008), 'Falling through the legal cracks: the pitfalls of using workers' compensation data as indicators of work-related injuries and illnesses', *Policy and Practice in Health and Safety*, **6**(2): 9–30.

Kendall, N. (2006), *Management and Governance of Occupational Health and Safety in Five Countries (United Kingdom, United States, Finland, Canada, Australia)*, National Occupational Health and Safety Advisory Committee: NOHSAC Technical Report 8, Wellington.

Nichols, T. (1997), *The Sociology of Industrial Injury*, Mansell, London.

Perspectives on occupational health and safety

Introduction

THE causes of occupational illness and injury have been examined from a number of disciplinary perspectives. The most prominent and influential have emerged from occupational medicine, engineering, occupational hygiene, ergonomics, work psychology, sociology, work relations, law and economics. These accounts vary widely in focus and frequently present conflicting pictures of the primary causes of injury and illness. Often there is little cross-disciplinary dialogue, with one perspective overlooking other valid and important considerations. These differences in focus frequently reflect underlying ideological differences between disciplines, and are most obvious where disciplines have become principally aligned to either the interests of workers or management. If we aim to develop a comprehensive and multidisciplinary perspective on OHS, we are faced with the problem of generating a workable synthesis of these conflicting views. Unfortunately, this is not an easy task.

Before we can integrate the knowledge from the various disciplinary perspectives we need to have a clear understanding of their history, current positions, strengths and limitations. Each of the major perspectives will now be examined in turn. A brief history of the origins and growth of each discipline will be provided before its current perspective on OHS issues is examined. It should be noted that the exchange of both theory and practice between disciplines has increased in recent years, blurring boundaries and also positively contributing to more multidisciplinary research (see chapter 5). We shall attempt to outline the central concerns and practices of each discipline, but the boundaries that we place around them must be arbitrary to some extent.

Medical and health science perspectives

From the late nineteenth century, the medical profession has assumed a dominant role in the definition and treatment of illness and the control of health-related services in Western societies (Rose, 1971; Abrams, 2001; Gochfeld, 2005). Its influence in the sphere of OHS has been no less pervasive. Medical practitioners have controlled both the way in which occupational illnesses are defined and the means by which they are treated. This dominance has been supported by factors including the political power of the profession, authority bestowed by legislation, the undeniable success of medical technology in treating many acute illnesses, and a high level of community acceptance of medical treatment. It is important to understand the significant influence the medical perspective has had on health and the way it has shaped the perceptions of OHS among managers, legislators, the general public and workers. It is also important to acknowledge the influence and perspective of other health professions (such as occupational health nursing and physiotherapy) as well as divisions within the medical profession (for example between general practice and occupational medicine).

Occupational medicine

Before we can understand contemporary occupational medicine we need to first ask: 'What is the core orientation characterising research and practice in occupational medicine?' To answer this question, we need to examine the central role played by the medical profession in workplace healthcare since the time of the Industrial Revolution. Early in the nineteenth century a number of physicians used their access to learned societies and other forums to draw public attention to the social and physical degradation imposed on the working class by industrial development (Abrams, 2001; Gochfeld, 2005). Many of these physicians had been compelled by financial necessity to accept work as town or parish surgeons, treating the poor. As a result, they developed a more intimate understanding of the needs of the working class than other professionals and wealthy employers. While most did not attack the existence and growth of industrial capitalism, prominent physicians did take a reformist stance, pointing to urgently needed public health reforms, including improvements in sewage and hygiene, housing and basic working conditions. Charles Thackrah (1832), for example, observed in relation to industrial disease that 'Evils are suffered to exist, even where the means of correction are known and easily applied' (cited in Ferguson, 1986: 1). He and several colleagues, usually local general practitioners who had begun to visit workplaces to provide medical services, fought hard to make the public aware of the social evils imposed upon many workers. In the UK public awareness and community and union campaigns led to legislation which, for example, required employers to provide limited medical services in trades identified as 'dangerous'. Unfortunately, the support of some medical practitioners for social reform had a less altruistic objective, forming part of a wider battle for professional power during a period in which physicians were struggling to achieve social recognition and control of healthcare (Rose, 1971; Russell and Schofield, 1989).

In Australia, organised examination of major occupational hazards began in the 1880s (although there is evidence of practice long before this; Quinlan, 1997) with investigations into lead exposure and lung disease in a variety of workplaces like mines. A few physicians began to be employed to deal with the high incidences of occupational disease and injury. A survey of large employers in 1925 identified only eight full-time occupational physicians, and a further thirty doctors, presumably general practitioners, providing part-time services (Ferguson, 1988). Their duties were limited, including pre-employment and periodic medical examinations, some treatment, public hygiene services and lectures on first aid. The first government unit specifically concerned with occupational health matters was the Division of Industrial Hygiene of the Commonwealth Department of Health, set up in 1921, followed by the opening of government units in several states and the commencement of the Commonwealth Munitions Medical Service in 1936 (Ferguson, 1986a). The Commonwealth Division of Occupational Hygiene produced an impressive range of reports on major occupational groups and hazards before its closure in 1932, and the work of Charles Badham in the NSW unit led the world in the recognition of pneumoconiosis among coal miners (Ferguson, 1988). The first private consultant in occupational medicine began practising in Sydney in the 1940s (Ferguson, 1988).

In New Zealand there are accounts of occupational medicine being practised as early as 1838 in the whaling stations and later among miners in the gold rush of the 1850s to 1860s. Indeed, New Zealand's first medical school at Otago University (second only to Melbourne in Australasia) was funded by money from the gold rush and the university still plays a major research and teaching role in occupational medicine. Although there are some examples of medical physicians undertaking work specifically in the area of occupational medicine, the development of occupational medicine in New Zealand and Australia was often an adjunct to public health or general practice. In New Zealand, local authority public health medical officers were responsible for health hazards of workers. With the enactment of the Social Security Act 1938, supervision of health hazards in factories and other places of work became the responsibility of the Department of Health. Unfortunately, the government services in both New Zealand and Australia established during the early 1900s were starved of staff and resources. These problems were compounded by inadequate research data, education, government policies and programs, and legislated health and safety standards. Consequently, in general, developments in occupational medicine lagged behind those in Europe and North America. Nevertheless, evidence was mounting regarding the widespread prevalence of a number of serious occupational diseases, including pneumoconiosis, lead poisoning and silicosis (Ferguson, 1988; Gochfeld, 2005).

World War II provided an important stimulus to the expansion of occupational medical services. High productivity was essential in the war industries at the same time that labour was scarce and often recruited from the less fit groups in the community. In the UK, wartime regulations requiring the appointment of a doctor in factories above a certain size demonstrated political acceptance that medical services could make a significant contribution to industrial productivity (Tyrer and Lee, 1979; Abrams, 2001). The postwar period saw these services gradually expand, usually through the part-time employment of general practitioners supported by occupational health nurses. Medical services developed in the munitions, mining, railways, and chemical industries, but achieved little penetration into the construction, agriculture and fishing industries

(Ferguson, 1988). In some cases at least, the expansion of medical services had less to do with the prevention of injury and ill health than with the time-savings and productivity benefits of treatment at the workplace (Tyrer and Lee, 1979). Nevertheless, it was only after World War II that the incidence of many severe occupational diseases of the nineteenth century substantially declined (Ferguson, 1986a). On the other hand, the legacy of exposure to asbestos and industrial noise is still with us and many of the old threats to health are being replaced by new ones.

Throughout its history the practice of medicine in the workplace has been dominated by non-specialist physicians who applied more general principles of clinical medicine to occupational problems. They traditionally emphasised clinical treatment and rarely visited the factory floor (Tyrer and Lee, 1979). Workplace visits by clinicians are still rare, and access to workplace medical services in Australia, New Zealand and other Western countries is probably restricted to less than 20% of the working population (Ferguson, 1986a; Cherry and McDonald, 2002; Gorman, 2004). Development of a recognised specialty in occupational medicine in Australia is a relatively recent phenomenon. The original professional association, the Australian and New Zealand Society of Occupational Medicine, was not founded until 1969 and full recognition of the specialty, through the formation of the Australasian Faculty of Occupational and Environmental Medicine, did not occur until 1983. The first postgraduate university qualification, the Diploma in Occupational Health at the University of Sydney, did not appear until 1974. Despite these developments, the majority of practitioners in the workplace are still general practitioners without even introductory training in occupational medicine (Ferguson, 1986a, 1988). This problem is not confined to Australia or New Zealand. In the 1980s only 66% of US medical schools taught occupational medicine and only 54% of the medical schools made the subject compulsory (Levy, 1984). In a recent editorial on the state of occupational medicine in the twenty-first century, Gorman (2004: 450) noted that:

> There are substantial problems in training occupational physicians ... some of these arise because of the role that occupational medicine has assumed as an escape discipline for dissatisfied practitioners from elsewhere. Unlike medicine and surgery in general, there are few real apprenticeships available in occupational medicine. Perhaps as a consequence of the failure to learn in such a master–apprentice relationship, there are very limited mechanisms available to manage problem occupational medicine trainees ... [In addition] there is frequently no or limited public funding of, or resource for either training or service delivery in occupational medicine. There has been a widespread capture of funds intended for occupational health research by epidemiologists.

In fact, general practitioners, who saw occupational physicians as a threat to their incomes, and other elements of the medical profession vigorously opposed the growth of occupational medicine as a recognised specialty (Ferguson, 1988). Yet general practitioners, as research shows, do not always have the expertise in occupational medicine

(Gorman, 2004). This concern was highlighted in a comprehensive review of the health of Britain's working age population, in which Black (2008: 16) observed:

> General Practitioners [GPs] have inadequate options for referral and occupational health provision is disproportionately concentrated among a few large employers, leaving the vast majority of small businesses unsupported … GPs often feel ill-equipped to offer advice to their patients on remaining in or returning to work. Their training has to date not prepared them for this and, therefore, the work-related advice they do give, can be naturally cautious.

Much remains to be done before occupational medicine is accepted as both an essential component of general medical training and an important area of specialisation. Indeed, recent trends in Australia, Canada, the US and elsewhere have not been positive in this regard.

The contemporary field of occupational medicine is often linked with environmental medicine, and research in this area can be found in both discourses. Occupational medicine also claims to encompass a very broad range of activities, including pre-employment and return-to-work medical screening, medical monitoring, biological monitoring, clinical medical treatment, health management and consultative services, health promotion, rehabilitation, and medical assessment for compensation and other purposes (Ferguson, 1988; Harrington and Gill, 1987; LaDou, 1997; Gochfeld, 2005). Individual practitioners, however, are generally involved in a limited range of these activities. In fact, occupational medicine maintains a strong emphasis on individual clinical treatment of illness and injury, and the diagnostic and therapeutic competence of most practitioners is not matched by their skill in illness prevention and health promotion (Ferguson, 1986a).

Medical screening is used to assess whether individual workers are fit to perform specific jobs (Mathews, 1985; Tyrer and Lee, 1979). It usually takes the form of pre-employment medicals and examinations before returning to work after illness. Pre-employment medicals may be used to assess whether applicants meet specific physical fitness standards required for particular jobs or if they are susceptible to specific hazards encountered on the job. For example, specific fitness standards may be required for fire-fighters or epileptics may be screened out of jobs as drivers or as high-rise construction workers. Pre-employment examinations are also used to establish health and biological baselines so later monitoring can assess whether health deteriorates after exposure to work hazards (Tyrer and Lee, 1979). For instance, hearing tests should be performed before workers enter noisy jobs and later used as an index of hearing loss and X-rays should be taken where exposure to dusts and fibres may lead to lung disease. On rare occasions, the taking of a more extensive medical history may be warranted if there are specific reasons for doing so. Return-to-work medicals provide a means of assessing whether workers have recovered sufficiently from illness or injury to recommence work without threatening their own health or that of other workers.

When used appropriately, medical screening can function to protect both workers and employers. Workers can be protected in two ways. First, they may be discouraged from entering employment that places their health at unreasonable risk. Second, they may be protected from threats to health and safety caused by unsuitable individuals being employed with them. Employers are protected from the costs of employing a worker who is unfit for the work required. However, employers often use pre-employment examinations more generally to minimise the risk of employing a worker likely to take sick leave frequently or make an unusually high number of workers' compensation claims; this is a particularly undesirable practice given the very limited ability of doctors to accurately predict such outcomes in most circumstances (Tyrer and Lee, 1979). We shall discuss other problems associated with medical screening and monitoring shortly.

Medical and biological monitoring both require ongoing checks of workers during their period of employment. Medical monitoring involves periodic examination aimed at identifying the clinical symptoms of occupational illness or disease (Mathews, 1985). Occupational physicians utilise information from a range of sources for this purpose, including general clinical examination, X-rays, lung function tests, hearing and eye tests, allergy tests and cytology screening. For example, lung function tests may be used to monitor changes in lung capacity and efficiency among workers exposed to dusts or fibres. Allergy tests are used to identify the development of sensitivity to particular substances in the workplace. Occupational asthma, for example, may arise from exposure to substances like platinum and isocyanates. Biological monitoring is performed to assess the level of specific substances, such as lead, in workers' bodies (Mathews, 1985; Rosenberg and Harrison, 1997). It is intended to identify the changes in the body that precede disease while they are still reversible. Samples of workers' blood, urine, nails, hair or exhaled breath may be analysed for evidence of the presence of the substance or its derivatives. The objective may be to assess simple exposure, for example by measuring lead levels in the blood; accumulated body burdens, such as the level of mercury in the hair; or derivatives of absorbed materials, such as coproporphyrins in urine after exposure to lead. In some circumstances, such as when workers are likely to be exposed to lead, medical or biological monitoring is a statutory requirement.

Occupational physicians perform a number of other health-related functions (see LaDou, 1997). Ferguson (1988) lists the following: prevention, recognition, treatment, and rehabilitation of work-related disease and injury, and the promotion of health, fitness and safe work design. Specialists in occupational medicine have long advanced the view that preventative practices have an important role in workplace health and safety, even though their practice has been predominantly concerned with medical examination and treatment. Unfortunately, their actual contribution to prevention programs is rarely spelled out clearly. For example, responsibility for preventative modification of the working environment is usually assigned to engineers, occupational hygienists and ergonomists. Although occupational physicians often claim to play a major role in the environmental design process, their contribution is generally confined to providing information on the medical effects of specific hazards rather than actually generating solutions. Since the 1980s occupational medicine has assumed a wider role in workplace health promotion (Ferguson, 1988). The approach to health promotion generally taken has focused on changing the behaviour of individual workers, dealing with health issues like drug and alcohol use, stress management, and diet and exercise programs. A more recent review by Horsley and Goddard (2007) has identified a shift in occupational medicine in Australia away from the workplace towards more community-based practice (reflecting changes in production such as downsizing and offshoring). Further, while traditional areas of treatment remain important, they identify evidence of a partial shift towards more proactive and preventative activity, including the prevention of disability in relation to musculoskeletal and stress-related disorders. The increased interest in health promotion along with the trends just identified (and a growing awareness of environmental health) have undoubtedly expanded the field's understanding of occupational illness.

There is growing recognition that the relationship between work and non-work illness is a complex one and that many diseases previously defined as 'non-occupational' may have partially or wholly arisen from work, or have been aggravated by work. A UK survey found that the rate of reporting work-related illness or injury to occupational physicians was eight times higher than that recorded by the government health surveillance schemes (Cherry and McDonald, 2002). Likewise, a Spanish study of a primary healthcare setting (Benavides et al., 2005) found a significant level of work-related diseases went unrecognised. There is also evidence that general practitioners still fail to inquire about patients' work practices and exposure to hazards (Gorman, 2004), perhaps because they have had little or no training in occupational medicine, as outlined above. Undoubtedly, as a result of this there are instances where a link between hazard exposure and occupational disease, such as exposure to dust or fumes leading to a respiratory condition, is not recognised and therefore, workers' compensation cannot be sought.

There is no doubt that medicine and medical practice have made, and will continue to make, an important contribution the field of occupational health. The expertise of medical practitioners to treat many ill and injured workers is beyond dispute. Medical research also has a vital role in refining our understanding of the physical aetiology of specific occupational illnesses. This work provides insights into the impact of various hazards on bodily functioning and provides a basis on which to develop prevention programs. Collection of detailed cumulative health records from periodic examination can provide an important source of information for the protection of workers exposed to health hazards. The accumulation of health data can also assist in broadening knowledge of the direct and indirect hazards associated with different jobs and processes. These records can be even more useful if they are regularly collated to provide information on the health status of identifiable groups of workers likely to be exposed to specific hazards.

Despite these important contributions, like all disciplinary perspectives, occupational medicine provides only a partial understanding of occupational health. Some of its limitations stem from the general shortcomings of what has become known as the 'medical model'. Others are more specific to the theory and practice of occupational medicine. We shall examine these limitations in terms of the potential of occupational medicine to contribute to comprehensive and effective occupational health practice.

Criticism of the medical model has been widespread for at least six decades (Davis and George, 1988). While the social causation of disease was well recognised by the nineteenth-century public health movement, in the twentieth and twenty-first centuries medicine has been dominated by a clinical model based heavily on the natural sciences. The clinical model is primarily concerned with the care of individuals rather than groups, with treatment rather than prevention, and with acute rather than chronic illness. It has led modern medicine to focus on curing disease through technological intervention, depending primarily on developments in chemotherapy and diagnostic and surgical procedures. The focus on individual, rather than collective, notions of illness has meant that modern medicine has devoted little attention to identifying and changing social and occupational factors with profound effects on health.

Emphasis on the identification and correction of biological pathology, and the collection of individual health data, such as that contained in medical histories, has inhibited recognition of the complex social factors impinging upon occupational health. It also does not facilitate the identification of hazards and illnesses to which groups of workers are exposed. The emphasis on treatment has also meant that scarce resources have been allocated to increasingly expensive individual cures, while even well-established and effective means of improving health through alterations to the physical and social environment have not received attention. Furthermore, the focus on acute conditions has meant that chronic injuries, such as repetitive strain injury (RSI) and back injury, and illnesses such as asbestosis and cancers, are less well understood than they should be. In general, the achievements of medicine have served selected categories of illness and selected elements of the population. This situation arose because medicine became preoccupied with curing sick workers rather than producing healthy working environments (a number of positive developments are examined in chapter 5).

On occasion, medical diagnosis and treatment have supported attempts by management to portray occupational illness as an individual problem rather than an outcome of the organisation of work. Hopkins and Palser (1984) observed that one means by which the 'blame' for injury and illness is shifted onto individual workers is to attribute them to malingering. Workers are accused of escaping work by falsifying or exaggerating injuries. Medical practitioners in Australia and New Zealand have sometimes propagated this idea by denying that an injury is 'real' or claiming that its incidence and disabling effects have been grossly exaggerated. Frequently, these judgments have been based on personal clinical impressions alone. Delays in the medical diagnosis of genuine illnesses and injuries, and delays in the recognition that medical conditions are occupationally related, have also provided misleading support for individualised accounts of occupational diseases and accusations of malingering. Delays of this nature are of particular concern in the current environment of increasingly rapid changes in work processes and the hazards to which workers are exposed.

Medical practitioners have also tended to support the view that workers' compensation claims are often fictitious or exaggerated by applying pseudo-diagnoses such as 'attitudinal pathos', 'compensation neurosis', 'bizarre hypochondrias', 'traumatic neurosis', and 'malingering' (Ellard, 1970). An image of the deviant and individualised nature of workers' suffering is clearly promoted by such terms. This image is rarely counter-balanced by recognition of the widespread sacrifices in health that many workers make to do their jobs, much of which results in no sick leave or workers' compensation and is consequently not reported in official statistics. Such viewpoints detract from attempts to explain the broader patterns of occupational illness for which their explanations are clearly untenable.

There are pressures for the medical profession to take a managerial orientation to health and safety issues. Medical practitioners generally espouse an admirable commitment to ethical and professionally independent care, supported by assertions that their first loyalty is to the health and wellbeing of the patient. With this orientation they can provide an important caring function which can benefit workers and help protect them from assaults on their health. Unfortunately, in occupational practice there are strong pressures for this ethic to be compromised. Most full-time occupational physicians are employed by industrial organisations, and consequently they have recognised an obligation to advance the economic interests of their employers as well as protect the individual and collective interests of the workers who are their patients (Ferguson, 1986b).

Professional societies, including the Australian and New Zealand Society of Occupational Medicine, have become aware of these dual loyalties and produced ethical standards for dealing with them. The guidelines are detailed and cover the circumstances and scope of prescribed examinations, the medical management of individual workers, certification of illness, disclosure of individual and organisational data, and professional communication (Ferguson, 1986b). Nevertheless, studies have indicated that being employed by the company can put medical doctors under pressure to support the interests of management (Kerr, 1981, 1990; Walters, 1982; Koh and Lee, 2003). Interviews with company doctors indicated that reliance on management for remuneration and resources limited their autonomy and constrained their ability to take the role of an objective third party (Kerr, 1981, 1990; Koh and Lee, 2003). Doctors reported contradictory pressures from labour and management which required them to simultaneously safeguard health and promote productivity and profit. The conflicting pressures were felt in four main areas: regulation of absenteeism, certification of workers' fitness to work, workers' compensation claims and control of workplace health hazards. The doctors indicated that they felt pressure to be cautious in classifying workers as fit, to be watchful for workers who might be 'cheating' the company through unwarranted sick leave or workers' compensation claims, and to place an emphasis on less-costly strategies for improving health and safety. They also reported frustration with what they saw as workers' tendency to overestimate hazards. This orientation clearly supported the interests of management more than of workers.

One factor leading to the development of occupational medicine as a recognised specialty was the growth of workers' compensation and common law claims in the occupational health arena. Once again, there may be explicit pressure for medical practitioners dealing with these claims to be oriented towards the protection of employers' interests rather than those of workers. As Tyrer and Lee (1979) observe, one of the initial reasons for the appointment of doctors in industry was to protect employers against claims at common law for industrial disease. Consequently, workers were often antagonistic to the doctors who they reasonably believed were employed to deny them their rights. Today, while many medical screening processes are ostensibly preventative and aimed at protecting the health of workers, unionists and others have argued that their primary function is to protect companies against compensation claims (Mathews, 1985). The central role played by occupational medicine in assessing the impact of health on the capacity to work may function in a positive way by authorising the absence of workers who are ill or providing certification of illness or injury for compensation purposes (Raffle, 1975). However, it may also promote attempts by employers to minimise workers' compensation and sick leave claims while affording workers little real protection from specific hazards (Mathews, 1985).

In addition to these immediate pressures, it has been claimed that the practice of occupational medicine has a class bias. It has been argued that the interests and ideology of professionals are those of the dominant class, and that professional expertise and authority serves to legitimate existing power structures and operates as a means of social control (Walters, 1982). In the case of occupational medicine, this social control function is particularly explicit in the regulation of workers' compensation and sick leave. Bartlett (1979) argued that other factors combining to limit concern for workers' health included doctors' training, expertise and professional self-interest that encouraged a curative rather than preventative orientation to healthcare. The middle-class background of most doctors means that they have little real experience and understanding of workers' needs and values, and they may consequently be less than sympathetic to workers' health problems.

As noted above, the focus of established medicine on life outside the workplace is further emphasised by the lack of specialist training in occupational medicine. Despite the efforts of the Australian Faculty of Occupational Medicine, specialist university training in occupational medicine has, like OHS training more generally, has stagnated since the 1990s (this problem is not confined to Australia or New Zealand). Limited specialist education programs flow onto research (note, however, recent efforts to establish a centre of occupational medicine research at the University of Western Australia). Occupational medicine has generally received little research funding and has been accorded little prominence in campaigns to raise the health standards of the community. More attention is paid, for example, to the road toll and non-occupational sources of cancer (see chapter 1).

Occupational medicine claims to encompass a very wide range of activities. Occupational physicians also frequently see themselves as the pre-eminent occupational health professionals and historically displayed a strong disposition to maintain control over the activities of other professionals. Tyrer and Lee (1979), for example, claimed that the occupational physician should be responsible for the provision of health services, coordinating and leading other professionals and having the ultimate power to make decisions. Raffle (1975) presented a similar model for occupational healthcare dominated by specialists in occupational medicine. These models effectively marginalised the input of other professionals by presuming that their expertise was secondary and rightly subject to medical control. A consequence is that the medical perspective, with its inherent limitations, dominates the provision of health services, and full and effective collaboration between professionals is discouraged. These attitudes appeared to have as much to do with the maintenance of professional control of healthcare by medical practitioners more generally as they do with the optimisation of health services (Rose, 1971; Russell and Schofield, 1989). Since the middle of last century the political activities of professional medical associations have been aimed at the effective exclusion of other professions from access to the wealth, prestige and power associated with medical practice (Russell and Schofield, 1989). This protection of professional privilege has been recently demonstrated in the vocal opposition of some members of the medical profession to the expansion of the training of nurses and ambulance officers into areas that had previously been the exclusive province of medical practitioners. The tension created by professional rivalry over the control of healthcare has also been a significant stumbling block in the development of effective and comprehensive health and safety management.

At the same time, some important distinctions within the medical perspective need to be acknowledged. Taken in its broadest sense (i.e. research and policy and not simply daily practice) occupational medicine has (like public and community medicine) far stronger historical roots in social medicine and public health than most areas of medicine (including general practice). As discussed in chapter 5, over the past 20 years research in occupational medicine has included a growing component that takes explicit account of the organisation of work, whether that be demand/control imbalance or the effects of particular actions or arrangements such as privatisation, hours of work and piecework payment systems (see, for example, Lacey et al., 2007). This research is also finding its way into 'mainstream' research journals such as *The Lancet* and more practitioner-orientated medical journals such as *The Journal of the American Medical Association* (see, for example, Ayas et al., 2006) as well as specialist occupational medicine and health journals. Increasingly this research has been undertaken by multidisciplinary teams and there is also evidence of less hierarchic multidisciplinary team-based approaches to occupational health (such as rural community-based health and safety initiatives). In short, taken as a whole occupational medicine adopts a more social and public health–orientated perspective than medicine more generally and there are a number of positive trends (although the field has also suffered a decline as a result of labour market changes such as offshoring and downsizing by larger public and private sector employers).

Returning to the question of practice, even though specific procedures like medical screening and monitoring often have an important role in a comprehensive occupational health program, they also have limitations. A particular concern is that employers may use them as a cheap alternative to environmental and engineering controls, which aim to identify health hazards, eliminate them and effectively protect workers from the primary sources of health risks. Optimally, medical screening and monitoring should be used as a secondary strategy to alert workers and management to the failure of environmental protection. Mathews (1985) argues that medical examinations should also satisfy several other important criteria before they are acceptable to workers. Most importantly, their paramount aim should be to offer genuine health protection to workers.

Unfortunately, as we noted earlier, medical examinations often appear to be intended to protect employers against claims for workers' compensation and sick leave. In all circumstances, the information collected should be directly relevant to health protection and not require invasion of workers' privacy. To ensure privacy is protected, the examination should only include questions and tests that can be used to assess susceptibility to a specific workplace hazard. Questions regarding smoking habits and previous workers' compensation claims may be unjustifiable, as may be routine back X-rays and general allergy tests. All questions and tests should provide information upon which the organisation can act to protect workers' health. Where specific hazards exist, pre-employment examinations should be used to establish baselines against which future biological and medical changes can be compared. Workers should have full access to their records but otherwise records should be strictly confidential. Where workers reach specific thresholds of biological contamination or disease development they should not be penalised, and their income and conditions of work should be maintained. Medical examinations should never be used as a means of removing workers who have succumbed to work hazards.

Occupational health nursing, occupational therapy and physiotherapy

At first glance it might appear that other health professionals operating alongside occupational physicians might have the same general outlook towards OHS. But is this the case? Aside from occupational physicians, there are a number of other health professionals, in particular occupational nurses, occupational therapists, physiologists, rehabilitation professionals and physiotherapists, who bring to OHS different perspectives of how the treatment and prevention of work-related injuries and illness should be managed. Often overlooked in the discourse on OHS, occupational nurses and physiotherapists play a pivotal role in the early detection and remedy of occupational issues and in the rehabilitation of injured or ill workers. Insufficient attention has been paid to the role and social impact of these and other professions (such as occupational therapists) even though each constitutes a significant component (and in combination the vast majority) of the broader healthcare workforce (for a study of nurses see Hart, 2003).

Occupational health nurses (also referred to as occupational and environmental health nurses) represent the largest single group of health professionals involved in delivering health services at the workplace and as such have an important role to play in workplace health management (see Whitaker and Baranski, 2001; Mellor et al., 2006). These registered nurses are typically working at the front line of prevention and treatment of workers' injuries or illnesses and are often involved in OHS interventions and promotions within the business as well as within the industry. A study by Mellor et al. (2006) found that the major areas of activity for OH nurses was in treatment, health assessment and rehabilitation, with managing OHS services being the only emergent area where substantial time was spent.

What differentiates occupational health nurses from general practice nurses is that they are frequently required to provide direct care to individuals and groups of workers in a variety of settings including business, industry, clinics, schools, and employee health in hospitals. However, the contribution that these occupational clinicians make to the field of OHS is often overlooked or diminished. In an open letter to the *American Journal of Public Health*, Kusnetz (1986: 465) argued that:

> The nurse in industry has always been a mainstay. Far more than the industrial hygienist or the occupational physician, it has been the nurse in the work place who has been the prime contact between the public health, and nursing professions and industrial practice. That they were omitted from this kind of review—particularly given the emphasis of the innovative nursing programs developed just before and after World War II—is, I think, an important oversight.

Since Kusnetz's plea for occupational health nurses to be included in the domain of OHS, the situation has not necessarily improved. Studies in both Australia and New Zealand show that there is still a lack of recognition of the value of occupational health nurses (Mellor and St John, 2007, 2009; Riegen and McAllister, 2008). This has major implications not only for the profession but also for OHS in general. Occupational nurses often find themselves on the periphery of important national and industry OHS strategy and policy initiatives. In New Zealand, for example, occupational nurses were not mentioned at all in OHS strategic documents such as Primary Healthcare Strategy, Workplace Health and Safety Strategy and the Nursing Workforce Strategy (Riegen and McAllister, 2008). Mellor and St John (2009: 86) warn that 'occupational health nurses must be prepared to constantly demonstrate their relevance'.

There is also a misconception regarding the range of professional skills they offer. There are indications that managers typically view the role of occupational health nurses as being one that focuses on containing OHS costs within the organisation, treating work-related injuries and illness as well as rehabilitating injured and ill workers (Riegen and McAllister, 2008; Mellor and St John, 2007). More recently a study undertaken by Mellor and St John (2009) revealed that increasingly important roles of occupational health nurses are injury prevention, health promotion, management and research (and work ability in the context of an ageing workforce; see Rossi et al., 2000; Naumanen, 2007). They caution, however, that fulfilling these expectations may place occupational health nurses in competition with other occupational health and safety personnel for particular responsibilities and may require negotiation to gain support for taking on these role activities (Mellor and St John, 2009). Moreover, fulfilling these emergent role activities effectively will require appropriate professional development and advanced education in areas such as OHS and work methods (Naumanen, 2007; Mellor and St John, 2009: 79). As with occupational physicians, changes in government policy with regard to preventative healthcare and public health may provide opportunities for occupational health nurses to undertake a broader (i.e. not organisation-specific) role in relation to health promotion (Wilkinson, 2008).

The contribution of occupational therapy has also often been overlooked. Occupational therapy has been defined by the American Occupational Therapy Association as the 'skilled treatment that helps individuals achieve independence in all facets of their lives. It gives people the skills for the job of living necessary for independent and satisfying lives' (cited in Gainer, 2008: 5–9). Gainer (2008) suggests occupational therapy shares a background with ergonomics but is more firmly ensconced within the healthcare industry. Others (Gutman, 2008) have noted that occupational therapy emerged earlier, namely in the early decades of the twentieth century, and took a strong interest in vocational re-education as part of the desire to assist persons with disabilities to function within their communities. Gutman (2008) argues that this link was broken as the field sought to avoid being subsumed by vocational technical training using strategies such as physician prescription of services and a focus on delivering services in hospital settings. Early pioneers like American Thomas Kidner (1866–1932) were also critical in carving out occupational therapy's role in return to work and its relationship to medicine (Friedland and Silva, 2008: 349–60). At the same time, Schemm (1994: 1082) has argued that founding members of the profession in both the UK and US

> all shared a core of humanistic beliefs while embracing the emerging paradigm of scientific medicine. The result has been an intellectual tension between the biological and psychosocial aspects of practice. For more than 75 years, occupational therapists struggled to balance the art and science of patient care. Recent debates on modalities, practice domains, and research indicate that the unifying core in the profession is occupation that considers a person's mind and body.

A major focus of occupational therapists is planning and coordinating the rehabilitation of injured or disabled workers to achieve the greatest level of personal and social functioning, and not simply a return to work. Nonetheless, the contexts occupational therapists operate in—including the imperatives of the workers' compensation system—shape their activities. Hooper (2006) has argued that the core epistemology of occupational therapy requires closer examination and change if the field is to actually implement occupation, participation and health as the focus of practice, research and education. She does, however, identify positive developments in this regard. The willingness to engage in critical and historically informed self-reflection is of itself a positive sign. As with a number of other health professions, evidence regarding the contribution and role of occupational therapy will be examined in chapter 8.

Like occupational nurses, occupational physiotherapists have made a significant contribution to OHS for over a century. In 1894, the UK recognised physiotherapy as a specialised branch of nursing regulated by a Chartered Society. In the succeeding two decades, formal physiotherapy programs were established, of which New Zealand's Otago University in 1913 was one of the first, followed by the US in 1914. The internationally renowned Australian nurse Sister Kenny, who developed physiotherapy techniques for polio victims, also greatly assisted in establishing and advancing the discipline. Today the increased reliance on physiotherapy (or physical therapy as it is also known) to assist in the rehabilitation of injured workers is common practice and it is not unusual for a series of treatments by an approved physiotherapist to be included in the workers' compensation payments. Physiotherapy is not only concerned with reducing pain and more or less restoring or maintaining optimal physical functioning of the worker, it has also been used successfully in OHS intervention and prevention strategies, especially in the prevention of back injury. Physiotherapy includes many specialties, such as cardiopulmonary, geriatric, neurologic, orthopaedic and pediatric to name some of the more common areas, and encompasses the physical, psychological, emotional, and social wellbeing of the patient. In addition, physiotherapists can apply a wide range of non-pharmacological treatments, including manual and electrophysical therapies, thermotherapy, hydrotherapy and graded exercise. As part of their assessment of a patient, a physiotherapist will examine relevant X-rays, laboratory tests, medical records and surgical notes. Based on this assessment and in consultation with the patient's doctor, the physiotherapist will then establish a diagnosis and, in collaboration with the patient, develop a treatment program.

Like a number of other health professions and OHS-related disciplines, there is evidence that physiotherapists are reconsidering or reflecting upon their research and practice, especially in the context of collaborating with other health sciences and integrating better with the promotion of health within society. Thus, for example, Dean (2009a & b) has argued that the clinical practice of physiotherapy needs to be better informed by and integrated with epidemiological research and other evidence on broader social and public health issues, although she has couched this mainly in terms of lifestyle behaviours rather than socioeconomic inequality or workplace conditions.

Taken as a group of healthcare professionals, occupational nurses, occupational therapists and physiotherapists face ethical issues similar to those of occupational medical physicians. In particular, they often find themselves as intermediaries between the medical specialist, the officer from the workers' compensation agency and the employer; each party may have different views on the appropriate treatment of the injured or ill workers. In many respects, these views are influenced by the costs involved in treating the injured or ill worker. For the employer and the workers' compensation agency, getting the worker back to work after they have suffered an injury, even if it is light duties, is less costly than having the worker remain off work. For the occupational nurse and occupational physiotherapist, sending a worker back to work prematurely may impede the worker's recovery.

Further, there is some disquiet about whose interests occupational nurses, occupational physiotherapists and other occupational health clinicians serve—employers or employees? By the very fact that their continued employment is reliant on the employer's and/or the workers' compensation agency's patronage, the health professional can be put in a difficult position. Multiple loyalties occur when the health professional has simultaneous obligations, either explicit or implicit, to a third party—usually a private employer or workers' compensation agency. The consequences may lead to adverse impacts on the patient and the patient's family (London, 2005: 324). This also presents a number of ethical issues surrounding patient rights and welfare, especially when it concerns patient confidentiality (see Triezenberg, 1996; Koh and Lee, 2003). For example, if a job applicant was found to have a history of depression, revealing this information without consent would be a breach of medical ethics and may have significant adverse consequences for the worker's rights in terms of stigmatisation and discrimination. An ethical framework, such as the one developed by the International Commission on Occupational Health, can minimise ethical conflicts, reduce potential infringements of the worker's rights, and promote non-maleficence and beneficence (Whorton and Davis, 1978; Sheldon, 2003; London, 2005).

The strengthening of a number of health professions by university-trained health science professionals over the past 30 years, including a parallel growth in postgraduate and research programs as well as academic journals, has brought with it more critical reflection on their education and role (including issues of ethics, independence and social responsibility). In professions such as nursing, academic journals now publish research into the OHS of nurses, especially regarding issues like work-related stress, burnout and the challenges posed by caring for the elderly (see, for example, Garrosa et al., 2008; Hansson and Arnetz, 2008; Verhaeghe et al., 2008). It is to be hoped that the latter will enhance understanding of OHS more generally among these professions, especially those actively involved in the provision of OHS services.

In spite of limitations and ethical issues, the medical and allied health professions have made a major contribution to our understanding of OHS. These professionals provide an array of skills to assist in the health and safety of workers and are more often than not at the forefront of highlighting OHS issues and developing solutions. However, the established dominance of the medical profession over healthcare does present the danger that OHS practice will be unduly dominated by medical thinking. In light of this danger, it is encouraging that occupational medical and health professionals are showing an increasing readiness to recognise the knowledge and expertise of professionals from other disciplines, such as occupational hygiene, ergonomics and work psychology. As Ferguson (1988) observed more than two decades ago, OHS is best managed and understood by multidisciplinary teams.

Occupational epidemiology

Epidemiology, a subdiscipline of medical science, has particular relevance to OHS. Epidemiology is generally defined as 'the study of the distribution and determinants of disease in human populations' (Christie, 1988: 2; also see Coggon et al., 2003). Established in the nineteenth century, the discipline of epidemiology was and still is concerned with the cause of epidemic diseases (see Terris, 2001 and Morris, 2007). Epidemiological research explores the frequency of occurrence of phenomena of interest in healthcare and relates measures of frequency to their determinants. Rather than being a coherent field of knowledge in itself, epidemiology provides a set of principles for research design and data analysis that can be used to demonstrate occurrence relationships. Occupational epidemiology aims to establish the existence or otherwise of causal relationships between work factors and illness that cannot be as clearly established using the traditional observational and clinical methods of occupational medicine. It also aims to provide a means of estimating the magnitude of a demonstrated risk of illness within a given occupational group and to assess how the risk is related to exposure to specific causal agents. In essence, epidemiology provides a means to establish the causes of disease, identify individuals at high risk and monitor the spread of disease.

Three primary features characterise epidemiological research and differentiate it from 'clinical' research in medicine (Christie, 1988; Pearce, 1996; Coggon, et al., 2003; Morris, 2007). First, it examines a postulated association between an occurrence and a 'cause' within a defined population. The occurrence, or phenomenon of interest, should be clearly measurable, in terms of presence, absence or magnitude. Examples of occurrences studied in occupational epidemiology include diseases such as coronary heart disease and lung cancer and states of health or injuries such as repetitive strain injury. The postulated association links the occurrence to a presumed cause or associated factor. In occupational epidemiology associations have frequently been postulated between the occurrence of specific cancers and the level of occupational exposure to specific substances. Second, epidemiological research attempts to measure the presumed 'cause' accurately and, if possible, devise a method of grading exposure to it. For example, in the case of the link between smoking and lung cancer, smoking could be simply graded as 'smoker/non-smoker'. However, stronger evidence of causality would be produced if a dose–response relationship could be established between exposure to smoking (for example, with the 'dose' measured in cigarettes smoked per day) and lung cancer (the response).

Third, the research designs are based on the clearest possible definition of the population within which the occurrence relationship is to be demonstrated. In occupational epidemiology, the purpose is to define a group of workers among whom there is an adequate range of potential exposure to the possible hazard under investigation. The population is often defined as all workers in a particular plant or industry during a particular time period. Frequently, the confined nature of the population studied means that results cannot automatically be presumed to generalise. It is essentially a matter of judgment, informed by experience and other data, as to whether a relationship between exposure to a particular occurrence and subsequent disease in one workplace will hold for all workers employed in similar circumstances (see Pearce, 1996; Pearce et al., 2007).

In brief, the concern of epidemiology is to study whether an occurrence of interest, usually an illness, is associated with one or more variables within a clearly defined population. Two terms are commonly used by epidemiologists to describe the occurrence of illness in a group of workers. The *prevalence* of an illness is the number of individuals suffering from the illness in a given population at a specific time (Christie, 1988; Mathews, 1985). The measure is more accurately known as the *point prevalence* as it refers the situation at a single point in time. If 45 of a group of 750 workers are found to experience severe sleep disturbance, then the point prevalence would be:

$$45/750 = 0.06 \text{ or } 45/750 \times 100 = 6 \text{ per } 100 \text{ at risk}$$

The *incidence* of an illness is the rate at which new cases of the illness appear over a specified period of time (Christie, 1988; Mathews, 1985). For example, among the 750 workers above, 705 individuals did not experience severe sleep disturbances. If those individuals were studied for a further 12 months and 36 developed severe sleep disturbances, there would be 36 new occurrences of the symptoms. The incidence would now be:

$36/705 = 0.051$ or $36/705 \times 100 = 5.1$ cases per 100 per year

This incidence rate would indicate the average 'risk' that a member of the population, who is free of symptoms, would run of developing those symptoms during the succeeding year (Christie, 1988). *Morbidity* is the incidence of an illness or disease and *mortality* is the incidence of death.

Before conclusions can be drawn from mortality rates calculated in this way it is necessary to decide whether they are abnormally high or low by comparing them to a suitable reference group. The most frequently used reference group is the relevant national population, which can usually be presumed to have not been widely exposed to the workplace variable being studied. However, the risk of dying is strongly associated with age, and sometimes with sex and other variables. It is therefore essential to take into account differences in age and other relevant variables between the population being studied and the reference group. This adjustment is achieved through 'standardisation' (Christie, 1988). In the case of age, standardisation can be achieved by dividing the worker population being studied into age ranges, usually of 5 or 10 years. Age-specific mortality rates can then be calculated for age ranges: 20–29, 30–39 and so on. The observed death rates in these ranges can then be compared with the expected death rates in the corresponding age ranges of the reference group. The result of such comparisons is usually reported as a standardised mortality ratio (SMR), which is calculated as follows:

$\text{SMR} = \text{observed death rate}/\text{expected death rate} \times 100$

The SMR calculated in this way provides an index of the proportion of mortality in the reference group that is experienced by the workers under investigation. An SMR of 100 indicates a mortality rate equal to that of the reference group, while SMRs above and below 100 indicate higher and lower mortalities respectively. For example, an SMR of 120 for coronary heart disease would indicate that death rates in the worker population were 20% higher than those in the reference group for this cause of death.

Epidemiologists generally use one of two approaches to establishing occurrence relationships (Christie, 1988). The first is commonly known as the *case-control study*, which involves comparing a group of people with the disease under investigation (cases) with a group that does not have the disease (controls). The objective is to examine differences between the groups in terms of exposure to a suspected causative agent (or agents). For example, in a study of RSI all employees who report RSI could be compared, on a range of relevant variables, with a random sample of employees who do not report symptoms. In case-control studies it is possible to collect information about a large number of variables at relatively low cost and consequently they are often used as a first step in examining suspected causal relationships.

The second approach is the cohort study. In these studies, comparisons are made between groups of people who are initially free of disease but are exposed to varying levels of the suspected causal agent. The groups are studied for sufficient time to determine if differences appear between them in the occurrence of the disease. Cohort studies can be either prospective or retrospective. Prospective studies start with a population as it exists in the present and follow it into the future. Retrospective studies define a point in the past as the starting point and follow the population through to a second nominated point in time, identifying occurrences using evidence such as organisational records and registrations of death and disease. Prospective studies are generally more time-consuming and expensive, and consequently they are less common. However, prospective studies provide clearer evidence of causal relationships and are the only means of calculating the actual risk of becoming ill through exposure to a causal factor (Bloom, 1988; Pearce, et al., 2007).

The occurrence relationships identified using these procedures may be either causal or descriptive (Miettinen, 1985). In a descriptive relationship an occurrence is related to another variable without any presumption of causality. Descriptive relationships may be of value for risk assessment, diagnosis and other applications in which the objective is to predict the probability of an occurrence, rather than isolate its cause or causes. For example, before the aetiology of a disease is clearly understood it may be useful for the purposes of risk assessment to know that the incidence of the disease is related to sex and age without ever presuming that the relationships are causal. However, an understanding of the aetiology of the disease is vitally important when the intention is to develop effective strategies of prevention and treatment. Consequently, the identification of causal relationships has become one of the primary concerns of epidemiology. Unfortunately, occupational illnesses often cannot be simply attributed to single causes and the epidemiologist must tease out relationships between complex clusters of causes.

The work of Hobbs et al. (1980) on lung disease among blue asbestos miners at the Wittenoom mine in Western Australia is one of the best-known examples of Australian occupational epidemiology. Using a retrospective design and data from a range of sources, including the Pneumoconiosis Board of Western Australia, cancer registries in several states and government death records, the researchers calculated the incidence of pneumoconiosis, mesothelioma and other respiratory cancers among ex-miners 12 years after the final closure of the mine. The results indicated that the incidence of all the diseases studied increased with duration of employment at the mine, the level of exposure to asbestos dust during the period of employment and the length of time since first employment at the mine. These findings provided telling evidence of a causal link between occupational exposure to blue asbestos at Wittenoom and the lung diseases studied, a link that had long been discounted by mining companies. In the case of mesothelioma, the evidence was particularly damning, as the occurrence of this disease is known to be negligible in the general community. The data from this study was considerably more compelling, and difficult to dispute, than previous clinical medical evidence, which could not clearly demonstrate cause–effect relationships.

In New Zealand, occupational epidemiologists have played a leading role in establishing a link between ill health among workers and their families and exposure to dioxin toxins (see McLean et al., 2002; Pearce, 2006). New Zealand has the dubious reputation of being the highest user per capita of dioxins in the world, ranging from phenoxy herbicide 2,4,5-T to pentachlorophenol (PCP) timber treatments. Exposure to dioxins, therefore, has been a lingering, widespread and devastating occupational health problem and there has been little or no compensation for those affected. Yet establishing causal links between specific diseases and dioxin exposures has not been without controversy in New Zealand and elsewhere, highlighting the different ways epidemiological findings are interpreted. This lack of consensus between and within epidemiology and occupational medical disciplines is most evident surrounding the research on the level of dioxin exposure of workers at the New Plymouth Ivon Watkins-Dow (IWD) chemical factory. On one hand, studies commissioned by the Ministry of Health and Ivon Watkins-Dow on dioxin exposure of workers at this plant were singled out as being conservative with their conclusions and containing a number of inherent biases—for example, not testing those workers potentially most affected (see Fowles et al., 2005; McBride et al., 2006). Critics also argued that funding agencies, namely Ivon Watkins-Dow and the Ministry of Health, had a conflict of interest in that both parties were subject to compensation claims by dioxin-affected workers, their families and neighbouring residents of the contaminated site. Research funded by industry, however, is not uncommon, and Dow Chemical Inc. has also funded research on the mortality of a cohort of male workers at their Ontario chemical plant in which the findings were similar to those in the Ministry of Health and New Zealand Ivon Watkins-Dow reports (see Burns et al., 2005).

On the other hand, the epidemiology research undertaken by researchers at Massey University's Centre for Public Health Research found that there were indeed higher death rates from cancer among the production workers at Ivon Watkins-Dow, particularly those in jobs with likely dioxin exposure. The Massey study also found that the risk of certain types of cancer was indeed higher for people who had worked in departments which probably involved the highest dioxin exposure: cancer mortality was not only 24% higher overall, but also 69% higher in synthesis workers, 64% higher in formulation and laboratory workers and 46% higher in maintenance and waste workers at the plant (Pearce et al., 2006). Moreover, unlike the Ministry of Health and Ivon Watkins-Dow research, the findings of the Massey University studies are consistent with those of the overall WHO study, which is the largest and most rigorous study conducted on this issue (see van den Berg et al., 2006).

Occupational epidemiology offers important advantages over the clinical and observational methods frequently used in occupational medicine, as highlighted by the above examples of asbestos and dioxin exposures. First and foremost, the use of more rigorous research designs provides stronger evidence of cause and effect relationships between workplace variables and specific illnesses. It is frequently used to follow up suggestive evidence produced by clinical research in an effort to confirm causality and to establish the strength of the causal relationship. This more convincing evidence can be critical in stimulating organisations and government authorities into action on occupational health issues. The more rigorous procedures of occupational epidemiology also provide a means of accurately monitoring trends in the mortality and morbidity of specific illnesses among different occupational groups, trends that are likely to be obscured by the focus of the medical model on individual treatment and diagnosis. For example, individual clinical treatment is less likely to bring to light an excessively high incidence of cancer among a group of workers exposed to a particular chemical and link cancer morbidity to this cause.

Epidemiology has also alerted researchers to a very important consideration in occupational health studies, the so-called 'healthy worker effect' (Pearce et al., 2007). Many epidemiological studies have demonstrated that mortality and illness rates for workers are lower than those for the general population. At first glance such results sound like good news for workers, but unfortunately they can be quite misleading. All epidemiological studies are comparative, and to ascertain whether a group of workers suffers from unusually high mortality or morbidity it is necessary to select an appropriate comparison group. Epidemiological studies in the workplace investigate samples strongly biased towards people who are fit enough to work (at least at the beginning of the study) and include a lower proportion of people who suffer from disabling and life-threatening illnesses than the general community (Mathews, 1985). Therefore workers will generally have lower mortality rates and experience lower levels of illness than the general population. If the intention is to assess the health impact of a particular workplace hazard, it is more enlightening to compare the workers' health with that of other workers who are similar in all respects (generally in terms of age, sex, occupation type and similar variables) but have not been exposed to the hazard being investigated. Alternatively, the rate for both groups could be standardised against the general community and their SMRs compared. In any case, the objective is to perform a meaningful comparison.

Occupational epidemiology has limitations as a means of understanding OHS problems. Epidemiological studies usually focus on relatively narrow sets of variables and direct causes of injury or illness. Epidemiologists prefer these variables to be clearly defined, easily measurable and limited in number (Christie, 1988; Clapp and Ozonoff, 2004). Global assessments of the prevalence or incidence of an illness within a target population may give little indication of the factors that determine why one individual and not another will fall victim to the illness under investigation. Further laboratory, clinical, or psychosocial research is often required to assess the reasons for individual susceptibility. As Quinn et al. (2007) observe, many studies evaluate a single exposure in relation to a particular disease, whereas workers typically experience multiple exposures simultaneously and exposure can also be influenced by socio-demographic and work process factors. In other instances the data has been examined too narrowly and important empirical and conceptual links have been underplayed or overlooked. For example, a recent review of how population-based cardiovascular research in the US used occupation data (MacDonald et al., 2009: 1411) found that studies rarely acknowledged known links between socioeconomic status, employment stability and working conditions, and that available data on workplace conditions was underutilised. Often the design of epidemiological studies is poorly suited to investigating the impact of broader aspects of the social organisation of work, such as management structures and power relations, on illness and injury. As the discussion of industrial sociology later in this chapter demonstrates, these factors can be important contributors to illness and injury. Nonetheless, over the past decade a growing number of epidemiologists (such as Roquelaure et al. (2007) who used Karasek's demand/control model to explore musculoskeletal disorders) have designed studies to consider these factors. These developments are discussed in more detail in chapter 5.

In common with all approaches to the collection of empirical data, epidemiological studies are subject to a number of methodological problems that must be avoided where possible in the design stage of a research project (see Christie, 1988: 46–52). For example, several problems can produce unrecognised 'healthy worker effects' including the biases that arise when there is a high level of self-selectivity among workers in particular groups, when there is high turnover in the population being studied, and when access to some workers is lost through death or illness during the period of the study (Christie, 1988). A major practical disadvantage of epidemiological studies is that they can take a long time to complete (Mathews, 1985). Prospective studies, as we have seen, provide the strongest evidence of causal relationships, but unfortunately they often take a decade or more to produce meaningful results. During this time many workers may suffer injuries, contract painful and deadly diseases, and perhaps die. As Mathews (1985) observes, leaving the identification of occupational disease entirely to epidemiology may amount to a policy of 'counting the victims' (p. 491). He argues that laboratory experiments and other methods of predicting the likely health impact of new chemicals, processes and technologies should be used in conjunction with epidemiological research. Further, as with occupational medicine, in practice occupational epidemiology can be subjected to industry and political influence, as illustrated by Tweedale's (2007; McCulloch and Tweedale, 2008) detailed examination of asbestos research and the role played by Sir Richard Doll. Such critical historical research should be an essential element in the education of epidemiologists and allied health professionals.

Despite these limitations, epidemiology provides a set of research tools that can help immensely in developing understanding of the health threats faced by workers. For this reason, it forms a significant component of a multidisciplinary approach to occupational health. Unfortunately, as we shall see later, convincing evidence regarding the causes of health problems frequently does not lead to rapid interventions to protect workers' health. We need to look to other perspectives to gain a more workable insight into the processes of intervention and prevention in the workplace.

A behavioural perspective: work psychology

The application of psychological knowledge to workplace problems has been an accepted part of management practice for some time. Psychologists have dominated social science research on occupational health for most of this century and this dominance persists today despite an upsurge in sociological research in the area. Psychologists have developed theories that attempt to explain and differentiate the causes of both occupational injury and occupational illness. Because of their widespread influence, it is vitally important to understand the strengths and weaknesses of these theories. The history of work psychology provides important insights into the factors that have shaped current psychological theories and wider community understanding of occupational injury and illness (Bohle, 1993). Psychology applied to the workplace has been known by several labels which have, at various times or in various contexts, denoted the whole field or specialisations within it, including industrial psychology, organisational psychology, industrial/organisational psychology, occupational psychology, and engineering (or human factors) psychology. 'Work psychology' is used here to refer to the theory and research encompassed by all of these labels.

During the period from the late nineteenth century until the beginning of World War I psychology emerged as an independent academic discipline and psychologists began to concern themselves with organisational issues such as personnel selection, industrial safety, work design and the efficiency of workers (Muchinsky, 1987). One of the most significant formative influences on the developing discipline was the work of the early industrial engineers, most notably Frederick Winslow Taylor. Since the 1890s Taylor had been developing management strategies aimed at maximising economic benefits to industry through increasing worker productivity, which he labelled 'Scientific Management' (see Taylor, 1947). Scientific Management had four basic objectives:

1 development of rigid work rules covering every motion of the worker, combined with standardisation and redesign of tools and working conditions to ensure maximum efficiency
2 selection and training of the most productive workers
3 instruction of workers in the most efficient working methods, and the payment of incentives to workers who worked fast and did what they were told
4 close and constant supervision of workers' activities.

The modification of work methods was achieved by observation and detailed analysis of workers' movements in what became known as 'time and motion studies'. These studies aimed to analyse the motions of workers in minute detail and to reduce the movements required for a given task to an absolute minimum. Quicker movements were then substituted for slower ones to minimise the total time required to complete the task. By breaking work down into narrow, clearly defined tasks which could be performed by relatively unskilled labour, Taylor hoped that the nature of work could be dictated and controlled by management. A major objective was to plan work so that initiative, autonomy and argument on the part of workers was impossible.

While Taylor was candid about his objective of maximising each individual worker's output, he also claimed that he pursued the maximum prosperity of each worker. However, he defined prosperity principally in terms of '… the development of each man to his state of maximum efficiency, so that he may be able to do, generally speaking, the highest grade of work for which his natural abilities fit him …' (Taylor, 1947: 9). Maximum efficiency was defined as 'turning out his largest daily output' (Taylor, 1947: 11). Taylor displayed little concern for the longer-term impact of this output level on health, and his methods deprived workers of the autonomy to make important decisions about their personal safety. Not surprisingly, his relationship with workers was plagued by hostility and conflict. Work psychology arose largely to deal with the problems of restriction of output, lack of cooperation, apathy and worker–management conflict that were generated by Taylor's methods (Bucklow, 1976). Ralph (1983) contends that the objective was to mitigate these effects without significantly changing production methods or reducing productivity.

With the advent of World War I psychologists grasped an opportunity to prove themselves by demonstrating how their discipline could contribute to the war effort. Their work was dominated by a philosophy of fitting workers to jobs and initially focused upon screening recruits for intellectual ability, assigning them to jobs and developing training strategies (Muchinsky, 1987). However, in 1915 the Health of Munitions Workers Committee (HMWC) in Britain began an influential research program which investigated the impact of factors such as fatigue and monotony on the productivity of women doing highly repetitive work in munitions factories. Health was generally treated as secondary to productivity and often examined only in terms of its effect on productivity. Later this research was expanded to investigate the causes of 'accidents' and to examine relationships between working hours, temperature, lighting, noise, humidity, ventilation, 'accidents' and industrial productivity (Mayo, 1933; Stephenson, 1929).

A pioneer of work psychology in Australia also became prominent at this time. The influence of Bernard Muscio, a professor of philosophy at the University of Sydney, was such that even CS Myers, the eminent director of the British National Institute of Industrial Psychology, praised his contribution to the field and proclaimed that Muscio's *Lectures on Industrial Psychology* (Muscio, 1917) were the source from which he 'first got to know anything about industrial psychology' (cited in Turtle and Orr, 1988: 13). Muscio's lectures covered several of the major interests of the time—fatigue, scientific management and work study methods, attitudes to work and injury causation. He argued that overtime and excessive work hours, machine-paced work, excessive noise, excessive work specialisation and monotony produced fatigue, which in turn increased injury rates and ill health. He attributed up to 90% of injuries to fatigue and saw more effective individual work practices as a primary solution to the problem. It is interesting that Muscio acknowledged the impact of fatigue on health but chose to devote his lectures to its effects on productivity and injury, topics of more immediate interest to employers.

Researchers after the war continued to examine injury rates. Early research by the successor to the HMWC, the Industrial Fatigue Research Board, had indicated that injuries were strongly affected by working hours, with one study demonstrating a 60% fall in accidents when the working day was reduced from 12 to 10 hours (Mayo, 1933). However, Greenwood and Woods (1919) argued that differences in the characteristics of individual workers, principally personality differences, were an 'extremely important factor' (p. 9) in injury causation. They also suggested that 'nervous or ultra careful' (p. 10) workers might appear to sustain more injuries, due to a tendency to report injuries that other workers would disregard. Later, in 1927, Smith, Culpin and Farmer (cited in

Rose, 1975: 81) identified the typical victim of 'telegraphist's cramp' as 'anxious, solitary, fearful, dependent and worried about his career progress'. The tendency towards injury was subsequently labelled 'accident proneness'. Stephenson (1929) claimed that the majority of injuries could be attributed to accident proneness arising from factors including 'nervous instability' (p. 132), poor motor coordination, bravado and a failure to perceive danger. While he acknowledged the contribution of environmental factors to injury, he considered individual factors to be much more important. Accident proneness is still a popular notion today, but as we shall see shortly there is no reliable evidence that it is a significant cause of injury.

Influential figures in work psychology at this time challenged the more extreme aspects of Taylorism, such as the notion of 'one best way' (Rose, 1975). Myers (1929) conveyed a genuine desire to introduce the 'best possible human conditions in occupational work' (p. 9) and argued that the aim of 'industrial psychology' was 'primarily not to obtain greater output but to give the worker greater ease at his work' (p. 14). Nevertheless, the bulk of psychologists' work remained oriented towards the needs of employers, placing heavy emphasis on improving productivity. It was widely presumed that if workers were appropriately selected, allocated to the right jobs, effectively trained and sheltered in carefully controlled physical working conditions they would remain both healthy and productive. For understandable reasons many workers were hostile to psychologists and suspicious of their methods. Mace (1954: 7) aptly summarised the philosophy of these early work psychologists:

> ... they somehow left the impression that the ultimate goal of these endeavours was the creation of an ideal factory fashioned in the style ... of a 'model cowhouse'—the milch cows of which were, of course, the industrial workers.

Some years after World War I, a series of studies conducted at the Hawthorne Works of the Western Electric Company by an expatriate Australian, Elton Mayo, and researchers from Harvard University stimulated a major re-evaluation of the field. The 'Hawthorne studies' were to become some of the most celebrated and influential investigations in work psychology. While it is not possible to describe the numerous experiments in detail here (see Mayo, 1933; Roethlisberger and Dickson, 1939), they do demand brief review.

The research began in 1924 with studies on the effect of illumination intensity on worker productivity. To the consternation of the researchers, productivity increased both when illumination was increased and when it was decreased. Even the control groups, for whom light levels had remained constant, increased their output. Faced with explaining these results, the Harvard researchers conducted three major research projects (Mayo, 1933; Roethlisberger and Dickson, 1939). The first project investigated a group of six women constructing and testing electrical relays. The second involved extensive interviews with over 1600 skilled and unskilled workers at the plant and the third involved detailed observation of 14 male operators in a 'bank-wiring room'.

In the relay-room studies the researchers attempted to assess the impact on productivity of changes in payment schemes, working hours, tasks and supervisory style.

They reported a 30% rise in productivity during the study and concluded that satisfaction arising from positive social relationships and friendly supervision had been a much more important cause of this improvement than changes in physical working conditions and pay. In the interview project the workers were encouraged to discuss complaints and sentiments about working conditions and supervision in unstructured sessions similar to personal counselling. The researchers concluded that the interviews had a therapeutic value arising from the opportunity they gave workers to express personal feelings and examine the links between other aspects of their lives and social relationships at work. In the bank-wiring room the researchers observed men performing coordinated tasks in which their output was dependent on that of other workers. After extensive observation, the researchers concluded that a strong set of informal rules and norms operated among the workers which, for example, set an accepted work rate and governed the nature of relationships between the workers and between the workers and their supervisors.

Mayo and his colleagues inferred from their findings that workers had strong social needs and that meeting these needs through positive social relationships at work was the key to high productivity, increased morale and improved health and wellbeing (Mayo, 1933). They believed that informal group relationships exerted strong controls over workers' behaviour and that managers wishing to increase productivity needed to be skilled enough in human relations to develop strong group cohesion and positive attitudes to management (Carey, 1976; O'Brien, 1984). A willingness to listen, rather than act upon workers' concerns, was seen to be sufficient to lift morale in many cases (Mayo, 1933: 96). In contrast, financial incentives and improvements in the physical working environment were seen to have little effect on worker behaviour. Widespread acceptance of these findings led to the emergence of the 'human relations school' in work psychology and management.

While Mayo displayed a paternalistic concern for the wellbeing of workers, he was guided by a strong conviction that work could be organised so that social harmony and productivity were simultaneously maximised (O'Brien, 1984). This view appears to have heavily coloured the interpretation of the Hawthorne data. Carey (1967, 1976) and others have persuasively argued that the evidence collected by Mayo and his colleagues did not support their conclusions. To start, major flaws in the research design and data collection meant the results had little scientific value. Furthermore, even if the evidence is accepted as reliable, it does not support the conclusion that social factors had the primary effect on productivity. Rather it indicates that financial rewards, directive leadership and discipline produced the greatest increases. Carey (1967: 416) concluded that 'only by massive and relentless reinterpretation' could the evidence be construed to suggest otherwise.

Despite the substantial deficiencies of the Hawthorne research, the human relations model dominated research and practice in work psychology for several decades. It had the positive effect of replacing the mechanistic notions of Taylorism with greater recognition of the social needs of workers, but the determinants of workers' efficiency, health and satisfaction were located very narrowly within their immediate working relationships. Behaviour was not considered to arise from rational responses to the workplace, but rather from emotion and irrationality moulded by complex social and interpersonal factors. The 'personal equilibrium' (Hollway, 1991: 82) of the worker, based substantially on past history and experiences outside work, was therefore seen as a major determinant of work behaviour and failure to respond positively to management interventions became evidence of the disturbed physiological and emotional state of the worker (Gillespie, 1991). For example, it was claimed that repetitive work did not itself cause negative responses, but merely provided an opportunity for 'pessimistic reverie' which would be discouraged if social exchange with other workers was possible (Roethlisberger and Dickson, cited in Hollway, 1991: 83–4). The emphasis placed on social harmony and a mutuality of interests between workers and management also diverted attention away from the effect of structural factors, such as inequities of power between workers and managers, on health and safety.

During World War II the armed services again made extensive use of psychological testing. The primary role of psychologists in Australia was to screen recruits for selection, job classification and training purposes (O'Neil, 1987). They were also employed to examine the factors affecting the physical performance of military personnel in action, such as heat tolerance in tanks (Turtle and Orr, 1988). Later, vocational guidance and rehabilitation services were developed, principally to aid the transition of military personnel with severe physical disabilities and psychiatric disorders back into the community and workforce (O'Neil, 1987). Psychologists were employed to maximise the productivity of the civilian workforce as well, once again through selection testing, training and equipment design.

The wartime development of selection tests stimulated research on emotional and interpersonal responses to frustration. Low frustration tolerance and an inability to work under pressure were seen to be major causes of industrial injury and illness (Brown, 1954). Brown (1954), in a highly influential book on psychology in industry, ascribed a vast range of illnesses to neurosis and psychological causes, including diabetes, dermatitis, gynaecological conditions and even venereal diseases. Some workers were said to be unduly susceptible to 'defects in social adjustment' (p. 266) arising from factors that included working more than 75 hours per week. Brown argued that campaigns to increase workers' awareness of occupational health threats contributed strongly to the creation of illness and injury by encouraging neurotic workers to develop illnesses or injure themselves as an expression of discontent with the workplace or as a means of attracting compensation (a tendency he labelled 'compensationitis' (p. 265)). Brown's analysis was strongly influenced by the paternalistic human relations approach, leading him to identify poor interpersonal relationships, low morale and negative supervisory styles as the principal organisational causes of the emotional disturbance underlying injury and illness. So, for example, differences in injury rates between two mines were attributed to 'variations in morale' (p. 259), and variations in geological conditions, equipment and work organisation were not examined. Ultimately, Brown argued that the major contributors to occupational neuroses included heredity, upbringing and non-work factors. This argument, and the use of stigmatising terms such as 'neurosis' and 'compensationitis' to describe workers' responses to demanding and stressful working environments, strongly supported the efforts of management to locate the causes of OHS problems, and hence their solutions, within the worker and not the workplace. Once again, the underlying assumption was that workers must adapt to jobs, rather than jobs to workers.

In the period since World War II several developments in psychology have been relevant to occupational health. They include new research on specific health problems and the growth of new specialties with different perspectives on occupational health issues. The new specialties include organisational psychology, engineering psychology and health psychology. Current research with particular relevance includes work on the causes of occupational stress and extensive investigation of the effects of work scheduling on physical and psychological wellbeing. We shall look briefly at the new specialties before we discuss the insights provided by current research in occupational stress (work scheduling is discussed in detail in chapter 6).

The wartime contributions of psychologists to the design of military equipment, such as tanks and aircraft cockpits, provided an impetus to the development of engineering (or 'human factors') psychology (Muchinsky, 1987). This specialist area deals with the interactions between humans and their physical working environment and with the design of equipment to enhance worker productivity and safety (Wickens and Kramer, 1985). It applies knowledge of human cognitive abilities, physical performance, reaction times, sensory acuity and coordination to the design process. Current areas of major interest in the area include human–computer interaction and human factors in the monitoring and control of complex, slowly responding production systems, such as nuclear power plants. In essence, engineering psychology aims to modify the working environment to be compatible with human capacities and skills, and can be seen as an extension of the work studies performed by early work psychologists.

Psychologists working in this area have made an important contribution to understanding of the factors leading to occupational injury (see Glendon and McKenna, 1995; Hale and Glendon, 1987; Reason et al., 1998). They have investigated the cognitive and perceptual processes required to monitor and respond to environmental threats and the effects that stress, workloads and environmental demands have on these processes. They have also examined the factors that encourage workers to accept danger and the processes that promote noncompliance with safety rules and procedures. An important factor is the perceived controllability of threats, including the extent to which workers attribute injury to a lack of skill, rather than just chance, and the degree to which they believe they can personally control the danger or trust others to do so. This work has been aimed at understanding human responses to dangerous situations and modifying the working environment to be compatible with human abilities and skills. Engineering psychology has made a major contribution to the field of ergonomics, which is discussed later in this chapter.

Work psychology was reshaped in the 1950s by the emergence of organisational psychology, which emphasises group processes and organisational change (see Hollway, 1991; Schein, 1988). The development of organisational psychology was heavily influenced by the human relations movement, which was reflected in a strong emphasis on interpersonal communication, group relationships and social influences on motivation. As psychologists delved into individual and group behaviour, the importance of understanding the organisation as a complex social system became apparent, and organisational psychology emerged. From this perspective, work methods and behaviour cannot be understood by simply studying individual workers but must be seen in terms of the complex demands of the organisational social system. The current concerns of organisational psychology include organisational communication processes, problem solving and decision making, inter- and intra-group conflict management, leadership, organisational culture and change processes in organisations. This systems approach is now widely used to examine the causes of injury and it is generally recognised that most injuries do not have a single 'cause' but rather arise from the interaction of multiple variables (Glendon et al., 2006). That is, the causes of injury are viewed as more complex phenomena than those portrayed by earlier psychologists. Psychologists have been prominent in identifying a wide variety of human characteristics, the lack of which may contribute to error, including attentiveness, perception of hazards, danger identification, motivation, and the processes involved in learning safe behaviour. In addition, the models of individual behaviour in dangerous conditions proposed by Hale and Glendon (1987), Reason et al. (1997, 1998), Glendon, et al. (2006) and others have extended this research. These authors have made a considerable contribution to our understanding of how and why accidents occur, as we will discuss in more detail in the following chapter.

Health psychology has contributed a new perspective on safety management and health promotion in the workplace. The field is broadly concerned with 'the scientific study of behaviour, thoughts, attitudes, and beliefs related to health and illness' (Bloom, 1988: 2) and takes a psychosocial orientation to health which emphasises its social determinants and focuses on the promotion and maintenance of health rather than treatment of ill health (see Holtzman et al., 1987; Krantz et al., 1985). Health psychology in the workplace has been most closely associated with health promotion programs which have aimed at changing lifestyle factors that lead to ill health such as smoking, excessive alcohol consumption, drug abuse, poor diet and insufficient exercise. In most cases they take a multi-method approach using combinations of educational interventions, health risk counselling, behavioural change programs, and stress management and lifestyle enhancement groups. Workplace interventions have usually emphasised stress management, aerobic exercise and smoking cessation programs. There is evidence that workplace programs can be more successful in achieving positive lifestyle changes than community-based ones (Bloom, 1988) but they are frequently marketed to management as a means of cost reduction and productivity improvement and must presumably be successful in these areas to be maintained. Like most psychological interventions they place a heavy focus on individual behavioural change. However, in an interesting recent development, psychologists have identified behavioural signs of workplace exposure to toxins and set up monitoring programs aimed at early identification and rectification of environmental exposures (see Seeber and Iregren, 1992).

Another aspect of health psychologists' work has been the application of 'behaviour modification' techniques to minimise occupational injury by promoting and maintaining safer individual behaviour (Reber and Wallin, 1984). Strategies used have included financial incentives, supervisory praise, goal setting and behavioural feedback. Managers and psychologists have, for example, negotiated goals for reducing unsafe behaviour or injury rates with workers and then provided regular feedback on progress towards these goals. Such programs have achieved some success in reducing injury rates, but this success relies upon a high level of individual control over injury and the elimination of contrary incentives to unsafe behaviour, such as piece-rate payment schemes and excessive production pressure.

In 1990 the term 'occupational health psychology' was coined by psychologist Jonathon Raymond, reflecting an attempt to synthesise work and health psychology and provide new insights as far as the effects of work on health were concerned. As noted by Quick (1999: 82) its emergence paralleled a growing and converging interest of those in public health and preventive medicine in the mental health problems arising from the social organisation of work. The *Journal of Occupational Health Psychology* edited by Julian Barling and *Work & Stress* edited by Tom Cox, together with a number of other journals, provided important vehicles for a wave of broader and more organisationally informed research into the effects of work (especially work-related stress) on the psychological wellbeing of workers and their families. For the past two decades excessive work-related stress has been widely recognised as a major contributor to occupational ill health, with negative effects on both physical health and psychological wellbeing. Work and health psychology have contributed to the development of psychological models of occupational stress. These models portray stress as a complex phenomenon with a range of individual, organisational and environmental causes. Organisational and environmental factors frequently identified as contributors include repetitive and machine-paced work, ambiguous and conflicting work roles, poor social relationships at work, shiftwork, excessively high or low work demands, low autonomy, physical danger and poor physical working conditions (Cox, 1988; Cooper et al., 2001). Individual factors commonly linked with lower stress resistance include limited job experience, insufficient training, ineffective coping strategies, poor diet, insufficient exercise and several personality and cognitive/perceptual characteristics (Mackay and Cooper, 1987; Schuler, 1980; Latack and Havlovic, 2006).

The negative health effects of occupational stress are as complex as its causes and vary greatly between individuals. These health effects are often divided into 'objective' and 'subjective' categories. Disease or pathology diagnosed by a medical practitioner is generally accepted as 'objective'. Although there is debate about the extent to which occupational stress causes disease, links have been proposed with conditions including high blood pressure, heart disease and ulcers. 'Subjective' health effects are those physical and psychological symptoms experienced and reported by workers themselves. Symptoms of stress frequently reported by workers include fatigue, anxiety, inability to concentrate, disturbances of mood and sleep disruption (Devereux et al., 2004). Although it is often claimed that self-reports of symptoms are unreliable, there is evidence that workers reporting more symptoms also have higher physiological indices of stress (Burke et al., 1993; Ang et al., 2008).

Extensive psychological research on stress has made several contributions to the occupational health field. It has provided a systematic examination of the mechanisms and processes through which organisational factors impinge on the health of individual workers and developed conceptual models to describe them. Psychological research is prominent in the development of robust scales to measure the extent of stress experienced by the individual (e.g. Hurrell et al., 1998; Spector, 2006). It has also drawn attention to the important and often overlooked subjective component of occupational ill health. Little recognition had previously been given to the debilitating effects of subjective symptoms, which are the most frequent and immediately disturbing health problems faced by most workers. By monitoring these subjective health effects and their physiological correlates, it is now possible to detect the early development of more severe physical illness.

Another important outcome of stress research has been a growing willingness of psychologists to recommend changes to the working environment and work organisation to improve workers' health. They have become increasingly critical of Taylorist principles of work simplification and have argued for job redesign to increase workers' control over their work and broaden skill utilisation (Wall and Martin, 1987). This position is based on strong evidence that repetitive, monotonous, de-skilled and machine-paced work is associated with marked psychological and physiological stress responses (Fletcher and Payne, 1980; Ganster and Fusilier, 1989; Johansson, 1989). Clegg and Wall (1990), for example, demonstrated that poorer mental health is associated with narrow, simplified jobs and that workers who feel they have few opportunities to use their skills may suffer most. On the basis of this research, psychologists have become more vocal critics of work characterised by low levels of stimulation, skill utilisation, autonomy and training (Johansson, 1989). They have also, with some support from other disciplines, focussed attention on the negative health effects of excessive working hours (see Sparks et al., 1997) and drawn attention to the detrimental effects of shiftwork on fatigue, subjective health, injury and domestic relationships (see chapter 6).

Psychologists have argued that individual stress management programs merely assist workers to cope with poorly designed working environments and should only be used to supplement job redesign intended to eliminate the primary sources of stress (Mackay and Cooper, 1987). This change in attitude has been slow to influence practitioners, however, and occupational stress management programs continue to focus heavily on individual coping skills (Reynolds and Shapiro, 1991). Nevertheless, stress research has considerably broadened the definition of occupational ill health and drawn it away from its focus upon physical injury and disease. The causes and effects of occupational stress, and its relationship to occupational illness, will be examined more extensively in chapter 5.

For much of its history work psychology focused on a small number of problem areas. In the days prior to the Hawthorne studies the underlying premise was that workers should be fitted to jobs, and that jobs were fixed by production imperatives.

Psychologists' work concentrated on personnel selection, the application of work study methods and the improvement of the physical environment. The health and safety of workers was often examined only in terms of its impact on productivity. With the advent of the Hawthorne studies, the emphasis shifted away from individuals and the physical working environment to the study of motivation, morale and social relationships within work groups. Certain psychosocial conditions of work such as monotony, poor interpersonal relationships, poor supervision, inappropriate selection and inadequate training were believed to have a crucial impact on worker health and wellbeing. With the more recent emergence of organisational and occupational health psychology, wider organisational influences on workers' behaviour and health were recognised. These developments expanded the range of variables of interest to psychologists and provided a basis from which stress research could consider complex interactions between individual and organisational variables. As a result, psychologists have become stronger advocates of job redesign and changes in work organisation to improve workers' health. Nevertheless, psychological research still focuses chiefly on two sets of causal variables, the characteristics and behaviours of individual workers (such as personality, training, experience and coping styles) and a restricted range of environmental and organisational factors (such as working hours, payment systems and the interpersonal environment).

The contributions of work psychologists to the field of occupational health have been widely criticised, often by psychologists themselves. Major criticisms include the undue emphasis placed on individualised explanations of injury and illness (and the consequent focus on preventative interventions on individual workers), the lack of evidence to support some psychological notions of injury causation, and the strongly managerial orientation of psychologists, both in terms of the problems they attempt to solve and the solutions they recommend.

The most conspicuous effect of psychological models has been to focus attention on individual explanations of occupational illness and injury or how workplace hazards are mediated by individual factors. Much psychological research has been concerned with identifying the characteristics and behaviours of individual workers that contribute to illness and injury. While the importance of some environmental factors is explicitly recognised, and many researchers concede that they are the primary causal variables, their impact is still assessed in relation to individual workers. Further, where psychologists have called for changes in aspects of the organisation of work, such as the abandonment of piece rates and increased worker autonomy, they have not systematically examined, or even recognised, the trade-offs between productivity and health that may be involved. Moreover, workplace factors are dealt with in a fragmented fashion which belies a broad understanding of the power structures and conflicts of interest within the workplace. Worker involvement in devising solutions to health and safety problems is minimised, and their interests are presumed to coincide with those of management. In most cases, the remedies suggested still concentrate upon individual behaviour change or relatively minor modifications to the working environment controlled by management.

Psychological theories derived from human relations particularly highlighted the contribution of worker characteristics and behaviour, such as accident proneness, to illness and injury. Selective focus on these factors provided a means for employers to locate the responsibility for injury with the individual worker and largely absolve themselves from responsibility for either injury or the worker behaviours that gave rise to it. This focus on the individual also provided a rationale for restricting interventions to relatively inexpensive activities such as improving selection procedures, upgrading training and introducing behaviour modification programs. These practices divert attention away from causes of injury associated with the organisation of work, such as production pressures and equipment design, that are potentially more costly to rectify.

Psychological theories have been used to support an understanding of injury and illness which 'blames the victim' rather than 'blaming the system'. For example, employers and managers have consistently emphasised the role of personality and poor coping strategies as the causes of stress and promoted individual stress management as the solution. Unions, on the other hand, have responded by emphasising environmental determinants and promoting interventions such as job redesign, physiological monitoring of workers, changed payment systems and increased penalty payments for stressful work. Clearly, it is optimal to intervene at both levels, but interventions aimed solely at the individual level are unlikely to be successful because they fail to act upon the underlying causes of the problem.

Psychological concepts are frequently misused by medical professionals, managers, insurers and the general public, even when psychologists themselves dispute their value. For example, the notion of accident proneness remained popular long after psychological researchers abandoned it due to a lack of supporting evidence and an acknowledgment that research had been based on methods and statistical techniques incapable of demonstrating clear cause and effect relationships (McKenna, 1983; Sheehy and Chapman, 1987). It was impossible, for example, to assess whether differences in personality and behaviour cause differential injury rates or whether the impact of injury causes changes in personality or behaviour. In addition, frequently no account was taken of differences in exposure to the risk of injury even though it would seem elementary to expect that workers employed on dangerous tasks would be injured more often than those exposed to less danger. The resilience of the term accident proneness or similar stigmatic concepts—for example, those applied to immigrant/foreign workers, such as 'Lebanese back', and to those suffering from repetitive strain injury, such as 'kangaroo paw' (see chapter 4)—can be more readily understood considering the attractiveness of 'victim-blaming' explanations to particular interest groups or the convenience of 'unexamined' prejudice over more careful assessment of the evidence. Psychologists have limited control over the distorted application of their concepts and research (Levy-Leboyer, 1998). On the other hand, the ongoing focus on individual worker characteristics and behaviour modification by many psychologists has provided fuel for 'victim-blaming' explanations (Hopkins and Palser, 1987), notwithstanding the sometimes strident criticism of such research emanating from other psychologists.

Over three decades ago Hale and Hale (1972) concluded that research on injury causation had focused too narrowly on a range of individual traits and behaviours and paid insufficient attention to the contribution of the social and physical environment. Sheehy and Chapman (1987) argued that this focus frequently led to a failure to collect adequate information about the situational and environmental determinants of injuries while characteristics and behaviours of workers were exhaustively examined and complex scales were developed to measure these phenomena. Sheehy and Chapman argued that injuries must be seen to result from the interaction of multiple causes, and as predictable processes rather than random events. More recently, *The Psychology of Workplace Safety*, a book edited by Julian Barling and Michael Frone (2004), has brought together much contemporary psychological theorising on occupational injury, including contributions on safety climate, teamwork, job insecurity/contingent work, drug use, payment systems, training, high-performance work systems and the vulnerability of younger workers. The chapters range from fairly conventional analysis of individual worker behaviour through to more explicit consideration of social and organisational factors, including the role of unions (see Kelloway, 2004). Taken as a whole it is fair to locate the book at the more progressive and organisationally informed end of the spectrum of psychological research into OHS, offering at times powerfully argued critiques of the more individually focused research.

In summary, psychologists have historically displayed a managerial orientation on occupational health issues. They rarely systematically examined health and safety problems from the point of view of workers and generally failed to promote solutions that could threaten productivity. Most uncritically assumed that a mutuality of interests existed between management and workers and that no significant conflict existed between health and productivity objectives. It is not surprising that psychologists have displayed this orientation. The nature of their employment has generally placed considerable pressure upon them to solve health and safety problems as understood by managers. Most psychologists working in OHS have either been employed as managers or as consultants for managers. Until the 1980s, the ability of psychologists to take an independent professional orientation to occupational health was also hindered by a shortage of practitioners with specialist training in the area (Henderson, 1981). While psychological theories explicitly recognise the organisational and environmental influences on injury and illness, psychologists have, in practice, rarely devoted much attention to variables outside the immediate working environment. Instead they have focused on aspects of individual behaviour that can be altered to improve individual health, wellbeing and productivity. Organisational control structures, production imperatives and managerial objectives are rarely examined, let alone questioned. This may be understandable given the focus of the psychological discipline on individual behaviour, but the unfortunate outcome has been that some psychologists, and many users of psychological theory and research, have perpetuated an indefensibly narrow view of the causes of occupational illness and injury. At worst, their work provided an intellectual foundation for 'victim-blaming' explanations of occupational illness. It is important to recognise these limitations when using psychological models to develop a more comprehensive understanding of occupational health.

Expert technical approaches: ergonomics, industrial hygiene and safety engineering

Several disciplines have what can be better described as an expert technical orientation to occupational health problems. Practitioners in these areas have had a pervasive influence on the way in which managers, administrators, legislators and the public understand and deal with health and safety problems in the workplace. Expert technical approaches share a strong focus on the physical nature of the workplace and the interaction between workers and their physical environment. While they have common interests, they have developed as separate fields that focus on particular problems and frequently recommend different interventions (see Pettersson-Strömbäck et al., 2006). We shall briefly describe the history and current practice of each one before analysing their strengths and weaknesses.

Occupational hygiene

Occupational hygiene is a long-established approach to occupational health management. It is concerned with the identification, measurement and evaluation of hazards, and the development of procedures for their control or elimination (Levine, 2006). The development of this field is often traced to the emergence of large-scale chemical manufacturing in the late nineteenth century when scientists and practitioners from medicine, engineering and chemistry were brought together to reverse the growth of industrial disease. However, Carter (2004: 299) contends the field has far older roots, arguing that industrial disease prevention practices in the workplace (such as wet grinding to reduce dust) that 'could be readily characterized as occupational hygiene' can be traced back to the 1720s in Britain—the very beginnings of the Industrial Revolution. By the early twentieth century occupational hygienists were at the forefront of identifying and establishing a list of hazardous substances together with their exposure limits. The development of the discipline was greatly stimulated by the advent of World War I, when early practitioners contributed to improvements in the productivity and health of the workforce, especially munitions workers (Europe led the US in this regard; Carter, 2004; Selby, 1925).

At this time, occupational hygienists tended to provide a secondary service to medical practitioners, being primarily concerned with the identification and control of the sources of health problems diagnosed by doctors, rather than active prevention through comprehensive periodic surveys and evaluations of the workplace. In the UK, for example, doctors carrying out periodic medical monitoring would be responsible for diagnosing the first signs of the absorption of toxins and the intervention of occupational hygienists would follow positive diagnoses. However, World War II saw a very rapid expansion of occupational hygiene services in the interests of 'manpower conservation'. Rules and regulations were developed for the handling of toxic substances and a more preventative orientation was taken through the design and coordination of various safeguards against harmful exposures. The discipline has now developed to the point where occupational hygienists are the first-line specialists responsible for the minimisation of occupational ill health in many workplaces.

Contemporary occupational hygiene is an environmental science which concerns itself with physical, chemical, and biological hazards to workers' health. It generally focuses upon physical illness and disease, and devotes comparatively little attention to subjective health and occupational injury. In their attempts to protect the physical health of workers, occupational hygienists address problems relating to toxicity, biohazards, airborne contamination, radiation protection, ventilation, and the control of noise, vibration, light and heat (Mikatavage, 1992; Burton, 2004; Ettinger, 2005; Levine, 2006). Hygienists also generally work closely with medical practitioners in the process of diagnosing health problems and identifying probable causes, but are expert in the management and control of physical hazards in the workplace. Since the 1980s hygienists have also collaborated with engineers and others to better manage explosions/fires, mass emissions and other serious incidents relating to major hazard facilities such as chemical plants, although this area has also generated a specialised literature (Rusch, 1993; Hu and Raymond, 2004).

The work of occupational hygienists can be roughly broken into three phases: identification, evaluation and control (Smith, 1983; Toohey et al., 2005). The identification phase involves the collection of information from a variety of sources. The overall work of the plant or organisation is usually broken down into its component processes and hazards associated with each process are specified. For example, welding and cutting may be one component process in an engineering plant. Hazards associated with this process could include inhalation of metal fumes and toxic gases and materials, noise from the torch, and eye and skin damage from infra-red and ultraviolet radiation.

Once all hazards are identified, an evaluation of the level of risk associated with each hazard is performed. This evaluation may be performed by collecting data from a number of sources. The sources could include background technical information on the processes and the hazards associated with them, sampling and environmental measurements to determine exposure levels, observation of work practices, and detailed physical analysis of the workplace to examine factors such as ventilation around workstations. In some cases, a full-scale organisational survey might be performed which would examine all facets of work activities including infrequent operations like maintenance and cleaning. The assessment of whether a significant hazard exists is generally based on scientific data defining exposure limits, government requirements set by statute, or consultation with other health professionals, especially medical practitioners, who have examined the workers themselves.

When hazards have been successfully identified and the associated risks evaluated, a control strategy is designed to reduce exposure to an acceptable level. The strategies employed by occupational hygienists include engineering controls, administrative controls, and protective clothing and equipment (Mathews, 1985; Roelofs et al., 2003). Engineering controls prevent disease by modification of tools, equipment (such as fume hoods and exhaust extractors) and processes (such as material substitution). It is generally concerned with physical hazards (such as noise, radiation, heat, humidity and vibration), chemical fumes, biohazards, and dusts and fibres. Control is generally achieved by source removal, source isolation and enclosure, pathway modification or worker enclosure. In source removal, strategies such as substitution of toxic chemicals with more benign ones are employed. Source isolation and enclosure involves protective practices such as enclosing chemicals in fume cupboards. Pathway modification interrupts transmission or transfer of dangerous by-products to workers by means such as ventilation, insulation or spraying. Worker enclosure involves confining workers to small, defined areas that are free of the hazard, for example by placing workers in sound-proofed booths for protection against excessively loud machinery. Enclosure should be applied as a last resort.

Administrative controls reduce hazards by modifying job procedures. They include job rotation, limited entry, permit-to-work systems, and job exclusion for certain groups of workers. Job rotation reduces the period during which individual workers are exposed to particular hazards, while limited entry areas minimise the number of workers exposed to a particular hazard. Permit-to-work systems require documentation to be issued to workers before they enter particular work areas. Exclusion is used to preclude specified groups of workers from performing particular jobs or entering particular areas. Women, for example, have been widely excluded from night work and from working with lead and other substances while of 'child-bearing age'. Protective clothing and equipment are generally used when engineering and administrative controls are not adequate to reliably protect workers' health. Protective clothing items include gloves, overalls, helmets and boots, and protective equipment includes respirators, goggles, ear muffs and welder's masks.

There are problems associated with a number of these controls (Mathews, 1985). In a meta-review of actual control practices, Roelofs et al. (2003: 62) found that almost three-quarters of the studies they reviewed discussed engineering controls, about half discussed administrative strategies, one-third discussed PPE and only a quarter considered primary prevention (such as material substitution). While the emphasis on engineering controls over administrative controls and PPE was laudable, the bulk of the former focused on localised and presumably cheaper solutions such as local exhaust ventilation (Roelofs et al., 2003: 62). Further, while exposure standards have an air of scientific objectivity as described in chapter 7, close attention needs to be paid to the data used to derive those standards as well as bargaining between employers and regulators (and less often workers) as to what standard will be implemented. Exclusion of particular workers is a highly discriminatory practice. It relieves management of responsibility for control of the hazard and transfers the full effect of hazard exposure to non-excluded workers. It may have little rational basis, place the health of workers who are not excluded at considerable risk and deny job opportunities to others who are excluded. Men, for example, may be just as vulnerable to lead toxicity, but have been widely exposed to these risks although they were banned for women. Protective clothing and administrative controls are relatively inexpensive solutions which shift the responsibility for maintaining health onto individual workers and disguise a failure on the part of management to effectively control the physical working environment. Protective clothing often places a hidden burden on the worker by hindering necessary movements, slowing performance, producing general discomfort and creating other hazards. For example, face masks may fog up and clog, hindering vision and making breathing difficult. Clothing may absorb toxins and fail to provide completely effective protection.

Further, the process of implementing controls can entail critical but opaque judgments, for example where lack of toxicity data in relation to chemicals is presumed to equate to lack of toxicity and a risk-neutral hazard default is not adopted (Hansson and Ruden, 2008). Other potentially contentious judgments apply at the identification and monitoring stages, including the selection of environmental measurement or biological monitoring (Harrison and Sepai, 2000); the full range of events (including maintenance) that may lead to exposures from equipment (Bowes, 2008); and the extent to which monitoring and control measures take sufficient account of actual work practices/usage patterns (Thomas, 2001) and what may shape this. Examples of the latter include a tendency for 'risk averse' land or aquatic farmers or forest plantation managers to overuse chemicals designed to control insect pests or parasites and the mixture of behavioural influences and demographic and employment structures in rural communities (Quandt et al., 2006).

After controls have been instituted the hygienist may recommend routine environmental monitoring to ensure that they are effective. Alternatively, monitoring may be used to provide an initial survey of health risks. In both cases, environmental monitoring involves measurement and evaluation of worker exposure to hazardous substances or materials (Mathews, 1985). Hazards monitored include noise, dust, chemical fumes, vibration and temperature. Data can be collected using a variety of methods. For instance, samples may be collected at specified points in time or collection may be continuous. Measurements may also be taken at one or more fixed points or by attaching personal monitors to workers. Each method has its strengths and weaknesses, but continuous monitoring on the person, if it is practicable, does offer a more reliable indication of the total exposure experienced by workers during normal work. The validity of non-continuous and fixed-point measures depends very heavily on the appropriateness of the timing of samples and the placement of meters.

Ergonomics

Ergonomics is another expert technical approach that has become increasingly influential in recent years. It can be broadly defined as the scientific study of the physical relationship between people, the equipment they use and their working environments (Karwowski, 2005). The principal objective of ergonomists is to modify the working environment to optimise this relationship. In practice, they are primarily concerned with the design of equipment and working environments to make best use of workers' potential without exceeding their physical and psychological capacities (see Bartlett, 1962; Sanders and McCormick, 1993; Kroemer and Grandjean, 1997; Karwowski, 2005; Brookhuis, 2008). Ergonomists generally assume that identification and elimination of problems in the design of tools, equipment, tasks and work systems is also the most effective and economic way to promote the safety and wellbeing of workers. In order to achieve its goals ergonomics draws together knowledge and practices from psychology, engineering, physiology, anatomy and anthropometry (the measurement of height, reach and bodily dimensions in different postures).

The field of ergonomics is a relatively recent development. The name was coined in the late 1940s to describe a new field concerned with the 'laws of work' (Brookhuis, 2008). The origins of the field lie largely in the time-and-motion studies of Taylor and of the research of early work psychologists on physical working conditions, work scheduling, fatigue and worker productivity. Ergonomics began to develop a separate identity during World War II when the armed services brought psychologists, engineers and physiologists together to explore the relationships between workers' physical and psychological capacities and their efficiency and health. The principal objective was to design equipment to ensure the maximum efficiency of personnel critical to the war effort, especially tank crews, pilots and munitions workers. Following the war the field was advanced by the explosive growth of the aerospace industry and the need to maximise the control of air crews over immensely expensive aircraft and armaments. There is little doubt that ergonomics developed primarily in response to pressures for increased worker efficiency and productivity, and consequently promotion of worker health and safety has assumed a somewhat lower priority among ergonomists than improving productivity. At the same time, the field has developed an array of methods for identifying and addressing hazardous working conditions, including the importance of comfort, posture and cumulative load as well as work and equipment design. It has also contributed to our knowledge of musculoskeletal disorders (Stubbs, 2000).

The underlying assumption of ergonomics is that occupational injury and ill health arise largely from a lack of fit between the capabilities of workers and the design of the physical working environment and work processes (Davis, 1988; Kroemer and Grandjean, 1997). The solutions to health and safety problems developed by ergonomists have primarily been concerned with the design of individual tools and equipment, the efficiency of individual work methods and the design of workstations. The design of tools and equipment is perhaps the activity for which they are most widely known. Ergonomists base this design process on extensive data concerning bodily dimensions, strength and the physical movement of workers. This data is used to produce design standards, which should ideally be classified by sex, age and working population. The standards are then used to design items such as hand tools and the mechanical controls for maximum efficiency. Ergonomic data is also widely used to develop standards for everyday tasks like determining the correct height of steps or the appropriate slope and width of ramps. Ergonomists have also played an important role in the minimisation of injuries arising from inherently dangerous work activities, such as manual handling of heavy loads. In an effort to develop solutions to manual handling problems, ergonomists have extensively examined the relationships between lifting technique, posture and load characteristics such as size, shape and weight.

Some ergonomists have also recognised the importance of behavioural factors in equipment design (Davis, 1988). For example, they have observed that protective clothing and equipment are often discarded because they are uncomfortable or they interfere with work efficiency. A number of design solutions have been developed to address these problems. For example, detailed anthropometric data about head and facial dimensions has been collected and used to improve the comfort and fit of head-mounted equipment. Other researchers have developed improvements in the design of safety goggles to minimise the misting that can diminish vision and contribute to injury in hot and humid environments. Ergonomists have also performed acoustic studies examining the effects of noise on speech recognition, error rates, hand–eye coordination, and thought and decision-making processes. This work has helped them to prescribe noise standards that not only are based on the thresholds of direct physical injury but also recognise the effects of noise on worker behaviours that are related to injury. Machinery can now be designed to meet these stricter standards.

The design of individual items of equipment has been an important part of ergonomists' work, but they have placed an equally strong emphasis on the integrated redesign of immediate working environments, or workstations. Ergonomists generally attempt to design workstations to match the size and capabilities of workers and to ensure that tools and machinery can be controlled with the minimum risk of injury or health problems (Davis, 1988). In order to optimise workstation design ergonomists observe workers performing specific tasks and analyse their interactions with their working environment. The final design takes into account a wide range of factors. It usually involves considerations such as the positioning of controls, provision of sufficient space for the physical movements required of the operator, and the design of controls to require forces within the safe capacities of the worker. It may also involve investigation of the body forces required for movements such as shifting levers; the forces impinging on muscles, joints and other parts of the body in various postures; and changes in bodily processes such as energy expenditure and oxygen consumption. Provision of special support equipment, such as effective protective clothing and first aid kits, may also be considered. The design of surrounding ramps, doorways, and corridors to ensure efficient movement of workers and materials may also be considered. The environment surrounding the workstation may be modified to ensure adequate ventilation and noise levels low enough to have minimal effect on communication and thought processes. The optimisation of vigilance has recently been identified as an important behavioural consideration in workstation design. This may require planning the workstation so that there is enough physical movement, perhaps by placing seats at a distance from consoles, so that workers have to move regularly and consequently find it easier to stay alert (Davis, 1988).

An example of this work with which most are familiar is the design of workstations for use with computerised visual display units (VDUs). The aim here is to achieve the optimal spatial and optical relationship between all components of the workstation including the chair, desk, monitor, keyboard and source document. The design must allow for differences in physical size between workers and this is generally achieved by the provision of various adjustments including chair height, keyboard height, monitor angle and position and source document position. Optimally, but less frequently in practice, consideration should be given to environmental factors like lighting and glare levels, noise levels, task organisation, work scheduling and temperature control where appropriate.

In recent times the electronic control equipment used in many workplaces has become increasingly complex, especially in aircraft cockpits, air traffic control stations, and nuclear power plants and similar high-technology environments. Ergonomists have been called upon to develop guidelines to optimise the efficiency of human interaction with this equipment. Their recommendations have focussed upon the qualities of visual displays and acoustic signals, and the spatial configuration of controls, monitoring devices and warning signals. Work on visual capacities, for example, has produced information on the effects of luminance, glare, flicker and colour on visual acuity in various conditions (Davis, 1988). The invasion of the workplace by computers and related technology has also drawn ergonomists into the design of 'software tools' (Mathews, 1985). In conjunction with cognitive and experimental psychologists they have contributed to the development of computer operating systems, word processors and computerised machinery controls. Specialists in the new area of 'cognitive ergonomics' have used knowledge of human sensory capabilities to understand the interface between humans and machines, especially the human–computer interface. They have developed design principles relating to the legibility and layout of text, the clarity of error and diagnostic messages, and the minimisation of human error in interacting with software programs.

Ergonomists have also begun to examine aspects of work organisation. They have built upon earlier interests in manual handling and the timing and duration of rest periods to become concerned with activities like job design, task allocation, work scheduling, the setting and monitoring of operating goals, the design of operating procedures and documentation, and safety training (Cullen, 1988; Grandjean, 1988). They have drawn heavily on recent work in work psychology, and the solutions they recommend are very similar. For example, ergonomists have pointed out that single-task, repetitive work is boring, stressful and a significant contributor to ill health and occupational overuse injuries (Mathews, 1985). They often recommend solutions drawn from the psychological literature, such as job rotation and an expansion of the variety of tasks performed by workers. However, their solutions also reflect their own expertise, for example in recommendations that tasks should be redesigned to ensure that workers use a variety of tools to minimise fatigue and monotony.

The activities that we have discussed to this point have mainly been concerned with the short-term impact of the working environment on health and safety. However, ergonomists have recently devoted increased attention to hazards with delayed effects (Davis, 1988). Gradual absorption of toxins, chronic radiation overdosage, cumulative musculoskeletal damage and long-term visual strain are all examples of hazards that present health threats but do not have obvious short-term signs and symptoms. There are many examples of ergonomists' contribution to the reduction of such hazards. They have redesigned tools and equipment to minimise spillage and long-term, low-level exposure to dangerous substances. They have also modified workstations and work areas to reduce radiation hazards. Safe limits have been revised for some repetitive tasks, allowing for the fact that physical stresses which are insignificant when they occur once may have serious effects when repeated over extended periods. Vibration white finger, tenosynovitis, cervical spondylosis and many back injuries arise in this way. In response to this problem ergonomists have produced standards that provide at least medium-term guidance on safe exposure to repetitive stresses. While it has long been accepted that inappropriate posture can contribute to pain and injury, there is a growing realisation that skeletal disorders can arise from prolonged maintenance of even correct posture. Ergonomists are now developing standards indicating safe tolerance times for correct postures.

Workplaces subjected to thorough ergonomic redesign should have had many health and safety hazards eliminated (see Hale, et al., 2007). Tools and equipment should be designed for efficient human use, controls should be well placed, and the forces required for their operation should be well within human capacities. Machines and equipment should be in optimal spatial relationships to each other. Materials should be at correct locations for safe handling, and all corridors, doorways, steps and ramps should be within design standards. Ventilation should be adequate, sufficient space should be available for the performance of all tasks and protective clothing should be comfortable and effective. Noise levels should be low enough to permit efficient communication and decision making, and the information displays on machinery should be clear and logical. Physical movement required should be sufficient to maintain vigilance and rates and times of work should not create unnecessary fatigue. This situation is of course an ideal, and often only some of these outcomes will be satisfactorily achieved.

Ergonomists have been for many years particularly interested in examining the link between OHS and increased workplace productivity (see Oxenburgh, 1991; MacLeod 1995; Shikdar and Sawaqed, 2003; Lahiri et al., 2005; Oxenburgh and Marlow, 2005). MacLeod (1995: 19) provides some insight into the reasons why ergonomists have been more active in this area than professionals in other fields of OHS and why they have been more successful in engaging with the business community over the links between OHS and productivity:

> Improving the fit between humans and tools inherently means a more effective match. Good ergonomic improvements often result in better ways of performing a task. An ergonomically designed workplace (or product) is a more productive workplace (or product). Not exceeding human capabilities does not mean reducing output or doing less. On the contrary, good design permits more output with less human effort.

Like the other expert technical approaches, ergonomics has an admirable preventative philosophy. Its strength is that it sets out to change the physical working environment to be maximally compatible with human operation. By fitting the design of equipment and work methods to the physical and cognitive capacities of workers, ergonomists act directly upon some important primary causes of occupational ill health and injury. They have also contributed significantly to the health and safety debate by promoting the notion that the extra effort required to maintain productivity in less-than-optimum working conditions directly contributes to short- and long-term health and safety effects. They have observed that increased effort may lead to injury through immediate error or overstrain, for example when over-reaching results in falls from ladders or scaffolding, or to long-term degradation of health and wellbeing, by producing, for example, overuse injuries (Cullen, 1988).

Nevertheless, narrow application of ergonomic interventions does have significant limitations. Ergonomists view injury at work as an aberrant event and seek to limit 'accidents' and errors by workers. In doing so they essentially treat workers as sophisticated machines whose limitations and potential for error must be circumvented or minimised for them to become more efficient components of the working environment. There is only limited recognition that aspects of the social organisation of work may contribute significantly to illness and injury. In practice, ergonomists have been remarkably silent regarding the role that organisational factors, like pressure for excessive output and incentive payment systems, play in injury and illness causation. They have been reticent to challenge managerial prerogative in such matters and have remained aligned to objectives of management (an orientation that they of course share with other professions). This managerial orientation is implicit in the words of Cullen (1988: 3) who observed that ergonomics would 'be of benefit to management decision-making in the design, installation and operation of plant and systems of work and also to the workers who are daily exposed to the effects of poor ergonomic design'. Although admirably eclectic in utilising knowledge from a range of different disciplines, ergonomists have traditionally placed little emphasis on actively involving workers in the problem-solving process. This reticence to consult with workers has resulted in many ergonomic interventions failing to resolve, or even address, threats to health and safety perceived by non-managers. It also partly explains failures by ergonomists to produce adequate standards for specific groups of workers, including women. Recent growth in the value placed on worker participation has therefore been encouraging (Stubbs, 2000). Cohen (1996), for example, provides practical advice on facilitating participation by workers in ergonomic problem solving. He describes several important considerations in promoting a team-based approach to participation, including obtaining management commitment, providing appropriate training to workers and management, tailoring the specific form of participation to the organisational context, promoting effective information sharing, selecting appropriate problem-solving activities to enhance motivation and evaluating outcomes. Similarly, Stubbs (2000: 277) examined the value of 'participatory ergonomics' in terms of understanding and solutions as well as emphasising the need for a multidisciplinary team approach and meeting the challenges posed by an ageing workforce.

Although the field has emerged relatively recently, ergonomists have had remarkable success in establishing their credibility in occupational health management. This has included influencing the suggested-expertise base of other OHS professions, such as post-injury interventions by occupational therapists (Bade and Eckert, 2008). Public acceptance of ergonomic design has been high enough for it to become a valuable marketing feature. We are often assailed by advertisements for 'ergonomic' desks, chairs and office equipment, much of which appears to be of dubious ergonomic value. Ergonomists themselves are often quick to point out that furniture is not universally 'ergonomic', but rather may be ergonomically appropriate for use in some contexts, or by some workers. So-called 'ergonomically designed' office furniture may well be no better than the old furniture it replaces (Mathews, 1985). Certainly evidence should be sought regarding the ergonomic suitability of furniture and equipment for the intended use, and preferably a suitably qualified person should be available to assess its suitability.

Ergonomists generally maintain a strongly expert approach. The aura of mystery and inaccessibility surrounding their esoteric, technical language has effectively discounted and marginalised more everyday accounts of the hazards created by work organisation. Consequently, ergonomic solutions have frequently been narrowly applied while unsafe work practices continue unchecked (Mathews, 1985). The introduction of ergonomic improvements to a workplace cannot overcome fundamental problems with the organisation of work. For example, no amount of ergonomic redesign will minimise occupational overuse injuries if workers are still required to perform repetitive work at a dangerous pace. Unfortunately, ergonomic intervention may be much more attractive to management because it avoids the immediate productivity impact that lowering work rates or otherwise altering work processes may entail. To be fair to ergonomists, they recognise the importance of improved work organisation, but in practice they tend to focus more heavily on modification of the physical working environment. There is therefore considerable scope for management to use ergonomic solutions as a means of diverting attention from more fundamental problems with work organisation.

Safety engineering

Safety engineering, a field related to occupational hygiene and ergonomics, also deserves brief mention. It is concerned with the design and modification of tools, equipment and work processes in order to minimise the probability of injury (Mathews, 1985). Safety engineers use three main means of injury minimisation: machine guarding, machine operating controls and lockout procedures. Safety engineering originated in the Industrial Revolution with the modification of machinery to protect workers by placing guards over moving parts and guarding remains one of its principal concerns. Blades, presses, rotors, gears and other mechanical sources of danger generally have guards fitted, at least initially, as the primary means of workers' protection. A later development was the introduction of controls to limit the possibility that machines could be operated inadvertently while parts of the operator's body were in dangerous positions. Levers, wheels, buttons, pedals and switches are frequently designed this way. Stamping machines, for example, often have dual-button controls that require two-handed operation in order to avoid fingers or other body parts being caught under the press. Lockout procedures are intended to ensure that controls are locked in the 'off' position while workers are in vulnerable situations, such as when performing maintenance on heavy machinery.

The line between the professions of safety engineering and ergonomics is often blurred, particularly around safety design and minimising errors. The intersection between these two disciplines has evolved into the subdiscipline of human factors and ergonomics (HFE) (see Karwowski, 2005; Cullen, 2007; Fadier, 2007; Hale et al., 2007).

The HFE discipline focuses on the understanding of interactions between people and systems, that is, everything that surrounds people at work and outside of their working environment. In particular, HFE professionals gather and apply information about human behaviour, their abilities and limitations and other characteristics in relation to the design of tools, machines, systems, tasks, jobs and environments for productive, safe, comfortable and effective human use (Sanders and McCormick, 1993; Karwowski, 2005). Based on such knowledge, HFE aims to optimise human wellbeing and overall system performance. Contemporary HFE is concerned with '… the systematic use of the knowledge concerning relevant human characteristics in order to achieve compatibility in the design of interactive systems of people, machines, environments, and devices of all kinds to ensure specific goals …' (Human Factors and Ergonomics Society, 2004, cited in Karwowski, 2005: 441). In this context, HFE deals with a broad scope of problems relevant to the design and evaluation of work systems, consumer products and working environments, in which human–machine interactions affect human performance and product usability.

The expert technical models have several general limitations. A major problem is that their technical language is incomprehensible to most workers and managers. This mystification encourages organisations to relinquish control over occupational health problems to experts. Unfortunately, the result is often that the solutions considered are limited to the changes in equipment or production processes about which the ergonomist, safety engineer or occupational hygienist is most knowledgeable. Equally important social and behavioural causes of injury and ill health may be left unaddressed. Safety engineers, for example, may design protection devices such as machine guards with no knowledge or understanding of the factors that may lead workers to remove them. Organisational factors, such as production deadlines or incentive payments that encourage workers to remove safety devices to increase the speed and efficiency of machines, remain in force. Similar problems exist with the solutions to repetitive strain injury often prescribed by ergonomists. These solutions have generally involved the introduction of specially designed furniture and equipment and the introduction of rest breaks and exercises for workers at risk. While these actions may do much to reduce the pain and discomfort of workers, they do not address more basic factors such as the widespread and continuing trend towards work intensification that have promoted overuse injuries across whole industries. As a general rule, it is important that expert technical solutions are not applied uncritically or in isolation from interventions that address important behavioural, organisational and social causes of illness and injury. Nevertheless, they do have an important role to play when applied as part of a comprehensive and balanced intervention program.

A critical perspective: sociology

Rather than limiting attention to individual workers and their immediate working environments, sociologists apply a wider lens to the study of OHS. In particular, sociologists have examined the ways in which organisational structures, payment systems, industrial conflict and other organisational, industrial and social factors can be used to explain and predict injury rates. Sociologists have also critiqued the way in which OHS government regulations and policies have been developed and enforced. As the literature in this area is extensive, we shall not to attempt to review it comprehensively, but rather to draw attention to important themes with direct relevance to occupational health and safety.

Although many sociological studies have focused principally on the causation of injury, largely disregarding the development of occupational illness and disease, several controversial but important observations have been produced that lie at the heart of the health and safety debate. First, the terminology used in the occupational health and safety arena frequently supports particular ideological positions regarding the causation of injury and illness. That is, the prevailing definitions of occupational injury and illness are value-laden and frequently based on medical or managerial constructs. Second, the preoccupation with increasing productivity has by and large been at the expense of workers' health and safety. There is a widespread subjugation of worker health and safety concerns to those of profitability within organisations. Third, there is emerging evidence indicating that some widespread forms of work organisation, such as shiftwork and subcontracting, have adverse effects on the health and wellbeing of many workers. Moreover, rather than being aberrant or unpredictable, injury is an inherent part of the social organisation of work. Fourth, there was an increasing body of evidence that programs of prevention based on existing models of occupational injury and illness had failed to effectively deal with the problem (Dwyer, 1983; Willis, 1989; Nichols, 1997). Finally, how OHS regulations are conceived and enforced is not straightforward but instead is subjected to outside influences from powerful interest groups. The way in which employers comply or do not comply with OHS regulations is again a complex process and often reflects the individual employer's attitude to occupational health and safety.

The first set of issues concerns how the terms 'occupational injury' and 'occupational illness' are defined and applied. Sociologists have drawn attention to the highly individualised and biologically prescriptive notions that dominate the contemporary Western view of health and medical care. Some sociologists and other writers have emphasised the active role of the medical profession in promoting these notions (Willis, 1984; Seale, 2008; Timmermans and Haas, 2008), while others see the profession's approach to treatment as simply obscuring the social causes of health problems (Taylor, 1979). In any case, the emphasis of the medical model on clinical methods and the identification of biological pathology have not been well suited to recognising the complex social factors that may impinge on occupational health. Medical practice has focused on treating individuals rather than groups, and the resulting collection of individual information, such as that contained in medical histories and death certificates, does not facilitate the identification of the hazards and illnesses to which groups of workers are exposed. For example, after their brief stints at Wittenoom, ex-miners became widely dispersed around Australia. For decades thereafter many received individual treatment for lung diseases from local doctors without their suffering being linked to work in the mine (or to the prospect of compensation).

These observations also help us to understand the 'diagnostic' debates that have surrounded occupational injuries such as repetitive strain injury (RSI). Medical practitioners have been prominent advocates of explanations that point to the origins of the various forms of RSI in individual behaviour and characteristics, such as poor posture. In one extreme case, a psychiatrist rejected explanations based on physical injury altogether, promoting her own unsubstantiated theory that the pain had its origins in psychiatric disturbance (Lucire, 1988). Such explanations divert attention from the contribution of organisational factors such as authority and control structures, job and equipment design and work rates and suggest a narrow range of prevention and treatment strategies. The RSI debate will be extensively examined in chapter 4.

The almost universal use of the term 'accident' again is not a neutral term. While 'accidents' often refers to the events that surround the occurrence of an injury, the term provides another means of supporting a managerialist interpretation of injury causation (James, 1987). It carries the implication that injuries are random events arising from largely unpredictable causes and directly supports efforts by managers to move the focus of attention for the solution of injury problems from organisational factors to individual ones. If injuries are not logical and predictable outcomes of the organisation of work, then the primary responsibility for their occurrence can be attributed to the workers who are injured. Injury prevention efforts should then logically focus on the behaviour of workers and not on work organisation. It is important to recognise that the terms used to refer to injury and illness, and the way in which they are customarily understood, can significantly affect perceptions of occupational health problems, and the range of potential solutions that are likely to be considered.

Building on these broader definitions of occupational injuries and illnesses, sociologists have endeavoured to link various indices of injury and disease to economic class and occupation. In general, the evidence is much more convincing for fatal injury than for illness due, at least in part, to the greater reliability of the available data. Indeed, a number of overseas studies have demonstrated a positive relationship between educational level, occupation and occupational disease and illness, and have linked broader measures of socioeconomic status to both precursors of cardiovascular disease and to negative behavioural and lifestyle factors (Davis and George, 1988). Oh and Shin's (2007: 2180) US study also shows that human capital—namely, education, occupation and work experience—are crucial determinants of non-fatal work injuries. Australia and New Zealand worker compensation claim statistics lend support to Oh and Shin's study, indicating that lower socioeconomic groups are over-represented in the occupational injury claims. Further, a general pattern emerges in that mortality ratios are higher for blue-collar unskilled and semi-skilled occupations (labourers, cleaners, etc.) and lower for professional, managerial and clerical occupations.

Occupational health problems are seen to be located within certain processes and within particular groups of workers. Shiftwork, for example, has become more common in recent years, especially with its growing penetration into white-collar work. This expansion appears to have been driven predominantly by the economic benefits of continuous or extended operation rather than 'technological necessity' in many industries

(Frank, 2000; Bohle et al., 2004). However, research into the health impact of shiftwork has produced increasingly persuasive evidence that shiftwork has a marked negative effect on the health and wellbeing of workers (see chapter 6). Night and early morning shifts, in particular, are now suspected to contribute to the development of physical diseases, such as coronary heart disease, and to a range of subjective health problems, such as fatigue, disturbances of mood and anxiety. Despite this evidence, shiftwork continues to grow in prevalence including particularly extreme work schedules, such as those requiring 28 or more consecutive days of 12-hour shifts in some long-distance commuting operations. In many cases, the health of workers has clearly become a secondary concern to the economic benefits of extended production.

Sociological research also draws attention to community, gender and ethnicity differences in the type and occurrences of occupational injuries (see McDiarmid, 1999; Mastekaasa, 2005; McGrath and DeFilippis, 2009). In New Zealand, for example, men accounted for more work-related injury claims than females in all occupation groups, with the exception of service and sales workers, clerks and professionals, where women made 60%, 57% and 51% of claims, respectively (Statistics NZ, 2008). Vis-a-vis injury claim indices can often reflect the labour market segmentation, whereby women workers are found in greater numbers in the service sector compared to male workers, who are employed primarily in the trades (see Crichton et al., 2005). In 2007, Māori had an incidence rate of 155 claims per 1000 FTEs, compared with 152 for Pacific Peoples and 111 for Europeans (Statistics NZ, 2008). This is consistent with figures showing that Māori were over-represented in the elementary occupations (that is, labourers and cleaners, etc.) as well as among plant and machine operators and assemblers occupations, which typically have high claim rates.

The evidence linking illness to economic status and occupation, however, is still ambiguous in both Australia and New Zealand. In their comparative study, Driscoll et al. (2004) attest to the fact that the extant research has yet to establish significant relationships between various measures of socioeconomic status and morbidity for a range of diseases. Attempts to establish causal relationships between occupation and morbidity in Australia and New Zealand are hampered by a paucity of research evidence and by the complexity of the health-related variables that are encompassed within occupational categories. Occupation tends to correlate with a range of factors that may independently affect health, including consumption patterns (dietary habits and alcohol intake), access to health services, education and housing. It is clear, however, that further research, including more specific collection of official data, is required before an adequate understanding of the impact of socioeconomic status and occupation on morbidity in Australia and New Zealand can be established.

Another important aspect of a wider sociological understanding of occupational injury and illness is the recognition that basic conflicts of interest may place workers at risk. A fundamental conflict of interest often exists between the maximisation of profit and the protection of health, irrespective of whether the organisation is located in so-called 'capitalist' or 'communist/socialist' countries. For centuries sociologists and others have noted that the need for capital accumulation and the drive to maintain competitiveness and increase productivity are often at the expense of workers' health and safety. Even if higher levels of production can be secured without sacrificing the health and safety of workers and the community, it is unlikely to occur when an overriding emphasis is placed on the former and the latter is treated as an afterthought (see Mayhew et al., 1997; Mayhew and Quinlan, 1999; Quinlan, 2001; Massey et al., 2007). Recent studies have dovetailed this analysis into particular settings. For example Hall's (2007) study of restructuring, environmentalism and farm safety in Ontario, Canada, argued that economic constraints and rationales represented an overriding basis for risk taking among farmers, irrespective of their level of OHS knowledge.

Willis (1989) observed that a significant aspect of the conflict over 'managerial prerogative' has been the extent to which employers have power to damage employees' health in the pursuit of profit. He argued that managerial practices in the occupational health arena have been dominated by the 'as far as reasonably possible' approach. In other words, health issues are treated as secondary to production imperatives and are only addressed where the solutions do not threaten production goals. Moreover, sociologists argue that while exposure to hazards associated with machinery and manual handling are being reduced, other risks associated with increases in labour productivity are on the rise. In examining the implications of the changing world of work on the health and safety of workers, James (2006: 11) notes that:

> The fact that over half of these new cases of work-related ill health stem from … stress, depression and anxiety, and musculoskeletal disorders, also raises an important issue of policy, particularly when account is taken of the further fact that, against a background of increasing work intensity and declining worker discretion, the prevalence rate for stress and related conditions has recently grown substantially … It also further suggests, given the way in which these conditions are intimately connected to workload levels and the nature of work tasks, that the achievement of reductions of this type will require employers to be placed under much greater pressure to design work tasks and establish workloads that are not detrimental to worker health.

Even readily available technology may not be used to reduce hazards. For example, in an analysis of back injury among nurses, Griffin (1986) concluded that financial constraints on the health industry had encouraged developments that significantly increased the probability of injury. These developments included changes in nursing practice that required more patient lifting and handling, understaffing which required each nurse to lift more frequently, inadequate lifting instruction and insufficient provision of lifting devices. The combined effect of these factors was to support a perception that back injuries were an inherent part of nursing work. In this occupation, and many others, dangerous work organisation has continued where it is profitable, and compensation, rather than prevention, has remained the dominant mode of dealing with injury problems. It is hardly surprising in these circumstances that Nichols (1990) identified an important link between management control over health and safety matters and injury rates.

Some sociologists have also argued that the development and maintenance of work structures that expose workers to danger are a reflection of an underlying value system in which economic productivity is valued more highly than the health and safety of workers. Where such values predominate, injury is only likely to be considered significant to the extent that it diminishes the productiveness of workers (James, 1987). Research is also clear that when economic productivity takes primacy over the health and safety of workers, compliance with occupational regulations will be poor (Lamm, 2002). Dwyer (1983) illustrates this point in his observation of a French building site where workers and their supervisor generally recognised that safety standards were sacrificed to production pressure. Management paid financial incentives to a gang of workers who took risks that other workers were unwilling to take. Insidiously, this lead gang was also responsible for setting the pace of work on the site. They professed to be little concerned by the lack of basic safety precautions, and benefited financially by their absence. When the failure to observe basic safety practices was pointed out to one worker he commented 'That's okay, a fall could happen to anyone … there'll always be accidents' (Dwyer, 1983: 150). Dissatisfied workers, on the other hand, who were paid lower wages, perceived the danger of injury to be excessively high and claimed that it arose predominantly from the pace of work and the authoritarian style of management. The comments of another worker illustrate how different their perceptions were:

> … they push us all the time … work, work—for them all that counts is concrete
> … if we ask for safety they don't give a stuff … who's going to die here? Not they!
> (p. 150)

In essence, social organisation of work is an important factor in explaining some of the causes of occupational injury and illness, in which the origins of OHS problems are located in social structures and processes, including the behaviour of particular groups. Sociologists are also increasingly concerned about the sweeping changes to the organisation of work in which the underpinning rationale is the drive to be more competitive in the global economy. There is strong evidence that these work organisation and labour market changes are having detrimental effects on the OHS of workers (see Quinlan, Mayhew and Bohle, 2001).

These changes can be in the form of organisational restructuring (e.g. downsizing and outsourcing); flexible and quality management initiatives (e.g. total quality management, lean production, modular manufacturing and high-performance work systems); and flexible, non-standard and precarious employment, all of which have consequential poor health and safety outcomes for disadvantaged groups of workers. Quinlan (1999: 427) summarises the impact of these recent changes:

> Over the past 20 years the labour markets of industrialised countries have undergone a series of profound changes. These changes have been associated with significant changes in work processes but until recently no attention was given to the consequences of this for occupational health and safety (OHS) … available evidence indicates that labour market restructuring is having a significant (adverse) but often

hidden impact on OHS. In many cases, these effects are compounded by competition, labour market and healthcare policies introduced since in the 1980s.

Johnstone et al. (2004: 2) also note the competitive pressures that induce businesses to adopt the work and organisational arrangements that can encourage corner-cutting on OHS, underbidding on contracts, the use of cheaper or inadequately maintained equipment, reductions in staff levels, speeding up of production or longer work hours. These organisational forms, particularly those which involve introducing third parties to work arrangements and creating multi-employer worksites, result in fractured, complex and disorganised work processes, weaker chains of responsibility and 'buck-passing', and a lack of specific job knowledge (including knowledge about OHS) among workers moving from job to job (Johnstone et al., 2004: 2). These fractured work arrangements also make it more difficult for worker interests in OHS to be effectively represented.

The changing organisation of work can also directly influence the level of exposure to physical and psychological hazards in the workplace. For example, workers with multiple jobs or extended work shifts might be at risk of exceeding permissible exposure concentrations to industrial chemicals. Long working hours and staff reductions may increase the risk of overexertion injuries. Increased public contact and alternative work schedules (e.g. night work), which are common in the growing service sector, may expose workers to heightened risk of violence in their jobs (NOHS, 2002; Shain and Kramer, 2004). Finally, OHS regulation, which traditionally has assumed factory work by full-time male workers in a continuing employment relationship governed by the contract of employment, has been slow to adapt to these new work patterns and organisational forms (Johnstone et al., 2004: 2).

In sum, sociological research has identified a range of organisational factors that can increase the probability of injury, including unusual work schedules, certain types of incentive payment systems, high levels of bureaucracy within organisations and highly directive and authoritarian management. Payment systems including piece rates or production bonuses, for example, can also encourage workers to work unreasonably fast in order to earn an adequate income, or the higher income to which they are encouraged to aspire by management (Dwyer, 1983; Robinson and Smallman, 2006). Safety devices (such as safety glasses, masks and gloves) may impede working at this pace, and consequently workers are encouraged to avoid using safety equipment and to ignore other safety procedures. Sociologists have argued that these aspects of work organisation are more important determinants of injuries than the more frequently blamed characteristics of individual workers, such as personality, carelessness or drug dependency. This perspective suggests quite different prevention strategies to the prevailing methods, such as abandoning of incentive payment schemes, increasing workers' autonomy, multi-skilling and job enrichment, and modification of supervisory practices.

Sociologists such as Charles Perrow (1999) have also scrutinised the different organisational settings in which industrial disasters and occupational injuries occur. As working environments obviously differ in the level of danger they present to workers, the injuries that arise in them cannot easily be passed off as random, unpredictable events. Rather, injuries are better seen as events with different probabilities in different workplaces and different levels of organisational complexity (Gerstein, 2008). In particular, Perrow (1999) argues that in complex organisations, predictably and inevitably major industrial disasters can be triggered by a simple component failure which in turn may lead to the consequential failure of other components. In essence, systems failure or so-called 'normal' accidents (to use his terminology) are those involving an interaction of multiple failures in systems with high-risk technologies. Instead of occupational injuries being unforeseen in these settings, Perrow (1999) observes that such events are part of the 'normal' existence of complex systems, such as the disaster at the Chernobyl nuclear power plant.

While this social rationality approach to injuries is not without its critics, particularly around the notion that disasters are inevitable in complex organisations, there are other grounds on which to argue that occupational injuries occur as a direct and predictable consequence of work organisation. As set out in chapter 1, injury rates vary from job to job, and consequently it is reasonable to conclude that exposure to a particular hazardous task will in itself be a key cause of the injury or illness and not the carelessness or other characteristics of workers. That is, injuries occur not only within a particular set of relationships (i.e. employer versus employee), but also arise from a complex range of factors that are determined in large part by work organisation. For example, James (1987) describes a work situation in which unskilled workers were employed in a hot and noisy area to service large pieces of moving equipment. Danger was constantly present in a work area characterised by pools of water on the floor, sparks from hot machinery and spots of grease. The dangerous nature of the work, and the perceived inadequacy of safety equipment, was recognised formally by a bonus payment system. Informally, the danger was compensated by an unofficial system of regulated absenteeism in which 'sickies' were taken by workers on a regular rotating basis. Lower-level management were clearly aware of this practice and gave it tacit acceptance. There is little doubt that, while there were differences of opinion regarding the origins of injury, the workplace was accepted to be dangerous by workers and management and formal and informal arrangements for compensation developed as a result. However, the social constraints were such that when production demands were high, and all hands were needed, the workers themselves suspended the absenteeism system. Workers appeared to use absenteeism as a means of avoiding injury and inherently hazardous and unpleasant working conditions, but suspended the practice when it began to interfere with productivity. This and other evidence led James to conclude that hierarchical control, the overriding emphasis upon production levels, and the reward system were the primary factors contributing to injury in this workplace.

Some workplaces present more dangers than others and hence there is a higher probability of injuries occurring within them. In most cases this probability should be assessable with a reasonable degree of accuracy if sufficient data is collected. Nichols (1997) conducted a detailed analysis of the 1990 Workplace Industrial Relations Survey in Britain to identify major determinates of injury. He demonstrated that the employing establishment being small, lack of trade union representation, and unilateral control of health and safety matters by management were associated with higher rates of injury. He concluded that these interrelated and mutually reinforcing components formed a structure that reliably increased workers' vulnerability to injury. Despite evidence of this nature, the dominant explanations of occupational 'accidents' continue to treat injury as aberrant or unusual. By focusing strategies for treatment and prevention upon the individual who is injured they obscure patterns in the susceptibility of different groups of workers to injury (James, 1987). Following on from Nichols' research, Robinson and Smallman's (2006) analysis of the British data from the Workplace Employee Relations Survey 1998 (WERS98) confirms that the changing world of work continues to have a detrimental impact on workers' health. Their analysis substantiates previous sociological research in that factors associated with flexible work and employment practices, such as precarious employment, are typically associated with a poor health and safety climate (Robinson and Smallman, 2006: 101).

Most theories, and the research methods associated with injury causation, however, examine limited sets of questions and variables and omit to examine important causes of injury. If a restricted range of theoretical models and methodologies are employed, an unnecessarily restricted range of prevention strategies is likely to be generated. The vast majority of studies to date have been based, at least implicitly, on theoretical models devised within occupational medicine, work psychology or the technical professions. These theories place little emphasis on the social organisation of work, and research derived from them fails to collect evidence that could demonstrate the importance of organisational factors in injury causation. An example is the research on accident prone-ness by work psychologists which explicitly denied the role of organisational causes of injury. A major omission of the dominant research paradigms has been their failure to systematically examine workers' understanding of the causes of injuries. Theories devised by 'experts' are tested using 'objective' research designs that intentionally obscure the knowledge and perceptions of the workers who act as their 'subjects'. Dwyer (1983) claims that the ineffectiveness of current injury prevention programs arises from these deficiencies and argues for a more intimate empirical studies of dangerous workplaces if a comprehensive and effective understanding of the causes of injury is to be derived. In order to address these problems, he conducted a study in which he developed an under-standing of the causes of injury on a building site through a series of semi-structured interviews with workers and supervisors, personal observation of work processes, and analysis of written records. In this way he was able to identify the causes of injury as they were perceived by the people actually doing the job. As we noted above, Dwyer's research identified two key factors causing injuries—authoritarian management and financial incentive systems. These factors have received little, if any, attention in the mainstream literature on occupational health and its management. It is probable that this omission is largely due to the managerial orientation of theory, research methods and researchers in this area. In any case, identification of relevant facets of the social relations of work is likely to assist us to develop more effective means of injury minimisation in the future. The resultant strategies may depart radically from current practices, however, and require significant changes in the social relations of production.

Not only has sociological research broadened our view of the underlying causes of work-related injuries and illness, the discipline has also provided a useful analysis of government policies and enforcement strategies, an area that is largely overlooked in the technical or psychology literature. In particular, research on OHS policy debates, the political process underpinning OHS legislation, and enforcement and compliance strategies are primarily located in sociology of law literature. In Wren's (2009) review of the literature exploring the origins of OHS regulation and the policy debates and causes of change in that area, he observes that there is a diversity of opinion on how to explain the OHS policy changes in New Zealand and Australia. Wren (2009) notes that some authors emphasise the determining influence of the level of political power that can be mobilised by the representatives of labour. Other authors highlight the functional role played by the state in maintaining the economic system. Some researchers focus upon the role of ideology in constraining the way OHS policy is thought about by policymakers, academics, practitioners and managers. It is also suggested that policies often reflect the current level of knowledge, values and beliefs of decision-makers, and emphasise the role of conflict over different values and ideas as the motivation behind change (Wren, 2009: 49). Still more authors have argued that most OHS law is only of symbolic value, while others have commented that even symbolic law can come to have a positive effect in the longer term.

The analysis of enforcement strategies has occupied sociologists as well as legal and political scientists. Research shows that the different styles of enforcement from deterrence to cooperative styles are applied in a contingent way, dependent upon the type of workplace, the level of hazard exposure and the attitude of the employer (see Beck and Woolfson, 2000; Lloyd, 2002; Haines and Gurney, 2002; Löfstedt, 2004; Johnstone and Sarre, 2004; Kagen et al., 2005; Wilpert, 2008). More recently, however, socio-legal scholars have turned their attention to OHS regulatory strategies within the context of diminishing government resources allocated to OHS enforcement and the increased use of more flexible work arrangements and the associated deterioration in occupational health and safety. Studies undertaken by Nossar et al. (2003) and Weil and Mallo (2007) showed that OHS regulatory agencies in Australia and the US have responded to a high rate of noncompliance and exploitation occurring in the textile and clothing industry and the ever-decreasing government resources by developing strategic enforcement approaches. In Nossar et al.'s (2003: 2) study, for example, the regulatory strategy developed in New South Wales sought to counter this lack of compliance via contractual tracking mechanisms to follow the work, tie in liability and shift overarching legal responsibility to the top of the supply chain. The process also entailed the integration of minimum standards relating to wages, hours and working conditions, OHS and access to workers' compensation. According to Nossar et al. (2003: 2) '… while home-based clothing manufacture represents a very old type of "flexible" work arrangement, it is one that regulators have found especially difficult to address.' They continue:

> … the elaborate multi-tiered subcontracting and diffuse work locations found in this industry are also characteristic of newer forms of contingent work in other industries

(such as some telework) and the regulatory challenges they pose (such as the tendency of elaborate supply chains to attenuate and fracture statutory responsibilities, at least in terms of the attitudes and behaviour of those involved). Thus, should it succeed, this regulatory strategy could serve as a model for intervention in relation to other industries with analogous work arrangements (and indeed some moves are already evident here) (Nossar et al., 2003: 2).

A great deal of attention has also been given to regulatory compliance. The socio-legal research has identified three broad reasons for noncompliance with OHS regulations, namely: economic, dissident and incompetency reasons (see Kagan, 1989; Lamm 2002). Noncompliance for *economic reasons* is motivated entirely by profit seeking to the detriment of the employees' health and safety. If the probability of being caught is small and the anticipated fine is negligible, it is almost certain that the OHS law will be disobeyed. On the other hand, noncompliance based on an expressive (rather than instrumental) *dissidence* against the OHS laws or enforcement actions occurs when the laws or their enforcement are perceived to be illegitimate. The employer in this instance will adopt a strategy of selective noncompliance when regulations impose unreasonable burdens and/or OHS enforcement agents treat them arbitrarily. *Incompetence*, however, occurs when the employer is either unaware of the OHS regulations or is unable to understand his or her obligations or implement the legal requirements.

In contrast to the existing descriptions of noncompliant behaviour there are compliance behaviours that can be arranged around the following three headings: social responsibility, strict conformity and professionalism. Compliance based primarily on *social responsibility* is one that favours an equal mix of social and profit concerns. Being socially responsible involves the notions of charity and stewardship whereby the welfare of the present and future labour force is not jeopardised. Compliance which is based on *strict conformity* to the law rests on the belief that health and safety standards can only be achieved and maintained if rules are implemented and obeyed. The twin concerns, namely that the law is designed to protect the employee and that lapses in compliance could result in prosecution, motivates the employer to digest the rules and regulations pertaining to his or her business. The compliance approach based on *professionalism* is one that extols competency and intellect. The employer's technical and professional training govern how he or she operates the business and how he or she applies OHS regulations. For the employer, owning a successful business goes hand in hand with being proficient in how the business is run, being knowledgeable about the various regulations and having the ability to implement them in the workplace (Lamm, 2002).

While it is evident that sociological scholarship has not only extended both the empirical and theoretical research in OHS but also alerted us to a range of variables previously omitted, there are still a number of shortcomings of the sociological perspective. First, the domain of sociology covers such a diverse range of topics that the subject itself has become fragmented, with no overarching theoretical framework and little or no integration of the different strands of sociology. For example, on one hand organisational sociology is concerned with the complexity of organisations and how these complexities contribute to workplace injuries, while on the other hand sociology of law focuses on how regulations are enacted and enforced, yet few studies have combined the useful aspects of each of the different strands. A second and related point is the relative scarcity of attempts by sociologists to investigate the causes of occupational illness and disease (notable exceptions include Thebaud-Mony's work on subcontracting and radioactivity exposure in the French nuclear industry, see chapter 5). There is still scant comprehensive re-evaluation of the dominant models of workplace injury causation, or of significant changes in safety practices. However, sociology does present persuasive arguments that organisation of work and social relations at work play a significant role in injury causation. We believe that the insights provided by sociology have much to contribute to the development of a comprehensive model of injury causation.

Third, there is still a failure to recognise any significant contribution of individual factors to occupational injuries and illness. With rare exceptions, sociologists have tended to entirely discount the individual dimension in occupational health. Although this stance is understandable given the current dominance of theory which focuses on the individual, it must be seen to be equally ideologically driven. Clearly some recognition of individual factors is required in a comprehensive model of injury causation, and work on individual behaviour and characteristics, particularly that drawn from work psychology, could be productively integrated into an extended sociological analysis. Research on the impact of work on psychological wellbeing has pointed to an aspect of occupational health that has great significance for workers but has been almost entirely overlooked by sociologists. Equally, the development of multidimensional models to explain the causes of occupational stress has pointed to the complexity of the aetiology of both the physical and psychological symptoms of stress and to the importance of the interaction between individuals and their environments. While there is no doubt that the current psychological theories overlook important aspects of the broader organisational, social and industrial environment there is great potential for sociologists to adapt these frameworks and place them within more comprehensive models of occupational illness. Interdisciplinary discourse in this area could be highly productive.

It is also unfortunate that the sociological literature has concentrated so heavily on physical injury at the expense of work on the more insidious development of occupational illness and disease. This emphasis has apparently arisen due to the easier measurement of industrial injury rates and the greater availability of injury records. The prevalence of disease is frequently more difficult to assess due to problems with diagnosis, long gestation periods and the inaccessibility of records. Sociologists may also have avoided examination of occupational illness because of the difficulty involved in adequately accounting for the contribution of factors outside the workplace to the development of illness and disease. While this problem is clearly complex, it is unlikely to disappear. In any case, external factors impinge on injuries as well. For example, back injuries are possible, and indeed common, outside the workplace, and injuries sustained at work can be exacerbated elsewhere (and vice versa). Such difficulties generate debate as to whether illnesses are more accurately defined as 'occupational illnesses' or merely 'job-related diseases'. Occupational illnesses are those that are directly caused by factors in the workplace, while job-related diseases are multifaceted in origin, having arisen not only from work-related hazards but also characteristics and behaviours of the individual worker (Rutenfranz et al., 1985). Decisions regarding the category into which an individual's illness falls are unlikely to be simple and objective. Clearly, it is in the interests of management to demonstrate that an illness is only job-related, and hence lessen their own responsibility for compensation, while it is frequently in the interests of workers that their illnesses are recognised as predominantly occupational in origin.

Finally, it is somewhat surprising that sociologists have failed to examine thoroughly important political and structural variables related to occupational health. Although they have attempted to take a broad social perspective, sociological theories have neglected to address the complex effects of state intervention and industrial resistance by organised labour on occupational health. The failure to recognise the broader industrial context in which relationships between employers and workers are ensconced detracts significantly from the richness of their analysis. Work organisation and conflict between the interests of management and workers do not develop within an industrial and political vacuum. These important contextual variables will be discussed in the following section dealing with the industrial relations of occupational health.

Work relations, legal and economic perspectives

Although orthodox OHS inquiry is firmly established in the disciplines of health and in medical as well as the expert technical approaches, other disciplines such as industrial relations, labour history, human resource management, law/criminology and economics have provided a fillip to OHS research by highlighting the interconnectedness of multiple factors. These fields plus sociology and politics can provide a deeper understanding of the context in which OHS operates—for example, the power relationship between the employer and employee, the differing interests of the main players, the contested terrain of regulatory law, as well as the social and economic consequences of work-related injuries and illnesses. These social sciences frequently occupy the same discourse although they are articulated through slightly different lenses. In this section we examine these differences and discuss the main themes and debates within employment relations, law and economics.

Work relations

A number of fields concerned with working relationships and workers have contributed to our understanding of OHS. Work has played a pivotal role in modern society—the emergence of free wage-labour is a defining characteristic of capitalist societies (compared to earlier feudal or ancient societies)—and the broader divisions associated with this have been a critical point of both conflict and collaboration. This, in turn, has been reflected in ideological/political divisions that have affected the scope and nature of a number of overlapping, if not competing, fields of academic research examining relations at work. Understanding this complexity calls for a brief explanation.

The poverty and inequality experienced by workers during the Industrial Revolution and the rise of the working class and unions (and later political parties) to represent them attracted the attention of both historians (such as Commons and Andrews, 1916, in the US) and social reformers (such as Sidney and Beatrice Webb, 1914, in Britain) in the late nineteenth/early twentieth centuries (not to mention earlier activists like Engels and Mayhew). Many made reference to the adverse health and safety effects of working conditions and efforts by unions, reformers and governments to combat this, and some like Commons devoted considerable attention to the issue. Over the course of the twentieth century a field of history devoted to work (social and labour history) emerged. Although OHS did not occupy an especially prominent place in the field (Quinlan, 1997) a number of scholars undertook detailed studies of working conditions and OHS-related issues (such as mine disasters, silicosis, pneumoconiosis, construction deaths, factory fires and factory legislation), often pointing to the critical (and complex) role of social mobilisations (community groups and unions) and vested interest groups (such as employers, insurers and the medical profession) in the recognition and response to serious hazards (see, for example, Derickson, 1998; Penrose, 1997, 1998). For example, Barbara Harrison (1991) has cast a critical eye over the role of the medical profession in relation to factory legislation and women's health in late nineteenth-century Britain. There were often (largely untapped) synergies between this research and critical historical research undertaken in the fields of epidemiology and occupational medicine (see, for example, Gochfeld, 2005; Tweedale, 2007).

Over the past decade historians have also provide a critical examination of management developments in OHS, including the Safety First Movement (and its connections to Taylorism and the promotion of non-union safety committees) and the role of occupational nurses (Esbester, 2008; Taksa, 2009). For example, Esbester's (2008: 217) critical examination of the use of company magazines in the period 1913–39 propagated 'a specific version of "safety" which attempted to extend managerial prerogative in the workplace'. Other studies have provided valuable insights into the complex interaction between attempts at regulation and economic forces. For example, Olmsted and Rhode's (2004) study found initial attempts to control the serious human and animal health problems of bovine tuberculosis in the US in the early 1900s were undermined by evasive interstate trade in diseased stock. An international study of working hours between 1870 and 1913—an earlier era of globalisation largely unknown to many of those who use the term authoritatively today—by Huberman (2004) found globalisation had at best an ambiguous effect on reducing working time, with national regulatory and institutional factors playing a key mediating role. These studies provide an important context for better understanding contemporary developments in OHS, especially when dovetailed with historical assessment of key professions. For example, in his assessment of occupational medicine in the US since the Industrial Revolution, Gochfeld (2005: 115) emphasises that the field has 'always been influenced by economics, politics and changing patterns of employment, and today these forces include managed care, weakened unions, outsourcing and contract labour, and a growing political and social conservatism, not to mention multinational corporations'.

The social compacts adopted by many countries at the end of World War II (to avoid depression and a re-emergence of fascism), in conjunction with the rise of unions and regulated collectivism at the workplace, was associated with the emergence of the new fields 'industrial relations' and 'labour law' to study union and employer behaviour, work laws, strikes and related matters. As with labour history, while both fields devoted relatively limited attention to OHS some important research was undertaken. Within industrial relations (and its close cousin labour studies) a number of researchers examined union action over OHS (including strikes) and, especially from the 1980s, the importance of workplace participatory structures in relation to OHS, including the logistical support unions provided to revised OHS laws (see the work of David Walters, 1996, 2004, 2006). Nonetheless, with the exception of wages, IR researchers displayed limited interest in substantive working conditions like OHS and took little notice of emerging research on structured inequalities at work and health (see the work of Karasek, Siegrist, Marmot and others discussed in chapter 5), even though it offered clear parallels with their own interest in workplace control and participation. The trifurcation of work legislation (into separate laws regulating industrial relations, OHS and workers' compensation) found in most countries was reflected in a similar trifurcation of researchers, with OHS and (even more so) workers' compensation representing a minority of the field. The latter research charted changes to OHS laws (including the substantial revisions that occurred in many countries between 1970 and the late 1980s) and the implementation/ enforcement of legal standards—an area where criminologists also made an important contribution (helping to build an often sophisticated socio-legal analysis of the nature and impact of social protection in this area).

Even though OHS and workers' compensation were subordinate streams of interest within labour history, industrial relations and labour law researchers in these areas made an important contribution to our understanding—helping to explain, for example, why knowledge of hazards has often taken so long to lead to a regulatory response; how interest groups shape knowledge of OHS; the role played by unions, employers and regulation; and what determines the effectiveness of regulatory protection. These issues are explored in more detail in chapters 7 and 10. Overall, these fields adopted a progressive and pluralist perspective that saw the role of collective representation among workers as valuable if not essential. In contrast to this a number of fields examining work relations tended to adopt a more individualised if not unitarist approach, including organisational behaviour and human resource management. Human resource management (HRM) emerged during the 1980s in part reflecting an ideological and economic shift away from collectivism and regulated markets towards individualism and unfettered markets, entailing 'new' business labour management practices and increased resistance to unions. Like organisational behaviour, HRM focused on micro-relations between workers and managers within the workplace whereas industrial relations and labour law adopted a more macro focus on institutions and regulation. However, as with IR, OHS tended to occupy a small if not smaller space within HR research with relatively few studies of employer approaches to OHS (and notably less interest in OHS laws or union activity in this area). Aided by governments embracing neo-liberalism, industrial relations went into decline as a field (though research activity continued) during the 1990s and HRM grew correspondingly. Whether the economic crisis and discrediting of neo-liberalism will reverse this trend is yet to be seen.

The picture just painted is by necessity generalised. In practice, IR and HRM researchers publish in each others' journals; some IR journals give considerable attention to OHS (notably *Relations Industrielles*); and the level of interest in OHS in these fields may rise over time (though no substantial shift is yet apparent). Nonetheless, the divisions are important and need to be borne in mind when assessing the impact and perspective of each field on OHS.

Some attempts have been made to merge industrial relations and human resources management, creating an overarching discipline 'employment relations' (Gardner and Palmer, 1992; Blyton and Turnbull, 1994; Boxall, 1995). This shift in definition has the advantage of extending the boundaries of traditional industrial relations and human resource management to include *all* aspects of the two approaches. Most importantly, it has incorporated both the macro approach of industrial relations and the micro or organisational approach of HRM. It is also recognised that OHS does not take place in isolation and can be found on many levels, each influencing the outcomes of OHS, either in a positive or negative way (see Boyd, 2003). For example:

- *the level of the employee*: work-related factors, such as the type of employment, level of pay, hours of work, level of day-to-day exposure to hazards as well as the degree to which the employee can participate in OHS matters
- *the organisational level:* the company's OSH policies and systems as well as its commitment to the health and safety of its workers
- *the level of the industry:* the characteristics of the industry and pressures from the key stakeholders, such as representatives from trade unions and employer associations operating in the industry to develop better OHS practices
- *the national level*: the legislation that governs occupational health and safety as well as the enforcement agency
- *the international level*: What occurs at the other levels is often influenced by international trends and events. International trade agreements, the operations of multinationals and the pressure to conform to international labour conventions and treaties all have an impact on the way OHS is conducted within the country.

Like sociology, employment relations is concerned with the study of *how* individuals, groups or organisations desire their interests to be represented (collectively or individually) and *what* these interests are, such as the amount of pay, the hours worked, the production output and safety procedures. Furthermore, employment relations laws and policies, including OHS, are influenced by a number of competing interest groups who in turn endeavour to manipulate how employment and OHS regulations are enacted and implemented. Indeed, some argue that national decisions concerning the occupational health and safety regulations and policies are essentially a compromise between powerful interest groups and the government. That is, the government is to be regarded as primarily serving the interests of those who they regulate, namely the employers and employees.

As each party will have different interests, conflict will inevitably arise and the extent to which this conflict is acknowledged and managed is the basis for the employment relations conflict frames of reference (Rasmussen and Lamm, 2002). Each of the conflict frames of reference, Marxist (or radical pluralist), unitarist and pluralist, can be aligned with the ideologies of the different parties—that is, the employee, the employer and the state, and as such provides a useful framework to analyse the different ways employers, employees and the state approach OHS, particularly worker participation. The fundamental differences between the conflict frames of reference are the ways conflict and power are viewed and the ways in which employees are treated. At one end of the spectrum is the Marxist dichotomous perspective which views conflict as inherent in the employment relationship and believes that under the current economic capitalist system, power and control over employees rests with employers. The only legitimate voice for employees is the trade union movement and the only counterbalance to the employers' power is collectivism. At the other end of the spectrum is the unitarist perspective in which conflict is viewed as pathological and not inevitable but the result of a misunderstanding. It views the organisation as a team, unified in a common purpose, namely the success of the organisation; with a single source of authority (management) and with all participants sharing the same goal, harmony and cooperation are the predicted outcomes. Trade unions are seen as an illegitimate intrusion into the unified and cooperative organisation, creating unnecessary conflict in an otherwise harmonious working environment. Finally, sitting in the middle of the spectrum (although leaning towards the Marxist perspective), the pluralist believes conflict and power are both inevitable and legitimate but must be tempered and controlled through formal structures and procedures. The potential conflict can be eased and stability achieved by recognising and involving trade unions, rather than outlawing them, and collectivism is a valid means by which individuals pursue their goals.

Efforts to redress the power imbalance between employers and employees have often been via worker participation mechanisms—an area that has received a great deal of attention from employment relations researchers. Formalised worker participation in occupational health and safety is not new and can be traced back to at least the Industrial Revolution. The development of worker involvement has varied among industry sectors: in the mining industry, legal provisions for worker inspections date back to 1872, while in other industries approaches have ranged from surreptitious deals over danger money to organised and long-fought struggles for collective bargaining rights (Page, 2002: 5). In addition, worker representation is more established in some countries than others. In Sweden, for example, the first law concerning elected workers' representatives was enacted in 1912 and in 1931 their position was reinforced, giving them the right to make complaints and propose changes to the regulatory agency.

More recently the increased number of health and safety committees and worker representatives are, in part, a result of several developments. The first and most obvious is that formalised health and safety representatives and health and safety committees are now a regulatory requirement in many jurisdictions, particularly those that have adopted a Robens model of OHS, as detailed in chapter 7. Second, increasing global competition has necessitated the search for techniques to increase productivity and reduce costs, including costs associated with workers' injuries and illnesses, and worker participation and the development of health and safety committees are one response to these pressures (Gunningham, 2008). Moreover, studies have confirmed that there is a link between workers' involvement and reduced injury and illness rates and ultimately reduced costs and increased performance (Weil, 1999; Popma, 2008). Third, the explosion of new technologies and the rapid changes in production have increased the need for flexible procedures, which in turn have implications for health and safety. Participation of workers on health and safety committees has been used to manage these changes and to reduce the level of tension between management and workers as a result of these changes (Lamm et al., 2007).

While employment relations studies have shown that health and safety committees and worker representatives can be effective in reducing the rate of injuries and disease, the successes have been varied (see Frick and Walters, 1998). First, research indicates that there are significant differences of opinion between the employers and employees as to the function of health and safety committees and worker representatives. Employers tend to rely more on the capacity of the formal health and safety management systems than do the safety representatives who put more emphasis on the need for daily and continuous health and safety consultations (Hovden, 2008; Trägårdh, 2008). Hovden (2008: 507) notes that the climate of participation and collaboration is assessed by the safety representatives as being less conducive to the overall objectives of the health and safety regulations than perceived by the managers. Second, studies in Australia, New Zealand and other countries show that scarcity of resources, including time, devoted to health and safety committees and representatives, the low priority given to the OHS and limited actual participation in key OHS decisions all contribute to undermining their success (Lamm, 1992; Nichols et al., 2007; Hovden, 2008; Trägårdh, 2008). Based on a recent analysis of the British WIRS dataset, Nichols et al. (2007: 222) argue that participative arrangements for health and safety are effective only when they have proper support. They conclude:

> But in doing … current regulatory provisions need to be consolidated and extended in ways that are relevant to the real world of work in the 21st century. Since the presence of trade union support cannot be relied upon to deliver effective arrangements for employee participation in health and safety where the regulatory framework for it is weak or absent, consideration needs to be given to the means with which this framework can be strengthened.

Trade union involvement in and endorsement of joint health and safety committees and worker representatives are essential ingredients in maintaining a safe and healthy working environment. This was acknowledged as early as 1890 in the New Zealand Sweating Commission Report which noted that wherever a union had been formed, working conditions improved and the hours of work were not excessive. Workers who are union members are more likely to exercise their rights to a safe workplace than their non-union counterparts. Unions also play an important role in initiating inspections and often can devote resources to monitoring and improving OHS conditions (Weil, 1999; Nichols et al., 2007). There is also substantial evidence that without trade union involvement, occupational injury and illness rates do not decline significantly and the individual workers who raise OHS issues with the employer may experience victimisation (Page, 2002; Strauss, 2006; Nichols et al., 2007; Gunningham, 2008).

However, even though most OHS statues in Australia and New Zealand support trade union involvement in OHS, the decline in trade union membership and density in Australia, New Zealand and other industrialised countries has meant that a proportion of joint health and safety committees and worker representatives will have little or no connection with trade unions (Gilson et al., 2002; Page, 2002). Moreover, the dominance of HRM and the trend towards the relegation of OHS under the HR manager's responsibilities have meant that there is more often than not an inherent managerial prerogative which undermines trade union employee participation initiatives. A few employment relations scholars, such as Boyd (2003), are beginning to question the extent to which HRM-related employee participation mechanisms are adequately represented and reconciled with employee interests and concerns over OHS. She argues that active employee participation (in which trade unions are an integral part) in OHS has been substantially diluted by employers to 'employee involvement' whereby team briefings become the only vehicle for employee contribution (Boyd, 2003: 164).

Given that there is an increasing dominance of HRM in OHS, the critique undertaken by Boyd (2003) is timely in that it provides evidence of the detrimental outcomes when OHS becomes the domain of HR. Based on international study of three industries, namely the airline, call centre and nuclear industries, she makes a number of important observations. First, as HRM derives much of its theory and practice from neo-classical and neo-liberal economic theories, there has been the inevitable substitution of trade union–backed collectivism with voluntarism and with it a general erosion of employee rights and apathy towards the enforcement of the OHS legislation. Second, her findings show that there has also been a major shift in HRM over the past two decades towards maximising and intensifying the output of labour via precarious employment arrangements, most likely at the expense of the employee's health and safety. Third, Boyd (2003: 163) observes that HRM polices and practices are mutating to fit contemporary workplaces and the pressures within them, which frequently are at odds with OHS standards. That is, managers are adapting a range of HR practices to meet the demands of customers, productivity and quality while sacrificing employee wellbeing. Finally, Boyd (2003: 166) is somewhat pessimistic regarding HRM's contribution to and support of the wellbeing of employees and concludes that HRM principles, policies and practices along with the notion of 'partnership' within a voluntaristic, self-regulatory framework are failing to provide the conditions that are required for responsible and high-quality health and safety management.

Although the employment relations perspective has been used successfully to expose the complexities of workplace relations and to incorporate other contextual factors, such as the particular industry, the jurisdiction and international pressures when examining OHS issues, and the incorporation of HRM under the employment relations discipline, creates an uneasy amalgamation. The fact that these same tensions between the more pluralist employment relations approach and the unitarist HRM approach are played out in the workplace between employers and employees is perhaps a weakness of the employment relations approach. That is, the employment relations perspective is so broad and straddles such a range of ideologies that it becomes difficult to identify a general unifying theory which can be applied to OHS phenomena.

OHS legal perspective

The amount of legislation that controls OHS practices and compensation as well as the level of enforcement are also contentious subjects in which employers and trade unions typically are on opposite sides. Nonetheless, OHS has for many years been treated as a matter for legal intervention. There is an expectation shared by trade unions, employers and the general community that some state intervention through legislation is necessary, if only to set minimum standards. It is not surprising, therefore, that the legal discipline has been a prominent feature of OHS and it is the contributions of this discipline that we will now briefly address.

This book is concerned with the array of OHS legal regulation whereby both the common law and legislation establish a series of requirements on employers/ managers, employees, the self-employed and subcontractors in relation to OHS. This legal framework establishes boundaries of behaviour with regard to what exposure standards are acceptable, what action or inaction on the part of an employer is not acceptable, which injured or diseased workers are entitled to compensation and what amount of compensation will be paid to them. As we will see in chapters 7 and 8, the determination of these boundaries raises important public policy questions that have often been the subject of strident debate. For example, it will be argued in chapter 8 that the determination of entitlements for the purpose of workers' compensation played a critical role in defining what occupational injuries and diseases were regarded as legitimate in terms of broader debates over OHS.

Given that the role of the law in relation to OHS is dealt with in some detail in two later chapters we do not propose to explore it in any detail here. Rather we will simply make one further point. The failure of preventative legislation to adequately protect workers has been the subject of considerable debate among legal scholars, criminologists and others. In particular they have sought to explain the ongoing absence of effective enforcement and the passive approach by Australian and New Zealand state agencies towards prosecuting for breaches of OHS law. As prosecution has always been a controversial element in the enforcement armoury of OHS regulators, the central question dominating the legal discourse is: what is the appropriate role of prosecution, and the criminal law more generally, in enforcing OHS offences? (see Johnstone, 1996, 2004) On the one hand, penalties are imposed that are intended by the courts to serve the functions of individual and general deterrence. If successful, these deterrent messages will provide disincentives to noncompliance and reduce levels of work-related injury and disease. On the other hand, criminal law often serves a much less pragmatic role, fulfilling moral, symbolic and retributive functions (see Gunningham, 2007: 361). To quote Gunningham (2007: 364), to overcome the 'paucity of prosecutions' there must be an alternative approach which focuses on risk rather than consequences, takes into consideration the company's previous OHS and emphasises that prosecution should not take place in the absence of culpability. For these purposes, it has been argued that culpability should mean a substantial falling short of reasonable expectations (a form of negligence), recklessness or intent. The actual decision to prosecute, it has been suggested, should be based on a calculus which takes account of all three of the above factors.

Other legal scholars have drawn attention to the political environment in which prosecutions take place (see Jamieson, 2005; Schofield, 2005; Armstong, 2008). They argue that such an environment is by no means neutral and often works against injured or ill workers, particularly vulnerable workers, in obtaining justice and compensation. Still others add that during OHS prosecutions, offences and the facts which constitute them are decontextualised by defence counsels or '… ripped out of the fabric within which they are embedded … thus making the breaches appear as though they were … "freak accidents", "catastrophes" or "tragedies", signifying that the event is something unusual and unexpected …' (Johnstone, 2004: 41). There is general agreement, however, that the low percentage of prosecutions compared to the number of breaches of OHS regulations is the result of a number of factors, namely limited resources of the inspectorate, the capture of enforcement agencies and a variety of other factors. However, some writers have suggested reasons that impinge more directly on fundamental understandings about OHS. Carson (1979, 1980, 1985, 1989) has argued that widespread regulatory breaches have been conventionalised to the extent they are not seen as criminal offences at all. He sees OHS legislation as largely a symbolic gesture which headed off the challenge of organised labour and built up a myth that criminal law was neither effective nor appropriate when it came to dealing with OHS infringements. Carson argues that the historical significance of intervention by the state to quarantine OHS from the terrain of industrial relations has been largely overlooked.

In seeking to reverse this separation and achieve a theoretical reintegration Carson contends that it is necessary to locate OHS regulation within a political economy perspective. According to this perspective, explanations of regulatory failure need to take account of conflicts between profits or production schedules and OHS and the pressure of declining product prices or threats to market shares. Other relevant factors include labour market characteristics (such as job insecurity and casual employment status), the relative strength of organised labour, conflicts of interest within regulatory agencies and the complicity of governments more concerned with maintaining employment levels or avoiding an adverse balance of payment figure than health and safety. In short, Carson's political economy perspective entails seeing regulation as only being comprehensible when analysed within a broader economic and employment relations context.

Economics of OHS

Finally, we need to address the economic context or what we might call the economics of OHS. At its broadest level there is a need to recognise that international patterns of trade and economic inequality affect OHS. As was noted in chapter 1, organisations in First World countries move their noxious industries offshore at the same time as the governments of debt-ridden Third World countries try to attract these and other industries through tax inducements and lower labour standards including wages, OHS and the suppression of unionism. Via trade competition and public protests these inequalities can then rebound on industries and workers in First World countries.

At the national and industry level similar processes can be seen to operate. Carson's study of the British North Sea oil industry demonstrates how the regulatory apparatus can be undermined by state-induced compromises that are driven by economic pressures. Periodic changes in economic activity associated with the business cycle may affect the incidence and reporting of occupational injury and disease by altering the experience/age profile of the workforce, the level of work intensity and competition for jobs, and a range of other factors (see, for example, Nichols, 1997). There is also a need to consider specific labour market structures, and changes which have occurred to them historically. Labour market structures based on migration/ethnicity, gender/family, geography and employment status can have a significant influence on OHS in a workplace, industry or region by shaping union organisation and the contours of competition for jobs and by influencing patterns of regulatory intervention. For example, gender segmentation in the labour market has been used to legitimate gender differentiation in the determination of OHS standards as well as gender-specific victim-blaming explanations of occupational injury. In chapter 1 we indicated that changing the characteristics of labour market structures could affect not only the incidence of injury and disease but also the impact of such injuries including worker access to compensation and rehabilitation. These issues will be expanded on in later chapters.

We should stress that the points we have just raised seldom figure in conventional neo-classical economic analysis of OHS. Although economists have largely ignored OHS for many years, conventional economic reasoning is important on at least two levels. First, even before economists became all that interested in OHS the lines of argument within what has become known as economic rationalism (or the resurgence of neo-classical economics based on notions of individual choice according to the dictates of the 'market') exerted a profound effect on public policies in many countries. Policies such as privatisation, self-regulation, competitive tendering/outsourcing, dismantling collective labour law regimes, minimising labour standards, removing tariff barriers/free trade agreements, changing taxation laws that redistribute wealth, and winding back public infrastructure and social security/unemployment benefits all have implications for OHS (Purse, 1997). The 'user-pays' principle in relation to the provision of services or the need to justify regulations in terms of often narrowly conceived cost–benefit analysis is also unlikely to be of great benefit to OHS (see chapter 1). Although OHS laws themselves have remained largely intact in countries like Australia and the UK (this is less true of New Zealand), the context in which the laws operate has changed significantly. We do not have space in this book to explore all the interconnections between dominant economic policy doctrines and OHS but will address a number in passing, highlighting if nothing else the considerable externalities these policies generally ignore (as in the case of home-based garment workers; see Mayhew and Quinlan, 1999). What is especially concerning is that the broader discourse of economic rationalism, with its notions of equal choice (i.e. no differentials of power), perfect information and the primacy of economic issues, has begun to shape at least some debates in OHS (Purvis, 1996: 395–7; Purse, 1997).

Second, an attempt has been made to insert orthodox economic reasoning into the realms of OHS in a more direct manner since the late 1970s and more especially from the 1980s onwards. This includes research into whether there were compensating wage differentials for workers in hazardous jobs and associated exploration of risk aversion among workers. To the mind of anyone with even the remotest knowledge of OHS, this is an entirely ridiculous line of intellectual inquiry based on the voluntary assumption of risk by individuals. It has been discredited by careful analysis (see Leigh, 1991; Robinson, 1991; Dorman, 1996) but the fact that it was even pursued says a lot about the state of contemporary economics (at least in the US where it was most popular). Another contribution, led by the Chicago School, has criticised OHS regulation as being ineffective and an impediment to market incentives, arguing that new forms of market-based deterrence need to be developed (for a discussion of these studies and additional contribution see Bartel and Thomas, 1985). There are a number of problems with this approach, including its failure to confront the weight of history on OHS regulation (see chapter 7), dependence on data that must be treated with considerable caution (see chapter 1) and presumptions about the information and choices available to the parties. A parallel argument has been run in relation to workers' compensation with subsidiary arguments about the greater efficiency of incentive systems and the private underwriting of workers' compensation insurance (for a recent evaluation of the latter see Neary, 1998). Again, some of these issues are taken up in chapter 8. We would not suggest that orthodox economists have made no contribution to OHS, as our use, albeit selective, of Industry Commission's (1994, 1995) inquiries into workers' compensation and workplace safety indicates (for a well-researched if controversial attempt at historical analysis by an economist see Aldrich, 1997). However, this form of economic discourse paints an essentially unrealistic and potentially dangerous picture of OHS and its potential role and assumptions need to be clearly recognised. In the US Peter Dorman's (1996) book *Markets and Mortality: Economics, Dangerous Work and the Value of Human Life* undertook a detailed review of conventional economic perspectives on OHS that shows that the 'real economics' of OHS are radically different. In his later report on the economics of OHS, Dorman (2000: 2) aptly notes that:

> When most people hear the word 'economics', they think it has to do with the management of money ... The economic perspective on occupational safety and health (OSH) encompasses both causes and consequences: the role of economic

factors in the etiology of workplace ill-health and the effects this has on the economic prospects for workers, enterprises, nations, and the world as a whole … [That is] it is a social science; its perspective is that of society as a whole, which includes workers, their families and their communities as well as enterprises, and it recognizes that not all the effects of ill-health show up in monetary transactions … It is therefore a very broad perspective, but it is not complete, because neither the causation nor the human significance of OSH can be reduced to its economic elements.

Dorman's comments reflect the tendency to concentrate on the costs of injuries and illness when discussing economics of OHS and the fact that this line of research has been a dominant feature in the OHS literature. Since the 1960s there have been a number of attempts to investigate the impact of workplace injuries and illnesses on productivity and the costs to both the company and the employee (Cutler and James, 1996; Evans, 2004). However, it is evident that such a task is complicated (Lofland, Pizzi and Frick, 2004) and this has stimulated a number of academic debates, as we will outline in more detail in the following chapter (McCunney, 2001). There is also a tendency to concentrate on the tangible, direct costs of injuries rather than the more ambiguous, indirect costs and the chronic costs associated with illnesses. Research in this area is often pursued in order to ascertain the extent of the OHS injury and illness and/or support arguments either for or against OHS improvements, even though obtaining reliable data on the costs associated with work-related injuries, illnesses and workers' compensation is highly problematic, as outlined in chapter 3. Discussions on the costs of injuries and workers' compensation claims can also be found in abundance in government reports, often generated to counter political attacks on the level of public sector funding in these areas. Although there are a few exceptions, such as Dorman (2000) and Pezzullo and Crook (2006), the discussions rarely extend to the cost of occupational disease and until lately the social costs of occupational injuries and illnesses were also ignored. Although developing tools to measure economic and social costs of occupational injuries and illness are still evolving (see Keller, 2001), to the victims and their families, these costs are all too real. The feeling of devastation was clearly evident in an interview with a widow participating in a New Zealand study who expressed the profound and lasting impact of her husband's injury on her:

> There was never a point to say goodbye to a marriage and that of all things of the whole lot I feel I have lost. I have lost my marriage … I always feel I live in the shade, I no longer live in the sun. (Ian's wife). (Adams, et al., 2002: 8)

In summary, the disciplines of employment relations, law and economics are not only complementary but also represent the core domains of OHS. Scholars within these fields are more often than not at the vanguard of debates surrounding the welfare of workers and their families. Their research has shown that a safe and healthy working environment is dependent upon a range of variables operating on a number of interdependent levels. At one end is the individual's workplace while at the other end are the international organisations, such as the ILO. Although their disciplines have made a significant contribution to our understanding of how OHS is managed and how it operates within the economic, legal and employment relations spheres, there are still relatively few OHS studies emanating from these disciplines and most concentrate solely on occupational injury with little attention given to occupational chronic diseases.

Conclusion

The discussion of perspectives in this chapter has been of necessity selective and abbreviated. A more comprehensive and nuanced explanation would require a book in its own right. Nonetheless, this chapter has sought to identify critical characteristics of how different disciplines have viewed OHS, including their origins and evolution as well as nuances, conflicts and tensions within each to the extent possible. The aim was to demonstrate that our knowledge of OHS is shaped by a number of different perspectives, that no single perspective provides a comprehensive understanding and that there are areas of compatibility and conflict among them.

The disciplines discussed present very different perspectives on OHS. Each perspective has strengths and weaknesses, and each can contribute significantly to our understanding of the origins of illness and injury in the workplace. The challenge is to successfully integrate these perspectives into a comprehensive framework. This framework needs to be coherent enough to provide a basis for informed and effective responses to OHS problems and it is difficult to integrate perspectives which differ in their focus, methods and ideological underpinnings. Further, re-conceptualisation needs to be combined with steps aimed at implementation. At the same time, a number of positive signs are identified in this and later chapters, including a growing interdisciplinary dialogue and some parallel developments in terms of understanding how OHS problems arise and are best addressed. For example, there is a growing recognition of the value of multidisciplinary teams in terms of identifying and assessing related hazards (such as cancer; see Thebaud–Mony et al., 2005), prevention (see Lippel, 2007) and also in terms of the management of chronic pain among injured workers, rehabilitation and return to work (see, for example, Fawcett and McCarthy, 2003).

Nonetheless, the challenge remains immense and is only likely to be resolved slowly. One valuable vehicle in this regard is education and public policy. Writing in the 1980s, Ferguson (1986, 1988) bemoaned the abysmal level of OHS training and the degree of inter-professional collaboration in the provision of OHS services. A number of the positive developments between the late 1980s and mid-1990s in this regard stalled if not went into reverse. If these developments are to be rebuilt and gain extended traction, governments, education institutions and the professions will all need to contribute (for example by governments funding programs that establish a strong nexus between research, policy and practice; de Leeuw et al., 2008). The development of multidisciplinary OHS education needs to be made a priority. Further, as is being more widely recognised within the health profession, education should include the promotion of cross–cutting competencies (such as communication and knowledge of

OHS law) and inter-professional programs at both undergraduate and postgraduate levels (Olson et al., 2005; Davidson et al., 2008). Attention also needs to be given to team-based and less hierarchical community-based delivery of services (Rossi et al., 2000; Fragar et al., 2008; Parry, 2008).

The process of identifying the strengths and weaknesses of the various disciplinary perspectives does not merely amount to trivial point scoring among theorists/researchers and practitioners with different training and mindsets. If intervention programs in occupational health are to achieve optimal effectiveness there must be a clear understanding of the primary variables that must be addressed, and the priorities that interventions at various levels should take. For example, a work-stress intervention that sees the pervasive practices of organisational restructuring/downsizing as aberrant interference or 'noise' is flawed and almost certainly doomed to failure because it has failed to take the context into account (Nytro et al., 2000). Similarly, medical studies of the hazards confronting young or immigrant workers that only recommend more 'education' display an ignorance of policy and labour market, institutional and regulatory factors that shape these hazards and should inform remedies. At a broader level, there is a need for a closer nexus between research and intervention studies, both in terms of design and evaluating their effectiveness. In general, there is insufficient policy and intervention evaluation research in OHS and, with notable exceptions, many of those studies that are undertaken are too narrowly focused in terms of what is assessed, the methods of assessment and the time frame. Notwithstanding this, some positive trends can be identified in terms of longer-term multidisciplinary research and practice and we will have more to say about this in later chapters.

Disciplinary divisions are historically contingent and reflect in part inter-professional rivalries. The rivalries form only one part of the political debate over OHS, but their impact is significant. One principal difference between disciplinary perspectives is the degree to which they focus attention on the characteristics or behaviours of individual workers, on physical characteristics of work or biomechanics, or upon social and organisational determinants of ill health and injury and their effects on workers and the community. The extent to which the focus is on workers as individuals or as groups has profound ideological and public policy implication. Knowledge and its application is shaped by social context. The role of interest groups needs to be recognised along with the potential for ideological distortions of knowledge whereby powerful groups selectively use theory and research to serve their own interests (see chapters 4 and 5). We should learn from this experience. At this stage in the development of knowledge in the occupational health area it is important to be cautious and circumspect in the application of specific theories and models, and to attempt to develop an eclectic and better-balanced understanding of the issues with which we are faced.

QUESTIONS FOR DISCUSSION

1 Describe the aspects of OHS most likely to be addressed by:
   a   an occupational physician
   b   an occupational health nurse
   c   a work psychologist
   d   an occupational hygienist
   e   a safety engineer
   f   an occupational therapist
   g   an ergonomist
   h   an industrial sociologist
2 To what extent can occupational injury and illness be attributed to the characteristics of individual workers?
3 To what extent do workers' and employers' interests coincide in OHS?
4 Is it reasonable to accept the advice of occupational health professionals as scientific and objective?
5 Discuss the strengths and weaknesses of two of the main disciplines in OHS.
6 What factors should receive first priority in the management of occupational illness and injury?

FURTHER READING

Barling, J. and Frone, M. (eds) (2004), *The Psychology of Workplace Safety*, American Psychological Association, Washington.

Carter, T. (2004), 'British occupational hygiene practice 1720–1920', *Annals of Occupational Hygiene*, **48**(4): 299–307.

Dorman, P. (1996), *Markets and Mortality: Economics, Dangerous Work and the Value of Human Life*, Cambridge University Press, Cambridge.

Horsley, R. and Goddard, D. (2007), 'Community occupational medicine in 2007 and beyond', *Journal of Occupational Health and Safety—Australia and New Zealand*, **23**(6): 531–8.

Kroemer, K. and Grandjean, E. (1997), *Fitting the Task to the Human: A Textbook of Occupational Ergonomics*, 5th edition, Taylor & Francis, London.

LaDou, J. (1997), *Occupational and Environmental Medicine*, 2nd edition, Appleton & Lange, Stamford, Connecticut.

Nichols, T. (1997), *The Sociology of Industrial Injury*, Mansell, London.

Explaining occupational injury

Introduction

CHAPTER 1 demonstrated that injury is a major but poorly recognised problem in the workplace. Chapter 2 described the historical contribution that several disciplines have made to research on the origins of occupational injury and disease. The aim of this chapter is to examine contemporary understanding of the nature of occupational injuries and to draw together the most prominent approaches to explaining their origins. To achieve this goal, the perspectives developed within ergonomics, safety engineering, psychology and sociology will be examined in detail and the debates surrounding the costs of injuries and the analysis of data will be explored. The injury problems faced by women and disadvantaged groups in the workforce will also be discussed. First, however, we shall briefly evaluate the usefulness of the term 'accident' in an occupational context.

To refer to 'accidents' in the workplace is frequently misleading and we prefer to use the term 'injuries' as an alternative. We have alluded to aspects of this important issue on several occasions, but it will be useful to briefly summarise the reasoning behind this preference before discussing explanations of injury in more detail. The term 'accident' has historically carried a strong implication that associated events occur randomly and cannot be avoided. Dictionaries certainly recognise this meaning, providing definitions such as 'event without apparent cause' (*The Concise Oxford Dictionary*, 1964) and 'anything that happens unexpectedly, without design, or by chance' (*The Concise Macquarie Dictionary*, 1982).

The view taken in this book is that most injuries are outcomes of a causal process and cannot reasonably be seen as chance or random events. Indeed, scientific enquiry into the causes of injuries would make little sense if they did not arise at least in part from predictable processes. There is enough evidence to show that injuries are more common in some jobs than others, and consequently they can be treated as a predictable outcome of a given work process (for example, Fosbroke et al., 1997; Feyer et al., 2001). Consequently, in a given job or workplace, injury has a probability and cannot be assumed to be a random event. For example, if a worker falls while working on a floor spattered with grease and oil, is it a chance event or can it be attributed, at least in significant part, to the machinery that sprayed the oil and grease onto the floor and other contributing factors?

Sheehy and Chapman (1987) point out that we generally see routine tasks as continuous, meaningful processes, but when an injury occurs the whole process is redefined and narrowly perceived as an event without a precipitating causal process. In many cases, with a change in perspective a process which could have been expected to lead to injury can be identified. It is reasonable to argue that the immediate circumstances surrounding most injuries involve two distinct events, an error and the injury itself (Hale and Hale, 1972). It is also possible that the error can be made without it leading to injury, even though the potential was there. For example, a fall from a ladder may result in an injury or it may not. Either event could be labelled an 'accident', but given the fact that the event was probably the result of a chain of causal events it is probably better identified as a 'dangerous incident' or something similar. In any case, most studies of occupational accidents have used reported injuries as their unit of analysis.

Hopkins and Palser (1987) point out that our understanding of the causes of injuries is often strongly flavoured by the type of questions that we ask about them. If we ask why a particular injury occurred, it is frequently difficult to move beyond an explanation that is primarily focused upon the characteristics of the victim or of the immediate environment in which the injury occurred. If, on the other hand, we ask why injury rates are higher in some workplaces than others, it is more likely that attention will be focussed on aspects of work organisation. For example, if a worker ignores safety procedures to secure a higher production bonus and is injured as a result, it is easy to blame the worker. However, if we are aware that injury rates are higher in organisations that pay production bonuses than those that do not, we are likely to see the bonus system as the cause of the injury.

The cost of occupational injuries

Since the 1960s there have been many attempts to investigate the costs of work-related near misses, injuries and fatalities to the company, the worker and the worker's family. There has also been a preoccupation, especially by compensation agencies, with developing quantitative estimates of the economic and social costs of occupational disease and injury to highlight the seriousness of the problems and to justify the allocation of resources for preventative measures (Brown et al., 2007). Typically estimates of the total annual costs of workplace injuries and fatalities are based on workers' compensation databases. However, making such estimates is complicated and has stimulated academic debate, as summarised by McCunney (2001). Arriving at a specific cost for any injury is complex and the means by which it is estimated is often not clear (see Cutler and James, 1996; Reville, 2001; Evans, 2004; Lofland, Pizzi and Frick, 2004; Lamm et al., 2007).

A more useful approach is to classify the different categories of costs involved in occupational injury (Andreoni, 1986; Roy, 1997; Dorman, 2000; Dennison, 2003;

Viscusi, 2004; Oxenburgh and Marlow, 2005). The same categories of costs can equally apply to occupational illness. The obvious direct costs of an occupational injury are: 1) accident costs; 2) medical costs; and 3) non-medical costs, as seen in tables 3.1 and 3.2, (Goodchild et al., 2002). Further, Pezzullo and Crook (2006) argue that these direct costs of injuries can be divided into production disturbance costs (12%); human capital costs (62%); health and rehabilitation costs (14%); administration costs (1%); transfer costs (5%); and other costs (6%).

Table 3.1   The composition of the total injury costs

Total injury costs	Individual	Family	Employer	Economy	Societal
Direct costs					
Accident costs*(i)*	✓		✓	✓	✓
Medical costs	✓		✓		
Non-medical costs	✓	✓	✓		
Indirect costs					
Absenteeism			✓	✓	
Productivity losses:	✓			✓	
reduced activity/ability	✓	✓		✓	
reduced participation					
Family worker substitution					
Worker replacement/ substitution			✓	✓	
Taxation					
Intangible costs					
Loss of life	✓	✓			✓
Loss of life expectancy	✓	✓			✓
Loss of quality of life	✓	✓			✓
Physical suffering	✓	✓			✓
Mental suffering					

Source: Goodchild, M., Sanderson, K. and Nana, G. (2002), *Measuring the Total Cost of Injury in New Zealand: A Review of Alternative Cost Methodologies*, Business and Economic Research Limited, Department of Labour, New Zealand Government.

Note: *(i)* not strictly a cost of injury

It is important to note that there are not only *direct* or *tangible costs* but also *indirect* or *intangible costs*, such as costs of lost production as a result of a decline in productivity, increased workers' compensation premiums, and pain, suffering or a reduction in quality of life, as outlined in table 3.2 (Klen, 1989; Dorman, 2000; Mossink and De Greef, 2002; Goetzel et al., 2003; Evans, 2004; De Greef and Van den Broek, 2004; Oxenburgh and Marlow, 2005).

Table 3.2   Intangible and tangible cost elements

	Intangible	Tangible
Victim	Pain and suffering. Moral and psychological suffering (especially in the case of a permanent disability).	Loss of salary and premiums. Reduction of professional capacity. Loss of time (medical treatments).
Family and friends	Moral and psychological suffering. Medical and family burden.	Financial loss. Extra costs.
Colleagues	Bad feeling. Worry or panic (in case of serious or frequent accidents).	Loss of time and possibly also of premiums. Increase of workload. Training of temporary workers.
Company	Deterioration of the social climate. Bad reputation. Weakening of human relations.	Internal audit. Decrease in production. Damages to the equipment, material. Quality losses. Training of new staff. Technical disturbances. Organisational difficulties. Increase of production costs. Increase of the insurance premium or reduction of the discount. Administration costs. Legal sanctions.
Society	Reduction of the human labour potential. Reduction of the quality of life.	Loss of production. Increase of social security costs. Medical treatment and rehabilitation costs. Decrease of the standard of living.

Source: De Greef, M. and Van den Broek, K. (2004), *Quality of the Working Environment and Productivity: Research Findings and Case Studies*, European Agency for Safety and Health at Work, Belgium.

Another broad approach of categorising the costs of injuries and fatalities is to link the costs with the different stages of managing the workplace risks. The categories are:

- *costs in anticipation:* the development, implementation and maintenance costs associated with OHS systems used to prevent or mitigate injuries. Underlying these costs are the principles of risk management.
- *costs as a consequence:* costs incurred by the employee, the employer and the public as a result of an injury. Examples include 'opportunity costs' such as employee 'down time', the loss of production and loss of time. Fines can also be incurred for negligent actions that caused the injury. Hidden costs are often the greatest proportion of consequential costs; for example, personal losses suffered by those injured, extra overtime, overemployment (extra staffing), training, employee turnover and lost production time. Other examples are damage to plant, product and equipment or higher insurance/compensation premiums.
- *costs in response:* the costs incurred by the organisation and the regulatory and compensatory agencies as a result of investigating the injury. Examples of these costs are lost time, diversion of scarce recourses and reporting (see Roy, 1997; Lamm et al., 2007).

Although it is difficult to accurately determine the scale of the problem in Australia and New Zealand, there are indicators. To estimate the social and economic costs associated with workplace injuries, the New Zealand Department of Labour (2002) investigated 15 cases of individuals who had suffered an injury or illness (Adam et al., 2002). The total documented costs of these 15 cases were $1 167 471 and the projected future costs of seven of the cases were expected to be $3 985 989 (although there is no indication of how many years this amount would cover). By 2004–05, the Accident Compensation Corporation had paid out compensation to workers amounting to $5 billion, 4% of GDP (Pezzullo and Crook, 2006). However, in their NOHSAC report, Pezzullo and Crook (2006) state that this figure is a gross underestimate and that only 2% of the full costs of occupational injury and illness are compensated ($20.9 billion in 2004–05).

There is also a tendency to concentrate on the tangible, direct costs of injuries rather than the more ambiguous, indirect costs and the chronic costs associated with long-term conditions, such as musculoskeletal injuries (Tappin et al., 2007). As Burton et al. (1999) note, the loss of worker productivity resulting from injuries is an indirect health cost to corporations that is largely unmeasured. They continue: 'Direct costs are much easier to quantify than indirect costs … When corporations do consider the impact of health costs, the losses considered are usually in the form of health insurance claims' (Burton et al., 1999: 863). It has been estimated that the hidden costs of workplace injury can vary between 0.5 and 20 times the wage or salary costs (Oxenburgh, 1991; William et al., 1997; Dorman, 2000; Viscusi, 2004; Butcher, 2004; Burton et al., 2005; Oxenburgh and Marlow, 2005; Pezzullo and Crook, 2006).

Some of the more difficult, though equally important, indirect costs to estimate are the social costs. Victims and their families argue that the social costs associated with being injured at work or losing a family member are the hardest to bear. The nature and breadth of social costs are aptly summarised by Keller (2001: 438):

> Social costs are typically described in losses or limitations in a person's ability to engage in major social roles and activities. These include working, parenting, or sharing leisure activities with or caring for friends and family. Impacts commonly discussed are the ability to perform tasks that are dictated by the work role (social consequences), as opposed to lost wages (economic consequences), or losing a range of motion (clinical consequences).

A study on the social costs of injury undertaken by New Zealand Department of Labour researchers (Adams et al., 2002) indicates that these social, cumulative costs are often incalculable as records are incomplete. In particular, their study shows that a considerable proportion of the indirect costs were borne by injured employees or their families. For example, the effects on their relationships were considerable. Loss of intimacy and increased distance between spouses or parents and children, or distance between employers and employees or between workmates, were common. Adams et al. note that injured employees felt '… isolated or self-imposed isolation put relationships under pressure—some broke down while others emerged from the difficult period strengthened through shared experiences' (Adams et al., 2002: 171). Their findings also showed that indirect, social costs have a ripple effect. For the employer, indirect costs included lost production, negative impacts on staff morale, bad publicity, the costs of replacing employees or equipment and, in some cases, legal costs. For the workplace, costs included the loss of friends and colleagues, possibly animosity towards injured or ill employees and even the immeasurable impact of feeling responsible for an injury or fatality. For the government sector, the impact on officials carrying out statutory functions was observed, including the psychological impact of investigating fatalities, dealing with recalcitrant employers and comforting bereaved or confused families. Other hidden costs included costs of medical retirement for government employees, plus education, injury prevention; and costs of investigation and appeals. Adams et al. (2002) also note that many costs are non-recoverable—for example, lost taxes, lost labour, voluntary and unpaid work, casual work (while this was also a loss to the individual, because it was not taxed, it was not compensated) and social capital. For the health sector, indirect costs observed included time, equipment and drugs, and rehabilitation costs.

While there is some use in providing estimates of injury costs and categories to capture all the different costs, Weil (2001: 419) argues that the first problem encountered in assessing the economic consequences of occupational injury and illness is defining the appropriate time dimension for analysis. Some economic consequences are immediate. Traumatic fatalities occur at a point in time and the consequences of the fatality can be evaluated at that time. On the other hand, exposure to some workplace hazards may not give rise to physical problems until a much later time. Consequently, the diagnosis of an injury may not necessarily signal the beginning of the economic consequences associated with that injury. The same is true for injuries where first return to work may not signal a long-term reattachment to the labour market.

Further, Weil argues that to capture these complexities, the economic consequences of occupational illness and injury can be usefully depicted as a flow or set of pathways, as outlined in figure 3.1. According to Weil (2001: 219) disability is the overall pathway while the inputs into the pathway are injuries or illness diagnoses. Workers leave the stream either by fatality or by returning to work on a permanent basis. In between entrances and exits to and from the pathway, workers will be distributed across a variety of states, each with associated economic consequences. Valuing the economic consequences of injury and illness can be thought of as summing the costs associated with the stream given the cross-section of workers in the stream at that point in time. In defining the state of injured workers, Weil (2001) makes important distinctions between impairments, functional limitations and disabilities, as outlined in figure 3.1. He maintains that 'an impairment' refers to a physiological or anatomical loss or abnormality. He adds, 'An impairment may in some instances give rise to a functional limitation, defined as a restriction of a person's capacities' (Weil 2001: 220). Functional limitations, according to Weil (2001) may lead to a disability if they limit the individual's ability to engage in activities in the home, the workplace or society.

Weil's work makes an important contribution in that he draws on the economic, public health and occupational medicine literature when estimating costs of occupational injuries. By combining the different perspectives, Weil is able to identify the different economic *and* social outcomes for injuries and fatalities, and thus provides a more sophisticated understanding of the *types* of costs involved; that is, he applies an ecological perspective used in public health which highlights the interrelation of various factors that influence such things as how functional limitations result in work disabilities. By incorporating an economic approach, he makes it clear that there are financial incentives to introduce OHS preventative measures for workers, employers and other institutional players.

Weil also illustrates how the locus and extent of social effects varies according to the extent of injury. Clearly, a serious disabling back injury can be expected to produce more substantial and varied social effects than a minor sprain (Dembe, 2001: 405). A prolonged occupational injury with extensive impairment requiring lengthy rehabilitation will probably have a greater social impact than one which is less severe. Disasters, and accidents resulting in multiple injuries and fatalities, may result in widespread psychological reactions within a community or population of workers. Investigators studying the social impact of occupational disorders must devise a way of classifying different types of workplace injuries and illnesses, and differentiating their severity and scope (Weil, 2001). Severe injuries and illnesses may also result in prolonged disability and rehabilitation, which are themselves social impacts that can subsequently produce additional social effects.

In summary, it is impossible to calculate the true economic and social costs of work-related injury and illness and, ipso facto, the Australian and New Zealand figures should be treated with caution as they are likely to be conservative (Roy, 1997; Dennison, 2003).

Figure 3.1   Disability pathways and economic outcomes

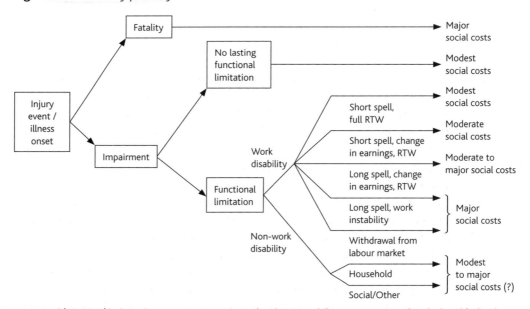

Source: Weil (2001: 420) 'Valuing the economic consequences of work injury and illness: a comparison of methods and findings', *American Journal of Industrial Medicine*, 40: 418–37.

Models of injury causation and investigation

While the costs of occupational injuries and fatalities are often used to bring attention to the scale of the problem, investigating the root causes of the injuries and fatalities is of equal importance. Occupational injury causation models and investigation methods have evolved over time and the focus in the injury causation literature has shifted from the sequence of events to the representation of the whole system. Injury investigation methods have also gradually evolved from searching for a single immediate cause to the recognition of multiple causes (Katsakiori et al., 2009). The development of theories to explain the causes of occupational injury, and the empirical research that has accompanied it, has been dominated by the disciplines of psychology, safety engineering and ergonomics. However, as we noted in chapter 2, in recent years most of this work has been subject to heavy criticism from industrial sociologists who have proposed very different models of injury causation. We shall now describe in more detail the explanations of injury causation presented by each of the disciplines, critically analyse each perspective, and then propose a means of integrating our understanding of injury causation into a strategy for assessing the causes of injuries. An understanding of the primary factors contributing to injury is a fundamental prerequisite to the development of effective safety management strategies. The methods to investigate injuries (commonly denoted as 'accident' investigation methods) will also be discussed here.

Expert technical explanations

The primary objectives of ergonomics and safety engineering are the same with regard to occupational injury. Both attempt to design aspects of the physical working environment to remove potential sources of injury (see Hale et al., 2007; Costella, 2008; Hollnagel et al., 2006; Driscoll et al., 2008). The underlying assumption is that the existence of injury risks within a work system will inevitably lead to injury. Both disciplines espouse a view that equipment and the working environment should be modified where possible to limit the exposure of workers to danger and hence minimise the need to rely on workers behaving safely (Thomas, 1988; Sanders and McCormick, 1993; Oxenburgh, 1991; Karwowski, 2005, Woods and Hollnagel, 2006). In theory at least, both disciplines take a commendable preventative orientation which locates the primary source of injury in environmental design.

Safety engineers are concerned with the design and modification of tools, equipment and work processes in order to minimise the risk of immediate physical injury (Woods and Hollnagel, 2006; Hale et al., 2007). Their work generally involves the design of machine guarding and operating controls to prevent workers coming in contact with dangerous parts, such as presses, blades, rotors and gears (Keyserling, 1983; Mathews, 1985; Jacinto and Aspinwall, 2003, 2004; Driscoll et al., 2008). Guarding is intended to achieve this goal by providing a physical barrier against contact with the dangerous part of machines or tools, such as drills, lathes, spindles, drive shafts, fans, rotors and belt drives. The moving shields on rotary saws that adjust to the cutting angle and protect the hands of the operator from contact with the blade are a common example. Operating controls, frequently used on presses, stamps, drills and saws, are installed to prevent workers from inadvertently operating the machine while parts of their bodies are in dangerous positions. Lockout procedures are also widely used to protect maintenance workers from injuries caused when other workers start machinery before they have completed their task. As stated in the previous chapter, safety engineers are in general concerned with the introduction of lockout procedures which require controls to be securely locked in the 'off' position when workers are likely to be in dangerous locations, especially with respect to heavy machinery.

The major problem with many of these engineering solutions is that they may interfere with the natural body motions required to efficiently perform tasks and consequently workers may seek to bypass them to get the job done. This problem is compounded in situations where workers are on piece rates or some other form of production bonus scheme and their incomes depend significantly on working quickly and efficiently. In fact, the interventions designed by safety engineers frequently do not pay sufficient attention to social, organisational and behavioural sources of injury.

As a way of overcoming the often narrow engineering approach to occupational injury, many safety engineers embraced a broader, systems approach in the 1980s (see Rasmussen, 1985). The view that injuries are a result of a combination of causes, arising from unreliable system components, whether human or technological, has gained a great deal of popularity, particularly in technically complicated industries such as aviation. More recently, safety engineers have recognised that to understand how occupational injuries and fatalities occur, we need to understand how complex systems succeed and sometimes fail. Safety engineers contend that occupational injuries which occur within socio-technological systems are due in part to unexpected dysfunctional interactions between system components, that is, human and machine, and are often related to external disturbances (Woods and Hallnagel, 2007). Organisations that have the ability to anticipate the changing shape of risk before failure and harm occur are more resilient than organisations that do not. Woods and Hallnagel (2007) argue that a resilient organisation treats safety as a core value, not a commodity that can be counted. Indeed, resilient engineering, as this approach has become known, is concerned with the ability in difficult conditions to stay within the safe envelope and avoid injuries (Hale and Heijer, 2006). Further, resilient organisations have the ability to keep, or recover quickly to, a stable state, allowing them to continue operations during and after a major mishap or in the presence of continuous significant stresses. Thus, resilience includes both the ability to avoid injuries and fatalities and the ability to respond effectively after these have occurred (Costella et al., 2008). However, Hale and Heijer (2006) argue that resilience should be considered against the background of the size of the risk; that is, organisations that are resilient in situations of very high risk may experience occupational injuries but not a substantial number. Equally the opposite can occur; that is, organisation may fail to be resilient in conditions of low risk and yet have no accidents (Hale and Heijer, 2006).

While orthodox safety engineering approaches to injury causation tend to focus on eliminating the problem by applying an engineering design solution, ergonomists take a broader approach. Ergonomics, as described in chapter 2, is an applied science concerned with the design of facilities, equipment, tools and tasks that are compatible with the anatomical, physiological, biomechanical, perceptual and behavioural characteristics of human beings (Sanders and McCormick, 1993; Karwowski, 2005; Pheasant and Haslegrave, 2006; also see the special edition of *Ergonomics*, 2008). The term 'ergonomics' is often used synonymously with the human factors approach in which the primary focus is on the interface between ergonomics, engineering, design, technology and the management of human-compatible systems and how individuals can use the technology safely and effectively (Karwowski, 2005: 436). The ergonomic approach to investigating workplace injuries is to systematically evaluate the tasks, equipment and work environment. Ergonomists generally focus their attention on risks in the physical environment, the handling of loads, the design of technical equipment, and workers' perceptions of hazards and responses to them (Leclercq et al., 2007; Drury, 2008).

Much of ergonomists' work is technical in nature. For example, to develop solutions to manual-handling problems ergonomists have extensively investigated the relationships between lifting technique, posture and load characteristics including size, shape and weight in an effort to reduce injuries such as occupational musculoskeletal injuries (see, for example, Kumar, 2001; Tappin et al., 2008). From this work they have developed standards for maximum safe loads and for design considerations such as the size and locations of handles on loads of various weights and dimensions. They have also widely investigated the physical interaction between workers and the working environment. For example, they have identified slips and falls as a major cause of occupational injuries and attempted to deal with the problem by examining the mechanics of walking, including the forces operating at the interface between the worker's shoe and the floor, and improving the slip characteristics of shoes and walking surfaces (Keyserling, 1983). Surfaces on platforms and scaffolds, in particular, are frequently modified to reduce the frequency of falls. Similarly, injuries on ladders have been approached by using anthropometric data and knowledge of the mechanics of ladder climbing to establish safe spacing between the rungs in order to reduce the risk of falls (Keyserling, 1983). However, in most instances ergonomists have tended to be more reactive towards technology (reactive design) rather than driving the technology (proactive design) (Karwowski, 2005: 439).

Ergonomists have also used physiological knowledge regarding the effects of physical work stress to assess the levels of energy expenditure that lead to excessive physical fatigue in different environmental conditions. Quantitative data of this kind has been used to establish appropriate rest cycles in different jobs. Much of the psychosocial and anatomical data collected by ergonomists has been used to design ergonomically sound tools and equipment. A good illustration of this type of research can be seen in the 2004 report on the role of work stress and psychosocial work factors in the development of musculoskeletal disorders undertaken by the Robens Centre for Health Ergonomics for the UK Health and Safety Executive (Devereux et al., 2004). Based on psychosocial and anatomical data collected from 3139 workers over approximately 15 months, Devereux et al. (2004) concluded that individual factors such as age and gender had no impact on the level of stress experienced by the workers. Instead, workers who were exposed to both physical and psychosocial work risk factors, that is, extrinsic effort, intrinsic effort, role ambiguity, role conflict and verbal abuse or confrontations with clients or the general public, had the greatest likelihood of reporting high levels of job stress.

As discussed in chapter 2, an important aspect of ergonomics is the integrated redesign of immediate working environments, or work stations (Hale et al., 2007). Typically, ergonomists observe the tasks performed by workers, analysing their interaction with their working environment in order to optimise work station design. In general, ergonomists attempt to design workstations to match the size and capabilities of workers and to ensure that tools and machinery can be controlled with the minimum risk of injury. Factors to be considered in a final design can include the positioning of controls and the provision of sufficient space for the physical movements required of the operator. The design process may also involve investigation of the body forces required for movements such as shifting levers or lifting weights; the forces impinging on muscles, joints and other parts of the body in various postures; and changes in bodily processes such as energy expenditure and oxygen consumption. In developing the final design, ergonomists also take into account the surrounding ramps, doorways and corridors to ensure efficient movement of workers and inflow and outflow of materials as well as the availability of effective protective clothing.

Ergonomic explanations of injury have also focused on the behaviour and perceptual processes of workers (Cacciabue, 2008). They have examined the contribution of a wide range of human behaviours to injury, including environmental perception, visual acuity, stress and subjective workloads, motor learning, data processing capacities and hazard perception. One study, for example, investigated the combined impact of factors such as annoying environmental distractions and stressors, hazards and adverse physical working conditions on injury rates (Melamed et al., 1989).

This work has alerted ergonomists to behavioural reasons why protective clothing and equipment may be discarded and safety standards ignored. Numerous design solutions have been developed to address these problems. For example, anthropometric data has been used to improve the comfort and fit of goggles and other head-mounted equipment. Design improvements have also been made to minimise the misting and diminished vision that have discouraged workers from wearing goggles when they should. This work has drawn very heavily on research from cognitive, experimental and work psychology. In common with psychologists working in this area, ergonomists tend to treat workers as sophisticated machines whose capacities must be exploited but not dangerously exceeded.

Finally, ergonomists have expanded their interests to include work organisation and in particular have turned their attention to the perennial quest of increasing performance (see chapter 2; Oxenburgh and Marlow, 2005). The solutions to increase performance and productivity proposed by ergonomists reflect their own expertise, for example in recommendations for task redesign to ensure workers use a variety of tools to minimise fatigue and monotony. Although the inclusion of worker participation mechanisms as a way of reducing the rate of workplace injuries was often overlooked by orthodox ergonomists, there is now a greater willingness among latter-day ergonomists to include such mechanisms in the mix of factors that have the potential to increase productivity (Wilson et al., 2005; Rivilis et al., 2006; Theberge et al., 2006; Pehkonen et al., 2009).

Psychological explanations

As we saw in chapter 2, work psychology has contributed to the debate regarding the origins of occupational injury since early last century. Some early theories have largely fallen into disrepute in scientific circles, such as the concept of 'accident proneness' and the pervasive use of the term 'accident' rather than 'injury'. Nonetheless, there is still a plethora of psychological studies that endeavour to explain risk-taking behaviour or 'sensation seeking' behaviour of individuals and how to modify risk-taking behaviour (see Zuckerman, 1971; Lawton and Parker, 1998). The so-called 'risk-taking behaviour' of employees is frequently cited as an important micro-level factor in the occurrence of near misses and injuries, and the inattention to (un)safe behaviour at work and a risk-taking tendency have been identified as significant risk factors (Landweerd et al. 1990; Glendon et al., 2006).

There is an underlying assumption underpinning risk-taking behaviour that while everyone has a propensity to take risks, this propensity differs from one individual to another depending on several factors, such as perception of the nature of the costs and benefits of taking the risk (Adams, 1995). Most of the studies concentrate on the relationship between the employee's attitude towards safety and their safety behaviour, including 'risk-taking tendency'. In a review of the literature on the relationship between accident liability and individual differences, focusing specifically on work-related injuries between 1970 and 1997, Lawton and Parker (1998) note that there are significant methodological problems with accident liability research in that most of the studies are retrospective. Also, differences between the accident-free and accident-involved groups are taken to provide evidence that the measured criterion characteristic is causally linked to work-related injuries, which may not necessarily be the case. They suggest that research into individual differences in accident liability should consider two possible routes to accident involvement via errors or violations. The first is the cognitive route, which involves failures in information processing or skill resulting in errors. This is the traditional realm of the psychologist in safety research. The second, social–psychological route involves a consideration of attitudinal and behavioural factors (1998).

Other psychologists have been critical of the narrow view of safety behaviour. Bradley (1989), for example, attacked what he considered to be misconceptions regarding the psychology of safety, particularly the tendency to categorise people and behaviours as either safe or unsafe. He considered this approach to be inappropriate for several reasons:

- Unsafe behaviour comes in various forms. It can range from an uncharacteristic omission to repeated acts of horseplay, from adoption of unsafe work methods and postures to failure to wear personal protective equipment, and from failure to identify, assess and respond to a hazard to intentional risk taking. These behaviours can all vary in terms of their frequency, duration, intentionality and danger.
- Unsafe behaviours are all multi-determined, being shaped by a series of physical, social and psychological factors.
- Solitary or isolated interventions are unlikely to be effective in dealing with the full range of unsafe behaviour. Instead, a comprehensive set of strategies is required.
- Contrary to much conventional wisdom, education and enforcement are not the most efficient means through which to improve safety performance.

Bradley (1989) argued that there is little value in trying to identify the accident prone and isolate them from dangerous situations. Rather, it should be accepted that no worker is immune from unsafe behaviour. All workers may, at some time or another, fall victim to the effects of fatigue, stress, boredom, frustration, intoxication and other injury-inducing factors. Bradley contended that susceptibility to injury is best seen as a function of workers' traits, their physiological and psychological states and the environmental circumstances. Great emphasis should be placed on the external and environmental determinants of behaviour, and explanations of unsafe behaviour should focus upon the environmental factors that encourage unsafe acts instead of the personality, inattentiveness or carelessness of the worker. The circumstances under which workers are likely to be encouraged to make speed–accuracy trade-offs, behave inappropriately, daydream, or become forgetful should be identified. Another potential negative effect is that workers may be discouraged from reporting injury when reporting may result in the loss of bonuses or other incentives. In other words, control of unsafe behaviour requires the identification and modification of those environmental conditions that encourage it.

This view is supported by Sheehy and Chapman (1987) who also recognised that injury causation must be seen as a multi-causal phenomenon. They asserted that the traditional emphasis placed on the role of worker characteristics, task characteristics and the design of the worker–machine interface is overly restrictive and overlooks the fundamental contribution of organisational factors to injury. They further observed that when high-risk industrial technologies are introduced the individual workers are often regarded as 'too inconsequential to justify a change in safety practices' (p. 210).

Bradley (1989) warned that work environments contain not only hazards but also factors that encourage unsafe behaviour. The impact of the environment on behaviour is frequently produced through its effect upon the workers' psychological state, including mood, cognitive functioning, energy levels and motivation. Bradley identified four aspects of the work environment that can affect unsafe behaviour. The first is *physical environment*, which is important not only in terms of the range of hazards it presents, but also in terms of their familiarity, identifiability and avoidability. It may also present barriers to safe behaviour, for example by the absence of adequate safety gear or safe routes through which to travel. Unsafe behaviour may also be encouraged by physical stressors and distractions. Physical stressors include heat, humidity, noise, dust, vibration and glare. Distractions include unpredictable and uncontrollable noises, odours and sounds. These conditions can cause workers to become uncomfortable, annoyed, frustrated and impatient. Second, several aspects of the *organisational environment* may contribute to improved safety performance. They include a high level of management commitment to safety, a stable and experienced workforce, an emphasis on safety in training, and employment of full-time safety personnel who report directly to top management. The third is *task structure*, which can induce unsafe behaviour by affecting workers' psychological state and imposing demands on workers' psychological resources. Extremes of task complexity, repetitiveness, variety, pace and load can have negative effects. Where demands are too low workers may become bored, lose concentration and daydream. Where demands are too high workers may become stressed, annoyed or anxious, which may lead to disorganised behaviour. Finally, aspects of the *psychosocial environment* can also influence whether workers take risks or avoid them. Supervisors, leading hands and experienced workers help to develop work group norms regarding safe and unsafe behaviour.

Having determined that many unsafe acts are reasonable responses to particular environmental conditions, Bradley (1989) concluded that changing unsafe behaviour must begin with environmental changes. The workplace should be changed to minimise physical hazards, stressors and distractions and to optimise ergonomic design. Tasks and jobs should be redesigned to be challenging but manageable. A positive organisational safety climate should be developed with effective safety policies, practices and personnel, and the active commitment of senior management. Work group structures and processes that support safety norms should be encouraged. The improvements in safety behaviour achieved by behaviour-change programs may well be greatly enhanced if they are combined with interventions to minimise physical hazards, redesign tasks and jobs to be more conducive to safety, encourage work group structures and processes that support safety norms, and develop a positive safety climate within the organisation.

Other efforts have been made to broaden explanations of injury beyond the characteristics and behaviour of individual workers. McKenna (1983) demonstrated the conceptual confusion and flaws in statistical reasoning inherent in the concept of 'accident proneness'. He argued that 'differential accident involvement' is a more appropriate term that makes fewer assumptions about the sources of injury. While a recognition that some workers are injured more often than others is implicit in the term, it does not imply that these differences necessarily arise from stable characteristics of the injured workers. McKenna accepted that differences in injury rates may frequently arise from differences in exposure to risk as well as from psychological and behavioural variables like reaction times and visual acuity. He contended that if perceptual, attentional and performance limitations of humans are discovered, the most appropriate solution may lie in the redesign of tasks, equipment or the working environment to take account of them. McKenna did, however, suggest that in certain conditions some individuals may temporarily display greater propensities to injury. Workers experiencing high levels of stress, including occupation stress, may be more likely to be injured, for example, while stress levels remain high. While most research psychologists have found arguments like those raised by McKenna persuasive, it must be acknowledged that some continue to pursue evidence that personality, maladjustment and 'neurosis' are linked to injury (see, for example, Hansen, 1989).

The concept of differential accident involvement suggests a much wider range of strategies to reduce injury than accident proneness did. A focus on accident proneness has an impact on the way staff are selected, dismissed or reassigned. The use of such section criteria as effective strategies for minimising injury rates is questionable, even if the right employee could be reliably identified. Differential accident involvement, however, suggests that equipment design, work organisation and environmental factors may be major contributors to injury and that appropriate intervention may reduce the injury rates of individuals who are temporarily at higher risk. McKenna has made an important contribution to the debate regarding individual differences in injury involvement, although in view of our concerns about the term 'accident', differential accident involvement would probably be better labelled 'differential injury involvement'.

After an extensive review of the literature, Hale and Hale (1972) noted several other relevant misunderstandings regarding the nature of occupational injury. It is widely assumed that different types of injuries arise from a set of common causes, but there is no evidence to demonstrate that this assumption is true. For example, it is not evident that minor and major injuries, or injuries in different industries, have the same causes. As a result of the failure to recognise the diversity of the causes of injury, there is a strong tendency to overgeneralise the results of research studies and ignore differences in tasks, industrial contexts, and the ages and skills of workers. Hale and Hale also concluded that researchers have failed to differentiate adequately between factors that are causally related to injury and those that are simply correlated. Causal relationships have often been assumed without considering their relative strengths. For example, is the causal relationship between particular aspects of work organisation and injury stronger than that between particular personality characteristics and injury? Hale and Hale considered that too much research effort has been devoted to the search for the causes of injury while evaluation of the effectiveness of prevention strategies has received little attention.

Recent psychological models have largely evolved in response to perceived deficiencies of earlier theoretical constructs and developments in broader theories of human behaviour. They portray injury as a much more complex phenomenon than the earlier models, generally recognising that most injuries do not have a single 'cause' but rather arise from the interaction of multiple variables (Glendon et al., 2006). Researchers have investigated a wide variety of human characteristics that may contribute to error, including attentiveness, perception of hazards, danger identification, motivation and the processes involved in learning safe behaviour. The models of individual behaviour in dangerous conditions proposed by Hale and Glendon (1987), Glendon and McKenna (1995) and Reason et al. (1998), for example, have extended this discourse.

Reason (1997, 1998) makes a distinction between: (a) accidents that occur to individuals and (b) organisational accidents that happen to systems or subsystems, as presented in table 3.3. Reason (1998) maintains that 'individual accidents' occur in circumstances where people work in close proximity to hazards and the 'defences' or protective measures against injuries or fatalities are superficial, limited or nonexistent. 'Organisational accidents', on the other hand, tend to occur within complex systems in which the defences against injuries and fatalities that have been developed over time become unwieldy, piecemeal or often redundant. In nuclear power plants, commercial aircraft and other contemporary high-tech systems, there is invariably a mixture of 'hard' and 'soft' defences. The former include engineered safety features—such as automatic controls, warning systems and shutdowns—together with various physical barriers and containments, while the latter comprise a combination of paper and people—rules and procedures, training, drills, administrative controls and, most particularly, front-line operators such as pilots and control room personnel. The result of these many layers of defence mechanisms is that these systems are largely impervious to single failures, either human or technical. For an accident to occur in such a system, Reason (1998: 295) argues, requires an unlikely combination of several different factors to penetrate the many protective layers and to allow hazards to come into damaging contact with plant, personnel or the environment.

Table 3.3 Distinguishing the characteristics of individual and organisational accidents

Individual	Organisational accidents
Frequent	Rare
Limited consequences	Widespread consequences
Few or no defences	Many defences
Limited causes	Multiple causes
Slips, trips and lapses	Product of new technology
Short 'history'	Long 'history'

Source: Reason, J.T. (1998), 'Achieving a safe culture: theory and practice', *Work & Stress*, 12: 296–306.

While dividing accidents into individual and organisational accidents is an important aspect of Reason's argument, it is his aetiology of an organisational accident represented by his 'Swiss cheese' model that has caught the imagination of many in the OHS profession (see figure 3.2). Here the defences, portrayed as cheese slices, are shown as intervening between the local hazards and potential losses. Each slice of cheese represents one layer of defence. In an ideal world, all of these layers would be intact. In reality, however, each layer has holes or gaps. These gaps are created by active failures—the errors and violations of those at the human–system interface—and by latent conditions arising from the failure of designers, builders, managers and maintainers to anticipate all possible scenarios (see Reason,1997, for a more detailed discussion). The holes due to active failures are likely to be relatively short lived, while those arising from latent conditions may lie dormant for many years until they are revealed by regulators, internal audits or by incidents and injuries. It is also important to recognise that, unlike the holes in Swiss cheese slices, these defensive gaps are not static, especially those due to active failures. They are in continuous flux, moving around and opening and shutting according to local circumstances. This metaphor also makes it clear why organisational accidents are rare events. For such a disaster to occur, it requires a lining up of the holes to permit a brief trajectory of accident opportunity.

Figure 3.2   Reason's Swiss cheese model

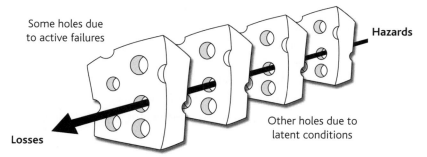

Source: Reason, J.T. (1998: 296), 'Achieving a safe culture: theory and practice', *Work & Stress*, 12: 296–306.

The Swiss cheese model serves to emphasise the importance of latent conditions and illustrate how, in combination with active failures, they may lead to accidents. Further, Reason's model is easy to comprehend and as such has been helpful in improving the understanding of accidents (Perneger, 2005). Yet its simplicity also means that some aspects cannot be easily described, or described at all, and that explanations based on the model therefore may be incomplete. Indeed, Hollnagel and Woods (2006) argue that the Swiss cheese model is a metaphor rather than a model and the metaphor itself oversimplifies the situation by referring to the organisation as a whole. There is ample practical experience to show that some parts of an organisation may be safe while others may be unsafe (Hollnagel and Woods, 2006). In other words, parts of the organisation may 'drift' in different directions. Further, the safety of the organisation does not necessarily derive from a linear combination of the parts, but rather depends on the ways in which they are coupled and how coordination across these parts is fragmented or synchronised (Perrow, 1999).

While some psychologists have expanded the focus on the individual to include organisational factors in injury causation, there is still a great deal of attention on the behaviour of the individual. It is not surprising, therefore, that psychological inter-ventions are primarily aimed at changing unsafe behaviour. Behaviour modification programs employ incentives, feedback or sanctions to encourage safer behaviour. In practice, psychologists have generally used various combinations of training, monetary incentives, prizes, graphic feedback, supervisory praise, feedback, and goal setting. Psychological research has often focused on identifying the most effective combinations of these strategies. Reber and Wallin (1984), for example, attempted to establish whether safety performance could be improved by training in safe behaviours followed by the setting of specific, difficult and accepted goals for improvement in the behaviours. They also attempted to assess whether safety performance would be further enhanced when workers received feedback concerning their department's performance in relation to its goals. The results indicated that training alone and training plus goal setting both had positive effects on safety behaviour, but the addition of feedback produced even greater increases in safety performance.

Behaviour modification programs, ever popular among employers as a means of enhancing safety and health, have been severely criticised because they generally place the prime responsibility for reducing harm on the individual employee, thus abdicating the employer's duty of care (Specht et al., 2006; Lamm et al., 2007). Another major drawback of behavioural modification programs is that they run the risk of assuming that unsafe behaviour is the only cause of injuries worth focusing on (Hopkins, 2006). Further, while research of this nature helps to refine the technology available to encourage safe behaviour, it ignores the impact of work organisation, equipment design and other social and organisational factors on injury, and transfers the responsibility for safety almost entirely onto the individual worker. The techniques used also emphasise immediate improvement rather than long-term changes in the incidence of injury. Thus, such approaches diminish or fail to recognise the importance of the sociology of work and to take into account the complexities of employment relationships and the influence of external economic, political and legal factors. Hopkins (2006a: 594) also states:

> The reality is that unsafe behaviour is merely the last link in a causal chain and not necessarily the most effective link to focus on, for the purposes of accident prevention ... unsafe acts are only one part of the story—unsafe conditions are the other—and any good safety management system must include vigorous programs aimed at identifying and rectifying unsafe conditions.

Although behaviour modification programs have been criticised, such programs have been seen as a useful vehicle for changing the entire safety culture and climate of the organisation to reduce mishaps, injuries and fatalities. While research on safety culture and climate can be found across several disciplines such as sociology or ergonomics, this area of OHS is dominated by the psychologists (for example, Reason, 1997; Cox and Flin, 1998; Glendon and Litherland, 2001; Parker et al., 2006). The emergence of safe culture and climate as a way of controlling injuries can be traced back to the International Atomic Energy Agency's (IAEA) initial report on the Chernobyl nuclear accident (IAEA, 1986). Since then it has been discussed in other major accident inquiries and analyses of safety failures, such as the Piper Alpha oil platform explosion in the North Sea and the Clapham Junction rail disaster in London. In both cases the Public Inquiry report argued that a poor safety culture within the operating company was an important determinant of the accident (Hidden, 1989). In these contexts the emphases were primarily on the perceived inadequacies of the prevailing safety cultures (Cox and Flin, 1998).

Researchers involved in safety research believe that safety culture and climate are key predictors of safety behaviour and performance (Reason, 1998; Cox and Cheyne, 2000; Glendon and Litherland, 2001; Mearns et al., 2000; Parker et al., 2006; Hopkins, 2006; Havold 2007, Mearns and Yule, 2009). In essence, safety culture and safety climate inhabit the same coin but different sides. Uttal's (1983) definition of safety culture captures most of its essentials: 'Shared values (what is important) and beliefs (how things work) that interact with an organisation's structures and control systems to produce behavioural norms (the way we do things around here)' (cf. Reason, 1998). The literature (Bate, 1992; Thompson et al., 1996) suggests at least two ways of treating safety culture: as something an organisation is (the beliefs, attitudes and values of its members regarding the pursuit of safety) and as something that an organisation has (the structures, practices, controls and policies designed to enhance safety). Both are essential for achieving an effective safety culture (Reason, 1998). Safety climate describes employees' perceptions, attitudes and beliefs about risk and safety, whereas safety culture is more complex and enduring and reflects fundamental values, norms, assumptions and expectations which to some extent reside in societal culture (Mearns and Flin, 1999).

However, Cox and Flin (1998), Hopkins (2006) and others rightly note that despite all that has been written about safety culture, there is still no agreement as to what the concept means. Attempts to study safety culture and its relationship to organisational outcomes have remained fragmented and underspecified in theoretical terms. More specifically, Guldenmund's (2000) extensive review of the literature reveals several limitations of safety culture and climate. First, the concepts of safety culture and safety climate are still ill-defined and not worked out well. Second, the relationship between safety culture and safety climate is unclear and there is considerable confusion about the cause, the content and the consequence of safety culture and climate. That is, the cause of safety culture and climate has not been addressed seriously, there is no consensus on the content of safety culture and climate, and the consequences of safety culture and climate are seldom discussed. Third, there is no satisfying model of safety culture or safety climate. Finally, the issue of the level of aggregation has not received the attention it warrants.

Moreover, like behaviour modification programs, initiatives to change the safety culture of the organisation have been captured by industry and are often code for blaming workers for health and safety failures. At the heart of safety culture initiatives is also a zero tolerance of injuries which can have the effect of perverting workplace safety by discouraging the reporting of injuries (Hopkins, 2006; Rosenberg, 2008). Hopkins (2006) notes that intolerance to injuries inherent in safety cultural initiatives may be counterproductive as companies are faced with a dilemma when it comes to information about safety problems. Should they seek out such information and learn from it, so as to reduce the risk of injuries, or should they suppress it, so that when an injury occurs they can not be held liable for failing to act on information in their possession? The disadvantage of suppressing such information is that it creates organisational learning disabilities.

In summary, within psychology discourse, approaches to injury and causation range from developing measures of individual risk-taking behaviour, and programs to change individual behaviour, to more sophisticated models that incorporate multiple causal factors. Unfortunately, recognition of organisational and environmental factors in psychological research is not frequently reflected in the prevention strategies psychologists propose in practice. For example, the depth of analysis of theory and research presented by Sheehy and Chapman is not systematically reflected in the workplace interventions that they propose. In common with most psychological solutions, their prevention strategies still focus predominantly on interventions at the level of the individual worker, such as training, feedback and counselling, and they do not challenge managerial prerogative in the implementation of these strategies. In particular, strategies to ensure that workers have the opportunity to negotiate effective safety policies and practices with management and to monitor and evaluate those policies and practices receive little attention. Little or no emphasis is placed on change at the industrial, policy or legislative levels.

Sociological perspectives

As sociologists tend to view occupational injuries and fatalities within a social, political, economic and legal context, their explanations often differ from those offered by ergonomists, engineers and psychologists. Indeed, they have been highly critical of some of the more dominant understandings of occupational injury (see Dwyer, 1991; Nichols, 1997; Perrow, 1999). Sociological explanations focus on aspects of the organisation of work as the primary determinant of occupational injury. In particular, sociologists have examined the way in which organisational structures, payment systems, industrial conflict and other organisational, industrial and social factors contribute to a process by which injury is socially produced. Sociologists also contend that, given the perennial tension between capital and labour, each with their different interests, there will always be debates over the causes of injuries and fatalities. By acknowledging that work is characterised by divisions of labour, sociologists also examine causes of injury by the delineation and distribution of roles and associated elements (e.g. how many hour are worked, who has the power to direct others, how are records kept, etc.) (Lloyd, 2002: 13). Sociologists have also contributed to understanding how OHS regulations are derived and why and how OHS regulations are followed and enforced.

While there is general agreement among sociologists that taking a multifaceted approach to explaining the causes of occupational injuries is important, there is also a lively debate about exactly how all these factors operate as explanatory variables (see Dwyer, 1991; Nichols, 1997; Daykin and Doyal, 1999; Perrow, 1999; Hopkins, 1999; Lloyd, 2002). One of the more robust debates centres on the 'normal accidents' theory developed by the sociologist Perrow (1999). In his book *Normal Accidents*, the emphasis is on the complexities of organisations as explanations and predictors of accidents (Perrow, 1999). Based on examples such as Three Mile Island (TMI), aircraft crashes, marine accidents, dams, and nuclear weapons research, he observes that the accidents are not only 'unexpected, but are incomprehensible ... ' to those responsible for the safe operation of those systems. Perrow argues that 'in part, this is because in these human–machine systems the interactions literally cannot be seen' (1999: 9) and for these reasons, he considers 'normal accidents' and 'system accidents' to be synonymous. He defines two related dimensions—interactive complexity and loose/tight coupling—which he claims together determine a system's susceptibility to accidents. Interactive complexity refers to the presence of unexpected sequences of events in a system which is either not visible or not immediately comprehensible (Perrow, 1999). A tightly coupled system is one that is highly interdependent: each part of the system is tightly linked to many other parts and therefore a change in one part can rapidly affect the status of other parts. Tightly coupled systems respond quickly to perturbations, but this response may be disastrous. Loosely coupled or decoupled systems have fewer or looser links between parts and therefore are able to absorb failures or unplanned behaviour without destabilisation. Further, 'normal accident' theorists claim that accidents keep occurring because companies with major accident hazards, such as the process industries, have increasingly complex technology and tightly coupled processes, which result in situations where accidents happen because the learning process is handicapped (Körvers and Sonnemans, 2008: 1066).

Perrow's theory, however, has been criticised on various points. Hopkins (1999: 93) argues that it applies to only a very small category of accidents. Second, its concepts are ill-defined, leading to serious ambiguities about just what the theory covers. Third, in some crucial respects it appears to be wrong. Fourth, recent attempts to reformulate the theory by expanding it in various ways—by incorporating basic insights from organisational sociology along with the concepts of interest group and power—actually replace rather than expand the theory. Finally, the theory is of very limited policy relevance. Nonetheless, Perrow's normal accidents theory is useful in that it places occupational injuries and fatalities within the context of complex, dynamic organisations.

Sociologists have also made several broad observations regarding the dominant views of occupational injury. As we noted in chapter 2, sociologists have argued that injury is an inherent part of the social organisation of work and that the safety of workers is widely accorded a lower priority than productivity. Moreover, they have argued that the popular explanations of occupational injury can be broadly categorised as 'blaming the victim' rather than 'blaming the system'. Explanations that blame the victim emphasise the characteristics and behaviour of workers as the causes of injury, while explanations that blame the system focus on organisation and emphasise the pressures placed on workers to engage in unsafe behaviour. Victim-blaming explanations suggest that prevention strategies should focus on the behaviour of individual workers, for example by training and behaviour modification, while explanations that blame the system imply a need for organisational and technical changes.

Attributing personal characteristics of the worker to the causes of the injury or fatality is common; for example, in rail and shipping disasters workers' 'carelessness' is frequently cited as the cause of the disaster. Sociologists, among others, argue that these simplistic and often inaccurate judgments are unhelpful in investigating the root causes of a mishap, injury or fatality. To highlight the patterns of victim blaming, Hopkins and Palser (1984) identified four popular 'victim-blaming' explanations of injury, namely accident proneness, ignorance/carelessness, machismo and malingering. Accident proneness, as we have already noted, has been heavily discredited on both conceptual and methodological grounds. However, the absence of reliable scientific support has not dampened the enthusiasm of employers, insurance companies and some health professionals for the notion. Accusations of accident proneness have also been associated with social and racial prejudice and difficulties in diagnosing and treating certain forms of injury. This tendency is exemplified in allegations that immigrants are more likely to suffer injury at work. In Australia, the terms 'Mediterranean back', 'Greek back', and 'Lebanese back' were coined during the 1960s and 1970s to highlight a perceived high incidence of back strain among immigrant workers. Such crude stigmatisation ignored the concentration of these ethnic groups in heavy or hazardous work and evidence demonstrating that the perceived differences were unfounded (see, for instance, White, 1980; Morrissey and Jakubowicz, 1980, both cited in Quinlan, 1987).

Explanations that attribute occupational injury to workers' apathy, carelessness or ignorance have been even more pervasive. Hopkins and Palser (1984) found in their study of coal mining that highly visible, but relatively cheap, practices adopted by management in line with this explanation, such as safety training and the appointment of safety officers, had little discernible effect on injury rates when applied in isolation. A somewhat less common explanation attributes injury to machismo, or the culture of masculinity which sees safety as a 'feminine' concern. Again, Hopkins and Palser found no evidence to suggest that machismo was a significant cause of injury. Although workers do behave in ways that breach formal safety rules, the reasons for this are complex and arise from more than a simple desire to live out a stereotype of reckless masculinity (Hopkins, 1988).

A final, extreme form of victim-blaming attributes injury to malingering. It is argued that workers either deliberately inflict minor injuries on themselves or falsify injuries to escape work. The theme of malingering is propagated in several ways. One means is to deny that an injury is 'real' or to suggest that its effects have been grossly exaggerated by workers. This strategy is aided by rapid changes in technology and work processes which introduce new hazards and may injure workers for long periods before the injury is recognised and legitimated. The discussion of RSI in chapter 4 highlights this phenomenon.

The malingering theme may also be supported by the accusations that workers' compensation claims are exaggerated or fictitious, a common charge from employers, insurance companies and some medical practitioners. Hopkins and Palser (1987) report that managers in their study 'time and again' suggested that 50% of injury claims were 'fake', 'bodgie' or 'bogus'. However, when asked for specifics the managers quickly dropped the percentage. One manager could only think of one bogus case in the last year and another manager expressed the opinion that the figure of 50% usually claimed by mining managers was wrong and in reality the figure was closer to 10%. As many injuries in the mining industry are sprains, strains and back injuries which may be relatively easy to fake, Hopkins and Palser did accept that some reported injuries were fictitious. However, they pointed out that it could not be assumed that the number of such injuries was significant without further investigation. Evidence used by managers as evidence of malingering was clearly inconclusive. For example, a sharp increase in the reported injuries after the introduction of the accident pay provision in the relevant industrial award was used as evidence of malingering on the basis that compensation substantially reduced the cost of injury to workers. However, an equally plausible explanation is that prior to the introduction of the scheme workers with genuine injuries could not afford to take time off work due to the inadequacy of the compensation available. They may therefore have continued to work when, from a medical point of view, they should have taken time off.

A preoccupation with malingering detracts, often intentionally, from attempts to explain the broader patterns of occupational injury for which the explanation is clearly untenable. And, as Nichols (1997) has poignantly observed:

> those who complain loudest about such behaviour are generally less anxious to emphasize the degree to which workers—honest workers, insecure workers, and workers who are just short of funds—struggle on, and keep on struggling day after day. And this despite minor injuries, gradually deteriorating health, and even work-induced mental illness, none of which shows up on the official record of work injuries.

In many cases it is clearly unreasonable to attribute responsibility for injury to the worker involved. Hopkins (1988) provides the persuasive example of a 16-year-old apprentice who was ordered to enter a cooker in a Sydney manufacturing plant and burnt to death by an unexpected release of steam. Often poor equipment design is a major contributor to injury. Sociologists have also associated various forms of work organisation with higher injury rates, including those that encourage excessive work rates and those in which workers are de-skilled and their autonomy to make decisions about their own safety is heavily curtailed (Dwyer, 1991; Nichols, 1997). Sociologists commonly argue that changes to work organisation, technology and the working environment are more likely to have lasting impact on injury rates than efforts to change the behaviours of individual workers, a point that is supported by evidence indicating that prevention strategies based on individual behavioural change have achieved only limited success (Nichols, 1997; Landsbergis, 2003; Bohle et al., 2004; Johnstone and Quinlan, 2006; Takahashi et al., 2008).

Nichols (1997) presented an extensive and persuasive analysis of occupational injury in Britain from the 1950s until the 1990s. After examining the historical development of notions of injury causation, including various interpretations of the concept of social production, Nichols developed a theoretical position, derived from political economy, which focused on the manner in which injury is influenced by broad economic and political relations. From this perspective, he attempted to describe the factors that determine the organisational determinants of injury, for example by examining the impact of politics and economics on injury rates in the French and British car industries. He reviewed historical trends in injury rates within the British manufacturing industry between 1960 and 1985, and used them to evaluate the efficacy of government regulation through the Health and Safety at Work Act of 1974. Nichols's focus on political economy has drawn attention to the wider influence of government on injury and highlighted the apparent relationship between the laissez-faire political economy of Thatcherism, and the associated shift of political power away from labour, and a decline in safety in the early 1980s. He concluded that the decline in injury rates in the second half of the 1970s, which had apparently signified the success of the 1974 legislation, and the subsequent rise in injury during in the early 1980s are best understood in terms of changes in the relative strengths of capital and labour during the two periods.

This historical and political investigation was complemented by a cross-sectional analysis of the third British Workplace Industrial Relations Survey (WIRS3). The WIRS3, conducted in 1990, had an important feature that the preceding WIRS surveys had lacked—it collected data on injury at the level of the individual industrial establishment. From this large set of data, Nichols identified three broad, interdependent institutional features—small size of the employing establishment, lack of trade union representation and unilateral management control over health and safety matters— that combined to create a structure of worker vulnerability to injury. Nichols's (1997) careful and detailed analysis of injury in Britain and the social, political and economic structures that influence it has undoubtedly made a very important contribution to knowledge of the origins of industrial injury.

In a later analysis of the next generation of the WIRS surveys, Workplace Employee Relations Survey 1998 (WERS98), Robinson and Smallman (2006: 89) identified issues surrounding the management of OHS within the changing world of work. Adding to Nichols's earlier sociological inquiry, Robinson and Smallman (2006) investigated the association between OHS and key features of change—new forms of work organisation, work flexibility, workforce characteristics and OHS systems. Their central premise is that work flexibility, an important component in work-related injuries, is not only solely about hours worked, but when and where one works, how such work fits in with one's wider responsibilities and whether the compression or smaller number of hours worked intensifies the nature of work. Further, they and others note that multi-skilling is likely to be associated with higher levels of injury because these systems rely upon the recruitment of inexperienced labour that is rapidly trained to be multi-skilled and may consequently lack the safety awareness of workers who have completed traditional apprenticeships or similar training (Beck and Woolfson, 2000; Robinson and Smallman, 2006). The pressures of multitasking also imply neither sufficient time for adequate training nor for familiarisation with new technology or work processes, and stress and poor health may ensue (Brannen et al., 2001). Another important feature of their study is that more substantial changes to work organisation, in the form of team working, can be effective in reducing OHS risk and, ipso facto, injuries—as long as they are properly conceived, configured and supported. Where more progressive forms operate, as with semi-autonomous work teams, their safety record is better; however, where 'weaker' forms exist, workers are more susceptible to injuries and ill health. Further, Robinson and Smallman's (2006: 90) strongest finding is that: '…OHS is at its best in larger workplaces, implying that effective OHS management is in part an issue of resources and expertise, factors that may be in shorter supply in small and medium-sized enterprises'. This finding is supported by other research on OHS in the small business sector undertaken by sociologists such as Eakin and MacEachen (1998), Walters (2002) and Hasle et al., (2009). In summary, Robinson and Smallman (2006) concur with Nichols's earlier work and argue that the uncertain and complex context of today's world of work is mirrored in its impact on OHS.

Dwyer (1983, 1991) has also attempted to develop a general model of injury causation. Dwyer's (1991) model divided work into four analytically distinct categories, namely rewards, command, organisation and the individual-member. Dwyer concluded that the first three categories are socially constructed. The rewards level refers to the process by which the productive resources of the organisation (labour and capital) are brought together for a cost below the price received for their product. The command level refers to the active control taken by the employers, or the management as their agents, over the actions of workers. The organisational level refers to the control taken by employers or management over the coordination of work and the knowledge required to perform it. The final category, individual-member, consists of the autonomy that is left to individual workers after they accommodate the effects of the other three.

Dwyer (1991) contended that the level of dominance exerted by employers over rewards, command and organisation affects the causation of injury. Growing employer dominance of the organisational level leads to them increasingly controlling knowledge of productive processes, producing a trend towards de-skilling of the workforce. As a result, workers may lack the knowledge necessary to carry out their jobs safely because management has not made it available. Increasing dominance of the command level by employers lowers workers' control over the tasks allocated to them. Workers' actions are directed to such an extent that they may be required to perform tasks that they consciously recognise to be against their own interest.

Dwyer's research suggested that employer authoritarianism was a key method of inducing high production from dissatisfied workers and a major cause of injury. Highly authoritarian management may limit workers' ability to communicate effectively with each other, and inexact or poorly understood communication may lead to injury in dangerous environments. As their dominance of the rewards level grows, employers increasingly attempt to push wage costs down and link pay to productivity. Workers may try to increase their incomes by seeking overtime or shift penalties, production bonuses, danger money and so on. Where workers rely on bonuses to increase income, they are under pressure to work fast, which may lead them to avoid using safety devices such as goggles and gloves that slow work rates. To support this argument, Dwyer (1983) cited the results of a study of a Swedish ore mine in which the abolition of incentive payment programs was followed by a 95% fall in severe injuries and a 70% fall in less-severe injuries.

At the individual-member level, the autonomy of workers is constrained by employer dominance of the other levels. Dwyer concluded that the individual-member level, in isolation from the other levels, is unlikely to contribute to the production of occupational injury. He draws attention to the lack of evidence to validate individual explanations of injury such as accident proneness and to the limited success of prevention strategies aimed at an individual level. Dwyer's model is an interesting attempt to provide a systematic framework for research on occupational injury, but has at least one significant limitation. Although it attempts to provide a comprehensive model of injury in the workplace it does not systematically address the collective industrial actions of workers. It fails to fully explain, for example, why workers have not made more concerted demands for safer working conditions.

In chapter 2 we noted that some sociologists have used labour process theory as a framework to examine injury causation. The labour process perspective enables a more dynamic and integrated consideration of the way in which work organisation interacts with worker health. This approach is particularly sensitive to the conflict between management and workers over the control of work (McIntyre, 2005). The introduction of technology, for example, can be seen as a change in the labour process which includes aspects of class struggle and is not technologically determined, but rather is the result of a series of choices about the organisation of work which are contested and socially shaped (Willis, 1989).

Hopkins and Palser (1987) and later McIntyre (2005) provided a good example of labour process research on injury. McIntyre's (2005) study on occupational injury and illness among Australian State Transit bus operators illustrates that viewing occupational injury and illness as an outcome of the labour process can provide useful contextual insights into occupational injury. Under labour process theory, different and conflicting interests between labour and capital create an inherent power imbalance which in turn has a detrimental impact on the occupational safety and health of workers. In essence, he and others argue that the managerial prerogative to control the labour process poses a major impediment to the advancement of better workplace safety and health. However, for managers there is also the unresolved tension between trying to balance a duty of care with the demands of production and the need to extract surplus labour from their workforce (McIntrye, 2005: 67).

In Hopkins and Palser's (1987) labour process research, they examined factors that could account for the high levels of injury in NSW underground coal mines. While finding no evidence to support psychological explanations, they did find a positive association between injury levels and both mine size and the amount of roof support work done. The finding regarding roof support work indicated that adverse geological conditions did not have a direct effect on injuries, but rather these conditions necessitated more construction work which, in turn, generated a higher number of routine construction injuries. With regard to mine size, they argued that the higher level of bureaucracy in large mines contributed to injury through reduced worker autonomy. Greater job specification and control by management gave workers less latitude to make responsible decisions relating to safety, such as when to stop production for further roof support work. Higher specialisation and rationalisation of tasks made it difficult to maintain concentration. Workers were given little opportunity to contribute ideas about how working conditions could be altered to reduce injury rates.

These findings indicated that higher injury rates in some mines were not inevitable, but were directly attributable to decisions about the size of the working unit, the structure of control and the organisation of work in more hazardous operations, especially roof support. These factors were all aspects of work organisation over which management exerted considerable discretion and on which individual workers' behaviour could have little effect. Despite this, management promoted a view that 'accidents' were caused by apathy, carelessness and malingering and developed safety programs that emphasised the role of safety officers. Although these activities had little practical effect, their symbolic role was to obscure the need for more fundamental changes in the conditions of work (Hopkins and Palser, 1984). Elsewhere, in another analysis of the link between the labour process and injury, Hopkins and Palser (1984) argued that breaches of safety standards by coal miners did not arise from carelessness but either represented acquiescence to managerial pressure to break safety codes or 'an attempt to assert the miners' own informally agreed safety standards' (page 2). In essence, miners were resisting efforts to reduce their autonomy and increase management control.

While the research done by Hopkins and Palser (1984) and McIntyre (2005) has implications outside state transport and coal mining, it is important to acknowledge that in some industries there may be no direct association between bureaucratised management and occupational injury. Important examples are the self-employed and subcontractors. The combination of output-based payment and intense competition among subbies has long been seen as a source of dangerous practices in the building industry, for example in the construction and use of scaffolding. Similarly, a New South Wales government study of owner-drivers in the road transport industry found that excessive hours behind the wheel, speeding and other breaches constituted a major safety hazard (*Sydney Morning Herald*, 24 November 1984). While the heavy financial commitments and low returns of drivers were often noted, the role of the major transport companies in promoting rate cutting among owner-drivers was generally overlooked. The pressure upon subcontractors may spill over to employed drivers, especially those in small companies where union representation is absent, where incentive payments are made for additional tasks (such as loading) or where drivers are compromised by heavy debts (incurred previously as an owner-driver) that have been taken over by the company (and are deducted from wages). In a similar way, little public recognition was given to the scheduling, staffing and rostering policies of bus companies as explanations of the spate of horrific collisions that occurred during 1989 and 1990. The pronounced expansion of subcontracting and casualised employment in many industries during the last two decades can be expected to have had significant effects on the prevalence of occupational injury. When Mayhew and Quinlan (1999) interviewed workers in the Australian clothing industry, for example, they found that outworkers employed exclusively on piece rates reported more than three times as many injuries as factory-based workers employed on time-based earnings or a combination of time-based earnings and productivity bonuses.

To summarise, the sociological studies outlined here have extended our understanding of why and how occupational injuries occur and to whom. The sociological research on occupation injury, however, is scarce compared to the research generated by psychologists, ergonomists and safety engineers, and most of the major sociological studies in this area were undertaken at least a decade ago. Nevertheless, the sociological perspective can been found in research from other disciplines, reflecting the current multidisciplinary approach to OHS. Moreover, it is important to note that sociological research on occupational injury has significant limitations, as we have outlined in chapter 2. It has had a gender bias, dealing predominantly with male-dominated industries and subjecting the experience of male workers to more detailed examination than that of female workers. Although sociologists have made the valid observation that there has been far too much emphasis placed on individual factors in injury causation, they have too readily dispensed with this level of analysis. A comprehensive model of injury causation requires a recognition of the contribution of individual behaviour and a systematic means of assessing its importance relative to other factors in specific contexts. At the opposite end of the spectrum, sociologists have, with some notable exceptions (see Nichols, 1997), also neglected the role of state intervention in the OHS arena and especially the impact of different forms and levels of regulation.

Accident investigation models

While the discourse on occupational injury can be located within a number of key disciplines, each with its own strengths and weaknesses, analysing the multiple causes of occupational injury is also an important component. The different methods used to investigate the causes of injury, commonly known as accident investigation, afford the opportunity to understand the circumstances and cause of the injury or near miss in question (Burgoyne, 1993: 401). Investigations into the causes of injuries should therefore extract as much information as possible and apply a rigorous scientific sequence of inquiry, deduction, induction, validation and finalisation. Unfortunately, this procedure is often thought to be unduly costly, in time and money, in relation to the importance of the occasion and all too frequently abbreviated procedures are used instead in order to serve partisan interests and profits (Burgoyne, 1993: 401). Moreover, there is a tendency to attribute injury to bad luck or the hidden self-destructive urges of workers. As we have discussed earlier, the 'pure chance' explanation suggests that there is no discernible pattern in the events leading up to injury and that all workers are exposed to the same risk, and therefore injury can be attributed to the individual worker's 'bad luck'.

In response to these difficulties, there have been numerous accident investigation methods developed over the decades, as summarised by Katsakiori et al. (2009) below. Each new accident investigation model has endeavoured to overcome the limitations of previous ones. The evolution of accident investigation and causation models over time shows a shift from the sequence of events to the representation of the whole system (Katsakiori et al., 2009: 1008). In particular, there has been a gradual shift from searching for a single cause, to the recognition of multiple causes, such as organisational and management weaknesses and their interactions with the working activities.

Accident investigation methods have been mainly developed for use in major accidents in technologically complex systems and the question is whether or not the models used to investigate injuries can provide effective diagnostic capabilities (see Leclercq et al., 2007). As Katsakiori et al. (2009: 1014) note, this constitutes a limitation to their use. Katsakiori et al. (2009: 1014) add that although a set of plausible requirements for evaluating accident investigation methods can be established, it is important that these can be attributed to the underlying accident causation model. In other words, the requirements established should help us verify that a specific accident investigation method fulfils the principles of the specific accident causation model, or give evidence to the degree of alignment between them.

Table 3.4 Overview of accident investigation methods

Accident investigation method	Description
Fault tree analysis (FTA)	Developed in the early 1960s by the Bell Laboratories, it looks at an undesired event (an accident) and all the possible things that can contribute to the event are diagrammed as a tree in order to show logical connections and causes leading to a specified accident. FTA is more an analytical tool for establishing relations; it does not give the investigator any particular guidance for gathering the information.
Management oversight and risk tree (MORT)	MORT was developed in 1973 for the US Atomic Energy Commission (Johnson, 1980). In MORT, the accident is defined as an unwanted energy transfer because of inadequate energy barriers and/or controls. The method follows the energy transfer and deviation concepts. Fact finding aims at identifying hazardous forms of energy and deviations from the planned and normal production process and the MORT diagram is a logic tree (the accident being the top event).
Multilinear events sequencing (MES)	Developed by Ludwig Benner in the 1970s, MES is a charting technique, which shows events chronologically ordered on a time line. It is based on the view that an accident begins when a stable situation is disturbed. A series of events can then lead to an accident. The method distinguishes between actors, actions and events.
Systematic cause analysis technique (SCAT)	The International Loss Control Institute (ILCI) developed SCAT in the late 1980s. It has its roots in Heinrich's domino theory (1941) and its updated version by Bird (1974). SCAT is presented as a chart which contains five blocks corresponding to five stages in the accident causation process.
Causal tree method (CTM)	Leplat (1978) originally developed CTM in the late 1970s for the French Institut National de Recherche et de Sécurité (INRS). It belongs to the category of tree techniques and the basic idea is that accidents result from variations in or deviations from the usual process. There are four classes of variations: those related to the individual, the task, the equipment and the environment.

Accident investigation method	Description
Occupational Accident Research Unit (OARU)	Kjellén and Larsson (1981) developed OARU for the Occupational Accident Research Unit (OARU) of the Royal Institute of Technology in Stockholm. The method has two levels of reasoning: describing the accident sequence and finding the determining factors.
TRIPOD	TRIPOD was developed in the mid-1990s in a joint project by the University of Leiden (The Netherlands) and the University of Manchester (UK) for use in the oil industry (Wagenaar et al., 1994). TRIPOD follows Reason's accident causation model. The idea behind TRIPOD is that organisational failures are the main factors in accident causation.
Accident evolution and barrier function (AEB)	AEB was developed in 1991 for the Swedish Nuclear Power Inspectorate (SKI) and the Netherlands Institute for Advanced Study in the Humanities and Social Sciences (Svenson, 2000). The AEB approach is a stand-alone method and addresses, as a central concept, safety barriers and their functions. An accident is modelled as a series of interactions between human and technical systems.
Integrated safety investigation methodology (ISIM)	ISIM was developed in 1998 by the Transportation Safety Board (TSB) of Canada and it follows Reason's (1990) accident causation model (Ayeko, 2002). The method starts with the collection of information regarding personnel, tasks, equipment and environmental conditions involved in the occurrence in order to determine the sequence of events and identify underlying factors and unsafe conditions.
Norske Statesbaner (NSB)	NSB was developed in the early 2000s by the Norwegian State Railways (Norske Statesbaner—NSB) for the analysis of accidents in the Norwegian railway sector. The method integrates the approaches of both Reason (1997) and Hollnagel (2002) and focuses on human, technical and organisational interaction (Skriver et al., 2003).
Work accidents investigation technique (WAIT)	WAIT was developed by Jacinto and Aspinwall (2003). It integrates the theoretical approaches developed by Reason (1997) and Hollnagel (2002).
Health and Safety Executive (HSG245)	HSG245 was developed in 2004 by the Health and Safety Executive (HSE) in order to provide a workbook for employers, unions, safety representatives and safety professionals (HSE, 2004). It follows Reason's accident causation model.
Control change cause analysis (3CA)	3CA was developed by Kingston et al. (2007) and was originally developed as an adjunct to a cooperative project run by Humber Chemical Focus and the UK HSE in 2000. Although it does not follow a specific accident causation model, it can be considered as systemic because it covers the management system. The 3CA investigator views an accident/incident as a sequence of events in which unwanted changes occur.

Source: Katsakiori, P., Sakellaropoulos, G. and Manatakis, E. (2009), 'Towards an evaluation of accident investigation methods in terms of their alignment with accident causation models', *Safety Science*, 47(7): 1007–15.

The most commonly used accident investigation models are event-based accident models, such as forward sequences (as in FMEA or event trees) or backward ones (as in fault trees). These models explain accidents in terms of multiple events sequenced as a chain over time. The chains may be branching or there may be multiple chains synchronised using time or common events (Leveson, 2004: 241). Other relationships may be represented by the chain in addition to a chronological one, but any such relationship is almost always a direct, linear one. Leveson (2004) argues that as a consequence, event-based models encourage limited notions of causality—usually linear causality relationships are emphasised—and it is difficult to incorporate non-linear relationships, including feedback. In addition, some important causal factors are difficult to fit into simple event models. For example, studies have found that the most important factor in the occurrence of accidents is management commitment to safety and the basic safety culture in the organisation or industry (see, for example, Smallman and John, 2001). Event-based models are also poor at representing systemic accident factors such as structural deficiencies in the organisation, management deficiencies and flaws in the safety culture of the company or industry (Leveson, 2004).

Choosing the most appropriate accident investigation model from the variety offered is a daunting task, even for the most experienced OHS practitioners. Moreover, each model has its limitations. As Katsakiori et al., (2009: 1014) rightly conclude, since different models sometimes approach accidents in entirely different ways, methods linked to these models can provide us with only fragmentary information regarding the accident. It is therefore expected that using a combination of model–method pairs, rather than a single one, could provide a better and more reliable platform for the investigation and analysis of accidents.

Occupational injury data

The essential ingredient of injury investigation and causation is the collection and analysis of injury data. The data collection can take the form of a survey (which is typically a single event) or an injury surveillance. Injury surveillance is the ongoing collection, analysis, interpretation and dissemination of injury data (see Rivara and Thompson, 2000). Generally it involves keeping records on individual cases, assembling information from those records, analysing and interpreting this information, and reporting it to others; that is, employees, managers and directors, medical practitioners, government officials, etc. It is universally acknowledged that the collection and classification of injury data is vital for describing the epidemiology of injury and developing injury indicators, and for injury surveillance (Cryer, 2006). Reliable and valid collection and measurement of injury severity data is also important for both the meaningful monitoring of trends and to assist in classifying information to meet specific injury policy prevention and control needs (Davie et al., 2007: 3).

There are a number of issues, however, surrounding occupational injury data. How injury data is collected, compiled and used is complicated and subject to a variety of interpretations and frequent misinterpretations. For example, if one business or jurisdiction records a higher number of injuries and fatalities than another, this does not necessarily mean that the working environment is less safe; instead it may indicate that the injury data collection mechanisms are more robust. The accessibility and usefulness of workplace or government injury data is another major issue not only for employers, trade unions and policymakers, but also for researchers.

The main sources of injury data are: the workplace, medical emergency clinics or hospitals, compensation claims and OHS regulatory and coronial agencies. Injury data collected at the workplace is frequently categorised by the number of days lost (lost time injury frequency rates or LTIFRs). LTIFRs are calculated as the number of occurrences of injury divided by the total number of hours worked by all workers in the recording unit, for each one million hours worked: LTIFRs/total hours $\times$ 1 000 000 (refer to AS 1885.1, 1990, WorkSafe Australia National Standard). Calculating the number and costs of injury workers' compensation claims is not only based on the severity of the injury but also on the ability of the injured worker to return to work in either full capacity or limited capacity, as discussed in more detail in chapter 8.

Table 3.5 Injuries resulting in fatalities and lost time

Country	Fatalities	Fatalities rate per 100 000 workers	Accident rate per 100 000 workers
Australia	275	3.2	2434
New Zealand	61	3.5	2699
Norway	72	3.2	2446
Denmark	90	3.4	2561
China	73 615	10.5	8028
Spain	1177	8.9	6803
Sweden	77	1.9	1469
United Kingdom	225	0.8	632
United States	6821	5.2	3959

Source: Hamalainen, P. Takala, J. Saarela, K. (2006), 'Global estimates of occupational accidents', *Safety Science*, 44(2): 137–56.
Note: An 'accident' is counted if it leads to three days' absence from work.

While it is acknowledged that injury data represented as LTIs provides useful indicators, they reflect the results of *past actions* (Blewett, 1994; Bottomley, 1994; Green, 1994; Shaw, 1994; Hopkins, 1994; Shaw and Blewett, 1995b; Riedel et al., 2001; Coglianese, Nash and Olmstead, 2002). That is, there is often a time lag between action taken by an organisation to improve performance and any change in actual performance. Riedel et al. (2001) also noted that using absenteeism figures as a result of either an injury or illness as a measurement of OHS performance is only valid for hourly paid workforces and is a dichotomous measurement of 'on the job'. Further, the use of LTIs

'… overlooks the gradations of impairment of workers who are present' (Riedel et al., 2001). They argue instead that there is a critical need to better quantify the loss of value produced by employees (Riedel et al., 2001: 168). Kletz (1993: 409) also states that:

> Lost Time Accident figures have only limited value … If senior managers pay great attention to the LTA rate and nothing else they are sending out the message that they do not really know why accidents occur and what should be done and, if this is so, safety cannot be very important … we obviously need some measure of performance in order to show up trends and compare one plant with another but no one parameter is adequate.

In distilling the key criticisms of LTI indicators, Shaw (1994: 17) notes that typically LTIs measure failure and not success; are subject to random fluctuations; do not measure the incidence of occupational disease; may under-report (or over-report) injuries and may vary as a result of subtle differences in criteria; and are particularly limited for assessing the future risk of high-consequence, low-probability accidents. In essence, outcome indicators may hide potential risks; for example, having a low incidence of injury does not necessarily mean that adequate safety systems and controls are in place.

The other sources of injury data are hospitals, emergency clinics and general practices. These sources have had long-established injury surveillance systems of collecting, categorising and analysing injury data. Hospital injury surveillance systems have been used effectively to identify industrial sectors carrying high risk of severe injuries, as illustrated in a study by Baarts et al. (2000). Hospital injury surveillance systems are also useful in that there is to some extent international standardisation in which international comparisons can be made, as seen for example in the research by Feyer et al. (2001), Benavides et al. (2003) and Dollard et al. (2007). The data is frequently classified under generic categories, namely the severity and type of injury/injuries as well as the cause of the injury and biographical details of the injured person, although the reliability of the information elicited from these last two categories is questionable. Moreover, there is international agreement that the indicators and the data on which they are based should have the following characteristics:

- completeness and accuracy of source data
- ability to measure changes over time
- measurement that is practicable
- ready comprehensibility (see Pearce et al., 2005; Cryer et al., 2006: 5).

Both the nomenclature and statistical classification of injury data, however, has been the subject of ongoing discussion, debate and continual reviews (e.g. Beahler et al., 2000; Hong, 2005; Pearce et al., 2005; Cryer and Langley, 2006). In particular, there has been debate in the international community over which codes within the WHO International Classification of Diseases (ICD) injury classification are in fact injuries. Injury severity can be measured on a number of dimensions and as such there has also been a deal of discussion around what scales are appropriate to use to measure the severity of injuries. Historically the focus in the literature has been on measures of severity in terms of damage to the body that have been validated against mortality outcomes (see Osler et al., 1996; Pearce et al., 2005; Cryer and Langley, 2008; Davie et al., 2008; Wong and Leung, 2008). There have been a number of scales proposed over the past thirty years, most notably the Abbreviated Injury Scale (AIS) severity score developed by the Association for the Advancement of Automotive Medicine (AAAM) in 1971 (Olser et al., 1996; Stevenson et al., 2001). In response to the inherent weaknesses in AIS, such as the inability to provide an overall score for patients with multiple injuries, Dr Susan Baker in 1974 developed the Injury Severity Score (ISS). However, this scale also has its critics who argue that it provides a limited scope for descriptions and restricts the number of patient's injuries to less than three. In order to overcome these weaknesses, most injury classifications and injury severity scales are derivatives of WHO's International Classification of Disease codes (ICD codes) or combinations of AIS and ICISS (Davie et al., 2008: 250). One such example is the WHO International Classification of Diseases–based injury severity score (ICISS) which involves estimating the probability of death directly from ICD injury diagnoses by examining a large set of cases for which survival status is known. Although the majority of research on the development of ICISS has been based on data collected in trauma centres, the same techniques have been successfully applied to national population-level statistics using injury hospitalisation databases (Davie et al., 2008: 250).

Coronial records are frequently included in injury surveillance systems. Such records are a rich but often overlooked source of work-related fatality data. Most coronial data research is preoccupied with farming and work-related road fatalities, although there are exceptions. For example, in a study investigating the contribution of design to the occurrence of fatal work-related injuries in Australia, Driscoll et al. (2008) analysed injury fatality records held by the Australian National Coroners' Information System. For Driscoll et al. (2008: 209), using the Australian National Coroners' Information System (NCIS) was essential because:

> … it is the only source that covers all work-related fatal incidents, regardless of the employment status of the injured person and the setting of the incident. It is the only accessible source likely to have detailed information on many of the deaths of interest.

Another reason for utilising coronial records is that such datasets are more consistent compared to other published omnibus statistics, as illustrated in Feyer et al.'s (2001: 22) international comparative study on the extent, distribution and nature of fatal occupational injuries across New Zealand, Australia and the US. Their results showed that New Zealand had the highest average annual rate (4.9/100 000), Australia an intermediate rate (3.8/100 000) and the US the lowest rate (3.2/100 000) of fatal occupational injury. The authors argue that much of the difference between countries was accounted for by differences in industry distribution. In each country, male workers, older workers and those working in agriculture, forestry and fishing, mining and construction were consistently at higher risk. In their concluding remarks, Feyer et al., (2001: 27) argue that when examining occupational injury and fatalities, it is critical to have consistent, reliable datasets across comparable jurisdictions.

The data information sheets used as the basis for injury surveillance are frequently the same as those used for compensation claims and are often completed by the same medical practitioner. However, as discussed elsewhere in this book, the injury data depicted as compensation claims is unreliable as it does not represent the true numbers of work-related injuries and fatalities. The main reasons are that there is the significant problem of under-reporting, not all workers are eligible for compensation (e.g. self-employed workers) and some injuries are either not covered or it is difficult to establish a causal link between the injury and a work activity. Not only are workers' compensation agencies a source of injury data, but OHS government agencies also have a statutory duty to collect, analyse and summarise injury data as part of their annual reporting. The injuries listed by regulatory agencies are primarily those that have been brought to the attention of the agencies, and the datasets, therefore, represent at best regulatory investigations. That is, the injury data supplied by OHS regulatory agencies can only be used, with caution, to indicate possible trends in certain sectors or work activities.

In spite of the problems with the injury data from workers' compensation and OHS regulatory agencies, the use of this type of injury data as the basis of OHS research has been very popular for several reasons. First, as we have noted, occupational injury data has been used to highlight hazardous sectors as well as identify dangerous processes. Industries such as manufacturing, construction and transport have more registered work-related fatalities than other industries and therefore it is understandable that researchers are keen to examine ways of making the working environment safer. Second, as these industries account for the bulk of compensation claims, there are great economic and social incentives to target these industries with a view to lowering the compensation claims. Third, because such hazardous industries have a high profile, research funding to investigate these industries is often more available and more lucrative than is the case for less-hazardous industries.

However, studies that concentrate on hazardous industries with reportedly high injury rates have a number of drawbacks. It is often the case that high-risk industries contain some of the world's largest multinational companies, which have little in common with, say, small businesses. Therefore, as most industry studies have a 'large business' bias, there is a strong likelihood that their conclusions need to be treated with caution when applied to small workplaces. Another problem arises where there is a growth in particular industries, such as tourism and hospitality, where risks are less well known and OHS control measures are less developed (Stevens, 1999; Lentz et al., 1999; Quinlan et al., 2001; Quinlan and Bohle, 2004; Quinlan et al., 2006; Weil and Mallo, 2007; Quinlan and Bohle, 2008).

Another danger of using industry injury and fatality indices is that they can present an illusion of simplicity. For example, Mayhew and Quinlan's (1998) study of workers in the clothing, textile and footwear industry highlights the pitfalls of using government injury and illness statistics as a basis for definitive conclusions. Their study shows that workers in industries with a high incidence of precarious employment are likely to be under-represented in the workers' compensation claims and injury or illness data, even though they may be experiencing similarly high levels of injury and illness as so-called 'high-risk' industries. In concordance, Thomas (1990) states that in order to provide in-depth explanations for disparities in the injury rate among different types of businesses, researchers cannot rely on government injury data alone, but should incorporate a range of data sources.

Nonetheless, inter-industry and intra-industry comparisons of injury rates have been used to expose wider OHS policy deficiencies as well as to identify hazardous industries that can be targeted by OHS regulatory agencies for prevention and enforcement measures (see, for example, the Heads of Workplace Safety Authorities (2004) report on Falls Prevention in Construction and the New Zealand Department of Labour (2007) report on Investigation of Causative Factors Associated with Summertime Workplace Fatalities). Benefits of comparative industry studies are outlined in the US National Institute for Occupational Safety and Health report entitled Identifying High-Risk Small Business Industries:

> Given the limited Federal, State and local resources available in the United States for occupational health and safety, public and occupational health practitioners must focus prevention activities on industries that have the greatest need. Identifying and understanding the risks associated with such industries will also prove useful to employers, employees and insurers involved in small business. (NIOSH, 1999: 3)

In addition, datasets containing injury figures, such as the discontinued Australian Workplace Industrial Relations Survey (1989–) and the UK's Workplace Industrial Relations Survey (1980–) have been used in studies of OHS in small businesses. For example, using the Workplace Industrial Relations Survey data (1980–) Nichols et al. (1995) examined the relationship between the size of firms and injury rates in the British manufacturing sector. Their study shows that manual workers in the manufacturing sector experience a higher injury rate than those working in other industry sectors. However, they stressed that the high rate of injury among manual workers employed in small manufacturing companies was more likely to be a consequence of a lack of resources and the inability to maintain a healthy and safe environment—problems that larger companies are more able to minimise. In a similar British study on workplace injuries in small and large manufacturing workplaces between 1994–95 and 1995–96, Stevens notes that:

> The profile of risk of workplace injury in small, medium and large workplaces is not the same for different severity or nature of injury suffered by employed people. Differences in injury rates between smaller and larger workplaces will probably reflect their different cultures, mix of occupations at risk, and processes, as well as any genuine differences in risk attributable to the management of safety. However, the factors that help explain the profile of relative risk for the bulk of reportable injuries cannot explain the relatively high risk of fatal and serious injury in small workplaces. (1999: 4)

As we have repeatedly stated, injury databases are imperfect and rarely capture the contingent labour force employed in precarious employment. Moreover, as Kendell

(2006: 19) rightly argues, neither employers nor employees feel encouraged to classify a problem as an 'injury' unless it is obviously so or serious in nature, as to do so will trigger a cascade of events that may include an investigation by the OHS inspectorate. In spite of the problems inherent in the collection and analysis of reliable injury data, such databases are essential tools in highlighting OHS trends and in developing preventative strategies.

Injury occurrence among vulnerable workers

In considering occupational injuries it is important to consider particular groups within the workforce, such as women, indigenous peoples and migrants, who are disproportionately represented in the injury data and who may be characterised as disadvantaged (e.g. Quinlan and Mayhew, 2001; Tucker, 2002; Wickramasekera, 2002; Nossar, et al., 2003; McLaren et al., 2004; Loh and Richardson, 2004; Walter et al., 2004; Jamieson, 2005; Hannif and Lamm, 2005; Siddiqui, 2006; Berdahl and McQuillan, 2008). Since the points below are relevant to an examination of occupational disease we intend to provide an overview of the issue in relation to injury and disease in this chapter.

The first point that needs to be made is that, given the existence of labour market segmentation in Australia, New Zealand and elsewhere, the incidence of work-related injury and disease is not spread evenly between male and female workers, or between those indigenous to Australia and New Zealand and various overseas-born groupings (such as southern European, Middle Eastern, Pacific Islanders and, more recently, South-East Asian migrants). This is because occupational health risks vary significantly between different industries and occupations, as mentioned previously, and the occupational distribution of these groups also varies significantly. For example, the incidence of work-related injury and disease among a particular group of migrants will reflect the occupations within which they are most heavily concentrated. It is therefore hardly surprising that those migrants who are overly represented in heavy manual tasks in construction, steel making, manufacturing, cleaning services and transport within postwar Australia and New Zealand also suffer a high prevalence of back strain and other injuries normally associated with such tasks. The tendency for migrants, and especially particular groups of them, to enter dangerous, dirty and enervating jobs at the bottom of the occupational hierarchy is by no means unique to Australia or New Zealand but has been a common feature of migration which became especially prevalent in the postwar period (see Lever-Tracy and Quinlan, 1988).

Despite this ready explanation for the variations in injury rates between ethnic groups, there has been a tendency to reach for explanations which suggest that certain groups are injury prone or deliberately rorting the workers' compensation system. The value of these victim-blaming explanations appears to lie primarily in the ideological role they perform. They have served as a basis for discriminatory employment practices on the part of management, the climate of fear arising from which has undoubtedly affected worker behaviour and injury reporting (Abrahams et al., 2004). In chapter 8 we will point out how discrimination has been practised against migrants and women with regard to the workers' compensation system.

The incidence of injury and illness among migrants has also been attributed to non-work factors in a more subtle and apparently benevolent fashion. There is mounting evidence that the greater level of injury and illness among the foreign-worker population was associated with the greater physical and psychosocial workload in the jobs they typically occupied and the stress associated with a greater risk of unemployment (Oppen, 1988; McLaren et al., 2004; Loh and Richardson, 2004; McKay et al., 2006; Siddiqui, 2006; CARAM Asia, 2007; Tinghög et al., 2007; Anya, 2007; Lay et al., 2007; Passel, 2007; Mirsky, 2008; Wong, 2008; Presmanes, 2008; Quinlan and Bohle, 2008). Popular explanations prefer to emphasise factors such as 'migration strain' or 'cultural distance' which placed the blame on the general alienation of migrants from the host society. In Australia and New Zealand reference has also been made to language problems as a precipitator of injury through, for instance, inability to read a safety notice or communicate a verbal warning in an emergency situation. While we do not doubt that this is a real possibility, the only available evidence indicates that it is not a major cause of injury (Maitra and Siddiqui, 1999; McKay et al., 2006; McDowell et al., 2008). More importantly, management's interest in the problem has been somewhat contingent in Australia and New Zealand; its importance was played down in the early 1970s when labour was in short supply, it was sometimes used as a reason for excluding non-English-speaking migrants in the late 1970s when English-speaking workers were readily available, and at no time was it conceded that management had the primary responsibility to ensure that suitable remedial steps were taken in terms of multilingual safety material or the provision of English classes on the job.

Gender divisions within the labour market perhaps raise even more fundamental issues. Historically, the female workforce has been concentrated in a narrow band of generally low-paid occupations in light manufacturing (such as food processing and the making of clothes), clerical and other office work, retailing, and other service areas, such as nursing and call centres. As noted in chapter 1, it is therefore not surprising that the pattern of occupational injury and disease in the female workforce varies significantly from that of the male workforce (the overlapping contours of segmentation based on migration also need to recognised here). There is, however, a need to acknowledge some special features.

First, more than for migrants, gender has become intertwined with the health and safety characteristics of particular jobs. As Carson (1989) and later Mayhew and Quinlan (1998), McDiarmid et al. (2000), Fotinatos and Cooper (2005) and Jamieson (2005) noted, sexist distinctions become part of a cultural hegemony with regard to OHS and women are relegated to 'detailed, boring and stressful low-paid work, while the macho attitudes of men encourage risk taking'. In other words, sexism is used to define the character of jobs and this carries certain OHS implications. It helps to legitimate the exposure of men to more overt risks associated with heavy loads, dangerous machinery and hazardous substances, and women to a less-recognised range of risks associated with, for instance, the highly specific loads associated with precise, rapid and repetitive tasks, and the pressure associated with incentive-based work systems, such as piecework and subcontracting. The study undertaken by McDiarmid et al. (2000) on the gender disparities in carpal tunnel syndrome (CTS) is a good illustration. There are significant gender disparities in US CTS rates in which three times more women suffer from CTS than men. Yet McDiarmid et al. (2000: 23) observe that it is too simplistic to emphasise the role of gender attributes in this risk disparity, and instead the multifactoral causes of CTS and the sex segregation of women into jobs with high-risk tasks, may be obscuring the work-related contributions to CTS risk. Indeed, their findings show that men and women doing the same work tasks will have similar rates of CTS.

Second, gender differentiation on the basis of perceived risks was formalised, at least in part, by the establishment of separate regulatory standards in relation to the exposure of males and females (and children and youths) to particular OHS risks from the first enactments of OHS laws in the nineteenth century. In some instances, such as in relation to lead foundries, women were excluded altogether by legislation. Differential weight-lifting limits, amenities requirements and other constraints had the same effect in other workplaces, either leading to gender-specific task structures or simply reinforcing existing gender-based job descriptions. Overall, the effect was to limit the employment opportunities of women, to leave some jobs as the preserve of males and to legitimate the exposure of males to a higher level of OHS risk. Current OHS legislation in both Australia and New Zealand has removed all mention of specific OHS regulatory requirements specific to women workers such as weight limits. However, Jamieson (2005: 70) argues that while there should not be a return to the laws based upon women's difference from men, the legislative reforms nonetheless have re-enforced the status quo by which the health and safety of women workers have become invisible to the State (Jamieson 2001).

Third, the general preoccupation with single-incident traumatic injuries in OHS research, practice and regulations has meant that the OHS problems of women have tended to be neglected. Even those trying to construct a sociological explanation of occupational injury and disease have tended to concentrate on male-dominated work situations such as coal mining. There are a number of reasons why gender needs to be taken into account in the development of a comprehensive explanation of the origins of occupational injury and disease. One reason is that gender-based relations at the workplace may affect the social processes which give rise to OHS problems, as well as the processes by which they are recognised and addressed. For example, gender roles will influence the type of supervisory pressures that women are subjected to where, as is often the case, the management structure is male dominated. This problem is compounded where the women are migrants or where the union is also male dominated. Overbearing male supervisors may constitute a direct source of stress.

Moreover, women typically occupy the front-line positions in the company, such as reception and call centres, liaising between the organisation and the client. Research on call centres, in which the labour force is predominantly women and/or new migrants, indicates that lack of control and the monotonous tasks performed in most call centres are also associated with negative heath and safety outcomes. In a number of recent studies on the health and safety of call centre employees, the findings draw a strong association between the unconventional working hours and long shifts and tiredness, fatigue and musculoskeletal injuries (Sprigg, 2003; Cook and Burgess-Limerick, 2004; Hannif and

Lamm, 2005; Gavhed and Toomingas, 2007; Robinson and Morley, 2007; Rainnie et al., 2008; Hannif et al., 2008; Hunt, 2008). Severe emotional stress suffered by employees as a result of extreme time-pressure to complete set tasks and dealing with disgruntled and abusive members of the public was a perennial theme in the studies. Cook and Burgess-Limerick (2004) show in their study that muscular strain and fatigue were also widely experienced by call centre employees as a result of using the keyboard for data entry for extended periods of time and the long periods of sedentary work. Employees attributed the strain and discomfort to the absence of ergonomically designed workstations and the use of 'one-size-fits-all' equipment which the manager claimed were sufficient given the casual nature of the work (Cook and Burgess-Limerick, 2004).

There is also evidence to indicate that gender relations affect the reporting of injury by women either as a result of direct pressures at the workplace (see, for example, Williams and Quinlan, 1988: 590) or because women are often concentrated in forms of employment where reporting is low, for example in casual/part-time work, family labour (in retail, restaurants and other small businesses) and various forms of self-employment including home-based labour, such as outwork in the clothing trades (on lower reporting among part-time workers see, for example, Cherry, 1984: 519–24). Again these factors can be seen to be reinforced by formalised discrimination in terms of the access and entitlements of married women to workers' compensation, unemployment benefits and other forms of social security (see chapter 8).

In addition, there are occupational health hazards which are specific to women and which are not simply related to the peculiarities of their occupational distribution. Lucas (cited in Williams and Quinlan, 1988: 592) and others (McKenzie and Shaw, 1979; Abbe, 2005; Krieger et al., 2006) have noted that the sexual harassment of females in the workplace—a phenomenon significantly underestimated partly because of the avoidance strategies developed by women—must be seen as an OHS hazard. Lucas questioned the adequacy of prevailing occupational health and safety models which are unable to address the specific risks encountered by women in paid employment and argued that patriarchal relations at the workplace should be incorporated into such models. In their recent study which documented the prevalence of workplace abuse, sexual and racial harassment at work among predominantly black, Latino, and white female and male low-income union workers in the US, Krieger et al. (2006) found that overall 85% of the cohort reported exposure to at least one of these three social hazards and that exposure to all three reached 30% among black women. They argue that from an occupational health perspective the conceptualisation of and research on psychosocial hazards at work should not be limited solely to job strain or perception of position within a social hierarchy, but instead should be expanded to include consideration of workplace abuse, sexual harassment and racial discrimination (Krieger et al., 2006: 81). Consideration should also be given to the impact of pressures arising from working women's domestic roles which have changed little despite the additional burden of paid employment. The conflicts and tensions associated with the attempt to balance work and domestic roles is exacerbated by the paucity of workplace-based childcare facilities and the failure of unions to pursue this as a major industrial issue.

Further, rigidities in the division of domestic labour can and do have an important bearing on injury impacts.

Finally, just as allegedly male behavioural dispositions have given rise to specifically masculine victim-blaming explanations of occupational injury, so too have alleged female characteristics been used to question both the origins and legitimacy of occupational injuries suffered by women. For example, the more emotional temperament attributed to women has formed the basis for suggesting that their injury symptoms have been exaggerated, are entirely imaginary or result from a neurosis rather than a physiological origin. A good example of this gender stereotyping can be found in the debate surrounding RSI, which is discussed in detail in chapter 4.

In sum, historical contours of labour market segmentation must be considered when developing an explanation of the origins and incidence of occupational injury (and disease). We have only primarily dealt with two disadvantaged groups here, women and migrants, but similar consideration needs to be given to other groups, such as indigenous and disabled workers, who also face restricted employment options. It has also been suggested that gender relations in the workplace assume such significance that they deserve special attention in terms both of policy and the development of more comprehensive models of injury and disease causation and impact. This includes recognition of formal differentiation in terms of legislation and more subtle and complex processes which affect the origin, reporting and treatment of injury and disease. One aspect of this would be to consider the extent to which unions have historically represented the OHS claims of male workers more effectively than those of women, the implications of this discrimination and the extent to which it is being redressed.

Conclusion

The material reviewed in this chapter provides some important insights into the costs and causes of occupational injury and the different methods used to investigate the causes of injuries. It suggests that injuries are better understood as the culmination of a process of causation that may include industrial, organisational, technical and human error components. This process varies from workplace to workplace, but in any specific industry or workplace there is a probability of injury that arises largely from the organisation of work. Unfortunately, this process view of injury is undermined by the widespread use of the term 'accident', which implies that injuries are unexpected, chance events without a clear causal process.

The disciplines of ergonomics, safety engineering, psychology and sociology have made important, and unique, contributions to knowledge of the processes of injury causation. In addition, various psychiatric explanations have from time to time attributed injury to forms of psychopathology expressed by workers, and numerous unsubstantiated but popular explanations, such as machismo and malingering, have focused on the behaviours and dispositions of individual workers and so can be broadly labelled 'pseudo-psychological'. Table 3.6 summarises the sources of injury emphasised by each of these perspectives.

Table 3.6 Perspectives on occupational injury causation

	Emphasis placed on various sources of injury			
	Ergonomics and safety engineering	Work psychology	Psychiatry and pseudo-psychology	Industrial sociology
Physical environment	Primary	Limited	Nil	Limited
Individual behaviour	Moderate	Primary	Primary	Nil/minimal
Immediate organisational factors	Low/moderate	Moderate	Nil	Moderate
Broader organisational factors	Nil	Minimal	Nil	Primary
State	Nil	Nil	Nil	Low/moderate
Worker participation	Minimal	Low/moderate	Nil	High

The expert technical disciplines of ergonomics and safety engineering have similar and complementary perspectives that are principally concerned with minimising injury through effective design and modification of the physical environment, equipment and work processes. Their interventions play a vital role in minimising the hazards to which workers are exposed. However, they tend to treat workers as sophisticated components of the production system whose capacities and limitations must be taken into account in the design process in a similar way to those of other components. As a consequence the interventions designed by engineers and safety engineers frequently do not pay sufficient attention to broader social and organisational sources of injury.

While psychologists have traditionally devoted most effort to identifying the human characteristics, capacities and behaviours that contribute to injury, there is now a stronger recognition that these factors must be balanced against organisational determinants. Most contemporary work psychologists portray injury as a multi-determined event with a complex causal process. They also recognise that organisational factors can contribute to states such as fatigue, frustration and stress that may, in turn, promote unsafe behaviour. There is growing acceptance that all workers are susceptible to the organisational and environmental causes of injury and that effective prevention requires change at this level. Unfortunately, most psychological interventions still focus on changing individual behaviour and pay little attention to broader organisational and social determinants of injury.

Sociologists have made several significant contributions to the understanding of occupational injury. First, they have highlighted the limitations of explanations that focus attention exclusively on individual behaviour or a mechanistic and technical understanding of work processes. They have observed that victim-blaming explanations rarely have real explanatory value and noted that the continued popularity of such explanations is best understood in terms of their attractiveness to vested interest groups. Second, they have developed an alternative approach that emphasises structural characteristics of the workplace in injury causation, especially the complex social processes that flow from the competing interests of management and workers. They have argued that, far from being aberrant incidents, occupational injuries are embedded in the dominant modes of work organisation and strongly influenced by powerful social and political structures. Third, attempts to integrate such explanations into the labour process literature have provided a more historically dynamic explanation both of the origins of occupational injury and management responses to it. From this perspective, the links between the emergence of Taylorism, the rising prevalence of occupational injury and the development of work psychology in the early twentieth century can be identified and understood.

On the other hand, this critical sociological research is still at a relatively early stage of development and has several limitations, most notably a gender bias and a tendency to entirely discount the role of individual worker behaviour in injury causation. This may reflect an understandable attempt to balance the dominant focus on individual factors and the often unsophisticated application of work psychology by OHS practitioners. Nevertheless, while structural factors need to be emphasised, some account must be taken of the individual level in a comprehensive model of occupational injury. Further, as we amplify in chapter 5, sociologists and psychologists have much to gain from engaging in a constructive discourse in relation to health and safety issues.

We have also endeavoured to present an overview of various often complex injury data collection and analysis systems as well as the different methods used to investigate injuries. To the average person the acronyms used to denote injury surveillance systems and accident investigation methods can be daunting and very confusing. It is important to have a basic understanding of the different methods and to recognise that each injury surveillance system and accident investigation method has strengths and weakness. In addition, there is a strong gender bias in explanations of occupational injury. For several reasons, we have argued that consideration of gender should be incorporated into wider models of injury causation and incorporated in strategies for injury reduction. The special position of other disadvantaged groups also needs to be considered, particularly the various migrant groups that constitute a major component of the Australian workforce.

In conclusion, the available evidence on injury causation suggests that it cannot be adequately understood in terms of the individualised and technical explanations that are now dominant. There is strong consensus, at least theoretically, between the major disciplines that the social and organisational factors contributing to injury deserve much greater recognition. However, much has yet to be done before a systematic and comprehensive model of injury causation can be developed. These new theoretical insights must also be transferred into practice. While the importance of multidisciplinary practice is now more widely recognised, it is often implemented ineffectively. Most often, practitioners with one disciplinary background attempt to integrate insights from other disciplines into their own work, rather than pursuing the establishment of genuine multidisciplinary cooperation. The result is frequently the unsophisticated application of knowledge and techniques in relation to which the practitioner has little, if any, formal training.

There is little doubt that effective multidisciplinary practice faces many barriers. The breaking of ideological divisions between the contributing disciplines is itself problematic. However, knowledge regarding occupational injury is also subject to ideological manipulation and reinterpretation by powerful vested interest groups, a problem that will be drawn into sharp relief in the next chapter as we examine the debate over repetitive strain injury (RSI) in detail.

QUESTIONS FOR DISCUSSION

1   There are a number of costs associated with work-related injuries. Identify these costs and how they impact on the employee, the employer and the wider community.
2   To what extent can occupational injuries be attributed to the individual characteristics and behaviour of workers?
3   You have been asked to suggest means of reducing the level of back injuries among nurses in a major public hospital. What factors would you need to investigate as possible sources of these injuries?
4   Briefly outline the explanations of occupational injury provided by ergonomists and safety engineers, psychologists and sociologists.
5   In what ways does the gender division of labour affect the origins and incidence of occupational injury?

FURTHER READING

Dorman, P. (2000), 'The economics of safety, health, and well-being at work: an overview', *InFocus Program on SafeWork, International Labour Organisation,* The Evergreen State College, Olympia, Washington.

Glendon, I., Clarke, S.G. and McKenna, E.F. (2006), *Human Safety and Risk Management,* Taylor & Francis, Boca Raton, FL.

Hopkins, A. (2006), 'What are we to make of safe behaviour programs?', *Safety Science,* **44**: 583–97.

Kendall, N. (2006), *Management and Governance of Occupational Health and Safety in Five Countries (United Kingdom, United States, Finland, Canada, Australia),* National Occupational Health and Safety Advisory Committee: NOHSAC Technical Report 8, Wellington.

Mearns, K.J. and Yule, S. (2009), 'The role of national culture in determining safety performance: challenges for the global oil and gas industry', *Safety Science,* **47** (2009): 777–85.

Nichols, T. (1997), *The Sociology of Industrial Injury,* Mansell, London.

Kroemer, K.H.E. and Grandjean, E. (1997), *Fitting the Task to the Human: A Textbook of Occupational Ergonomics,* 5th edition, Taylor & Francis, London.

Sheehy, N.P. and Chapman, A.J. (1987), 'Industrial accidents', in Cooper, C.L. and Robertson, I.T. (eds) *International Review of Industrial and Organisational Psychology 1987,* John Wiley & Sons, Chichester, UK: 201–27.

4

Case study: work-related musculoskeletal injuries

Introduction

WORK-RELATED musculoskeletal injuries are one of the main causes of occupational injuries in Australia, New Zealand and overseas, affecting workers employed in all occupations who typically undertake strenuous and repetitive tasks (Punnett and Wegman, 2004; Driscoll et al., 2005). Both the ILO and the WHO note that the rate of musculoskeletal injuries has reached epidemic proportions, with no sign of declining (Luttmann et al., 2003). It is generally acknowledged that the rise in the number of work-related musculoskeletal injuries is a result of the increased exposure to workplace risk factors, more segmented and repetitive work, increased mechanisation, intensification of work, longer working hours and shifts in working practices towards the service and information sector (Boocock et al., 2006: 291). Musculoskeletal injuries typically occur when physical and psychosocial demands are too great, resulting in discomfort, pain or functional impairment and cause workers to suffer debilitating neck, shoulder and arm pain as well as lower-back pain (Luttmann et al., 2003; Tappin et al., 2008). The preferred generic term 'musculoskeletal injury' used by OHS and workers' compensation agencies in Australia, New Zealand and elsewhere incorporates a broad range of injuries and disorders, such as cumulative trauma disorder and repetitive strain injury (RSI) or occupational overuse syndromes (OOS), and covers a wide range of conditions that affect muscles, tendons, nerves, bones and joints (see, for example, the NZ *Injury Prevention, Rehabilitation, and Compensation Act, 2001* and the Australian Safety and Compensation Council *Compendium of Workers Compensation Statistics*, 2008c).

However, the definition, diagnosis, treatment and compensation of work-related musculoskeletal injuries have attracted a level of political and community attention rarely accorded to other workplace health and safety issues. The debate has been characterised by highly divergent views regarding the origins of the pain reported by workers and the means by which it should be managed. The conflict over work-related musculoskeletal injuries, particularly repetitive strain injuries, reflects genuine confusion about the aetiology of musculoskeletal injuries. The conflict has also been fuelled by the selective use and distortion of evidence by vested interest groups promoting their own objectives. Furthermore, work-related musculoskeletal injury is often described as a purely biomechanical problem that is best treated by ergonomic intervention (Cutlip et al., 2009). However, this view overlooks important industrial and social influences on its definition, development, impact and management.

This chapter has three objectives. The first is to examine the nature and history of work-related musculoskeletal injury and dispel some popular myths about it. The second is to describe the major disciplinary perspectives on the injury and examine the different solutions they promote. The third objective is to illustrate how vested interest groups have polarised the scientific debate regarding the origins of musculoskeletal injury and the ways that it should be managed. This discussion of the musculoskeletal injury debate illustrates how information can be selectively employed or actively distorted to serve the interests of different players in the health and safety arena, including workers, employers, insurers, politicians and health professionals. While there are numerous interventions employed to reduce the rate of work-related musculoskeletal injury, there are scant quality reviews of the level of expertise involved in implementing the interventions and the methods used.

Defining musculoskeletal injury

While the terms 'work-related musculoskeletal injury' (WMSI) and 'work-related musculoskeletal disorder' (WMSD) are commonly used as generic phrases to refer to a variety of diseases or injuries to bones, muscles, tendons, joints, nerves and blood vessels that may occur in the workplace, the terms are somewhat ambiguous. For example, the 2004 report from the American Academy of Orthopaedic Surgeons and American Association of Orthopaedic Surgeons defines MSD no more specifically than the '... loss of the sense of well being in a body part'. Other vague catch-all terms used to describe diseases and injuries that may occur in the workplace include: cumulative trauma disorder, repetitive stress disorder, repetitive stress injury and work-related disorder. Boocock et al. (2009: 296) point out that while musculoskeletal injury appears to have become the preferred nomenclature, unlike other terms it precludes assumptions about possible causative factors. Further, grouping divergent pathologies into a single term has caused more confusion among employers, employees, healthcare providers, insurers and policymakers, particularly when dealing with workers' compensation claims and maintaining injury surveillance databases. To add to the confusion, the different disciplinary perspectives and the competing interests of the employers, employees and the state have often worked against developing a generally agreed definition for musculoskeletal injury or disorder (see Luttmann et al., 2003; Boocock et al., 2009; Karjalainen et al., 2009).

Another inherent problem in defining musculoskeletal injury or musculoskeletal disorder is the way in which the terms 'injury' and 'disorder' appear to be interchangeable (see Lötters and Burdorf, 2006). There are nonetheless distinctions in which onset of an injury is sudden while a disorder is a gradual progression, mediated by some pathogen or pre-pathological progression. Workplace musculoskeletal injuries can also be broadly divided into two categories: (1) idiopathic and (2) traumatic. On one hand, the idiopathic injuries resulting in the biomechanical degradation of some part of the body cannot be assigned to a specific act or incident (although they can be confounded by other factors) (Kumar, 2001: 20). The fact that it is difficult to link the disorder with a specific incident has enormous ramifications and complicates workers' compensation claim outcomes, as outlined later in the chapter. The traumatic injuries, on the other hand, can be clearly associated with an incident or an action. Since idiopathic injuries are not assignable to any factor, their further differentiation into subcategories is difficult. However, the traumatic injury category is an assembly of a variety of mechanisms through which injuries occur. Among these are: (a) overexertion, (b) sudden imbalance, (c) pulling apart, (d) crushing, (e) impact, (f) slip and fall, (g) cut, (h) abrasion and laceration, etc. (Kumar, 2001: 20). In both of the two main categories and in all subcategories, a dominance of biomechanical factors is obvious. In short, in spite of the differences between 'injury' and 'disorder', the universal term 'musculoskeletal injury' has been adopted by workers' compensation agencies in Australia and New Zealand and, in order to avoid confusion, is the term used most frequently in this chapter.

A term associated with musculoskeletal injury that requires some explanation and illustrates how it is often difficult to classify injuries is repetitive strain injury (RSI) or as it is known in New Zealand, 'occupational overuse syndrome' (OOS). RSI is widely used as an umbrella term which encompasses tendon-related disorders (such as tenosynovitis, epicondylitis and tendinitis), peripheral-nerve entrapment (such as carpel tunnel syndrome and radial tunnel syndrome), neurovascular/vascular disorders (such as hand–arm vibration syndrome) and joint/joint-capsule disorders (such as bursitis and synovitis) (Yassi, 1997; Cole et al., 2005). Unfortunately, even the causes of some of the well-defined disorders, such as carpal tunnel syndrome and tenosynovitis, are unclear and several are known to have causes outside the work environment (Ferguson, 1984). However, controversy has really centred on the existence or otherwise of an unclearly defined disorder that has been included in injury checklists as 'RSI—other' or 'RSI—not further specified' (Mullaly and Grigg, 1988). Sufferers in this category report aching, weakness and tenderness of muscles without observable signs of injury (Ferguson, 1984; Higgs and Mackinnon, 1995; Barbe and Barr, 2006). Mullaly and Grigg (1988) noted that RSI proponents tend to use the umbrella definition of RSI, while those who question its medical existence use the term narrowly to refer to the less-defined disorder. As Ferguson (1984) noted, compensation cases have been reported in disease categories, such as 'synovitis, bursitis, and tenosynovitis' and 'other diseases of the musculoskeletal system, and connective tissue', and injury categories, such as 'sprains and strains'. McDermott (1986) argues that terms such as repetitive strain injury are unsatisfactory labels for several reasons. First, they imply that an injury has been caused by repetitive movement when for many workers the condition is induced by a static muscle load. Second, it is not clear whether 'strain' is the cause of the condition. Third, no injury or abnormality is apparent on clinical examination in many cases. The shortcomings of the label have led to a search for alternatives, probably the most accepted of which in Australia and New Zealand have been 'occupational overuse syndrome' and 'regional pain syndrome'. Unfortunately, these labels have also proven to be controversial and have not received widespread acceptance, especially in the general community where RSI is readily recognised.

The lack of suitable operational definitions for work-related musculoskeletal injuries has two major and related implications—namely, classification difficulties and the ability to access workers' compensation. First, as discussed in the previous chapter, injury surveillance databases are plagued by inaccuracies and more specifically have inherently poor classifications, including those for musculoskeletal injury, which creates major problems for researchers. These problems are not confined to Australian and New Zealand injury surveillance databases but can also be found in other countries. For example, although the UK Health and Safety Executive is reliant on the Labour Force Survey as their single most comprehensively reported data source for information about work-related illness and workplace accidents, the agency recognises the significant limitations in the methods and the classifications used to ascertain musculoskeletal injury (Gerr, 2008; Palmer et al., 2008). Second, the ambiguity around the definition and diagnosis of work-related musculoskeletal injury has often led to problems in understanding both the causative factors and the most effective strategies for prevention (Boocock et al., 2009: 296). In particular, this ambiguity has the effect of introducing doubt over whether or not a musculoskeletal injury is work-related, and in turn can jeopardise the worker's ability to obtain workers' compensation. As we outline in chapter 8, establishing the link between work activities and a musculoskeletal injury is often contentious with the burden of proof left to the worker. In New Zealand, for example, most musculoskeletal injuries were defined as 'diffuse muscle conditions' rather than 'accidents' and therefore under the previous legislation sufferers were not eligible for compensation because injuries, and not illnesses, were compensable (Wigley, 1992; Driscoll et al., 2004). There is evidence to show that workers in precarious employment suffering from work-related musculoskeletal injuries are also unlikely to seek or obtain compensation (Quinlan and Mayhew, 1999; Fan et al., 2006). As Lippel (2006: 251) states:

> Recognition of occupational disease claims is far more problematic, particularly for multiple-job holders who have, either simultaneously or over a period of years, been exposed to risks while there are holding various forms of employment—some of which are covered and others are not.

In spite of the ongoing debates over defining and diagnosing work-related musculoskeletal injuries, it is still generally accepted that the term describes a wide range of inflammatory and degenerative injuries and disorders resulting in pain and functional impairment (Tappin et al., 2008). Moreover, the relationship between the performance of work and musculoskeletal injuries is now well documented (Buckle and Devereux, 2002; Plouvier et al., 2008; Boocock et al., 2007; Boocock et al., 2009). It is this relationship between performance of work and musculoskeletal injuries and how the different disciplines view musculoskeletal injuries which we will now turn our attention to.

Explanations of musculoskeletal injuries

As we have observed, 'work-related musculoskeletal injury' is not a neutral term and therefore can be viewed in a number of different ways. Moreover, acknowledging the different disciplinary constructs of work-related musculoskeletal injury is important as it has implications for the way the injury is treated, the process of rehabilitation and the likelihood of obtaining compensation. In this section we shall focus on the more dominant explanations—namely the medical, ergonomic and sociological explanations. However, before we do so, comment needs to be made about how work-related musculoskeletal injuries have been viewed and the ensuing debate that has taken place over the past few decades.

Although often portrayed as a modern epidemic there are good grounds for believing work-related musculoskeletal injury have been a serious but under-reported OHS problem for centuries. Indeed, in his pioneering book published in the early eighteenth century, Ramazzini (1964, reprint) describes an injury among notaries that sounds remarkably like RSI and his suggestions as to its causes are prescient. Tenosynovitis was first reported in 1825 (McDermot, 1986). Work-related musculoskeletal injuries, including overuse injuries, have been regularly reported in the UK for well over a century, for example documented in a paper on 'telegraphist's cramp' in *The Lancet* in 1875, and reports of other overuse injuries, such as 'beat knee' of British low-seam coalminers, were well documented in the *British Medical Journal* from 1882 onwards (Thun et al., 1987). In fact, papers on overuse injuries have appeared regularly in international medical journals since that time. The different labels given to repetition injuries include 'housemaid's knee'; 'telegraphist's cramp', 'packer's wrist', 'writer's cramp', 'Ericsson's arm' and 'process worker's arm' (Quintner, 1991; Willis, 1986: 212). It is also interesting to note that as early as 1925 the British Industrial Fatigue Research Board recommended rest breaks for workers involved in repetitive work. More detailed accounts of the history of overuse injuries in Australia and overseas are provided in the NOHSC report on RSI (NOHSC, 1986) and by Quintner (1991). The historical evidence is convincing enough to have led a prominent occupational physician, Professor David Ferguson, to conclude in 1984 that, despite dramatic increases in the reporting of RSI in Australia in the 1980s, the injury was probably a longstanding endemic rather than an epidemic.

While Ferguson's assessment is accurate, the dramatic rise in the number of compensation claims for work-related musculoskeletal injuries and disorders, particularly RSI, in Australia and New Zealand during the 1980s and early 1990s fuelled a widespread belief that such injuries were an 'epidemic'. The increased rate of compensation claims gave rise to the stigmatising appellation 'kangaroo paw'. In New Zealand, RSI or occupational overuse syndrome was viewed as a 'women's syndrome' because, as in Australia, many of the claimants were women clerical workers employed in the public service or finance sector (Taylor, 2005). The women's movement in both Australia and New Zealand, including groups such as the Women's Repetition Injury Support Team (WRIST) (Reilly, 1995), also identified RSI as an important issue of gender inequality. These influences, accompanied by changes in legislation, combined to make occupational health and safety an important industrial relations issue. At the same time, economic changes increased the prominence of RSI (Willis, 1986). High unemployment meant less mobility between jobs, effectively thwarting a traditional blue-collar response to repetitive work, which had been to escape by changing jobs. The rate and duration of female participation in the paid workforce also increased, encouraging a sharper focus on occupational health matters associated with women's work. Simultaneously, the rapid introduction of new technology changed the sexual and ethnic mix of RSI victims. For example, keyboard technology was rapidly introduced into male and traditionally strongly unionised occupations such as the printing trade, and into white-collar clerical workplaces such as the public service. These groups wield significant industrial power and express their concerns articulately. Consequently, it was much more difficult to pass off the injury as malingering than it was when the victims were predominantly migrant workers.

Interestingly the belief that there was an epidemic of RSI cases was largely confined to industrialised countries. In her study on the rise and fall of the RSI epidemic in the 1980s and 1990s, MacEachen (2004) argues that RSI might have declined, not simply in the context of tighter legislation, better ergonomic work conditions and improved labour relations, but also through being controlled or managed out of the workplace in different ways. That is, the strategies used by managers reflected their views of RSI, namely that workplace aches and pains were considered a relatively mundane problem located in a type of worker rather than in a type of physical work environment. MacEachen (2004: 509) concluded that these practices of controlling RSI were '... the minutiae of occupational health relations; they become apparent not in policy or stated ideals and objectives of organisations, but in the governing rationalities of managers'.

In his critique of the Australian experience, Awerbuch (2004: 418) also noted that at one time or another many physical factors were mooted as causal of the Australian RSI epidemic, but not a single controlled scientific study was ever published demonstrating that correction of any notional factor in a workplace setting made a difference to the number of reports of arm pain. Indeed, Awerbuch (2004: 418) highlighted the fact that millions of dollars were spent on workstation redesign, ergonomic furniture and keyboards, functional capacity evaluations, physical therapies, ill-conceived surgery and rehabilitation of workers with no evidence of physical injury; safe hourly keystroke rates were prescribed, rest breaks implemented and job rotation and multi-skilling were introduced. Yet to this day a level of repetitive human activity deemed to be physically harmful, if indeed such a level exists, remains undefined and, indeed, unidentified. As Awerbuch, (2004: 418) concluded: 'The Australian RSI epidemic burnt out not because any one notional cause or series of causes was identified and successfully addressed. It burnt out because in the end doctors stopped certifying as physically injured large numbers of uninjured workers'.

To complicate the matter further, workers' compensation statistics in Australia and New Zealand do not provide an adequate picture of the incidence of work-related musculoskeletal injuries, including RSI. The first problem is that RSI was not treated as a separate injury category for workers' compensation purposes. The majority of cases appeared to fall into five disease categories, but the number of cases reported in other categories is unknown (NOHSC, 1986; Australian Safety and Compensation Council, 2008). Moreover, many of the muscle, ligament and other soft tissue problems reported in these categories were unrelated to RSI. Reported statistics were consequently approximations, generally based on the categories into which the majority of RSI claims were believed to be classified. A second major problem is that workers' compensation statistics excluded the self-employed, Commonwealth employees, casual employees, workers who took fewer than three days off work (in NSW) and eligible workers who did not make a claim.

Finally, there is considerable widespread under-reporting of RSI and musculoskeletal injuries in general. Under-reporting musculoskeletal injuries or disorders has economic implications for both employees and employer—namely cost shifting from workers' compensation to employees and private sector insurers, productivity losses, and increased rates of 'unexplained' turnover of experienced, trained workers (Morse et al., 2005: 48). In an analysis of seven years of workers' compensation and physician reporting data, Morse et al., (2005: 48) maintains that there is a high degree of under-reporting of upper extremity musculoskeletal injuries and disorders. An important inference from their findings is that most injured workers with musculoskeletal injuries and disorders choose not to pursue workers' compensation claims, but instead seek treatment for their injuries on a private basis. Their research also shows that workers tend not to inform employers of their condition. This perspective contrasts sharply with the recent assertion that there is a 'moral hazard' from workers' compensation insurance that results in applications for benefits from workers who do not in fact have work-related musculoskeletal injuries and disorders, or makes employees in high-insurance-benefit states less likely to work safely. The bulk of employees with these injuries, however, appear to be reluctant to enter, much less take advantage of, the workers' compensation insurance system (Morse, 2005: 49).

Medical and ergonomic explanations

Physicians and ergonomists generally view the causes of musculoskeletal injury in similar ways; the study of the biomechanical relationship between workers and their working environment is central to medical and ergonomic explanations of musculoskeletal injury. The focus is primarily upon the exposure of biomechanical factors that lead to overloading of particular muscle groups and ultimately produce pain and injury (see Higgs and Mackinnon, 1995; Yassi, 1997). The introduction of new technology is generally identified as a major factor responsible for the recent rise in the incidence of musculoskeletal injury, particularly lower-back pain and RSI. It is argued that the expansion of mechanised and partly automated processes has often led to lighter physical work, but has required increased regularity of physical movement and has concentrated workloads in very specific parts of the body (McDermott, 1986). These changes, combined with poorly designed equipment and inappropriate work practices, are believed by many ergonomists and medical practitioners to produce muscular strain and injury. The importance of a limited range of psychosocial factors in the causal process is often recognised, although the mechanisms through which they contribute to injury are rarely specified. In fact, the pathological process through which strain may produce injury remains very unclear (American Academy of Orthopaedic Surgeons, 2009; Karjalainen et al., 2009), although detailed explanations have been proposed in respected medical and ergonomic journals, such as the *Annual Review of Medicine and Economics* (Higgs and Mackinnon, 1995; Kumar, 2001).

Biomechanical research and analysis can be conducted on multiple levels, from the molecular to the tissue and organ levels (Garg and Kapellusch, 2009). There is also a wide range of variables that constitute biomechanical factors—for example, heavy manual work, exposure to vibration and poor ergonomically designed sitting arrangements have all been reported as associated with lower-back pain injury. Biomechanical research focuses on posture required from workers, the types of movement they must perform, the physical forces they must exert to perform movements, the frequency of repetitive movements and the bodily locations where workloads are concentrated. Biomechanical research has also been useful in determining the long-term effects on workers' health. For example, in a recent study on the effects of exposure to long-term work-related biomechanical strains of French workers, Plouvier et al. (2008) concluded that there is a high probability that lower-back pain can be related to a workers' past occupational history. In particular, they found that handling heavy loads over a long period of time and years of driving are more closely associated with lower-back pain in later years (Plouvier et al., 2008: 273).

Research on VDU operators provides another good example. Observation has indicated that these workers may perform well in excess of 80 000 key strokes per day and that the workload is heavily concentrated on the arms and shoulders (McDermott, 1986). While each keystroke requires little effort, it is suspected that the high-speed movements repeated over many hours cause fatigue and ultimately RSI. Ergonomic assessment has shown that certain types of movement and postural positions are associated with RSI in these circumstances and these findings have led to investigation of the potential for poor computer workstation design to contribute to injury. This work has identified three critical operator–workstation interfaces: between the hand and keyboard, between the body and the chair, and between the eye and the screen and other documents. If any of these relationships is not optimal, stressful posture may result. However, it was clear very early on that equipment design was not the only source of RSI. Consideration had to be given to other demands of the job, especially the volume and intensity of work. In general, the attention of medical and ergonomic researchers has been confined to these two sets of factors: the physical relationship between workers and equipment and the organisation of work tasks.

Despite having relatively limited systematic research to support it, the medical/ ergonomic model has dominated the management of musculoskeletal injury from the start. Preventative strategies have predictably concentrated upon biomechanical problems and work organisation. They have usually entailed the introduction of ergonomic equipment designed to meet standards concerning the most effective physical and spatial relationships between workers and their equipment. Changes to work organisation have often been recommended to complement ergonomic interventions, generally including a combination of some of the following measures: alternation of repetitive and non-repetitive work, rest breaks and exercise at regular intervals, reductions in work rates and abolition of production incentives. More innovative practitioners and researchers have also actively involved shop-floor workers in participatory ergonomic redesign processes, achieving considerable improvements in injury rates (Cohen, 1996; Haukka et al., 2008).

In VDU work, ergonomic design of computer workstations and reorganisation of work have generally been recommended to alleviate the problem. Solutions often prescribed have included providing ergonomic furniture, introducing 10-minute rest breaks each hour, limiting key stroke rates (usually to less than 10 000 strokes per hour), limiting keyboard work to less than four or five hours a day and dispensing with incentive payment systems. Ergonomically designed equipment is often introduced as well. Workstations are designed to optimise the spatial and optical relationship between the chair, desk, monitor, keyboard, source document and other components. These designs should allow for differences in physical size between workers, which is usually achieved by the provision of a range of adjustments to the chair and other equipment. Ideally, but less frequently in practice, consideration should be given to environmental factors such as lighting and glare levels, noise levels and temperature control. Unfortunately, some organisations invested in ergonomic equipment and task redesign only to find that the rate of workers' compensation claims stabilised or even continued to increase (Kiesler and Finholt, 1988; NOHSC, 1986). Possible reasons for this lack of success will become apparent as we examine the perspectives offered by other disciplines.

In addition to preventative practices, medical practitioners have employed an extensive range of treatments for musculoskeletal injury, including rest, immobilisation, exercise, hypnosis, relaxation, counselling, work modification, electrical nerve stimulation, physiotherapy, drug therapy and surgery (McDermott, 1986; NOHSC, 1986; Yassi, 1997; Foye et al., 2007). Browne and his colleagues (1984) outline a treatment program based on the stage of development the RSI has reached. At Stage 1 they consider there is a high probability of reversing the condition and recommend modification of equipment, changes to work organisation and monitoring of the worker's condition. At Stages 2 and 3 they recommend that the worker be rested from work until symptoms subside. Where RSI is advanced, and the worker is unable to resume work, they recommend commencement of symptomatic medical treatment, which may include a selection of the treatments listed above. Despite attempts like this one to systematise the selection of treatments, the diversity of the treatment strategies employed by medical practitioners suggests they have had difficulty identifying effective methods and have engaged in a considerable degree of experimentation. Evidence from a 'phone-in' conducted for RSI sufferers supports this impression (Task Force Report, 1985). When asked which of a list of treatments helped them the most, the most frequent response was 'none at all' (reported by over one-third of callers), followed by 'rest'. Typically, only a small proportion (approximately 20%) of sufferers who had received other treatments reported them to be 'most effective'.

While medical physicians and ergonomists have been at the forefront of devising preventative practices and a range of treatments for musculoskeletal injury, medical physicians in particular have been criticised over their inconsistent diagnoses of musculoskeletal injuries and resistance by some physicians to establish a link between the patient's injury and his or her work activities (see Panagos et al., 2007). The history of workers' compensation is littered with examples of workers being denied workers' compensation for work-related musculoskeletal injury in which the medical profession have played a major role as assessors for workers' compensation agencies. However, as mentioned elsewhere in the book, physicians are often placed in an invidious position between the worker, the employer and the compensation agency while at the same time having to operate within the constraints of the continually changing terminology and regulations pursuant under compensation legislation which dictate how musculoskeletal injury will be defined and under what circumstances the injured worker will or will not be compensated (Rennie, 1995; Campbell, 1996; Driscoll et al., 2004). In addition, medical physicians have often been called on to represent different conflicting interests of the workers or employers and/or the workers' compensation agencies in the diagnosis and rehabilitation of musculoskeletal injuries, which has in many instances resulted in bitter disputes (Levenstein, 2008). In response, a number of medical associations have drafted guidelines for non-treating doctors who perform medical assessments of patients for compensation agencies. Support groups for sufferers of musculoskeletal injury have also been established with the aim of putting pressure on both the medical fraternity and the government and their agencies to act ethically and to provide fair compensation and adequate rehabilitation.

The medical criteria used to diagnose work-related musculoskeletal injuries or disorders, particularly RSI, have also been criticised. Spillane in particular disputes the medical/ergonomic model of RSI, preferring a pain-patient model and arguing that the management and treatment of RSI has amounted to a medicalising of work behaviour (Spillane and Deves, 1987; Spillane, 2008). He argues that RSI represents an example of the progressive medicalisation of work behaviour in which notions of 'illness', 'treatment' and 'patienthood' figure prominently. He (2008: 94) concludes:

> The legally sanctioned use of the medical model in Australian working life has had unfortunate consequences. By medicalising conflicts in work relations, constructive work reform has given way to therapeutic paternalism which replaces moral conflicts with medical 'conditions' frequently 'diagnosed' in the absence of signs. Two consequences are the increasing power of medical practitioners to determine who is healthy and who is ill, and the increased dependency of those who adopt or are placed in the role of patient.

While the debate within medical discourse over diagnosis of musculoskeletal injuries and disorders and the link between musculoskeletal injuries such as RSI or OOS and work activities may appear to have subsided, it has not vanished by any means. In their report, Work Related Gradual Process, Disease or Infection (2005), the Ministerial Advisory Panel, noted that that:

> … many claimants have been denied cover because of their inability to prove they have suffered physical injuries notwithstanding the fact they have been disabled by reason of their work. This problem is perhaps best highlighted by reference to three groups in our community, namely: those who suffer regional pain syndrome (RPS) which is a type of condition that is more commonly known to fall under the umbrella term of occupational overuse syndrome (OOS); those who suffer multiple chemical sensitivity (MCS); and those who suffer serious injuries and illnesses caused by stress (2005: 25).

Yet over the past decade there have been a number of systematic reviews of more than 6000 studies all of which have established that there are reliable relationships between workplace characteristics and work-related musculoskeletal injury or disorders (for example, see Westgaard and Winkel, 1997; Bernard, 1997; Karsh, 2006; Boocock et al., 2007; Boocock et al., 2009). Examining musculoskeletal disorders, the many reviews have focused chiefly on disorders of the neck, shoulder, arm and wrist. It was found that these disorders were convincingly linked to work factors including repetition, forceful movement and posture, or a combination of the three. The evidence was persuasive enough for Linda Rosenstock, Director of the US National Institute for Occupational Safety and Health (NIOSH), to assert that: 'On the basis of our review of the literature, NIOSH concludes that a large body of credible epidemiologic research exists that shows a consistent relationship between MSDs and certain physical factors, especially at higher exposure levels' (Rosenstock, 1997: iii).

Not only is there evidence linking workplace characteristics with certain work-related musculoskeletal injuries or disorders, there are also a wide range of underpinning theories of causation. Karsh's (2006) detailed examination of nine theories is a good illustration of the diverse range of work-related musculoskeletal injury causation theories within the ergonomic literature. The theories were selected by Karsh (2006) on the basis that each represents different populations and settings, as outlined in the table below. That is, some focused on biomechanical mechanisms while others focused on psychological mechanisms. Some were derived from office workers and others were derived more from biomechanical laboratory studies of lifting. Nonetheless, the theories and models highlighted by Karsh (2006: 80) have many commonalities. First, the theories and models showed that physical or psychological exposures could impact on work-related musculoskeletal injury or disorders. Second, most of the models contained feedback mechanisms or cascading effects in which responses to one exposure or dose lead to another exposure, which in turn led to new exposures. Third, common to all of the theories and models was that there was no indication of specific magnitudes, durations of exposure or latency periods.

Table 4.1 Ergonomic theories of work-related musculoskeletal injuries and disorders

Author	Model or theory
Armstrong et al. (1993)	The model defined the relationships between exposures, doses, capacity and responses for neck and upper limb WMSDs and showed how there was a cascading effect.
Hagberg et al. (1995)	Authors presented a generic model of WMSD prevention in their book on that same topic. Their model further refined theories about WMSD causation by showing how workplace features and generic risk factors could impact pathophysiology outcomes.
Sauter and Swanson (1996)	In the ecological model, which was specific to office environments, a proposed relationship between psychological and biomechanical strain was shown, as was the detection and labelling of sensations. That model is conceptually similar to the model proposed by Carayon et al. (1999).
Feuerstein (1996)	Author proposed a work-style model of WMSD causation whereby proposed behavioural mechanisms were explained.
Carayon et al. (2000)	This ecological model was designed to illustrate that job stress mechanisms and the work system (e.g. work organisation, job design, work environment and technology) have a direct impact on short-term emotional, physiological and behavioural responses.
Kumar (2001)	1 The multivariate interaction theory of musculoskeletal injury precipitation which highlights the interactions between genetic, morphological, psychosocial and biomechanical factors impacting the individual's musculoskeletal system. 2 Differential fatigue theory proposed that different activities differentially loaded on different joints and different muscles. 3 Cumulative load theory recognises that while biological tissue is capable of self-repair, the tissue can suffer from degradation if loadings are repeated. 4 Overexertion theory suggested exertion, which was defined as a function of force, duration, posture and motion, that exceeds the limits of tissue could cause the tissue to fail.
National Research Council and Institute of Medicine (NRC/IOM) (2001)	The model showed the relationship between work factors, external loads, organisational factors, social context, individual characteristics and outcomes. In particular, the model showed that three interacting workplace factors—external loads, organisational factors and social context—could directly impact biomechanical loading as well as outcomes such as pain and impairment.
Karsh, (2006)	The integrated model is a combination of the theories and models to form a composite model that incorporates the various paths and mechanisms that have been proposed. This composite model illustrates the complexity of WMSD aetiology by describing 35 proposed pathways between the 12 major constructs that have been proposed in previous models.

Source: Karsh, B. (2006), 'Theories of work-related musculoskeletal disorders: implications for ergonomic interventions', *Theoretical Issues in Ergonomic Science*, 7 (1): 71–88.

There is no doubt that the medical and ergonomic professions have been prominent in the prevention, treatment and rehabilitation of work-related musculoskeletal injuries and have made a significant contribution to understanding the underlying causes and the development of interventions. However, the role that the medical physicians and ergonomists have played in the decisions regarding workers obtaining compensation or their rehabilitation have sometimes been seen by employers and employees as controversial.

Psychological explanations

Seeking explanations for musculoskeletal injuries and in particular repetitive strain injuries has generated a number of psychology studies, many of which have focused on the personality traits of the individual (see Karwowski et al., 2003 and Gielo-Perczak et al., 2005). The key question driving this controversial stream of research is: are there some workers more susceptible to musculoskeletal injuries than others, and if so why? A central feature of this research has been the development of complex inventories of personality traits. These personality inventories measure characteristics such as emotion and temperament, cognitive variables (e.g. intelligence and achievement) and psychomotor skills (Aiken, 1999; Morgan, 2007). Personality assessments, for example Friedman and Rosenman's (1974) Type A and Type B personality categories, have also been used to mark workers suffering with musculoskeletal injuries from non-suffers (Chen et al., 2005; Sudhakaran and Mirka, 2005). This form of categorising (or some would say stigmatising) workers with musculoskeletal injuries gained considerable popularity during the so-called 'RSI epidemic' of the 1980s and 1990s in which workers with RSI were often described as having personalities that were competitive, ambitious, high performing and who had the ability to complete tasks rapidly (refer Sudhakaran and Mirka, 2005; Morgan, 2007).

Authors who pursue this line of inquiry have been criticised for their narrow focus on the attributes of the individual and for fostering a 'victim-blaming ideology' rather than recognising other sources of musculoskeletal injuries and investigating underlying problems and solutions that incorporate a wider number of factors (Kenny, 2000; Cole et al., 2005; Morgan, 2007). Furthermore, the research linking musculoskeletal injuries, including RSI, with the personality of the individual is inconclusive. The few studies that were undertaken in the 1980s suggested a positive relationship between neck–shoulder disorder and personality type but all acknowledged a need for more investigation (Karwowski et al., 2003). Still other researchers argue that while individual differences can contribute to the variance in exposure to musculoskeletal injuries, there remains a great deal of confusion over the mechanisms by which individual characteristics affect these type of injuries (Cole and Rivilis, 2004). More recently, researchers have replicated earlier studies but have found little or no evidence of an association between specific personality traits and workers with musculoskeletal injuries (Sudhakaran and Mirka, 2005; Morgan, 2007).

While psychological explanations of musculoskeletal injury based entirely on personality inventories have been criticised as being narrow and lacking any substantial empirical evidence, there has been a greater acceptance of research that incorporates a broad range of psychosocial factors (Malchaire et al., 2001; Lanfranchi and Duveau, 2008). In particular, a number of psychologists have turned their attention to the characteristics of the job tasks together with other psychosocial aspects of the working environment, including changes to work processes and elements (repetition, constrained posture, machine-pacing, high attitudinal demands and supervisory pressure) conducive to stress as contributing to these disorders (Mullaly and Grigg, 1988; Kiseler and Finholt, 1988; Johnston et al., 2007). However, this is not the sole domain of psychology as the literature on psychosocial factors provides an intersection for multiple disciplines including sociology, ergonomics and medicine (see Sprigg et al., 2003). Nor is this research new; for example, the psychologists Andersen and Williams (1988) developed their multi-component theoretical model of stress and musculoskeletal injury in the 1980s. The central hypothesis of their model is that workers are at greater risk of musculoskeletal injuries when put in a stressful, demanding, monotonous work situation and when other factors come into play, such as an accumulation of stress and fatigue, a lack of coping resources and certain personality characteristics (trait anxiety, locus of control, sensation seeking). More specifically, when placed in a stressful situation, these workers are more likely to exhibit greater muscle tension, which in turn heightens the risk of injury (Williams, 1996). Research undertaken primarily by psychologists also reveals that workers with a work-related musculoskeletal injury will likely suffer concurrent depression which, in turn, impedes their rehabilitation (Sullivan et al., 2008). Many of the studies linking psychosocial factors with musculoskeletal injury are set within the nursing profession as nurses have a very high rate of work-related musculoskeletal injury, especially lower-back pain and injury (see, for example, Daraiseh et al., 2003; Gillen et al., 2007; Morgan, 2007; Stichler, 2009). Further, nurses are likely to work extended schedules (long hours, on-call, mandatory overtime, working on days off) and literature shows a strong link between overtime and extended work schedules and an increased risk of musculoskeletal injuries (Dembe et al., 2005; Trinkoff et al., 2006; Morgan, 2007).

In spite of efforts by some researchers to broaden the psychology discourse to include other key factors such as the pace and intensification of work and the design of the workstation when explaining the causes of musculoskeletal injuries, the myopic preoccupation with attributing certain personality traits to sufferers of musculoskeletal injuries continues. As a result the interventions proposed by psychologists are essentially about changing the behaviour of the individual and equipping them with coping mechanisms. The implication is that the employee, rather than the employer, is solely responsible for reducing their risk of musculoskeletal injuries, which is not only contrary to the legislation, but also assumes that the employee has the power to make the changes to their working environment, which in most cases is simply impossible.

Sociological explanations

In contrast to the psychological approach to musculoskeletal injuries, sociologists have examined broader determinants of the dramatic growth of work-related musculoskeletal injuries, investigating both the organisational and social sources of the injury and the industrial, social and political factors influencing whether workers report pain and seek compensation for it (Nichols, 1997). Unlike other experts, sociologists have also acknowledged the relationship between the growth in work intensification and the rise in the number of work-related musculoskeletal injuries. Their explanations have not denied the contribution of physiological and ergonomic factors to work-related musculoskeletal injury, or attempted to deny the symptoms and suffering associated with the injury, but have argued that occupational injuries and illnesses can only be fully understood by examining the social and industrial context in which they occurred.

One reason why work-related musculoskeletal injury emerged as a major issue in the past decades is the ongoing resistance to methods of work organisation that have negative effects on workers health and safety. That is, debates over work-related musculoskeletal injuries have provided the focal point for resisting managerial prerogatives of piece rates, incentive systems and other forms of work organisation affecting the health and safety of workers. It was because work-related musculoskeletal injuries carried such serious ramifications for the interests of both workers and employers that the negotiation about its definition and political meaning has been so intense. Moreover, the clearer it became that these types of injuries were not necessarily restricted to clerical workers but instead were found across a range of occupations and industries, such as health, meat processing, transport, construction, printing and engineering, the more powerful trade unions were stirred into action. Trade unions challenged the alienating and dehumanising direction in which the labour process was going and intensified the pressure on management to introduce mechanisms such as worker participation, work enrichment and industrial democracy as ways of reducing the rate of work-related musculoskeletal injuries.

Traditional employer responses to occupational health hazards, which aim to fit the worker to the job, were ineffective in coping with musculoskeletal injury. Attempts to devise biomechanical tests to identify workers predisposed to such injuries at pre-employment screenings were opposed by the National Health and Medical Research Council (1985) on the basis that there was no technical equipment adequate for the task. On the other hand, employers were faced with rapidly increasing workers' compensation premiums and the escalating costs associated with rehabilitation. Because of the intensity of the debate and the high stakes, occupational health professionals were called upon to mediate. Unfortunately, their frequently contradictory evidence only served to embroil them in the controversy. The result was that the definition of RSI became the object of hotly contested political negotiation and mediation (MacEachean, 2004).

The dominant medical and psychological paradigm is that work-related musculoskeletal injuries or disorders are in some way linked to the characteristics of the individual worker, such as personal traits, gender and race, rather than the job itself.

This view is also common among employers, as MacEachen (2004: 507) noted: '... RSI was conceived as a problem located in certain types of workers (rather than types of work environments), and the disability, 'RSI', was fragmented and subordinated to issues relating to worker character and broader organisational culture and mandates' (also see Tappin et al., 2008a). However, this perspective is being challenged by an emerging sociological inquiry. While not ignoring the other factors, sociological research indicates that it is more useful to look first at the work task or tasks as well as the hours worked as the primary sources of work-related musculoskeletal injuries and disorders, rather than attributing the cause of the injury entirely to the victim (see Dembe et al., 2004). Zhang et al.'s (2009: 35) study on comparing the rate of musculoskeletal injuries between US-born and foreign-born workers is an interesting example in that although migrant workers typically suffer a higher rate of injury and illness compared to the non-migrant workers, their study indicates that when both groups of workers are employed in the same hazardous industries, they will suffer comparable injuries irrespective of their immigration status. Further, in a study investigating the combined effect of socioeconomic status, education, income and occupation, Gillen et al. (2007) concluded that occupation was a key risk factor for musculoskeletal injuries. Based on their sample of healthcare workers, it appears that '... the qualities inherent in the 'job' itself matter more than other socioeconomic factors per se, recognizing that any given occupation in a hospital setting represents a set of job-specific exposures encompassing both physical and psychosocial factors' (Gillen et al., 2007: 257).

However, once workers have suffered a musculoskeletal injury there will be negative social and economic consequences for the worker, their family, employer and broader community (Adams et al., 2002; Brown et al., 2007; Li-Tsang et al., 2008). Guy and Short's (2005) study of the relevance of the type of work and socioeconomic status on the experiences of pain rehabilitation for Australian workers with musculoskeletal injuries also found chronic pain is strongly associated with socioeconomic disadvantage, high levels of unemployment and social costs. In addition, they argue that the adverse effects of injured workers' experiences of compensation systems have potential to further disadvantage them if they have blue-collar backgrounds (Guy and Short, 2005: 8). That is, their study's results show that workers from blue-collar backgrounds experience a double jeopardy in relation to disabling work injury and its management. First, the type of heavy and repetitious work performed by blue-collar workers is more likely to predispose them to musculoskeletal injury. Second, because they have fewer resources on which to draw, such as education and job skills, their capacity to retrain and to regain full employment as required by current compensation and rehabilitation programs is severely constrained. Their experience of work-related rehabilitation is unlikely to be an empowering one.

It would be misleading, however, to suggest that the sociology literature offers definitive causes of musculoskeletal injuries. Instead, the research suggests that explanations of musculoskeletal injury aetiology are more nuanced, particularly around factors of gender and age. In their study of age and gender differences based on workers' compensation claims, Breslin et al. (2003) reveal that even though work hazards were the primary determinant of musculoskeletal injuries, maturational and gender factors may be relevant in musculoskeletal injuries and disorders if tied to the type of work and the length of work (also see Albert et al., 2007; Zuhosky et al., 2007). In particular, chronic musculoskeletal disorders constituted a smaller proportion of adolescent claims which the authors suggest is due to the fact that young workers have had less time to show a history of impaired work functioning, an essential part of the assessment to determine permanent impairment (Breslin et al., 2003).

Furthermore, there are a number of external factors which, combined with the working conditions and employment relationships, form a more complex picture of musculoskeletal injuries. In an in-depth study of the causes and interventions of musculoskeletal injuries in the New Zealand meat processing industry, Tappin et al. (2007; 2008a & b) argue that consideration should be given to both internal and external contextual factors when examining causes of musculoskeletal injuries. Their conceptual model, outlined below, indicates the direction of influence for contextual factors and their role in increasing exposure to physical and psychosocial risk factors. The complexity of the problem is further increased because all of these factors interact and vary over time and from one situation to another. Tappin et al. (2008a & b) and others (see National Research Council, 2001), however, state that research is needed to clarify such relationships. Notwithstanding, Tappin et al.'s research is important as it has implications for other, similar industry settings where the work is relentless and repetitive and where there is a need to confront prevailing attitudes of 'blaming the

Figure 4.1   Multiple factors of musculoskeletal injuries

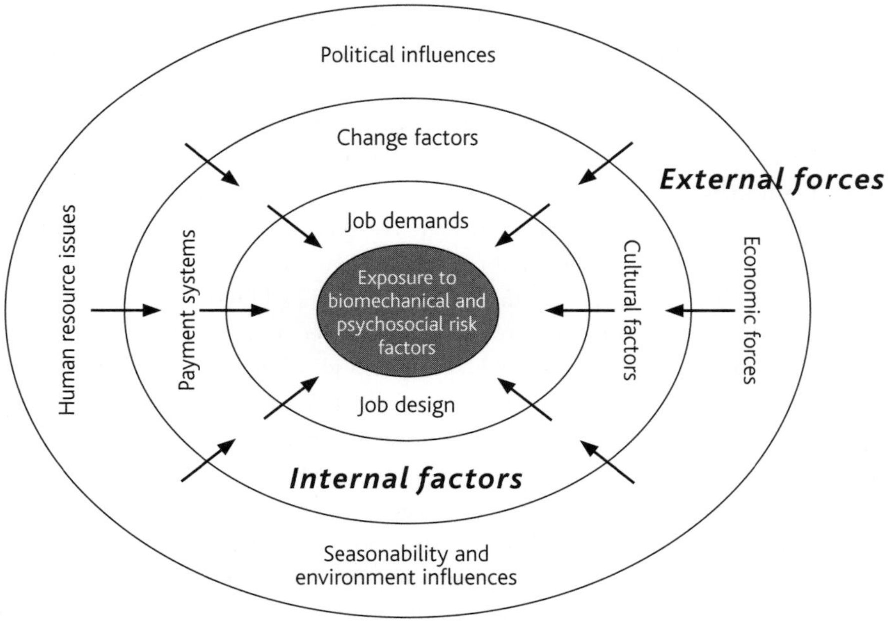

Source: Tappin et al. (2008: 1581)

worker' for musculoskeletal injuries which, in turn, hinder prevention strategies. It is also important as it debunks the myth that upper-body musculoskeletal injuries are typically prevalent in female-dominated occupations and thus are essentially a 'women's problem'. Instead, such injuries are just as widespread in male-dominated occupations such as transport, meat processing, carpentry, and agriculture and forestry.

Intervention measures

There are a plethora of interventions designed to reduce the rate of musculoskeletal injuries, ranging from medical solutions to regulatory intervention and ergonomically designed workstations. There are also a vast array of treatments and rehabilitation programs aimed at injured workers. The standard intervention process begins with a preliminary analysis of the work situation, followed by the diagnostic stage in which the causes, or determinants, are identified. In the fourth stage of the process, solutions are developed and changes implemented and the final stage requires a complete review (see Denis et al., 2008).

The various interventions for the management of musculoskeletal injuries can also be divided into three main categories—mechanical exposure interventions, production system interventions and modifier interventions—and often reflect the employers' attitude and approach towards musculoskeletal injuries (see Boocock et al., 2005). Mechanical exposure interventions typically focus on altering the design of tools, such as the computer mouse or keyboard. Production systems interventions often implement changes to the material production and/or the organisational culture of a company. An example would be team building and increased worker participation in solving problems of workplace production (i.e. participatory ergonomics). Studies that investigate the effect of specific training of workers to manage exposure levels are termed 'modifier interventions', examples of which would be exercise or training programs. In spite of the fact that there is a surfeit of interventions (Boocock et al., 2005; Denis et al., 2007), unfortunately, extensive reviews of the literature undertaken by Boocock et al. (2005), Denis et al. (2008), Jordon et al. (2009) and Karjalainen et al. (2009) all lamented the paucity of rigorous studies on the effectiveness of the interventions, treatment and rehabilitation of musculoskeletal injuries.

As a way of overcoming this lack of scrutiny of the many interventions, some of which have very little or no scientific merit, the Cochrane Bone, Joint and Muscle Trauma Group have produced a number of systematic reviews of interventions, treatments and the rehabilitation of musculoskeletal injuries. The multidisciplinary Cochrane Bone, Joint and Muscle Trauma Group is one of approximately 50 collaborative review groups within the international Cochrane Collaboration, and includes both researchers and healthcare professionals. Aside from providing an important forum to discuss the prevention, treatment and rehabilitation of musculoskeletal injuries, the reviews undertaken by the Cochrane Bone, Joint and Muscle Trauma Group are updated and published in *The Cochrane Library* (see <www.bjmtg.cochrane.org>).

Although there is a lack of rigorous evaluation of the many intervention methods, there is nonetheless general consensus over which type of interventions are most effective. As mentioned in the previous chapter, many of the interventions touted are essentially about getting the worker to take responsibility for their actions—for example, changing their behaviour, managing their stress and undergoing training and education. However, as we have seen, effective interventions are those that address the type of work undertaken and the working conditions, such as the number of hours worked and the arrangement of the workstation, as well as acknowledging a range of other factors, for example the intensification of work, economic conditions and regulatory enforcement of OHS standards (Hignett, 2003). There also appears to be no single intervention strategy that could be effectively applied for all types of industrial settings. Therefore multidimensional interventions, including a participatory approach and individual, technical and organisational measures, seem to be an appropriate strategy for reducing the physical demands and the symptoms of musculoskeletal injuries (Roquelaure, 2008). The amount of time, resources and thought devoted to the assessment of the problem, the development of the solution, the implementation of the changes and the subsequent review will determine the success of the intervention (Anema et al., 2004; Denis et al., 2008). Finally, most agree that the level of competency of those implementing the interventions as well as support from management and internal and external experts are essential ingredients (Legg et al., 2008).

Putting debates surrounding musculoskeletal disorders into context

To better understand work-related musculoskeletal disorders and the sometimes fierce debate surrounding diagnosis, treatment and preventative interventions a number of contextual points need to be recognised.

First, the belated and contested recognition of RSI, and associated debates about treatment, prevention, compensation and rehabilitation measures during the 1980s and 1990s are by no means unique or even exceptional. The history of OHS is littered with examples where musculoskeletal and other work-related health disorders have undergone a similar process of contestation and social debate, as well illustrated by Allard Dembe's book (1996), to mention but one study. A more historically informed and multidisciplinary examination of musculoskeletal disorders (see below) is required.

Second, the same point applies to stigmatisation of particular groups of workers as susceptible or manipulative. During the 1980s debate over RSI in Australia, women and public servants were stigmatised, conveniently ignoring the concentration of women in particular jobs as well as social factors (such as job security and the presence of unions) that affect reporting. The epithet 'kangaroo paw' also overlooked an earlier 'epidemic' in Japan and was quietly dropped (without apology or explanation by those who used it) when similar problems became apparent in the US, Britain and elsewhere. What was also overlooked was that similar stigmatisation was widely used in relation to immigrant workers suffering back injuries during the 1970s, with epithetic terms such as 'Greek back', 'Lebanese back', 'Mediterranean Back' and 'Turkish Back'. Once again, these terms detracted attention from the concentration of these workers in manufacturing and construction jobs where there was a high risk of musculoskeletal injury. Nor, again, did those using these terms admit fault in the face of evidence that fraudulent compensation claims were a relatively minor problem more than offset by under-reporting and that immigrant workers on average fared worse under workers' compensation (Hemerik and Cena, 1993; Morrison et al., 1993).

Third, when dealing with injuries or disorders that are widespread (if not pervasive within particular jobs or more generally) there is a need to recognise 'normalisation' and other social influences on reporting. Some injuries are so common—and musculoskeletal injuries often fit into this category—that they are not even perceived as an injury, or at least not a noteworthy one, but simply part of the job. These responses reflect not simply peer opinion but also power imbalances at work. For example, a Canadian study (Breslin et al., 2007) found the tendency of younger workers to see injuries as 'part of the job' reflected their perceived lack of control over their conditions of work, although it also noted gender differences, with females emphasising that their complaints were disregarded by supervisors while male workers said they stifled complaints 'in order to appear mature among their (older) co-workers.' Factors shaping the reluctance to report injuries, along with the need for effective mechanisms, can help to explain why injuries may remain unreported (and then suddenly appear as an 'epidemic') or become chronic injuries over time without any intervention. In this regard, it also needs to be borne in mind that evidence indicates that half of all work-related injuries and illnesses do not result in a workers' compensation claim (see chapters 1 and 8).

Fourth, Ramazzini (1964, reprint) recognised over 300 years ago that work-related injury and disease can only be fully understood when a close examination is made of actual work processes. However, this critical element is often missing (in the case of medicine) or compromised by selective observation (as in the case of ergonomics and psychology) in the examination of musculoskeletal or other disorders. For example, a number of studies have pointed to an association between piecework payment systems and poor psychosocial working conditions and musculoskeletal pain and injury (Lacey et al., 2007; Premji et al., 2008c). While an approach that includes an examination of work processes is becoming more popular it is still by no means an integral part of the examination of musculoskeletal disorders. Further, many of the conditions giving rise to musculoskeletal injuries are not unique and appear to be shared by other work-related illness. Therefore, much can be learnt by examining studies of the role played by work organisation and processes on other types of work-related health problems and there is also a case for examining multiple OHS indices (Barling et al., 2003; Myers et al., 2007). This may help to identify the most critical causal factors as well as develop remedies that simultaneously resolve several hazards such as work-related stress, occupational violence and musculoskeletal disorders. These observations again highlight the need for more multidisciplinary research into musculoskeletal disorders.

Conclusion

There has been intense controversy regarding the nature and origins of musculoskeletal injury. There is, however, no doubt that large numbers of workers have experienced a cluster of symptoms involving severe and debilitating pain of the neck, shoulders, back and upper and lower limbs. It is also indisputable that there was a dramatic rise in workers' compensation claims for the condition in Australia and New Zealand during the 1980s and 1990s and that this upsurge in reporting corresponded with major changes in work organisation in many of the workplaces affected. However, despite the public attention that it has attracted, musculoskeletal injury has not been clearly defined. It is in fact used as an umbrella term encompassing both recognised disorders with clear physical signs and more diffuse conditions characterised by severe symptoms but no discernible physical signs. Controversy over the definition of the condition has been fuelled by medical ideology, which separates illness and disease and presumes that physical pathology does not exist where observable physical signs are not present. This ideology has particular difficulty accommodating conditions like RSI and back injury that appear to arise from strain, are cumulative and are characterised by severe subjective pain and other symptoms without physical signs. In fact, there are strong parallels between the RSI debate and the one concerning back strain that preceded it in Australia and New Zealand.

The lack of understanding of the pathology of some forms of musculoskeletal injury has provided the opportunity for the various vested interest groups to define and reinterpret the condition to meet their own needs. This uncertainty has led to unsubstantiated accusations that musculoskeletal injuries, especially RSI, are the result of mass hysteria and suggestions that many workers seeking compensation are neurotic and malingering, despite considerable evidence that musculoskeletal injuries have been reported for centuries and are widespread elsewhere. Fuelling the controversy have been different, and sometimes conflicting, explanations of the origins and dramatic emergence of musculoskeletal injury, generated by the disciplines of medicine, ergonomics, psychiatry, psychology and sociology.

Fierce public and legal debate has enhanced the ability of interest groups to selectively, and sometimes misleadingly, exploit explanations of musculoskeletal injuries to promote their own objectives. The courts became a forum in which the debate was thrashed out, with the protagonists generally having more concern for legal victory than the development of an accurate understanding of the problem. A sensationalised debate simultaneously raged in the mass media. The debate over musculoskeletal injuries, especially RSI, provides a stark illustration of the processes of conflict, negotiation and accommodation that surround the definition and management of many occupational health issues. The polarised nature of the debate and many of the specific arguments over definition and aetiology are especially characteristic of injuries that are not amenable to clear medical diagnosis. Ultimately, the conflict over the definitions and origins of the different musculoskeletal injuries produced considerable confusion and argument regarding the strategies that should be used for its management, although ergonomic redesign of equipment and work stations combined with limited task and job redesign have been the most widely accepted strategies. Throughout the debate the real losers have been the many sufferers of musculoskeletal injuries who endure pain, stigma, fear of unemployment and unnecessary delays in the identification and implementation of solutions to their problems.

QUESTIONS FOR DISCUSSION

1 What are the major difficulties in defining musculoskeletal injury? Is it likely that consensus will be reached about a definition?
2 Repetitive strain injury or RSI can be viewed through a number of lenses. Examine the strengths and weaknesses of the way four different disciplines view RSI.
3 Who are the major groups with vested interests in RSI? How did they influence the debate over the origins of RSI in Australia?
4 Outline the more useful approaches used to prevent musculoskeletal injury.

FURTHER READING

Boocock, M.G., Collier, J., McNair, P.J., Simmonds, M., Larmer, P.J. and Armstrong, B. (2009), 'A framework for the classification and diagnosis of work-related upper extremity conditions: systematic review', *Seminars in Arthritis and Rheumatism*, **38**(4): 296–311.

Hopkins, A. (1989), 'The social construction of repetition strain injury', *Australia and New Zealand Journal of Sociology*, **25**(2): 239–59.

Karsh, B-T. (2006), 'Theories of work-related musculoskeletal disorders: implications for ergonomic interventions', *Theoretical Issues in Ergonomics Science*, **7**(1): 71–88.

Kumar, S. (2001), 'Theories of musculoskeletal injury causation', *Ergonomics*, **44**(1): 17–47.

Quintner, J. (1991), 'The RSI syndrome in historical perspective', *International Disability Studies*, **13**: 99–104.

Sudhakaran, S. and Mirka, G.A. (2005), 'A laboratory investigation of personality type and break-taking behavior', *International Journal of Industrial Ergonomics,* **35**(3): 237–46.

Trinkoff, A., Le, R., Geiger-Brown, J., Lipscomb, J. and Lang, G. (2006), 'Longitudinal relationship of work hours, mandatory overtime, and on-call to musculoskeletal problems in nurses', *American Journal of Industrial Medicine*, **49**: 964–71.

Williams, J.M. (1996), 'Stress, coping resources, and injury risk', *International Journal of Stress Management,* **3**(4): 209–221.

Yassi, A. (1997), 'Repetitive strain injuries', *The Lancet,* **349**: 943–7.

5

Occupational disease, stress and illness

Introduction

IN chapter 1 we noted that the World Health Organization/International Labour Organization have defined health as a complete state of physical, psychological and social wellbeing and not simply the absence of disease and deformity. Given our discussion in chapter 2, we would clearly endorse the application of this broad notion in relation to the sphere of work. At the same time it was noted that much of the OHS literature and the institutional apparatuses that deal with OHS are predicated on a more narrow conception of health, namely physiologically verified injuries and disease.

This chapter focuses on occupational disease, stress and illness. We cannot pretend that this is a straightforward task. The boundary between disease and injury is by no means an unambiguous one. Even leaving this issue aside, it seems clear to us that the medical notion of disease, although important in its own right, is not sufficiently broad to encompass all the health effects of work not covered by occupational injury. Psychologists and other behavioural and social scientists have tried to widen the terrain of health effects, most notably through the notion of stress but also through more generalised terms such as sickness and illness. From our perspective, the notion of stress is not an illness in itself but a process of interactions that may affect health. However, while the notion of stress has won a degree of acceptance from other disciplines such as medicine and sociology, its precise meaning remains the subject of vigorous debate within the ranks of psychologists. It has been increasingly recognised that psychological stress can affect the onset of disease and self-reported health problems can be a good predictor of 'objective' physiological effects (Singh-Manoux et al., 2006). It has also been increasingly recognised that harassment and bullying in the workplace, including sexual harassment, represent an important threat to the health and wellbeing of workers. However, there is no agreed framework for categorising the various health effects of work just described into some more comprehensive and systematic understanding of occupational health. Thus, we are left with categories that overlap and interact—

apart from disease, there is no general agreement as to their meaning. It is confusing terrain but it cannot be ignored for this reason.

The chapter begins with a general discussion on the incidence and nature of occupational disease, highlighting its importance, the complex interaction between work and disease, and the difficulty of obtaining meaningful statistics that can be used to guide prevention strategies. Given what has already been said, we make no effort to do the same for stress or illness. However, a number of efforts to measure changes in psychosocial working conditions in Europe and elsewhere are discussed. The chapter then looks at how a range of relevant disciplines, including occupational medicine/ epidemiology, other health sciences, occupational hygiene, psychology and sociology (and related fields) have sought to identify, assess, explain and control work-related disease, stress and illness. Of course, the fields do not address all aspects. Occupational medicine and epidemiology have been largely concerned with disease whereas psychologists and sociologists have been more concerned with stress, worker wellbeing and more generalised notions of illness. In the last section of the chapter we look at how regulatory infrastructure and interest groups are shaping research and standard setting in relation to the hazardous substances that give rise to disease.

Some of the discussion in this chapter is necessarily tentative, demonstrating if nothing else the immensity of the task of understanding the health effects of work in anything like a comprehensive sense. Nevertheless, we hope to indicate the value of a multidisciplinary approach. The survey of the available evidence on the health effects of hours of work in chapter 6 will reinforce this point.

Occupational disease—a brief overview

Disease and work

Occupational diseases are a significant and often grossly underestimated problem in the workplace. Occupational diseases entail a wide range of complaints including:

- mild and acute skin disorders (such as dermatitis arising from contact with an organic solvent or other chemical)
- viral and bacteriological infections such as AIDS and hepatitis C among healthcare and emergency workers (see, for example, Stevens and Coyle, 2000; Chen and Jenkins, 2007), brucellosis among meat workers and Legionnaires Disease among retail and office workers
- respiratory complaints including asthma-like conditions brought about by inhaling airborne pollutants such as organic and inorganic dust, fumes, pollen, smoke and chemical residues
- cancers resulting from exposure to the sun, radiation, carcinogens such as asbestos and other harmful substances
- the malfunction/deterioration of organs and body functions due to the accumulation of toxic substances or progressive exposure to a harmful physical agent
- nervous disorders and coronary heart disease induced by stress.

Many of these are insidious because:

- they are subject to a long gestation period (more than 30 years after exposure in the case of some cancers such as mesothelioma; Leigh, 2005)
- they develop slowly and often imperceptibly in their early stages but are degenerative and irreversible once the symptoms become apparent
- symptoms may only be recognised in cases of acute exposure
- they may lead to intermittent bouts of chronic suffering
- health effects are complicated by multiple exposures to toxic substances or complex interactions with physical factors (temperature, humidity, etc.) and the organisation of work (workloads, production pressures, job insecurity, etc.). For example, in their study of dermatitis among aircrews, Leggat and Smith (2006) found aircrews were exposed to an array of skin irritants (including sealants used in aircraft manufacture and jet fuel) and dermatitis appeared to be exacerbated by low humidity on long-haul flights. The situation is even more complex in cases where multiple exposures give rise to different diseases or have synergistic effects.

The distinction drawn between injury and disease is a medical one, but one fraught with complexities. Ferguson (1986a: 1) argued that the

> … mechanism and outcomes of acute trauma and long-term exposure to noxious agents are distinct enough to justify separation of occupational disease and injury as pathological and clinical entities. The distinction is less obvious at other points along what is clearly a spectrum. Acute chemical and physical burns, for example, can be seen as injuries whereas acute and sub-acute internal effects from radiations or inhalations may not. Irritant contact eczema results from repeated minor mostly chemical burns. However, sensitising contact eczema as a consequence of such irritation may more readily be called a disease. Similarly, an acute intervertebral disc lesion after heavy lifting may be an injury, whereas intervertebral joint degeneration after repeated minor physical trauma over many years may not. The same may be said about acute and cumulative cochlear damage from noise. And is hepatitis B contracted in a laboratory from an accidental needle prick disease or injury?

In practice, specific exposures, events or activities can simultaneously give rise to a range of injuries, diseases and other health risks. Respiratory diseases, a number of cancer-related deaths and chronic impairment of mental health have now been recorded among persons (including rescue, recovery and clean-up workers) exposed to the 9/11 bombing of the World Trade Centre in New York (Prezant et al., 2008; Stellman et al., 2008). Stimulant drug use by truck drivers can lead to increased risk of injury (through crashes) as well as short- and long-term health effects (such as cardiac arrhythmia). Chronic health problems such as asthma may also predispose workers to illness or injury although there are few high-quality studies of this connection (Eisner et al., 2006; Palmer et al., 2008).

Another complexity concerns the nature and degree of work-relatedness. Non-occupational factors can impact on work-related injuries but the interaction of work and non-work factors is arguably more widespread, complex and difficult to disentangle in the case of disease. Ferguson (in Douglas et al., 1986: 21–2) identifies four levels of work-relatedness in relation to disease, namely:

1 those diseases such as lead poisoning among foundry workers where the source of exposure is either exclusive to the workplace or so significant as to overwhelm other sources of exposure

2 those diseases which result from both occupational and non-occupational factors

3 those diseases which are non-occupational in origin but which are aggravated by work

4 those diseases not related to work but which inhibit the capacity of workers to carry out their tasks.

Ferguson recognised that this taxonomy was flawed in the sense that the same disease may by found under all four categories. Further, the identification of disease and attributing the respective contributions of work and environmental factors occurs in a dynamic environment (see the discussion below relating to occupational asthma for evidence of an allocation of causality in this regard). For example, the growth of temporary work involving frequent changes to jobs (if not occupations) in many countries over the past 20 years will make the identification of exposures to hazardous substances more difficult (and the same applies to the increased use of subcontractors). Aside from changes to work itself (in terms of technology, substances used and organisation), the last 30 years have witnessed significant demographic changes (in terms of gender, ethnicity and age) in the workforce as well as large intra- and international movements of labour. Climate change will also affect the pattern of disease exposure by, for example, affecting patterns of rainfall and prolonged heat, the location of both subtropical and arid conditions, and the seasonal vectors within which parasites can survive (Albin et al., 2009).

It is also important to recognise that disease risks originating at work can also affect family members of workers and the broader community. Perhaps the best know example is asbestos—the children and wives of asbestos workers suffered mesothelioma as a result of contact with asbestos-laced clothing and communities also suffered risks due to asbestos in the air or on the ground (in some cases asbestos tailings were even used as road fill) near mines (McCulloch and Tweedale, 2008). Other recent examples include lead levels affecting children living near the Mount Isa mine in Queensland and a Taiwanese study of cancer among the children of female electronic workers (*CCH OHS Alert*, 22 & 26 May 2008; Sung et al., 2008: 115–19). Such cases highlight the close intersection of occupational health and public health that may need to be borne in mind when devising preventative intervention. As McCulloch and Tweedale (2008) have shown, banning asbestos was the only sensible policy response to the insidious health threat posed by this material. The asbestos example raises a final issue, namely the critical role community mobilisations and institutions play in disease recognition. As noted by Albin et al. (2009: 3) international institutions concerned with consumer health and safety are generally stronger than those dealing with workers' health and this is likely to remain the case. In short, complexities confronting the identification of occupational disease are not likely to diminish in the foreseeable future.

The distinction between occupational injuries and occupational diseases has been modified by the legal system, especially workers' compensation (see chapter 8). Although the introduction of workers' compensation systems helped to sponsor research into occupational diseases, the original focus of these schemes was on 'accidents' or occupational injuries and, despite efforts to redress this, a fundamental imbalance remains. Figlio (cited in Weindling, 1985: 10) argued that in resolving disputes over the attribution of liability the legal system has reduced diseases to the status of accidents, a misleading concept that continues to exert far too much influence in OHS (see chapter 3). As more recent studies demonstrate (Cox and Lippel, 2008), these problems have not been remedied and, indeed, the gaps in recording occupational illness in workers' compensation claims data have widened due to labour market changes, the failure to recognise chronic work-related stress and the legal obstacles to having a claim recognised as work related.

The administrative process for recognising disease has varied between countries and sometimes (as in Australia and Canada) even within countries (Cox and Lippel, 2008). In some jurisdictions diseases were designated as 'injuries' for the purpose of compensation while in others specific diseases were certified as work related for those undertaking particular jobs. There are interjurisdictional complexities even in relation to well-recognised health problems. For example, health complaints normally grouped under the appellation of RSI are listed as injuries in some states, as diseases in others, or can be found under both categories. In states such as New South Wales and Queensland all deafness, including that due to acute exposure of a short duration, is listed as a disease (accounting for a significant proportion of total disease claims). Even if such problems could be overcome it still needs to be recognised that injuries, disease and stress may interact in complex fashions which may not be easily disentangled.

For both the medical profession and the legal system a critical element in distinguishing between occupational injuries and occupational diseases appears to be the notion that the former arise from a discrete incident or event. We will have more to say about this below. At this point it is important to note that while the distinction drawn between disease and injury is by no means unproblematic a separate discussion of disease can still be justified. It does allow us to focus on more insidious occupational health risks—risks which warrant greater attention not only for policy reasons but also because an examination of them will contribute to the development of more sophisticated understanding of the origins of occupational ill health.

The extent and incidence of occupational disease and ill health

Knowledge of the incidence of occupational disease (both in an aggregate sense and in relation to particular diseases) is fragmented and inadequate and this has significant implications for any attempt to identify causal factors. In 1986, Elling (1986: 97) argued that the reporting of occupational diseases was abysmal although some countries fared worse than others. Despite initiatives in a number of countries in the more than 20 years since this statement was made, the observation remains valid. Available evidence indicates that occupational disease is responsible for far more deaths than traumatic injury. As noted by Sokas and Sprince (2008), a group of Finnish researchers (Hamalainen et al., 2007) applied attributable occupational fractions to seven major categories of global disease (communicable diseases, malignant neoplasms, respiratory diseases, circulatory diseases, neuropsychiatric conditions, digestive system diseases and genitor-urinary diseases), resulting in a estimate of two million deaths annually, including 346 000 from traumatic injury.

Knowledge regarding the extent of occupational ill health not defined or grossly under-reported as a disease, such as heat-related illness (see Bonauto et al., 2007), work-related depression and other types of mental distress is, if anything, worse. Systematic collection of information on psychosocial working conditions at national level is exceptional although some relevant information (such as sickness absence and hospital visits) has been included in large panel studies undertaken in a number of countries (the Nordic countries in particular). Since the early 1990s the European Foundation for Improvement in Living and Working Conditions (EFILWC) has conducted five-yearly surveys of working conditions (1000 workers from each EU country) that include psychosocial working conditions. As noted by a Finnish speaker at an EU Presidency Conference on the Quality of Work in 2001, this information and a set of work quality indicators (including OHS) developed by the EFILWC provided a valuable tool for identifying and addressing gaps in work health policies. Unfortunately, broader development and application of this approach within the EU was stymied by employer opposition and neo-liberal policymakers. In Australia an attempt to measure and address psychosocial risk factors by the Victorian Department of Health encountered similar opposition (for a description of this development, see LaMontagne et al., 2006). In the US, the National Occupational Research Agenda (NORA) initiated within NIOSH during the Clinton presidency also entailed an explicit recognition of the need to address organisational factors in occupational health but again it failed to realise its potential after the election of George W Bush (Goldenhar et al., 2001).

Even where a growing body of international research has identified that work-related health problems are important or widespread, such as bullying and occupational violence (see Mayhew et al., 2004; Mayhew and Chappell, 2007), little if any attempt has been made by governments to collect and publish statistics on their incidence. Occupational violence resulting in workers' compensation claims, while of value (see McCall and Horwitz, 2004), capture only a fraction of even the most overt cases (and completely miss the low-level occupational violence that studies find to be most prevalent). Even government-sponsored surveys of these problems are comparatively rare. From a prevention perspective it is important to try and identify emergent risks. In the EU the European Agency for Safety and Health at Work (2005, 2006, 2007) has produced a series of reports on emerging physical, biological and psychosocial risks. In New Zealand, the National Occupational Health and Safety Advisory Committee commissioned a series of scoping reports as well as an overview of emerging OHS risks (Bohle et al., 2009) drawing on a wide range of international evidence. Such information, as well as assessments of current interventions, is of critical value in terms of guiding policy development especially in the context of demographic, technological and other changes to work. No similar exercise has been undertaken in Australia, or in many other countries for that matter.

In sum, in all the countries with which we are familiar, the official datasets so often quoted as authoritative with regard to indices of OHS outcomes consist of a flawed set of work-related injury statistics, statistics on occupational disease that are more conspicuous for what they omit than what they include, and in some cases fragmentary sets of other work-related health data (such as sickness absence statistics in a number of the Scandinavian countries or household panel data in the US and Australia). The remainder of this section will explore the issue of work-related disease in a little more detail.

A number of reasons for the poor statistics on disease were identified in chapter 1, notably the under-representation of disease in workers' compensation claims which form the basis for the official occupational illness statistics of Australia and many other countries (see also chapter 8). The development of a coronial database has improved the recording of work-related deaths due to trauma but not disease. Recognition of diseases as work related might be expected to improve data over time. However, such recognition is often belated and, as discussed elsewhere, new chemicals and other potential hazards to health are being introduced in workplaces without prior vetting. Further, the datasets—whether they were derived from workers' compensation claims, requirements on employers to report or nationwide surveys—have not necessarily improved. Just as a number of governments 'massaged' unemployment data in the 1970s to 1990s (invariably reducing the number recorded as jobless) so too, in at least some cases, changes in the basis for recording workers' compensation claims, reporting or survey methods have reduced the recording of occupational injuries and illnesses (see chapter 3). In the US, for example, changes to OSHA's record-keeping regulations have been severely criticised (see, for example, Cullen, 2004) as representing a deliberate attempt to understate the extent of occupational illness. This criticism has received support from a careful time series analysis undertaken by Friedman and Forst (2007) which found that 83% of the much vaunted decline in occupational injuries and illnesses between 1992 and 2003 was attributable to changes in OSHA's record-keeping rules.

Reference has been made to complexities that almost certainly affect statistics on work-related disease, including the different types and levels of association between disease and work. Structural features of the healthcare system compound these problems. Elling (1986: 18–19) has observed that the

> trouble for the clinician, especially the one not trained to pay attention to OSH diseases and not able to take a work history as well as a family history, is that metal dust asthma looks like a pollen-caused asthma; a solvent-caused skin rash looks like a rash from some home cleaning agent; a lung cancer caused by asbestos looks like one caused from smoking.

Over twenty years later the issue remains. A study of medical records by Politi et al. (2004) found that while physicians obtained gender and age histories in 99% of cases an occupational history was only completed in 27.8% of cases. There have been repeated calls for medical education programs to be redressed in this regard and to reinforce the message after graduation (see, for example, Storey et al., 2001). Practical methods for recording work and environmental exposure histories as well as key questions (e.g. What is the riskiest part of your job?) have also been proposed (Abelsohn et al., 2002; Marshall et al., 2002; Sanborn et al., 2002; Golstein, 2007). Nonetheless, occupational hazards are still a comparatively small component of medical education and the failure by physicians to take detailed occupational histories remains common and a major impediment to the detection of work-related diseases.

A point not mentioned by Elling is the additional problem of workers with complex employment histories, something that is becoming more rather than less common with the growth of contingent employment in many industrialised countries (Leigh, 2005). In Australia, and probably most other industrialised countries, primary healthcare providers such as general practitioners receive minimal training in the area of occupational medicine and disease and the general thrust of their training would militate against them attributing a workplace origin to such complaints (Ferguson, 1988: 484). Ferguson (1988: 485) believed that, given their prominent role in both on-site and off-site care of workers, this lack of training has probably led to a significant level of misattribution of illness. Ferguson (1986a: 1–2) also argued that as a whole the medical profession has displayed little interest in either taking action on behalf of workers or adjusting its practices to the more general needs of industrial society. It had not sought to address infrastructural problems such as the inadequate information provided by death certificates (for a recent assessment of the value of death certificates see Bidulescu et al., 2007) and the failure of hospital records (with some exceptions) to include occupational history details. Ferguson (1986a: 1–2) noted that workplace visits by clinicians are uncommon, and in countries such as the US the overwhelming emphasis has been on remedial treatment rather than prevention. Although these problems affect both injuries and diseases the impact with regard to disease management is liable to be more profound given the insidious nature of many disease risks. In 1986 Elling (1986: 19) argued that the financial linkages which flow from the heavily privatised US healthcare system and the starving of resources to the public healthcare sector, including agencies such as the Occupational Safety and Health Administration (OSHA), have rendered the situation especially acute in that country. The situation did not improve over the next 20 years but instead arguably worsened.

As in many other countries, occupational medicine remains a highly specialised substratum of medicine in Australia with a relatively small number of qualified practitioners/researchers and limited policy clout to exert significant influence on the broader healthcare agenda. Specialists in occupational medicine have been operating in Australia since the early twentieth century but significant academic training in the area only commenced in the 1970s. In 1988 there were 456 members of the (then) Australian College of Occupational Medicine (Ferguson, 1988: 485) and a decade later the number had increased to around 600. Reviewing the situation in the late 1980s, Ferguson (1988: 485) concluded the 'great majority of workplaces provide no on-site health care of any kind, let alone specialised care'. As far as we are aware this remains the situation in Australia today, with most physicians employed by industry (either directly or via consulting arrangements) lacking specialist training in occupational medicine. Ferguson (1988: 484–5) argued that unlike in many other countries, in Australia there has been greater emphasis on preventative occupational medicine rather than the practice of clinical medicine in industry. Similar points can be in relation to other professional groups with a particular focus on occupational disease, notably epidemiology (largely drawn from the ranks of occupational medicine), occupational hygiene and toxicology.

In the 1980s and the first half of the 1990s there was an expansion in tertiary education programs and a consequent growth in the number of trained professionals in these and other OHS-related fields in Australia (coinciding with legislative initiatives and a greater level of government and community interest in the area). However, the combination of labour market restructuring and less interested governments stymied further growth (if not effecting a decline) after this time. As a result the trend had only a very limited impact on the recognition of occupational disease risks. LaDou (2002) has offered a similarly sober account of occupational medicine in the US, noting that government agency efforts to build the field in 1970 (again coinciding with major changes to OHS legislation) had limited success (attempts to bring occupational medicine into medical schools failed) and then went into reverse as the number of corporate positions for occupational physicians declined. Gochfeld (2005) added further context, noting that occupational medicine in the US had suffered as a field as a result of the growth of contingent work arrangements and outsourcing, managed care and weakened unions; as well as globalisation of manufacturing which, with its seemingly limitless supply of cheap labour, diminished interest in hazard controls and OHS more generally. With the exception of managed care, the issues identified by Gochfeld would apply to most developed countries.

Other aspects of healthcare infrastructure will affect the recognition of occupational disease. For example, where countries have comprehensive national population registries (as is the case with the Nordic countries) this can both facilitate epidemiological research and enable these studies to overcome practical difficulties such as control bias (NIEHS Working Group, 1998: 107). Unfortunately, such registries are not found in many countries, including Australia. Comprehensive and specific cancer registries can also be a powerful aid to epidemiological research (Calman, 1996). The types of epidemiological research that are funded to use them will influence the value of these registries, and in Australia occupational exposure has long been the poor cousin of cancer research funded by government and other agencies. As far as we are aware, the only relatively comprehensive cancer register in Australia with a clear occupational focus is the Australian Mesothelioma Register (Leigh et al., 1998). Even apparently small administrative changes and cost-saving measures may have important effects. For example, in recent years there has been a decline in autopsy rates in the US and this may well have a not-insignificant effect on the number of undiagnosed cancers, including those that are work related.

It is fair to say that there is presently no systematic effort to identify occupational disease risks in Australia and New Zealand and government agencies with responsibilities in this area have been starved of resources. The Industrial Hygiene Unit of the federal Department of Health in Australia did important work in the first decades of the twentieth century but was wound up before World War II. No real effort was made to fill this gap until the establishment of the National Occupational Health and Safety Commission (NOHSC) in the mid-1980s. The research arm of NOHSC (including both intramural programs and the funding of external research) started to fill some gaps (such as a study estimating exposure to silicosis; see Nurminen et al., 1992: 393–9) but was all but abolished by changes to NOHSC under the Coalition government elected in 1996 (Quinlan, 2000). The Mesothelioma Register—one of the most accurate registers of its type—was retained in a diminished form. Since the defeat of the Coalition government and the election of a federal Labor government in 2007 considerable funding has been directed to asbestos diseases and at the time of writing the Australian Safety and Compensation Council (itself to be restructured by the new government) was looking to restart the register. The National Industrial Chemical Notification and Assessment Scheme (NICNAS) continues to operate but, while valuable, it is unable to cope with the proliferation of new chemical products in industry (see chapter 1). While many states long operated occupational medical units these bodies could never fill the gaps just mentioned and several have also been recently downsized as part of the restructuring of OHS agencies. In short, infrastructural support for occupational disease detection is woefully inadequate.

Australia relies on information from overseas agencies (such as NIOSH) and professional standard-setting bodies, as well as international research. Although this may make sense, in many respects there is a need for research to ensure this information is relevant to Australian conditions (for example, where climate and differences in production or usage of chemicals affect exposure). Further, research in the other industrialised countries will reflect their industry mix. Winder (1991: 356) has argued that crucial similarities with the US make comparisons possible. Nevertheless, there are areas of industry/employment and climate that are sufficiently distinct to warrant specialised research. For example, Australia is rare if not unique among industrialised countries in having large-scale subtropical and tropical agriculture (pineapples, bananas, sugar, tea, macadamia nuts, mangoes, lychees and other exotic fruit) and beef production (New Zealand occupies a similar position regarding some other widely exported products like kiwi fruit). These agricultural products are mostly produced in developing countries. The chemicals used in these countries are not always identical to those used in Australia and research into the occupational health effects of pesticides and other chemicals used is minimal (for an account of high exposure to pesticides among workers in the Costa Rican banana industry see Wesseling, 1997). Even if research was available for these countries, differences in regulatory arrangements and production units (for example, where production was undertaken by large plantations as opposed to family-owned farms) might make it difficult to apply in the Australian context.

Elling (1986: 19) has argued that the political economy of production, including conflicts and interdependencies between capital and labour, will affect the reporting and gathering of information on occupational disease. As with health infrastructure, we can identify international differences that result from the historically contingent capital–labour nexus that has developed in particular countries, and the regulatory apparatus associated with this. In Australia, over the past 100 years there have been a series of disturbing examples of complicity by state agencies in the suppression of information on occupational disease risks in relation to lead (Gillespie, 1990), silicosis (James, 1993), asbestos (McCulloch and Tweedale, 2008) and steelmaking (Quinlan, 1997). We will return to this issue in a later section of this chapter.

One major area of occupational disease is respiratory and lung diseases. According to the International Agency for Research on Cancer (IARC, cited in Firth et al., 1997: x), 95% of known human lung carcinogens have been detected in workplace settings. Lung cancer is the largest single form of work-related cancer (Firth et al., 1997: x). The United States Centers for Disease Control has undertaken periodic surveillance of work-related lung disease, using information obtained from a number of government agencies, including the National Centre for Health Statistics, OSHA, the Mine Safety and Health Administration and the Bureau of Mines. The 2007 report (Centers for Disease Control, 2007: xxiii–xxv) identified 13 000 asbestosis deaths in the period 1995–2004 (with little recent movement in the annual average) and 15 000 malignant mesothelioma deaths in the period 1999–2004 (again with little evidence of trend improvement). The report noted trend improvements in mortality with regard to coal workers' pneumoconiosis (with annual deaths declining from 2500 in the early 1980s to less than 1000, 20 years later) and silicosis (from over 1000 deaths annually in the 1960s to less than 200, 40 years later). Nearly 20% of the mesothelioma deaths were females, women constituted almost one-third of byssinosis deaths, and healthcare had significantly elevated proportionate tuberculosis mortality in 1990–99. The top five occupations in terms of chronic obstructive pulmonary disease mortality were washing, cleaning and pickling machine operators; helpers, mechanics and repairers; textile cutting machine operators; mine machine operators and construction trades. Further, half of the 22 occupational groups identified in the 1990–99 data as being associated with significantly elevated risk of asthma-related death were related to healthcare and education (other at-risk industries were agriculture and livestock)—demonstrating that exposure risks to serious disease are not a male preserve (Centers for Disease Control, 2007: xxiii–xix). At a more disaggregated level, the report (Centers for Disease Control, 2007: xxvi) also noted that public health surveillance programs in four states (California, Massachusetts, Michigan and New Jersey) identified 4000 cases of work-related asthma in 1993–2002, of which 68% were caused by occupational exposure while 20% 'represented pre-existing asthma aggravated by occupational exposure'.

While the CDC reports contain valuable data on the significant toll of death due to work-related disease—data not matched in Australia, New Zealand or many other countries—they are by no means comprehensive and nor do they provide a detailed measure of incidence or frequency rates. The 2007 and earlier CDC reports (such as

Centers for Disease Control, 1996) acknowledged a series of limitations in the data, including relocation by persons with long latency disease, changes in employment patterns by industry and the absence of morbidity data (see also Leigh, 2005). While the CDC report includes data on hypersensitivity pneumonitis, a study of this disease among metal workers due to exposure to metal-working fluids (Gupta and Rosenman, 2006) found it was under-recognised by healthcare providers and current surveillance systems failed to provide an accurate estimate of its occurrence. As has been noted already, the recognition of work-related disease is affected by societal and regulatory factors, not simply the state of medical research. In its 1996 report the Centers for Disease Control (1996: 4–5) noted that recognition of pneumoconiosis had been enhanced by the passage of compensation and OHS laws but even here understatement was possible due to, for example, the relocation/retirement of mine workers to non-mining regions such as Florida and California. It is therefore hard to draw more than tentative (and conservative) conclusions about the overall incidence of occupational disease and trends with regard to a particular disease. With regard to work-related asthma, a review (Vandenplas et al., 2003) noted that there was accumulating evidence that the work environment made a significant and socioeconomically costly contribution to the general burden of asthma in the community. This and later reviews of the epidemiological evidence (Bardana, 2008) have estimated that those suffering work-related asthma account for between 9 and 15% of the total asthmatic population.

With regard to several important disease categories, available evidence is so fragmented that it is difficult to speculate on the overall proportion of the disease due to occupational exposure. Establishing a clear association between exposure and disease requires detailed knowledge of exposure, worker tasks and histories. With no systematic approach or resourcing (see below), in many instances there can be a considerable delay between the first suggestions of a link and the accumulation of evidence to establish (or refute) this. An example is the association between diesel exhaust and lung cancer where studies suggesting a link began to be published from the early 1980s. These results were confirmed by a meta-review in the late 1990s (Lipsett and Campleman, 1999), with more recent research clarifying the relationship between lung cancer and vehicle exhaust exposure in truck industry workers (Garshick et al., 2008). A 20- to 30-year lag is not atypical to accumulate the number of confirmatory studies required before an association is accepted. Even longer lags are common in relation to long-latency disease (Leigh, 2005). Since multiple exposures are also common, more systematic information is required on the predominant chemicals used and on other exposures in particular industries and types of workplace. In the US the National Institute of Occupational Safety and Health conducted national surveys of workplace exposure to hazardous substances in 1972–74 and 1981–83 as part of its hazard surveillance program (Greif et al., 1995: 264–9). In Denmark a national survey of the distribution of hazardous chemicals used in a stratified sample of businesses was carried out in the late 1980s (Brandoff et al., 1995) as an integral part of measures aimed at better regulating occupational exposures. Such studies appear to be exceptional and we know of no similar research in Australia. As noted below, occupational hygienists have also made an important contribution to our knowledge of hazard exposures in particular industries. Overall, however, information on hazard exposures and occupational disease remains fragmented and incomplete.

In several areas the link between disease and occupational exposures, and indeed other sources of exposure, remains ambiguous despite, in some instances, numerous studies over a long period of time. A good example is the scope of the occupational disease problem that can be attributed to exposure to electromagnetic fields. In 1998 a working group from the National Institute of Environmental Health Sciences conducted an extensive review of the available research literature (stretching over 30 years) on the health effects of exposure to powerline-frequency electric and magnetic fields in a range of settings including occupational exposures. With regard to the latter, the NIEHS Working Group report (1998: 286,132) concluded that the evidence was inadequate for an array of health effects apart from chronic lymphocytic leukemia where there was 'limited evidence that occupational exposure to extremely low-frequency magnetic fields is carcinogenic to adults'.

It is not uncommon for hazardous materials to give rise to a number of diseases and other health effects, including behavioural effects (such as increased aggression, depression and even suicide) although research into these multiple effects is often patchy. There is, for example, quite an extensive body of research into the neuropsychological effects of workers exposed to organophosphate pesticides including those used in sheep dips, banana plantations and a wide range other agricultural activities (for recent studies see Steenland et al., 1994 and Stephens et al., 1995). Another problem is the very limited amount of research that considers combinant effects. The overwhelming majority of existing epidemiological research focuses on a single or confined set of causal agents although in most workplaces workers are exposed to a wide array of chemicals and other potentially harmful agents, and in at least some cases the combined effects may be significant. Morata et al. (1994: 359–65) found a significant number of workers in the US were exposed to ototoxic organic solvents such as toluene that could alone, or in combination with noise, result in hearing loss but research into the impact of these effects (much less regulatory action and monitoring) was lacking. Even studies like this one identifying such gaps are relatively rare.

Further, there are areas of exposure and disease mechanisms that have attracted attention only comparatively recently and for which the collection of evidence is either at early stage or the findings remain inconclusive or contradictory. Examples of this include the long-term exposure of pilots to ionising radiation (Yong et al., 2009), nanotechnology (Ostiguy et al., 2008), chemicals such as 1-bromopropane (a replacement for chlorofluorocarbons; see Centers for Disease Control *MMWR* 2008, 75(48): 1300–2) and indoor air quality. In some cases, health risks may go unrecognised for many years. For example, retrospective analysis traced the first outbreak of legionnaires disease to the 1940s although it was not recognised until the 1976 outbreak that gave the disease its name. In other cases, research has identified a complex set of highly specific mechanisms that may affect health. For example, Ostiguy et al. (2008) observed that while toxicological data specific to nanoparticles remained limited it could be 'seen that each product, and even each synthesised NP batch, can have its own toxicity'. In yet other cases, such as Multiple Chemical Sensitivity and Chronic Fatigue Syndrome, the very existence of the problem let alone any occupational association has been the subject of vigorous and unresolved debate. Research has also identified potentially important disease mechanisms. In a recent review Albin et al. (2009: 4) identified four examples of this, namely oxidative stress implicated as the action of toxicity of compounds like cadmium; epigenetic (non-mutational) changes which can be transgenerational and increase susceptibility to a multitude of disorders (arsenic has been linked to this effect); alterations to miRNA that could represent a new epigenetic mechanism; and intra-uterine 'priming of sensitivity to postnatal exposure (cancer, attention disorders)'.

In other areas the hazard may be well known but comparatively little research has been carried out in workplace settings. An obvious example is the issue of the health effects of passive smoking at work. Although this deficit is being addressed, one problem is that among the most at-risk groups are hospitality workers, and the high labour turnover and casual employment practices common in this industry will make epidemiological tracking extraordinarily difficult (it is also an industry most resistant to placing bans on smoking). Another example relates to biological agents. Some biological risks, such as anthrax, have been recognised for over 100 years. However, in the last decade far more attention has been given to biologically induced diseases resulting from workplace exposure, including blood-borne pathogens such as HIV, hepatitis, salmonella poisoning among food processing workers, exposure to the hantavirus among workers coming into contact with rodents, and exposure to the hendra virus in those dealing with horses (such as trainers and veterinary staff). The occupations exposed to various categories of hepatitis are still being charted (Stevens and Coyle, 2007). Research has also been comparatively recent even in relation to some rather obvious and long-existing 'candidates' for biological assaults, such as sewage and mortuary workers (see McCunney, 1986; Levin et al., 1996). Overall, it can be argued that an array of biological risks have only been belatedly recognised. In the US, there were 5000 cases of hepatitis B infections among healthcare workers in 1990—a figure that declined to 800 in 1995 following the promulgation of the Bloodborne Pathogens Standard. (Jeffress, 1998a). According to OSHA (Jeffress, 1998b: 48250) there were an estimated 600 000 percutaneous injuries each year at work, with potentially serious consequences in terms of hepatitis, HIV and other diseases (for a discussion of blood-borne pathogen exposures see Gershon, 1996).

There are other important gaps and problems to do with our knowledge of occu-pational disease. One such problem is the ambiguous boundary between occupational exposure and disease, and environmental exposure and disease (Russell, 1995: 3–4). There are several elements to this problem. Hazardous substances—especially those that are soluble in water or airborne—do not respect workplace boundaries or the legal status of those they encounter. Hazardous airborne substances may spread from the workplace to the surrounding community where workers live, complicating the detec-tion of occupational exposure, or like dioxins, pesticide residues and other substances they may invade the soil or water table and be collected in animal fats with flow-on effects to humans. The extent of these effects is unknown but may be substantial, especially in particular communities. Hazardous substances such as benzene are emitted from an array of others sources such car exhaust and cigarette smoke. It is also well known that smoking exacerbates the impact of work-related exposure to hazardous substances such as asbestos. Other transmission mechanisms warrant recognition. For example, the relocation of work (and hazardous substances used in this) to the home and smaller, less regulated work settings that has resulted from the growth of telework, outsourcing and other forms of labour market/work re-organisation will make the detection of work-related disease more difficult. In some cases, hazardous materials adhering to workers' clothing, etc. may be a source of contamination in the home. In the US, a study by NIOSH (1996) found this was a serious problem with, for example, children of construction workers exposed to lead being six times more likely to have blood lead levels over the recommended limit than those whose parents did not work in lead-exposed jobs. An Italian study (Aggazzotti et al., 1994) found significantly higher levels of perchloroethylene—a compound used in dry cleaning—in the homes of dry cleaning workers. There is also evidence on the transmission of fatal levels of asbestos exposure to the wives, if not the children, of asbestos industry workers in a number of countries, including Italy (see Magnani et al., 1993: 779–84; McCulloch and Tweedale, 2008). The last point raises the question as to whether occupational disease statistics should include those persons suffering disease indirectly as a result of workplace exposure to a family member.

A related issue is the question of the reproductive effects of occupational exposures to hazardous substances. Even a decade ago, NIOSH estimated there were over 1000 workplace chemicals shown to have reproductive effects on animals (most have not been assessed in relation to humans) while most of the four millions chemicals in commercial use remain untested. Assessing reproductive risk is not simple since there are a number of possible effects (infertility, increased risk of spontaneous abortion, stillbirth, birth defects and childhood diseases such as leukemia and non-Hodgkin's lymphoma) and animal tests cannot be simply correlated to workplace exposure. Aside from chemicals, physical hazards such as X-rays, biological hazards (from the handling of animals by process workers or contact with childhood diseases such as German measles among teachers and childcare workers) and strenuous or stressful work may present a problem for working women who fall pregnant (Chamberlain, 1991: 1070–3). Another complicating factor is that human male fertility is lower than test animals, which may make the former more susceptible to damage (EPA Office of Research and Development, 1996: 55). Despite these complexities, by 1996 the US Environmental Protection Agency (EPA Office of Research and Development, 1996) was sufficiently concerned to produce detailed guidelines on risk assessment.

There is a (slowly) growing body of evidence on the reproductive risks associated with particular chemicals such as toluene, pesticides and a range of other substances (Messing, 1998: 137–51). The bulk of this research has focused on transmission via exposure to female workers (Figa-Talamanca, 2006) rather than via the sperm of exposed male workers, even though documents produced by NIOSH and the EPA recognised male exposure as a major problem (for an exception see Berry, 1995). The EPA Office of Research and Development (1996: 19) argued that, unless there was evidence to the contrary, chemicals should be assumed to affect both sexes because mechanisms controlling reproduction were similar and there was a pronounced imbalance in research. Further, in spite of the latter, there was evidence of toxicity resulting from male exposures. Limited evidence on reproductive effects almost certainly contributes to an understatement of the impact of occupational exposures to hazardous substances.

In highlighting the gender imbalance in research on reproductive risks, Messing (1998: 138–9) noted that for many years research concentrated on the health of the foetus rather than the health problems experienced by pregnant workers. Messing correctly saw the focus on female reproductive risks as reflecting an isolated exception to the general paucity of research into the occupational health problems of female workers and a widespread but questionable presumption that women's work was less hazardous (see also Messing, 1992: 1–9). There are a number of elements to this problem. One aspect was the neglect of occupational health problems in industries and occupations (such as service tasks) where female workers were concentrated. It is arguable women were neglected even where they were employed in workplaces that were traditional focal points for research, such as factories (for an exception see the study of women exposed to 1,1,1-trichloroethane by House et al., 1994). There are signs of change, including studies of heat stress among female laundry workers and hepatitis A among childcare workers (Brabant, 1992; Tranter, 1998; Jacques et al., 1994; Messing et al., 1995). Recent research on the health effects of precarious employment and psychosocial working conditions has increasingly explored gender and has commonly identified significant differences in terms of outcomes (see, for example, Kim et al., 2008; Wieclaw et al., 2008). Notwithstanding some positive trends, a significant gender imbalance remains with regard to occupational health research (Messing, 2002) and consequently our knowledge of occupational disease risks among women is even more fragmentary than the inadequate evidence pertaining to men. There are relatively few studies of disease, health and hazard exposures with regard to self-employed workers or those working from isolated situations like homes—both areas where women are conspicuously represented (Sasaki and Matsumoto, 2005). While the structured health inequalities confronting men also warrant attention (Williams, 2003), meeting the urgent need for more systematic research into occupational disease and health issues would necessitate redressing the longstanding gender imbalance. Further, care needs to be taken so that research undertaken is properly contextualised so that it is not misinterpreted (for example, studies of menstrual disorders and their adverse symptoms at work; see, for example, Smith, 2008).

Another factor contributing to the imbalance in knowledge regarding occupational health among women is—as a recent Canadian study has shown (Le Jeune et al., 2008)—the serious gaps in government data sources.

Other complicating factors in relation to work-related disease and other health problems experienced by women require attention. Notable here is the imbalance of domestic duties that means women workers must cope with a 'double burden' of trying to meet both work and domestic demands, and the complex combined effects this has for their health. While some research has examined the impacts on non-occupational diseases like rheumatoid arthritis (Reisine and Fifield, 1995), far more recent research has been directed at the impact of work/non-work conflicts on health impairment (van Hooff et al., 2005) and more especially psychological wellbeing (see, for example, Allan et al., 2007; Haines et al., 2008; Innstrand et al., 2008). Other potential influences on health include the subordinate jobs women occupy and the patriarchal management structures they must confront, bullying and sexual harassment and greater reluctance or inability to report health problems at work (Walters et al., 1995: 127–8; Quinlan, 1996: 412–4). Evidence pertaining to several of these issues is discussed later in this chapter.

Demographic factors such as age and immigrant status can also affect the recognition of occupational disease and ill health. For example, tracking exposures among the hundreds of millions of foreign-born workers who now form a significant proportion of the labour force in Australia, the US and other countries represents a significant challenge, especially when these workers are mobile or relocate, change jobs or are part of the growing army of foreign temporary workers (guest workers, backpackers and students). The question of age raises a number of complications. With regard to younger workers there is the problem that many will typically have held a series of jobs of short duration by the time they reach their early thirties, making the linking of exposure to disease difficult. The substantial numbers of students who work part time also raises complexities in measuring health effects (Santana et al., 2005). Older workers raise a number of other issues. This includes the difficulty of disentangling work-related components of diseases and chronic illnesses also related to ageing (Wegman and McGee, 2004). Another set of challenges arise from the contradictory demands of trying to maintain the labour force participation of older workers to address the ageing population of many countries while at the same time trends to work intensification and contingent work (described elsewhere in this book) diminish their health and work ability (Wegman and McGee, 2004; Sluiter, 2006; Schofield et al., 2008). Another aspect of this contradiction is that repeated rounds of downsizing/restructuring have impacted more heavily on the health of older workers (who survive the restructuring) while forcing others into premature retirement (with associated health effects), onto disability pensions or into more precarious and health-damaging (both directly and via the health effects of reduced socioeconomic status) forms of employment (Gallo et al., 2004; Vahtera et al., 2005; Sacker et al., 2008; Bohle et al., 2010). Job losses and labour market 'skidding' associated with economic recessions such as the severe one occurring at the time of writing will only serve to sharpen these contradictions and make hazard exposures, diseases and other health effects even more difficult to track (Gardiner et al., 2007; AARP, 2009).

In addition to the points just made there is a need to recognise the effect that organisational factors within the workplace as well as broader social structures may have on the development and reporting of disease and other health indicators. However, as the discussion of gender demonstrates, other factors may affect the onset of disease.

In our discussion thus far attention has focused on problems mapping the relationship between work and diseases due to exposure to hazardous substances. Of course, as occupational hygienists have shown (see below) different production processes and methods for handling hazardous materials can have profound effects on exposure levels. However, demographic factors such as age may also have an effect. The population and workforces of most industrialised countries are aging. This may have implications for both exposure and the medical care of exposed workers but there has been little if any attempt to assess this (for an OHS nursing perspective on this issue see Hart and Moore, 1992: 36–40). Some groups of workers may be especially vulnerable to exposures, including children and adolescent workers (see Forastieri, 1997: 22–3). The employment of children and adolescents may be an issue most significant for developing countries. However, it also has relevance for industrialised countries where children are employed in agriculture, where increasing use has been made of adolescents in fast-food and service jobs, and where increased employment of children has been linked to the re-emergence of home-based work and the informal economy. In short, work organisation and social structures can affect the extent and impact of exposure to hazardous substances. However, there is also evidence that organisational factors may be a source of disease in their own right. In a later section we present epidemiological evidence that suggests the organisation of work, including demands placed on workers, their place in the job hierarchy and the degree of control they exercise, have significant measurable effects on the risk of myocardial infarction and other health indicators. As yet, little or not attempt has been made to incorporate this evidence into calculations about the extent of occupational disease.

Overall, there is relatively reliable evidence on the number and incidence of particular occupational diseases (including some types of work-related lung disease) as well as the association between disease and certain production processes/hazardous substances (such as vinyl chloride). Since the 1980s new reporting systems and databases have increased the amount and quality of information on occupational disease. However, information on the extent and incidence of occupational disease remains a fractured patchwork with many gaps (Carter, 1991: 289–91). For the reasons just mentioned it is not possible to construct aggregate data or patterns of incidence of occupational disease by industry/occupation with the degree of comprehensiveness and accuracy that is the case with occupational injuries. Nevertheless, available evidence indicates that occupational disease is a substantial problem and attempts to produce aggregate data, even if somewhat speculative, reinforce this point. In the US for example, Leigh et al. (1997) estimated that the civilian workforce experienced around 6500 job-related fatal traumas and 13.2 million job-related non-fatal injuries each year compared with 60 300 fatalities due to occupational disease and 862 000 non-fatal illnesses. Driscoll (1993: 164–6) has supported this pattern, where occupational disease is seen to result in higher mortality but lower levels of morbidity in comparison to occupational injuries.

In Australia, Kerr et al. (1996) made the most systematic attempt to measure the magnitude of death due to occupational exposures to hazardous substances and compare this to other common sources of death (see table 5.1). Table 5.1 (Kerr et al.,

1996: 60) indicates that in 1992 exposure to hazardous substances at work was responsible for more deaths than all other selected causes, with the exception of suicide, and this was more than four times the number of deaths due to injury at work. Among males, the incidence of deaths due to occupational exposures to hazardous substances far exceeded all other selected causes. The estimate that work-related disease was responsible for around 2200 deaths annually initially aroused considerable controversy and some trenchant criticism (Christophers and Zammit, 1997: 331–9). Evaluating this criticism, Gun supported Christophers and Zammit's point about chemical-related death from non-malignant diseases but noted that their estimate did not include deaths due to acute chemical injuries or pneumoconiosis (see CDC report on US data above). Driscoll (1997: 341–52) argued that many of the attacks on Kerr et al. were ill-founded and the furore largely arose from the apparently abrupt increase in the level of work-related fatal disease which could more accurately be viewed as rectifying a gross level of understatement in the past. We would endorse both observations. It is worth noting that the controversy proved to be short-lived and updated figures based on Kerr et al.'s estimates are now widely quoted. Indeed, the furore now looks distinctly odd. In the US, government agency estimates suggesting that occupational disease was responsible for a far higher number of fatalities than occupational injury can be traced back to at least the early 1970s (Elling, 1986: 19–20). Further, the Australian Mesothelioma Register indicated that this one form of overwhelmingly occupationally induced disease was alone responsible for around 400 deaths annually by the early 1990s (and is still yet to peak; Leigh et al. 1998: 8). In other words, the annual toll from just one form of occupational disease fell not far short of the annual number of all work-related traumatic deaths. Even if the CDC data for the US discussed earlier was used in heavily discounted fashion it would suggest that the Kerr et al. figures may yet prove to be an underestimate.

Table 5.1 Comparison of deaths due to occupational exposure to hazardous substances with those from other selected causes, Australia, 1992[1] (frequency and rate)

Condition	Number of deaths	Death rate (per million)
Motor vehicle accidents	2066	120
Suicide	2294	130
AIDS	643	36
Homicide	319	20
Work-related traumatic death Male Female Persons	483 32 515	121 13 81
Hazardous substances Male Female Persons	1752 487 2239	255 69 161

Source: Kerr et al. (1996: 60)

[1] All data is for 1992 except for those concerning work-related traumatic fatalities, which are the yearly average for 1982–84.

As far as we are aware, no comprehensive attempt has been made to estimate the extent of morbidity associated with work-related disease in Australia. Data on morbidity is, if anything, even more inadequate that that pertaining to disease-related fatalities, and this represents a major barrier to better understanding the origins and prevalence of occupational disease. Sim (2007: 557–72) has argued for the introduction of an occupational disease surveillance system in Australia to be used in conjunction with other tools such as hazard exposure databases (for a recent initiative in this regard see Creaser et al., 2007: 563–70). For comparatively rich countries like Australia and New Zealand these initiatives are in our view long overdue. The development of such systems will need to be informed by recognition of changes to technology, work organisation and exposed populations, including vulnerable groups such as temporary and seasonal workers (Bohle et al., 2009).

In chapter 1 reference was made to the rapid proliferation of chemicals and other hazardous substances in the workplace—a proliferation subject to only minimal regulatory controls. It is no loose analogy to suggest that we may have seen only the tip of the iceberg of occupational diseases that could impact on workers in Australia, New Zealand and other countries over the next few decades.

Explaining occupational disease, stress and illness: the contribution of particular disciplines

Occupational medicine and epidemiology

Role and history

Occupational medicine has played a critical role in the identification and treatment of occupational disease, not simply in the sense of dealing with individual workers but also in shaping our understanding of the extent and nature of such diseases, their causes and the broad solutions that should be adopted. The origins of occupational medicine can be traced back 400 years to a number of physicians who published their findings linking particular occupations, such as miners, with specific ailments. However, as was noted in chapter 2, occupational medicine primarily grew up in an ad hoc fashion during the Industrial Revolution from the clinical experience of physicians employed within industrial towns and regions where they were called on to deal with what were clearly distinctive patterns of disease and injury. It was further bolstered by the development of workers' compensation legislation and the demands it created in terms of linking illness to work (Ferguson, 1994).

A number of early observations on the relationship of work to disease were especially perceptive and have not lost their saliency. In 1713, Bernado Ramazzini (1964, reprint: 15), a general physician often dubbed the founder of occupational medicine, wrote:

> Various and manifold is the harvest of diseases reaped by certain workers from the crafts and trades they pursue; all the profit they get is fatal injury to their health.

That crop germinates mostly, I think from two causes. The first and most potent is the harmful character of the materials they handle, for these emit noxious vapours and very fine particles inimical to human beings and induce particular diseases; the second cause I ascribe to certain violent and irregular motions and unnatural postures of the body, by reason of which the natural structure of the vital machine is so impaired that serious diseases gradually develop there from.

Ramazzini's methods of diagnosis remain instructive. He did not rely simply on clinical observation but directly investigated workers, observing their tasks and the working environment (Milles, 1985: 59–60).

Clinical diagnosis based on establishing a causal association between exposure of workers to a specific physical agent and a disease through a detailed occupational history played a dominant role in the development of occupational medicine. Clinical diagnosis remains central although it has been increasingly augmented by epidemiology. It would be wrong to characterise the mainstream of occupational medicine as remaining entirely unaware of the need to take account of legislation and social problems, or even to reflect on its own history (there is an extensive literature on the history of occupational medicine). Weindling (1985: 3) notes that almost one-third of Hunter's *The Diseases of Occupations*—for many years a standard text on occupational medicine—was devoted to history, including case studies illustrating 'the limitations of medical science, particularly in the face of social problems'. However, Weindling (1985: 3) argues that Hunter's use of history lacked critical awareness, tending to eulogise progress in legislation and medicine without reference to the difficulties of effecting improvements in OHS practice.

Using clinical observation or epidemiological methods, occupational medical research has largely focused on identifying or evaluating physical agents (chemicals, mineral fibres and even drugs such as alcohol) that have a one-off or cumulative health effect, as measured by the presence/extent of disease or its immediate precursors. Occupational epidemiology represented a major development in terms of identifying and measuring health risks with the application of quantitative methods in the twentieth century (Stellman, 2003). Nonetheless, most studies evaluate a single or closely related group of substances in relation to a restricted category of workers and in terms of a confined range of health outcomes whereas most workers will be subjected to multiple exposures (accentuated in the case of some socio-demographic groups; Quinn et al., 2007). The detection of occupational cancer using epidemiology is difficult, requiring the elimination of a range of possible confounding factors and some degree of caution in interpreting results (Doll, 1985: 22–31). Limited access to employee records, or their destruction by employers, also presents difficulties for historical cohort studies and case control studies (Betts and Rushton, 1998; Rushton and Betts, 2000), as do industries and occupations marked by significant levels of labour turnover. The occupational disease risks faced by women remain under-researched within epidemiology (Artazcoz et al., 2007), including the role of occupational exposures in major disease risks such as breast cancer (for a recent exception see Shahm et al., 2006).

Notwithstanding this, medical research has been immensely important in identifying diseases and connecting them to an array of hazardous substances, some examples of which are to found in this and other chapters of this book. Like a number of the expert technical approaches to occupational injury discussed in chapter 3, occupational medicine has a commendable focus on the physical working environment and, as such, has provided important insights into the origin of diseases that might otherwise have gone unrecognised. It has provided crucial evidence on the need to control or ban certain materials from the workplace as well as support for changes in production processes. Yet the preoccupation with physical characteristics and disease has also been a source of weakness, leaving other causal factors and other evidence of ill health under-researched. Addressing particular hazardous substances is important but, in the absence of a more holistic approach, unlikely to achieve a healthy working environment. Further, given its detached clinical focus, occupational medicine has been less capable of suggesting an array of measures to control exposure to harmful substances than is the case with occupational hygiene (see next section). Moreover, despite the development of more sophisticated techniques, recognition of disease risks is still often belated, restricted to extreme cases and requires appropriate responses both on the part of state agencies and organised labour.

Overall, prior to the 1980s clinical occupational medicine and epidemiological research took little account of the organisation of work as a cause of injury and disease and much research within the field continues to follow this paradigm. We are not suggesting that this research is not valuable. Identifying hazardous substances used in the workplace and their impacts on health is critical. At the same time, it needs to be recognised that exposures can be affected by work organisation and the extent and enforcement of regulatory standards (see below). Further, as the next section shows, over the past 20 or more years a growing body of evidence from researchers in the field of medicine and epidemiology (drawing on work by scholars in other fields) has demonstrated that the way work is organised can be a source of illness and disease in its own right.

Recognition of work organisation by medicine and epidemiology and the growth of multidisciplinary research

From the 1980s a growing body of medical research began to examine the health effects of particular work arrangements, including shiftwork, long or irregular working hours and the specific effects of this on pregnant workers (Xu et al., 1994; Spurgeon at al., 1997: 367–75; Liu and Tanaka, 2002; Dembe et al., 2005; Boivin et al., 2007; Erren, 2009). The health effects of working time arrangements have attracted considerable attention from researchers in other fields, such as psychology, with recent studies looking at the effects of control of working time as well as work–family interference (see, for example, Hughes and Parkes, 2007). The health effects of working time are explored in depth in chapter 6.

Other areas of growing interest among medical researchers include the health of particular groups of workers, such as immigrants and women, and the health of specific occupations, such as bus and truck drivers. With regard to the latter, a number of European and then US studies explored the link between work demands and heart disease among bus and truck drivers (Netterstrom and Laursen, 1981; Hartvig and Midttun, 1983; Krause et al., 1997a & b). A review of 22 epidemiological studies of bus drivers (Winkleby et al., 1988: 255–62) found that, irrespective of methodology and other variations, the studies consistently reported that bus drivers experience higher rates of mortality, morbidity and illness-related absence than workers in a wide range of other occupations. In their own study of 1449 urban transit operators (Krause et al., 1997b:179–86) they found that physical workload and psychosocial factors were simultaneously and independently associated with back and neck pain. The psychosocial factors identified as influential included extended uninterrupted driving periods, frequency of job problems, high psychological demands, high job dissatisfaction and low supervisory support (Krause et al., 1997: 179). They concluded that the study supported the role of psychosocial job characteristics in the aetiology of occupational back and neck pain. It followed that these issues could be addressed through reorganisation of work processes. The same survey also revealed that alcohol consumption was also related to occupational factors including specific worksite and shift times as well as reported job stressors (Ragland et al., 1995: 635–45). Further research by the same team on San Francisco bus drivers revealed that the pressure of a largely unachievable scheduling and linked bonus/penalty system was the overwhelming factor contributing to high blood pressure and the longer they drove the higher it got. What is also noteworthy about this research was the active involvement of the union in all stages of the project.

There were a number of interconnections and critical researchers in what was to become a significant development in occupational medicine and epidemiological research. In the US, Len Syme and June Fisher played a critical role in the urban transit study just mentioned and some years earlier Syme had supervised Michael Marmot's PhD. Marmot (who was English born and had studied medicine at the University of Sydney) took a position at University College, London, where, with a talented team of associates, including Jane Ferrie, he pioneered researched into the impact of social gradients at work on health (Marmot, 1998), principally via a large longitudinal study of workers within the British civil service, known as the Whitehall II study. Clustering the surveyed workforce into four broad groups differentiated on the basis of socio-economic status and job control (administrators at the top followed by professionals, clerical workers and others), Marmot et al. found a clear ranking of health outcomes. In Finland researchers, including Jussi Vahtera, Kivimaki and Marianne Virtanen, undertook work (most notably a longitudinal study of local government workers) that in many ways paralleled and complemented Whitehall II. Taken as a whole, this work has helped to inspire a large and growing body of medical and epidemiological research on the social determinants of workplace health internationally.

To some degree, the growing interest of medical researchers in the impact of social characteristics of work on health was inspired by and drew on the work of several researchers in other disciplines, providing a tangible example of the benefits of the multidisciplinarity advocated throughout this book. Most notable here was the work of Robert Karasek, a psychologist, and Johannes Siegrist, a sociologist.

Karasek (1979) and his colleagues (Karasek et al., 1981, 1982, 1988; Theorell et al., 1987; Schnaul et al., 1990, 2000) argued that there was a strong association between job strain and coronary heart disease, myocardial infarction and elevated blood pressure. Karasek's notion of job strain—the combination of high job demands with limited control or latitude for independent decision making—has been the source of considerable further research. Marmot et al. (1997), for example, explored the contribution of job control and other social factors to coronary heart disease, emphasising the importance of the former in explaining variations in health. With some qualifications, a large body of subsequent research (amounting to well over 100 studies and growing steadily) undertaken in many countries and across a wide range of different occupations (from farmers, factory workers and truck drivers to public servants and call centre workers) has endorsed the value of the demand–control/job strain model. For example, a study of Swedish farmers (Thelin, 1998: 139–45) found that male farmers had a significantly higher authority over work in comparison to that for other occupations and this, together with lifestyle factors, was probably related to their low risk of coronary heart disease. A more recent study of call centre workers (Croidieu et al., 2008) found that demand–control imbalance increased with seniority, low decision-latitude increased with firm size and psychological demands were higher on workers handling both incoming and outgoing calls. The demand-control or job strain model has also acted as a stimulus for medical researchers to start exploring areas of organisations and work that would have once been seen as the preserve of industrial relations and organisational behaviour, such as notions of organisational justice and more recently leadership. A high level of justice in managerial behaviour has been found to have a positive effects on worker health while abusive, passive-avoidant and laissez-faire leadership has been associated with increased psychological distress and increased risk of cardiovascular disease (for a recent exploration of leadership effects, see Nyberg et al., 2009).

The demand-control model has been subject to some criticism. Karen Messing has argued that the model conflates physiological and psychosocial workload. The model has also been seen as too task-focused, ignoring broader organisational and environmental factors (such as labour market conditions and available social support). Johnson (2008) notes the model was developed before Keynesian policies and an interest in workplace democratisation in Europe (and Australasia) were supplanted by global neo-liberalism with its emphasis on 'flexible' (including labour) markets and removing social protection which has led to rising social inequality and power imbalances. Nonetheless, Johnson (2008: 15) concludes that the 'core elements, namely, the intensification of effort, power, and collectivity, continue to provide important ways of viewing the human impact of neoliberal globalisation'. Other potential limitations identified by subsequent studies include that the psychological demand dimension within the model is too generic (Sundin et al., 2008) and that the inclusion of older workers within study cohorts dilutes the association between job strain and heart disease (Kivimaki et al., 2008). Karasek has responded to perceived limitations by making revisions to the model, the first step being the job demand–control–support model (DCS), though criticisms of physiological mechanisms remain (see Shirom et al., 2008).

The other major contribution to medical research on the social determinants of health at work was the effort/reward (ERI) imbalance model developed by German sociologist Johannes Siegrist (1996). In essence, the model argues that imbalances in efforts and rewards (both intrinsic and extrinsic) will adversely affect the health and wellbeing of workers. As with Karasek's model, a considerable body of medical research using the instrument developed by Siegrist has found that it has value in terms of explaining a range of health outcomes (both physiological and psychological) at work. For example, a body of studies (see, for example, Willis et al., 2008) has found the model is a good predictor of the work-related stress associated with work–family conflict and burnout. Further, a study involving Marmot and Siegrist (Chandola et al., 2007) found the effort/reward imbalance model can also be used to explain the health effects of close social relationships of workers (in terms of failed reciprocity in partnership, parent–children and general trusting). This indicates the model may have value in guiding counselling and stress interventions outside the sphere of work.

Karasek's demand-control-support (DCS) model and Siegrist's effort reward imbalance model (ERI) should not be seen as separate realms of research but rather two important attempts to explain how the organisation of work affects health. A number of researchers (including Marmot et al.) have used both models and the findings have often been complementary. For example, a Finnish study of local government workers by Ala-Mursula et al. (2005) found that employee control over working time moderated the effects of job strain and effort-reward imbalance on sickness absence.

Both models have provided important insights into the health effects of workplace change and the job insecurity associated with organisational restructuring/downsizing and the growth of contingent forms of employment. A now extensive body of research (see, for example, Ferrie et al., 1995, 1998; Vahtera et al., 1998, 2005; Niedhammer et al., 2006; Labbe et al., 2007) has found that downsizing and job insecurity are associated with increases in psychological distress, sickness absence, cardiovascular disease, disability and even drug use among 'surviving' workers. Other medical researchers have explored analogous concepts. For example, a longitudinal Swedish study (Petterson et al., 2005) of hospital employees found redundancies/restructuring were associated with increased work demands and deteriorating mental health while decreased time to plan work was associated with increased long-term sick leave. Assessing the health effects of downsizing is difficult because these changes to processes are complex and mixed in with other changes such as outsourcing; conventional OHS indicators such as absenteeism and workers' compensation/disability claims may be distorted by institutional and reporting effects (such as those linked to presenteeism); and there may also be a 'healthy worker' effect if pre-existing health status influences those targeted for retrenchment (Arrighi and Hertz-Picciotto, 1994). However, a number of the larger longitudinal studies such as the Whitehall II study of Ferrie et al. have adopted methodologies (including multiple morbidity and health behaviour measures) that overcome most if not all of these limitations. Downsizing and organisational change may have other effects on OHS, including influencing employer practices relevant to the detection of occupational and other diseases. For example, a survey by the Centre for Disease Control (1997: 421–4) found fewer US worksites conducted cancer screening in 1995 than three years earlier with corporate downsizing being identified as one of three possible causal factors. Interestingly, recent research (Ferrie et al., 2008: 98–110) indicates that labour force expansion can also have adverse effects of health, suggesting that it is the change process and not simply the direction of change that damages health.

Studies of the health effects of part-time and temporary work have progressively included a broader spectrum of countries (Kim et al., 2008). More recent studies have also investigated the gender effects of precarious employment. What is also of benefit are an ongoing series of critical reviews of the research literature, weighing the evidence and pointing to gaps for further research (see, for example, Ferrie et al., 2008; Quinlan and Bohle, 2008, 2009). Thus, while much of the research on presenteeism (see below) has focused on its effects on psychological distress and burnout, such workplace practices also have implications for chronic injuries, infections, allergies and arthritis (Schultz and Edington, 2007).

Recent research and the growth of precarious employment has highlighted the need for the Karasek model in particular to take account of broader labour market and social factors, something that Karasek has begun to undertake. The application of the DCS and ERI models to workplace change has also been imbalanced, largely focused on the effects of downsizing/job insecurity on employees in large organisations and, to a lesser extent, comparing health outcomes for temporary, part-time and permanent workers. Even research into the latter group is at present not sufficiently extensive or conceptually refined (between different categories of temporary or part-time workers, or to consider spillover effects or exposure effects arising because temporary workers may work fewer hours/have intermittent work sequences). For example, a number of studies have found significant gender-based differences in the health effects arising from factors such as the dual burden or double load on women arising from their care activities in the home (Gash et al., 2006). Recent studies (Schweder, 2009) also suggest there may be distinct causal trajectories for health and safety outcomes so that temporary workers may experience higher injury-rates but not worse health outcomes than permanent workers. With regard to spillover effects it needs to be recognised that the presence of temporary workers (or subcontractors for that matter) can affect the health and wellbeing of permanent workers due to the shifting of supervisory, administrative loads, training responsibilities and the like (Mayhew and Quinlan, 2006). Changes to interpersonal relationships may also be important. A Quebec study of adult education teachers (Siefert et al., 2007: 299) found precarious work contracts adversely affected mental health through not only job insecurity but also negative effects 'on the ability to do one's job and take pride in one's work, as well as weakening the interpersonal relationships on which successful, productive work depends'. Further, there is growing evidence that the spillover effects of downsizing/understaffing and use of contingent workers (such as contractors and temporary workers) can extend to the health and safety of clients and customers (Quinlan and Bohle, 2008: 496). For example, a study by Stegenga et al. (2002) found an association between nurse understaffing and nonsocial viral gastrointestinal infections on a general pediatrics ward.

Important areas of change to work organisation such as outsourcing/subcontracting, self-employment (including micro businesses, home-based work and franchising arrangements) have received little attention (for a review of research on the OHS effects of privatisation, see Egan et al., 2007). Among those medical and epidemiological studies of these changes only a few try to apply either the DCS or ERI models. Nonetheless, some of the research is worthy of mention. A Danish study of privatisation/ outsourcing of bus drivers (Netterstrom and Hansen, 2000) found that outsourced drivers experienced deterioration in their psychosocial work environment, as well as a variety of physiological symptoms of stress, including increased systolic blood pressure. Medical researchers such as Suruda (1992), Bull et al. (2002) and Sorensen et al. (2007) have also undertaken research into hazard exposures and health in enterprises of different sizes, with most finding that smaller enterprises (including those that are part of a larger enterprise) tend to be more hazardous even when industry is controlled (though most ignore whether the small firm is part of a subcontracting network). These findings are in accordance with similar work undertaken by sociologists and industrial relations researchers, although the latter are able to provide additional insights on how workplace relations differ in smaller workplaces and the meanings that workers attach to their experiences (Eakin and MacEachen, 1998; Mayhew, 2000; Walters, 2001a). There is also a series of medical studies of home-care providers (for a review see Quinlan and Bohle, 2008). Again, their contribution is by no means exclusive. Psychologists such as Julian Barling and Michael Frone (Barling and Mendelson, 1999; Barling and Frone, 2003) have also made important contributions in this area, examining the effects of home-based work, intergenerational effects on families and the vulnerabilities of younger workers (who are concentrated in contingent jobs). Barling and Tom Cox, as editors of the *Journal of Occupational Health Psychology* and *Work & Stress* respectively, have been well attuned to the challenges posed by changing work arrangements. As noted below, researchers in other disciplines have recently tried to develop models to explain how precarious employment affects health.

At the same time, growing interesting among medical and epidemiological researchers in the effect of profound changes to work organisation over the past 30 years, as well as equally profound demographic changes to the workforce, is reflected in studies of gender differences in the health effects of precarious employment (Menendez et al., 2007). It has also been increasingly dovetailed with research into the problems encountered by foreign workers, including undocumented/illegal immigrants (Lipscomb et al., 2008). It has been reflected in research into precarious employment and the informal sector such as street vendors, domestic workers and small businesses that are largely unregulated in poor countries and which can account for half the workforce in some countries (EMCONET, 2007). An epidemiological study by Santana et al. (1997: 1236–42) of women workers in the informal sector in Brazil found evidence to suggest that informal work had adverse effects on mental health and this was exacerbated by imbalances in the allocation of domestic tasks. Another Brazilian study (Iriat et al., 2008) highlighted the importance of the absence of legislative protection in shaping the attitudes of informal workers to occupational health hazards in their jobs.

The issues and nuances of constructive debate among researchers working in these areas should not detract from several fundamental observations.

First, over the past 15 years a significant and growing cohort of medical and epidemiological researchers have not only embraced the concept of work organisation but, particularly through the work of Marmot et al. and the application of models developed by Karasek and Siegrist, have demonstrated that the way work is organised has profound effects of health and wellbeing. Indeed, in contrast to a number of other areas of OHS research discussed in this book (such as behaviour-based safety), there is now a large and compelling body of evidence documenting which aspects of work organisation damage people's health and, in so doing, suggesting what changes or remedies are needed. These parallel and extend the workload and organisational justice themes that marked industrial relations research (with notable exceptions, more so than that found in human resource management or organisational behaviour). The problem is that this evidence is largely incompatible with the major trends in work organisation (including management labour strategy and neo-liberal government policy) that have marked the last 30 years and have yet (at the time of writing) to be seriously reconsidered. For those seeking to manage OHS more effectively this disjunction represents a major challenge.

Second, although medical scholars such as Marmot (and others too numerous to list) have played a critical role in promoting this new research agenda, the research has both drawn on the work of scholars in other fields such as psychology and sociology (most notably Karasek and Siegrist) and encouraged more multidisciplinary research (in terms of conception, the teams involved and methodology). It has provided a new methodological basis for linking work organisation to occupational health. Further, we can identify other developments in medical/epidemiological research that are helping to build a more multifaceted explanation of occupational disease and variations in health indices among different groups of workers (especially vulnerable groups such as immigrants). In many respects this represents an important step towards the multidisciplinary approach to OHS this book has advocated since the first edition (1991). Important challenges remain, notably how to transform this evidence into concrete practices, policies and laws—areas where the contribution of fields such as industrial relations and law are critical. Even here, however, there is evidence of some progress. For example, occupational medicine and epidemiological journals have begun to publish research on the effects of representative structures, laws and legislative compliance while in 2009 the *American Journal of Public Health* published a special issue on community struggles and occupational health.

Third, the reference to public health raises another critical point. The growing recognition among medical and epidemiological researchers that work is a form of social organisation and the specific ways work is organised affect health outcomes—profoundly—reflects similar trends (although more a rediscovery) in terms of the social determinants of health more generally. It has long been recognised that those in lower socioeconomic groups experienced significantly higher levels of morbidity and mortality than those groups near the top. However, research was unable to explain finer gradations (for example, why doctors should die younger than those at the very top) and it was also recognised that classical risk factors (diet, alcohol, tobacco and exercise) explained less than half the individual variation in coronary heart disease (Dixon, 1999: 17). An increasingly influential group of researchers (such as Marmot, 1998) argued that although classical biomedical factors remain relevant, class and working and living conditions are more important risk factors. McMichael (1989: 12) argued '… social structural and biomedical risk factors do not necessarily represent competing, alternative explanations; rather they suggest different stages in the underlying causal chain and they suggest different, potentially complementary, preventive strategies.' Further, the social determinants of health with regard to work both influence and are affected by other social determinants of health such as the poverty, education, urban living conditions, access to and nature of healthcare, organisational participation, migration, gender structures within society and the like (see, for example, Caperchione et al., 2008; Najman et al., 2008). As the obsequious devotion to neo-liberalism over the past 20 years demonstrates, government policies and business practices may impact on health in all these areas simultaneously (Bird, 2001; Labonte and Schrecker, 2007; Florey et al., 2007; Krieger, 2008). Any attempt to address the social determinants of health must recognise these interconnections (Blas et al., 2008). There has recently been an ambitious attempt to address this. In 2005 the World Health Organization established a Commission for the Social Determinants for Health (CSDH) which, in turn, established around a dozen knowledge networks (composed of a mix of experts and representatives of government, organisations and community groups) with the task to report on problems and remedies in relation to areas such as urban living conditions, children's health, gender and employment. In 2007 each of the networks published a report while the CSDH also produced a general report, with a focus not as much on remedies as problem identification. The network dealing with employment conditions (EMCONET, 2007) examined five broad categories of work with regard to health that were seen to pose particular challenges requiring attention (unemployment, insecure and precarious employment, the informal sector, forced labour and child labour).

As will be seen below, there are strong parallels and potential synergies between some streams of recent medical and epidemiological research by Marmot and others and the research of sociologists and other social scientists into occupational health. Since 2000 there is far more evidence of multidisciplinary research and discourse. It is essential that this trend continue to gain momentum because it will, in our view, lead not only to more compelling explanations of how work affects health but also—by drawing on knowledge of interest groups (and their practices), professions, institutions, policies and law—to more effective interventions or remedies to the problems that are identified. In keeping with our earlier criticism of injury interventions the process will also need to be participatory rather than 'expert' driven. Examples of the latter include medical researchers joining employers, unions and local community groups to identify and address health problems confronting immigrant day labourers and homecare workers (Zanoni et al., 2006; Cho et al., 2007).

Other health sciences, ergonomics and built environment perspectives

Researchers in a number of health sciences have also made a contribution to our understanding of the links between work and health although, as with medicine, this contribution has sometimes been problematic. For example it is critical that those studying addiction behaviour take account of occupational or work organisation factors such as shiftwork that have been found to be associated with drug use (Marchand, 2008). Otherwise the analysis and suggested interventions could lose sight of critical causal factors.

A number of health science researchers have drawn on social science concepts to help explain the impact of workplace demands on interprofessional collaboration, health and wellbeing—a notable example being the embracing of the notion of 'emotional labour' in the fields of nursing (Miller et al., 2008). For example, a study by de Jonge et al. (2008) found a relationship between emotional job demands and health/wellbeing and that could be moderated by compensatory changes to job resources.

As was noted in chapter 3, by and large ergonomists have been very circumspect in addressing work organisation issues such as workload, restructuring/downsizing and the use of contingent workers. There are some notable exceptions which demonstrate the potentially valuable contribution they can make, with a notable example being the outstanding work of Karen Messing and colleagues in Quebec. For example, Siefert and Messing's (2006) study of hotel cleaners examined ergonomic load through detailed observation of tasks. The study showed how changes in the ergonomic load flowed from a combination of casualisation (use of temporary workers) and outsourcing (it was also influenced by a shift to immigrant labour that affected lines of worker solidarity and resistance).

The design of workplaces can have a critical impact on worker health and wellbeing. Some important aspects of this, such as ventilation, air conditioning and extraction/exhaust systems, are addressed by engineers and occupational hygienists (discussed below) while others, such as the design and position of equipment and equipment–human interactions, are addressed by ergonomists.

Workplace design must address all types of workplaces, not simply factories and offices but a wide range of other settings including ships, aeroplanes, mines, farms, forestry coops, trucks and roads. Changes in work—even those that appear incremental such as extending a mine—as well as changes in production methods (such as the shift to mechanical harvesting in forestry; see Rickards, 2008) can create significant workplace design issues in terms of maintaining the occupational health, safety and wellbeing of workers. For example, reductions to staffing levels in healthcare facilities, the use of halfway houses and increases in home-based care have placed more workers in isolation (and more at risk of client assault). The shift to open-plan office design has been seen to increase worker stress (*OHS Alert*, 14 January 2009), hardly surprising given that it enhances supervisory oversight of work activity and removes the personal space of workers. Even within semi-open-plan settings the arrangement of work-stations may affect the degree and nature of inter-worker communication and morale. The personal space allocated to workers can affect their health and wellbeing as it may impede their capacity to fulfil their tasks (due to disruptions/noise or their incapacity to store the tools or materials they need ready to hand), further inhibit control over how tasks are accomplished, or affect coping strategies and how work is perceived. For example, the ability to place a stamp of individuality on a workplace (by having a space to put family photos and the like) can be important, especially where tasks are monotonous (we are aware of a case where an employer went so far as to prescribe the number of photos permitted in a work space). It is increasingly common for work spaces to be regimented in size, layout and content even with regard to highly skilled professionals, with managerialist cost-based size reductions justified on the spurious grounds that this is the new standard; that access to computers means that professionals don't require as many books/journals; and that employers shouldn't provide space for 'personal property'. One result is that some personal work materials are moved home, thereby affecting the work–home divide. These practices, as well as others like 'hot-desking' and 'hoteling' (where work teams essentially 'rent' space), all require research in terms of their health effects but have been ignored by ergonomists and other fields that claim expertise in the area of workplace design.

As noted elsewhere, in practice the overriding objective of ergonomic interventions is to promote efficiency rather than enhance health because these are management's priorities. While ergonomic principles are commonly considered in the design of large industrial workplaces this is by no means the case with those in the service sector or small to medium workplaces. Even in large industrial settings, workplace design and 'no hazardous product use' protocols are seldom an integral part of the OHS management system, health surveillance/management or workplace health promotion (Hiller, 2003). This needs to change if health and safety hazards are to be identified and progressively designed out of the workplace.

In the past, research by hygienists, ergonomists and engineers tended to overlook organisational aspects of workplace design. Despite evidence of a growing awareness of the need to consider the interaction between work organisation and workplace design this remains largely the case. Over the past decade, there have been signs of more promising research, especially emanating from multidisciplinary research teams (composed of medical/health researchers, engineers/ergonomists and social scientists) in the Nordic countries. Examples include a study of call centres in Sweden (Norman et al., 2008) and a Danish review of indoor office environment research (Schneider et al., 1999). Simultaneously addressing work organisation and workplace design in terms of interventions offers the opportunities to reshape work in ways that promote health and wellbeing, including integrating non-sedentary activities and providing a pleasant internal and external environment. Such redesign could usefully draw on the knowledge of other health-related disciplines such as exercise physiology and human movements. Unfortunately, as yet efforts to encourage exercise at work tend to overlook both organisational and design constraints and rely on psychological promotion of the type that has had mediocre success in other areas of OHS (Cooley et al., 2008). There is a growing recognition of how changes in workforce anthropometrics (due to factors such as migration from countries with different anthropometric profiles or rising levels of obesity) should be incorporated into workplace design (see, for example, Australian Safety and Compensation Council, 2009). But again, a broader multidisciplinary discourse is needed. For example, in the area of obesity some consideration also needs to be given to how both workplace design and work organisation (concentrated sedentary tasks, shiftwork, long hours and demand/control imbalance) contribute to obesity (see, for example, Schulte et al., 2007, 2008).

Although sociologists and other social scientists have largely ignored workplace design a number of the studies that do exist provide valuable insights. For example, in their examination of sick building syndrome, Bain and Baldry (1995) argued that the built working environment was not a neutral factor but a critical element in the labour process because the way buildings are constructed and maintained encapsulates judgments about cost efficiency, the regulation of energy use and the legitimacy of worker input, and these in turn have significant implications for the health and wellbeing of the latter. Boyd (see Boyd and Bain, 1998, 1999) extended this work by looking specifically at the impact of market deregulation and associated changes to jobs and labour management practices in the international airline industry. They found that deregulation resulted in a number of measures by airlines to cut costs and intensify work among airline cabin crews that had adverse effects on the latter's health. This included introducing recirculated air and then significantly increasing the level of recirculated air on planes (from 20% to a now standard 50%) with detrimental effects on the health of crew (Boyd and Bain, 1999: 2).

Aircraft, their maintenance and use provide a useful exemplar of current limits in terms of workplace design when it comes to health. Considerable attention has been given to the safety engineering of aircraft but this has largely been driven by public safety considerations and far less attention has been given to the workplace health aspects. This has been illustrated by a number of cases. One was the maintenance design of the F-111 requiring maintenance workers to crawl within the fuel tanks of the aircraft to undertake resealing, which a commission of inquiry undertaken by the Royal Australian Air Force (RAAF, 2001) ultimately found (after more than a decade of complaints from workers) was an extremely hazardous procedure. Another case, carefully documented by Vakas (2007), involved cabin fume concerns (including MCS) with regard to the British Aerospace 146 passenger aircraft—a problem also encountered to a lesser degree in other commercial aircraft such as the McDonald Douglas MD-80, Airbus A320 and Boeing 737 and 757. The design/manufacturing limitation was exacerbated, in some airlines, by poor maintenance practices. Vakas found that industry interests and complicit regulators rebuffed, deflected and minimised these concerns (and related concerns about Mobil Jet Oil) over a number of years. Examining government inquiries into the issue undertaken in the UK, US and Australia, Vakas (2007: 248) found that only the latter adopted a proactive preventative approach that 'acknowledged the short- to medium-term health effects as well as the reports of aircraft crew, unions and the media which documented these problems'. Vakas (2007: 250) argues health research and professionals had played a limited role in assisting the debate, with some more concerned with acting as gatekeepers to the term MCS.

The discipline that is most conspicuously absent from the workplace design, health and wellbeing issue is the field of built environment/architecture. This is the field that designs the general structure and layout of buildings that become workplaces, including the materials used, aspect, landscape/screening, relationship to the surrounding environment and often many features of the internal design. As far as we have been able to determine university programs in this area devote little or no attention to this issue. While some aspects of human activity in work spaces are considered in workplace design (such as lighting, acoustics or thermal comfort), the process is highly circumscribed, is normally addressed as a series of discrete issues and does not consider organisational factors (Mahdavi and Unzeitg, 2005). Worker input into the design process is the exception and the consultation is generally superficial even when it occurs.

Like other aspects of workplaces that affect health, workplace design can be influenced by the social/institutional and regulatory context. In Denmark, for example, the requirement for occupational health services has provided an avenue whereby the consultancies providing these services can facilitate learning in the workplace design process (Broberg and Hermund, 2007).

Occupational hygiene

Occupational hygiene is concerned with the recognition, evaluation, monitoring and control or elimination of environmental agents that are hazardous to workers including liquid chemicals, dusts (organic and inorganic), fumes and particulates. As noted in chapter 2, it is an expert technical approach to OHS which had its origin early this century when scientists and practitioners from medicine, engineering and chemistry were brought together to reverse the growth of industrial disease. In Europe, in particular, occupational hygiene grew up as a response to the growth of chemical industry and the numerous acute chemicals to which workers were being exposed (Gerhardsson, 1988: 1). Thus, from its very outset occupational hygiene can be seen as especially concerned with occupational disease risks. This remains a key focus although the discipline was broadened to consider the interaction of workplace efficiency and health, and aspects of the environment which give rise to injury as well as disease.

Though often portrayed as simply a subdiscipline of medicine, occupational hygiene can be more accurately described as an environmental science, relying heavily on disciplines such as chemistry (and especially toxicology) and environmental engineering. Environmental chemistry/toxicology assesses the impact of chemicals on the environment and living organisms, including genetic and reproductive effects on male and female workers (for a examination of this, see Winder, 1993). Toxicology has developed a number of important tools for measuring and evaluating the toxicity of hazardous materials including lethal dosage. In the case of harmful substances that are flammable or explosive (and may be designated as dangerous goods like LPG or petroleum), or where the release of large quantities (such as ammonia) could have catastrophic consequences, the concerns of occupational hygienists also intersect with the major hazard and emergency response focus of disciplines such as safety/process engineering, disaster response/control and emergency risk management. In the light of the history of serious disasters since the 1970s as well as more recent events there is a growing body of literature addressing these issues (see, for example, Rusch, 1993; Hu and Raymond, 2004; Proust, 2006).

Ferguson (1986: 3) argues that, reflecting the general lag in the development of a multidisciplinary approach to OHS management within Australia, professional training for occupational hygienists was only introduced in the late 1970s and before this time they 'were almost non-existent in industry'.

With regard to occupational disease, occupational hygienists have been principally concerned with the measurement of exposure to toxic substances in the workplace and devising appropriate remedial strategies. With regard to measuring exposures, hygienists have undertaken important work across a wide range of industries, ranging from specific chemicals used in particular industries (see, for example, Hines et al., 2009) and workplaces or leaks/emissions from equipment (Bowes, 2008) through to more broad-ranging assessments of occupational hazards in industries or areas of activity such as offshore oil and gas installations (Gardner, 2003). One strength of some these studies is the close examination of work processes in trying to determine the level, nature and reasons for exposures, including why actual practices may exceed recommended procedures (see, for example, Lebailly et al., 2009). Further, as a study of particulate exposure in the US trucking industry demonstrates (Smith et al., 2006), other disciplines such as epidemiology can contribute to more nuanced studies of exposure that incorporate job histories and size and location of workplaces.

The hygiene profession and particularly its bodies—most notably the American Conference of Government Industrial Hygienists (ACGIH)—has played a critical role in developing exposure standards for chemicals and other hazardous substances that have become the basis for regulatory standards in the US, Australia and other countries (Vincent, 1998; Topping, 2001).

Other areas of activity include biological exposure markers (see, for example, Gori et al., 2009) and critically evaluating or reviewing evidence on the adequacy of measurement or sampling procedures (see, for example, Harper, 2006) or usage monitoring in relation to pesticides or other chemicals, including assessments associated with government legislation (Thomas, 2001). The interest of occupational hygiene is not restricted to hazardous substances but also examines dose–response relationships and the health effects of work processes such as hand–arm vibration (Sauni et al., 2009), as well as setting standards with regard to hand activity (Franzblau et al., 2005). Hygienists have also collaborated with epidemiologists, toxicologists and other researchers to provide valuable reviews of the industry use of and exposure to particular substances like tetrachloroethylene and trichloroethylene (Bakke et al., 2007; Gold et al., 2008).

With regard to remedies, the array of practices is too complex to summarise here. However, central to these interventions has been the notion of a hierarchy of control procedures (Grantham, 1992: 53), namely:

- elimination of the hazard
- substitution of the hazard with a safer alternative
- engineering out the hazard by isolation
- engineering out the hazard by ventilation
- administrative controls
- personal protective equipment (PPE).

In short, occupational hygiene places a commendable emphasis on removing hazardous materials from the workplace altogether if possible followed by various forms of engineered controls and with administrative devices and PPE being seen as the last line of resort. As noted by Maynard (2006), the knowledge of hazardous substances and a range of 'good' hygiene practices for managing exposure developed over a long period of time provides the basis for dealing with new or emerging substances and technologies that may prove to be harmful such as nanomaterials. On the other hand, occupational hygiene has displayed a limited recognition of how work organisation can affect exposure to hazardous substances although work scheduling and practices do get some recognition as part of administrative controls (Grantham, 1992: 77). In some circumstances it is entirely appropriate for PPE and administrative controls to be used while a more fundamental solution is being devised and implemented. However, in some cases the latter is delayed and it is not uncommon for occupational hygienists to be put under implicit pressure to devise the most 'cost-effective' solution, usually based on a short-term and narrow interpretation of costs.

There is limited evidence reviewing the nature and balance of occupational hygiene interventions at industry or broader levels (as opposed to workplace specific studies). A study (Roelofs et al., 2003: 62–7) that reviewed 92 studies of chemical hazard prevention and controls in peer-reviewed hygiene journals found that almost three-quarters discussed engineering controls (mostly exhaust ventilation); about half discussed administrative controls (housekeeping, personal hygiene and surveillance); one-third considered PPE; and only one-quarter considered primary prevention strategies such as material substitution. While these categories are not mutually exclusive and an array of different measures may be appropriate in particular situations, this study indicates that interventions were targeted at the least costly and 'bandaid' end of the spectrum rather than with fundamental reorganisation/primary prevention. For their part, Roelofs et al. (2003: 62) recommended improvements in the evaluation and promotion of effective prevention strategies. Like other expert technical approaches to OHS, occupational hygiene has seldom sought to involve workers in the development of solutions to exposure problems. Hygienists have developed self-assessment tools for workers to measure exposure. Studies have indicated that workers can make valid measurements but according to a recent Swedish study (Pettersson-Stromback et al., 2008: 663–71) workers needed more support to use these tools on an ongoing basis and to take preventative actions.

As industrial hygiene has moved from dealing with acute poisoning to the more insidious effects associated with the myriad of hazardous substances used by industry (or even a particular workplace), the task of assessing and controlling hazard exposures has become increasingly complex and demanding (Harrison, 1986). A particular challenge is also applying these techniques in small to medium-sized firms. One method of doing this—which originated from a program initiated in the UK Health and Safety Executive (HSE)—was control banding, which refers to a set of strategies offering 'simplified solutions for controlling worker exposures to constituents often encountered in the workplace' (Zalk and Nelson, 2008: 330). While control banding is now applied globally, Zalk and Nelson's (2008) review identified a number of strengths and weaknesses in the practice, suggesting the need for further assessment and refinement. As a recent examination of control banding by Tischer et al. (2009) observed, even assessing the effectiveness of control banding is no simple matter. It should be noted that the development and assessment of interventions in relation to hazard exposure is by no means the sole preserve of hygienists. Epidemiologists and other health professions (often in multidisciplinary teams) have also made a valuable contribution (see, for example, LaMontagne et al., 2005), including groups such as nurses and dentists essentially trying to safeguard themselves (Walsh, 2000).

Industrial hygienists have used a number of means of exposure monitoring including environmental exposure monitoring and biological exposure monitoring (for a discussion, see Harper, 2004). While biological exposure monitoring of workers has been seen to avoid some of the measurement problems associated with environmental exposure monitoring, technical problems remain, such as the selection of biomarkers (King, 1990: 315–22; Harrison and Sepai, 2000). More importantly perhaps, biological monitoring of workers (including pre-employment screening) raises significant ethical issues as well as having a tendency to draw attention to the worker, and susceptible individuals in particular, rather than the workplace environment (Harrison, 1986: 10). The occupational hygiene profession has emphasised that biological monitoring is primarily undertaken to assist in the control of exposures, not health surveillance, with the latter viewed more as a way of detecting failure of control (King, 1990: 318). Nonetheless, ongoing prominence of the issue is indicative of pressures to misuse this technique, especially when the hygienist is directly employed by a firm and preferable control measures are seen as too expensive.

On a more positive note, occupational hygienists have been developing more comprehensive frameworks for simultaneously addressing an array of hazards and other factors influencing workplace health. For example, Schulte et al. (2008) have proposed a framework for concurrently considering occupational hazards and obesity. The proposed framework is not only concerned with investigating the relationship between obesity and other hazards and the impact on absence and disability. It also entails assessing the workplace for prevention programs, promoting a comprehensive approach to worker health and addressing legal, social and ethical issues (Shulte et al., 2008). The role of hygiene professional associations in developing exposure standards to guide regulation has also had important benefits, though with a number of equally important qualifications discussed in the last section of this chapter.

Like several other disciplines, such as ergonomics, occupational hygiene has the potential to make a valuable contribution in terms of better understanding how work organisation affects health or mediates exposures to hazardous substances (through the application of new research methods or insights), especially when part of a multi-disciplinary research approach. Journals such as *Annals of Occupational Hygiene* have published a number of papers on this area. For example, Gardner's (2003) review of hazards in offshore oil and gas installations identified lower staffing levels and an ageing workforce as requiring further attention. At the same time, the ways in which workplace behaviour, labour market structures and the like can affect exposure to hazardous substances are seldom explored. A review of research into pesticide exposures of farmworkers (and their families) by Quandt et al. (2006b) found few studies tried to directly test the association between behavioural or psychosocial and environmental factors with exposure, even though seasonal and temporary labour and immigrant family work teams are a prominent feature of the industry.

Occupational hygienists have also played a critical role in developing exposure limits or benchmarks which seek to differentiate safe and unsafe exposure levels. Harrison (1986: 8) notes that relationships between the extent of the exposure or dose and its effects are often difficult to quantify and are, in any case, based on the assumption that there is a harmless level of exposure which can then be practically distinguished from a harmful level of exposure. Despite such problems the determination of exposure limits has formed the basis for standard setting and associated state regulation. A number of different approaches to exposure standards have been developed. However, over the last 50 years threshold limit values (TLVs) developed by the American Conference of Government Industrial Hygienists (ACGIH)—a private professional organisation—have influenced formal exposure standards not only in the US but also in many European countries, Japan and Australia (Castleman and Ziem, 1988: 531; Vincent, 1998; Topping, 2001). TLVs represent upper limits to exposure which are deemed sufficient to protect 'most workers most of the time' (Harrison, 1986: 11) although a practice of minimising exposure should be pursued. TLVs have been expressed in a number of different ways. Most notably they are expressed as a time-weighted average exposure limit based on standard working hours (i.e. eight hours). The time-weighted average forms the basis for most standard setting. However, it has been augmented by a short-term exposure limit to deal with brief exposures of a more hazardous nature and a TLV ceiling which sets an exposure level that should not be permitted even briefly (Harrison, 1986: 11). The influence of industry in the development of TLVs has been subject to considerable debate over the past decade and this is addressed in a later section.

Overall, occupational hygiene has made a significant contribution to the management of occupational disease risks in the workplace. The measurement of known or suspected hazards has become more sophisticated, the profession has contributed to our knowledge of such hazards, and it has been responsible for more systematic programs for establishing exposure standards and dealing with them. The employment of occupational hygienists by industry in Australia and New Zealand has lagged behind some other countries and they still are a rarity even in larger firms. More active government involvement in chemical regulation, research and promoting OHS education would be likely to lead to more interest in employing hygienists. A larger community of trained hygienists, as with a number of other OHS professions, would be of benefit to both Australia and New Zealand.

On the negative side, while occupational hygienists focus their attention on environmental aspects of the workplace their vision of the environment is a limited one. In terms of workplace or industry practice occupational hygiene has been preoccupied with personal monitoring and measurement (Gerhardsson, 1988: 19). In combination with a desire to minimise costs, this has tended to lead to remedial strategies that emphasise protecting the worker rather than control of the environmental hazard. Human and organisational factors have also received scant attention. Some occupational hygienists are aware of these limitations and have advocated a broader approach (see Gerhardsson, 1988). However, even here control is still viewed in terms of particular hazards such as noise and ventilation and of specific and rather narrowly defined human and organisational aspects. As such, occupational hygiene can be seen to constitute a partial approach to the control of occupational disease. Like ergonomists, occupational hygienists have generally steered clear of issues of work organisation, especially those likely to prove contentious by infringing on management's decision making. There have been some conspicuous exceptions. In 2001 the American Industrial Hygiene Association (AIHA) issued a position statement on sweatshops that identified the connection between long hours, low earnings, piecework payment schemes, child labour, discrimination, and multiple violations of OHS, workers' compensation/social security and environmental laws as serious threats to health. A white paper that accompanied the statement addressed issues such as the importance of workers' rights, employer and contractor responsibilities, codes and standards, and the role of industrial hygienists and the AIHA.

Psychological perspectives

The contribution of psychology to the understanding of disease and illness in the workplace differs significantly from that of occupational medicine and occupational hygiene. Work and health psychologists have placed relatively little emphasis on exploring the aetiology of specific diseases, preferring to examine the broader processes through which biological, psychological, social and organisational variables impinge on the health and wellbeing of workers. Psychological research has made an important contribution by drawing attention to the effects of work on the subjective health of workers. It has stimulated much greater interest in workers' experience of physical and psychological symptoms than the biologically prescriptive approaches of medicine and occupational hygiene. The contribution of psychologists to our understanding of occupational health issues such as occupational violence/bullying has already been mentioned in earlier sections of this chapter and the following chapter will examine their contribution to knowledge of the health effects of working hours. Hence, in this section we will principally focus on psychological research with regard to work-related stress.

While work-related stress has attracted a degree of controversy including suggestions it is essentially a socially constructed 'disease' of rich countries, the World Health Organization (Houtman et al., 2007) has recognised it as a serious hazard even in the traditional working environment of developing countries. A recent Welsh study (Barnes et al., 2008) found that among common health problems, work-related depression and stress were consistently reported by workers as having a high impact on their lives. As noted in the earlier section on occupational medicine, in recent years there has been a growing research 'dialogue' between some psychologists, most notably Robert Karasek, and medical researchers such as Michael Marmot in terms of trying to explain how work organisation shapes health outcomes. Karasek's DCS model has proved increasingly popular with work stress researchers from a wide range of disciplines (see, for example, Verhaeghe et al., 2008).

Health psychology has had a significant influence on research into illness and disease in the workplace. Health psychologists generally argue that ill health is caused by the combined effects of many social, environmental, behavioural and biological factors (Krantz et al., 1985). They have broadened the understanding of occupational illness and disease by describing the ways in which social and psychological factors can contribute to the development of physical disease. First, they have drawn attention to the direct role that psychophysiological processes play in disease development. They have investigated the processes through which psychological and social variables stimulate various psychophysiological responses that may in turn produce pathological changes in the body. For example, research evidence indicates that the experience of stress may produce hormonal changes which in turn suppress immunological processes and increase susceptibility to disease.

Second, health psychologists have drawn attention to behavioural and lifestyle variables that may be directly damaging to health, including tobacco smoking, excessive alcohol consumption, lack of exercise and poor diet. Importantly, they have recognised that the origins of these behaviours frequently lie in deeply rooted cultural and psychosocial influences. Third, health psychologists have observed that behaviour may aggravate physical disease when individuals ignore or fail to recognise the significance of symptoms, delay reporting illness and seeking medical care or fail to comply with treatment or rehabilitation regimes. They have begun to investigate the social and psychological variables governing perceptions of symptoms, reactions to pain and illness, reporting of illness and compliance with treatment.

Health psychology has stimulated a growth in psychologists' interest in workplace health promotion. Health promotion programs generally involve a range of diagnostic, educational and behavioural change activities designed to support the attainment and maintenance of positive health (Matteson and Ivancevich, 1988). Specific areas of concern include physical fitness, weight control, dietary and nutritional counselling, smoking cessation, stress management, blood pressure monitoring and control, alcohol and drug control and general lifestyle improvement. Psychologists predominantly offer services to assist in smoking cessation, weight control, hypertension control, stress management and drug and alcohol control. They usually employ a multi-method approach, using a combination of individual counselling, education, behaviour change programs, relaxation, hypnosis, biofeedback and lifestyle enhancement groups.

Unfortunately, health psychologists' wider theoretical appreciation of the social causes of illness and disease is rarely put into practice. To date, workplace programs offered by psychologists have focused heavily on individual behavioural change. This shortcoming may partly result from the constraints placed on health promotion activities by employers. There is little doubt that the motives of employers in supporting health promotion programs frequently lie in the potential productivity and profitability advantages that they offer, rather than a direct concern for the health of their workforce (Matteson and Ivancevich, 1988). As a result, in order to be maintained or expanded, programs often have to prove their value in terms of improvements in absenteeism, punctuality, turnover, injury rates and workers' compensation claims. Immediate costs of this nature can often be minimised by focusing on individual behavioural change.

Occupational stress management has been a major focus of workplace health promotion programs. However, research and practice in this area extend outside the boundaries of health psychology. In fact, occupational stress research had its origins early this century in studies predominantly concerned with the effects of boredom, monotony and various characteristics of the physical working environment on fatigue and injury rates. As we noted in chapter 2, an Australian academic, Bernard Muscio, published a widely acclaimed series of lectures examining this work in 1917. During the 1940s, Selye (1946) was the first to attempt to explain the psychophysiological processes through which environmental stressors produce illness and disease. Work on the relationship between occupational stress and health expanded steadily from then until the 1970s when research interest rose dramatically, and occupational stress became a major concern of work psychologists. The massive volume of material written since that time is impossible to summarise adequately here, but many reviews are available (see, for example, Cooper, 1985; Seward, 1997).

In this overview we shall limit our attention to examining the definition of stress, discussing the major causal variables, and identifying some of the current issues in occupational stress research and intervention. It is important to acknowledge at this point that psychology has by no means been the only discipline to contribute to under-standing of occupational stress. Major contributions have also been made by researchers from medicine, physiology, epidemiology and management. However, psychologists have performed the largest volume of research in this area and have strongly influenced the way in which the field has been conceived.

The first problem to arise in dealing with occupational stress is to identify an appropriate definition. The variety of ways in which stress is understood by both researchers and the general public makes this task confusing to say the least. Mackay and Cooper (1987) simplified the problem somewhat by identifying the four major ways in which stress has been conceived: as a stimulus, as a response, as a perception and as a transaction. The stimulus approach portrays stress as a noxious characteristic of the environment. Excessive noise, for example, is seen as a stress which produces strain in the worker. The response approach depicts stress as a bodily reaction to externally imposed demands. The response is usually described in terms of disturbances of behaviour (e.g. avoidance of threatening situations), emotions (e.g. anxiety), physiology (e.g. raised hormonal levels), or the presence of a stress-related disease. The perception approach depicts stress as arising from perceptual or cognitive processes that produce physiological and psychological signs and symptoms. According to this view, stress does not arise from the objective nature of the working environment but from the worker's subjective appraisal that work is excessively demanding or threatening.

The transactional approach does not view stress as a fixed component of either the environment or the individual worker. Instead, it is seen as a process that involves a complex set of relationships between aspects of the working environment and the capacities and behaviours of the worker. Mackay and Cooper (1987) noted a number of important characteristics of this process. First, it involves a discrepancy between the demands placed on the person and their skills and resources to deal with them. Both the objective nature of these demands and the person's perception of them are important. Second, perceptions of demands depend upon the discrepancy between the characteristics of the person and the resources provided by the working environment. Third, the person's appraisal of this discrepancy will determine whether they apply coping strategies and whether these strategies are cognitive, behavioural or physiological in nature.

Although a host of definitions have been proposed (see Schuler, 1980), the majority of researchers now agree that occupational stress is best understood as a transactional process. It is widely agreed that this process includes a complex interaction between many organisational, psychological and biological variables. Although many models have been proposed to describe the variables involved and the way that they interact, a reasonable level of consensus has been reached regarding the categories of variables that contribute to the process.

There are marked differences between workers in the stress symptoms that they report in similar work situations. Schuler (1980) divides symptoms into physiological, psychological and behavioural categories. Immediate physiological symptoms include increases in heart and respiration rates and blood pressure, and 'butterflies'. All of these responses appear to result from the release of adrenaline and other hormones into the bloodstream. Long-term physiological outcomes that have been associated with occupational stress include diseases like coronary heart disease and peptic ulcers, although the evidence linking these diseases to stress is often disputed. Psychological symptoms include tension, anxiety, depression, fatigue and boredom. Although research on behavioural symptoms is limited, there is some evidence that stress is related to organisational variables including increased absenteeism and turnover, and to individual variables including changes in appetite and increased tobacco and alcohol consumption.

Many organisational variables have been identified as sources of stress. Cooper (1985) divides them into six categories:

1 *Factors intrinsic to the job.* Many job characteristics may promote stress, including poor physical working conditions, shiftwork (which we examine in detail in chapter 6), work overload, work underload, physical danger and a lack of fit between workers' psychosocial characteristics and the work environment.

2 *Relationships at work.* Positive interpersonal relationships at work and social support from co-workers and supervisors/bosses are associated with lower job stress.

3 *Role in the organisation.* Several aspects of an individual's role in the organisation have been linked with increased stress, predominantly among clerical workers and managers/professionals, including role ambiguity (the lack of clarity in a person's job), role conflict (conflicting demands between different aspects of the job) and responsibility for people and their safety.

4 *Career development.* Factors related to career development can be significant stressors, including over-promotion, under-promotion, status, lack of job security and thwarted ambition. An incongruence between status and skills and other symptoms of career blockages are a particular problem faced by women.

5 *Organisational structure and climate.* The aspects of organisational structure and climate that are most strongly associated with stress are insufficient participation in decision making and lack of autonomy. Workers are likely to become stressed when they are not given legitimate opportunities to contribute to decisions directly related to their work.

6 *Home–work interface.* Conflict between domestic and work roles, especially in terms of time, can be a major source of stress. Pressures experienced in each sphere are additive.

The last category, home–work interface, has been a focus of occupational stress research only since the 1980s. Conflict between work and non-work roles can arise from both structural and emotional interference (Jackson et al., 1985). Structural interference occurs when the timing of activities in one domain constrains participation in the other; it reflects conflicts in the scheduling of work and other activities. Emotional interference occurs when emotional reactions in one domain affect emotions and behaviour in the other; it arises from effects on mood, health and behaviour. Structural conflict clearly contributes to the stressful effects of long working hours that have recently attracted renewed attention from researchers (Sparks et al., 1997). Some forms of work organisation may create particularly intrusive forms of structural conflict. Research on shiftwork, in particular, has demonstrated that the demands of shift schedules produce significant negative effects on fatigue, physical symptoms and psychological wellbeing (Bohle and Tilley, 1989; Pisarski et al., 1998). Recent theoretical models of work–non-work conflict have emphasised the complex and reciprocal nature of the relationship between work and non-work roles and the important part played by social support from supervisors, co-workers and family in reducing negative effects (Frone et al., 1997; Pisarski et al., 1998). Interventions in this area are rare as yet, but should focus on increasing social support from supervisors and co-workers, reducing excessive workloads and increasing the flexibility of working hours.

Contrary to popular belief, the organisational characteristics most highly associated with stress are concentrated at the bottom of the work hierarchy (Karasek, 1979). Workers in lower-status jobs are exposed to more physical and chemical stressors and experience more physiological strain than those in more privileged positions. They generally have more boring, monotonous, machine-paced, physically demanding, dangerous and highly routine jobs that require limited skill and initiative. This work provides little autonomy and fulfilment, and often offers less job security. Karasek (1979) demonstrated that jobs with high demands and low discretion, which are characteristically concentrated at the lower end of the occupational hierarchy, are associated with more stress symptoms than either jobs with low demand and low discretion or those with high demand and high discretion. This work generated the Demand–Control Model of occupational stress in which jobs can be classified according to two dimensions: the level of decision control, or autonomy, and the level of job demand. Jobs with low decision-control and high job-demand are most stressful. This model suggests that managerial and professional jobs with high demands and high discretion, requiring higher-order intellectual functions, creativity and problem solving, usually produce the lowest level of stress symptoms. In general, workers lower in the occupational hierarchy have less control over their work and less power to effectively modify or remove sources of stress in their workplace. The combination of these factors with high job demands often results in lower-status occupations being more stressful than higher status ones. It has often been asserted that the solution to this stress lies in enriching jobs and allowing workers greater autonomy to make important decisions in relation to their work.

Subsequent research by psychologists suggested more complex relationships between control, autonomy, stress and other workplace variables. It indicates that the relationship between job scope and stress is curvilinear, such that jobs with both very low and very high levels of complexity are highly stressful (Jia Lin Xie and Johns, 1995). Highly complex jobs are most stressful when workers perceive a mismatch between the demands of the job and their ability to satisfy those demands (Jia Lin Xie and Johns, 1995; Schaubroeck and Merritt, 1997). Further, decision-making authority may itself be a source of stress if it is not complemented by enough organisational influence to exercise genuine control (Baker et al., 1996). Consequently, the effects of decision-making authority may be more positive at higher levels of the organisational hierarchy. In addition to hierarchical position, social support may affect an individual's ability to exercise control. Social support from supervisors and co-workers in particular may interact in complex ways with job demands and control to buffer the effects of stress and reduce symptom levels (Daniels and Guppy, 1994; Schaubroeck and Fink, 1998). Finally, genuine participation by workers in job redesign processes may have important positive effects on subsequent control and attitudes, including organisational commitment (Nytro et al., 2000). In general, this evidence suggests that job control interventions should promote active involvement by workers in the redesign of their own jobs and take into account their skills and training levels, constraints on their ability to exercise control and influence, and the social support available to them.

Understanding of the effects of work organisation on stress levels and health has relied heavily on reports of symptoms from workers themselves. It has been suggested that these reports are unreliable, being affected by extraneous factors such as personality, job dissatisfaction and the quality of relationships between management and workers. However, evidence from a number of sources indicates that conclusions derived from this data correlate well with those from more 'objective' data. For example, Spillane (1984) described Australian research that has examined the physiological costs of work by monitoring the secretion of hormones such as adrenaline and cortisol and increases in heart rate and blood pressure. High physiological costs maintained over long periods of time can be expected to lead to stress reactions, reduced psychological wellbeing and possibly chronic diseases such as coronary heart disease. One study showed that women working on machine-controlled production processes had more marked stress responses, demonstrated by higher hormone levels, than workers on manually operated machines that allowed greater control over work pace and greater utilisation of skills. Another study compared a group of women paid by piece rates with one paid a fixed wage. Both groups worked on similarly mechanised processes, but the women on piece rates had higher levels of stress hormones. Spillane's (1984) interpretation of these results was that the stress on the mechanised production system resulted from qualitative underload (it was boring and unstimulating) and from quantitative overload (it encouraged overwork) on the piece-rate system. This physiological evidence, combined with similar research from Sweden (Frankenhauser and Gardell, 1976; Karasek, 1979), strongly supports the conclusion that externally controlled and highly paced work is very stressful.

More recent stress research has picked up on changes to psychosocial work environments, notably increased workloads and intensity, that have affected many private and public sector organisations as a result of management practices such as 'lean production', outsourcing and cost-cutting changes to infrastructure support, staffing ratios and staffing mixes (i.e. the numbers of particular occupational groups, such as registered nurses and nursing aides in a hospital). For example, Winefield et al. (Winefield and Jarrett, 2001; Winefield et al., 2003; Gillespie et al., 2001) undertook a series of studies that found that, notwithstanding the autonomy exercised by university staff and the support of colleagues, changes to staff–student ratios and declining facilities resulted in high levels of psychological stress, with outcomes being worst in newer universities. In a similar vein, a growing body of research has examined the impact of restructuring, changes to work demands and role conflicts (itself sometimes an outcome of understaffing) on stress, and in some cases presenteeism, among homecare providers and healthcare workers, especially nurses, in nursing homes and hospitals (see, for example, Aust et al., 2007; Ron, 2008; Verhaeghe et al., 2008). Other studies point to complex interactions between work-related stress, burnout and substance abuse, such as Chen and Cunradi's (2008) study of urban transit operators. A recent cross-cultural study of Canada and Pakistan (Jamal, 2008) found that self-employed workers reported significantly higher burnout and emotional exhaustion than employees. Yet other studies have examined the role of stressors on temporary employees—a growing phenomenon given change to labour markets affecting most countries (Slattery et al., 2008).

At the same time, a considerable body of the psychological research into the relationship between stress and changes in work organisation focuses on mediating factors including how the change process is conducted—an approach that tends to at best only moderate the harmful aspects of these changes (Tveldt et al., 2009). This reflects the broader thrust of stress intervention literature that usually evaluated relatively confined changes to the work environment and often regarded major organisational change like restructuring or downsizing as disruptive 'noise' to the intervention rather than a pervasive and characteristic feature of working life in the late twentieth and early twenty-first century (Nytro et al., 2000). The inconclusive or ambiguous results of work stress management interventions led to attempts to develop better assessment tools or measures of workers' responses, and more rarely a questioning of the general thrust and value of such interventions (Randall et al., 2009).

Further, despite the growing evidence of the effects of organisational factors, the characteristics of individual workers are still widely believed to play a major role in the stress process. It has been argued that individuals' perceptions of threats, demands and opportunities at work are determined to some extent by personal qualities such as their needs, values, abilities, experience and personality (Daniels and Guppy, 1994; Jia Lin Xie and Johns, 1995; Schaubroek and Merritt, 1997). There is evidence to suggest that stress responses are affected by dispositional differences between individuals, such as the degree to which they value achievement, feedback, self-control, interpersonal recognition and acceptance, challenge, responsibility and stimulation. There is also evidence that relevant abilities and experience in the form of familiarity with stressful situations, or training in dealing with them, diminish stress responses. Personality is probably the individual characteristic that has been most widely proposed to influence susceptibility to stress. 'Hardiness' is a prominent example. Hardiness is characterised by an optimistic cognitive appraisal of stressful events and a willingness to take decisive action to minimise the impact of stressors (Kobasa et al., 1981). Kobasa (1979) claimed hardy people possess three crucial personality traits: commitment, control and challenge. These people easily commit themselves to what they are doing, generally believe that they can at least partially control important events and consider change to be a normal challenge or impetus to development (Kobasa and Puccetti, 1983). Kobasa (1979) acknowledged, however, that hardiness is a learnt characteristic. It therefore appears likely that an individual's work history will strongly affect the extent to which they display the traits associated with hardiness. Managers and professionals who have autonomous, interesting and challenging jobs might reasonably be expected to develop greater senses of control, challenge and commitment than workers in jobs that are externally controlled, unstimulating and monotonous. The concept of hardiness continues to be used (Garrosa et al., 2008) although its popularity appears to have waned.

During the late 1970s and early 1980s a string of studies suggested that individuals with high hardiness levels respond to a variety of occupational and social stressors with less marked deterioration in physical and psychological wellbeing than individuals who are low in hardiness (Kobasa, 1984; Kobasa et al., 1981; Kobasa and Puccetti, 1983). However, concerns have recently been raised about the meaningfulness of the three hardiness dimensions, how effectively they buffer stress and how strongly hardiness is related to another personality variable, neuroticism (Funk, 1992). There is also relatively little to demonstrate that hardiness genuinely predicts stress resistance over time. For example, a longitudinal study found little evidence that high levels of commitment, control and challenge provided special resources for resisting the stress associated with rotating shiftwork (Bohle, 1997). More generally, personality variables have demonstrated stronger and more consistent relationships with stress when measured concurrently than when genuinely used to predict stress outcomes in longitudinal studies. In most cases, they appear to have relatively limited predictive validity and hence provide a poor basis for identifying workers most at risk in stressful conditions.

Individuals also differ in terms of the strategies that they use to cope with occupational stress. Generally, active strategies of coping with stress that are aimed at removing the source of the problem are more effective than more passive strategies such as psychological withdrawal/disengagement, apathy or resort to drugs (Chen and Cunradi, 2008). The use of various forms of individual relaxation strategies has been found to have significant value for increasing general wellbeing and combating non-work stress problems (Mackay and Cooper, 1987). The problem with these approaches is that they are solely designed to help the worker mitigate the effects of poorly designed working environments. Mackay and Cooper (1987) argue that such stress management training should only be used to supplement organisational change and job redesign programs aimed at dealing with the source of stress, or to help workers deal with stressors that genuinely cannot be designed out of the job (such as ambulance officers having to deal with death and trauma). Unfortunately, the mediating role of coping behaviour remains a significant focus of stress research even though some recent studies indicate some coping behaviours represent a transmission belt to ill health rather than a remedy to the problem (Chen and Cunradi, 2008).

Not surprisingly, stress research has been interpreted in widely different ways by employers and workers. Employers have frequently attempted to avoid the issue altogether or to focus attention upon the personalities and coping styles of workers as the primary determinants of stress. Employers are generally inclined to promote stress management programs that involve counselling, exercise or relaxation training. Where job redesign and worker participation programs have been introduced, economic and industrial factors have usually stimulated them (Spillane, 1984). Rarely have attempts been made to bring about the changes in organisational power structures and management practices that are necessary to significantly reduce work stress in many cases. In contrast to employers, workers and trade unions have emphasised the environmental determinants of stress, and have generally sought changes in the organisation of work, greater autonomy and participation in decision making for workers, and penalty payments for stressful work.

There are several significant limitations of stress research and stress management practices. Burke (1986) noted important shortcomings of research in the mid-1980s and his criticisms are largely valid today. Initially, studies of occupational stress predominantly focused on men and male-dominated occupations despite evidence that men and women experience different stressors, even in the same job or workplace. In addition to the demands of the job itself, women face unique stressors including sexual discrimination, sexual harassment and lower status than male colleagues. Since the 1990s this imbalance has begun to be addressed. A related issue is that stress research has been biased towards managers and executives rather than industrial workers and those in lower clerical and service positions. This is unfortunate given the strong evidence that occupational stress is concentrated at the lower end of the occupational hierarchy. More generally, there has been little research concerning the relationships between social class and stress. In a recent review (Kelloway et al., 2008) noted that stress intervention assessment studies remained sparse (in comparison to studies of stressors) and relied too heavily on cross-sectional data.

Burke (1986) also drew attention to the significant gap between knowledge of the causes of stress and the practices of psychologists and management consultants who deliver stress-management programs. Research has clearly established the importance of organisational variables in creating stress and demonstrated that individual coping may contribute little to diminishing it (Shinn et al., 1984). Sadly, however, practitioners rarely emphasise interventions directed at changing attributes of the working environment. Reynolds and Shapiro (1991) argued that this focus reflects the influence of clinical psychologists and, with them, the individualised and treatment-focused orientation of the medical model. The result has been the dominance of individualised stress-management programs based on treatment methods drawn heavily from clinical psychology. Reynolds and Shapiro note the ethical problems inherent in selecting the individual employee as the target for change, arguing that individual-level interventions imply that stress problems reside primarily in the individual and that organisations are only responsible for providing assistance for workers to change. Attempts to reduce or remove stressors from the environment are rare and most interventions amount to little more than attempts to increase employee tolerance to noxious job characteristics. A reasonable assessment of the situation would suggest that individual stress management training should be used only when environmental stressors cannot be modified, or in conjunction with the removal or modification of stressors. A good example of the latter is isolated groups of workers like farmers, where community network–based support can try to moderate the effects of work and related financial and family stressors (Fragar et al., 2008). However, even here ways of addressing root causes need to be sought.

Reynolds and Shapiro (1991) argue in favour of interventions drawn from work psychology that are characterised by two complementary strategies: technostructural intervention and human-process intervention. Technostructural strategies focus on changes in job design, organisational structure, control, information and reward systems. Human-process interventions address problems with interpersonal and group processes. Reynolds and Briner (1994: 75) later intensified the argument, concluding that stress management interventions had failed to deliver effective solutions and attributing this failure to 'inadequate and oversimplistic theories which obscure the many conflicting interests of employees, employers and researchers'.

As noted earlier, a number of sociologists have been highly critical of stress research. This issue has been pursued forcibly by Otto (1985), who has attacked what she calls 'stress management ideology'. She has argued that intrinsic to this ideology is a denial of knowledge which perpetuates an understanding of stress that favours dominant interest groups (especially employers) to the neglect of others. The ideology is exemplified by the prominence given to 'executive stress' in the mass media and the promotion of individual stress management at the expense of the structural changes to the organisation of work that are required if occupational stress is to be effectively addressed. The notion that managers and executives are the most exposed to stress is clearly untrue, and the promotion of individual coping strategies is an extension of the 'victim-blaming' ideologies (discussed in chapter 3) that can be used to deflect responsibility for ill health away from the organisation of work and locate it within the characteristics and behaviours of individual workers. For employers and managers interested in cost minimisation individual stress management also presents a cheap and simple alternative to comprehensive reorganisation of work.

Otto (1985) argued that the primary source of occupational stress is the failure of the work environment to match people's needs and capacities rather than in the inability of workers to tolerate what may be intolerable conditions. She observes that individual differences in the effectiveness of coping strategies may reflect the cumulative impact of workplace stressors. Workers with little control over their work and a sense of powerlessness are likely to use less active coping strategies that leave the source of the stress untouched, such as daydreaming and psychological withdrawal, and resort to drugs to help them ease work pressures. Managers and professional workers who have a high degree of control over their work, and whose work problems are more amenable to resolution, are more likely to cope in an active way by confidently attempting to solve problems and remove sources of stress. In general, the more intense the stressors and the stronger the perception that the situation is unalterable, the greater the likelihood that coping strategies will be passive and directed at psychological withdrawal.

Rather than rejecting the notion of stress outright, a number of sociologists and other social scientists have sought to modify the concept and apply it in a non-managerialist fashion to the examination of work organisation and health. In part, this entails recognition on their part that, irrespective of its misuse, the notion of stress does provide a vehicle for introducing workers' subjective experiences into the examination of health effects of work. Houben (1991: 309–27), for example, has explored the link between production control and chronic stress among workers. In a later study, Houben and Nijhuis (1996) argued that one effect of chronic work-related stress was burnout. This, in turn, could be linked back to economic–technical rationalisation and technocratic control in work organisations, and specifically the use of systematic control based on principles of flexible specialisation with regard to blue-collar production workers and professional workers in human services. In critically reviewing the entire work stress literature from a sociological perspective, Peterson argues that studies adopting a labour process approach provide the 'most comprehensive framework for understanding the causes and consequences of stress' (Peterson, 1995: 495. For a detailed examination see also Peterson, 1998). In this regard, his argument closely parallels what we saw to be the most impressive sociological theorising on the origins of occupational injury in chapter 3. At the same time, Peterson (1995: 495) argues there is a need to counterbalance the preoccupation of the labour process literature with the point of production and extend the analysis to include the effects of stress on management's control over work at a number of different levels. The latter include management decisions affecting market growth, customer service and competitiveness (Peterson, 1995: 512). If regulatory policies affecting the latter are included there are some potentially interesting tie-ups with Boyd's study of the airline industry and a number of others discussed in this chapter. There is also the question as to how institutional factors mediate these effects. Lerner (1982) argued that collective consciousness, especially through trade unions, could afford workers with a more effective means of addressing stress than the individualised or heavily circumscribed group facilitation processes promoted in much of the psychological literature. At the same time, for unions to achieve this may require some significant rethinking on their part. A study by Lowe and Northcott (1995: 420–40) found that for workers in the most stressful working conditions dissatisfaction with the job was more likely to have a negative effect on their attitude towards the union rather than leading them to take the issue to the union. In recent years unions in Australia and elsewhere have sought to take up the issue of stress (see chapter 9) but if Lowe and Northcott's finding is confirmed by subsequent studies then unions will need to overcome this stumbling block and demonstrate their relevance.

Earlier we described positive interchanges between psychologists and other social scientists relating to health. Psychological models provide several important insights into occupational stress and illness. Significantly, they have recognised that the subjective health and wellbeing of workers is a legitimate focus for research. Transactional models also draw attention to the complex interactions between social, organisational, psychological and biological variables that lie at the heart of occupational stress. These models capture important aspects of the development of occupational illness that are missing from the medical model. Unfortunately, the knowledge derived from stress research has not been effectively applied in the workplace. The interests of employers and other powerful interest groups have been reflected in a 'stress management ideology' which diverts attention from the organisational determinants of stress and illness and transfers responsibility for dealing with the problem onto the individual worker. This ideology also focuses unwarranted attention on 'executive stress' and ignores strong evidence that the burden of work stress falls most heavily on workers at the bottom of the occupational hierarchy. Interestingly, this phenomenon illustrates a major shortcoming of psychological theory. As we noted in chapter 2, psychological models deal with the social and organisational determinants of ill health in a fragmented fashion that fails to deal systematically with critical power structures and value systems operating in the workplace. Sociologists, on the other hand, have focussed heavily on these issues.

Sociological and related social science perspectives

Since the early 1980s sociologists and social scientists in 'neighbouring' fields, such as industrial relations, have produced a now substantial body of research that attempts to show that patterns of work organisation and related institutional and regulatory influences provide significant explanatory insights into occupational injury (Dwyer, 1991; Hopkins, 1999; Nichols, 1990, 1997). Attempts by the same fields to provide a comparable contribution to understanding occupational disease and other forms of ill health initially lagged behind, in part because initial research focused on de-mythologising workplace 'accidents'.

Sociologists, political scientists and others have provided detailed examinations of major incidents at industrial plants that had wide-ranging health ramifications both for workers and the nearby community, such as the explosion at the Union Carbide plant at Bhopal in India. A number of these studies identify the underlying causes in terms of industry influence and the political economy of regulation (Carson, 1989). Examining a diverse array of incidents giving rise to injury or disease risks, including the high injury toll in the British North Sea oil industry, disasters such as Piper Alpha and Bhopal and the slow mass poisoning of workers in the asbestos industry, Carson (1989) identified many similarities. These included pressures to cut costs or push ahead with production, compromised or ineffectual enforcement agencies, industry pressure and complicit governments, as well as relatively simple but sometimes catastrophic decisions on staffing and maintenance levels. Thanks to historians such as Alan Derickson (1998) and health researchers interested in history such as Allard Dembe (1996), we have detailed accounts of how the prolonged and problematic interaction of medicine, organised labour, industry, government and other interest groups shaped recognition of diseases such as 'black lung' and noise-induced hearing loss. As yet, however, limited efforts have been made to use this work for more general theorising on work-related disease and illness by sociologists and other social scientists. This task is important not just because it would add to our understanding of the origins of disease and ill health. It would also contribute to the development of a broader sociological understanding of occupational injury and disease.

While sociological and industrial relations researchers have tended to concentrate on occupational injury or major hazards rather than health, there are important exceptions. Annie Thebaud-Mony's (1999) study of subcontracting and hazard exposures in the French nuclear industry found that while subcontractors made up only a tiny fraction of the workforce they were engaged in especially hazardous tasks and were subjected to 90% of all irradiation dosages. In Quebec, a narrative study of career paths by Malenfant et al. (2006) explored how intermittent work affected the life and health of male and female workers, and how these could be grouped in terms of age, occupation and a variety of other factors. Other researchers have explored both the injury and health effects (using the GHQ and other measures) associated with multi-tiered subcontracting and supply chains in the road transport and food processing industries (Mayhew and Quinlan, 2006; Lloyd and James, 2008). Another study involving Thebaudy-Mony and SCOP 93 (2005) highlights the strengths of a sociologically informed but multidisciplinary and participative research approach to ill health that also entails a proactive intervention. The research team, which included unions, sought to indentify work-related cancers in a Paris suburb by compiling detailed job histories between 2002 and 2003 (the first stage of a long-term study). Of the 127 workers providing job histories 74% of men and 70% of women were deemed to have occupational cancers, and compensation claims were prepared on behalf of 26 (mostly for asbestos-related cancers) of these, under the rigid rules of the French system.

A number of studies indicate that specific aspects of work organisation are associated with increased risk of injury and ill health. Paralleling sociological/IR research linking incentive payment systems to higher injury rates among garment workers (Mayhew and Quinlan, 1999), a Quebec study by Brisson et al. (1992) found pieceworkers were more likely to take medication for stomach problems and there was an increased prevalence of severe disability among long-term pieceworkers. In a similar vein, the use of stimulant drugs by long-haul truck drivers to combat excessive hours/fatigue (itself a response to remuneration systems) entails a risk of injury as well as long-term health effects that include an increased risk of myocardial infarction (Quinlan et al., 2006, Williamson, 2007; Quinlan and Wright, 2008). These findings parallel research by psychologists and others on the association between piecework or incentive-based payment systems and adverse health and safety outcomes (Sundstrom-Frisk, 1984; Lacey et al., 2007; Williamson, 2007).

Industrial relations and other social science researchers have also begun giving attention to the impact of precarious employment on health, safety and wellbeing in ways that may extend the insights of Karasek and Siegrist by developing models that integrate labour market and broader social factors. This includes the employment strain model (Clarke et al., 2007; Lewchuk et al., 2008) and the economic/reward pressure, disorganisation and regulatory failure (PDR) model of Quinlan et al. (2001). The employment strain model takes explicit account not only of the job insecurity associated with precarious employment but also its consequences (notably the regularity of jobs/periods of unemployment, the time and energy spent on job search and the social support resources available to the worker). Clarke, Lewchuk et al.'s model has the advantage of seeing precariousness as the culmination of a trajectory of experiences, so that the work–life histories of workers need to be traced. These latter models can also be used to explain work-related injury—an area not addressed by either the demand-control-support or effort-reward models (though a potential link through effects on cognitive function has begun to be explored; see Elovainio et al., 2009). However the employment strain and PDR models are in their early stages and will require rigorous testing.

Returning to a more general consideration of sociological research on OHS we would argue that in many though not all circumstances specific forms of work organisation will give rise to both injury and disease risks simultaneously. This provides links not only with medical research (notably that of Marmot and others) already mentioned but also with the work of safety engineers, ergonomists and occupational hygienists, whereby social scientists can provide a critical organisational context for explaining recurring problems with work design. Indeed, despite the disciplinary divides among technical experts it is easy to cite examples where poor work design contributes to both disease and injury risks. In this respect we can cite two workplaces we have visited. At one, a large food processing factory, the layout and movement of materials was poorly organised, requiring a relatively large number of forklift trucks to operate in a confined area. This arrangement not only increased the risk of injuries due to collisions between trucks, and trucks and pedestrians, it also posed problems in terms of the stress on the drivers and the level of vehicle emissions. Further, at an experimental farm we observed a number of hazardous aspects to the work process, entailing both injury and disease risks. One concerned the auger used to mix grain and various additives for the feed lot. While molasses was added to reduce the dust created during the mechanical mixing process, considerable dust levels were created, especially during the initial stages when the various ingredients were added. There was no guard at the top of the mixer to reduce the dust level and to prevent a worker's arm from coming into contact with machinery or prevent a worker from falling in during the stage of mixing additives. The molasses used created cleaning problems—itself a dangerous task given that most workers found it easier to clean the mixer by climbing in. A worker doing this would be invisible to any workmates and there was no emergency switch within reach of the mixer. Similarly, a hammer mill used to shred chaff subjected the operators to excessive noise, and since the feeder did not operate properly workers were required to feed the bales into the rotating teeth of an initial shredder by hand. In both cases the machinery and the work process associated with it entailed both disease and injury risks which had received little or no attention at either the design or operation stage. From a sociological perspective it also needs to be asked how decision making at the level of the employer and broader societal level allows such situations to arise frequently and remain unaddressed.

With several qualifications, the available evidence indicates there is little need for a distinctive sociological explanation of occupational disease and injury. The qualifications mainly relate to recognition and regulatory responses. The insidious character of many diseases (and the combination of long gestation with job changes by workers) means that adverse health outcomes are usually far less socially conspicuous—though it is important not to lose sight of belated and contentious recognition in relation to some types of injury (see chapter 4). The healthcare system, especially medicine, plays an arguably more critical role in recognition of work-related disease. It may also be argued that the insidious nature of occupational diseases has provided a ready excuse for them being less adequately dealt with by the regulatory system.

On the other hand, it is more difficult to construct 'victim-blaming' or individualistic explanations of work-related disease than injury. Such arguments or approaches have been developed in relation to pre-employment health testing, health surveillance, biological monitoring, genetic susceptibility—including misusing the expanded scope for DNA testing—and the use of PPE (Draper, 1986). As occupational hygienists are quick to point out, PPE is a cheap but last-resort and second-best solution that creates its own OHS problems, and may be discarded by workers because it is inadequate, uncomfortable or interferes with the carrying out of the task. Workplace health promotion (WHP) and alcohol and other drug policies can also form the basis for individualising worker responsibility for their health (Blum and Roman, 1986; Levy and Wegman, 1988: 13; chapter 10). Sociologists have contributed to a critical analysis of manipulative and individualised interventions as well as identifying why low-paid and insecure workers may eschew WHP for fear the information will be used to target them for retrenchment (Draper, 1986; Blum and Roman, 1986; Daykin, 1997).

In much the same vein, Otto (1986) argued that much of the stress literature was managerialist, focusing on individualised aspects (such as coping strategies) and failing to emphasise the subordination of workers as a potentially critical causal factor. In an effort to move the narrow stress discourse, Bellaby (1986: 52) proposed a model where attention focused on the social process of sickness whereby 'illness is dramatized or a disease is diagnosed and treated'. Bellaby's study highlighted significant differences in the ways management and workers viewed the origins of sickness in the workplace and the tacit negotiations that occurred with regard to breaks from the line and absence. Bellaby also emphasised the impact on sickness of the introduction of more stringent control of task time that accompanied mechanical control of work and Taylorist job design. Bellaby's historical perspective is valuable. We need more historically informed studies so that changes in management strategy and production methods, and changes in the nature of worker resistance, can be more systematically related to patterns of occupational illness.

More sociological research is required on often value-laden public debates about high and costly levels of sickness absence which fail to give any recognition to the changes in work organisation (including work intensity and working hours) that underlie this. On the other hand, sociologists have contributed new insights into working arrangements. Notable here is the concept of presenteeism (Simpson, 2000) whereby workers feel obliged to be at work longer than standard hours, including unpaid overtime and even attending when they are ill. Presenteeism has become a widespread phenomenon in the context of organisational restructuring/downsizing and job insecurity, as well as forms of task organisation where sickness absence results only in a backlog of work or the redistribution of work onto already busy colleagues. Its pervasiveness has been sufficient to affect even management discourse on work (and counterbalance to some extent the obsession with sickness absence costs). Researchers from a number of other disciplines, such as psychology (Aronsson et al., 2000) and occupational medicine (Hansen and Anderson, 2008) have picked up the concept and have examined its impact on worker health and wellbeing.

Another important contribution that sociologists and other social scientists have made to our knowledge about worker health and wellbeing has been in the areas of harassment, bullying and aggressive behaviour in the workplace. One of their important contributions in this regard has been to provide both a gender perspective and a work organisation perspective on the origins and incidence of occupational violence (see, for example, Zapf, 1999; Mayhew and Quinlan, 2002; Mayhew et al., 2004). They have also noted that while sexual harassment is not confined to the workplace and therefore cannot be uniquely attributed to the social relations of production it appears to be the most common location for sexual harassment. Lucas (1991) argued that sexual harassment at work is an OHS problem almost entirely confined to women and, as such, it highlights the need to modify theoretical explanations of occupational injury and disease to include explicit recognition of gender. An overlapping contribution has been their research—along with that of psychologists—into the origins and effects of mobbing, bullying and aggressive behaviour in the workplace. There is growing evidence that occupational violence that takes the form of harassment and bullying rather than actual physical assault is relatively widespread, can be affected by the nature of or changes to work organisation and can have serious long-term effects on worker health and wellbeing, even to the point of suicide in extreme cases. Sociological and other researchers have also provided evidence that harassment and violence is more prevalent or difficult to manage with regard to a contingent workforce, young workers and shift/night workers (Mayhew and Quinlan, 2000, 2001; McCall and Horwitz, 2004). Consistent with this, a recent epidemiological study found rates of unwanted sexual advances were far higher among contingent workers than permanent workers. Other research (see, for example, Gascon et al., 2009) suggests high levels of aggression towards healthcare workers, especially in accident/emergency and psychiatric treatment areas, which may be linked to restructuring and neo-liberal policy-inspired cost-cutting within the healthcare sector—something that requires further research.

The contribution of sociologists and social scientists in industrial relations has entailed identifying other potentially important connections and consequences with regard to occupational violence. For example, in a large Quebec study undertaken by Marchand (2008) workplace harassment was an important factor in alcohol use and abuse. As with presenteeism, psychologists and researchers in other fields have undertaken considerable research in the field of mobbing, bullying and occupational violence (see, for example, Glaso et al., 2007; Saunders et al., 2007; de Pedro et al., 2008). A study by Hauge et al. (2007) found that bullying at work was associated with stress in organisations and laissez-faire leadership styles, and adversely impacted on the perceived wellbeing of bystanders, not just those who are targeted. The importance of concepts of fairness and justice, as well as abusive behaviour by supervisors, to understanding bullying and violence has been identified by researchers such as Saunders et al. (2007) and Dupre et al. (2006). In their study, Dupre et al. (2006) found that financial and personal fulfilment reasons moderated aggression among young part-time employees. Other research has linked workplace harassment with both distress and alcohol use (Richman et al., 2004). The latter finding highlights the fact that, as with exposure to multiple hazardous substances, exposure to bullying, harassment, or indeed, other indicators of poor psychosocial working conditions can have synergistic or cascading effects on worker health and wellbeing. Further, while reporting these issues a number of cases indicate that they can also lead to escalated victimisation/retribution or the additional stress associated with management denial of the problem or lengthy litigation (Richman et al., 2004; Quinlan, 2007).

Sociologists and industrial relations researchers have also drawn on Hochschild's (1983) concept of emotional labour—management's control of worker emotions as an element of their tasks so that it becomes an additional and demanding aspect of their labour—to examine the health and wellbeing of workers. Hochschild developed the concept in the context of high-pressure service work delivered by predominantly female workers (flight attendants). Boyd (2002) for example, used the concept to explore the relationship between customer violence and employee health and safety. Bolton and Boyd (2003) and Claire Williams (2003) used the concept to examine the work of flight attendants, though both seek to modify it in the light of their findings. Emotional labour has been applied to other service occupations such as call centre workers (Russell, 2008). The notion that the emotional labour or prescribed forms of behaviour within particular jobs or organisations may pose a threat to health and wellbeing has attracted the attention of researchers in other fields. As noted earlier, the concept has attracted significant attention from researchers in a number of service professions with a reputation for placing strenuous emotional demands on workers, such as nursing.

While research on emotional labour has been concentrated on service sector work, Townsend (2008) has argued that production employees may also be subject to this form of manipulation by management, especially in the context of groups or team-based production. In addition to the link with occupational violence suggested by Boyd (2002) there may be synergies between emotional labour and other concepts currently applied to worker health and wellbeing, including the DCS and ERI models as well as the notions of burnout and emotional exhaustion developed by psychologists. While the proliferation of concepts with the potential to explain aspects of workers' health and wellbeing might be seen as the product of specific disciplinary perspectives, two points are worth bearing in mind. First, in a sense these concepts share a recognition of the intensity (psychological and physical) and imbalance in modern systems of work. Second, constructive engagement, debate and borrowing have the potential to yield a more compelling or overarching explanation of how work organisation shapes health outcomes.

Social scientists have also explored the effect of particular management regimes, especially those designed to intensify work such as lean production, on health. A Canadian study of the auto components manufacturing industry (Lewchuk and Robertson, 1996) found lean production had led to heavier workloads and increased workers' concerns over their health. They (Lewchuk and Robertson, 1996: 9) found 51% of workers reported high levels of workplace health risks, 40% reported pain or discomfort in half the days in the previous month and 37% reported working in awkward positions. Compared to two years earlier, 41% felt work had become less healthy, 44% reported that their current job was more tense than two years ago and 45% reported being more tired after work. Another Canadian study (Eakin and MacEachen, 1998: 896–914) argued that particular features of working life in small workplaces, including more personalised social relations and low polarisation of employer–employee interests, shaped workers' perceptions of health and injury. Whereas epidemiological research has portrayed the relationship between psychosocial factors and objective indicators of health status as lineal and causal (see above), Eakin and MacEachan (1998: 912) argued the relationship has subjective and contingent elements that need to be recognised. Yet another Canadian study, this one dealing with the public health sector (Skillen, 1996: 111–46), found that workers perceived organisational factors as inseparable from the hazards in their physical and psychosocial work environments. Skillen (1996: 135) emphasised the importance of power and dependency (including the subordination of women) as factors shaping occupational health within organisations and concluded '... a sociological perspective informed by organisational theory was required for the study of the production and reproduction of occupational hazards'.

In comparison to theorising on occupational injury, sociological research on occupational disease, stress and illness is still at early stage of development although we can note a distinct improvement over the past decade. A recurring theme in most of the studies discussed in this section is the critical impact of job control and social control, with the clear and often explicit conclusion that democratising the workplace was essential to creating a healthy working environment. Of course, as a number of studies also recognised, moves to achieve this were likely to encounter significant structural barriers (see Johnson, 1989). Indeed, in some countries at least, it is arguable that the trend is in the other direction (due to factors such as the growth of contingent work, declining union membership, weakening of industrial relations regimes and concepts such as lean production). Nonetheless, given evidence presented elsewhere in this chapter and the book, we believe the sooner this issue is confronted the sooner concrete steps can be made towards a healthier working environment. There are some positive signs in some countries. For example, in the Netherlands and Sweden, Terry (1996: 545) argues that legislative provisions for employee empowerment have been expanded in '... key areas of workplace decision-making that may influence work-related stress'. The Swedish Act, for example, requires employers to adapt work to people. On the other hand, while Terry sees this approach as in keeping with the EU framework directive, Britain has continued to rely on the top-down and reactive approach of statutory duty of care provisions. This has also been the approach adopted in Australia (see chapter 7). In New Zealand, unlike in Britain and Australia, there are no regulatory provisions for worker involvement in OHS whatsoever (see chapter 10). While the Occupational Health and Safety Service has issued advice to employers on preventing work-related stress and fatigue the government has ruled out any legislative initiatives (*Occupational Health Newsletter*, No. 394 15 May 1997: 5). In the next section we will look at important ways the regulatory and healthcare infrastructure has shaped our knowledge of and ability to prevent occupational disease.

The political economy of research, standard setting and regulation of disease, illness and stress

Chapter 3 argued that an adequate explanation of occupational injury must contain reference to the ways that state intervention has shaped work processes and their consequences (further evidence on this is presented in chapters 7 and 9). We have also shown how interest groups have shaped understandings of occupational injury. The same points can be made in relation to occupational disease.

Research infrastructure and value-free research?

Research into hazardous substances and occupational disease is liable to be controversial because the findings may have significant financial consequences for industry as well as health consequences for workers. Quite apart from limitations that may arise from disciplinary 'blinkers'—and we are in no way gainsaying the vital contribution of research by epidemiologists, toxicologists and others—structural influences on the provision of information on occupational disease also need to be recognised.

Most obviously, research into hazardous substances is affected by infrastructure and resourcing. In most countries governments establish the infrastructure through scientific agencies and universities that conduct research into occupational hazards. Government scientific agencies distil local and foreign research, issue alerts on newly recognised hazards, recommend standards or revised standards in relation to hazards, and make critical decisions or recommendations in relation to the prioritisation and funding of research activities. While politically motivated interference in these critical scientific decisions has a long history, it has become especially prominent in the last 20 years where neo-liberalism has dominated policy discourse. In Australia, the neo-liberal Howard government (1996–2007) abolished the research component (internal expert staff and external grant funding) of the National Occupational Health and Safety Commission (NOHSC was eventually replaced by a narrower and more compensation-focused Australian Safety and Compensation Council or ASCC)—a move opposed by OHS professional bodies. The loss of over 100 scientists employed by NOHSC and around one million dollars (small though this was) annually in external research project and postgraduate research support funding had a substantial negative effect on the nation's OHS research capacity, and the capacity for industry-independent research in particular. It also meant the ASCC lacked a credible core of scientists to undertake research or review overseas research In Sweden, the incoming neo-liberal government abolished the internationally regarded National Institute of Working Life in 2007—a move that drew international condemnation in scientific circles. In the US, the George W Bush administration did not abolish the National Institute for Occupational Safety and Health (NIOSH) but it did make changes to key personnel. Further, in 2004 (Weiss, 2004) the Bush administration reorganised it as a mid-level coordinating centre within the Centers for Disease Control—a move that drew opposition from a wide range of groups (including those often at loggerheads) who valued 'good science'.

A critical policy presumption that guides standard setting and risk management with regard to chemicals and other hazardous substances also affects research as well as the standards themselves, notably the failure to apply the precautionary principle. As Hansson and Ruden (2008: 964) have observed: 'In many risk management decisions concerning industrial chemicals, including decisions on classification and labelling, lack of toxicity data is interpreted as (or has the same implications as) absence of toxicity'. In essence, chemicals used at work are presumed healthy and safe until proven otherwise. The time lapse while evidence on toxicity accumulates means that the burden of risk remains as much with workers as it was at the beginning of the Industrial Revolution.

Those who believe that the risk of subsequent litigation will be sufficient incentive for industry to pre-empt this should read McCulloch and Tweedale's (2008) careful assessment of the history of asbestos. The absence of a requirement on industry to pre-vet chemicals shapes not only how and when research is undertaken but also who undertakes it and the evaluation of this evidence. Further, where the chemical concerned is traded across international borders, neo-liberal–dominated agencies like the World Trade Organisation and NAFTA can be, and have been, inserted into the equation on the basis that action taken by one country in relation to a hazardous substance amounts to 'hidden protectionism'. To this may be added bodies established by hazardous industries to question unfavourable research or attempt to capture international agencies responsible for evaluating research (see, for example, McCulloch and Tweedale, 2008).

Further, how governments respond to research cannot be treated as a given. The apparatus of the state, and the infrastructure for health research and the healthcare system more generally are subjected to a range of interest groups and shifting alliances. Specific interest groups may reshape the response to research to secure more favourable outcomes. For example, while the dangers of tobacco have long been accepted the gambling industry and especially casinos (based on the importance of foreign 'high-roller' clientele and claims of competitive undercutting by less-regulated rivals) waged a war against the proscribing of smoking in their venues, achieving a degree of success (such as exemption from laws) in some quarters. As research has demonstrated (Pilkington et al., 2007), second-hand smoke is a serious hazard for casino workers for which a universal ban on smoking in these and other public premises is the only viable remedy. In Australia, as in some other countries, the cost threat of common law litigation payouts ultimately proved more instrumental than research in causing government to act.

With regard to the resourcing of research, significant imbalances between particular interest groups need to be acknowledged. Fagin and Lavelle (1996) found that in the area of weed science (including chemical weed killers) in the US, the federal government employed 75 scientists, universities another 180 and chemical corporations 1400. No comparable figures are available for Australia and New Zealand, but even given these countries' smaller (and predominantly overseas-owned) chemical industries, the ratio is unlikely to be better. Since the proprietary products of many US chemical companies (including weed killers) are either imported or produced (by subsidiaries or under license) in Australia and New Zealand the imbalance in research resources will flow on to Australia. In the US, if not Australia, chemical companies provide a major source of research funding for those scientists working in universities. Without impugning the independence of these scientists, it would be naive to believe that the availability of funding in no way shapes research agendas (for example, in promoting a focus on chemicals rather than other forms of weed control).

There is evidence to suggest that funding affects research findings. Fagin and Lavelle (1996) assessed the research literature on four hazardous substances, namely atrazine, alachlor (both weed killers), perchloroethylene (a chlorinated solvent used in dry cleaning) and formaldehyde (used in glue, insulation and a range of other areas). They found that of the 43 studies funded by corporations, 32 (or 74%) reached a favourable finding on the chemical involved, five studies were inconclusive and six (or 14%) had negative findings. Of the 118 studies funded by government, universities and charitable organisations, only 27 (or 23%) reached favourable conclusions on the substances, 20 were inconclusive and 71 (60%) reached negative findings (Fagin and Lavelle, 1996: 51). In 1980 William Gaffey, employed by the chemical producer Monsanto, co-authored a paper with Judith Zack on workers at Monsanto's Nitro West Virginia plant that found no evidence of increased cancer risks among workers exposed to dioxin over many years (Zack and Gaffey, 1983: 571–91). The paper was influential in regulatory debate and litigation until 1984 when, during a worker suit against Monsanto, Zack conceded that four workers classified as 'unexposed' to dioxin had been classified as 'exposed' in an earlier study she co-authored (the issue was subsequently debated in the British journal *Nature*; Hay and Silbergeld, 1985, 1986; Gough, 1985). Similar problems of industry-influenced research have been identified with regard to other hazardous materials, notably asbestos.

Researchers can be placed in a difficult position by confidentiality conditions attached to research and by their consultancy relationship with firms, both of which may be essential to obtain access to workers' and company records. A recent case highlights these and other issues. In the early 1990s a number of workers employed in nylon flocking (a manufacturing process used to produce velour-type material) at a Microfibres Inc plant in Ontario, Canada, developed a rare form of interstitial lung disease (now known as flock workers' lung). When workers reported similar symptoms at the company's Rhode Island plant in 1994–95, Microfibres asked David Kern, an occupational physician, to investigate the potential causes (NIOSH was also involved), with Kern being asked to sign a confidentiality agreement. (For a detailed account of events see Shuchman, 1998: 341–4). In 1996, while investigations were taking place, Kern submitted an abstract of his findings to the 1997 meeting of the Thoracic Society in order to alert other physicians to a new occupational disease and to obtain information as to whether the disease had been identified elsewhere in the world. Upon discovering this, Microfibres demanded that the abstract be withdrawn, threatening legal action. In response, Dr Kern withdrew from his consulting relationship with the company and consulted officials of Brown University and its affiliate Memorial Hospital of Rhode Island (where he was employed in the occupational medicine clinic). The university and hospital offered Kern no support, both recommending that he comply with the company's request and later informing him that the occupational health service had been closed, effectively dismissing him. The journal *Annals of Internal Medicine* subsequently published Kern's findings showing that the incidence of interstitial lung disease among workers in the nylon flocking industry was at least 50 times higher than that for the general population (Kern et al., 1998: 261–72). The journal also published an account of the events (Shuchman, 1998: 341–4) and an editorial (Davidoff, 1998: 327–8). The incident aroused widespread debate (and alarm) in the journal and among occupational health researchers more generally. It is worth noting that, amid heated debate between officials from the university, hospital and Kern and others over whether the events resulted from a breach of research etiquette/mutual misunderstandings or an infringement of scientific freedom, the rigour of the study has not been questioned. In concluding his own account, *Annals* editor Frank Davidoff (1998: 328) observed '… the story is a sobering reminder that the practice of medicine, even at its scientific best, is always a social act'. As Davidoff's editorial entitled 'New disease, old story' makes clear, problems concerning confidentiality clauses, industry influence, research protocols and scientific independence are far from exceptional. Since most problems undoubtedly go unreported (even being insidiously inculcated into the research process), they are seldom raised in discussions of the origins of occupational disease.

There is also evidence of more blatant forms of intervention, including an attempt to persuade the then editor (Schilling) of the *British Journal of Industrial Medicine* to suppress publication of Doll's (1955) now classic study of the link between asbestos workers and lung cancer. The long-term efforts of the asbestos industry to suppress information and manipulate debate on asbestos has been well documented, as has the belated and less-than-vigorous role of government agencies in Australia and the US (Castleman, 1990; McCulloch and Tweedale, 2008). McCulloch and Tweedale's (2008) book *Defending the Indefensible* carefully traces the long and, indeed, ongoing history of industry efforts to reinterpret and obfuscate results, 'capture' researchers (including Doll himself), orchestrate attempts to discredit critical researchers (notably Irving Selikoff), and use global trade agreements to oppose the banning of asbestos in the developed world and continue its operations in developing countries. In Quebec—a major asbestos producer—the Quebec Chrysotile Institute has funded research that the evidence in relation to chrysotile is inconclusive, contrary to the now generally accepted view that exposure to any type of asbestos increases the risk of lung cancer, mesothelioma and other lung and pleural disorders (Pezerat, 2009).

The asbestos issue has usually been presented in isolation and has thus been seen as an isolated case. However, very similar allegations with varying levels of supporting evidence have been made, and continue to be made, in relation to other hazardous substances, including vinyl chloride and benzene (Morris, 1998; Huff, 2007a & b). According to Huff (2007b: 213), benzene-induced cancer in humans was first reported in the late 1920s but carcinogenesis findings were not reported conclusively until 50 years later—a 'discrepancy' exploited by industry 'to discredit the use of animal bioassays as surrogates for human exposure experience'. In poor countries it is easier for companies to withhold information, provide less than full explanations of even severe exposures to hazardous materials and resist claims for compensation, as the incident at Union Carbide's Bhopal plant in 1984 well illustrates (Mathur and Morehouse, 2002). In a commentary drawing on dozens of detailed studies, Huff (2007a: 107–16) argued that industry influence on occupational and environmental health—including the conduct of scientific research, access to information and deliberation of standards/recommendations by international agencies—was both a global issue and one where influence had become increasingly brazen.

It also needs to be recalled that Richard Doll's influence extended well beyond asbestos-related cancer. In 1981 Doll and Peto published a study estimating that only about 4% of cancer deaths in the UK over the past few decades were attributable to occupational exposures, well below the estimates of others. The paper was subject to a number of criticisms (see, for example, Stellman and Stellman, 1996), including the averaging of unexposed population in with the exposed population and the limited number of carcinogens considered (only 16, while the International Agency on Research on Cancer classifies 89 substances as definite carcinogens, 64 as probable carcinogens and 264 as possible human carcinogens). Nonetheless, the paper was enormously influential, being regularly quoted by government OHS agencies in the UK, Australia and elsewhere, as well as in the research literature. At the end of Doll's career it was revealed that his Oxford college had received a substantial donation from an asbestos producer and that Doll had accepted a substantial and longstanding (since 1976) retainer from chemical multinational Monsanto (McCulloch and Tweedale, 2008: 138). This tarnished Doll's reputation and his death brought a series of further allegations—for example, that he had made dismissive attacks on researchers who identified a more significant occupational-exposure contribution to cancer-related deaths and morbidity.

As already noted, attempts by industry to influence research are not restricted to occupational disease (see Shuchman, 1998). Deyo et al. (1997: 1176) argued in the US the 'lead industry hobbled the work of Needleman and colleagues on the health risks of low-level lead exposure and intimidated others through coordinated attacks at scientific meetings and skilful manipulation of the procedures for investigating scientific misconduct'. Nor is industry the only special-interest group to try and influence health researchers or public debate and policy responses to their findings (see Deyo et al., 1997: 1176–80). Research by historians has even identified instances where union connivance (to maintain jobs) with management slowed the recognition of serious health risks (Stern, 2003) although such cases appear exceptional, with unions more typically involved in prolonged struggles to secure recognition of a particular disease as work related (see, for example, Rennie, 2005; Vergara, 2005).

There are no easy remedies to the problems just identified. Obvious steps include government regulation to deal with attempts to influence research/researchers, the withholding of vital OHS information and conditions that companies can attach to research on their workforce. Increased funding from non-aligned sources and protocols about disclosing funding sources in publications (many journals already have these) would also assist. A number of these problems are likely to remain hidden and therefore difficult to address in all but extreme cases. Nonetheless, governments must abandon neo-liberal ideology and provide direct and meaningful support to independent publicly orientated research and preventative practice. Scientists, clinicians, other professions, workers, unions and community groups must also combine to pursue collaborative research and interventions (including those with progressive employers) and place pressure for accountability on both government and international agencies (Huff, 2007a).

The debate over threshold limit values (TLVs)

In developing a critical understanding of occupational disease, it is important to recognise that the development of exposure standards on hazardous substances and the implementation of regulatory measures have often been contentious processes, as a variety of different groups, including the professions, have sought to exert an influence. These debates are only occasionally made public and so seldom occupy a conspicuous place in OHS policy debates. Nevertheless, it is important to recognise that the problematic features of standard setting in relation to hazardous substances cannot be simply attributed to the difficulties of conducting scientific research but are also shaped by competing interests and inequalities of power (these also affect the resources dedicated to resolving particular problems). A long-running debate over threshold limit values (TLVs) provides some insights into these aspects.

As was noted earlier, TLVs, developed by the American Conference of Government Industrial Hygienists (ACGIH)—a private professional organisation—have formed the basis for hazardous substance exposure standards in many countries, including Australia. As such, they were viewed as neutral and scientific. However, while many TLVs have remained uncontroversial, from the late 1980s there was growing criticism of the development and application of TLVs. Criticism of individual TLVs was not new. This criticism was led by Barry Castleman. In a detailed study of medical and legal aspects of asbestos, Castleman (1990) documented how the TLV committee of the ACGIH resisted mounting criticism of the asbestos TLV from an array of eminent sources until 1971. The committee's chair during this period (and for over 20 years in total), Herbert Stokinger, had expressed scepticism about the carcinogenicity of asbestos in the 1950s—a minority viewpoint even at this time (Castleman, 1990: 266). Castleman's interpretation has been supported by a more recent assessment of the ACGIH's decision making in relation to asbestos. In their own review, Egilman and Reinert (1995: 667) conclude that the proposed asbestos guideline was '… known to be inadequate when it was first proposed, was severely criticised between 1946 and 1968, but nonetheless was promulgated annually and remained unchanged until 1971'.

In the course of his research, Castleman had become concerned about the ACGIH's reliance on industry input and the effect this might have on the independence of the TLVs developed. In 1969 Stokinger had expressed the view that:

> The TLVs are industry's values … industry has the sole responsibility to develop data on its own products; government is not in a position to develop enough facilities to handle the problem in total, nor should it, when reliable toxicological consultants are now available … There is no question that inability to obtain industrial hygiene data is one of the greatest problems facing the committee today. (Stokinger, 1969, cited in Castleman, 1990: 266).

Together with Grace Ziem, Castleman undertook a more wide-ranging assessment of the development of TLVs. Castleman and Ziem (1988: 531–59) found that unpublished corporate communications played an important role in the development of TLVs for 104 substances (for 15 substances they represented the only data source and attempts to obtain this information was mostly unsuccessful). Case studies of lead and seven carcinogens revealed various types of corporate influence, including corporate representatives acting as consultants with primary responsibility to develop TLVs for proprietary chemicals of the companies, such as Dow and Dupont, that employed them (Castleman and Ziem, 1988: 531). Castleman and Ziem (1988: 555–6) concluded that, despite the reputation of TLVs as being scientifically based, they were neither particularly scientific nor did they provide an adequate level of protection for workers. While conceding that the TLV committee's limited financial resources had hampered the development of TLVs, Castleman and Ziem argued that the problem was more fundamental than this. Castleman and Ziem (1988: 556) contended that the ascription of numerical values for acceptable exposure limits for workers by a group of experts 'is very much a political as well as a scientific process'. The only means of countering this, they suggested, was to open the information and processes for arriving at exposure limits to public scrutiny and to establish clear guidelines to preclude manipulation by corporations and other financially compromised interests. They also advocated that a significant decision-making role be accorded to representatives of those exposed to the hazards, namely workers (a similar argument has been made in the Canadian context; see Sentes, 1989: 719–22). In another paper, Ziem and Castleman (1989: 910–18) reported that of 376 air concentration exposure limits mandated by the US Occupational Safety and Health Administration in 1989, 350 were derived from the ACGIH's 1987 TLV list. They reiterated their criticism that the TLV development process had been 'gravely flawed by lack of scientific rigour, inadequate medical input, and lack of attention to financial conflicts of interest' (Ziem and Castleman, 1989: 910). Tracing the development of TLVs, they noted that, among other things, as late as 1988 the TLV committee would not permit interested scientists to attend its meetings (Ziem and Castleman, 1989: 914).

Other researchers have echoed Castleman and Ziem's concerns. In their study, Egilman and Reinhart (1995: 667–8) argued that an examination of the procedure used to develop the asbestos TLV revealed that the ACGIH failed to thoroughly consider all published (and therefore critically reviewed) research and uncritically accepted unpublished research data from financially interested companies. Egilman and Reinhart also found companies had suppressed internal studies that indicated the guidelines were inadequate and had sought to modify medical articles in ways that minimised concerns about health effects. They argued that these three factors were not unique to asbestos but had '… influenced the determination of many other ACGIH guidelines' (Egilman and Reinhart, 1995: 667).

Not surprisingly, the ACGIH rapidly responded to Castleman and Ziem, labelling their criticism as imbalanced. The ACGIH Board of Directors (1990: 340–4) argued that Castleman and Ziem had misrepresented OSHA's use of TLVs and had dealt with only a minority of the TLVs developed. The board also suggested the TLV debate detracted attention from more fundamental questions about whether governments and other bodies should promulgate health standards both in the US and internationally. At the same time, the board implicitly conceded there were problems by outlining new measures to be undertaken in the development of TLVs. These included a major effort to improve TLVs, the allocation of more internal resources to this task, adopting a more open approach to the review process and developing procedures to handle conflicts of interest (ACGIH Board of Directors, 1990: 344). In 1991 the ACGIH vigorously resisted strong pressure, including threatened legal action, from the Formaldehyde Institute (a body representing the formaldehyde industry) when it revised the TLV for formaldehyde to 0.3 ppm (*ACGIH Bulletin Board*, 1991: 1–2; for a critical discussion of the activities of the Formaldehyde Institute and similar industry bodies see Fagin and Lavelle, 1996).

In a later study, Castleman and Ziem (1994: 133–43) continued to express doubts that the ACGIH had fully addressed the conflict of interest issue on the pivotal TLV committee. They noted that TLV committee members were not required to disclose income from consulting (a requirement for members of scientific committees to US government agencies). The conflict of interests policy amounted to an understanding that a committee member who felt they might have a conflict would raise it with the chair so it could be resolved. Castleman and Ziem (1994: 133) argued that the 'ACGIH declined to explicitly prohibit committee members from being involved in developing TLVs for substances produced by firms with which they have financial relationships'.

The TLV debate raises a number of important issues aside from the more obvious questions about the ethics of corporate influence on standard-setting bodies and the maintenance of independence by professional bodies that by their very nature will have close ties to industry. The debate highlights the fact that standard setting always involves normative judgments about risk and, with regard to many hazardous substances, assessing a scientific research literature that is sparse, ambiguous or includes entirely contradictory sets of findings. Further, when flaws in decision-making processes have been identified the ensuing debate barely enters the public domain. These observations establish the basis for two points. First, where governments use standard-setting information prepared by independent professional bodies they must take steps either to vet the information or to establish guidelines on the development of that information so as to preserve the public interest. Countries such as Norway have sought to make socioeconomic considerations an explicit part of the standard-setting process. Second, where normative judgments are being made it is critical that all the key stakeholders have input, but most especially representatives of workers because it is they (and their families) who bear the most direct, severe and usually irreversible consequences of what are deemed to be acceptable levels of risk. At present, the regulatory infrastructure in the US makes no provision for tripartite processes to evaluate standards and there appears little prospect of change in the near future. This is not the case in other countries such as Australia, which has tripartite bodies at national level and in some states (see chapter 7). Nevertheless, possessing tripartite bodies has not necessarily led to critical consideration of TLVs. The debate over TLVs received some attention from OHS professionals in Australia but was not, as far as we are aware, addressed at a public policy level even though this country makes considerable use of TLVs to guide its standard setting.

Regulatory failure

One of the major problems confronting attempts to explain occupational disease is the complete inadequacy of existing regulatory controls. Despite the insidious character of many diseases, new substances (including new combinations of existing chemicals) can be introduced into the workplace with minimal if any risk assessment of their potential health effects. In general, regulations also fail to ensure that there is a comprehensive record of those substances being used in specific industries or particular types of workplace. Without such controls it is possible for hazardous substances to enter the workplace and for the health effects to accumulate over time. Acute poisoning, epidemiological or clinical research and even chance will result in some, but undoubtedly by no means all, being identified. Until the late 1990s there was no attempt in the US to record statistics on chemical incidents (a report carried out at this time estimated that there had been over 600 000 such incidents between 1987 and 1996; Chemical Safety and Hazards Investigation Board, 1999: 1). As far as we are aware there are no comparable statistics for Australia. For substances that don't result in acute incidents the process may take many years (the disease chloracne was first described in 1897 and linked to pesticide manufacturing workers in the 1930s but dioxin was not identified as the underlying cause until 1960). In some cases, the evidence will remain inconclusive and subject to considerable debate. In other words, the regulatory framework establishes rules on the introduction and use of potentially hazardous substances that make it virtually impossible to systematically detect their health effects. A regulatory framework based on the vetting and licensing of all new chemicals or, at least, a precautionary-principle approach (see Freestone and Hay, 1996) together with the maintenance of a comprehensive register of their use might have had rather different consequences.

Not only is the regulatory framework on hazardous materials largely reactive in approach, in many countries it is also incredibly complex because the vast array of hazardous materials, including radioactive substances, is subject to a number of different bodies of legislation and regulatory agencies with overlapping coverage. The situation is made even worse in Australia by a dual system of state and federal laws (for a discussion of the unsatisfactory regulation of hazardous and radioactive substances, see Gun, 1994: 523–7; Rosen, 1998: 395–400). In the US the federal government has taken a more decisive role but even here the overlapping roles of federal agencies, most notably the EPA and OSHA, has caused problems requiring careful attention. For example, it was not until 1997 that the EPA and OSHA developed a formal protocol on the investigation of chemical incidents (see Patterson, 1997).

The regulation of a potentially vast array of hazardous substances presents a major challenge and may require strategies specific to a particular substance or a particular industry. For example, in relation to substances where there can be no doubt as to their toxicity, such as tobacco and asbestos, it would be more effective to ban their use entirely rather than deal with them at a workplace level. In both cases there would be significant industry opposition to these measures (and consumer opposition as well in the case of tobacco). In Australia and a number of other countries, a combination of strong public health campaigns and litigation by workers affected by passive smoking has resulted in the banning of smoking in government buildings, almost all public transport and many large commercial workplaces. Yet there are conspicuous limits to this approach due to the vigorous opposition of particular industries who feel their business will be damaged, such as hospitality and gambling. The casualised nature of much of the workforce in these industries diminishes the prospect of expensive litigation. Further, the option of more efficient air conditioning may be defeated by the practice of keeping premises warm to encourage additional alcohol consumption. In this case, creeping environmental controls and programs designed to reduce smoking in general seem essential (see Baker, 1991).

In other cases, the characteristics of the industry make regulation difficult and demand specific responses. For example, Q fever is a significant health problem for those working with or near cattle and sheep (or materials such as straw these animals have been in contact with), entailing perpetual flu-like symptoms that have been known to drive some of those infected to commit suicide. The only effective protection is vaccination and it would be reasonable to regard this as essential for abattoir workers (see Bell et al., 1997). However, vaccination should only be carried out on individual workers once (second vaccinations can be dangerous) and to achieve this would require a management plan covering the whole industry due to the transient nature of the workforce in Australia if not elsewhere. In Queensland, for example, both the union and larger employers are in favour of compulsory vaccination but smaller employers have resisted these moves on the grounds of costs, and attempts at addressing this well-known and serious problem by direct regulation were still unresolved in April 1999. In general, regulatory control measures will be expensive and difficult to implement in industries where there is an atomised workforce consisting of numerous small businesses, self-employed workers or subcontractors using highly hazardous substances. Examples of such industries are not hard to find and include farming and lawn care/gardening services, both of which use dangerous pesticides (for a discussion of this in relation to the latter, see Gadon, 1996: 794–9). Major regulatory problems are by no means confined to such atomistic industries. Even industries such as healthcare with a highly trained workforce can present major problems due to the sheer array of biological threats and changing work practices.

As with research and standard setting there is also a question of corporate and broader industry influence on regulation at both the national and international level. In relation to the latter, concerns have been recently raised about corporate influence on a number of international organisations that are important sources of information on toxic substances (see Castleman and Lemen, 1998: 53–5). A notable example is the International Program on Chemical Safety (IPCS) that is jointly funded by the WHO (where it is located), the ILO and the UN Environment Program. In 1993 Watterson (1993: 131–2) raised concerns about the IPCS's credibility, reporting that manufacturers (ICI, Hoechst and DuPont) had prepared the first drafts of its reports on chlorofluorocarbon refrigerants and the fungicide benomyl. Further, little if any effort had been made to balance the presence of industry observers at IPCS task meetings with non-industry representatives. Following Watterson, Castleman and Lemen (1998: 53–5) reported a similar pattern of industry involvement in drafting IPCS documents on methylene chloride (drawing a strongly hostile response from NIOSH) and chrysotile asbestos (which the Collegium Ramazzini refused to review). Castleman and Lemen (a former Assistant Surgeon General with the US Public Health Service) also document increasingly vocal protests by scientists about corporate influence on these and other IPCS activities (including a Berlin workshop on multiple chemical sensitivity which decided to rename it as idiopathic environmental intolerances).

Castleman and Lemen (1998: 53–5) also identified corporate influence on ILO activities, including X-ray training workshops held in Latin America and a proposed monograph on the hazards of fibrous materials submitted to the ILO by the International Commission on Occupational Health (ICOH) Scientific Committee on Fibres. In the latter case, the author of the chapter on asbestos was a former director of health and environment for the Asbestos Institute (an industry body). Stunned by this, three long-time experts on asbestos declined to review chapters for the report and this, together with criticism from other scientists and unions in the Nordic countries, the UK and the US, caused the ILO to withdraw the monograph from consideration as an ILO publication. The International Commission on Occupational Health (ICOH), a professional body listed by agencies such as the ILO as an affiliated non-government organisation, and which has prepared scientific documents for them, was drawn into the criticism of being subject to industry influence (Giannasi and Thebaud-Mony, 1997: 150–7). Indeed, in a scathing editorial for the journal *Archives of Environmental Health*, LaDou (1998: 248) documented a series of apparent conflicts of interest within ICOH and questioned its purported independence, labelling it '... a club whose members represent the private sector'. There is also evidence of industry using other international bodies to try and circumvent regulatory controls on hazardous materials. Castleman and Lemen (1998: 54–5) report alleged moves by the industry to block an EU ban on asbestos through the World Trade Organisation. Canada, the world's largest exporter (with seven of the 10 biggest markets being developing countries), had already challenged a French ban on asbestos (10 EU members have bans and the UK and Ireland are considering this). It took the matter to the World Trade Organisation (WTO) as an unfair trade practice. Following unanimous evidence from scientific reviewers that chrysotile is a carcinogen and controlled use was impractical, the WTO's Dispute Resolution Panel upheld France's right to ban asbestos in September 2000 (McCulloch and Tweedale, 2008: 248).

Quite apart from the issue of establishing standards there are also problems in relation to enforcement. The limited evidence available indicates that non-compliance with regulatory standards on exposure to hazardous substances is by no means uncommon. In the US, sampling carried out by OSHA and Mine Safety and Health Administration inspectors between 1985 and 1994 found silica levels exceeded the Permissible Exposure Limit (PEL) in about 15% of cases. For other pneumoconiotic agents, samples exceeded the PEL in around 7% of cases (Centre for Disease Control,

1996: 3). Even fairly rigorous enforcement can be manipulated with, for example, the use of contractors to do hazardous maintenance (Thebaud-Mony, 1999) or workers being rostered onto high-exposure tasks immediately prior to taking annual leave (to minimise the risk that adverse results can be detected by biological monitoring). The extent of these sorts of practices is unknown. However, the larger issue is that rigorous auditing of exposures by regulatory agencies is very exceptional, confined to only the most hazardous workplaces (such as nuclear power plants) and often then in particular circumstances, such as in cases where an unplanned discharge of hazardous chemicals or materials occurs (such as the breach of a retaining dam at a uranium mine or in response to a cancer cluster at a building).

Changes to government policies over the past two decades may actually be having adverse effects on the extent of occupational illness. As the report of the Commission for the Social Determinants of Health of the World Health Organization (2007) and it knowledge network component reports (such as EMCONET, 2007) clearly showed, the pursuit of neo-liberal policies has had significant adverse effects on health outcomes globally through changes to healthcare and urban infrastructure, increases in socioeconomic inequalities within and between countries and, of most direct relevance to this book, via the changes it has effected on employment and working conditions (see also Benach and Mutaner, 2009). As noted already in this book (including this chapter), a substantial body of international research indicates that job insecurity and growth of contingent or precarious forms of employment has resulted in a deterioration in OHS (Quinlan, 1999). However, the regulatory response to these new health threats remains fragmented and muted at best. Some areas, such as the mental health problems associated with downsizing/restructuring and job insecurity, have been almost entirely ignored by regulators and policymakers even where the capacity to intervene already exists (Quinlan, 2007a).

If lessons are to be drawn from the belated recognition and partial response to health hazards at work they are that a more proactive/early intervention and precautionary approach is required. Reviewing the recognition and control of occupational disease from ancient times Leigh (2007: 529) concluded:

> Whatever else society may have learnt from silica and asbestos by the end of the 20th century, one stark lesson is that, if it fails to recognise the health risks of materials and chemicals and fails to take action at the earliest possible stage to prevent them occurring, then, even without considering legal liability issues, the human cost can be beyond anything that a society should be asking its members to pay for manufactured products—the price of which can never reflect their true cost to those that produced them … Changes in technology and in the organisation of work, and in the acceptability of harm or of uncertainty about harm mean that the end of the agenda is never reached. New problems create new challenges, and the solutions to them may well have a major influence on the developments of patterns of work in the 21st century.

Conclusion

Unlike occupational injury, there is nothing even remotely like accurate information on the extent of occupational disease and other health-related problems. It is clear that exposure to hazardous substances and other sources of occupational disease results in the death of far more workers than do injuries in the workplace. Beyond this the evidence is very fragmentary. The precautionary principle does not operate with regard to workplace health. Exposure to substances such as chemicals, nanotechnologies and exposure to ionising radiation can occur, in large part, without any prior assessment of their health effects. The same applies to changes to work organisation including hours of work, workloads, job security, effort/reward balance and the like. The proliferation of inadequately regulated and potentially (if not known) hazardous materials should be cause for concern, as should growing evidence on the hazardous effects of particular types of work organisation.

More specifically, the contribution of a number of disciplines to our understanding of the origins, extent and methods of dealing with occupational disease risks was assessed. In relation to occupational medicine/epidemiology it was noted that this discipline has played a critical role historically in bringing recognition to the diseases associated with particular types of industry and the hazardous substances used by workers in them. More recently medical researchers have looked at the impact of work organisation and especially job control on the onset of disease and health indices. Both bodies of research are important in terms of prevention, but the latter has been far less influential in terms of affecting employer and government practices. These distinct bodies of research are potentially complementary but integration requires a deal of attention and the role played by regulation needs to be incorporated into this. At the same time, we identified a number of limitations with medical/epidemiological research, including a neglect of health effects on women and weakness in terms of proffered solutions. We also examined the role played by occupational hygienists in the management of exposure to harmful substances and the setting of exposure standards at workplace, industry and national level. It was noted that occupational hygiene certainly brought a more systematic approach to hazard measuring, monitoring and management. As with occupational medicine, Australia has tended to lag behind other countries in both the training and employment of occupational hygienists. On the one hand, occupational hygiene has been far more focused on devising practical solutions to hazards than occupational medicine. On the other hand, we noted problems, including occupational hygiene's neglect of organisational factors and pressures on hygienists to use suboptimal control measures.

Psychological research on occupational stress and illness has identified aspects of the development of occupational illness that are heavily discounted by the medical model. In particular, psychologists have drawn attention to the importance of recognising the impact of work on the subjective health and wellbeing of workers. They have also attempted to disentangle the complex interaction between social, organisational, psychological and biological variables that is at the heart of occupational illness.

Unfortunately, while there are signs of some very positive research by psychologists (including Tom Cox, Julian Barling and Michael Frone to name a few, and not to forget Robert Karasek) a substantial body of writing and research still adheres to a 'stress management' approach that transfers the responsibility for stress away from the organisation and onto the individual worker. Turning to sociologists and other social scientists, it was noted that historically these groups tended to be preoccupied with occupational injury but in recent years there have been more positive signs of the important contribution they can make to understanding health and illness. Even leaving the important work of Johannes Siegrist to one side, there are also some clear synergies between the work of medical researchers such as Marmot and sociological research that emphasise the importance of job control, subordination and (to a lesser extent) reward factors, as well as the potential to build on the institutional and regulatory insights of social science researchers, including industrial relations and law/criminology. Like psychologists, sociologists have emphasised the importance of subjective as well as objective measures of health and wellbeing. Recognition of the subjective is essential if workers are to be seen as playing more than a passive role. There are also signs that the potential for effective collaboration between researchers in these two fields is growing.

As has been argued throughout this book, a multidisciplinary and participatory approach is essential to understand the origins, incidence and effective interventions with regard to health problems at work.

Finally, it is an unfortunate but critical observation that the belated recognition of and attention to even the most dangerous substances cannot be seen as entirely 'accidental' or the product of inadequate knowledge (itself socially mediated). A number of dimensions of this were identified in the introductory discussion of disease and the final section of this chapter looked more specifically at instances where powerful interest groups sought to shape understanding and action on hazardous materials in the workplace. Without suggesting every problem identified is typical, they do raise critical issues that cannot be ignored when discussing occupational disease and ill health. A number of the regulatory issues will be taken up in more detail in chapters 7 and 8.

QUESTIONS FOR DISCUSSION

1   What is meant by the terms occupational disease and illness?
2   What role should occupational hygienists and other professional bodies play in devising occupational exposure standards?
3   What does the notion of stress contribute to our understanding of occupational health and illness?
4   Is it either useful or desirable to develop separate sociological explanations of occupational injury and disease?
5   There have been longstanding criticisms of the way in which occupational diseases have largely been overlooked in OHS legislation and enforcement policies. Explain the reasons why this situation continues and what can be done to improve it.

FURTHER READING

Ferrie, J., Westerlund, H., Virtanen, M., Vahtera, J. and Kivimaki, M. (2008), 'Flexible labour markets and employee health', *Scandinavian Journal of Work Environment and Health*, (Supp No.6): 98–110.

Grantham, D. (1992), *Occupational Health and Hygiene: Guidebook for the WHSO*, Merino Lithographics, Brisbane.

Huff, J. (2007), 'Industry influence on occupational and environmental public health', *International Journal of Occupational and Environmental Health*, **13**(1): 107–16.

LaDou, J. (1997), *Occupational and Environmental Medicine*, 2nd edition, Appleton & Lange, Stamford, Connecticut.

Marmot, M. (1998), 'Contribution of psychosocial factors to socioeconomic differences in health', *The Millbank Quarterly*, **76**(3): 403–48.

Petersen, C. (ed.) (2005), *Work Stress: Studies in the Context, Content and Outcomes of Stress*, Baywood, New York.

Sim, M. (2007), 'The need for an occupational disease surveillance system in Australia', *Journal of Occupational Health and Safety—Australia and New Zealand*, **23**(6): 557–62.

Weindling, P. (ed.) (1985), *The Social History of Occupational Health*, Croom Helm, London.

Zalk, D. and Nelson, D. (2008), 'History and evolution of control banding: a review', *Journal of Occupational and Environmental Hygiene*, **5**: 330–46.

Case study: working hours and health

Introduction

WORKING hours can present a significant but under-recognised risk to health. Research on the topic has mainly concerned shiftwork but recently irregular hours have also attracted scientific attention. Although shiftwork has a long history, it increased in prevalence during the second half of last century, reaching into the white-collar and professional sectors where it had previously been rare. Similarly, in recent years irregular hours have become pervasive across a wide range of industries and occupations, a development that is linked to the growth of precarious employment. Unfortunately, work outside daylight hours, especially during the middle of the night and the early hours of the morning, often produces upheaval to physiological processes, subjective health, and social and domestic life. Predictably, it is distasteful to most workers.

The physiological disruption, disturbance of eating and sleeping patterns, and social isolation caused by working hours may have marked negative effects on health. Shiftworkers widely report sleep disturbances, fatigue, gastrointestinal complaints and diminished wellbeing. These short-term effects have been recognised for some time. However, recently persuasive evidence has emerged to indicate that night work has significant longer-term disease risks. Further, the effects of working hours are superimposed on those of other health hazards in the workplace and in some cases exacerbate them. At present, knowledge of the mechanisms through which these effects are created is incomplete. Nevertheless, several disciplines have made important, often complementary, contributions to understanding of this topic. Before exploring the health effects of working hours we shall briefly examine historical developments in shiftwork and working hours.

A brief history of shiftwork and working hours

Work outside daylight hours is not new (see Scherrer, 1981). There is little doubt that it existed before recorded history, for example when sentries worked through the night to protect communities from attack. Sheep, cattle, horses and fire were probably tended throughout the night in early times. In Europe during the Roman era, night work became widely established for commercial, military, religious, and social purposes. A law passed by Julius Caesar forbidding the movement of most horse-drawn vehicles in city streets during the day was ultimately extended to all cities in the empire. As a result, workers transported all manner of goods into cities at night. Riders dispatched urgent imperial mail, the vestals guarded sacred fire and Roman armies marched and fought at night. Sailors, reliant on the stars for navigation, took all but short coastal journeys after dark. Just as today, many births occurred during the night and midwives attended them.

Despite this activity, the proportion of the population working at night was very small. During the Middle Ages nocturnal activity further decreased due to diminished trade in the cities and prohibitions on many types of work at night. It was not until the Renaissance that night work began to expand again with increased trade and improvements in maritime and road transport. Continuous, 24-hour mining operations using three rotating shifts had also appeared by the sixteenth century.

The arrival of the Industrial Revolution in the mid-eighteenth century saw a dramatic leap in work outside daylight hours (Scherrer, 1981). Rapid scientific and technological development was largely responsible. Gas lighting and mechanisation of work in urban factories made around-the-clock production economically attractive. Continuous operations became common in workplaces such as mines, shipyards, sugar refineries, paper factories, glass foundries and oil refineries. In factories, work days of between 12 and 13 hours were common for adults and children. Workers employed in their homes on a subcontract basis, sometimes known as the 'domestic system', frequently worked between 14 and 16 hours per day. Their workplaces were widely known as 'sweatshops'.

Early in the nineteenth century two 12-hour shifts were common in blast furnaces, forges, rolling mills, metallurgical establishments, paper mills and glass works (Kogi, 1985). Later, three teams working eight-hour shifts gradually replaced the two-shift system in manufacturing industries, with shifts typically worked from 0800 to 1600, 1600 to 2400, and 2400 to 0800, or thereabouts. In addition to manufacturing, shiftwork became much more common in service industries, including medical services and the police. However, towards the close of the Industrial Revolution, the proportion of the population involved in shiftwork decreased somewhat, especially with the banning of night work for women and children in many countries.

During the twentieth century technology again considerably expanded the range of occupations requiring night and evening work. Marked accelerations in this trend, arising largely from changes in economic conditions, occurred in the mid-1950s and the early 1970s (Anonymous, 1980; Gordon et al., 1986; Kogi, 1985). By the 1980s, between 15 and 30% of the workforce in industrialised countries were employed on some form of shift schedule, and in some industries the percentage was substantially higher (Bosworth and Dawkins, 1980; Copsey and Corlett, 1985; Department of Science and Technology, 1980; Gordon et al., 1986; Kogi, 1985). Gordon et al. (1986) found that the proportion of the workforce employed on shiftwork during a 12-month period appeared higher than these estimates, approximately 36% for men in the US. Elsewhere, it was estimated that night workers represented between 7 and 15% of the workforce in industrialised countries by the mid-1980s (International Labour Office, 1988).

Australian Bureau of Statistics figures (ABS, 1982) indicate that by the early 1980s 25.7% of all employees worked on weekends, at night or on rotating shiftwork and 9.4% were night workers. Shiftwork was very common in manufacturing, occurring in 53% of manufacturing workplaces (Department of Science and Technology, 1980). It was particularly widespread in the food, engineering, textiles, printing, tobacco and vehicle construction industries. Marked growth was also apparent in private and public sector service industries, including postal services, telecommunications, broadcasting, transport, power supply, health services, security and entertainment (Department of Science and Technology, 1980). By 1976, shiftworkers were employed in approximately 60% of organisations in the industry category encompassing hospitals and other service providers (Department of Science and Technology, 1980: 7).

In addition to technological changes, economic and social factors have played important roles in the expansion of working hours. Many industrial plants, for example, are operated continuously for economic rather than technical reasons (Kogi, 1985), and the profit advantages of more intensive utilisation of expensive capital equipment encourage growth in shiftwork. Profitability is increased by more rapid depreciation of expensive capital items, reduced costs per production unit and greater capacity to meet rapid changes in demand. With rapid technological innovation, obsolescence is an important incentive to depreciate and replace plant and equipment more quickly. Political factors have also contributed at various times, such as a belief that shiftwork may help reduce unemployment (Kogi, 1985). As noted earlier, community needs or desires to increase the availability of services have also contributed, especially in relation to transport, communication, entertainment and health (Costa, 2003a; Kogi, 1985).

More recently, the marked growth of precarious employment and flexible work since the 1970s (see chapters 1 and 5) has been accompanied by a similar expansion in irregular working hours. Work has spread more extensively into the evenings, nights and weekends while hours have become more variable (Costa, 2003a). For example, by 2002 only 24% of the working population in Europe was engaged in 'standard' day work—that is, work beginning no earlier than 7.30 or 8.00 in the morning and finishing no later than 5.00 or 6.00 in the evening Monday to Friday (Costa, 2003a). At that time, 18.8% of European workers were doing shiftwork that included night work and the proportion of males (24%) was substantially higher than females (12%). Most workers are now engaged in some form of 'non-standard' hours, such as shiftwork, compressed working weeks, part-time work or irregular hours. Irregular hours encompass various forms of unpredictable and variable hours, which usually spread into evenings and weekends, and sometimes night work. For example, a recent study of casual workers in five-star hotels in Sydney, Australia, indicated that working hours ranged from 0 to 72 hours per week and shift lengths ranged from 2 to 18 hours (Bohle et al., 2004).

As a result of the growth of non-standard hours, the borders between work and leisure time are much less rigid than they once were. A much wider spread of working hours is common in industries where day work once dominated and, significantly, both long and irregular hours have more deeply infiltrated white-collar and professional occupations, when previously they had been largely confined to unskilled and semi-skilled occupations. The associated social costs have often been overlooked, but effects on workers' health and quality of life should be considered when the desirability of changes in hours is assessed. Before we examine these effects we shall briefly explore the meaning of the term 'shiftwork'.

What is shiftwork?

Shiftwork can be broadly defined as any form of work scheduling in which workers are divided into two or more groups working at different times of day. Unfortunately, the term is generally used without further qualification to refer to a diverse array of work schedules (Akerstedt, 1988; Costa, 2003a). Taylor and Pocock (1972: 202), for example, defined shiftwork as 'any system of working hours other than regular day work', and pooled all workers satisfying this criterion into one group. Such broad categorisation fails to recognise important differences between schedules.

Shift schedules vary in many ways, including the length of shifts, the timing of shift changes, the rapidity of rotation between shifts, the regularity of progression from shift to shift, the extent to which they cover 24-hour operations (particularly at night) and the number of days of operation per week. They frequently require seven-day, 24-hour coverage, such as three-shift schedules with eight-hour morning, evening and night shifts. Workers may be permanently assigned to one shift or they may be required to rotate between shifts. Shift rotations vary from rapid, for example every two or three days, to slow, perhaps every week or every month. Recently, two-shift rosters with rapid rotations through 12-hour shifts, or a combination of 10-hour and 14-hour shifts, have become common. Emergency services, for example, have often adopted schedules that rotate through two day shifts, two night shifts, and four days off.

Over the past few decades there has been marked growth in the prevalence of 12-hour shifts in the Australian mining and petrochemical industries. The schedules vary from relatively rapid rotation, for example with four days at work followed by four days off, to very slow and unbalanced rotations, such as 21 days at work followed by seven days off. Schedules requiring many consecutive days at work are characteristic of a form of work organisation known as fly-in fly-out (FIFO) or 'long-distance commuting'. FIFO involves work that is so isolated from workers' homes and other residential communities that work schedules are designed to require blocks of days on site followed by blocks of days at home (Storey and Shrimpton, 1991). In most cases, workers are transported to and from work by air. On 'symmetric' schedules, time on and off the site is evenly distributed, for example with seven days on and seven days off. On 'asymmetric' schedules, workers spend more time on site than off, for example 14 days on and seven days off or, in an extreme case, 63 days on and 12 days off.

Long periods spent doing intensive and physically demanding work at vast distances from home have special implications for the domestic lives, and probably the health, of many FIFO workers.

In other industries rosters are discontinuous, usually not requiring work on weekends or in the middle of the night. Common examples include 'discontinuous three-shift rosters' in which weekends are usually free and 'double-day shifts' which usually involve eight-hour morning and afternoon/evening shifts Monday to Friday. 'Split shifts', where work is divided into two stints of three or four hours with a break of several hours in between, are common in the tourism and hospitality industry. In some industries, predominantly female workers are employed part time to work a shift of approximately four hours in the evening after the conclusion of the 'normal' working day.

The shift schedules described above are among the most widely used, but there are so many different rosters that it is impossible to list them all. In view of this diversity, researchers have developed classification criteria to describe and differentiate roster systems more clearly. Kogi (1985), for example, identified four basic criteria:

1 whether the schedule requires work at night
2 whether the schedule is continuous (covering the full week) or discontinuous (omitting one or more days, usually weekends)
3 whether shifts are permanent or rotating
4 whether the day is divided into two, three, four or more shifts.

Within these categories other potentially important factors should be specified, including the frequency of night shift, the rapidity and direction of shift rotation, the starting and finishing times of shifts, the number of consecutive shifts worked and the number of days off between shifts (Costa, 2003a; Rutenfranz et al., 1985). As we shall see, particular characteristics of some rosters are likely to have negative effects on health. However, as few researchers have precisely described the shift rosters they have investigated, there is often limited direct evidence to demonstrate these effects.

Health effects of working hours

Shiftwork

There is now extensive evidence that shiftwork and non-standard hours are growing in prevalence and have adverse effects, particularly when night work is required (Barnes-Farrell et al., 2008; Costa, 2003a & b). The negative impact of shiftwork has been recognised for some time (see, for example, Dunham, 1977; Gordon et al., 1986) and includes effects on physical health, mental health, physiological functioning, sleep, work performance and family and social life. Night work conflicts with the circadian (daily) rhythms of most human physiological, behavioural and performance variables. Night shift requires work when most circadian rhythms are in an early-morning trough, between 2.00 am and 6.00 am. It also requires daytime sleep, which is disrupted by circadian factors.

Historically, the negative effects of shiftwork have been widely acknowledged. They are explicitly recognised by the widespread practice of paying shiftworkers penalty rates for working outside normal hours. This compensation is paid for the ill health and other inconveniences that accompany shiftwork, a practice intended to translate the negative effects of undesirable work organisation into purely monetary terms. While it provides a way to summarise the complex and multidimensional effects of shiftwork, this practice has significant limitations (Thierry, 1981). Unfortunately, financial compensation does little, if anything, to improve the health of shiftworkers, and may even conceal negative effects. Penalty rates tend to sustain the status quo and discourage redesign of work schedules to reduce negative health effects. Indeed, shift penalties provide a direct economic incentive to risk health and wellbeing, as financial benefits are often major factors encouraging workers to begin and continue shiftwork. The incentives offered to risk health and the growing prevalence of shiftwork have made it increasingly important to better understand the effects of different work schedules on health and wellbeing.

It is important to sound a note of caution before discussing research on the health effects of shiftwork. Unfortunately, although hundreds of shiftwork studies have been conducted, our knowledge of the health impact of specific roster arrangements is still very incomplete, largely due to the limitations of the methods used to conduct much of the research. In 1986, these limitations led Akerstedt and Knutsson (1986: 403) to conclude that practically all studies suffer from 'major methodological flaws that seriously affect the validity of the conclusions'. Although substantial improvements have become apparent since that time, methodological limitations still present a barrier to the expansion of knowledge in this field. One promising development has been the emergence of more compelling theoretical frameworks. For many years there was little sufficiently detailed theory to guide the design and interpretation of research, but the more complex models developed since the 1990s offer more effective frameworks to guide research in the future.

Two methodological problems are very common in shiftwork research. The first is that the majority of studies are cross-sectional. They usually examine a group of workers at a single point in time and attempt to compare the health of shiftworkers with that of day workers in different organisations or to simply link biological, psychological or behavioural characteristics of workers to assessments of their health. Relatively few include appropriate control groups with which to compare the shiftworkers' health. Such studies provide little hard evidence of cause and effect relationships between variables. For example, many researchers have concluded that certain biological characteristics of workers may determine their ability to adapt to night work, when it is plausible that biological differences between workers were produced by exposure to shiftwork. Other researchers have found that shiftworkers' health is as good as that of the general community and concluded that shiftwork has no discernible negative effect on health, overlooking the 'healthy worker' effect discussed in chapter 2.

The second problem is that field studies of shiftwork have almost exclusively examined workers with previous shiftwork experience, and often many years of it. There is evidence that many people leave shiftwork, however, and several studies have indicated that those who do leave are less healthy than those who stay (Angersbach et al., 1980; Czeisler et al., 1983; Knutsson et al., 1986; Koller, 1983; Verhaegen et al., 1986). Indeed, many avoid shiftwork from the start (Akerstedt and Knutsson, 1986) or are screened out by physicians (Haider et al., 1981). Such evidence suggests that studies of experienced shiftworkers may be sampling a self-selected and relatively robust group of workers who either have better resources to cope with shiftwork or are more determined to do so. These methodological limitations undoubtedly reflect genuine difficulties in conducting sound research in organisations, but they must be kept in mind when attempting to interpret the shiftwork literature. Ultimately, only studies that monitor shiftworkers over time and compare changes in their health with those of non-shiftworkers doing the same type of work will convincingly establish health effects.

It has been argued that workers' perceptions of their health are as important as so-called 'objective' indices of ill health (Harrington, 1978). There has been strong evidence for some time that most shiftworkers report chronically impaired subjective health and wellbeing (Akerstedt, 1980, 1988; Frese and Semmer, 1986; Verhaegen et al., 1986). Commonly reported symptoms include sleep disruption, gastrointestinal discomfort, disturbances of appetite, dizziness and psychological symptoms, such as sleepiness, persisting fatigue, anxiety, irritability, mild depression and mood disturbances (Akerstedt, 1980; Frese and Semmer, 1986; Reinberg et al., 1983; Rutenfranz et al., 1985; Tasto et al., 1978). There is also evidence that these subjective symptoms are very significant to shiftworkers (Akerstedt and Torsvall, 1978; Meers et al., 1978), and that they are more prevalent among shiftworkers than permanent day workers (Akerstedt, 1980; Angersbach et al., 1980; Frese and Semmer, 1986; Verhaegen et al., 1986). Night work and rotating shifts appear to have the most marked negative impact (Akerstedt, 1980, 1988; Tasto et al., 1978), but elevated symptoms have also been associated with early morning shifts (Akerstedt, 1980; Reinberg et al., 1975). While there is some evidence that day workers may experience some subjective symptoms more often than shiftworkers, the balance of the evidence indicates that shiftworkers experience a wide range of symptoms more often, and more intensely, than day workers.

The negative subjective effects of shiftwork become apparent early. Kundi et al. (1979) found that shiftwork has its strongest influence on subjective health and well-being during the first five years. Conversely, Tasto et al. (1978) found few differences on a range of physical, psychological and behavioural variables between workers with less than six months of shift experience and those with a year or more of experience. They concluded that the critical variable affecting health was the type of shifts worked, not the amount of shiftwork experience. Longitudinal research by Meers et al. (1978) also indicated that subjective health declined significantly after six months of regular night work, and that continuing deterioration was apparent four years later. Another follow-up after seven years led the researchers to conclude 'there has been a continuous increase in subjective health complaints, in neuroticism, in somatic neurotic complaints, in fatigue, and in digestive symptoms' (Verhaegen et al., 1981: 281). The final follow-up after 12½ years indicated that shiftworkers had higher symptom levels on a range of health variables than a matched group of day workers, with the most marked difference emerging in fatigue (Verhaegen et al., 1986). A controlled longitudinal study by Bohle and Tilley (1989) also demonstrated that nine months of infrequent night work had substantial negative effects on nurses' psychological wellbeing. Together, these studies provide persuasive evidence that rotating shiftwork, particularly when it includes night work, has negative effects on subjective health and that symptoms appear shortly after workers begin doing shifts.

Shiftwork also has acute effects on mood and wellbeing. Bohle and Tilley (1993) examined day-to-day variations in mood when nurses completed their very first block of night shifts. Night work did not affect four of the six dimensions of mood measured but it did have substantial negative effects on vigour and fatigue. Interestingly, vigour and fatigue deteriorated markedly on the first night, but then remained stable across four subsequent nights, indicating that night work had an immediate negative effect but it did not accumulate from night to night thereafter. Several other studies have produced similar results in relation to fatigue (see Knauth, 1995). Prizmic et al. (1995) identified shiftwork-tolerant and shiftwork-intolerant workers using self-reports of psychosomatic and digestive symptoms and sleep quality. They then examined differences in mood changes during the day between shiftwork-tolerant and shiftwork-intolerant workers and a group of workers with no shiftwork experience. All three groups displayed similar patterns of variation in mood and fatigue across the day, but the shiftwork-intolerant group had consistently lower positive mood scores and higher fatigue scores than the other two groups, suggesting that there are substantial individual differences in the short-term impact of shiftwork on mood.

In addition to these acute effects, there is now persuasive evidence that shiftwork has longer-term effects on disease. Until recently, there was vigorous debate about the extent to which it contributes to the development of physical disease. While some reviewers concluded that it did (Moore-Ede and Richardson, 1985), others argued that there was little conclusive evidence (Harrington, 1978; Rutenfranz et al., 1985). Certainly, the methodological limitations of much of the relevant research made it unclear whether the incidence of particular medical and psychiatric conditions was higher among shiftworkers than permanent day workers (Rutenfranz et al., 1985).

In recent years, evidence has accumulated to link shiftwork requiring night work to gastrointestinal and cardiovascular disease, psychosomatic complaints and various forms of cancer (Costa, 2003a; Knutsson, 2003). In relation to breast cancer, for example, Hansen (2001) reported the results of a population-based study of 7035 women with breast cancer and individually-matched controls without breast cancer. The results indicated that, after controlling for socioeconomic status, age and reproductive history, the risk of breast cancer for women who had worked for at least six months in an occupation in which at least 60% of respondents worked at night was 50% higher than for those who had not. There was also a tendency for increased risk with increasing duration of night-time employment. Similarly, Davis et al. (2001) studied 813 women with a new diagnosis of breast cancer and 793 age-matched controls. They found that women who had worked night shift had a 60% higher risk of breast cancer and that the risk increased significantly with each additional hour per week of night work (averaged over a 10-year period). Women who worked at least 5.7 hours per week had 2.3 times greater risk. Various other studies have identified elevated risks of breast cancer among night workers (Pukkala et al., 1995; Rix and Lynge, 1996).

This increased risk may be explained by women who work at night being exposed to artificial light, which suppresses melatonin secretion by the pineal gland and may induce continuous production of oestrogen, which is associated with elevated risk (Davis et al., 2001; Hansen, 2001). After a review of available evidence, the World Health Organization International Agency for Research on Cancer Monograph Working Group concluded in 2008 that shiftwork involving circadian disruption is a Group 2A carcinogen (probably carcinogenic to humans) (Straif et al., 2008). They also noted the apparent pathway through light exposure at night, the pineal and melatonin suppression, which can also lead to compromised immune function.

There is also growing evidence regarding an elevated risk of cardiovascular disease. In the 1980s, Knutsson (1989) argued that, although many reviews concluded that shiftwork is not related to coronary heart disease (CHD), a careful examination of previous research identified widespread methodological limitations. Studies conducted by Knutsson and his colleagues indicated that the risk of CHD increased with increasing experience of shiftwork, that shiftworkers had higher levels of important risk factors for CHD, and that changes in diet associated with shiftwork appeared to have led to increases in serum triglyceride levels that increase the risk of CHD (see also Knutsson et al., 1986). Elsewhere, ex-shiftworkers had also been found to have high levels of cardiovascular disease (Koller, 1983). Subsequent studies have also found that shiftwork that includes night work is a risk factor for cardiovascular disease (e.g. Boggild and Knutsson, 1999; Fujino et al., 2006; Kawachi et al., 1995; Tuchsen et al., 2006). Using data from 80180 participants in the Nurses Health Study, Brown et al. (2009) also found a modest (4%) increase in the risk of ischaemic stroke among female nurses for every five years of rotating shiftwork with night shifts.

Evidence has also accumulated in relation to gastrointestinal disease. A longitudinal study of 640 workers by Angersbach et al. (1980) indicated that gastrointestinal diseases were more common and more severe among shiftworkers than day workers doing the same job. Elsewhere, workers who leave shiftwork to return to day work have been found to have up to twice the level of gastrointestinal disease experienced by those who remain on shiftwork (Moore-Ede and Richardson, 1985), supporting the view that many workers leave shiftwork for health reasons. Tuchsen et al. (1994) used Danish national data to compare the rate of first hospital discharge for gastric ulcer of 122116 men in occupations with at least 20% non-daytime work and 593281 men in occupations requiring only daytime work. Using standardised hospitalisation ratios, they found that men in the non-daytime group had a 30% higher overall risk and that the group with late-evening work had the highest additional risk (136%). They attributed the higher risks to physiological, psychological and social/domestic factors.

The contribution of shiftwork to the development of other diseases is less clear. General evidence suggests that night workers may have less resistance to some diseases than day workers. Various immunological functions appear to be depressed among night workers, who may be more susceptible to some diseases as a result (Kogi, 1985). Interestingly, Akerstedt et al. (2004) examined data from a large, representative sample in Sweden and found that shiftwork was unrelated to mortality among blue-collar workers and only associated with a significantly higher mortality rate among female white-collar workers, for whom the prevalence of shiftwork was relatively low. However, the shiftwork category included many different work schedules and the impact of schedules requiring night work, in particular, could not be separately evaluated.

In summary, there is strong evidence that shiftworkers experience more subjective health problems than day workers and recently evidence has considerably strengthened that shiftwork that includes night work significantly increases the risk of developing several life-threatening conditions, particularly cardiovascular and gastrointestinal disease and various cancers. The key challenge to researchers has been to identify the mechanisms through which shiftwork has these negative effects, and hence ways to alleviate them.

Irregular working hours

Since the 1980s there has been strong and vocal support for the expansion of 'flexible employment', particularly from politicians and business leaders. They often claim that these 'flexible' forms of work are 'family friendly' and offer workers greater freedom to accommodate the conflicting demands of work and domestic roles. It is certainly true that workers can benefit from the opportunity to adjust working time to their commitments away from work, especially in dual-income or single-parent families with high work hours (Golden, 2001; Russell and Bowman, 2000). However, a weak labour market position and tenuous employment mean that many workers in flexible employment have less control over their hours than more securely employed workers (Golden, 2001; Hipple, 2001). They are more likely than permanent employees to work extremely short or extremely long hours (Mayhew and Quinlan, 1999)

Unfortunately, most forms of workplace flexibility, including flexible hours, have been driven principally by employers' desire to reduce labour costs and make product supplies and services more responsive to markets. In the US, access to flexible hours is largely restricted to full-time workers on more than 50 hours per week or the least privileged who work short, irregular or antisocial hours (Golden, 2001). In fact, Golden (2001) concluded that flexibility often appears to come 'at the dear price of lost leisure time, significantly lower earnings, a checkered career progression or stresses associated with irregular work' (page 65). In Australia, rather than being family-friendly, flexible employment has often placed heavy pressure on workers to juggle work and family life in inconvenient and stressful ways (ACIRRT, 1999). Unfortunately, the growth of flexible work, and the associated expansion of irregular and unpredictable hours, frequently has negative effects on domestic and leisure activities and increases work–life conflict more generally (Härmä and Ilmarinen, 1999; Costa and DiMilia, 2008).

A study of permanent and casual employees in five-star hotels reported by Bohle et al. (2004) provides an illustration of the irregular hours that may be imposed upon flexible workers. Casual employees reported much greater variation in working hours than full-time staff. Their hours ranged from 0 to 73 hours per week and shift lengths ranged from two to 18 hours. Many casuals were only advised of the starting times for their shifts, with finishing times being decided by a manager or supervisor during the shift. They could be sent home within a few hours of starting a shift and asked to return several hours later. By contrast, most full-time employees reported much more regular hours, often fixed shifts of eight hours with limited overtime. Variability, unpredictability and a lack of control over working hours were significant sources of work–life conflict for casuals. One reported that the work schedule could 'change three or four times a week'. Others reported negative effects of increased work–life conflict including poor sleep, irregular exercise, unhealthy and irregular meals, interference with tertiary study and disrupted social and family lives. One casual reported 'I don't have a life at all' and another claimed '… it's bad here. Poor rostering … and, also, … the inflexibility of working hours … There's complaints every day. Hours are crazy'.

If flexible hours are to benefit workers, they must genuinely have the opportunity to adjust working time to accommodate important commitments outside work. The timing of many domestic, social, sport and leisure activities is inflexible and the scheduling of work critically affects workers' ability to participate meaningfully in those activities. There is good evidence that workers' control over work scheduling, or even over work tasks more generally, affects the impact of shiftwork. Several studies (see Bohle and Tilley, 1989; Pisarski et al., 1998, 2006, 2008) have illustrated how increased control reduces work–life conflict which, in turn, leads to fewer physical and psychological symptoms and more positive attitudes to work. An important aspect of control is the capacity to accurately predict work commitments for a reasonable period into the future. This predictability allows workers to plan and organise social and domestic activities more effectively.

Long hours

While not exclusively associated with shiftwork or irregular hours, long weekly working hours are often found in conjunction with long shifts (10 hours or more) and evening or weekend work, especially when irregularity is combined with multiple jobs. In fact, it is almost impossible to do very long hours (50 or more per week) within the confines of 'standard' Monday to Friday day work. The negative health effects attributable to long hours are also likely to compound the negative effects of both shiftwork and irregular hours.

Over the final two decades of last century, average full-time working hours increased dramatically while the number of low-income, part-time workers similarly surged, producing a division between the 'work rich' and the 'work poor' (ACIRRT, 1999; Golden, 2001). In Australia, the proportion of the full-time workforce working more than 48 hours per week increased from 19% in the late 1970s to 32% in the late 1990s (ACIRTT, 1999). Most of those working very long hours are managers and professionals but some skilled and semi-skilled workers, such as truck drivers and miners, may also have greatly extended working weeks. While average full-time working hours in Australia are very high by the standards of other developed economies (Campbell, 2001), the proportion of the workforce working very long hours also rose in North America and parts of Europe at the same time (Quinlan, 1998). In the US work increasingly spread into the early morning and the evening (Golden, 2001) and one aspect of the trend to longer working hours was a widespread extension of workdays from eight hours to 10, 12 or more hours.

Over the past two decades there has been increasing agreement among scientists that long working hours have negative effects on health and safety. The array of outcome variables on which these effects have been found includes injury, cardiovascular disorders, pre-term birth, musculoskeletal discomfort, insufficient sleep, work–life conflict, stress, sickness absence and general health (Ala-Mursula et al., 2006; Dembe, 2009; Grosch et al., 2006; Raediker et al., 2006; Sparks et al., 1997). Sparks et al. (1997), for example, conducted an extensive review of international evidence and concluded that long working hours are associated with negative health outcomes including depression, anxiety, stress, physical symptoms and, most strongly, coronary heart disease. Unfortunately, most of the available evidence on the impact of long working hours concerns males, who are disproportionately represented among those doing long hours in paid employment.

In an interesting recent paper, Ala-Mursula et al. (2006) examined the effects of all working hours (domestic, paid and commuting) on sickness absence in a sample of 25 703 public sector employees in Finland. Long domestic and total (paid + domestic + commuting) hours were linked to more medically certified sickness absence for both females and males, but long paid working hours were associated with less self-certified absence, perhaps reflecting greater presenteeism pressure. Long commuting hours were linked to more sickness absence of both types. Low control over daily hours predicted medically certified absence for females and males and self-certified absences for males. This research clearly demonstrates the value of considering the impact of all forms of work and work-related activities.

Much of the research on the impact of long hours has been conducted in single organisations, industries or occupations. However, Grosch et al. (2006) reported an analysis of data from 1744 respondents from the nationally representative 2002 General Social Survey in the US. The respondents were divided into five groups according to working hours, from part-time (1–34 hours per week) to 'higher overtime' (70+ hours per week). Overtime work (41 or more hours per week, reported by 41% of the sample) was associated with self-employment, salary-based pay, more than one job, working as an independent contractor or consultant, working split or irregular shifts or on call, and mandatory overtime. The overtime groups reported greater job demands, such as 'working very fast' or 'too much work to do', and having less time for activities away from work, such as 'difficulty taking time off' or fewer hours of relaxation each day. On the positive side, they reported more participation in workplace decision making and more opportunity to develop their own abilities. Results such as these add credence to similar findings from other studies not based on nationally representative samples.

Similarly, Raediker et al. (2006) analysed data from a representative sample of 17 821 participants in the third European Union survey on working conditions, in 2000. Their analysis identified an upward trend in both musculoskeletal disorders (e.g. backache, limb pain) and psycho-vegetative complaints (e.g. heart disease, sleep problems) as weekly working hours increased from less than 20 to more than 60. This relationship became more pronounced when various individual (e.g. age) and situational (e.g. shift-work) moderating or confounding factors were controlled. There was also a general trend to increasing psycho-vegetative and musculoskeletal disorders with age but it was not linear.

Trends towards flexible work, longer hours and work intensification have contributed to an increase in irregular or fragmented working hours and extreme forms of shift work (ACIRRT, 1999; Quinlan, 1998). Labour cost minimisation may, for example, necessitate the temporary rostering of additional staff during peak periods and produce a proliferation of irregular work schedules designed to fill gaps (Omura, 2001). Work has increasingly encroached on 'normal', highly valued family time (ACCIRT, 1999). For example, split shifts may require employees, often women, to work both in the early morning and the evening, when domestic demands are frequently at their greatest, and take time off during the middle of the day, while children are at school or in child care.

A growing proportion of shift schedules combine antisocial hours with very long working weeks. Those found in FIFO mining operations may be particularly extreme. FIFO schedules generally require work every day while on site and rotations of 14 to 21 consecutive 12-hour shifts are common. In the most extreme cases, 12-hour working days can exceed leisure days by more than three to one, even when the extensive commuting between the work site and home, arguably an integral part of the working regime, is counted as leisure time. To date, there has been too little rigorous research on FIFO schedules to adequately understand their impact on health or to be able to identify satisfactorily the threshold at which the imbalance between work and leisure time leads to a significant escalation in health risks.

Many researchers warn that extended working hours should be introduced with great care and that health and safety effects should be systematically and carefully evaluated (see, for example, Raediker et al., 2006). Dembe (2009) also warns that long working hours raise a range of ethical questions and implications that also warrant careful consideration. Examples include the potential existence of mandatory or unpaid overtime, the possibility of employer coercion, potential limits on the voluntary assumption of risk by workers, the possible presence of gender-based inequalities and the politics of government intervention and regulation.

Influences on shiftworkers' health

The evidence above demonstrates that shiftworkers as a group experience more health and wellbeing problems than their counterparts in day work. However, the magnitude of these negative health effects also varies considerably between shiftworkers. It is not surprising that this should be so, as various physiological, psychological, behavioural, organisational and social variables may all affect health outcomes. At present the mechanisms through which these variables influence adaptation to shiftwork are not clear, but our knowledge is expanding rapidly.

Shiftwork research has been dominated by the disciplines of occupational medicine, physiology and psychology. Sociologists and other social scientists have also made significant contributions. Each discipline has tended to focus upon specific aspects of adaptation and particular sets of variables, although in recent years there has been a productive exchange of ideas between disciplines. The result is that, while the various disciplines have maintained primary areas of interest, shiftwork research is more eclectic than research on many other aspects of occupational health. Medical and physiological research has focused most heavily on efforts to assess the extent to which shiftwork contributes to the development of physical disease, and on understanding the processes of physiological adjustment to work at different times of the day and night. Psychological research has been predominantly concerned with identifying the factors that affect individual shiftworkers' adaptation to shift rosters. In doing so it has examined a range of biological, psychological, social and organisational variables. Adaptation has usually been measured in terms of the extent to which workers' sleep and biological functioning is disrupted by shifts, workers' reports of physical and psychological symptoms, and attitudes to various shifts. Sociologists have principally examined the effects that shiftwork has on the performance of social roles and the burden it places on the spouses and families of shiftworkers. Because the level of discourse between disciplines is high, and their research has overlapped, there is little point in dealing with their separate contributions. Instead, we shall discuss the contribution that the major categories of variables make to adaptation.

Physiological rhythms

Most physiological and psychological variables display regular 24-hour oscillations known as circadian rhythms. An illustration of a typical human body temperature circadian rhythm is presented in figure 6.1. These rhythms differ between individuals in terms of their acrophase (the time of day at which they reach their peak), their amplitude (the difference between the peak of the rhythm and its mean) and their mean level. The characteristics of the rhythm are determined by both endogenous (biological) and exogenous (environmental) factors. The endogenous component of the rhythm is widely considered to be genetic (Brown, 1980; Ehret, 1980) and is frequently attributed to the action of one or more biological 'clocks', although their exact location and functioning is the subject of debate (Wever, 1985). Supporting evidence indicates that the body temperature rhythm and many other physiological rhythms persist when experimental subjects are kept on constant bed rest in complete isolation from any time cues (Wever, 1979).

Environmental variables that affect the form of circadian rhythms are known as time cues or 'zeitgebers'. They include changes in the physical environment, such as the daily alternation of light and dark, and social cues such as meal times, clock time and domestic and leisure activities (Minors and Waterhouse, 1985a; Wever, 1979). However, circadian rhythms will only synchronise with zeitgebers within a limited 'range of entrainment' of between 23 and 27 hours (Wever, 1979, 1985). In other words, the normal 24-hour rhythm will only shorten by approximately one hour per day or lengthen by approximately three hours per day. Consequently, the rhythm adjustments of between eight and ten hours often required to adjust to shift changes should, at best, take many days to complete. When the changes required exceed the range of entrainment, the circadian system is likely to become disrupted. This disruption may lead to symptoms such as sleep disturbances, persisting fatigue and gastrointestinal disorders (Reinberg et al., 1983)

Figure 6.1   The human circadian rhythm of body temperature

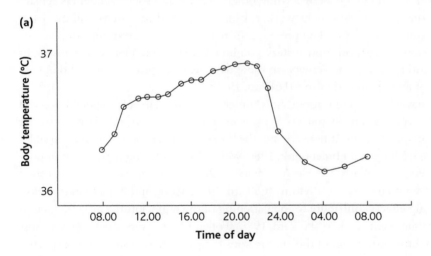

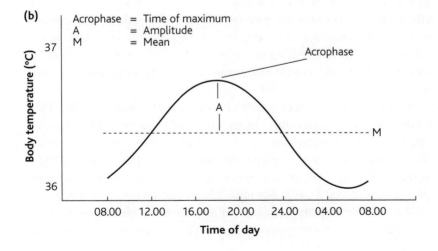

Most studies of circadian rhythms and shiftwork have either attempted to assess how effectively rhythms adjust to shift changes or tried to identify the rhythm characteristics that distinguish the workers who most readily adapt to shiftwork. We shall restrict our attention to the most widely researched circadian variable, the body temperature rhythm. The available evidence suggests that shiftworkers' circadian rhythms rarely adjust more than partially to shift changes (Costa, 2003a). Several studies have demonstrated that the temperature rhythms of night workers do not fully adjust to a nocturnal orientation, even after up to 21 consecutive shifts without days off (Akerstedt, 1985; Folkard et al., 1978; Knauth et al., 1981; Rutenfranz et al., 1981). These studies reveal a general trend towards partial phase adjustment and reduction in the amplitude of the rhythm over successive night shifts, with rapid reversion to day-oriented rhythms on days off. It appears that rhythms only fully invert when complete isolation from conflicting social and physical zeitgebers is achieved. However, for most night workers only work schedules are altered while other physical and social zeitgebers remain the same. Consequently, few night workers can be expected to achieve full inversion (Wegmann and Klein, 1985). The provision of rest days after a maximum of seven or eight consecutive nights on most rosters, combined with the tendency of most night workers to revert to daytime activity on these days, tends to produce very little phase adjustment of endogenous rhythms (Folkard, 1988).

Doubts have been raised about how much the circadian adjustment observed among night workers actually reflects changes in endogenous rhythms. There is strong evidence that apparent adjustments reflect the 'masking' effects of exogenous variables (Folkard, 1988; Moog and Hildebrandt, 1986; Wever, 1985). During night work important zeitgebers, particularly the sleep–activity cycle and eating patterns, are pushed into conflict with endogenous rhythms (Folkard, 1988; Moog and Hildebrandt, 1986). These masking effects contribute to the flattening of the temperature curve frequently observed among night workers (Folkard, 1988). Folkard (1988) proposed that, for most shiftworkers, little movement of the endogenous temperature rhythm can be expected over the normal maximum of six or seven consecutive night shifts. Masking effects provide an alternative explanation for the more marked circadian adjustment to night shift observed among permanent night workers. These workers frequently display a stronger commitment to orienting their sleep, eating patterns and social lives around night work (Adams et al., 1986; Verhaegen, Cober et al., 1987), and their apparently greater rhythm adjustment may largely reflect the stronger masking from this more thorough change in routine.

More recently, significant streams of research have investigated strategies for achieving more effective circadian adjustment to night work and enhancing the alertness of workers on night shift or irregular hours. One has examined the effects of carefully timed exposure to bright light. For example, a laboratory study by Bougrine et al. (1995) demonstrated that exposure to bright light between 2.00 am and 5.00 am during the first three night shifts produced a rapid resetting of the melatonin circadian rhythm to a nocturnal orientation. The quantity and quality of daytime sleep after night work was equal to that recorded by the participants during the nights immediately prior to the stint of night shift. Bright light exposure was also associated with an improvement in night-time performance on several cognitive tasks. In a subsequent study, Bougrine et al. (1998) confirmed that stable synchronisation to nocturnal work could be achieved after three nights of bright light exposure and that rapid re-synchronisation to a diurnal orientation could be achieved using daytime administration of bright light. These changes were observed among participants on a six-nights-on, two-nights-off schedule but less effective synchronisation was achieved by participants on a more rapid three-night-on, one-day-off schedule. Bougrine et al. also noted that the optimal timing of bright light exposure may be influenced by differences in circadian rhythms between workers.

Interestingly, Costa et al. (1995) reported a field study in which bright light had more limited effects. Among nurses working on a rapid rotation schedule with only two consecutive night shifts, bright light exposure had small positive effects on mood and performance variables but it did not move circadian rhythms of body temperature, cortisol and melatonin. Costa et al. observed that this failure to produce circadian re-synchronisation appeared to arise partly from the practical constraints placed on the intensity, timing and duration of bright light exposure in a working environment. However, they also noted that circadian adjustment is undesirable on rapid rotation rosters and bright light exposure should be adjusted to produce the observed positive effects on mood and performance without resetting the circadian systems. This study highlights the importance of establishing whether promising results obtained in the laboratory can be replicated in the workplace.

Other researchers have investigated the effects of the hormone melatonin on circadian adjustment. Research has demonstrated that carefully timed administration of melatonin has predictable phase-shifting effects on circadian rhythms in humans, particularly in relation to temperature, fatigue and sleepiness rhythms (Arendt et al., 1995). These properties have been used successfully to treat the effects of jet lag and sleep disturbances associated with blindness. Although there have been relatively few studies specifically examining the use of melatonin by shiftworkers, the available evidence suggests that administration of melatonin immediately before daytime sleep produces improved sleep duration and quality, higher night-time alertness and greater circadian rhythm synchronisation, at least in workers on seven-day rotating rosters (Arendt et al., 1995).

An important ethical issue is highlighted by the research on bright light and melatonin. It concerns the acceptability of manipulating workers' biological functioning to satisfy the demands of work rather than modifying work to better match the adaptive capacities of workers. Many consider it unacceptable for workers to be pressured, even expected, to accept the use of bright light, melatonin or other interventions to adapt to physiologically inappropriate working hours. There is particular concern regarding the lack of knowledge about the effects of these strategies beyond the very short term. Little is know about the effects of frequent and rapid resetting of circadian rhythms on shiftworkers' health and wellbeing over relatively short periods of months, much less over many years of shift changes (Arendt et al., 1995). This knowledge is required before concerns about the application of bright light and melatonin can be adequately resolved. In any case, it is appropriate to expect that shift schedules are optimised from a health and safety point of view before intrusive procedures for active resetting of shiftworkers' circadian rhythms are instituted (Costa et al., 1995).

The evidence discussed to this point has concerned mean changes in the rhythms of groups of shiftworkers. It has not taken into account individual differences in circadian characteristics that may affect the responses to the displacement and disruption of sleep and activity caused by night work (Folkard and Monk, 1981; Moog, 1987). In the 1970s and 1980s, the effects of differences in the rhythm phase and amplitude were widely investigated. Several studies indicated that individual differences in the acrophase of the temperature rhythm affect responses to night work (Folkard and Monk, 1981; Hildebrandt, 1980; Moog, 1987). For example, Hildebrandt and Stratmann (1979) found that night nurses whose oral temperature rhythms peaked relatively late exhibited less disturbance of circadian rhythms, smaller sleep deficits and fewer subjective complaints than those whose rhythms peaked early. Moog (1987) controlled masking effects and found that the earlier the acrophase of an individual's temperature rhythm, the less rapidly the rhythm would adjust to shift changes. Individuals whose rhythms peaked very late could adjust their circadian systems to permanent night shifts and weekly rotating shift systems, but not rapidly rotating systems. The rhythms of individuals whose acrophases were neither late nor early adjusted to permanent night shifts but not to either weekly or rapidly rotating shift systems. The rhythms of individuals with very early acrophases did not even adjust successfully to permanent night shifts.

This research was generally based on the assumption that it is desirable for circadian rhythms to adjust to changes in the timing of sleep and activity so that there is less pressure for shiftworkers to work against the dictates of their circadian rhythms (Monk, 1988). Proponents of this view often suggest that shift rosters should be designed to rotate slowly from day to afternoon to night shifts to optimise circadian adjustment. However, Moog's results suggest that such adjustment will still be impossible for many workers.

Other researchers suggested that differences in the amplitude of the temperature rhythm predicted tolerance to night work. Reinberg and his colleagues found that as rhythm amplitude increases, the rate at which the rhythm changes phase in response to shift changes decreases (Reinberg, 1979; Reinberg et al., 1983). This result was replicated in both field and experimental studies (Knauth et al., 1978; Minors and Waterhouse, 1983). Experienced shiftworkers with large-amplitude, stable rhythms have also been found to report fewer symptoms of intolerance, such as persisting fatigue, sleep disturbance and gastrointestinal disorders (Reinberg et al., 1979; Reinberg et al., 1981).

However, Reinberg et al. (1984) demonstrated that the temperature rhythms of most shiftwork-intolerant individuals tended to be more easily disrupted than the rhythms of shiftwork-tolerant individuals. Intolerant individuals were those who displayed more symptoms of sleep disturbance, persisting fatigue, mood and behaviour change, and digestive disorders. These findings suggest that rhythm amplitude may not be the primary determinant of tolerance, but that intolerance arises from circadian disruption and reduced rhythm amplitude is an outcome of this disruption (Kerkhof, 1985). The conclusion generally drawn from the work of Reinberg and his colleagues is that shift rosters should be designed to restrict the degree of circadian adjustment required from workers and minimise disruption to the circadian system. Consequently, rapidly rotating rosters with a minimum of night work are recommended instead of more slowly rotating rosters. By limiting the number of consecutive night shifts, rapidly rotating rosters should have the additional benefit of minimising accumulated sleep deficits (Folkard, Minors and Waterhouse, 1985).

Researchers have disputed the desirability of circadian stability or adjustment. To some extent, the desirability of one or the other may depend on the shift schedule. It is now widely agreed that stability is an advantage for workers on rapidly rotating rosters, but some researchers argue in favour of phase adjustment for workers on permanent night work or slow-rotation rosters. However, for some time there has been a strong body of opinion that regular, rapid-rotation schedules with fewer consecutive night shifts should be favoured over schedules with slow rotations or fixed shifts, largely because they do promote greater circadian stability (Akerstedt, 1985; Folkard, 1988; Kogi, 1985). Several studies have attributed improvements in subjective health to rapid-rotation rosters. For example, Williamson and Sanderson (1986) found reductions in digestive disorders, headaches, anxiety and sleep disturbances after a weekly rotation, three-shift roster was replaced with rapid rotations and a maximum of three consecutive night shifts. Unfortunately, most early studies were not effectively controlled and must be interpreted with caution. An exception is a small controlled study of the transition from weekly rotations to more rapid rotations by Knauth and Kiesswetter (1987), which showed a reduction in sleep disturbances on night shift, but no change in gastrointestinal and neurovegetative symptoms.

The evidence in favour of rapid rotation is not clear-cut, however, and various negative findings have been reported. Verhaegen, Cober et al. (1987) found that permanent full-time night nurses reported better subjective health and more favourable attitudes to night work than younger nurses who worked between one and four consecutive night shifts every four to 10 weeks. Minors and Waterhouse (1985b) also found that nurses on rapid rotations reported more subjective complaints (headache, nausea, etc.) during night shift than those on slower rotations. Once again, however, these studies were cross-sectional and not well controlled, limiting their interpretability. For example, the rapid-rotation group studied by Minors and Waterhouse (1985b) was older and had more experience of night work and greater family commitments, each of which may have contributed to the differences in symptoms. Nevertheless, Frese and Semmer (1986) recently found no significant difference in physical and psychosomatic complaints or irritation/strain between workers on rapid rotation 12-hour shifts and those on slower rotation eight-hour shifts when confounding variables such as age, workplace and environmental stressors and union membership were controlled. Of course, self-reports may also be affected by confounding factors such as a greater acceptance of fatigue and reduced wellbeing among regular night workers and a tendency for occasional night workers to expect that they will not adjust. The issue regarding rapid or slow rotation remains unresolved. However, after reviewing the available evidence, Knauth (1995) concluded that intermediate speeds of rotation are worst in relation to performance and fatigue and that there is insufficient evidence to decide whether rapid rotations or permanent shifts are best in relation to fatigue, performance and injury.

Research on circadian rhythms and shiftwork has several limitations. Many studies have used uncontrolled cross-sectional designs, defined adaptation primarily in terms of the responses of circadian rhythms to shift changes, or failed to systematically separate endogenous changes from masking effects. Cross-sectional studies do not provide conclusive evidence of causal relationships, and longitudinal studies have cast doubt on the effectiveness of circadian characteristics as predictors of subjective health. Early evidence suggested that circadian amplitude measured prior to shiftwork does not predict individual differences in phase change to shift changes (Minors and Waterhouse, 1983). Vidacek et al. (1987) found that neither the phase nor the amplitude of the temperature and heart rate circadian rhythms prior to shiftwork predicted various physical symptoms after three years of shiftwork. A subsequent publication (Vidacek et al., 1993) reported more evidence of a link between characteristics of the body temperature and heart rate rhythms and measures of shiftwork intolerance, but the evidence was still relatively weak and inconsistent. Later, Bohle (1997b) reported that neither the phase nor the amplitude of the oral temperature circadian rhythm prior to the commencement of shiftwork predicted subsequent psychological wellbeing or attitudes to shiftwork.

As this brief review indicates, there is still much to be learnt about the relationships between circadian factors and shiftworkers' health. It is clear that work at night is performed largely in conflict with the circadian system and at considerable cost to workers, both in terms of acute effects on mood and subjective health and longer-term effects on disease risks. However, there is presently little evidence that individual differences in circadian characteristics prior to the commencement of shiftwork influence subsequent shiftwork tolerance. The issue as to whether, in general, rapid rotations or permanent shifts are more desirable from a circadian point of view is still yet to be conclusively resolved.

Sleep

Displacement and disruption of sleep are unavoidable consequences of many work schedules, and it is not surprising that sleep disturbances are widely reported to be the major complaint of shiftworkers (Akerstedt, 1985; Koller, 1983). The most common complaints concern reduced duration and quality of sleep and associated fatigue. Most studies indicate that daytime sleep after night shift averages between one and four hours less than normal night-time sleep, and that night workers take more naps during leisure hours (Akerstedt and Gillberg, 1982; Knauth, Landau et al., 1980; Tilley et al., 1982). Permanent night shift workers have also been found to sleep significantly less, on average, than afternoon and rotating shift workers (Tasto et al., 1978). This sleep deficit accumulates over successive nights, as even permanent night workers sleep less after work than on days off (Folkard, Minors and Waterhouse, 1985). Curtailed sleep is not unique to night work, and several studies have demonstrated that early morning shifts (starting prior to 0700) can also produce significant reductions in sleep length and severe fatigue (Akerstedt, 1995). Excessive sleepiness is, in turn, associated with a heightened risk of injury (Dinges, 1995).

Many studies have demonstrated that shiftworkers report poorer sleep quality and greater dissatisfaction with sleep patterns than permanent day workers (e.g. Akerstedt, 1985; Knauth and Rutenfranz, 1981; Tepas, 1982). Tasto et al. (1978) found that permanent night workers and rotating shift workers reported more awakenings after sleep onset, more trouble falling asleep after being awakened, and more tiredness and sleepiness on awakening than day and afternoon shift workers. Night shift workers were more tired at work than the other groups. Rutenfranz et al. (1981) reported that 90% of a group of shiftworkers complained of sleep disturbances while working night shifts, and that less than 20% had similar complaints after transferring to day shift. For rotating shift workers, sleep quality appears to vary according to shift. Akerstedt (1980) found that three-shift workers reported similar sleep quality to day- and two-shift workers on corresponding shifts. Interestingly, three-shift workers reported more sleep complaints on night shift than on early morning shift, even though sleep length was the same. Sleep complaints were lowest on afternoon shifts.

The nature of the work schedule appears to directly affect the extent to which shiftworkers can adapt their sleep to night shift (Akerstedt, 1988; Frese and Harwich, 1984; Minors and Waterhouse, 1985b). Nurses whose shifts rotate rapidly (one or two successive nights) have been found to adjust their sleep to night work less well than those doing longer blocks of nights (Minors and Waterhouse, 1983, 1985b; Verhaegen, Cober et al., 1987). For example, in one study permanent night nurses recorded similar daytime sleep length to nurses on rotating shifts but their sleep quality was higher (Verhaegen, Cober et al., 1987). Smith (1979) found that average sleep length across all shifts and day sleep after night shift were lower on rapid rotations than on weekly rotations. He concluded there is a trade-off between the requirement to work more night shifts after extended wakefulness on rapid rotations and the requirement to carry sleep losses over more consecutive nights on weekly rotations.

Disturbances of sleep length and quality caused by night shift appear to be responsible for the elevated sleepiness and fatigue which is the major element of the poorer subjective health reported by almost all night workers (Akerstedt, 1988, 1995; Monk and Folkard, 1985). This increased sleepiness, particularly among night workers, can be inferred from several aspects of behaviour, including a greater tendency to fall asleep while at work, more frequent naps during leisure hours, extended sleep during days off and complaints of sleepiness (Folkard, Minors and Waterhouse, 1985). Sleepiness increases during night shift and reaches a pronounced peak during the second half of the night (Akerstedt, 1988), even among permanent night nurses (Folkard et al., 1978). The sleepiness of night workers would be considered pathological during the day and has been found to fall below that arising from moderate intakes of alcohol and hypnotics (Akerstedt, 1995). After reviewing the available evidence, Akerstedt (1995: 19–20) concluded that sleepiness on night shift 'afflicts virtually all individuals almost without exception and will reach severe performance incapacitating levels in a majority of subjects and outright incidents of sleep in a large minority'.

Akerstedt (1988) tentatively estimated that 75% of night workers experience sleepiness on every night shift. Self-reports and physiological data indicate that many night workers have brief, involuntary sleep episodes at work (Akerstedt, 1995; Wedderburn, 1987), and it has been estimated that at least 20% of workers on night shift are sleepy enough to fall asleep (Akerstedt, 1988). Although experiencing extreme sleepiness, workers may be unaware of falling asleep or may severely underestimate the length of naps (Akerstedt, 1988). Even in the absence of sleep, the severe sleepiness associate with night shift is associated with major performance lapses (Akerstedt, 1995). These findings have major implications for the safety of workers employed at night, especially in dangerous environments.

Differences in 'natural' sleep duration and quality may also predict whether workers adapt to night work. Benoit et al. (1981) reported that short sleepers (who slept less than six hours a night) maintained more stable circadian rhythms when deprived of night-time sleep than long sleepers (who slept more than nine hours a night). Long sleepers also tend to sleep less, and have less REM sleep, after sleep-deprived nights (Benoit et al., 1980). However, a longitudinal study indicated that pre-shiftwork sleep quality and duration were poor predictors of psychological symptoms when nurses began working shifts (Bohle, 1997b). Sleep duration did not predict psychological symptoms after six or 15 months of shiftwork, and sleep quality was related to symptoms after six months of shiftwork, but not after 15 months. It is possible, of course, that the sleep variables predict other symptoms of shiftwork intolerance, or that they predict longer-term adaptation, and more research is required to establish whether, and when, they are effective predictors.

Although researchers usually examine the impact of shiftwork on sleep, sleep behaviour may also affect shiftwork tolerance. For example, there is a marked interdependence between circadian rhythms and sleep duration after night work. Sleep is shortest when it begins in the trough of the body temperature circadian rhythm and longest when it begins close to the peak of the rhythm (Akerstedt, 1995). Consequently, the time at which shiftworkers try to sleep during the day is likely to affect the amount of sleep they get and, in turn, their level of adaptation to night work.

After reviewing evidence on naps and work performance, Rosekind et al. (1995) concluded that strategic napping can positively affect alertness and performance at work. Naps can be used preventatively, before the start of the shift, or operationally, while at work. Napping can, however, have negative effects through 'sleep inertia', the grogginess and disorientation sometimes experienced for 10 or 15 minutes after waking, or disruption of subsequent sleep if naps are long. Research on other aspects of 'sleep hygiene', behavioural strategies for improving sleep length and quality, indicates that adherence to some guidelines for shiftworkers have little effect on sleep after night shift. Greenwood et al. (1995), for example, tested the effects of six practices often recommended for night workers, such as exercise and strategic timing of alcohol and caffeine consumption. Only restricting tobacco intake during the six hours prior to sleep had a positive effect on daytime sleep duration. More research is required to identify effective sleep hygiene practices for shiftworkers and to define the conditions in which they are effective.

Another recent research development has been the evaluation of alertness-enhancing drugs to assist workers to adapt to disturbed sleep and excessive sleepiness caused by night work and variable hours. Although caffeine has long been used widely by shiftworkers to counter fatigue and enhance alertness, systematic research on its effectiveness, and that of other alertness enhancers, in shiftwork has only emerged since the 1990s (see Akerstedt and Ficca, 1997). However, there is substantial evidence that caffeine is effective for postponing sleep and for reducing fatigue in boring and repetitive tasks, but that repeated consumption may reduce hand steadiness. The structure of sleep stages across the night is not strongly affected, but tension and anxiety are increased and side effects or dependence could result at high doses (6–9 mg/kg) (Akerstedt and Ficca, 1997).

Modafinil is an alternative to caffeine that has attracted considerable attention since the late 1990s. Much of the data on modafinil has been drawn from studies of patients with sleep disorders, such as narcolepsy or sleep apnoea (Walsh et al., 2004), and studies directly relevant to shiftwork have often employed laboratory-based simulations of night work, not actual night workers in their work context. Walsh et al. (2004), for example, examined the effects of modafinil on the alertness, psychomotor performance and neuropsychological functions during a four-night simulated night shift schedule. The results indicated that a group that received 200 mg doses of modafinil had significantly better alertness and neuropsychological functions than a control group that received a placebo. Modafinil had no clinically meaningful negative effect on sleep during daytime sleep after night shift and the participants reported no other side effects. However, in the absence of evidence regarding the effects of modafinil on cardiovascular conditions, Walsh et al. recommended that it should not be prescribed to anyone with such conditions.

Subsequently, Czeisler et al. (2006) investigated the effectiveness of 200 mg doses of modafinil for shiftwork sleep disorder, a combination of excessive sleepiness and daytime insomnia estimated to affect 5 to 10% of night shift workers. They found a modest improvement in night-time sleep latency (the time between attempting to fall asleep and sleep onset). Also, a higher proportion of patients treated with modafinil had improvements in clinical symptoms than in the (placebo) control group. Patients who received modafinil had better vigilance at night and reported fewer 'accidents' or 'near-accidents' when commuting home. However, despite these benefits, patients on modafinil still experienced excessive sleepiness and impairment of night-time performance. As testing was performed in a laboratory setting, it is also unclear how the results would transfer to a work setting.

Overall, modafinil has been found to have positive, although sometimes modest, positive effects on alertness and performance, sleep latency, and other health and safety measures. There is no evidence of significant negative effects on subsequent sleep, even when taken over relatively long periods, or other major side effects (Akerstedt and Ficca, 1997; Czeisler et al., 2006; Walsh et al., 2004), although research evidence is still limited. Nevertheless, similarly to bright light and melatonin treatments, an ethical question arises as to whether it is appropriate to encourage shiftworkers to use alertness enhancers or other pharmaceutical agents to adapt to physiologically undesirable working hours (Akerstedt and Ficca, 1997; Walsh et al., 2004).

Personality characteristics

Many studies have examined relationships between personality and shiftwork tolerance, although interest in the topic has diminished in recent years. The most widely investigated variables have been introversion/extroversion, neuroticism and diurnal type (Akerstedt, 1980; Costa, 2003a). Introversion/extroversion and neuroticism have also been correlated with shiftwork tolerance. Tasto et al. (1978) found higher symptom levels were reported by shiftworkers who were high in neuroticism and introversion. Nachreiner (1975) also found that neurotic introverts were more likely to be dissatisfied with shifts and to transfer to day work. Akerstedt (1980) reported that neuroticism was strongly associated with reports of physical and psychological symptoms among regular night workers, and Iskra-Golec et al. (1987) found a strong negative correlation between neuroticism and shiftwork tolerance. Both personality dimensions have also been linked with physiological adjustment. Colquhoun and Folkard (1978) found neurotic extroverts exhibited the most marked adjustment of circadian rhythms across successive night shifts. Colquhoun and Condon (1981) found that the oral temperature rhythm adjusted more rapidly to night work in extroverts than introverts, even when all subjects were low on neuroticism. Of course, as we have seen, it is not clear whether rapid re-entrainment is necessarily adaptive.

These studies of extroversion/introversion and neuroticism were cross-sectional and could not clearly establish causal relationships. Neuroticism, in particular, could be expected to correlate with reported symptoms whether or not workers did shiftwork. Indeed, Bohle and Tilley (1989) found that neuroticism correlated strongly with psychological symptoms prior to shiftwork, but failed to predict symptoms after 15 months of rotating shifts. Similar results were reported by Vidacek et al. (1987) for physical symptoms. There is also evidence that shiftwork intolerance increases neuroticism (Meers et al., 1978; Vidacek et al., 1987).

Diurnal type, or 'morningness/eveningness', questionnaires have been developed to distinguish the behavioural manifestations of early or late phase circadian rhythms (Horne and Ostberg, 1976, Smith et al., 1989, Torsvall and Akerstedt, 1980). 'Morning types' identified with these questionnaires tend to display characteristics associated with shiftwork intolerance, including earlier phase and lower amplitude circadian rhythms and less positive responses to sleep disruption (Kerkhof, 1985). Indeed, several cross-sectional studies have suggested that morning types do adapt less well to shiftwork. They have been found to be more sensitive to delays in night-time sleep (Hildebrandt, 1986), to wake earlier after morning sleeps (Hildebrandt and Stratmann, 1979; Kerkhof,

1985), to report less satisfaction with night work (Hildebrandt, 1986; Nachreiner, 1975), to be more likely to transfer from shifts to day work (Akerstedt and Torsvall, 1978; Hauke et al., 1979; Hildebrandt, 1976) and to have lower scores on a measure of shiftwork tolerance (Iskra–Golec et al., 1987). Ostberg (1973) reported that morning types adapted less well to night work, in terms of sleep disruption, time estimation performance, meal timing and physical fitness.

These findings have been supported by longitudinal studies. Vidacek et al. (1987) found that scores on two morningness questionnaires completed before workers started shiftwork predicted symptoms after three years in rapid rotation shiftwork. In a similar longitudinal study, Bohle and Tilley (1989) found that morningness predicted psychological wellbeing after 15 months of shiftwork. It is presently unclear, however, to what extent the link between morningness and symptoms is a reflection of a primary relationship between symptoms and circadian characteristics (Monk and Folkard, 1985; Hildebrandt, 1986).

Research on diurnal type has identified two other behavioural characteristics that are proposed to influence adaptation to shiftwork: vigour and rigidity of sleep. Vigour is defined as the ability to overcome drowsiness (Folkard et al., 1979). Vigorous individuals claim to be relatively unaffected by lack of sleep, and to be able to wake up easily at unusual times (Folkard et al., 1979). Initial evidence indicated that vigorous shiftworkers experience less disruption of health, sleep and sexual activity (Folkard et al., 1980). Vigour was also associated with a higher overall level of alertness and a less steep drop in alertness during night shift (Folkard et al.,1979). The rigidity of sleep variable is concerned with differences between individuals in the extent to which they prefer to sleep and eat at regular times (Folkard et al., 1979). Early evidence suggested that sleep flexibility was associated with lower anxiety and fewer digestive problems among shiftworkers (Folkard et al., 1980). On night shift, flexible sleepers reported a faster rise in alertness over the day, higher alertness at night and higher quality day sleep (Folkard et al., 1979).

Vidacek et al. (1987) tested the predictive validity of these measures by collecting baseline scores from industrial workers before they commenced shiftwork and using them to predict various aspects of health after three years on a rapidly rotating, three-shift roster. Vigour predicted psychosomatic and respiratory problems, alcohol consumption and general health. Rigidity also predicted digestive problems, respiratory problems and general health. However, a similar longitudinal study, admittedly using an early version of the questionnaire, found that neither vigour nor rigidity predicted the psychological wellbeing of nurses after 15 months on rotating shifts (Bohle and Tilley, 1989). This inconsistency may, in part at least, reflect the limitations of the questionnaires developed to measure vigour and rigidity of sleep (Smith et al., 1989; Smith et al., 1993).

The extent to which these personality variables actually predict shiftwork tolerance remains unclear. In the case of neuroticism, in particular, an inability to cope with shift-work may produce changes in personality scores as much as personality affects tolerance. The evidence regarding extroversion/introversion is also unconvincing. Although there is more substantial evidence that diurnal type predicts tolerance, and the theoretical rationale for it doing so is clearer, any predictive relationship may simply reflect the fact that diurnal type indirectly measures circadian rhythm characteristics that affect adaptation. More longitudinal research is needed to identify the direction of causality in the relationships between personality variables and shiftwork tolerance and also to assess whether personality predicts tolerance independently of circadian variables.

Social and organisational factors

Many social and organisational factors may influence adaptation to shiftwork. The inability to conform to socially valued time schedules often produces a sense of alienation from the wider community that may have marked negative effects on the health and wellbeing of shiftworkers (Costa, 2003a; McGrath et al., 1984; Walker, 1985). Schedule design is probably the major variable governing the impact of shiftwork. Different shift schedules can be expected to have very different effects on health and wellbeing. As we have seen, characteristics such as the speed and direction of rotation, the frequency of night shifts and the timing of shift changes may all have an impact on subjective health.

Rutenfranz et al. (1985) argued that only night shift should produce a significant decline in health and wellbeing. They asserted that this decline results mainly from disruption of physiological circadian rhythms and disturbance of sleeping and eating rhythms, and that only night work induces enough conflict between these rhythms and the rest–activity cycle to significantly diminish health. Consequently, other relevant social and organisational variables should only have a marked negative effect on health and wellbeing when shiftwork includes night work. There is certainly evidence indicating that night shift has a more marked negative effect on symptoms than other shifts. In a large-scale study, Tasto et al. (1978) found that experience of night work was a better predictor of symptoms than experience of shiftwork in general. Other studies indicate that greater frequency and duration of night shifts, and a higher number of consecutive nights on duty, are linked with higher symptom levels (Kogi, 1985; Rutenfranz et al., 1985).

Nevertheless, shiftwork without night duty may also have negative effects on health and wellbeing. Other shifts may present adaptation problems through dislocation of social and domestic life, and alienation from community patterns of business, social, recreational and domestic activity (Jackson et al., 1985; Mott et al., 1965; Walker, 1985). Rotating shiftworkers, in particular, often have little opportunity to take part in regular activities outside work. This disruption is principally felt through constraints on contact with family and friends, organisational and institutional membership, participation in organised sport and other leisure activities (Gordon et al., 1986; Walker, 1985). Tasto et al. (1978), for example, found that both fixed and rotating shiftworkers were less satisfied than day workers with their overall work schedule and with the time available for personal, social and sporting activities. Shiftworkers and their families were also less satisfied with the time they spent together than day workers and their families. Evening and weekend shifts tend to be most disliked as they infringe on highly valued time that is usually devoted to domestic, social and leisure activities (Knauth, 1987; Walker, 1985).

Working at these times is often particularly disliked by young, single adults who tend to value evening and weekend social activities very highly (Walker, 1985).

Supporting evidence indicates that symptom levels are related to actual and perceived interference between work and other activities (Bohle, 2002; Jackson et al., 1985; Kinnunen and Mauno, 1998; Knutsson, 2003; Walker, 1985). For example, Jackson et al. (1985) found that shiftworkers who were most dissatisfied with conflict between work and family activities had the most negative scores on an index of physical health, psychological mood and behavioural adjustment. Kogi (1981) found that complaints of insufficient time for rest and leisure were lowest for day workers and highest for workers on discontinuous day–night and irregular shifts. Similar differences were found in complaints about fatigue, feeling unhealthy and sleeplessness. These cross-sectional studies cannot convincingly establish cause and effect relationships, but they have recently been supported by longitudinal research. Studies by Bohle and Tilley (1989, 1993, 1998) during nurses' first 15 months of shiftwork demonstrated that work–life conflict predicted psychological wellbeing, fatigue on night shift and attitudes to shiftwork more consistently than sleep, circadian, personality and social variables. Subsequent studies in nursing also demonstrated relationships between work–life conflict and reports of symptoms (Loudoun and Bohle, 1997; Pisarski et al., 1998; 2006, 2008).

Unusual working hours may also have advantages. Those who like shiftwork often report that time off during the day is convenient for shopping, medical consultations and other social and domestic activities (Folkard, Minors and Waterhouse, 1985). When valued by shiftworkers, these advantages are likely to diminish perceived work–life conflict. More generally, differences between shiftworkers in their preferred social and domestic activities, and the extent to which those activities are solitary or flexible in their timing, appear to influence work–life conflict and consequently shiftwork tolerance more generally (Thierry and Jansen, 1982; Walker, 1985).

The negative effect of work–life conflict on shiftwork tolerance suggests that more flexible shift schedules that allow workers an appropriate level of shift allocations may improve shiftworkers' health. It is interesting to note that when Taylor, Folkard and Shapiro (1997) compared various benefits offered by shift schedules, benefits to family life were most strongly related to several measures of shiftwork intolerance, including psychological wellbeing, anxiety, chronic fatigue and digestive and cardiovascular symptoms. More directly, Barton et al. (1993) found that greater control over work hours, through flexible rostering or the opportunity to choose permanent night work, was associated with more positive outcomes on several measures of shiftwork tolerance, including chronic fatigue, sleep disturbances, psychological wellbeing, social and domestic disruption and job satisfaction. Various flexibility strategies have the potential to increase shiftworkers' control over their work schedules, including self-rostering, choice of a permanent shift, flexitime and job sharing (Barton et al., 1993; Kogi, 1995). There are, however, significant challenges in devising management systems to ensure that each worker has fair and equitable access to the benefits offered by flexibility.

Other social and organisational factors may also moderate the negative effects of shiftwork. Thierry and Jansen (1982) argued that social support is particularly critical for shiftworkers, due to the social isolation they often experience. The limited evidence available confirms that social support at work and at home is associated with better health among shiftworkers (Bohle and Tilley, 1989, 1993; Jackson et al., 1985; Pisarski et al., 2006, 2008). Pisarski et al. (1998) tested a detailed model of the relationships between various forms of social support, work–life conflict and health among nurses on rotating shiftwork. The results demonstrated that social support from co-workers and family both had direct positive effects on symptom levels. Support from supervisors, on the other hand, had indirect effects achieved by reducing work–life conflict and increasing the support offered by co-workers. Jackson et al. (1985) found that shiftworkers who reported poor health, negative mood and poor behavioural adjustment also reported high dissatisfaction with work–life conflict, and their spouses reported lower quality of family life and greater dissatisfaction with the shiftworker's job. These negative effects on the family may, in turn, affect the level of support shiftworkers receive from their families.

General health

Several medical and psychiatric conditions may predispose individuals to respond poorly to shiftwork, including diabetes mellitus, thyrotoxicosis, epilepsy, severe depression, narcolepsy and chronic respiratory, cardiovascular and renal disorders (Akerstedt, 1980; Angersbach et al., 1980; Kerkhof, 1985; Koller et al., 1984; Rutenfranz et al., 1985; Winget et al., 1978). Most of these conditions have marked circadian variations, and symptoms may therefore be exacerbated when individuals are subjected to rapid shift rotations that disrupt the circadian system (Winget et al., 1978). Workers with these conditions may benefit from closer health surveillance, especially during the period immediately after they commence shiftwork.

Combined and interactive effects of other health threats

Unfortunately, the effects of shiftwork, complex in themselves, cannot be considered in isolation from those of other health and safety risks. Hazards present in day work may be more dangerous in conjunction with shiftwork; examples include noise, climatic conditions, lighting, vibration and various toxic substances. Rutenfranz and Knauth (1986) found shiftworkers were exposed to excessive noise, vibration and unfavourable lighting conditions more often than day workers. In most cases, shiftworkers were exposed to two or more of these threats at once and night workers were exposed to unfavourable climatic conditions even more often than other shiftworkers. Little is currently known about the long-term effects of shiftwork in warm climatic conditions. However, Rutenfranz and Knauth (1986) do note that conditions for daytime sleep in the tropics and subtropics are particularly negative, an observation that is especially relevant to Australia.

There has been little research examining the effects of hazards at different times of day. Experiments on animals indicate that the effects of many potentially noxious agents, both physical and chemical, vary according to the point in the circadian cycle at which exposure occurs (Reinberg et al., 1986). Fixed doses of some toxins that are well tolerated during one phase of the circadian cycle may have negative effects during another phase. Kiesswetter and colleagues (Kiesswetter et al., 1995, 1997) have performed several controlled laboratory and field studies to examine the relationships between organic solvent exposures and shiftwork. Kiesswetter and Seeber (1995) reported that acetone exposure below the 'maximum allowable concentration' in Germany (2400 mg/m^3) had negative effects on acute symptoms (discomfort, irritation and difficulty breathing) and fatigue, and that these effects were greater on night shift. They concluded that threshold levels of exposure to acetone, previously considered harmless, could add to fatigue and acute symptoms on critical shifts, particularly night shift. Later, Kiesswetter et al. (1997) examined how shiftworkers' sleep was affected by three solvents: ethanol, ethyl acetate and acetone. In laboratory studies they found that short-term exposure to ethyl acetate and acetone, and a mixture of the two, produced a deepening of subsequent sleep. However, a field study of acetone-exposed shiftworkers indicated that daytime sleep was less deep, probably due to long-term exposure to the solvent. The researchers concluded that the impact of solvent exposure on sleep varies according to the time of day that exposure occurs and recommended further research to distinguish between short-term, long-term and time-of-day effects.

For some time, researchers have argued that circadian effects must be considered when exposure standards are established (see Reinberg et al., 1986; Kieswetter et al., 1995), but there is little evidence that these warnings have been taken seriously. There is a pressing need for more research on the additive and interactive relationships between shiftwork and a wide range of workplace hazards.

Women and working hours

Early research on shiftwork was dominated by studies of males, most often in heavy industry (Monk and Folkard, 1985). This sex bias was significant, as the evidence now available suggests that the social and domestic demands and constraints placed on many women may make adaptation to shiftwork more difficult than it is for men. Conflict between work and non-work activities presents a particular concern for female shiftworkers who are employed full-time and have partners and dependent children (Brown and Charles, 1982; Gadbois, 1981; Loudoun and Bohle, 1997). Women generally have more extensive family and domestic responsibilities than males, and female shiftworkers appear to receive little relief from this workload. Gadbois (1981) found that female night workers routinely attended to family and domestic tasks at the expense of daytime sleep, with the married women taking 1 hour and 20 minutes less daytime sleep than their unmarried counterparts. After an extensive study of female shiftworkers in several industries, Charles and Brown (1981: 696) concluded that night work takes place 'without any fundamental transformation of the sexual division of labour and at considerable cost to the women themselves'.

Since the 1990s there has been considerably more research involving female shift-workers, particularly in nursing (Barton et al., 1995; Bohle, 1997a & b; Bohle and Tilley,

1989, 1993, 1998; Loudoun and Bohle, 1997; Olsson et al., 1987; Pisarski et al., 1998, 2006, 2008). Loudoun and Bohle (1997) highlighted the relationship between domestic responsibilities and work–life conflict for female shiftworkers. Women with partners and dependent children reported higher work–life conflict than single women without dependants. Time budget diaries revealed women with partners and dependent children were disadvantaged with regard to leisure time, domestic work and sleep after night shift in comparison to women without dependants. Although there was no difference between married women and their male partners in total (paid and unpaid) work time, the women spent more time on domestic work and less time on leisure activities than their partners. In a direct comparison of females and males working in the same setting, Olsson et al. (1987) found that females reported more musculoskeletal, gastrointestinal and psychological symptoms than males. Unfortunately, both of these studies were cross-sectional and did not clearly establish whether the differences identified arose from shiftwork or other factors.

Despite the growth in the number of studies focussed on women in shiftwork, too few have directly examined sex differences in shiftwork tolerance. Such comparative research should be a priority and particular emphasis should be placed on longitudinal studies of women and men employed under the same working conditions. Only systematic comparisons of his nature can clearly establish the impact of sex and sex roles on adaptation.

Effects on older workers

European data indicates that the prevalence of shiftwork with night work only diminishes slightly over the age of 45 and that 24% of men and 12% of women in this age group work at night (Costa, 2003a). Unfortunately, little is known about how the effects of working hours vary with age, and researchers have yet to adequately disentangle the impact of working hours from other factors associated with ageing. There has, nevertheless, been valuable research on the topic.

It has been known for some time that shift-related sleep and health disturbances increase with age, especially among night workers (Akerstedt and Torsvall, 1981b; Foret, Bensimon, Benoit and Vieux, 1981; Koller, 1983; Rutenfranz et al., 1985). Koller (1983), for example, found that physical and psychological symptoms rose steeply in the early years of shiftwork, tapered off for a period of time, and rose steeply again after the age of 40. No equivalent trend was observed among day workers. A steep rise in symptoms of intolerance in the 40s was documented in several other studies (Monk and Folkard, 1985). There is also longstanding evidence that fatigue, gastrointestinal symptoms and sleep disturbances increase with age among shiftworkers (Akerstedt and Torsvall, 1981a; Koller, 1983). The exception appears to be sleep length before early morning shifts, which can improve with age (Akerstedt and Torsvall, 1981b). Koller (1983) found that age effects were not related to length of experience of shiftwork, suggesting they may arise from age-related changes towards earlier phase, decreased amplitude and greater instability of circadian rhythms (Akerstedt and Torsvall, 1981b; Kerkhof, 1985).

Recent findings confirm that the negative effect of shiftwork and irregular hours increase with age, particularly if they include night work (Bohle et al., 2009; Costa, 2003a). Ageing is associated with changes in the form and synchronisation of circadian rhythms and slower circadian adjustment to night work (Härmä and Ilmarinen, 1999, Costa and Sartori, 2007). These changes appear to contribute to a shortening of sleep after night shift and a greater risk of sleep disorders among older shift workers (Costa and DiMilia, 2008) while enhancing sleep before morning shifts (Costa and Sartori, 2007). Härmä and Ilmarinen (1999) reviewed evidence regarding links between age and the gastrointestinal, cardiovascular, psychosomatic and psychosocial health effects of shift work. For gastrointestinal disorders, mean time between beginning shiftwork and the diagnosis of peptic ulcers is five to six years, but when all digestive disorders are included, the highest prevalence is among shift workers with the longest experience (23–40 years). Coronary heart disease has been demonstrated to increase for the first 20 years of shiftwork exposure, after which its prevalence falls. A similar finding has been reported for depression. The extent to which the increased prevalence of disorders with age and experience reflects longer exposure or a greater susceptibility is unclear. Similarly, the impact of healthy worker effects and self-selection on these patterns of results is not well understood. Nevertheless, the critical age for increasing intolerance to night work appears to be between 45 and 50 (Costa and DiMilia, 2008).

Relatively little is known about the specific nature of the work–life conflict encountered by older workers or its effects on health. Research demonstrating negative effects of conflict on health, wellbeing and social and domestic life (Kinnunen and Mauno, 1998; Knutsson, 2003) has tended to focus on younger workers with dependent children. Unlike younger workers, those over 45 may favour free time during weekday mornings, and place less emphasis on free evenings and weekends. The work–life issues faced by older workers may also differ in important ways from those confronted by their younger counterparts. One example is the tension between paid employment and simultaneous caring responsibilities for both dependent children and parents or older relatives. Primary carers have been found to have poorer physical, mental and emotional health and substantially lower labour force participation than non-carers (de Vaus, 2004; Edwards et al., 2007). The age groups most likely to receive carers' payments from the Australian Government are in the age groups from 45 to 64 years and carers in paid employment are significantly more likely to be dissatisfied with their level of face-to-face social contact, which is associated with poorer health status, than those not in paid employment (Edwards et al., 2007). The dual role of caregiver and worker has been found to have negative effects on mental health elsewhere (Sparks et al., 2001). The total time devoted to employment and caring may leave very little opportunity for social contact outside the household. This evidence suggests older workers with caring responsibilities are disadvantaged in terms of work–life conflict and health but more research is urgently needed.

Conversely, a recent study suggests that the interaction between work and family for older workers can be more positive than negative. Gordon, Whelan-Berry and Hamilton (2007) reported that older women made deliberate choices about work and life responsibilities, and revised their definitions of success to incorporate more personal achievements, allowing them to balance work and family in more satisfying ways. This study did not measure health effects, however, focusing instead on work outcomes, such as job satisfaction and organisational commitment, which may be unrelated to health. Further, the participants often had well-established careers and seniority, with favourable access to paid time off work and flexible working hours. The experience of less-privileged or contingently employed older workers is likely to be less positive.

Shiftwork and irregular working hours may also have negative effects on the work ability of older workers. Costa (2005) reports findings that, across various work contexts, shiftworkers have lower work ability than day workers and that the effect is most pronounced among older workers. He attributes the reduced tolerance to shift and night work of older workers to four sets of factors: 1) changes in circadian rhythms; 2) 'psycho-physical conditions', such as physical fitness and sleep efficiency; 3) working conditions, such as workloads; and 4) social conditions, such as commuting. Costa et al. (2005) also found that the work ability scores of female shift workers in the health care sector deteriorated more markedly over time than those of their counterparts on day work. Ilmarinen and Rantanen (1999) argue that the need for recovery time increases with age and the physical demands of work. Work schedules should therefore allow older workers to pause after peaks in workload to prevent cumulative fatigue. Flexible schedules that respond principally to the needs of the worker, rather than those of the employer, may be particularly effective in reducing work–life conflict for older workers.

Unfortunately, evidence regarding the relationship between age and injury in shiftwork is very limited and any tentative conclusions rely on indirect evidence. Folkard (2008: 195) recently reviewed the available evidence and observed that there is a 'complete lack of studies that have directly examined the combined effects of age and shiftwork on occupational injuries and accidents'. However, he concluded there is clear evidence that, irrespective of the age of the worker, injury rates are higher on night shift and they increase over successive night shifts more rapidly than over successive day shifts. He also noted evidence that, while injuries are less frequent among older workers, they tend to be more severe. Finally, he cited evidence from objective studies of physical and cognitive performance and sleepiness suggesting older workers are less able to maintain performance over both the course of a single night shift and over several successive night shifts. Based on this evidence, Folkard inferred that it appears likely older workers may be subject to a greater risk of injuries and accidents on night shift. He identified a 'clear need' for quality epidemiological studies to examine the combined effects of ageing and shiftwork and to separate effects of ageing alone from those arising from shiftwork.

Costa (2005) makes several recommendations for shift workers over the age of 45:

1 night work should be limited or avoided
2 permanent night work should be voluntary and transfer to day work should be assisted
3 workers should have greater scope to choose preferred shifts
4 workload should be reduced
5 working hours should be shortened

6 rest pauses should be more frequent and short naps should be allowed

7 health checks should be more frequent (at least every two years)

8 greater counselling and training on coping strategies should be provided.

Unfortunately, while these recommendations are based on working hours research, there have not been sufficient rigorous scientific studies to be confident that they all have the desired positive effect on the health of older workers or to identify the magnitude of the effects that do exist.

Current knowledge of working hours and health

There is still much to be learnt about the health impact of working hours. Unfortunately, the findings of many studies conflict, which may be attributable either to limitations in research methods or to genuine differences between the workers and workplaces investigated. A contributing factor has been the paucity of sound theoretical models to guide the design and interpretation of shiftwork research. Early models, such as the 'stress and strain' model proposed by Colquhoun and Rutenfranz (1980), were very simple and of limited explanatory value. However, later contributions are more complex and more comprehensively describe the factors affecting shiftwork intolerance (see Folkard, 1993; Knutsson, 1989; Pisarski et al., 1998, 2006, 2008; Scott et al., 1997). Folkard's (1993) model offers important conceptual insights by identifying the major clusters of variables influencing shiftwork tolerance and attempting to describe the relationships between them. This model has not been systematically tested and its validity has yet to be fully established. However, recent studies using path analysis have examined relationships between some of the variable clusters described by Folkard, inevitably adding extra layers of detail and suggesting modifications to the model (see, for example, Barton et al., 1995; Pisarski et al., 1998). This is the process by which better understanding gradually develops.

It is important to recognise the limitations of knowledge when considering strategies for more effective management of work schedules. If organisations and shiftworkers are to have the information necessary to design optimal rosters, researchers must develop valid and detailed information about the effects of different roster systems. The prospects for dealing effectively with the health problems posed by shiftwork therefore rely on the quality of future research. This research should be based on explicit models of adaptation and employ sound research methods. While such research is important internationally, it is particularly critical in Australia, where industrial and climatic conditions are very different from those in the European countries where most research has been done to date.

Conclusion

Work during evenings, weekends and the night is not a new phenomenon, but technological, economic and social pressures have driven its widespread expansion since the 1950s. While social and technological demands have driven this extension of working hours in some workplaces, in others it exists principally to improve profitability and is often introduced with little attention to its health and social costs. Work schedules are often designed with more concern for profit and administrative convenience than for the health of the workers whose lives must conform to them. This is the case despite substantial evidence that the disruption of sleep, physiological rhythms and social and domestic life caused by shiftwork and irregular hours, particularly when they include night work, produces negative effects on health, including persisting fatigue, sleep disruption, gastrointestinal discomfort, disturbances of appetite, dizziness, anxiety, irritability and disturbances of mood. Until relatively recently, evidence regarding the contribution of working hours to the development of disease was equivocal, but it has become much more compelling, particularly in relation to cardiovascular and gastrointestinal disease and various cancers.

Unfortunately, knowledge of the mechanisms through which working hours affect health is far from complete. This situation reflects the inherent complexity of the causal processes and methodological limitations of much of the research. However, there is strong reason to believe that biological, behavioural, organisational and social variables all play a role. The balance of the evidence suggests that physiological circadian rhythms rarely adjust more than partially to night work. Sleep disturbances are the major complaint of shiftworkers and they often suffer from extreme sleepiness, fatigue and depressed mood. Night and early morning shifts are the main culprits in this regard, but differences in 'sleep hygiene' may contribute to individual differences in adaptation. Many social and organisational variables also appear to affect the health and wellbeing of shiftworkers, who are often severely alienated from social and domestic activities. The extent of this alienation is largely determined by the nature of the shift rosters being worked and the availability of social support from supervisors, co-workers, family and friends. Domestic responsibilities can directly affect adaptation, for example where they curtail sleep after night shift, and women with dependent children are particularly vulnerable to these effects. Some medical conditions also diminish workers' ability to adapt to night work. Despite much research on personality and shiftwork, the evidence currently available does not convincingly demonstrate that personality variables substantially affect shiftwork tolerance. Even diurnal type, which has been the most strongly linked to tolerance, may merely be an indirect measure of differences in the circadian rhythm characteristics that actually affect adjustment to shift changes.

The complexity of the variables influencing the health of shiftworkers ensures that no ideal or universal shift schedule can be devised. Although many researchers support rapidly rotating schedules with a minimum of night work there is evidence that permanent shifts can also have advantages. Rapid rotations can be highly disruptive to social and domestic life unless they are regular and predictable, allowing workers to plan their activities outside work well in advance. In all cases, the desirability of a particular schedule in any organisation will be determined by many factors, including the nature of the work being performed, the climatic conditions, the physical working environment, the facilities provided for shiftworkers, the demographic characteristics of the workforce and the level of community support for shiftworkers. Recognition of the conflict between shiftwork and life outside work suggests that scheduling should be made as flexible as possible, allowing workers the maximum opportunity to accommodate social and domestic activities. Given the importance of social and domestic factors in determining the health impact of shiftwork, it is also important that the design of work schedules is not left to managers and occupational health professionals. The workers themselves should be active participants in the development of their schedules. Ultimately, of course, recognition of the unnatural nature of night and early morning work and their undoubted negative effects implies that organisations should limit them to a minimum, especially where they are not necessary for persuasive social or technical reasons.

QUESTIONS FOR DISCUSSION

1   To what extent can the growth of shiftwork be seen to have arisen out of technological necessity?
2   Briefly describe the contributions of the major disciplines that have contributed to our understanding of the health effects of shiftwork and working hours.
3   Describe the major sets of factors that affect adaptation to shiftwork.
4   Why is it unlikely that an 'ideal' roster system will be devised?
5   To what extent are the health and safety effects of irregular hours that extend into the evening, weekend or night likely to be similar to, or different from, those of regularly rotating shiftwork?

FURTHER READING

Costa, G. (2003), 'Shiftwork and occupational medicine: an overview', *Occupational Medicine*, **53**: 83–8.

Grosch, J.W., Caruso, C.C., Rosa, R.R. and Sauter, S.L. (2006), 'Long hours of work in the US: associations with demographic and organisational characteristics, psychosocial working conditions, and health', *American Journal of Industrial Medicine*, **49**: 943–52.

Straif, K., Baan, R., Grosse, Y., Secretan, B., El Ghissassi, F., Bouvard, V. et al. (2007), 'Carcinogenicity of shift-work, painting, and fire-fighting', *Lancet Oncology*, **8**(12), 1065–6.

Tuchsen, F., Hannerz, H. and Burr, H. (2006), 'A 12 year prospective study of circulatory disease amongst Danish shift workers', *Occupational and Environmental Medicine*, **63**(7), 451–5.

7

Law and prevention

Introduction

WITHIN industrialised societies like Britain, the US, Australia and New Zealand the need for government to intervene in the area of OHS has long been accepted. In essence government intervention has pursued three broad policy goals, namely:

1 the prevention or minimisation of occupational health risks

2 ensuring medical treatment and monetary compensation for injured workers

3 facilitating the rehabilitation of those with severe or permanent disabilities.

This chapter addresses the first of these objectives. In most countries, including Australia and New Zealand, separate bodies of legislation have been developed to deal with prevention on the one hand and workers' compensation and rehabilitation on the other hand. Chapter 8 will examine law and policy debates in relation to workers' compensation and rehabilitation. At the very outset it is worth noting that under Australia's federal political structure the states and territories currently hold primary responsibility for both types of legislation. Like Canada and unlike the US, federal government OHS legislation performs a largely residual role (i.e. to cover otherwise excluded groups such as federal public servants, the defence forces and seamen) apart from some measures of national coordination through the National Occupational Health and Safety Commission (NOHSC). Unlike many other Commonwealth countries, such as Australia, the UK and Canada, New Zealand has a unicameral political structure based on the Westminster model, in which statues are introduced, refined (or rejected) and passed by one house of parliament.

This chapter is divided into a number of sections. Section 2 identifies the complex array of state intervention in OHS. The importance of looking beyond the formal structure of legislation and examining the policies by which it is implemented as well as the impact of other forms of regulation and infrastructure is emphasised. Section 3 provides a brief history of OHS legislation in Australia and New Zealand and indicates why these laws underwent a substantial revision between 1973 and 1989. Section 4 describes and evaluates the current framework of OHS legislation, and in so doing it seeks to place Australian and New Zealand law into an international context and examine a number of important policy debates relating to OHS regulation. Section 5 examines the implementation of post–Robens legislation including the role and activities of OHS inspectorates. Section 6 discusses a number of major challenges to existing regulatory regimes, most notably profound changes to labour markets/work organisation and difficulties regulating high-hazard workplaces. In the final section (7) we make a number of concluding observations about OHS regulation.

The nature and scope of state intervention in OHS

Within most if not all industrialised countries OHS is the subject of a complex array of state intervention. Unfortunately, too often discussion of legal intervention into OHS is confined to those general laws that directly pertain to OHS, overlooking influential bodies of law and the complex interactions between them (for an important exception, see Ashford, 1976 and Ashford and Caldart, 1996). Further, as is more generally recognised in the literature, the discussion of OHS law cannot be restricted to a detailed examination of legislative provisions. It must also consider how these requirements are implemented, a process influenced by politics, the administrative tools and resources of OHS agencies, union and employer attitudes, court practices and a host of other factors (for an examination of Australian OHS law that tries to do this, see Johnstone, 1997). To overcome the latter limitation this chapter will consider the policy debates associated with OHS law in some detail. We will also use the term regulation to describe the broad scope of state intervention. Regulation refers to the control of social behaviour by some mechanism or apparatus of authority and encapsulates the form these controls can take, the processes by which they are implemented and the outcomes of this implementation. With these general points in mind a number of sources of regulation can be identified.

Regulation via the common law

The common law is a non-codified body of law originally based on custom and developed by the courts in English-speaking countries like Australia, Britain, Canada, New Zealand and the US. Under common law the contract of employment contains a number of implied duties that apply to both the employer and employees. After a struggle lasting around 100 years from the mid-1830s, courts in Britain, the US, Australia, New Zealand and elsewhere conceded that the contract of employment incorporated a duty of care on the part of the employer to provide a reasonably safe workplace. Breaches of this implied duty resulting in injury or death could form the basis of an action for damages by or on the behalf of the worker (also see chapter 8 on workers' compensation). A tort of negligence with much the same effect was also developed. The awarding of damages arising from actions at common law (i.e. breach of contract or tort) could be seen to fulfil both compensatory (by the payment of damages to the worker or their family) and deterrent functions (by placing additional costs on negligent employers) by internalising otherwise externalised costs. In practice, common law actions proved too restricted to achieve either outcome satisfactorily, requiring legislative intervention. Nevertheless, the common law continues to play a regulatory role in OHS, and one that has changed over time.

Regulation via statute

A second and more pervasive form of intervention has been the introduction of legislation or statutes that specifically (in whole or part) addressed the health and safety of workers. Within the broad ambit of statutory regulation we can distinguish a number of different categories. First, we can distinguish statutes principally or significantly concerned with OHS (such as the prevention and workers' compensation laws just mentioned) from those where OHS provisions are incidental to the main purpose of the Act (such as laws dealing with food and health standards, road transport, the environment and accommodation of rural workers). One notable body of incidental legislation is the general criminal statutes. In the 1980s and early 1990s there was a debate over whether employers whose negligence caused the death of a worker should be charged with manslaughter, murder or a special class of offence (workplace homicide under criminal or OHS statutes; Von Ebers, 1986; Bergman, 1991; Carson and Johnstone, 1990; Gobert, 2008). Another body of legislation which has often been viewed as having, at most, an incidental role in OHS regulation is collective labour laws (i.e. those laws providing the framework for union recognition and dispute settlement by collective bargaining, conciliation, arbitration or other means). As chapter 9 shows, collective labour laws have important if often unrecognised effects on OHS and can be used to directly regulate safety although this option has often been utilised only in a limited fashion.

A further distinction can be made between primary Acts of parliament and delegated legislation where parliament has ceded its power to make regulations to a non-parliamentary body (such as a minister). Regulations (as distinct from the broader notion of regulation) contain specific technical standards, penalties or procedural requirements that must be followed in order to satisfy general obligations found under the primary Act. They can be altered without reference to parliament thereby avoiding the delays that would otherwise be entailed. The major OHS laws of countries such as Australia, New Zealand, Canada and Britain are essentially enabling legislation that make use of subordinate legislation (regulations) or codes to flesh out performance standards set down in general duty of care provisions. The use of regulations was a longstanding device, usually enunciating detailed or specification standards and identifying a single mode of compliance. The reform of OHS laws in the last 20 years often entailed attempts to rationalise and develop a more comprehensive set of OHS regulations. The character of regulations also underwent change as a consequence of the national uniformity push in Australia and New Zealand (see below), with regulations now incorporating performance standards (such as requirements for risk assessment). A breach of regulations is a criminal offence with a set penalty that is, because of its status as subordinate legislation, usually set at a lower level than penalties pertaining to offences under provisions of the principal Act. However, in New Zealand and some Australian jurisdictions, such as Victoria, a breach of regulations is held to be a breach of the principal Act (i.e. the Occupational Health Safety and Act, 1985). Regulations are to be found in most industrialised countries although they go under a variety of labels.

Third, the legislative changes influenced by the British Robens report of 1972 (see below) included the introduction of a new instrument—codes of practice—in Britain, Australia, New Zealand and a number of other countries. Unlike old-style regulations, codes do not specify one mode of compliance with a legislative standard but rather present ways in which a standard, say, on manual handling, can be met. Typically the language applied to codes of practice is similar to the language used in guidance notes or best practice materials, which is not always the case with regulations. Since the methods of compliance indicated in a code of practice are not exclusive, failure to comply with a code may not constitute an offence of itself. The precise legal ramifications of failing to comply with a code differ among the various Australian jurisdictions (See Johnstone, 1997: 284–94). In South Australia, Victoria and New Zealand a court will find failure to comply with a relevant code as a contravention of the relevant duty provision of the Act unless the duty holder can demonstrate that the method they used was as good or better than the method specified in the code. In NSW the Occupational Health and Safety Act provides that compliance with a code is evidence of compliance with the legal duty. The Western Australian and the Australian Capital Territory Acts are silent on this issue, the effect of which according to Johnstone (1997) is to adopt the NSW position. The Queensland Workplace Health and Safety Act, 1995 explicitly states that compliance with an advisory standard (the Queensland term for performance standard) is compliance with the legal duty. Where the duty holder fails to comply with an advisory standard, this is taken as evidence of a breach of the legal duty. The burden is then on the duty holder to prove either that they did comply with the advisory standard or some better method as a defence. Codes of practice have been seen to be a more flexible tool than regulations. However, this argument should not be overstated, as the distinction between the two instruments appears to have narrowed over time. Even accepting this distinction, both have strengths and weaknesses (see below). In Australia, while there has been a general shift towards codes of practice the degree to which they have replaced regulations within specific jurisdictions varies widely.

Aside from regulations and codes of practice government agencies and other bodies may also develop standards and guidance notes in relation to OHS that do not, by themselves, constitute formal regulatory instruments. Standards related to substances, work processes or other matters developed by bodies such as the National Health and Medical Research Council (NHMRC), NOHSC or the Standards Association of Australia can be adopted under a statute, regulations or codes of practice. Where standards are not incorporated into legislation or codes they will have the status of recommendations that are not directly enforceable but may be used as evidence of acceptable practice in court proceedings. The same applies to guidance notes that are normally issued to provide advice to employers on how they can best meet their OHS obligations (say, in regard to a specific guidance note on machine guarding).

Fourth, quite apart from standards developed within national boundaries, recognition must also be given to international bodies that either set standards, such as the International Labour Organization (ILO), or whose activities may be seen to set standards, such as the International Agency for Research on Cancer (IARC). Professional bodies may also affect international standards, the most obvious example being the American Conference of Government Industrial Hygienists (ACGIH), whose exposure limits have been widely adopted internationally (see chapter 5). Legal recognition of international OHS standards, such as those developed by the ILO, requires a two-stage process, namely formal ratification by governments as well as measures to actually implement this. For some countries (Australia included) ratification is often a pro-tracted process, although it is usually followed by genuine efforts at implementation (not the case with some countries that readily ratify ILO standards). Another poten-tially important vehicle for uniform standards and supra-national laws is regional trade blocs/communities such as the European Union and the CER agreement between New Zealand and Australia. Thus far no effort has been made to incorporate OHS and other labour standards into agreements reached under the auspices of the World Trade Organization (WTO). The absence of regulations setting minimum global/ international standards in OHS represents a serious and growing deficiency that is discussed (albeit briefly) later in this chapter.

Regulatory infrastructure

State intervention in OHS cannot be seen simply in terms of the enactment of laws that directly or indirectly address OHS. It is necessary to consider the administrative, research and enforcement agencies that service these laws.

Administrative practices, enforcement practices and dominant policy directions can affect the extent and nature of OHS regulation, the types of penalties used (for example the emphasis on economic or criminal sanctions) and enforcement strategies. Dominant policy discourses can also lead to inconsistent or even contradictory govern-ment policies. Notably, while now coming under some scrutiny, neo-liberal ideas—that unfettered markets, self-regulation and a minimum of government intervention in economic activity provide optimal social outcomes—have dominated global policy discourse (especially in English-speaking countries) over the past 30 years. As already noted, there is clear evidence that the downsizing, privatisation and outsourcing prac-tices promoted by labour market 'flexibility' under this policy mantra have had adverse OHS effects which present a serious challenge to OHS regulation and inspectorates (including attempts to maintain OHS standards within government employers). As noted by Broom et al. (2006) among others, government labour market or industrial relations policies that facilitate particular types of work arrangements cannot be viewed as neutral in their health effects. Neo-liberalism has also provided the justification for international economic and trade relationships whereby OHS and other labour standards are excluded (and where the public health and safety standards of some countries have also been compromised). At the national level, it is characterised by ongoing 'concerns' with regulatory overburden on business and OHS regulation has been a key target of this (see Productivity Commission, 2008, 2009).

As has just been indicated, OHS may be affected by governments pursuing policies that seem to have nothing to do with OHS or where the OHS impacts are not considered. For example, a now substantial body of evidence indicates that downsizing/ restructuring, outsourcing/competitive tendering and the use of temporary/agency workers—all common practices among government agencies over the past two decades—have substantial adverse effects on OHS (Quinlan and Bohle, 2008, 2009) and as such pose an additional burden on OHS regulatory agencies. Inconsistent and even contradictory policies within government are common despite popular references to (and commendable examples of) the need for a 'whole of government' approach. On a more positive note we can point to examples of government policies that are designed to reinforce OHS standards, such as including OHS in procurement policies.

It should be emphasised that OHS regulation needs to evolve in order to address changes to OHS hazards (due to changes in chemicals, work processes and the like) and just stalling or delaying this process will open gaps over time. In Australia neo-liberal ideas had a limited direct effect on OHS regulation in the period 1980 to 2010. There is no evidence that state agencies found themselves unable to issue new standards although the level of activity slowed markedly between 1996 and 2007 at federal level. While neo-liberalism didn't prevent some genuinely innovative regulation at state level (such as laws dealing with supply chains in trucking and clothing manufacture), these followed significant community campaigns, inquiries and research, and neo-liberal opposition made it more difficult to translate these initiatives to the federal level. As described below, following its election in 1996, the neo-liberal–inspired Howard federal government downsized then abolished Australia's federal OHS research and standards coordination agency (NOHSC). The agency which regulated federal public servants and workers employed by ex-federal agencies, such as Telstra, also became notable for its lack of enforcement even though its coverage was expanded to include a number of large national private employers. Even following the defeat of the Howard government in November 2007 (and the election of a prime minister who formally disavows neo-liberalism), a danger remains that measures to harmonise OHS laws (discussed below) and Productivity Commission (2008, 2009) reviews of chemical regulation and regulatory burdens with regard to OHS regulation could lead to a lowest-common-denominator approach. However, at the time of writing it is too early to assess whether this will occur.

In the US, an effect is even more clearly discernable. During the entire Bush administration, the Occupational Safety and Health Administration (OSHA)—the federal agency responsible for OHS—promulgated only one new OHS standard (for hexavalent chromium and then under court order) and OSHA officials issued 86% fewer economically significant rules and regulations than under the previous Clinton (Democrat) administration. Under the stewardship of the George W Bush–appointed Secretary of the Department of Labor (of which OSHA forms a part), Elaine Chao, OSHA was the subject of considerable criticism for being inactive from a range of quarters, including the president of the American Industrial Hygienists Association (AIHA), Lindsay Booher. Booher pointed to the urgent need to update permissible exposure limits (PELs), some of which had been written in the 1960s. Chao claimed the credit for a decline in reported injuries and illnesses during her tenure although a study undertaken by Friedman and Forst (2007) found that changes to record-keeping rules in 1995 and 2001 accounted for 83% of the reduction (and note other issues about injury/illness reporting discussed elsewhere in this book). Subsequent reports of the Office of Inspector General of this Department of Labor (2009a & b) were highly critical of OSHA's enforcement activity with regard to employers experiencing fatalities and its use of consultants. Complaints about OSHA inactivity had been reported in the press over a number of years (see, for example, Smith, 2008). While problems with OSHA predated the Bush era (and indeed some were longstanding; see Silverstein, 2008) the non-interventionist approach adopted between 2000 and 2008 magnified concerns about the agency's ineffectiveness. Through strategic staff 'redeployments' and other influences, the Bush administration also exerted a narrowing influence on the federal government's OHS research and scientific advisory agency, the National Institute for Occupational Safety and Health (NIOSH), which is part of the Centers for Disease Control (Silverstein, 2008). Following its election in November 2008, the Obama administration made significant changes to key personnel within the Department of Labor and OSHA, including the appointment of Hilda Solis as Secretary of the Department of Labor and Jordon Barab as Deputy Assistant Secretary of OSHA. Barab, for example, had long been an unapologetic advocate of worker safety with a background of OHS activity within the union movement as well as stints with the US Chemical Safety and Hazard Investigation Board (an independent federal agency) and as a federal policy advisor.

The US experience highlights how subtle and not-so-subtle policy shifts can be implemented through the selection/appointment of senior administrative appointments 'sympathetic' to particular policy directions. Despite its convention of public sector independence, Australia has not been immune from such practices. More broadly it needs to be recognised that neo-liberal economists dominate many influential federal government agencies, such as Finance and Treasury, the Productivity Commission and the Australian Consumer and Competition Commission. As far as we are aware, no person with substantial OHS expertise (to the point of being viewed as a national or international expert) has ever occupied a key position in Industry/Productivity Commission inquiries into OHS or workers' compensation.

Research funding and infrastructure also plays a key role because it provides evidence on new and existing hazards that can form the basis for revising OHS standards. As noted in chapter 1, while workers' compensation claims records provide some OHS data to inform interventions including regulatory activities, it suffers from serious deficiencies with regard to occupational disease, mental illness, new/emerging hazards and effective coverage of the growing contingent workforce. There is also a growing recognition that the OHS effects associated with changes in work organisation have not been captured by conventional datasets. In the European Union one response to this was to undertake a five-yearly survey of working conditions (including psychosocial conditions) in member countries since the early 1990s. These surveys provided insights into changing conditions and hazards as well as enabling OHS components of quality of work indicators (see, for example, European Foundation for the Improvement of Living and Working Conditions, 2009). Efforts to utilise these elements as part of an agenda to develop quality of work policies in 2001 were stymied by neo-liberal interests within the EU (EMCONET, 2007). Nothing comparable has even been attempted in Australasia or North America (although a work stress survey undertaken for the Victorian Department of Health demonstrated the value of this approach; LaMontagne et al., 2006). Despite this, there is a critical need for more broadly based OHS indicators to guide policy in the future.

Beyond the question of enhancing our knowledge of broad shifts in safety, health and wellbeing at the workplace, research can also play a critical role in producing more specialised knowledge. Again, infrastructure is critical to this. Countries such as Finland, Denmark and the US have national OHS research agencies to both undertake and collate knowledge (including overseas research). In Australia, state OHS agencies have funded some research. The National Occupational Health and Safety Commission (established in the mid-1980s) initially included a major research function (both internal and funding external research) but this was largely eliminated by downsizing/restructuring after 1996, a situation that carried over to its successor organisation (the Australian Safety and Compensation Council or ASCC). It is as yet unclear what role the new federal body—Safe Work Australia—will undertake with regard to research. In New Zealand the National Occupational Health and Safety Advisory Committee, an independent government agency responsible for providing advice directly to the Minister of Labour on OHS issues, sponsored some important scoping research but was abolished following the election of a neoliberal government.

OHS regulation is underpinned by a broader societal infrastructure. This includes the general healthcare infrastructure, such as whether there is a universal publicly funded healthcare system (like Medicare in Australia and found in almost all rich countries and some poor countries), public hospitals, rehabilitation clinics and community health centres; as well as government-funded research and standard-setting agencies such as the Australian National Health and Medical Research Council, Australian Research Council and New Zealand National Occupational Health and Safety Advisory Committee as well as universities. The health infrastructure also includes government funding and controls on the training of doctors, nurses and other health professionals (including OHS); general health education; and promotion programs. Not least it also includes healthcare services access/financing policies such as Medicare, and government require-ments or decisions with regard to the recording of health statistics and incidents (such as the issuing of death certificates and the conduct of coronial inquiries, mining warden's courts, royal commissions and other investigatory apparatuses). Healthcare infrastructure may have profound effects on OHS. For example, the provision of compulsory health insurance and a strong public health system will set a baseline for the healthcare of injured workers, including those who may receive inadequate treatment or assistance under workers' compensation schemes (such as contingent workers or those suffering a 'non-recognised' occupational disease). As noted in chapter 1, inadequate recognition of occupational disease has been a problem pertaining to workers' compensation sys-tems in many countries. On the other hand, workers' compensation made a valuable contribution to healthcare infrastructure (for a study of the role of healthcare services on workplace injury impacts, see Mustard and Hertzman, 2001). The introduction of workers' compensation schemes stimulated recognition of and attention to work–related injuries and health by the healthcare system, encouraging the development of industrial medicine (funding university posts, research and government occupational disease units) as well as providing a statistical knowledge base on occupational illness.

Beyond the healthcare system we should recognise other areas where government intervention provides infrastructure that affects OHS. Obvious examples include unemployment benefits and other forms of social security, including those applying in the case of long-term or permanent disability. The scope and level of unemployment entitlements will affect attitudes to work, including the risks workers may be willing to take to get a job and the pressure on family members, including children, to find employment. Where unemployment benefits are especially inadequate this can encourage a desperate search for work and encourage informal and even illegal forms of employment marked by comparatively higher OHS risks. The increased popularity in some countries of linking unemployment benefits to some form of work activity (known as work for the dole, workfare, etc.) also raises issues about OHS, including the legal rights of these workers (for example, the right to refuse unsafe tasks). More importantly perhaps, there is a complex, significant but seldom explored relationship between workers' compensation and other forms of social security. In some countries, such as France (see Mialon, 1990), workers' compensation constitutes an integrated part of the social security system while in others, like Australia and the US, workers' compensation operates independently of the social security system. In both Australia and the US, workers compensation developed prior to a more general welfare safety net and remains largely a matter regulated by state governments whereas social security is handled federally. In many countries the social security system acts as a safety net for those workers who (for a variety of reasons) miss out on workers' compensation. In Australia and other countries, like Canada, there is also a significant gender-biased movement of the long-term injured from state/territory workers' compensation systems into the federal social security system (Stewart, 1991; Hertzman et al., 1999; Quinlan and Mayhew, 1999). The safety-net role of social security has consequences for the burden on OHS costs respectively borne by industry, workers (and their families) and the community and the policy decisions that may flow from this. Further, since the shift is usually accompanied by a general reduction in the level of benefits it may have long-term consequences for the economic security, health and wellbeing of affected families. We will have more to say on these issues in chapter 8.

With notable exceptions (See Elling, 1986, 1989; Gillespie, 1987, 1990), the important role of regulatory infrastructure is understated or ignored in discussions of OHS regulation.

The interaction between different forms of regulation

It is useful to identify the array of ways that state intervention affects OHS because these are seldom systematically addressed in the OHS literature. This also means that important interconnections are often ignored in policy debates (Wren, 2008). For this reason it is worth providing some examples of interactions and overlap.

First, there is an interaction between statutes that directly address OHS. Although most countries have separate bodies of legislation dealing with prevention and compensation it does not follow that the provision of compensation has had no effect on employer and worker attitudes in relation to prevention. Indeed, when workers' compensation laws were first introduced and again more recently, this has been an area of considerable debate (see chapter 8). In a number of countries the rationalisation of OHS legislation after 1970 still left separate bodies of law covering worksites deemed to be exceptional such as mines (in Australia and the US) and offshore oil rigs (in Britain and Australia). In some instances these laws can overlap when, for example, a mine is being built or is undergoing major construction work.

Second, there are interactions and overlaps between OHS statutes and other bodies of legislation. The most notable examples include legislation dealing with (other) employment standards such as minimum wages, anti-discrimination/equal employment opportunity (EEO) and collective bargaining or arbitration (see chapter 9) as well as those dealing with the environment, mine safety, oil and gas production and transport (road, rail, maritime and air). For example, it is quite possible for an incident involving a truck to give rise to a prosecution under both OHS and road transport legislation. In countries like Australia and New Zealand there are often conventions among government agencies to coordinate enforcement activities and to determine which law will be used in terms of compliance. In New Zealand this aspect has been particularly contentious as informal or formal conventions have tended to apply weaker statutes to prosecutions of employers instead of applying the more stringent ones. Concern over this practice has resulted in ministerial inquiries (see Wilson, 2000) and submissions to parliamentary select committees. In Australia a complex situation has arisen with regard to mining. In some jurisdictions (notably Tasmania) mining has been absorbed into OHS legislation; others have integrated the relationship between OHS and mining laws (notably NSW) while in yet other jurisdictions (such as Queensland and Western Australia) entirely separate bodies of laws have been retained (although mining laws have been revised to be more consistent with the post-Robens model of OHS legislation; Gunningham, 2007). Further, those responsible for developing nationally consistent mining legislation opposed incorporation into OHS law as part of the national OHS law-harmonisation process. Another area where international researchers have identified a complex overlay of OHS and other laws (as well as gaps in the regulatory framework) is offshore fishing (see Windle et al., 2008). A complex overlap between OHS and industrial relations (IR) legislation is also to be found in Australia, New Zealand and other countries, such as Canada. For example, in Australia right of access to the workplace for union officials on OHS issues can be found under both OHS and IR laws (depending on the jurisdiction) and on occasion industrial awards and agreements may extend to issues already addressed in OHS legislation. It is not possible to explore all these interactions in this book; however, a number will be explored later in this chapter and in chapter 9. At this point it is worth noting that there are not simply questions of overlapping jurisdictions here but also important differences in the regulatory environment, including the resourcing and the activity of enforcement agencies (for evidence of this, see Grabosky and Braithwaite, 1986;

Carson, 1989; Quinlan, 2001; Wran and McLelland, 2005). Again, we will return to these issues later in this chapter.

Third and finally, there are interactions between statute law and the common law where, as in Australia and New Zealand, both bodies of law exist. The most obvious area of interaction is between workers' compensation and common law. In some countries, such as Australia, a dual system is maintained whereby injured workers may pursue claims under either workers' compensation or a claim for damages at common law. 'Double-dipping' is not permitted and some Australian jurisdictions also place a series of procedural limits on common law actions (see chapter 8). In other countries, such as the US, the provision of workers' compensation by statute has entailed precluding common law actions altogether. In New Zealand, however, the right to sue for injury was removed in 1974 and replaced with a universal no-fault compensation system (see chapter 8). There are also less-recognised interactions between preventative legislation and common law. In some countries (including Australia), common law actions for damages can be based on statutory breaches as well as breaches of common law duties in tort or contract. In Australia such actions became significantly more prevalent in the 1980s (Brooks, 1988a: 3). The borrowing has not been one-sided. The revised OHS laws of Britain, New Zealand and most Australian states and territories contain duty of care provisions significantly modelled on those found within the common law, including the extension of liability to manufacturers, designers and suppliers. Finally, there are even more subtle interactions with regard to court decision-making practices. The interpretation by courts of statutory requirements and common law claims is seen to involve quite distinct processes but in practice the common law training of most judges results in a drift of concepts and reasoning from the latter into the former.

The development of OHS law prior to 1970

Having identified the array of means by which state intervention affects OHS, it is important to provide a brief account of the origins and development of OHS legislation in Australia and New Zealand along with some reference to other countries. This will help to explain why OHS laws became fragmented and the limitations with early forms of regulatory intervention. This, in turn, provides a context for examining the current legislation and the extent to which it has overcome these problems.

The first OHS laws were enacted in Australia and New Zealand when these countries were still independent British colonies. As such, the model for early OHS legislation in Australia and New Zealand was drawn from Britain and hence there is a need to briefly mention legislative development there. Even after federation in 1901, Australian OHS largely remained a state jurisdiction and state laws continued to be influenced by British developments well into the twentieth century. However, contrary to some suggestions (see Gunningham, 1984), even during the colonial period local laws were never complete clones of British legislation and the extent of differences tended to grow over time. Indeed, by the 1890s radical employment legislation in New Zealand was influencing laws in both Australia and Britain.

In Britain the first OHS legislation was a response to the appalling working conditions associated with the Industrial Revolution. The Health and Morals of Apprentices Act (1802) banned the employment of young children and required that factory walls be limed regularly to prevent outbreaks of disease, as had occurred at Sir Robert Peel's Radcliffe mills in 1784. This and subsequent Acts focused on children, whose misuse attracted a larger body of middle-class outrage. From 1844 women were another target of legislative protection and, indeed, as Sass (1999) has documented, women played a pivotal role in the development of OHS laws. Early factory laws had little effect and it was not until 1833 that a government inspectorate was created to monitor compliance and initiate prosecutions. It is not coincidental that this reform occurred at the height of the labour movement's push for reduced working hours and parliamentary reform. The push was assisted by evidence from a number of physicians who documented the health of workers in the new industrial towns, including Charles Thackrah. From the 1840s onwards factory legislation was periodically expanded and new laws were introduced to deal with hazardous industries, most notably mining and construction. Overall, the growth of British legislation can be most accurately portrayed as a series of ad hoc responses to periodic campaigns to address specific hazards (resulting in detailed and prescriptive regulations on machinery, ventilation, etc.) and not the logical outcome of far-sighted reformers like Lord Shaftsbury or growing technical knowledge. Indeed, knowledge and outcomes were shaped by the interaction between various interest groups, with periodic regressions (as evidenced by changes to medical understanding of the role of dust in lung diseases among miners between the 1860s and 1930s).

In sum, the predominant model of legislative intervention adopted was detailed specification in relation to certain physical characteristics of the workplace (such as requiring guarding of specific machinery, ventilation, hygienic amenities, regular inspection of boilers, etc.). By and large, the legislation limited its constraints on employer behaviour to these detailed requirements and set no more general performance standards (although a moral code might be read into the detailed requirements). In other words it was a legislative framework that focused on certain physical artefacts of work rather than the general behaviour of employers or the social organisation of work processes (apart from measures to limit the employment or tasks performed by women and children). The legislation has been labelled as paternalistic because it afforded no formal opportunity for collaboration between interested parties (though tacit negotiation often occurred between employers and inspectors and employers and courts; see, for example, Carson, 1970) and certainly no means of input for workers and their representatives. Rather, the state assumed control of a specific set of matters with other OHS issues being left for employers to decide. This model of legislation has also been labelled as punitive because of its focus on setting minimum standards with accompanying penalties for any breaches that were detected. In practice, however, administration of the legislation bore little resemblance to its apparent punitive character. Nonetheless, as already noted, the Australian and New Zealand colonies largely copied this legal framework. The replication of laws was particularly apparent between New Zealand and the state of Victoria and it was not uncommon to see facsimiles of early

OHS laws, for example the 1873 legislation regulating the employment conditions of women and children.

Given its relative importance it is not surprising that, unlike Britain, the first colonial OHS laws in both Australia and New Zealand addressed the mining industry. New South Wales, the dominant coal producer up until the 1960s, introduced a single-page Act in 1854 dealing with the inspection of coal mines. In 1862 an expanded Act was introduced (among other things it banned children under 13 years from working in pits), with further legislation in 1876. While largely copying British laws the timing of changes to legislation, and some issues of substance, was influenced by local events, especially major coal disasters such as occurred at Bulli in 1889 and the Brunner Mine in 1896. Legislation dealing with metalliferous mining was introduced by most colonies in the second half of the nineteenth century. However, it was not until the 1880s that this law significantly addressed OHS, requiring the inspection of mines and reporting of accidents, and detailing minimum standards in relation to machinery, equipment, etc. (see, for example, the Tasmanian Regulation of Mines Acts of 1881 and 1884). Although Queensland was the second most important coal producer it regulated both metalliferous and coal mines under a single Mines Regulation Act introduced in 1881. Separate coal mining legislation was not introduced until 1925, in the aftermath of the Mount Mulligan mine disaster in 1921 when 74 men were killed in a methane explosion—the third worst such disaster in Australian history (after Bulli, 1889 and Mount Kembla, 1905). As with coal mining, legislative change was often triggered by the public outcry and union pressure arising from a particular incident, such as a roof collapse, the crashing of a cage carrying miners or flooded workings.

While the risk of explosions was greatest in coal mines, dust was a major issue in all mines. This issue drew attention from a number of local physicians from the 1870s onwards and it was one area where Australians made a contribution to both occupational medicine and the reform of mine conditions. Even so, it was not until the first decades of the twentieth century that a combination of industrial pressures (including the famous 1908 Blackball Miners' Strike in New Zealand and an 18-month strike by Broken Hill miners in 1919–20), political changes (election of a Labor government) and consequent initiatives in OHS research and regulation altered work practices that had killed thousands of Australian and New Zealand miners. In practice, some gains were undermined in the 1930s depression, but in the postwar period the Coal Miners' Federation in particular was able, in conjunction with bodies like the Joint Coal Board in NSW, to improve working conditions. Further, in both Queensland and New South Wales coal mining legislation gave workers and unions rights in relation to OHS that were unique and are still superior to those found within the post-Robens OHS laws.

While the colonies legislated on mining in a serious fashion from the early 1880s and were also relatively quick to copy British employers' liability legislation around the same time, they took longer to adopt factory legislation. The obvious explanation is that manufacturing was small scale and relatively unimportant, compared to agriculture, fishing, forestry and mining. However, while occupational medicine grew in a slow and fragmented fashion (with most attention focusing on diseases affecting miners and rural workers), colonial physicians were making observations about the effects of long hours and hazardous substances on tradesmen and other workers from the 1840s (Gandevia, 1971). Indeed, in colonial New Zealand death rates from workplace accidents were higher than those in Britain and higher than most states in Australia (95.7 per 100 000 population) (Armstrong, 2008: 10). As Eldred-Grigg (1990: 66) noted:

> Work caused spectacular accidents and disease … Timber felling, which crushed dozens of men every year in the late nineteenth century, was probably the most dangerous job. Death from other forms of crushing in mines and quarries, or road and railway works, were almost as common.

The treatment of child and female labour, hazardous working and living conditions were also being raised in a series of government inquiries from the 1860s onwards. Further, while manufacturing was small scale, on occasion the risks were only too apparent. For example, a boiler explosion at the Union Saw Mill in Maryborough, Queensland, in August 1872 killed the manager and seven workers. Two related factors may help explain the lag, namely that the small scale of operations was not conducive to union organisation which could press for these measures. On the other hand, craft workers (who were unionised at a level at least comparable to Britain) secured the eight-hour working day far earlier and more completely than their British counterparts. In New Zealand the eight-hour working day was first introduced as early as 1840 by the carpenter Samuel Parnell. Thus, the hours issue only became a critical rallying point for factory reform with the rise of semi-skilled factory labour (including women) in larger establishments during the 1880s and the organisation of long-suffering retail workers around the same time.

New Zealand and Victoria, which had the most manufacturing, led the introduction of factory legislation in 1873 with a law which, like earlier British legislation, was directed at female workers. The Victorian legislation was expanded in the 1880s. Tasmania, too, introduced laws restricting the employment of females and children in workrooms and factories (1884) and requiring the inspection of machinery (1884, 1889). By 1890 the growing union movement was pressing for legislative intervention on the sweating of female factory and shop workers, boiler inspection and a range of other issues. Despite copious evidence collected from inquiries and other sources, factory legislation was only introduced into New Zealand in 1890 and Queensland and NSW in 1896, with Western Australia following with a boiler inspection law in 1897. Some colonies incorporated early closing provisions in their factory legislation while others introduced separate Acts. In Queensland the political pressure of the rural producers meant that they were exempted from many provisions, including machinery inspection, enabling substandard boilers to be relocated to country districts. Subsequently, a separate and less demanding rural machinery law was introduced—a situation that persisted until 1990!

Following federation in Australia most areas of OHS, except maritime/air transport and federal employees, remained within state jurisdiction. In the first decades of the twentieth century the legislation just mentioned was consolidated and other laws were introduced to deal with construction hazards, lifts and scaffolding. This process of accretion continued and by the 1960s the result was a complex legislative maze of well over 150 federal, state and territory statutes and regulations covering mines, factories, construction, other workplaces (such as ships) and specific hazards. New Zealand mirrored the situation in Australia and by the 1960s OHS legislation was covered by no less than 31 Acts supported by some 100 regulations and codes of practice and administered by five government departments.

Judging the overall effectiveness of these legislative developments is by no means simple and the limited research undertaken suggests a complex picture. On the one hand, the laws in combination with union activity, government inquiries and the establishment of occupational medicine units by the Commonwealth Government (1921), NSW (1923) and Victoria (1937), did affect changes within factories, mines and some other workplaces. Robertson (1927) was right to see factory legislation as an important social development. Ferguson (1994) documented the important role played by occupational medicine units and physicians such as WT Nelson and Charles Badham in providing information to affect changes. Major improvements were made in relation to silicosis, although this needs to be balanced against setbacks such as the undermining of Badham's work on lead poisoning at Port Pirie by company/ state government collaboration (see Gillespie, 1990). However, while it is probably safe to say OHS legislation made an important contribution to safeguarding workers, it did not secure this without an input from trade unions and other interested parties, and the impact was far short of preventing occupational injury and disease. The role of employment shifts and changes in management is unclear. Aldrich (1997) has argued major improvements in a number of US industries during the early twentieth century were due to shifts in employment away from dangerous jobs, regulation and, more controversially, the 'safety first' movement led by a group of safety professionals, who advocated that management take responsibility for OHS. In New Zealand this 'safety first' philosophy was credited with an almost unblemished safety record during construction work on the Manapouri power station in 1997–2000 in which there were over 300 workers who worked over 1 500 000 man-hours without any loss of life or permanent disability injuries. The 'safety first' movement has also had a presence in Australia (in the railways and some manufacturing activities) but available research has not supported Aldrich's interpretation, seeing it rather as a largely symbolic part of the manipulative welfare policies of the time (see Patmore, 1985). Aldrich's argument warrants further investigation, although it should be treated with caution given potential distortions in the datasets on which he relies (and notwithstanding his scholarly use of these statistics).

With some exceptions (Maconachie, 1988) the impact of early factory legislation in Australia has been subject to little detailed investigation. However, in New Zealand (Campbell, 1987; Wren, 1997), Canada (see Tucker, 1990), Britain (Carson, 1979, 1980; Bartrip and Fenn, 1980, 1983) and other countries with a similar framework, quite detailed research has been undertaken. Carson's research, including his debate with

Bartrip and Fenn, offers a number of insights not only into factory legislation but also more general problems affecting OHS legislation right up to the present time. Examining British factory Acts in the 1830s and 1840s, Carson (1979) argued the introduction and administration of these laws involved a complex interchange of class interests which ultimately rendered them largely symbolic. Despite a view that evasion of the legislation would be confined to a few operators, the early inspectorate found breaches were extremely widespread. This, and the unsympathetic attitude of the courts to prosecutions of this 'middle-class' crime, meant that, after a brief effort at enforcement, inspectors evolved elaborate practices to avoid prosecution. In essence, Carson argues factory crime (and OHS Acts were and remain criminal statutes) was conventionalised or treated as a less important offence warranting, in most instances, cajoling and education of all but the most recalcitrant employers. In sum, factory legislation was used to buy off the challenge of an emerging union movement but its administration constituted a largely symbolic accommodation of class interests. Three Australian studies of factory legislation in Victoria and Queensland found support for Carson's conventionalisation thesis (see Maconachie, 1988; Johnstone, 1994; Quinlan and Goodwin, 2005).

Bartrip and Fenn (1980) challenged Carson's conventionalisation thesis, arguing that the inspectorate's preference for persuasion over litigation was essentially a pragmatic response based on logistical constraints (education was far cheaper than court proceedings). Bartrip and Fenn's argument is appealing and, as the 2006 rockfall at the Beaconsfield goldmine and other more recent events demonstrates, not without contemporary relevance. However, it fails to explain why, relative to other regulatory agencies, OHS inspectorates remained chronically under-resourced over many years. This implies something about the political will of governments and the balance of social forces that influence the scope of regulatory activities more consistent with Carson's explanation. Further, a now substantial body of international research on the recognition and regulation of hazardous substances, both historically and more recently, has identified the key role played by interest groups (such as employers, unions, insurers, community mobilisations and the medical profession) in shaping state responses (see, for example, Rosner and Markowitz, 1989, 1991; Bowden and Penrose, 2006; Tucker, 2006; Hunter and LaMontagne, 2008). Much of this research—while often painting a complex picture—is broadly consistent with Carson's interpretation of what influences regulation and its enforcement (though generally focusing more on the former).

The foregoing debate raises a number of important questions. Clearly, the development and implementation of legislation needs to be viewed in a dynamic social context. Further, as Grabosky and Braithwaite argue (1986), persuasion and prosecution are not complete alternatives and most regulatory agencies use a mixture of both, the real question being how to select a mix that will have optimal effect. There is also the question of how to garner more resources for OHS agencies and how to shift longstanding attitudes to prosecutions. We will return to these and related questions later in this chapter.

Problems with pre-Robens legislation and an agenda for reform

Australia, Britain and New Zealand were by no means the only countries to adopt an ad hoc, fragmented and paternalistic approach to legislating on OHS. From the late 1960s onwards there was increasing recognition among policymakers, unions, academics and others that this approach suffered from a number of fundamental flaws, namely:

■ The multiplicity of laws—exacerbated in Australia by the federal political structure—created confusion among employers, unions and other key groups. Even within the same state or jurisdiction separate OHS laws might establish different standards in relation to the same hazard. Further, often a number of pieces of legislation applied to a single workplace. Finally, the laws were administered by a number of departments, some with their own inspectorates who adopted quite different approaches to enforcement.

■ This complex array of laws did not afford protection to all workers or all types of hazards. There were many gaps in coverage including a tendency of legislation to focus on safety problems rather than hazards to health (through chemicals, biological agents, dusts, etc.), and to be preoccupied with physical artefacts of the workplace (machines, etc.) rather than work processes and organisation.

■ The laws were reviewed only irregularly, often as the result of a particular incident, change of government or union/community campaign. This meant that the provisions became anachronistic or failed to keep up with changes at the workplace—a major problem as changes accelerated in the later postwar period.

■ The laws usually only set very minimal standards and even these standards were often not rigorously enforced by over-stretched and prosecution-shy inspectorates. Further, when prosecutions occurred, the penalties imposed by court were often low, both because the maximum penalties were set low and because courts tended to impose heavily discounted penalties even in the case of repeat/serious offenders.

■ Although workers bore the brunt of failure to meet minimum OHS standards they, or their representatives, had no direct say in setting these standards.

During the 1970s and 1980s the governments of a number of industrialised countries undertook a major overhaul of their OHS laws in response to union and community pressure and a growing recognition of limitations with existing laws. In the US for example, a coal mine disaster in West Virginia was the catalyst for the introduction of federal mine safety legislation in 1969 and a more general OHS law (the Occupational Safety and Health Act or OSH Act) was enacted in the following year. The Scandinavian countries of Norway, Sweden and Denmark all introduced comprehensive work environment legislation in the 1970s. Both the US developments and those in Scandinavia had some influence in Australia over the next decade or so. The US OSH Act created a national OHS research institute (NIOSH) which served as a partial model for a similar body (part of NOHSC) established by federal OHS legislation in 1984. The strong powers granted to employee health and safety representatives under Scandinavian work environment laws (especially the right to order a halt to work processes they believed posed an imminent threat to health) influenced revised OHS laws in a number of Australian states (notably Victoria and South Australia).

There was strong local pressure to reform OHS legislation in Australia and New Zealand and the overhaul of state and territory laws, which mostly concluded between 1973 and 1989, as well as the introduction of Australian federal OHS legislation in 1984 and New Zealand OHS law in 1992, cannot be seen simply as an effort to mimic overseas developments. In some instances, legislators drew on features in local legislation, such as the safety officer role provided for under the Queensland Construction Safety Act. In other cases, they experimented with new structures largely without reference to overseas experience, such as the development of tripartite industry committees in Queensland (a version of which was introduced into NSW in 1998). Nevertheless, when it came to deciding the form legislative reforms should take, overseas models did play a critical part, especially that developed by the Robens Inquiry. The inquiry chaired by Lord Robens was set up in 1970 to investigate why OHS did not appear to be markedly improving in Britain and reported two years later. The model it proposed not only formed the basis for the British Health and Safety at Work Act (1974) but also shaped laws in Australia (in states where independent inquiries were held the recommendations largely endorsed the Robens model) and a number of other countries. Indeed, key Robens principles became the foundation for ILO Convention No. 155 'Concerning Occupational Safety and Health and the Working Environment' of 1981. Because of its profound influence it is worth briefly examining Robens' major findings and recommendations.

Robens argued that the complex array of paternalistic and punitive laws had failed to minimise injuries and had exerted a narcotic effect on employer activity. To rectify this, Robens' recommendations had two principal objectives. First, a more unified and integrated system of legislation and administration was to be created, that is, the multiplicity of Acts was to be replaced by a single Act, setting broad procedures and standards, and with a single administering agency and inspectorate. Second, a more effectively self-regulating system was to be created where employers and workers were jointly involved in the formulation and implementation of health and safety policy at the workplace (Johnstone, 2004). Robens proposed a number of mechanisms for achieving this including the bipartite negotiation of codes of practice at industry and workplace level.

The key mechanisms for achieving this was replacing much of the maze of existing regulation with a single overarching law, an enabling Act that established broad standards, decision-making structures and procedures rather than directly specifying the detailed standards that might apply to particular workplace, machine or work process. The new law would contain new general duty provisions that imposed broad principle-based standards on employers, designers, manufacturers, workers and other parties. These were articulated to a more systematic set of specification standards, performance standards or compliance guides expressed either in terms of codes or regulations made under the legislation. Significant avenues for employer and union/worker involvement also underpinned the approach, notably tripartite standard-setting bodies, bipartite workplace committees and employee health and safety representatives. At the same time, Robens urged a number of changes to enforcement including increased inspectoral powers and new sanctions (most notably, improvement and prohibition notices).

The Robens approach and the legislation it gave rise to had a number of clear advantages over earlier laws, namely:

- rationalisation of laws, regulatory standards and inspectoral agencies
- giving employers and unions/workers the right to participate in standard setting at national/state, industry and workplace level
- providing for a regular review process of OHS standards
- giving employees or their representatives the right to information as well as monitoring and enforcement functions
- the introduction of new enforcement mechanisms of issuing improvement and pro-hibition notices. These had the advantage of immediately addressing a risk (unlike a lengthy prosecution) and placing the burden of compliance on the employer.

Notwithstanding these strengths, the Robens report contained a number of questionable or ambiguous arguments that weakened its overall analysis of the problem of regulating OHS. Two of these deserve particular mention.

The first concerns the overlapping arguments that there was too much law, the punitive approach to enforcement had failed and detailed regulation had narcotic effect on employers and workers, encouraging complete dependence. The contention about too much law is only valid as far as the complexity and fragmentation of earlier laws was concerned. These laws still left significant gaps in coverage and from this perspective it could be argued there was actually too little law (Brooks, 1988). Further, both Brooks (1988) and Carson (1979, 1980) make the important point that, far from having failed, punitive enforcement had never been really tried. This undermines the narcotic effect argument of Robens. The reasons for management and workers not taking a more proactive role were far more complex than simply the style of legislation. Further, the relationship between punitive regulation by the state and self-regulation was far more complex than Robens presumed (Dawson et al., 1988).

A second set of arguments by Robens requiring scrutiny was that there was a greater natural identity of interests between workers and employers in relation to OHS than in other matters and there was no legitimate scope for bargaining over OHS (Johnstone, 2004). Robens contended primary responsibility for prevention should reside with those most directly affected, namely employers and workers. Both arguments formed important planks for Robens's advocacy of a self-regulating system, but the first was incorrect and the second was too simplistic. While there are important opportunities for worker/manager collaboration over OHS, and these should be encouraged, to suggest there is a natural identity of interest and bargaining can be excluded flew in the face of 150 years of history as well as a considered interpretation of the present situation. Evidence attesting to this was presented in earlier chapters and further evidence will be presented later in this chapter, along with chapter 9. Robens's point about placing primary responsibility for OHS with employers and workers recognises their immediate interest in the matter and the important normative judgments that are invariably involved in deciding acceptable risk levels. However, interest does not equate to power. The relationship between employers and workers is essentially an unequal one, and the power imbalance is at best partially offset where workers belong to a union. Hence, the state must provide infrastructure to ensure joint decision-making is meaningful (such as the powers and logistical support given to health and safety representatives). It must also provide other avenues where participatory mechanisms are weak or impractical (such as small businesses). It appears that Robens was only partly aware of this.

The Robens notion of a self-regulating system was framed at a time when the union movement and collective regulation of employment standards was stronger in countries like Britain and Australia than is the case today. While denying a role for bargaining over OHS, the Robens model presumed this context because unions provided critical logistical support for the participatory structures and processes envisaged. In the Scandinavian countries, there was stronger regulatory support for participatory mechanisms and greater recognition of the critical role of unions. Further, changes to union density were less pronounced, making the effects of this on the infrastructural support unions provide less of an issue. The US represents the other extreme. In that country union density was already low in the 1970s (and has declined further) and, unlike all the countries just mentioned, OHS law reforms of 1969–70 contained no significant mechanisms for worker or union involvement (even though unions played a critical role in securing this legislation).

The relevance of these limitations in Robens' understanding of OHS regulation will be made clear in later sections of this chapter. At this point it is important to identify the main features of the post-Robens OHS legislation adopted in Australia.

Main features of principal OHS laws

In broad terms, Australia and New Zealand both adopted Robens-model legislation, though more belatedly in the case of New Zealand. Between 1973 and 1989 federal, state and territory governments in Australia all enacted laws based on the Robens model but with a variety of local and other international influences. Several jurisdictions, such as Victoria and South Australia, made significant amendments to their laws during the 1980s while in other jurisdictions, such as Queensland, important changes were made after 1989. Following two major reviews in the late 1990s, NSW introduced a revised OHS Act in 2000 (and a risk assessment regulation in 2001). Following some political pressure (including employers unhappy with the general duty provisions) two further reviews were undertaken but as at March 2009 the government had not revised legislation. A number of other states undertook reviews of their OHS legislation after 2000 (notably Victoria, Western Australia, Tasmania, the Northern Territory and ACT). While not altering the overall structure of the legislation, these reviews led to changes to general duty provisions, risk assessment requirements, participatory mechanisms, penalties and enforcement procedures.

At the federal level, OHS legislation introduced by the then Labor government in the 1980s did not (as in the US) establish an overarching regulatory framework with which states and territories had to comply. Rather, aside from directly covering Commonwealth employees (including the armed forces and ex-government business enterprises like Telstra), federal legislation was limited to creating a tripartite national standards coordination and research agency—the National Occupational Health and Safety Commission (NOHSC). After its election 1996, a neo-liberal federal government cut NOHSC's budget, effectively eliminating its research functions before later cutting back on its standards development activity (Quinlan, 2000). In 2005 NOHSC was abolished altogether and replaced with a new federal body—the Australian Safety and Compensation Council or ASCC—which, while nominally still tripartite, was under closer ministerial control and was responsible for both prevention and workers' compensation. This body pursued rather narrower and cost-focused objectives. The federal government also made changes to federal OHS and compensation laws that enabled some national private-sector employers to move to the federal system (for an examination of federal legislative changes during the 1996–2007 period see Quinlan and Johnstone, 2009). Although ostensibly a response to employer calls for greater uniformity in OHS legislation, these measures actually resulted in a more fractured system of state and federal OHS laws.

Nonetheless, the bipartisan objective of a more consistent regulatory environment with regard to economic activity has created ongoing policy momentum for national uniformity in OHS legislation. Unlike in Canada, all jurisdictions in Australia drew on a similar regulatory heritage and the structure of the post-Robens laws were broadly similar. At the same time, there were many differences in legislation and associated regulations/codes of practice. These ranged from different plant and equipment certification requirements (with regard to cranes and forklift trucks, for example) through to differences in general duties and participatory mechanisms. For example, only Queensland included risk assessment requirements in its general duty provisions (in other jurisdictions this is contained in regulations) and required health and safety officers to be appointed in workplaces with more than 30 employees. Several jurisdictions reversed the onus of proof in terms of parties meeting their obligations under general duty provisions. Similarly, only in NSW were unions empowered to take a prosecution. In recent years the Council of Australian Government (representing the ministers of federal, state and territory governments) has become more active in promoting uniformity (New Zealand has also been involved in these ministerial processes as part of the Closer Economic Relations or CER agreement). In 2008 a federal Labor government (elected in November 2007) announced the establishment of a National Review into Model OHS Laws with a view to recommending a legislative template that would be adopted in all jurisdictions. After considering numerous submissions addressing a range of issues (including legislative objectives, the nature of general duty provisions, risk assessment and participatory mechanisms/union involvement) the review team issued two reports (2008, 2009).

While Australia and Britain were implementing Robens-type models during the 1970s and 1980s, New Zealand directed its attention to a comprehensive 'no-fault' system of compensation of occupational injury and disease. As a consequence,

New Zealand failed to address the issue of its scattered and often ineffectual OHS legislation and it was not until 1988 that the Labour Government established the tripartite Advisory Council for Occupational Safety and Health (ACOSH), chaired by the then Minister of Labour, the Hon. Stan Rodger. ACOSH committee issued a report, Occupational Safety and Health Reform: A Public Discussion Paper (1988), which proposed radical changes to the original structures. Similar to the British Robens report, it recommended the replacement of those structures by one Act, implemented and administered by a single authority, namely the OSH Service of the Department of Labour. The report also stated that workers should participate in the decisions affecting their safety and health. The sentiments of 'one Act, one authority' were strongly endorsed by the New Zealand Employers Federation (NZEF) and supported by the bulk of public submissions on the ACOSH report. Although the New Zealand Council of Trade Unions (NZCTU) supported the principle of 'one Act, one authority', they were also adamant that worker participation be included in the Labour Government's Occupational Health and Safety Bill, 1990. The report and the subsequent Bill signalled a radical departure from the traditional prescriptive legislation and enforcement to a more unfettered approach to the employment relationship between the state and business. Indeed, the 1980s policy debates surrounding the OHS reforms have subsequently been seen as a *prelude* to the policy shifts associated with other pieces of employment-related legislation (e.g. Employment Contracts Act, 1991, Industry Training Act, 1992, Human Rights Act, 1993 and Privacy Act, 1993). As a result in part of CER and in part because of their shared history, New Zealand OHS legislation shares a number of similarities with Australian state legislation but until recently had not included any formalised worker representation in the Act.

Notwithstanding differences addressed by Australian national uniformity OHS laws, Australia and New Zealand share a number of important features, notably:

■ A principal OHS Act covers almost all workers and all types of hazards and is administered by a single department and inspectorate. In New Zealand, workers in all industries are now covered by the Health and Safety in Employment Amendment Act, 2003. In Australia a number of areas were either entirely exempted from OHS legislation or subject to dual/overlapping regulatory regimes, namely transport, mining and oil and gas exploration/production (including offshore facilities). Safety in road transport is subject to both transport and OHS legislation (with coordination of enforcement achieved via interagency protocols and agreements as well as the National Transport Commission). Maritime and air transport are the subject of separate legislation although federal OHS legislation also has coverage over airline workers. As in Britain, offshore oil and gas production is subject to specific legislation and an independent regulatory authority. In the case of mining the situation is complex. In Tasmania mining was (as in New Zealand) incorporated within OHS legislation (although the implications of this in terms of inspectorate resourcing and regulations were criticised by the findings of the coronial inquest into the April 2006 rockfall at the Beaconsfield goldmine; Chandler, 2009). In jurisdictions such as Queensland and Western Australia mining remains the subject of independent separate legislation whereas in NSW mining legislation has been retained (as well as a separate inspectorate) but sits below the overarching duties established in that state's OHS Act. Even in jurisdictions where separate mining safety laws have been retained, moves have been made to make these laws more compatible with the Robens model (for example, by incorporating general duty provisions) and recent developments in OHS regulation (notably an emphasis on risk assessment and management systems). Efforts to secure greater national uniformity in mining legislation preceded the national review into model OHS laws. For a number of reasons (including the Beaconsfield findings, as well as stronger worker involvement and risk assessment provisions in some jurisdictions) it seems unlikely that mining will be incorporated into OHS legislation in the foreseeable future.

- OHS laws incorporate general duty provisions specifying the responsibilities of employers, contractors, suppliers, designers, manufacturers, occupiers and workers in relation to OHS. These provisions set a general set of principles in relation to the behaviour of the parties. For example, a primary duty for employers is to maintain a healthy and safe working environment, including safe plant/equipment, safe handling of hazardous substances, properly inducted/trained and supervised workers and a safe system of work. Unlike earlier laws which overwhelmingly specified the precise measures to be taken by employers (such as the installation of guarding in particular machinery)—specification standards—the general duty provisions established broad performance standards. Performance standards are framed so as to reflect the degree of control that various parties such as employers, principal contractors, subcontractors and workers exercise in relation to the workplace and their responsibility in relation to a particular hazard. Appropriately, those with greater or more direct control or responsibility in relation to the control of hazards carry a heavier burden of responsibility. The inclusion of duties on what may be termed upstream duty holders, such as the designers, manufacturers and importers/suppliers, was a critical shift beyond the narrow focus of earlier legislation and a recognition of the complex origin of some hazards, such as plant or equipment with serious design flaws, poorly engineered work settings or equipment supplied (or expert advice) without due concern for its safety or appropriateness. After some lag there is now a growing level of attention being devoted to design issues and upstream duty holders by both regulatory/standard-setting agencies and inspectors in the field (see below). This is a significant shift although it represents modest progress towards addressing a very large gap.

- The general duty provisions (and associated regulations) also contained procedural requirements—process standards—including requirements to undertake risk assessment (say, with regard to manual handling) and to consult with workers and their representatives. Regulations and codes of practice have been introduced to provide guidance on how these performance and process standards can be met. In sum, post-Robens legislation marked a shift to performance and process standards—a shift reinforced by subsequent changes in regulation and enforcement strategy (including the increased emphasis on management systems and risk management).

At the same time, while specification standards were rationalised they were by no means abandoned. Rather, specification standards governing exposure to asbestos, lead or noise and a range of other areas have been retained within subordinate legislation (or regulations) attached to the principal OHS Act or within associated legislation (such as mining legislation). Indeed, while performance and process standards were seen as more comprehensive, flexible and proactive, specification standards were still being developed where this was seen as the most effective remedy to a particular hazard. The result is that in many if not most industries there is mix of specification, process and performance standards. This complexity does not diminish the significance of the shift in OHS legislation that has flowed from the introduction of general duty provisions.

- The new OHS Acts incorporated new remedies or enforcement tools, notably prohibition and improvement notices as well as significantly increased financial penalties for breaches of the key duties by individuals as well as corporations. There was also provision for jailing offenders in some states (such as Victoria and Queensland), provisions yet to be used. As the name implies, improvement notices require a matter to be rectified within a specified time frame while prohibition notices ban the use of a particular item of plant or work process deemed an imminent and serious risk to health or safety until the latter is addressed. The movement to the issuing of notices was seen as part of developing a more proactive approach to enforcing OHS legislation. Improvement and prohibition notices need to be seen in the context of other remedies at inspectors' disposal. In some jurisdiction inspectors are also able to issue verbal directions if a matter can be rectified while they are on site. Since the 1980s a number of other remedies have been added to the inspectorate's armoury in most jurisdictions, notably infringement notices (on-the-spot fines) and enforceable undertakings. Enforceable undertakings empower the inspectorate to accept a written undertaking about remedial measures for a detected contravention of the OHS Act, rather than proceeding with the prosecution. If the undertaking is breached, a court may make appropriate orders (Johnstone and Quinlan, 2008). As noted below, inspectorates have also made use of a number of other innovative enforcement options, including adverse publicity orders.

- The reformed OHS legislation also incorporated Robens's recommended mechanisms for ensuring employers and workers had a more direct say in deciding OHS standards and also ensuring the regular review of these standards. These included the establishment of tripartite councils/commissions to review and advise on OHS standards in each state and the federal jurisdiction. New Zealand has periodically established advisory bodies, most notably the tripartite Workplace Health and Safety Council established in 2006 and the National Occupational Health and Safety Advisory Committee (NOHSAC). As in Australia the existence of these bodies, however, is at the whim of the prevailing government. In the 1990s the election of conservative state governments ideologically opposed to tripartism resulted in the abolition of these bodies in Victoria and South Australia. In NSW the body was abolished and then reactivated. In Queensland, 12 tripartite industry committees (the number has since been cut to eight) were also established to develop OHS policies at an industry level and in 1998 NSW adopted a similar model (called industry reference groups). Another participatory mechanism has been the provision for the establishment of joint employer/employee OHS committees at the workplace (there is a minimum size requirement). Finally, in all jurisdictions except New South Wales and the Northern Territory the principal OHS legislation provided for the election of employee health and safety representatives (representatives are proposed by the 1998 review and are under consideration). Unlike joint workplace committees, whose role was to address OHS problems and seek improvements, health and safety representatives had the role of safeguarding the health of employees and ensuring legislative standards were being met. The rights and powers of representatives vary considerably from the relatively minimal powers given in Queensland to the right to call a stop to dangerous work processes in the Commonwealth jurisdiction, Victoria and South Australia.

Beyond these broad generalisations it is important to identify and briefly discuss the main provisions of the legislation (for a more detailed examination, see Johnstone, 2004).

Objects, coverage and general duties

Unlike earlier laws, the post-Robens Acts contain a clear statement of their objectives in terms of safeguarding workers and adopt a wide definition of key terms such as occupational health and safety, workplace and workers. The Acts also extend their coverage to include persons other than employees who may enter an employer's workplace, including volunteers, customers/clients and subcontractors.

All the OHS Acts contain a set of general duty provisions for an array of identified parties. Although broadly similar, variations in wording of the provisions among the jurisdictions can affect court proceedings and have impeded the push for national uniformity. One distinction affecting legal proceedings is to be found in the NSW and Queensland Acts in relation to the burden of proof concerning the practicality of measures to comply with the general duties. As in the UK, but unlike in other Australian jurisdictions, the Queensland and NSW Acts place the burden of proof with the defendant rather than the prosecution (Johnstone, 1997). In other words, it would be incumbent on an employer being prosecuted to show that control measures were impractical not for the prosecuting OHS agency to demonstrate that practical controls were available to the employer.

Notwithstanding some variations, the duty provisions of all jurisdictions specify a range of responsibilities on employers and employees plus a number of other parties. The latter include building occupiers, designers, manufacturers, suppliers, installers and subcontractors (see, for example, s15–18 of NSW Occupational Health and Safety Act and s21–25 of the Victorian Occupational Health and Safety Act). In other words, those who design, produce, introduce or market equipment, substances and work processes should recognise and act on an obligation that these machines, processes, etc.

do not harm the health of workers. The inclusion of specified duties in relation to manufacturers, suppliers and importers may be seen as a potentially important effort to address the extended and complex chains of responsibility for occupational hazards. As yet there have been relatively few prosecutions of designers and others more remotely connected to hazardous incidents, although a number of OHS agencies are becoming more active in this area. In Victoria there have been a series of cases of equipment hire firms being prosecuted after incidents where the equipment proved faulty or insufficient care was taken to ensure those operating it had appropriate knowledge or qualifications (see Director of Public Prosecutions v Ancon Travel Towers Pty Ltd, 1998; *Department of Labour v. Waste Management N.Z. Ltd*, 1995).

The duties for each category are structured to recognise their differing degrees of control over the workplace and are therefore most extensive in relation to employers, manufacturers and others introducing equipment, substances or new work processes. Thus, for example, s21 of the Victorian OHS Act, 1985 requires employers to maintain a safe system of work and a safe workplace, protect workers against hazardous substances and provide adequate information, training and supervision. Correspondingly, employees' duties are confined to obeying lawful instructions and not acting in a fashion that would endanger themselves or others at the workplace.

In terms of structuring responsibilities, a number of Acts give some recognition to the problems posed by contractors or multi-employer workplaces. Indeed, a number of Acts (such as the Victorian Occupational Health and Safety Act) expressly refer to the duty owed by employers to independent contractors. The Victorian Act also includes a provision that employees of an independent contractor are deemed employees of the host employer. In Queensland the problems posed by contractors has been partially addressed via special duties applying to designated projects. Under the New Zealand Health and Safety in Employment Act, 1992, both the principal contractor and the subcontractor have duties of care (see s18). Responsibility for subcontractors can also be derived from other employer/self-employed person's duties, most notably the need to maintain a safe system of work and to safeguard those other than employees on their premises. In combination, these duties establish a clear responsibility of the host employer or major contractor for both those they directly engage as employees and others engaged indirectly via a subcontracting arrangement. In recent years more use has been made of these provisions as OHS agencies have responded to serious incidents associated with the increased use of outsourcing. Finally, it is arguable that where the duties of employers/self-employed persons are broadly drafted, as is the case in Queensland and Victoria, it may extend to other contingent work arrangements such as the relationship of franchiser to franchisee (Johnstone, 1999)

Putting the last two points together it can be seen that the interrelationship between the duties of different parties is not only hierarchic (as between employer and subcontractor or worker) but can also follow a sequential chain of responsibilities (i.e. from design to manufacture to supply to actual use). It is also important to note that the duties or the parties to them are not mutually exclusive when it comes to determining breaches and launching prosecutions. In other words, OHS agencies may charge a single party (say, an employer) with breaching a number of general duties or lay charges against a number of parties (say, an employer, two subcontractors and a worker) for breaches arising from the same incident or inspector's report.

The inclusion of the general duty provisions in revised OHS legislation has been seen to perform three functions:

1 to clearly establish the responsibilities of different parties in terms of the Act and to do so in a more structured and encompassing fashion than envisaged in pre-reform laws (i.e. coverage of manufacturers, etc.)

2 to provide a framework of designated responsibility that would remain viable even in the context of rapid changes to work processes and the hazards associated with them

3 by formally enunciating and extending common law duties, to have an educative role.

Despite some problems (see below) and criticism (for a discussion, see Johnstone, 2004), a balanced assessment of experience over the past 30 years is that the general duty provisions have performed these functions. Contrary to early concerns, the general duty provisions have not proved to be either too ambiguous or unenforceable. The shift, however, was neither unproblematic nor immediate. Rather, it entailed a gradual learning process on the part of inspectorates as well as employers and other duty holders—something the Industry Commission (1995) identified in the mid 1990s and which has been reinforced by more recent research (Johnstone and Quinlan, 2008). It should be recognised that the shift to general duties was consistent with (and indeed contributed to) other developments affecting OHS, including a growing interest in management systems and influence of risk management concepts. Parallel though by no means identical shifts can be found in other countries, including the introduction of systematic management/internal control in Scandinavian work environment legislation and the introduction of the process control standard in the US (even though the OHS legislation of that country remained largely wedded to specification standards).

It should be stressed that the introduction of duties imposing general performance standards (and process standards within regulations and codes of practice) did not result in the complete removal of specification standards. Rather, specification standards were revised/rationalised and incorporated into regulations or codes of practice. Again, this generally occurred over a number years with some avenues for consideration of where specification standards should be retained. Although regulations are normally associated with specification standards and codes of practice with process standards, a number of jurisdictions have adopted different practices in this regard and it is not uncommon for a generic or industry regulation or code to include both specification and process standards. On occasion Australian and New Zealand unions both expressed concerns that regulations had been removed injudiciously. In part reflecting concerns that the general duty provisions would prove ineffective there were nonetheless instances where the changeover resulted in serious omissions. A conspicuous example was the removal of all specification standards pertaining to the mining industry in Tasmania when (unlike most other states) this industry was incorporated under the Workplace Health and Safety Act, 1995. This decision, made without due assessment of its implications, was the subject of criticism by two coronial inquests into the death of miners in rockfalls (Chandler, 2009). While the precise balance and appropriate use in particular circumstances is open to ongoing debate, a mixture of standards represents not so much a failure to fully implement change as a recognition that no one type of standard best addresses all hazards. Specification standards can have a precision and simplicity that makes them ideally suited to certain types of hazards where the hazard is well known and a single clear method of addressing this can be stated. Performance and process standards are more flexible and can cover a wider array of related hazards, including organisational and behavioural aspects (such as risks associated with shiftwork or using contractors), with a set of identification, assessment and control procedures. They are also better suited to situations where hazards are less well understood and a complex array of factors means that no single remedy or limit is feasible or even desirable (as with manual handling). Gunningham (1996: 221–46) argued that while these instruments were conceptually distinct they could and should be used in combination (although he suggested less reliance should be placed on specification standards).

Tripartism and standard setting

The establishment of tripartite bodies to review and make recommendations on OHS standards was a central feature of the post-Robens legislative reforms. Establishing a tripartite body to review OHS standards and procedures in New Zealand is largely left to the Department of Labour to initiate, sometimes at the request of the Minister of Labour. In Australia, however, initially the principal OHS laws of all states made provision for the establishment of a major tripartite body to review OHS standards and procedures generally and to advise the minister of appropriate changes when these are considered necessary. This usually meant a mixture of representatives nominated by government, union and employer peak councils (and sometimes appointed experts). After 1992 the election of conservative governments hostile to tripartism led to the abolition of these bodies in several states (notably Victoria, South Australia and Tasmania). This approach was not adopted by conservative government in all states (e.g. Queensland and Western Australia), nor federally (although significant changes were made after 1996—see below), and even in those states affected tripartite bodies were generally re-established when Labor returned to office.

Tripartite bodies cannot mandate new standards or implement new procedures. Rather, they undertake a review and advisory role, assessing the effectiveness of existing standards; recommending changes to OHS standards, codes and the like; promoting OHS education and training; coordinating intra-government policies on OHS; and reviewing accreditation and licensing requirements. Initially there was some debate about the level of different categories of membership (notably of government representatives), appointment processes and the role of expert members (see Quinlan and Bohle, 1991: 210–11) but many of the concerns appear to have been allayed. Professional OHS associations such as the Safety Institute of Australia and the Ergonomics Society of Australia have made repeated calls for direct representation on these bodies, but without much success.

In addition to jurisdiction-wide standard-setting bodies in Australia, the principal OHS laws of most jurisdictions make provision for tripartite committees to tender specific advice on a particular area. Some of these committees (such as those advising on ethnic and gender-related aspects of OHS) may assume an ongoing role while others (such as those advising on a particular hazard or activity such as diving) are disbanded after completing their allotted task.

In Queensland the Workplace Health and Safety Act established ongoing tripartite committees at industry level (originally 12 but this number was then reduced). These committees have functions similar to the peak Workplace Health and Safety Council but their role is confined to a particular industry or related set of industries (such as retailing and hospitality). Industry committees meet bimonthly (though working groups they establish may meet more regularly) and may direct their recommendations either to the minister directly or to the Queensland Workplace Health and Safety Council. Representation on these committees is more heavily weighted towards employer and unions (whose nominees can include experts) with only one government representative. In 1998 NSW adopted a similar system of tripartite industry committees (called Industry Reference Groups) following recommendations by the Grellman inquiry into workers' compensation and a report on workplace safety by the Legislative Council Standing Committee on Law and Justice (1998).

Once established, industry committees have been allowed to develop their own priorities. The relevant OHS agency does provide a level of coordination (in Queensland the chairs of committees also meet on regular basis) and supporting infrastructure as well as resources to complete particular tasks (such as the provision of expertise or the publication of guidance material produced by the committee). Industry committees have engaged in a wide range of activities. These include developing specific industry codes or guidance notes on particular hazards (such as a guide to manual handling in retail establishments), conducting forums for small business or specific campaigns, reviewing statistics and compliance programs and linking vocational training to OHS. Other activities have included promoting OHS in remote areas and, as has recently occurred in NSW, getting key parties to sign memorandums of understanding on OHS. In Queensland, industry committees have facilitated a number of improvements in agency documents, most notably the production of materials that can be more readily used by small business. This has often entailed productive exchanges with inspectors. A good example is a machine-guarding guide for the manufacturing industry that was produced in Queensland in a short (20 pages) and non-glossy A4 format (so it could easily be torn apart, pinned to walls or faxed) with simple diagrams. Systems messages (such as the links between guarding and other OHS problems) were inserted in an unobtrusive manner and the guidance note was promoted in a new range of venues (including not just the internet but the second-hand machinery sale columns of newspapers).

Despite teething problems and the need to accept that some committees will prove less effective than others, the industry committee model has made a valuable contribution to OHS. Industry committees have a number of features that enable them to perform some tasks more effectively than wider-ranging tripartite bodies or single-issue/limited duration committees. In general, their representatives have a closer knowledge of what is occurring in the workplaces they cover and can devise practical and industry-specific solutions. Thus, for example, a construction industry committee can not only prioritise outsourcing but also devise a strategy that takes account of the particular forms of subcontracting found in the industry (a similar argument would apply to occupational violence in the hospitality industry). Unlike short duration committees, these industry committees are able to build a base of shared knowledge and collaboration over time although we are in no way suggesting that conflicts of interest will or even should evaporate. The industry committee structure also represents a means for improving standards across the entire jurisdiction. Finally, industry committees are well situated to get their products out into the field, to gain feedback from employers and to devise new ways of promoting products. Overall, the industry committee system can form an effective interim level between jurisdiction-wide standard-setting bodies and joint health and safety committees located at workplace or enterprise level. It is a pity more jurisdictions have not followed the Queensland and NSW example. At the same time, even in jurisdictions without this structure there is evidence of the benefits of industry-level collaboration in terms of the development of industry codes of practice (see, for example, the forestry code developed in Tasmania).

Workplace health and safety officers

One feature of the Queensland regulatory system that had not been adopted elsewhere (except in a non-mandatory basis under the 2000 NSW OHS Act) but is worthy of mention is the position of the workplace health and safety officer (WHSO). Under the Queensland Workplace Health and Safety Act all workplaces with 30 or more employees are required to appoint a WHSO. This is not a form of employee participation but a managerial position (modelled on provisions in an earlier Queensland law, the Construction Safety Act). The WHSO does not assume the legal responsibilities of the employer and is subject to the supervision of the employer or principal contractor (unless, of course the employer/principal contractor takes on the role of WHSO). Importantly, the Act prescribes a set minimum of qualifications to be held by WHSOs (including a sound knowledge of the legislation, relevant codes and regulation, OHS practices and investigation procedures). To ensure this, the Act requires that WHSOs undergo a specified two-stage training/accreditation process (stage one is general and stage two industry specific) with an approved provider.

The functions of the WHSO identified in the Queensland Act include advising the employer; conducting inspections and education programmes; investigating injuries, illnesses and dangerous occurrences; assisting inspectors; and assisting with workplace

OHS committees. The WHSO is not empowered to order a halt to the work process where they believe there is an imminent danger to workers' health. Rather they are required to report such matters to the employer.

Under the Queensland Workplace Health and Safety Act the employer is required to:

- give the WHSO access to all information they possess on actual or potential hazards or the OHS of employees
- allow the WHSO to be present at any interview concerning OHS between the employer and an employee (after approval of the employee has been obtained)
- consult the WHSO on all changes to the workplace, plant or substances likely to affect OHS
- provide such facilities as the WHSO requires to carry out their tasks
- permit the WHSO to seek appropriate advice on OHS matters.

The Act does not and, given the variations in workplace size, could not specify whether the WHSO is to be full time or part time. Where a group of firms is too small to appoint a specialist officer they may appoint an existing employee or manager as WHSO. There appears to be no barrier to an employer engaging a consultant in this capacity or a number of firms may engage a single person to service their needs. A firm with many workplaces may engage either single or multiple WHSOs so long as they can demonstrate that the arrangement will enable regular site visits. Nor is there anything to stop the employer from designating themself as the WHSO.

Although the WHSO model has not been adopted elsewhere (except on a non-mandatory basis in NSW) it has yielded a number of benefits that make it worthy of consideration in other jurisdictions. First, designating such a position has encouraged more organisations to appoint a person or persons (depending on the number of workplaces) with some professional understanding of OHS. Second, the legislative requirements for formal training (offered by a range of providers, including employer organisations, Safe Work Queensland and tertiary education institutions) strengthened the link between education and prevention. Several universities have included training modules within degree programs thereby ensuring an increasing supply of better informed and qualified OHS managers. These benefits could be enhanced if accreditation requirements were progressively lifted over time. Third, even where employers are too small to require a WHSO, as in the case of many builders, it has been found that a number still undertook WHSO training. Thus, the measure has reached into small business where many other regulatory measures have failed to gain access. In its report on OHS, the Industry Commission (1995) argued that the measure had proved to be effective and worth emulating in other jurisdictions. Fourth and finally, in practice it has been found that WHSOs work closely with employee health and safety representatives on workplace OHS committees (to which both are required members) and in everyday problem solving. While there was some initial fear that their role would be conflated with that of the representatives, this has largely been avoided. Overall, the WHSO provisions appear to have encouraged a more coordinated approach to OHS at workplace level.

Avenues of worker involvement at workplace level

Involving workers in OHS was a key principle in the Robens report. Post-Robens legislation included mechanisms to promote worker (or more generally employee) involvement at workplace level. The two most critical mechanisms were workplace health and safety committees and employee health and safety representatives. In some jurisdictions a more generic requirement that employees be consulted in certain circumstances can be found under regulations. For example, in Tasmania, Regulation 15 of the Workplace Health and Safety Regulations, 1998 requires consultation with employee safety representatives, committees and employees regarding identification of hazards, risk assessment and control provisions or if 'a proposed change in the workplace is likely to have a significant detrimental effect on the health, safety or welfare of any person'. In other words, the obligation to consult is not restricted to situations where a committee or health and safety representative (HSR) is present. It should also be noted that a number of OHS statutes in Australia empower union officials to enter workplaces for OHS purposes and that NSW also enables unions to initiate a prosecution for breaches of the legislation. We will return to the question of residual consultation requirements and the role of unions later in this chapter (while the role of unions is considered in some detail in chapter 9). At this point attention will focus on committees and HSRs, which remain the key participatory mechanisms within the legislation.

Joint workplace health and safety committees

The principal OHS Acts of all Australian jurisdictions and latterly the New Zealand Health and Safety in Employment Amendment Act, 2002, have sought to promote collaborative decision making through provisions for the establishment of joint employer/employee health and safety committees. In most cases (with the partial exception of NSW) these provisions contain few specific requirements with regard to the structure and functioning of these committees. Rather, they identify procedures for their establishment, a general array of functions and set some limits on composition and meeting times (Queensland and NSW legislation requires committees to meet at least once every three months). With regard to establishment, the laws of all jurisdictions anticipate that in most circumstances committees will be established after a vote by employees, or following a request by the health and safety representative. Most jurisdictions set a minimum workplace size, for example 20 employees, for these procedures. Typical functions include collaboration with management to maintain safe systems of work, including education, investigation of injuries/illnesses, formulation of procedures, etc. (in appropriate languages); maintaining records; and resolving OHS issues (Queensland Workplace Health and Safety Act, 1995). In terms of committee composition there are few requirements although almost jurisdictions require that at least half the membership be employees. This is designed to prevent committees being 'stacked' with managers although it does not prevent more subtle forms of manipulation on the part of employers.

Overall, the laws provide scope for committees to take on a wide range of structures and activities. This appears to be based on two considerations. First, and most obviously, broadly framed provisions recognise the wide diversity of employment situations (in terms of size and nature, e.g. steelworks or small warehouse) and enable employers and employees to develop structures appropriate to their specific needs. Second, it also reflects the greater prominence most principal Acts accord to the role of employee health and safety representatives (generally abbreviated to the acronym HSR although in Tasmania they are referred to as employee safety representatives and the acronym is ESR) in terms of monitoring and enforcement. In short, the splintering of functions between committees and HSR representatives was seen as critical. Committees were concerned with devising new OHS standards and procedures at workplace level (a problem-solving function) whereas the prime role of HSRs was to safeguard employee interests and ensure regulatory requirements were met (a monitoring and enforcement function). In practice, representatives are usually involved in committees and, indeed, their membership is mandated in some jurisdictions. However, the distinction was designed to afford a formal protection from the conflict of interests that might arise if an HSR was asked to overlook a regulatory breach in return for an improvement in another area of the workplace.

The workplace committee provisions in OHS legislation have had a significant effect on the extent of formal processes for worker consultation in Australia. The first Australian Workplace Industrial Relations Survey in 1990 found 41% of Australian workplaces with 20 or more employees had a joint OHS committee and five years later the figure had risen to 43% (Morehead et al., 1997). The presence of committees probably promoted other changes such as the development of formal OHS policies, the maintenance of injury records and the facilitation of the role of OHS managers (Morehead et al., 1997; Pragnell, 1995: 9). Nonetheless, the impact of committee requirements should not be overstated. The presence of committees and their role depends on a number of contextual factors, including the overlapping impact of HSRs in most jurisdictions (see below). Committees are open to manipulation, including the promotion of acquiescent members, inadequate training of members, restricted budgets, circumscribed agendas and delays/limits on implementation of committee decisions (Wyatt, 1987, Hovden, 2008; Trägårdh, 2008). Pragnell's study (1995: 8) noted that 92% of all workplaces with committees in NSW reported that the committee was management-dominated. These problems (including whether committees exist) appear to be worst where there are no unions present, their presence or input is contested or the relevant union has not taken sufficient interest in OHS (Pragnell, 1995: 9–10). These findings are also consistent with a more recent survey (Holland et al., 2009) that found that joint consultation committees were more likely to operate where unions were present and management had a positive attitude to unions. Weak regulatory provisions and the more hostile industrial relations climate that has emerged since the 1980s have reduced the presence and activities of workplace OHS committees, even in high-risk industries such as construction and mining. For example, prior to the 2006 rockfall (after which the inspectorate—Workplace Standards Tasmania—directed that a committee be established) the Beaconsfield goldmine only had one short-lived OHS committee (called the Zero Committee) in its decade of operations. There was even some dispute as to whether the Zero Committee constituted a workplace OHS committee under Tasmanian OHS legislation.

The positive role joint workplace committees can play is reinforced by international evidence. For example, writing on the US, Weil (1999) argued that committees can improve OHS outcomes by prevention education and training, by providing a forum for identifying and resolving problems and by enhancing enforcement. It is noteworthy that while regulators in the US have largely eschewed a participatory approach to OHS, joint workplace committees are a partial exception to this. They are encouraged in a number of states (in Pennsylvania, for example, the Workers' Compensation Act provides an incentive discount for employers with a certified committee) and are even mandated in some, such as Oregon (under that state's Workers Compensation Reform Act, 1990). A study of the Canadian province of Ontario (Lewchuk and Robertson, 1996) found the introduction of mandated joint health and safety committees helped to reduce the number of lost-time injuries in a range of industries (by up to 18%). A notable exception was retailing, where committees were not mandated and no improvement occurred in the period studied. A number of British studies (Reilly et al., 1995; Walters, 2006) point to the positive effects of workplace committees, especially where unions are involved. Looking at the issue from another perspective, poor communication and worker involvement has been identified as a contributory factor to a number of major hazard incidents in Australia, New Zealand and other countries (see chapter 10). Evidence on the value of worker involvement is considered in more detail in chapter 9.

In concluding this section about the legislation governing workplace OHS committees several final observations need to be made. First, these provisions marked an important departure from pre-Robens legislation and had positive effects although the extent of these effects has been inhibited by limitations within the legislative and external changes. Second, the provisions on committees should have been augmented with provisions requiring consultation where a committee was not present (mainly but not exclusively in small workplaces). This gap has not been addressed in either Australia or New Zealand. Third, committee provisions have not been modified to address the challenges posed by profound changes to work organisation, including the growth of smaller workplaces and the increased use of contingent workers (self-employed subcontractors, temporary workers and home-based/remote workers). Fourth, as Walters's study of the UK ably demonstrates (2006), the regulatory climate that has prevailed in countries under the sway of neo-liberalism (including Australia and New Zealand) has eschewed new regulation promoting the effectiveness of workplace committees and other forms of worker involvement in favour of promoting voluntary approaches. This approach has, if anything, accelerated the erosion of genuine worker involvement. The third and fourth points just raised will be examined in more detail later in this chapter.

Employee health and safety representatives (HSRs)

One of the most critical innovations in OHS laws was the empowering of employees to take on a monitoring and enforcement role—a task earlier laws (apart from those relating to coal mining) left entirely in the hands of state-appointed inspectors. All jurisdictions make provision for the appointment of employee health and safety representatives (HSRs) to carry out this function It is worth noting that other laws, notably those relating to seafarers and coal miners also provide for the appointment of HSRs (although usually under another title, such as check inspector in the case of miners). Indeed, under NSW and Queensland coal mining legislation these representatives have wider-ranging powers than is the case with the principal OHS laws (and a similar gap exists in relation to rights of ordinary workers to information and to make complaints).

There are considerable variations between jurisdictions in terms of selection, functions and rights of HSRs and their removal from office. Several debates about the functions of and powers granted to HSRs are worth addressing because they raise important issues about how OHS laws establish a climate for genuine worker input.

First, in terms of the appointment process the principal OHS laws of all jurisdictions make it clear that this decision rests with employees, with the normal appointment mechanism being via an election conducted among employees at the workplace or designated work group. In Victoria unions were initially given a direct role in the appointment process but this was removed by a conservative government in 1993. The role of unions in the appointment of HSRs was controversial because during some parliamentary debates of the 1980s a number of politicians painted it and the appointment of HSRs more generally as a route to establishing mini 'soviets' in the workplace whereby industrial relations warfare would compromise OHS—claims that now look laughable given the experience of the past 20 years. It is worth noting that in Britain HSRs are appointed by recognised unions.

Arguments about union involvement are worth presenting because they highlight more general issues about the role of HSRs. On the one hand, employers and others opposed to a union role argued that it was more democratic for all employees to be involved in the election rather than only union members, that not all workplaces are unionised and that multi-union workplaces could present difficulties. On the other hand, unions and others argued that unions were the accepted representatives of employees and attempts to bypass them could lead to management manipulation or tokenism. It was also argued that unions were the only bodies that could provide crucial resources and logistical support for HSRs to carry out their tasks, and arrangements could be made for both non-union and multiple-union workplaces. At one level, debates over the formal rights of non-union members misrepresent reality. In practice, workers in non-union workplaces seldom appoint HSRs and even when they do these representatives often face major difficulties carrying out their role (Walters, 1996). Studies in Britain (James, 1992; Walters and Nichols, 2007) and Australia (Biggins et al., 1988, 1989, 1991) have indicated that strong union organisation at the workplace was a major factor underpinning effectiveness of health and safety representatives. This supports the argument that unions provide the logistical support to make this form of worker involvement meaningful, including training, information provision and protection from victimisation. There is also Australian and international evidence that OHS training of HSRs (or their equivalents) is more effective when provided by unions than other bodies, such as private educators/consultants (Culvenor et al., 1996; Kurtz et al., 1997). In chapter 9 the union role in OHS is explored in more detail (see also Quinlan and Johnstone, 2009).

Second, the scope of the functions that health and safety representatives are able to undertake also varies considerably under the OHS laws of different jurisdictions. Some (such as South Australia, Western Australia, Victoria and New Zealand) give HSRs wide-ranging powers compared to others jurisdictions, such as Queensland, NSW, and Tasmania. Research (see, for example, Biggins and Phillips 1991a & b; Culvenor et al., 1996) indicates that the scope of HSR powers and the training they receive to undertake these tasks have a critical bearing on their effectiveness. Critical to the HSR fulfilling their role effectively is the right to information about workplace changes that may affect OHS and the right to make inspections, investigate complaints, make representations to the employer, hold discussions with employees and draw on outside assistance. By far the most controversial power granted to HSR in some jurisdictions (fewer than half) was the right to issue provisional improvement notices (PIN) or order a cessation of work in circumstances of imminent risk. This power in Australia may only be exercised under specific conditions and according to a prescribed set of procedures, although the procedure is less restrictive in New Zealand. The power to halt work in situations of imminent risk was one aspect of revised OHS legislation in Australia and New Zealand that drew more on Scandinavian work environment laws (where it had operated for some time) rather than Robens, although there were local precedents for this power in the mining laws of NSW and Queensland and federal maritime legislation.

Providing HSRs with the power to issue notices entailed recognition that, contrary to Robens's arguments about mutuality, the representative's role as an independent safeguard of workers' interests could involve instances of conflict with employers as well as consensual interactions. In essence, the legislation contained dispute-settling procedures, with the HSR having a remedy to deal with serious situations where attempts at an agreed solution failed. The Western Australian legislation did not grant this power to HSRs but did provide a means whereby a cessation of work could occur if the matter could not be resolved after reference to the workplace OHS committee. Granting representatives a right to order improvements to work processes or a cessation of work was initially controversial, drawing considerable criticism from employers and conservative politicians, with repeated claims that the power would be abused or used to pursue 'industrial relations' issues. However, as the South Australian Occupational Safety, Health and Welfare Steering Committee (1984) pointed out, a legal right to refuse unsafe work was unexceptional (and already existed at common law) and unions exercised similar powers within the industrial relations arena. The ethical right of workers to safeguard their safety cannot be ignored. At a more pragmatic level, evidence from Scandinavian countries, Australia and Canada over more than 20 years indicates that these powers have been used in a responsible manner and have not been abused (Hebdon and Hyatt, 1998: 592). It should also be emphasised that there are a series of practical and procedural protections against the misuse of notices. In Australia and New Zealand, if not elsewhere, the issuing of a notice (especially one of a more serious nature) invariably leads to a workplace visit by a government OHS inspector who can make a determination and, if necessary, cancel the notice (for a case appealing such a cancellation, see Cameron, G. and Alchin, M., *Australian Industrial Relations Commission* C2005/2494, 16 April 2007). As with notices issued by inspectors, the employer may also lodge an appeal against notice. Finally, all Australian OHS Acts contain provisions for the removal of HSRs who abuse their post, while in New Zealand more emphasis is on conflict resolution through mediation. In sum, the granting of such powers is justified, evidence indicates it has overwhelmingly been used responsibly and there are more than adequate safeguards to deal with isolated cases of abuse. A more critical issue is that absence of HSRs in most workplaces means that most workers lack this important protection.

Looked at with the advantage of 20 years of hindsight it can be stated that the HSR provisions formed a critical component of revised OHS laws. The need to grant workers the right to information, the right to involvement in monitoring and standard setting and the right to halt the work process where they believe their health is endangered is recognised internationally. It can also have important and positive effects on the management of OHS at the workplace. Studies by Biggins in Australia (Biggins et al., 1991; Gaines and Biggins, 1992), Walters and Nichols (2007) in the UK and Hovden et al. (2008) in Norway found the presence of HSRs had a beneficial impact on OHS attitudes and practices at the workplace. At the same time, Hovden et al.'s (2008) study of the oil and gas industry found differences in perception, with management placing considerable emphasis on OHS management systems while HSRs placed more reliance on daily consultations. HSRs were also more negative about the climate of collaboration and participation than management, especially with regard to meeting the objectives of OHS regulations. Overall, available research and our own observations (during numerous workplace visits) indicate that HSRs are most successful where management adopts a positive attitude to OHS, values representatives' input and gives them enough time to carry out their functions (including training and updating their knowledge). Unfortunately, the role and supports provided (for training time and the like) to HSRs remain too circumscribed in some Australian jurisdictions for these benefits to be fully realised. As discussed in chapter 9, recent changes in industrial relations in Australia have weakened the framework for worker participation in OHS. Fewer unionised workplaces have meant fewer HSRs and a climate where more employers are hostile to worker rights seems to have resulted in more cases of alleged victimisation of HSRs for carrying out their activities (Quinlan and Johnstone, 2009). The critical role of the immediate regulatory framework (under OHS law) and the broader context of institutional and regulatory relations (in terms of union presence and policies, industrial relations and politics) are reinforced by international studies. For example, Tucker's (1992) comparison of worker participation in OHS in Sweden and Canada found that the more supportive structure in Sweden had tangible effects on the quality of worker participation, including resolving ambiguities arising from bipartite structures of representation (i.e. HSR and union) at the workplace. Comparing HSRs in Britain and Sweden, Walters (1996b) reached similar conclusions. These findings should form the basis for a more informed and constructive policy debate in Australia and New Zealand.

Sweden is also noteworthy with regard to the regional safety representative system developed to deal with small and medium workplaces lacking their own HSR. In 1998 over 1500 union-affiliated (and union-supported, though costs were reimbursed by the state) regional safety representatives (equivalent to 300 full-time officers) covered 700 000 workers in 160 000 workplaces with fewer than 50 employees (Frick and Walters, 1998). Regional safety representatives can be appointed to a number of workplaces. Notwithstanding a need to further enhance their training, Frick and Walters (1998) found regional representatives were an extremely important source of practical OHS advice and generally enjoyed good relations with both management and government inspectors. The regional safety representative system provides an innovative and practical means of providing OHS help to smaller firms, as well as extending worker representation to cover a far wider number of workplaces. An analogous but much smaller scale system already applies in the NSW and Queensland coal mining industry where union-appointed district check inspectors (partly government funded) provide an independent monitor on safety in all mines within their jurisdiction. This system has worked well for a number of years. However, there are strong grounds for introducing a more extensive regional representative system along Swedish lines. Such an approach would make an important contribution to the critical problem of improving OHS in small business and the representative gap by changes in work organisation discussed later in this chapter.

Penalties, enforcement powers and processes

The Robens report was ambivalent about the use of criminal law as a means of enforcement but did advocate more direct forms of enforcement, namely empowering inspectors to issue improvement and prohibition notices. In Australia and New Zealand, legislators were less ambivalent about the need to enhance conventional punitive enforcement mechanisms. Further, there was a significant upgrading of penalties attached to convictions for serious offences under the legislation in both countries. This process of increasing financial penalties has been extended since, although the actual level of maximum penalties varies substantially between jurisdictions. For example, in 2008 maximum fines that could be imposed on corporations ranged from $150 000 in Tasmania to $500 000 in New Zealand, $750 000 in Queensland and up to $1 020 780 in Victoria. Several jurisdictions (NSW, South Australia and Western Australia) impose more severe penalties for repeat or aggravated offences ($825 000, $600 000 and $625 000 respectively). The laws of two jurisdictions (NSW and the

Northern Territory) contain penalties higher than the Victorian maximum where a reckless or intentional breach caused death ($1 650 000 and $1 375 000 respectively; Johnstone and Quinlan, 2008).

Fines for breaches of subordinate legislation, namely regulations made under the Acts, were also progressively increased (though these remain well below those applying to failure to comply with a provision of the principal Act). The principal OHS laws of most jurisdictions adopted the practice of expressing fines in terms of penalty points or units, the monetary value of which were designated in regulations. In keeping with the enabling character of much post-Robens legislation, this meant the level of penalties could be adjusted without requiring the matter to be brought before parliament (regulations are subordinate legislation and can be altered by ministerial advice to the Governor in Council).

As with earlier legislation, in practice maximum penalties are seldom imposed by courts and the latest figures indicate that this remains the case (Workplace Relations Ministers' Council, 2008). However, the higher penalties applying to breaches by both corporations and individuals establish a context for assessing the significance of the law to society. It also sets a range within which courts set fines and over time it does appear that courts have been prepared to impose heavier penalties on a selective basis. In most jurisdictions prosecutions may be initiated in either a lower court (usually before magistrates or an industrial magistrate) or a higher court (the Supreme Court or Industrial/Employment Court in most jurisdictions apart from Victoria where it is a County Court) depending on the gravity of the offence. The great majority of cases are tried before a lower court and this helps to explain why the average penalties remain a fraction of the maximum penalty applying to offences. Notwithstanding a trend to increases, even the penalties imposed by superior courts for serious offences by recidivist employers seldom attract anywhere near the maximum penalty.

Importantly, the laws draw a distinction between offences by individuals and corporations, with significantly higher financial penalties (often by an order of 10) being attached to the latter. This does not preclude simultaneous prosecution of both individuals and a corporation (or several bodies) held to have breached their respective duties (or regulations) in relation to a single or closely related series of events. Indeed, a number of Acts, such as the Queensland Workplace Health and Safety Act, 1995, made the possibility of dual prosecution quite explicit as well as defining those individuals (notably, the managing director and others responsible for managing the business) that might be held liable for a corporate breach. As in a number of other countries, the principal OHS Acts of most jurisdictions require that corporate officer holders demonstrate due diligence in preventing a contravention by the organisation, its employees or contractors (see the NSW Occupational Health and Safety Act, 2000). This means managers and directors must take reasonable care to lay down a safe system of work, to implement the system (induction, training, monitoring and supervision) and to enforce it (including acting immediately if the system fails). Managers can delegate functions but not their legal responsibilities. Where activities are delegated, managers must ensure reporting procedures are in place so they remain fully informed.

Provisions dealing with directors/managers were an attempt to overcome the combination of legal technicalities (such as proximity and mens rea) and organisational complexities (including complex management structures and the corporate veil) that historically made it difficult to prosecute managers (other than small business owners/managers) for serious acts or omissions in relation to OHS.

More recent changes to OHS legislation have reinforced this trend, expanding the duties of directors (Harpur, 2008). As a general rule, the focus of OHS legislation is on senior management. More subordinate managers have responsibilities—something a number of less reputable employers have sought to exaggerate in their internal communications—but there are good public policy reasons not to prosecute such managers apart from exceptional cases. Indeed, the selection of individual managers for prosecution more generally requires careful consideration to ensure the correct 'messages' are sent. This was highlighted by the Gretley case where the prosecution of a number of managers (itself arguably a response to a lack of prosecution for OHS breaches in the past) following an inrush of water that drowned five miners arguably sent mixed messages (for a discussion of the prosecution and subsequent appeal by the company involved, see Foster, 2008). In a number of jurisdictions (such as Tasmania) OHS laws identify parties holding particular responsibilities in hazardous workplaces. As noted elsewhere, these provisions have been subject to some 'manipulation' which should be guarded against to ensure they only apply to managers with the overall responsibility and ultimate power to make decisions affecting safety on those worksites.

As criminal legislation, a number of OHS Acts (such as in NSW, the Northern Territory, Queensland and New Zealand) also provide for imprisonment of individuals in the cases of serious or repeated offences, although there are considerable variations with regard to the maximum term and whether imprisonment is an additional or alternative penalty. Despite an increased willingness by most Australian and New Zealand inspectorates to prosecute over the past 20 years, the pursuit of a jail penalty remains almost unknown even in the most flagrant cases. During the 1980s there were a number of prosecutions in the US where directors/managers were convicted of homicide/manslaughter and jailed (Reiner and Chatten-Brown, 1989). While attracting worldwide publicity—in no small part because it was so unusual—it failed to presage any trend towards such actions. The failure to jail even the most negligent manager causing death when even those in charge of a motor vehicle now face this penalty (including 'ordinary' motorists as well as truck drivers, but not those employing the latter even where their actions have been found to contribute to the fatal crash) provides contemporary support for Carson's conventionalisation thesis. This is not a reflection of community attitudes, with public surveys repeatedly placing death through negligence at work as among the most abhorrent offences.

In Australia and other countries, the failure to impose a jail penalty on managers responsible for flagrant breaches of OHS standards causing death has become a source of concern to family members of those killed (and their representatives) and a source of public debate, highlighted by a number of government inquiries (such as that conducted in NSW into the death of a number of young workers; Nile, 2004). There seems to be no justifiable public policy grounds for precluding unlawful killing or manslaughter at work from the penalty that is normally imposed for this offence in other circumstances. Indeed, used selectively for the 'worst of the worst' cases—as the strategic enforcement strategies and limited resources of inspectorates would dictate in any case—such action would have both deterrent and symbolic value. Prosecution of senior managers might also serve to remind CEOs and their equivalents that delegating responsibility, or establishing procedures which imply middle-managers carry the burden of responsibility for OHS, will be to no avail if they cannot demonstrate they have carried out their own legislative duties of oversight and control in this regard. It is worth noting in passing that as a result of the death of two cleaners who fell 26 storeys from a Gold Coast building when their swing stage scaffold failed on 21 June 2008 (and referred to in chapter 1), the Queensland Division of Workplace Health and Safety laid charges against three companies and an executive officer of one of those companies (*CCH OHS Alert*, 5 June 2009). The case and its outcome is unknown at the time of writing of this book.

Over the past decade a parallel and, if anything, more conspicuous public debate involving calls for corporations to be charged with manslaughter or causing unlawful death has occurred in Australia, the UK and elsewhere (Ridley and Dunford, 1997; Haines, et al., 2002; Johnstone, 2004; Johnson, 2008). Repeated calls and union/public campaigns for special legislative provisions (in OHS or general criminal codes) dealing with workplace death or industrial manslaughter yielded positive responses in the UK, Canada and a number of Australian jurisdictions (those in the Australian Capital Territory even included supply chain provisions affecting upstream duty holders). However, as with the prison penalty for individual managers, little if any use has been made of these legislative provisions even in the most extreme cases. Indeed, an assessment (Gobert, 2008) of the UK Corporate Manslaughter and Corporate Homicide Act, 2007—introduced after 13 years of deliberation and struggle—found that it was largely symbolic, being narrow in scope and entailing attenuated and potentially politicised procedures.

With regard to new penalties/enforcement tools, the OHS laws of all jurisdictions adopted the improvement and prohibition notice techniques advocated by Robens and used to such good effect under the UK Health and Safety at Work Act. As the name implies, improvement notices require the employer or other responsible party to rectify an identified problem (this may relate to plant, equipment or a work process) within a specified time period. Prohibition notices, on the other hand, are designed to address situations where there is an imminent and serious risk to health by placing an immediate ban on a piece of equipment, specified work method, etc.

At the same time, Australian and New Zealand jurisdictions continued to take an innovative approach to enforcement, developing new remedies. In most jurisdictions inspectors now have the power to issue verbal directions (to rectify a hazard when this can be achieved before they leave the site) and to issue infringement notices (on-the-spot fines). For example, in 2008 a $5000 infringement notice was issued against an ACT employer who failed to provide information on the use of chemicals or sufficient PPE to a worker (*SIA Safety Week* Issue 150, 16 June 2008). Other recently used penalties include 'naming and shaming', or adverse publicity court orders, whereby the court orders the convicted defendant to publicise the offence, conviction and penalty (NSW, Victoria, SA and the ACT). Other examples include court orders requiring the offender to participate in an OHS-related project (NSW, Victoria and SA); to undertake remedial measures or training (NSW, SA and the ACT); or requiring the defendant to give an undertaking not to reoffend within two years and to engage a consultant, develop systematic OHS management and have the OHS management approach monitored by a third party (Victoria). As noted above, most jurisdictions also have the capacity to issue enforceable undertakings. Finally, a number of Acts include provisions permitting a range of additional and targeted actions by inspectorates. For example, in response to the 2006 fatal rockfall at the Beaconsfield mine the Chief Mines Inspector imposed more stringent reporting requirements with regard to rockfalls and, under s39 of the Workplace Health and Safety Act, Workplace Standards Tasmania (WST) required the mine to prepare what amount to a safety case that had to be approved by WST before mining operations could recommence.

The principal OHS laws also sought to address problems of earlier OHS laws in relation to enforcement (including ambiguities with regard to inspectoral powers) and upgrade penalties for obstructing an inspector and the like. For example, the Queensland Workplace Health Safety Act, 1995 clarified and extended the powers of inspectors, though a warrant was still required in the case of domestic premises. Similar legal or administrative limitations apply to the entry to domestic premises in other jurisdictions. However, as a NSW inquiry recognised (Standing Committee on Law and Justice, 1997), such restrictions are problematic given the significant expansion of home-based work in new activities (telework) as well as traditional areas (such as clothing outwork). Other powers include the right to call assistance (including the police), to control movement by members of the public where a serious incident has occurred, to question employees or former employees, to require production of documents and to take copies of documents and collect materials (including photos and measurements). Inspectors could also require the names and address of persons (with reasonable cause) and institute proceedings under the Act. The Queensland Act empowers inspectors to seize any premises, plant or substance. Other sections of the Act reinforced these powers by identifying the obligations owed to inspectors by the owner, occupiers, etc. and made any attempt to hinder an inspector a serious offence. Finally, like the legislation of other jurisdictions, the Queensland Act empowered inspectors to issue improvement and prohibition notices. Notwithstanding some variations, the powers afforded to inspectors in Queensland are broadly similar to those found in other jurisdictions.

The beefing up of traditional avenues of enforcement plus the addition of new methods was not seen as contrary to the development of self-regulation. Indeed, it has been argued that effective enforcement mechanisms establish the environment essential for constructive collaboration between employers and employees.

In terms of initiating prosecutions the dominant approach in Australia and New Zealand has been to leave this power in the hands of the inspectorate, although in some jurisdictions (such as Tasmania), recommendations for prosecutions are referred to the

DPP rather than being undertaken by the inspectorate itself (as is the case in NSW, for example). Under the NSW Occupational Health and Safety Act, 2000, union secretaries are also able to initiate prosecutions under the Act, so unions have the option of taking their own prosecutions where the responsible OHS agency (WorkCover NSW) has failed to take legal action against an employer. Under the 2002 amendments of the New Zealand Health and Safety in Employment Act, 1992, the Crown monopoly on prosecutions was removed and private prosecutions are now possible but only once the Department of Labour has decided not to prosecute and has not issued an infringement notice or sought a compliance order for the same matter. However, critics argue that the Department of Labour is abdicating its statutory responsibility and that New Zealand's low rate of prosecutions will worsen. In comparable jurisdictions the rates of prosecutions for breaches of the OHS legislation are much higher. For example, Queensland's Workplace Health and Safety inspectorate carried out 214 prosecutions in 2005, with offenders ordered to pay fines and costs totalling more than $4.76 million, compared to New Zealand's Department of Labour which undertook only 154 prosecutions, netting a total of $633 300 (Queensland Department of Employment and Industrial Relations, 2005; New Zealand Department of Labour, 2005).

Given the time and expense of launching private prosecution, this option has been used selectively in both Australia and New Zealand (to our knowledge there have been fewer than 20 such prosecutions). However, the details of these cases and their success indicate the power has been used judiciously and to good effect. For examples, in the 1990s the Nurses Union successfully prosecuted several government health services in relation to failure to provide a safe system of work with regard to back injuries and breach of protocol in relation to needlestick injuries (*Moatt v Mid Western Health Service*, 1996 and *White v Illawarra Health Service*, 1996). Similarly, in the early years of the current decade the Finance Sector Union successfully prosecuted several banks for failing to provide adequate robbery protection for tellers, resulting in the installation of security screens. In these and other cases we are aware of, the prosecutions followed unsuccessful attempts by the union concerned to negotiate improvements in relation to the hazard.

The implementation of post-Robens legislation

Beyond formal changes in legislation, it is critical to consider changes to policies and enforcement practices that have occurred over the past 20 or more years. To some degree these changes were a logical outcome of the legislation itself. For example, the introduction of general duty provisions including reference to healthy working environment and safe systems of work encouraged a broader, more systematic and proactive view of employers' responsibilities to manage their OHS. At the same time, other developments fed into these changes, including the growing influence of 'systems' and 'risk management' within the realms of both industry and regulators. Similarly, changes in enforcement tools provided inspectors with avenues to change their practices and the laws required them to consider a broader range of issues. However, the activities of inspectorates were also influenced by broader changes in the workforce and society as well as evolving ideas about how to maximise enforcement outcomes in the context of limited resources. In this section, the evolution of systematic OHS management and enforcement activities of inspectors will be considered in turn.

Risk assessment and systematic OHS management

From the 1990s OHS inspectorates in Australia and New Zealand (and many other developed countries for that matter) displayed a growing interest in promoting a more systematic approach to managing OHS on the part of employers via the use of risk assessment/risk management and OHS management systems. Rather than simply responding to known hazards—as was often the case in the past—regulators sought to encourage employers (and subsequently other duty holders such as designers, manufacturers and suppliers) to establish a set of structures and procedures for identifying, assessing and controlling OHS risks. While management systems figured little in the Robens report or related debates about legislative reform in Britain, Australia and New Zealand, this approach could be seen as a logical outcome of Robens's model legislation with its focus on performance standards and establishing safe systems of work. It was reinforced by inspectorates who sought to encourage employers to pursue a more proactive and comprehensive approach to hazard assessment and control measures because they saw it as a more effective use of their limited resources than past enforcement practices.

At the same time, there were wider factors at work including the growing global popularity or influence of risk management (that grew out of the fields of engineering and insurance) and 'systems' approaches within management and the development of international standards (notably ISO9000 and ISO14000) requiring a systematic approach to quality and environment (Frick et al., 2000). Norway introduced an internal control regulation that required employers to adopt a systematic approach to OHS (with Sweden adopting a similar measure) in part as a response to the conspicuous failures of the past, highlighted by the Alexander Kjelland oil rig disaster (Frick et al., 2000). For its part, the European Union issued a directive on risk assessment, requiring employers to undertake risk assessment in relation to work-related hazards. The value of a systematic approach to OHS even impacted on countries that remained largely wedded to specification standards–based OHS legislation. In both France and Quebec, for example, inspectorates drew on risk assessment ideas in terms of their enforcement while, in the US, OSHA promoted a systematic approach to OHS via its Voluntary Performance Program (VPP).

Before examining the application of systematic OHS management and risk assessment/management under Australian and New Zealand OHS legislation, several important points of clarification need to be made. First, the promotion of systematic OHS management by regulators is often used interchangeably with OHS management systems—or the formal devices used by individual employers to manage OHS. However, an employer (especially a small one) may meet the regulatory requirements of adopting a systematic approach to OHS without having an elaborate paper-based system and, further, even possession of a formal system may not guarantee that it complies with the regulators' requirements. As discussed in chapter 10, OHS management systems can contain serious flaws. In short, systematic OHS management is not the same as OHS management systems. Second, on the other hand the interchangeable use of the terms risk assessment and risk management is justified in our view because use of the former in legislation often includes specific directions to take appropriate control measures once the risk associated with a hazard has been assessed, the assessment process needs to include a review of control measures currently in place and, at a level of logic, there would seem little point to undertaking a risk assessment without also addressing the appropriate management of that risk. Third, risk assessment constitutes a critical component of a systematic approach to OHS and, in our view, an essential component of an effective OHS management system (although this system will also include other things such as objectives, policies and accountabilities, participatory processes, monitoring and auditing practices). In essence, risk assessment involves considering both the likelihood/frequency and consequences/magnitude (impact and costs) of a hazard or event as a basis for determining appropriate responses (and prioritising activity with regard to a range of hazards).

Fourth, as evident in the observations of experts (see Cross, 2000), as well as well-accepted guidance standards (such as Australian/New Zealand Standard 4360) risk assessment/management entails a number of steps and guiding principles. The key steps in risk assessment are:

■ establish the context (of the organisation and events where the process is to occur)
■ identify the risks (including all hazards or components of a hazard)
■ analyse the risks (gathering information about the hazard, the mechanisms leading to injury/illness and its magnitude)
■ evaluate the risks (often entailing a ranking based on relative likelihood and consequences using a risk matrix)
■ treat the risks (implement suitable control measures, according to the hierarchy of control)
■ monitor, review/modify (assess the effectiveness of controls and if necessary revise).

While risk assessment may be quantitative or qualitative the latter is more typical in OHS (though still drawing on quantitative data) because work-related hazards are complex/dynamic (as are workplaces) and multi-causal and not all relevant information (or evidence pertaining to the quality of that information) is quantifiable. Risk matrices can provide a useful basis for summarising and ranking information as part of the evaluation process (Cross, 2000: 368). As Cross (2000), and standards such as ANZS4360 emphasise communication and workforce consultation is critical during all stages of the process.

Leaving these important clarifications aside, the role played by regulation in systematic OHS management and risk assessment has varied between countries but these differences are nuanced and have changed over time. As already indicated, Scandinavian countries like Norway and Sweden essentially mandated systematic OHS management while in the US the approach was entirely voluntary via VPP (employers also adopted their own systems, some purchasing off-the-shelf products such as the DuPont scheme). In Britain and Australia (and to a lesser extent New Zealand) the situation was more nuanced. Legislation in Australia did not directly mandate a systematic approach. Employers (especially large ones) tended to voluntarily embrace a 'systems' approach (aided by active OHS consultants) and Australia and New Zealand pioneered the adoption of a standard on OHS management systems (AS4801 and AS/NZS4804). At the same time, regulators also played an influential role. A systematic approach was encouraged by inspectorates (including Comcare) in their codes and guidance material (including the production of OHS management self-audit tools, such as SafetyMAP in Victoria and Worksafe Plan in Western Australia), augmenting what was already found within the general duty provisions as well as their enforcement activities. Further, mandatory requirements for risk assessment (including circumstances where the workplace changed or new knowledge became available) similar to the EU directive were introduced by Australian jurisdictions, largely under regulation (such as the NSW OHS Regulation 2001) but in some instances by incorporation into general duty provisions (notably the Queensland Workplace Health and Safety Act and the ACT Work Safety Act 2008). Typical requirements include the need to adopt a hierarchy of control approach to controlling risks and to consult workers or their representatives (requirements as to documenting the process can vary with the hazard). The ACT Work Safety Act 2008 has extended the obligations from 'employees' to 'workers' thereby covering contractors, and the duty extends not only to employers but designers, franchisees and others conducting a business or undertaking.

This impetus was reinforced in the courts, with decisions evolving to indicate that in order to meet their general duties employers needed not simply to respond to hazards and comply with legal requirements on an ad hoc basis but to adopt a structured and proactive approach that identified and addressed all foreseeable risks, to ensure workers were suitably trained and supervised and to monitor/review systems over time (Johnstone, 2004; Johnstone and Quinlan, 2008). Failure to carry out risk assessment has also been incorporated into prosecutions. For example, in 2002 a demolition and asbestos-removal company in NSW was prosecuted after an employee fell through a roof and sustained significant injuries. The employer was convicted under general duty s15(1) of failing to provide a safe system of work; failing to carry out risk assessment on the task and complete a work method statement; failing to ensure use of fall protection; and failing to provide instruction, training and adequate supervision (*WorkCover (Inspector Stewart) v the Crown in the Right of the State of NSW Department of Education and Training, Department of Juvenile Justice and TAFE* [2002]) NSWIRC 259, 3466 of 2001). In a similar vein, in 2008 a diving company was convicted of failing to manage risks in relation to a novice diver (*Marfleet v Kaptive Pty Ltd* [2008] QIC, 6 October 2008).

The trend towards emphasising systematic OHS management and risk assessment has received additional impetus from mining legislation and reviews into mine safety (Gunningham, 2008). Following serious rockfalls in October 2005 (six months before and in the same levels as the falls that included one killing Larry Knight), the independent investigation (Quinlan, 2007) and coronial inquest (Chandler, 2009) devoted considerable attention to OHS management and risk assessment. Both found that the mine had failed to undertake a systematic and thorough risk assessment (including reviewing all control measures already in place and monitoring new interventions). Mine management had not consulted with workers as part of the risk assessment process and key deliberations and decisions were not documented. Documenting deliberations is valuable in terms of ensuring all relevant issues are considered and in terms of guiding future action (including future risk assessments). Drawing on the independent inquiry as well as his assessment of the evidence presented during the inquest, the coroner concluded that a thorough and systematic risk assessment would have significantly reduced the likelihood of the fatal events of April 2006. The coroner also observed that in other jurisdictions regulators responsible for mining had produced specific guidance material on risk assessment and recommended the provision of similar guidance in Tasmania. It is unfortunate that these reports were not released in time to be considered by the national review on harmonising OHS laws.

The promotion of systematic OHS management and requirements to undertake risk assessment represent a generally positive step in OHS regulation. International and Australian evidence indicates that these developments have coincided with greater management awareness of and involvement in OHS, and some studies—such as those of internal control in Norway—have been able to directly chart the role regulation has played in this (Frick et al., 2000; Gallagher et al., 2001; Saksvik and Quinlan, 2003; Geldart et al., 2005; Torp and Moen, 2006; Robson et al., 2007). A Norwegian study (Saksvik et al., 2003) found internal control had led to higher levels of OHS training, risk assessment and action plans but statistics did not allow an evaluation of the effects on OHS (due to changes in employment levels and registration procedures in the 1990s). Several studies found an association between mandating systematic OHS management with improvements in OHS, although a Swedish study (Dellve et al., 2008) concluded better developed systems led to higher reporting of disorders. As with voluntarily adopted OHS management systems (see chapter 10), there is a need for research into the effects of mandating systematic OHS management on OHS outcomes, if only to identify limitations and areas for improvement. At the same time, such assessments need to be viewed in context. As discussed in chapters 9 and 10, the potential benefits of systematic OHS management have been weakened by changes in work organisation and the industrial relations climate.

There are also other challenges in implementing systematic OHS management, including the danger of 'paper compliance'—a disconnect between documented procedures and actual practice—or where objectives are not matched by implementation procedures and accountabilities (a problem well identified by the NSW Standing Committee on Law and Justice inquiry, 1998 Volume II: 7–31). As noted in a number of jurisdictions, regulators developed OHS management audit tools to enable employers to assess the scope and effectiveness of their OHS policies and practices, establish benchmarks, plan improvements and gain recognition for standards achieved. Audit documents were divided into a number of critical elements (such as building commitment, purchasing, safe work systems, monitoring, reporting and correcting deficiencies) and the Victorian audit system, known as SafetyMAP, was divided into three levels of achievement (initial, transitional and advanced) so as to provide a mechanism for progressive improvements over time. While such measures are still valuable, enthusiasm for them among regulators has tended to wane (Johnstone and Quinlan, 2008) as evidence of paper compliance emerged. This was symptomatic of a more general problem with OHS management systems marked by a proliferation of checklists that although valuable if used selectively are prone to 'tick and flick'. This problem was also marked by incidents (both relatively small-scale and large-scale like Longford and BP Texas City) where even elaborately documented systems were either critically flawed or not implemented (Hopkins, 2002; Baker, 2007). Although the guidance material produced by Australian regulators includes excellent material it often shies away from highlighting the lessons to be learnt from 'failed systems' or areas employers might find a more confronting infringement on their prerogative, such as work organisation (this is changing albeit slowly).

Moreover, as international research attests (Hasle et al., 2009), the systematic approach was problematic for small business, which commonly found it difficult to implement such an approach to OHS (due to resource and other constraints) or undertake risk assessment as part of this. Problems common to small business (see Tuskes and Key, 1988; Eakin, 1992; Lamm, 1997; Hasle and Limborg, 1997 and Mayhew, 1997; Hasle et al., 2009) include a low level of OHS awareness and training of workers, a tendency for managers to place responsibility for OHS with workers and limited knowledge of and compliance with OHS laws. Prior to the last decade, the latter problem was often exacerbated by a 'top-down' approach from most OHS regulators (whereas small business preferred a 'bottom-up' hazard-focused approach), producing generic materials in a language and style that was comprehensible to large firms but not small employers with few resources and often under economic pressure. However, over the past decade regulators in Europe, Australia and elsewhere have undertaken extensive steps to overcome these limitations, including the provision of advisory support (direct and indirect), repackaging of guidance materials and their distribution methods, and targeted industry programs (some such as the safe building plan in Queensland and the REACH program in the EU indicate that small employers can develop 'systems'; Farber, 2008).

Some cautionary observations are also required with regard to risk assessment where the value of the process can be critically affected by the underlying assumptions used; the time and resources devoted to the process, the inexperience/expertise of those involved, the degree of worker involvement, risk/hazard habituation and a tendency for managers to place too much confidence in existing controls until these demonstrably fail, à la Beaconsfield (*CCH OHS Alert*, Issue 1, 13 February 2009). As with systematic OHS management, evidence indicates small business finds risk assessment challenging. A Danish study of worker participation in risk assessment (Jensen, 2002) found larger employers but not small employers had complied with legislation implementing the 1989 EU Framework Directive—and even larger employer compliance fell short of meeting the objectives of the law. As with OHS management 'systems', regulators need to provide further critical guidance on risk assessment, including common pitfalls. In the UK the Health and Safety Executive (2003) has produced a report on the latter and such information deserves wider dissemination in Australia and New Zealand.

At the same time, as a number of inspectorates are already aware, universalistic approaches to promoting risk assessment and systematic OHS management have limitations and what is needed is a more adaptive approach that may, for example, focus on 'chain of responsibility' (and many small businesses operate in a supply chain) where this seems more effective (Steve Hyam, ex-manager Workplace Standards Tasmania, personal communication, 8 February 2007). Size is not the only issue and, as a Danish OHS expert Per Langaa Jensen (see NSW Standing Committee on Law and Justice, 1998) argued, strategic inspectorate enforcement activity needs to take account of both the willingness and capacity of employers to comply with legislation.

Overall, the shift to systematic OHS management can be viewed as a positive development but one with limitations and potential risks. On the positive side, systematic OHS management provides a means of managing complex and dynamic work environments, something that an approach focusing on particular hazards or particular remedies (such as behaviour change) will invariably fail to do. A systems approach can be a vehicle for greater recognition of organisational factors that affect OHS, including the degree of involvement by workers, although not all systems will do this. It requires careful consideration of the processes of identification, assessment, control and performance measurement. There is evidence indicating that the regulatory promotion of systematic OHS has improved OHS awareness and processes, but there is too little research on the impact on OHS outcomes. The systematic approach also had the potential to enable OHS inspectorates to make better use of their limited resources by internalising the burden of compliance processes on employers and other duty holders (such as suppliers)—where they should be. This would allow inspectorates to focus on auditing the system (including its implementation) rather than the entire workplace, as well as targeting employers not using a systematic approach. Unfortunately, recent research indicates this 'freeing up' of resources has not occurred (Johnstone and Quinlan, 2008) and there is value in comparing other countries' experience in this regard (especially the Nordic countries) to see if they have had more success (and if so how).

Changes to inspectorate training and enforcement activities

Formal changes to enforcement powers and processes cannot be discussed without reference to infrastructural influences on compliance. Widening the powers of inspectors, altering the basis of offences to include performance standards and increasing the size and array of penalties available created a series of challenges as well as opportunities for OHS agencies. It was also associated with a series of administrative decisions relating to the merging of previously separate inspectoral agencies, reorganisation of task and operational command, the creation of separate prosecution units and decisions about compliance strategies. The latter included targeted campaigns to raise public awareness of OHS (via television, radio and roadside billboards) which were carefully assessed and adapted over time—creating an invaluable community context for inspectorate activities—as well as those directed at employers, workers and other duty holders.

The post-Robens legislation placed a series of new demands on inspectorates and this, in turn, raised issues about recruitment/selection, training/qualifications, experience, resourcing, inspection and enforcement activities. Post-Robens legislation required inspectors to undertake a wider array of tasks and take account of a wider array of factors because assessing compliance was no longer confined to specification standards but included wide-ranging general duty provisions and related process standards. Inspectors had to ensure both specification standards and performance standards were met, and their area of discretionary judgment was widened with regard to the determination of priorities and appropriate remedies. In some jurisdictions, such as Queensland, the magnitude of the change was even greater because the inspectorate had previously been divided into specialised units (such as machinery inspection). Historically, the vast majority of inspectors were males with a trade background or qualification, supplemented by inhouse training after they joined the inspectorate. This provided an arguably good grounding for enforcing specification standards in industries with significant plant- and structure-related physical hazards. However, it was less well suited to making decisions about compliance with general duties, including what constituted a safe system of work across a wide range of industries.

Initially, the transformation of the inspectorate was a slow and sometimes difficult process, but an extensive study of four Australian inspectorates (Johnstone and Quinlan, 2008) found that by 2004 a major shift had occurred. From the late 1980s, and more especially over the past decade, there were changes to recruitment to inspectorates with a shift to engaging more women and persons with formal OHS qualifications (TAFE and university diplomas or university degrees). In part, this was a response to the broader coverage of industries/workplaces (such as retailing, childcare, education and other service sector activities) and hazards (including manual handling and work organisation). Inspectorates were also able to draw recruits from a number of excellent undergraduate and postgraduate degree programs in OHS (although availability suffered from financial stringency within the university system over the past decade). At the same time, trade qualifications were still emphasised in areas such as construction, and in other areas, such as manufacturing and transport, industry experience was still seen to count in the selection process (inspectors could also obtain relevant qualifications such as a forklift truck licence after appointment). A major exception to this pattern is Comcare, which appears to have recruited largely from the ranks of ex-police since its coverage began to expand into the private sector after 2005.

Over the past 15 years most inspectorates have also undertaken measures to formalise and professionalise the training of inspectors, mostly through extended inhouse programs (with external expert input) and replacing reliance on shorter/less formalised training and the 'buddy' system. For example, programs used by jurisdictions such as Western Australia and Victoria are of three to six months' duration, including on-the-job components (aided by digital technology) and supervised learning with experienced inspectors. The formal education component covers not only traditional areas of investigation and legal compliance (but now dealing with the framework of general duties) but also includes a stronger focus on OHS (including hazard identification and risk assessment). Some smaller jurisdictions (such as Tasmania) found it difficult to mount their own formal programs and continued to rely on a mixture of in-sourced courses and the 'buddy' system. Another exception was Comcare which (as of 2008) continued to rely on a short course in government without any notable OHS components.

After initial training, most inspectorates supported (through time off and covering course costs) further education and skills upgrading with short courses as well as degrees and diplomas. Again, resource constraints in smaller inspectorates as well as travel costs for inspectorates remote from the east coast (such as Western Australia and the Northern Territory) are an inhibiting factor that the federal government could usefully address as part of its OHS law harmonisation process.

An extended study of four inspectorates (Johnstone and Quinlan, 2008) found that the new training regimes were (notwithstanding some criticism) viewed positively by both inspectors who had undertaken them and older inspectors who had not. Nor was there a notable conflict between trade- and OHS-related qualifications. Inspectors in areas such as construction saw trade qualifications and experience as essential but having OHS qualifications as well was also seen as valuable. The study also found that in general inspectors made adept use of their skills, including their knowledge of OHS and OHS law, to identify and address serious hazards in the workplace in a wide range of areas (such as plant, manual handling and hazardous systems of work). It is also worth noting that the growth of tertiary qualifications among inspectors reflects a professionalising of the occupation in Australia, a trend already underway for some time in Western Europe and North America.

Not surprisingly, the formal training and upgrading of inspectors' skills as well as their knowledge of OHS legislation has made them highly attractive to employers. A not insignificant number have been poached, resulting in a loss of able personnel, additional training costs and the disruption associated with labour turnover for inspectorates. The relatively low salary levels of OHS inspectors (mining inspectors earn about 20% more) and lack of extended career structure has made it comparatively easy to poach inspectors. The problem remains despite efforts by some jurisdictions to improve pay and career structures so that they are more in keeping with the professional nature of modern inspectors' tasks. Johnstone and Quinlan (2008) found inspectors were generally highly committed to their jobs, with some returning to the inspectorate after a stint in the private sector (despite the pay cut). It also needs to be acknowledged that the recruitment of inspectors by private employers and others (including unions and other government agencies) has more general benefits for OHS. Nonetheless, the additional costs associated with depletion and ensuring effective retention levels within the inspectorate require further attention.

The issue of inspectoral effectiveness was not simply one of recruitment and training but also of the number of inspectors and the logistical support available to them as well as the effective deployment of available resources. From the mid-1990s inspectorates of many Australian jurisdictions as well as New Zealand underwent significant structural changes. Most notably, there was a move to organise the inspectorate into industry (or often multi-industry) based teams (dovetailed into regional organisation), often with (as in the case of Victoria and Western Australia) a high-hazard team that included technical specialists such as ergonomists or hygienists (and whose services could be called on by other teams as required). Overall, the industry team structure facilitated a more effective deployment of resources to meet the wider array of hazards and workplaces now covered by OHS legislation (including previously neglected areas—parts of the service sector such as healthcare and aged care facilities, prisons, offices, schools and child care centres). It also enabled the development of industry-specific knowledge and enforcement as well as the mentoring of more inexperienced inspectors.

Another important change occurred with regard to enforcement and workplace visits. Until the mid-1990s inspectorates conducted a large number of random inspections, in which inspectors worked their way through their districts, in addition to accident investigations, responses to complaints and programmed visits. However, since this time there has been a pronounced shift towards using 'proactive' workplace visits as part of targeted programs or campaigns initiated at regional, state or national levels. For example, in 1998 WorkCover NSW undertook a two-month blitz in relation to sawmills, inspecting over 100 mills and issuing 630 notices, most for inadequate machine guarding. There has also been progressive targeting of particular industries and subsectors with information gathering followed by selected provision of OHS materials, publicised audits and the use of on-the-spot fines, prohibition and improvement notices, and follow-up prosecutions for employers found to have made no attempt to rectify major defects. In Queensland, for example, the inspectorate developed OHS profiles on a number of industry subsectors and these were used in the production of material as well as targeted enforcement. In some cases, specific research and stakeholder consultation is undertaken to better identify the problems and focal points for intervention (for example, this was done with regard to the road transport industry in Victoria in 2008). The shift to a more proactive approach to enforcement and use of research appears to be a common trend among OHS regulators in Europe and North America if not elsewhere. For example, in the US a major initiative has been undertaken with regard to trucking in the state of Washington while at the national level NIOSH has developed priority research/intervention programs in construction and transport and warehousing (Rauser et al., 2008). Further, it is now more common for regulators to undertake/commission research on the effectiveness of particular campaigns or types of interventions (see, for example, Cox et al., 2008).

Relatively recent examples of state level campaigns in Australia include the targeting of specific hazards (such as dangerous goods, occupational violence and workplace traffic systems) and industry subsectors (such as call centres, schools/child care centres, warehouses, recycling/waste-handling facilities). Examples of proactive visits connected to nationally coordinated campaigns include a 'fall from heights' campaign in construction, a campaign on forklift trucks and a campaign targeting the suppliers of agricultural machinery. The shift to more proactive enforcement and workplace visits is seen to make more effective use of limited inspectoral resources. Johnstone and Quinlan's (2008) study included 118 'typical' workplace visits highlighting this shift (see table 7.1), although overstating it to some degree as interviews indicated that OHS inspectorates struggle to ensure that reactive inspections and investigations (in response to complaints and injuries and fatalities) do not exceed proactive inspections. In some industries, such as transport and warehouse, and some regions inspectors stated that they found it difficult to meet a backlog of complaints/information while also achieving the proactive visit targets set by agencies.

Table 7.1   Workplace visits: type of visit

Type of visit	2004	2006	total
Proactive/targeted campaign	39	37	76 (64.4%)
Response to complaint	12	10	22 (18.6)
Investigation	9	10	19 (16.1%)
Other/unclear	1	0	1 (0.85%)
Total	61	57	118

Source: Johnstone and Quinlan (2008).

Notwithstanding these changes, the growing emphasis on systematic OHSM did not free up resources, and changes to work organisation, including the growth of elaborate supply chains, subcontracting and small business and greater use of contingent workers (including labour hire), actually exacerbated the enforcement problems confronting inspectors. Another exacerbating factor was the weakening of unions and retreat of industrial relations regulation from a number of key areas with OHS implications, such as hours of work and rest breaks (Quinlan and Johnstone, 2004). In sum, over the past two decades the role of inspectors has become more challenging and even with more effective deployment required a combination of more inspectors and greater logistical back up.

In the mid-1990s the Industry Commission's (1995: 131, 423–33) review of inspectoral resources and activities found wide inter-jurisdictional variations in the expenditure on enforcement and the size of the inspectorate. During the 1990s inspectorate numbers and other resources in Australia did not keep pace with workforce growth and broadened responsibilities under post-Robens legislation. The situation, if anything, was more acute in New Zealand. More recent data (table 7.2) indicates that the absolute number of inspectors grew between 2001 and 2006 in most jurisdictions. The number of inspectors per 10 000 employees—a more accurate measure of relative resourcing—indicates just over one inspector for every 10 000 employees in the larger jurisdictions (except Queensland which is better resourced) with most smaller jurisdictions enjoying a higher ratio. This does not mean smaller jurisdictions are better resourced, because they do not have the advantages accruing to a critical mass available to larger inspectorates (in terms of task specialisation and the like). The major exception again is Comcare—a small jurisdiction that didn't even match larger jurisdictions in terms of resourcing as its coverage expanded. That increases in inspectoral resources overwhelmingly occurred in jurisdictions during periods where Labor was in government seems more than coincidental.

It should be observed that one inspector for every 10 000 employees means that the average inspector is responsible for hundreds if not thousands of workplaces (in industries with many small operators, such as retailing). One consequence is that the vast majority of workplaces will not be visited in any given year or even within five-yearly intervals. Workplace visits take time (including travel time which is often lengthy in regional areas), inspectors' tasks extend well beyond visiting workplaces (including data collection and interviews as part of investigations) and even small workplaces may require repeat visits after a problem has been identified (to check that issues have been resolved). In short, raw numbers alone cannot answer whether resourcing is adequate. Johnstone and Quinlan's (2008) study of four state jurisdictions found inspectors were generally satisfied with the level of logistical support, including the provision of vehicles, laptop computers (and even portable printers so notices could be printed off on site), mobile phones, wireless internet connections, digital cameras (to record incidents) and a centralised network for recording workplace visits, accessing information on past visits and the like. However, the vast majority of inspectors interviewed indicated that they believed their industry team was under-resourced by an order that averaged around 50%. This level of under-resourcing was not framed in terms of the capacity to visit even half the workplaces covered on an annual basis but rather to achieve enough workplace visits (combining proactive and reactive visits) to achieve a satisfactory level of compliance.

Any assessment of the resourcing and effectiveness of inspectorates needs to consider the responsibilities of and actions taken by inspectors. Prior to a visit it is common for inspectors to view records of prior visits to that workplace (if these have occurred) and other relevant information held by the agencies (in both digitalised form via a central databank and in hard copy files for non-digitalised material). During a visit the inspector may need to examine a wide range of potential hazards and work arrangements covered by the legislation (see table 7.4). As well as undertaking a 'walk round', forms of observation include detailed examination of plant or work systems; talking to managers, workers and other parties (such as consultants); examining documents (such as machinery maintenance or training/induction records); and possibly taking photographs. Prior to or after a visit an inspector may need to research or seek advice on relevant standards. The level of detail sought will depend on whether there are outstanding issues and the nature of the workplaces (for example, major hazard facilities such as chemical plants or refineries are normally subjected to very thorough inspections of physical plant, work systems and OHSM system documentation).

Table 7.2 Number of OHS inspectors and actions taken, 2001–06, by jurisdiction

	Year	NSW	Vic.	Qld	WA	SA	Tas.	NT	ACT	Aust. Govt*	Total Aust.	New Zealand
Number of field active inspectors	2001–02	301	226	127	70	57	n/a	10	12	16	820	158
	2002–03	301	236	148	70	57	n/a	10	12	16	852	161
	2003–04	301	236	155	94	89	25	12	12	16	945	168
	2004–05	301	236	189	94	89	27	12	12	16	979	165
	2005–06	301	236	206	103	89	29	12	12	22	1013	157
Number of field active inspectors per 10000 employees	2001–02	1.1	1.1	1.0	0.9	1.0	n/a	1.1	1.0	0.7	1.0	0.9
	2002–03	1.1	1.1	1.1	0.9	0.9	n/a	1.1	1.0	0.7	1.0	0.9
	2003–04	1.1	1.1	1.1	1.2	1.4	1.4	1.4	1.1	0.7	1.1	0.9
	2004–05	1.1	1.1	1.2	1.1	1.4	1.4	1.4	1.0	0.6	1.1	0.9
	2005–06	1.1	1.1	1.3	1.2	1.4	1.5	1.4	1.0	0.8	1.1	0.8
Number of infringement notices issued	2001–02	1471	n/a	99	n/a	n/a	n/a	71	0	n/a	1641	
	2002–03	1289	n/a	289	n/a	n/a	n/a	242	0	n/a	1820	
	2003–04	915	n/a	488	n/a	n/a	n/a	31	0	n/a	1434	
	2004–05	1652	n/a	462	n/a	n/a	n/a	7	8	n/a	2130	
	2005–06	1195	n/a	499	n/a	n/a	n/a	47	28	n/a	1769	
Number of improvement notices issued	2001–02	10517	11922	6246	9818	1025	420	19	77	8	40065	
	2002–03	12646	14964	11136	10263	1977	346	22	80	18	51452	
	2003–04	17927	12492	16200	11848	2748	198	29	202	17	61662	
	2004–05	18213	12117	13348	12391	4688	423	17	163	12	61381	
	2005–06	14832	11168	16463	11891	3573	297	49	427	12	58517	
Number of prohibition notices issued	2001–02	786	3102	1188	887	191	109	25	39	2	6331	
	2002–03	779	2904	1256	895	364	131	56	48	9	6444	
	2003–04	1139	2308	1886	870	814	87	14	50	6	7020	
	2004–05	1421	2308	1788	963	899	266	14	66	20	7751	
	2005–06	1212	1876	2223	708	623	125	54	88	10	6918	
Number of prosecutions resulting in conviction	2001–02	455	115	114	41	8	11	2	0	0	746	132
	2002–03	443	105	101	38	22	24	0	2	0	735	119
	2003–04	399	110	120	43	30	7	0	5	0	714	100
	2004–05	384	93	156	48	31	7	0	11	0	731	119
	2005–06	340	70	143	41	51	12	0	5	0	662	79

Source: Workplace Relations Ministers' Council, (2008), *Comparative Performance Monitoring Report: Comparison of Occupational Health and Safety and Workers' Compensation Schemes in Australia and New Zealand,* 10th edition, Office of Australian Safety and Compensation Council, Canberra.

* Comcare, covering federal government workers (including ex-agencies) and some national private employers

Johnstone and Quinlan's (2008) study found that most workplace visits involved discussions with senior managers and at least one other party (table 7.3). What was surprising was that in less than half the visits undertaken (42.4%) did inspectors speak to workers beyond a simple greeting (and even then discussions were often of fairly short duration). One issue here, raised by inspectors themselves, was the fear of workers that those identifying OHS problems might be subject to victimisation—something that would constitute a clear breach of OHS legislation but was often difficult to prove. While this is a significant issue requiring attention (see Quinlan and Johnstone, 2009), OHS agencies themselves have acknowledged that it is critical that inspectors spend more time obtaining the views of workers. Concerns about victimisation have also drawn a regulatory response. In 2008 Victoria introduced the Occupational Health and Safety (Employee Protection) Bill to create a civil cause of action for employees or prospective employees discriminated against on OHS grounds.

Table 7.3 indicates that in just over one-third of visits inspectors spoke to HSRs. In some instances the workplace was simply too small to have a HSR but in other cases there was no HSR present because the workplace was not unionised and HSR presence is strongly linked to unionisation (because unions provide critical protection, training and other forms of logistical support for the HSR). Some jurisdictions (like Victoria) require the inspector to make contact with a HSR if one is present (on some occasions the HSR was off shift when the visit occurred) and this practice appears to be gaining support in other jurisdictions. However, beyond the need to revise inspectorate practices, the limited contact with workers and HSRs is symptomatic of problems arising from changes to work organisation (with more contingent workers and small workplaces, often in a subcontracting chain) and the industrial relations climate (away from collectivisation) over the past 30 years. We will return to these issues later in this chapter and in chapter 9.

Table 7.3   Who was spoken to by inspector during visit*

	2004	2006	Total (percentage)
Manager/owner	41	39	80 (67.8%)
Other supervisors	30	25	55 (46.6%)
Workers	25	25	50 (42.4%)
Health and safety representatives	24	19	43 (36.4%)
Contractors	8	4	12 (10.2%)
OHS consultant	3	2	5 (4.2%)

Source: Johnstone and Quinlan (2008).

* Since visits often entail multiple discussions totals exceed 118 and percentage totals exceed 100%.

Another critical issue is what sort of issues inspectors examined. Post-Robens OHS laws require inspectors to consider a wide array of potential hazards and arrays of regulatory compliance. In their study, Johnstone and Quinlan (forthcoming) examined six broad areas of OHS standards, representing both those that were covered by pre-Robens laws (such as plant and machinery) through to areas where new process standards had been developed (such as ergonomics/manual handling) or other areas (such as suppliers, designers and other upper-stream duty holders and changes to work arrangements such as labour hire, occupational violence, working hours and the use of subcontractors) where the general duty provisions now provide regulatory coverage. As indicated in table 7.4, while there are differences in activity across industry the most commonly examined issue by OHS inspectors during visits was plant and equipment—a traditional area of inspectoral activity. At the same time, inspectors also devoted considerable attention to hazardous substances and changing work arrangements, followed by manual handling. The latter would have ranked higher but for a relatively low level of attention during inspections on construction sites (which one inspector indicated was due to the need to focus on 'more pressing' hazards such as falls from height). Even upstream duty holders received a surprising level of attention (typical cases included faults or hazards with equipment supplied to an employer). The level of attention given to OHSM documentation needs to be treated with caution. With the notable exception of major hazard facilities, in most cases the documents examined pertained to specific elements of a system (such as maintenance or training records) rather than the overall system and a number of inspectors expressed concern about 'tick and flick' documentation and the broader issue of 'paper' compliance (i.e. documentation that didn't match actual practices). Leaving this point to one side, Johnstone and Quinlan (2008) found inspectors examined a wide array of OHS standards even though inspectors acknowledged a number of these areas (such as hazardous substances) required more attention.

Table 7.4 What was examined by industry: numbers and ranking

OHS standard	Construction	Services	Retail	Manufacturing	Transport	Total
Plant/equipment	17(1)	21(1)	6(1)	25(1)	6(1)	75(1)
Manual handling	2(5)	14(5)	3(2)	11(5)	6(1)	36(5)
Hazardous substances	7(3)	16(3)	3(2)	18(3)	4(5)	48(3)
Changing work arrangements	6(4)	15(4)	1(5)	16(4)	5(4)	43(4)
Upstream duty holders	6(4)	14(5)	2(3)	11(5)	2(6)	35(6)
OHSM documentation	9(2)	20(2)	2(3)	19(2)	7(3)	57(2)
Totals	47	100	17	100	30	294

Source: Johnstone and Quinlan (2008).

Speaking to a range of parties and examining a number of issues at a workplace takes time, not to mention the time spent on prior research or in travelling to the workplace (often a considerable distance in the case of country/regional inspectors). As the nature of the workplace and the type of visit varies considerably so can the duration of the visit, as indicated by table 7.5 taken from Johnstone and Quinlan (2008). At one extreme, the inspector may arrive to find the workplace has closed for the day due to some unforeseen event or find critical parties are not present, while at the other extreme an investigation into a serious incident may entail lengthy observation, interviews and data collection (often with follow-up interviews as more evidence is obtained or needs to be tested). Beyond the actual time spent at the workplace it should be noted that investigation is an iterative process and even in a relatively simple case it may take a number of months to collect and assess the relevant material before recommending a course of action.

Table 7.5   Duration of inspector visits by industry

	Mean	Median	Range
Construction	1 hr 55	1 hr 15	15 to 240 minutes
Services	1 hr 00	0 hr 45	15 to 300 minutes
Manufacturing	1 hr 40	1 hr 30	0 to 350 minutes
Retail	1 hr 00	0 hr 10	10 to 260 minutes
Transport	1 hr 50	1 hr 30	0 to 225 minutes

Source: Johnstone and Quinlan (2008).

Table 7.2 summarises enforcement activity by jurisdiction between 2001 and 2006. Compared to Industry Commission (1995) data from the early to mid-1990s this indicates that, overall, inspectorates issued a far higher number of improvement notices and a somewhat higher number of prohibition notices (infringement notices are a relatively new option and so no comparisons can be made). For example, in 1992–93 Australian inspectorates issued 18 070 improvement notices and 4767 prohibition notices (Industry Commission, 1995: 438–9) whereas the comparable figures for 2005–06 were 58 517 and 6918. The growing use of improvement notices in particular is more than commensurate with the growth of the workforce during this period. While the level of enforcement activity varies between jurisdictions, again the real outlier is Comcare where activity of all types is below even comparably small jurisdictions such as the Northern Territory and the Australian Capital Territory.

It needs to be recognised that the issuing of notices is only part of a raft of actions an inspector may take, including issuing verbal directions when the matter can be resolved while the inspector is on site. Further, as already implied, regular contact and repeat visits can be used to good effect to improve OHS in conjunction with formal enforcement activity. Johnstone and Quinlan's (2008) study found inspectors often spent considerable time talking to managers about how they could improve OHS. Their observations of workplace visits suggested that inspectors tend to take informal measures during inspections and use improvement notices relatively frequently, with occasional resort to prohibition notices (see table 7.6). Table 7.6 indicates no formal action was taken in 50% of visits, although in several cases information was being collected as part of an investigation (and in at least one case a successful prosecution was subsequently launched).

Table 7.6   Enforcement action taken during visits: numbers and ranking

	2004	2006	Total (%)*
None/information or entry report	34 (1)	25 (1)	59 (50%)
Verbal directions	17 (3)	13 (3)	30 (25.4%)
Improvement notice	19 (2)	21 (2)	40 (33.9%)
Prohibition notice	7 (4)	7 (4)	14 (11.9%)
Dangerous goods licence granted	6 (5)	1 (5)	7 (5.9%)
Total workplaces visited	61	57	118

Source: Johnstone and Quinlan (2008).
*Since visits often entail multiple actions totals exceed 118 and percentage totals exceed 100%.

Another issue is the extent to which inspectors have embraced the move towards process and performance standards. Overall, table 7.7 (taken from Johnstone and Quinlan, 2008, who asked inspectors what standard they used to take an action) indicates that inspectors make extensive use of both specification and process/performance

Table 7.7   Standards called up in each industry: number and percentage breakdown

	Construction	Services	Manufacturing	Retail	Transport	Total
Only specification	5 (25)	5 (26.3)	2 (11)	0	0	12 (17.9)
Mostly specification	4 (20)	4 (21)	6 (33.3)	1 (16.7)	2 (50)	17 (25.4)
Mixed (50/50)	4 (20)	3 (15.8)	7 (38.9)	2 (33.3)	2 (50)	18 (26.9)
Mostly process/ performance	2 (10)	3 (15.8)	2 (11.1)	1 (16.7)	0	8 (11.9)
Only process/ performance	5 (25)	4 (21)	1(5.6)	2 (33.3)	0	12 (17.9)

Source: Johnstone and Quinlan (2008).
Note: spread of standards called up across all industries

standards with a slight bias towards specification standards (which may reflect agency preferences where there is an option of using either a specification standard–based regulation or the general duty provisions). Small numbers make it difficult to compare industries. Nonetheless, the greater reliance on specification standards in construction and manufacturing (where longstanding and extensive specification standards have been retained) compared to services and retailing (where there was little by way of specification standards historically) is not surprising. At the same time, inspectors in all industries made regular use of process and performance standards.

In sum, evidence indicates that inspectorates have undergone significant changes in terms of recruitment/selection, qualifications/training and patterns of inspection and enforcement since the shift to post-Robens OHS legislation—a shift that Johnstone and Quinlan's (2008) study suggested had small beginnings but has gained in momentum over the past 15 years. Evidence from other countries such as Sweden, Denmark, Canada, France and Britain indicates that many of these changes reflect more general trends. This is not to say the pattern of inspection is identical. For example, a Swedish study (Frick, forthcoming) indicated inspectors there generally spent less time talking to managers, more time examining OHSM and more time talking to workers or their representatives. In Quebec and France, the move from specification-based OHS legislation has been less pronounced although the increased influence of risk management concepts has affected inspectorate practices in ways not too dissimilar from those identified in Australia. In New Zealand limited evidence on inspectorate activity suggests trends similar to Australia but a system facing greater resource constraints and with less government support for vigorous enforcement. Leaving these nuances to one side, there does appear to have been a general shift towards a better educated and more OHS 'savvy' inspectorate and more proactive forms of workplace monitoring and enforcement (and in a number of countries the use of a wider array of enforcement tools or remedies).

Putting the enforcement of OHS legislation into a broader context

Meaningful discussion of enforcement needs to be placed in the context of a broader debate on regulatory compliance. The vast literature on regulatory compliance cannot be summarised here but a number of observations can be made.

In addition to questions of regulatory style (notably whether compliance activities rely more on legal sanctions/punishment/deterrence or persuasion/education/consultation) and inspectoral training/resources already discussed, compliance is shaped by a number of factors. A framework for analysing regulatory enforcement proposed by Kagan (1989) identifies three sets of factors.

First, there are legal design factors including the degree of stringency in the regulatory mission, legal powers (and the emphasis placed on ex-ante or ex-post methods of compliance) and the specificity of legal rules and remedies (such as the contrast between specification and performance standards already discussed). One distinctive characteristic of OHS regulation is its limited use of ex-ante methods such as licensing and safety case regimes and greater reliance on ex-post methods of detecting and investigating breaches—something that, given the number of workplaces, places a heavy logistical burden on the inspectorate. This is a burden few if any OHS inspectorates we are familiar with have the resources to meet (Johnstone and Quinlan, 2008). Regulators placing greater responsibility on employers (especially those of medium to large size) to develop their own systematic approaches to OHS has had positive effects but it has not freed up inspectorate resources (Geldart et al., 2005; Johnstone and Quinlan, 2008). Investigation of incidents (Johnstone and Quinlan, 2008) is also often time-consuming and resource intensive, involving detailed collection of evidence (including often-repeated rounds of interviews as further information emerges), careful assessment and judgments about the appropriate action to be taken or recommended (in some jurisdictions proposed prosecutions are subject to a referral and review process). Even a relatively uncomplicated investigation may take several months and serious incident/fatality investigations even longer: those at two Tasmanian mines (following deaths from rockfalls) took well over 12 months. The result of overextended inspectorates and an ex-post approach is that insufficient workplaces are visited and not all serious incidents are investigated (especially those involving truck drivers; see Perrone, 2000).

Second, there are regulatory environment factors including the visibility of violations, something affected by the frequency of interaction between the agency and the regulated entities as well as the activities of complainants such as workers, unions and the public. Kagan notes that a collaborative approach is easier when there is frequent contact. As already noted, this can involve questions of resourcing as well as intent. Another environmental factor is the regulated enterprise's willingness to comply. Relevant here is the size and sophistication of the enterprise (large organisations are liable to be more sensitive about their public image but may also be more adept at manipulating inspectors) as well as the cost of compliance and the economic resilience of regulated units. Over the past decade or more, inspectorates in Australia, Europe and elsewhere have made increased use of targeted campaigns to improve OHS in small business, including new forms of information dissemination (such as OHS advisors) and periodic blitzes (including graduated actions and the use of infringement notices/on-the-spot fines). At the same time, while many studies of small business identify lack of knowledge and logistical constraints as inhibiting their compliance with OHS legislation, a number point out that noncompliance may also represent a calculated response to competitive pressures and their subordinate position in a supply chain (Mayhew and Quinlan, 1997; Hasle et al., 2009). Acute economic pressure is not confined to small companies and financial pressures have been linked to noncompliance and serious incidents at medium to large workplaces (Jobb, 1994; Bell and Healy, 2006). On a more positive note, the increasing focus on upstream duty holders provides one basis for addressing this problem.

Third, there is the political environment, including dominant policy discourses, struggles between competing interest groups and the possibility that the regulatory agency may be 'captured' by the entities it seeks to regulate. Examples of the effect of neo-liberal policies and government policies with regard to enforcement have already been given. Changes in inspectoral activity can be achieved in covert ways through new appointments to senior agency posts; budgetary or staff cuts; reorganisation of staff training, tasks or administrative control; or subtle messages delivered about the desirability of prosecutions. Other studies have found that dangerous compromises can arise from a desire by governments to avoid political controversy or to promote what are regarded as economically urgent projects. For example, Carson (1989) argued that state collusion in the subordination of OHS to economic considerations that weakened regulatory activities played a critical part in Bhopal, Piper Alpha and a number of other major OHS disasters (for studies making similar points, see also Tucker, 2006). On the other hand, significant incidents can create strong community pressure for more stringent state intervention, including formal inquiries and new laws. Even here, however, studies suggest that in at least some instances the response is symbolic or corrodes relatively soon after public outrage wanes (Hopkins, 1999a & b; Tucker, 2006).

In practice, the three sets of factors identified by Kagan interact and cannot be seen as mutually exclusive. For example, the political environment can affect regulatory design. The dominance of neo-liberal ideology in public policy during the past two decades was associated with a generally 'light touch' approach to corporate criminality that emphasised collaboration, self-regulation, a focus on individual responsibility (often a vehicle to blame-shifting) and the use of incentives rather than punitive action (Snider, 2000; Gray, 2006; Howe and Landau, 2007). As indicated by the introduction of workplace death provisions and several other regulatory initiatives (such as supply chain regulation) in some jurisdictions already discussed, along with the rapid discarding of more naive notions of self-regulation, OHS regulation in Australia and some other countries did not entirely embrace these changes with the enthusiasm evident in other areas of regulation. Nonetheless, it was not entirely immune to these influences or their effects in other areas (such as industrial relations). One instance of this influence that did impact on OHS regulation was the growing influence of cost–benefit analysis (CBA)—and the need to prepare regulatory impact statements as part of the standards development process. Although appearing to be a 'neutral' process that will promote optimal community welfare, CBA comes with considerable baggage. As already demonstrated in chapter 1, estimating the extent and costs of occupational hazards is at best a complex and difficult process and the same point applies to measuring socioeconomic impacts of regulation on the community. In practice, the application is often crude (OHS problems are often complex and scientific knowledge can change significantly over time), can differ markedly between jurisdictions (important in a global context) and can result in socially unacceptable outcomes, especially where risks appear expensive to mitigate (for example, how would CBA have balanced health effects against the widespread use of asbestos products in the 1970s?). Despite these concerns (for a discussion, see 'Health and safety at work: a question of costs and benefits?' 1999) CBA has been strongly pushed by agencies dominated by neo-liberal ideas such as the European Commission.

Current challenges to the regulatory framework

The impact of changes to work organisation and labour markets

Over the past 30 years a series of profound changes have occurred in work arrangements and labour markets in Australia, New Zealand and most, if not all, countries. These changes, including growing job insecurity, increased use of contingent workers, subcontracting and the like have already been described earlier in the book. What needs to be noted here is that, quite apart from their direct effects on OHS already discussed, these changes have also had a significant effect on OHS regulatory regimes. The most apparent manifestation has been a number of serious incidents, particularly ones involving contractors, such as an engine room fire that killed four sailors on the *Westralia* in May 1998, that have required extensive investigation and a regulatory response. These incidents are symptomatic of more wide-ranging problems these work arrangements pose for OHS legislation.

First, the general duty provisions (and the multiple parties they apply to) in post-Robens OHS legislation provide a far better framework for dealing with complex multi-employer worksites, elaborate subcontracting and supply-chain arrangements than earlier specification standard–based laws. Inspectorates in Australia have employed increasingly astute enforcement strategies (from the interventions of individual inspectors through to targeted campaigns and prosecutions) to discourage any belief that these arrangements can be used to evade regulatory responsibilities. A growing body of guidance material clarifying responsibilities of various parties and indicating appropriate control measures has also been produced. Indeed, in the areas of subcontracting and agency labour Australian regulators appear to have been more active than their counterparts in Europe and North America (Johnstone et al., 2001; Hasle, 2007). This includes some genuinely innovative regulatory regimes governing supply chains/outsourcing in the clothing (notably home-based workers) and long-haul truck industry, as well as more generic supply chain regulation (James et al., 2007). These provide models that reinforce emerging international recognition of the importance of supply-chain regulation in safeguarding OHS and other labour standards (Weil and Mallo, 2007; Lloyd and James, 2008). Nonetheless, these measures represent only the first steps in solving a larger problem which continues to grow as elaborate supply chains become more pervasive (both nationally and globally). Available evidence indicates that the use of labour hire (temporary agency workers), direct-hire temporary workers and subcontractors has led to confusion—if not deliberate attempts at 'risk shifting'—with regard to the obligations of particular duty holders (Quinlan, 2004a; Johnstone and Quinlan, 2006; Quinlan and Bohle, 2008).

Second, the growth of small often subcontracted workplaces (including homes), remote and mobile workplaces, complex and sometimes fluid work arrangements (such as turnover among contractors or fixed-term workplaces), together with often equally complex business configurations (using the corporate veil) increase the logistical difficulties facing inspectorates in terms of monitoring workplaces, investigating incidents/

hazards or launching legal proceedings (Quinlan, 2004b). While often making good use of their limited resources (with targeted campaigns and the like) it is not unfair to say that inspectorates have found it extremely difficult to cope (amid many other competing demands) with the scope of the problems now posed by more fractured work arrangements. Some important areas have virtually escaped any regulatory attention. For example, downsizing/restructuring almost always entails changes to work organisation that can (and evidence suggests often does) affect OHS, and general duty provisions, risk assessment and consultative requirements impose obligations on employers in this regard. While aware that downsizing/restructuring affects OHS, and that even large employers seldom meet the obligations just identified, inspectorates have failed to monitor or undertake enforcement with regard to this (Quinlan, 2007a). Rather, like their counterparts in most other countries with which we are familiar, inspectorates have largely been restricted to addressing occupational violence or bullying that can be a consequences of the reduced staffing level and altered management climate associated with such changes.

Third, the growth of small business, subcontracting and the use of contingent workers has weakened both the extent and effectiveness of participatory mechanisms in OHS legislation. It has meant more remote work (such as in homes) or small workplaces falling below the size threshold for establishing a committee, more temporary/labour hire and subcontract workers on site who are unlikely to be involved in/represented by workplace committees or HSRs and more non-unionised workplaces (Johnstone et al., 2005). OHS agencies are aware of these problems and in some cases revisions have been made to regulatory requirements (for example, worker consultation guidance associated with the NSW OHS Risk Assessment Regulation of 2001 requires employers to take account of the use of contingent workers and other special features of their workforce such as ethnic composition). Residual provisions (or a general duty) requiring consultation even where no formal mechanisms (committee or HSR) are in place have been used on occasion. For example, in 2007 a scaffolding subcontractor in northern NSW was successfully prosecuted by WorkCover NSW for breaching both its duty to ensure a safe working environment and its obligation to consult after a casual worker fell and was injured while dismantling scaffolding (Taylor, 2007). However, these cases are too rare to exert a wide-ranging effect. While workplace inspections by unions represent another option to provide worker representation—and one that unions should put more resources into—even under the best circumstances they lack the logistics to visit many workplaces and access may be restricted unless they already have members on site. Further, changes to the industrial relations climate since the 1990s have resulted in more cases where employers have challenged such access (see, for example, *Jim Pearson Transport and Transport Workers' Union of Australia*, Australian Industrial Relations Commission, RE2007/2418, 6 July 2007).

Further, participatory provisions in most OHS legislation in Australia and New Zealand (and other countries too) continue to be framed largely in terms of 'employees' rather than workers, and inspectoral activities seldom focus on participatory mechanisms, let alone the challenges posed by changing work arrangements (Johnstone and Quinlan, 2008). As in the UK, several Australian jurisdictions have considered or experimented with the option of 'roving safety representatives' to provide employee representation on smaller or non-represented worksites—drawing on the highly successful experience of regional safety representatives in Sweden already discussed (Frick and Walters, 1998). However, the experiments have been short-lived, in no small part due to the prevailing neo-liberal regulatory climate referred to earlier rather than the intrinsic merits of the schemes (Walters, 2006).

It is worth noting that a number of well-documented submissions to the national model OHS legislation review of 2008–09 made extensive reference to these problems and proposed solutions, including strengthening supply-chain provisions in OHS legislation and establishing a system of roving safety representatives. For some reason (not explained) the issue was largely ignored by the review panel except to the extent that it might be captured by a recommended broadening of the definition of 'worker'. However, the problem of worker involvement mechanisms—a pivotal part of post-Robens OHS legislation—being weakened if not bypassed by changes to work arrangements will not disappear. If anything, the economic recession experienced by Australia (and globally) at the time of writing is likely to accentuate these shortcomings. Ultimately, the challenge will need to be addressed if worker involvement is to remain a meaningful feature of OHS legislation. Evidence of the last 20 years indicates no reliance can be placed on voluntarism in this regard. Rather, governments will need to take a more decisive role in mandating a more effective framework for worker involvement in decision making on OHS.

It should be noted that the implications of these omissions affect some groups within the workforce more than others. Most notably, women constituted the vast majority of contingent workers even prior to the recent expansion. Further, they were concentrated in a number of industries (such as healthcare, retailing and personal services) and work arrangements (including home-based work and homecare) most affected by the current expansion. This includes work arrangements (such as home-based work) where an extremely complex interplay between different regulatory regimes (governing industrial relations, OHS, workers' compensation and taxation) is conducive to confusion, evasion and serious compliance issues. With some notable exceptions (Bernstein et al., 2001; Lippel, 2005) the gender implications of the growth of precarious employment for OHS regulatory regimes has been largely ignored. This reflects, in part, both past priorities and major knowledge gaps with regard to OHS research into work arrangements such as home-based work where women are concentrated (for a scoping exercise carried out in the UK, see O'Hara, 2002). Moreover, in countries such as Australia and the US there is also an almost complete disconnect between political rhetoric about the importance of work–family balance and evidence on how different types of flexible work (temporary work, part-time permanent work and home-based work) have affected this, and no serious consideration of policies that would deliver this outcome (Price and Burgard, 2006).

The growth of precarious employment/contingent work and other changes to work arrangements just described represent a serious challenge to all OHS regulatory regimes, not simply those drawing on the Robens model, such as Australia and New Zealand (see, for example, Silverstein, 2008). Further, the growth of flexible employment and other changes to work arrangements have presented difficulties not only to OHS legislation and OHS inspectorates but also regarding the role of law relating to work and labour standards and its relationship to other bodies. Several significant examples are worth citing.

First, the growth of temporary employment in industries such as hospitality and retailing as well as the growth of self-employment and home-based work has been associated with increased employment of younger workers and even the re-emergence of significant levels of child labour within industrialised countries like Australia (Quinlan et al., 2001b). In Australia this has led to a number of reviews of and revisions to state child labour laws and new child employment principles being established by industrial tribunals that include references to OHS (see, for example, Mourell and Allan, 2005; Child Employment Principles Case 2007 [2007] *NSWIRComm* 110, IRC 3579 of 2006). For their part, over the past decade or more OHS inspectorates in Australia, the US, Canada and other countries have developed guidance material, information/advisory mechanisms and campaigns targeting younger workers as a vulnerable group. Unfortunately, with some exceptions this activity—while undoubtedly valuable—fails to take sufficient consideration of the fact that the vast majority of young workers are concentrated in contingent jobs.

Second, over the past 25 years there has been a significant revival of large-scale international movements of workers (especially from poorer to richer countries such as Australia, the US and New Zealand) not only via formal migration but also—and this distinguishes it from earlier periods—large numbers of temporary workers (guest workers) and illegal/undocumented immigrants. Again, these workers tend to be concentrated in contingent work arrangements and, indeed, guest workers (such as s457 visa holders in Australia) represent a mechanism for contingent work. The vulnerability of newly arrived foreign workers (often with language difficulties and unsure of their legal rights/entitlements) becomes double jeopardy in the generally more hazardous contingent work arrangements. For foreign guest workers (especially those relying on employer sponsorship and industrial relations entitlements that do not match those of 'local' workers performing the same tasks) and illegal/undocumented immigrants (where any complaint could lead to discovery and deportation) the situation is even more acute. Studies in Australia, the US and Europe (Guthrie and Quinlan, 2005; Toh and Quinlan, 2009; Cho et al., 2007; Sokas and Sprince, 2008) have identified both greater vulnerability of these workers in relation to OHS and the limited attention given to this by OHS regulators. Some positive steps have been taken. For example, from 2008 onwards WorkSafe Victoria launched a number of prosecutions following a series of serious incidents involving s457 workers. In one case, Lakeside Packaging Pty Ltd was convicted for failing to provide a safe system of work, training and supervision following incidents involving several Chinese s457 visa holders (the company had also demanded two return to work with broken arms, *SIA Safety Week* Issue 153, 7 July 2008). Nonetheless, more proactive action is required, including the federal government reconsidering legislation and policies associated with the introduction of such workers. Unfortunately, a federal government review of the s457 scheme in 2008 largely sidestepped the OHS issue, seeing it primarily in terms of language difficulties (and even this was dealt with in a simplistic manner; see Premji et al., 2008a) despite submissions pointing to the broader issues of vulnerability and contingent work arrangements.

Third, the shift to more flexible work and the removal of industrial relations provisions (in awards) has been associated with significant changes to working hour arrangements, including longer shifts, split shifts, removal of rest breaks and minimum call-back periods, more irregular shifts and the like. As described in chapter 6, there is a substantial and growing body of international evidence that working hour arrangements, including a number of those just described such as atypical shifts, have significant OHS effects. In Australia growing concern at the OHS implications of extended hours of work, especially in the mining industry and trucking, were the subject of a number of government inquiries and the introduction (in New South Wales, Tasmania and Western Australia, for example) of new OHS codes or regulations designed to limit hours of work and combat fatigue. In essence, OHS regulators have been obliged to start remedying problems arising from the retreat of industrial relations regulation—a retreat resulting from the influence of neo-liberal ideas among policymakers. Lack of rest breaks and other 'flexible' working hour arrangements have become a growing source of concern to OHS inspectors across a range of industries. Further, in heavy vehicle road transport at least, a combination of industry influence and a preference for 'light touch' regulation has led to fatigue management regimes that actually permit longer hours of work 'if managed', contrary to the sustained evidence of Professor Ann Williamson and other experts. In sum, as with the other changes mentioned, OHS regulators are finding it difficult to meet challenges associated with changes to working hours. Again, these problems are not confined to Australia.

Regulating high-hazard workplaces and hazardous substances: still a work in progress

An overlapping set of challenges confronting regulators over the past 30 years has been how to best address the potentially disastrous incidents in major hazard facilities and other high-hazard workplaces as well as dealing with the proliferation and use of chemicals.

Major hazard facilities are workplaces that refine, manufacture, use or store large quantities of hazardous substances or dangerous goods, including oil and gas refineries, offshore oil rigs, gas-fired and nuclear power stations, chemical plants and explosives manufacturers and stores. Serious, indeed disastrous incidents resulting in multiple deaths (both workers and nearby residents) involving such workplaces have occurred for over a century. However, it was a series of incidents from the 1970s (including Flixborough in the UK, Seveso in Italy, Bhopal in India, Phillips 66 in the US, the

Alexander Kjelland oil rig in Norway, Longford in Australia, AZF Toulouse in France and BP Texas City in the US) that resulted in the introduction of significantly tighter regulatory regimes to govern major hazard facilities in the European Union, North America, Australia and elsewhere. In Norway, the Alexander Kjelland oil rig disaster led to the introduction of the internal control regime of systematic OHS management and control of subcontractors (Frick et al., 2000). In the US, the Phillips 66 explosion/ fire and similar incidents at other chemical plants led to the introduction of a new process safety standard that also included tighter control on contractors (Johnstone et al., 2001). In Europe, the Flixborough and Seveso incidents provided the impetus for a new regime to manage major hazard facilities called the safety case regime (SCR). A number of Australian jurisdictions adopted a similar approach. Victoria adopted a safety case regime approach to major hazard facilities after a serious explosion and fire at the Esso Longford refinery in Gippsland in 1998. A safety case regime was also imposed by federal legislation governing offshore oil and gas production.

Like the process safety standard regime in the US, the safety case regime (SCR) is designed to prevent low-frequency catastrophic events in major hazard facilities. Under the safety case regime, there is an obligation on the operator to demonstrate to the regulator that they have implemented a regime that has identified hazards, assessed risks and has effective control measures in place. Regulatory scrutiny and acceptance is a prerequisite to operate. The regulator accepts but does not formally approve the SCR because the onus for operations, including hazard identification, risk assessment, control measures and monitoring remains with the operators who have the knowledge to adapt these measures on a regular, even daily basis as conditions change (as is the case with regard to blasting and mucking out operations at a mine). The safety case regime covers the construction/recommencement, operation and closure phases. The SCR places a strong onus on a highly trained and adequately resourced inspectorate. For example, in Victoria each inspector in the major hazard facilities team has received dedicated training and is only responsible for around six workplaces compared to the literally hundreds of workplaces an OHS inspector is normally responsible for.

Research into the effectiveness of safety case regimes indicates that they improve overall hazard identification and control, due to the need to review systems and processes. There is some evidence that the potential for further improvements corrodes over time, although this problem also applies to OHS management systems and other regulatory interventions such as the process safety standard in the US (Vectra Group, 2003: 3). With regard to the latter, the explosion at BP's Texas City refinery in 2005 (which killed 15 workers and injured 180 others) highlighted the problems of a management focus on individual safety rather than serious hazards, lack of regulatory oversight and poor industrial relations/low worker input climate (Baker, 2007). A survey undertaken by the United Steelworkers Union (2007) found highly hazardous conditions were common at other refineries, neither the letter nor spirit of the process safety standard had been achieved and a combination of understaffing and poor work organisation increased the risk of disasters.

The imposition of SCR is normally contingent on a minimum size threshold (for example, based on the amount of hazardous material stored on site) and there is evidence that some companies have tried to evade the regime by manipulating their storage arrangements.

It is beyond the scope of this chapter to discuss specialist health and safety legislation covering air, sea and road transport and mining and gas production in any detail (for a detailed examination of mining regulation in Australia, see Gunningham, 2006). However, it is worth noting that extending the SCR approach to workplaces that are not deemed major hazard facilities but are widely viewed as highly hazardous is a current focus of policy consideration. The most notable example has been in relation to mines, where it has been seen as a logical extension of risk-based regulation in the mining industry—a means of addressing the limitations in systems design and implementation (Heiler, 2006; Gunningham, 2006b). In Western Australia SCR has been imposed on a number of mines and this approach was also adopted by Workplace Standards Tasmania in relation to the recommencement of mining operations at the Beaconsfield goldmine following the fatal rockfalls of April 2006. As Beaconsfield was not a large mine (with fewer than 200 workers as employees or contractors), this case demonstrated the wide applicability of SCR to mining operations. Given growing awareness of limitations in OHS management systems and Australia's already favourable international reputation in terms of mining safety, this development warrants wider attention. Evidence on the limitations of OHSMS with regard to high-hazard workplaces and the failure to learn from 'repeat' disasters is discussed in chapter 10 (see also Hopkins, 2008).

In concluding this discussion of the regulation of hazardous industries a number of further points can be made. First, there can be a number of investigatory and regulatory responses even in relation to incidents within the same industry and jurisdiction. For example, a serious incident resulting in death at a mine may give rise to a coronial inquest, an investigation by the relevant inspectorate (or inspectorates in the case of dual regulatory coverage), an independent government inquiry/royal commission or almost any combination of these. With regard to transport safety, the US, Canada and Australia have established special investigative agencies. In the US there is also an independent government agency to investigate hazardous incidents involving chemicals—the Chemical Safety Board. The duality of regulatory investigation has both strengths (in terms of review and approaching the event from different perspectives/expertise bases as well as gearing the investigation to the scale and nature of the event) and weaknesses (notably, fragmentation). For example, major events are generally multi-causal and therefore there may be lessons to be learnt by a range of disciplines/professions involved in safety, such as engineers as well as regulators (Cooke and Durso, 2007). Second, the community concerns associated with major events (or a series of them) and the limitations revealed by investigations continue, as in the past, to act as an important impetus for regulatory action. This can even apply in less than democratic societies. In 2008 Chinese officials responded with a crackdown on privately operated coal mines following a series of disasters in the run-up to the Beijing Olympics (*The Age*, 4 August 2008). Third, on a less positive note, as noted by Haines (2009), these responses may sometimes be driven more by symbolism than a desire to address the underlying causes. Further, the highly focused investigatory response can lead to fragmentation or decontextualisation and a failure to identify where the problems identified played a part in previous incidents—something which may hold important clues to more effective responses in the future (for a useful example of an exception in relation to truck driver fatalities see Pinch, 2004). While there is a growing recognition of the need to look at other events (including those in other countries)—aided in no small part by readier access via information technology—steps in this direction remain relatively timid at least as far as government investigations are concerned.

Consideration of how to regulate the use of highly hazardous materials in major facilities needs to be seen in the context of the pervasive threat posed by the proliferating use of chemicals across a wide range of work settings—many where chemical use is seen as so incidental to work activity that the hazards largely escape recognition. Of the many tens of thousands of chemicals in commercial use in Australia and New Zealand only a fraction are subjected to rigorous health testing. The same applies to countries like the US where even more chemicals may be in commercial use and the problem extends to public health as well as occupational health (Lin, 2009). Further, as noted by Linda Birnbaum, director of the US National Institute for Environmental Health Sciences and the National Toxicology Program (Washington DC), in 2009, the failure to consider additive or synergistic effects (see chapter 1) has resulted in significant gaps even where testing has been conducted. The precautionary principle—that where there are serious environmental or health threats precautionary measures should proceed prior to full scientific confirmation—has not been applied to this area.

In 1989 the National Industrial Chemical Notification and Assessment Scheme (NICNAS) was established under the supervision of NOHSC (later the ASCC). NICNAS was one of four federal agencies established by the early 1990s to deal with chemicals, assisted by state governments ceding some of their powers over chemicals within their domain (the others dealt with agricultural pesticides and veterinary medicines, therapeutic goods/human medicines, and food products and additives). NICNAS required the potential risks of all new industrial chemicals to be assessed prior to importation or manufacture so the information could enable companies introducing them, workers and the community to implement appropriate safeguards. Between 1989 and early 1999, 597 chemicals were notified, and a Material Safety Data Sheet (MSDS) prepared for each, under NICNAS legislation. Around this time it was estimated that 20 000 chemicals were imported and another 700 manufactured in Australia (in 1999 there were also 38 500 single substances included in the Australia Inventory of Chemical Substances) so, at best, NICNAS was a fractional approach to notification. The sheer scale of the task meant NICNAS had to deal with existing chemicals on a priority basis. The national MSDS repository received data sheets on almost a daily basis (by early 1999 it contained over 15 000 MSDSs). However, this can still be regard as a drop in the ocean of potentially hazardous chemicals and, as far as we are aware, largely ignores additive, potentiate or synergistic effects associated with substances that combine a number of chemicals.

Exposure to some hazardous substances (such as asbestos, lead and mercury) is directly regulated under OHS and environmental protection legislation, and the ASCC (and presumably its replacement Safe Work Australia) can effectively ban a substance by adding them to schedule 2 of the National Model Regulations for the Control of Workplace Hazardous Substances (Productivity Commission, 2008: 144). However, such actions only affect a tiny fraction of those substances known to be harmful (let alone those suspected of being harmful). The same point applies to chemicals identified as hazardous substances under regulations of the OHS statutes of various state and territory jurisdictions (and New Zealand). The general duty provisions in Australian and New Zealand OHS legislation also impose a more generic obligation with regard to hazardous substances on employers, suppliers, manufacturers, importers and other parties. However, with regard to this all jurisdictions rely on the MSDS 'as a reference document for risk assessment and risk control' (Killey et al., 2009). Further, unless the chemical is specifically regulated inspectorates are unlikely to take action except in the clearest circumstances where a hazard has been detected (and then mainly in relation to serious exposure, poor handling or storage rather than more insidious effects of exposure).

This is not to suggest that OHS inspectorates have been entirely reactive. Training of inspectors with regard to hazardous substances has been improved, monitoring of chemicals appears to have increased and agencies have produced targeted guidance material (some targeted at small businesses such as printers) and campaigns. As has occurred in other countries, specific interventions (such as those relating to the use of chemicals in agriculture and manufacturing) have been devised, though more independent scrutiny (see LaMontagne et al., 2005) is required in this regard. Taken as a whole, while there are positive trends the scope of activity by under-resourced inspectorates does not match the scale of the problem.

In essence, NICNAS represents a national notification and information provision scheme, not a scheme for regulating exposure to hazardous chemicals. Even where MSDSs are required in a workplace, ensuring they have been obtained and appropriate work practices adopted on the basis (itself limited) of this information represents a significant logistical challenge to already over-stretched OHS inspectorates. While most medium to large firms may be diligent in regard to obtaining and displaying MSDSs, workplace visits in a range of industries undertaken by Johnstone and Quinlan (2008) found this could not be presumed and even this level of activity was absent in many small workplaces (including those using significant amounts of hazardous chemicals). For example, at one workplace spray-painting metal products and using a range of hazardous painting materials, solvents and the like, there was not a single MSDS (even though the paint packages warned the product was not to come into contact with human skin) and the work practices and emergency procedures showed no appreciation for the hazards involved. Although this was an extreme case, serious deficiencies in the storage and handling of hazardous chemicals were commonly encountered by inspectors (see table 7.4). Further, a recent study of pesticide use in agriculture (Killey et al., 2009: 127) found that while the vast majority of pesticides could be presumed to represent 'hazardous substances' under OHS regulations, there were problems with the coverage and content of MSDSs, with the information being in the authors' view 'erroneous in at least 15% of cases'.

Further, as in other areas of regulation consideration has to be given to the effect of the currently still dominant neo-liberal policy discourse. In July 2008 the Productivity Commission (2008)—a federal agency dominated by neo-liberal economists committed to reducing regulatory 'burdens'—produced a research report on chemicals and plastics regulation for an Australian Council of Governments review on harmonising chemical and plastics regulation. In reviewing all regulatory regimes in relation to chemical safety the Productivity Commission report (2008: xxv) concluded that 'the current institutional and regulatory arrangements are broadly *effective* in management of risks to health and safety, but are less effective in managing risks to the environment and national security'. In a breathtaking illustration of ignorance, the report (2008: 138–9; 148–50) relies on workers' compensation data to indicate the case for compliance, and to compare Australia's performance with other countries, without acknowledging either the well-recognised and substantial deficiencies in this data when it comes to disease-related claims or the equally significant limitations in assessing trends or comparing inter-country performance due to the effect of changing work arrangements and different data recording conventions. These limitations and others relating to the measurement of work-related disease have been extensively documented in this book (see chapters 1, 3, 7 and 8).

The commission also assessed moves to establish a single regulatory framework for workplace chemicals. It noted (Productivity Commission, 2008: 156) that in 2002 NOHSC had initiated a review of hazardous substance regulatory frameworks and NOHSC's successor (ASCC) drafted a consolidated system of national standards and codes of practice for hazardous workplace chemicals. The Productivity Commission detailed the costs of implementing the system, including industry misgivings in this regard and costs to the inspectorates (somewhat ironic given that these were also indicative of the deficiencies already experienced by inspectorates in terms of regulating hazardous substances). After raising a series of concerns that costs might exceed benefits, the Productivity Commission (2008: 164–5) recommended that pursuit of a national scheme of hazardous substance regulation be subject to a regulatory impact assessment by the ASCC (and a favourable outcome). Subsections describing the conduct of the study for the report are also indicative of the Productivity Commission's philosophy and approach. For example the 20-page discussion of compliance and administrative costs includes subheadings on how compliance costs can reduce firm profitability, how regulatory arrangements can be anti-competitive, how the introduction of safe/more effective chemicals can be impeded and how reforms can add to the regulatory burden.

The major recommendations of the Productivity Commission (2008: xlii) report recommended that the Australian Government impose a statutory duty on NICNAS to ensure the cost of chemical assessments is commensurate with the risks posed and assessment priorities are directed to the most efficient management of aggregate risk of industrial chemicals. Another critical recommendation was that the role of NICNAS should be limited to scientific assessment of chemical hazards and its power to ban or phase out chemicals be removed. As others have observed (Rae, 2008), the chemical industry would have cause to be pleased with the positive response to their input into the review. Untrammelled by a consideration of the evidence of disastrous incidents arising in major hazard facilities (see above and chapter 10) or the serious issues confronting inspectorates actually dealing with hazardous substances (see Johnstone and Quinlan, 2008), the Productivity Commission also recommended that the ASCC should determine whether there was a case for major hazard facilities regulation beyond generic OHS and environmental regulation on a 'cost–benefit' basis and, if so, how greater national consistency could be achieved. Another key recommendation was that implementation of the globally harmonised system (known as GHS) of classifying and labelling chemicals for the workplace sector only proceed when it could be shown to demonstrate net benefits, including consideration of the actions of major trading partners like the US and China (Productivity Commission, 2008: xlv). Tying chemical regulation to China presents an interesting prospect given that country's very poor record of regulating OHS more generally. It is also worth noting that the European Union—another major trading partner—brought its GHS regulation into force in January 2009, complementing its REACH (registration, evaluation, authorisation and restriction of chemicals) Regulation that extends to subcontracted and small operators—something Australia could also do well to emulate. In practice, costs are a lot easier to measure or estimate than benefits and the effect of these recommendations, if implemented, would almost certainly be to delay and narrow the scope of regulation of chemicals in the workplace. History is littered with what have eventually proved to be extremely costly (in economic and human terms) examples of belated recognition of and responses to hazardous substances at work (see, for example, the deseal/reseal maintenance program on the F-111).

Harking back to our earlier discussion of regulatory infrastructure, it is important to note that efforts to regulate hazardous substances in Australia have been hampered by the erosion of research funding and infrastructure as well as a lack of epidemiological databases (apart from the mesothelioma register). The shortage of specialist technical advice within the federal government since the downgrading/abolition of NOHSC have also weakened the exchange of information with similar bodies in other countries. As a rich country, Australia should be adopting a leadership role in terms of research to meet its own needs, stand on an equal footing with other rich countries in terms of sharing information, and assist poorer countries—especially those in the Asia-Pacific region.

The problems just described are by no means unique to Australia although the Productivity Commission's recent input is especially disturbing. The size and complexity of the chemical industry and the rapid innovation within it have outstripped resources for notification, assessment and regulation in Australia and many if not all other industrialised countries, especially in the absence of stringent licensing requirements like those which apply to food (but which also have been watered down in some respects due to a combination of neo-liberal policy and industry influence—membership of the food standards authority of Australia and New Zealand is currently dominated by industry representatives). It is important to note that research into and regulatory responses to hazardous exposures affecting women workers (due to their concentration in jobs such as hairdressing), as well as chemicals affecting reproduction, have in general lagged well behind even the muted response described here (for an exception see Fudge and Tucker, 1993). As yet regulators have also given limited attention to the problems posed by new technologies such as nanotechnology.

The challenges in effectively regulating chemicals in the workplace do not constitute a case for inaction. Despite their limitations, MSDSs represent a valuable step towards both recognising exposures and beginning the process of controlling them. Nonetheless, the deficiencies of reactive approaches (including the issues of costly screening and treatment described in chapters 7 and 8), and the multiplicity of exposure sources (both within and outside the workplace) indicate a more proactive and public health–focused approach is needed (Sokas and Sprince, 2008). As Sokas (2008: 171) has argued, what is needed is an integrated national and international regime of environmental and work-place protection that is based on collaboration with (rather than the marginalising of) community and worker movements that are currently springing up over this issue.

National uniformity in OHS regulation and the global regulatory gap

A significant feature of the regulatory framework in Australia has been the fragmentation arising from its multi-jurisdictional character. Most countries (such as New Zealand, Sweden, Japan, China and Britain) have a unitary political structure and a single set of OHS laws. Even among those countries with a federal political structure, most (such as the US, Germany and Malaysia) have enacted laws providing for overarching federal government control of OHS. After 1970 only Canada remained close to the Australian approach of relying on state/provincial or territory legislation. Prior to 1985 federal OHS laws in Australia were largely confined to those areas clearly within the federal constitutional domain (maritime and air transport, federal employees and the defences forces). In the 1920s and early 1930s an Industrial Hygiene Unit established within the federal Department of Health made a significant contribution to attempts to minimise silicosis in the mining industry as well as several other occupational diseases. However, this body was wound back during the Great Depression. A revival of interest during World War II (the Munitions Medical Service and Factory Welfare Division of the federal Department of Labour and Industry) was also short-lived despite a recommendation for an increased Commonwealth role in OHS (Gillespie, 1987).

By the 1980s the limitations of this fractured approach were becoming increasingly apparent. Large employers, in particular, encountered difficulties coordinating their national operations in a context where different legislative standards applied in specific states and territories. This affected matters such as training and certification requirements for the operators of plant and equipment, the guarding of particular types of machinery, the existence and rules relating to health and safety representatives and workplace committees and a host of other matters. The Australian Council of Trade Unions (ACTU) was also keen for a more active national approach to OHS as part of its broader concerns with the social wage and quality of life (incorporated into an Accord signed with the Australian Labor Party promising wage restraint).

In 1985 the federal Labor government (elected two years earlier) established a national OHS agency—the National Occupational Health and Safety Commission (NOHSC) and its corporate entity Worksafe Australia to promote a more coordinated approach to OHS standards/policies, training/education and research. In keeping with government philosophy, the commission was tripartite with representatives of federal, state and territory governments as well as peak employer (the Australian Chamber of Commerce and Industry or ACCI) and union organisations (notably, the ACTU). The commission was a collaborative structure with limited powers to make decisions. It had the power, staff (including a considerable number of scientists and technical experts) and funding to initiate research, collect statistics, encourage professional development and develop and assess national standards. The National Institute or Worksafe Australia established under the auspices of the commission (with a staff of around 180 at its peak in the early 1990s) was loosely modelled on NIOSH in the US. However, the adoption and implementation of national standards remained dependent on state and territory governments. Further, the commission was not even responsible for administering OHS laws pertaining to federal employees, which remained the province of a separate federal government agency—Comcare.

It is worth noting in passing that the collaborative approach adopted by the federal government was not its only option. While apparently lacking constitutional power to impose OHS legislation on states and territories (a High Court decision on the corporation's power in 2006 largely sidestepped this obstacle), the federal government could have ratified ILO Convention 155 and then used this as a basis for overarching OHS legislation under its external treaties power (the government had indeed used the power to block a dam on the Franklin River in Tasmania). For different reasons, both Labor and the conservative side of Australian politics (the Liberal–National Coalition) were reluctant to assume direct federal control of OHS. In short, the barriers to federal OHS legislation were primarily political not legal (Lee and Quinlan, 1994). However, to add impetus to its uniformity push the federal government commissioned major inquiries into OHS and workers' compensation by its economic performance agency (the Industry Commission, 1994, 1995) that documented the complexity, inefficiencies and problems arising from the existing fractured system and strongly advocated a more coordinated national approach.

Notwithstanding the limitations on its role, some teething problems (including poor leadership/strategic direction) and ongoing interest group struggles (especially on the part of state governments which felt under-represented) NOHSC made a valuable contribution to a more national approach to OHS. National codes for RSI and manual handling developed in the 1980s were rapidly adopted by states and territories. The first genuinely national research and statistics infrastructure was established (including staff, a library and international linkages with comparable agencies such as NIOSH).

NOHSC also promoted OHS research and training/education within universities and colleges by funding research and PhD scholarships and producing guidance material on OHS education and the like. In 1991 NOHSC established a National Uniformity Taskforce to pursue its strategic priority of national coordination in OHS standards and mutual recognition of OHS-related operator qualifications. Progress towards national uniformity was achieved but the process was slow and sometimes problematic due to complexity in the way standards were framed in different jurisdictions, differences in approach and differences in the level of standards (with some states concerned about a lowest common denominator approach while others feared the impost on industry of higher standards).

The defeat of Labor and election of a federal Coalition government in 1996 wrought significant changes on NOHSC. Its budget was slashed by a third and staffing by half, virtually obliterating research capacity and creating internal turmoil as the senior leadership was changed; some administrators sought to reposition the agency to be more akin to the neo-liberal philosophy of the government, and a number of remaining talented staff resigned when the agency was relocated from Sydney to Canberra. Ostensibly the commitment to national uniformity was continued and, indeed, cuts to other activities were partly justified on the grounds that from now standards would be a priority. In practice, a review of existing national standards was abandoned (before finalising its first review, that of manual handling) and development of new national standards largely stalled as the standards area too was wound back.

In 2005 the federal government replaced NOHSC with the Australian Safety and Compensation Council (ASCC) as its advisory body to coordinate efforts to prevent workplace death, injury and disease, and improve workers' compensation, rehabilitation and return to work arrangements. While the ASCC was a tripartite body composed of representatives of state and federal governments as well as three representatives from employers and unions, its structure was more closely tied to the federal minister than to NOHSC. The ASCC's dual focus on prevention and workers' compensation also represented an important shift. The greater emphasis on workers' compensation and especially the costs associated with this, and adopting a 'partnership' approach with industry (rather than an emphasis on setting and enforcing regulatory standards) was more in keeping with the thinking of the federal government. In terms of infrastructure, the ASCC relied heavily on the web-based materials produced under NOHSC, although it was responsible for producing a number of reports in its own right during its relatively short existence (2005–08). There was little development in terms of new national standards. Some revision and extension was undertaken, such as a new code of practice declared for the prevention of musculoskeletal disorders from performing manual tasks (2007). In February 2009 the ASCC (2009) issued a discussion paper on safety requirements for the design, manufacture and conformity assessment of plant with its successor organisation (Safe Work Australia) taking over the development process in relation to this standard.

It needs to be stressed that sluggish development in terms of uniform national standards did not mean that there was not an increasing level of cooperation between state and territory agencies in terms of operational campaigns during this period. The Heads of Workplace Safety Authorities (HWSA) which represents general managers of OHS inspectorates in Australia and New Zealand conducted a number of nationally coordinated campaigns in relation to agreed high-priority hazards after 2004 (with different state agencies acting in a leadership role). Between 2004 and 2006 this included manual handling in hospitals and manufacturing, labour hire in manufacturing and prevention of falls in construction; and more recent examples (2007–08) included new and young workers in hospitality, manual tasks in retail/wholesale and transport, managing aggressive behaviour in healthcare and machine guarding. This and other evidence of growing operational cooperation between inspectorates (see Johnstone and Quinlan, 2008)—something worthy of more federal funding support—needs to be borne in mind when considering the movement to a more nationally consistent OHS regulatory system.

For its part, the Coalition government had developed a growing interest in pushing its own vision of national uniformity and responding to calls from national employers. In 2003 the report of a Productivity Commission (the successor to the Industry Commission) inquiry into workers' compensation had found that state and territory governments were reluctant to give up their own workers' compensation regimes for a mixture of institutional, financial and political reasons. However, one option suggested by the report was to extend coverage to national employers to become self-insured under the Comcare scheme (which now included federal corporations, such as the Commonwealth Bank and Telstra that had been privatised). The federal government amended the Comcare legislation to provide this option and subsequently (in 2005) amended legislation so that any employer joining Comcare would henceforth be exclusively covered by federal OHS legislation, not state or territory OHS laws. A small but growing number of large private employers (including construction and transport firms) took advantage of this option. This move proved controversial, drawing criticism not only from state governments but unions who alleged the move was at least partly inspired by employers wanting to move into a environment that provided less union access to workplaces and where the level of enforcement of OHS standards (by Comcare) was conspicuously lower than state or territory jurisdictions. Leaving this to one side, the process would not secure national uniformity in the foreseeable future (unless state regimes felt obliged to cut a deal with the federal government) and it actually caused greater complexity on some worksites. Notably, where joint ventures or contractors were involved these would still be covered by state/territory inspectorates leading to a situation where state and federal OHS inspectors had to cover the same workplace.

In November 2007 the federal Coalition government was defeated and replaced by a Labor government that rapidly announced an inquiry into Comcare (and a moratorium on new employers joining the scheme), a national review into model uniform OHS laws and the replacement of the ASCC with a new body, Safe Work Australia (established in early 2009). The Comcare review (which considered both federal OHS and compensation aspects of the agency) was completed in May 2008 but was not publicly released by the minister until August 2009. However, public submissions to the review from a wide range of parties (including law societies) made a number of strident criticisms of the recruitment/selection/training and operations of Comcare inspectors and pointed out its low level of enforcement activity when compared to virtually every other OHS inspectorate in Australia.

In its first report (Crompton, 2008) the Review Panel on Model OHS laws recommended that an overarching duty of care be owed to workers (the definition of which was expanded) by those conducting a business or undertaking; that office-holders be required to exercise due diligence in terms of compliance with the model act; and that both new offences and increased penalties for breaches of the act be introduced. In its second report (Crompton, 2009) the Review Panel on Model OHS laws argued that hazard-specific legislation (such as that covering mining, dangerous goods and transport) should only continue where 'objectively justified' (the panel should read the February 2009 findings of the coroner into the 2006 rockfall at the Beaconsfield goldmine in this regard), suggested a set of objectives based on current OHS Acts and recommended the inclusion of a number of definitions such as 'health'. With regard to worker involvement and consultation, the panel recommended a broad obligation be placed on those undertaking a business in this regard, that provisions be included for workers to elect HSRs and that HSRs be given a range of powers (including the right to direct a cessation of unsafe work). The panel did not support the inclusion of risk management within the general duty provisions of the legislation but did support a requirement that primary duty holders should monitor health and workplace conditions. Recommendations in relation to the powers of inspectors and the capacity to use enforceable undertakings largely reflected the state of play in existing laws (or recent and general trends with regard to them). The panel recommended a right-of-entry power governing union officials and employees so they could access workplaces but did not support the right of unions to initiate prosecutions (as is the case under NSW OHS legislation).

Within the confines of this book it is impossible to unpackage and critically assess these and other recommendations of the review panel in any detail, and as the final outcome of the review is unclear at the time of writing any attempt could well prove a bootless exercise. Nonetheless, some basic points are worth making. At one level the review has managed to distil key aspects of model OHS legislation in Australia and propose a workable set of arrangements that also address some problems identified in existing laws (in relation to definitions and the like). The review panel recognised the critical role of worker involvement and the right to refuse unsafe work. On the other hand, on some issues the panel appears to have adopted an overly conservative approach even where the balance of evidence did not support this (even if the assertions of some submissions to the panel would have suggested otherwise). For example, the panel chose not to recommend that risk assessment be incorporated into the general duty provisions even though Queensland had already done this successfully (it would have been consistent with existing trends in court decisions relating to employer duties and the value of such guidance has been highlighted by incidents such as the 2006 rockfall at the Beaconsfield goldmine—the draft act does refer to risk management). Further, the panel's recommendation that the right to prosecute be limited to inspectorates (and the DPP in some circumstances) was not supported by convincing argument or evidence. In NSW, where unions have the right to initiate prosecutions, they have used this option selectively (costs providing a deterrent to frivolous actions) and successfully (virtually all of the fewer than 20 cases have resulted in convictions), and the results have complemented, not interfered with, enforcement activities by inspectorates. Both the examples just cited also highlight another issue, namely the risk that uniformity will be achieved by a levelling down or lowest common denominator approach to legislative requirements. At the level of regulations or subsidiary legislation—an area less than fully addressed by the panel review—the danger of adopting uniform but lower standards is if anything more direct. For example, in NSW innovative regulations dealing with supply chains in clothing manufacture and trucking are likely to be lost in such an exercise even though they present a model that deserves wider application in the context of changing work arrangements and labour markets (see James et al., 2007)—itself an area largely neglected by the panel despite well-substantiated submissions on this subject. Such an approach is not consistent with the maintenance of the highest OHS standards and is likely to prove divisive in the longer term.

Overall, while progress has been made in terms of national uniformity, even under an optimistic scenario the issue is unlikely to be fully resolved within the next five years. As indicated at several points already, it is not simply a question of achieving formal consistency in OHS standards but also securing this in an operational sense through closer alignment of inspectoral resourcing, training and strategic enforcement. Again, generally parallel trends are already apparent in most Australian jurisdictions along with a growing level of collaboration at both management and inspector level between the different state and territory agencies. At a more formal level regular meetings of the Heads of Workplace Safety Authorities in Australia (the heads of inspectorates) have agreed on national campaigns (such as an audit of OHS in the cleaning industry and a campaign targeting road freight supply chains), the harmonisation of guidance material as well as the adoption of a code of conduct for inspectors and the development of a national OHS compliance and enforcement policy. For its part, the model OHS legislation review panel was cognisant of infrastructural issues relating to the inspectorate but while it could make some recommendations in this regard was unable to recommend federal funding to promote greater operational collaboration.

Finally, it is important to place the issue of national uniformity in a global context. One way of viewing this issue is the extent to which Australian OHS law should bind the activities of Australian businesses operating overseas. For example, is it ethical for an Australian firm to adopt lower OHS standards in a poorer country because the regulatory standards and level of enforcement is lower? A more generic question is the extent to which increasingly globalised production and service provision require a more uniform or international approach to OHS regulation. Before proceeding to deal with the last question, it is worth noting that the problems of fragmentation/uniformity are by no means confined to Australia. In the US the formal requirements of federal

OHS legislation do not always reflect wide disparities in terms of implementing these standards among the states (or the exclusion of areas from OSHA regulation such as the public sector in Florida). Further, in the European Union implementation of the EU Framework Directive (and other OHS-related directives) varies markedly among member countries, a problem that was exacerbated by the accession of a large number of new member states in Eastern Europe after 2004—many with a poor record on OHS and limited regulatory infrastructure (Woolfson and Calite, 2007, 2008). As the EU example highlights, the issue of regulatory uniformity readily leads to questions of uniformity at international level, especially where free trade agreements on the movement of goods and services are involved. As far as we can judge, the harmonisation of OHS standards has received no real consideration by the parties to the North American Free Trade Agreement (NAFTA). The same applied to the Closer Economic Relations (CER) pact between Australia and New Zealand until around 2005 when the Workplace Relations Minister's Council established a comparative OHS performance monitoring system (including inspectorate resourcing and activity) covering Australian jurisdictions and New Zealand, forming a basis for further harmonisation measures.

Beyond supra-national entities like the EU and free trade zones/agreements (like NAFTA and CER), it is important to note that the globalisation of commercial arrangements and breaking down of trade 'barriers' by the World Trade Organization has not been accompanied by any international agreement or regulation of OHS standards or any related labour standards (covering child labour, minimum wages, maximum hours and the like) for that matter. The International Labour Organization (a body representing government and employers as well as workers) has been given no official standing in critical decisions about global trading arrangements, and the standards it sets (which may be compromised by opposition from representatives) are essentially unenforceable with no penalties for noncompliance (unlike the WTO). Similarly, the World Health Organization (WHO) is also unable to make enforceable rulings on health standards and is excluded from decisions about trade and commercial arrangements that have a critical bearing on workplace health. The activities of the ILO and WHO also need to be viewed in a context where the social compact on human rights (including health) adopted by the United Nations essentially endorses the voluntarist and inadequate (in terms of coverage and enforcement) nature of corporate social responsibility. Further a number of agencies and bodies that influence scientific and policy documents—such as the International Commission on Occupational Health (ICOH), a private non-profit organisation of OHS experts—have been subject to criticism in relation to undeclared conflicts of interest and industry/corporate influence (Ashford et al., 2002). Ashford et al. (2002) argued that recognition of ICOH compromised the credibility of ILO and WHO although it should be noted there is no evidence of undue corporate influence on a report (and component reports) prepared by the Commission for the Social Determinants of Health in 2007.

As Rosenstock et al. (2005) observed, 80% of the world's workforce reside in developing countries and they experience a disproportionate burden of occupational injury and disease (in Latin America occupational fatalities alone are estimated to account for 2–4% of GDP), much of which could be readily prevented but for a lack of private investment and regulatory intervention (that also leads to widespread under-reporting; Santana et al. 2007). International supply chains provide a clear connection between these working conditions and goods and services consumed in developed countries but the mantra of the inevitability of globalisation remains conspicuously silent on the associated logic of bringing OHS standards into alignment. This pattern of using globalisation to evade regulation and unwind OHS standards was arguably pioneered by the shipping industry. Flags of convenience (registering ships in countries like Liberia that were the safety equivalent of a tax haven) were used by operators to escape regulatory standards pertaining to the seaworthiness of vessels and labour/OHS standards of seamen. Regulated shipping fleets collapsed (by 2008 there were only 40 'Australian-flagged' commercial ships; *CCH OHS Alert*, 28 October 2008) and, as noted in chapter 1, losses or mishaps (such as oil spills) involving old/poorly maintained ships mounted while crews were drawn from impoverished countries under exploitative and often dangerous conditions.

Not surprisingly, collaborative efforts by the ILO and WHO to advance OHS have failed (Rosenstock et al., 2005). As a recent report prepared for the Commission on the Social Determinants of Health of WHO observed (EMCONET, 2007), the international regulatory gap in labour standards has been a recipe for a 'race to the bottom' in employment conditions with often disastrous consequences for OHS. The time is now long overdue for serious efforts to internationalise the regulation of OHS standards (without compromising higher standards in some countries) utilising, for example, supply chain regulation and a commitment to improve OHS standards (both assisted and duly monitored) as a prerequisite for international trade agreements.

Conclusion

This chapter has concentrated on the principal OHS legislation found in Australia and New Zealand, including comparing these laws and their enforcement to other countries. Although some mention was made of other OHS legislation (such as that relating to transport, mining, oil and gas) it is beyond the scope of this book to consider them at length (see further reading, below, for guidance to mining laws). It can be noted that in relation to mining and transport, efforts have been made over the past decade to make these laws more compatible with the principal OHS legislation and there have also been initiatives to coordinate enforcement activities. Indeed, in some areas such as road transport a number of regulatory developments (such as those pertaining to supply chains) in Australia are innovative and provide a guide to global developments in OHS regulation in the future. Having said this, a number of general observations can be made about OHS legislation.

Overall, the move to post–Robens model legislation and process/performance standards can be viewed as a positive development, especially in the context of a better trained and more strategically focused inspectorate. These laws provide more comprehensive coverage of workers and hazards (including the capacity to deal with complex and dynamic working environments) and the parties whose actions affect OHS; a mixture of standards and remedies/penalties that can address a complex array of hazards; and a recognition of the important and valuable input workers should have in relation to OHS. The effectiveness of these laws was enhanced by the strategic use of enforcement and changes within inspectorates (in terms of recruitment, training and organisation). The proactive and strategic approach adopted by OHS inspectorates set a model for mines inspectorates (where these remained separate) and stands in sharp contrast to other labour inspectorates (such as those responsible for industrial relations) where a more reactive complaint-based approach has (with some exceptions) remained the norm (Goodwin and Maconachie, 2005).

Further, over the past decade or more state and territory governments in Australia have generally provided a supportive environment where inspectorates have been able to determine and pursue enforcement strategies. A number (such as South Australia and Western Australia) also increased the overall size of the inspectorate although research (Johnstone and Quinlan, 2008) indicates they remain seriously under-resourced (though this problem is by no means confined to Australia). A conspicuous exception to this was the growing federal jurisdiction (Comcare) where all types of enforcement activity (ranging from issuing notices to prosecutions) were minimal. Overall, the level of prosecution appears to have increased since the 1980s and generally astute use is being made of other remedies. Whether this will alter after the change of government and review of Comcare will bear watching.

Notwithstanding this generally positive picture, a number of serious and some longstanding challenges need to be addressed in the future. A number of these have already been discussed at some length (such as changes to work organisation, hazardous substances, the interaction of different bodies of law and national/global uniformity) while others were only mentioned in passing. Examples of the former include changes to work organisation (including the effects on OHS indicators), the weakening of avenues of worker involvement (exacerbated by a more hostile industrial relations environment and union decline) and the challenges posed by hazardous substances. An example of the latter is gender. While the legislative framework covers female workers and the hazards they encounter far more comprehensively than earlier laws and there have been a number of positive developments (such as the introduction of standards in relation to ergonomics and chemicals in hairdressing), the implementation of OHS laws (including research/guidance material and enforcement on OHS hazards) still gives insufficient recognition to female workers and the jobs they are concentrated in (Quinlan, 1996).

While a number of government agencies have sought to address this issue much remains to be done. For example, there is still a limited regulatory focus on home-based work—a work arrangement where women are disproportionately represented. The key role of regulatory infrastructure also needs to be recognised. As Premji et al. (2008b) demonstrate in relation to musculoskeletal disorders, ambiguity and gender 'imbalances' in scientific research can affect both prevention and compensation. Historical imbalances in research on reproductive hazards also shaped public policy responses although efforts have been made to counter this (Winder, 1993). By default, the data gaps in relation to women's OHS shape regulation and policy. At the same time, drawing on a range of sources even existing information may suggest new areas for focusing interventions. For example, a Canadian study that not only detailed data gaps but also tried to distil available information identified three common sources of suffering, namely ambiguous job requirements, multiple low-level hazards and isolation (Le Jeune et al., 2008) The ongoing gender gap in relation OHS regulation is a global issue though some countries probably fare worse than others in this regard (Messing, 1992, 1998, 2002).

In a similar vein, over the past decade OHS regulators in Australia, North America and elsewhere have devoted greater attention to younger workers but efforts on behalf of other large groups of vulnerable workers, notably foreign/migrant workers and persons with disabilities, has been more muted (Centers for Disease Control, 2008; Australian Safety and Compensation Council, 2007a). Another serious challenge only briefly mentioned in this chapter is the need to adapt legislation and enforcement to better address psychosocial working conditions that are hazardous to the health and wellbeing of workers, including problematic working hour arrangements, poor security/work intensification and harassment/bullying (Quinlan, 2007).

QUESTIONS FOR DISCUSSION

1 What are the key features of the revised Robens model OHS laws in Australia? Critically evaluate the strengths and weaknesses of two of these features in the light of changes to work organisation over the past 30 years.

2 Compare and contrast specification, process and performance standards. Should all specification standards be dispensed with?

3 Identify and discuss a serious challenge confronting preventative OHS law in Australia or New Zealand.

4 What are the strengths and weaknesses of a focus on risk assessment or systematic OHS management in OHS regulation?

FURTHER READING

Gunningham, N. (2007), *Mine Safety: Law, Regulation and Policy*, Federation Press.

Gunningham, N. (2008), 'Occupational health and safety, worker participation and the mining industry in a changing world', *Economic and Industrial Democracy*, **29**(3): 336–61.

James, P., Johnstone, R., Quinlan, M. and Walters, D. (2007), 'Regulating supply chains for safety and health', *Industrial Law Journal*, **36**(2): 163–87.

Johnstone, R. (2004), *Occupational Health and Safety Law and Policy*, 2nd edition, Law Book Company, Sydney.

Johnstone, R. and King, M. (2008), 'A responsive sanction to promote systematic compliance? Enforceable undertakings in occupational health and safety regulation', *Australian Journal of Labour Law*, **21**: 280–315.

Le Jeune, G., Belisle, A. and Messing, K. (2008), 'The data gap in Canadian women's occupational health', *Policy and Practice in Health and Safety*, **6**(2): 51–81.

Quinlan, M., Johnstone, R. and McNamara, M. (2009), 'Australian health and safety inspectors' perceptions and actions in relation to changed work arrangements', *Journal of Industrial Relations*, **51**(4): 559–75.

Quinlan, M. and Johnstone, R. (2009), 'The implications of de-collectivist industrial relations laws and associated developments for worker health and safety in Australia, 1996–2007', *Industrial Relations Journal*, 40(5): 426–43.

Workers' compensation and rehabilitation

Introduction

THE introduction of workers' compensation regimes in Australia, New Zealand and most other industrialised countries around the late nineteenth and early twentieth centuries represented a large-scale experiment in social welfare and these regimes continue to operate as critical mechanisms for dispensing mass social justice. As with preventative legislation, this achievement was the result of many years of political struggle on the part of workers, unions and other interested parties. Further, the prevention of injury and disease is a part (but not the main objective) of workers' compensation legislation in which the broad sets of policy objectives pursued by workers' compensation schemes have been the following:

- provide medical treatment and income security to injured workers (and their dependants)
- ensure employers meet the costs associated with injuries and diseases which arise at workplaces under their control
- encourage rehabilitation of injured workers
- encourage greater preventative measures on the part of employers.

In practice the simultaneous pursuit of these broad policy objectives is difficult. The pursuit of one objective may have the effect of undermining the chances of achieving another. For example, the spreading of risks via workers' compensation premiums needed to achieve the first objective may interfere with the task of encouraging employers to take preventive measures by penalising employers who have accidents. In part because of this and because of their political origins, the tenor of workers' compensation schemes reflects the accumulative compromises made by progressive governments and the political priorities of the government of the day. And while the removal of fault as a basis for compensation diminished some adversarial aspects of workers' compensation, the schemes are still frequently a source of conflict between workers (and their unions) and employers. There may be consensus on the need to ensure that workers have safe and healthy workplaces, but there is still disagreement on many aspects of workers' compensation. When it comes to compensation for injury and disease, the interests of workers and employers differ. Injured workers' interests lie principally in obtaining income security and rehabilitation, while employers' interests lie with ensuring efficiency and lower costs for workers' compensation overall. The extent of coverage, the amount and duration of benefits and the administrative and appeal structure remain political issues.

In this chapter we review the development of workers' compensation schemes in Australia and New Zealand and describe the main elements of workers' compensation in each of the jurisdictions. In particular, we examine who is covered, what is covered, the level of compensation, rehabilitation and disputes processes. While the Australian and New Zealand basic structures are similar, there are important differences in details of coverage and entitlement. We conclude with a discussion of outstanding issues.

The development of workers' compensation schemes

In spite of the horrendous working conditions typified by the Industrial Revolution and the resultant high rates of occupational injuries, diseases and fatalities, there were few options available for injured or ill workers or their dependants to obtain compensation. More often than not workers and their families were reliant on the charity of their employer or the community. Although substantial public collections were taken up after disasters involving significant worker fatalities, such as the 1896 Brunner Mine Disaster on the west coast of New Zealand and the explosion at the Union Saw Mill in Maryborough, Queensland in 1872, such support was restricted to highly visible incidents and even then financial assistance was by no means guaranteed. Such work-related disasters in both Australia and New Zealand galvanised workers and their families for years afterwards to push for a fair, straightforward and no-fault workers' compensation scheme. A number of compensation levies, (for example, the one administered by the New Zealand Department of Mines), sickness funds and subsidised medical schemes were established by a few government agencies and employers who felt an obligation to their workers. However, such practices were by no means typical and some employer responses were less than benevolent. There is also evidence that many of the accident funds and medical schemes were poorly administered and often exploitative, requiring workers to make contributions that far exceeded any services provided (Maconachie, 1997: 83–5; for the US situation see Butler and Worrall, 2008). In short, relying on employer or community sympathy was liable to prove inadequate at best.

Workers could also take out a form of mutual insurance by joining a friendly society (such as the Oddfellows) or a trade union which offered sickness, funeral and other friendly or social benefits—a major function of many early unions. Although in nineteenth century Britain, Australia and New Zealand mutual insurance was the most common form of protection insurance, only the best paid workers, such as craftsmen, could afford this type of insurance and even this was often inadequate compensation for debilitating injuries. Lower paid workers and those in precarious jobs could not afford the payments, or were forced to cease payments when unemployed. Thus, early attempts to address workers' compensation were piecemeal, complex and inadequate and placed the entire burden to obtain compensation with workers rather than with their employers, who controlled the workplaces and work processes.

Another largely ineffectual option available for injured workers was to seek redress by suing their employer for negligence or breaching their implied duty of care via common law under contract of employment. The first widely acknowledged attempt occurred in England in 1837 (Johnstone, 2004) when a butcher's assistant named Charles Priestly, aged 15 at the time of his accident, tried unsuccessfully to sue his employer after falling from an overloaded butcher's cart. However, at the same time a railway worker in the US named Gilham Barnes was successful in a claim he made after sustaining serious injuries in a derailment where two other workers were killed. Soon after this, in an almost identical case, another employee (Nicholas Farwell) of the same company had his claim rejected, and it was this second case that set a precedent for later litigation (Tomlins, 1988).

The fact that the tort systems of Britain, the US, Australia and New Zealand during the nineteenth and early twentieth centuries rarely provided any compensation to the injured worker or, in the case of a fatality, to their families was as a result of three pernicious sets of legal doctrines—the so-called 'unholy Trinity'—namely: (a) common employment (b) contributory negligence; and (c) *volenti non fit injuria* (Purse, 2005). The first doctrine, *common employment*, rejected the employer's liability on the basis of the negligence of a co-worker (i.e. where the injury was seen to arise from the actions of a fellow worker). This could readily be achieved by a narrow interpretation of the complex social processes that often give rise to injuries. In many early cases the courts omitted to recognise the master's duty let alone whether it had been breached. The second doctrine, *contributory negligence*, held that where careless behaviour by an employee contributed to their injury this mitigated if not annulled the employer's negligence (Rennie, 1995). Indeed, even if a very small degree of blame could be attached to the worker this contributory negligence could be enough to defeat the claim entirely. Brooks's (1993: 18) examination of early Australian cases argued that antipodean courts closely followed the English path although she detected a 'little more flexibility' in their application of the doctrine of common employment. The third doctrine, *volenti non fit injuria*, (clearly a product of Priestley v Fowler) held that servants must bear the consequences of risks voluntarily assumed. In one English case (*Senior v Ward*, 1859, cited in Brooks, 1988), the court rejected a claim by the family of a miner who fell down a shaft on the grounds that the deceased was aware the company habitually neglected to follow regulations requiring the testing of cages prior to use! In other words, the worker's knowledge that the company regularly breached its legislative duties abrogated the family's right to common law damages.

There are several explanations for the courts' restrictive approach to common law claims by injured workers. Schwartz (1989) sought to explain the defeat of many early claims in the US in terms of the slow evolution of tort law. However, this argument fails to explain why the doctrine of vicarious liability (which already existed) was not used in preference to the doctrine of common employment or why Scottish courts immediately adopted the 'modern' approach of ignoring the doctrine of common employment and giving little recognition to *volenti* doctrine (Brooks, 1993: 15). The class-orientated subsidy thesis provides another explanation whereby the judiciary were motivated by a desire to insulate industry from the economic costs of a flood of prosecutions from injured workers and other claimants (such as those whose homes were set alight by passing trains) arising from industrial activities (Abel, 1981). Certainly, it appears more than coincidental that the bulk of worker claims emanated from railways, maritime transport, mining, construction and manufacturing industries that were not only dangerous but also key engines of trade and industrial development in the nineteenth and early twentieth centuries. A third argument postulated by Tomlins (1988) is that the courts were determined to preserve managerial prerogative and the existing social order in the workplace, something which an avalanche of compensation claims would undermine. Witt (1998: 1470) also criticises the subsidy thesis and supports Tomlin's contentions, arguing that the master/servant rule (or the doctrine of common employment) preserved the hierarchy of control/status at the workplace. Indeed, Witt (1998: 1501) and later Purse (2005) and Armstrong (2008) argue that the law of workplace accidents both reflected the laissez-faire ideology of the times and helped to shape the organisation of work during the period between 1842 and 1910. While the approaches of the courts towards injured workers may still be debated, it is generally accepted that the courts were not entirely neutral in workers' compensation disputes (for an illustration of this see *Wilsons and Clyde Coal Co v English*, 1938, cited in Brooks, 1993: 21). Workers' suspicion of the courts continued throughout much of the twentieth century even though workers in Britain, Australia and New Zealand eventually achieved a relatively unambiguous right to sue their employer at common law. This suspicion arguably was in part the reason administrative tribunals were established to hear appeals of workers' compensation disputes in the 1970s in some jurisdictions (although other factors were sometimes pivotal, such as the adoption of monopoly insurance in Canada).

From the 1880s agitation by unions over the manifest failings of the common law option in Britain, Australia and New Zealand led to legislative initiatives. At first, these simply sought to remedy some aspects of the common law approach. An Employers' Liability Act was introduced into Britain in 1880 and over the next decade this legislation was copied by the various Australian colonies and New Zealand, though with some variations (for example, the coverage of seamen and domestic servants was debated in several colonies; see Cowan, 1997: 94). In essence, employers' liability Acts set grounds for establishing negligence in a limited number of situations and provided a capped level of payments (up to three years' wages under the UK Act) for specified classes of manual workers (in dangerous occupations such as mining, although seamen were excluded). In practice, although the Acts made small inroads into the *volenti* and common employment doctrines, they offered a very restricted remedy and often proved ineffective even for those workers who were covered (Brooks, 1993: 16). Workers still needed to establish negligence on the part of the employer and courts tended to adopt a narrow interpretation of liability and entitlements (Campbell., 1996: 10; Cowan,

1997: 94–7). In her study of the building of the Cairns–Kuranda railway in north Queensland, Maconachie (1997: 77) found that of the 23 workers killed and hundreds seriously injured, only one worker was recorded as receiving compensation under the Queensland Employers' Liability Act. Maconachie's (1997: 87–8) study also drew attention to the lack of awareness of the law among a workforce that was remote from Brisbane and included many immigrants. Further, employers pressured workers into signing opting-out agreements whereby they waived their rights to take action under the legislation (it is worth noting that, unlike the first British Act, several colonial laws banned these clauses).

The conspicuous failure of employers' liability legislation to address the increasingly visible toll of injury, disease and death brought with it increased agitation from the labour movement and other interest groups as well as community pressure for new forms of legislative intervention (Bartrip and Fenn, 1983 and Cass, 1983). This culminated in the passage of the Workers' Compensation Act in the UK in 1897, and the passage of similar though by no means identical laws over the next 30 years in Australia, the US, Canada and New Zealand (Campbell, 1996; Cowan, 1997; Plumb and Cowell, 1998; Purse, 2005). These laws were partly modelled on the German and Austrian comprehensive, no-fault insurance system which can be traced back to 1854 when '… Prussia required employers in certain industries to contribute to accident funds administered by statutory associations' (Carr, 1998: 417). In the 1880s a compulsory mutual liability scheme was introduced into Germany by Chancellor Bismarck which set the broad model for a 'no-fault' comprehensive system of compensation for injured workers (see Engelhard, 2007 for an overview of the history of early workers' compensation). However, the English-speaking countries—Britain, Canada, Australia, New Zealand and the US—lagged well behind these developments (Bartrip and Burman, 1983; Cass, 1983; Campbell, 1996; Cowan, 1997; Purse, 2005; Armstrong, 2008). Moreover, unlike in New Zealand (which has a unicameral political system), in Australia, the US and Canada the main workers' compensation schemes were (and remain) a state/territory/province responsibility. In each country, federal governments perform a largely residual role covering their own employees (including the military) and several special categories of workers employed beyond the boundaries of state jurisdictions (notably merchant seamen).

As was the case with other OHS legislation in both Australia and New Zealand, the introduction of workers' compensation laws was often bitterly contested by groups of employers, private insurers and other interested groups. It often took several attempts, underpinned by the increased franchise and mobilisation of working-class voters and over a decade of struggle (if not considerably longer), before viable and comprehensive schemes were achieved. South Australia was the first Australian state to legislate in 1900 while in Western Australia laws were introduced in 1902 and 1912. In Victoria it took several legislative efforts before a workable scheme was established in 1914. A more prolonged struggle occurred in NSW that was not resolved until the 1926 law was enacted. In Queensland opposition from pastoral interests torpedoed the first three workers' compensation Bills introduced into parliament (1899, 1900 and 1901).

Pastoral interests then attempted to undermine the first inadequate law (1905) but were finally defeated in 1916 when a more durable law was introduced by the Labor Government (Cowan, 1997). Ironically, as a result of what many saw as incompetence on the part of the Upper House of Queensland Parliament, a government monopoly over workers' compensation insurance was enshrined. Labor governments in other states failed to achieve this, although it was proposed again in the 1980s and 1990s (Plumb and Cowell, 1998: 243).

While New Zealand's reforming Liberal Government of the 1890s and early 1900s saw the benefit of a workers' compensation scheme along the lines of the German and Austrian schemes, it was the Brunner mine disaster in which 67 miners, many of them Australians, lost their lives that galvanised public opinion for a comprehensive, no-fault compensation scheme. An early attempt was the enactment of the Workers' Compensation for Accidents Act, 1900—a modest Act that provided 50% of the loss of earnings with a maximum of £2 per week (Campbell, 1996). Interestingly, in New Zealand, workers who campaigned for a no-fault workers' compensation scheme were equated with being 'warriors' for social justice (see Campbell, 1996; Armstrong, 2008), as the following quote illustrates:

> The artisan and the mechanic are like the soldier, in that both run a risk of death or horrid maiming, and that in the interests of others—of the community at large. The soldier has his pension; the industrial soldier should have his. The employer can insure his building … [and] … machinery … why should not the workman insure the only instrument of production he possess—namely his life and limbs. (cited in Campbell, 1996: 15)

With their common reference point to the German system, workers' compensation systems in Australia, Britain, the US, Canada and to some extent New Zealand (which moved to a universal compensation system in 1981 as discussed below) share a number of features, namely:

■ *No-fault compensation and broad coverage.* In order to receive payments covering medical expenses and lost income, workers do not need to demonstrate employer negligence but rather that their injuries arose out of and (latterly changed to 'or') during the course of employment. This opened the compensation option to a wide range of claims and claimants that were previously excluded under the common law or employers' liability Acts. In many jurisdictions the coverage is implicit in definitions of what constitutes 'a worker' and recognition of medical conditions was progressively widened over time to include some self-employed workers and volunteers as well as a greater array of occupational diseases. Nevertheless, with regard to the last point it is important to note that the schemes began very much as injury compensation schemes and as such the under-recognition of disease remains a significant limitation. The elimination of the concept of fault also applies to contributory negligence by workers and although most Australian jurisdictions now contain contributory negligence provisions (see table 8.1), as far as we are aware these have rarely been invoked.

- *Specified compensation entitlements.* Unlike common law, workers' compensation legislation specifies the entitlements of injured workers (such as medical and hospital costs, payment in lieu of lost wages and lump sum benefits in the case of death or permanent disability). In general, compensation is calculated on the basis of the workers' earning capacity and degree of work incapacity (or disability) arising from the injury and disease. Compensation is intended to replace the worker's earnings, not to cover his or her loss as understood at common law. That is, there is generally no compensation for pain and suffering in and of itself, or for loss of the amenities of life. The injury schedules of most jurisdictions (such as Western Australia) include claims for physical scarring but generally do not include compensation for emotional suffering. The scale of entitlement for permanent disability is determined on the basis of an assessment of loss of physical function. Often workers' compensation authorities may use what some refer to as the 'meat chart' which sets out the amount payable for the loss or impairment of body parts (fingers, toes, etc.) to determine the appropriate percentage loss of function represented by a damaged or missing body part (for a discussion of the origins and development of the latter, see Blackmore, 1993: 59–63). Workers' compensation schemes are generally said to have the objective of providing 'fair' compensation. However, the definition of what is fair often begins with a description of the workers' compensation as a bargain or compromise, as injured workers gave up their right to compensation as measured by the common law in return for a no-fault administrative compensation scheme. Defenders of the scheme argue that injured workers gave up the extent of compensation as measured by the common law in exchange for faster and more certain compensation. No-fault administrative compensation schemes allowed workers to avoid the delays and uncertainties inherent in the common law tort and court-based system. Injured workers may not receive as much compensation as they might have if successful under tort, but they would receive compensation regardless of who or what caused the injury and regardless of the financial situation of their employer. This said, compensation in all jurisdictions is to be 'fair'. While the determination of actual compensation differs among jurisdictions, in general injured workers rarely receive recompense for the full economic cost of their injuries when all of the 'costs', such as pre-injury earnings, rehabilitation and retraining, lost opportunities, pension entitlements and loss of enjoyment of life, are taken into account.
- *Mandatory coverage and collective liability.* All employers were required to take out workers' compensation insurance with an accredited private or government agency (Plumb and Cowell, 1998: 244). In some jurisdictions self-insurance is also an option once certain conditions are met. In general, workers (with the exception of self-employed workers), are not required to contribute to funding the system. Employers who fail to take out cover are subject to penalties and most schemes include a residual fund to cover injured workers in the situation where the employer has failed to do so or where the employer is no longer in business. Employer premiums are normally calculated on an industry by industry basis, reflecting the overall

incidence of claims, and requiring all employers to contribute to fund the system (in some cases bonus discounts or penalty premiums are applied according to the performance of individual firms).

- *Right of appeal.* Most workers' compensation schemes have since the 1970s provided both workers and employers with a right to appeal decisions made by insurers or government compensation agencies although in some jurisdictions there are procedural and other restrictions placed on this right (such as time limits or the grounds upon which appeals can be based).

While New Zealand's workers' compensation incorporated the above features, it developed its own distinctive universal, no-fault injury and rehabilitation compensation scheme in the 1970s. In New Zealand, workers' compensation is a major component of a larger comprehensive accident compensation scheme. Therefore a brief commentary is necessary (see Luntz, 2004, 2008 for New Zealand and Australian comparisons).

The origins of the New Zealand scheme lie with the Report of the Royal Commission commonly referred to as the Woodhouse Report after its chairman who presented the report in 1967. At the time the Woodhouse Report was something of a 'bombshell' as its recommendations went far beyond simply recommending changes to the workers' compensation scheme. The Woodhouse Report recommended a compensation scheme which would provide all accident victims with 24-hour no-fault compensation regardless of where the accident occurred (at work, at home or on the roads) and what the individual was doing at the time (working, playing sport or driving). The rationale for a comprehensive accident compensation scheme was that the existing compensation schemes, common law action for damages (in tort) and social welfare benefits, were costly and inefficient. Common law actions for damages which require proof of fault before compensation is payable were described in the Woodhouse Report as a 'forensic lottery'. In 1974 an accident compensation scheme was adopted in New Zealand. Anyone who suffers a personal injury by accident is covered under the accident compensation scheme, administered by the Accident Compensation Corporation (ACC). Therefore, in New Zealand it is not necessary to prove that an injury arose out of or in the course of employment to receive compensation. However, a distinction between work and non-work accidents continues to be made for the purposes of funding the scheme. An outline of the five 'Woodhouse' principles is set out in table 8.1, (see Woodhouse Report, 1967: 39–41).

The current Injury Prevention, Rehabilitation, and Compensation Act, 2001 differs from previous law in that it establishes *injury prevention* as a primary function of the Accident Compensation Corporation. The Act specifies a new *rehabilitation* principle—namely, that rehabilitation is to be provided by the corporation to restore the claimant's health, independence and participation to the maximum extent practicable and can make available a lump sum payment for permanent impairment. The intent of this change is to provide fairer compensation for those who, through impairment, suffer non-economic loss. This includes both physical impairment and mental injury (caused by a physical injury or sexual abuse). The Act further provides a more *flexible assessment* of loss of earnings, a new formula for setting a minimum level of weekly compensation,

Table 8.1 Woodhouse principles

1 Community responsibility	In the national interest, and as a matter of national obligation, the community must protect all citizens (including the self-employed and the housewives) who sustain them from the burden of sudden individual losses when their ability to contribute to the general welfare by their work has been interrupted by physical incapacity.
2 Comprehensive entitlement	All injured persons should receive compensation from any community-financed scheme on the same uniform method of assessment, regardless of the causes which gave rise to their injuries. (In other words, it should not make any difference to the compensation available if a person is injured at work or at home.)
3 Complete rehabilitation	The scheme must be deliberately organised to urge forward the physical and vocational recovery of these citizens while at the same time providing a real measure of money compensation for their losses. (In other words, restoring the worker's earning capacity through rehabilitation was as important as monetary compensation.)
4 Real compensation	Real compensation demands for the whole period of incapacity the provision of income-related benefits for lost income and recognition of the plain fact that any permanent bodily impairment is a loss in itself regardless of its effect on earning capacity.
5 Administrative efficiency	The achievement of the system will be eroded to the extent that its benefits are delayed, or are inconsistently assessed, or the system itself is administered by methods that are economically wasteful.

Source: Woodhouse (1967).

more flexible provisions for self-employed people and simplified regulations concerning premium payment procedures. The Act also incorporates a Code of ACC Claimants' Rights and allows for the disclosure of information to the Department of Child, Youth and Family Services and for the reporting of medical errors to the relevant professional body and the Health and Disability Commissioner.

Since 2001, there have been a number of amendments, such as extending the no-fault principle to medical misadventure and compensation for self-employed as well as greater discretion for rehabilitation. The amendment to the Act also bypasses the normal requirement to prove causation which is required for gradual process injuries or diseases. It also lists 25 additional conditions or diseases to be added to Schedule 2. Although many of the occupational diseases are rare, some are more common, such as noise-induced hearing loss, dermatitis and some types of asthma caused by sensitising agents or irritants inherent in the work process, for example sawdust (ACC, 2005). This change will have the greatest affect on industries where employees may be exposed to the risk of certain diseases.

In summary, in the past century workers' compensation legislation has addressed, more or less, the issues relating to compensation, rehabilitation and prevention. Over the last 30 years the domain of workplace safety has been bifurcated as issues relating to the prevention of workplace injury and disease have been largely removed from the purview of workers' compensation and placed into the domain of occupational health and safety. Workers' compensation schemes are now focused on the task of determining compensation for injured workers, their rehabilitation and return to work. Prevention, depending on the jurisdiction, is dealt with through OHS legislation and administrative structures, as discussed in more detail in the next section.

Workers' compensation—an overview

In principle all workers who are injured while working in Australia and New Zealand receive workers' compensation. As workers' compensation is a state and national responsibility, the nature and extent of compensation differs from state to state as well as from Australia to New Zealand. There are a total of 10 different workers' compensation schemes in Australia and New Zealand; each jurisdiction has its own workers' compensation scheme. While all workers' compensation schemes have much in common, there are differences in the legislative and administrative structure of the compensation scheme as well as the level of coverage, entitlement and compensation payments. These differences reflect political or ideological perspectives on the issues of worker and employer responsibility for compensation and prevention of injury. Parties to the right and left of the political spectrum accept the need for workers' compensation, but a similar consensus on issues such as the appropriate level of compensation or the role of the private sector in administering and funding the scheme has not yet been achieved.

In each jurisdiction, the workers' compensation scheme is established by legislation. While each scheme is different, they all share certain features. Below we provide a general overview of the basic features of the Australian and New Zealand workers' compensation schemes and highlight principal jurisdictional differences.

Workers' compensation schemes—private or public

Workers' compensation provides the second largest area of insurance cover after motor vehicle insurance. It is not surprising, therefore, that private insurers who are eager to extend their business and employers who believe that private insurance will reduce their insurance costs strongly resist the move to make it a government monopoly. This resistance has been successful, to varying degrees, in ensuring a role for private insurers. Unlike Queensland, South Australia, the Australian Capital Territory and to a lesser extent New Zealand, the Australian states and the Northern Territory privatised some aspects of workers' compensation in the 1990s. During this period the election of conservative neo-liberal governments in Australia and New Zealand with strong ideological commitments to the private sector legislative change was associated with changes that introduced a self-insurance option into most jurisdictions (see table 8.2). A change of governments, however, resulted in a shift back to public insurance schemes. This seesaw shift from state-funded insurer to a mixture of public and private sector insurers and back again was most evident in New Zealand. Eager to introduce a self-insurance option and competition into the state-run workers' compensation scheme, the New Zealand National Government enacted the Accident Insurance Act in 1998. This Act in effect disengaged the government from workers' compensation altogether by creating a new Crown-owned enterprise in late 1998 specifically for workplace injury insurance called @ Work Insurance. However, this foray into a private and semi-private insurers mix for worker' compensation was short-lived and after the 2000 election, the Labour Coalition Government returned to the country's unique government monopoly of a no-fault universal compensation scheme.

In most jurisdictions, employer representatives continue to argue that competitive premiums offered by private insurers are beneficial, especially for small business employers (Purse, 2005; Lamm, 2008). Not only is there debate over whether or not compensation schemes should be controlled by a state monopoly agency or multiple agencies, but there is also debate over how workers' compensation schemes should be funded and administered. That is, should workers' compensation schemes be administered by the state, private insurers or self-insurers and should they determine

Table 8.2   Agencies responsible for workers' compensation in each jurisdiction

	Cwlth	Vic.	NSW	SA	WA
Policy	Comcare: Dept of Education, Employment and Workplace Relations	Victorian WorkCover Authority (WorkSafe Victoria)	WorkCover NSW	WorkCover SA	WorkCover WA
Premium	Comcare	Victorian WorkCover Authority	WorkCover NSW	WorkCover SA	Insurers subject to WorkCover WA oversight
Claims	Comcare/self-insurers	6 private sector agents	7 private sector agents	1 private sector agent	10 private sector agents
Current legislation	Safety, Rehabilitation and Compensation Act 1988	Accident Compensation Act 1985 and Accident Compensation (WorkCover Insurance) Act 1993	Workplace Injury Management and Workers Compensation Act 1998 and Workers Compensation Act 1987	Workers' Rehabilitation and Compensation Act 1986 and WorkCover Corporation Act 1994	Workers' Compensation and Injury Management Act 1981

Source: Safe Work Australia (2009a), *Comparison of Workers' Compensation Arrangements in Australia and New Zealand*, Commonwealth of Australia, Barton, ACT: 30–1.

who is eligible to claim? Other questions include: how should claims be processed and what is the appropriate level of care and rehabilitation for injured workers? Quite apart from the range and level of entitlement, the effectiveness and equity of workers' compensation regimes is also determined by the speed and manner in which claims are handled, including how problematic claims are identified and adjudicated. The overall costs of the administrative processes, including the review and appeal process, are significant but necessary costs of a compensation scheme. Part of the original rationale for workers' compensation schemes was the need to ensure that injured workers had a more certain and quicker remedy than that provided by either the common law or employers' liability Acts (Wood et al., 1995).

For workers living from pay cheque to pay cheque, waiting weeks or months for the adjudication of their claims was not a viable option. Since the introduction of workers' compensation schemes, administrative problems have arisen from time to time, particularly among private insurers and self-insurers, including problems relating

Qld	Tas.	NT	ACT	NZ
Department of Employment and Industrial Relations	Department of Justice and WorkCover Tasmania	Department of Employment, Education and Training	Office of Industrial Relations	Department of Labour
WorkCover Queensland	Licensed private sector insurers subject to WorkCover oversight	Private sector agents	Private sector agents	Accident Compensation Corporation
WorkCover Queensland and self-insurers	8 private sector insurers	5 private sector agents	7 approved insurers 9 self-insurers	Accident Compensation Corporation
Workers' Compensation and Rehabilitation Act 2003	Workers' Rehabilitation and Compensation Act 1988	Work Health Act 1986	Workers' Compensation Act 1951	Injury Prevention, Rehabilitation, and Compensation Act 2001

to delays in the processing of workers' claims. Other administrative issues such as those involving inequitable or discriminatory judgments in relation to particular groups of claimant workers, the excessive costs of administering claims, the seemingly increasing bureaucratic and technical complexity of the system as well as the role of lawyers and litigation in protecting workers' and employers' rights have also been the subject of debate. In most jurisdictions, workers' compensation schemes have been continually reviewed and reformed. Despite the numbers of issues on the table, in recent years and in most jurisdictions in Australia and New Zealand, the debate over workers' compensation has included a discussion of the costs of the scheme to employers and, in this context, the benefits of private versus public administration of the scheme.

Centralised state-owned workers' compensation insurance has a number of administrative advantages over private insurer schemes in terms of rationalising and better coordinating claims handling, claim/cost investigation and containment (including the use of computers to investigate claims patterns and frauds). Recent efficiencies introduced into state-owned compensation agencies have meant that processing of claims has become quicker, thus reducing the cost of containment and rehabilitation. Typically, state-owned compensation agencies pursuant under the legislation also have the advantage of linking prevention with rehabilitation. For example, the New Zealand Injury Prevention, Rehabilitation, and Compensation Act, 2001 establishes injury prevention as a primary function of the Accident Compensation Corporation. To this end, the Accident Compensation Corporation is required to promote measures to reduce the incidence and severity of personal injury. Generally, private provision of services only results in improvement where 'there is room for the private organisation to provide a more cost-effective service delivery' (see Gunderson and Hyatt, 1999: 547). The problem with privatisation of workers' compensation is that as a general rule less than 15% of overall expenditure is related to the costs administering the scheme. Most of the expenditure, over 80%, is paid out in the form of compensation. Thus opponents of privatisation argue that as there is little scope for cost-cutting, private firms will only make money to the extent that they reduce benefits or limit entitlement to compensation.

The form of workers' compensation adopted in Australia was by no means identical to that introduced in other English-speaking countries. One important area of difference was in relation to the rights of workers to pursue common law claims. In New Zealand, Canada and the US this option was severely curtailed if not entirely excluded by the introduction of compulsory workers' compensation schemes (Plumb and Cowell, 1998: 244). In Australia, on the other hand, most jurisdictions permitted workers to pursue common law claims (and in Queensland this was included in the monopoly workers' compensation cover). This was an attractive option where there was clear evidence of negligence and where workers felt the broader basis for determining damages at common law would result in a larger payout. 'Double dipping' also precludes any settlement having to be adjusted to deduct payments made under the workers' compensation scheme. Since the 1980s reforms to workers' compensation schemes, however, a number of Australian jurisdictions have placed limitations on worker access to common law action.

While it is beyond the scope of this chapter to discuss the differences in the various schemes, even in relation to the differences among Australian jurisdictions, table 8.2 provides a summary of the basic features of the various Australian schemes. As illustrated in the table, there are a number of other potentially significant differences that can be identified not only in relation to the workers' compensation schemes which operate in different countries but also within countries with largely state/province-based schemes such as Australia, the US and Canada. Differences include definitions of 'workers' and medical conditions covered; the type and level of benefits, waiting periods and maximum wage payments; the determination of industry premiums and employer specific bonus/penalties; how appeals are handled; and the emphasis placed on prevention or rehabilitation activities (Plumb and Cowell, 1998: 243).

There are attempts to minimise these interstate differences in the form of the Australian Safety and Compensation Council (ASCC) and Comcare (see Kendall, 2006: 140). While the ASCC was not itself a regulatory authority, it was clearly created to influence policy development and policy harmonisation between the states and territories. Established in 2005 to replace the National Occupational Health and Safety Commission, it was a tripartite body, with members currently representing federal, state and territory governments; the Australian Chamber of Commerce and Industry; and the Australian Council of Trade Unions. Its role was to provide national standards and codes of practice with the expectation that the states and territories will adopt them. Comcare is a Commonwealth statutory authority established under the Safety, Rehabilitation and Compensation (SRC) Act, 1988 and is also covered by the Commonwealth Authorities and Companies Act, 1997. It aims to reduce the human and financial costs of workplace injuries and diseases in each of the jurisdictions. Comcare administers the Commonwealth's workers' compensation scheme under the SRC Act and also administers the Occupational Health and Safety (Commonwealth Employment) Act, 1991. How successful these agencies have been in reducing the level of complexity and confusion of Australian workers' compensation is demonstrated in the following sections by variances between who and what is covered and the level and degrees of compensation and rehabilitation.

Coverage

Who is covered?

One of the main benefits of current workers' compensation legislation over the common law and various employers' liability Acts is that it broadens the scope of workers who can claim compensation and the nature of personal injury and disease accepted under the various schemes. Today in Australia and New Zealand, workers' compensation schemes provide coverage to most, if not all waged workers for work-related personal

Table 8.3 Synopsis of all the jurisdictions' workers' compensation schemes

	Cwlth [5]	Vic.	NSW	SA
Employees covered for workers' compensation 2006–07[1]	323 225	2 303 890	2 944 890	673 760
Number of serious claims with 1 week or more incapacity 2006–07[1]	2669	28 030	41 050	10 860
Incidence of serious claims per 1000 employees 2006–07[1]	8.3	12.2	13.9	16.1
Compensated deaths per 100 000 employees 2006–07	5.9	2.5	1.9	1.3
Scheme funding	Central fund	Hybrid fund	Hybrid fund	Central fund
Standardised average premium rate[2]	1.55% (2007–08)	1.61% (2006–07)	1.94% (2006–07)	3.14% (2006–07)
	1.77% (2006–07)	1.76% (2005–06)	2.35% (2005–06)	3.06% (2005–06)
Funding ratio	113% (June 08)	120.2% (June 08)	105% (June 08)	65% (June 07)
Excess/unfunded[4] (30 June 08)	$157m excess	$1.557 billion excess	$625m excess	$843m unfunded
Access to common law	Yes for 3rd party. Limited against employer/other employee	Limited	Limited	No

Source: Safe Work Australia (2009a), *Comparison of Workers' Compensation Arrangements in Australia and New Zealand*, Commonwealth of Australia, Barton, ACT: 32–3.

1   Source: Workplace Relations Ministers' Council, Comparative Performance Monitoring Report, tenth edition, August 2008.

2   Source: Workplace Relations Minister's Council, Comparative Performance Monitoring Report, 2005–06 ninth edition, February 2008, 2006–07 tenth edition, August 2008.

3   For New Zealand this figure includes self-insurers and self-employed persons who are covered by the scheme.

4   Assets and liabilities for centrally funded and privately underwritten schemes are calculated differently, see 'Funding ratio'.

5   Comcare data only.

WA	Qld	Tas.	NT	ACT	NZ
962 160	1 704 850	196 390	95 010	98 830	1 604 170 [3]
12 670	30 790	3390	1250	1780 (2006–07)	25 220
13.2	18.1	17.3	13.2	14.4	15.7
2.3	4.5	2.0	2.1	0.0	5.9
Privately underwritten	Central fund	Privately underwritten	Privately underwritten	Privately underwritten	Central fund
1.51% (2006–07)	1.18% (2006–07)	1.71% (2006–07)	1.98 (2006–07)	2.58% (2006–07)	0.94% (2006–07)
1.67% (2005–06)	1.36% (2005–06)	1.84% (2005–06)	2.17% (2005–06)	2.87% (2005–06)	0.94% (2005–06)
120.1% (June 07)	163.7% (June 08)	168% (2005–06)	100% (June 06)	Not available	129.5% (June 08)
Not available	$1.22 billion excess	Not available	Nil	Not available	NZ$495.8m excess
Limited	Yes	Limited	No	Unlimited	No

injury and disease. Compensation includes compensation for the costs of the medical treatment and income support in the event of injury and, to a lesser extent, disease, as well as rehabilitation and pension entitlement. Coverage, which initially included only industrial male workers who were disabled by accidents, was extended over the course of the twentieth century to include all employees—men and women involved in manual and non-manual or managerial work—and some categories of self-employed workers, independent contractors and volunteers (such as church and charity workers).

While the objective for workers' compensation legislation is to ensure that most of the workforce is covered, there remain some significant omissions in coverage, which unless addressed through legislation will increase the number of workers without coverage. Further, as the number of workers employed in certain forms of non-standard or contingent work grow in Australia and New Zealand, the risk is that more workers will be uninsured or inadequately insured against workplace injury. As the Australian Industry Commission (1994: 90–4) inquiry into workers' compensation found, moves to extend coverage are liable to encounter strong opposition from influential interest groups (notably small business and industry organisations) who perceive economic benefits in retaining a narrow definition of a contract *of* service, thus excluding many workers who are only nominally independent contractors (or engaged under a contract for services). Moreover, opposition to limiting employers' and independent contractors' ability to arrange their own coverage has been reinforced by free market ideologists over the past decades. In this section, who exactly is covered by workers' compensation will be examined, followed by a discussion on the issue of the uneven uptake of workers' compensation by certain groups of workers.

Although table 8.3 shows the numbers of workers presently covered in the 10 jurisdictions in Australia and New Zealand, it does not portray the complexities of who exactly is eligible for full workers' compensation cover. The extent and form of coverage is determined largely by the definition of 'worker' in the relevant legislation (see the Australian Productivity Commission Report, 2004). A worker is most commonly defined as a person employed under a contract *of* service and thus is classified as an 'employee'. An 'employee' is distinguished from an independent contractor or self-employed worker, who has a contract *for* service. Common law tests used to ascertain whether or not an individual is 'an employee', 'an independent contractor' or 'a self-employed worker' take into account the nature of the work and other factors, such as whether the employer or worker provides the tools, sets the hours of work and directs the activities. Differentiating between 'employee' on one hand and 'self-employed/ independent contractor' on the other hand has enormous implications for the amount of workers' compensation received and rehabilitation assistance given and whether or not the worker has to pay levies to cover the cost of claims arising from work-related injuries and disease, as is the case under the New Zealand Injury Prevention, Rehabilitation, and Compensation Act, 2001. Moreover, ignorance or confusion about eligibility for coverage, because of the differences in definitions of 'an employee', can mean an injured worker becomes the responsibility of the Australian Government under its Medicare or social security programs (Australian Productivity Commission, 2004).

Difficulties arise in industries where subcontracting and contracting out work is the norm, such as construction and road transport, and where employees and independent contractors frequently work side by side and have similar working conditions (see NOHSC, 2004: 11; Johnstone and Quinlan, 2006; Turner, 2006). Independent contractors or self-employed workers may have work practices and remuneration similar to those of employees, but under employment and compensation law these workers are likely to be treated differently and as such they may not have the same cover as employees (or may not be covered at all). That is, as self-employed workers, their eligibility for workers' compensation may be limited and may seem, at times, arbitrary. For example, in Queensland for a number of years self-employed building workers were covered for workers' compensation so long as they only brought hand tools on site. This meant that lending the contractor a utility vehicle or wheelbarrow for the day would have removed their eligibility—something many workers were unaware of. Also, in industries such as construction and road transport individual workers could easily and often did alter their employment status (i.e. from subcontractor to employee or vice versa), making the assessment of their eligibility for compensation more complicated. The ongoing challenge of determining who is a worker for the purpose of workers' compensation coverage is not confined to Australia. A report by the Workers' Compensation Board of British Columbia (WCB of BC, 1997: 18) argued that adjudicating the eligibility of claimants on the basis of their employment status had become an administrative burden and an increasingly controversial issue due to the expansion of non-standard or precarious forms of employment. New Zealand, however, differs from most other jurisdictions in that under the Injury Prevention, Rehabilitation, and Compensation Act, 2001, the no-fault principle has been extended to cover medical misadventure and compensation for self-employed workers as well as greater discretion for rehabilitation.

Restricting compensation coverage for groups of workers such as self-employed workers is problematic for a number of reasons. First, among the self-employed, there is a tendency to underinsure by underestimating earnings (see Egger, 1997: 8; WCB of BC, 1997: 17; Mayhew, 1999b: 105–15; Fan et al., 2006). Second, under most schemes the self-employed can arrange for their own insurance coverage; however, it requires an understanding of the need to provide workers' compensation coverage as well as how to arrange coverage. Even when the need and means for some level of workers' compensation coverage is understood, the self-employed worker has to accept the cost. The third problem with optional coverage for the self-employed is that there are a growing number of self-employed workers who are working in dangerous jobs, including farming, forestry, fishing, road transport and construction. A narrow definition of 'contract of service' allows employers, through subcontracting or contracting out risky work, to minimise the costs of workers' compensation. Excluding independent contractors from coverage can also affect the overall number of claims and OHS indices for these industries. Any change which widens the definition of 'contract of service' to include workers who are nominally independent contractors would presumably affect premiums where the affected category of workers were in a subcontract relationship.

The inclusion or exclusion of independent contractors can be seen, therefore, as an effective externalisation of OHS costs from the employer to the workers and to his or her community if the injured worker fails to obtain adequate coverage. Because a number of these jobs are dangerous and result in a significant number of serious injuries, and because fatalities or severe disabling injuries may have long-term effects on the income, education and health expenditure of dependent families, the externalised costs are probably quite substantial (Waehrer et al., 2007).

To add to the confusion, the definition of 'worker' (and thus the extent of coverage) differs from state to state. For example, on one hand in the Northern Territory coverage is largely restricted to employees using pay-as-you-earn (PAYE) while on the other

Table 8.4 Workers' compensation coverage for independent contractors and labour hire claims

	Cwlth	Vic.	NSW	SA
Are individual contractors covered under legislation?	Comcare: No, if employed under contract for service. Seacare: No, compensation only through employment of employees MRCS: only if a 'declared member' (s8)	No, if employed under contract for service. Yes, if they enter into any form of contract of service	No, if employed under contract for service. The legislation also does not cover a contractor who entered into contract of service where the employment is for less than five days	No, if employed under contract for service. Yes, if they undertake prescribed work or work of a prescribed class
Are labour hire workers covered under legislation?	Comcare: Possibly, according to definition of nature of cantract Seacare: No MRCS: only if a declared 'member' (s8)	Yes, labour hire firm held to be employer	Yes, labour hire firm held to be employer	Yes, generally liability rests with labour hire firm

Source: Safe Work Australia (2009a), *Comparison of Workers' Compensation Arrangements in Australia and New Zealand*, Commonwealth of Australia, Barton, ACT: 123–4.

hand coverage is wider in New South Wales as certain types of independent contractors may be covered. Moreover, universal coverage is yet to be achieved. Domestic and agricultural workers were initially not covered by workers' compensation, and although agricultural workers are now covered there is still patchy coverage for domestic workers. Inconsistent coverage remains an issue particularly given the emergence of new forms of work arrangements, such as multiple job holding, franchising, telework and leased labour. The growth of hitherto insignificant types of work, including the re-emergence of home-based work, further blurs traditional distinctions between work under a contract of service and work under a contract for service. The introduction of 'work for the dole' schemes in Australia and New Zealand in the late 1990s (and

WA	Qld	Tas.	NT	ACT	NZ
No, if employed under contract for service	No, if employed under contract for service	No, if employed under contract for service. Exception where contract is for work not related to a trade or business (s4B)	No, if ABN supplied, otherwise yes	No, if employed under contract for service. However, there are provisions for the coverage of regular contractors	Yes
Yes, labour hire firm held to be employer	Yes, labour hire firm held to be employer	Yes, labour hire firm held to be employer	From 1 August 2007, all labour hire firms will have to purchase workers' compensation insurance for their workers, including those let on hire	Yes, where the individual is not an executive officer of the corporation and: – has been engaged by the labour hirer under a contract for services to work for someone other than the labour hirer – there is no contract to perform work between the individual and person for who work is to be performed – the individual does all or part of the work	Yes, labour hire firm held to be the employer

the use of similar schemes such as Workfare in Canada), as well as the use of prison labour in private prisons, has also raised questions and a great deal of debate as to the compensation entitlements of these workers. As Laing (2002: 89) concludes:

> A reasonable question arising … is perhaps why each category of person (employee, contractor, employee of contractor, etc) needs to be referred to at all when it is intended that all those in the workplace be protected. By specifying each category of person it leaves open the possibility for the creation of other (work) arrangements, which could be entered into in order to avoid the obligation. It seems the most effective course is to protect everyone and provide them with duties to protect themselves and others at the workplace. In that regard the employer might be specified as the co-ordinating agency or principal.

Under-reporting of workplace injuries and subsequent failures to make compensation claims as well as general ignorance of workers' compensation entitlements are significant and widespread issues that are not restricted to Australia and New Zealand (Productivity Commission, 2004; NOSHAC, 2006). Indeed, research shows that lack of information about workers' compensation and fear about the consequences of making a claim are more important factors in the uptake of compensation than the ineligibility of the worker to obtain workers' compensation. In addition, under-reporting workers' compensation claims has a negative effect on preventive health and safety measures in the workplace and is more damaging than the financial consequences (Fan et al., 2006; Thompson, 2007). That is, employers are guided by injury and illness statistics in designing and implementing workplace health and safety programs, and if employers are not fully aware of the events that occur in their workplace, preventive efforts may become less of a priority. This is particularly important with respect to occupational diseases, because the timely identification of causal factors for diseases such as asthma and dermatitis can have a drastic effect on individual outcomes (Thompson, 2007: 343).

While obtaining reliable data on the level of under-reporting is difficult, the level of ignorance about workers' compensation schemes, including information on coverage and rehabilitation entitlements, is staggering, with some reports estimating 40–50% of those surveyed stating that they were unaware of the specific scheme (Australian Government Productivity Commission, 2004; Sager and James, 2005; Parrish and Schofield, 2005; NOSHAC, 2006; Fan et al., 2006; Presmanes, 2008). Younger or migrant workers may be particularly ill informed. As discussed in chapter 1, there is evidence to suggest that those most at risk of being unaware of or afraid to exercise their rights to compensation are already vulnerable groups of workers. They include adolescent, female, immigrant (especially illegal or non-English speaking immigrants) and precariously employed workers often in small and/or non-unionised workplaces, engaged in seasonal work (such as fruit picking) or in remote locations (Quinlan and Mayhew, 1999, Quinlan, 2004). James also found under-reporting was highest among four categories of workers, namely those who were unskilled, occupationally mobile, self-employed or geographically isolated (James, 1993: 48–53). There is also research indicating that as a consequence of the combination of lesser industrial bargaining power, lower wages and differing forms of injury and disease, women working in Australia, Canada and elsewhere often receive less than men in compensation payments, struggle to obtain equity in the dispute resolution process and experience greater difficulties in returning to work following injury or disease (Lippel, 1989, 1999a, 2003; Calvey and Jansz, 2005; Guthrie and Jansz, 2006).

The difficulties contingent workers (i.e. subcontractors, casuals, outworkers and small business operators) have in obtaining workers' compensation are highlighted in studies undertaken by Quinlan, Mayhew, Burgess and others. In one of the earlier studies in this area, Quinlan and Mayhew (1999) surveyed workers from a range of industries and occupations across three Australian jurisdictions in which they were asked to identify what form of injury insurance they were covered by (including workers' compensation). Overall, around 50% of the almost 1300 workers surveyed believed they were covered by workers' compensation while 20% felt they had no formal entitlements to workers' compensation or other form of entitlement (including private insurance cover). Further, although some of those surveyed accurately perceived that they were not entitled to workers' compensation, a considerable proportion of eligible workers were ignorant of their entitlements. Both factory and home-based clothing workers are formally entitled to workers' compensation. However, only 7% of home-based workers were aware of this, 13% were unsure and more than 70% believed they were excluded from cover. Indeed, clothing outworkers had the poorest knowledge of their workers' compensation entitlements of all the occupational groups surveyed. Among factory-based clothing workers, 59% correctly believed they were covered, 26% were unsure and 12% believed they were not covered (the low figures even for this group probably reflect the significant proportion of non-English-speaking background immigrants employed in this industry). Although all fast-food workers were covered by workers' compensation only 52% were clearly aware of this. Most other fast-food respondents fell into the not sure category (39%) rather than believing they had other forms of cover (8.2%) or had no cover whatsoever (2%).

Providing comprehensive and inclusive workers' compensation can alleviate the failure to lodge compensation claims, especially among young and inexperienced workers and new migrant workers. Comprehensive cover under the workers' compensation system is also a simpler and more effective way to provide for injured workers than a scheme of compulsory private insurance which lacks sufficient enforcement mechanisms, as highlighted in the Woodhouse Report some 40 years ago. Further, comprehensive workers' compensation schemes are necessary to ensure that the costs of workplace injuries are met by industry. With globalisation and increased competition from low-waged countries, there is a temptation to shift the cost of injured workers from employers to social or public welfare and medical schemes. Therefore, the concerns of vulnerable workers, especially migrant labour, need to be addressed systematically as well as individually. Ongoing workforce education is also needed to ensure that eligible workers file claims for compensation and are able to do so without fear of employer reprisal.

What is covered?

Beyond the issue of whether or not workers are eligible, aware and willing to make claims, there are also important questions concerning what type of work-related injury and illness claims are covered. It is important to observe at the outset that the introduction of workers' compensation schemes had the effect of significantly extending the range of medical conditions for which workers could obtain compensation and that this coverage was widened over the course of the twentieth century. At first glance, what is covered under compensation statutes appears to be straightforward. The relevant legislation sets out the basic parameters for coverage beginning with definitions of 'personal injury', 'accident' and 'disease'. Although it is clear to most claimants what injuries and diseases are covered, there is still a level of ambiguity concerning a significant number of claims. One problem is that 'occupational injury' and 'occupational disease' are complex conditions which result from a number of causes. Another is that the understanding of the nature of both the condition and its various causes continues to evolve. What is covered under compensation criteria is often linked to the OHS laws and these laws change as OHS improves. For example, the introduction of stress and fatigue as identifiable hazards in the amendment to the New Zealand Health and Safety in Employment Act, 1992 should mean that those claims lodged in which work-related stress and fatigue are factors are now more likely to be successful. Administrators of workers' compensation typically treat definitions of occupational injury and disease

Table 8.5 Definition of injury

	Cwlth	Vic.	NSW	SA
Definition of 'injury' for purposes of coverage	'... a physical or mental injury arising out of, or in the course of, the employee's employment ...'	'... an injury arising out of, or in the course of, any employment ...'	'... personal injury arising out of, or in the course of, employment ...'	'... disability arises out of, or in the course of, employment ...'
Employment contribution	To a significant degree (for diseases)	A significant contributing factor for heart attack or stroke, disease, a recurrence, aggravation, acceleration, exacerbation or deterioration of any pre-existing injury or disease	No compensation is payable under this Act in respect of an injury unless the employment concerned was a substantial contributing factor to the injury	Substantial cause (for psychiatric disabilities only)

Source: Safe Work Australia (2009a), *Comparison of Workers' Compensation Arrangements in Australia and New Zealand*, Commonwealth of Australia, Barton, ACT: 34–5.

as unambiguous, but may still allow some degree of discretion in individual cases. In particular, the issue of how chronic injuries and diseases are determined to be work-related, whether as the result of exposure to a specific *workplace hazard* (as opposed to a hazard outside the workplace) or as linked to a *particular workplace*, remains contentious and a perennial issue in workers' compensation.

The focus of workers' compensation in both Australia and New Zealand, however, has been on *occupational injury* while compensation of *occupational disease* has been severely restricted and generally ignored (Bohle and Quinlan, 2000; Oliphant, 2008). Yet when the injury has been determined to be work-related, the criteria for compensation are confusing and continually changing, meaning coverage is frequently restricted to a narrow set of parameters and likely to be related to the politics of the day. Although Australian jurisdictions recognise work-related injury, some occupational diseases (such as occupational deafness and asbestos-induced diseases) and work-related stress and fatigue, there are numerous interstate differences, as outlined in table 8.5. For example, some states make specific reference to mental illness, some refer to injury by accident, some include a specific definition of disease and South Australia specifically excludes coronary heart disease. Jurisdictions make varying provisions for particular diseases, such as dust-related disease, stress-related conditions, repetitive strain injury and hearing loss (Australian Government Productivity Commission, 2004). In short, what is specifically covered under workers' compensation is confusing, particularly for those workers who

WA	Qld	Tas.	NT	ACT	NZ
'… a personal injury by accident arising out of or in the course of the employment …'	'… a personal injury arising out of, or in the course of, employment …'	'An injury, or a disease, arising out of, or in the course of, employment'	'… a physical or mental injury … out of or in the course of employment…'	'a physical or mental injury … includes aggravation, acceleration or recurrence of a pre-existing injury … arising out of, or in the course of, the worker's employment'	'A work-related personal injury is a personal injury that a person suffers: (a) while he or she is at any place for the purposes of his or her employment'
To a significant degree (for diseases only)	Significant contributing factor	Employment is the 'major or most significant factor' (for diseases only)	To a material degree (for diseases and gradual process)	A substantial contributing factor	No requirement (except for work-related gradual process, disease, or infection suffered by the person)

reside in one jurisdiction and work in another. Further, coverage for occupational disease is by no means exhaustive and a number of longstanding problems exist. The problems include: inadequate mechanisms for the recognition of diseases as caused or triggered by work activities; lengthy delays associated with the acceptance of claims for occupational disease, even where the disease is recognised as an occupational disease; and the often arbitrary recognition of stress-related illnesses.

Below we deal with each of these problems in turn. We discuss the issues surrounding compensating occupational injury before turning to a discussion of occupational disease.

Occupational injury

'Occupational injury' is generally defined under compensation law as a personal injury that is some form of physical or mental harm, caused by an incident, usually characterised as an accident, which occurred at work and/or during working hours (Campbell, 1996; Parrish and Schofield, 2005; Oliphant, 2008). There are, however, different interpretations and views of occupational or work-related injury within each of the workers compensation laws in Australia and New Zealand, as outlined in table 8.5. In addition, as workers' compensation rests on whether or not the injured worker's condition was directly related to his or her employment activities, the recognition of particular types of injury as work-related for the purposes of compensation has been by no means a simple or uncontested process. In some cases recognition of certain forms of injury has occurred only after a fierce struggle among interested parties, including the medical profession, unions, employers and compensation agencies.

The process of making a workers' compensation claim for injury is fairly straight-forward. The worker notifies the employer of an injury and the employer, or the injured worker's representative, then notifies the compensation authority or insurance company. In several jurisdictions (notably South Australia and New South Wales) the worker can receive provisional payments while his or her claim is being considered. Provisional payment allows the injured worker to receive both an income and medical treatment while the compensation authority or insurance company gathers evidence to either support or dispute the claim. Once the claim is accepted, benefits are paid to the injured worker. If the claim is declined, where provisional payments are made, the insurer makes no further payments. In all jurisdictions, the injured worker has the right of appeal to a higher authority (Parrish and Schofield, 2005). The time taken between the date of injury and the date of adjudication of the claim varies greatly from jurisdiction to jurisdiction. However, research indicates that management of the claims process throughout Australia and to a lesser extent New Zealand has attracted criticism, especially over the delays in payment to injured workers. Delays related to claims administration have been found to hinder worker recovery from injury as they act as barriers to treatment and rehabilitation programs which might facilitate a quick return to work (Parrish and Schofield, 2005; Sager and James, 2005; Guthrie and Jansz, 2006;

Duncan, 2008). Based on their qualitative study, Parrish and Schofield, (2005) identified the following limitations of the New South Wales compensation for injury:

1 the complete lack of information regarding rights and entitlements following an injury
2 significant delays in every aspect of the claims process
3 irregular, inconsistent and non-existent payments for wage replacement and expenses incurred for treatment
4 relationships with claims officers that were characterised by constrained access, deception, inefficiency and miscommunication, and demeaning and hostile attitudes of claims officers
5 the invisibility of New South Wales WorkCover services designed to assist injured workers with the claims process
6 exclusion from participation in the management of their medical treatment and rehabilitation
7 abuse by therapeutic professionals involved in the claims process, especially those employed by insurance companies.

While most adjudication of claims rests on the facts of individual cases, there remain a number of areas of controversy. Two of the most controversial areas of compensation for occupational injury concern a category of injuries or disorders known as as occupational overuse injury (OOI) or repetitive strain injury (RSI) and the issues related to 'mobile workers'.

Occupational overuse injury (OOI) and repetitive strain injury (RSI):

Work-related musculoskeletal disorders or 'WMSDs', a term adopted by the World Health Organization, have been the subject of debate regarding the causal links (as such disorders occur over time and it is therefore difficult to pinpoint the actual cause) and the pejorative use of terms to describe these disorders. Some of terms to denote work-related musculoskeletal disorders include: 'cumulative trauma disorder', 'repetitive strain injury', 'repetitive motion disorder', 'occupational overuse syndrome', 'occupational cervicobrachial disorder' and 'hand/arm syndrome'. While each of these terms is used to describe a range of soft tissue disorders which may or may not be caused or aggravated by employment activities, they remain contested. From the perspective of the insurers, the terms can be misleading in that such terms imply the presence of repetition, trauma, motion or work-relatedness as the main cause or significant cause of the condition or disorder. Moreover in some jurisdictions, work-related musculoskeletal disorders are treated as occupational injury and in others as occupational disease. It is not uncommon for musculoskeletal injuries to be termed 'syndromes', as this can signify an illness rather than an injury and therefore it will be more difficult to obtain compensation. Even where the condition is accepted either as an occupational injury or as a disease covered by compensation, it is often difficult to establish a causal link between the work activity and the condition in individual situations.

In Australia and New Zealand work-related musculoskeletal disorders are referred to as occupational overuse injury (OOI) or repetitive strain injury (RSI). These injuries include forms of epicondylitis and carpal tunnel injuries which epidemiological studies have shown are likely to have been caused by work-related, repetitive activities. During the late 1970s through to the 1990s there was a prevailing attitude that musculoskeletal injuries were not real injuries or, if they were real, were not sufficient by themselves to be disabling, therefore workers suffering from these types of injuries were not eligible for compensation. The difficulty in appreciating the impact of repetitive strain was compounded by the fact that many of the injured workers were employed in female-dominated occupations involving clerical, word processing and data processing tasks, which implied that these types of injuries were related more to gender than to the work. Such conditions came to be seen as 'a woman's problem'. However, RSI claims are also to be found in male-dominated occupations such as meat processing and transport. Further, by the 1990s, there was a great deal of talk of 'an epidemic' of RSI claims. A critical observation is that the apparent epidemic proportions of compensation claims in relation to particular types of injury may have more to do with belated recognition of these types of injuries than changes in the actual level of incidence.

There is also evidence that most workers diagnosed with an occupational musculo-skeletal injury do not readily apply for workers' compensation because of the difficulties in obtaining workers' compensation (Rosenman et al., 2000). Quinter (1995: 256) summarises the vehement debate over RSI which took place in Australia and New Zealand in the 1980s and 1990s:

> … RSI was remarkable for the accompanying social commentary offered by many of the medical participants. This commentary was to have a profound effect on relationships between individual doctors and their patients with RSI. It reflected and reinforced the prevailing stereotypes within Australian society, not only of working women, but also of recipients of workers' compensation payments. On the other hand, some of the medical responses to the epidemic were severely criticised by social scientists who analysed the epidemic. In the process of such criticism, a number of stereotypes of doctors were also reinforced.

A number of writers including Willis (1986) have argued that social processes mediate the recognition and provision of compensation in relation to occupational injuries such as those grouped under the label of RSI or similar terms. These social processes are historically contingent, and this helps explain why a particular injury or group of injuries may be recognised more belatedly in some countries. As we have also noted, the debate over RSI is by no means an especially new or unique case. There are some clear parallels between the RSI debate and a debate over occupational back strain that occurred in Australia and New Zealand a decade earlier. Indeed, strain-type injuries that are difficult to conclusively diagnose using the conventional medical model and, due to the number of workers involved, entail potentially significant costs to employers and insurers have been subject to debate over many years in a number of (if not most) industrialised countries. In the US, Dembe (1996) has extensively documented how social factors shaped understandings of both cumulative trauma disorders of the hands and wrists and back disorders over more than 100 years. He refers to attempts to depict telegraphist's cramp earlier this century in terms of occupational neuroses and allegations about the susceptibility of Jews and women, the low reporting of hand disorders between 1920 and 1980 and the role of labour activism in altering this (Dembe, 1996: 24–101). Australian and New Zealand readers familiar with the RSI debate will recognise similarities with Dembe's (1996: 102–59) examination of the debate surrounding the evolving recognition of occupational back pain. It is worth noting in passing that he provides a comparable analysis of a significant occupational disease, namely noise-induced hearing loss (Dembe, 1996: 160–228).

The modern-day equivalent of 'telegraphists' cramp' can also be found in emerging forms of work, such as call centres, which are not necessarily as injury-free as first contemplated and where compensation coverage is varied. Call centre workers are reporting injuries that range from back strain to carpal tunnel injuries as well as suffering from airborne and contact diseases from working within confined, air-conditioned offices and handling bacteria-ridden headsets and telephone systems (Hunt, 2008). Indications are that the level of under-reporting of compensation claims among these workers is high as most call centre workers are in non-standard, contingent work and identifying the exact time and place where the injury occurred is difficult for these workers, thus reducing the rate of success of lodging a claim (Hannif and Lamm, 2006).

Mobile workers

The other emerging form of employment is mobile work, which by its very nature has significant workers' compensation issues. Workers are increasingly expected to travel interstate and to other countries as part of their work. Inquiries into the safety and health of workers in the transport industry in a number of countries, including Australia and New Zealand (see Wilson et al., 2000; Quinlan, 2001; Jones, 2003; Saltzman and Belzer, 2007), have reported an above average injury, illness and fatality rate among these workers in spite of the fact that there is a significant level of under-reporting of workers' compensation claims (Quinlan, 2001). Findings from a survey of New South Wales truck drivers undertaken by Mayhew and Quinlan (2000) as part of the Report of Inquiry into Safety in the Long Haul Trucking Industry showed that over a quarter of drivers reported an acute injury or illness and over half the drivers reported a chronic injury, while over one-third of owner-drivers and small fleet operators reported a chronic back injury. The survey also revealed that workers' compensation claims data seriously understates the extent of work-related injury and disease in the road transport industry due to reporting/claim problems and the fact that most owner-drivers do not take out workers' compensation cover (and a not insubstantial number have no insurance cover whatsoever) (Quinlan, 2001: 3). Not only is there a problem of under-reporting workers' compensation claims for injuries sustained while travelling but there is also a lack of standardisation between Australian jurisdictions of who and what is covered by compensation, as illustrated in table 8.6 below.

Table 8.6   Coverage of journey claims

	Cwlth	Vic.	NSW	SA
Journey to and from work	Comcare: No (some exceptions) Seacare: Yes MRCS: Yes	No (journeys are covered under separate statutory no-fault transport accident scheme)	Yes (some restrictions)	Generally no. Only in very limited circumstances may be covered—most journey accidents would not be covered
Journey undertaken for work purposes	Comcare: Yes Seacare: Yes MRCS: Yes	Yes (some restrictions)	Yes—covered by s4 definition of 'personal injury arising out of or in the course of employment', not under s10 'journey claims'	Yes

Source: Safe Work Australia (2009a), *Comparison of Workers' Compensation Arrangements in Australia and New Zealand*, Commonwealth of Australia, Barton, ACT: 35–6.

Including workers travelling to and from work was one of the first significant ways that coverage under workers' compensation was broadened. Although it has led to many complicated cases (in terms of determining what constitutes a normal journey and a host of other matters) the general principle went largely unchallenged until the 1990s. However, the Industry Commission (1994: 94–7) provided a focus for employer criticisms that journey claims were not sufficiently work-related (and similar arguments about injuries during breaks/free time at work). This pressure from employers resulted in changes to journey entitlements in a number of jurisdictions, despite union arguments that these claims were not only low but also were only undertaken because of work and were covered under ILO convention 121 (which Australia has ratified). The debate over journey claims highlights the role of interest groups and cost considerations in determining what types of claim are covered by workers' compensation. It is likely that the very same influences have shaped recognition of occupational disease. Ultimately, the only real solution to this problem may be better preventative measures.

In summary, obtaining compensation for work-related acute injury has traditionally been more straightforward than is the case for chronic occupational disease as the link between cause and effect is easier to establish. Nonetheless, there is still a significant under-reporting of claims, especially among contingent workers in non-standard employment, and given that there is a growing trend towards this form of employment, under-reporting will continue to be an issue.

WA	Qld	Tas.	NT	ACT	NZ
No	Yes (some restrictions)	No (some exceptions)	No (some exceptions)	Yes	Yes (some restrictions)
Yes	Yes	Yes	Yes	Yes	No

Occupational disease

Perhaps the most significant limitation to the workers' compensation system in Australia and New Zealand as well as all other countries is the inadequate recognition of occupational disease. Even though knowledge of occupational disease stretches back hundreds of years (for example, scrotal cancer among chimney sweeps and recognition of scurvy among seamen in the eighteenth century) the workers' compensation schemes introduced in Australia and New Zealand were essentially *injury* compensation schemes (Barth and Hunt, 1980: 2–3, 6–7). The Victorian Act of 1914, for example, prescribed only six diseases, with claims for any other disease being treated in the same way as injuries arising from an 'accident' and, accordingly, very difficult to substantiate (Foenander, 1956: 26). During the course of the twentieth century the schemes were modified to take more account of occupational disease (for example, including specific reference to disease in the definition of injury). In New Zealand, the 1967 Woodhouse Report went even further and recommended the move towards a universal compensation scheme which included illnesses and disability. However, this was not to be, and as Oliphant (2007: 3) states '… the failure of past attempts to extend the scheme to sickness and disability provide no grounds for confidence that this goal will ever be achieved'. He adds '… that the present scheme so manifestly fails to give effect to the Woodhouse principles, because of the exclusion of sickness and disability, that it becomes easy to view those principles as irrelevant: at best, they are paid lip-service and their content devalued; at worst, they are ignored, and cost considerations are given decisive importance (rather than merely acting as practical constraints on the pursuit of principled goals)' (Oliphant, 2007: 3).

There are a number of examples, nonetheless, of extremely belated recognition for compensation purposes of conspicuous occupational diseases. Asbestos is an obvious case in point. Concerns at the health effects of asbestos exposure can be traced back to Roman times (Castleman, 1990: 1) and by the early years of the twentieth century the dangers were sufficiently clear to Canadian insurance companies that they refused to issue life policies to asbestos miners. By the 1930s there was good clinical evidence on dangers of asbestos exposure and by the 1950s research by Doll and others had clearly linked asbestos to lung cancer (Castleman, 1990: 83–4). Given that asbestos has been manufactured and used widely, particularly in construction and engineering, in both Australia and New Zealand since 1888, the number of people exposed is estimated to be in the millions (Haigh, 2006).

Despite the knowledge that exposure to asbestos was extremely hazardous, compensation agencies either refused to compensate for asbestos-related diseases or placed severe restrictions on the amount received or the right to sue. For example, asbestos-related diseases were not recognised by the NSW workers' compensation authority until the mid 1970s but (due to its extensive use and the lagged effects) rapidly became one of the most important categories of compensated disease. In Western Australia, the other state with asbestos mines, lung cancer was made compensable in 1981 (McCulloch, 1986: 197–8). Under New Zealand's no-fault accident compensation scheme, the right to sue for all injuries sustained and for those diseases where exposure to asbestos occurred after 1974 was removed. For workers exposed to asbestos after 1974 and whose compensation was paid out by the ACC, weekly payments were paltry (e.g. $67 per week in the 1990s) and receiving lumps sum payments, until recently, was not an option (Armstrong, 2008). To make matters worse, for those Australian and New Zealand workers affected by asbestos and whose only option was to sue their employer for compensation, often at great financial cost to themselves and their families, the prospect of still being alive when and if their case succeeded was minimal.

The under-recognition of occupational disease in workers' compensation schemes may be attributed to a number of factors, several of which we discussed in our more general discussion of occupational disease in chapter 5. This includes limited knowledge on the aetiology of many diseases, the complication of multiple exposure to hazardous substances (some with unique combinant effects) from a range of sources in and outside the workplace and the problem of measuring lagged effects and long-term low-level exposures (see Barth and Hunt, 1980: 11–15; NOHSAC Technical Report (2), 2002; Leigh and Robbins, 2004). While many (though by no means all) injuries may be traced back to a single or closely related set of incidents at the workplace, the same cannot be said for many occupational diseases where causal exposures have been insidious and long-term, in spite of the fact that there is a large medical literature documenting the prevalence of chronic fatal diseases linked to occupational exposures (see Leigh and

Robbins, 2004). At best, a number will only be revealed via the statistical associations and risk probabilities of expensive and consequently often scarce epidemiological analysis. There is also a lack of epidemiological research compounded by the limited capacity of this tool where exposed workers are in transient jobs or they are widely dispersed in small groups (as in the case of tick dip workers).

Further, a number of researchers have pointed to the comparative difficulty that both workers' compensation agencies and the judicial system appear to have evaluating scientific evidence generally. An understanding of expert scientific evidence, whether epidemiological or from other medical specialties, requires not only a basic appreciation of the specialty, but a fundamental grasp of statistics. Epidemiological evidence may support the finding of a link between a work-related exposure and disease (see Schroeder, 1986 and Blessman, 1991), but this link is evidence only of risk or of the likelihood of a connection between the work activity or workplace and the individual worker's condition. It is not proof that the work activity or exposure caused the worker's illness. In other words, epidemiological evidence is evidence as to general risks of exposure and is not evidence as to the particular cause of an individual worker's illness. Most workers' compensation schemes overcome this difficulty by recognising or accepting that certain diseases are likely to be the result of workplace exposure in certain circumstances. There is then a legal presumption that the activity or exposure caused the disease. This means, however, that unless the condition is recognised as an occupational disease, there is very little chance that the worker's claim will be accepted. And even where the condition is recognised as an occupational disease, the worker may still have considerable legal challenges in proving that there was sufficient exposure or activity to warrant the benefit of the presumption. Most significantly, it is often very difficult to have new conditions or forms of exposure accepted as occupational diseases or causes of occupational diseases.

A number of US studies (see Blessman, 1991; Barth and Hunt, 1980) have found occupational disease claims experienced a far higher rate of rejection than injury-based claims (Blessman also found disease claims were almost three times as costly to adjudicate). We are aware of no similar Australian or New Zealand studies but it is likely that the situation is not dissimilar. Examining the NSW compensation system in the mid 1980s, Brooks (1987b: 38–66) found the legislation failed to clearly distinguish between disease and injury but the more difficult criteria applied to establishing disease claims had encouraged attempts to 'fit' some diseases within the injury category and consequential definitional debates. It should be acknowledged that the introduction of workers' compensation played no small part in the development of occupational medicine and epidemiological research from the 1920s onward. Nonetheless, the preoccupation of workers' compensation schemes with the notion of 'accidents' (Figlio, 1985; Wilson, 1982)—and the intellectual baggage associated with this—provides an important clue to understanding the focus on injury.

The fact that workers' compensation schemes have failed and/or limited compensation for disease cannot be explained only in terms of the technical difficulties of researching these links and institutional blinkers within workers' compensation agencies and the judicial system. Rather, recognition also involves sociopolitical processes that include the struggle between competing interest groups along similar lines to that described in relation to some types of injury. Just as was the case in terms of defining who is covered, determination of what should qualify as a work-related injury, disease or illness has significant but rather different implications for workers, employers, government and insurers. As the Industry Commission (1994: 94–9) observed, these interest groups express quite distinct positions on the issue, and similar debates occur in other countries. This is made clear by O'Loughlin's (2005: 21) examination of the political debate over 1987 workers' compensation 'reforms' in New South Wales (NSW). The reforms mainly involved restricting injured workers' rights to common law action and lump sum settlements and obliging them to return to work. Such an outcome required the transformation of workers' status from industrial citizens to clients of intensified therapeutic management, authorised and overseen by the state. This development was underpinned by a significant change in the political culture associated with the formulation of workers' compensation policy. O'Loughlin (2005: 21) observed that: 'central to it was the virtual disappearance of class-based parliamentary discourse, and its replacement by a neo-liberal discursive consensus in identifying the needs of injured workers and in developing strategies to address them'.

Within workers' compensation schemes, criteria have been developed for classifying compensable diseases in an effort to make compensation more accessible for workers suffering work-related diseases and where a relatively clear link to a particular occupation has been established. One way of doing this is to designate certain types of diseases as honorary 'injuries' or to apply internationally recognised criteria of work-related diseases, such as those outlined in the ILO Convention 42, Workmen's Compensation (Occupational Diseases) Convention. The workers' compensation authorities will accept a work association (i.e. the disease is compensable) for such a disease if the worker can show they suffer a particular disease and work in a nominated occupation for which that disease is prescribed (e.g. lead poisoning among lead foundry workers). Once this is established the onus of proof to dispute such a claim rests with the insurer or compensation authorities, not with the claimant. This can still lead to somewhat arbitrary distinctions in terms of what are nominated occupations. For example, Q fever and brucellosis may be prescribed diseases for abattoir workers but not veterinarians (even those working in primary industry). Where a disease is not prescribed it is up to the claimant to establish a causal link between their work activities and their disease, which is more often than not a difficult task, as outlined above. In many of the Australian jurisdictions, the list of prescribed diseases is limited and accounts for only a fraction of the harmful substances and work activities which have been linked to particular diseases by medical and epidemiological research. Moreover, in Australia and New Zealand there have been periodic efforts to narrow the compensation categories even further as a way of restricting compensation entitlements, particularly those related to long-term claims.

Unlike regulations in most other countries, the New Zealand Injury Prevention, Rehabilitation, and Compensation Act, 2001 bypasses the normal requirement to prove causation which is required for gradual process injuries or diseases. It also lists 25 additional conditions or diseases to be added to Schedule 2 (see NOHSAC Report, 2005 for a more detailed critique). Although many of the occupational diseases are rare, some are more common, such as noise-induced hearing loss, dermatitis and some types of asthma caused by sensitising agents or irritants inherent in the work process, for example sawdust (ACC, 2005). This change has had the greatest affect on industries where employees may be exposed to the risk of certain diseases. There are still a number of instances when a work-related disease may not be covered. For example, cover does not extend to viruses, bacteria or fungi. It is possible that a person could be infected with tuberculosis in a workplace setting but not be covered by the ACC scheme, even though exposure occurred in the workplace. The Ministerial Advisory Panel on Gradual Process, Disease or Infection is currently undertaking work to review the ACC scheme's boundaries regarding workplace exposure (Allen and Clarke, 2006: 49).

In spite of the fact that compensation has gradually been extended to cover more work-related diseases, the rate of success is still relatively low (NOHSAC, 2005). Stress, like asbestos, is a good illustration of how difficult it is to receive compensation even though it has been compensable for a number of years in Australia and New Zealand (Guthrie, 2007). Initially, successful claims were overwhelmingly concentrated in a number of occupations that were viewed as particularly stressful— for example, workers in the police force, prisons and emergency services, air-traffic controllers, managers, teachers and public servants. This pattern has only slightly broadened over time despite evidence that it in no way reflects the actual incidence of work-related stress in the community (Keegel et al., 2009). As with RSI and some occupational diseases, compensation proceedings over stress have also been complicated by experts and others suggesting that the origins of depression and the like primarily lie outside the workplace (Ellashof and Streltzer, 1992). It is perhaps not too cynical to see the restricted recognition of stress-related claims as being influenced by such concerns and the cost implications of a more expansive interpretation. Indeed, noting that work-related stress constituted the most expensive form of claim in all Australian jurisdictions, a study by Guthrie (2007: 528) found that over the past decade efforts were made to reduce these costs 'by imposing noted special legislative thresholds on such claims'. In other words, agencies adopted what Guthrie accurately describes as a 'back-ended' approach to cost minimisation by limiting access to compensation. Interestingly, in New Zealand, successful compensation cases for stress have been achieved through the employment courts under personal grievance provision, rather than through the ACC, and most of the employment cases have involved public servants (for example, Brickell v A-G [2000] 2 ERNZ 529), as discussed in more detail in relation to the disputes process.

Workers' compensation schemes of Australia, New Zealand and other countries have yet to fully throw off the shackles of their origin as acute trauma or injury compensation schemes. Progressively greater recognition has been given to disease but recognition is still very restricted in terms of the diseases for which an occupational association is readily accepted. Nor has access to tort action under common law (where available) done much to remedy this imbalance. As Schroeder (1986: 159) has observed, these actions must surmount legal doctrines (establishing 'foreseeability', causation and statutes of limitations) '… just as formidable as those presented by the workers' compensation system'. Further, employers or insurers can use legal techniques to prolong the period between the time a claim is filed and the time it finally reaches court to increase the financial burden on the claimant and increase the chance they will drop proceedings or even die before the case can be heard. Allegations of the use of such tactics have been made in relation to cases brought by asbestos-exposed workers with mesothelioma. However, even without such tactics, common law actions take considerable time and, because of the other problems just mentioned, will benefit only a minority of workers at best.

Compensation—an overview

Every year thousands of Australians and New Zealanders suffering occupational injuries or diseases receive some form of compensation. In all 10 jurisdictions, workers' compensation covers medical and hospital expenses as well as costs of rehabilitation (including artificial limbs and related expenses such as house or workplace modification and travelling expenses). Workers' compensation payments also come in a variety of forms, that is, short-term weekly or biweekly payments in lieu of lost earnings as well as compensation for permanent disability, which includes long-term pensions and, in some jurisdictions, lump sum payments. There is also provision for compensation in the event of a worker's death payable to his or her dependent spouse and children.

While current schemes are more generous than those available in the early years of workers' compensation and compensation remains more predictable and timely than damages available at common law, a number of issues remain. The main issue is that the level of compensation varies depending on the jurisdiction. Some current schemes provide what can be described as minimal income support, placing injured workers and their families into economic hardship. The second issue is the level of compensation entitlements. Although over much of the course of the twentieth century the scope and level of entitlements was gradually increased to include advanced medical treatment and rehabilitation services, such services are not available in all jurisdictions. Moreover, common law damages for similar but non–work-related injuries often exceed worker's compensation entitlements (see Wood et al., 1995).

In spite of the fact that workers' compensation schemes in each of the 10 jurisdictions offers different levels of compensation, the basic categories for compensation benefits are, however, similar. The categories include:

- costs of medical treatment
- short-term income replacement
- long-term compensation
- lump sum payments
- death benefits.

Costs of medical treatment

Workers' compensation schemes in both Australia and New Zealand typically fund medical expenses of injured workers, although these entitlements are subjected to fluctuating budget constraints. The injured worker might also be eligible for medical care funded either publicly or privately, but medical costs of injury or disease accepted as compensable are paid or reimbursed by the scheme. Coverage by workers' compensation is thus more important in jurisdictions where publicly funded medical treatment is limited. For example, under a workers' compensation scheme an injured worker may be eligible for specialist treatment, physiotherapy or rehabilitation services which may not be available under a publicly funded medical service. Studies indicate coverage is low among lower paid workers and those in small business and that even reduced premiums have only a modest incentive effect on the taking out of such cover (see Chernew et al., 1997; Leigh and Robbins, 2004; Fan et al, 2006). It hardly needs to be said that the group just mentioned include many workers facing a significant risk of work-related illness and who are most likely to experience problems obtaining workers' compensation. A lesson also to be drawn from this is that a shift to voluntary health insurance is liable to compound the impact of gaps in coverage and entitlements within the workers' compensation system.

Short-term income replacement

All workers' compensation schemes provide short-term income replacement. The nature or level of compensation over the short term is determined by how much the worker is paid and by how long the short-term period lasts. With respect to the amount of payment, the injured worker generally receives an amount calculated on the basis of pre-injury earnings. In jurisdictions where the compensation is not taxable, the calculation can be done on the basis of the worker's net earnings. In addition, the level of compensation for the short term is usually intended to replace all of the worker's lost earnings. However, in some jurisdictions (notably in Canada) the short-term income replacement is set lower than earned income in order to ensure that the injured worker has an 'incentive' to return to work. The level of compensation over the short term also takes into account the worker's ability to work. Over the short term the income replacement may be calculated on the basis of total disability or on the basis of partial disability if the worker is, for example, able to work two hours a day.

The length of time for which the short-term income replacement is paid also differs from state to state. Table 8.7 sets out basic compensation periods, including short-term compensation. The determination of 'short-term' is generally intended to reflect the period of time the worker needs to recover from his or her injury. Most injured workers recover within weeks and return to work without difficulty. However, some injuries are intractable and others leave the worker with permanent disability. These workers are entitled to long-term compensation and, where appropriate, rehabilitation assistance. Furthermore, the level of entitlements was never especially generous and for many if not most workers, it was arguably inadequate. Supporting payments (made in lieu of wages) and lump sum settlements were never designed to maintain workers in exactly the same economic position that they would have been in if injury or disease had not occurred. Even leaving aside delays to payment, most workers will still incur a net cost as a result of a lost-time injury or disease. Based on work incapacity, workers' compensation payments do not commodify all the losses that could be considered in a common law claim (including disfigurement, pain and suffering, effects on quality of life, lost promotion opportunities, etc.).

Long-term compensation

After a period of convalescence the worker's condition may stabilise. At the point where the medical evidence suggests that there is little likelihood of further improvement, the worker may be assessed to determine his or her functional impairment resulting from the compensable injury or disease. If the worker is assessed as having a permanent functional impairment as a result of the compensable injury, then they still receive compensation payments, but the amount of payments over the long term is usually different from the amount paid over the shorter recovery period. The long-term or permanent compensation, (often referred to as a pension), is usually calculated on the basis of the worker's pre-injury earnings taking into account the level of the assessed functional impairment. The resulting amount is intended to compensate the worker for loss of income over the long term and may include top up for loss of pension entitlement. The payment of long-term compensation may continue for the worker's whole life but is usually greatly reduced when the worker retires or when he or she reaches the designated retirement age. In some jurisdictions, the payment may even end when the worker reaches retirement. Also in some jurisdictions the long-term benefits are paid out in a lump sum rather than periodic payments.

Table 8.7   Period of near-full income replacement of pre-injury earnings for workers who cannot earn

	Cwlth	Vic.	NSW	SA *	WA	Qld	Tas.	NT	ACT	NZ
100% wage replacement (number of weeks)	45	13 (95% replacement)	26	52	13	26	13	26	26	Week 2–5: 80% of short-term calculation

Source: Safe Work Australia (2009a), *Comparison of Workers' Compensation Arrangements in Australia and New Zealand*, Commonwealth of Australia, Barton, ACT: 37–8.
* Significant legislative amendments were made to the South Australian scheme with effect from 1 July 2008.

The amount of compensation an injured worker who has suffered permanent impairment receives varies considerably depending not only on the jurisdiction but on the cause and type of accident, that is, whether work-related, traffic-related, medical negligence, bad luck or misadventure. For example, an injured person working in Australia unable to return to work can receive under (a) all workers' compensation schemes: no-fault periodic payments, with common law lump sums available in Queensland, Western Australia, Tasmania and the Australian Capital Territory (b) public liability (including medical indemnity): common law lump sums and (c) compulsory third party schemes: no-fault payments in Victoria, Tasmania and Northern Territory and common law lump sums in other jurisdictions (Australian Government Productivity Commission, 2004: 145).

Long-term compensation is expensive. In most jurisdictions there is concerted effort to reduce the number of long-term claimants given the costs to the compensation authority. In Australia and New Zealand injured or ill workers may have to resort to other welfare benefits in those jurisdictions where the compensation structures do not include long-tail claims. Premature exhaustion of lump sum compensation can leave no alternative other than to fall back on the Australian Government's social security programs (Australian Government Productivity Commission, 2004). In New Zealand this was clearly illustrated when, at the end of the 1990s, the ACC attempted to purge itself of its long-term claimants, such as those involving occupational overuse injuries, in order to make the proposed transition from public sector to private sector insurer operating in a competitive workers' compensation market. As a result, each person with a significant injury became the responsibility of an individual ACC staff member and greater emphasis was placed on rehabilitation and returning injured workers to the workforce. However, there was widespread criticism of this approach on the basis that it did little to reduce the number of long-term claimants and instead moved many of the claimants onto other sickness and disability benefits.

Lump sum payments

In most states in Australia and in New Zealand the worker may also receive a lump sum amount in addition to or in lieu of a long-term compensation award. Lump sum compensation awards may also provide compensation for loss described in common law as 'loss of amenities of life' or sometimes referred to as 'non-economic loss'. Loss of amenities of life is a measure of the impact of the injury on the worker's lifestyle, namely pain and suffering, permanent impairment, disfigurement and reduced expectation of life. Some schemes (the Australian Government, New South Wales and Victoria) compensate pain and suffering separately from other loss of amenities of life. Others provide one lump sum payment for all loss of amenities of life. In 2003–04, maximum payments for non-economic loss ranged from $135 531 in Western Australia to $347 890 in Victoria. The average across all schemes was around $211 000 (Australian Government Productivity Commission, 2004).

Table 8.8 Final step-down incapacity payments

Parameter	Cwlth	Vic.	NSW	SA [1]	WA
Final step-down (after week …)	45	13	26	52	13
Minimum amount	75%	75%	$287.40	80%	85%
Variation	More for dependants, less capacity to earn	Less capacity to earn	Increases for dependent spouse and/or children	Less capacity or deemed capacity to earn	Subject to award rates
Financial Limit	150% of AWOTEFA [3]	$1210 per week	—	—	—
Time limit	—	2.5 years	2 years	—	—
Age limit	65 unless worker is over 63 years at time of injury, in which case max. 2 years	65 unless worker over 62.5 years at time of injury, in which case max. 2.5 years after incapacity	Retirement age + 12 months	65 unless worker is over 64.5 at time of injury, in which case max. 6 months. Payments cease at 70	65 unless worker is over 64 at time of injury, in which case max. 1 year

Source: Safe Work Australia (2009a), *Comparison of Workers' Compensation Arrangements in Australia and New Zealand*, Commonwealth of Australia, Barton, ACT: 37–8.
1   Significant legislative amendments were made to the South Australian scheme with effect from 1 July 2008.
2   If the work related impairment is over 15%
3   Average weekly ordinary time earnings of full-time adults

Table 8.9 Permanent impairment thresholds and entitlements

Permanent impairment	Cwlth	Vic.	NSW	SA
% of impairment	10% WPI 5% hearing >0% fingers, toes, taste, smell	10% except for total losses compensated under different table. 5% for Chapter 3 musculoskeletal injuries with a date of injury on or after 2 December 2003. 30% for psychological injuries	1% Hearing loss 6% Psychological injury 15%	None except hearing loss 5%
Lump sum *	$146 016	$384 180	$231 000	$136 000
Additional	$54 756	$462 720 (less any statutory impairment benefit paid)	$50 000	$91 800

Source: Safe Work Australia (2009a), *Comparison of Workers' Compensation Arrangements in Australia and New Zealand*, Commonwealth of Australia, Barton, ACT: 40–1.
* Significant legislative amendments were made to the South Australian scheme with effect from 1 July 2008.

Qld	Tas.	NT	ACT	NZ
104	78	26	26	5: 80% of long-term calculation
65% [2]	80%	75%	65%	NZ$360
—	Less capacity to earn	More for dependants, less capacity to earn	More for dependants, less capacity to earn	Less capacity to earn
$227 565	—	—	—	NZ$1 583.41
5 years	9 years	2 years	2 years	—
—	65 unless worker is over 64 at time of injury, in which case max. 1 year. If a worker's employment would allow the worker to continue beyond age 65 the tribunal may determine that weekly payments may continue for a specified period	65 unless worker is over 64.5 at time of injury, in which case max. 6 months	65 unless worker is over 63 years at time of injury, in which case max. 2 years	65 unless: – if a worker is between 63 and 64 years at time of injury, max. 2 years – if a worker is 64 at time of injury, max. 1 year. All subject to an election to be entitled to compensation rather than superannuation

WA	Qld	Tas.	NT	ACT	NZ
1% Hearing loss initial 10% and subsequent loss 5%	1%	5% WPI >0% fingers and toes 10% psychiatric impairment	5%	1%	1%
$159 091	$227 565	$222 267.15	$215 030	$170 719.51	NZ$113 363.92
—	$227 565	—	—	—	—

Lump sum payments were originally paid in lieu of weekly benefits in the case of death or permanent disablement. The level of payment was calculated according to the degree of incapacity (set out in a table of maims) or, in the case of death/total incapacity, up to a maximum amount depending on age and the number dependants. The latter entitlement operated in a gender-biased fashion because females were seldom the primary breadwinners (Guthrie and Jansz, 2006). Lump sum payments can also come from sources other than the compensation authority or insurer, namely the courts. That is, the worker may also be entitled to sue for further damages in certain circumstances. There is also a propensity for the courts in Australia and New Zealand to award lump sum payments, appropriated from fines, to workers as compensation for injuries they have sustained. When the New Zealand Accident Compensation Corporation abolished its lump sum payments to victims of injury (although this remedy has been restored), the courts began to regularly award to workers at least 50% and up to 90% of the fines. However, it has been argued that these compensatory payments should not be seen as a 'de facto compensation system to replace the ACC lump-sum award' (Judge Saunders, *Masters* v. *Wanaka Tourist Craft Ltd*, Unreported, DC, 28 May 1996, CRN 500200415849). There have been a number of cases where the court, under section 28 of the Criminal Justice Act, 1985, has paid part of the fine to the victims of the offence, for example, in prosecutions against David Spencer Ltd and Fletcher Challenge Steel Makers. As the court noted in Department of Labour v Alexandra Holdings Ltd [1994] DCR 50:

> This unfortunate man, in trying to be a good employee, has suffered a serious loss for which, one has to say, accident compensation will not adequately compensate him. Whereas, in earlier years, accidents of this sort normally attracted very substantial common law damages or, later on, resulted in quite sizeable lump sum payouts of accident compensation, such payouts have now ceased or become reduced, in many cases, to a level which many sections of the community regard as almost contemptuous.

Although lump sums paid in the case of death or disablement can vary widely across different jurisdictions, the maximum lump sum payouts are seldom sufficient to offset financial loss or indeed comparable to other areas of compulsory insurance (such as third-party motor accident insurance) (see the Australian Government Productivity Commission's Report on National Workers' Compensation and Occupational Health and Safety Frameworks, 2004). Prior to the reforms of the 1980s a number of schemes allowed private insurers, and even self-insurers, to commute weekly payments into a lump sum settlement. This was open to abuse. It was in the interests of insurers to delay proceedings, stop weekly payments and limit payouts (and could be seen as a direct conflict of interest for self-insurers), and a mixture of ignorance, emotional strain and the financial pressure of accumulating debt often placed workers in a very poor bargaining position. A study of lump sum settlements to workers suffering back injuries (Encel and Johnson, 1972) found that, contrary to popular belief, workers did not make a rapid and 'remarkable' recovery once the claim was settled and the settlement was largely used to pay accumulated debts rather than to generate future income. A second NSW study of both common law and workers' compensation lump sum settlements (Bass, 1983) found that both groups suffered a decline in income and employment status with the latter faring worse because of the generally lower awards made under workers' compensation. An inquiry into the Victorian workers' compensation system (Cooney, 1984: chapter 10) was also highly critical of the lump sum settlement process. It raised a number of criticisms already mentioned (such as those relating to delays and financial insecurity) as well as pointing to the inability of some workers to manage lump settlements and problems when the level of disability increased some time after final settlement. Reforms made to workers' compensation schemes in virtually every jurisdiction during the 1980s sought to address these issues by removing the option to commute, increasing weekly payments and, in some cases, introducing a lump sum payout for pain and suffering. However, as was the case with weekly payments, in the 1990s (and somewhat earlier in Victoria) a number of the enhanced benefits were wound back as part of the push to contain workers' compensation costs.

A related issue is the time limit on payments and the relationship between workers' compensation and social security. Initially, workers' compensation schemes set fairly rigid limits on the period that weekly payments could be received, after which time the only option available to workers was a lump sum settlement for permanent disability. In practice, limits to payments meant that workers with long-term injuries or permanent disabilities, or whose lump sums had proved inadequate to maintain income, shifted onto the social security system. As a study by Stewart and Doyle (1988) (see also Stewart, 1991a) showed, this had two effects. One was a substantial cost-shifting away from predominantly state-administered workers' compensation schemes (funded by employers) to the federal social security system (funded by taxpayers). The second effect was a further reduction in entitlements because—unlike workers' compensation payments—social security payments were means-tested and also set at a far lower level (workers' compensation lump sum payments are also not taxable). As we have noted elsewhere, the shift also entailed a significant gender bias because, as most female workers were not the primary breadwinners, they were excluded from social security payments in all but the direst circumstances. Of course, the inadequate workers' compensation coverage of particular groups of workers as well as disease and some illnesses (such as those related to stress) mentioned earlier compounds both effects (see Stewart, 1991b). The converse is also true. In a longitudinal study of construction industry workers' compensation claims data in Canada, Fortin et al., (1999) conclude that if workers' compensation payouts are more generous than unemployment benefits, there will be an increase in the duration of claims due to severe accidents that are difficult to diagnose. Moreover, the duration of spells on workers' compensation is much higher when an accident occurs in December, a month which corresponds to the beginning of the lay-off season in the construction sector.

Although the restricted time limits on payments were addressed by reforms to workers' compensation during the 1980s cost-shifting remains a major problem and was the subject of attention by the Australian Government Productivity Commission's

Report on National Workers' Compensation and Occupational Health and Safety Frameworks, (2004: 271) in which it was noted that:

> Cost shifting towards workers' compensation schemes undermines scheme afford-ability and limits the ability of schemes to provide for those suffering from a work-related injury or illness. Some injuries or illnesses which are compensable under workers' compensation schemes may have been caused or aggravated by conditions outside the workplace. Musculo-skeletal injuries, which may be exacerbated by ageing, are a notable example.

Despite this, the matter has received little attention and this is understandable. State and territory governments keen to keep workers' compensation premiums low are unlikely to push for action on cost-shifting, while successive federal governments have seen little benefit in raising an issue where the costs to the taxpayer are hidden and which would arouse considerable hostility from the states.

Death benefits

Where a worker is killed while employed or dies as a result of an occupational disease, his or her dependants may receive compensation benefits, as outlined in table 8.10. These benefits vary but generally provide for income replacement for dependent spouses and children calculated as either a fixed amount or on the basis of the deceased worker's earnings. This can be related to pre-injury earnings (Victoria, South Australia and Tasmania), average state earnings (Queensland) or an indexed amount (currently ranging from $50.75 per week for each dependent child in the Australian Capital Territory to $86.60 per week in New South Wales).

Rehabilitation and return to work

The principal objective of workers' compensation schemes is often seen as compensation. However, since the 1970s increased attention has been given to the objective of rehabilitation and return to work. Rehabilitation encompasses medical/physiological, vocational and psychosocial elements of restitution of worker health and wellbeing, including minimising/managing permanent disability and adverse effects on social interactions (such as those within the family) that arise from this. Return to work—where possible—can be seen as an important element of the rehabilitation process, although for policymakers, insurers and other interested parties it is often seen as the overarching objective.

Complete rehabilitation was set out in the Woodhouse Report as the third principle of a comprehensive administrative compensation scheme and a central benefit of the proposed compensation scheme. In tort, loss due to injury was quantified and measured in monetary terms. However, it was felt that injured workers lost more than just wages; that is, an injured worker also lost his or her livelihood. As the report noted, the worker, their family and their community lost the benefit of the worker's 'productive capacity'

(Woodhouse Report, 1967: 40). Complete rehabilitation would ensure that every injured worker recovered 'the maximum degree of bodily health and vocational utility in a minimum of time' (Woodhouse Report, 1967: 40). The explicit goal of the compensation scheme in terms of rehabilitation was to ensure that the worker either returns to his or her pre-injury employment or to another job without a loss of earnings.

For policymakers, complete rehabilitation is often seen to mean that the injured worker received medical treatment, compensation for lost wages and help to restore their earnings capacity over the long term. The nature of rehabilitation offered in each jurisdiction is set out in the relevant statute (e.g. Australian Safety, Rehabilitation and Compensation (SRC) Act, 1988, and New Zealand Injury Prevention, Rehabilitation, and Compensation Act, 2001). In most jurisdictions, the level of rehabilitation is linked to the workers' pre-injury earnings. The more the worker earned prior to their injury, the greater their earning capacity and thus the greater the effort that is dedicated to their rehabilitation. While physical rehabilitation is an important component of complete rehabilitation, vocational rehabilitation may be the most difficult. Vocational rehabilitation requires a return to work and is to a large extent dependent upon whether the employers are willing and able to re-employ the worker. The willingness of employers to accept injured workers in turn may depend on the costs of them not doing so. Some jurisdictions impose a duty to accommodate on employers who may face fines or increased costs if they fail to find some work for returning workers. Also, compensation agencies wield a great deal of influence over the costs involved in rehabilitation and extent of coverage. The Australian vocational rehabilitation industry is influenced at the federal level by the Commonwealth Rehabilitation Service and Comcare, while in New Zealand it is influenced by the Accident Compensation Corporation.

As with specific measures aimed at prevention, until relatively recently workers' compensation schemes in Australia and New Zealand were overwhelmingly concerned with providing monetary compensation (or commodifying injury and disease) and there was little effort to encourage rehabilitation of injured workers. Although a number of jurisdictions introduced rehabilitation provisions into their workers' compensation Acts, these were usually short, ambiguous and offered little to support the rehabilitation process (Sager and James, 2005; Purse, 2005; Kendall et al., 2007). For example, there was no obligation on the employer to maintain a job for an injured worker (and workers with permanent disabilities were commonly dismissed in the lead up to offering a lump sum settlement) and delays in processing claims often undermined the rehabilitation process. Those employers who retained disabled workers often assigned them to a restricted set of functions that understated their capabilities and went under the demeaning title of 'light duties'. Further, few resources were given over to rehabilitation activities.

Reviews and subsequent reforms of workers' compensation schemes on both sides of the Tasman from the 1980s onwards sought to address at least some of these issues and provide a far greater emphasis on and a broad view of rehabilitation although the precise measures adopted varied widely among the different jurisdictions. In NSW, for example, reforms to the Workers' Compensation Act in 1987 required employers to

Table 8.10 Death benefits

Death benefits	Cwlth	Vic.	NSW	SA *	WA
Lump sum	$219 024	$257 210	$337 700	$230 983	$218 095
Weekly payments per child	$72.98	% of pre-injury earnings for dependent spouse and/or children to max. $1210 per week	$106.20	25% of deceased's notional weekly earnings	25% of deceased's notional weekly earnings if child is 'orphan', or 12.5% if 'dependent, non-orphaned' or a child's allowance of $41.70 per week (subject to LPI) for each dependent child up to age 16 or 21 if a student, whichever an arbitrator determines as likely to be in the best interests of that dependent.
Funeral	$9297	$9000	$9000	$7100	$7813
Other	—	Counselling for family $5000 max.	Counselling for family	Weekly payments of up to 50% of notional weekly earnings for a totally dependent spouse or domestic partner, less depending on degree of dependency	—

* Significant legislative amendments were made to the South Australian scheme with effect from 1 July 2008.

Source: Safe Work Australia (2009a), *Comparison of Workers' Compensation Arrangements in Australia and New Zealand*, Commonwealth of Australia, Barton, ACT: 41–4.

Qld	Tas.	NT	ACT	NZ
$426 260	$222 267.15	$268 788	$170 720	Spouse: NZ$5469.34 Each child or other dependant: NZ$2734.68 s381
10% of 'ordinary time earnings' payable weekly to each dependent family member until 16 or a student (where spouse is totally dependent)	A dependent child is entitled to 10% of the basic salary, commencing on the expiration of 13 weeks after the date of death.	$103.38	$56.91	Spouse: 60% of the long-term rate of weekly compensation that the earner would have received. Each child and other dependant: 20% of the weekly compensation
Reasonable	Reasonable cost of burial or cremation	$5375	$4553	NZ$5101.38
$11 385 paid to totally dependent spouse—reduced by the total amount of weekly payment of compensation	Spouse is entitled to weekly payments calculated at the same rate as the deceased would have received if he/she became totally incapacitated: – first 13 weeks: 100% of weekly payments – 14–78 weeks: 85% of weekly payments – 78 weeks–2 years: 80%of weekly payments	—	—	Child care payments: NZ$116.30 for a single child, NZ$69.78 each if there are more than two children, and a total of NZ$162.82 for 3 or more children

establish a rehabilitation program in consultation with unions and in accordance with guidelines issued by the Occupational Health, Safety and Rehabilitation Council of NSW. Each program needed to specify an accredited rehabilitation team (of relevant professionals) providing services on site (in the case of large employers) or at regional rehabilitation centres. From January 1989 employers with more than 20 employees had to have a rehabilitation coordinator. In Victoria the 1985 WorkCare legislation created the Victorian Accident Rehabilitation Council to oversee the development of a network of government and licensed private rehabilitation centres. The Victorian system also placed an obligation on employers to hold a job for injured workers undergoing rehabilitation for a period that was increased from six to 12 months in 1989. In South Australia the new emphasis on rehabilitation found recognition in the retitling of the Act in 1987 (to place rehabilitation ahead of workers' compensation), the provision of a clearly defined set of rehabilitation standards and the offer of reduced insurance premiums for employers with approved rehabilitation facilities. A Workers' Rehabilitation Advisory Unit was established to directly engage in the rehabilitation activities and facilitate independent activities by employers. In Queensland a large rehabilitation centre was established in South Brisbane in 1987, initially based on a narrow medical model of rehabilitation but gradually widening its approach. The needs of workers outside Brisbane and widely dispersed across this vast state were addressed through a network of regional rehabilitation personnel. At the federal level, Comcare promoted Case Management Plans, designed to facilitate a return to work, and the Commonwealth Rehabilitation Reform Bill of the 1990s paved the way for the corporatisation and competitive neutrality of Australia's first and largest rehabilitation service, the Commonwealth Rehabilitation Service (now known as CRS Australia). As Kendall et al. (2007: 818) notes:

> Despite federal government assurances that the reforms would not alter existing rehabilitation policies or services, there has been a marked change in referral patterns, rehabilitation activities and program duration as a result. Many people cautiously welcomed the possibility of a more cost effective rehabilitation service in Australia, but this change also symbolized the end of social rehabilitation models and the rise of a privatized business model of vocational rehabilitation.

While most of the structures described above have remained largely unaltered since the 1990s, there have been some changes. One critical area where changes were made was in relation to the employment security of injured workers. The Victorian WorkCare legislation had set reasonably stringent procedures in this regard (followed to some degree by South Australia) compared to other states and territories (such as NSW). In the first half of the 1990s there were halting efforts to enhance employment security in some jurisdictions (notably Comcare, Western Australia, Tasmania and the Northern Territory). Rehabilitation professionals and others have viewed retaining a right to continued employment as critical to effective rehabilitation. On the other hand, employment security provisions have attracted criticism on the grounds that they are ineffective (see Ison, 1990: 857), are costly to employers and the scheme, and—as far as neo-liberal policy advisers are concerned—send the wrong signal to workers and thereby distort the labour market. Purse (1998, 2005) and Kendall et al. (2007) argue that employment security provisions could actually reduce costs by preventing employers simply shifting the costs onto workers' compensation schemes and the community as well as encouraging more effective rehabilitation and the retention of people in meaningful and productive work. While conceding that more research is needed, Purse (1998b: 256) cites a 1991 South Australian study that argued that vigorous enforcement of employment security provisions would result in substantial savings of $106 million. The main problem, according to Purse (1998: 252–9), was that there was substantial noncompliance with the employment security provisions and new measures were required to address this.

In the Australian Government Productivity Commission's 2004 report on the inquiry into National Workers' Compensation and Occupational Health and Safety Frameworks, it was noted that the duration of rehabilitation has tended to increase in recent years, with the average number of days of paid compensation rising from 52 in 1998–99 to 57 in 2002–03. Associated with this has been an increase in the average nominal cost of claims from $7532 to $10 102, although jurisdictions that privately underwrote insurance experienced a decrease in claims costs (Australian Government Productivity Commission, 2004). In New Zealand, the duration of rehabilitation for workers has been gradually increasing since 2003, although the rehabilitation rates during 2007–08 at 3, 6, 9 and 12 months were all lower than in 2006–07 (ACC Annual Report, 2008). However, both Australian and New Zealand figures should be treated with caution as the true extent of injured or ill workers unable to return to work for a period of time is masked by a number of factors, including the lack of sophisticated data collection methods and the substitution of other benefits for compensation.

Although there has been an increase in the duration of rehabilitation as well as some advances in terms of resources, time, planning and multidisciplinary expertise, given the low baseline set by previous activities in rehabilitation, even a modest improvement would be relatively substantial. It is also important to put the Australian and New Zealand initiatives into a broader context. Overall, these efforts to promote rehabilitation are relatively modest compared to a number of European Union countries, especially those (such as Finland) where governments have mandated extensive occupational health services. Even in these countries, major challenges remain. For example, a Finnish study (Kivisto et al., 2008) found that less than half of their occupational health services provided return-to-work services and those offered varied widely in quality, with many diverging from current scientific evidence. The latter problem is also relevant to any assessment of policy developments in Australia.

Furthermore, even highly developed rehabilitation schemes face major constraints. This is not simply due to factors such as employer resistance already mentioned. The impact of injury and prospects for rehabilitation can vary widely due to factors such as the type of injury/illness, the type of job and other labour market factors, and even gender and geography. The impact of injury is complex, involving an array of physical, psychological and social effects, and not simply physiological incapacity or disfigurement. For example, an amputation often has less effect on return to work than a chronic strain injury even though the latter is far less visible. A number of studies have found that sprain and strain injuries, including RSI, were both the most costly and of longest duration (see Morrison et al., 1993: 117–30; Larsson, 1994: 71–5). These complaints are such a widespread OHS problem that they pose a severe challenge to both compensation and rehabilitation. As Larsson's assessment of the Swedish experience concludes, effective solutions to this problem lie more in the realms of prevention. Within this complex mix are fundamental issues, namely the ability to get workers back to work within an appropriate period of time and to deliver a vocational rehabilitation service accessible to all workers.

Achieving this also requires a critical assessment of the role of various professions engaged in medical treatment and rehabilitation. Unfortunately, this is an issue that has received only limited attention even in relatively recent reviews of workers' compensation (Hanks, 2008). On occasion astute observations are made. For example, in his review of the Tasmanian Workers Rehabilitation and Compensation Act, 1988 Alan Clayton (2007: 7) recommended that medical practitioners be encouraged to visit workplaces in order to familiarise themselves with the working environment and opportunities for alternative duties. This recommendation is consistent with earlier observations made about the role of medical practitioners in OHS (chapter 5).

Finally, the provision of rehabilitation with regard to work-related injury and illness needs to consider permanent impairment/disability. This in turn should be related to the provision of disability employment services more generally, not only because a significant proportion of those in receipt of disability-based social security were disabled as a result of workplace injury or disease (Hertzman et al., 1999; Albertsen et al., 2007) but also to ensure overall coordination in terms of policy. In 2008 the federal government announced a review of disability employment services in Australia and released a discussion paper examining the provision of services, employment incentives and vocational rehabilitation (Department of Education, Employment and Workplace Relations, 2008). Framed in a context where Australia was seen to be experiencing labour shortages (especially with regard to skilled labour), the model proposed emphasised flexibility and targeted support for job seekers, as well as enhanced remote and regional incentives. We would suggest future policy developments will need to pay closer attention to job security and to coordinate initiatives with others designed to address the considerable wastage of older workers within the Australian labour market.

Moving beyond immediate policy debates it needs to be recognised that rehabilitation and return to work has been the subject of considerable international research, with contributions from a number of disciplines and professions involved in the provision of services such as rehabilitation, rehabilitation medicine, occupational therapy, physiology/exercise science and physiotherapy. As in other areas already discussed, the perspectives of particular disciplines shape their understanding of the problem and remedies/interventions recommended. Some adopt a more clinical approach—such as the development of clinical rules and practices for workers with persistent musculoskeletal pain (Hewitt et al., 2007)—although tensions between this and the need to take account of psychosocial factors is to be found, to a greater or lesser degree, within a number of professions as well as between different professions. Each discipline represents a partial insight, with both strengths and weaknesses. Over the past two decades there has been a growing acceptance—and practice—of a multidisciplinary approach to rehabilitation (Anema et al., 2007; Michel et al., 2007). Although a detailed examination of each discipline and its role is beyond the scope of this book it is worth summarising some findings of recent research.

Research suggests the successful integration of the injured or ill worker back into the workforce, including the length of time between being injured or ill and returning to full-time work, is reliant on a number of factors. With regard to return to work, influences identified include the nature of the injury/illness, age, pain intensity, self-assessed work ability, worker beliefs/expectations, and industry/sector and psychosocial risk/organisational factors (Reiso et al., 2003; Post et al., 2005; Schultz et al., 2005; Schroer et al., 2005; Heymans et al., 2006). Studies have found that employer/supervisory behaviour, including support afforded and communication with injured workers, can affect return to work, and may be especially important for workers absent due to mental health problems (Nieuwenhuijsen et al., 2004; Butler et al., 2007; Holmgren and Ivanoff, 2007; Aas et al., 2008). A Norwegian study of long-term sick workers (Landstad et al., 2009) found that—in addition to the competing logics of the medical profession, government and employers—earlier work experience, age and other members in the household influenced the rehabilitation process and return to work. Among employers and some practitioners contrasts are commonly drawn between rehabilitation outcomes among those experiencing work injuries and those with non–work-related injuries (such as sporting injuries); the role of the level of benefits has also been studied. However, such observations are often decontextualised (for example, ignoring age effects) and the research evidence is mixed (Zella et al., 2005; Hou et al., 2008). For example, a Taiwan study (Hou et al., 2008) found the likelihood of return to work was similar for workers' compensation and non–workers' compensation groups with orthopaedic injuries, while a Spanish study (Benavides et al., 2009) found sickness benefits had a limited effect on the time taken to return to work.

Account needs to be taken of the nature of the injury and illness (for example, whether the injury is acute or chronic). In this regard, the research is more extensive in some areas than others. Thus, there is a considerable body of research on return-to-work rehabilitation for workers with musculoskeletal disorders and occupational back pain (see, for example, Baril et al., 2003; Baldwin et al., 2007; Bültmann et al., 2007). On the other hand, there is less comparable research on those suffering from mental health problems or respiratory ill health even though these disorders also commonly result in long-term disability (Briand et al., 2007; Peters et al., 2007; Blank et al., 2008). Further, a recent review (Briand et al., 2008: 2007) found that most return-to-work interventions for musculoskeletal disorders did not address the multi-causality of work disability, with the authors advocating interventions that involved 'the work environment and concerted action by the various parties'. A Swedish study (Norrefalk et al., 2008) found that multi-professional rehabilitation programs offered the greatest net economic benefits when dealing with return to work for those experiencing persistent musculoskeletal pain.

Other studies (Kominski et al., 2008) have found that the behaviour of treating physicians can also affect return to work outcomes, again highlighting the need for a more thorough understanding of OHS among general practitioners as well as specialists. As already implicit in earlier discussion, government policies and key stakeholders such as employers and unions, or other interest groups in the compensation process such as the legal profession, can affect the broad policy framework governing return to work as well as their implementation—and these interactions can be complex, as illustrated by a study of the NSW coal mining industry (Pelham, 2005). Work organisation and labour market factors also affect return to work (Hansson et al., 2006).

The factors just identified interrelate and this needs to be considered when planning interventions. While there is growing recognition of the need for a nuanced, consultative and multidisciplinary approach (Pransky et al., 2005) professional perspectives are still often based on a partial rather than holistic understanding of the problem. As with professions dealing with prevention, many professions involved in rehabilitation have a limited understanding of the OHS context. Many studies continue to place too much emphasis on individual (including health promotion) factors, a narrow range of interventions such as motivation and counselling, or ergonomic interventions—although the latter has the advantage of potentially addressing the underlying causes of disability, especially if entailing a participatory approach (Bonde et al., 2005; Anema et al., 2003, 2004). Inadequate recognition has been given to psychosocial, work environment and other organisation factors (for exceptions, see Gimeno et al., 2005; Janssen et al., 2003; Iles et al., 2008). This may not be surprising given that the latter require not only an understanding of recent trends in OHS research (see chapter 5) but also a willingness to question management decisions about working environments. To their credit, other studies, such as Dellve et al.'s (2003) study of Swedish homecare workers, highlight the critical role of basic work system characteristics in the onset of permanent work disability, indicating that return to work policies need to be integrated with attention to eliminating the sources of disability if interventions are to be more than 'bandaid' operations.

The process of integrating workers back into the workforce after suffering an injury or illness is fraught with difficulties. There is a need to critically evaluate specific strategies, such as return to work coordination (Shaw et al., 2007), and also to give due consideration to the latest evidence drawn from both quantitative and qualitative studies (MacEachen et al., 2006). In their study on injured workers' perspectives of their rehabilitation process, Sager and James (2005: 113) commented that workers ultimately want to return to their meaningful, productive worker role. They, and other researchers, also found a lack of support from key stakeholders, unfulfilling return to work duties and the negative attitude of co-workers can have a detrimental effect on the experiences and return to work outcomes of injured workers (Kenny, 1995a, 1995b; Williams and Westmorland, 2002; Westmorland et al., 2002). Moreover, although assigning workers to 'light duties' or 'modified duties' is a common (albeit contentious) approach in rehabilitation, it is often unavailable for workers (Purse, 2005; Sager and James, 2005; Guthrie and Jansz, 2006; Kendall et al. 2007). A recent meta-review of quantitative return to work intervention studies (Franche et al., 2005) identified only 10 quality studies, the majority indicating that work disability duration was significantly reduced although evidence on quality of life outcomes was much weaker.

There has long been a presumption that minimising absence duration following an injury/illness or securing an early return to work where possible is desirable because it limits negative psychological effects and social disruption. A large body of research has addressed rehabilitation strategies in this context (Franche et al., 2007). A study by Galizzi and Boden (2003) found that capacity to return to the pre-injury employer was an important determinant—a result that supports the need for more job security protections for injured workers as already discussed—as were the challenges posed by increased precarious employment (discussed below). This raises a broader contextual point. Without questioning the value of appropriately organised early return to work (see Pransky et al., 2005) there is also a need to recognise that job insecurity can encourage workers to stay at work after experiencing an injury or illness—a form of presenteeism—that may aggravate their condition. The capacity of laws to reshape behaviour was demonstrated in Sweden where exempting smaller enterprises from the Employment Security Act resulted in a 13% decline in sickness absence in those firms, especially those employing relatively few women or temporary workers (Olsson, 2008).

There is also a body research evaluating the role of interventions, including the contribution of particular professions. For example, ergonomics- and physiotherapy-based interventions play a significant role with regard to musculoskeletal disorders and chronic lower-back pain (see, for example, Critchley et al., 2007; Landau et al., 2007). Despite this, a review (Verhagen et al., 2006) found there was limited evidence for the effectiveness of interventions in keyboard redesign, exercises, rest breaks and manual therapy. A number of studies (Anema et al., 2007; Bade and Eckert, 2008; Hoffman and Cantoni, 2008) have also evaluated interventions by occupational therapists in relation to musculoskeletal, neurological and other disorders. As with ergonomics and other disciplines there have been calls for greater use of meta-reviews, including the Cochrane Collaboration, to better assess the evidence pertaining to the effectiveness of interventions by occupational therapists (Martin et al., 2008).

Research has also identified significant barriers to returning to work for injured or ill workers. The first is the inability to access clear, accessible and consistent information related to rehabilitation and the lack of open communication pathways between key stakeholders in this regard (Quinlan, 1996; Sengupta et al., 2005; Sager and James, 2005; Bültmann et al., 2007). Second, the cost structure of rehabilitation in Australia and New Zealand has also created problems. Kendall et al. (2007: 29) noted that, in Australia, the demise of non-profit and socially-based rehabilitation in favour of fixed funding models (e.g. managed care or case-based funding), coupled with the growing emphasis on cost containment, has placed many vocational rehabilitation providers in an unfamiliar environment dominated by bureaucratic, legal, economic and political imperatives. They concluded that although it was expected that vocational rehabilitation would address rising injury costs, its inability to do so has jeopardised its existence (Kendall et al., 2007: 29). Third, the growth of more precarious forms of employment presents a major challenge to return to work and occupational rehabilitation more generally. There is evidence that self-employed workers are more likely to continue working with injury or disease, and thereby risk exacerbating their disability to the point where they must leave the workforce altogether (Mayhew and Quinlan, 1997, 1999). Further, temporary employment or job insecurity is not conducive to meaningful rehabilitation, as illustrated by a Victorian study that identified a poor return-to-work experience among labour hire/temp agency workers (Underhill, 2008). Fourth, high unemployment at regional or societal level (as in a recession) may discourage rehabilitation due to the ready pool of replacement labour and lengthening periods of unemployment among workers that can affect post-injury employment prospects (Galizzi and Boden, 2003). Sixth, as already noted, long-term and effective rehabilitation with regard to some work activities and workplaces will require attention to the underlying causes of injury and disease (and not the provision of alternative duties). As yet this aspect has received little if any attention from policymakers although some researchers are beginning to draw attention to this issue. For example, a Quebec study (St-Arnaud et al., 2007) of return to work following mental health problems found improving working conditions could be a major determinant of health recovery and job retention.

It is also more difficult to establish effective rehabilitation programs in relation to small business because these employers have fewer resources to devote to rehabilitation, less knowledge of support mechanisms and few activities or jobs that be adjusted to meet the needs of disabled workers. Again, the growth of microbusiness as a consequence of outsourcing and privatisation has exacerbated this problem. A Danish study (Andersen et al., 2007) indicated the need for different return to work strategies within small enterprises, including building on social networks within them.

The overarching goal of rehabilitation is not only return to work where possible. Other critical if overlapping considerations include how to manage both temporary and chronic pain and the management of disability. It is also important to understand the psychosocial and socioeconomic impacts of injury and illness.

There is an important body of research and practice on pain, including the management of long-term or chronic pain by workers, emanating from a number of fields including rehabilitation and clinical medicine, nursing, physiology and health psychology. Particular areas of focus are lower-back pain arising from work and non-work sources affecting work ability (especially among older workers), return to work and ongoing work engagement (Nguyen and Randolph, 2007). Chronic pain, and coping with it, raises psychological issues. A recent meta-review of research (Hoffman et al., 2007: 1) concluded that multidisciplinary approaches to dealing with chronic lower-back pain that included a psychological component 'had positive short-term effects on pain interference and positive long-term effects on return to work'.

Turning to the issue of injury impacts, it needs to be recognised that injury or illness at work can entail a range of effects on both work and non-work activities, including relationships with family and friends and future income security/prospects. Some of the economic costs on workers and their dependants have already been mentioned in this chapter and chapter 1 (see also Boden et al., 2001; Weil, 2001). Permanent or prolonged incapacity arising from a work-related injury or illness can have profound effects on socioeconomic status, interfering with career progression, requiring a job change or leading to unemployment (Desmarez et al., 2007). In the case of permanent disability it can also require a partner, parent or offspring to take on a major and ongoing caregiving role. Only in the most extreme cases is this likely to attract compensation (via legislation or a common law settlement) and even then disputation and inconsistencies in access are common (for a recent US case raising some of these points see *Sabino v The Industrial Commission of Arizona and others*, Supreme Court of Arizona, CV-08-0359-PR, 2009). Differential access to compensation even among workers in the same industry due to employment status or in the case of undocumented immigrants (for a US study, see Waehrer et al., 2007) can have long-term implications with the additional cost burden affecting financial security and their dependants' access to healthcare and education (and with it career options).

There are other social and human impacts. As with non-work situations (such as war, criminal assault or automobile crashes), workplace injuries or traumatic incidents (such as a bank teller or retail worker threatened during a robbery) can be associated with post-traumatic stress disorders (PTSD). Such disorders can affect return-to-work outcomes and need to be addressed as part of the rehabilitation process (the same applies to return to work from non–work-related PTSD). This includes not only targeted support but also careful assessment of symptom severity, work functioning, employability and other established risk factors (Mathews 2005, 2006; Mathews and Chinnery, 2005). It should be noted that severe injury and particularly the death of a worker (following a traumatic incident, including work-related suicide) can have significant psychological impacts on their family (partners, parents and children) and colleagues. This area has largely been overlooked in terms of research and policy. However, our own preliminary research indicates that employer and government (including the inspectorate responsible for investigating the incident and workers' compensation authorities) policies appear poorly geared to deal with these circumstances in terms of recognising the psychological, social and economic impacts of workplace death and having appropriate protocols (regarding contact/communication and ongoing support) in place. In Australia, Canada and elsewhere community groups have been established to provide mutual support and to campaign for improvements in both OHS and workers' compensation laws, and a number of unions have also been active in the area, such as the Construction, Forestry, Mining and Energy Union (see chapter 9).

Research has identified a number of influences on injury impacts including type of injury/illness, type of work, socioeconomic status, location and gender (James, 1989; Guthrie and Jansz, 2007). For example, James (1989) found those in lower socio-economic groups were most adversely affected while males were less adaptable than females when a disabling injury necessitated a change to the conventional allocation of domestic tasks. In particular, driving a car played a strong role in male identity and having to give this up often proved extremely traumatic. A more recent Danish study (Hannerz et al., 2007) found that differences in the consequences of an injury, especially for women, were more significant than the risk of injury in explaining the social inequality of injury-related disability retirement. Geographic factors, such as the distance from rehabilitation services and the array of alternative jobs in the area, as well as community features may also affect the impact of injury, including the prospect of returning to work. Injury impacts can flow both ways or have compounding effects. For example, a work-related injury or illness that inhibits activity may impose additional responsibilities on others in the worker's household to assist the worker with routine tasks at home. As a study of workers with musculoskeletal disorders by Franche et al. (2006) found, it may also impact adversely on that worker's caregiving activities (not only with regard to children but aged parents or disabled/chronically ill siblings).

Finally, there is also an extensive literature on the management of disability, including the establishment of programs to address prolonged physical and psychological injury and permanent impairment or disability (see, for example, Rose, 2006). There is also an overlap with studies of pain management or studies that use specific pain and disability as preferred indicators of health (rather than more generic indicators) among workers on sickness-related absence (van Duijin et al., 2004). While reviews have tended to support the efficacy of disability management interventions (see, for example, Tompa et al., 2008) other studies (Williams et al., 2007) point to wide variations in the content, quality and effectiveness of such practices even within the same industry and region.

While worker rehabilitation in Australia and New Zealand has changed dramatically in the last few decades and is now almost unrecognisable, this discussion has only addressed a few of the issues. Overall, it would seem fair to say that the 1980s reforms represented a major advance over the almost complete neglect of the issue (especially prior to the 1970s). Nevertheless, rehabilitation remains a second-order policy objective and one whose success rests of a number of complex factors, including particular types of jobs—jobs that have been in relative decline over the past 20 years. To address this issue requires measures well beyond the realms of making more amendments to rehabilitation procedures. Other challenges will continue to confront the discipline of rehabilitation in the next few decades, including the ageing workforce, technology, globalisation and the subsequent changing nature of work. Further, rehabilitation practice and to some extent research, as Kendall et al. (2007) argue, has been captured by an economic agenda. In this new context, rehabilitation in Australia and New Zealand may need to find its identity all over again. Over the last decade there have been several calls for a new approach to rehabilitation that is more in line with the emancipation movement.

Dispute resolution—administrative and common law solutions

As disputes in any compensation scheme are inevitable, all workers' compensation legislation provides a process for the administration of claims, including dispute resolution. In some ways, workers' compensation schemes can be seen as the result of dissatisfaction with the common law process of settling injured workers' claims in the late nineteenth and early twentieth centuries. Workers' compensation schemes were designed with a view to reducing the number of disputes, in particular the number of disputes between workers and employers. With the adoption of workers' compensation whereby the cost of the compensation schemes was shared by all employers, workplace injuries were compensated regardless of fault, thus removing the need for a worker to sue and prove negligence in order to obtain compensation. In effect the implementation of workers' compensation eliminated many disputes between injured workers and their employers, but disputes still remain. Instead, disputes now arise between injured workers and the workers' compensation authority. The objective, however, is to provide a dispute resolution process which resolves disputes in an equitable and cost-effective manner. The process has to be efficient and fair.

Before workers' compensation systems were adopted, workers had to rely on common law and court-adjudicated claims in tort law. The courts remain a possible forum for resolution between workers and the workers' compensation authorities. The problem, however, is that the court process is expensive and often very slow. Further, the courts offer a sophisticated level of adjudication which many feel is unnecessary for most workers' compensation disputes. Most workers' compensation authorities seek a process which is quicker and less expensive than the courts in terms of administrative and legal costs for the authority as well as for workers, their unions and employers. The need for speedy resolution of disputes is seen as particularly important where the injured worker has been denied compensation for lost wages. Delays caused in the resolution of disputes create uncertainty and frustration for both workers and employers and increase the financial and human costs of injury.

To a large extent, the structure of each workers' compensation scheme determines the types of disputes that may arise. Typically, if the compensation scheme is a no-fault scheme, proving negligence will not be a major source of dispute. At the same time, all but the South Australian and Northern Territory schemes have a common law option where the question of fault is relevant and where the resolution of the issue of negligence can incur high costs. Also, many schemes have established a rating system (often known as an 'effectiveness rating') as an integral part of the structure whereby every employer is given a rating which determines their compensation costs. Such rating systems are perceived as either an incentive for injury prevention or a penalty for careless employers. Those employers who have a high record of worker injuries may find that their compensation rating is poor and, ipso facto, their workers' compensation premiums increased. Thus fault continues to play a role in the funding of most compensation schemes. The use of bonus/penalty premium incentives has been a source of considerable debate internationally. Problems that have been identified include the incapacity of smaller firms to calculate their risk of serious incidents and the capacity of employers to manipulate claims (through measures such as claim suppression, premature return to work, selective shift re-rostering and attendance pressure) in ways that disguise rather than reduce injury and illness at work. This can interfere with the social protection role of workers' compensation. The schemes can also have other unintended and undesirable consequences. For example, a Canadian study (Harcourt et al., 2007) found an association between experience rating and discriminatory hiring practices by employers.

Most disputes for both employers and workers are with the workers' compensation authority. Employer disputes may arise when there is disagreement about whether they adequately met the requirements of the scheme. For example, disputes can arise over whether the workers should be classified as employees or independent contractors as this will determine the employer's premiums and the level of acceptable provisions for return to work. As premiums are also determined on the basis of the industry classification of the employer's business and how the employer pays his or her staff, these kinds of disputes will inevitably arise. Other disputes between the employer and the authority may concern safety or other work practices. For workers, disputes can arise over the acceptance of a claim, whether or not an injury or illness was work-related and the extent of injury or the impact on the worker's ability to work. Disputes can arise over every decision made by the authority concerning worker entitlement, fitness for a return to work, rehabilitation and so on.

The two main types of disputes are administrative and substantive. Administrative disputes are those involving mistakes or misinformation which may have occurred in processing the claim. Substantive disputes are the result of disagreements over the level or form of entitlements. In theory, administrative disputes can and should be easily and quickly resolved through a process of review, while more substantive disagreements require a more sophisticated appeal process. It is difficult to classify decisions as administrative or substantive before they are made as almost all decisions involve administrative and substantive issues. For example, it is necessary to establish that the injury (or disease) is related to employment activities before any compensation is payable. A claim may be denied as a result of an administrative error involving the time or place of the incident. The claim may also be denied for what might be termed substantive reasons involving disagreement as to the time or the place and thus whether activity resulting in injury was work-related. Injury resulting from a fall in a parking lot often raises these kinds of problems. Similarly, a dispute over the level of compensation or over the period of disablement may arise as a result of a mistake in the recording of actual earnings or, more substantively, as a result of a disagreement over what earnings should be included in the calculation. Claims may be problematic and lead to disputes for any number of other reasons. There may be uncertainty over the nature and extent of the injury or disease, questions about coverage under the legislation or questions as to the legitimacy of the claim itself. While the dispute is between workers and the workers' compensation authority, workers and employers often view themselves as adversaries. Adversarial tendencies seem inevitable (despite the fact that it is a no-fault system), given that employers fund the scheme (and are often subject to effectiveness ratings) and workers receive compensation benefits.

The nature of the disputes and the dispute resolution process are determined by the relevant legislation in each jurisdiction. As each jurisdiction in Australia and New Zealand is unique, the disputes and the dispute resolution process are also different. The level of dispute claims varies widely between jurisdictions (figure 8.1). Nonetheless,

Figure 8.1 The proportion of claims with disputes in Australia and New Zealand, 2002–07

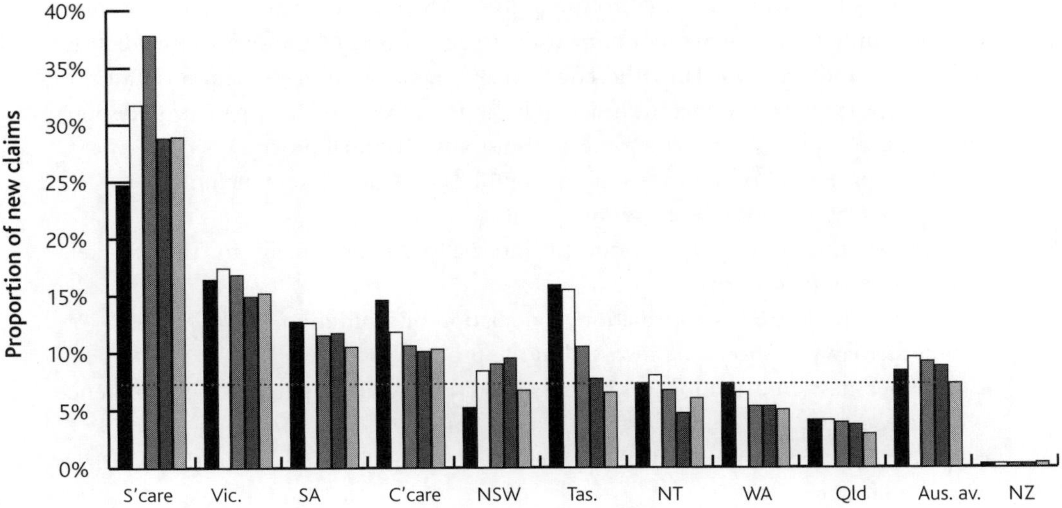

	S'care	Vic.	SA	C'care	NSW	Tas.	NT	WA	Qld	Aus. av.	NZ
2002–03	24.7%	16.4%	12.7%	14.6%	5.2%	15.9%	7.3%	7.3%	4.1%	8.4%	0.3%
2003–04	31.7%	17.4%	12.6%	11.8%	8.4%	15.5%	8.0%	6.5%	4.1%	9.6%	0.3%
2004–05	37.8%	16.8%	11.5%	10.6%	9.0%	10.5%	6.7%	5.3%	3.9%	9.2%	0.3%
2005–06	28.8%	14.9%	11.7%	10.1%	9.5%	7.7%	4.7%	5.3%	3.7%	8.8%	0.3%
2006–07	28.9%	15.2%	10.5%	10.3%	6.7%	6.5%	6.0%	5.0%	2.9%	7.3%	0.4%
2006–07 Australian average											

Source: Workplace Relations Ministers' Council, (2008) *Comparative Performance Monitoring Report Comparison of occupational health and safety and workers' compensation schemes in Australia and New Zealand,* 10th edition, Barton ACT: 28.

the overall percentage of administrative and substantive disputes over claims is relativity low, especially in New Zealand, and averaging about 8.5% in Australia.

Viewing the different dispute processes on a spectrum, at one end is a dispute resolution which typically involves an internal review, perhaps involving the initial decision maker or supervisor reviewing the decision. At the other end of the spectrum, the process can involve an appeal heard in an independent administrative tribunal, in common law court or some combination of the two. The process may involve an administrative tribunal rather than a court as administrative tribunals are seen as a more cost effective and efficient means of dispute resolution. The process may also be independent of the workers' compensation authority in that the decision makers involved are not employed by the workers' compensation authority. The right to appeal the authority's decisions to a body independent of the authority arguably ensures the integrity of the scheme. The workers' compensation authorities are structured in such a way as to be independent of government or employer involvement. Their governing officers, however, are usually appointed by the government of the day and are often regarded as having allegiances to either employers or trade unions. With respect to the role of the courts, while the right to sue in tort for workplace injury was either eliminated or limited under workers' compensation legislation in a number of jurisdictions in Australia and New Zealand, the courts may retain a role in the administration of worker's compensation, either for hearing the appeal of workers' compensation disputes or for hearing appeals concerning the administrative tribunal process.

The dispute resolution process raises a number of issues. These include:

- whether the process is a review or appeal
- whether the process is conducted internally or externally to the workers' compensation authority
- whether the process is a mediation, conciliation or arbitration
- whether lawyers should be involved in the process
- whether new information on injury and disease will be permitted to influence outcomes
- how the decisions in individual disputes are used to inform the institutional process and policy.

The first issue is whether or not the dispute is best formulated as a review or as an appeal of the original decision. A review suggests a less formal and possibly quick examination and reconsideration of the disputed decision. An appeal connotes that something more than a review is involved. For some, the prospect of an appeal means that adjudication, possibly with the benefits of a hearing, is involved. Of course the nature of the review or appeal also depends upon who conducts it and how it is conducted. Related to this is the issue of whether the review or appeal is conducted internally, (that is, by employees of the workers' compensation authority) or whether the review or appeal is addressed by someone working independently of the authority. A third issue concerns the nature of the process—whether the process is a mediation, conciliation or arbitration, and if it is an arbitration involving adjudication, whether the process is inquisitorial (i.e. an investigation conducted by the decision maker) or adversarial (i.e. where the decision maker decides on the basis of information or evidence provided to him by the parties). Other questions concerning the process include whether there would be some form of a hearing and what evidence and evidentiary rules would apply, if any. Also related are questions regarding the participation of the worker and employer in the process as well as issues relating to the accessibility of the process.

Another issue concerns the involvement of lawyers in the process. Debate over the role of the legal profession and the level of litigation in processing workers' compensation claims is by no means confined to Australia (for reference to this in the US, see Boden, 1995: 206). It needs to be recognised that adversarial relations have arisen in workers' compensation proceedings even in jurisdictions where input by the legal profession has long been restricted, such as Queensland. Irrespective of the system used, workers' compensation will always involve accommodating the competing interests of insurers, employers, claimant workers and unions. Compensation agencies have also been keen to minimise the overall costs of the system, especially in federal multi-jurisdictional schemes such as Australia, Canada and the US where compensation and other labour costs have become the subject of competition to attract/retain business and employment. As the Queensland experience showed over many years, the latter is a powerful driver to minimise claims exposure even where private insurers are absent. Changes to the policies of workers' compensation agencies can also directly contribute to the number of disputed claims and there is evidence of a tougher line being taken by a number of agencies, including Queensland WorkCover in recent years. Having said all this, it still seems clear that the involvement of the legal profession has exacerbated the degree of adversarial relations and claims costs. One Australian study found that legal representation in the claim settlement process increased the cost of compensation claims fourfold (Morrison et al., 1995: 16). Without restrictions on the role of lawyers, these problems may have been even greater given the shift to contingency fees and an over-supplied legal profession (in the US it has been argued that a litigious appeals process has resulted in considerable additional costs being borne by the compensation schemes; see Plumb and Cowell, 1998: 247). It is more than coincidental that in NSW, where the legal profession retained a significant role, a Workers' Compensation Resolution Service was established in response to concerns about the cost and lengthy delays involved in disputed claims. In May 1998 this service was expanded to deal with all disputed workers' compensation claims (*Industrial Relations in NSW*, 1999: 7).

In defending their role, the legal profession has pointed to the expertise they bring to proceedings and their capacity to better represent claimants in a difficult situation, including vulnerable workers. In Canada there is some evidence that community legal centres have played a positive role in this regard. Such activities parallel to some degree (for non-union workers) the role of lawyers retained by unions to assist their members—a critical but little-discussed aspect of the role of unions in OHS (see chapter 9)—and may be worthy of consideration in Australia. Moreover, the removal of lawyers does not automatically result in a more equitable process but depends very much on the mechanisms adopted. A study of the introduction of an informal dispute resolution process that excluded lawyers in Western Australia by Guthrie (2003: 229–68) argued this actually aggravated pre-existing power imbalances.

Nonetheless, the input that lawyers might have on behalf of vulnerable groups is at best a mitigating argument in favour of their inclusion. Irrespective of the presence of lawyers, there is substantial evidence of discriminatory treatment of particular groups of workers, notably women and non-Anglophone migrants. There is evidence that female workers, especially migrants and those engaged in insecure jobs in catering, retailing, factories, childcare, cleaning, seasonal fruit picking, etc., are reluctant to lodge a workers' compensation claim for RSI, back strain or other complaints for fear of losing their jobs and that they experience discriminatory treatment when they do make claims (Calvey and Jansz, 2005; Guthrie and Jansz, 2006; Lippel, 1989, 1999a, 2003). Alcorso (1989) argued that making a compensation claim presents difficulties to Australian-born workers but for non-Anglophone immigrants these problems are magnified. As far as we are aware, no compensation authority has taken more than minimal steps (most notably the production of multilingual information) to remedy these problems. It should also be noted that many workers in casual and other precarious jobs do not belong to unions and this can have a significant effect on compensation claims. North American studies (see, for example, Meng and Smith, 1993) indicate that union members are more likely to obtain workers' compensation and, while we have no comparable studies in Australia, it is likely the situation is similar.

A further issue arises as different kinds of injury and disease emerge over time from new work patterns and new medical information on the relationship between work and workers' health may also emerge. The question that arises is to what extent should the new information be acknowledged by the authority before it can be considered on review or appeal? Ongoing epidemiological research continues to improve understanding of the relationship between injury and disease and the work activities and work environment. For example, in Western Australia there was a 114% increase in claims relating to stress between 1995–96 and 1999–2000 (Guthrie 2001: 73). The increase in the number of stress-related claims reflects the changing nature of employment and changing social attitudes regarding psychological injury, although, as noted above, accepted claims still represent a small fraction of the potential number of claimants. The difficulty is that the criteria for entitlement for RSI, stress or other occupational diseases are set out in legislation and thus are generally fixed. The basis for the legislated inclusion, or exclusion, of any conditions is expert opinion, namely medical epidemiological evidence of causation. For example, in some jurisdictions the criteria for the acceptance of certain repetitive strain injuries to the shoulder might require demonstrated use of the shoulder at over 60 degrees abduction. This means that even if an injured worker establishes that her work involved significant use of her shoulder and that there was no other activity which might have caused the injury, if the use did not require 60 degrees abduction, the worker's claim is likely to be refused. If the worker on appeal of the denial of the claim then produces new epidemiological evidence concluding that 60 degrees abduction was not required, the question is whether or not the review or appeal panel could accept that information as sufficient and accept the claim.

Part of the problem is that in order to determine the 'work-relatedness' of the injury or disease there needs to be sufficient evidence to show that the work activity or environment was the cause or a significant cause of the injury or disease. However, at the heart of this problem is the nature of work. People rarely work 24 hours a day, seven days a week; instead, work usually occupies less than 30% of a worker's time on a daily basis, and over the period of a year work may only occupy 25% of the worker's time. Workers typically spend most of their time away from workplaces where they may suffer injury or be exposed to some disease. In addition, some workers may have a genetic predisposition to certain types of injury or occupational diseases or over time workers may develop a predisposition to injury. Older workers are generally seen as more susceptible to injury arising over time with activity, although younger workers are more likely to be injured. Recreational activities, whether needlework or rugby, may contribute to the development of the injury or disease; however, linking these activities as the main origin of the injury or disease will invariably cause differences of opinion.

Claims for psychological injury are particularly difficult to prove and are a continual source of disputes. In particular, compensation for stress is complicated by the lack of agreement over the causes of the condition. The origins of depression, for example, are likely to be multi-factorial in which case the cause may not be entirely work-related (Ellashof and Streltzer, 1992). That is, issues relating to the worker's family and/or their lifestyle may (or may not) be important factors in their illness. The restricted view of stress-related claims is influenced by such concerns and is reflected in the ongoing debate surrounding work-related stress. Notwithstanding, successful compensation cases for stress have been achieved through the New Zealand employment courts under the *personal grievance provision*, rather than claiming through the ACC. Many of the employment cases have involved public servants (for example, Brickell v A-G [2000] 2 ERNZ 529). One of the most notable cases was that of Mr Gilbert, a probation officer who was forced to leave his job of over 30 years on medical grounds as a result of years of overwork. In the subsequent court case in June 2000, Judge Colgan upheld the claims of breach of contract and personal grievance and awarded Mr Gilbert:

- a lump sum for loss of income from the date of resignation for the 14 years of working life before he became entitled to New Zealand superannuation
- $75 000 as general damages for humiliation, anxiety and distress
- $50 000 for loss of career, employment status and employability
- $14 000 approximately, for medical expenses
- $50 000 exemplary damages.

Arguably, given that a dispute resolution process must deal appropriately with claims for personal injury and disease, the process should have the capacity to accept new medical or epidemiological evidence. With respect to stress claims, the dispute process may need to involve, for example, the use of independent psychologists/psychiatrists to provide an initial assessment of the worker's condition and the relationship of that condition to the work activity. This is linked to a final issue related to the dispute resolution process and that is how the decisions in individual disputes are used to inform the institutional process and policy. There is an ongoing need in any dispute resolution process to evaluate the nature of the disputes and the decisions in the context of overall policy. The relationship between decisions made on individual claims and the authority's policy regarding such matters is important if there is to be consistency between claims. The challenge for a compensation authority is to determine the balance between using policy to determine individual disputes and using decisions arising from individual disputes to develop policy.

The resolution of disputes has been seen as critical to the system (Plumb and Cowell, 1998: 244). As set out in table 8.11, in Australia and New Zealand, the process involves an initial process and then an appeal to an administrative tribunal or, as in the case of New Zealand, a specialised court at the District Court level. Appeal to the courts is limited.

Table 8.11   Dispute resolution

Appeal rights	Commonwealth	Vic.	NSW	SA
Initial	Reconsideration	Conciliation	Arbitrator of Workers Compensation Commission	Reconsideration
Then	Administrative Appeals Tribunal, then Federal Court, then High Court	Courts	Presidential member of Workers Compensation Commission	Conciliation, arbitration, judicial review, appeal to full bench of tribunal
Access to common law	Yes, for third party. Limited against employer/other employees	Limited	Limited	No

Source: Safe Work Australia (2009a), *Comparison of Workers' Compensation Arrangements in Australia and New Zealand,* Commonwealth of Australia, Barton, ACT: 44–5.

Longstanding issues and future trends

In the numerous business surveys conducted on the key issues facing employers, the issues surrounding workers' compensation are always high on the list. However, workers' compensation issues are more complex than just premium levies, compensation payments and rehabilitation. The vagaries of government policies, the decline of certain industries and the rise of others, and changes in working arrangements all have an impact on the number of workers' compensation claims, workers' compensation regulations and the administering institutions. Moreover, as outlined above, an increasingly diverse labour force—namely an increasingly ageing workforce, with increased female participation, increased hire labour (labour contractors), increased immigration, etc.—will continue to add layers of complexity to already complex workers' compensation schemes. In this section we will explore some of the key issues that impact on workers' compensation outcomes.

Underpinning the debates concerning workers' compensation and rehabilitation is the recognition that there are links between the perceived need to increase productivity and performance/cut costs, global changes to employment practices and the level of payment and number of workers covered by some form of compensation. As noted in chapter 1 there have been international changes to working arrangements that have resulted in the decline of full-time employment, the rise in precarious work and casualised labour,

WA	Qld	Tas.	NT	ACT	NZ
Conciliation	Internal review	Conciliation, Workers Rehabilitation and Compensation Tribunal	Mediation	Conciliation	Review and mediation, conducted by an independent reviewer or mediator
Dispute Resolution Directorate, (arbitration), Commissioner, District Court	Q-COMP, Industrial Magistrate or Commission Industrial Court	Arbitration by tribunal, appeal to Supreme Court	Work Health Court	Arbitration	A review decision can be appealed to the District Court. Appeals on questions of law can be taken to the High Court and the Court of Appeal
Limited	Yes	Limited	No	Unlimited	No

and consequential irregular workers' compensation coverage for disadvantaged groups (Walters, 2001; Campbell and Burgess, 2001; Tucker, 2002; Quinlan et al., 2001; Quinlan, 2002, 2004c; Lewchuk et al, 2003; Frick, 2003; Shain and Kramer, 2004; Hannif and Lamm, 2005; Johnstone et al., 2005; James, 2006). National and international changes to the organisation of work and their implications for workers' compensation have also come to the attention of governments and their agencies. In its 2002 report, the US National Institute for Occupational Safety and Health (NIOSH) described a range of new organisational practices that employers have implemented to compete more effectively in the global economy but which have negative workers' compensation outcomes, including flexible and quality management initiatives (e.g. total quality management, lean production, modular manufacturing and high performance work schemes) and the use of temporary and contingent labour. Reviewing one consequence of these changes, the US Government Accountability Office (2007) noted that a significant growth in the proportion of the workforce employed as independent contractors (from 6.7% in 1995 to 7.4% in 2005) had in part resulted from the misclassification of employees as independent contractors, with implications for the administration of workers' compensation, taxation and unemployment insurance regimes.

Another significant trend in the past two decades among industrialised countries is the restructuring/downsizing of large organisations and the accelerated growth of the small business sector, which now represents over 90% of the business population in both Australia and New Zealand; in New Zealand over 60% of the population work in this sector. The implications of having a preponderant small business sector on workers receiving compensation are threefold. First, the OHS regulatory and compensation agencies have typically found it difficult to infiltrate the small business sector as it is heterogeneous, geographically scattered and lacks cohesive representation. Small businesses also have short life cycles of only three to five years, making it difficult to implement preventative strategies or follow through on long-term worker rehabilitation. In spite of these difficulties, Australian and New Zealand government compensation authorities have developed a plethora of compensation-related strategies aimed at supporting the small business sector. For example, Australian WorkCover authorities have introduced initiatives aimed at reducing levies for small businesses. How successful these small business initiatives are is sill unclear as there are few, if any, evaluations. A second, related point is that managing workers' compensation claims within small businesses can be more resource-intensive than in larger organisations. Case study research shows that the relationship between case manager and small business employer and/or employee is frequently fraught (Legg et al., 2008). Finally, there is evidence that under-reporting of workers' compensation claims is not unusual in the small business sector (Quinlan, 2002). That is, there is a propensity for small business employers, many of whom are financially stretched, to sidestep the formal procedures of workers' compensation and to deal with their workers' injuries and illnesses 'in house'. The key reasons why small business employers do not wish to engage with the workers' compensation agencies directly is that their premiums may increase as a consequence of an injured worker, other OHS regulatory agencies could be alerted resulting in possible fines for the employer, and the workforce could be undocumented or illegal migrants.

Another concern identified in a number of countries, including Australia and New Zealand, is the burgeoning costs of workers' compensation. This concern appears to be the result of a combination of factors, including escalating medical costs, increased lump sum and common law settlements, improvements to benefits and a broadening of the array of allowable claims. It should be stressed that the impact of particular factors on workers' compensation schemes has been the subject of considerable debate (itself influenced by the perspective of specific interest groups) and may not be identical for each country or jurisdiction, thereby precluding a universal remedy. In Australia, with its mixture of private and public healthcare, there has been far less concern with medical costs. Rather, policy attention has tended to focus on coverage and entitlement levels, including access to common law settlements (not really an issue in the US). The critical drivers in moves to reduce costs from the late 1980s onwards were not only concerns with the increase in compensation costs incurred by employers but also concerns at the level of unfunded liabilities within the schemes. Employer pressure on governments and compensation authorities to contain costs will continue as part of their more general campaign to reduce labour costs and regulatory burdens and replace compulsion with voluntary choice of workers' compensation. Responses by government to rein in compensation costs vary widely but include attempts to reduce costs by capping coverage and entitlements (including restricting access to common law settlements), an increased focus of risk management/prevention and reducing the cost of claims processing (including altering the input of lawyers and the organisation of medical treatment), as well as vigorous attempts by compensation agencies to reduce compensation fraud.

These pressures also explain the delicate balancing act performed when considering improvements to the scope and level of benefits (including the duration of weekly benefits and lump sum payments) both within government reviews of workers' compensation (see, for example, Clayton, 2007; Hanks, 2008) and government response to these reviews. For example, the government of South Australia proposed a number of cost-cutting measures (including reducing weekly payments and economic disincentives for appealing decisions) following a review by Alan Clayton (*CCH OHS Alert*, 7 April 2008). In Victoria the government's response to the Hanks (2008) review included improvements to lump sum benefits and superannuation contributions for injured workers but unions claimed the proposed changes discriminated against workers suffering stress-related injuries and did nothing to enhance return to work *(CCH OHS Alert*, 18 June 2009). The level and adequacy of benefits will remain a source of ongoing policy debate. Ultimately, while costs savings may be made in the provision of healthcare, improved administrative processes and enhanced rehabilitation (including enhanced inter-professional collaboration; Bernacki, 2004), a more fundamental pathway would be to reduce the overall incidence of injury and disease to enable a more generous compensation regime for those who are injured.

For many years there has been pressure to harmonise the different approaches to workers' compensation, not only within Australia but also between Australia and New Zealand as part of bilateral agreements. Australian reviews into workers' compensation in the main have recommended a national strategy to harmonise the state systems as a way reducing both the costs of compensation and the level of complexity, particularly for those businesses operating across different jurisdictions. The 2003 report of the Royal Commission into the Building and Construction Industry, for example, recommended that the Australian Government encourage the states and territories to continue efforts to harmonise the key definitions of their various workers' compensation systems, particularly the definition of 'worker' (RCBC, 2003: 271). Established in 2005, one of the main objectives of the Australian Safety and Compensation Council is to enhance the harmonisation between the state systems across a range of factors that include data collection and standards and codes. At their inaugural meeting the Council agreed to the harmonisation of key areas of occupational health and safety (OHS) and workers' compensation schemes, and also agreed to develop proposals to harmonise the administration of these schemes

In New Zealand attention has been on the standardisation of the country's workers' compensation data and in particular the injury claims. Pursuant under the Injury Prevention, Rehabilitation, and Compensation Act, 2001, part 8, Statistics New Zealand was appointed Injury Information Manager. This involves coordinating the production of official injury statistics across agencies that produce injury data. It should be noted that New Zealand's injury data comprises almost entirely Accident Compensation Corporation claims. The legislation also requires the Injury Information Manager to provide a program of statistics and information services based on an integrated database of injury information. Statistics New Zealand is charged with producing and publishing injury statistics. The Injury Surveillance Ministerial Advisory Panel (ISMAP), whose members report directly to the Minister of the ACC, was also established to ensure that these duties are carried out in a timely and rigorous manner.

What is not conspicuous in the public and political debates over workers' compensation are a number of significant longstanding problems related to equality of access and treatment. First, as already observed, the growth of precarious employment or contingent work arrangements has reduced both the formal and effective coverage of workers' compensation. This has meant two classes of workers often working in the same job and even alongside one another—one with access to the protection of workers' compensation and one without it. The result is not only social and health inequity but the creation of a socially costly set of incentives to further shift the burden of work-related injury and disease onto the community, workers and their families. It undermines the social protection role of workers' compensation as well as the objective of obliging employers to bear the costs of work-related injuries and disease. We would argue that this represents an outcome that is inefficient at the macro level and demonstrates a lack of foresight on the part of policymakers besotted with neo-liberal ideology.

Second, amid the debates about costs, questions as to whether existing payment levels and coverage are adequate seems to be a second-order consideration. As has already been observed, in the US the effects of economic crises such as the one at the time of writing are likely to tip the balance more towards cost containment (and reduced reporting by workers) and even further away from the question of social justice and equity. This also applies to the recognition of new sources of occupational ill health as a basis for claims as well as full recognition of existing areas where evidence shows current access to compensation in no way reflects the full burden of work-related illness within the community. Stress and mental health problems (including suicide) arising from work provide one of the clearest examples of this (Walters, 2007). The highly selective recognition and compensation of workers suffering mental health problems (and musculoskeletal disorders too), especially women, has been documented for over 20 years by researchers such as Katherine Lippel (1989, 2003). It seems clear the selectivity is driven not just by complexities in establishing a connection (especially when non-work factors may also play a part), but by concern that broader access would lead to a 'blow-out' in workers' compensation costs. However, it could equally be posited that if workers' compensation regimes were to give more recognition to these claims then employers would need to give more attention to psychosocial conditions of work.

The belated and selective recognition of occupational disease provides another example of where it can be argued that current workers' compensation regimes are not providing an adequate level of social protection. While low reporting of occupational disease by physicians contributes to this, it also seems clear that workers' compensation regimes are themselves deficient in recognising disease and may themselves even affect physician reporting (Verger et al., 2008). A number of examples were given in earlier chapters, including chemical exposures relating to the deseal/reseal maintenance program of the F-111 and asbestos (see also *OHS Alert*, 21 July 2008). The case of asbestos illustrates belated recognition of worker exposure but also wider community impacts that affected not just mining communities (such as Barraba in NSW and Libby, Montana in the US) but those living in areas associated with asbestos use such as communities surrounding the power generation industry in the Latrobe Valley of Victoria (Hunter and LaMontagne, 2008). In June 2009, for example, the US Environmental Protection Agency (*New Release*, 17 June 2009) announced a public health emergency in Libby, Montana, to organise a more aggressive clean-up of longstanding asbestos material in the town (the mine closed in 1990) and to assist residents with medical care. Similar worker and community exposures and belated compensatory responses (under both workers' compensation and civil compensation schemes, via the common law or via special government schemes or ex gratia payments) can be identified with regard to other hazardous substances such as lead (see, for example, debates about lead residues in the town of Mount Isa, including child care facilities).

What is also notable about these cases and more generally (such as an improvement in the death benefit in NSW for the families of construction workers killed on the job, *CCH OHS Alert*, 24 November 2008) is that responses were not only belated but a direct response to often prolonged community agitation. Hunter and LaMontagne's (2008: 361) study of community asbestos exposure in the Latrobe Valley found the belated and contended response reflected not only 'the reluctance of authorities to acknowledge the problems arising from the extensive use of asbestos in power stations' but also the political nature of the definition of 'community'. This highlights both the interface between work and community health and the key role played by vested interest groups. Other examples of the latter point include the use of prolonged legal proceedings/appeals and technicalities to defeat, delay and minimise claims. Another disturbing trend is the use of the corporate veil to evade or minimise corporate liability, as highlighted by the case of James Hardie who relocated to the Netherlands (a move to low-tax Ireland was mooted in 2009), leaving an inadequately funded compensation scheme to cover asbestos sufferers—something defeated only by a strident union–community campaign led by Bernie Banton (see chapter 5). Evidence of these problems can be identified in other countries, highlighting among other things the need for global business regulation and greater international collaboration regarding the recognition of compensable disease (Souza et al., 2008). They represent the extreme tip of a much larger iceberg as far as compensation for work-related disease and mental illness is concerned.

The overlap between work and community health, the complexity in distinguishing work-related from non–work-related factors for both disease and mental health in particular, the failure to cover workers who are not employees (including the self-employed and volunteers) and the role played by powerful interest groups raise a very fundamental policy question. That is, would it be better to move away from a workers' compensation model to a public health model that is broader than the New Zealand approach? Such a move, which has been advocated by Ladou (2006), would entail far more than just the integration of workers' compensation into social security as has already occurred in a number of European countries. It would require a more general rethinking of how OHS is approached in the community, including the role of professional groups. A number of other 'developments', such as growing evidence of environmental impacts on health, the health threats posed by climate change and the broader evidence linking social inequalities to health outcomes, are supportive of a broad public health-driven rather than fragmented approach based around particular silos of causation/responsibility. There is likely to be significant opposition to a change in this direction. Nonetheless, it warrants serious consideration.

Third, another significant and longstanding issue only briefly alluded to thus far concerns the equity of treatment of those making claims. As noted earlier, there is a body of evidence that women, immigrants and the precariously employed have more trouble accessing workers' compensation, receive fewer or lower benefits on average, are more likely to have their entitlements disputed and do not receive the same level of support in terms of rehabilitation and return to work (Lippel, 1989, 1999a; Quinlan and Mayhew, 1999; Scherzer et al., 2005; Guthrie and Jansz, 2006; Walters, 2007; Nicholson et al., 2008; Underhill, 2008). For example, a Canadian study by Lippel (1999a) found that while access to compensation for psychological disability related to stress was difficult for all workers, it was most difficult for women. A later study on musculoskeletal disorders by Lippel (2003: 253) found women were significantly less likely to have their claim accepted by the appeal tribunal. Importantly, Lippel pointed to the misuse of scientific evidence in appeal proceedings. While the evidence is fragmentary, it is sufficient to indicate there are serious problems of systemic discrimination that have not been addressed by efforts at more equitable administration in the 1980s and warrant far more attention. That most governments appear not even to have taken the step of more thoroughly investigating the issue is telling as to the importance of this issue in policy terms.

There are broad social issues that warrant attention here. Workers' compensation schemes operate in a social context alongside other laws, policies and practices, including industrial relations, and the interaction between them is critical. These interconnections, such as those providing for maternity leave or the reassignment of pregnant workers to different tasks (Bretin et al., 2004), are often not recognised or inadequately addressed. Responses have also been shaped by the dominant neo-liberal policy discourse—that relocates the balance of responsibilities between individuals on the one hand, and the state and corporations on the other—even where this has detrimental effects. For example, while the workers' compensation legislation of all Australian states tries to secure a degree of employment security for workers disabled by injury or disease, in practice the limited effectiveness of these provisions (including opt-outs where it is not reasonably practicable to provide suitable duties) arguably weakens the effectiveness of vocational rehabilitation schemes (Purse, 2000; Guthrie, 2002). The commodification of workers (into temporary workers, foreign guest workers and the like) is not consistent with building the ongoing reciprocal relationships essential for meaningful rehabilitation and return to work programs (Toh and Quinlan, 2009). Similarly, MacEachen (2000) has argued that neo-liberalism has affected the administration of workers' compensation by shaping the ways that managers view and respond to RSI.

The post-2007 economic crisis—itself a product of the 'unshackled' and deregulated markets—will, if sustained over a number of years, exacerbate these problems, especially for the growing number of older workers (part of the ageing workforce), many already with chronic injuries and health problems, who lose their jobs. With regard to the last observation it should also be noted that the implications of an ageing workforce for workers' compensation regimes and rehabilitation practices have received inadequate attention (Evans et al., 2008; Lynch, 2009). There is evidence that injury outcomes for older workers are by no means worse than for younger workers but this can become problematic if employers fail to reciprocate on the higher levels of work attachment typically found among older workers (Pransky et al., 2005c). Similarly, the growing popularity of applying the concept of work ability to an ageing workforce will have little meaning unless it is combined with appropriate multimodal rehabilitation (Kuoppala and Lamminpaa, 2008) and a suitable policy framework is put in place, including employment incentives/options and security safeguards. The healthcare workforce, including physiotherapists, is itself by no means immune to the challenges of an ageing workforce that will need to be addressed over the next 20 or more years (Schofield and Fletcher, 2007).

Fourth, yet another longstanding issue is the effects of the compensation process on worker health and wellbeing. In other words, the compensation process itself can have significant consequences for the health and wellbeing of workers suffering an injury or illness as a result of work. As with equity of treatment, evidence that caseworkers; physicians (both general practitioners and specialists); other occupational health and rehabilitation specialists such as physiotherapists, psychiatrists and psychologists; compensation agency staff and appeals tribunals; supervisors/managers/employers; and lawyers can have positive or negative effects on the health and wellbeing of claimant workers has been around for some time (Lippel, 1999b; 2007). It has implications for OHS and legal professional practice; employer, government and union policies; as well as researchers. In Victoria, WorkCover is assisting a research project that follows an earlier (2002) project on work-related suicide that will compare suicide among those on WorkCover benefits with those in receipt of other benefits. Unfortunately, research into the effects of the compensation process (either in specific or generic terms) remains exceptional. For their part, government reports have largely addressed this issue only insofar as it pertains to timely settlement of claims, transparent dispute resolution and early return to work (Hanks, 2008). Overall, the matter has received inadequate or even ill-considered (such as the use of disparaging terms like 'compensation neurosis') attention that ignores underlying causes such as stigmatisation and power imbalances between claimants and those who 'treat' them (again there may be important nuances in the experience of workers in relation to different professions such as physicians and physiotherapists; James, 1989). One reason for this is that workers' compensation remains very much the poor cousin in terms of work-related health research, receiving comparatively limited attention even among law, sociology and industrial relations researchers. For example, the effect of mistrust and surveillance of claimants has largely been ignored by researchers and policymakers (for an exception, see Lippel, 2005), especially when compared to alleged fraudulent claims.

Ultimately, the long-term implications of workers' compensation systems that are more strongly driven by a financial loss-control philosophy are unclear but it is hard to see the changes to entitlements and the like as a benefit to workers. The balancing of potentially conflicting goals is liable to remain as elusive as ever. Ultimately, the development of fair and cost-efficient workers' compensation systems probably depends on the capacity to reduce the incidence of injury and disease. However, we are yet to be convinced that the workers' compensation system can be more than a marginal driver here. While neo-liberal economists, and the policymakers and professionals they influence, display a fascination (some would say fixation) with market incentives the history of OHS shows that market signals are, at best, a crude device. Employers do not have perfect information and can respond to pressure to reduce claims in ways that have nothing to do with reductions in injury and disease. The move to a more market-driven workers' compensation system may reduce costs to employers but increase externalities borne by the community. There are already lessons about the limits of a more market-sensitive legal remedy in the common law which, as Leigh (1998) has observed, has conspicuously failed to adequately compensate injured workers or to induce dramatic improvements in OHS from employers.

Conclusion

The development of workers' compensation represented a pioneering form of social security that addressed some of the adverse consequences of the widespread and severe burden of work-related injuries and (to a far lesser extent) disease and mental ill health. It remains a critical and essential mechanism for protecting workers and their families—one that should be extended to all workers and all societies that regard themselves as civilised. At the same time, attempts to secure the four major aims of workers' compensation regimes require careful balancing, and recognition that affording protection and enhancing rehabilitation should remain the overarching goals. The integration of workers' compensation with prevention regimes may seem attractive—and a degree of collaboration has clear benefits (Parsons, 2002). However, we remain firmly of the view that there are persuasive policy and logistical grounds for maintaining separation, including potential conflicts of interest and focus, and the limitations of workers' compensation data as a measure of OHS outcomes. There are more compelling grounds for aligning or incorporating workers' compensation into a more general public health insurance scheme, and the New Zealand approach can be seen as one step in this direction. At the very least, if workers' compensation is to continue to play a role in the twenty-first century at least as significant as in the second half of the twentieth century (and preferably an enhanced one) then it will need to address some serious challenges, such as those posed by changes to work arrangements, demographics and labour markets; inadequate treatment of disease and mental illness; and the provision of more effective rehabilitation.

QUESTIONS FOR DISCUSSION

1 Identify the major objectives of reforms to workers' compensation schemes in Australia or New Zealand since the mid-1980s. Did these reforms entail contradictions or inconsistencies?
2 Compare and contrast the different Australian and New Zealand workers' compensation schemes and argue either for the Australian schemes or the New Zealand universal no-faults scheme.
3 Identify three major challenges confronting workers' compensation regimes and suggest ways in which these might be addressed.
4 Evaluate the case for incorporating workers' compensation into social security or into a national accident insurance scheme.
5 Discuss recent efforts to enhance the scope for rehabilitation for workers suffering a debilitating injury or disease.
6 Discuss the impacts of an injury or disease on a worker, their family and friends, identifying factors that influence these impacts.

FURTHER READING

Armstrong, H. (2008), *Blood on the Coal: The Origins and Future of New Zealand's Accident Compensation Scheme*, Trade Union History Project, Wellington.

Briand, C., Durand, M., St-Arnaud, L. and Corbiere, M. (2008), 'How well do return-to-work interventions for musculoskeletal conditions address the multi-causality of work disability?', *Journal of Occupational Rehabilitation*, **18**: 207–17.

Campbell, I. (1996), *Compensation for Personal Injury in New Zealand: Its Rise and Fall*, University of Auckland Press, Auckland.

Guthrie, R. (2007), 'The Australian legal framework for stress claims', *Journal of Law and Medicine*, **14**(4): 528–50.

Guthrie, R. and Jansz, J. (2006), 'Women's experience in the workers' compensation system', *Journal of Occupational Rehabilitation*, **16**(3): 474–88.

Johnstone, R. (2004), *Occupational Health and Safety Law and Policy: Text and Materials*, LBC Information Services, Sydney.

Krause, N. and Lund, T. (2004), 'Returning to work after occupational injury', in Barling, J. and Frone, M. (eds) *The Psychology of Workplace Safety*, American Psychological Association, Washington: 249–64.

Lippel, K. (2007), 'Workers describe the effect of the workers' compensation process on their health: a Quebec study', *International Journal of Law and Psychiatry*, **30**: 427–43.

St-Arnaud, L., Bourbonais, R., Saint-Jean, M. and Rheaume, J. (2007), 'Determinants of return-to-work among employees absent due to mental health problems', *Relations Industrielles*, **62**(4): 690–713.

Worker communication and involvement in occupational health and safety

Introduction

THIS chapter examines the issue of worker involvement in OHS. As noted in the chapter on regulation, OHS legislation in Australia and New Zealand, like that of a number of other countries, provides a number of mechanisms for worker involvement, notably workplace health and safety committees and health and safety representatives.

The term 'worker' is used rather than 'employee' in this chapter because not all workers are employees (some are self–employed contractors) and not all employees are directly engaged by an employer (some are employees of contractors or labour hire firms). Historically, participatory mechanisms in OHS legislation focused on employees directly engaged by an employer. However, in recent years OHS agencies have begun to recognise these changes to work arrangements, as discussed elsewhere in the book (Johnstone et al., 2006), and have attempted to address the narrow approach to worker involvement in OHS. There are ethical and practical arguments for an approach to worker involvement that is not confined to employees. For example, if an organisation makes significant and ongoing use of contractors they should be incorporated into its OHS program, including opportunities to raise problems and participate in problem solving. Contractors and their employees have a right to be informed of OHS issues and contribute to workplace committees. There is also a practical consideration in that these workers can have knowledge of the organisation's work processes that would otherwise be excluded.

An assessment of worker involvement cannot be disembodied from another sphere of regulation and institutions, namely industrial relations. Historically, mobilisations of workers, especially through unions (but also through political organisations and other bodies) have, in combination with broader community alliances, played a pivotal role in the development and enhancement of OHS and workers' compensation laws. As this chapter will show, unions help workers raise OHS issues, provide logistical support for health and safety representatives (HSRs) (such as training; see Walters et al., 2001) and have increasingly used collective bargaining and industrial tribunals to address OHS issues. In so doing unions (as presumed if not envisaged by the Robens report) provide the infrastructure that supports participatory mechanisms in the workplace. At the same time, developments over the last decade have demonstrated that declining union membership and legislation that erodes collective negotiation/awards and union rights (notably the right to enter workplaces and represent workers) can have serious adverse effects on OHS.

There is a growing recognition among policymakers and the public at large that since workers (and their families) bear the most direct consequences of any failure in relation to occupational health and safety they have a number of basic rights. These are rights

- to know about the hazards they may encounter
- to be involved in devising solutions
- to refuse tasks that pose an imminent threat to their health and wellbeing
- to have a say in deciding what OHS standards are acceptable because these standards seldom specify an absolute level of safety and invariably entail normative judgments about acceptable levels of risk.

These rights have been increasingly accepted, at least in principle, internationally (see International Labour Organization Convention No.155, cited in Creighton, 1993). Procedural avenues for worker access to information and involvement include 'right to know' provisions, employee health and safety representatives and joint workplace health and safety committees. One or more of these mechanisms can be found in the OHS legislation of most advanced industrial countries. Of course, the mechanisms are far more extensive in some countries (notable examples include the Nordic countries of Denmark, Finland, Norway and Sweden) than in others (such as the US where worker have a 'right to know' about hazards but virtually no legislative right to participate). The participatory mechanisms found under current Australian and New Zealand OHS legislation would place it in the mid to upper range of this spectrum.

In most countries prescribed avenues for worker involvement in safety and health are a comparatively recent phenomenon (i.e. of the last 20–30 years) and mark a significant departure from earlier OHS legislation. Prior to the post-Robens reforms, OHS legislation in Australia and New Zealand (apart from several coal mining laws) afforded workers or their representative unions few if any opportunities to participate in deciding OHS standards, to consult and negotiate with employers or to ensure OHS laws were enforced. Further, the notion of worker involvement received little if any recognition in either the literature or practice of OHS management. Workers had a common law right to refuse dangerous work but the power imbalance between employers and workers meant this right could rarely be exercised. In Australia and

New Zealand strike activity has been heavily restricted and traditionally confined to health and safety matters and unions could and did pursue these issues. However, industrial conflict over poor conditions tended to be spasmodic or confined to some very dangerous occupations (such as coal mining and stevedoring) although there were some notable examples, such as the Blackball Miners' Strike of 1908 and the lockout of Waterside Workers in 1951 in which health and safety issues were used by unions to ignite social change and resolve other grievances. Industrial tribunals were reluctant to make rulings on OHS matters which went beyond those laid down in legislation and most unions confined their activity to lobbying for better laws and looking after the workers' compensation or common law claims of their members. In sum, OHS was largely seen as the prerogative of management and the relevant state agencies.

As noted in the chapter on preventative legislation, changes to principal OHS laws in Australia between 1972 and 1989 established the rights of workers to information and involvement, and included a series of participatory mechanisms to give effect to this. Tripartite standard-setting and policy-making bodies were established at industry, state, territory and national level to encourage a more constructive and proactive approach to OHS standard setting from both management and unions (although these bodies have since been abolished by conservative governments in several states). At the workplace level, the laws provide for joint workplace OHS committees to address OHS problems and for employee OHS representatives to monitor conditions to ensure that workers' health is being safeguarded. For instance, s77(1) and s81(f) of the Queensland Workplace Health and Safety Act, 1995 require that the employer must consult with the HSR regarding any changes to work processes or substances that may affect OHS. In Victoria and South Australia HSRs may order a temporary halt to the work process in situations where they perceive an immediate and significant danger to workers' health.

In some states and territories the principal OHS legislation fails to ensure that employee HSRs have the training, powers and functions that would enable them to carry out their activities effectively and to make employee involvement meaningful. Both international and Australian evidence indicates that where HSRs have been given significant powers, notably the authority to issue a provisional prohibition or improvement notice (where there is an imminent and serious danger to workers' health), these powers have not been abused (see Peppard, 2007). On the other side, changes to the industrial relations climate appear to have been associated with an increasing number of instances of discrimination against HSRs (see Warren-Langford et al., 1993: 604; Quinlan and Johnstone, 2009). The large number of such cases is a worrying trend given the key role played by HSRs in safeguarding employee interests.

New Zealand deviated from the Robens model, unlike Australia and other countries that had adopted the model, in that it did not stipulate the participation of workers in decisions affecting their health and safety. Instead, it only made vague reference to the involvement of workers in health and safety issues (see section 12, Health and Safety in Employment Act, 1992). The fact that formalised worker participation failed to materialise in the legislation was not surprising, given the National Government's preference for employment relations' policies that favoured individualism and self-interest. The Health and Safety in Employment Amendment Act, 2002 now requires employers to ensure that their employees have a reasonable opportunity to participate in work-related health and safety matters. 'Reasonable opportunity' is determined by the particular circumstances of each workplace, including things such as the number of employees employed, the number of workplaces and the distance between them, the potential sources of harm in the place or places of work, the nature of the employment arrangements (e.g. the extent and regularity of seasonal employees) and the overriding duty to act in good faith as set out in the Employment Relations Act, 2000.

It also needs to be recognised that unions play a critical role in terms of facilitating effective employee involvement (see Trägårdh, 2008). Unions provide the training for these representatives (via state ACTU OHS training units), support material and industrial backup (including protection from unfair dismissal). Studies in both Britain and Australia (cited in Quinlan, 1993) have demonstrated that the effectiveness of HSRs is contingent upon union support (and the granting of meaningful powers under the legislation). For example, Leopold and Beaumont (1983) found that participatory structures for OHS were only effective in highly unionised workplaces. Available evidence (see below) indicates a similar situation in Australia.

Following on from the last point, reference needs to be made to significant changes that have occurred in the industrial relations climate in Australia, New Zealand and other industrialised countries. These changes include a rapid growth of non-regulated or weakly unionised forms of work (subcontracting, franchising, agency labour, casualisation, etc.), a decline in union membership, widespread union amalgamations and the development of a sharp policy focus on the relationship between industrial relations and workplace productivity. In Australia and New Zealand the latter has given rise to enterprise bargaining and associated changes to industrial relations legislation (including award simplification in Australian and the abolishment of the award system altogether in New Zealand). It might be suggested that participatory mechanisms afforded by OHS laws and the shifting locus of industrial relations provide opportunities for innovative workplace reforms that enhance both productivity and employee health and wellbeing. However, this requires real commitment and planning by the parties. It also requires a regulatory framework that encourages trust by ensuring genuinely representative negotiations, the maintenance of minimum standards and notions of equity. Without these prerequisites there is a real danger that workplace reforms may undermine OHS performance rather than enhancing it. The remainder of this chapter will elaborate on this and other issues just identified.

The dimensions of worker involvement in OHS

As already noted, worker involvement in OHS may take on a number of forms. It also originates from a number of different sources, although in practice these can often interact.

Involvement mechanisms under OHS and workers' compensation legislation

One source of worker involvement already discussed is that prescribed by OHS legislation in Australia, New Zealand and other countries. Specific mechanisms include formal worker/union representation on bodies advising government on OHS standards (at state/territory and federal level), requirements for joint workplace committees to address OHS, the appointment of employee HSRs to safeguard worker interests, mandated employee notification of certain hazards and mechanisms for resolving management–worker disagreements over imminent risks. A number of states (notably New South Wales and Queensland) also have an array of industry-level bipartite advisory committees. Overall, joint workplace committees and employee HSRs are the most pervasive form of worker involvement afforded under OHS legislation in Australia and the same applies to the Nordic countries.

These requirements represent a significant source of worker involvement, especially at a time where other forms of worker participation (i.e. via unions or those associated with industrial democracy schemes) have been in decline. While it is difficult to know exactly how many HSRs there are in New Zealand, it has been estimated that the Council of Trade Unions (CTU) has trained on average 6000 health and safety worker representatives annually since 2003. Unfortunately, government funding to train HSRs in New Zealand has recently been severely curtailed and the number of trade union–trained representatives will be reduced to 2000 per annum for the foreseeable future. In Australia we estimate there are over 30 000 worker HSRs. Changes to the OHS legislation that occurred in NSW also provided for the appointment of HSRs. Extensive federal government workplace surveys in 1990 and 1995 revealed that mechanisms of worker involvement associated with OHS (and in particular formal legislative requirements relating to committees and representatives) were the single most important source of workplace participation by employees. As table 9.1 indicates, both the absolute number and proportion of workplaces with OHS committees grew between 1990 and 1995. As might be expected, committees and representatives were more likely to be present in larger workplaces and more highly unionised industries such as mining, manufacturing, electricity, construction, transport, communication, government, education and health services (table 9.1). The last point is indicative of the important infrastructure role played by unions. The Australian Workplace Industrial Relations Survey undertaken in 1995 included a number of additional questions. The results indicated an association between the presence of representative structures and indicators of a more systematic approach to OHS management at the workplace, including the carrying out of audits, risk assessments and the presence of an injury/disease reporting system. Although this association did not establish causality a number of studies of employee HSRs have found that their presence encouraged a more planned and effective approach to OHS on the part of management (see Biggins et al., 1991). These are important observations.

Table 9.1 Presence of OHS committees, elected OHS representatives and OHS indicators at the workplace, as indicated by Australian Workplace Industrial Relations Surveys (AWIRS) in 1990 and 1995

	1990		1995							
	A %	Wp '00	A %	Wp '00	B %	Wp '00	C %	D %	E %	Wp '00
All workplaces	41	305	43	367	66	371	39	52	88	356
Number of employees										
20–49	23	147	25	185	55	188	31	42	82	179
50–99	45	83	52	99	73	100	36	59	91	98
100–199	62	44	69	51	80	51	57	67	97	49
200–499	83	22	81	22	91	22	66	68	97	21
500+	82	9	91	10	93	10	77	85	100	9
Sector										
Private	35	216	37	262	58	265	36	53	86	256
Public	55	89	59	105	87	106	48	52	93	100
Organisational status										
Part of larger organisation	46	243	48	290	72	293	43	55	90	279
Single workplace organisation	20	62	27	77	46	78	25	43	79	77
Industry										
Mining	43	3	62	4	80	4	56	68	96	4
Manufacturing	54	67	57	64	73	65	45	55	92	63
Electricity, gas and water supply	75	6	75	4	85	5	69	70	100	4
Construction	47	13	48	10	67	10	37	49	90	10
Wholesale trade	28	19	38	21	57	21	34	56	79	20
Retail trade	33	37	38	51	66	52	30	57	86	49
Accommodation, cafes and restaurants	12	21	13	31	35	31	32	47	81	30
Transport and storage	46	12	55	15	71	15	45	53	91	14
Communication services	88	8	55	6	90	6	63	66	95	6
Finance and Insurance	13	14	15	13	33	13	39	43	86	13

	1990		1995							
	A %	Wp '00	A %	Wp '00	B %	Wp '00	C %	D %	E %	Wp '00
Property and business services	21	19	23	27	39	27	27	39	67	27
Government administration	69	15	69	21	85	21	58	59	99	20
Education	29	32	44	49	80	50	28	42	90	48
Health and community services	56	25	62	29	87	29	53	65	98	27
Cultural and recreational services	34	5	28	9	52	9	41	53	81	8
Personal and other services	26	9	41	13	69	13	51	57	87	13
Union and delegate presence										
No union	13	60	19	97	41	98	25	40	70	97
Union, no delegate	29	83	36	80	60	81	41	52	91	76
Union and delegate	57	162	59	190	82	192	46	59	95	184

Source: Morehead et al. (1997: 453).

Notes:
Population: all workplaces with 20 or more employees.

Estimates were based on 'yes' responses by management to the following questions:
A   Are there any specialist occupational health and safety committees at this workplace? (1990 and 1995)
B   Are there any elected occupational health and safety representatives at this workplace? (1995 only)
C   Has this workplace undergone an occupational health and safety audit in the last year? By audit I mean the evaluation of OHS management systems, records and procedures—it is different from an inspection. (1995 only) Prompt: an audit can be done internally or externally.
D   In the last year, has this workplace undertaken a formal risk assessment of existing hazards? (1995 only)
E   Does this workplace have a formal injury and/or disease reporting system? (1995 only)

Wp = number of workplaces

Unfortunately it is impossible to track developments with any precision after 1995 because the then federal government abandoned carrying out Australian Workplace Industrial Relations Surveys (hopefully this matter will be reconsidered). In New Zealand, the general paucity of employment relations data means that we do not know how many functioning health and safety committees there are or how many HSRs have been elected, although data on trade union membership and collective bargaining are compiled by Victoria University of Wellington's Industrial Relations Centre. What can be said is that these mechanisms were largely constructed around the notion of permanent ongoing employment and widespread union presence in the workplace.

The growth of contingent work, outsourcing/subcontracting and declining union density has led to a weakening of these involvement and representative mechanisms in Australia, and other countries such as Canada for that matter. These changes have led to the growth of non-union workplaces and workplaces where large numbers of temporary and self-employed subcontractors are present (Johnstone et al., 2005; Lewchuk et al., 2008). At this time, jurisdictional attempts to modify requirements with regard to consultation and worker involvement (such as the NSW Risk Assessment Regulation, 2001) are exceptional and their effects can only be guessed at since OHS inspectorates seldom undertake systematic audits of participatory mechanisms. A study of Australian OHS inspectors (Johnstone and Quinlan, 2008) found that of 118 workplace visits undertaken by researchers with OHS inspectors in 2004 and 2006, HSRs were only found in unionised workplaces and that many workplaces lacked a union presence.

Examining the UK context, Walters (2006) has argued that despite neo-liberal resistance to any new regulation there was a strong argument for greater legislative support for participatory mechanisms, including the training and powers of HSRs and the use of 'roving' HSRs to provide representation in non-unionised workplaces. Similar arguments have also been mounted in Australia and one response of the Tasmanian government to the Beaconsfield mine rockfall was to trial trained union safety officers able to visit workplaces in the mining and construction industries (the trial, which was not extended, was flawed because officers could only visit workplaces in response to a complaint). On the other hand, a similar scheme of appointed safety representatives has operated successfully in Queensland and NSW mines over many years. Regional or roving safety representatives offer one solution to the weakening of worker involvement mechanisms worthy of careful consideration. At the same time, it is a partial remedy. As Frick (2008) has observed, even in Sweden where the scheme originated and is well established, global production and labour market changes have resulted in more fragmented and diffused employer responsibility and OHS activity that has led to more isolated and resource-hampered regional safety representatives less able to reach and assist workers in the worst small enterprises.

In the 1990s the decline of unions and growth of non-unionised workplaces was used by some employer groups to question the relevance of union involvement in worker participation mechanisms mandated under some Australian OHS legislation and to call for more generic procedures. This resulted in the amendment of some laws, notably in Victoria, although the law was later amended to also permit union-appointed safety officers to have workplace access. The debate about remodelling worker involvement provisions and the role of unions is not unique to Australia. A similar debate has occurred in Britain where James and Walters (2002) have argued that in practice unions perform a critical supporting role to worker involvement mechanisms so this needs to be enhanced rather than diminished through legislation (with residual provisions and roving representative mechanisms for non-union workplaces). In our view this argument has equal resonance in Australia. In New Zealand the situation was more extreme whereby under the 1990s employment legislation trade unions and any form of worker representation was written out. Since 2000 the trade unions have been an integral part of the employment relationship but their presence in law may be subsequently reduced as a result of the election of the National Government in 2008.

Finally, as noted in the chapter on OHS legislation, there are requirements for workers to be consulted in specific circumstances such as where there is proposed change at work that may affect OHS. While most laws specify contact with an HSR or workplace health and safety committee some state laws (notably that of Tasmania) include a more generic requirement for consultation that would seem to cover circumstances where neither a committee nor an HSR is present. Further, in a number of countries, and in several Australian jurisdictions, there is also provision for formal worker representation under workers' compensation legislation. In some cases this fills a gap not covered by preventative legislation while in other cases, such as in New South Wales, the peak body represents both streams because the two functions have been merged into a single agency (in this case WorkCover NSW).

Employer-initiated forms of worker involvement

Some forms of employee involvement are provided voluntarily by employers and not in response to a legislative requirement (or significantly reshaped by legislation, as in the case of an existing workplace OHS committee that did not comply with legislation). Employer-initiated forms of worker involvement in OHS have a long history but have been the subject of ongoing controversy. For example, the Safety First movement, which originated in the US and then spread to other countries such as Britain and Australia in the early twentieth century, 'sought to reduce accidents through the adoption of non-union safety committees and re-engineering techniques, based on various aspects of scientific management' (Taksa, 2009; see also Aldrich, 1997). Closely tied to Taylorism it was viewed as an attempt to subvert union organisation under the guise of promoting safety. More recently efforts to promote individualised direct worker involvement schemes or workplace surveys and interventions based on Behaviour Based Safety (BBS) have been the subject of similar criticisms, as outlined in the next chapter. It is not suggested that all attempts by employers to promote worker involvement have been viewed as an attempt to subvert more collective worker input. However, this context needs to be recognised.

Current forms of employer-initiated worker involvement include a wide array of informal activities such as consultation in the course of walk-arounds by managers or the raising of OHS issues at lunches and other meetings. There are also formal mechanisms such as suggestion schemes; surveys of worker attitudes; worker involvement in risk assessment or job safety analysis; toolbox, pre-start and workplace OHS committees; and structured consultation processes.

The quality of these mechanisms varies widely and in ways that cannot be simply equated to a distinction between formal and informal activities. Regular informal discussions may be a highly effective tool in small workplaces but such an approach is unlikely to be effective in a larger organisation. We have little direct evidence on the extent and quality of these voluntary mechanisms although it is likely some of the factors identified in studies of legislatively prescribed mechanisms such as management commitment also apply (Milgate et al., 2002). A study (Brown et al., 2007) of determinants of employee involvement schemes (autonomous groups, quality circles, joint consultative committees and task forces) based on the 1995 Australian Workplace Industrial Relations Survey (AWIRS) data found these schemes were associated with the presence of longer tenure employees, complementary human resource management practices (such as formal training), unionisation and larger workplaces. As noted elsewhere in this chapter, changes to work organisation, employer practices and union density over the past 20 years have weakened the presence of a number of these critical determinants. Examples cited elsewhere (such as the Beaconsfield mine) also call into question the effectiveness of these mechanisms where they exist.

Mechanisms of work involvement via industrial relations institutions and laws

Finally, there are mechanisms for employee involvement in OHS afforded under the institutional mechanisms of industrial relations. Attempts by workers to redress safety concerns through collective action including strikes, bans and bargaining represent a well-established convention stretching back at least 150 years in Australia, New Zealand and other countries with a longstanding union movement. The introduction of collective labour law had a not insubstantial effect on OHS by establishing minimum labour standards (covering minimum wages, maximum hours of work, sick and recreation leave, rest breaks and the like); granting unions legal rights to organise, enter workplaces and bargain; and regulating the form, contents and enforcement of collective agreements. However, as we will show below, the scope for explicitly bargaining over OHS matters was often circumscribed in practice. Nevertheless, the realm of industrial relations has provided a series of formal mechanisms for worker input into OHS, including workplace- and industry-level agreements on standards and procedures and special rules dealing with strikes or disputes over safety matters.

Industrial relations laws also provide a right if not a mechanism (in addition to those found in OHS laws) for workers to refuse unsafe work—a basic protection with regard to OHS. In Australia the awards governing some industries (see below) rendered imminent risk posed by a hazard as grounds for bypassing the steps laid out in a grievance procedure. Further, until changes were introduced by the Howard Coalition government (1996–2007), federal industrial relations law stipulated that workers stopping work (or striking, in effect) with regard to a genuine concern that they faced an imminent risk could do so without loss of wages. The onus of proof in such action rested on the employer to demonstrate that the concern was not reasonable. However, under its WorkChoices legislation in 2005 the Howard government shifted the onus of proof to workers.

Although the right to refuse unsafe work is critical in a society that values the health and wellbeing of its citizens and should also be regarded as a fundamental human right, the exercise of this right is not unproblematic, especially in the case of insecure, non-unionised or other vulnerable workers. For their part, some have expressed concerns that the right could be misused to increase union bargaining power or harass employers. These concerns generally lack a persuasive evidentiary base. For example, Australian and Canadian studies (Carson et al., 1990; Hebdon and Hyatt, 1998) found that while the exercise of these rights was more likely in an adversarial industrial relations climate there was little evidence it was used to harass employers. Tribunals also appear to take a very conservative approach to such actions. Another study (Harcourt and Harcourt, 2000) that examined 272 Canadian arbitration and labour relations board decisions involving employees who refused work on safety grounds found that these employees had to meet rigid conditions to qualify for protection from discipline, based on beliefs that OHS was an area of managerial prerogative and the need to retain management authority over production. As discussed elsewhere, there is clear evidence that many workers feel apprehensive about raising OHS issues for fear they could be subject to some form of discrimination, discipline or retribution.

In addition to options for direct bargaining over OHS and formal input prescribed under legislation, workers may also obtain representation via community mobilisations and the political lobbying of unions for improvements to OHS legislation (including workers' compensation) and other laws and policies that affect OHS.

The nature, quality and effectiveness of worker involvement

In addition to the different sources of worker involvement, important distinctions can be made in terms of the form and quality of involvement. One important distinction is between representative and direct forms of participation. In the former, worker input is channelled through formal structures, with elected/appointed spokespersons, a designated scope and procedures to govern decision making. On the other hand, direct participation entails more immediate input by individuals into work organisation that is often more informal although it may be organised to some degree through the functions of human resources and OHS management at the workplace. While not discounting direct worker participation in OHS, Walters and Nichols (2007) identify a number of reasons for placing greater emphasis on representative forms of participation. Walters and Frick (2000: 49) question much of the research on direct participation, arguing it ignores the industrial relations context of OHS and pointing to studies questioning whether direct participation is a reality for workers subject to new managerial methods. On the other hand, they argue that a focus on representative participation is justifiable because there is a body of subjective and objective evidence in relation to its effectiveness and, unlike direct participation, it can be linked back to specific statutory measures and collective agreements. Further, it is more amenable to including broader societal context. Finally, Walters and Frick (2000) argue that evidence indicates direct participation is often best achieved in workplaces where the institutions of representative participation are well established.

Evaluating the quality or effectiveness of worker participation involves more than a distinction between direct and indirect participation. The different measures for involving workers need to be examined more closely, including the context in which they are applied. For example, while workers have a right to know about hazards that may affect their health, the communication of such information by itself cannot be construed as meaningful worker participation. Rather, it is a necessary part of the foundations upon which a participation process can be built. The same applies to formal joint consultation or suggestion/problem reporting schemes where workers and managers exchange views but where the latter are under no obligation to act on this advice or incorporate it into their subsequent decisions. A suggestion/problem identification scheme where management must demonstrate a response still represents an individualised form of participation where management ultimately controls the agenda. It is superior to a one-way consultation process but still represents a very constrained form of participation.

Events at the Beaconsfield goldmine prior to the fatal rockfall on Anzac Day 2006 highlight a number of the issues just mentioned. Although the mine had an array of mechanisms for workers to raise safety concerns (including periodic worker surveys and toolbox meetings), apart from a short-lived safety committee (which did not operate effectively) these mechanisms were direct and individualised. The independent investigation found that a significant number of workers held serious concerns about seismicity and rockfalls in the mine for some time prior to the incident (and more especially after a serious set of rockfalls in October 2005) but were frustrated by the inability to communicate these concerns or have them treated seriously by management. Following the October 2005 rockfalls, management changed mining methods but the 'consultation' process primarily involved telling workers about these changes. There was no evidence workers were asked for input or even that their views were sought and recorded. The circumstances at Beaconsfield are not unique. A number of investigations into major disasters have identified poor communication and consultation with workers as a factor contributing to the event, including the Piper Alpha oil rig disaster in the North Sea in 1988 that killed 167 workers, and the explosion and fire at BP's Texas City refinery in 2005 that killed 15 workers and injured many others (Woolfson et al., 1997; Baker 2007). In both Piper Alpha and Texas City a key recommendation of the official investigations was to improve worker communication and consultation (Woolfson et al., 1997: 270; Baker, 2007: xxii).

Research into participatory mechanisms has identified a number of factors that affect their effectiveness. A review of research into committees and HSRs by Milgate et al. (2002) identified a number of factors as fundamental to effective performance, including management commitment, communication, training and information, union involvement, organisation infrastructure, committee processes and the involvement of experts (see also Weil, 1999). A report on HSRs undertaken for the UK Health and Safety Executive by Walters et al. (2005: xi), including specific studies of the chemicals and construction industry, found the prerequisites for effective worker representation and consultation on OHS were strong legislative support and effective external inspection, demonstrated management commitment to both OHS and participation, competent hazard/risk evaluation and control, autonomous worker representation at the workplace and external union support, and consultation and communication between worker representatives and their constituencies. Similarly a report prepared for the European Trade Union Technical Bureau for Health and Safety (Menendez et al., 2007: 58–9) concluded that the key factors making HSRs effective were union empowerment (through appropriate labour market polices, regulatory provisions and enforcement); union support for HSRs and strategies to support contingent workers; as well as HSRs' coverage and resources (including minimum levels of representation); knowledge and consciousness (including training and capacity to generate their own views and information); and rights and capacity to exercise influence (including respect and recognition). In a similar vein, a study (Garcia et al., 2007) of Spanish HSRs found that while they were active in providing information and advising workers this was insufficient for genuine participation in decision making on OHS at the workplace and participatory mechanisms needed to be reinforced. In Australia, pioneering research on HSRs by David Biggins and colleagues (1988, 1989, 1991a & b) highlighted the importance of training and the powers granted to them by legislation. Unfortunately, this work has not been updated and extended.

Beyond these broad observations a number of studies have pointed to more micro factors such as the importance of how worker representatives obtain and apply their knowledge and the scope of and training associated with workplace OHS committees. For example, a Canadian study of worker representation in OHS committees (in unionised settings) by Hall et al. (2006) argued that while many representatives understood their role in political terms, the most effective were those who could autonomously collect and strategically apply legal, technical and medical knowledge as tools in this political activity. A US study (Eaton and Nocerino, 2000) of the health and safety committees in public sector workplaces found that committee scope and training affected perceptions of committee effectiveness. In other words, to be effective, committees needed a meaningful scope of activities (not just trivial, routine or housekeeping matters) and those involved needed training to carry out their tasks. This finding closely matches our own observations of workplace OHS committees in Australia and New Zealand. The US study (Eaton and Nocerino, 2000) also found that workplaces with committees having greater worker involvement reported fewer illnesses and injuries.

In sum, meaningful participation must involve some form of joint decision making where the issues raised are not trivial, workers involved are representative of workforce opinion (not those least liable to offend), their views are treated seriously and their input can materially affect outcomes. Thus, while a joint workplace committee may generally offer a more effective avenue for worker participation than a narrow joint consultation process (however well-intended) the degree of participation offered by committees will itself vary widely. Representative structures, including how members are selected, the balance of power between managers and workers, designated functions and meeting times, budgetary and other resources, training of members and the procedural aftermath of decisions reached will all help to determine whether the committee offers genuine input or is largely symbolic. Legislative frameworks and union input set important baselines for committee operations. Essentially the same points about resources and the like can be made in connection with the effectiveness of HSRs.

Worker involvement and OHS management

A strong theme throughout this book is that workers can and should have a significant level of involvement in addressing the hazards they face at work. At various points we have identified arguments to support this contention in addition to the ethical ones just referred to. These included the important role that workers and their representatives can play in relation to monitoring and encouraging compliance with OHS regulations. We have also tried to show that organisational factors are a critical factor in the origins of OHS problems and, accordingly, solutions must be sought that draw on the full resources of the organisation, especially its workforce. In the next chapter on management approaches to OHS we will develop this argument further, identifying how workers can be integrated into an effective OHS management program and also examining the limitations of approaches that preclude such involvement. Without pre-empting this, it is important to identify a number of very practical reasons for worker involvement in OHS management as part of the more general examination of worker involvement in OHS being undertaken in this chapter. The involvement of workers in decision making over OHS has four general benefits to management.

1 *Contribution to knowledge of hazards*   First, as those most intimately associated with the work process, employees have a store of otherwise untapped knowledge that is valuable in identifying and addressing hazards. They can inform management of hitherto unknown risks and also provide insights into health effects which are not apparent at work such as interruptions to sleep and antisocial behaviour. Psychologists have found that subjective reporting of symptoms among shiftworkers is a good predictor of later physiological problems (Frese and Semmer, 1986). As incidents such as the rockfall at the Beaconsfield mine in 2006 highlight, workers' direct and intimate knowledge of the workplace and work processes is important to the identification of hazards and risk assessment processes.

2 *Contribution to solutions*   Second, their knowledge also allows them to suggest solutions—and often innovative and cost-effective solutions to OHS problems. For example, in the Ipswich railway workshops workers devised and built a number of trolleys for shifting heavy maintenance equipment and also simply-erected steel trestles to support rail carriages while maintenance was being carried out. These innovations effectively addressed a number of manual handling problems and have now been adopted at other railway workshops throughout Queensland.

3 *Contribution in terms of commitment*   Third, the involvement of workers will strengthen an OHS program because they more clearly become stakeholders in the venture. Their involvement will facilitate more effective dissemination of OHS information and will encourage a better understanding of risk exposures and need for protective

devices, workplace equipment, changed work practices, etc. on the part of employees. Research in Australia (Biggins and Phillips, 1991) and other countries (Hovden et al., 2008) has indicated how the presence of employee HSRs has promoted a more proactive and comprehensive approach to OHS management. At the same time, this contribution can be influenced by the prevailing industrial relations climate, the resources made available to HSRs and OHS and the mechanisms for participation at key stages (such as the planning of changes to work processes). Even in highly union-ised countries such as Norway, with a history of collaborative industrial relations, recent studies (see Hovden et al., 2007) point to tensions and gaps in the relationship between management and HSRs. While embracing worker involvement is not with-out challenges to management (including role dilemmas) these need to be viewed firmly in the context of the problems that the alternative poses. Worker exclusion, the failure to provide information or simply treating workers as the recipients of OHS advice generated by management is likely to result in cynicism and distrust which can undermine an OHS program. Failure to provide full and meaningful OHS information to workers can prove costly in terms of an eventual blow-out in workers' compensation or common law damages claims, soured industrial relations and adverse publicity. This has been illustrated by incidents such as the prolonged disputes over cancer risks to coke-oven workers at the Port Kembla steelworks in the late 1970s/early 1980s, the bitter dispute over the use of DCB at Hoechst Australia's Altona plant in Melbourne (Berger, 1993) and the asbestos exposures to workers employed by James Hardie. Even where there is no industrial dispute, as in the case of explosions at the Simsmetal factory at Laverton North in Melbourne (1986) and the explosion at Esso's Longford refinery (1998), adverse publicity arising from the incident and later court proceedings can be very damaging.

4 *Contribution to OHS program evaluation*   Fourth, feedback from workers can provide critical evidence as to how effectively an OHS strategy or program is operating and where it might be improved. The diffusion of knowledge on OHS and the impact of training measures can only really be assessed via such mechanisms. Quantitative measures of OHS performance, such as lost-time injury incidence, are at best partial measures that are open to manipulation via changes to practices which affect reporting (such as changing shift or leave arrangements, bringing injured workers on site, etc.). Formal and informal feedback from workers can provide an important qualitative check on how OHS programs are working in practice. As the NSW Mine Safety Review (Wran and McClelland, 2005) found, there can be a serious disconnect between the formal procedures outlined in an OHS management plan and the practices that actually occur at the coalface.

Other benefits

In addition to the benefits just identified, worker involvement in OHS can have other benefits. As noted elsewhere in the book, studies have indicated that the presence of HSRs lifts the standard of OHS management (Biggins and Phillips, 1991). Further, worker involvement can help implement change processes in the workplace and secure benefits in terms of both quality and productivity (Oxenburgh, 1993: 40–2; Oxenburgh and Marlow, 2005). Direct links have been made between production errors (such as breakdowns and defect rates) and OHS problems—both indicate disorganisation. OHS problems also represent a barrier to productivity via their costs and interruptions to production or service delivery. There are less tangible effects such as the impact of management's seeming indifference as to OHS on employee attitudes and morale. Kuorinka and Patry (1995: 365–70) argued that the combination of a participatory approach to ergonomics can be an effective means of promoting OHS in a context of rapidly changing technologies, production and marketing strategies. In short, recognition of OHS and a participatory approach to problem solving is seen as a means of both promoting and maximising the benefits of workplace reform.

During the 1990s Worksafe Australia (NOHSC) and some state OHS agencies promoted benchmarking and 'best practice' models as a means of assisting employers to enhance OHS performance. While it is difficult to generalise from these best-practice examples and schemes, key features that repeatedly emerged in the cases were a strong senior management commitment to OHS (and building a productive and equitable culture at work), stable industrial relations marked by a good working relationship with unions and a participatory approach that encouraged workers to be involved and make innovative suggestions. Some employers stumbled on the connection between OHS, quality and productivity accidentally, as in the case of an Australian multinational leasing transport equipment that initially sought to improve OHS in its maintenance depots. After gaining cooperation from the union and reassuring workers about job security it brought a safety engineer on site to discuss changes in the work process with workers and to devise solutions on the basis of their suggestions. As a result of this ongoing process, major changes to the work process cut workplace injuries and led to more interesting and skilled tasks (as far as employees were concerned), substantial and unpredicted boosts to productivity and the development of state-of-the-art tool technology which could be exported. Synergies between improved OHS and quality or production improvements are by no means automatic and usually require careful planning and implementation (but not a mountain of paperwork) and an integrated management system (Blewett and Shaw, 1996: 481–7; Massey et al., 2006: 15–20).

It is hard to judge the impact of the formal best practice programs. After 1996 the schemes lost favour following the election of a neo-liberal conservative federal government that eschewed tripartism/bipartism and pursued a de-collectivist agenda with regard to workplace legislation and policy. Further, calls to involve workers (in a real sense as opposed to carefully constrained work teams) and enhance OHS ran counter to a number of influential management strategies of work reorganisation, such as lean production, outsourcing and engineered standards—strategies that all had authoritarianism and work intensification at their core. An example of this was the introduction of engineered standards into the warehousing industry in the US, Sweden and Australia, which entailed an intensification of work associated with computer-assisted task measurement and monitoring of workers involved in making up orders (as well as temporary workers; see Wright and Lund, 1996, 1998). In Australia an extensive inquiry into this change following a protracted industrial dispute (Industrial Relations Commission of NSW, 1996) heard evidence of adverse OHS effects (including increased lifting and other manual handling problems, greater stress from performance pressures and speeding by forklift trucks). Management made few efforts to anticipate these effects, let alone address them once they became apparent. Further, the Crown submitted (Industrial Relations Commission of NSW, 1996: 211) that neither workers nor the union had been consulted about the changes despite their significant impact on work arrangements. Worksafe Australia submitted (Industrial Relations Commission of NSW, 1996: 218) that employers and managers in the industry understood little of their current legal obligations in relation to manual handling. The Industrial Relations Commission of NSW (1996: 322) concluded employers had not taken any real steps to redress the impact of an increase of efficiency achieved at the expense of human labour and called for a change of attitude. The commission recommended greater collaboration that entailed specific recognition of regulatory codes on manual handling and overuse injury when addressing the problem of measured work performance, but its findings did not result in significant changes to work organisation.

The case just cited raises more general questions about the role of worker and union input. Unions and the opportunities for collective bargaining afforded by the industrial relations framework can provide another valuable mechanism of worker involvement in OHS. It is to this subject that attention will now turn.

Union activity and bargaining over OHS

Unions may play a significant role in improving OHS and, indeed, have done so at times in the past. As the most representative and independent organisations of workers they can seek to change the policies and practices of both employers and government. There are seven main methods by which unions may seek to safeguard the OHS of their members and other workers, namely:

1   negotiate or bargain with employers to eliminate OHS risks
2   provide OHS information and logistical assistance to workers
3   conduct OHS education and training programs to workers, job delegates, etc.
4   protect workers active on OHS issues from victimisation
5   campaign for improvements in OHS standards and legislation
6   take part in the administration and enforcement of OHS legislation
7   provide advice and legal or other assistance to injured workers in terms of workers' compensation claims, rehabilitation and common law actions for damages.

In the past unions have tended to place more emphasis on some activities than others. For example, in Australia unions have devoted considerable energy to ensuring injured workers are properly represented in workers' compensation and common law damages claims. This activity has received little recognition although for large numbers of injured workers and their families it is an absolutely crucial role, especially when eligibility is unclear or claims are contested. This activity raises important policy questions about large numbers of injured workers who do not belong to unions and lack access to their support. In recent years several unions, such as the Construction, Forestry, Mining and Energy Union (CFMEU), have sought to provide more broadly-based support to injured workers and their families, including non–union members. The CFMEU has provided assistance (information on entitlements and legal avenues, pressure on regulators and employers as well as financial and social support) to non-union workers and their families (especially in the case of fatalities), including vulnerable groups such as foreign guest workers. It has also drawn community and government attention to these problems and policies (such as the poorly regulated federal guest worker scheme) that have given rise to them. In 2007 the CFMEU facilitated the establishment of a support group/network of the families of workers killed on the job—the Workplace Tragedy Support Group. In addition to providing support and information the group has campaigned with some success for improvements in OHS and workers' compensation laws. Similar bodies exist in a number of other countries, such as Canada.

In New Zealand, trade unions have led a number of OHS campaigns, including successfully agitating for a Ministerial Inquiry into the health and safety practices of Tranz Rail in 2000. The New Zealand Department of Labour stated that between 1993 and 2000 Tranz Rail recorded over eight times the national average of work-related fatalities (Wilson, 2000). To complicate matters, many New Zealand employers and workers, including those working in the railways, were not covered by the Health and Safety in Employment Act, 1992, as recommended in the UK's Robens report. More recently trade unions were instrumental in getting the Health and Safety in Employment Act, 1992 amended to include formalised worker participation and representation as well as ensuring that New Zealand employers and workers, with rare exceptions, are now covered by the Act. In spite of the recent successes in New Zealand, the efforts of unions to directly negotiate improvements in OHS have met with varying degrees of success over time and in relation to different countries. Reasons for this include the relative strength of the union movement, the specific regulatory apparatus governing collective negotiations (including the attitudes of industrial tribunals, governments and courts), the response of employers and the priorities and strategic preferences of unions.

Union activity over OHS also needs to be viewed in the context of community organisation and responses. A few examples illustrate this. In the 1880s and 1890s broadly based community alliances, including anti-sweating leagues composed of social reformers, religious groups and unions, played a pivotal role in the introduction of social protection legislation (including OHS laws) in Australia, New Zealand, Europe and North America. Over a longer period up to the present, public outrage at major OHS disasters—especially in the mining industry but also with regard to factories (such as the 1913 Triangle Shirt Waist fire in the US and the Kader fire in Thailand), refineries (such as the explosion at Esso Longford in Victoria in 1998 and that at AZF in Toulouse, France in 2001) and maritime disasters—has created a climate where governments have felt the need to introduce stronger OHS legislation (Tucker, 2006). In the 1970s and 1980s bodies such as workers' health centres and action groups and women's community health centres located throughout Australia and New Zealand played a major role in raising community awareness about OHS and encouraging unions to play a more active role in the area. In the 1980s and 1990s other bodies emerged, including a number established by bereaved parents (Fran Kavanagh founded Advocates of Workplace Safety in NSW, Dr Tord Kjellstrom established the Trade Union Health and Safety Centre in New Zealand and similar bodies have also emerged in Canada and other countries) that put pressure on governments by highlighting the human toll and impact of injury and death. An alliance between the asbestos sufferers groups (led by Bernie Banton) and unions ultimately thwarted efforts by James Hardie to minimise its liability to compensate victims of asbestos exposure (moving its headquarters offshore and using an under-funded scheme). Finally, in the Australian clothing and trucking industries union–community alliances were successful in gaining legislative, tribunal and policy interventions by government to better protect the health and safety of these vulnerable workers. Again, similar examples of important community-based campaigns can be identified in other countries, such as a campaign for workers' compensation protection for informal workers in Brazil and campaigns to protect immigrant day labour in the US (Quinlan and Sokas, 2009).

Reference to unions and community mobilisations raises the broader question of the relationship of unions to public health. This is an important question though one largely beyond the confines of this book. Two observations are, however, worth making. First, as we have noted elsewhere (Quinlan and Bohle, 2008) there is a growing body of international evidence that the growth of work arrangements such as subcontracting or outsourcing (in industries such as transport) and downsizing/reduced staffing levels (in healthcare) can have adverse health and safety effects on the community. Unions have tended to oppose these arrangements and in a number of instances, such as trucking and healthcare, have made explicit reference to the adverse community health effects conspicuously ignored by neo-liberal policy makers. Other areas, such as transport security and the safety of food and other products produced through a combination of elaborate supply chains and contingent workers, require further investigation in this regard. Second, there is some evidence that the presence of unions is associated with better community health outcomes (see, for example, Seago, 2004) though far more research is required in this area.

It is beyond the scope of this book to examine the whole array of union activity with regard to OHS in depth (for a historical comparison of union involvement in OHS in Australia and the US, see Quinlan, 1993: 154–66). Several aspects were referred to in earlier chapters. The remainder of this chapter will focus on the industrial relations of OHS and union bargaining over OHS.

The industrial relations of OHS

Union involvement in OHS opens broader questions about the relationship between industrial relations and OHS—a relationship that has frequently been misunderstood or misrepresented. As the relationship has been examined in detail elsewhere (Carson and Henenberg, 1988; Robinson, 1991; Quinlan, 1993: 140–69; Rennie, 2005) our primary concern here is to make some basic points of clarification.

Occupational health and safety and industrial relations have often been viewed as entities that can and should be kept distinct. A common perception of occupational health and safety is of a largely technical area where there are no major differences of interest among workers, managers, governments and professionals in terms of seeking improvements. Industrial relations, on the other hand, is seen as an area for which competing interests are the raison d'être, with institutional processes seeking to reconcile conflicts over wages, job security and a host of other matters. In essence, we are presented with two quite separate visions of the world of work, each sustained by its own field of knowledge, professional apparatus and regulation. The clearest demonstration of the desire to separate the two fields was the oft-repeated phrase that 'safety shouldn't be bargained over'. Over the past 20 years the separation has been blurred at the edges due to OHS legislative changes affording union input and greater acceptance of organisational aspects of OHS (such as psychosocial factors). However, despite this the separation has by no means vanished at policy level or in other arenas. Therefore, it is important to make a number of basic points, evidence for which was provided in earlier chapters.

OHS and other workplace matters are inexorably intertwined

It is impossible to distinguish OHS from other aspects of the working environment, because these factors interact in complex ways that cannot be unpacked to provide separate arrays of remedies. Changes to staffing levels in a workplace can raise a multiplicity of issues, including job security, seniority, career development, earning, task changes and OHS. In practice, it is often impossible to disentangle these issues and any solution is liable to have ramifications for all. There is now a considerable body of research demonstrating that payment rates and systems, authority structures, job security, staffing levels and a host of other employment matters can affect OHS. Recognition of the link can even be found in government reports on OHS that, for example, have recommended against piecework payment systems on safety grounds or have found that failure to enforce minimum wage or hours requirements has undermined OHS (Nevada Commission on Workplace Safety and Community Protection, 1998: 10; Motor Accidents Authority, 2001; NOHSAC, 2007; National Transport Commission, 2008).

Correspondingly, health-related outcomes at work, such as death, serious injury or the onset of disease, impact on other aspects of the work environment and can influence the character of management/worker relations. Not only is OHS intertwined with other employment conditions, there is also evidence to indicate worker organisation in the form of unions has positive effects on OHS and, correspondingly, a weakening of union representation can have negative effects. Walters and colleagues (Walters and Nichols, 2007; Nichols et al., 2007), for example, have identified a series of British, US, French, Australian and Norwegian studies undertaken since the 1970s that found union presence/strength, and the participatory approach to decision making this promotes, had positive and measurable benefits in terms of OHS outcomes. Other studies have pointed to positive effects. For example, a study by Gillen et al. (2002) that compared union and non-union workers found the former were more likely to perceive their supervisors as caring about safety, be made more aware of dangerous work practices, have received OHS training when hired, have regular safety meetings and view taking risks as not part of their job. At the other extreme, as noted elsewhere in this book, a poor industrial relations climate where union input is not valued has been identified as a contributing factor in a number of OHS disasters (Tucker, 2006; Baker, 2007).

The question then is not how to separate OHS from other issues (or by implication how to exclude unions from OHS) but how to accommodate the interactions between, say, a wage claim or a debate over work restructuring and OHS to optimise outcomes. As we will show below, failing to address the linkages can result in socially harmful outcomes.

Bargaining over OHS is inevitable

It follows from the last point that some degree of bargaining over OHS is inevitable. Health and safety matters have long been a source of worker mobilisation and industrial disputation. A database on worker organisation in Australia between 1795 and 1900 found that health and safety ranked as the fourth most frequently cited union objective (wages and hours ranked top) and that working conditions (including health and safety) was the fourth most commonly cited issue involved in strikes and disputes (Anderson and Quinlan, 2008: 117–18). While the Australian Bureau of Statistics and Statistics New Zealand have published data on industrial disputes since the early twentieth century these statistics make it difficult to identify the number of disputes that are primarily concerned with OHS. Nevertheless, as we noted in an earlier edition, a breakdown of unpublished data for the years 1985–88 indicated that—even using a conservative approach—almost 10% of disputes were primarily concerned with OHS (Quinlan and Bohle, 1991: 338). Since 2003, Statistics New Zealand commentaries on work stoppages have typically ranked health and safety issues, such as long work hours, overtime and shiftwork, as the third major reason for industrial disputes (Statistics New Zealand, 2008). Further, it is no coincidence that within the Australian and New Zealand health and education sectors there has been a dramatic increase in the past decade in the level of work intensification and a parallel rise in the number and length of industrial disputes over increased workloads and hours worked (Australian Bureau of Statistics, 2008b; Statistics New Zealand, 2008; see also Hyslop and Maré, 2007). Since most disputes are multi-causal, figures on the causes of disputes represent an understatement of the number of times OHS was an issue in an industrial dispute. While the data just cited is fragmentary it is indicative that OHS has long been a common source of industrial disputation in Australia and New Zealand.

Strikes and disputes provide only one indication of the extent to which OHS is bargained over. In many instances issues are raised by workers or their union delegate and addressed at the workplace without a formal dispute being notified. Evidence on this sort of activity is even more fragmentary than disputes data but does suggest that OHS matters are being addressed by conventional industrial relations mechanisms in the workplace on a significant and ongoing basis. For example, the 1995 AWIRS survey (Morehead et al., 1997: 167) found that union delegates in 45% of the workplaces reported that monitoring and dealing with OHS issues was one of their tasks. In a smaller proportion of workplaces (15%) delegates reported spending a lot of time on this activity in the previous year. Delegates in 19% of workplaces identified OHS as an issue frequently raised with management over the previous year (Morehead et al, 175).

Bargaining over OHS is not confined to the industrial relations arena

Bargaining over OHS does not just occur in the conventional industrial relations arena. We have already shown that interest groups influence the development of OHS knowledge, the speed and manner with which such knowledge is used to amend OHS laws and the extent and nature of compliance activities. This web of interest groups extends far beyond workers and employers and not all their interactions should be labelled as bargaining (for studies of influence in relation to OHS disasters see Tucker, 2006). Nonetheless, bargained exchanges of both a tacit and explicit nature occur. For example, in recent years there has been an ongoing struggle between the European Union and Australian and New Zealand employer organisations and peak union bodies over the extent to which OHS agencies and regulators should address the OHS implications of precarious employment. In Australia, New Zealand and the UK unions have sought more stringent laws with regard to death in the workplace, while some employers have argued that existing OHS laws are too onerous. Other interest groups, such as the medical profession, insurers, regulators and think tanks, have also sought to exert an influence. Further, as noted in previous chapters OHS standards often represent a compromise rather than the highest possible level of protection based on scientific knowledge (itself not immune to the influence of interest groups).

Again, there is nothing especially new about interest group bargaining about OHS standards and practices. Indeed, in Australia, New Zealand, the US, France and other countries there is an extensive body of historical research documenting these struggles and the critical role workers and unions had to play to persuade the state to intervene on a wide array of OHS issues, often in the face of equally vigorous opposition from employers (see, for example, Dembe, 1996; Campbell, 1996, 1998; Derickson, 1998; Quinlan, 1997; Rasmussen and Lamm, 2002; Armstrong, 2008). Australian research includes Gillespie's (1990) study of lead poisoning at Port Pirie, Penrose's (1997, 1998) studies of lead poisoning at Mount Isa and Weil's disease among north Queensland canecutters in the 1930s, and Oliver's (1997) study of wharf labourers and forestry workers in post–World War I Western Australia. In New Zealand, historians have chronicled the many bitter conflicts between trade unions, employers and the state, over exposure to hazards such as coal dust, asbestos fibres, etc. (see Scott, 2001; Nolan, 2006; Armstrong, 2008). More recently trade unions have been at the vanguard of obtaining compensation for New Zealanders exposed to dioxin and pentachlorophenol (PCP), as detailed in the next chapter (see Purnell et al., 2005; McLean et al., 2007). In the US and Canada, studies include Richard Rennie and Alan Derickson's extensive research on struggles over silicosis among metalliferous miners and coal miners' black lung (Derickson, 1998; Rennie, 2005), and Rosner and Markowitz's (1991) more wide-ranging study of silicosis (see also studies in Rosner and Markowitz, 1989). Virtually all the studies just mentioned identify a complex and shifting relationship between professional groups, regulators, unions, employers and community groups. For all this it is important to recognise than many important OHS standards that are now taken for granted were not simply a rational response to accumulated knowledge but the outcome of sometimes bitter and protracted struggles. As McCulloch and Tweedale's (2008) study of asbestos highlights, industry was able to delay effective intervention over many years, withholding information, influencing research and drawing on allies in government, insurance and the medical profession. Even now, the banning of asbestos in most rich countries is being subverted by the industry moving its operations to developing countries. While asbestos may represent an extreme case it is easy to identify more recent struggles similar to those mentioned above, including debates over cancer clusters in particular buildings, work overload/staffing levels in healthcare and transport, and latex (see, for example, Gordon et al., 2008).

We are not suggesting bargaining occurs in relation to every workplace hazard, simply that the way society is organised provides an underlying basis for interest group mobilisation over OHS. Further, the absence of bargaining should not be seen as indicating that a less-subjective and more impartial outcome is likely. Bargaining presumes that interested parties can obtain information, mobilise and have avenues for presenting and resolving their differences and, as the case of Baryulgil asbestos miners indicates (McCulloch, 1986), this is not always the case. The absence of effective organisation among workers will leave the determination of OHS standards in the hands of government, professional groups and industry. As noted in an earlier chapter, these interactions can involve influences and exchanges that are neither transparent nor necessarily in the community interest (Castleman and Ziem, 1988; Ziem and Castleman, 1989).

The bifurcation of OHS and industrial relations is historically contingent

Most importantly perhaps, the historical separation of OHS from industrial relations was not predetermined or the result of a reasoned debate but a historically contingent outcome that arose from the separate development of OHS legislation, workers' compensation regimes and industrial relations laws and institutions. In short there has been a trifurcation of regulation governing working conditions and the rights of workers. Carson has argued that the separation was not accidental and nor were the factors sustaining it. Referring to the development of early British factory legislation—the first OHS laws that set the model for legislation in many countries—Carson and Henenberg (1988: 3) state the separation '… accomplished two crucial and related things: it signalled an ideological separation of occupational health and safety issues from the war-torn terrain of industrial relations; and it achieved this not insubstantial feat by indicating that these matters were now the business of the state'.

OHS was excluded from the realms of collective negotiation and unions were denied direct input. Where matters were not prescribed by the state they were deemed to be the prerogative of management. As we demonstrate below, the existence of OHS laws was used to circumscribe union efforts to negotiate improvements in safety through industrial relations institutions of collective bargaining or its equivalent, although other factors also played a part. Employers saw the separation as a means of circumscribing union activity and supported it. In sum, the separation was largely ideological, although in turn this shaped the evolution of knowledge, academia and the professions. By and large this separation of OHS and industrial relations remained unchallenged until the introduction of more participatory or Robens-style OHS legislation. Even this legislation only partially bridged the now extensive institutional divide. While the separation seems to exist in all industrialised countries it is more pronounced in some countries (especially the US where OHS legislation still affords little or no formal union input) than others. The gap appears least in the Nordic countries (Sweden, Norway, Finland and Denmark) where, despite the separation of OHS and collective labour laws, the term 'work environment' was used to encapsulate all aspects of employment conditions, including OHS. This term that pervaded research and policy debate has recently come under attack from neo-liberal parties, especially in Sweden. In Australia attempts to develop similar bridges have not occurred, at least not in an overarching policy sense, though legislative reforms introduced recently to protect clothing outworkers and truck drivers actually integrate the different spheres (OHS and IR) of regulation (Quinlan and Sokas, 2009).

Union bargaining over OHS

The industrial relations regimes adopted by Australia, New Zealand and other industrialised countries have a number of profound yet little-recognised effects on OHS. Developed over a long period of struggle these systems—the main regulatory and institutional architecture—were not secured in industrialised countries until the early twentieth century (or even later in the case of the US). Although varying considerably in scope and form, the regimes all established legal minimum employment conditions (covering child labour, minimum wage rates, annual leave and maximum working hours) and the right of unions to collectively bargain (resulting in widespread collective determination of working conditions). The setting and enforcement of minimum labour standards as well as improvements to pay levels and employment conditions secured through collective negotiation had significant implications for OHS. Prior to this, overwork and even malnutrition—both a consequence of low-paid and insecure work as much as unregulated hours—were a major source of occupational ill health even in countries like Australia, New Zealand and the US that had secured relatively high per capita income and living standards by the second half of the nineteenth century. Indeed, in the last quarter of the nineteenth century anti-sweating leagues were formed in Australia, New Zealand, Europe and the US to campaign against the combination of low pay and long hours that marked occupations such as bootmaking, the baking trade, tailoresses and needlewomen. It became a prominent issue for early factory inspectors and government inquiries. Elizabeth Rogers (a needlewoman from Bowden) told the 1892 Royal Commission in Adelaide:

> I could mention six (young girls) now whose lives are worked out through working so hard at the shirt trade. It is hard work to make a dozen shirts in a day and some have had to work, oh, so hard. One girl is at home now, and is being attended to by the doctor. She had to make a dozen shirts in a day to get her wages. (cited in Williams, 1997: 37)

In New Zealand in 1890, and later in Australia in the early twentieth century, the introduction of state and federal systems of compulsory arbitration brought with it union recognition and a pervasive system of tribunal-administered awards detailing wages, hours and a host of other conditions for particular industries and occupation. These awards were legally enforceable and soon covered the great bulk of New Zealand and Australian employees, setting a benchmark for the community that, by and large, removed sweated labour conditions. Moreover, in the course of the twentieth century union campaigns on issues such as working hours, piecework, casual employment, shiftwork and other work practices had important effects on OHS. Gains were either inserted into new awards covering the industry/occupation or became part of industry, workplace or enterprise agreements that sat alongside or above awards. For example, the elimination of the bull system of casual hiring among wharf labourers (whereby persons seeking work turned up each day with a number of the fittest looking being selected by the supervisor) in 1942 had important consequences for the health and wellbeing of these workers. A medical examination of 130 wharf labourers in the following year by specialist Dr Ronald McQueen (undertaken as part of the Stevedoring Industry Commission) identified the health consequences of previous employment practices, exacerbated by the Great Depression. Expecting malingerers, McQueen instead found men who were prematurely aged and seriously disabled in many cases (not through alcohol). McQueen (cited in Nelson, 1957: 119) concluded:

> The endless search for the infrequent job which would keep them and their families from the precarious borderline of malnutrition had taken its devastating toll. The feverish high tension work performed when the job is secured in order to ensure its repetition had been paid for at the shocking price of premature old age and physical calamity.

It is worth noting in passing that in 1996–98 the then federal government lent active support to attempts to reshape the stevedoring industry by weakening if not eliminating the influence of the Maritime Union of Australia (MUA), altering work practices and reintroducing casual labour—the latter part of an international effort by employers that had been successful in countries such as New Zealand and the UK

(Dabscheck, 2007: 10). While efforts to eliminate the union failed, more intensive work practices (higher productivity and lower staffing levels) were introduced in a 1998 enterprise agreement. In 2004 the MUA initiated a prosecution against the stevedoring company at the centre of the dispute (Patrick Stevedores) under the NSW OHS Act, arguing the new system of work placed straddle carrier operators (especially those who were older and less physically fit) at greater risk of incurring repetitive strain injury (RSI). The charges laid by the union were largely upheld with the presiding judge (Haylen) imposing a substantial fine on the company (*Coombs v Patrick Stevedores Holdings Pty Ltd [2005]*, esp. at paras 79–80). However, the new work system remained with minor modifications.

It is also worth noting in passing that the hazards posed by overwork/long hours, low pay and malnutrition are not confined to an earlier historical phase. They are still widespread in developing countries, with a large informal sector of insecure employment/self-employment (often around half the workforce) and a weak industrial relations system—little union presence or minimum standards legislation (Santana et al., 1997; Lowenson, 1999). Further, as discussed below, the problems of long hours and low pay (if not malnutrition) are re-emerging in pockets of the workforce of industrialised countries (notably some home-based and self-employed workers).

Leaving these observations to one side, it can be noted that by the 1980s even a relatively basic industry or occupational award contained 60–70 provisions covering not only wages and hours but shift breaks/minimum call-back times, rest breaks, meal allowances, the provision of clothing and a host of other matters, including OHS. A number of these provisions, like those relating to hours and rest breaks, had positive benefits for OHS. On the other hand, there was also a tendency—in some industries especially—to commodify hazardous or unhealthy conditions into additional pay in the form of special allowances or 'danger' money. As Jeffrey (1995: 168) noted, the overriding contribution of the New Zealand system of awards operating within the compulsory conciliation and arbitration framework was the willingness of employers to throw money at workplace hazards and of employees to accept it, rather than attempting to overcome the health and safety problems. The same problem was conspicuous in Australia until the 1980s.

Unlike in Australia, the New Zealand award system, together with all the accumulated conditions, was abolished in 1990 and workers were once again vulnerable to exploitation. Harbridge and Street (1995), McLaughlin (2000) and Geare (2001) provide evidence linking the abolition of the award system with the deterioration of conditions, highlighting particularly the trend of working longer hours for less pay. Like wages and hours, a number of these additional conditions of employment, such as rest breaks and minimum call-back times, had implications for OHS. However, with some notable exceptions, the introduction of these award conditions was seldom secured on the basis of arguments or decisions explicitly addressing safety or health. Early tribunals occasionally commissioned inquiries into OHS, especially in relation to women workers (Quinlan, 1997: 9–10, 26), but this practice was exceptional and became progressively narrower in scope. OHS improvements were usually a subsidiary issue or an unintended outcome of changes introduced for another purpose, such as more secure employment or an improvement in working conditions. Award provisions or clauses in collective agreements that did explicitly focus on OHS were generally limited in scope. Examples included provisions on first aid, amenities, PPE, accident pay (to bridge the gap between earnings and workers' compensation entitlements), generic statements about the importance of safety, the publication of safety rules and the need for workers to obey safety rules (Quinlan and Bohle, 1991: 351). As already noted, more disturbingly some 'OHS' provisions involved a reinterpretation or commodification of risk and discomfort through 'danger money', 'height' pay and similar types of allowances.

A detailed examination of the evolution of federal tribunal decisions on OHS identified a number of exceptions to this pattern. In several industries, most notably the mining and maritime industries, a combination of conspicuous hazards and strong unions with a strong interest in OHS resulted in more far-reaching provisions on OHS. These included agreements relating to roads on mines sites and a clause in the federal waterfront award that excluded work stoppages connected to safety from a general requirement that work continue while a disagreement was being handled by the grievance procedure (Quinlan and Bohle, 1991: 354). The federal tribunal also approved special OHS provisions in circumstances where coverage by OHS legislation was manifestly inadequate, ambiguous or complicated by overlapping state/federal coverage. Examples of this include detailed OHS provisions in a federal award covering deep-sea divers employed in the offshore oil industry (introduced after a strike in 1969) and special clauses dealing with journalists and film crews working in dangerous locations overseas (Quinlan and Bohle, 1991: 350–1).

Some OHS clauses, such as the one exempting safety-related strikes from the no-stoppage requirement in grievance procedures, spread to a number of other Australian and New Zealand awards. This reflected an acceptance of the principle that workers should have an unambiguous right to withdraw their labour if confronted with what they believed to be an imminent and serious risk to their health. This was reinforced by employment court decisions in New Zealand (Rasmussen and Lamm, 2002) and amendments to Australian federal industrial relations legislation in 1988, inserting a provision (s124 of the Industrial Relations Act) that gave workers the right to recover lost wages where the stoppage was occasioned by a genuine concern about risks to their health or safety. By the 1970s the federal tribunal was also adopting a more critical approach to the commodification of risk into allowances. For example, a full bench of the commission rejected a claim by the Ships, Painters and Dockers' Union for an allowance for handling asbestos, with Mr Justice Staples in particular lambasting the union for the ghoulishness intrinsic in its proposal (176 CAR 1041). The commission continued to award allowances for hazardous conditions especially under the euphemistic label of a disability allowance. In the 1980s the removal of asbestos was the subject of a series of decisions involving building workers (see, for example, 293 CAR 272; 298 CAR 188; 301 CAR 505). However, in these cases the allowances were given in conjunction with requirements for additional protective clothing and adherence to approved removal procedures. It appears that the allowance was made in recognition of the degree of discomfort involved in the task (including the wearing of elaborate protective clothing) rather than in exchange for residual danger.

Without losing sight of these exceptions a central question remains as to why explicit bargaining over OHS was so circumscribed in the conventional industrial relations arena. A number of factors appear to have contributed to this.

With regard to the federal jurisdiction, at least up to the 1980s there was some question as to whether OHS was an 'industrial matter' (i.e. the legitimate subject of a tribunal ruling). A number of union claims were rejected on this basis, including claims relating to hours of work in the stevedoring and mining industries, and clothing and baking trades, between 1913 and 1920 (Brooks, 1988: 688–9; Bennett, 1984: 32–3). This restricted approach carried through to the 1960s. In 1962 the High Court prohibited a manning requirement in relation to Melbourne buses inserted in the award by Commissioner Taylor on the basis of stress and danger (99 CAR 264). However, from the late 1970s onwards, federal tribunals showed a greater willingness to make judgments on OHS issues. By the 1980s, judgments on asbestos removal, outwork and an OHS award for auto workers meant there was no longer any question that OHS was an industrial matter. A similar approach was adopted by state tribunals although their capacity to deal with OHS was never subject to a constitutional limitation. That state tribunal decision making was largely consistent with that of the federal tribunal indicates that the constitution was not the primary reason behind limited direct involvement in OHS issues.

A more compelling explanation of the circumscribed approach of state and federal tribunals can probably be found in a combination of other factors. We would suggest there was a self-imposed predilection by industrial tribunal members to stay out of the field of OHS as far as possible. Tribunal judges or commissioners were selected from the ranks of industrial relations practitioners (unions and employer organisations), the public service and the legal profession. Few had any detailed knowledge or expertise in OHS. Reinforcing this was the repeated indication in tribunal decisions that they should not interfere with the standards laid down in OHS legislation unless these could be shown to be manifestly inadequate—an approach endorsed by at least some state governments (Quinlan and Bohle, 1991: 344). In other words, tribunal activity was shaped by the legislative and ideological bifurcation of OHS and industrial relations discussed earlier. For their part, employers reinforced this bifurcation, arguing that OHS issues or standards beyond those laid down in relevant OHS legislation were a matter of managerial prerogative and therefore not open to collective negotiation or tribunal determination. Where tribunals did make rulings (as in the 1962 decision on the manning levels of Melbourne buses) employers lodged appeals to higher courts.

However, beyond the reluctance of tribunals and resistance of employers, the unions and their approach also played an important role. Without ignoring the impact of the defeat of a number of early union claims in relation to OHS (see above), it needs to be acknowledged that for most of the twentieth century attempts by Australian and New Zealand unions to negotiate substantive improvements in OHS using the industrial relations arena were sporadic and piecemeal, and ongoing attempts to bargain improvements in OHS were largely confined to unions covering miners and maritime and construction workers. Moreover, as stated above, the introduction of the Employment Contracts Act, 1990, with its emphasis on individual contracts and the dismantling of the award system, handicapped New Zealand trade unions negotiating health and safety matters within collective agreements. Despite reverting to more of a collective bargaining model of employment relations in 2000, New Zealand trade unions have never fully recovered and the health and safety of workers continue to be compromised.

Most unions in both Australia and New Zealand saw their OHS obligations to members principally in terms of lobbying for more stringent legislation and supporting workers' compensation claims. In Australia, like tribunal members, many union officials probably felt they lacked expertise to pursue OHS and conventional expert discourse on OHS made their task even more difficult. Even those who, like waterside union official Tom Nelson, overcame this barrier expressed considerable resentment at the way allegedly impartial but actually value-laden expertise was brought to bear in disputes over OHS (Nelson, 1957: 114–19). A lack of expertise and sympathetic experts hampered union efforts to negotiate OHS improvements in other countries. In the US a Worker's Health Bureau established in the 1920s by sympathetic experts such as Alice Hamilton to help unions take a more proactive approach on OHS was short-lived and partially successful (Nugent, 1985). Similarly, studies by Noble (1986) and Robinson (1991) found limited bargaining over OHS by US unions—but with an upward trend, as in Australia from the 1970s—something only partly explained by the even more difficult situation US unions faced with regard to employer opposition and the approach of both government and the courts. In sum, the reluctance of many Australian unions to consistently mount OHS claims as part of the normal industrial relations negotiation process—while not unique—legitimated (by default) the bifurcation of OHS and industrial relations.

Catalysts of change: growing union interest in OHS from the mid-1970s

As in the UK and a number of other countries, Australian and New Zealand unions demonstrated a growing interest in and more proactive approach to OHS from the mid to late 1970s. This change was apparent at all levels. At the national level, the peak union organisations—the Australian Council of Trade Unions (ACTU) and the New Zealand Council of Trade Unions (NZCTU)—each formulated their first OHS policy in the late 1970s and have progressively expanded and revised their polices since. The ACTU established an Occupational Health and Safety Unit to act as a conduit for information and education for unions and health and safety representatives as well as an OHS committee (with representatives of individual unions) that meets on a regular basis. The ACTU's OHS Unit produced regular compendiums or digests of material on particular hazards and recent research drawn from a wide range of sources which became a valuable tool for unions and others (including overseas usage). In 1998 the ACTU responded to concerns about work intensification linked to organisational restructuring (such as downsizing) by launching high-profile campaigns on bullying and work-related stress (backed by its own workforce survey). Several years later, annual conferences on OHS were organised. Unfortunately, a restructuring of the OHS unit in 2004 led to the departure of three experienced staff members and lapsing of the regular digests, although the practice of annual OHS conferences has continued. The ACTU prepared submissions to government inquiries and reviews, including federal reviews of Comcare and OHS legislation in 2008. State branches of the ACTU (such as Unions NSW) have also established OHS committees and engaged in a parallel range of activities. In 2008 the ACTU launched a campaign on work and environmental cancer and called on the federal government to implement a complete ban on asbestos (as well as conducting an inquiry into asbestos).

In the 1960s and 1970s a great deal of New Zealand trade unions' focus was on forming a no-fault, universal accident compensation scheme. The trade union representatives, especially Des Dalgety who represented both the law society and the railway unions, played a pivotal role in the establishment of the Accident Compensation Corporation. Agreeing to a no-fault compensation scheme, however, meant that workers had to forfeit their right to sue under tort. The introduction of new technology and, in particular, the liberal (mis)use of toxic chemicals and the consequent impact on workers' health also became an increasing concern for many of the trade unions. This concern resulted in policy formulation and the development of claims addressing the negative outcomes of specified hazards. In addition, Wren's (2002: 54) study of New Zealand OHS policy shows that by the late 1970s and early 1980s the CTU was the prime mover in changing New Zealanders' approach to OHS from one that was essential reactionary to one that was more aligned to the Robens model. The CTU supported any reform that promised the maintenance of existing standards, gave workers the right to participate and held out the hope of reinvigorating official government action over OHS (Wren, 2002: 55). Wren (2002: 55) continues:

> It was the Council's action in presenting a list of demands for OHS policy change on 27 November, 1984 to the new Labour Government that led to opening up the discussion about change beyond the confines of officialdom through the formation of ACOSH [Advisory Committee on Occupational Safety and Health].

Parallel changes are apparent among individual unions in Australia and New Zealand, with virtually all of them developing OHS policies and including OHS matters in their journals/bulletins/internet homepages (several, such as the Australian Workers Union and the New Zealand EPMU, published separate OHS magazines as well as publications on particular topics such as stress and chemical exposure). A growing number have appointed specialist OHS officials, developed codes of practice in relation to particular hazards and undertaken member OHS surveys (e.g. for those working under labour hire arrangements or in call centres). In addition to the provision of information there have been a number of conspicuous waves of industrial action in connection with OHS, beginning with asbestos in the late 1970s and struggles of RSI among clerical and other workers in the 1980s and more recently campaigns in relation to deaths in the road transport industry and cancer clusters (most notably at the ABC studios in Brisbane which resulted in a relocation). Other examples of recent union activity in relation to OHS include airport baggage handlers' complaints about staffing levels, rosters and poorly maintained equipment; Queensland electricity maintenance workers striking due to an overloaded network; and a complaint from the Australian Manufacturing Workers Union that workers at the Ranger mine in the Northern Territory had been contaminated with uranium (*CCH OHS Alert*, 18 March 2008, 7 April 2008, 21 November 2008)

Industrial action and campaigns have had an educative effect, reinforcing the capacity and willingness of workers to take action on other OHS problems. Although still generally restricted to overt hazards, the array of hazards over which unions have made demands, imposed bans and undertaken campaigns has increased. Activity remains predominantly reactive, responding to the OHS threats associated with changes to work organisation by employers but proactive and well-orchestrated campaigns using multiple pressure points (community awareness/mobilisation, political/government and industrial) can be identified in a number of industries. Examples include the Australian Nurses Federation campaign on hospital staffing levels, the Transport Workers' Union campaign on trucking safety and the CFMEU's campaign on construction safety.

Growing union interest in OHS since the 1970s has not been confined to Australia and New Zealand. Comparable or even earlier trends can be identified in the US, Britain, Finland, Norway, Denmark, Sweden and a number of other industrialised countries. In the UK, the Trades Union Congress produces a regular online bulletin (Risks) while information on hazards and campaigns is also disseminated by *Hazards* magazine (edited by Rory O'Neil). The European Trade Union Congress also has an Institute for Research, Education and Health and Safety which, among other things, produces a newsletter, hosts conferences and lobbies governments.

While country-specific factors played some part in these developments during the 1970s and 1980s (such as the massive economic and labour market reforms in New Zealand and the limitations on wage bargaining in Australia), a number of global factors also need to be recognised, including the emergence of community mobilisations on women's, environmental, race and health issues in the 1970s. In Australia manifestations of this included the pioneering 'green ban' movement implemented by the Builders' Labourers Federation (that preserved critical heritage and green space in Sydney). With regard to OHS, women's community health centres established with federal government funding in the mid-1970s, workers' health action groups and workers' health centres formed in the late 1970s in Sydney, Brisbane, Newcastle, etc. and in the main cities in New Zealand, acted as a focal point for raising awareness, especially with regard to hitherto neglected groups of workers and hazards. While the relationship between the latter and unions were not without tensions (some unions embraced these bodies and a number depended on union funding) they provided an important adjunct to the OHS infrastructure in terms of collecting, reinterpreting and disseminating OHS information and mobilising activity (Le Nevez and Strange, 1989). Even unions that were initially suspicious (a minority) often responded by increasing their own activity over OHS. More participatory OHS laws introduced in the 1970s and 1980s—a product of union struggle—also provided important mechanisms that directly and indirectly reinforced union involvement in OHS.

The impact and role of workers' health centres tended to fade in the 1990s (some still operate) although this gap has been partly filled by other community-based bodies such as Advocates for Workplace Safety (established by Fran Kavanagh in NSW), Asian Women at Work, Concerned Families of Australian Truckies, the Asbestos Disease Sufferers Association and the Workplace Tragedy Support Group referred to earlier in this chapter. While there will always be turnover among bodies representing community mobilisations over OHS this does not represent grounds for understating their historical and contemporary importance. The impact of Bernie Banton and other asbestos disease sufferers in their alliance with the ACTU to wring justice from a reluctant and powerful corporation in the past decade is evidence of this.

In recent years a growing number of unions have made astute use of independent research and government inquiries to bolster their pursuit of OHS issues. Examples include a study of the OHS effects of outwork (undertaken in the late 1990s) that was used by the Textile, Clothing and Footwear Union to support its claims for a mandatory code and supply chain regulation while the Transport Workers Union made similar use of a study and inquiry into long-haul trucking in 2000–01. In most of these cases, such as the CFMEU's campaign with regard to construction safety and guest workers, there is a dovetailing of industrial action, community support/mobilisation (including the provision of help to affected workers and their families even when the former was not a union member) and calls for research and government inquiries. Similar activity can be identified in other countries. For example, in the US the United Farmworkers of America secured a pioneering study of cancer incidence (1987–97) among its mobile and largely Hispanic membership, undertaken by the Cancer Registry of Central California and funded by the Centers for Disease Control and California Cancer Research Program (Mills and Kwong, no date). The San Francisco–based Hotel and Employment/Restaurant Employees Union used research to negotiate a reduction in workload and improved conditions for hotel cleaners (Lee and Krause, 2002). In the UK Holder and O'Brien (2007) argue that a grassroots campaign using organised protests and media exposure contributed to a substantial reduction in injuries in the construction industry.

Since the 1990s in particular, profound changes in the labour market and work organisation described in chapter 1 have spurred greater union interest in OHS. These changes have brought with them serious threats to OHS while also presenting opportunities for unions to negotiate over work organisation. The imperative for unions to take a stronger interest in OHS in Australia, New Zealand, the US and elsewhere has been accentuated by a growing if still partial recognition that this is an area around which workers can be mobilised to arrest a long-term decline in membership (due in no small part to labour market changes and more aggressively anti-union policies among employers). The last subsection of this chapter will turn to these issues.

Changes to industrial relations regimes and OHS, 1988–2008

As in a number of other countries, a combination of changing employment patterns and shifts in industrial relations regulation in Australia pose a major threat to the ability of unions to safeguard the health of their members, let alone negotiate improvements in OHS. The growth in precarious employment (casuals, part-timers, etc.), the enactment of laws weakening union rights to organise and represent workers, and more frequent resort to anti-union tactics by employers have played a part in weakening unions in a number of countries, including the US, New Zealand, Britain, Canada and Australia. In Australia union density fell from 51% in 1976 to 19% in 2006. In New Zealand the fall in union membership was staggering—there was a 30% drop between 1990 and 2000. Quite apart from any other change, such a dramatic decline in union density and membership has had a significant impact on the extent to which unions have been able to bargain over a range of issues, including OHS. As US evidence shows, union presence in the workplace affects the willingness of workers to raise OHS issues with government inspectors and agencies as well as enforcement activities (Weil, 1991, 1992; Robinson, 1991).

Bennett (1994) and Wren (2002) have observed that the particular legal and institutional framework under which collective bargaining occurs critically affects not only bargaining processes but also outcomes (including what matters even make it on to the agenda). As noted above, while arbitration tribunals were generally reluctant to make substantial and explicit determinations on OHS, the system contained a number of important features helping to safeguard worker interests. This included an array of legally enforceable minimum standards (not just on wages and hours but shift breaks and penalties; casual/permanent staff ratios; training requirements; relatively unproblematic legal recognition of unions and their right to enter workplaces, monitor compliance and bargain; provisions giving—qualified—preference to union members; and compulsory arbitration of matters that could not be resolved that discouraged outright union avoidance among employers).

However, from the late 1980s changes to industrial relations legislation, especially at federal level—often under the banner of promoting flexible and enterprise-based bargaining—eroded a number of these critical features of the arbitration system. In New Zealand the changes were even more abrupt with the arbitral model being all but abandoned. The shift to enterprise bargaining transformed Australian industrial relations into a more differentiated realm of the strong and the weak in terms of working conditions. While it was suggested that a more 'decentralised' (in many cases this aspect proved illusory) enterprise bargaining system could be more conducive to bargaining over OHS than the arbitration system, evidence indicated that this did not occur—at least in any substantive way (Bohle and Quinlan, 2000). There was more evidence to show that enterprise bargaining was associated with work intensification, the substitution of pay for non-monetary conditions that had relevance for OHS (such as rest breaks and call-back times) and the introduction of longer or bifurcated (split shift) hours of work (Department of Industrial Relations, 1996; ACIRRT, 1999).

In the Australian federal sphere—the most important jurisdiction in terms of coverage—the changes were first initiated under a Labor government (1983–96). They entailed promoting bargained agreements rather than awards (although awards continued to set a wide-ranging baseline of employment entitlements) and from 1993 permitting a non-union bargaining (and agreements) stream. Upon its election in 1996 a conservative federal Coalition government introduced the Workplace Relations Act which went considerably further in promoting non-union agreements, including individual contracts similar to those found under the New Zealand Employment Contracts Act. Union rights to enter the workplace, organise and represent workers were significantly curtailed. Any one of these changes is likely to have significant implications for OHS. The 2005 WorkChoices legislation decisively shifted the focus of Australian industrial relations from a system with a strong protective function, focusing on fair work with a central role for the public interest, to a system privileging individual rights and private economic interests. Beyond de-collectivising the federal system it sought to supplant state and territory industrial relations laws (in Australia dual federal and state systems operated with regard to industrial relations). Encouraging individual contracts was one major change brought about by the New Zealand Employment Contracts Act (1990) and the Australian Workplace Relations Act (1996) and the subsequent WorkChoices (2005) reforms. As stated earlier, under the Employment Contracts Act awards were replaced by employment contracts and trade unions were written out and instead replaced by 'bargaining agents'.

While in New Zealand the Employment Relations Act, 2000 reversed many of the punitive aspects of the Employment Contracts Act (ECA) and the amendments to the Health and Safety in Employment Act, 1992 strengthened worker representation as well as incorporating stress and fatigue, evidence shows that many employers, most of whom operate in the small business sector, practise employment relations and health safety as though these changes never occurred. As a consequence of this, OHS issues such as stress and fatigue are prevalent and are unlikely to be addressed (Lo and Lamm, 2005; Hannif and Lamm, 2005). Nonetheless, under the New Zealand Labour Coalition and with support from the trade unions and other OHS activists, a number of OHS initiatives were generated between 2000 and 2008, including the advisory Workplace Health and Safety Council (WHSC), the strategy implementation committee, the Workplace Health and Safety Strategy (WHSS) and the National Occupational Health and Safety Advisory Committee (NOHSAC). NOHSAC's function was to provide expert, independent and often hard-hitting advice based on commissioned research directly to the Minister of Labour (or Associate Minister of Labour) on major OHS issues. The tripartite WHSC has also rolled out a number of initiatives; many of them are community-based, aimed at high-risk occupations such as farming, and many are linked to other government research programs such as increasing performance and productivity. For the first time in decades, government agencies were directed to fund research into wide-ranging OHS issues—for example, managing OHS within culturally diverse, small workplaces and the effects of precarious employment on OHS—which went beyond simply analysing ACC injury data. Recently trade unions have been more successful in raising issues around occupational disease than was previously the case and having initiatives launched, such as inquiries into chemical exposure (e.g. Ministerial Inquiry into the Management of Certain Hazardous Substances in Workplaces 2003) and the Gradual Process and Occupational Disease Panel chaired by the CTU representative Hazel Armstrong. Trade union executives have also been prominent on key OHS committees and boards, for example Ross Wilson was not only President of the CTU but also chair of the Accident Compensation Board. With the recent election of the National Government it is unclear, however, if any or all of these initiatives will continue.

In Australia the legislative reforms have diminished the role of awards and collective agreements, and have made it easier to convert from awards to individual agreements. Under the Workplace Relations Act, 1996 awards were to be stripped back to 20 'allowable award matters' (prior to this even a very basic industry award might set 60–70 employment conditions). While unions could negotiate with employers on other issues they could not insist these matters (including OHS) were incorporated into a legally binding award. Although union efforts to insert OHS provisions into awards had been relatively circumspect in the past (mainly in relation to training times, safety-related grievances and the like), the scope for such actions was narrowed just as it was becoming more attractive as a means of defending existing conditions or looking for gains in a difficult climate.

The WorkChoices legislation placed further limits on the role of unions to negotiate, take industrial action and enter workplaces. Further, the scope of awards was pared back even further from their traditional position as the major regulator of terms and conditions at work. The WorkChoices legislation provided for minimum statutory entitlements for individual employees, referred to as the Australian Fair Pay and Conditions. These conditions governed wages, ordinary hours of work, annual leave, personal/carer's leave and parental leave, and were expressed as a 'guarantee' that the standard could not be undercut by other regulatory instruments such as workplace agreements. While awards continued to set out minimum standards, their scope was confined to 15 'allowable matters' (section 513(1)). These 'allowable matters' were also narrowly expressed as ordinary time hours of work, incentive-based payments and bonuses, annual leave loadings, ceremonial leave, observance of public holidays, some monetary allowances, loadings for overtime or shiftwork, penalty rates, some forms of redundancy pay, stand-down provisions, some types of dispute-settling procedures, types of employment (such as full-time, casual, regular part-time and shiftwork) and conditions for outworkers (but only to the degree necessary to ensure their conditions of work were fair and reasonable in comparison with persons performing the same work at an employer's business or commercial premises). Notably, wages, classification of employees and OHS were not allowable award matters.

The WorkChoices reforms also restricted the capacity of the federal arbitral tribunal—the Australian Industrial Relations Commission (AIRC)—to administer awards, make awards and resolve industrial disputes. The AIRC's power to make new awards was removed and its role limited to varying or updating existing awards. The AIRC's major roles now were to implement the award simplification process (of stripping out non-allowable matters) and resolve disputes referred voluntarily to it by disputing parties (i.e. not compulsory arbitration but following model dispute resolution processes set out in the WorkChoices Act). A new Australian Fair Pay Commission was established to set wages—including a federal minimum wage, and minimum wages, piece rates and casual loadings for different award classifications.

Under WorkChoices, the principal mechanism for determining terms and conditions at work was workplace agreements, the most important of which were Australian Workplace Agreements (AWAs). AWAs were statutory individual agreements first introduced in the Workplace Relations Act, 1996. Because they were made under federal statute, their provisions overrode the common law and the provisions of any state statutes. Collective agreements could be made either with a union or directly with employees (provided a majority of employees approved the agreement).

A number of these changes—notably the introduction of individual agreements and exclusion of unions from agreement-making processes—significantly affected the role of trade unions in the federal industrial relations system. The system also prohibited provisions in awards or agreements facilitating trade union membership. While ostensibly retaining state industrial relations laws on right of entry for OHS purposes, Part 15 of the Workplace Relations Act imposed more restrictive requirements and procedures on entry by union officials. Union officials seeking to enter a workplace must hold both federal and state entry permits, give 24 hours' notice and obey reasonable employer requests to comply with site OHS requirements. The Workplace Relations Act provided civil penalties if officials entering a workplace obstructed any person or acted in an improper manner (Workplace Relations Act section 767(1) and Part 14 Division 3; Hooker, 2006: 61–72).

The federal IR legislation did not override state or territory OHS and workers' compensation laws, including powers of government OHS inspectors to enter workplaces (Workplace Relations Act 1996 section 16(3)), although there may be ambiguities where these OHS laws deal with issues such as hours of work (as is the case in several states).

The Workplace Relations Act, 1996 (Part 9) prohibited any form of industrial action, unless such action was taken during a properly notified 'bargaining period'. The WorkChoices legislation required a secret ballot of union members before industrial action could be taken (unless action was in response to a lockout). Further, Division 9 of Part 9 made it unlawful for an employer to make a payment to an employee in relation to any period during which the employee was engaged in 'industrial action'. Section 420(1) defines 'industrial action' broadly, and retains an exception that action by an employee is not prohibited 'industrial action' if the action was based on a reasonable concern by the employee about an imminent risk to his or her health and safety, but then shifts the onus of showing the concern was unreasonable from the employer, so that it now rested on the union or employees to prove these concerns were reasonable.

While largely targeting collectivist industrial relations the federal Coalition government also undertook measures with regard to OHS. The government did not abolish the federal tripartite OHS research, policy and standards coordination agency—the National Occupational Health and Safety Commission (NOHSC)—as it had proposed prior to the 1993 election but did slash its budget by a third. NOHSC lost half its staff (including most of its scientists and research capacity) and had its role narrowed to focus on more immediate ministerial interests (Quinlan, 2000). A number of senior administrative staff resigned or were not reappointed and the decision to move the agency's office and the library from Sydney to Canberra resulted in the loss of additional staff. In 2005 NOHSC was replaced by the Australian Safety and Compensation Council (ASCC) which retained tripartite representation but was subject to more direct ministerial control and had workers' compensation as well as prevention roles, resulting in a stronger cost containment focus (Quinlan, 2006). Other measures undertaken included the introduction of a bill (not passed) to prevent the industrial manslaughter provisions of the Australian Capital Territory Crimes Act from applying to Commonwealth employers and employees. More importantly, changes to the Commonwealth Safety, Rehabilitation and Compensation Act, 1988, in 2005, enabled large national employers to self-insure under that Act rather than state and territory workers' compensation laws. In 2007 amendments to the Commonwealth OHS Act, 1991 provided that employers licensed to self-insure under the Commonwealth workers' compensation regime (Comcare) were to be regulated by the Commonwealth OHS Act, rather than state and territory OHS laws. While calls for a unified OHS workers' compensation regime had been made over a number of years, this measure bypassed the need for state government cooperation (or a formal constitutional takeover), resulting in a more fractured process (in 2008 the newly elected Labor federal Minister for Employment and Workplace Relations announced a moratorium on self-insurance licences and initiated a Review of Comcare, the findings of which are yet to be released). The federal government also initiated a review of the federal OHS Act to better meet 'needs' at enterprise level in response to employer complaints of excessive red tape. Discussion paper 'issues' included the application of employer duties to overseas operations, removing the power of HSRs to issue provisional improvement notices (PINs), avenues for recovering damages caused by HSR actions and employer/ employee 'agreed' arrangements regarding representation of HSRs.

One major effect of the federal IR changes after 1996, especially WorkChoices, was to diminish job security and make it easier for employers to reorganise work arrangements. The 2005 amendments eliminated unfair dismissal protection for employers with fewer than 100 employees, and expanded the scope for uncontested dismissal (in particular, a dismissal that was made 'for genuine operational reasons' by larger organisations). WorkChoices specifically prohibited some matters being part of the content of agreements, including terms regarding the engagement of contractors and labour hire (temporary agency) workers—both areas where inspectorates have identified serious OHS problems (Johnstone and Quinlan, 2006). The narrowing of the 'allowable award matters' removed other award protections relevant to health and safety, such as provisions on minimum wages, maximum hours, rest breaks and minimum call-back times (between work shifts). By seeking to override state and territory industrial relations laws (see Workplace Relations Act sections 16 and 17), the legislation removed job security and OHS protections enshrined in these laws. Overall, the changes diminished job security even among nominally permanent workers and enhanced the capacity of employers to use fixed contracts, leased jobs, restructuring, outsourcing/use of subcontractors, multiple job holding, long shifts and unpaid overtime. A substantial body of international research already attests to the adverse effects of job insecurity and changed work arrangements (use of temporary workers and subcontractors) on worker health (mental and physical), safety and wellbeing (Strazdins et al., 2004; Quinlan et al., 2001). These changes have also been linked to presenteeism where workers are afraid to refuse work or take leave when sick for fear they may lose their job (Aronsson et al., 2000; Dew et al., 2005). Relevant to the latter point, WorkChoices amendments included more stringent certification requirements regarding workers taking sick leave.

The Workplace Relations Regulations 2006 prohibited agreements relating to union training and paid stop-work meetings, including training and meetings relating to OHS. This prohibition can be seen as a capstone on a range of measures designed to inhibit collective negotiation and union activity with implications for OHS. For example, restricted right of entry provisions made it more difficult for unions to identify, address and monitor exploitation and risk exposure among short-term workers, especially those on temporary work visas, backpackers, student workers and illegal foreign workers (Guthrie and Quinlan, 2005). Revised IR laws also weakened the presence and effectiveness of HSRs who are largely confined to unionised workplaces and depend on unions for training (for example, on hazard recognition) and protection from victimisation (see below). In some industries lower wages flowing from the reforms constituted a safety issue because they encouraged work overload and corner-cutting on safety. For example, a state government inquiry into long-haul trucking uncovered evidence that AWAs in trucking were based on average speeds that effectively required drivers to break road rules (Quinlan, 2001: 139–40). Other government inquiries received evidence that non-union workers, workers on individual contracts, agency workers and self-employed subcontractors were less likely to know their OHS legal rights, speak out on OHS or have their concerns treated seriously (Wran and McClelland, 2005). This evidence needs to be viewed in the context of substantial international evidence of the positive role unions play with regard to OHS (Walters and Nichols, 2007).

WorkChoices was part of a raft of federal regulatory initiatives affecting OHS. The Federal Independent Contractor Act, 2006 (Cth) paralleled the Workplace Relations Act and prevented contractor access to award protection, such as minimum wage rates. Only clothing outworkers and short-haul truck drivers were given specific exemption from the provisions of the Act following strong lobbying from community groups and unions. Further, in 2001 the federal government established a royal commission into the building and construction industry. In their submissions, unions repeatedly raised concerns about serious breaches of OHS legislation. However, of 179 inappropriate acts identified in Commissioner Cole's final report, 166 were committed by unions, nine by government agencies under pressure from unions and four (all related to OHS) by employers (Dabscheck, 2005: 184). Commissioner Cole collected detailed information on union activities, but not on unlawful and inappropriate OHS practices, stating that while OHS was important he was concerned with the future (Dabscheck, 2005: 188–9). The commission's final report made a number of OHS-related recommendations, including national uniformity of OHS regulation, consideration of supply-chain and design regulation, funding of more OHS inspectors, establishment of an Office of the Commissioner for OHS and measures to prevent the 'misuse' of OHS by unions for industrial relations purposes (Cole, 2003). In 2005 the federal government responded by introducing the Building and Construction Industry Improvement Act, establishing a new body (the Australian Building and Construction Commission) with wide-ranging inquisitorial and enforcement powers in the construction industry. Very few of the OHS recommendations were implemented. Commission activity focused on 'misbehaviour' by unions. Some pre-existing collective mechanisms for addressing OHS fell into disuse and there is little evidence of the commission investigators pursuing this matter.

State and territory governments did not meekly surrender to the federal government initiatives described previously. Indeed, in one sense WorkChoices was a response to the unwillingness of Labor-dominated state and territory governments to abandon collectivist regimes that, while accommodating 'flexibility', still accorded a central role to awards, tribunals and unions. Even as they launched an (ultimately unsuccessful) challenge to the constitutional validity of the WorkChoices legislation, virtually every state government also initiated an inquiry into the implications of the legislation. These inquiries uniformly found that workers would fare worse under WorkChoices, with a number (such as Queensland and New South Wales) making specific reference to adverse effects on OHS. Governments like NSW have strengthened the regulatory protection of children/younger workers where the states still have unambiguous jurisdiction (Riley, 2007), while Queensland, Victoria, the Australian Capital Territory and the Northern Territory amended their OHS legislation to strengthen the rights of union officers to enter workplaces to investigate suspected safety contraventions (Nickless, 2005: 1–4; Creighton and Rozen, 2007: 291–2). In 2006 Tasmania, responding to the Beaconsfield mine rockfall that killed one miner and trapped two others, trialled a scheme enabling trained union officers to visit mines and construction sites (though only in response to worker complaints). The scheme was criticised by employer organisations as breaching ILO conventions although similar arrangements had been operating in Queensland and NSW coalmines over many years. While by no means a direct response to WorkChoices, several state governments reviewed their OHS laws and enforcement policies/practices to address the flexible work arrangements, clarifying legal responsibilities with regard to subcontracting and agency labour arrangements (Maxwell, 2003). Actions were taken to better protect workers reporting OHS problems from victimisation (see, for example, Western Australia) and a number of cases were pursued in this regard (see below).

Just prior to the introduction of WorkChoices reforms, the New South Wales government introduced legislation—the Industrial Relations (Ethical Clothing Trades)

Act—that sought to protect home-based clothing workers (mostly recently arrived immigrants) from industrial exploitation and OHS hazards by integrating industrial relations, OHS and workers' compensation entitlements and adopting a mandatory code that focused legal responsibility at the top of the supply chain (Nossar et al., 2004). Similar measures were adopted in other states (Rawling, 2007). Strong community-based campaigns also meant this group was exempted from the wind-back in federal award protection under the Workplace Relations Act, WorkChoices and the Independent Contractors Act, 2006 (similar efforts were made with truck drivers; Australian Senate Employment, Workplace Relations and Education Legislation Committee, 2006: 17–18).

As the New Zealand experience of the 1990s shows, the federal government's IR laws posed a double threat to unions with regard to OHS because they made it harder for them to negotiate over these issues federally and because they tried to override state and territory IR laws, threatening any gains or agreements made at this level. For employers wanting to take a more aggressive approach to unions the laws offered new opportunities. For example, in 2006 a provision providing a taxi voucher for bank workers finishing after 8 pm—a measure to protect them from the risk of assault—was abolished (Finance Sector Union of Australia v National Australia Bank Ltd, 6 October 2006). Employers also exploited new provisions in relation to industrial action in Part 9 of the Workplace Relations Act (discussed earlier in this chapter). In January 2004 the AIRC ordered mineworkers at Anglo Coal (Capcoal Management) Pty Ltd's Southern Colliery back to work following a 48-hour stoppage over safety concerns, arguing that while management had failed to undertake regular safety checks prescribed under the Queensland Coal Mine Health and Safety Act it could not condone protest action which inflicted financial loss on the employer. In another case, 107 workers building a railway line south of Perth in Western Australia who went on strike (in a prohibited period and against the recommendation of their union) following the dismissal of their job delegate who had been active in OHS were prosecuted by the Australian Building and Construction Commission. In October 2007, following negotiations with the Construction, Forestry, Mining and Energy Union, charges against 11 workers who were not involved in the strike were dropped, and charges against four other workers were downgraded. The remaining workers are charged with contravening the Building and Construction Improvement Act, 2005, and each faces fines of up to $22 000. In addition, 82 workers were charged with contravening an order of the Australian Industrial Relations Commission in December 2005 'to not take industrial action' (Leighton Kumagai Joint Centre and Construction, Forestry, Mining and Energy Union, 2005), facing a fine of up to $6000 each.

The IR climate created by the federal government also emboldened employer groups, especially the mining industry, to challenge general duty provisions in the NSW OHS Act where the duties are expressed in absolute terms but subject to a defence imposing the onus on the duty holder to show that measures to avoid or reduce risks were not reasonably practicable. In 2005 the Swiss company Xstrata unsuccessfully challenged prosecutions arising from four work deaths at the Gretley colliery which it had purchased (Foster, 2008). Nevertheless, this pressure influenced a review of that legislation in 2006, which recommended the general duty provisions in NSW be amended so that the onus of proving all elements of a general duty offence—including reasonable practicability—lay with the prosecution. A subsequent review of the NSW OHS Act by Paul Stein QC recommended that the qualification of 'reasonably practicable' be included in the statement of the general duty but the onus of proving measures were not reasonably practicable remain with the duty holder.

There is also evidence that restrictions on union right of entry into workplaces in both Australia and New Zealand had serious implications for OHS. For example, in April 2007 the Transport Workers Union (TWU) gave Jim Pearson Transport written notice it wanted to inspect the premises and access employment records regarding suspected breaches (relating to fatigue and maintenance) of the OHS Act, 2000 (NSW). However, when union officers asked for access to Global Positioning System (GPS) records (used to track driver movements and hours) the company challenged the TWU's right of entry before the AIRC. The company argued the union had not provided reasonable grounds for suspected breaches (section 754 of the Workplace Relations Act), had not fully complied with section 748 of the Act and officials intended to inspect records of workers who were not members of the union (section 457 of the Act). The TWU ultimately obtained an order securing access (*Jim Pearson Transport v Transport Workers Union of Australia* [2007]). In November 2008, Unions NSW accused John Holland (an employer with Comcare) of repeatedly refusing to grant union officials access to the Sydney desalination plant construction site—the accusation followed a wall collapse that injured two workers (*CCH OHS Alert*, 21 November 2008). These and other cases indicate that WorkChoices created both confusion and deliberate obstruction with regard to union right of entry.

Employers alleged unions were using OHS access as a stalking or 'Trojan horse' to pursue other issues, a concern to which the Australian Building and Construction Commissioner, John Lloyd, responded to by issuing an alert (*Thompson Occupational Health News*, 17 October 2007: 6). The Victorian Secretary of the Construction, Forestry, Mining and Energy Union (CFMEU), Martin Kingham, rejected the claims, stating the union would continue to respond to requests from HSRs to 'make jobs safer'. In August 2007, a CFMEU organiser, Adrian McLoughlin, had his federal right of entry permit suspended for two months and was required to undergo training. The permit was re-issued in October 2007 (Senior Deputy President Watson *Supplementary Decision*, [2007]).

Union right of entry performs a critical role in monitoring compliance with OHS legislation. No OHS inspectorate in Australia or New Zealand (or in other country we are familiar with for that matter) has the capacity to visit more than a tiny fraction of the total workplaces it covers in any given year. Unions report issues to inspectors (including alerting them to problems at non-union workplaces) but even so the 'reach' of inspectorates remains limited. In this regard, union OHS activities enhance monitoring and compliance with the legislation. Unions perform a critical role in monitoring compliance, providing an avenue for workers to report problems anonymously, resolving

OHS problems with management and identifying serious breaches of OHS legislation requiring intervention. Without right of entry union officers would be unable to access workplaces and evidence of what has been found during such visits on occasion indicates that serious breaches would go undetected (resulting in injury and even death).

The OHS statutes in the Australian Capital Territory, New South Wales, Queensland and Victoria each contain union entry provisions but there are no union entry provisions in the federal OHS Act, nor those of the Northern Territory, South Australia, Tasmania or Western Australia. A number of states have moved to fill this gap following careful consideration of the issue. For example, the Maxwell Report (at pages 215–21) examined the issue (including the New South Wales experience with union right of entry provisions) and concluded that such a right should be included in the Victorian OHS Act. Further, a number of public submissions to the federal Comcare Review in 2008, including those from several state governments or their OHS agencies, stated that the current federal arrangements inhibited union input into OHS. Reference was also made to other laws granting union or district safety representatives access and special powers in particular industries (notably district check inspectors in Queensland under the Mining and Quarrying Health and Safety Act, 1999 and the Coal Mining Safety and Health Act, 1999. NSW mining legislation contains similar provisions).

Several examples highlight the importance of workplace access in terms of union input into OHS. In the construction industry the Construction, Forestry, Mining and Energy Union (CFMEU) has undertaken numerous inspections of construction worksites while the Community, Electrical and Power Union (CEPU) has undertaken member surveys in relation to OHS issues at particular workplaces (CEPU Communications Division, Victorian Branch, *Survey & Body-Mapping Exercise at Dandenong Letters Centre May/June 2007*). For its part, the Financial Sector Union (FSU) used workplace access in its campaign to have security barriers erected in bank branches to protect staff from violence and emotional trauma associated with robberies. Following unsuccessful approaches to a number of banks the union gained access to bank sites following robberies to collect information (including photographs) that were then used to launch four successful prosecutions against the banks concerned under the NSW OHS Act. (As noted elsewhere, NSW is the only jurisdiction to permit unions to prosecute for breaches of OHS legislation. We are aware of other instances where unions have used this option successfully—such as the Maritime Union of Australia and the Nurses Union—and it is seen as important but only in particular circumstances. As unions acknowledge themselves, there have been relatively few cases and the logistical and financial costs associated with pursuing a prosecution means this is unlikely to change.) The union believed these actions were instrumental in bringing about a change in response, the adoption of enhanced security measures and a substantial drop in the number of NSW branches subjected to robbery attempts from 7.9% in 2002 to 1.3% in 2006 (Finance Sector Union, 2008).

Right of entry needs to be viewed in the context of the fear of victimisation of workers who raise an OHS issue referred to elsewhere in this report. Right of entry enables unions to investigate an OHS issue which workers are afraid to raise or pursue directly with an inspectoral agency or to gather evidence when a worker or HSR has been victimised. As noted in the chapter on legislation, there is clear evidence that OHS inspectors see fear of victimisation as an important factor inhibiting worker reporting of OHS. Victimisation of a worker for raising an OHS issue is a clear breach of every major state and federal OHS law, but proving such cases is difficult and the few cases where action has been taken overwhelmingly involve employee health and safety representatives—but see *Boylan Distribution Services Pty Ltd* (unreported, Sunshine Magistrates Court, Victoria, 29 July 2003), which involved the dismissal of a casual truck driver for refusing to drive an unsafe truck. For example, an HSR at a Victorian factory successfully sought reinstatement from the Federal Court when he was dismissed after complaining to his union (CFMEU) that constant surveillance of his activities and discussions with other workers by the manager amounted to bullying and harassment (*Claveria v Pilkington Australia Ltd* [2007] FCA 1692). It cannot be presumed that cases coming before the courts represent the totality of the problem.

A number of employers tried to use the Workplace Relations Act to defeat complaints of victimisation. For example, when a crane driver in NSW who was dismissed after he had raised concerns about the OHS risk assessment process in a job-site risk analysis required by his employer, sought reinstatement, the employer attempted to defeat the application by arguing that relief from victimisation was excluded by the operation of s16 of the Workplace Relations Act. The bench rejected the challenge, making reference to the Road Transport Mutual Responsibility judgment and endorsing a submission by the NSW Minister for Industrial Relations (who had intervened in the case) regarding the public interest in protecting the freedom of workers to raise health and safety issues in the workplace and their participation as HSRs or in workplace committees (*CFMEU (NSW) (o/b of Hemsworth) v Brolrik Pty Ltd t/as Botany Cranes & Forklift Services* [2007] NSWIRComm 205, 21 September 2007). The judges stated (at para. 71) that establishing

> statutory remedies to prevent and to respond to instances of victimisation which might occur where employees seek to engage in those very processes which are aimed at improving and promoting health, safety and welfare at work is vital … It is clear that consultation with, and participation by, employees is certainly seen as an integral component in ensuring that workplace health and safety objectives, as set out in s3 of the OHS Act, are achieved.

While this decision clearly affirmed the rights of workers to participate, instances of victimisation and use of federal workplace relations legislation to oppose remedies highlight how changes in the IR climate influenced the behaviour of parties. Worker fear of reporting OHS is a longstanding issue affected by an array of factors, such as declining union density, the growth of contingent work arrangements and alternative job opportunities. Nonetheless, WorkChoices accentuated the problem by facilitating de-collectivist strategies among employers and weakening job security. A study of OHS inspectors in Australia identified a number of cases illustrating this point. For example, at a factory specialising in spray painting metal products the owner/operator told the inspector his visit arose because on 27 March 2006 (when WorkChoices came into effect) he had dismissed his entire workforce and he believed these workers had lodged a complaint about OHS by way of revenge. The employer went on to state that over the next three weeks he had hired a succession of young and relatively inexperienced workers. The workers were not using protective clothing/equipment (apart from face masks for spray painting). The inspection revealed a series of serious breaches of OHS legislation (including inadequate induction and training, open vats of acid and an inoperative emergency shower). Since the workplace had been visited by an inspector previously the employer should have been aware of at least some of these issues (Quinlan and Johnstone, 2009). The cascading effect of such actions on worker perceptions via community networks also needs to be acknowledged.

For its part, the Australian union movement strenuously resisted the workplace relations/WorkChoices reforms and when this failed mounted a large and persuasive political campaign that played a significant role in the electoral defeat of the federal Coalition government in November 2007.

Prior to the election, unions tried to continue their role in relation to OHS notwithstanding the difficulties now posed. Before the passage of WorkChoices in particular several unions secured major victories on OHS issues. Notable here was the campaign of the Victorian Nurses Union for minimum staffing levels in hospitals. Another notable, though far less publicised, victory occurred when the CEPU opposed a proposal by Australia Post to introduce a new mail delivery system that would have required postal delivery workers to ride their small bikes for eight hours instead of the current four-hour shifts (mixed with other duties). The CEPU hired its own OHS experts to challenge the risk assessment process undertaken by Australia Post and ultimately the proposal was rejected on ergonomic grounds (with evidence from one of Australia Post's own expert consultants).

Following the passage of WorkChoices, some unions sought to bypass WorkChoices and use the state award system to enhance worker security and OHS protection. This has included a number of 'test cases'—cases setting general requirements in awards with the potential to also flow on to other jurisdictions. In 2004, Unions NSW lodged a claim for award provisions enabling long-serving casual (temporary) workers to convert to permanent jobs, placing limits on contracting out and agency work and inserting clauses identifying employer OHS obligations (such as induction and training) to temporary agency workers. The NSW Industrial Relations Commission judgment acceded to the union's OHS claim (Secure Employment Test Case [2006]). Rejecting employer arguments that the matter should be left to OHS legislation the judgment stated (at para. 545) that since 'the provisions, in most cases, will have largely a communicative, clarifying and thus an important educational, effect, we consider it appropriate that the application in this regard should be granted'.

The challenge of WorkChoices to state systems was explicitly considered by another NSW test case in 2005 when the Transport Workers Union sought an industrial award and contract determination that would introduce OHS obligations to extend require-ments under the NSW Occupational Health and Safety (Long Distance Truck Driver

Fatigue) Regulation 2005 (Jamieson, 2006). The union claim sought the introduction of safe driving plans (to replace logbooks), a contractual tracking mechanism to facilitate supply-chain regulation, a drug and alcohol usage policy and mandatory OHS training. In its February 2006 decision the NSW Industrial Relations Commission had to consider the implications of WorkChoices, which employers argued excluded the operation of the NSW IR Act. The bench rejected employer objections, finding the exclusion of OHS coverage under section 16 of the Workplace Relations Amendment Act (WorkChoices) left unions open to pursue OHS-related claims before state industrial tribunals (Transport Industry—Mutual Responsibility for Road Safety (State) Award and Contract Determination (No. 2), Re [2006]).

In 2008 a newly elected federal Labor government started to dismantle elements of the previous government's industrial relations laws, abolishing provisions for statutory individual employment contracts (Australian Workplace Agreements). However, this process will take time and the government has not committed itself to reinstituting the arbitration regime. Issues such as restricted union right of entry, a wider raft of minimum award conditions (including OHS) and readier access to compulsory arbitration have not been addressed. At the time of writing, unions are still campaigning for return to a more forthrightly collectivist industrial relations regime.

Overall, as Gunningham (2008) has identified in the mining industry, the combination of changes to employer labour strategies, work arrangements and neo-liberal policies has significantly weakened unions in Australia and most other countries over the past 20 years. This has had significant adverse effects for worker involvement in OHS notwithstanding the mechanisms in OHS legislation. Indeed, far from being an alternative to traditional forms of collective worker organisation (i.e. unions) these mechanisms depend in no small measure on the latter for their effectiveness. Declining union density has had more profound effects on already vulnerable groups such as younger workers and immigrant guest workers (Haynes et al., 2005; Toh and Quinlan, 2009). Further, as James and Walters (1997, 2002) have demonstrated, expanding non-union forms of representation does not represent an effective or practical remedy to this gap because of the critical logistical and protective role that unions play. The provision of critical public goods by unions—including enhanced worker input into OHS—needs to be recognised and enhanced by policymakers and employers. For their part, all unions need to accept that OHS is fundamental to representing their members' interests and to learn from those unions who have adopted more proactive strategies in this regard.

Conclusion

Worker involvement in decision making over OHS is critical to the ethical and effective management of OHS. It can also be an integral part of enhancing productivity and quality at the workplace. As examples cited in this book highlight, a participatory approach to improving OHS can act as a catalyst for retaining essential health-promoting work arrangements and for initiating workplace reforms. These may occur as a result of both formal and informal processes. Nonetheless, in Australia and New Zealand (and other countries too) there has been a fundamental policy contradiction between efforts to enhance worker involvement under OHS legislation and changes to the industrial relations climate (in terms of both laws and work arrangements) that have undermined unions and collective negotiation over working conditions. The result has often been crude forms of work intensification and changes to working hours and employment standards that have undermined OHS. Many groups of workers are too weakly organised to defend existing conditions let alone have a realistic chance of negotiating superior standards.

Opportunities for employees and employers to devise and negotiate work arrangements that simultaneously enhance productivity and OHS still exist but the current environment does not encourage this approach let alone the long-term pursuit of improvements in work quality. Indeed, there is a significant disconnect between public pronouncements about the importance of securing work–life balance, better quality child care and the like and evidence pertaining to the experience of most workers (as discussed elsewhere in this book). The shift to a contractualist labour law regime in Australia, New Zealand and elsewhere has effectively reduced employee input into OHS and increased the likelihood of adverse OHS effects through lower minimum standards and reduced union bargaining rights. It has also discouraged the trust and involvement essential for more innovative consideration of how to reshape work arrangements to enhance productivity, health and wellbeing.

QUESTIONS FOR DISCUSSION

1 Australia and New Zealand had different approaches towards worker participation in OHS during the 1990s. What were these differences and why did they exist?
2 Make a list of the benefits of worker participation in OHS decisions. List the ways of implementing these benefits and any barriers to implementation.
3 Is the linking of industrial relations and occupational health and safety something that should be avoided?
4 Identify and evaluate the strengths and weaknesses of different sources of worker involvement in OHS. Suggest specific ways in which governments, unions, employers and others may improve the effectiveness of worker involvement.

FURTHER READING

Gunningham, N. (2008), 'Occupational health and safety, worker participation and the mining industry in a changing world', *Economic and Industrial Democracy*, **29**(3): 336–61.

Johnstone, R., Quinlan, M. and Walters, D. (2005), 'Statutory occupational health and safety workplace arrangements for the modern labour market', *Journal of Industrial Relations*, **47**(1): 93–116.

Nichols, T., Walters, D. and Tasiran, A. (2008), 'Trade unions, institutional mediation and industrial safety: evidence from the UK', *Journal of Industrial Relations*, **49**(2): 211–25.

Quinlan, M. (1993), 'The industrial relations of occupational health and safety', in Quinlan, M. (ed.), *Work and Health*, Melbourne, Macmillan: 140–69.

Walters, D. and Nichols, T. (2007), *Worker Representation and Workplace Health and Safety*, Palgrave Macmillan, Basingstoke.

Weil, D. (1999), 'Are mandated health and safety committees substitutes for or supplements to labor unions?', *Industrial & Labor Relations Review*, **52**(3): 339–60.

10

Approaches to managing occupational health and safety

Introduction

THIS chapter provides an overview of the strategies currently being applied to the management of occupational health and safety (OHS) at enterprise level, including an evaluation of recent developments in the area. It then discusses a number of critical issues that should be considered in the development of an occupational health and safety program. The chapter concludes with an attempt to describe policies and organisational structures that can be employed to promote effective and genuinely participatory health and safety management.

There is a plethora of OHS prevention and intervention programs and approaches ranging from Bird and Germain's work on loss control and rating systems commencing in the 1960s to best practice, zero harm, behaviour-based safety, risk-management and health and productivity management approaches. OHS legislation in Australia and New Zealand incorporates many of the principles of conventional OHS prevention and intervention programs. Ideally the management of OHS should aim at the absolute minimisation of illness and injury at work. However, as we have seen, a number of competing explanations of occupational injury and illness suggest quite different strategies for their minimisation. Most focus upon unsafe behaviour and poor design of the physical work environment as the major causal variables. Management strategies based on these explanations can be roughly divided into three groups. The first group is broadly concerned with modification of the physical working environment, such as the provision of machine guarding or the containment of toxic substances. The second group is concerned with the medical and biological condition of individual workers and includes the screening, monitoring and treatment strategies aimed at identifying workers who are susceptible to illness and treating those who succumb to it. The third group is concerned with changing workers' behaviour and includes a variety of educational and behaviour modification strategies. These strategies are strongly based on expert models and management must generally enlist the services of specialist professionals to both plan and implement them.

A final set of strategies addresses broader organisational determinants of ill health and injury and is concerned with the establishment of organisational structures to deal with health and safety issues. Some of these structures facilitate genuine participation by workers in policy formulation and the implementation of management programs, an approach that is discouraged by the expert models employed in the first three groups of strategies. Table 10.1 presents a summary of the major strategies in each of the four categories. We shall now briefly discuss the strategies in each category.

Table 10.1   Major occupational health and safety management strategies

Environmental modification and monitoring	Individual screening and monitoring	Individual behaviour change	Organisational strategies
Hazard identification Engineering controls Ergonomic intervention Protective clothing and equipment Environmental monitoring Risk assessment	Pre-employment examinations Return-to-work examinations Medical monitoring Biological monitoring Alcohol and other drug screening	Health and safety education Training Behaviour modification Administrative controls (SWP and JSA) Stress management	Workplace committees and consultation Health surveys and audits Work reorganisation Workplace health promotion and on-site OHS centres OHS management systems Risk management

Environmental modification and monitoring

A number of OHS interventions are aimed at altering the physical working environment in order to make it less hazardous. Many of the solutions provided by engineers, ergonomists and occupational hygienists fall into this category, such as machine guarding, source isolation or removal, and workstation redesign. These interventions generally share a strong preventative orientation and often focus on linking OHS interventions with increasing productivity (e.g. Sanders and McCormick; 1987; Simpson, 1990; Oxenburgh, 1991; MacLeod, 1995; Frick, 1997; Shikdar and Sawaqed, 2003; Lahiri et al., 2005). As we have already discussed these interventions in earlier chapters this section will primarily focus on issues that arise during their implementation.

The strategies in this category include hazard identification, engineering controls, many ergonomic interventions, and the use of protective clothing and equipment. Hazard identification, an important component of Australian and New Zealand OHS legislation, involves breaking down the overall technology of the organisation into its component processes and specifying the hazards associated with each (Cater and Smith, 2006). Once the hazards are identified, the level of risk associated with each one is assessed (see below). The outcome of an effective hazard identification or hazard surveillance should result in action to reduce harmful exposure in the workplace and should complement health monitoring or surveillance (Koh and Aw, 2003). Engineering controls are one means of minimising the impact of known risks. They are designed to prevent disease and injury by the modification of tools, equipment, and physical processes. They are generally concerned with physical hazards (such as noise, heat, vibration, dangerous machinery, etc.), chemical fumes, biohazards, and dusts and fibres. They achieve control by removing, isolating or enclosing hazards or by interrupting the pathways through which dangerous by-products are transferred to the worker.

An alternative to engineering and administrative controls (see below) is personal protective equipment (PPE) which is designed to protect the worker from hazards in their environment. Personal protective equipments (PPE) consists of clothing items such as gloves, overalls, helmets, and boots as well as protective equipment such as respirators, goggles, earmuffs, and welder's masks. As was noted earlier, occupational hygienists rightly regard PPE as significantly inferior to engineering and other controls and consider that it should be used only on a temporary protective basis or as a measure of last resort. This is because PPE does nothing to eliminate or reduce the presence of the hazard, cannot always provide complete protection, can be cumbersome and uncomfortable, and is a source of problems in its own right (as in cases where the wearing of earmuffs or plugs hinder communication). For example, a helmet will only protect against relatively small/light falling objects and will do nothing to protect a miner from rocks that burst horizontally from walls or the face due to pressure. Similarly, a study of the use of safety footwear by women across a range of Australian industries found many wearers believed the footwear caused problems with their feet. They also reported that the '… hot, inflexible soles impeded specific work tasks and some women stated that the steel caps pressed on their toes' (Marr, 1991: 437). In a few fortunately exceptional cases some types of purported PPE have proved useless, a notable example being back belts for lifting (Thomas et al., 1999)—and quite distinct from the positive role played by safety belts. Keeping these qualifications in mind, PPE can still perform a critical adjunct role, especially in high-hazard workplaces (such as the wearing of high-visibility vests in road transport, warehouses and on construction sites and the use of helmets and foot protection in mining and construction) and for emergency workers such as the police, SES and firefighters.

The effective use of PPE requires careful hazard assessment, determination of ergonomic and other task constraints, careful selection (and a range of products in the case of hearing protection as some workers will find plugs more comfortable than muffs), training/motivation, surveillance of compliance and maintenance of equipment. Where PPE is essential, quality counts and continuous improvement should be sought. For example, a US study (Prezant et al., 1999) found the introduction of improved firefighting protective uniforms had a significant impact on the incidence and severity of burn injuries. A similar point can be made with regard to heat- and chemical-resistant clothing (and compressed breathing apparatus) used by emergency workers. The PPE option is more complex and expensive than it may first appear and it is not uncommon for companies to omit or inadequately implement some of the points relating to quality, a selection of options, maintenance, etc. just mentioned. Workers are more likely to be persuaded of the importance of PPE where employers undertake other measures indicative of a strong interest in OHS. On the other hand, incentive-based payments/production deadlines and protective equipment that inhibits the work process can discourage PPE use (or effective use such as the failure to anchor safety harnesses).

Ergonomic interventions are aimed at designing the physical working environment and work processes to fit the capacities of workers (Davis, 1988). Ergonomists design tools, equipment and workstations to comply with standards derived from extensive research on the bodily dimensions (see also anthropometry), strength and physical movements of workers. These standards provide a basis on which to design items such as hand tools and the controls on machinery for maximum compatibility with human capabilities. Ergonomic design of workstations takes into account a wide range of factors, including the positioning of controls, the spatial relationship between components, and the forces required to operate controls. In the case of the computer workstation, for example, ergonomists attempt to achieve the optimal spatial and optical relationship between all components including the chair, desk, keyboard, monitor and source document. Allowance must then be made for adjustment to allow for differences in the physical size between workers. Ergonomists may also provide advice on suitable modifications to the environment surrounding the workstation, including optimal levels of light, noise, ventilation and temperature. Changes to ramps, doorways and corridors may also be recommended to facilitate safe movement around the workstation. Thorough ergonomic redesign should ideally result in health and safety hazards being eliminated from the workplace. Tools and equipment should be designed for efficient use, controls should be well placed and the forces required to operate them should be within safe limits. Workstation components should be in optimal spatial relationship to each other and there should be adequate space for work tasks and movement of materials. Lighting, ventilation, noise and temperature should be at appropriate levels.

As discussed in chapters 2–4, ergonomic interventions do not simply entail changes to workplace design but also changes to work organisation, although the latter tends to be restricted in scope, such as recommending limits to particular tasks, rest breaks and exercise. As with a number of expert areas the adoption of particular interventions is not always well-informed by the evidence. For example, a review of research on interventions to prevent musculoskeletal disorders among computer users (Brewer et al., 2006) found that evidence did not support the effectiveness of workstation adjustment, rest breaks and exercise—responses commonly adopted by management—but did point to a positive effect from alternative pointing devices.

The narrow application of environmental interventions has significant limitations of which managers should be aware. Their scientific and technical nature tends to mystify the causes of injury for most workers and managers, encouraging them to relinquish much control over health and safety management. The expert approach favoured by most professionals in the area further discourages the active participation of the workers, and often management, in the diagnosis of problems and the development and implementation of solutions. Consequently, many interventions fail to address, let alone resolve, major threats to health and safety perceived by workers and managers. Important social and behavioural causes of injury and illness are frequently left unaddressed. Ergonomic redesign of equipment and workstations, for example, may help to reduce the pain and discomfort of workers, but it cannot overcome fundamental problems with the organisation of work. Redesigning workstations may have only marginal effects at best (Brewer et al., 2006) if factors such as work rates and job design are not adequately addressed.

Further, as stated above, ergonomic solutions are frequently linked with the employers' desire to increase productivity, often overlooking the negative outcomes for workers. MacLeod (1995: 19) provides some insight into the reasons why ergonomists have been more active in this area and why they have been more successful in engaging with the business community over the links between OHS and productivity than professionals in other fields of OHS:

> Improving the fit between humans and tools inherently means a more effective match. Good ergonomic improvements often result in better ways of performing a task. An ergonomically designed workplace (or product) is a more productive workplace (or product). Not exceeding human capabilities does not mean reducing output or doing less. On the contrary, good design permits more output with less human effort.

Based on his recent study, James (2006), however, observes that while exposure to hazards associated with machinery and manual handling are being reduced, other risks associated with increases in labour productivity are on the rise. He continues:

> The fact that over half of these new cases of work-related ill health stem from … stress, depression and anxiety, and musculoskeletal disorders, also raises an important issue of policy, particularly when account is taken of the further fact that, against a background of increasing work intensity and declining worker discretion, the prevalence rate for stress and related conditions has recently grown substantially … It also further suggests, given the way in which these conditions are intimately connected to workload levels and the nature of work tasks, that the achievement of reductions of this type will require employers to be placed under much greater pressure to design work tasks and establish workloads that are not detrimental to worker health. (James, 2006: 11)

Thus, it would appear that efforts to increase productivity through ergonomic interventions can have contradictory results.

Many environmental strategies rely heavily on risk assessment procedures which provide estimates of the likelihood and impact that a particular injury or illness will arise in the workplace (Knight, 2002; Glendon et al., 2006). While it is important to know whether a toxic substance or work practice has the potential to cause harm, it is equally important to know the probability of that harm occurring. Risk assessment, a key component of risk management, provides a process for estimating the probability that a specified undesirable outcome will result from a specific duration of exposure to a specific hazard. It can be applied to both the probability of harm to individuals as the result of exposure to particular hazards and to the likelihood of particular hazardous events occurring. Risk assessment techniques can be used to analyse the safety performance of a department or organisation over time using its past performance as a baseline. The relative health and safety performance of different departments or organisations in controlling similar hazards can also be compared. This information can then be used to direct attention to problem areas.

When used carefully, and with due consideration to its limitations, risk assessment provides an important aid to decision making. It is important, however, to avoid allowing the apparent objectivity of figures produced by risk assessment to obscure their uncertain and largely subjective nature (see Pearce, Checkoway and Kriebel, 2007, for a critique of assessment and control selection bias). They are often based on very loose definitions of both the 'doses' of hazards absorbed by workers and the subsequent 'effects'. Moreover, the standards used to determine the permissible levels of exposure, namely 'threshold limit values' (TLVs) and 'biological exposure indices' (BEIs), should also be treated with caution as there are no guarantees that the risk assessment of substances and the analytical methods used are reliable or accurate (see below). That is, doses are frequently measured in terms of environmental exposures, such as the concentration of asbestos fibres in the air, which do not accurately measure the amount of the substance absorbed by the worker. In addition, the effects of exposure are often inadequately differentiated in terms of whether they are biological or health effects, and whether they are short-term or long-term. However, there are obviously important differences between biological disturbances without clinical effects, immediate health effects, longer-term health effects and behavioural effects. Exposure standards usually take no account of the long-term effects of work at maximum exposure limits. It is also widely assumed that workers are only exposed to one hazard at a time and that short-term effects are reversible. For example, a cumulative dose–effect curve for noise exposure indicates that the legislative standard of 85 dBA (current in Australia and many other countries) can be expected to result in hearing damage for many workers. Pearce et al. (2007: 563) also warn that risk assessments are flawed if the wrong group of workers is examined for exposure to hazards. For example, if white-collar workers are more likely to be selected for (or participate in) a study than manual workers who have had the greater exposure, then the results will be biased.

Further, no effort is generally made to directly link exposure standards to clear dose–effect relationships, and managers widely assume that adherence to the standards will result in workers being protected from any adverse effects. The reality is quite different. That is, the hazards (such as a chemical compound) depend not only on toxicity, but also on the levels of exposure. A good illustration of this is the controversy surrounding the contamination of workers of the phenoxy herbicide 2,4,5-T. In New Zealand this herbicide was manufactured at the Ivon Watkins-Dow plant in New Plymouth until 1987 when production ceased, and during the last few years of its production the Ivon Watkins-Dow factory was the last in the world to still be producing 2,4,5-T (Purnell et al., 2006; Burns et al., 2005). It is well established in animal studies that tetrachlorodibenzodioxin (TCDD) exposure in high doses can cause birth defects and cancer. Epidemiological studies of workers with very high exposures have also clearly demonstrated increased cancer risks. Accordingly, TCDD was classified as a proven human carcinogen by the World Health Organization's International Agency for Research on Cancer (IARC) in 1997 (Pearce, 2006: 7). However, in New Zealand and Australia there have been bitter arguments between, on one hand, workers and their families and, on the other hand, the employers and government agencies over whether or not TCDD can cause detectable numbers of cancer cases or other health effects in workers with moderate levels of exposure, and/or in members of the general public with low levels of exposure. The scientific debate, and the public controversy, has not been helped by the neglect of the issue by various government agencies, particularly in the 1980s when the tendency was to dismiss the risks as 'trivial' or 'unproven' (Pearce, 2006: 7).

Probably the most contentious aspect of risk assessment is the decision concerning what constitutes an 'acceptable risk' of illness or injury. Even though the setting of exposure standards is strongly reliant on technical data, the final specification of a 'safe' or 'acceptable' exposure limit involves a value judgment which cannot be satisfactorily resolved on scientific grounds alone (Mathews, 1993; Harrison, 1986; Burgess-Limerick, 2003 for a detailed outline of issues surrounding 'acceptable risk' in Australian workplaces). Consequently, it is vitally important that the technical and scientific task of identifying, analysing and measuring risks is clearly separated from the broader social task of judging the acceptability of particular risk levels. The final designation of an acceptable risk level should emanate from a social and political process involving governments, employers, unions, health professionals and the wider community. Social decision processes should consider the rights of workers not to be exposed to unnecessary pain and suffering, likely levels of pain and suffering, potential social costs inflicted on the families of affected workers and estimated demand for medical and social services to care for affected workers and their families. These individual and community costs are balanced against the costs to industry of reducing exposure levels. If exposure standards are too stringent, the costs may result in firms being forced to close down and workers being laid off. Ultimately, the costs of unemployment have to be weighed against those of ill health, at least in the short term. Complex value judgments of this nature should not be made without the involvement of all major interest groups. Tripartite forums involving governments, employers and unions provide some level of assurance that these important decisions are not controlled by powerful vested interests. Lang Hancock's celebrated statement that 'you can't make an omelette without breaking eggs' (Hills, 1989: 172), when referring to the victims of asbestos at Wittenoom, provides a graphic illustration of the extreme views that must not be allowed to dominate debate concerning occupational exposure standards.

Clearly, the exposure standards (e.g. TLVs and BEIs) which provide managers with reference points for environmental monitoring and intervention, such as 'permissible exposure limits' or 'maximum acceptable concentrations', are not the objective figures that they may appear to be at first glance. Managers should be especially cautious about accepting as 'objective' the determinations of risk supplied entirely by technical experts. These determinations rely to a significant degree on the subjective perceptions and judgments of professionals whose training and experience may lead them to see problems and solutions in a different way to other groups who have a legitimate role in the setting of safety standards.

Wherever possible, the effectiveness of engineering controls in protecting workers from toxic exposure should be assessed by environmental monitoring. Certainly, exposure standards provide little protection to workers if the workplace is not regularly monitored to ensure compliance. The aim of environmental monitoring is to obtain measurements that are as close as possible to the true total exposure of workers to a specific hazard (Harrison, 1986). It can be used for radiant fields, such as noise and various forms of radiation, and airborne contaminants, including gases, vapours, mists and dusts.

A number of factors affect the accuracy of environmental monitoring, particularly the location of sampling devices and the timing and duration of sampling. Environmental samples can be taken from two types of source: fixed sampling devices located somewhere within the workplace, or personal sampling devices which are attached to, or closely follow, the worker being monitored (Harrison, 1986). Often the concentration of the hazard being measured can vary substantially within the workplace and in these circumstances personal sampling devices are likely to be more accurate in assessing true exposure. The timing and duration of sampling are also critical and must be matched to the process concerned. Sampling may be continuous, periodic or occasional and analysis of samples may be immediate or delayed (Heederik and Rooy, 2008). Continuous monitoring provides the most information about exposure, and should generally continue through at least one complete production cycle. If the substance being monitored presents an immediate threat to life, sampling should be continuous and analysis should be automatic and immediate, setting off alarms when the exposure level exceeds a clearly defined threshold.

Individual screening and monitoring

In this section we shall examine strategies used to assess and monitor the physical health of individual workers, namely screening and monitoring, both of which are very widely used occupational health management strategies. The rationale for medical screening and monitoring is to detect adverse health effects resulting from occupational exposures at as early a stage as possible, so that appropriate preventive measures can be instituted promptly. More precisely, screening procedures are principally aimed at identifying workers who are susceptible to occupational hazards before they enter the workplace, while monitoring involves regular tests and examinations intended to detect biological or medical evidence of exposure to toxins or deteriorating physical health. Monitoring of workers for exposure is also a fundamental part of Australian and New Zealand health and safety legislation. Screening and monitoring data can be used to identify trends or emerging patterns in workplace hazards and illnesses.

Medical screening and monitoring can take a variety of forms, from pre-employment health screening or periodic clinical assessments of individuals to public health reviews on the health status of groups of workers (Koh and Aw, 2003: 706). In order to be effective, however, screening and monitoring have to be followed by preventive action and evaluation of the effectiveness of the intervention (Sorgdrager, 2004).

Screening, pre-employment and return to work examinations

Medical screening and monitoring do not necessarily involve full clinical examinations. Some require as little as the completion of a simple questionnaire (Bradshaw et al., 2003; Mortelmans, 2008) while others involve a selected medical examination supplemented by specific tests, such as lung function tests. The less-frequently used screenings are full clinical examinations, including physiological and biochemical tests. The less-extensive assessments can often be carried out by a trained occupational health nurse, who may only need to seek assistance when the worker does not satisfy established criteria (Kho and Aw, 2003). A consultant physician may then interview or examine the worker.

The most common form of screening is the *pre-employment* which is used to determine the level of fitness of applicants. Pre-employment examinations should be treated only as an evaluation of the individual's capacity to work without risk to their own or others' health and safety and should be carried out to prevent future health and safety risk for the worker or candidate, co-workers and the public (Bateman and Finlay, 2002; Bonanni et al., 2004; Serra et al., 2007). For example, firefighters may be required to meet explicit strength and fitness requirements, and epileptics may screen out of construction work at heights (Sluiter and Frings-Dresen, 2007). In all cases the characteristics or conditions that absolutely exclude workers from doing a particular job should be clearly defined. The question is, however, which pre-employment methods are most effective? In an attempt to resolve this issue, Moshe et al. (2008) compared three methods of medical screening of workers: 1) examination by an occupational physician; 2) examination by a general practitioner whose medical records were subsequently evaluated by an occupational physician; and 3) the applicant filled out an occupational health questionnaire which was evaluated by an occupational physician. They concluded that a self-administered health questionnaire evaluated by an occupational physician as pre-employment assessment was more efficient and less costly than previously used protocols which included a physical examination and laboratory tests performed for each applicant. In particular, it was the most preferred method of pre-employment evaluation for non-hazardous occupations (Moshe et al., 2008).

Health screening, including pre-employment screening, raises a number of ethical as well as practical issues. Medical testing is by no means unproblematic, even in relation to well-known complaints, such as colour vision or illicit substance use, and the tests themselves are often inadequate as a guide to overall employment suitability (see, for example, Sorgdrager et al., 2004; Bailey, 2008). Advances in knowledge in recent years have expanded the scope for genetic testing of workers with regard to predisposition for illness or a family history of particular illnesses. While there may be legitimate grounds for genetic testing in specialised circumstances (Palmer et al., 2004), the growing use of this form of testing, and its potential misuse, has been a source of controversy and a matter for legal intervention (see Andrews and Jaeger, 1991; Holtzman, 1996; Murray et al., 2001; Palmer et al., 2004). For example, in the US, the House of Representatives in 2007 held a hearing on a bill that would ban companies from using genetic information to make employment decisions (Schoeff, 2007). Schulte (2007) also notes that although increasingly workplace exposures are being controlled to lower concentrations, workers with susceptible genetic profiles may still be at unacceptably high risk. There is a broad range of published evidence, for example, showing that genetic polymorphisms can lead to differential occupational disease risks in exposed workers (see Schulte, 2007). From an OHS perspective, however, the main danger is that genetic screening can divert attention from the need to remedy exposures at source in the workplace. As Palmer et al. (2004: 452) argue, in sensitive areas such as genetic testing, the onus should be on the employer to justify plans for pre-placement screening.

Another contentious area of health screening is with regard to workers with infectious diseases such as HIV-AIDS and hepatitis (Botes and Otto, 2003). Movements of workers from countries or locations with different exposure levels to infectious disease may bring with it new risks, as in the case of immigrant workers from countries with endemic tuberculosis who have been employed extensively in the US poultry industry (Kim et al., 2003; Gulati et al., 2005). This aspect of the international movement of workers has often been addressed in only a fragmented fashion and is especially problematic in the case of undocumented/illegal immigrants and temporary workers (backpackers, tourists and guest workers). While exclusion from the workplace is sometimes required, in the vast majority of cases the situation can be addressed through the provision of adequate protocols. Ethical and non-discriminatory health surveillance measures require careful planning and appropriate interventions to manage exposures (Kim et al., 2003).

In an editorial reviewing findings on the ethical use of genetic information in the workplace, Geppert and Roberts (2005: 518) stated that genetic testing should be used only with worker consent, workers should control access to the information, testing is justified only when the information is required to protect the worker or a third party and genetic testing should not be used to shift responsibility for a healthy working environment from the employer to the employee. These observations provide an ethical framework to guide the use of pre-employment screening and return to work assessments more generally.

As noted in chapter 7, one of the problems here is a lack of regulatory guidance in Australia, New Zealand and other countries in relation to the use of pre-employment and other forms of health screening as well as the complex interaction between OHS, anti-discrimination and privacy law (Rasmussen and Lamm, 2002). There is evidence that pre-employment screenings are used to discriminate against job applicants (Bateman and Finlay, 2002). In New Zealand just under half of all complaints to the Human Rights Commission concerned discrimination arising from pre-employment screening processes, and a quarter of all employment-related complaints were as a result of being discriminated against on the basis of disability (Human Rights Commission, 2008). In Australia, claims of discrimination on the basis of pre-employment screening or disability are also common.

It is also common for organisations to require workers to satisfactorily complete a medical examination before returning to work after illness or injury. Return-to-work medicals provide a means by which to assess whether workers have recovered sufficiently from illness or injury to resume their work without risking their own health and wellbeing or that of other workers (MacKenzie et al., 1998; Staal et al., 2003; Kapoor, et al., 2006; Holtslag et al., 2007). For example, where workers have suffered from an infectious disease such as hepatitis, it is clearly important that they do not return to work too early and risk the health of other workers. If workers are not allowed to return to work on medical grounds, employers should be able to demonstrate that the nature of the work made a risk to their health, or that of others, inevitable. They should also be able to demonstrate that it is not practicable to modify the work environment or the task to eliminate the risk.

Finally, there are problems with inconsistency in the application of testing and there is evidence of wide disparities of practice not only in a single employer but also among employers in closely related activities (Lanyon and Goodstein, 2004). Moreover, there is a concern that pre-employment tests have not been standardised and that there is a lack of predictive validity data on the selection measures (Piotrowski and Armstrong, 2006). In short, testing should be selective, consistent and, as far as possible, non-exclusionary.

Medical and biological monitoring

There are two main reasons why medical and biological monitoring are applied in work situations: first, where the presence of the hazard is essential or inherent to the work process, and no other feasible alternatives are available, and second, if the causal relation between the exposure and the health effect is not well defined, as in exposure to sensitisers and carcinogens (Koh and Aw, 2003; Larsen et al., 2007). Koh and Aw (2003: 706) note that there may be an ethical dilemma involved in considering what constitutes an essential part of an industrial process versus the extent of acceptable risk to those who have to be exposed in the course of their work. Moreover, as stated above, in many countries, periodic medical and biological monitoring are statutory requirements for workers exposed to prescribed hazards. For example, in Australia and New Zealand standards require employers to provide employees with access to medical screening examinations when they are exposed to designated substances.

Although medical and biological monitoring have similar purposes, there are differences. Medical monitoring involves regular examinations intended to detect the clinical symptoms of occupational illness and disease. A number of different sources of information may be used for this purpose, including general clinical examinations, allergy tests, X-rays, lung function tests, hearing and eye tests and tests of cellular abnormalities (Koh and Aw, 2003). For example, X-rays may be used to check for signs of scarring of the lungs among workers previously exposed to dust or asbestos or to check for clubbing of the fingers (acro-osteolysis) among workers previously exposed to vinyl chloride. Of course, although workers may have been exposed to high levels of these hazards in the past, environmental containment and monitoring should now ensure that these exposures no longer occur. In any case, lung function tests may provide a less invasive means of testing for lung damage arising from dusts and fibres (Mastrangelo et al., 2008). These tests are designed to test variables including lung volume, ventilatory capacity (the ability to move air in and out of the lungs) and the gas-transfer performance.

Biological monitoring is performed to assess the level of specific toxins, or their by-products, in the body or to detect structural or functional effects of exposure to toxins (refer to Koh and Aw, 2003 for a more detailed explanation). The intention is to detect abnormalities that precede disease while there is a possibility that their effects can be reversed, rather than to identify overt symptoms of disease (Mathews, 1993). For example, regular monitoring of blood lead levels may detect lead exposure before symptoms of lead poisoning appear, facilitating early intervention (Taylor et al., 2007). The measurement of the substance, or a metabolic by-product, may be achieved by analysing samples of blood, urine, nails, hair and exhaled air. Medical and biological baselines should be established at pre-employment examinations to provide a means of assessing whether deterioration has occurred as a result of occupational exposures. The common practice of establishing baselines after the worker has been on the job for a period of time should be avoided, especially in the case of variables that may deteriorate rapidly, such as hearing (Mathews, 1993: 476).

Biological monitoring can potentially provide a more accurate index of exposure than environmental monitoring, but it has practical and ethical limitations (see Tomicic and Droz, 2008). It is likely to be more accurate than environmental monitoring in assessing exposure to hazards because all routes of exposure are accounted for and uncertainties regarding rates of absorption, biotransformation, retention and excretion are avoided. It also provides an index of total exposure that includes both occupational and non-occupation exposures. Unfortunately, several difficult preconditions must be met if biological monitoring is to be a viable proposition (Purnell et al., 2005). An adequately sensitive and specific biological indicator of exposure must be known, and reliable and sufficiently sensitive analytic methods for detecting the indicator must exist. Samples for analysis must be obtainable without imposing unreasonable danger, inconvenience or discomfort on the workers involved. As yet, these preconditions have been met for few substances.

Even if these technical problems can be solved, there are more general concerns with biological monitoring. It relies upon recognised exposure standards, or 'biological limit values', as a signal to take action. As we have previously pointed out, these exposure limits are frequently decided as much by political and industrial negotiation as by objective scientific research. Consequently, they partially reflect the power balance between various vested interest groups. The interpretation of abnormal results is also subject to a number of other uncertainties (Burgess-Limerick, 2003). The results may be unreliable due to poor quality control in the analytic process, and they may reflect changes that are occupational or non-occupational in origin. It may also be quite normal for some individuals to be outside the normal range on some tests. There are also ethical problems with compulsory biological testing. Further, heavy dependence on this form of monitoring can lead to an undue emphasis on the biological effects of exposure, and the removal of individual workers from the source of the problem, instead of direct reduction of environmental risks.

As is the case with screening, regulatory requirements for health surveillance vary widely between countries and are, at present, quite limited in Australia and New Zealand. Gaps in surveillance may only become apparent in the most extreme cases. For example, Lin et al. (2005) describe the case of a young female laboratory worker in Taiwan whose exposure to dangerous levels of chloroform was only discovered when her family consulted the workplace material safety data sheet after she was admitted to hospital (in a coma) suffering acute hepatic encephalopathy. Subsequent air sampling indicated she had been exposed to chloroform concentrations over 15 parts per million for two weeks. Even where such requirements exist, available evidence indicates implementation is poor. A study in the US by Silverstein (1994: 283–95) identified 21 OSHA standards requiring some form of surveillance but found problems in relation to quality control and scope. A more recent study of health surveillance of exposure to hazardous substances in the UK semiconductor industry (Kinoulty and Williams, 2006: 100) found surveillance was reactive (even where there was specialist occupational health input) and poorly targeted 'with limited interpretation and feedback to management'.

Alcohol and other drug surveillance

One area of individual health screening that warrants particular attention is the issue of alcohol and other drug surveillance. The level of drug surveillance by employers has grown over the past 20 years and is now relatively widespread in the US (*Workers' Comp Insider*, 11 January 2005; Stump, 2008) and common in hazardous industries such as mining in Australia. Since the 1980s the issue of drug use in the workplace has attracted prominent concern, mainly among employers/business groups and the media (though some unions have also become more active in this area, such as the Transport Workers Union). The public debate has often entailed repeated claims that drug use is a major cause of injury and lost productivity along with calls for rigorous surveillance regimes including random drug testing of workers. In some countries, regulations mandating drug testing of workers in hazardous industries or those where there are concerns over public safety have become more common. In the US, for example, Department of Transport regulations have long required companies to undertake mandatory drug testing of truck drivers they employ. More recently, the Executive Order 12564 on the Drug Free Federal Workplace was introduced mandating each executive agency to establish a program to test for drug use by federal employees in 'sensitive' positions (Levine and Rennie, 2004).

Issues surrounding drug and alcohol screening are complex (see Evans et al., 2004; Holland et al., 2005; Cowan et al., 2005). However, while evidence suggests drug use is a major problem in particular industries, such as long-haul trucking and prostitution (Williamson, 2007), more general claims about the extent of alcohol and illicit drug use and its connection to serious injuries in the workplace are frequently exaggerated. According to International Labour Organization (ILO) estimates, between 3 and 15% of fatal work accidents in Australia are related to drug and alcohol use (cited in Holland et al., 2005: 327) and even these figures must be treated with caution. The problem is that there have been very few large-scale surveys on drug use within the workforce (see Hoffmann and Larison, 1999; SAMHSA, 1999; French, Roebuck and Alexandre, 2004; George, 2005; Frone, 2006; Carpenter, 2007); most studies are small-scale surveys (limited sample or a single site) that suffer from a number of methodological problems. Holland et al. (2005) also note that, in Australia, the comparatively few studies undertaken have largely focused on illicit drug use in healthcare and road transport. In the UK, however, there have been two independent government reviews on drug testing in the workplace (see Evans et al., 2004; Cowan et al., 2005). The Report of the Independent Inquiry into Drug Testing at Work (2004: 2002), chaired by Ruth Evans, concluded that for the majority of businesses, investment in management training and systems is likely to have a more beneficial impact on safety, performance and productivity than the introduction of drug testing at work.

Despite a plethora of oft-quoted figures, the evidence of a connection between drug use and workplace is fragmented (and mainly deals with alcohol) and suggestive rather than compelling (see Holland et al., 2005; Carpenter, 2007). In their review of the literature, Hutcheson et al. (1995: 14) and later Holland et al. (2005) identify a number of methodological and other problems and offer the tentative conclusion that 'alcohol does appear to be implicated in a number of accidents'. The only relatively reliable evidence on a connection between drug use and workplace health relates to fatal injuries (see those cited above, gathered via autopsies). Even here other factors may have contributed to death. In their study, Berry et al. (2007: 1399) found that risky drinking occurred at least occasionally in 44% of Australian workers. Workers in the hospitality, agriculture, manufacturing, construction and retail industries, workers in blue-collar occupations and young workers were identified as at-risk subgroups. The authors also note that their data provides evidence that patterns of consumption differ between occupational and industry groups, and highlights the pressing need to develop policies and prevention and intervention strategies to reduce harmful alcohol use in Australia, particularly among young adults. In sum, alcohol is an important contributor to serious work injuries in some industries, but arguably less important than other causal factors (such as employment status/subcontracting, irregular working hours and fatigue), a number of which attract far less media/public and management attention (see Jones et al. 2003).

Currently, testing for common drugs and alcohol in the workplace is usually undertaken as a two-step process. The first step normally involves a simple and inexpensive screening test while the second step is a more specific and definitive identification test (called a confirmatory analysis). The analytical techniques used for drug detection also depend on the chemical and physical properties of each substance or its breakdown products. In their technical report, Cowan et al. (2005: 4) state that the time spans over which drugs can be detected in different tissues may be influenced by a number of factors. These include the state of health of an individual, presence of disease, age, the properties of the drug and its distribution within the body, the quantity of drug taken, whether drug intake involved single or chronic dosing and the sensitivity of the analytical methods used. Consequently, there is no universal test that can be applied to detect the presence of a drug and it is necessary to employ a range of different tests for different drugs. Cowan et al. (2005: 32) argue that although there has been a reliance on urine testing as it is easier to collect, blood, oral fluid, sweat and hair are now being used with increasing frequency as a consequence of improvements in analytical technology.

The use of drug testing, however, has raised a number of critical issues. First, there has been considerable debate over the accuracy (including quality control) and scientific validity of various forms of workplace drug testing, with the general consensus of a series of studies being that testing is a complex and problematic process (Evans, 2004; Cowan, 2005). Second, there is mounting US and UK evidence that drug testing has little positive impact on prevention and rehabilitation (Kesselring and Pittman, 2002; Wickizer et al., 2004). In their review, Evans et al. (2004) reach a similar conclusion and make the additional point that a comprehensive and carefully administered drug-testing program can be extremely costly to implement. Third, the implementation of a drug-testing regime raises a series of legal issues in relation to privacy, disability and discrimination/equal employment opportunity. Drug testing of workers has been the subject of strenuous debate and legal action both in Australia and New Zealand, as well as overseas (for example, see BHP Iron Ore Pty Ltd v. Construction, Mining, Energy, Timberyards, Sawmills and Woodworkers Union West Australian (WA) Branch, West Australian Industrial Relations Commission, (WAIRC) 130, 19 June (1998) and NZ Amalgamated Engineering Printing and Manufacturing Union Incorporated v Air New Zealand, Judgment Number: AC 22/04 File Number: ARC 42/03, Employment Court (2004)).

Fourth, there is an overlap between these legal questions and ethical issues, including the rights of the individual as well as the potential for arbitrary or improper use of testing that has drawn attention from government bodies in Australia, New Zealand and overseas. Rasmussen and Lamm (2002) noted a trend in New Zealand whereby employers are implementing surveillance and drug-testing regimes as health and safety measures in order to offset the likelihood that they will be prosecuted if a worker is injured while under the influence of drugs or alcohol, or observed to have committed a hazardous act. However, unions state that drug testing and surveillance contravene the principles and the tenets of the Privacy Act 1993. Unions and workers argue that, on the one hand, employers, particularly those in the health sector, are invoking the principles of the Privacy Act and are reluctant to divulge information pertinent to workers' health and safety, yet on the other hand, they are ignoring the Privacy Act when implementing drug-testing and employee surveillance schemes to mitigate health and safety fines. Fifth, as the Evans report (2004) clearly shows, implementing drug testing has had damaging effects on worker morale and employment relationships. In Australia, New Zealand and elsewhere, unions have been sceptical about widespread drug testing, arguing that testing should only occur in situations where there is a clearly established risk and involving agreed procedures (see Labor Council of NSW, 1995; Holland et al., 2005). Even then, testing should be just one part of a comprehensive program that addresses the entire workplace (and working environment) and treats alcohol and substance abuse as an illness, providing information, counselling and other support for workers, with punitive measures being left as a final resort.

As the foregoing suggests, a number of ethical and practical judgments need to be made if workplace drug testing is to be justified and effective. This includes assessing the costs of a testing program and the threats posed to workers, customers, the organisation and the community. Due consideration also needs to be given to managing the consequences of positive test results and providing an appropriate mixture of support and last-resort sanctions. The reasons underpinning drug use are complex and treating it only as a behavioural failing is unlikely to bear positive results. Some companies have adopted a comprehensive approach which is applied with commendable restraint and discretion while others use it in a punitive and blame-shifting sense even if the conditions of work (such as fatigue and excessive hours) are a causal factor promoting drug use. Unfortunately, we have almost no evidence on the scope, nature and implementation of drug testing and management regimes. In terms of managing drug use, a mixture of temporary workplace exclusion, counselling and employee assistance programs with termination in the case of repeated 'offences' appear common. As recently noted by the Alcohol and Drugs Council of Australia (*CCH OHS Alert* 24 April 2009), if drug use is to be genuinely treated as an illness then serious consideration needs to be given to the provision of appropriate treatment by suitably trained health providers. Employee assistance programs, or EAPs, are used as a human resource management technique for managing individual worker problems that may affect the enterprise, and their use in relation to alcohol or substance abuse has been endorsed in both Australia and New Zealand (see Hansen, 2004). However, like drug testing, while EAPs may have a role to play they address symptoms rather than the underlying problem and are open to being used in a manipulative and unethical fashion.

The last point is critical. A number of studies have identified work-related stress, irregular or late shifts and other job characteristics as causal factors in alcohol and drug use—factors that can and should be addressed (see Head et al., 2004; Moore et al., 2007; Frone, 2008). In other words, it is important to see whether aspects of the workplace (including geographic isolation for miners and several other groups of workers) or the work process itself contribute to substance abuse. For example, in the road transport industry there is evidence to suggest that the use of drug stimulants is linked to punishing schedules, trip-based remuneration and intense competition for work (Williamson et al., 2004; Williamson, 2007). Another study (Midford et al., 1997) found the higher level of binge drinking at one of two mine sites surveyed could be linked to shift cycles. The connection between work organisation or job characteristics such as shiftwork and drug use is too little explored. However, a recent Australian study (Brown et al., 2008) concluded that alcohol and drug (AOD) policies not only have to be adequately designed and fair but part of a more holistic approach to impairment that engages in workplace design to reduce AOD use and send a consistent health message to employees and the community.

In our view, alcohol and drug testing should be used very selectively and only in the context of a clear and comprehensive alcohol and substance abuse program that has been devised in consultation with workers/unions. Further, this program should be implemented as part of a broader OHS agenda to ensure it does not become a diversionary issue.

Summary

When used appropriately, screening and monitoring can have benefits for employers and workers. Workers can be discouraged from taking jobs in which they are placed at an unreasonable risk of ill health or injury. They can also be protected from the risks that arise when unsuitable individuals are employed to work with them. In some circumstances, unions and workers may seek regular biological and medical monitoring as a safeguard to check the effectiveness of environmental controls. For example, ACTU policy specifies that there should always be medical and biological monitoring where workers are required to wear protective clothing or where control of a hazard is believed to be ineffective (Mathews, 1993). Data from regular examinations can be used to develop a cumulative health profile for individual workers which can chart any deterioration in health status and provide a basis for preventative intervention (Ferguson, 1986b). This data should be strictly confidential and workers should have full access to their own records so that they can monitor changes in their own health. On the other hand, employers can be protected from the economic and social costs of employing a worker who has a high probability of suffering ill health and injury from their work. Systematic aggregation of data from screening and monitoring processes can also provide an important source of information on the direct and indirect health hazards associated with different jobs and processes (Mathews, 1993). These records can be very useful if they are regularly collated to provide information on the health status of groups of workers who may be exposed to particular health hazards. Effective monitoring procedures can provide important information for preventative environmental modification and work design.

Screening and monitoring also have significant limitations as OHS management strategies. When used in isolation, or as part of a narrow range of health and safety strategies, they can divert attention away from organisational hazards and onto the coping capacities of workers. They often appeal to management and employers because they represent a cheap alternative, at least in the short term, to the engineering controls, environmental monitoring and work reorganisation that may be required to effectively eliminate hazards from the workplace. However, over-reliance on screening and monitoring raises significant ethical and legal issues (Johnstone, 1993). Mathews

(1993: 478) lists a number of conditions that should be met if these procedures are to be used. He believes that they should offer the individual worker real protection over and above the group protection provided by environmental controls. They should also not expose workers unnecessarily to additional hazards, as is the case with routine X-rays. Individual screening and monitoring should only be employed as a second line of defence that alerts workers and managers to the failure of environmental protection. They should also provide the workers and managers with information that they can act upon to protect health. Some investigations, such as cytological tests for cancer, may only provide evidence of a condition that is incurable, providing little help to the victim.

As we noted in chapter 2, general examinations and health assessments are rarely effective in predicting whether a worker will perform poorly on the job, take frequent sick leave or make an unusually high number of workers' compensation claims (Ferguson, 1986b; Low and Holz, 1987). Ferguson (1986b) claims that such examinations are no more effective than a self-administered questionnaire in determining the probability of injury or survival to normal retirement age. X-rays, for example, are ineffective predictors of the probability of back injury and in addition carry a risk of genetic and other damage. Low and Holz (1987) suggest that much greater benefit is likely to result from the modification of work tasks than from pre-employment health assessments. They suggest that the high emphasis placed on pre-employment health assessments in some organisations may arise from a lack of knowledge of other techniques for assessing and reducing the risk of illness and injury. As yet, relatively few specific examinations or tests have been shown to be valid predictors of fitness for work (Ferguson, 1986b). Collection of general health information without direct relevance to occupational hazards, such as family histories, is not appropriate and constitutes an invasion of the worker's privacy. Questions such as 'Do you smoke?' or 'Do you drink?' that require a yes or no answer provide quite meaningless information and should definitely be avoided.

As we have noted, screening procedures should be designed to assess whether the job applicant or other workers would be put at an unacceptable risk if the applicant were placed in the relevant job. If it is not possible to modify the job to reduce this risk, it should only be used as one of the criteria taken into account in the employment decision. Questions and tests should be designed only to assess susceptibility to specific hazards likely to be encountered on the job. Frequently, X-rays and general allergy tests are unjustifiable, as are questions regarding smoking habits and previous workers' compensation claims (Mathews, 1993). Periodic chest X-rays, for example, are often used to detect the development of lung cancer, but they are an inefficient way of doing this at the time it can be easily cured, and are useless for predicting who is going to develop the cancer in the future (Kelman, 1985). Even where screening tests validly assess whether workers are sufficiently fit to meet current job requirements, they may still be discriminatory if the job has not been modified so that a reasonably high proportion of the population could do the job without being at increased risk (Low and Holz, 1987). In essence, they reflect a philosophy of fitting workers to jobs, rather than fitting jobs to workers. Where workers do reach a specified threshold of biological contamination or disease development they should not be penalised, and their income and conditions of work should be maintained (Mathews, 1993). Medical examinations should not be used as a means of identifying and disposing of workers who have become the victims of work hazards.

Individual behaviour change strategies

Procedures designed to assess physical health and biological exposure are not the only management practices that focus predominantly on the individual worker. In fact, many of the most widely applied OHS practices are primarily aimed at individual behavioural change (see Mullen, 2004). The most common of these interventions are safety education and training, behaviour modification programs, administrative controls and stress management programs. The first three strategies are usually aimed at injury prevention, while stress management usually focuses on the prevention or moderation of illness and disease. We shall briefly examine each of these forms of intervention.

OHS education and training

The use of training as a means of changing behaviour has been a prominent theme in OHS management for a long time (Glendon and McKenna, 1995; McQuiston, 2000; Mukherjee et al., 2000; Copper and Cotton, 2000). Research indicates there are benefits to integrating OHS training within formal vocational qualifications and industry training (Baker and Wooden, 1995: 109). Many organisations concentrate a large part of their health and safety effort on education and training. Even so, it is important to put this in perspective. In both Australia and New Zealand the percentage of training offered by employers is below 10% and the time devoted to training is only approximately 90 minutes per employee per annum (Australian National Training Authority, 2005; de Bruin et al., 2005). In Canada, Smith and Mustard's (2007) study found only 20% of Canadian employees received safety training in their first year of a new job. They also noted that the provision of safety training did not appear to be more prevalent among workers in occupations with increased risk of injuries. While studies on the level of safety education and training are few and government statistics are patchy, the evidence does indicate that this important and mandatory aspect of OHS still amounts to a tiny fraction of total employer activity. There is also evidence that small businesses are less likely to provide OHS training compared to medium-sized and large businesses (Lamm and Walters, 2004). Given that small businesses constitute a significant proportion of both the Australian and New Zealand business population, this is of concern. Other important areas where there is evidence or claims of neglect in terms of training include temporary and part-time workers, subcontractors and temporary agency/labour hire workers (see, for example, *SIA Safety Week* Issue 146 19 May 2008).

Safety education is aimed at making workers aware of hazards in the workplace and the behaviours necessary to avoid them. Educational interventions include general instruction on hazards and more specialised advice and instruction on safety rules, first aid facilities, and procedures for workers' compensation claims (Mukherjee, 2000; Lingard, 2002; Woods et al., 2004; Pidd, 2004). Workers should also be familiarised with the operation of the workplace health and safety committee, the role of safety representatives and the availability of other health and safety services, such as health promotion programs and on-site health centres. Educational programs often concentrate on discouraging unsafe behaviours by placing posters and signs. These may warn against high-risk behaviour such as running or smoking (especially near flammable materials) or draw attention to the presence of dangerous substances such as toxic and corrosive chemicals, dusts, fumes and inflammable substances and to hazards such as slippery floors and high-voltage equipment. Posters and signs may also be used to identify the location of vital protection equipment (such as safety showers) and procedures to be followed in emergencies. In some cases safety education uses marketing techniques to build on broader public health issues, as illustrated by the efforts of a number of Australian employers in relation to smoking and skin cancer (see Godkin, 1991: 477–82). In other situations the intervention is designed to raise OHS awareness and priorities among isolated workers—for example, community-based campaigns in Australia and New Zealand in relation to the handling of agricultural chemicals and the use of ag-bikes on farms (see also a study of group-based interventions among farmers and farmworkers in Sweden; Stave et al., 2008).

The basic aim of safety training is to ensure that workers have the skills to follow safety procedures and perform their work in a safe manner (Burke et al., 2007). Training should initially be provided during the induction period, including both formal training sessions and on-the-job training from supervisors and experienced staff selected as trainers. Training sessions may provide instruction on the use of protective clothing and safety equipment as well as instruction in skills such as manual handling and machine operation. In hazardous environments, or where complex safety procedures are required, revision sessions should be completed periodically. Follow-up sessions may also be used to extend training as the worker's experience and responsibilities increase. Appropriate supplementary training should also be provided where workers are moved into new jobs. Workers in some jobs may be required to have completed training courses or tests and obtained official certification before they can legally perform certain types of work. For example, in jobs involving the operation of cranes, forklifts and other load lifting equipment special training (including safety procedures) and certification is required in most states in Australia and in New Zealand.

The safety training needs of employees vary according to their position within the organisation (McQuiston, 2000). Workers generally require training in safety behaviours and procedures that are directly relevant to their work. Supervisors need additional training in skills relevant to direct safety management. Personal accountability for the safety of the workers under their direction means that supervisors require a detailed knowledge of the hazards in the workplace and a broader understanding of injury causation (Mukherjee et al., 2000). They should also be aware of the supervisor's role in eliminating injury. For these reasons, supervisors should benefit from more extensive formal training in occupational health and safety, either through in-house courses and seminars or those run by external consultants. Supervisors are often responsible for much of the safety training provided to shopfloor staff and they should receive appropriate instruction in training strategies. As there is some evidence that experienced workers can be more effective safety trainers than supervisors (Swuste and Arnoldy, 2003; Walters and Nichols, 2007; Popma, 2008), it may also be desirable to extend this instruction to a chosen group of such workers. Higher level managers have a major responsibility for setting standards in health and safety, and consequently their induction and training should also include education on the organisation's safety rules and procedures. This education may also be supplemented by attendance at selected outside seminars and courses. The content of all OHS training courses should be documented and regularly reviewed and updated to respond to changes in technology and work organisation. Records should be kept of the training completed by all staff and used for regular assessments of individual training needs.

Despite the popularity of training and education as a tool for managing OHS there have been comparatively few rigorous evaluations of their effectiveness in terms of reducing the incidence of injury (for a recent review of the evidence, see Mukherjee et al., 2000; Anlezark, 2006; Legg, et al., 2008). Education and training programs are often developed without sufficient attention being given to the array of risk factors in the workplace and the underlying causes of occupational injury. Even where training is targeted at unsafe behaviour the focus is often on correct measures (such as safe lifting techniques) that take no account of the factors that may encourage such behaviour (such as workload/staffing limitations, poor organisation and emergency situations). Like other behaviour modification programs, training and education tend to concentrate on hazardous incidents and safety, rather than on health aspects of OHS. In the light of this, it is perhaps not surprising that a British study of line and senior managers in manufacturing found they had '... a much sounder understanding of their role in injury prevention than that related to illness prevention' (Falconer and Hoel, 1996: 151).

The literature on training and education largely overlooks the small business sector and, if it is mentioned, there is a general view that small business employers tend to adopt a reactive, ad hoc approach to employee training and education (Walters, 2001; Hasle and Limborg, 2006). Instead, research on training and education in this sector tends to be incorporated with other aspects of managing a small business. This is not surprising as it is impossible to separate training and education from other aspects of running a small business. Moreover, training and education practised in small businesses differs from that practised in large organisations in that the lines of communication are shorter, the structure is simpler (Wojcik et al., 2003; Lamm and Walters, 2003; Kitching, 2008; Hasle and Kines et al., 2009). The interrelationships between the functions of operating a small business are so tight that a shift in one area will have immediate consequences in another. Typically, resources (i.e. finance, staff, time, etc.) in a small business are stretched. The application of the most basic training practices in small workplaces has to be considered alongside the weekly cash flow because commercial pressures are felt more keenly and immediately.

The foregoing generalisations do not entirely portray the assortment of small business approaches to OHS training and education. For example, a recent UK study undertaken by Kitching (2008) notes that training and education policies among small businesses are highly diverse and range from strategic and tactical to restrictive policies. He adds that in employer-led systems such as that of the UK, employers exert a dominant influence on training, with few institutional pressures to train, other than those related to regulatory requirements—for example, health and safety. This contrasts with consensus-led and developmental state systems where social or legal norms sustain high levels of skill formation. For example, in Norway the Internal Control Regulation within OHS legislation mandates that firms must have (and document) an OHS management system and this has encouraged OHS training among managers that extends to small to medium firms. A study of small to medium vehicle repair garages in Norway by Torp (2008) found managers who had undertaken OHS management training reported a significantly greater improvement in that OHS management system than a control group. Training also had a positive effect on how workers regarded their working environment.

Although there have been few studies specifically on training and education in the small business sector, there has been a plethora of government-supported training and education interventions aimed at the small businesses located in hazardous industries such as forestry, fishing and the agriculture sector (Wojcik et al., 2003; for a more in-depth review, see Legg et al., 2008). The rationale for implementing training and education programs targeted at small businesses in hazardous industries is the belief such programs can reduce the level of injuries and illnesses and make a positive difference in small workplaces. There is also the fact that most small business employers do not have the time, resources or the level of competency required to adequately train their employees. However, in a recent review of evaluations of OHS initiatives for small business, including training and education, a number of problems were identified (Legg et al., 2008). First, the choice of which industry to target was based entirely on the less than reliable government injury statistics. That is, the industries that had the highest officially registered compensation claims were chosen, irrespective of the fact that these figures do not necessarily indicate the true level of injury and illness rates. Second, there is a lack of rigorous evaluations on OHS programs and interventions, primarily because when the initiative is developed there is little or no provision for any evaluation to be undertaken. In addition, most of the OHS programs and interventions were designed around industry-specific workplace hazards and thus the focus of the resultant evaluation (if indeed there ever was one) was on the success or failure of injury and illness reduction rather than the uptake of the initiative by the small business community. The third problem in determining the success or failure of small business OHS programs and interventions is the frequent absence of intervention research principles (see Goldenhar et al., 2001; La Montagne et al., 2004). While there are distinct phases in the process of implementing an OHS intervention and its evaluation, it is crucial that an intervention and its evaluation be planned simultaneously and that the evaluation design and its methods be decided before the intervention is introduced (Robson et al., 2001: 6). Moreover, the evaluation must take place in tandem with the implementation of the initiative in order to inform the development of the initiative; that is, there must be an integrated approach to evaluation/effectiveness research.

Acknowledging these limitations does not mean that OHS training shouldn't be facilitated if not mandated for workers and owners/managers in hazardous workplaces, especially smaller operators where resourcing constraints might otherwise discourage such activities. Lamm (1997) noted that the compulsory inclusion of OHS in trade training in Australia had distinct benefits when it came to tradesmen managing their own workplaces. Similarly, the mandating of a workplace health and safety officer position in Queensland OHS legislation resulted in the owners of small construction firms undertaking the training required to assume this post. At the same time, the effectiveness of training must be viewed in the context of other interventions designed to address critical issues pertaining to OHS in small business (see Mayhew et al., 1997). In road transport, the Transport Workers Union and other bodies have advocated requirements for both operator and worker training on both OHS and public safety grounds (Transport Industry—Mutual Responsibility for Road Safety (State) Award and Contract Determination (No. 2), Re [2006]). However, this action was seen to accompany rather than substitute for action on the OHS problems posed by intense competition/subcontracting and poor/incentive-based remuneration.

Aside from largely overlooking the small business sector, available research fails to address the challenges posed in terms of providing training on complex multi-employer worksites (for an exception see Des Dorides et al., 2006); transitory/seasonal or high labour turnover workplaces (often found in agriculture and hospitality); and with regard to remote workers (such as teleworkers and home-based workers). Research also deals mostly with the training/education of workers and supervisors rather than senior management, even though some studies (see Hakkinen, 1995; Smallman and John, 2001; Luria et al., 2008) indicate programs for top management can increase their interest and awareness in OHS—surely the logical precursor to other types of change. Finally, the literature usually focuses on training/education initiated by employers. This ignores legally mandated/union-sponsored training of employee health and safety representatives and health and safety officers. There is some evidence that this external and independent education input may play an important but often overlooked role in those countries and jurisdictions where it operates (Mukherjee et al., 2000; Swuste and Arnoldy, 2003; Thomson, 2006).

Although education and training have an important place in a comprehensive approach to health and safety management, they should only constitute one part of an OHS program that acts upon organisational as well as individual causes of illness and injury. Further, education and training can only be effective where the desired forms of behaviour are not discouraged by the nature of the work. For example, simply making workers aware of dangers and tutoring them in safe practices in a work situation characterised by chaotic work peaks and dangerous physical conditions, such as a commercial kitchen, is likely to have little effect if more effective work organisation is not simultaneously introduced.

Behavioural modification programs

One means of reducing unsafe individual behaviour is to introduce programs based on the psychological principles of behaviour modification, which we discussed in chapters 2 and 3. Behavioural psychologists point out that the work environment usually provides little direct reward for safe behaviour and rarely sanctions unsafe behaviour, either through injury or reprimands from supervisors (Johnson, 2003; Luria et al., 2008). The objective of behavioural change programs is to encourage safe behaviour and discourage unsafe behaviour through the judicious use of incentives, feedback and sanctions. In practice, the programs usually consist of various combinations of training, monetary incentives and prizes, graphic feedback, supervisory praise, goal setting, information and motivational feedback. Considerable research has been devoted to identifying the most effective combinations of these strategies (see Glendon and McKenna, 1995: 36–69; Mullen, 2004; Wirth and Sigurdsson, 2008).

The rationale for behavioural change programs is the desire to curtail 'risk-taking behaviour' (Glendon et al., 2006). There is an underlying assumption that this behaviour is one of the main causal factors of workplace injuries and fatalities. There is also the assumption that everyone has a propensity to take risks and that this propensity differs from one individual to another depending on a number of factors, such as perception of the nature of the costs and benefits of taking the risk (Adams, 1995; Landweerd et. al., 1990; Glendon et al., 2006). Most of the studies concentrate on the relationship between the employee's attitude towards safety and their safety behaviour, including 'risk-taking tendency' and the need to change the individual's behaviour and ultimately the safety culture of the organisation (Lawton and Parker, 1998; Nicholson et al., 2005). However, more recently there has been an effort to link behavioural change programs with changing the safety culture of the organisation (Guldenmund, 2000; Cooper, 2000; Reason, 2000). In an attempt to marry these two concepts, Glendon et al. (2006: 367) note that when defining safety culture, the premise of some researchers is to focus on *attitudes*, where others emphasise safety culture being expressed through their *behaviour* and work activities (Guldenmund, 2000). In other words, the safety culture of an organisation acts as a guide as to how employees will behave in the workplace. Their behaviour will also be influenced or determined by what behaviours are rewarded and acceptable within the workplace. For example, Clarke (2006: 278) states that the safety culture is not only observed within the 'general state of the premises and conditions of the machinery but in the attitudes and behaviours of the employees towards safety'.

Because of its linear approach that has the potential to encompass both individual behaviour and organisational culture, behavioural change programs have been used for many purposes, including reducing violations of mining regulations, increasing use of protective eye apparatus, increasing ear plug use and reducing traffic-related injuries among police officers (Sheehy and Chapman, 1987). There is evidence that behavioural change programs can produce improvements in safety performance, at least in the short term; however, whether or not they can significantly reduce the level of injuries is still unclear (Robson et al., 2001; Wirth and Sigurdsson, 2008). Assessments over a longer time frame or studies of why schemes lapse are extremely rare. Further, the extent to which the improvements identified in studies reflect a reduction in unsafe behaviour or merely a reduction in the reporting of injury is also unclear. Some behaviour modification schemes discourage injury reporting and this may be a major problem, as the following discussion will show.

Behaviour modification programs have also been criticised because in general they place the prime responsibility for reducing harm on the individual employee, thus abdicating the employer's duty of care (Lamm et al., 2007). Another major drawback of behavioural modification programs is that they run the risk of assuming that unsafe behaviour is the only cause of accidents worth focusing on (Hopkins, 2006a: 594). Moreover, such approaches fail to recognise or diminish the importance of the sociology of work and to take into account the complexities of employment relationships and the influence of external economic, political and legal factors. Hopkins (2006a: 594) also states:

> The reality is that unsafe behaviour is merely the last link in a causal chain and not necessarily the most effective link to focus on, for the purposes of accident prevention … unsafe acts are only one part of the story—unsafe conditions are the other—and any good safety management system must include vigorous programs aimed at identifying and rectifying unsafe conditions.

In spite of these criticisms, behaviour modification programs are popular, particularly among employers as a means of enhancing safety and health. Two of the more common examples of behaviour modification programs are incentive schemes and behaviour-based safety. We will discuss each of these in turn.

Safety incentive, reward and penalty systems

One longstanding method to modify individual worker behaviour has involved the use of incentives. Incentives typically take the form of some form of reward for appropriate behaviour although they can also include attempts to penalise 'unsafe' behaviours. Safety incentive systems were first popularised in the early twentieth century, especially in the US. The nature of the schemes and the array of rewards or penalties involved vary enormously. For example, the schemes can entail individual or group competitions (for developing a safety poster or lowest injury record, etc.), individual or group rewards for specified periods (a month, a year, etc.) without injury or the use of safety indicators in the determination of pay or bonuses. Prizes or rewards range from as little as a mug, T-shirt or certificate through to free meals, paid breaks (from a doughnut break to an entire shift off), paid trips, electronic goods and direct monetary payments (ranging from small amounts to substantial sums). For example, at the Beaconsfield goldmine, management operated a system whereby workers identified by supervisors and other managers as having excelled in safety (such as reporting a problem) were given the equivalent of a small 'scratchie' prize ticket with the opportunity to be part of a large draw. Penalties can include verbal and written warnings, compulsory counselling/retraining, the issuing of tickets/fines by other workers (a US practice unlikely to work in Australia given strong social norms against 'dobbing'), pay cuts, suspension and even dismissal. In most schemes, penalties play a distinctly secondary role and it is recognised that they contribute little to affecting change unless organised into a graduated system ranging from verbal and written warnings up to counselling, suspension and termination.

As with a number of other management interventions in OHS there has been little research into the effectiveness of safety incentives. The research that exists tends to be equivocal. For example, a study by Haines et al. (2001) found that safety incentive programs were more likely to be effective when implemented in settings with positive supervisor/worker relationships and independent teams sharing safety norms. The use of such incentives has been raised as problematic by a number of government inquiries or reviews in the mining industry (Wran and McClelland, 2005; Quinlan, 2007). At the Beaconsfield goldmine interviews with workers, supervisors and managers revealed sharp divisions about the effectiveness of the scratchie scheme. Some workers and managers believed it raised awareness of safety although this was tempered by the view that receiving scratchies had become an expectation (and was being manipulated to some degree). A number of experienced mineworkers and several supervisors were more openly critical of the need for such measures, arguing safety was a matter of 'climate', not incentives (Quinlan, 2007). In the mining industry, evaluating the role of safety incentives must also take account of the potentially serious adverse effects on worker behaviour of the widespread use of production incentives (such as productivity bonuses based on tonnage or ore quality). These issues are not confined to mining. It also needs to be observed that like a number of behavioural interventions, the focus of incentives is workplace safety rather than workplace health.

While incentive schemes appear to work as far as managers are concerned, they suffer from a number of problems. The problem with those based on outcome performance measures (often lost time injuries or compensation claims) and rule observance indicators is that these can be manipulated and, indeed, the system provides an incentive for this, thus defeating the purpose of the exercise. In other words, the system may buy silence or encourage forms of deviant behaviour rather than a genuine improvement in OHS performance. For example, workers' compensation claims can be 'converted' into sickness claims and injuries can be hidden through the manipulation of shift rosters (so injured workers are rostered off) or having injured workers at work even though they are unable to undertake any tasks. In short, such systems are open to abuse (Walters et al., 1995: 286–90). This manipulation may occur at both a tacit and organised level. For example, where incentives are paid to a group there may be strong informal pressure on individuals not to report injury. In other cases, the collective effect on reporting may become apparent in bizarre ways. For example, in one Australian business when a serious injury occurred in one section of the workplace, depriving it of any chance of achieving the incentive bonus, a flood of generally minor injury claims followed. It is reasonable to assume that many of these claims had been held back while there was still a prospect of the bonus being achieved. The problems with injury and compensation claims data has to some extent been recognised, leading to the use of other additional measures including the use of PPE, the number of hazards identified and point systems linked to specific practices such as completing safety orientations, auditing lockout procedures and undertaking OHS training. However, incentive systems that are tied to elaborate performance measures can be problematic as their very complexity diffuses motivation, the purpose of the incentive systems. Leaving this issue aside, reporting effects remain a major limitation of incentive schemes.

A second and overlapping problem relates to the underlying rationale of incentive systems. Even where incentive systems are based on group performance (as in the case of a particular workplace or section thereof), the presumption is that incentives will succeed by inducing individual workers to modify their behaviour. This, in turn, assumes that individuals or groups are in control of their behaviour and changes in behaviour will secure improvements. Both assumptions are problematic. Health and safety problems are not simply the result of unsafe behaviour but rather a mixture of organisational, technical and behavioural factors, with the former two affecting the latter. Poorly designed equipment, poorly planned work processes, pressures to rush work and inadequate attention to hazardous substances will not be addressed by incentive systems. In some cases the management command system will be contradictory where production pressures are not reconciled to pressures to act safely. Where these and other inconsistencies occur it is likely workers will be unable to maintain the performance measures specified in safety incentives. Further, there is a very practical problem in terms of specifying safe behaviour in all situations a worker may encounter. In practice workplace rules can only cover a fraction of the working activities in any workplace and obeying all these rules is not always conducive to production or service delivery. It is common to find cases where production or service delivery is actually achieved by the deliberate breaching of such rules (for example, the emergency lift on a nursing home patient who has collapsed in a shower and where the attending nurse has no help immediately at hand). Incentive systems cannot address these situations. Given all that has just been said it follows that if incentive systems do not address the underlying origins of OHS risks, the changes in behaviour they specify are unlikely to secure a significant long-term improvement in OHS. Often these schemes can have a short-term effect in terms of awareness-raising but the real crunch is to provide compelling evidence that the scheme has achieved tangible results in isolation of other measures over an extended period of time (say, several years). We are yet to see compelling evidence of such long-term success.

Finally, once established, incentives can become an expected part of the reward system, something that may both restrict their motivating effect and make them difficult to remove. In Australia, BHP for many years operated a system of offering prizes to sections of its steelworks that achieved the best record in terms of recorded injury over a period of time. Ultimately, although they became disenchanted with this scheme, it still took management some years to remove it.

The overall level of interest in safety incentive schemes has waxed and waned over the past century but has remained a more popular tool in the US (Barr, 1997: 53–5) than in countries like Australia. Nonetheless, as the foregoing discussion of Australian mining indicates, it remains a resilient option even in the latter. Like other behaviour modification measures, the ongoing appeal of incentive schemes can probably be best explained in terms of their relative cheapness to implement and their individualising effect on OHS.

Behaviour-based safety

Since the early 1980s a new form of behaviour modification program known as behaviour-based safety (BBS) or behaviour-based management systems has been promoted in the US and since the 1990s has gained attention in other countries, such as the UK, South Africa, Australia and New Zealand. For example, it was introduced at the Alcoa Pinjara refinery in Western Australia (see *Safety WA* Autumn, 1992; Massey et al., 2007). In 2008 the New Zealand Department of Labour commissioned research into this area. In the US, the founder of BBS, E Scott Geller, has championed it to business leaders, while in Australia it has been heavily promoted by a number of conferences (such as periodic 'Behaviour Based Safety Now!' conferences) and consultants (such as those engaged by the Beaconsfield goldmine from 2004 onwards). Geller and colleagues (Williams and Geller, 2000; Boyce and Geller, 2001; Geller, 2001, 2005; Wiegand and Geller, 2004) have published a number of articles in safety and psychology journals outlining BBS, including key elements such as observational-based intervention, positive reinforcement of behaviour, feedback and response maintenance (note our earlier discussion of the corrosion commonly associated with behaviour modification).

As the name implies, behaviour-based safety systems focus on unsafe behaviour in the workplace but try to do so in a rather more comprehensive and systematic fashion than most other individual behaviour change programs. Behavioural-based safety is an approach designed to improve safety performance directly through peer observations of safe behaviours, goal setting, performance feedback and celebrations or incentives for reaching safety goals (Ryan and John, 2001; Johnson, 2003; Don and John, 2005). Interventions target supervisors and managers as well as workers although much of the former is directed at enabling managers to provide more supportive 'leadership'.

Behavioural-based safety has been conceptualised by Wirth and Sigurdsson (2008: 590) as fitting into any level of the hierarchy whenever implementation or evaluation of a control depends on behaviour change. In an attempt to illustrate the generic behavioural-based safety process, Wirth and Sigurdsson (2008: 591) have mapped out the involvement of key participants at different stages of the process, as seen in figure 10.1. Some elements of the process are more common than others, but elements 13–15 are especially highlighted as they represent what most behavioural-based safety experts agree are crucial to a successful behavioural safety process. Wirth and Sigurdsson (2008: 591) add that as line employees are often well represented on safety committees, for the purposes of the model, their additional contributions to the development of the process are captured in the related 'swim lane'. Although their main contributions are depicted during the initial development and design stage only, safety consultants should also be involved in many of the process activities. During this stage, the importance of establishing a safety committee is perhaps the single most important practice linked to improved safety performance. Whether this process actually occurs in reality, especially at the level of worker involvement, and how applicable it is for the small business sector is debatable (see Champoux and Brun's (2003) study on the applicability of interventions for small businesses).

The central goal is to specify appropriate modes of behaviour for each work process and every individual within the organisation. There is an emphasis on inculcating behaviour modification into a continuous improvement process, along with elaborate statistical tracking of behaviour patterns (Sulzer-Azaroff and Austin, 2000; Geller, 2001; Thomas, 2001). For example, in their ideal form the programs deal with the commitment, expectations and accountability of line managers; the involvement of all employees; goal setting and action plans; technical and regulatory requirements; safe work practices; training and resource capability; behaviour observation and feedback; and performance tracking. As well as a strong emphasis on goal setting, observation and training, their implementation involves the listing of behaviours within various sections of the workplace, the appointment of 'inspectors' to observe workers and a scoring system to measure performance and guide feedback (Hurst and Palya, 2003). Behaviour-based safety programs often emphasise the importance of a supportive management approach whereby great efforts are made to provide feedback to workers in positive ways (listening, consistency, use of praise, etc.) and to involve workers via teams, meetings and other mechanisms. However, the consultation occurs in a tightly controlled context and even close attention to providing management support may appear manipulative. In a more overtly negative vein, the notion has also encompassed hiring practices (i.e. hiring workers with 'safe' behaviours) as well as the close tracking of 'accident repeaters'. As with much recent human resource management literature, there are frequent references to creating a 'culture' within the organisation which tend to mask the very contrived forms of participation that are legitimated (Krause, 2001).

To the extent that it focuses on behaviour throughout the organisation, behaviour-based safety can be seen to mimic some features of 'legendary' successful schemes such as DuPont. However, behaviour-based systems lack the emphasis on senior management commitment that marks the DuPont model. They also fail to recognise that the emphasis on behaviour in DuPont followed considerable attention to physical aspects of the working environment. In some cases, behaviour-based programs have

Figure 10.1 A generic behavioural-based safety process map showing the involvement of key participants at different stages of the process in their respective 'swim lanes'*

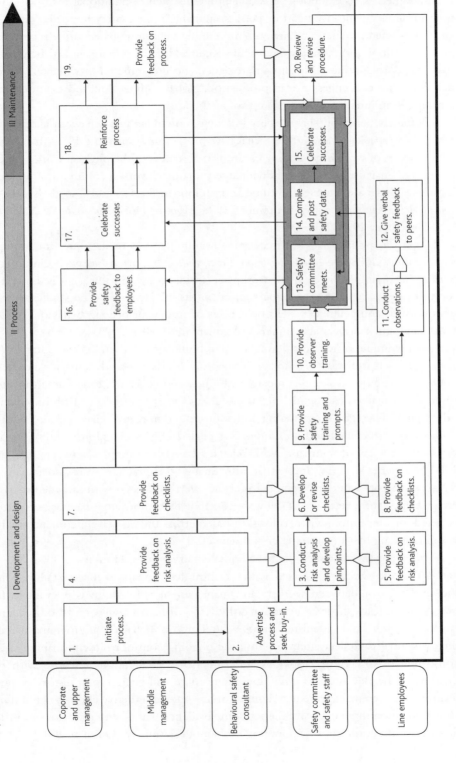

Source: Wirth and Sigurdsson (2008: 591)

* Activities that span more than one swim lane indicate multiple or shared involvement in that activity.
Arrows indicate the flow of information, and lines with open pentagons indicate feedback. Elements 13–15 represent core activities that drive the process.

been adopted as an extension of earlier programs such as traditional forms in injury prevention (accident investigation, posters, etc.) and linking safety to quality via TQM and team-based production. However, more often behaviour-based safety is promoted as a stand-alone program. Further, while Krause (2001) explicitly linked behaviour-based safety to continuous quality improvement, he also argued it may help enterprises deal with the challenges of lean production, global competition and environmental concerns—an intriguing set of claims to say the least.

Ultimately, behaviour-based safety still focuses on individual behaviour and, as such, recycles or repackages a set of ideas that have been around since the 1930s. It does not address issues of work organisation, hazardous substances or the physical work environment. This narrow focus and individualised forms of worker communication (such as surveys) have also aroused hostility from unions in the US and Canada (see *UAW On-the-Job Health and Safety*, September 1998; *Workers' Health International Newsletter*, July–December 1998: 26).

Despite its popularity with management and claims as to its value (for example, on 20 August 2008, the *Health Insurance Email Bulletin* reported Norwich Union Risk Services as stating BBS could cut workplace accidents by up to 85%), it is difficult to locate evidence assessing let alone supporting its effectiveness. The studies that do exist are not compelling. For example, a set of studies of driving behaviour among short-haul truck drivers and miners (Hickman and Geller, 2003a & b) are based on very small samples of workers (less than 40 in both cases) and limited time frames (i.e. seven weeks in the case of miners). Similarly, a Malaysian study (Shariff and Keng, 2008) was based on a single company case study and covered a time frame too short to draw any really meaningful conclusions about the effectiveness of BBS in reducing injury rates. These are longstanding limitations found in many behaviour intervention studies more generally (see, for example, Ray et al., 1997; Cox and Jones, 2008). A study based on a review of traumatic work-related fatalities in Australia between 1982 and 1984 by Feyer et al. (1997) found that individual worker practices were associated with skill-based errors while management practices were associated with knowledge-based errors. Importantly, Feyer et al. (1997: 55) conclude that 'knowledge-based errors can be targeted for prevention, whereas for skill-based errors the only avenue for prevention lies in targeting the surrounding circumstances'.

Reviewing the evidence on behavioural interventions, Hopkins (2006a: 593–4) argues that the evidence is mixed, with a critical determinant of success/failure being the level of trust between workers and management. This point is relevant to the observation already made about union attitudes to BBS. In a review of major incidents, Anderson (2005a & b) identified another limitation of behavioural programs, namely their potential to deflect attention from the ongoing control of low probability/high consequence risks. Both Hopkins's and Anderson's observations resonate with the incident at the Beaconsfield goldmine where there had been a long history of poor relations between management and mineworkers (including active efforts to limit if not eliminate union influence), and there is some evidence that the attention given to BBS did detract attention from the looming problem of seismicity (Quinlan, 2007).

In sum, we remain unconvinced about the value of BBS and would urge management to approach it with guarded scepticism. As has already been argued, behaviour modification does have a place in the management of OHS but this should be firmly located in a broader approach that emphasises work environment and organisation.

Administrative controls

Administrative controls are methods of reducing the probability of illness or injury by modifying job procedures (Bulzacchelli, 2007). As we noted in chapter 2, the strategies included under this label include job rotation, permit-to-work systems, limited entry regulations and job exclusion for specified groups of workers. Job rotation reduces the amount of time that each worker is exposed to a particular hazard. Limited entry areas control the number of workers exposed to a hazard, as does job exclusion by precluding certain groups of workers, such as women, from performing particular jobs or entering particular areas. Common examples include floor marked lines to isolate pedestrians from mobile equipment or to designate restricted entry zones (temporary taping is also used to designate hazardous or 'no-go' zones). Permit-to-work systems (for hazardous activities such as welding) are meant to ensure that workers are fully aware of hazards and appropriate safety procedures by requiring that they read or carry special documentation before entering specified areas.

Although administrative controls play a role in managing OHS there are limitations in their application. In implementation they tend to focus on safety rather than risks to health (though rules can be developed in relation to chemical exposures and the like). Common limitations with administrative controls include arrays of rules that are too complex, flawed or poorly developed (in terms of language or content); rules devised without reference to workers affected by them or not explained to workers; inadequate monitoring and auditing; and a failure to take account of workplace change or a failure to understand the underlying sources of work hazards, including pressure or incentives that encourage hazardous work practices (Laurence, 2005).

For example, rules about the movement of supermarket trolleys by collectors may be of little value unless the reasons why these are often breached are addressed, and rigid rules governing on-site behaviour may be flouted by workers if adherence to them is seen to make completing the task far more difficult. Further, administering even well-established controls such as work permit systems can be a demanding task in practice, especially if there are numerous subcontractors on site, there are pressures to complete tasks and those using the permits lack the information and capacity to query faulty permits. The failure of a work permit system through poor implementation/enforcement and the like has contributed to death or serious injury. For example, a coronial inquest (Cotterell, 1991: 4–5) into the death of Charlie Portelli, a subcontract welder, following an explosion at a Melbourne petroleum refinery on 16 February 1990 found not only that the Hot Work Permit he was issued was defective in crucial respects and that this was not an isolated event but also that this reflected a pattern of repeated short cuts and difficulties due to lack of manpower physically able to carry out the inspection required. At the very least, administrative controls require careful development, thorough induction and training of those involved, vigorous supervision/monitoring and periodic independent auditing. As the Portelli case demonstrates, they also require attention to workloads (in this case those of supervising managers) and work organisation.

Used in isolation, administrative controls do nothing to modify the hazards that are the primary causes of illness and injury. Where they are used as an adjunct to modifications to the working environment they are far more likely to be successful. For example, at the BHP Wire Works, Newcastle, administrative controls were used to complement substantial changes to the roadway system (guard rails, re-routing, etc.) to isolate pedestrians from vehicle traffic. In combination, this achieved a significant reduction in injury despite the narrow road widths of a factory laid out more than 100 years ago. However, all too often administrative controls are not utilised in conjunction with environmental modifications. Like protective clothing, they often present a substantially less expensive means of minimising injury and illness than the implementation of engineering controls and other physical modifications of the working environment. In the process they shift the responsibility for minimising risks away from management and directly onto workers. Consequently they are generally a less desirable and higher risk strategy than environment controls. Job exclusion is also a highly discriminatory practice in most cases. For this reason administrative controls should be seen as a secondary or temporary solution that is used until effective environmental control methods are available.

Administrative controls are often linked to *systematic process standards*. Typically, these standards are applied to the management of nominated hazards or to key arrangements for managing OHS (Brooks, 2001; Buff and Gunningham, 2003: 13). For example, the national standards for manual handling, plant, hazardous substances, major hazardous facilities, the storage and handling of dangerous goods and certification for hazardous occupations all incorporate systematic processes. The most important characteristic of the OHS regulations or evidentiary standards (i.e. approved codes of practice/advisory standards) resulting from this initiative is their consistent approach to managing hazards by incorporating the three fundamental steps of hazard identification, risk assessment and risk control. Thus, duty holders are obliged to assess risks, and to regularly evaluate and improve control measures (Buff and Gunningham, 2003: 13).

Stress management

As we have already discussed stress management in chapter 5, this section will only briefly discuss some of the specific techniques used in stress management programs and reiterate our comments about the limitations of individual stress management. A large number of coping strategies are taught under the general banner of stress management (Lo and Lamm, 2005). They include physical and psychological relaxation methods, lifestyle management and general health enhancement strategies. Physical relaxation methods include strategies such as progressive muscle relaxation, biofeedback, yoga and tai chi. Psychological strategies for altering perceptions of stress and demand include meditation, hypnosis, self-hypnosis and various forms of psychotherapy. A range of popular 'positive thinking' programs, many of which are of very dubious long-term value, fall into this category. Consultants often market lifestyle management strategies such as time management as a means of stress reduction. General health enhancement strategies, such as improved diet and regular physical exercise, are often advocated as indirect means of reducing stress. All of these strategies are presented as a means through which the individual worker can learn to cope effectively with work-related stress. Training in the use of these techniques, or at least an introduction to them, is usually provided by internal or external health consultants in one-off seminars or in a series of short workshops. In some cases, professional emotional counselling may also be offered to supplement this training. Stress management is rarely linked in a systematic way to other aspects of the organisation's health and safety management program.

While stress management can provide a means of coping with crises at work, we consider it is an ineffective organisational strategy unless used in combination with strategies that address the structural causes of stress. Consistent with this, an international review of 90 job stress intervention evaluation studies undertaken between 1990 and 2005 (LaMontagne et al., 2007) found that individual interventions were beneficial at the individual level but not the organisational level while organisationally focused interventions had favourable effects at both the individual and organisational level. As we noted in chapter 5, some job characteristics are strongly linked to physiological and psychological stress responses. Monotonous, machine-paced, physically demanding, dangerous or highly routine jobs are likely to be highly stressful for most workers. Similarly, work overload affects many workers but these interventions usually focus on assisting workers to 'manage' their workloads, not alter them (Randall et al., 2007). Individual stress management does not alter any of these job characteristics and is only likely to be successful as a short-term, 'stopgap' response to them. In fact, there is evidence that individual coping may not reduce the strain produced by these stressors at all (Kenny, 2000). Stress management is also usually delivered as an 'expert' intervention with limited if any scope for worker input. A study of a stress management intervention relating to nurses by Randall et al. (2007) found that nurses' perceptions provided important insights into the intervention's impact—something commonly overlooked by the dominant evaluation paradigm used. A Danish study (Nielsen et al., 2008) reinforced this finding about the importance of worker assessments of interventions. A Japanese study (Kobayashi et al., 2008) found evidence supporting the effectiveness of a participatory approach to stress management, albeit still in the context of a relatively restricted range of interventions to the work environment. Again, evidence supports more active worker involvement—a recurring theme in this book.

This selective treating of symptoms issue was taken up by Otto (1985), who attacked what she labelled as 'stress management ideology' that involved a denial of knowledge and perpetuated an understanding of stress that favours dominant interest groups (especially employers) to the neglect of others. The ideology is exemplified by the promotion of individual stress management at the expense of the changes to the organisation of work that are required if occupational stress is to be effectively addressed. Promotion of individual coping strategies is an extension of the 'victim-blaming' strategies (discussed in chapter 3) that can be used to deflect responsibility for ill health away from the organisation of work and locate it within the characteristics and behaviours of individual workers. For employers and managers interested in cost minimisation, individual stress management presents a cheap and simple alternative to comprehensive reorganisation of work. Otto believed that the primary source of occupational stress is the failure of the work environment to match people's needs and capacities rather than in the inability of workers to tolerate what may be intolerable conditions.

Otto's critique of stress management interventions remains valid over 20 years later, despite greater recognition of the importance of participatory processes. As burnout and emotional exhaustion have emerged as issues, interventions have continued to focus on the provision of individual or group support and to ignore underlying causal issues such as workload/staffing levels, presenteeism and organisational restructuring (Aronsson et al., 2000; Le Blanc, Hox, Schaufeli, Taris and Peeters, 2007). Further, there often seems to be a disconnection between the provision of stress management support and other aspects of the working environment hardly conducive to this, such as poor work–life balance or a climate of bullying. For example, while the NSW ambulance service has support mechanisms to deal with stress, a parliamentary inquiry in 2008 received widespread complaints of a bullying culture within the service, fatigue and widespread resignations ('Bullying rife in ambulance service, inquiry told', *CCH OHS Alert* 7 July 2008). Bullying and other forms of occupational violence have been found to be common, especially in industries and sectors such as healthcare (see, for example, Fleming and Harvey, 2002). While medium to large employers have increasingly adopted programs to address occupational violence, these interventions seldom entail significant changes to work organisation that underpin these problems (such as inadequate staffing levels, working in isolation and just-in-time work systems).

Summary

Individual behaviour change programs suffer from a number of significant limitations, some of which were discussed at length in the chapter on injuries. With the exception of stress management, these programs focus on safety to the exclusion of health and are preoccupied with 'accidents', incidents or unsafe acts. Like most other behaviour change strategies, they are based on the notion of identifying and remedying unsafe behaviour. The notion of unsafe practices can be traced back to Heinrich (1931: 68–72). Heinrich's unsubstantiated assertion that human error/unsafe practices (often simply labelled as behaviour) were responsible for 80 to 90% of all injuries in the workplace has been repeated to the point of folklore in some OHS management circles. Judgments about the importance of behaviour depend critically on how broadly the term is defined and how it is applied. If, as appears often to be the case, behaviour is interpreted to mean that some independent human action (often an error) preceded an incident then it is hardly surprising that behaviour will appear to play a role in, if not underpin, most incidents and injuries. However, as we have reiterated throughout this book, the behaviour of individuals is but one of a number of contributing factors, and is itself shaped by organisational and other influences. In other words, behaviour may only appear important because the definition used excludes most other causal factors. To be fair to Heinrich (1931: 38–63), it must be acknowledged that he recognised both a multiplicity of causal factors and a chain of causation (the so-called domino theory). However, as Slappendel has observed (1995: 216), Heinrich's domino model analyses accidents as chains of discrete causes rather than taking an integrated approach. Similarly, more recent versions of behaviour modification such as BBS emphasise behavioural intervention to break an implicitly discrete chain of causation and we can see little evidence of even fairly conventional root cause analysis within them.

Probably the greatest shortcoming of behaviour change strategies is that they over-emphasise the role of individual behaviour and downplay if not entirely ignore the impact of work organisation, equipment design and other physical and organisational factors on injury. The limitations of this have been repeatedly acknowledged by psychologists, sociologists and others over the past 20 years (Sheehy and Chapman, 1987; Bradley, 1989; Ford and Tetrick, 2008). Overcoming this limitation is not simply a matter of combining behavioural interventions with efforts to find and remove hazards, as some have suggested (Ford and Tetrick, 2008: 1482). The underlying presumptions and implementation of some, if not many behavioural interventions (such as BBS), are incompatible with more organisationally and environmentally focused interventions. Further, there is also a question as to the level or prioritising of invariably limited management resources (in terms of time, money and the like) to these respective activities. In high-hazard workplaces such as mines, refineries or construction sites, individual behaviour will often represent the last and potentially inadequate line of defence ('safe behaviour' may be of limited use if a rockfall occurs or a crane collapses), so priority needs to be given to engineering, environmental and work organisation interventions. We would argue that even in less hazardous workplaces the appropriate role of behaviour modification is to support more fundamental controls (in terms of workplace design/organisation and the like). We would also suggest that improvements in safety behaviour can be greatly enhanced if they are accompanied by physical and organisational interventions to improve the work environment.

Organisational strategies

A number of broader strategies and arrangements can be used by management to structure OHS activities. Increasingly, management of medium to large organisations have used risk management and OHS management systems (OHSMS) to inform their OHS practices. Common organisational components of OHSMS include workplace health and safety committees, workplace health surveys and safety monitoring, OHS audits and the development of inhouse health promotion programs and on-site health and safety centres. Less commonly used strategies include job redesign and changes to the broader organisation of work, though, as noted earlier, these have the potential to significantly reduce ill health and injury. We shall briefly examine each of these strategies.

Workplace OHS committees and other participative mechanisms

One common and potentially important organisational strategy is the establishment of consultative and collaborative mechanisms at the workplace or enterprise level. Mechanisms for worker input on OHS include shift, pre-start and toolbox meetings as well as formal OHS committees. While surveys of workers have value they are not of themselves a participative mechanism and are dealt with in another section of this chapter. Although toolbox, shift and pre-start meetings offer an avenue for workers raising OHS issues these mechanisms tend to be time-constrained, individualised and focused on routine, housekeeping or immediate areas of concern rather than more fundamental OHS issues (including those involving major budget expenditures). While of value, the opportunity to raise OHS issues at toolbox or shift meetings is not a substitute for a formally constituted OHS committee. At the same time, where a workplace is too small to justify the establishment of an OHS committee, employers can seek worker involvement or feedback on OHS by setting aside time (say, a lunchtime) every six months or so to discuss OHS (and encouraging feedback at other times).

Participatory OHS committees provide a structure through which workers and management can cooperate and share responsibility for the development and implementation of strategies to protect the health and safety of workers (see Weil, 1999; Walters, 2004; Nichols et al., 2007; Popma, 2008; Gunningham, 2008). They are generally responsible for formulating organisational policies, procedures and practices relating to OHS, and for monitoring their implementation. In effect, their role is both to review health and safety performance and to develop new policies and practices. In addition, they often play an educational role, coordinating the dissemination of information regarding workplace hazards and the provision of health and safety training to workers. As indicated in chapter 7, in Australia, New Zealand and many other countries there are statutory requirements regarding the provision of workplace committees and safety representatives. In this section we shall discuss more general managerial considerations regarding the structure and functions of workplace committees.

The membership of OHS committees varies between organisations. However, several characteristics are generally desirable. First, the number of workers' representatives should at least match the number of management representatives (this is a legislative requirement in some jurisdictions), and workers should be the ones to elect their representatives. Where present, elected HSRs or their equivalent should be members of the committee. Excluding them invites friction and undermines the credibility of the committee, and OHS laws tend to mandate HSR membership in any case. A basic philosophy underlying participatory OHS committees is that employees should be actively involved in hazard assessment, the setting of safety standards and policy formulation (Nichols et al., 2007). Balanced representation between management and workers is vital to ensure that workers can genuinely influence these processes. Second, rather than being full voting members, health professionals and specialist health and safety staff should act as consultants to the committee. In this capacity they can furnish reports and provide professional advice, but they do not have undue influence over decision making that is normative in nature. This role also protects the professional integrity of such people and allows them to express opinions without them necessarily being construed as those of management. Third, some management representatives on the committee should be of sufficient seniority to have the authority to make decisions and influence the implementation of organisational policies or in other ways demonstrate their commitment (Hodson, 2002).

The functions of the committees may differ in detail between organisations, but, once again, some roles are generally desirable. The committee should have a number of important review functions. It should receive regular reports on injuries and their causes. It should also regularly consider the results of any environmental monitoring, hazard identification or risk assessment conducted in the workplace. The committee should also have input into how these activities are carried out. Where there is no HSR, a delegated committee member should be able to participate in workplace inspections carried out by government inspectors or 'walk around' OHS monitoring exercises by management. Finally, it should review aggregate data from all medical and biological monitoring programs. Associated with these review functions is an investigatory role. The committee should investigate any evidence that comes to its attention concerning practices, working conditions or equipment that are considered unsafe or a risk to health. The committee should also have policy-making functions. In addition to contributing to the formulation of the organisation's overall OHS policy, it should also be involved in the development of detailed procedures and codes of practice governing the way in which work is performed. Unions would generally see legal regulations and standards as representing a minimum set of policy guidelines beyond which policies and procedures should be developed by joint committees rather than unilaterally by management (Johnstone et al., 2005; Gunningham, 2008). Providing OHS committees with a significant budget and enabling the committee to prioritise its expenditure is one way of promoting a constructive and proactive role.

The effectiveness of OHS committees is influenced by a range of factors. One major factor is the skills and knowledge base of the members (Hodson, 2002; Swuste and Arnoldy, 2002). Members should receive training that provides them with a basic understanding of the magnitude of health and safety problems in the workplace, the types of hazards present, the potential effects of these hazards, preventative strategies appropriate to these hazards and sources of relevant technical information and advice. They should also have basic research skills, including knowledge of theories of injury and illness causation, investigation methods and the interpretation of data. A second important factor is the provision of adequate information, and financial and human resources for the committee to perform its work. It is fundamental that the committee is not seen as a token gesture by management and is supported and funded accordingly. In their study, Wyatt and Sinclair (1998: 91–6) found that factors influencing the effectiveness of OHS committees were senior management commitment and consultative management style, infrastructural supports (funding and support staff), the integration of OHS with everyday management practices, time to undertake tasks and the competence of individual members. A French study (Bernard and Nicolay-Stock, 2007) of OHS committees established in the agricultural sector found that 75% had established prevention programs but 30% of members believed their committee lacked sufficient information. As noted in the previous chapter, the performance of OHS committees will also be affected by industrial relations. Johnstone et al. (2005) note that, with some exceptions, the principal mechanisms establishing worker participation under OHS statutes in Australia, New Zealand and other industrialised countries—namely OHS representatives and OHS committees— take little or no account of changing work arrangements. Rather, they argue, the workforce is an identifiable and relatively stable group of employees located together or in very regular contact and working for a single employer (Johnstone et al., 2005: 95).

While OHS committees provide an important forum, they should not be seen as a replacement for union-appointed health and safety representatives who can provide direct lines of communication between workers and management (see Hovden et al., 2008; Trägårdh, 2008). While the responsibilities of OHS committees lie in the areas of data collection and policy formulation and implementation, the function of safety representatives is to safeguard the interests of workers and to enforce health and safety standards. Unions would generally be very resistant to structural arrangements that compromised the independence of safety representatives and their ability to deal directly with management regarding the enforcement of health and safety standards. For example, representatives should not be placed in the position of being asked to forestall requests for the rectification of an existing fault in return for a promised improvement in another aspect of health and safety.

Health and safety surveys and audits

The efficiency of workplace committees, and health and safety management in general, depends very heavily on the collection of information regarding current conditions and practices within the organisation. Health and safety surveys and audits are an important source of this information. Surveys can be used to develop a broad information base across the organisation or within designated work areas, while independent audits can provide more precisely quantified data on specific aspects of health and safety performance or the OHS management system as a whole.

Health and safety surveys may be used to collect information on a range of factors (for a general discussion, see Toohey et al., 2005 and Glendon et al., 2006). Information on the incidence of illness and injury is usually collected, including minor injuries (from first aid records), lost time injuries (from workers' compensation claims) and absenteeism (from personnel and pay records). Information may also be gathered on current levels of training, skills and work experience among workers in different job designations. Aggregation of this data may assist in the development of education and training programs. However, the common practice of collecting data on individual characteristics, such as personal disabilities and age, is generally unacceptable. As we have previously indicated, these characteristics are often very poor predictors of later health and safety outcomes and, consequently, collection of the information is discriminatory in many cases. Generally, individual data of this nature is best collected during the process of medical monitoring with appropriate protection of confidentiality. Much more useful and important information is usually derived from surveys of workplace design and work organisation. Attention should be paid to both broad work organisation factors, such as payment systems and production pressures, and the details of job design. Data should also be collected on the types of equipment, raw materials and physical processes in the workplace, with particular emphasis on threats arising from toxicity, flammability and other direct health hazards.

The information derived from the survey can be compiled to provide a summary of the health and safety risks in the organisation (Glendon et al., 2006). This information base can be used as an empirical foundation from which health and safety programs can be developed to meet the particular needs of the organisation. Specific health and safety problems may be brought to light which require further investigation, and perhaps assistance from outside experts. Examples include specific work processes such as spray painting; the presence of dangerous or harmful substances; barriers to effective communication (such as the combination of excessive noise with inhibitive protective clothing); hazardous working conditions, such as intense heat or cold; and potentially dangerous work organisation, such as piece rates.

It is vital that the health and safety survey is devised in cooperation with people who have expertise in health and safety and thorough knowledge of research in organisations. To do otherwise is to risk expending considerable time and expense on the collection of data which may be meaningless or, at least, provide a very limited basis for action. Depending on the nature of the survey and the availability of on-site expertise, it may be advisable to secure the services of an external consultant to provide input to the process. The objective is to achieve an appropriate balance between expert input and the development of skills within the organisation. It is particularly important that an effort is made to develop basic data-collection skills among the members of the workplace health and safety committee. It should also be recognised that surveys are only as good as the questions asked or, indeed, not asked.

Most research into OHS problems at the workplace still takes the form of obtaining and interpreting accident/incident reports although hazardous process and near-miss reporting systems are now more common. Most accident reporting systems were not systematically designed for effective data gathering, having usually developed in unplanned ways to meet a range of organisational, medical and legal demands (Sheehy and Chapman, 1987). Many organisations employ highly structured accident or incident reporting schedules that provide large amounts of discrete and easily understood data, although the quality of this data will vary according to factors such as management's response to reporting (Clarke, 1998). Sheehy and Chapman (1987) point out that the apparent precision of this information may be deceptive. The categories are often difficult to accurately define and consequently give a false sense of reliability. Further, investigators are encouraged to use only the simple categorical labels provided, such as 'misjudgment'. Consequently, only information that supports the theories of injury causation on which the schedule is based is collected while other equally valid information is ignored. Sheehy and Chapman describe two accident surveillance systems based on an implicit theory of injury causation that emphasises victim culpability. These systems concentrate on collecting information concerning victim characteristics and overlook other factors that may be significant contributors to the incident. Such data collection methods are very likely to generate biased and misleading information on injury causation.

A further problem with categorical reporting systems is that they do not treat injuries as processes, but rather as discrete events without meaningful antecedents or consequences. The collection of categorical data is relatively simple and provides an impression of completeness, but creates arbitrary discontinuities in the injury process. A more desirable and realistic approach is the elicitation of process data, for example through the collection of structured verbal reports. Such methods provide a better understanding of the causal process leading to the injury (increasing use is being made of causal root tree analysis). This knowledge should provide a more valid and practically useful basis for intervention, although it may be more complex and difficult to interpret and vary in its level of explicitness (Sheehy and Chapman, 1987).

Health and safety audits are management tools that are intended to accurately measure compliance with a range of OHS-related matters, including safety procedures and the safety of items of equipment. They can take a number of forms, including single issue, legal or technical compliance audits with specific checklists in which each item is rated against a measurable standard (CCH Australia, 1987; Glendon, 1995; Pybus, 1996). They provide accurate measurement of compliance to noise, dust and other standards and clearly quantify the performance of health and safety equipment and controls. Audits should be performed regularly, although the exact timing will depend on the nature of the audit and the workplace. For example, where audits are stand-alone exercises they may need to occur more often (such as every three to six months). Where a two-tier auditing process is used entailing a substantial and formal audit augmented by more regular but less formal audits, the former may occur at less regular intervals of, say, once per year. Regular informal but systematic walk-around audits have much value in identifying problems and reinforcing the formal auditing process.

Health and safety surveys and audits perform related but distinct functions. Surveys are used to collect general information and are often very exploratory in nature, aiming to identify areas that require closer attention. Audits are designed to collect very specific information about performance in previously identified and clearly defined areas of health and safety performance. Audits should be conducted on a regular basis, while surveys are generally conducted when a need is perceived, for example when there have been significant changes in technology or staffing. Areas of concern identified in surveys may later be defined and converted into a measurable index for regular audit.

Work reorganisation and organisational climate

An alternative and less widely applied approach to illness and injury minimisation is to change the ways in which work is organised. As we noted in earlier chapters, sociologists and psychologists have identified various aspects of work and task organisation that contribute to injury and illness. Psychologists have usually confined their attention to the design of individual jobs and tasks, while sociologists have advocated more fundamental changes to the way that labour is organised across firms and industries. The strength of these approaches is that they attempt to act on structural causes of unsafe behaviour and illness rather than attempting to adapt workers' behaviour to stressful and dangerous working conditions.

Taylor's (1947) scientific management principles have dominated job design practices for most of this century. Taylor's approach emphasised an extreme division of labour, work simplification and direct management control over the execution of work. Today, despite academic discussion of high-involvement and knowledge-based work, Tayloristic work simplification together with more recent efforts to intensify work arrangements (such as lean production and outsourcing) remains the most widely applied job design paradigm. Paul Landsbergis and colleagues (1999) have explored the links between employer work strategies, such as lean production, and OHS (for an exceptional piece of parallel research involving collaboration between an OHS and an IR researcher, see Wright and Lund, 1996, 1998). This basic observation needs to be borne in mind when discussing work reorganisation even though there is longstanding evidence as to the adverse OHS effects of simplification and work intensification.

Turning to the work of psychologists, it can be noted that since the 1920s psychological research has frequently demonstrated that highly simplified and repetitive work can have negative health, performance and attitudinal effects (Wall and Martin, 1987). For many years psychologists have advocated reversal of the trend towards work simplification and recommended that jobs should be designed to include a wider range of tasks and to offer workers a greater level of control over their labour. Psychologists now use the term 'job redesign' to signify the movement away from the dominant model of work simplification. From the 1950s psychological research on work design was dominated by two approaches, namely job enrichment and the creation of autonomous work groups or teams. The concept of autonomous work groups evolved within the socio-technical systems approach developed by the Tavistock Institute in the UK (Trist, 1981). A key feature of autonomous work groups is that they give workers considerable freedom to organise their everyday work activities (Wall and Martin, 1987). The group is typically delegated control over the pace of work, the allocation of tasks within the group and the timing and organisation of breaks. Group members may also participate in the recruitment and training of new members. Often the groups require, and receive, little direct supervision. The proponents of autonomous work groups also strongly advocate the direct involvement of workers in the design and redesign of their own jobs. Team-based production systems have become commonplace but the focus has largely been productivity enhancement and many lack the autonomy or authority to make meaningful decisions about their jobs.

There is some evidence on the impact of work groups on OHS. A Canadian study (Simard and Marchand, 1995: 113) of 1061 work groups in 97 manufacturing plants found a significant correlation between lost time injury rates and the propensity of work groups to take initiatives on safety. The propensity of work groups to raise safety issues was largely influenced by factors internal to the workplace (most notably, supervisory participative management of safety) although the socioeconomic context of the secondary labour market could act as a significant constraint on management commitment (Simard and Marchand, 1995: 113,125). Similarly, Caple et al. (1997: 243–5) found the introduction of natural work groups into the Australian automobile industry resulted in a substantial reduction in the number and severity of injuries in those plants where senior management demonstrated commitment (including the provision of adequate planning, training, regular meetings and resources).

There is little research on the effects of job enrichment on OHS and this is perhaps not surprising given that the dominant trend in work practices has not been in this direction. Work restructuring, including the use of work groups, has sometimes been associated with an increase in the range of tasks undertaken by workers but, in practice, management interventions under this label often amount to multi-tasking to maintain production rather than genuine multi-skilling. Limited research into work reorganisation has sometimes yielded unexpected results. For example, a Canadian study (Lanoie and Trottier, 1998) of warehouse packers found a shift from a mechanical to a manual handling system reduced injuries and was also cost effective.

Since the 1990s there has been a growth in research by psychologists and others into interventions that extend beyond stress management and involve some element of work reorganisation or redesign. Workplace change is often the norm rather than 'noise'. A Norwegian study by Saksvik et al. (2007) sought to develop the criteria for 'healthy organisational change', including paying attention to the norms and diversity of local employees and empowering individuals to restore their sense of control and job security.

As noted in chapter 5, a number of innovative models have tried to address those aspects of work organisation that adversely affect health and in so doing offer directions for intervention in terms of work organisation. Notable here has been the work of Karasek (1979), Marmot (1998) and Siegrist (1996) that was discussed in some detail in that chapter. Recently health researchers have also examined the effects of organisational justice on workers' health and wellbeing (Elovainio et al., 2002; Sutinen et al., 2002). The implications of this research are that employers need to give more attention to redressing demand–control and effort–rewards imbalances in the workplace. Landsbergis and Cahill (1994) document ways a number of unions in the US have promoted stress interventions that are more consistent with the Karasek model, including surveys and medical studies of workers, stress committees and collective bargaining on this issue. Unfortunately, this activity seems to have remained exceptional in the US and other countries.

As was noted in chapter 5, other social science researchers have pointed to harmful aspects of work organisation, including overarching production imperatives, hierarchy within the workplace, piecework and contingent work arrangements (Nichols, 1997; Mayhew and Quinlan, 1999). Like the research just mentioned, several studies identify concrete steps that management might take to address OHS. A study of lost time injuries in Canadian manufacturing firms (Shannon et al., 1996: 258–68) found that lower rates were associated with concrete management concern for the workforce, greater worker involvement in general decision making, greater willingness of OHS committees to solve problems internally and a more experienced workforce. Profitability and financial performance were not significant. The linking of safety to participation, long job tenure and experience that this and other studies have identified suggests clear strategic responses.

Another body of research has explored how organisational climate or characteristics shape OHS outcomes. Some of this research mirrors earlier behavioural research and seems as much concerned with productivity or performance as with health outcomes (Cotton and Hart, 2003). Other studies perceive organisational climate or 'culture' (an ill-defined and ambiguous concept at best) in terms of perceptions or a shared or consensual view about OHS among managers and workers (Wadsworth and Smith, 2009). Though not without value—highlighting the importance of worker perceptions and management trust and support or developing measures of 'safety climate' that move beyond engineering systems (Dodsworth et al., 2007; Hoivik et al., 2007)—the studies are often restricted in scope and fail to consider industry-specific hazards. Hopkins (2006b) argues that the result is often a superficial analysis where researchers spend too much time on narrow 'climate' measurement devices and fail to immerse themselves in the organisation and its history. Similarly, Atonsen (2009) states that the organisational culture studies tend to ignore the reality of power and conflict in organisations. Other studies (DeJoy et al., 2004) have found that 'safety climate' only exerted a limited mediating role. As Clarke (2002) has observed, researchers and managers also needs to recognise the disruptive effects on 'organisational safety culture' brought about by downsizing and the widespread use of contingent workers. There are important exceptions. A number of studies have used a broad approach to organisational climate where institutional, labour market and power relationships are not ignored (see Lowe et al., 2003; Harenstam et al., 2006).

In sum, there is now an extensive body of research indicating that significant improvements in OHS require a substantial reorganisation of work and a critical examination of day-to-day management practices that are now taken for granted. Work reorganisation represents one of the more challenging ways of trying to improve OHS but equally offers the best prospects for building a healthier and productive workplace in the future.

Workplace health promotion, wellness and on-site OHS centres

Over the past two decades there has been a growing awareness of preventative health practices in Western societies. This awareness has been reflected in greater concern regarding obesity, diet, physical fitness, work–life balance and cessation or moderation of unhealthy habits such as smoking and alcohol consumption. One manifestation of this change has been an increase in the number of company-sponsored programs designed to improve employee health and wellbeing—what has been commonly labelled as workplace health promotion (WHP) and the more recently fashionable concept of 'wellness'. These programs are intended to encourage workers to make behavioural and lifestyle changes that are believed to be conducive to good health. A combination of diagnostic, educational and behavioural-change activities are usually provided at the workplace (Matteson and Ivancevich, 1988). The goal of WHP is attitudinal and behavioural change, leading to changes in mechanisms that mediate chronic disease (such as cholesterol, sun exposure and drug use) and injury (via exercise) as well as promoting mental wellbeing (Abrams et al., 1986; Pritchard and McCarthy, 2002).

Workplace health promotion (WHP) programs can be divided into either narrow or broad spectrum activities (Matteson and Ivancevich, 1988). Narrow spectrum programs consist of only one or two components, while broad spectrum programs may include six or more activities. Narrow 'wellness' programs have been criticised (Koh, 1995). Even multi-component programs generally concentrate on behaviour change rather than organisational or structural issues at the workplace (though some use group as well as individual approaches; see Bergstrom et al., 2008). Programs typically offer health assessments (often via a survey rather than medical examination); medical and educational counselling; behaviour change; access to information (via web portals and the like); wellness literature and referral services (see, for example, Mills et al., 2007). The most common targets of these programs are smoking cessation, blood pressure screening and control, stress management, nutrition and obesity, exercise and fitness, and drug and alcohol programs (Abrams et al., 1986). Originally WHP tended to emphasise cheaper strategies based on information provision, but while this remains important (even if the vehicles of delivery have changed) there has been a trend to more active attempts at behavioural change.

Employers have pursued workplace health promotion for a number of reasons. These include presumed benefits to efficiency and productivity from reductions in sickness-related absenteeism, labour turnover, injury and health-related costs (such as workers' compensation and other insurance premiums); increased organisational commitment of staff; improved corporate image; a competitive advantage in recruitment; and enhanced industrial relations (see, for example, Mills et al., 2007; Cooper and Patterson, 2008). The cost effectiveness of WHP has been the subject of longstanding research and debate (Jacobson et al., 1990: 655–6; Goetzel, 2008). A US review by Goetzel (2008) concluded that while properly designed WHP could increase both employee health and productivity, only 7% of employers used all the program components required for successful interventions. A Dutch study (Robroek et al., 2007) of a cardiovascular disease intervention found that the intervention needed to be individually tailored and long-term to be cost effective.

Organisations have also responded to direct pressure from employees and unions for the provision of a range of health and fitness services. In a number of European countries, such as the Netherlands, Sweden, Finland and Norway, the law requires some health promotion services. Within the EU this has a more organisational and public health focus than is found elsewhere, although the type and level of implementation still varies significantly among member countries (Hamalainen, 2006). The greater organisational focus and regulatory/policy content has resulted in the development of network relationships and partnerships between OH service providers, inspectors and other government agencies, insurers, employers, unions and professional bodies (Hamalainen and the ENWHP network, 2007). Indeed, WHP is given a far broader meaning in the European context when compared to the more internalised and individualised approach to WHP in North America, Australia and New Zealand. In the US employer interest in workplace health promotion was as a logical extension of the healthcare support large firms already provided due to the absence of a universal healthcare insurance system (like Medicare in Australia or the NHS in the UK). In Australia and New Zealand neither of these incentives applied. This helps explain why health promotion proved less popular with employers (apart from international companies such as Ericsson). While a growth of interest can be detected from the late 1980s (Williams, 1991: 489–94), if surveys undertaken for the superannuation industry and other bodies are to be believed (see, for example, 'Most bosses ignore workers' mental health: survey' *CCH OHS Alert* 8 October 2008), programs to support employee wellbeing remain exceptional for Australian workers. It appears that employee assistance programs (EAP) are the most common activity (Kirk and Brown, 2003). In New Zealand the smaller average size of employers was an additional impediment. It should also be noted that the global shift to downsizing, outsourcing and the like over the past two decades has acted as a more general impediment to the growth of WHP.

Despite strong convictions that WHP activities lead to positive individual and organisational outcomes, and a body of research that has grown over the past 20 years, the evidence as to their value remains far from conclusive and more rigorous and consistent research is required. For example, an extensive review of workplace interventions to promote mental wellbeing in the workplace by Graveling et al. (2008: x) found general inconsistency in definitions used to describe mental health; a wide array of methodologies and outcome measures; and similar diversity in the interventions— ranging from sending out leaflets on stress, training, counselling, recreational music and massage to organisational measures addressing the source of stress. They identified enough papers to suggest that these programs might have tangible benefits but evidence was insufficient to make unequivocal statements. A meta-review by Kuoppala et al. (2008: 1216–27) found that activities involving exercise, lifestyle and ergonomics were potentially effective but the application of education and psychological interventions in isolation was not. They argued (Kuoppala et al., 2008: 1216) that WHP 'should target both physical and psychosocial environments at work'.

Our own reading of studies indicates that like, much intervention literature, the results need to be treated cautiously due to a number of recurring methodological limitations, including the often short time frame of the study and the absence of follow-up to see whether results held over the longer term (Kristensen, 2008). Context is also critical. For example, there is a case for extolling the virtues of improved diet and exercise to long-haul truck drivers. However, any intervention needs to recognise that they are frequently absent from home for long periods, drive long hours (especially late at night), and are often under considerable pressure to meet schedules, resulting in inadequate sleep and cumulative fatigue (Mayhew and Quinlan, 2006). Unless these underlying issues are addressed, any intervention is at best partial, if not tokenistic, and unlikely to prove effective over the longer term.

There are few assessments of WHP schemes in Australia. A small Australian study (based on a survey of management) undertaken by Williams (1991: 489–94) identified a number of factors affecting the implementation of WHP, including management commitment, coordination, communication with and involvement by employees, and union and community support (see also an attempt to model the costs and benefits of health promotion by Hocking, 1992: 511–15). A review of EAPs by Kirk and Brown (2003: 138) concluded that evidence did not 'fully support' their effectiveness but they were valued by employees and appeared to 'impact positively on employee mental health'. In their review, Blewett and Shaw (1995b: 461–5) emphasise the problematic relationship between OHS and personal health promotion, arguing that WHP should not detract from conventional prevention practices. Indeed, there has been a recurring debate internationally about the relationship between OHS and WHP and wellness programs (Kohte, 2003). While the two may operate in a synergistic way, this depends on the conception of WHP—especially the extent to which broader organisation factors are addressed (see below)—and the motives of employers for pursuing it.

More extensive research has been undertaken in the US and Europe. However, in the 20 years since Matteson and Ivancevich (1986) wrote their review a number of key issues they identified remain unresolved. WHP programs are more likely to be found in large firms and to benefit the permanent employees (a bias that will favour male workers) and there is also evidence that the programs are insensitive to the needs of ethnic minorities or immigrants (Aguirre-Molina and Molina, 1990: 789–806). Studies have often found that WHP programs focus on issues of individual health behaviour (notably smoking and nutrition) that are indirectly connected to work and give far less attention to combined work and environmental exposures to harmful substances (Heimendinger et al., 1990; Weisbrod et al., 1991). Programs have been criticised as being too narrow to achieve results even in relation to nutrition and other lifestyle changes; it has been argued that WHP programs need to be broadened to involve family members and the community (McCauley and Mirin, 1990 and Katz and Showstack 1990).

Bellingham (1990: 666–7) criticises individual health promotion, arguing schemes typically have a short-term focus involving essentially fragmented sets of activities that downplay employee involvement and collective/environmental factors. He argues that management commitment to modifying the work environment is critical to developing effective WHP programs. This is not an isolated criticism. Chapman Walsh et al. (1991) argue that WHP, and especially more narrowly conceived 'wellness programs', can be seen as just another method of individualising and blame shifting that amounts to a new form of corporate social control. The individualised approach has also been labelled as ineffective. Petersen and Stunkard (1989: 821–2, cited in Dixon, 1999: 23) argued that the success of workplace health promotion programs depended on '… the extent to which labor and management formed a coherent group with a strong sense of personal and collective control. Collective control cannot exist if there is no collectivity …'.

Other studies highlight the need for planning, expenditure and accommodation to workers' interests if programs are to be made effective. For example, a study of barriers and incentives in relation to worker involvement in WHP (Kruger et al., 2007) found the most frequently stated barrier was time constraints while the incentive workers wanted was the provision of programs in a convenient time and location and as employer-paid time off during the workday. Other studies identify a need to consider the context of workers when undertaking WHP (an issue also raised by Randall et al., 2007). For example, as a Canadian study (Tavares and Plotnikoff, 2008) showed, a major barrier to attempts to promote physical activity among female workers was the family obligations and time pressures on women with young children. Consistent with the last point, WHP programs seldom consider issues of job design or work organisation that impact on their effectiveness. While evidence suggests physical activity programs have benefits (Dugdill et al., 2008), few consider how work can be reorganised so that such activity becomes part of the job rather than a supplement. A Dutch study (Alavinia et al., 2009: 55) found that the degree of job control exercised by workers was important to maintaining productivity and concluded 'health management at the workplace should consider interventions that increase the possibility for workers with health problems to continue working according to their abilities'. In short, WHP needs to move from adapting people to jobs to adapting jobs to people.

A more general limitation already alluded to is that WPH and wellness programs cannot be viewed in isolation from rapid and often profound changes in organisations and work, such as downsizing/restructuring, work intensification, changes to working hour arrangements, outsourcing and the increased use of contingent workers that have already been described extensively elsewhere in this book. Nytro et al. (2000) have observed these endemic changes undermine work stress interventions because they are a source of stress in their own right. As Kristensen (2008) has observed in a critical review of psychosocial intervention studies, the organisational flux that researchers often saw as disruptive to their assessment was not incidental 'noise' but the norm of working life and organisational experience—and something that should have been integral to their research. The move away from large organisations with relatively stable workforces also means fewer workplaces where WHP can be implemented. The network approach in Europe does provide opportunities for WHP in small business but efforts in this regard appear exceptional (Hamalainen and the ENWHP network, 2007: 46–9; Klatt and Ollman, 2007). The challenge of providing WHP or wellness programs to subcontractors, teleworkers or home-based workers is seldom if ever acknowledged in the literature, let alone addressed (although it helps to explain why WHP programs are uncommon in industries such as construction where contingent work arrangements are pervasive; see Pritchard and McCarthy, 2002).

The criticisms just made indicate not just that WHP applied in isolation has significant limitations but that there are also broader reasons for concern. Like screening and surveillance, the use of WHP can raise important ethical issues. In some instances, individual risk assessment (using sickness absence records and the like) associated with WHP programs can provide the basis for targeting the behaviour of individuals and groups in ways that are not only ineffective but should be cause for concern (Taimela et al., 2008). Further, while WHP programs have a laudatory preventative orientation, the objectives are generally restricted to changing individual attitudes and behaviour. As a result these programs suffer from the same limitations as other individual behavioural strategies already discussed, including an inability to sustain outcomes (Abrams et al., 1986; Weisbrod et al., 1991). Such observations have led to suggestions that health promotion should be addressed to achieving organisational change as well as individual change so that the organisation becomes health oriented (Abrams et al., 1986). However, Abrams et al. still portray health promotion as primarily an expert, management-controlled strategy. Later in this chapter further evidence will be provided to show that such non-participatory models of occupational health management have significant limitations. At the same time, a Danish researcher Kamp (2009: 85–102) has argued that WHP can be reconfigured along more collectivist lines—similar to some other areas of public health—and integrated with OHS in ways that not only focus on the underlying sources of ill health but also empower workers to genuinely participate in addressing this.

Some larger organisations support on-site OHS centres, providing first aid, OHS induction/training, medical screening and monitoring services, as well as a range of injury prevention and health promotion activities and post-injury rehabilitation services. The provision of occupational health services is mandated in the EU (although the level of implementation varies widely between countries) but not in Australia and therefore is confined to only some of the largest employers in the latter. Nonetheless, even within the EU the provision of these services has been adversely effected by changes to work arrangements (Husman and Husman, 2006).

Among the functions of on-site OHS centres are the coordination of emergency procedures (evacuation/refuge points and procedures, rescue teams, first aid and emergency showers); maintaining medical and OHS records, including records of screening and health surveillance; induction; training competency/currency; OHS KPIs; injury and hazard exposure records; near miss and dangerous incident reports; workers' compensation claims and return to work; EAP usage; compliance with SWPs, JSAs and the like; employee health and wellbeing surveys; OHS program monitoring; and maintaining copies of investigations and external audit or consultant reports. Where medical screening and monitoring is performed, the detailed health records of individual workers should be maintained in strict confidentiality by the centre. Notwithstanding this, maintenance of an archive of medical records can provide a valuable database for retrospective research. Other functions include establishing effective working relationships with the workplace health and safety committee, other departments in the organisation, safety representatives and the relevant unions, local hospitals and clinics, and outside professional consultants.

The collection of OHS data is critical; so too are strategic judgments about what information is most appropriate given the array of hazards and challenges to worker health and wellbeing in the workplace and ensuring the data collected is analysed and used effectively. Advances in information technology have provided enhanced means of collecting, storing (using a variety of databases and often customised packages), analysing and communicating information (via email, intranet and the internet for example). While little research has been undertaken on how effectively OHS centres manage their information, some specific incidents suggest the need for improvement. For example, at the Beaconsfield mine, while seismicity was recognised as a critical issue by management the only two OHS indicators nominated as KPIs were lost time and medically treated injuries. The mine recorded rockfalls but there is no evidence these were systematically analysed (for trends, frequency, cause and location) until after the fatal incident on 25 April 2006.

On-site OHS centres can play a valuable role in the coordination of rehabilitation services for workers who have suffered injury or illness at work. As general issues associated with rehabilitation and return to work were examined at some length in the chapter on workers' compensation, attention here will be restricted to the provision of services in the workplace. These services are generally designed to return workers to their maximum potential performance after occupational illness or injury and to minimise workers' compensation costs. Where possible, an attempt is made either to maintain staff at work or to facilitate their rapid return to the workplace. Workplace rehabilitation generally involves redesign of tasks and equipment so that staff can continue to work while recovering from illness or injury. For this reason ergonomic assessment, aimed at fitting the job to the worker, plays an important role in rehabilitation (CCH Australia, 1987). Aspects of the job that should be evaluated include work organisation, job design, workstation and equipment design and the worker's level of autonomy and control. Appropriate physical modifications should be made to equipment and the working environment, and in some cases the injured worker may have to be moved to a more suitable job. These changes may have to be complemented by additional education and training, so that the worker has the appropriate skills to adapt to changed tasks and equipment, and to avoid further injury (training in lifting and handling techniques may be necessary, for example). It is common for workers to initially return part time and gradually build up to full-time work.

A number of other factors may contribute to the success of rehabilitation programs (see chapter 8). Early intervention is vitally important so that the factors contributing to the problem can be identified, and appropriate intervention commenced, before the illness or injury becomes more serious or chronic. Workers should also be actively involved in decision making about their own rehabilitation program. In general, they should be given the opportunity to maintain a significant level of responsibility for, and control over, both the rehabilitation strategy employed and the pace of their return to the workforce. It is also crucial that the primary organisational authority and responsibility for rehabilitation is clearly delegated, ideally to the health centre if one exists. Clear delegation is necessary if the services provided are to be timely, well coordinated and appropriately resourced.

The provision of effective rehabilitation services (see chapter 8) represents a considerable improvement over post-injury procedures that were previously oriented to negotiating payouts and did little to address the underlying causes of injury and ill health or to facilitate a successful return to meaningful work (CCH Australia, 1987). Instead of being banished from the workforce and sanitised out of public view, even the seriously disabled can often be returned to active and fulfilling work for relatively low capital outlays. For example, one organisation of which we are aware has purchased voice-actuated computer equipment for workers whose injuries preclude them from using keyboards. For the organisation, expenditure on such equipment can be balanced favourably against costs such as turnover, training and the loss of valuable expertise that may be incurred if experienced staff are forced out of work. For the worker, a return to meaningful work, and the financial security and independence that accompanies it, often represents a cherished alternative to dependence on charity and social security. The wider community is relieved from social security and healthcare costs, and it benefits from the continued contribution of the workers to their organisation and to community life in general. Further, the return of injured workers serves as a reminder to the organisation and its employees of the human cost of injury, which contrasts favourably with the more common practice of excising the permanently disabled from the work environment and rapidly forgetting them. It also highlights the organisation's acceptance that injured workers have rights to employment where possible—an acceptance that undoubtedly enhances employer/employee relations generally. Handled sensitively, rehabilitation services provide an important means of reducing the costs, both financial and social, of occupational injury and illness.

Critical issues in OHS management

Throughout our examination of the various strategies that management can use to address OHS we have identified a number of critical points.

First, we identified the shortcomings of strategies that focused on workers as individuals and argued that organisation-level interventions were far more likely to address the underlying causes of occupational ill health. For many years the focus of health and safety management was largely on individual behavioural change, an approach that can be characterised as aiming to fix the worker, not the workplace. Policy responses consistent with this approach include attempts to screen out or redeploy workers, closer supervision, stricter safety rules, the development of safety awareness and education programs and behaviour modification. In the 1980s and 1990s cruder forms of victim blaming fell into disfavour and there was a growing recognition that the physical and organisational working environment needed to be addressed. However, as the emergence of BBS and narrow applications of safety 'culture' demonstrate, behavioural approaches have proved remarkably resilient. The problem with these approaches is their preoccupation with modifying individual behaviour. We do not entirely discount the value of behaviour change strategies but such policies need to be designed as an adjunct to a more comprehensive approach to health and safety that addresses the underlying environmental and organisational origins of injury, illness and disease.

A second important theme developed throughout this chapter was in relation to the value of expert technical models for modifying the physical work environment. Occupational health and safety management practices have historically been strongly influenced by an expert model of intervention. Professionals, including physicians, nurses, occupational hygienists, psychologists, physiotherapists, occupational therapists and ergonomists, have been employed by management to provide expert advice and services deemed to be appropriate. We praised the preventative focus of many of these models and their recognition of the need to modify the work environment, while also noting that the models used were too narrow, frequently applied in a fragmented or decontextualised fashion, or shaped by management interests and priorities. Their limitations included a tendency to oversimplify the behavioural interactions between workers, supervisors and their physical environment. The organisational context is usually ignored. At the same time, the policies contain the worst features of an expert approach, being dressed up in technocratic language designed to impress upper management but confusing many of those who will be directly affected. To some extent this problem has been compounded by the proliferation of OHS consultants, some excellent, but others peddling what can only be described as slickly packaged but narrow and inflexible programs (this appears to be an even greater problem in the US). Generally, workers and lower supervisory management are not genuinely consulted and are not seen to offer worthwhile input into the creation of more effective strategies.

The last point flows on to another theme developed throughout the chapter, namely the need to see worker participation as critical to the process of resolving health and safety problems at work. In chapter 9 we identified both ethical and practical reasons for this. In this chapter we have presented further evidence to this effect, namely that worker involvement improves the quality of OHS management (see also Arocena et al., 2008). Worker input represents an important source of information for both managers and consultants and it is especially critical given increasingly rapid changes that often occur within workplaces. One of the disturbing findings of the investigation into the 2006 rockfall at the Beaconsfield goldmine was that no consultant spoke to workers about ground conditions prior to the incident and they were, therefore, unaware of workers' experiences and concerns in this regard (Quinlan, 2007). This is another example of the danger of narrowly constructed OHS expertise that doesn't draw on all available sources of information. The role of unions is also critical in terms of worker involvement. Although it is sometimes suggested (as was the case at the Beaconsfield mine) that direct communication between management and its workforce offers a (superior?) alternative to communication via unions this is not supported by evidence. Indeed, a large survey of workplaces in Denmark and Britain (Croucher et al., 2006) found direct communication between HRM managers and employees was positively affected by union presence.

A similar point can be made in relation to the role of line management in OHS. In the past, line managers have typically received insufficient training in OHS and have not had it included in their performance appraisal. Not surprisingly, many saw it as a nuisance and an obstruction to efficiency and productivity or not really an issue at all. This often became a barrier to implementing OHS changes although, in fairness to line managers, it should also be noted that, like workers, they were often excluded from participating in critical decisions over OHS. Sheehy and Chapman (1987) argue that in companies that have successful safety programs there is generally a high level of management commitment to safety and the programs are integrated into other work programs and practices. It is clear that if a participatory approach to health and safety management is to be effective it must involve line management. Their support is vital for the successful implementation of many interventions and any resistance from them is a major impediment to the development of an effective organisational OHS program. Consequently, if health and safety is to be fully recognised and supported, it needs to be seen as part of the line manager's role and not an intrusion upon it. Further, any fear among managers that a participatory approach to OHS will undermine their authority in other areas needs to be addressed in education and training programs. Research has indicated that one of the strongest barriers to effective management involvement in safety is a reluctance to accept safety as an important performance criterion (Sheehy and Chapman, 1987). To reinforce the importance of their responsibilities in this area, OHS management should be formally included in performance appraisals for all managers.

In sum, an effective approach to managing OHS must have an informed understanding of the extent, origins or causes of occupational ill health. Understanding the causes of occupational injury and disease is by no means a simple task. Even a cursory reading of this book should indicate that the causes of occupational injury and illness are complex. Work organisation, equipment design and other aspects of the physical working environment, administrative practices and social and psychological processes may all interact in a single causal process. In view of this complexity, it is essential that health and safety management be approached in a systematic and comprehensive manner. It also is important to ensure the maximum breadth of input and action in all phases of the diagnosis, intervention and evaluation process. Effective diagnosis will depend on collection of data from a variety of sources. Expert knowledge should not be utilised in isolation, but combined with information gathered from workers and supervisors who have everyday experience with the hazards.

After an accurate diagnosis has been achieved, comprehensive intervention must be pursued at all relevant levels. As we have previously argued, the interventions considered should not be narrow and limited to a particular range of strategies. While it is possible that behavioural programs or equipment redesign may provide adequate solutions to a particular problem, interventions that tend to be overlooked, such as changes in work organisation or job redesign, must be considered and implemented where appropriate. Following successful intervention there should be ongoing monitoring of health and safety performance. Once again, accurate evaluation of this performance relies on collection of data from the widest possible range of sources. Regular health and safety audits provide an important source of data for evaluation. Effective lines of communication must be kept open between management, the workplace health and safety committee and workers. The health and safety committee, in particular, should play an active investigatory role. It should not only encourage staff to report new and potential hazards, but also actively instigate diagnostic surveys and audits as necessary. The successful achievement of each of these goals is dependent on the development of appropriate organisational structures for health and safety management. The next section will consider OHS management systems as a vehicle for doing this.

OHS management systems and risk management: panaceas to past problems?

Past attempts by management to deal with OHS suffered from a number of recurring problems, namely:

- an overemphasis on individual behaviour change, monitoring and protection strategies
- a failure to comprehensively and systematically review and assess hazards. Typically management dealt with a select number of known hazards.
- policy objectives, structures and practices were often not well connected or articulated
- while policies often purported to be proactive, in reality they were commonly reactive and static and failed to address major changes in the workplace till well after these changes were made
- the policies in place addressed only some hazards and typically did so in a partial and fragmented manner that ignored important connections (for example, between work organisation and 'unsafe' work practices).

Over the last 20 years the limitations of this approach, especially in the context of complex and changing workplaces, has been increasingly recognised. A number of factors, including regulatory changes discussed in chapter 7 and a growing interest in risk management/loss control and systems (Frick et al., 2000), led to a growing interest in more systematic approaches to managing OHS, and in particular the notion of OHS management systems (OHSMS). The term OHS management systems is used in a wide variety of ways, and goes under a number of different labels—something complicated by confusion with systematic OHSM and the differing terminology used by OHS agencies in various countries (e.g. Internal Control in Norway and OHS programs in the US; Frick et al., 2000). Systematic OHSM generally refers to the efforts of government agencies to secure a more proactive and planned approach to OHS by employers while OHSMS refers to the internal systems that employers develop to manage OHS.

In principle, OHS management systems provide the opportunity to secure enhanced OHS outcomes. From a management perspective the systems approach can be seen to have a number of distinct advantages. Most obviously, OHS management systems can enable management to:

- identify, assess and address all significant hazards
- prioritise OHS activities

- address some hazards at the entry point or design stage
- address changes to the workplace and hazards
- monitor and audit OHS processes and outcomes
- meet ethical as well as legal requirements in relation to OHS.

Additionally, it has been claimed that OHS management systems can deliver improvements in labour/management relations, profitability and productivity (see, for example, Mottel et al., 1995) although evidence from government reviews and research suggest aspects of this causal connection may operate in the other direction—namely, that good industrial relations is a pre-condition for effective OHSMS (Gallagher, 1997; Gallagher et al., 2001; Saksvik and Quinlan, 2003; Wran and McClelland, 2005). The latter interpretation is also more consistent with evidence that trust and trusted information sources are essential to effective risk communication (Conchie and Burns, 2009). Where there is a lack of trust between workers and managers, two-way communication of information breaks down and, as a number of major incidents like that at the Beaconsfield mine in 2006 attest, a poor industrial relations climate is not conducive either to trust or communication.

International corporations (Dotson, 1997), or firms with widely dispersed work-places, can use the systems model to secure a consistent approach to OHS. The systems approach has been portrayed as the natural corollary of management systems developed in the area of quality, chemical management, major hazards engineering and the environment (Celik, 2009; Reniers et al., 2009). These arguments, along with a growing interest in performance management, also help explain why the notion of OHS management systems has become so popular.

In practice, many systems fail to come close to achieving these ambitious goals. Common limitations with systems include:

- a focus on or preoccupation with safety rather than health
- a focus on or preoccupation with individual behaviour and routine hazards
- inadequate hazard identification and risk assessment
- inadequate OHS and OHSM performance indicators
- paper compliance (including tick the box) and a 'disconnect' in terms of implementation
- inadequate systems monitoring and independent auditing
- inadequate feedback loops (management and workers)
- inadequate attention to changes to work organisation and changes in work processes
- poor use of consultants or the purchase of 'package' systems.

Several observations serve to illustrate the importance of these limitations (other examples are cited below).

First, behaviour-based controls and currently fashionable/highly promoted interventions based on this, notably behaviour-based safety (BBS), do not constitute a comprehensive OHSMS. Behaviour-based strategies are an element but subsidiary to environmental and work organisation interventions in terms of a comprehensive OHSMS. As a scheme, BBS has been criticised for focusing too much on individual behaviour at the expense of devoting attention to physical working conditions (including plant and equipment), management practices and work organisation (Hopkins, 2006a). In our view, BBS can deflect attention and resources from more critical hazards. In a hierarchy of controls, behaviour is the last line of defence (and one not especially suited to minimising many health-related hazards such as toxic exposure to chemicals and the like). Further, as an individualised approach, BBS detracts attention from the collective input of workers through health and safety committees, HSRs and unions.

Second, risk management plays a critical role in an OHSMS by establishing procedures to govern hazard identification, risk assessment, the introduction of new control measures and review. At its most basic, the process of risk assessment seeks to assess the magnitude and likelihood of an incident or exposure in the workplace in order to form a basis for deciding the urgency and resources that should be devoted to particular problems. The assessment process follows the identification of all relevant hazards. This information is then used to devise a response or intervention, and the effectiveness of the latter is then assessed to inform (and if need be, modify) future responses thereby closing the loop. As already noted, the dimensions for assessing risk revolve around trying to assess, on the one hand, the magnitude (seriousness and consequences) of being exposed to the hazard and, on the other hand, the likelihood (or frequency) of exposure. Thus, for example, a hazard which is rarely encountered and entails minimal costs may be assessed as a minimal risk requiring limited intervention whereas a hazard exposure that is relatively infrequent but has very serious consequences (causing serious injury or death) would require a significant response. As noted by the Standards Australia/Standards New Zealand *Handbook Risk Management Guidelines Companion to AS/NZS 4360: 2004*, the benefits of risk management include fewer unexpected events/surprises; better exploitation of opportunities; improved planning, performance and effectiveness; economy and efficiency; enhanced reputation/improved stakeholder relationships; improved information for decision making; and enhanced accountability and governance.

However, risk management is a component of an OHSMS—not an OHSMS of itself—and must be implemented with care. Given its origins in insurance and engineering there can be a tendency to overemphasise what can be readily measured or 'costed' in a risk assessment process. This approach has limitations in OHS where, as we have noted elsewhere, workers' compensation claims (the most obvious source for costing OHS outcomes) seriously understate particular types of claims, such as exposures to hazardous substances. While measurement clearly has value, a qualitative approach to risk assessment is both acceptable and, indeed, essential where key risks cannot be readily quantified (they can still be ranked based on the available information). Further, as made clear in AS4360 as well as numerous government regulations and guides, a key element in risk assessment is communication and consultation with key stakeholders (notably workers). Too often in our experience this element has been either missing or dealt with in a perfunctory or inadequate manner. At the Beaconsfield goldmine, for example, workers were told about management's intentions following serious rockfalls in October 2005 (six months before the fatal fall in April 2006). However, they were not consulted—a two-way process—and nor were their views sought by consultants assessing the seismicity and ground conditions at the mine (Quinlan, 2007).

These observations illustrate that while risk assessment has been increasingly embraced in OHS management a number of serious limitations have been identified with regard to its application. For example, the NSW Department of Primary Industries' (1997b: 4–5) *Guide to Reviewing a Risk Assessment* identified a number of common faults in risk assessment to be guarded against, including the omission of credible accidents or incidents, unwarranted optimism about safeguards implemented (something the guide noted could also ensnare 'independent' consultants working closely with the organisation), unstated or unsupported assumptions and use of risk assessment to justify a predetermined position. In a similar vein, a report on good practice in risk assessment prepared for the Health and Safety Executive (HSE) in the UK (Gadd et al., 2003: viii) identified a number of common pitfalls in risk assessment, including:

- dividing the time spent on hazardous activity between several individuals—the 'salami' approach to risk estimation (the term 'salami' approach is taken directly from the HSE report)
- not involving a team of people in risk estimation or not involving employees with practical knowledge of the process/activity being assessed
- ineffective use of consultants
- failure to identify all hazards associated with a particular activity
- not doing anything with the results of this assessment
- not linking hazards with risk controls.

Other common limitations (see also Gadd et al., 2004) include a failure to document the risk assessment process, especially in the context of major changes. Following the major rockfalls of October 2005 the Beaconsfield goldmine did not document an overarching risk assessment process as distinct from collecting hazard-related information (Quinlan, 2007). In this case interviews with managers indicated no overarching assessment had occurred. Documenting major risk assessment processes in sufficient detail to show how the process was approached, what was considered and how final decisions were arrived at is critical, not simply to demonstrate compliance with relevant OHS legislation and regulations. This documentation will provide information for reassuring the workforce, guidance for future reviews (especially given lapses of time/memory or the departure of key personnel involved) and for making revisions in the light of new information or experience.

Given evidence of limitations in OHS management and the application of risk management as part of this, it is important to examine what are the critical components of an effective OHS management system.

What constitutes an effective OHS management system?

There is now a flood of published material on OHS management systems (OHSMS), including books and articles, government publications (brochures, guides and self-audit manuals) as well as marketed packages of consultants, professional associations and individual companies such as DuPont. Much, though by no means all, of this material is narrowly prescriptive and lacks the critical focus that would allow management to evaluate the strengths and weaknesses of particular system models so as to better inform their own endeavours. Overall, research on the effectiveness of OHSMS has generally drawn positive conclusions, but this is heavily qualified by acknowledgment of the heterogeneity of OHSMS, and critical provisos about these effects, including the institutional and regulatory context and role of unions (Frick et al., 2000; Saksvik and Quinlan, 2003; Robson et al., 2007; Bottani et al., 2009).

Like any popular idea, the notion of OHS management systems encompasses a wide array of different meanings and interpretations, with each discipline and interest group trying to put its own spin on it. At one level, there is a surprising level of agreement internationally about the key features of an effective management approach to OHS. We have summarised these features from a New Zealander's perspective (see Pringle 1995), although similar sentiments can be drawn from a wide range of government, academic and consultant literature on OHS management and OHS management systems. Pringle (1995: 271) argues that organisations that perform best in OHS have the following four characteristics:

- a strong and demonstrable management commitment to OHS
- efficient hazard identification and evaluation followed by engineering, training and other control responses
- effective employee communication and involvement
- an OHS program integrated into the larger management system.

At another level, these widely accepted principles mask a range of critical questions and more contentious issues. For example, what is precisely meant by senior management commitment and, even more critically, how can it be secured? There is clear agreement that management commitment amounts to more than a clear expression of this sentiment in policy statements but must be demonstrated by actions. The latter might include senior management involvement in OHS committees, the dedication of significant budget and time resources to OHS, making OHS a lead agenda item at management meetings, the clear articulation of policies and making OHS a significant aspect of all management training, role specification and performance appraisal. How to actually secure senior management commitment often receives at best cursory attention. In the 1990s much of the rhetoric in government publications and prescriptive books on OHS management systems was that OHS is good for business. While it may have validity, it is not an especially new argument, raising the obvious question of why this line of reasoning has not driven all managers to prioritise OHS in the past. We are not suggesting cost–benefit arguments cannot be used to persuade senior managers about the OHS consequences of a particular course of action. However, relying on economic motivations alone is problematic because the situation is rather more contingent than this argument would suggest and it also presumes rationality and clear market signals (see Frick, 1995, 1996). Reliance on an 'OHS pays' argument amounts to confining the discourse on OHS to a neo-liberal agenda rather than one where social and human consequences also have importance. One of the few to devote considerable attention to the issue of management commitment is Hopkins (1995) who is highly critical of productivity and profitability-based arguments and argues OHS should be presented in terms of ethics. He argues this cannot and should not be left as a choice or voluntary decision for managers to make. Rather, the state has a strong role to play in terms of providing a regulatory framework that encourages managers to treat OHS seriously (by, for example, rigorously pursuing due diligence). For those managers who have already adopted such an approach this intervention will present no problem. We endorse Hopkins's argument about the need for a rather more proactive role by regulators, both by providing the materials that will assist them to implement OHS management systems and by adopting a compliance strategy that targets those employers whose actions indicate an unwillingness to take OHS seriously.

Another critical point of disagreement is the content and thrust of the OHS management system in terms of hazard identification, assessment and control. Throughout this book we have strenuously argued that to effectively manage OHS it is essential that the physical work environment, work organisation and the behaviour of management and workers be simultaneously addressed. We have also endeavoured to show that all three factors interact but organisational factors exert a critical influence on behaviour as well as shaping decisions in relation to the use of hazardous substances, plant and equipment, etc. Finally, it has also been an essential tenet of this book that, on both ethical and practical grounds, workers must play a significant role in identifying hazards, developing solutions and auditing their effectiveness. Although an OHS management system is a logical way to achieve these objectives many individual programs or packages with which we are familiar are too narrow in scope or conception to do this. For example, some systems focus on ensuring that employees, subcontractors, etc. are properly trained for their tasks and maintaining safe plant and equipment, completely ignoring work organisation. Some system packages contain elaborate checklists of hazards or risk factors but the approach is more taxonomic than integrated. In others, the input of workers is tightly circumscribed (for example, only occurring through teams or work groups with narrowly defined responsibilities).

Most commonly, the system models place an overriding emphasis on behaviour. This is especially the case with the US and British literature (see, for example, Cox and Cox, 1996), reflecting in part the relative attractiveness of this approach to management (see chapter 3), and it is worth noting that behaviour occupies a conspicuous role in the much-heralded DuPont system. It also probably reflects the discourse among psychologists who continue to dominate much of the management debate about OHS. Many work and organisational psychologists appear to have perceived systems as largely entailing a better and more comprehensive approach to managing attitudes and behaviour (see, for example, Donald and Young, 1996; Cabrera, 1998; Fahlbruch and Wilpert, 1999). A systems approach largely preoccupied with behaviour is, given what we have tried to demonstrate throughout this book, more of dead-end alley than a genuine advance in our understanding of OHS. Not all psychologists have adopted this interpretation. A number of Scandinavian psychologists have presented an interpretation that is essentially consistent with our own. For example, in their study of the Norwegian

Internal Control system, Nytro et al. (1998) make a number of critical observations about the organisational prerequisites for effective OHS management systems. They identify the critical role the regulatory and institutional context plays in promoting a situation where management takes a serious interest in OHS, where there is sufficient educational and other infrastructure for change to occur and where workers have a meaningful input. Nytro et al. (1998) emphasise the importance of worker involvement and argue a critical future challenge is to break down the ideological divide between the collective negotiation of wages and the working environment so work can be addressed in a more holistic fashion, rather than with the present fractured approach.

The third and final contentious issue we wish to discuss in relation to OHS management systems is the question of measuring performance. Part of the whole rationale for implementing the systems approach is that it will lend itself more to measurable improvements in OHS. It has also been argued that measuring OHS performance will itself contribute to OHS being treated in a serious manner by management (see Dotson, 1996: 669). Thus, a critical prerequisite for implementing an effective OHS management system is having a set of performance measures by which to judge the system and, if necessary, to modify it. Indeed, performance measures are essential to any structured approach to OHS. One of the limitations with even widely used OHS management systems is that they rely on a narrow band of measures that are open to manipulation or fail to fully reflect the enterprise's performance. For example, the notion of zero injuries, zero accidents, no lost-time compensation claims and the like are the most frequently touted goals of many OHS management systems, but as we have already indicated, these measures have limitations (see also Shaw, 1994: 17).

It has been increasingly recognised that a far wider range of performance indicators is available, including both negative and positive indicators, as well as indicators of both outcomes and processes. A by no means comprehensive list of potential performance measures would include the following:

Outcome measures
- total, average or cost per man-hour of workers' compensation claims
- frequency and severity of injuries
- benchmarking injury performance against industry averages or other firms
- number of incidents or near misses reported
- total or average OHS-related costs (direct and indirect)
- number of noncompliance incidents identified, rules broken or 'unsafe' behaviour
- number of inspectorate investigations/prosecutions
- contractor injury records
- number of emergency incidents
- number of worker OHS suggestions/complaints
- audit results including government and self-administered audits
- external consultant evaluations

Process measures
- OHS problems identified
- OHS problems addressed

- OHS innovations introduced
- training/induction programs completed
- level of supervisor/management/worker communication/participation
- OHS audits completed
- safety committee initiatives
- staff attitudes/perceptions of OHS

As indicated, workplace audits are a means of measuring OHS performance but they can also be used to test the validity of other indicators and identify limitations in the system requiring modification. Rigorous auditing is an essential component in any effective OHS management system (Waring, 1996).

Andrea Shaw (1994) has made a number of points about the characteristics of meaningful performance measures, namely that they should:

- include an array of positive and negative measures, not simply one. An array of measures helps to mitigate against the bias and manipulation that may occur in relation to any single or narrow group of measures. At the same time, the number of measures should not be so numerous as to be confusing.
- include both process measures and outcome measures since an effective OHS management system will need to connect the former to the latter if it is to have any real understanding of how improvements are achieved
- include both quantitative and qualitative measures. This will give a more rounded feel for performance and qualitative measures are often a good way of checking the veracity of quantitative measures.
- be transparent, reliable/consistent and readily understood. Measures that are opaque or too complicated to comprehend are unlikely to contribute to informed analysis or be able to be presented to the workforce in an meaningful way.
- include avenues for worker feedback and even informal mechanisms. Informal networks are often a rich source of information about what is actually happening at the shop-floor level and can provide important clues for critically investigating numbers that suggest a radically difference picture.

We would endorse these points as key principles for selecting performance measures. One implication of these principles is that organisations should devise and modify performance measures to suit their particular workplace and should resist the temptation to adopt only measures that are easily benchmarked against other employers. Equally, while the use of computer tracking systems and other measurement packages has value (see Dotson, 1996, 1997; Hondros, 1991) we would caution against uncritical use of them. These systems often if not always contain presumptions about the nature of OHS problems which are not made explicit. The preoccupation with quantitative forms of measurement in many systems is an additional limitation.

Summary

Drawing the foregoing discussion together, it can be seen that while OHS management systems represent a potentially significant development, many of the programs promoted under this label represent, at best, a slight modification of pre-existing practices.

Enterprises should be cautious about buying and using systems 'off the shelf' without serious consideration to their strengths and limitations as well as the modifications that may need to be made. Equally, just as in the area of the audit systems promoted by OHS agencies, there is a danger of 'paper compliance' unless adequate efforts are made to audit results. The independent monitoring role that workers can play is critical in this regard (see Saksvik and Nytro, 1996). In Australia, Gallagher (1997) undertook a detailed study of the characteristics of OHS management systems across a range of employers and industries to try to identify those characteristics associated with effective systems. Drawing on her findings and others presented in the book we would suggest that an effective OHS management system requires a number of key components or, to put it another way, must be founded on the following key principles:

- OHS (including rehabilitation) must be integrated into normal production/service activities.
- There must be demonstrated commitment and leadership from senior management.
- Work organisation, equipment and the environment as well as behaviour with a particular focus on the first three factors must be addressed.
- The system must identify and assign responsibilities at all levels of the organisation (with appropriate training, powers and other forms of facilitation).
- It must recognise and address change with a view to enhancing OHS over time.
- It must utilise an appropriate mix of qualitative and quantitative/positive and negative performance indicators, monitored via an effective auditing regime.
- It must place great value on worker input into designing the system, identifying risks, planning remedies and auditing the system.

The point about change is one that is insufficiently recognised. While the OHS management systems literature often contains reference to continuous improvement or similar terms, there is another side to change in the workplace that is generally omitted but which we have referred to elsewhere in this book. We are referring to changes in the size and composition of the workforce as well as work organisation due to downsizing, the increased used of casual workers and outsourcing. These and other changes (such as those discussed in chapter 9) may have significant impacts on OHS. A fractured and contingent workforce, for example, may represent a serious threat to a well-conceived OHS management system (Quinlan and Mayhew, in Frick et al., 2000).

The book now turns to how management can approach OHS in two very different situations, namely the management of major hazards and OHS management in small business.

Managing high-hazard workplaces and facilities

Major-hazard facilities and workplaces—such as refineries, mines and chemical plants and storage facilities—present particular challenges in terms of managing OHS. On the one hand, controlling for infrequent but potentially catastrophic events such as a chemical explosion are very different from the controls that may be employed to manage more routine but low-level risks such as slips and trips (where even in the case of serious injury only one worker is liable to be affected). On the other hand, it is important that the management of very different types of hazards be integrated into an overall OHSMS (and major-hazard facilities should be presumed to have an OHSMS). Evidence of a number of disasters indicates that the need to meet this dual challenge has been misunderstood.

Measures employed in relation to major hazards include:

- catastrophic risk assessment/planning
- emergency response/evacuation procedures
- induction/training, SWP, JSAs and supervision protocols
- behaviour modification (worker and management)
- scenario planning (major-hazard plans)
- near miss and incident reporting and investigation
- performance indicators/monitoring
- independent system auditing and risk assessment.

In a previous subsection we identified a number of common flaws in OHSMS, namely:

- focus on safety, not health
- focus on individual behaviour/routine risk
- inadequate hazard identification and risk assessment
- inadequate performance indicators
- paper compliance and 'disconnect' in implementation
- inadequate systems monitoring and independent auditing
- inadequate feedback loops (management and workers)
- inadequate attention to changes to organisation/processes
- poor use of consultants.

A number of disastrous incidents indicate that several of these flaws play an especially critical role in relation to the failure of OHS at major-hazard facilities. As the work of James Reason (2000), Andrew Hopkins (1999a & b) and Eric Tucker (2006) demonstrates, important lessons can be learnt from these incidents. Unfortunately, there has been a tendency by government inquiries to look at these incidents in isolation rather than try to identify and address systemic failings. Further, official investigations have used a number of different methods and (often implicitly) relied on different theoretical models about causation (Roed-Larsen et al., 2004; Le Croze, 2008).

James Reason (2000) has examined failures in a range of contexts. He is critical of approaches that focus on individual human behaviour and has sought to identify the factors that make for reliable organisations, as well as the circumstances where multiple defences, barriers and safeguards can be pierced by an 'accident' trajectory—the Swiss cheese model (for a critique of this model—or at least people's understanding of it—see Perneger, 2005). A number of researchers have sought to draw on the Swiss cheese model and to develop the characteristics of high-reliability organisations to minimise human and organisational failures in high-hazard workplaces such as offshore oil installations (Bea, 1998; Hee et al., 1999; Ren et al., 2008). Reason rejects arguments that organisational complexity or technology is at the root of serious incidents—these challenges can be managed by high-reliability organisations so long as there is sufficient flexibility within them to adapt to new challenges (see also Le Coze, 2005).

Serious incidents can seldom be tied to a single reason, event or decision but have multiple causalities, including a chain of events that defeats the safeguards in place (amounting to aligned holes in Reason's Swiss cheese model). Nonetheless, while the investigations are too often taken in isolation (see above) and use different methods, the reported findings often reveal a recurring pattern of failures. In a recent review of major incidents (not all work-related) Wearne (2008) identified a recurring set of institutional failures preceding the event, notably problems with prioritising, responsibilities, procedures, expertise, attention to unusual operations, lack of inspection, lack of checking and lack of attention to warning signs. With regard to serious incidents at major-hazard workplaces our own perusal of the records identified a not dissimilar list of 'repeat' or recurring causal factors including (the examples cited in the list are illustrative and by no means exhaustive):

- design, engineering or planning flaws (e.g. Westgate Bridge collapse, Melbourne, 1970; Piper Alpha, UK, 1988; Beaconsfield mine, Tasmania, 2006)
- complexity and cumulative disorganisation by decisions—isolation/trees (e.g. Esso Longford, Victoria, 1998)
- fragmentation of work and authority (e.g. use of subcontractors—Valujet flight 592, Florida, USA, 1996; AZF, Toulouse, France, 2001)
- poor communication, IR and feedback loops (e.g. Esso Longford, Victoria, 1998; BP Texas City Refinery, USA, 2005; Beaconsfield mine, Tasmania, 2006)
- inadequate risk assessment and poor system auditing (e.g. Moura mine disaster, Queensland, 1994; Beaconsfield mine, Tasmania, 2006)
- political/regulatory compromises/failure (e.g. Bhopal, India, 1984; Kader Toy Factory Fire, Thailand, 1993; Georgia Sugar Refinery Explosion, 2008)
- poor performance indicators/ignored warning signals (numerous examples, see below)
- financial pressures (e.g. Westray mine disaster, Nova Scotia, 1992; BP Texas City Refinery, USA, 2005)
- inadequate attention to processes and changes to work organisation/processes (e.g. Bhopal, India, 1984; BP Texas City Refinery, USA, 2005).

It is beyond the province of this book to discuss all these limitations in detail but a number are worthy of discussion, especially as several highlight themes already raised in this book about how management should approach OHS.

Poor communication and inadequate worker consultation is an area that has been linked to major-hazard incidents. Poor communication within the organisation and between management and workers (including the absence of feedback loops for reporting problems) has been repeatedly identified as a contributing factor to major occupational disasters (Hopkins, 2000: 54–67). Communication problems, in terms of both horizontal and vertical flows of information, and resulting failures to obtain, transmit or react to knowledge within the organisation, have been identified as significant and recurrent contributors to serious incidents in high-hazard workplaces since the late 1970s (Turner, 1978; Hopkins, 1999b; Baker, 2007). For example, a key recommendation of the official inquiry into the 1988 Piper Alpha disaster (an explosion on a offshore oil rig in the North Sea that killed 167 workers) by Lord Cullen (1990, Vol. 2, Recommendation 27, cited in Woolfson et al., 1996: 270) was for workforce involvement in the reconstruction of safety in the offshore oil industry. Cullen stated (1990: Ch. 18: 48, cited in Woolfson et al., 1996: 270) that it was

> essential that the whole workforce is committed to and involved in safe operations. The first-line supervisors are a key link in achieving that, as each is personally responsible for ensuring all employees, whether the company's own or contractors, are trained to and do work safely and that they not only know how to perform their jobs safely but are convinced they have the responsibility to do so. Possibly the most visible instrument for the involvement of the workforce in safety is a safety committee system.

Lord Cullen also noted the important role of HSRs (Cullen, 1990: Ch. 21: 84 cited in Woolfson et al., 1996: 278)—the appointment of health and safety representatives by unions 'could be of some benefit in making the work of safety representatives and safety committees effective, mainly through the credibility and resistance to pressures which trade union backing would provide'.

A related issue is the need to involve workers in the risk assessment process regarding major-hazard incidents. As the *Guide to Reviewing a Risk Assessment* prepared by the New South Wales Department of Primary Industry (1997: 1) for the mining industry observes, 'it is not possible to check the standard of safety achieved in relation to major accidents by counting the frequency of them' and therefore attention needs to be given to methods that will lead to high-quality inputs into safety, and risk assessment is 'a proven technique for improving the quality of input to safety management, aiming to prevent accidents by "debugging" designs and operating methods etc before accidents occur, rather than responding to accidents which have happened and aiming to prevent recurrence'. Essential features of risk assessment identified in the guide (at page 2) include use of a team with varied and relevant experience, detailed and systematic risk identification, use of a comprehensive checklist of possible problems, definition of key questions to be answered prior to risk assessment, definition of the safety standard to be reached as well as monitoring and auditing programs.

An imbalance or deficiency with regard to focusing on individual and routine hazards on the one hand and catastrophic risks on the other has been identified in connection to mine management safety regimes and OHS management systems more generally in high-hazard workplaces (Hopkins, 1999b; Baker, 2007; United States Chemical Safety Board, 2007b). The importance of a process safety focus rather than focus on individual/personal safety or injury has been highlighted by recent investigations into a number of OHS management system failures that had catastrophic consequences, such as the explosion at BP's Texas City refinery that resulted in the death of 15 workers. In assessing BP's approach to safety in connection with the incident the *Report of the BP US Refineries Independent Safety Review Panel* (Baker 2007: xii) stated

> BP has an aspiration goal of 'no accidents, no harm to people.' BP has not provided effective leadership in making certain its management and its US refining workforce understands what is expected of them regarding process safety performance. BP has emphasised personal safety in recent years and has achieved significant improvement in personal safety performance, but BP did not emphasize process safety. BP mistakenly interpreted improving personal injury rates as an indication of acceptable process safety performance at its US refineries. BP's reliance on this data, combined with inadequate process safety understanding, created a false sense of confidence that BP was properly addressing process safety risks.

One of the key recommendations of the panel (No.7 at page xvii) was the need for both leading and lagging performance indicators. In addition to several already mentioned, 'near misses' have been viewed as a valuable predictor of actual injuries or serious events. In his study of the Esso Longford gas plant explosion in 1998, OHS expert Andrew Hopkins (1999a: 70–1) makes reference to the potential danger of focusing on lost-time injuries in high-hazard workplaces, including mines:

> … firms normally attend to what is being measured, at the expense of what is not. Thus, a focus on LTIs can lead companies to become complacent about their management of major hazards. This is exactly what seems to have happened at Esso … Precisely the same phenomenon contributed to the explosion at Moura. By concentrating on high frequency/low severity problems Moura had managed to halve its lost-time injury frequency rate in four years preceding the explosion, from 153 injuries per million hours worked in 1989/90 to 71 in 1993/94. By this criterion, Moura was safer than many other Australian coal mines. But as a consequence of focusing on relatively minor matters, the need for vigilance in relation to catastrophic events was overlooked.

Deficiencies in safety management systems auditing have been identified as a significant contributing factor to a number of major-hazard events in workplaces (Hopkins, 1999b, 2000; Baker, 2007). It needs to be noted that auditing is often confused with monitoring. Monitoring refers to internal processes that management puts in place to evaluate the implementation of OHS management systems on an ongoing basis. Auditing can be understood as an external process whereby the effectiveness of the management system is independently reviewed periodically. Thus monitoring and auditing are distinct processes although the terms are frequently confused. Both processes are essential to ensure that the system is operating as designed and that procedures are actually being implemented (i.e. avoiding common problems such as 'paper compliance' where documented procedures do not reflect actual practices or there is a significant level of noncompliance). The need for effective system auditing has been identified by recent investigations into disastrous incidents in high-hazard workplaces, such as the explosion at the BP's Texas City refinery in the US in 2005. The Report of the BP US Refineries Independent Safety Review Panel (Baker, 2007: xvii) recommended that 'BP should establish and implement an effective system to audit process safety performance at its US refineries'. Hopkins (1999b: 146–7) has observed that inquiries into a number of occupational disasters (including the Piper Alpha offshore oil platform explosion in the North Sea in 1988, the 1994 Moura mine disaster in Queensland and the 1998 explosion at Esso's Longford plant in Victoria) identified defective monitoring/auditing of management systems that failed to identify critical problems—but problems that were readily uncovered by an investigation following the incident. Reasons for these deficiencies include an unwillingness to pass on bad news, failure to seek the views of or listen to key personnel, failure to anticipate the consequences of organisational restructuring/work reorganisation, failure to maintain the currency of high-hazard scenarios, and practices that are fragmentary (looking at components of a system but not its sum) or target routine tasks but fail to interrogate areas or practices with the potential to have catastrophic consequences. Risk assessment, monitoring and auditing complex and hazardous workplaces require careful prioritising. It may also require reconsideration and modification of assessment and auditing/monitoring tools (Le Croze, 2005).

Financial pressures have also been linked to a number of major-hazard incidents and proving such an association is often difficult. For example, the allegation was made that corners were being cut in relation to safety by workers at Beaconsfield goldmine (which was then under administration) following the rockfall on 25 April 2006. This was by no means the first time a mine in financial difficulties has experienced a serious hazard event, and where these pressures were later found to have compromised OHS management in ways that directly contributed to the incident (see, for example, Glasbeek and Tucker, 1993; Jobb, 1994). A recent review of the causes of major-hazard incidents undertaken by the Health and Safety Laboratory of the UK Health and Safety Executive (Bell and Healy, 2006: iii) noted that there was some evidence that productivity pressures could adversely affect management commitment to safety.

This connection is not confined to mines or organisations experiencing financial difficulties (see also United States Chemical Safety and Hazard Investigation Board, 2007b; Hopkins, 1999a: 91–7). It may be a product of a push for higher profits or strategic decisions about global activities. An ex-operator at the Union Carbide plant at Bhopal, India (Chouhan, 2005: 205) stated

> I know how the (December 1984) disaster happened. The merciless cost-cutting, severely affecting materials of construction, maintenance, training, manpower and morale resulted in the disaster that was waiting to happen. Significant differences between the West Virginia, USA plant and the Bhopal, India plant show the callous disregard of the corporation for the people of developing countries.

Others, such as Carson (1990) note the complicity of government authorities in this outcome. It might be presumed that the huge economic costs (if not public outrage) associated with such disasters would motivate management to take great precautionary measures. However, Hopkins (1999b) observes that in spite of the many notorious examples, such as the Zeebrugge ferry disaster (1987), Bhopal (1984), Piper Alpha (1988) and Moura mine disaster (Queensland, 1986), the consequences of these disasters seem not to impact on key decision-makers and makes a mockery of the argument that 'safety pays'. It is worth adding that in the case of the Beaconsfield mine the results of the rockfall were a long-term cessation of mining operations, large legal expenses as the mine responded to the subsequent independent investigation and coronial inquest and the potential for costs associated with extensive civil litigation, and the refusal of the mine's insurer to cover expenses associated with the disaster.

With regard to warning signals it can be noted that investigation into serious incidents frequently uncovers clear evidence that there were warning signals or issues that should have caused management concern sometime before the fatal incident. For example, prior to the explosion at the Moura No. 4 coalmine, Queensland, in 1986, management knew the gas build-up behind a sealed panel would go through the explosive range (at 2330–2400 hrs) while men were underground. At the Gretley coal mine a number of deputies noticed abnormal water in the weeks prior to the inrush that drowned a number of miners. Prior to the Valujet crash into a Florida swamp there had been a pattern of repeated maintenance faults and also poor contractor maintenance prior to the incident. Prior to the fatal explosion at the Esso Longford refinery on 25 September 1998 there had been a similar cold-temperature incident about one month earlier, on 28 August 1998. Finally, there had been 24 unplanned rockfalls at the Beaconsfield goldmine prior to the fatal rockfall on 25 April 2006, a pattern of about a fall every five weeks (or a fall over 50 tonnes every 10 weeks) with no tailing off despite interventions after a dangerous set of rockfalls in October 2005. On the morning of 25 April 2006 a small rockfall occurred in the 925-metre level in the vicinity of where the large and fatal falls of ground occurred 12 hours later.

A key question then becomes: why in these cases management did not respond to these warning signals? What should be concerning to those designing and implementing OHS management systems, and those responsible for regulatory oversight of them, is the apparent inability to learn from the errors identified in past cases (see Hopkins, 1999b; Baker, 2007; United States Chemical Safety Board, 2007b and others identified earlier in this report) where a combination of communication problems, deficiencies in auditing systems and a preoccupation with individual/personal safety and routine risks have contributed significantly to the failure of OHS management systems in mines and other high-hazard workplaces, with catastrophic consequences. For example, giving evidence before a US House of Representatives Subcommittee, the chair of the Chemical Safety Board—a US federal agency that investigates serious chemical-related incidents—stated she found striking similarities between the explosion at BP's Texas City refinery in 2005 and a failure at the same company's pipeline in Prudhoe Bay, Alaska, in 2006. Chair Carolyn Merritt stated virtually all the seven root-causes identified at Texas City had applied to Prudhoe Bay. In addition to those already noted earlier in this report (such as poor communication and auditing), Merritt referred to the 'significant role of budget and production pressures in driving BP's decision making—and ultimately harming safety' and 'a normalization of deviance where risk levels gradually crept up due to evolving operating conditions'.

The issue becomes how to best address problems relating to high-hazard workplaces. With regard to this a number of responses can be identified, namely:

- safety case regime (SCR)
- major hazard plans
- independent rigorous auditing of OHS management systems and major-hazard plans
- integration and continuous focus review re balancing routine and non-routine risks
- identification of performance indicators, red flag protocols
- enhanced communication, worker information, empowerment and triple-feedback loops
- multiple input into risk assessment, controls and carefully documented risk assessment/review process.

This book cannot discuss all these options in detail. Rather, a number of critical observations will be made. The safety case regime (SCR) or what is sometimes referred to as the Seveso standard was adopted in the European Union after an explosion at a chemical plant in the Italian town of Seveso in the late 1970s resulted in widespread exposure to dioxins. In Australia a number of state governments mandated the safety case regime for high-hazard workplaces, beginning in Victoria as a specific response to the Esso Longford refinery explosion in 1998 (though other hazardous events also played a part) and more recently it has been imposed on a number of mines in Western Australia (it was also imposed on the Beaconsfield goldmine—with the mine having to justify how it would safely recommence production after the Anzac Day incident). Under the safety case regime, there is an obligation on the operator to demonstrate to the regulator that they have implemented a regime that has identified hazards, assessed risks and has effective control measures in place. Regulatory scrutiny and acceptance is a prerequisite to operate. The regulator accepts but does not formally approve the SCR because the onus for operations, including hazard identification, risk assessment, control measures and monitoring, remain with the operators who have the knowledge to adapt these measures on a regular (even daily) basis as conditions change (as is the case with regard to blasting and mucking out operations at a mine). The safety case regime covers the construction/recommencement, operation and closure phases.

The safety case regime has been widely used to manage high-hazard facilities in Europe, not only chemical plants and refineries but offshore oil rigs and the like (SCR is also applied in the Australian offshore oil industry). Use of the safety case approach in mining has also received consideration in other Australian jurisdictions and has been seen as a logical extension of risk-based regulation for the mining industry—a means of addressing the limitations in systems design and implementation (Heiler, 2006; Gunningham, 2006b). One of the strengths of the safety case approach is the emphasis it places on the initial design of workplaces and systems—a higher order intervention that will affect the demands placed on downstream interventions or safeguards (for a study of the application of this approach in the maritime industry, see Wang, 2002). For example, in the mining context a better planned mine may require less reliance on ground support activities (such as roof bolts) than a poorly designed mine. Research into the effectiveness of safety case regimes indicates that they do improve overall hazard identification and control, due to the need to review systems and processes, but there is some evidence that the potential for further improvements corrodes over time (Vectra Group, 2003: 3). It is worth noting that corrosion is a problem affecting OHSMS too.

For managers of high-hazard workplaces there are also lessons to be learnt, namely:

- Design a system to do the job, not just one you are most comfortable with or least threatened by.
- Study/keep in mind why apparently 'good' systems failed.
- Expect systems to degrade over time (OHS not central?).
- Be alert that changes to work organisation can weaken even the best OHSMS.
- Use regulators and benchmark (but don't rely on industry benchmarks or see compliance as a goal).
- Remember that integration and expert systems are only as strong as their weakest link. Knowledge at all levels needs to be valued in hazard identification, remedies and warning signals.
- System auditing and triple-feedback loops are essential.

Small businesses

While the notion of OHS management systems has considerable appeal for medium to large enterprises there has been considerable debate as to the appropriateness of this approach to small business, or indeed, what approach to OHS best suits small business more generally. Most prescriptive OHS texts, and much OHS research, have focused on the experience and needs of medium and more-especially large enterprises and workplaces. In this book we have sought to remedy this imbalance, at least in part, by referring to small business and associated categories such as self-employed workers and subcontractors (many of who can be equally designated as small businesses) in virtually every chapter. However, this still leaves the issue of how to manage OHS within small, often culturally diverse, workplaces. Given that small businesses account for well over 90% of all employers in most industrialised countries, such as Australia and New Zealand, and depending on the precise cut-off adopted (usually 30–50 workers) around 40–60% of total employment, effective management of OHS within small businesses cannot be overlooked.

One of the problems in trying to implement the different management approaches to OHS, as discussed above, is that this sector is heterogeneous and the standard of OHS differs considerably, therefore applying one standard approach will be problematic. For example, a self-employed worker is qualitatively different to a firm with 30 employees, and a small business in the road transport sector may operate in a far different regulatory environment from comparably sized operations in pharmaceutical manufacturing, electrical repairs or even air transport. Workforce characteristics (including training levels, age, experience and stability), physical hazards and other factors may also vary widely. As an aside, it is worth noting that industry characteristics are commonly ignored by the OHS literature generally. This literature continues to focus on 'high-risk' industries such as manufacturing, construction, mining, forestry and agriculture with a corresponding neglect of the service sector even though it accounts for an increasingly greater share of total employment in most developed countries (Legg et al., 2008).

With all these qualifications in mind we can still make a number of tentative assumptions. First, the great majority of small businesses do not have a formally documented OHS management system and many rely almost entirely on informal processes. In small firms at least, documentation may not be an essential (if still insufficient) condition for the existence of an OHS management system. Hence it is possible for some small businesses to operate a satisfactory OHS system without specifically recognising it as such. On the other hand, characteristic features of many small businesses, including limited resources and specialist expertise, lack of training and rapid turnover (of labour and the business itself), make it more likely that such informal systems will not exist. As research by Eakin (1992), Lamm and Walters (2004) and others has found, the approach to OHS is far more likely to be ad hoc, haphazard and reliant on workers. To the extent that OHS is recognised, it is more likely to be in the area of safety than occupational health (Bradshaw et al., 2001).

Even where a small business such as a restaurant has no explicit or formal approach to OHS, the way that decisions are made in relation to staff training, deployment and potentially hazardous work processes (such as spills, knives and slippery floors) will still amount to an approach by default. In the case of a restaurant this may amount to seeing hazardous incidents or injuries in terms of careless behaviour (and ignoring issues of rushing/workload, failure to keep floors clear of spills, poor control of swinging doors and the like). In other words, even where a small workplace appears to have no approach to OHS, an approach can almost always be deduced from interview and observation that will fit into one or more of the four major strategies we identified in this chapter.

Small businesses can adopt a more systematic approach to OHS drawing on some of the principles discussed in this chapter. For example, the greater level of personal contact in a small business has been seen to obviate the need for more formal communication channels with employees. However, as some small business researchers have observed (see Lamm, 1997; Lamm and Pio, 2008; Martin, 2008), the readily encountered opinion of many small business owners that they have a close understanding of their employees is not always shared by their employees, particularly if the workforce is culturally diverse. While a business may be too small to establish a formal OHS committee, similar ends can be achieved via lunchtime meetings. Similarly, a relatively simple and regular walk-around audit process may be effective for a small business.

Further, even relatively small firms can adopt a systematic approach to managing OHS risks even if they cannot develop elaborate 'paperwork' systems. A small niche builder, for example, identified the major hazards associated with using subcontractors and addressed these by adopting three rules to guide all activity along with daily site visits by the manager knowledgeable about OHS (obviating the need for more elaborate monitoring measures). The provision of hazard information specific to the industry subsector where the small business is located, by either government agencies or professional bodies, can assist operators to focus their activities. Makin and Winder (2008) argue that hazard profiling can be used to enable small businesses to develop OHSMS that they can comprehend and apply.

In this and other chapters the ways in which government agencies have driven initiatives to improve OHS in the small business sector have been discussed. In particular, a great deal of emphasis has gone into safety education in areas such as agriculture/farm safety but, as a recent study (Legg et al., 2008) observed, there is almost no evidence on the effectiveness of these activities in terms of eliminating hazards. Further, Eakin et al. (2000) and later Legg et al. (2008) have identified a number of key principles of which government agencies need to be cognisant. First, OHS strategies for the small business sector should have an underpinning evidence-based rationale, incorporate a rigorous evidence-based approach for evaluating the efficacy of OHS strategies and should be designed to be sustainable in the long term. Second, an OHS management approach to injury/illness prevention that accommodates small business employers on their own terms, adapting to and taking cues from 'below'—the community and the workplace—is more likely to be successful than a top-down externally imposed regulatory approach. Moreover, approaches that embrace positive reinforcement of existing (good) OHS practices, legitimisation of the owner's concerns and an accommodative posture towards workplace 'reality' and the employer's frame of reference will be more effective than negative enforcement approaches. Third, while strategies of social integration and social influence should be used to engage employers, financial arguments and techniques used to motivate the small business employer to engage are likely to be more successful in improving OHS management practices. Solutions for small business OHS problems must be conceived in relation to the owner's perspectives, such as low/no cost—or better real (i.e. substantial) financial incentives—non-threatening, enhancement of business performance and sensitivity to business needs.

Fourth, the positive aspects of OHS management resident within small businesses should be mobilised, rather than just focusing on the removal of apparent 'barriers'. This will require the application of an approach that provides for gaining a thorough business-specific understanding of the organisational, business and cultural realities of the 'small business life'. The prevailing education-centred 'through the front door' approach to small business OHS promotion is unlikely to adequately address the needs of many of the small business employees (e.g. casual/part-time, migrant, youth). Eakin et al. (2000) argue that behavioural change strategies, such as community and organisational development, and alternative approaches to dissemination of knowledge such as the use of public media channels, should be considered. In addition, worker participation in OHS management practices should generally be encouraged in principle, but since the evidence relating to the efficacy of this approach is uncertain, there should be national support for systematic study of this approach. Finally, the success of small business OHS promotion initiatives appears dependent on the relationship established between an OHS professional and the owner/manager and the workplace. Thus not only will it be necessary to provide sufficient numbers of appropriately trained and qualified OHS professionals, but the nature of their training will need to reflect the need for relationship management as well as the usual appropriate technical OHS qualifications.

In sum, managing OHS within small, culturally diverse workplaces is at least as complicated as in medium-sized and large companies. Yet in spite of the complications, we see no reason why our assessment of the strengths and weaknesses of the key approaches to OHS management raised in this chapter are not applicable to small business even if some of the specific techniques described are not.

Conclusion

Several important conclusions can be drawn from our discussion of management strategies. Probably the most fundamental is that a more holistic approach must be taken to health and safety management. The approaches that have dominated practice in the area to date have been too fragmented and narrow. Indeed, selection of a management strategy has often had more to do with ideology and the consultant's disciplinary background than with an impartial evaluation of the strategy's efficacy. In any case, any narrow disciplinary approach applied in isolation is likely to provide only partial amelioration of complex health and safety problems. A thorough multidisciplinary approach to OHS management is urgently needed.

We have also argued that OHS management should be based on a genuinely participative model. The complexity of OHS problems makes it vital that the development of health and safety policies and practices is built upon the broadest possible knowledge base. It is therefore important that workers and supervisors who have the closest day-to-day experience of hazards should add their knowledge to that of health professionals, consultants and more senior managers in the formation of policies and practices. The active involvement of all levels of staff in the development and implementation of the OHS program also helps to promote greater organisational commitment to health and safety. However, a participatory management strategy will only operate effectively if it is supported by clearly defined organisational structures with policy-making, review, and investigatory functions. These structures should be a central and integral part of the organisation's operational decision-making processes and have clearly defined lines of responsibility and accountability. A participatory approach to OHS supported by appropriate organisational structures provides a long-term capacity for the organisation to adapt to a changing hazards array and to review and revise management strategies.

Finally, what is the overall trend in terms of OHS management? The answer here is mixed. On the positive side some of the cruder forms of behaviour control have lost influence over the past 20 years and medium to large employers are more likely to have an OHS management system in place that takes some cognisance of environmental and organisational factors. In some industries a more proactive approach to OHS can be found even among small operators. On the negative side, behaviour modification remains unjustifiably popular (for example, BBS) and workplaces have been subjected to a series of fracturing changes so the appearance of formal systems can too often mask disorganisation. In a review of Canadian developments during the 1990s, Geldart et al. (2005) found increases in OHS training and increased management interest in OHS but the latter was also associated with a reduction in worker involvement. Similar trends can be identified in Australia and New Zealand. This represents the result of not only changes in the labour market, regulatory and industrial relations context but also the 'top-down' and limited feedback loops symptomatic of most OHSMS. As we have already noted, OHSMS require worker involvement to be effective so flaws need to be recognised and remedied.

QUESTIONS FOR DISCUSSION

1   Compare and contrast the strengths and limitations of any two of the following sets of OHS management strategies: environmental modification and monitoring; individual screening and monitoring; individual behaviour change; organisational strategies.

2   Assess the arguments for and against OHS management systems. What is required for these systems to work effectively?

3   What level of control should management exert over OHS? In what specific areas should management assume primary responsibility?

4   Discuss the ethical issues surrounding pre-employment screening and return to work examination.

FURTHER READING

Gadd, S., Keeley, D. and Balmforth, H. (2004), 'Pitfalls in risk assessment: examples from the UK', *Safety Science*, **42**: 841–57.

Geldart, S., Shannon, H. and Lohfeld, L. (2005), 'Have companies improved their health and safety approaches over the last decade? A longitudinal study', *American Journal of Industrial Medicine*, **47**: 227–36.

Hopkins, A. (2006), 'What are we to make of safe behaviour programs?', *Safety Science*, **44**: 583–97.

Kamp, A. (2009), 'Bridging collective and individual approaches to occupational safety and health: what promises does workplace health promotion hold?', *Policy and Practice in Health and Safety*, **7**(1): 85–102.

Robson, L., Clarke, J., Cullen, K., Bielecky, A., Severin, C., Bigelow, P., Irvin, E., Culyer, A. and Mahood, Q. (2007), 'The effectiveness of occupational health and safety management system interventions: a systematic review', *Safety Science*, **45**(3): 329–53.

Smallman, C. and John, G. (2001), 'British directors' perspective on the impact of health and safety on corporate performance', *Safety Science*, **38**(3): 227–39.

Swuste, P. and Arnoldy, F. (2003), 'The safety adviser/manager as agent of organisational change: a new challenge to expert training', *Safety Science*, **41**(1): 15–27.

Bibliography

AARP (2009), *A Year-End Look at the Economic Slowdown's Impact on Middle-Aged and Older Americans*, AARP, Washington DC.

Aas, R., Ellingsen, K., Lindoe, P. and Moller, A. (2008), 'Leadership qualities in the return to work process: a content analysis', *Journal of Occupational Rehabilitation*, **18**(1): 335–46.

Abbe, O.O. (2008), 'Modeling the relationship among occupational stress, psychological/physical symptoms and injuries in the construction industry', *The Department of Construction Management and Industrial Engineering*, Master of Science Degree in Industrial Engineering, Louisiana State University, Louisiana: 72.

Abel, R. (1981), 'A critique of American tort law', *British Journal of Law and Society*, **8**: 199–231.

Abelsohn, A., Gibson, B., Sanborn, M. and Weir, E. (2002), 'Identifying and managing adverse environmental health impacts: 5. persistent organic pollutants', *Canadian Medical Association Journal*, **166**(12): 1549–54.

Abrahams, D., Haigh, F. and Pennington, A. (2004), *Policy Health Impact Assessment for the European Union: A Health Impact Assessment of the European Employment Strategy Across the European Union*, report for Health & Consumer Protection Directorate General, European Commission, Brussels.

Abrams, D., Elder, J., Carleton, R., Lasater, T. and Artz, L. (1986), 'Social learning principles for organizational health promotion: an integrated approach', in Cataldo, M. and Coates, T. (eds) *Health and Industry: A Behavioural Medicine Perspective*, John Wiley and Sons, New York: 28–51.

Abrams, K. (2001), 'A short history of occupational health', *Journal of Public Policy*, **22**(1): 34–80.

ABS (1982), *Working Hours Arrangements, Australia, February to May 1981*, Catalogue No. 6338.0, Sydney.

ABS (2004), *Mature Age Persons Statistical Profile: Labour Force*, Australian Bureau of Statistics 4905.0.55.001.

ABS (2005), *Australian Labour Market Statistics, Jan 2005*, Australian Bureau of Statistics 6105.0

ABS, (2006), *Population by Age and Sex, Australian States and Territories*, Australian Bureau of Statistics 3201.0.

ABS (2008a), *Employee Earnings and Trade Union Membership, Australia*, Australian Bureau of Statistics 6310.0.

ABS (2008b), *6321.0.55.001—Industrial Disputes*, Australia, Dec 2008, <abs.gov.au/AUSSTATS>

ABS (2009), *Work-Related Injuries 2005–06*, Australian Bureau of Statistics Catalogue No.6324.0, Canberra.

Access Economics (2006), *The Economic and Social Costs of Occupational Disease and Injury in New Zealand: Technical Report 4*, NOHSAC, Wellington.

Accident Commission Corporation (2008), *Annual Report 2008*, Wellington.

Accident Compensation Corporation (2005), *Briefing to the Incoming Minister for ACC*, Wellington.

ACGIH Board of Directors (1990), 'Threshold limit values: a more balanced appraisal', *Applied Occupational and Environmental Hygiene*, **5**(6): 340–4.

ACGIH Bulletin Board (1991), **36**(5): 1–2.

ACGIH (1999), *Threshold Limit Values and Biological Exposure Indices for 1999*, American Conference of Governmental Industrial Hygienists, Cincinnati.

ACIRRT (1999), *Australia at Work: Just Managing*, Prentice Hall, Sydney.

ACOSH (1988), *Occupational Safety and Health Reform: A Public Discussion Paper*, Advisory Council for Occupational Safety and Health, Wellington.

Adams, J. (1995), *Risk*, UCL Press, London.

Adams, J., Folkard, S. and Young, M. (1986), 'Coping strategies used by nurses on night duty', *Ergonomics*, **29**(2): 185–95.

Adams, M., Burton, J., Graham, S., McLeod, A., Rajan, R., Whatman, R., Bridge, M., Hill, R. and Johri, R. (2002), *Aftermath: The Social and Economic Consequences of Workplace Injury and Illness*, The Department of Labour & The Accident Compensation Corporation, Wellington.

Aggazzotti, G., Fantuzzi, G., Righi, E., Predieri, G., Gobba, F., Paltrinieri, M. and Cavalleri, A. (1994), 'Occupational and environmental exposure to perchloroethylene (PCE) in dry cleaners and their family members', *Archives of Environmental Health*, **49**(6): 487–93.

Aguirre-Molina, M. and Molina, C. (1990), 'Ethnic/racial populations and worksite health promotions', *Occupational Medicine: State of the Art Reviews*, **5**(4): 789–806.

Ahonen, E. and Benavides, F. (2006), 'Risk of fatal and non-fatal occupational injury to foreign workers in Spain', *Journal of Epidemiology and Community Health*, **60**: 424–6.

Aiken, L.R. (1999), *Personality Assessment: Methods and Practices*, 3rd edition, Hogrefe & Huber Publishers, Seattle.

Akerstedt, T. (1980), 'Interindividual differences in adjustment to shiftwork', in Colquhoun, W. and Rutenfranz, J. (eds) *Studies of Shiftwork*, Taylor and Francis, London.

Akerstedt, T. (1985), 'Adjustment of the physiological circadian rhythms and the sleep–wake cycle to shiftwork', in Folkard, S. and Monk, T.H. (eds) *Hours of Work: Temporal Factors in Work-Scheduling*, John Wiley, Chichester.

Akerstedt, T. (1988), 'Sleepiness as a consequence of shiftwork', *Sleep*, **11**(1): 17–34.

Akerstedt, T. (1995), 'Work hours, sleepiness and the underlying mechanisms', *Journal of Sleep Research*, **4**(Supp. 2): 15–22.

Akerstedt, T. and Ficca, G. (1997), 'Alertness-enhancing drugs as a countermeasure to fatigue in irregular work hours', *Chronobiology International*, **14**(2): 145–58.

Akerstedt, T. and Gillberg, M. (1982), 'Displacement of the sleep period and sleep deprivation: implications for shift work', *Human Neurobiology*, **1**: 163–71.

Akerstedt, T., Kecklund, G. and Johansson, S.E. (2004), 'Shift work and mortality', *Chronobiology International*, **21**(6): 1055–61.

Akerstedt, T. and Knutsson, A. (1986), 'Shift work, disease and epidemiology', in Haider, M., Koller, M. and Cervinka, R. (eds) *Night and Shift Work: Longterm Effects and their Prevention*, Verlag Peter Lang, Frankfurt Am Main.

Akerstedt, T. and Torsvall, L. (1978), 'Experimental changes in shift schedules—their effects on wellbeing', *Ergonomics*, **21**: 849–56.

Akerstedt, T. and Torsvall, L. (1981a), 'Shift work, shift-dependent well-being and individual differences', *Ergonomics*, **24**: 265–73.

Akerstedt, T. and Torsvall, L. (1981b), 'Age, sleep, and adjustments to shift work', in Koella, W. (ed.) *Sleep 1980*, Karger, Basel.

Ala-Mursula, L. (2006), 'Employee Worktime Control and Health', Faculty of Medicine, Department of Public Health Science and General Practice, University of Oulu, ACTA Universitatis Ouluensis, D Medic, A894, Oulu.

Ala-Mursula, L., Vahtera, J., Kouvonen, A., Väänänen, A., Linna, A., Pentti, J. and Kivimaki, M. (2006), 'Long hours in paid and domestic work and subsequent sickness absence: does control over daily working hours matter?', *Occupational and Environmental Medicine*, **63**: 608–16.

Ala-Mursula, L., Vahtera, J., Linna, A., Pentti, J. and Kivimaki, M. (2005), 'Employee worktime control moderates the effects of job strain and effort–reward imbalances on sickness absence: the 10-town study', *Journal of Epidemiology and Community Health*, **59**: 851–7.

Alavinia, S., Molenaar, D. and Burdoff, A. (2009), 'Productivity loss in the workforce: associations with health, work demands and individual characteristics', *American Journal of Industrial Medicine*, **52**: 49–56.

Albert, W.J., Currie-Jackson, N. and Duncan, C.A. (2008), 'A survey of musculoskeletal injuries amongst Canadian massage therapists', *Journal of Bodywork and Movement Therapies*, **12**: 86–93.

Albertsen, K., Kauppinen, K., Grimsmo, A., Sorenson, B., Rafnsdottir, G. and Tomasson, K. (2007), *Working Time Arrangements and Social Consequences: What Do We Know?*, Nordic Council of Ministers, Copenhagen.

Albertsen, K., Lund, T., Christensen, K., Kristensen, T. and Villadsen, E. (2007), 'Predictors of disability pension over a 10 year period for men and women', *Scandinavian Journal of Public Health*, **35**(1): 78–85.

Albin, M., Broberg, K. and Jackobsson, K. (2009), 'Research challenges in occupational and environmental medicine until 2030', *Occupational and Environmental Medicine*, **66**(1): 3–5.

Albury, D. and Schwartz, J. (1983), 'Why the safety lamp increased accidents', *New Scientist*, 10 February: 362–4.

Alcorso, C. (1989), 'Migrants and the workers' compensation system: the basis of an ideology', *Australian and New Zealand Journal of Sociology*, **25**(1): 46–65.

Aldrich, M. (1997), *Safety First: Technology, Labor and Business in the Building of American Work Safety, 1870–1939*, The Johns Hopkins University Press, Baltimore.

Allan, C., Loudon, R. and Peetz, D. (2007), 'Influences on work/non-work conflict', *Journal of Sociology*, **43**(3): 219–39.

Allen and Clarke Policy and Regulatory Specialists Ltd (2006), *Occupational Health and Safety in New Zealand: Technical Report Prepared for the National Occupational Health and Safety Advisory Committee: NOHSAC Technical Report 7*, National Occupational Health and Safety Advisory Committee, Wellington.

Allen, D. and Kazan-Allen, L. (eds) (2008), *India's Asbestos Time Bomb*, International Ban Asbestos Secretariat, London.

American Academy of Orthopaedic Surgeons and American Association of Orthopaedic Surgeons (2004), *Defining Musculoskeletal Disorders in the Workplace*, Position Statement 1165, <www.aaos.org/about/papers/position/1165.asp>

Andersen, L., Kines, P. and Hasle, P. (2007), 'Owner attitudes and self-reported behaviour towards modified work after occupational injury absence in small enterprises: a qualitative study', *Journal of Occupational Rehabilitation*, **17**: 101–21.

Andersen, M.B. and Williams, J.M. (1988), 'A model of stress and athletic injury: prediction and prevention', *Journal of Sport and Exercise Physiology*, **10**: 294–306.

Anderson, G. and Quinlan, M. (2008), 'Regulating work arrangements in Australia and New Zealand 1788–2006', *Labour History*, **95**: 111–32.

Anderson, M. (2005a), 'Behavioural safety and major accident hazards: magic bullet or shot in the dark?', *Process Safety and Environmental Protection*, **83**(B2): 109–16.

Anderson, M. (2005b), *Behavioural Safety and Major Accident Hazards: Magic Bullet or Shot in the Dark?*, Health and Safety Executive, UK.

Andreoni, D. (1986), *The Cost of Occupational Accidents and Diseases*, International Labour Office, Geneva.

Andrews, L. and Jaeger, A. (1991), 'Confidentiality of genetic information in the workplace', *American Journal of Law and Medicine*, **17**(1 & 2): 75–108.

Anema, J.R., Cuelenaere, B., van der Beek, A.J., Knol, D.L., de Vet, H.C.W. and van Mechelen, W. (2004), 'The effectiveness of ergonomic interventions on return-to-work after low back pain; a prospective two year cohort study in six countries on low back pain patients sicklisted for 3–4 months', *Occupational and Environmental Medicine*, **61**: 289–94.

Anema, J., Steenstra, I., Bongers, P., de Vet, H., Knol, D., Loisel, P. and van Mechelen, W. (2007), 'Multidisciplinary rehabilitation for subacute low back pain: graded activity or workplace intervention or both?', *Spine*, **32**(3): 291–8.

Anema, J., Steenstra, I., Urlings, I., Bongers, P., de Vroome, E. and van Mechelen, W. (2003), 'Participator ergonomics as a return to work intervention: a future challenge', *American Journal of Industrial Medicine*, **44**(3): 273–81.

Ang, H.B., Lamm, F. and Tipples, R. (2008), 'The impact of stressors on psychological well-being of New Zealand farmers and the development of a conceptual model', *Policy and Practice in Health and Safety*, **6**(1): 79–96.

Angersbach, D., Knauth, P., Loskant, H., Karvonen, M.J., Undeutsch, K. and Rutenfranz, J. (1980), 'A retrospective cohort study comparing complaints and diseases in day and shift workers', *International Archives of Occupational and Environmental Health*, **45**: 127–40.

Anlezark, A., Dawe, S. and Hayman, S. (2005), *An Aid to Systematic Reviews of Research in Vocational Education and Training in Australia*, National Centre for Vocational Education Research, <www.ncver.edu.au>

Anonymous (1980), 'Shiftworking: the general picture', in Colquhoun, W.P. and Rutenfranz, J. (eds) *Studies of Shiftwork*, Taylor and Francis, London.

Anya, I. (2007), 'Vulnerable migrants have a right to health', *Lancet*, **370**: 1–2.

Arendt, J., Deacon, S., English, J., Hampton, S. and Morgan, L. (1995), 'Melatonin and adjustment to phase shift', *Journal of Sleep Research*, **4**(2): 74–9.

Armstrong, H. (2008), *Blood on the Coal: The Origins and Future of New Zealand's Accident Compensation Scheme*, Trade Union History Project, Wellington.

Armstrong, T.J., Buckle, P., Fine, L.J., Hagberg, M., Jonsson, B., Kilbom, A., Kuorinka, I.A.A., Silverstein, B.A., Sjogaard, G. and Viikari-Juntura, E.R.A. (1993), 'A conceptual model of work-related neck and upper-limb musculoskeletal disorders', *Scandinavian Journal of Work Environment and Health*, **19**: 73–84.

Arocena, P., Nunez, I. and Villanueva, M. (2008), 'The impact of prevention measures and organizational factors on occupational injuries', *Safety Science*, **46**: 1369–84.

Aronsson, G., Dallner, M., Lindh, T. and Goransson, S. (2005), 'Flexible pay but fixed expense: personal financial strain among on-call employees', *International Journal of Health Services*, **35**(3): 499–528.

Aronsson, G., Gustafsson, K. and Dallner, M. (2000), 'Sick but yet at work. An empirical study of sickness presenteeism', *Journal of Epidemiology and Community Health*, 54: 502–9.

Arrighi, H. and Hertz-Picciotto, I. (1994), 'The evolving concept of the healthy worker survivor effect', *Epidemiology*, **5**(2): 189–96.

Artazcoz, L., Borrell, C., Cortas, I., Escriba-Aguir, V. and Cascant, L. (2007), 'Occupational epidemiology and work related inequalities in health: a gender perspective for two complementary approaches to work and health research', *Journal of Epidemiology and Community Health*, **61**: 39–45.

Artazcoz, L., Cortès, I., Escribà-Agüir, V., Cascant, L. and Villegas, R. (2009), 'Understanding the relationship of long working hours with health status and health-related behaviours', *Journal of Epidemiology and Community Health*, **63**: 521–7.

Arup, C. (1993), 'A critical review of workers' compensation', in Quinlan, M. (ed.) *Work and Health*, Macmillan, Melbourne: 263–83.

Ashford, N. (1976), *Crisis in the Workplace: Occupational Disease and Injury*, MIT Press, Cambridge, Mass.

Ashford, N. and Caldart, C. (1996), *Technology, Law and the Working Environment*, Island Press, Washington.

Ashford, N., Castleman, B., Frank, A. and Giannasi, F. (2002), 'The International Commission on Occupational Health (ICOH) and its influence on international organisations', *International Journal of Occupational and Environmental Health*, **8**(2): 156–62.

Ashton, D., Sung, J. and Raddon, A. (2005), *A Case where Size Matters: A Preliminary Investigation into the Institutionalisation of Skill Formation and Firm Size*, Centre for Labour Market Studies, University of Leicester, Research Paper No. 60.

Atonsen, T. (2009), 'Safety culture and the issue of power', *Safety Science*, **47**: 183–91.

Aust, B., Rugulies, R., Skakon, J., Scherzer, T. and Jensen, C. (2007), 'Psychosocial work environment of hospital workers: validation of a comprehensive assessment scale', *International Journal of Nursing Studies*, **44**: 814–25.

Australian Department of Education, Science and Training (2005), *Skilling Australia—New Directions for Vocational Education and Training*, Australian National Training Authority, <www.dest.gov.au/sectors/training_skills/default2.htm>

Australian Industry Commission (1994), *Workers' Compensation in Australia: Report No. 36 4 February 1994*, Commonwealth of Australia, Melbourne.

Australian Institute of Health and Welfare, (2008), *Occupational Asthma Workshop: A Brief Overview*, 14–15 August, Australian Government, Canberra.

Australian National Occupational Health and Safety Commission (NOHSC) (2002), *Extending the Use of OHS Positive Performance Indicators in Australian Industry: Epidemiology*, Canberra.

Australian Productivity Commission (2004), *National Workers' Compensation and Occupational Health and Safety Frameworks: Productivity Commission Inquiry Report No. 27, 16 March 2004*, Commonwealth of Australia, Melbourne.

Australian Safety and Compensation Council (2007a), *Are People with Disability at Risk at Work? A Review of the Evidence*, Australian Government, Canberra.

Australian Safety and Compensation Council (2007b), *Comparison of Workers' Compensation Arrangements in Australia and New Zealand 30 June 2007*, Australian Government, Canberra.

Australian Safety and Compensation Council (2008a), *Occupational Disease Indicators: April 2008*, Australian Government, Canberra.

Australian Safety and Compensation Council (2008b), *Work-Related Traumatic Injury Fatalities, Australia 2004–05*, Australian Government, Canberra.

Australian Safety and Compensation Council (2008c), *Compendium of Workers' Compensation Statistics Australia 2005–06*, Australian Government, Canberra.

Australian Safety and Compensation Council (2009a), *Sizing up Australia: How Contemporary is the Anthropometric Data Australian Designers Use?*, Australian Government, Canberra.

Australian Safety and Compensation Council (2009b), *Public Discussion Paper: Safety Requirements for the Design, Manufacture and Conformity Assessment of Plant*, Australian Government, Canberra.

Australian Senate Employment, Workplace Relations and Education Legislation Committee (2006), *Provisions of the Independent Contractors Bill 2006 and the Workplace Relations Legislation Amendment (Independent Contractors) Bill 2006*, Canberra.

Australian Workplace Industrial Relations Surveys (AWIRS) 1990 and 1995.

Awerbuch, M. (2004), 'Clinical perspectives. Repetitive strain injuries: has the Australian epidemic burnt out?' *Internal Medicine Journal*, **34**: 416–9.

Ayas, N., Barger, L., Cade, B., Hashimoto, D., Rosner, D., Cronin, J., Speizer, F. and Czeisler, C. (2006), 'Extended work duration and the risk of self-reported percutaneous injury in interns', *Journal of the American Medical Association*, **296**(9): 1055–62.

Ayeko, M. (2002), 'Integrated safety investigation method (ISIM)—investigating for risk mitigation', paper presented at the Workshop on Investigation and Reporting of Incidents and Accidents, Glasgow, July: 115–26, in Katsakiori, P., Sakellaropoulos, G. and Manatakis, E. (2009), 'Towards an evaluation of accident investigation methods in terms of their alignment with accident causation models', *Safety Science*, **47**(7): 1007–15.

Azaroff, L., Lax, M., Levenstein, C. and Wegman, D. (2004), 'Wounding the messenger: the new economy makes occupational health indicators too good to be true', *International Journal of Health Services*, **34**(2): 271–303.

Baarts, C., Mikkelsen, K.L., Hannerz, H. and Tüchsen, F. (2000), 'Use of a national hospitalization register to identify industrial sectors carrying high risk of severe injuries: a three-year cohort study of more than 900 000 Danish men', *American Journal of Industrial Medicine*, **38**: 619–27.

Bade, S. and Eckert, J. (2008), 'Occupational therapists expertise in work rehabilitation and ergonomics', *Work*, **31**(1): 1–3.

Bailey, K. (2008), 'The use of evidence-based clinical tools in occupational medicine', *Occupational Medicine (London) 1–5*, **58**(8): 556–60.

Bain, P. and Baldry, C. (1995), 'Sickness and control in the office—the sick building syndrome', *New Technology, Work and Employment*, **10**(1): 19–31.

Baker, E., Israel, B. and Schurman, S. (1996), 'Role of control and support in occupational stress: an integrated model', *Social Science & Medicine*, **43**(7): 1145–59.

Baker, J. (2007), *Report of the BP US Refineries Independent Safety Review Panel*, United States of America.

Baker, M. and Wooden, M. (1995), 'Formal training for employees of small businesses', *Journal of Small Enterprise Association of Australia and New Zealand*, **4**(12): 108–25.

Bakke, B., Stewart, P. and Waters, M. (2007), 'Uses of exposure to trichloroethylene in US industry: a systematic literature review', *Journal of Occupational and Environmental Hygiene*, **4**(5): 375–90.

Baldwin, M., Butler, R., Johnson, W. and Cote, P. (2007), 'Self-reported severity measures as predictors of return to work outcomes in occupational back pain', *Journal of Occupational Rehabilitation*, **17**(4): 683–700.

Bambra, C., Gibson, M., Sowden, A., Wright, K., Whitehead, M. and Petticrew, M. (2009), 'Working for health? Evidence from systematic reviews on the effects on health and health inequalities of organisational changes to the psychosocial work environment', *Preventive Medicine*, **48**: 454–61.

Barbe, M.F. and Barr, A.E. (2006), 'Inflammation and the pathophysiology of work-related musculoskeletal disorders', *Brain, Behavior, and Immunity*, **20**(5): 423–9.

Bardana, E. (2008), 'Occupational asthma', *Journal of Allergies and Clinical Immunology*, **121**(2): S408–S411.

Baril, R., Clarke, J., Friesen, M., Stock, S., Cole, D. and the Work-Ready group (2003), 'Management of return to work programs for workers with musculoskeletal disorders: a qualitative study of three Canadian provinces', *Social Science & Medicine*, **57**: 2101–14.

Barling, J. and Frone, M. (eds) (2004), *The Psychology of Workplace Safety*, American Psychological Association, Washington, 2003.

Barling, J., Kelloway, E. and Iverson, R. (2003), 'High-quality work, job satisfaction, and occupational injuries', *Journal of Applied Psychology*, **88**(2): 276–83.

Barling, J. and Mendelson, M. (1999), 'Parents' job insecurity affects children's grade performances through the indirect effects of beliefs in an unjust world and negative mood', *Journal of Occupational Health Psychology*, **4**(4): 347–55.

Barnes, M., Buck, R., Williams, G., Webb, K. and Aylward, M. (2008), 'Beliefs about common health problems at work: a qualitative study', *Social Science & Medicine*, **67**: 657–65.

Barnes-Farrell, J.L., Davies-Schrils, K., McGonagl, A., Walsh, B., Di Milia, L., Fischer, F.M. et al. (2008), 'What aspects of shift work influence off-shift wellbeing of healthcare workers?', *Applied Ergonomics*, **39**: 589–96.

Barr, J. (1997), 'The merits of safety incentive programs', *Occupational Health and Safety*, **66**(6): 52–5.

Bartel, A. and Thomas, L. (1985), 'Direct and indirect effects of regulation: a new look at OSHA's impact', *Journal of Law and Economics*, **28**(1): 1–25.

Barten, F., Santana, V., Rongo, L., Varillas, W. and Pakasi, T. (2008), 'Contextualising workers' health and safety in urban settings: the need for a global perspective and integrated approach', *Habitat International*, **32**: 223–36.

Barth, P. and Hunt, H. (1980), *Workers' Compensation and Work-Related Illnesses and Diseases*, MIT Press, Cambridge, Mass.

Bartlett, F.C. (1962), 'The future of ergonomics', *Ergonomics*, **5**: 505–11.

Bartlett, B. (1979), 'The politics of occupational health', *New Doctor*, **13**: 12–18.

Bartley, M., Sacker, A. and Clarke, P. (2004), 'Employment status, employment conditions, and limiting illness', *Journal of Epidemiology and Community Health*, **58**: 501–6.

Barton, J., Smith, L., Totterdell, P., Spelten, E. and Folkard, S. (1993), 'Does individual choice determine shift system acceptability?', *Ergonomics*, **36**(1–3): 93–100.

Barton, J., Spelten, E., Totterdell, P., Smith, L. and Folkard, S. (1995), 'Is there an optimum number of night shifts? Relationship between sleep, health and well-being', *Work and Stress*, **9**(2 & 3): 109–23.

Bartrip, P. and Fenn, P. (1980), 'The conventionalization of factory crime—a re-assessment', *International Journal of the Sociology of Law*, **8**: 175–86.

Bartrip, P. and Fenn, P. (1983), 'The evolution of regulatory style in the nineteenth century British factory inspectorate', *Journal of Law and Society*, **10**(2): 201–22.

Bass, C. (1983), *Lump-Sum Accident Compensation*, NSW Law Reform Commission Reference Research Paper, Government Printer, Sydney.

Bate, P. (1992), 'The impact of organisational culture on approaches to organisational problem-solving', in Salaman, G. (ed.) *Human Resource Strategies*, Sage, London.

Bateman, B.J. and Finlay, F. (2002), 'Long term medical conditions: career prospects', *Occupational and Environmental Medicine*, **59**(12): 851–2.

Bea, R. (1998), 'Human and organization factors: engineering operating safety into offshore structures', *Reliability Engineering and System Safety*, **61**: 109–26.

Beahler, C.C., Sundheim, J.J. and Trapp, N.I. (2000), 'Information retrieval in systematic reviews: challenges in the public health arena', *American Journal of Industrial Medicine*, **18**: 6–10.

Beck, M. and Woolfson, C. (2000), 'The regulation of health and safety in Britain: from old Labour to new Labour', *Industrial Relations Journal*, **31**(1): 35–49.

Bell, J. and Healey, N. (2006), *The Causes of Major Hazard Incidents and How to Improve Risk Control and Health and Safety Management: A Review of the Existing Literature*, Health and Safety Laboratory, Harpur Hill, Buxton Derbyshire.

Bell, M., Patel, M. and Sheridan, J. (1997), 'Q fever vaccination in Queensland abattoirs', *Communicable Diseases Intelligence*, **21**(3): 29–31.

Bellaby, P. (1986), 'Stress and coping discourse: please boss, can I leave the line? A sociological alternative to explaining sickness, injury and absence at work in terms of stress and coping', *International Journal of Sociology and Social Policy*, **6**(4): 52–68.

Bellingham, R. (1990), 'Debunking the myth of individual health promotion', *Occupational Medicine: State of the Art Reviews*, **5**(4): 665–75.

Benach, J. and Muntaner, C. with Solar, O., Santana, V. and Quinlan, M. (2009), *Employment, Work and Health Inequalities: A Global Perspective*, World Health Organization, Geneva.

Benavides, F.G., Benach, J., Muntaner, C., Delclos, G.L., Catot, N. and Amable, M. (2006), 'Associations between temporary employment and occupational injury: what are the mechanisms?' *Occupational Environmental Medicine*, **63**: 416–21.

Benavides, F.G., Castejon, J., Gimeno, D., Porta, M., Mestres, J. and Simonet, P. (2005), 'Certification of occupational diseases in a primary health care setting', *American Journal of Industrial Medicine*, **47**: 176–80.

Benavides, F.G., Delclos, G.L., Cooper, S.P. and Benach, J. (2003), 'Comparison of fatal occupational injury surveillance systems between the European Union and the United States', *American Journal of Industrial Medicine*, **44**: 385–91.

Benavides, F., Serra, C., Dominguez, R., Martinez, J., Plana, M., Despuig, M., Sampere, M. and Gimeno, D. (2009), 'Does return to work occur earlier after work-related sick leave episodes than after non–work-related sick leave episodes? A retrospective cohort study in Spain', *Occupational and Environmental Medicine*, **66**: 63–7.

Benner, L. (1975), 'Accident investigation: multilinear events sequencing method', *Journal of Safety Research*, (7): 67–73, in Katsakiori, P., Sakellaropoulos, G. and Manatakis, E. (2009), 'Towards an evaluation of accident investigation methods in terms of their alignment with accident causation models', *Safety Science*, **47**(7): 1007–15.

Bennett, L. (1984), 'Legal intervention and the female workforce: the Australian Conciliation and Arbitration Court 1907–1921', *International Journal of the Sociology of Law*, **12**: 23–36.

Bennett, L. (1994), 'Women and enterprise bargaining: the legal and institutional framework', *Journal of Industrial Relations*, **36**(2): 191–212.

Benoit, O., Foret, J., Bouard, G., Merle, B., Landau, J. and Marc, M. (1980), 'Habitual sleep length and patterns of recovery sleep after 24-hour and 36-hour sleep deprivation', *Electroencephalography in Clinical Neurophysiology*, **50**: 77–85.

Benoit, O., Foret, J., Merle, B. and Bouard, G. (1981), 'Diurnal rhythm of axillary temperature in long and short sleepers: effects of sleep deprivation and sleep displacement', *Sleep*, **4**(4): 359–65.

Berdahl, T.A. and McQuillan, J. (2008), *Occupational Racial Composition and Nonfatal Work Injuries*, University of Nebraska, Lincoln.

Berdahl, T.A. and McQuillan, J. (2008), 'Occupational racial composition and nonfatal work injuries', *Social Problems*, **55**(4): 549–72.

Berger, Y. (1993), 'The Hoechst dispute: a paradigm shift in occupational health and safety', in Quinlan, M. (ed.) *Work and Health: The Origins, Management and Regulation of Occupational Illness*, Macmillan Australia, Melbourne: 116–26.

Berger, Y. (1997), *Occupational Stressors and Stress: A Few Facts, Fictions and Fixes*, Executive Media, Melbourne.

Berggren, C. (1993), 'Lean production—the end of history?', *Work, Employment and Society*, **7**(2): 163–88.

Bergman, D. (1991), *Deaths at Work: Accidents or Corporate Crime?*, Workers' Education Association, London.

Bergstrom, G., Bjorklund, C., Fired, I., Lisspers, J., Nathell, L., Hermansson, U., Helander, A., Bodin, L. and Jensen, I. (2008), 'A comprehensive workplace intervention and its outcomes with regard to lifestyle, health and sick leave: the AHA study', *Work—A Journal of Prevention Assessment and Rehabilitation*, **31**(2): 167–80.

Berkowitz, M. (1979), *The Economics of Work Accidents in New Zealand*, Industrial Relations Centre, Victoria University of Wellington.

Bernacki, E. (2004), 'Factors influencing the costs of workers' compensation', *Clinical Occupational and Environmental Medicine*, **4**(2): 249–57.

Bernard, B.P. (1997), *Musculoskeletal Disorders and Workplace Factors: a Critical Review of Epidemiologic Evidence for Work-Related Musculoskeletal Disorders of the Neck, Upper Extremity, and Low Back*, National Institute for Occupational Safety and Health, Cincinnati.

Bernard, C. and Nicolay-Stock, S. (2007), 'Workplace health and safety committees of the agricultural sector: a pluridisciplinary approach', *Archives des Maladies Professionnelles et de l'Environnement*, **68**(5 & 6): 494–502.

Bernstein, S., Lippel, K. and Lamarche, L. (2001), *Women and Homework: The Canadian Legislative Framework*, Status of Women Canada, Ottawa.

Berry, J., Pidd, K., Roche, A-M. and Harrison, J.E. (2007), 'Prevalence and patterns of alcohol use in the Australian workforce: findings from the 2001 National Drug Strategy Household Survey', *Addiction*, **102**(9): 1399–410.

Berry, R. (1995), 'Preconception paternal occupational radiation exposure and risk of childhood leukemia: a paradox within an enigma', *Occupational Medicine*, **45**(1): 5–10.

Betts, D. and Rushton, L. (1998), 'The feasibility of conducting occupational epidemiology in the UK', *Occupational Medicine*, **48**(7): 433–9.

BHP Iron Ore Pty Ltd v. Construction, Mining Energy Timberyards, Sawmills and Woodworkers Union West Australian (WA) Branch, West Australian Industrial Relations Commission, (WAIRC) 130, 19 June (1998).

Bidulescu, A., Rose, K., Wolf, S. and Rosamond, W. (2007), 'Occupation recorded on certificates of death compared with self-report: the Atherosclerosis Risk in Communities (ARIC) study', *BMC Public Health*, **7**: 229.

Biggins, D. (1986), 'Focus on occupational health: what can be done', *New Doctor*, **47**: 6–10.

Biggins, D., Abrahams, H., Farr, T. and Kempnich, B. (1989), 'The role of the workers' health centre', *Journal of Occupational Health and Safety—Australia and New Zealand*, **5**(4): 317–25.

Biggins, D. and Phillips, M. (1991a), 'A survey of health and safety representatives in Queensland, part 1: activities, issues and information sources', *Journal of Occupational Health and Safety—Australia and New Zealand*, **7**(3): 195–202.

Biggins, D. and Phillips, M. (1991b), 'A survey of health and safety representatives in Queensland, part 2: comparison of representatives and shop stewards', *Journal of Occupational Health and Safety—Australia and New Zealand*, **7**(4): 281–6.

Biggins, D., Phillips, M. and O'Sullivan, P. (1988), 'A survey of health and safety representatives in Western Australia', *Journal of Occupational Health and Safety—Australia and New Zealand*, **4**(6): 527–32.

Biggins, D., Phillips, M. and O'Sullivan, P. (1991), 'Benefits of worker participation in health and safety', *Labour and Industry*, **4**(1): 138–59.

Bird, F.E. (1974), *Management Guide to Loss Control*, Institute Press, Division of International Loss Control Institute, Atlanta.

Bird, F. and Germain, G. (1986), *Practical Loss Control Leadership*, Institute Publishing, Loganville, USA.

Black, D.C. (2008), *Review of the Health of Britain's Working Age Population: Working for a Healthier Tomorrow*, Secretary of State for Health and the Secretary of State for Work and Pensions.

Blackmore, K. (1993), 'Law, medicine and the compensation debate: part 1', *Journal of Occupational Health and Safety—Australia and New Zealand*, **9**(1): 59–63.

Blank, L., Peters, J., Pickvance, S., Wilford, J. and McDonald, E. (2008), 'A systematic review of the factors which predict return to work for people suffering episodes of poor mental health', *Journal of Occupational Rehabilitation*, **18**(1): 27–34.

Blank, V., Andersson, R., Linden, A. and Nilsson, B. (1995), 'Hidden accident rates and patterns in the Swedish mining industry due to the involvement of contract workers', *Safety Science*, **21**(1): 23–35.

Blas, E., Gilson, L., Kelly, M., Labonte, R., Lapitan, J., Muntaner, C., Ostlin, P., Popay, J., Sadana, R., Sen, G., Schrecker, T. and Vaghri, Z. (2008), 'Addressing the social determinants of health inequities: what can the state and civil society do?', *The Lancet*, **372**: 1684–9.

Blessman, J. (1991), 'Differential treatment of occupational disease v occupational injury by workers' compensation in Washington State', *Journal of Occupational Medicine*, **33**(2): 121–6.

Blewett, V. (1994), 'Summary of proceedings', in *Beyond Lost Time Injuries: Positive Performance Indicators for OHS*, WorkSafe Australia, Australian Government Publishing Services, Canberra.

Blewett, V. and Shaw, A. (1995a), 'Enterprise bargaining—supporting or hindering OHS best practice?', *Journal of Occupational Health and Safety—Australia and New Zealand*, **11**(2): 139–44.

Blewett, V. and Shaw, A. (1995b), 'Health promotion, handle with care: issues for health promotion in the workplace', *Journal of Occupational Health and Safety—Australia and New Zealand*, **11**(5): 461–5.

Blewett, V. and Shaw, A. (1996), 'Quality occupational health and safety?', *Journal of Occupational Health and Safety—Australia and New Zealand*, **12**(4): 481–7.

Bloom, B.L. (1988), *Health Psychology: A Psychology Perspective*, Prentice Hall, Englewood Cliffs, New Jersey.

Bluff, E. and Gunningham, N. (2003), *Principle, Process, Performance or What? New Approaches to OHS Standards Setting*, National Research Centre for OHS Regulation, Working Paper 9, <ohs.anu. edu.au>

Blum, T. and Roman, P. (1986), 'Occupational health and safety programmes for alcoholism in the United States and Australia: dilemmas in technology transfer', *International Journal of Sociology and Social Policy*, **6**(4): 40–51.

Blyton, P. and Turnbull, P. (1998), *The Dynamics of Employee Relations*. Macmillan, London.

Boden, L. (1995), 'Workers compensation in the United States: high costs and low benefits', *Annual Review of Public Health*, **16**: 189–218.

Boden, L., Biddle, E. and Spieler, E. (2001), 'Social and economic impacts of workplace illness and injury: current and future directions for research', *American Journal of Industrial Medicine*, **40**: 398–402.

Boggild, H. and Knutsson, A. (1999), 'Shift work, risk factors and cardiovascular disease', *Scandinavian Journal of Work Environment & Health*, **25**(2): 85–9.

Bohgard, L., Akselsson, R., Holmer, I., Johansson, G., Rassner, F. and Swensson, L. (2009), 'Physical factors', in Bohgard, L. et al. (eds) *Work and Technology on Human Terms*, Prevent, Stockholm: 191–306.

Bohgard, L. and Albin, M. (2009), 'Chemical health risks', in Bohgard, L. et al. (eds) *Work and Technology on Human Terms*, Prevent, Stockholm: 307–37.

Bohle, P. (1993), 'Work psychology and the management of OHS: an historical overview', in Quinlan, M. (ed.) *Work and Health: Critical Readings on the Origins of Management and Regulations of Occupational Health*, Macmillan, Melbourne.

Bohle, P. (1997a), 'Does "hardiness" really predict adaptation to shiftwork?', *Work and Stress*, **11**(4): 369–76.

Bohle, P. (1997b), 'Sleep and circadian rhythm characteristics as predictors of adjustment to shift-work', *International Journal of Occupational and Environmental Health*, **3**(2) (Supp.): S30–S34.

Bohle, P. (2002). 'Work–life conflict: the issues and implications for OHS', in *CCH Master OHS and Environment Guide 2003*, CCH Australia, Sydney: 477–93.

Bohle, P., Buchanan, J., Considine, G., Cooke, A., Jakubauskas, M., Quinlan, M., Rafferty, M. and Rose, R. (2008), *The Evolving Work Environment in New Zealand: Implications for Occupational Health and Safety*, National Occupational Health and Safety Advisory Committee (NOHSAC) Technical Report No.10, Wellington.

Bohle, P., Cooke, A., Jakubauskas, M., Quinlan, M. and Rafferty, M. (2009), *The Changing World of Work and Emergent Occupational Disease and Injury Risks in New Zealand: A Benchmark Review*, prepared for National Occupational Health and Safety Advisory Committee (NOHSAC), Wellington.

Bohle, P., Pitt, C. and Quinlan, M. (in press, 2009). 'Time to call it quits? The safety and health of older workers', *International Journal of Health Services*.

Bohle, P. and Quinlan, M. (2000), *Managing Occupational Health and Safety: A Multidisciplinary Approach*, 2nd edition, Macmillan, Melbourne.

Bohle, P. and Quinlan, M. (2005), Editorial: 'Long working hours and OHS: what have we learned?', *Journal of Occupational Health and Safety—Australia and New Zealand*, **21**(4): 275–8.

Bohle, P., Quinlan, M., Kennedy, D. and Williamson, A. (2004), 'Working hours, work–life conflict and health: a comparison of precarious and "permanent" employment', *Revista de Saúde Pública*, **38**(Suplemento): 19–25.

Bohle, P., Quinlan, M. and Mayhew, C. (2001), 'The health effects of job insecurity: an evaluation of the evidence', *Economic and Labour Relations Review*, **12**(1): 32–60.

Bohle, P. and Tilley, A. (1988), 'Early experience of shiftwork: influences on attitudes', *Journal of Occupational and Organizational Psychology*, **71**: 61–79.

Bohle, P. and Tilley, A. (1989), 'The impact of night work on psychological well-being', *Ergonomics*, **32**(9): 1089–99.

Bohle, P. and Tilley, A. (1993), 'Predicting mood change on night shift', *Ergonomics*, **36** (1–3): 125–34.

Boivin, D., Tremblay, G. and James, F. (2007), 'Working on atypical schedules', *Sleep Medicine*, **8**: 578–89.

Bolton, S. and Boyd, C. (2003), 'Trolley dolly or skilled emotion manager? Moving on from Hochschild Managed Heart', *Work, Employment & Society*, **17**(2): 289–308.

Bonanni, C., Drysdale, D., Hughes, A. and Doyle, P. (2006), 'Employee background verification: the cross-referencing effect', *International Business & Economics Research Journal*, **5**(11): 1–8.

Bonauto, D., Anderson, R., Rauser, E. and Burke, B. (2007), 'Occupational heat illness in Washington State', *American Journal of Industrial Medicine*, **50**: 940–50.

Bonde, J., Rasmussen, M., Hjollund, H., Svendsen, S., Kolstad, H., Jensen, L. and Wieclaw, J. (2005), 'Occupational disorders and return to work: a randomized controlled study', *Journal of Rehabilitation Medicine*, **37**(4): 230–5.

Boocock, M.G., Collier, J., McNair, P.J., Simmonds, M., Larmer, P.J. and Armstrong, B. (2009), 'A framework for the classification and diagnosis of work-related upper extremity conditions: systematic review', *Seminars in Arthritis and Rheumatism*, **38**(4): 296–311.

Boocock, M.G., McNair, P.J., Larmer, P.J., Armstrong, B., Collier, J., Simmonds, M. and Garrett, N. (2005), *OOS Prevention Literature Review: Report to the Accident Compensation Corporation*, Physical Rehabilitation Research Centre, Auckland.

Boocock, M.G., McNair, P.J., Larmer, P.J., Armstrong, B., Collier, J., Simmonds, M. and Garrett, N. (2007), 'Interventions for the prevention and management of neck/upper extremity musculoskeletal conditions: a systematic review', *Occupational and Environmental Medicine*, **64**(5): 291–303.

Bosma, H., Peter, R., Siegrist, J. and Marmot, M. (1998), 'Two alternative job stress models and the risk of coronary heart disease', *American Journal of Public Health*, **88**(1): 68–74.

Bosworth, D. and Dawkins, P. (1980), 'Shiftworking and unsocial hours', *Industrial Relations Journal*, **11**: 32–40.

Botes, A. and Otto, M. (2003), 'Ethical dilemmas related to the HIV-positive person in the workplace', *Nursing Ethics*, **10**(3): 281–94.

Bottani, E., Monica, L. and Vignali, G. (2009), 'Safety management systems: performance differences between adopters and non-adopters', *Safety Science*, **47**: 155–62.

Bottomley, B. (1994), 'Means of encouraging best practice in occupational health and safety', in *Beyond Lost Time Injuries: Positive Performance Indicators for OHS*, WorkSafe Australia, Australian Government Publishing Services, Canberra.

Boufous, S. and Williamson, A. (2002), 'Work-related injury in NSW hospitalization and workers' compensation datasets: a comparative analysis', *Australia and New Zealand Journal of Public Health*, **27**(3): 352–7.

Bougrine, S., Mollard, R., Ignazi, G. and Coblentz, A. (1995), 'Appropriate use of bright light promotes a durable adaptation to night-shifts and accelerates readjustment during recovery after a period of night-shifts', *Work and Stress*, **9** (2 & 3): 314–26.

Bougrine, S., Mollard, R., Ignazi, G. and Coblentz, A. (1998), 'Days off and bright lights: effects on adaptation to night work', *International Journal of Industrial Ergonomics*, **21**(3 & 4): 187–98.

Bowden, B. and Penrose, B. (2006), 'Dust, contractors, politics and silicosis: conflicting narratives and the Queensland Royal Commission into Miners Phthisis, 1911', *Australian Historical Studies*, **128**: 89–107.

Bowes, S. (2008), 'Equipment, exposure, emission review—specification of process equipment for worker exposure control', *Journal of Occupational and Environmental Hygiene*, **5**(12): 797–806.

Boxall, P. (1995), *The Challenge of Human Resource Management*, Longman Paul, Auckland.

Boyce, T. and Geller, E. (2001), 'Applied behaviour analysis and occupational safety: the challenge of response maintenance', *Journal of Organisational Behaviour Management*, **21**(1): 31–60.

Boyd, C. (2002), 'Customer violence and employee health and safety', *Work Employment & Society*, **16**(1): 151–69.

Boyd, C. (2003), *Human Resource Management and Occupational Health and Safety*, Routledge, New York.

Boyd, C. and Bain, P. (1999), 'What kind of "new working life" for airline cabin crews?', paper presented to Health Hazards and Challenges in the Working Life Conference, Stockholm, 11 January 1999.

Boylan Distribution Services Pty Ltd (unreported, Sunshine Magistrates Court, Victoria, 29 July 2003).

Brabant C. (1992), 'Heat exposure standards and women's work: equitable and debatable?', *Women and Health*, **18**(3): 119–30.

Bradley, G.L. (1989), 'The forgotten role of environmental control: some thoughts on the psychology of safety', *Journal of Occupational Health and Safety—Australia and New Zealand*, **5**(6): 501–8.

Bradshaw, L., Barber, C., Davies, J., Curran, A. and Fishwick, D. (2007), 'Work-related asthma symptoms and attitudes to the workplace', *Occupational Medicine*, **57**: 30–35.

Bradshaw, L., Curran, D., Eskin, F. and Fishwick, D. (2001), 'Provision and perception of occupational health in small and medium-sized enterprises in Sheffield, UK', *Occupational Medicine*, **51**(1): 39–44.

Brandorff, N., Flyvholm, M., Beck, I., Skov, T. and Bach, E. (1995), 'National survey on the use of chemicals in the working environment: estimated exposure events', *Occupational and Environmental Medicine*, **52**: 454–63.

Brannen, J., Lewis, S., Moss, P., Smithson., J. and McCarraher, L. (2001), *Workplace Change and Family Life. Report on Two Case Studies*, Work-Life Research Centre, Manchester Metropolitan University, Manchester.

Breslin, C., Koehoorn, M., Smith, P. and Manno, M. (2003), 'Age related differences in work injuries and permanent impairment: a comparison of workers' compensation claims among adolescents, young adults, and adults', *Occupational and Environmental Medicine*, **60**(9): e10.

Breslin, C., Polzer, J., MacEachen, E., Morrongiello, B. and Shannon, H. (2007), 'Workplace injury or "part of the job": towards a gendered understanding of injuries and complaints among young workers', *Social Science & Medicine*, **64**: 782–93.

Breslin, F., Day, D., Tompa, E., Irvin, E., Sudipa, B., Clarke, J. and Wang, A. (2005), *Systematic Review of Factors for Work Injury among Youth*, Institute of Work and Health, Toronto.

Breslin, F., Day, D., Tompa, E., Irvin, E., Sudipa, B., Clarke, J., Wang, A. and Koehoom, M. (2006), *Systematic Review of Factors Associated with Occupational Disease among Young People*, Institute of Work and Health, Toronto.

Breslin, F. and Smith, P. (2006), 'Trial by fire: a multivariate examination of the relation between job tenure and work injuries', *Occupational and Environmental Medicine*, **63**: 27–32.

Bretin, H., De Koninck, M. and Saurel-Cubizolles, M. (2004), 'Conciliation travil/famille: Quel prix pour l'emploi et le travil des femmes? A propos de la protection de la grossesse et de la maternitie en France et au Quebec', *Sante Societe et Solidarite*, **2**: 149–60.

Brewer, S., Van Eard, D., Amick, B., Irvin, E., Daum, K., Gerr, F., Moore, J., Cullen, K. and Rempel, D. (2006), 'Workplace interventions to prevent musculoskeletal and visual symptoms and disorders among computer users: a systematic review', *Journal of Occupational Rehabilitation*, **16**: 325–58.

Briand, C., Durand, M., St-Arnaud, L. and Corbiere, M. (2007), 'Work and mental health: learning from return-to-work rehabilitation programs designed for workers with musculoskeletal disorders', *International Journal of Law and Psychiatry*, **30**: 444–57.

Briand, C., Durand, M., St-Arnaud, L. and Corbiere, M. (2008), 'How well do return-to-work interventions for musculoskeletal conditions address the multicausality of work disability?', *Journal of Occupational Rehabilitation*, **18**: 207–17.

Brickell v Attorney-General [2000] 2 ERNZ 529, High Court.

Brisson, C., Vezina, M. and Vinet, A. (1992), 'Health problems of women employed in jobs involving psychological and ergonomic stressors: the case of garment workers in Quebec', *Women and Health*, **18**(3): 49–77.

Broberg, O. and Hermund, I. (2007), 'The OHS consultant as a facilitator of learning in workplace design processes: four explorative case studies of current practice', *International Journal of Industrial Ergonomics*, **37**: 810–16.

Brookhuis, K.A. (2008), 'From ergonauts to infonauts: 50 years of ergonomics research', *Ergonomics*, **51**(1): 55–8.

Brooks, A. (1987a), 'Flaws of a committee based participatory system', *Journal of Occupational Health and Safety—Australia and New Zealand*, **3**(3): 224–30.

Brooks, A. (1987b), 'The concepts of "injury" and "disease" in workers' compensation law—a re-examination in the light of recent reforms', *University of New South Wales Law Journal*, **10**: 38–66.

Brooks, A. (1988), *Guidebook to Australian Occupational Health and Safety Laws*, 3rd edition, CCH Australia, Sydney.

Brooks, A. (1993), *Occupational Health and Safety Law in Australia*, CCH, Sydney.

Brooks, A. (2001), 'Systems standards and performance standard regulation of occupational health and safety: a comparison of the European Union and Australian approaches', *The Journal of Industrial Relations*, **43**(4): 361–86.

Broom, D., D'Souza, R., Strazdins, L., Butterworth, P., Parslow, R. and Rogers, B. (2006), 'The lesser evil: bad jobs or unemployment? A survey of mid-aged Australians', *Social Science and Medicine*, **63**: 575–86.

Brown, D. and Charles, N. (1982), *Women and Shiftwork: Some Evidence from Britain*, European Foundation for the Improvement of Living and Working Conditions, Dublin.

Brown, D.L., Feskanich, D., Sanchez, B.N., Rexrode, K.M., Schernhammer, E.S. and Lisabeth, L.D. (2009), 'Rotating night shift work and the risk of ischemic stroke', *American Journal of Epidemiology*, **169**(11): 1370–7.

Brown, D. and Hyam, S. (2007), *Safe from Injury and Risks to Health: Review of Workplace Health and Safety in Tasmania—Interim Report*, Department of Justice, Hobart.

Brown, F. (1980), 'The exogenous nature of rhythms', in Scheving, L. and Halberg, F. (eds) *Chronobiology: Principles and Applications to Shifts in Schedules*, Sijthoff and Noordhoff, Alphen aan den Rifn, Netherlands.

Brown, J. (1954), *The Social Psychology of Industry*, Penguin, Harmondsworth.

Brown, J.A., Shannon, H.S., Mustard, C.A. and McDonough, P. (2007), 'Social and economic consequences of workplace injury: a population-based study of workers in British Columbia, Canada', *American Journal of Industrial Medicine*, **50**: 633–45.

Brown, M., Geddes, L. and Heywood, J. (2007), 'The determinants of employee-involvement schemes: private sector Australian evidence', *Economic and Industrial Democracy*, **28**(2): 259–91.

Brown, S. (2009), *A Year-End Look at the Economic Slowdown's Impact on Middle-Aged and Older Americans*, AARP, Washington.

Brown, S., Bain, P. and Freeman, M. (2008), 'Employee perceptions of alcohol and drug policy effectiveness: policy features, concerns about drug testing, and the key role of preventative measures', *Drugs: Education, Prevention and Policy*, **15**(2): 145–60.

Browne, C., Nolan, B. and Faithfull, D. (1984), 'Occupational repetition strain injuries: guidelines for diagnosis and management', *Medical Journal of Australia*, **140**: 329–32.

Buckle, P. and Devereux, J. (2002), 'The nature of work-related neck and upper limb musculoskeletal disorders', *Applied Ergonomics* **33**: 207–17.

Bucklow, M. (1976), 'A new role for the work group', in Munro, J. (ed.) *Classes, Conflict and Control: Studies in Criminal Justice Management*, Anderson Publishing Co., Cincinnati.

Buff, L. and Gunningham, N. (2004), 'Principle, process, performance or what? New approaches to OHS standards setting', in Buff, L., Gunningham, N. and Johnstone, R. (eds) *OHS Regulation for a Changing World of Work*, The Federation Press, Sydney.

Bull, N., Riise, T. and Moen, B. (2002), 'Work-related injuries and occupational health and safety factors in smaller enterprises—a prospective study', *Occupational Medicine*, **52**(2): 70–4.

Bültmann, U., Franche, R.L., Hogg-Johnson, S., Côté, P., Lee, H., Severin, C., Vidmar, M. and Carnide, N. (2007), 'Health status, work limitations, and return-to-work trajectories in injured workers with musculoskeletal disorders', *Quality of Life Research*, **16**(7): 1167–78.

Bulzacchelli, M., Vernick, J., Webster, D. and Lees, P. (2007), 'Effects of the occupational safety and health administration's control of hazardous energy (lockout/tagout) standard on rates of machinery-related fatal occupational injury', *Injury Prevention*, **13**(5): 334–8.

Bunch, K. (1981), 'Combustibles in mines' in Hargraves, A.J. (ed.) *Ignitions, Explosions and Fires*, Australian Institute of Mining and Metallurgy, Wollongong.

Bureau of Labor Statistics, (1998), *National Census of Fatal Occupational Injuries, 1997*, United States Department of Labor, Washington.

Bureau of Labor Statistics, (2006), *Workplace Injuries and Illnesses in 2005*, United States Department of Labor, Washington.

Bureau of Labor Statistics, (2008), *National Census of Fatal Occupational Injuries in 2007*, United States Department of Labor, Washington.

Burgess, J. and Campbell, I. (1998), 'The nature and dimensions of precarious employment in Australia', *Journal of Labour and Industry*, **8**(3): 5–22.

Burgess, J., Connell, J. and Rasmussen, E. (2005), 'Temporary agency work and precarious employment: a review of the current situation in Australia and New Zealand', *Management Revue*, **16**(3): 351–69.

Burgess, J. and Strachan, G. (1999), 'The expansion of non-standard employment in Australia and the extension of employers control', chapter 7 in Felstead, A. and Jewson, N. (eds) *Global Trends in Flexible Labour: Critical Perspectives on Work and Organisations*, Macmillan Press, Hampshire.

Burgess-Limerick, R. (2003), *Issues Associated with Force and Weight Limits and Associated Threshold Limit Values in the Physical Handling Work Environment*, UniQuest Pty Ltd, Issues paper commissioned by NOHSC for the review of the National Standard and Code of Practice on Manual Handling and Associated Documents.

Burgoyne, J. H. (1993), 'Reflections on accident investigations', *Safety Science*, **16**: 401–6.

Burke, M., Chan-Serafin, S., Salvador, R., Smith, A. and Sarpy, S. (2008), 'The role of national culture and organizational climate in safety training effectiveness', *European Journal of Work and Organizational Psychology*, **17**(1): 133–152.

Burke, R.J. (1986), 'The present and future status of stress research', *Journal of Organisational Behaviour Management*, **8**(2): 249–67.

Burns, C., Harrison, K., Jammer, B., Zuccarini, D. and Lafrance, B. (2005), 'A cancer incidence and mortality study of Dow Chemical Canada Inc. manufacturing sites', *Occupational Medicine (London)*, **55**(8): 618–24.

Burton, D.J. (2004), Donald E. Cummings Memorial Award Lecture: 'Industrial hygiene in decline— what can we do?', *Journal of Occupational and Environmental Hygiene*, **1**: 148–52.

Burton, W.N., Chen, C.Y., Conti, D.J., Schultz, A.B., Pransky, G. and Edington, D.W. (2005), 'The association of health risks with on-the-job productivity', *Journal of Occupational Environmental Medicine*, **47**(8): 769–77.

Burton, W.N., Conti, D.J., Chen, C.Y., Schultz, A.B. and Edington, D.W. (1999) 'The role of health risk factors and disease on worker productivity', *Journal of Occupational Environment Medicine*, **41**: 863–77.

Butcher, F. (2004), 'Aftermath: using research to understand the social and economic consequences of workplace injury and illness', *Social Policy Journal of New Zealand*, (23): 181–94.

Butler, R., Johnson, W. and Cote, P. (2007), 'It pays to be nice: employer–worker relationships and the management of back pain claims', *Journal of Occupational and Environmental Medicine*, **49**(2): 214–25.

Butler, R. and Worrall, J. (2008), 'Wage and injury response to shifts in workplace liability', *Industrial & Labor Relations Review*, **61**(2): 181–200.

C^2 Technologies (2008), *Firefighter Fatalities in the United States in 2007*, US Department of Homeland Security and Federal Emergency Management Agency, Washington.

Cabrera, D. (1998), 'Safety climate and attitude', in Hale, A. and Baram, M. (eds) *Safety Management and the Challenge of Organisational Change*, Elsevier, Oxford.

Cacciabue, P.C. (2008), 'Role and challenges of ergonomics in modern societal contexts', *Ergonomics*, **51**(1): 42–8.

Calman, K. (1996), 'Cancer: science and society and the communication of risk', *British Medical Journal*, 313(7060).

Calvey, J. and Jansz, J. (2005), 'Women's experience of the workers' compensation system', *Australian Journal of Social Issues*, **40**(2): 285–311.

Cameron, G. and Alchin, M. *Australian Industrial Relations Commission* C2005/2494 16 April 2007.

Campbell, I.B. (1987) *Legislating for Workplace Hazards in New Zealand*, Massey Univeristy, Palmerston North.

Campbell, I.B. (1996), *Compensation for Personal Injury in New Zealand: Its Rise and Fall*, University of Auckland Press, Auckland.

Campbell, I.B. (1998), *Health and Safety in Employment Act: An Overview*, Uni-Osh Publishing, Palmerston North.

Campbell, I. (2001), *Cross National Comparisons: Work Time Around the World*, Australian Council of Trade Unions, Melbourne.

Campbell, I. and Burgess, J. (2001a), 'Casual employment in Australia and temporary work in Europe: developing a cross national comparison', *Work, Employment and Society*, **15**(1): 171–84.

Campbell, I. and Burgess, J. (2001b), 'A new estimate of casual employment?', *Australian Bulletin of Labour*, **27**(2): 85–108.

Caperchione, C., Lauder, W., Kolt, G., Duncan, M. and Mummery, W. (2008), 'Associations between social capital and health status in an Australian population', *Psychology, Health & Medicine*, **13**(4): 471–82.

Caple, D., Grieg, J. and Cordingley, R. (1997), 'Ability of workplace teams to manage OHS: report on the Worksafe Australia project integration of OHS into natural work groups (NWG) in the automobile industry, June 1995', *Journal of Occupational Health and Safety—Australia and New Zealand*, **13**(3): 243–5.

CARAM Asia (2007), *State of Health of Migrants 2007: Mandatory Testing*, Kuala Lumpur, CARAM Asia Berhad.

Carayon, P. and Smith, M. J. (2000), 'Work organization and ergonomics', *Applied Ergonomics*, **31**: 649–62.

Carey, A. (1976), 'Industrial psychology and sociology in Australia', in Boreham, P., Pemberton A. and Wilson P. (eds) *The Professions in Australia: A Critical Appraisal*, University of Queensland Press, St Lucia.

Carpenter, C.S. (2007), 'Workplace drug testing and worker drug use', *Health Services Research*, **42**(2): 795–810.

Carr, J. (1998), 'Workers' compensation systems: purpose and mandate', *Occupational Medicine: State of the Art Reviews*, **13**(2): 417–22.

Carson, W. (1979), 'The conventionalisation of early factory crime', *International Journal of the Sociology of Law*, **7**: 37–60.

Carson, W. (1980), 'Early factory inspectors and the viable class society—a rejoinder', *International Journal of the Sociology of Law*, **8**: 187–91.

Carson, W. (1982), *The Other Price of Britain's Oil: Safety and Control on the North Sea*, Martin Robertson, Oxford.

Carson, W. (1989), 'Occupational health and safety: a political economy perspective', *Labour and Industry*, **2**(2): 301–16.

Carson, W. and Hennenberg, C. (1988), 'The political economy of legislative change: making sense of Victoria's new occupational health and safety legislation', *Law in Context*, **6**(2): 1–19.

Carson, W.G., Henenberg, C. and Johnstone, R. (1990), *Victorian Occupational Health and Safety: An Assessment of Law in Transition*, The La Trobe/Melbourne Occupational Health and Safety Project. Department of Legal Studies, La Trobe University, Bundoora.

Carson, W. and Johnstone, R. (1990), 'The dupes of hazard: occupational health and safety and the Victorian sanctions debate', *The Australian and New Zealand Journal of Sociology*, **26**(1): 126–41.

Carter, G. and Smith, S.D. (2006), 'Safety hazard identification on construction projects', *Journal of Construction Engineering and Management*, **132**(2): 197–205.

Carter, J. (1991), 'There's a lot of it about?', *British Journal of Industrial Medicine*, **48**(5): 289–91.

Carter, T. (2004), 'British occupational hygiene practice 1720–1920', *Annals of Occupational Hygiene*, **48**(4): 299–307.

Caruso, C., Hitchcock, E., Dick, R., Russo, J. and Schmit, J. (2004), *Overtime and Extended Shifts: Recent Findings on Illnesses, Injuries and Health Behaviors*, US Department of Health and Human Services, Cincinnati.

Cass, G. (1983), *Workers Benefit or Employers' Burden: Workers' Compensation in New South Wales, 1880–1926*, Industrial Relations Research Centre Monograph, University of New South Wales.

Castleman, B. (1990), *Asbestos: Medical and Legal Aspects*, 3rd edition, Prentice Hall, Englewood Cliffs, New Jersey.

Castleman, B. and Lemen, R. (1998), 'The manipulation of international scientific organisations', *International Journal of Occupational and Environmental Health*, **4**(1): 53–5.

Castleman, B. and Ziem, G. (1988), 'Corporate influence on threshold limit values', *American Journal of Industrial Medicine*, **13**: 531–59.

Castleman, B. and Ziem, G. (1994), 'American Conference of Government Industrial Hygienists: low threshold of credibility', *American Journal of Industrial Medicine*, **26**: 133–43.

CCH OHS Alert, various issues.

Celik, M. (2009), 'Designing of integrated quality and safety management systems (IQSMS) for shipping operations', *Safety Science*, **47**: 569–77.

Centers for Disease Control (1996), *Work-Related Lung Disease Surveillance Report 1996*, National Institute for Occupational Safety and Health, US Department of Health and Human Services, Cincinnati.

Centers for Disease Control (1997), 'Cancer screening offered by worksites—United States, 1992 and 1995', *Morbidity and Mortality Weekly Report*, **46**(19): 421–4.

Centers for Disease Control (1998), *Atlas of Respiratory Disease Mortality, United States: 1982–1993*, National Institute for Occupational Safety and Health, US Department of Health and Human Services, Cincinnati.

Centers for Disease Control (2007), *Work-Related Lung Disease Surveillance Report 1996*, National Institute for Occupational Safety and Health, US Department of Health and Human Services, Cincinnati.

Centers for Disease Control (2008a), 'Work-related injury deaths among Hispanics—United States, 1992–2006', *MMWR Weekly*, **57**(22): 597–600.

Centers for Disease Control (2008b), 'Neurological illness associated with occupational exposure to the solvent 1-bromopropane—New Jersey and Pennsylvania, 2007–8', *MMWR*, **57**(48): 1300–2.

Centers for Disease Control, *MMWR* 2008, **75**(48): 1300–2.

CEPU Communications Division, Victorian Branch, *Survey & Body-Mapping Exercise at Dandenong Letters Centre May/June 2007*.

CFMEU (NSW) (o/b of Hemsworth) v Brolrik Pty Ltd t/as Botany Cranes & Forklift Services [2007] NSWIRComm 205, 21 September 2007.

Chamberlain, G. (1991), 'Work in pregnancy', *British Medical Journal*, **302**(6784): 1070–3.

Champoux, D. and Brun, J-P. (2003), 'Occupational health and safety management in small size enterprises: an overview of the situation and avenues for intervention and research', *Safety Science*, **41**: 301–18.

Chandler, R. (coroner) (2009), *Findings in the Matter of an Inquest Touching the Death of Larry Paul Knight*, Magistrates Court of Tasmania, 26 February.

Chandola, T., Marmot, M. and Siegrist, J. (2007), 'Failed reciprocity in close social relationships and health: findings from the Whitehall II study', *Journal of Psychosomatic Research*, **63**: 403–11.

Chapman, W.D. (1991), 'Costs of illness in the workplace', in Green, G. and Baker, F. (eds) *Work, Health and Productivity*, Oxford University Press, New York: 217–39.

Chapman, W.D., Jennings, S., Mangione, T. and Merrigan, D. (1991), 'Health promotion versus health protection? Employees perspectives and concerns', *Journal of Public Health Policy*, **12**(2): 148–64.

Charles, N. and Brown, D. (1981), 'Women, shiftwork and the sexual division of labour', *Sociological Review*, **29**: 685–704.

Chau, N., Mur, J., Benamghar, L., Siegried, C., Dangelzer, J., Francais, M., Jacquin, R. and Soudot, A. (2004), 'Relationships between certain individual characteristics and occupational injuries for various jobs in the construction industry: a case control study', *American Journal of Industrial Medicine*, **45**: 84–92.

Chen, G. and Jenkins, E. (2007), 'Potential work-related exposures to bloodborne pathogens by industry and occupation in the United States part II: a telephone interview survey', *American Journal of Industrial Medicine*, **50**(4): 285–92.

Chen, M. and Cunradi, C. (2008), 'Job stress, burnout and substance abuse among urban transit operators: the potential mediating role of coping behaviour', *Work & Stress*, **22**(4): 327–40.

Chen, W.Q., Yu, I.T.S. and Wong, T.W. (2005), 'Impact of occupational stress and other psychosocial factors on musculoskeletal pain among Chinese offshore oil installation workers', *Occupational and Environmental Medicine*, **62**(4): 251–6.

Cheng, Y., Chen, C-W., Chen, C-J. and Chiang, T. (2005). 'Job insecurity and its association with health among employees in the Taiwanese general population', *Social Science and Medicine*, **61**: 41–52.

Chernew, M., Frick, K. and McLaughlin, M. (1997), 'The demand of health insurance coverage by low-income workers: can reduced premiums achieve full coverage?', *Health Services Research*, **32**(4): 453–70.

Cherry, N. (1984), 'Women and work stress: evidence from the 1946 birth cohort', *Ergonomics*, **27**(5): 519–26.

Cherry, N.M. and McDonald, J.C. (2002), 'The incidence of work-related disease reported by occupational physicians, 1996–2001', *Occupational Medicine*, **52**(7): 407–11.

Child Employment Principles Case 2007 [2007] *NSWIRComm* 110, IRC 3579 of 2006.

Cho, C., Oliva, J., Swertzer, E., Neuvarez, J., Zanoni, J. and Sokas, R. (2007), 'An interfaith workers' centre approach to workplace rights: implications for workplace safety and health,' *Journal of Occupational and Environmental Medicine*, **49**(3): 275–81.

Chouhan, T. (2005), 'The unfolding of the Bhopal disaster', *Journal of Loss Prevention*, **18**: 205–8.

Christie, D. (1988), *A Guide to Occupational Epidemiology*, CCH International, North Ryde, NSW.

Christophers, A. and Zammit, M. (1997), 'Critique of the Kerr Report: best estimate of the magnitude of health effects of occupational exposure to hazardous substances', *Journal of Occupational Health and Safety—Australia and New Zealand*, **13**(4): 331–9.

Clapp, R. and Ozonoff, D. (2004), 'Environment and health: vital intersection or contested territory?', *American Journal of Law & Medicine*, **30**(2004): 189–215.

Clarke, M., Lewchuk, W., de Wolff, A. and King A. (2007) '"This just isn't sustainable": precarious employment, stress and workers' health', *International Journal of Law and Psychiatry*, **30**: 311–26.

Clarke, S. (1998a), 'Organisational factors affecting the incident reporting of train drivers', *Work and Stress*, **12**(1): 6–16.

Clarke, S. (1998b), 'Safety culture on the UK railway network', *Work & Stress*, **12**(3): 285–92.

Clarke, S. (2002), 'The contemporary workforce: implications for organizational safety culture', *Personnel Review*, **32**(1): 40–57.

Clarke, S. (2006), 'Contrasting perceptual, attitudinal and dispositional approaches to accident involvement in the workplace', *Safety Science*, **44**(6): 537–50.

Claveria v Pilkington Australia Ltd [2007] Federal Court of Australia 1692.

Clayton, A. (2007), *Review of the Tasmanian Workers' Compensation System: Report*, Government of Tasmania, Hobart.

Clegg, C. and Wall, T. (1990), 'The relationship between simplified jobs and mental health: a replication study', *Journal of Occupational Psychology*, **63**: 289–96.

Clifford, D. (2003), *Ministerial Inquiry into the Management of Certain Hazardous Substances in Workplaces*, for the Minister of Labour, Hon. M. Wilson, Wellington.

Cochrane Bone, Joint and Muscle Trauma Group—*The Cochrane Library*, (see <www.bjmtg.cochrane.org>—chapter 4).

Coggon , D., Harris, E.C., Poole, J. and Palmer, K.T. (2003), 'Extended follow-up of a cohort of British chemical workers exposed to formaldehyde', *Journal of the National Cancer Institute*, **95**: 1608–15.

Coglianese, C., Nash, J. and Olmstead, T. (2002), 'Performance-based regulation: prospects and limitations in health, safety and environmental protection', Regulatory Policy Program Report No. RPP-03, Harvard University, Cambridge Massachusetts.

Cohen, A. (1996), 'Worker participation: approaches and issues', in Bhattacharya, A. and McGlothlin, J.D. (eds) *Occupational Ergonomics: Theory and Applications*, Marcel Dekker, New York.

Cole, D.C. and Rivilis, I. (2004), 'Individual factors and musculoskeletal disorders: a framework for their consideration', *Journal of Electromyography and Kinesiology*, **14**: 121–7.

Cole, D.C., Ibrahim, S. and Shannon, H.S. (2005), 'Predictors of work-related repetitive strain injuries in a population cohort', *American Journal of Public Health*, **95**(7): 1233–7.

Cole, T. (2003), *Final Report of the Royal Commission into the Building and Construction Industry*, Australian Government, Canberra.

Colquhoun, W. and Condon, R. (1981), 'Introversion-extraversion and adjustment of the body-temperature rhythm to night work', in Reinberg, A., Vieux, N. and Andlauer, P. (eds) *Night and Shift Work: Biological and Social Aspects*, Pergamon Press, Oxford.

Colquhoun, W. and Folkard, S. (1978), 'Personality differences in body-temperature rhythm, and their relation to its adjustment to night work', *Ergonomics*, **21**(10): 811–17.

Colquhoun, W. and Rutenfranz, J. (1980), 'Introduction', in Colquhoun, W. and Rutenfranz, J. (eds) *Studies of Shiftwork*, Taylor and Francis, London.

Committee on the Health and Safety Implications of Child Labour and others (1998), *Protecting Youth at Work: Health, Safety, and Development of Working Children and Adolescents in the United States*, National Academy Press, Washington.

Commons, J. and Andrews, J. (1916), *Principles of Labour Legislation*, Harper and Bros, New York.

Concha-Barrientos, M., Nelson, D., Fingerhut, M., Driscoll, T. and Leigh, J. (2005), 'The global burden due to occupational injury', *American Journal of Industrial Medicine*, **48**: 470–81.

Conchie, S. and Burns, C. (2009), 'Improving occupational safety: using a trusted information source to communicate about risk', *Journal of Risk Research*, **12**(1): 13–25.

Construction Forestry Mining and Energy Union (CFMEU)—*Survey & Body-Mapping Exercise at Dandenong Letters Centre May/June 2007*.

Cook, C. and Burgess-Limerick, R. (2004), 'The effect of forearm support on musculoskeletal discomfort during call centre work', *Applied Ergonomics*, **35**(2004): 337–42.

Cooke, N. and Durso, F. (2007), *Stories of Modern Technology Failures and Cognitive Engineering Successes*, CRC Press, Boca Raton.

Cooley, P., Foley, S. and Magnussen, C. (2008), 'Increasing stair usage in a professional workplace: a test of the efficacy of positive and negative message prompts to change pedestrian choices', *Health Promotion Journal of Australia*, **19**(1): 64–7.

Coombs v Patrick Stevedores Holdings Pty Ltd [2005] NSWIRComm 56 3 March 2005.

Cooney, B. (1984), *Report of the Committee of Inquiry into the Victorian Workers' Compensation System*, Government Printer, Melbourne.

Cooper, C. (1985), 'The stress of work: an overview', *Aviation, Space and Environmental Medicine*, **56**(7): 627–32.

Cooper, C.L., Dewe, P.J. and O'Driscoll, M.P. (2001), *Organizational Stress: A Review and Critique of Theory, Research, and Applications*, Thousand Oaks, Sage.

Cooper, D. (2001), 'Treating safety as a value', *Professional Safety*, **46**(2): 17.

Cooper, J. and Patterson, D. (2008), 'Should business invest in the health of its workers?', *International Journal of Workplace Health Management*, **1**(1): 65–71.

Cooper, M. (2000), 'Towards a model of safety culture', *Safety Science*, **36**: 111–36.

Copper, M. and Cotton, D. (2000), 'Safety training: a special case?', *Journal of European Industrial Training*, **24**(9): 481–90.

Copsey, S. and Corlett, E. (1985), '*Shiftwork Review: Research of the European Foundation* 1981–1984, European Foundation for the Improvement of Living and Working Conditions, Dublin.

Corn, J. (1989), *Protecting the Health of Workers: The American Conference of Government Industrial Hygienists 1938–1988*, ACGIH, Cincinnati.

Costa, G. (2003a), 'Shiftwork and occupational medicine: an overview', *Occupational Medicine*, **53**: 83–8.

Costa, G. (2003b), 'Factors influencing health of workers and tolerance to shift work', *Theoretical Issues in Ergonomic Science*, **4**(3 & 4), 263–88.

Costa, G. (2005), 'Some considerations about aging, shift work and work ability', in Costa, G., Goedhard, W. and Ilmarinen, J. (eds) *Assessment and Promotion of Work Ability, Health and Well-Being of Ageing Workers: Proceedings of the 2nd International Symposium on Work Ability, Verona, Italy, 18–20 October 2004*, Elsevier, San Diego, CA: 67–72.

Costa, G. and DiMilia, L. (2008), 'Ageing and shift work: a complex problem to face', *Chronobiology International*, **25**(2): 165–81.

Costa, G., Gaffuri, E., Ghirlanda, G., Minors, D. and Waterhouse, J. (1995), 'Psychophysical conditions and hormonal secretion in nurses on a rapidly rotating shift schedule and exposed to bright light during night work', *Work and Stress*, **9**(2 & 3): 148–57.

Costa, G. and Sartori, S. (2007), 'Ageing, working hours and work ability', *Ergonomics*, **50**(11): 1914–30.

Costa, G., Sartori, S., Bertoldo, B., Olivato, D., Antonacci, G., Ciuffa, V. et al. (2005), 'Work ability in health care workers', in Costa, G., Goedhard, W. and Ilmarinen, J. (eds) *Assessment and Promotion of Work Ability, Health and Well-Being of Ageing Workers, 1280: Proceedings of the 2nd International Symposium on Work Ability, Verona, Italy, 18–20 October 2004*, Elsevier, San Diego, CA: 264–9.

Costella, M.F., Saurin, T.A. and de Macedo Guimarães, L.B. (2009), 'A method for assessing health and safety management systems from the resilience engineering perspective', *Safety Science*, **47**(8): 1056–67.

Costello, A., Abbas, M., Allen, A., Ball, S., Bell, S., Bellamy, R., Friel, S., Groce, N., Johnson, A., Kett, M., Lee, M., Levy, C., Maslin, M., McCoy, D., McGuire, B., Montgomery, H., Napier, D., Pagel, C., Patel, J., de Oliveira, J., Redclift, N., Rees, H., Rogger, D., Scott, J., Stephenson, J., Twigg, J., Wolf, J. and Patterson, C. (2009), 'Managing the health effects of climate change', *The Lancet*, **373**: 1693–733.

Cotterell, B. (1991), *Record of Investigation into Death of Charlie Portelli 16 February 1990*, 4 July, State Coroner's Office, South Melbourne.

Cotton, P. and Hart, P. (2003), 'Occupational wellbeing and performance: a review of organisational health', *Australian Psychologist*, **38**(2): 118–27.

Cowan, D., Osselton, D. and Robinson, S. (2005), 'Drug Testing', *Foresight Brain Science, Addiction and Drugs Project, UK*, Office of Science and Technology, London.

Cowan, P. (1997), 'From exploitation to innovation: the development of early workers' compensation legislation in Queensland', *Labour History*, **73**: 93–104.

Cox, A., O'Regan, S., Denvir, A., Broughton, A., Pearmain, B., Tyers, C. and Hillage, J. (2008), *What Works in Delivering Improved Health and Safety Outcomes: A Review of the Existing Evidence*, Health and Safety Executive Research Report RR654, Norwich.

Cox, R. and Lippel, K. (2008), 'Falling through the legal cracks: the pitfalls of using workers' compensation data as indicators of work-related injuries and illnesses', *Policy and Practice in Health and Safety*, **6**(2): 9–30.

Cox, S.J. and Cheyne, A.J.T. (2000), 'Assessing safety culture in offshore environments', *Safety Science*, **34**(1–3): 111–29.

Cox, S. and Cox, T. (1996), *Safety Systems and People*, Butterworth-Heinemann, Oxford.

Cox, S. and Flin, R. (1998), 'Safety culture: philosopher's stone or man of straw?', *Work & Stress*, **12**(3): 189–201.

Cox, S. and Jones, B. (2006), 'Behavioural safety and accident prevention: short-term "fad" or sustainable "fix"?', *Process Safety and Environmental Protection*, **84**(B3): 164–70.

Cox, T. (1988), 'Organizational health', *Work and Stress*, **2**: 1–2.

Creaser, W., Miller, P., Hogan, A., Kyaw-Myint, S., Hill, J., May, B. and Stavreski, B. (2007), 'The Australian hazard exposure assessment database project', *Journal of Occupational Health and Safety—Australia and New Zealand*, **23**(6): 563–70.

Creighton, B. and Rozen, P. (2007), *Occupational Health and Safety Law in Victoria*, Federation Press, Sydney.

Crichton, S., Stillman, S. and Hyslop, D. (2005), *Returning to Work from Injury: Longitudinal Evidence on Employment and Earnings (Update)*, Statistics New Zealand, Wellington.

Critchley, D., Ratcliffe, J., Noonan, S., Hones, R. and Hurley, M. (2007), 'Effectiveness and cost-effectiveness of three types of physiotherapy used to recognize low back pain disability', *Spine*, **32**(14): 1474–81.

Croidieu, S., Charbotel, B., Vohito, M., Renaud, L., Jaussaud, J., Bourboul, C., Ardiet, D., Imbard, I., Guerin, A. and Bergeret, A. (2008), 'Call-handlers' working conditions and their subjective experience of work—a transversal study', *International Archive of Occupational and Environmental Health*, **82**: 67–77.

Crompton, R. (chair) (2008), *National Review into Model Occupational Health and Safety Laws: First Report to the Workplace Relations Ministers' Council*, Commonwealth of Australia, Canberra.

Crompton, R. (chair) (2009), *National Review into Model Occupational Health and Safety Laws: Second Report to the Workplace Relations Ministers' Council*, Commonwealth of Australia, Canberra.

Cross, J. (2000), 'Principles of risk management in OHS', in Bohle, P. and Quinlan, M. *Managing Occupational Health and Safety: A Multidisciplinary Approach*, 2nd edition, Macmillan, Melbourne: 364–72.

Croucher, R., Gooderham, P. and Parry, E. (2006), 'The influences on direct communication in British and Danish firms: country, "strategic HRM" or unionization?', *European Journal of Industrial Relations*, **12**(3): 267–86.

Cryer, C. (2006), 'Severity of injury measures and descriptive epidemiology', *Inj Prev*, **12**(2): 67–8.

Cryer, C. and Langley, J.D. (2006), 'Developing valid indicators of injury incidence for "all injury"', *Injury Prevention*, **12**(3): 202–7.

Cryer, C. and Langley, J.D. (2008), 'Studies need to make explicit the theoretical and case definitions of injury', *Inj Prev*, **14**(2): 74–7.

Cullen, E. (1988), 'The advantages of ergonomics intervention', in Nicholson, A. and Ridd, J. (eds) *Health, Safety and Ergonomics*, Butterworths, London.

Cullen, L. (2004), *A Job to Die For*, Common Courage Press, Monroe, ME.

Cullen, L. (2007), 'Human factors integration—bridging the gap between system designers and end-users: a case study', *Safety Science*, **45**: 621–29.

Culvenor, J., Cowley, S. and Else, D. (1996), *Evaluation of Health and Safety Representative Training in South Australia*, WorkCover Corporation of South Australia, Adelaide.

Cutler, T. and James, P. (1996), 'Does safety pay? A critial account of the health and safety exective document: the costs of accidents', *Work, Employment and Society*, **10**(4): 755–65.

Cutlip, R.G., Baker, B.A., Hollander, M. and Ensey, J. (2009), 'Injury and adaptive mechanisms in skeletal muscle', *Journal of Electromyography and Kinesiology*, **19**: 358–72.

Czeisler, C., Moore-Ede, M. and Coleman, R. (1983), 'Resetting circadian clocks: applications to sleep disorders medicine and occupational health', in Guilleminault, C. and Lugaresi, E. (eds) *Sleep/Wake Disorders: Natural History, Epidemiology, and Long-Term Evolution*, Raven Press, New York.

Czeisler, C.A., Walsh, J.K., Roth, T., Hughes, R.J., Wright, K.P., Kingsbury, L., Arora, S., Schwartz, J.R.L., Niebler, G. and Dinges, D.F. (2006), 'Modafinil for excessive sleepiness associated with shift-work sleep disorder', *New England Journal of Medicine*, **353**(5): 476–86.

Dabscheck, B. (2005), 'Two and two makes five: industrial relations and the gentle art of doublethink', *Economic and Labour Relations Review*, **15**(2): 181–98.

Dabscheck, B. (2007), 'The contract regulation club', *Economic and Labour Relations Review*, **16**(2): 3–24.

Daniels, K. and Guppy, A. (1994), 'Occupational stress, social support, job control, and psychological well-being', *Human Relations*, **47**(12): 1523.

Daraiseh, N., Genaidy, A.M., Karwowski, W., Davis, L.S., Stambough, S. and Huston, R.L. (2003), 'Musculoskeletal outcomes in multiple body regions and work effects among nurses: the effects of stressful and stimulating working conditions', *Ergonomics*, **46**(12): 1178–99.

Davidoff, F. (1998), 'New Disease, Old Story', *Annals of Internal Medicine*, **129**: 327–8.

Davidson, M., Smith, R., Dodd, K., Smith, J. and O'Loughlan, M. (2008), 'Interprofessional pre-qualification clinical education: a systematic review', *Australian Health Review*, **32**(1): 111–20.

Davie, G., Cryer, C. and Langley, J. (2008), 'Improving the predictive ability of the ICD-based injury severity score', *Injury Prevention*, **14**(4): 250–5.

Davis, A. and George, J. (1988), *States of Health: Health and Illness in Australia*, Harper and Row, Sydney.

Davis, P. (1988), 'The contribution of ergonomics to present and future industrial safety and health', in Nicholson, A. and Ridd, J. (eds) *Health, Safety and Ergonomics*, Butterworths, London.

Davis, S., Mirick, D.K. and Stevens, R.G. (2001), 'Night shift work, light at night, and risk of breast cancer', *Journal of the National Cancer Institute*, **93**(2): 1557–62.

Dawson, D. and Brooks, B. (1999), *Report of the Longford Royal Commission: The Esso Longford Gas Plant Accident*, Government Printer, Melbourne.

Dawson, S., Willman, P., Bamford, M. and Clinton, A. (1988), *Safety at Work: The Limits of Self-Regulation*, Cambridge University Press, Cambridge.

Daykin, N. (1997), 'Workplace health promotion: issues and strategies for an insecure workforce', paper presented to 12th Employment Research Unit Conference, Cardiff Business School, 11–12 September.

Daykin, N. and Doyal, L. (1999), *Health and Work: Critical Perspectives*, Macmillan, London.

Dean, E. (2009a), 'Physical therapy in the 21st century (part I): toward practices informed by epidemiology and the crisis of lifestyle conditions', *Physiotherapy Theory and Practice*, **25**(5 & 6): 330–53.

Dean, E. (2009b), 'Physical therapy in the 21st century (part II): evidence-based practice within the context of evidence-informed practice', *Physiotherapy Theory and Practice*, **25**(5 & 6): 354–68.

de Bruin, A., McLaren, E. and Spoonley, P. (2005), 'Labour demand in a tight labour market: a survey of employers', Research Report No. 2, Labour Market Dynamics Research Programme, Albany, Auckland.

De Greef, M. and Van den Broek, K. (2004), *Quality of the Working Environment and Productivity: Research Findings and Case Studies*, European Agency for Safety and Health at Work, Belgium.

de Jonge, J., Le Blanc, P., Peeters, M. and Noordam, H. (2008), 'Emotional job demands and the role of matching job resources: a cross-sectional study among healthcare workers', *International Journal of Nursing Studies*, **45**(10): 1460–9.

Dejoy, D., Schaffer, B., Wilson, M., Vandenberg, R. and Butts, M. (2004), 'Creating safer workplaces: assessing the determinants and role of safety climate', *Journal of Safety Research*, **35**: 81–90.

De Leeuw, E., McNess, A., Crisp, B. and Stagnitti, K. (2008), 'Theoretical reflections on the nexus between research, policy and practice', *Critical Public Health*, **18**(1): 5–20.

Dellve, L., Lagerstrom, M. and Hagberg, M. (2003), 'Work-system risk factors for permanent work disability among home-care workers: a case control study', *International Archives of Occupational and Environmental Health*, **76**: 216–24.

Dellve, L., Skagert, K. and Eklof, M. (2008), 'The impact of systematic occupational health and safety management for occupational disorders and long-term work attendance', *Social Science & Medicine*, **67**: 965–70.

Dembe, A. (1996), *Occupation and Disease: How Social Factors Affect the Conception of Work-Related Disorders*, Yale University, New Haven.

Dembe, A.E. (2001), 'The social consequences of occupational injuries and illnesses', *American Journal of Industrial Medicine*, **40**(4): 403–17.

Dembe, A.E. (2009), 'Ethical issues relating to the health effects of long working hours', *Journal of Business Ethics*, **84**: 195–208.

Dembe, A., Erickson, J., Delbos, R. and Banks, S. (2005), 'The impact of overtime and long work hours on occupational injuries and illnesses', *Occupational and Environmental Medicine*, **62**, 588–97.

Dement, J. and Lipscomb, H. (1999), 'Workers' compensation experience of North Carolina Residential Construction Workers, 1986–1994', *Applied Occupational and Environmental Hygiene*, **14**: 97–106.

Denis, D., St-Vincent, M., Imbeau, D., Jetté, C. and Nastasia, I. (2008), 'Intervention practices in musculoskeletal disorder prevention: a critical literature review', *Applied Ergonomics*, **39**: 1–14.

Dennison, S. (2003). *The Economic Cost of Fire: Estimates for 2000*, Office of the Deputy Prime Minister, London, <www.odpm.gov.uk>

Department for Business Innovation and Skills (1998), *Workplace Employee Relations Survey (WERS98)*, <www.berr.gov.uk/whatwedo/employment/research-evaluation/wers-2004>

Department of Education, Employment and Workplace Relations, (2008), *The Future of Disability Employment Services in Australia: Discussion Paper*, Australian Government, Canberra.

Department of Industrial Relations (1996), *Annual Report 1995: Enterprise Bargaining in Australia*, Australian Government Publishing Service, Canberra.

Department of Industrial Relations (1999), *Industrial Relations in New South Wales*, **2**(1): 7.

Department of Infrastructure, Transport, Regional Development and Local Government, (2009), *Road Deaths Australia: 2008 Statistical Summary*, Road Safety Report No. 4, Australian Government, Canberra.

Department of Labour v Alexandra Holdings Ltd [1994] DCR 50.

Department of Labour v. Waste Management N.Z. Ltd (1995), CRN No. 40040511262 (Dist. Ct, Auckland).

Department of Science & Technology (1980), *Shiftwork in Australia: A Study of its Effects*, Australian Government Publishing Service, Canberra.

de Pedro, M., Sanchez, M., Navarro, M. and Izquierdo, G. (2008), 'Workplace mobbing and effects on workers' health', *Spanish Journal of Psychology*, **11**(1): 219–27.

Derickson, A. (1998), *Black Lung: Anatomy of a Public Health Disaster*, Cornell University Press, Ithica, New York.

Des Dorides, A., Corradino, R., Onnis, A. and Verdesca, D. (2006), 'On the job training in construction sites of the hospital corporation of Careggi', *G It Med Lav Ergon*, **28**(1 Supp.): 77–80.

De Serres, G. (1995), 'Need for vaccination of sewer workers against leptospirosis and hepatitis A', *Journal of Occupational and Environmental Medicine*, **52**: 505–7.

Desmarez, P., Godin, I. and Renneson, B. (2007), 'The impact of occupational accidents on injured workers' socioeconomic status', *Travail Humain*, **70**(2): 127–52.

De Vaus, D. (2004), *Diversity and Change in Australian Families: Statistical Profiles*, Institute of Family Studies, Melbourne.

Devereux, J., Rydstedt, L., Kelly, V., Weston, P. and Buckle, P. (2004), *The Role of Work Stress and Psychological Factors in the Development of Musculoskeletal Disorders: The Stress and MSD Study*, report for Health and Safety Executive 2004, Robens Centre for Health Ergonomics, Surrey.

Dew, K., Keefe, V. and Small, K. (2005), '"Choosing" to work when sick: workplace presenteeism', *Social Science and Medicine*, **60**: 2273–82.

Deyo, R., Psaty, B., Simon, G., Wagner, E. And Omenn, G. (1997), 'The messenger under attack—intimidation of researchers by special interest groups', *New England Journal of Medicine*, **336**(16): 1176–80.

Dinges, D.F. (1995), 'An overview of sleepiness and accidents', *Journal of Sleep Research*, **4**(Supp. 2), 4–14.

Dingsdag, D. (1993), *The Bulli Mining Disaster 1887: Lesson from the Past*, St Louis Press, Sydney.

Director of Public Prosecutions v Ancon Travel Towers Pty Ltd, unreported, County Court of Victoria, Judge Mullaly, 16 December 1998.

Dixon, J. (1999), *A National R and D Collaboration on Health and Socioeconomic Status for Australia*, Discussion Paper, National Centre for Epidemiology and Population Health, Australian National University, Canberra.

Dodsworth, M., Connelly, K., Ellert, C. and Sharratt, P. (2007), 'Organisational climate metrics as safety, health and environment performance indicators and aid to relative risk ranking within industry', *Process Safety and Environmental Protection*, **85**(B1): 59–69.

Doll, R. (1955), 'Mortality for lung cancer in asbestos workers', *British Journal of Industrial Medicine*, **12**: 81–6.

Doll, R. (1985), 'Occupational cancer: a hazard for epidemiologists', *International Journal of Epidemiology*, **14**(1): 22–31.

Dollard, M., Skinner, N., Tuckey, M.R. and Bailey, T. (2007), 'National surveillance of psychosocial risk factors in the workplace: an international overview', *Work & Stress*, **21**(1): 1–29.

Don, N. and John, A. (2005), 'Behavior-based safety: improvement opportunities in hospital safety', *Professional Safety*, **50**(2): 33.

Donald, I. and Young, S. (1996), 'Managing safety: an attitudinal-based approach to improving safety in organisations', *Leadership and Organisation Development Journal*, **17**: 13–20.

Dong, X. and Platner, J. (2004) 'Occupational fatalities of Hispanic construction workers from 1992 to 2000', *American Journal of Industrial Medicine*, **45**: 45–54.

Dorman, P. (1996), *Markets and Mortality: Economics, Dangerous Work, and the Value of Human Life*, Cambridge University Press, Cambridge.

Dorman, P. (2000), *The Economics of Safety, Health, and Well-Being at Work: An Overview, InFocus Program on SafeWork, International Labour Organisation*, The Evergreen State College Olympia, Washington.

dos Santos Antao, V., Pinheiro, G. and Wassell, J. (2009), 'Asbestosis mortality in the USA: facts and predictions', *Occupational and Environmental Medicine*, **66**: 335–8.

Dotson, K. (1996), 'An international safety and health measurement strategy: corporate programs, systems and results', *Journal of Occupational Health and Safety—Australia and New Zealand*, **12**(6): 669–78.

Dotson, K. (1997), 'Development of international corporate health and safety guidelines', *Applied Occupational and Environmental Hygiene*, **12**(2): 889–95.

Douglas, D., Ferguson, D., Harrison, J. and Stevenson, M. (1986), *Occupational Health and Safety*, Australian Medical Association, Sydney.

Draper, E. (1986), 'High-risk workers or high-risk work: genetic susceptibility policies in the hazardous workplace', *International Journal of Sociology and Social Policy*, **6**(4): 12–28.

Driscoll, T. (1993), 'Are work-related injuries more common than disease in the workplace?', *Occupational Medicine*, **43**(3): 164–6.

Driscoll, T. (1997), 'Health effects of occupational exposure to hazardous substances in Australia: putting criticisms of the Kerr report into perspective', *Journal of Occupational Health and Safety—Australia and New Zealand*, **13**(4): 341–52.

Driscoll, T. (2006), *Review of Australian and New Zealand Workplace Exposure Surveillance Systems*, Prepared for Australian Safety and Compensation Council and National Occupational Safety and Health Advisory Committee, Commonwealth of Australia, Canberra.

Driscoll, T., Dryson, E., Feyer, A-M., Gander, P., McCracken, S., Pearce, N. and Wagstaffe, M. (2005), *Review of Schedule 2 of the Injury Prevention Rehabilitation and Compensation Act, 2001 (IPRC Act)*, NOHSAC, Wellington.

Driscoll, T., Harrison, J., Bradley, C. and Newson, R. (2008), 'The role of design issues in work-related fatal injury in Australia', *Journal of Safety Research*, **39**(2): 209–14.

Driscoll, T., Mannetje, A., Dryson, E., Feyer, A-M., Gander, P., McCracken, S., Pearce, N. and Wagstaffe, M. (2004), *The Burden of Occupational Disease and Injury in New Zealand: Technical Report*, NOHSAC, Wellington.

Drury, C.G. (2008), 'The future of ergonomics/the future of work: 45 years after Bartlett (1962)', *Ergonomics*, **51**(1): 14–20.

Dugdill, L., Brettle, A., Hulme, C., McCluskey, S. and Long, A. (2008), 'Workplace physical activity interventions: a systematic review', *International Journal of Workplace Health Management* **1**(1): 20–40.

Duncan, G. (2008), 'Boundary disputes in ACC and the no-fault principle', in *Accident Compensation Forty Years On: A Symposium to Celebrate the Woodhouse Report*, Auckland University Law School, 13 December 2007, <www.auckland.ac.nz/uoa/about/research/units/accgroup/symposium.cfm>

Dunham, R.B. (1977), 'Shiftwork: a review and theoretical analysis', *Academy of Management Review*, **2**(4): 624–34.

Dupre, E. K. (2006), Michelle, I, Connelly, C.E., Barling, J., Hoption, C. 'Workplace aggression in teenage part-time employees', *Journal of Applied Psychology*, (91)5, 987–997.

Duxbury, L. (2007), *Keynote Address to Emerging Health and Safety Issues from Changing Workplaces—A Canadian Discussion, Symposium Sponsored by the Canadian Centre for Occupational Health and Safety*, 18–19 September, Vancouver.

Dwyer, T. (1983), 'A new concept of the production of industrial accidents: a sociological approach', *New Zealand Journal of Industrial Relations*, **8**: 147–60.

Dwyer, T. (1991), *Life and Death at Work: Industrial Accidents as a Case of Socially Produced Error*, Plenum Press, New York.

Eakin, J. (1992), 'Leaving it up to the workers: sociological perspectives on the management of health and safety in small workplaces', *International Journal of Health Services* 1992; **22**: 689–704.

Eakin, J., Lamm, F. and Limborg, H.J. (2000), 'International perspective on the promotion of health and safety in small workplaces', in Frick, K., Jensen, P.L., Quinlan, M. and Wilthagen, T. (eds) *Systematic Occupational Health and Safety Management: Perspectives on an International Development*, Pergamon, Oxford: 227–50.

Eakin, J. and MacEachen, E. (1998), 'Health and the social relations of work: a study of the health-related experiences of employees in small workplaces', *Sociology of Health and Illness*, **20**(6): 896–914.

Eaton, A. and Nocerino, T. (2000), 'The effectiveness of health and safety committees: results of a survey of public sector workplaces', *Industrial Relations*, **39**(2): 265–90.

Edling, C., Lindberg, A. and Ulftberg, J. (1993), 'Occupational exposure to organic solvents as a cause of sleep apnoea', *British Journal of Industrial Medicine*, **50**: 276–9.

Edwards, B., Higgins, D.J. and Zmijewski, N. (2007), 'The families caring for a person with a disability study and the social lives of carers', *Family Matters*, **76**: 8–47.

Egan, M., Pettigrew, M., Ogilvie, D., Hamilton, V. and Drever, F. (2007), '"Profits before people"? A systematic review of the health and safety impacts of privatizing public utilities and industries in developed countries', *Journal of Epidemiology and Community Health*, **61**: 862–70.

Egeland, G., Sweeny, M., Fingerhut, M., Wille, K., Schnorr, T. and Halerin, W. (1995), 'Total serum testosterone and gonadotropins in workers exposed to dioxin', *American Journal of Epidemiology*, **141**(5): 477–8.

Egger, P. (1997), 'Contract labour and employment: some proposals for further consideration', in Egger, P. and Poschen, P. (eds) *Contract Labour: Looking at Issues—Nine Country Cases*, Labour Education 1997/1-2 Nos 106/7, International Labour Organisation, Geneva.

Egilman, D. and Reinert, A. (1995), 'The origin and development of the asbestos threshold limit value: scientific indifference and corporate influence', *International Journal of Health Services*, **25**(4): 667–96.

Ehret, C. (1980), 'On circadian cybernetics, and the innate and genetic nature of circadian rhythms', in Scheving, L. and Halberg, F. (eds) Chronobiology: *Principles and Application to Shifts in Schedules*, Sijhoff and Noordhoff, Alphen aan den Rijn, Netherlands.

Eisner, M., Yelin, E., Katz, P., Lactao, G., Iribarren, C. and Blanc, P. (2006), 'Risk factors for work disability in severe adult asthma', *American Journal of Medicine*, **119**(10): 884–91.

Eldred-Grigg, S. (1990), *New Zealand Working People 1890 to 1990*, Dunmore Press Ltd, Palmerston North.

Ellard, J. (1970), 'Psychological reactions to compensable injury', *Medical Journal of Australia*, 22 August: 349–55.

Ellashof, B. and Streltzer, J. (1992), 'The role of "stress" in workers' compensation claims', *Journal of Occupational Medicine*, **34**(3): 297–303.

Elling, R. (1986), *The Struggle for Workers' Health: A Study of Six Industrialised Countries*, Baywood Publishing Company, New York.

Elling, R. (1989), 'The political economy of workers' health and safety', *Social Science and Medicine*, **28**(11): 1171–82.

Elovainio, M., Ferrie, J., Singh-Manoux, A., Gimeno, D., De Vogli, R., Shipley, M., Vahtera, J., Brunner, E., Marmot, M. and Kivimaki, M. (2009), 'Cumulative exposure to high-strain and active jobs as predictors of cognitive function: the Whitehall II study', *Occupational and Environmental Medicine*, **66**: 32–7.

Elovainio, M., Forma, P., Kivimaki, M., Sinervo, T., Sutinen, R. and Laine, M. (2005), 'Job demands and job control as correlates of early retirement thoughts in Finnish social and health care employees', *Work and Stress*, **19**(1): 84–92.

Elovainio, M., Kivimaki, M. and Vahtera, J. (2002), 'Organizational justice: evidence of a new psychosocial predictor of health', *American Journal of Public Health*, **92**(1): 105–8.

EMCONET (2007), *Employment Conditions and Health Inequalities: Final Report to the WHO Commission for the Social Determinants of Health*, Employment Conditions Knowledge Network, <www.who.int/social_determinants/resources/articles/emconet_who_report.pdf>

Encel, S. and Johnson, C. (1972), *Workers' Compensation, Redemption, Settlement and Rehabilitation*, School of Sociology, University of New South Wales.

Engelhard, E. (2007), 'Shifts of work-related injury compensation. Background analysis: the concurrence of compensation schemes', *Tort and Insurance Law Yearbook*, Springer Vienna, **20**: 9–82.

Environmental Protection Agency (2009), *New Release*, 17 June, US Department of Health and Human Services, Washington. EPA Office of Research and Development, (1996), *Guidelines for Reproductive Toxicity Risk Assessment*, US Environmental Protection Agency, Washington.

EPA Office of Research and Development (1996), *Guidelines for Reproductive Toxicity Risk Assessment*, US Environmental Protection Agency, Washington.

Erren, T. (2009), 'Identifying research challenges for occupational and environmental medicine until 2030: an initiative', *Occupational and Environmental Medicine*, **66**(1): 5–6.

Esbester, M. (2008), 'Administration, technology and workplace safety in Britain in the early 20th century', *Yearbook of European Administrative History*, **20**: 95–118.

Esltad, J. and Vabo, M. (2008), 'Job stress, sickness absence and sickness presenteeism in Nordic elderly care', *Scandinavian Journal of Public Health*, **36**(5): 467–74.

Ettinger, H.J. (2005), Henry Smyth Jr. Award Lecture: 'Occupational exposure limits: do we need them? Who is responsible? How do we get them?', *Journal of Occupational and Environmental Hygiene*, **2**: 25–30.

European Agency for Safety and Health at Work (1999), 'Health and safety at work: a question of costs and benefits?', *Magazine of the European Agency for Safety and Health at Work*, 20 December 1999.

European Agency for Safety and Health at Work (2005), *Expert Forecast on Emerging Physical Risks Related to Occupational Safety and Health*, European Communities, Bilbao.

European Agency for Safety and Health at Work (2006), *Expert Forecast on Emerging Biological Risks Related to Occupational Safety and Health*, European Communities, Bilbao.

European Agency for Safety and Health at Work (2007), *Expert Forecast on Emerging Psycho-Social Risks Related to Occupational Safety and Health*, European Communities, Bilbao.

European Foundation for the Improvement of Living and Working Conditions (1998), *Working Conditions in the European Union*, Dublin.

European Foundation for the Improvement of Living and Working Conditions (2009), *Working Conditions in the European Union*, Work Organisation, Dublin.

Evans, D., Conte, K., Gilroy, M., Marvin, T., Theysohn, H. and Fisher, G. (2008), 'Occupational therapy—meeting the needs of older adult workers', *Work: A Journal of Prevention Assessment and Rehabilitation*, **31**(1): 73–82.

Evans, R. (chair), Burgin, Y., de Rosas, V. and Roberts, M. (2004), *Drug Testing in the Workplace: The Report of the Independent Inquiry into Drug Testing at Work*, Joseph Rowntree Foundation, The Homestead, 40 Water End, York YO30 6WP, <www.jrf.org.uk>

Fabiano, B., Curro, F. and Pastorino, R. (2004), 'A study of the relationship between occupational injuries and firm size and type in the Italian industry', *Safety Science*, **42**: 587–600.

Fabiano, B., Perantini, I., Ferraiolo, A. and Pastorino, R. (1995), 'A century of accidents in the Italian industry: relationship with the production cycle', *Safety Science*, **21**: 65–74.

Fadier, E. (2007), 'Editorial', *Safety Science*, **45**: 541–44.

Fagin, D. and Lavelle, M. (1996), *Toxic Deception: How the Chemical Industry Manipulates Science, Bends the Law and Endangers your Health*, Carol Publishing Group, New Jersey.

Fahlbruch, B. and Wilpert, B. (1999), 'System safety—an emerging field for I/O psychology', *International Review of Industrial and Organisational Psychology*, **14**: 55–93.

Falconer, L. and Hoel, H. (1996), 'The perceptions of line and senior managers in relation to occupational health issues', *Occupational Medicine*, **46**(2): 151–6.

Fan, Z.J., Bonauto, D., Foley, M. and Silverstein, B. (2006), 'Underreporting of work-related injury or illness to workers' compensation: individual and industry factors', *Journal of Occupational Environmental Medicine*, **48**(9): 914–22.

Farber, D. (2008), *Five Regulatory Lessons from REACH*, Public Law Research Paper No. 1301306, School of Law, University of California, Berkeley.

Faucett, J. and McCarthy, D. (2003), 'Chronic pain in the workplace', *Nursing Clinics of North America*, **38**(3): 509.

Ferguson, D. (1984), 'The "new industrial epidemic"', *The Medical Journal of Australia*, **140**: 318–19.

Ferguson, D. (1986a), 'Historical perspective', in Douglas, D., Ferguson, D., Harrison, J. and Stevenson, M. *Occupational Health and Safety*, Australian Medical Association, Glebe, NSW: 1–3.

Ferguson, D. (1986b), 'Practice of occupational medicine', in Douglas, D. Ferguson, D., Harrison, J. and Stevenson, M. *Occupational Health and Safety*, Australian Medical Association, Sydney.

Ferguson, D. (1988), 'Occupational medicine in Australia: the past, the present and the future', *Journal of Occupational Health and Safety: Australia and New Zealand*, **4**(6): 481–8.

Ferguson, D. (1994), 'Eighty years of occupational medicine in Australia', *Medical Journal of Australia*, **161**: 35–8.

Ferrie, J., Martinkainen, P., Shipley, M., Marmot, M., Stansfeld, S. and Smith, G. (2001), 'Employment status and health after privatization in white collar civil servants: prospective cohort study', *British Medical Journal*, **322**: 1–7.

Ferrie, J., Shipley, M., Marmot, M., Stansfeld, S. and Smith, G. (1998), 'An uncertain future: the health effects of threats to employment security in white collar men and women', *American Journal of Public Health*, **88**(7): 1030–6.

Ferrie, J., Westerlund, H., Virtanen, M., Vahtera, J. and Kivimaki, M. (2008), 'Flexible labour markets and employee health', *Scandinavian Journal of Work Environment and Health*, (Supp. No.6): 98–110.

Feuerstein, M. (1996), 'Work style: definition, empirical support, and implications for prevention, evaluation, and rehabilitation of occupational upper-extremity disorders', in Moon, S.D. and Sauter, S.L. (eds) *Beyond Biomechanics: Psychological Aspects of Musculoskeletal Disorders in Office Work*, Taylor & Francis, Bristol, PA: 177–206.

Feyer, A., Williamson, A. and Cairns, D. (1997), 'The involvement of human behaviour in occupational accidents: errors in context', *Safety Science*, **25**(1–3): 55–65.

Feyer, A-M., Williamson, A.M., Stout, N., Driscoll, T., Usher, H. and Langley, J.D. (2001), 'Comparison of work related fatal injuries in the United States, Australia, and New Zealand: method and overall findings', *Injury Prevention*, **7**: 22–8.

Figa-Talamanca, I. (2006), 'Occupational risk factors and reproductive health of women', *Occupational Medicine*, **56**: 521–33.

Figlio, K. (1985), 'What is an accident?', in Weindling, P. (ed.) *The Social History of Occupational Health*, Croom Helm, London.

Finance Sector Union of Australia (2008), *Submission to the Comcare Review*, Department of Employment and Industrial Relations, Canberra.

Finance Sector Union of Australia v National Australia Bank Ltd, Australian Industrial Relations Commission (AIRC), C2006/2938 PR974260, 6 October 2006.

Firth, M., Brophy, J. and Keith, M. (1997), *Workplace Roulette: Gambling with Cancer*, Windsor Occupational Health Information Services, Toronto.

Fitzgerald, E., Weinstein, A., Youngblood, L., Standfast, S. and Melius, J. (1989), 'Health effects three years after potential exposure to the toxic contaminants of an electrical fire', *Archives of Environmental Health*, **44**(4): 214–21.

Fleming, P. and Harvey, H. (2002), 'Strategy development in dealing with violence against employees in the workplace', *Journal of the Royal Society for the Promotion of Health*, **122**(4): 226–32.

Fletcher, B. and Payne, R.L. (1980), 'Stress and work: a review and theoretical framework', *Personnel Review*, **9**(1): 19–29.

Florey, L., Galea, S. and Wilson, M. (2007), 'Macrosocial determinants of population health in the context of globalization', in Galea, S. (ed.) *Macrosocial Determinants Population Health*, Springer, New York: 15–51.

Foenander, O. (1956), *Developments in the Law Governing Workers' Compensation in Victoria*, Law Book Company, Melbourne.

Folkard, S. (1988), 'Circadian rhythms and shiftwork: adjustment or masking?', in Hekkens, W., Kerkhof, G. and Reitveld, W. (eds) *Advances in the Biosciences: Trends in Chronobiology*, Pergamon Press, Oxford.

Folkard, S. (1993), 'Editorial', *Ergonomics*, **36**(1–3): 1–2.

Folkard, S. (2008), 'Shift work, safety, and ageing', *Chronobiology International*, **25**(2): 183–98.

Folkard, S., Minors, D. and Waterhouse, J. (1985), 'Chronobiology and shiftwork: current issues and trends', *Chronobiology*, **12**: 31–54.

Folkard, S. and Monk, T. (1981), 'Individual differences in the circadian response to a weekly rotating shift system', in Reinberg, A., Vieux, N. and Andlauer, P. (eds) *Night and Shift Work: Biological and Social Aspects*, Pergamon Press, Oxford.

Folkard, S., Monk, T., Lewis, E. and Whelpton, C. (1980), *Individual Differences in Adjustment to Shiftwork*, Laboratory of Experimental Psychology, University of Sussex, Brighton.

Folkard. S., Monk, T. and Lobban, M. (1978), 'Short-and long-term adjustment of circadian rhythms in "permanent" night nurses', *Ergonomics*, **21**(10): 785–99.

Folkard, S., Monk, T. and Lobban, M. (1979), 'Toward a predictive test of adjustment to shiftwork', *Ergonomics*, **22**(1): 79–91.

Forastieri, V. (1997), *Children at Work: Health and Safety Risks*, International Labour Organisation, Geneva.

Ford, M. and Tetrick, L. (2008), 'Safety motivation and human resource management in North America', *International Journal of Human Resource Management*, **19**(8): 1472–85.

Foret, J., Bensimon, G., Benoit, O. and Vieux, N. (1981), 'Quality of sleep as a function of age and shift work', in Reinberg, A., Vieux, N. and Andlauer, P. (eds) *Night and Shift Work: Biological and Social Aspects*, Pergamon Press, Oxford.

Fortin, B., Lanoie, P. and Laporteis, C. (1999), 'Is workers' compensation a substitute for unemployment insurance?', *Journal of Risk and Uncertainty*, **18**(2): 165–88.

Fosbroke, D.E., Kisner, S.M. and Myers, J.R. (1997), 'Working lifetime risk of occupational fatal injury', *American Journal of Industrial Medicine*, **31**: 459–67.

Foster, N. (2008), 'Mining, maps and mindfulness: the Gretley appeal to the full bench of the Industrial Court of NSW', *Journal of Occupational Health and Safety—Australia and New Zealand*, **24**(2): 113–29.

Fotinatos, R. and Cooper, C. (2005), 'The role of gender and social class in work stress', *Journal of Managerial Psychology*, **20**(1): 14–23.

Fowles, J., Gallagher, L., Baker, V., Phillips, D., Marriott, F., Stevenson, C. and Noonan, M. (2005), *A Study of 2,3,7,8-Tetrachlorodibenzo-p-dioxin (TCDD) Exposures in Paritutu, New Zealand: A Report to the New Zealand Ministry of Health*, Institute of Environmental Science and Research Limited, <www.esr.cri.nz/Pages/default.aspx>

Foye, P.M., Sullivan, W.J., Sable, A.W., Panagos, A., Zuhosky, J.P. and Irwin, R.W. (2007), 'Work-related musculoskeletal conditions: the role for physical therapy, occupational therapy, bracing, and modalities', *Industrial Medicine and Acute Musculoskeletal Rehabilitation*, **88**(Supp. 1): S14-7.

Fragar, L., Kelly, B., Peters, M., Henderson, A. and Tonna, A. (2008), 'Partnerships to promote mental health in NSW farmers: the New South Wales farmers blueprint for mental health', *Australian Journal of Rural Health*, **16**: 170–5.

Franche, R., Cullen, K., Clarke, J., Irvin, E., Sinclair, S. and Frank, J. (2005), 'Workplace-based return-to-work interventions: a systematic review of the quantitative literature', *Journal of Occupational Rehabilitation*, **15**(4): 607–31.

Franche, R., Pole, J., Hogg-Johnson, S., Vidmar, M. and Breslin, C. (2006), 'The impact of work-related musculoskeletal disorders on worker' caregiving activities', *American Journal of Industrial Medicine*, **49**(9): 780–90.

Franche, R., Sevein, C., Hogg-Johnson, S., Cote, P., Vidmar, M. and Lee, H. (2007), 'The impact of early workplace-based return-to-work strategies on work absence duration: a 6-month longitudinal study following occupational musculoskeletal injury', *Journal of Occupational and Environmental Medicine*, **49**(9): 960–74.

Frank, A.L. (2000), 'Injuries related to shiftwork', *American Journal of Preventive Medicine*, **18**(4, Supp. 1): 33–6.

Frankenhauser, M. and Gardell, B. (1976), 'Underload and overload in working life: outline of a multidisciplinary approach', *Journal of Human Stress*, **2**: 35.

Franzblau, A., Armstrong, T., Werner, R. and Ulin, S. (2005), 'A cross-sectional assessment of the ACGIH TLV for hand activity level', *Journal of Occupational Rehabilitation*, **15**(1): 57–67.

Freestone, D. and Hay, E. (eds) (1996), *The precautionary Principle and International Law: The Challenge of Implementation*, Kluwer Law International, Boston.

French, M., Roebuck, M. and Alexandre, P. (2004) 'To test or not to test: do workplace drug testing programs discourage employee drug use?', *Social Science Research*, **33**: 45–63.

Frese, M. and Harwich, C. (1984), 'Shiftwork and the length and quality of sleep', *Journal of Occupational Medicine*, **26**(8): 561–6.

Frese, M. and Semmer, N. (1986), 'Shiftwork, stress and psychosomatic complaints: a comparison between workers in different shiftwork schedules, non-shiftworkers and previous shiftworkers', *Ergonomics*, **29**(1): 99–114.

Frick, K. (1995), 'Reconciling the divergent goals of high productivity and occupational health and safety: the Swedish Working Life Fund's integration of work environment and industrial policies', unpublished paper, National Institute for Working Life, Stockholm.

Frick, K. (1996), 'Why can't managers see any profit in health and safety at work? Contradictory views and their penetrations into working life', unpublished paper, National Institute for Working Life, Stockholm.

Frick, K. (1997), 'Regional safety representatives for small companies: a Swedish anomaly', *IEA '97 Conference Proceedings*, International Ergonomic Committee, Tampere.

Frick, K. (2004), 'Organisational development for occupational health and safety management', in Bluff, E. Gunningham, N. and Johnstone, R. (eds) *OHS Regulation for the 21st Century*, Federation Press, Sydney.

Frick, K. (2008), 'Swedish regional safety reps support OHS in small firms—a success threatened by labour market changes', unpublished paper.

Frick, K., Jensen, P., Quinlan, M. and Wilthagen, T. (eds) (2000), *Systematic Occupational Health and Safety Management: Perspectives on an International Development*, Pergamon, Amsterdam.

Frick, K. and Walters, D. (1998), 'Worker representation on health and safety in small enterprises: lessons for a Swedish approach', *International Labour Review*, **137**(3): 367–89.

Friedland, J. and Silva, J. (2008), 'Evolving identities: Thomas Bessell Kidner and occupational therapy in the United States', *American Journal of Occupational Therapy*, **62**(3): 349–60.

Friedman, L. and Forst, L. (2007), 'The impact of OSHA recordkeeping regulation changes on occupational injury and illness trends in the USA: a time-series analysis', *Occupational and Environmental Medicine*, **64**: 454–60.

Friedman, M. and Rosenman, R.H. (1974), *Type A Behavior and your Heart*, Alfred A. Knopf, Inc., New York.

Frone, M. (2006), 'Prevalence and distribution of illicit drug use in the workforce and in the workplace: findings and implications from a US National Survey', *Journal of Applied Psychology*, **91**(4): 856–69.

Frone, M. (2008), 'Are work stressors related to employee substance use? The importance of temporal context in assessments of alcohol and illicit drug use', *Journal of Applied Psychology*, **93**(1): 199–206.

Frone, M., Yardley, J. and Markel, K. (1997), 'Developing and testing an integrated model of the work-family interface', *Journal of Vocational Behaviour*, **50**: 145–67.

Fudge, J. and Tucker, E. (1993), 'Reproductive hazards in the workplace: legal issues of regulation, enforcement and redress', in *Royal Commission on New Technologies, Legal and Ethical Issues in New Reproductive Technologies: Pregnancy and Parenthood*, Volume 4, Research Studies, Royal Commission on New Reproductive Technologies, Ottawa.

Fujino, Y., Iso, H., Tamakoshi, A., Inaba, Y., Koizumi, A., Kubo, T. and Yoshimura, T. (2006), 'A prospective cohort study of shift work and risk of ischemic heart disease in Japanese male workers', *American Journal of Epidemiology*, **164**(2): 128–35.

Funk, S.C. (1992), 'Hardiness: a review of theory and research', *Health Psychology*, **11**(5): 335–45.

Gadbois, C. (1981), 'Women on night shift: interdependence of sleep and off-the-job activities', in Reinberg, A., Vieux, N. and Andlauer, P. (eds) *Night and Shift Work: Biological and Social Aspects*, Pergamon Press, Oxford.

Gadd, S., Keeley, D. and Balmforth, H. (2003), *Good Practice and Pitfalls in Risk Assessment*, prepared by the Health and Safety Laboratory for the Health and Safety Executive, Sheffield, UK.

Gadd, S., Keeley, D. and Balmforth, H. (2004), 'Pitfalls in risk assessment: examples from the UK', *Safety Science*, **42**: 841–57.

Gadon, M. (1996), 'Pesticide poisonings in the lawn care and tree service industries', *Journal of Occupational and Environmental Medicine*, **38**(8): 794–9.

Gainer, R. (2008), 'History of ergonomics and occupational therapy', *Work: A Journal of Prevention Assessment and Rehabilitation*, **31**(1): 5–9.

Gaines, J. and Biggins, D. (1992), 'A survey of health and safety representatives in the Northern Territory', *Journal of Occupational Health and Safety—Australia and New Zealand*, **8**(5): 421–8.

Galizzi, M. and Boden, L. (2003), 'The return to work of injured workers: evidence from matched unemployment insurance and workers' compensation data', *Labour Economics*, **10**: 311–37.

Gallagher, C. (1997), *Health and Safety Management Systems: An Analysis of System Types and Effectiveness*, research report to the National Occupational Health and Safety Commission, Sydney.

Gallagher, C., Underhill, E. and Rimmer, M. (2001), *Occupational Health and Safety Management Systems: A Review of their Effectiveness in Securing Healthier and Safer Workplaces*, National Occupational Health and Safety Commission, Sydney.

Gallo, W., Bradley, E., Falba, T., Dubin, J., Cramer, L., Bogardus, S. and Kasl, S. (2004), 'Involuntary job loss as a risk factor for subsequent myocardial infarction and strokes', *American Journal of Industrial Medicine*, **45**: 408–16.

Gandevia, B. (1971), 'Occupation and disease in Australia since 1788: part one', *Bulletin of the Postgraduate Committee in Medicine*, University of Sydney, **27**(8): 157–97.

Ganster, C. and Fusilier, M. (1989), 'Control in the workplace', in Cooper, C. and Robertson, I. (eds) *International Review of Industrial and Organizational Psychology, 1989*, John Wiley, Chichester, UK.

Garcia, A., Lopez-Jacob, M., Dudzinski, I., Gadea, R. and Rodrigo, F. (2007), 'Factors associated with the activities of safety representatives in Spanish workplaces', *Journal of Epidemiology and Community Health*, **61**: 784–90.

Gardiner, J., Stuart, M., Forde, C., Greenwood, I., McKenzie, R. and Perrett, R. (2007), 'Work–life balance and older workers: employees' perspectives on retirement transitions following redundancy', *International Journal of Human Resource Management*, **18**(3): 476–89.

Gardner, M. and Palmer, G. (1992). *Employment Relations: Industrial Relations and Human Resource Management in Australia*, Macmillan Education, South Melbourne.

Gardner, R. (2003), 'Overview and characteristics of some occupational exposures and health risks in offshore oil and gas installations', *Annals of Occupational Hygiene*, **47**(3): 201–10.

Garg, A. and Kapellusch, J.M. (2009), 'Applications of biomechanics for prevention of work-related musculoskeletal disorders', *Ergonomics*, **52**(1): 36–59.

Garrosa, E., Jimenez, B., Liang, Y. and Gonzalez, J. (2008), 'The relationship between socio-demographic variables, job stressors, burnout, and hard personality in nurses: an exploratory study', *International Journal of Nursing Studies*, **45**: 418–27.

Garshick, E., Laden, F., Hart, J., Rosner, B., Davis, M., Eisen, E. and Smith, T. (2008), 'Lung cancer and vehicle exhaust in trucking industry workers', *Environmental Health Perspectives*, **116**(10): 1327–32.

Gascon, S., Martinez-Jarreta, B., Santed, M., Gonzalez-Andrade, J. and Casalod, Y. (2009), 'Aggression towards healthcare workers in Spain: a multi-facility study to evaluate the distribution of growing violence among professionals, health facilities and departments', *International Journal of Occupational and Environmental Health*, **15**(2): 30–6.

Gash, V., Mertens, A. and Romeau Gordo, L. (2006), 'Are fixed-term jobs bad for your health? A comparison of West Germany and Spain', *IAB Discussion Paper No. 8/2006*, Berlin.

Gavhed, D. and Toomingas, A. (2007), 'Observed physical working conditions in a sample of call centres in Sweden and their relations to directives, recommendations and operators' comfort and symptoms', *International Journal of Industrial Ergonomics*, **37**(9 & 10): 790–800.

Geare, A. (2001), 'The Employment Contracts Act 1991–2000: a decade of change', *New Zealand Journal of Industrial Relations*, **26**(3): 287–306.

Geldart, S., Shannon, H. and Lohfeld, L. (2005), 'Have companies improved their health and safety approaches over the last decade? A longitudinal study', *American Journal of Industrial Medicine*, **47**: 227–36.

Geller, E. (2001a), 'Behaviour-based safety in industry: realizing the large scale potential of psychology to promote human welfare', *Applied and Preventive Psychology*, **10**(2): 87–105.

Geller, E. (2001b), 'Sustaining participation in a safety improvement process: 10 relevant principles from behavioral science', *Professional Safety*, **46**(9): 24–9.

Geller, E. (2005), 'Behaviour-based safety and occupational risk management', *Behaviour Modification*, **29**(3): 539–61.

George, S. (2005), 'A snapshot of workplace drug testing in the UK', *Occupational Medicine*, **55**: 69–71.

Geppert, C. and Roberts, L. (2005), 'Ethical issues in the use of genetic information in the workplace: a review of recent developments', *Current Opinion in Psychiatry*, **18**: 518–24.

Gerhardson, G. (1988), 'The future of occupational hygiene—an international overview', *Annals of Occupational Hygiene*, **32**(1): 1–19.

Gerr, F. (2008), 'Surveillance of work-related musculoskeletal disorders', *Occupational and Environmental Medicine*, **65**(5): 298–9.

Gershon, R. (1996), 'Bloodborne pathogen exposure among health care workers', *American Journal of Industrial Medicine*, **29**(4): 418–20.

Gerstein, M. (2008), *Flirting with Danger: Why Accidents are Rarely Accidental*, Union Square Press, New York.

Giannasi, F. and Thebaud-Mony, A. (1997), 'Occupational exposures to asbestos in Brazil', *International Journal of Occupational and Environmental Health*, **3**(2): 150–7.

Giatti, L., Barreto, S. and Comini Cesar, C. (2008), 'Household context and self-rated health: the impact of unemployment and informal work', *Journal of Epidemiology and Community Health*, **62**: 1079–85.

Gielo-Perczak, K., Karwowski, W., Hancock, P.A., Parasuraman, R. and Marras, W.S. (2005), 'Are we ready to consider individual differences in human capabilities in our workplace designs?', *Proceedings of the Human Factors and Ergonomics Society 49th Annual Meeting*: 1220–3.

Gillen, M., Baltz, D., Gassel, M., Kirsch, L. and Vaccaro, D. (2002), 'Perceived safety climate, job demands, and coworker support among union and nonunion injured construction workers', *Journal of Safety* Research, **33**: 33–51.

Gillen, M., Yen, I.H., Trupin, L., Swig, L., Rugulies, R., Mullen, K., Font, A., Burian, D., Ryan, G., Janowitz, I., Quinlan, P.A., Frank, J. and Blanc, P. (2007), 'The association of socioeconomic status and psychosocial and physical workplace factors with musculoskeletal injury in hospital workers', *American Journal of Industrial Medicine*, **50**: 245–60.

Gillespie, N., Walsh, M., Winefield, A., Dua, J. and Stough, C. (2001), 'Occupational stress in universities: staff perceptions of the causes, consequences and moderators of stress', *Work & Stress*, **15**(1): 53–72.

Gillespie, R. (1987), 'The limits of industrial hygiene: Commonwealth Government initiatives in occupational health, 1921–1948', in Atwood, H. and Kenny, J. (eds) *Reflections on Medical History and Health in Australia*, Medical History Unit, University of Melbourne.

Gillespie, R. (1990), 'Accounting for lead poisoning: the medical politics of occupational health', *Social History*, **15**(3): 303–31.

Gillespie, R. (1991), *Manufacturing Knowledge: A History of the Hawthorne Experiments*, Cambridge University Press, Cambridge.

Gilson, C.H.J., Wagar, T.H. and Brown, M. (2002), 'The adoption and retention of joint participation programs: preliminary evidence from New Zealand', *New Zealand Journal of Employment Relations*, **27**(3): 269–81.

Gimeno, D., Amick, B., Habeck, R., Ossmann, J. and Katz, J. (2005), 'The role of job strain on return to work after carpel tunnel surgery', *Occupational and Environmental Medicine*, **62**: 778–85.

Glasbeek, H. and Tucker, E. (1993), 'Death by consensus: the Westray story', *New Solutions*, **3**: 14–41.

Glaso, L., Matthiesen, S., Neilsen, M. and Einarsen, S. (2007), 'Do targets of workplace bullying portray a general victim personality profile?', *Scandinavian Journal of Psychology*, **48**: 313–19.

Glendon, A.I., Clarke, S.G. and McKenna, E.F. (2006), *Human Safety and Risk Management*, 2nd edition, Taylor & Francis, Boca Raton.

Glendon, A.I. and Litherland, D.K. (2001), 'Safety climate factors, group differences and safety behaviour in road construction', *Safety Science*, **39**(3): 157–88.

Glendon, A.I. and McKenna, E.F. (1995), *Human Safety and Risk Management*, Chapman & Hall, London.

Glendon, A.I. and Stanton, N.A. (2000), 'Perspectives on safety culture', *Safety Science* **34**(1–3): 193–214.

Glendon, I. (1995), 'Risk management for the 1990s: safety auditing', *Journal of Occupational Health and Safety—Australia and New Zealand*, **11**(6): 569–75.

Gobert, J. (2008), 'The Corporate Manslaughter and Corporate Homicide Act, 2007', *Modern Law Review*, **71**(3): 413–33.

Gochfeld, M. (2005), 'Occupational medicine practice in the United States since the industrial revolution', *Journal of Occupational and Environmental Medicine*, **47**: 115–31.

Godkin, G. (1991), 'Changing workplace behaviour ... skin cancer protection', *Journal of Occupational Health and Safety—Australia and New Zealand*, **7**(6): 477–82.

Goetzel, R.Z., Hawkins, K., Ozminkowski, R.J. and Wang, S. (2003), 'The health and productivity cost burben of the "top 10" physical and mental health conditions affecting six large US employers', *Journal of Occupational Environment Medicine*, **45**(1): 5–14.

Goetzel, R. (2008), 'The health and cost benefits of work site health promotion programs', *Annual Review of Public Health*, **29**: 303–23.

Gold, L., De Roos, A., Waters, M. and Stewart, P. (2008), 'Systematic literature review of the uses and levels of occupational exposure to tetrachloroethylene', *Journal of Occupational and Environmental Hygiene*, **5**(12): 807–39.

Golden, L. (2001), 'Flexible work schedules: what are we trading off to get them?' *Monthly Labor Review*, March, **124**: 50–67.

Goldenhar, L.M., LaMontagne, A.D., Katz, T., Heaney, C. and Landsbergis, P. (2001), 'The intervention research process in occupational safety & health: an overview from the National Occupational Research Agenda Intervention Effectiveness Research Team', *Journal of Occupational Environmental Medicine*, **43**(7): 616–22.

Goldsmith, C. (2007), 'Nanotechnology: keeping up to speed on small', *National Safety*: 18–23.

Goldsmith, D. (1998), 'Uses of workers' compensation data in epidemiological research', *Occupational Medicine: State of the Art Reviews*, **13**(2): 389–415.

Goldstein, B. (2007), 'The second question of the occupational history: what is the riskiest part of your job?', *Journal of Occupational and Environmental Medicine*, **49**(10): 1060–2.

Goodchild, M., Sanderson, K. and Nana, G. (2002), *Measuring the Total Cost of Injury in New Zealand: A Review of Alternative Cost Methodologies*, Business and Economic Research Limited, Wellington, The Department of Labour.

Goodwin, M. and Maconachie, G. (2005), 'Employer evasion of worker entitlements 1986–1995: what and whose?', paper published in proceedings of AIRAANZ Conference: 239–46.

Gordon, J.R., Whelan-Berry, K.S. and Hamilton, E.A. (2007), 'The relationship among work-family conflict enhancement, organizational work-family culture, and work outcomes for older working women', *Journal of Occupational Health Psychology*, **12**(4): 350–64.

Gordon, N., Cleary, P., Parker, C. and Czeisler, C. (1986), 'The prevalence and health impact of shiftwork', *American Journal of Public Health*, **76** (10): 1225–8.

Gordon, S., Buchanan, J. and Bretherton, T. (2008), *Safety in Numbers: Nurse-to-Patient Ratios and the Future of Health Care*, ILR Press, Cornell, Ithica.

Gori, G., Carrieri, M., Scapellato, M., Parvoli, G., Ferrara, D., Rella, R., Sturaro, A. and Bartolucci, G. (2009), '2-methylanthraquinone as a marker of occupational exposure to teak wood dust in boatyards', *Annals of Occupational Hygiene*, **53**(1): 27–32.

Gorman, D. (2004), Editorial: 'Where to for occupational medicine?', *Internal Medicine Journal*, **34**: 449–450.

Gough, M. (1985), 'Dioxin exposure at Monsanto', *Nature*, 12 December, **318**: 504.

Grabosky, P. and Braithwaite, J. (1986), *Of Manners Gentle: Enforcement Strategies of Australian Business Regulatory Agencies*, Oxford University Press, Melbourne.

Grandjean, E. (1988), *Fitting the Task to the Man: A Textbook of Occupational Ergonomics*, Taylor and Francis, London.

Grantham, D. (1992), *Occupational Health and Hygiene: Guidebook for the WHSO*, Merino Lithographics, Brisbane.

Graveling, R., Crawford, J., Cowie, H., Amati, C. and Vohra, S. (2008), *A Review of Workplace Interventions that Promote Mental Wellbeing in the Workplace*, Institute of Occupational Medicine, Edinburgh.

Gravina, N., Huang, Y-H., Robertson, M., Blair, M. and Austin, A. (2008), 'Promoting behavior change', *Professional Safety*, **53**(11): 30.

Gray, G. (2006), 'The regulation of corporate violations', *British Journal of Criminology*, **46**: 875–92.

Green, R. (1993), 'Analysis and measurement of productivity at the workplace', *Labour and Industry*, **5**(1 & 2): 1–15.

Green, R. (1994), 'A positive role for OHS in performance management', in *Beyond Lost Time Injuries: Positive Performance Indicators for OHS*, WorkSafe Australia, Australian Government Publishing Services, Canberra.

Green, R. (no date), 'A positive role for OHS in performance measurement', unpublished paper, Employment Studies Centre, University of Newcastle.

Greenwood, K., Rich, W. and James, J. (1995), 'Sleep hygiene practices and sleep duration in rotating-shiftworkers', *Work and Stress*, **9**(2 & 3): 262–71.

Greenwood, M. and Woods, H.M. (1919), A *Report of the Incidence of Industiral Accidents and Individuals with Special Reference to Multiple Accidents*, Reports of the Industrial Fatigue Research Board 4, HMSO, London.

Greif, A., Young, R., Carroll, M., Sieber, W., Pedersen, D., Sundin, D. and Seta, J. (1995), 'National Institute for Occupational Safety and Health general industry occupational exposure databases: their structure, capabilities and limitations', *Applied Occupational and Environmental Hygiene*, **10**(4): 264–9.

Griffin, V. (1986). 'The social production of occupational injury: a case study of nurses' work-related back injuries', unpublished Masters' dissertation, Griffith University, Brisbane.

Griffiths, A. (2000), 'Designing and managing healthy work for older workers', *Occupational Medicine*, **50**: 473–4.

Griffiths, A. (2007), 'Healthy work for older workers: work design and management factors', in Loretto, W., Vickerstaff, S. and White, P. (eds) *The Future for Older Workers: New Perspectives*, Policy Press, Bristol: 121–37.

Grosch, J.W., Caruso, C.C., Rosa, R.R. and Sauter, S.L. (2006), 'Long hours of work in the US: associations with demographic and organisational characteristics, psychosocial working conditions, and health', *American Journal of Industrial Medicine*, **49**: 943–52.

Gulati, M., Liss, D., Sparer, M., Holt, E. and Rabinowitz, P. (2005), 'Risk factors for tuberculin skin test positivity in an industrial workforce: results of a contact investigation', *Journal of Occupational and Environmental Medicine*, **47**(11): 1190–9.

Guldenmund, F.W. (2000), 'The nature of safety culture: a review of theory and research', *Safety Science*, **34**(1–3): 215–57.

Gun, R. (1994), 'The Worksafe model regulations for chemical safety: how much benefit?', *Journal of Occupational Health and Safety—Australia and New Zealand*, **10**(6): 523–7.

Gun, R. (1998), Letter to the editor: 'Critique of the Kerr Report', *Journal of Occupational Health and Safety—Australia and New Zealand*, **14**(1): 26–8.

Gunderson, M. and Hyatt, D. (1999), 'Privatization of workers' compensation: will the cure kill the patient?', *International Journal of Law and Psychiatry*, **22**(5 & 6): 547–65.

Gunningham, N. (1996), 'From compliance to best practice in OHS: the roles of specification, performance and systems-based standards', *Australian Journal of Labour Law*, **9**(3): 221–46.

Gunningham, N. (2005), 'Safety regulation and the mines inspectorate: lessons from Western Australia', *Journal of Occupational Health and Safety—Australia and New Zealand*, **21**(4): 299–309.

Gunningham, N. (2006a), 'Best practice mine safety regulation: are we there yet?', *Journal of Occupational Health and Safety—Australia and New Zealand*, **22**(3): 237–49.

Gunningham, N. (2006b), 'Safety, regulation and the mining industry', *Australian Journal of Labour Law*, **19**(1): 30–58.

Gunningham, N. (2007), *Mine Safety: Law, Regulation and Policy*, Federation Press.

Gunningham, N. (2008), 'Occupational health and safety, worker participation and the mining industry in a changing world', *Economic and Industrial Democracy*, **29**(3): 336–61.

Gupta, A. and Rosenman, K. (2006), 'Hypersensitivity pneumonitis due to metal working fluids: sporadic or under reported?', *American Journal of Industrial Medicine*, **49**: 423–33.

Guthrie, R. (2001), 'Report on the implementation of the Labor Party direction statement in relation to workers' compensation', report to the Workers' Compensation and Rehabilitation Commission for the Hon Minister for Consumer and Employment Protection.

Guthrie, R. (2002), 'The dismissal of workers covered by return to work provisions under workers compensation laws', *Journal of Industrial Relations*, **44**(4): 545–61.

Guthrie, R. (2003), 'Negotiation, power and conciliation, and review of compensation claims', *Law and Policy*, **24**(3): 229–68.

Guthrie, R. (2007), 'The Australian legal framework for stress claims', *Journal of Law and Medicine*, **14**(4): 528–50.

Guthrie, R. and Jansz, J. (2006), 'Women's experience in the workers' compensation system', *Journal of Occupational Rehabilitation*, **16**(3): 474–88.

Guthrie, R. and Quinlan, M. (2005), 'The occupational health and safety rights and workers compensation entitlements of illegal immigrants: an emerging challenge', *Policy and Practice in Safety and Health*, **3**(2): 69–89.

Gutman, S. (2008), 'Occupational therapy's link to vocational reeducation, 1910–1925', *Work: A Journal of Prevention Assessment and Rehabilitation*, **51**(10): 907–15.

Guy, L. and Short, S.D. (2005), 'Rehabilitation of workers with musculoskeletal injury and chronic pain', *Health Sociology Review*, **14**: 77–83.

Hagberg, M., Silverstein, B., Wells, R., Smith, M.J., Hendrick, H.W., Carayon, P. and Perusse, M. (1995), *Work-Related Musculoskeletal Disorders (WMSDs): A Reference Book for Prevention*, Taylor & Francis, London.

Hagg, G., Ericson, M. and Odenrick, P. (2009), 'Physical load', in Bohgard, L. et al. (eds) *Work and Technology on Human Terms*, Prevent, Stockholm: 129–81.

Haider, M., Kundi, M. and Koller, M. (1981), 'Methodological issues and problems in shift work research', in Johnson, L., Tepas, D., Colquhoun, W. and Colligan, M. (eds) *Biological Rhythms, Sleep and Shiftwork*, MTP Press, New York.

Haigh, G. (2006), *Asbestos House: Secret History of James Hardie Industries*, Scribe Publications Pty Ltd, Carlton North, Victoria.

Haines, F. (2009), 'Regulatory failures and regulatory solutions: a characteristic analysis of the aftermath of a disaster', *Law and Social Inquiry*, **34**(1): 31–60.

Haines, F., Gurney, D. and Jaques, M.S. (2002), 'The shadows of the law: contemporary approaches to regulation and the problem of regulatory conflict', paper published in the proceedings of Current Issues in Regulation: Enforcement and Compliance Conference, Australian Institute of Criminology, Melbourne: 1–7.

Haines, V., Marchand, A., Rousseau, V. and Demers, A. (2008), 'The mediating role of work-to-family conflict in the relationship between shiftwork and depression', *Work & Stress*, **22**(4): 341–56.

Haines, V., Merrheim, G. and Roy, M. (2001), 'Understanding reactions to safety incentives', *Journal of Safety Research*, **32**: 17–30.

Hakkinen, K. (1995), 'A learning-by-doing strategy to improve top management involvement in safety', *Safety Science*, **20**: 299–304.

Hale, A.R. and Glendon, A.I. (1987), *Individual Behaviour in the Control of Danger*, Elsevier, Amsterdam.

Hale, A. and Hale, O. (1972), *A Review of the Industrial Accident Research Literature*, HMSO, London.

Hale, A. and Heijer, T. (2006) 'Defining resilience', in Hollnagel, E., Woods, D. and Leveson, N. (eds) *Resilience Engineering: Concepts and Precepts*, Ashgate Publishing Company, Burlington, VT.

Hall, A. (2007), 'Restructuring, environmentalism and the problems of farm safety', *Sociologica Ruralis*, **47**(4): 343–68.

Hall, A., Forrest, A., Sears, A. and Carlan, N. (2006), 'Making a difference: knowledge activism and worker representation in joint OHS committees', *Relations Industrielles* **61**(3): 408–36.

Hale, A., Kirwan, B. and Kjellén, U. (2007), 'Safe by design: where are we now?', *Safety Science*, **45**: 305–27.

Hamalainen, R. (2006), *Workplace Health Promotion in Europe—The Role of National Policies and Strategies*, Finnish Institute of Occupational Health, Helsinki.

Hamalainen, P., Takala, J. and Saarela, K. (2006), 'Global estimates of occupational acidents', *Safety Science*, **44**(2): 137–56.

Hamalainen, P., Takala, J. and Saarela, K. (2007), 'Global estimates of work-related diseases', *American Journal of Industrial Medicine*, **58**: 28–41.

Hamalainen, R. and the ENWHP network (2007), Value of partnership for workplace *Health Promotion—Guideline for Partnership Building*, Finnish Institute for Occupational Health, Helsinki.

Hanks, P. (2008), *Accident Compensation Act Review: Final Report*, Government of Victoria, Melbourne.

Hannerz, H., Mikkelsen, K., Nielsen, M., Tuchsen, F. and Spangenberg, S. (2007), 'Social inequalities in injury occurrence and in disability retirement attributable to injuries: a 5 year follow-up study of a 2.1 million gainfully employed people', *BMC Public Health*, 7; 215, doi:10.1186/1471-2458-7-215.

Hannif, Z., Burgess, J. and Connell, J. (2008), 'Call centres and the quality of work life: towards a research agenda', *Journal of Industrial Relations*, **50**(2): 271–84.

Hannif, Z. and Lamm, F. (2005), 'When non-standard work becomes precarious: insights from the New Zealand call centre industry', *Management Review*, **16**(3): 324–50.

Hansen, C. (1989), 'A causal model of the relationship among accidents, biodata, personality, and cognitive factors', *Journal of Applied Psychology*, **74**(1): 81–90.

Hansen, C. and Andersen, J. (2008), 'Going ill to work—what personal circumstances, attitudes and work-related factors are associated with sickness presenteeism?', *Social Science & Medicine*, **67**: 956–64.

Hansen, J. (2001), 'Increased breast cancer risk among women who work predominantly at night', *Epidemiology*, **12**(1): 74–7.

Hansen, S. (2004), 'From "common observation" to behavioural risk management workplace surveillance and employee assistance 1914–2003', *International Sociology*, **19**: 151–71.

Hansson, H. and Arnetz, J. (2008), 'Nursing staff competence, work strain and satisfaction in elderly care: a comparison of home-based care and nursing homes', *Journal of Clinical Nursing*, **17**: 468–81.

Hansson, M., Bostrom, C. and Harms-Ringdahl, K. (2006), 'Sickness absence and sickness attendance—what people with neck and back pain think', *Social Science & Medicine*, **62**: 2183–95.

Hansson, S. and Ruden, C. (2008), 'A risk neutral default for chemical risk management', *American Journal of Industrial Medicine*, **51**: 964–7.

Harbridge, R. and Street, M. (1994), 'Labour market adjustment and women in the service industry: a survey', *New Zealand Journal of Industrial Relations*, **20**(1): 23–34.

Harcourt, M. and Harcourt, S. (2000), 'When can an employee refuse unsafe work and expect to be protected from discipline? Evidence from Canada', *Industrial and Labor Relations Review*, **53**(4): 684–703.

Harcourt, M., Lam, H. and Harcourt, S. (2007), 'The impact of workers' compensation experience-rating on discriminatory hiring practices', *Journal of Economic Issues*, **41**(3): 681–99.

Harenstam, A., Markland, S., Berntson, E., Bolin, M. and Ylander, J. (2006), *Understanding the Organisational Impact of Working Conditions and Health*, National Institute for Working Life, Stockholm.

Harma, M. and Illmarinen, J. (1999), 'Towards the 24-hour society—new approaches for ageing shift workers?', *Scandinavian Journal of Work Environment & Health*, **25**(6): 610–15.

Harper, M. (2004), 'Assessing workplace chemical exposure: the role of exposure monitoring', *Journal of Environmental Monitoring*, **6**: 404–12.

Harper, M. (2006), 'A review of workplace aerosol sampling procedures and their relevance to the assessment of beryllium exposures', *Journal of Environmental Monitoring*, **8**: 598–604.

Harpur, P. (2008), 'Occupational health and safety issues and the boardroom: criminal penalties for directors for company's lack of safety', *Corporate Governance eJournal*: 1–7.

Harrington, J. (1978), *Shift Work and Health: A Critical Review of the Literature*, HMSO, London.

Harrington, J.M. (1994), 'Shift work and health—a critical review of the literature on working hours', *Annals of the Academy of Medicine Singapore*, **23**: 699–705.

Harrington, J. and Gill, F. (1987), *Occupational Health*, Blackwell Scientific Publications, Oxford.

Harrison, B. (1991), 'Women's health or social control? The role of the medical profession in relation to factory legislation in late nineteenth century Britain', *Sociology of Health & Illness*, **13**(4): 469–91.

Harrison, J. (1986), 'Occupational hazards and their control', in Douglas, D., Ferguson, D., Harrison, J. and Stevenson, M. *Occupational Health and Safety*, Australian Medical Association, Glebe, NSW: 5–13.

Harrison, J. and Sepai, O. (2000), 'Should control measures be based on air measurements or biological/biological effects monitoring?', *Occupational Medicine*, **50**(1): 61–3.

Hart, B. and Moore, P. (1992), 'The aging workforce: challenges for the occupational health nurse', *AAOHM Journal*, **40**(1): 36–40.

Hart, C. (2003), *Nurses and Politics: The Impact of Power and Practice*, Macmillan, Basingstoke.

Hartvig, P. and Midttun, O. (1983), 'Coronary heart disease risk factors in bus and truck drivers: a controlled cohort study', *International Archives of Occupational and Environmental Health*, **52**: 353–60.

Hasle, P. (2007), 'Outsourcing and employer responsibility: a case study of occupational health and safety in the Danish public transport sector', *Relations Industrielles*, **62**(1): 96–117.

Hasle, P., Kines, P. and Andersen, L.P. (2009), 'Small enterprise owners' accident causation attribution and prevention', *Safety Science*, **47**(1): 9–19.

Hasle, P. and Limborg, H.J. (2006), 'A review of the literature on preventive occupational health and safety activities in small enterprises', *Industrial Health*, **44**(1): 6–12.

Hauge, L., Skogstad, L. and Einarsen, S. (2007), 'Relationships between stressful work environments and bullying: results of a large representative study', *Work & Stress*, **21**(3): 220–42.

Hauke, P., Kittler, H. and Moog, R. (1979), 'Inter-individual differences in tolerance to shiftwork related to morningness-eveningness', *Chronobiologica*, **6**: 109.

Haukka, E., Leino-Arjas, P., Viikari-Juntura, E., Takala, E-P., Malmivaara, A., Hopsu, L., Mutanen, P., Ketola, R., Virtanen, T., Pehkonen, I., Holtari-Leino, M., Nyka¨nen, J., Stenholm, S., Nykyri, E. and Riihimäki, H. (2008), 'A randomised controlled trial on whether a participatory ergonomics intervention could prevent musculoskeletal disorders', *Occupational and Environmental Medicine*, **65**(12): 849–56.

Havold, J. (2007), 'National cultures and safety orientation: a study of seafarers working for Norwegian shipping companies', *Work & Stress,* **21**(2): 173–95.

Hay, A. and Silbergeld, E. (1985), 'Assessing the risk of dioxin exposure', *Nature*, 9 May, **315**: 102–3.

Hay, A. and Silbergeld, E. (1986), 'Dioxin exposure at Monsanto', *Nature*, 17 April, **320**: 569.

Haynes, P., Vowles, J. and Boxall, P. (2005), 'Explaining the younger-older worker union density gap: evidence from New Zealand', *British Journal of Industrial Relations*, **43**(1): 93–116.

Head, J., Stansfeld, S.A. and Siegrist, J. (2004), 'The psychosocial work environment and alcohol dependence: a prospective study', *Journal of Occupational Environmental Medicine*, **61**(3): 219–24.

Heads of Workplace Safety Authorities (2004), *Falls Prevention in Construction: An Australian and New Zealand Joint Compliance Project*, WorkSafe Victoria, Melbourne.

'Health and safety at work: a question of costs and benefits?' (1999), *Magazine of the European Agency for Safety and Health at Work*, Bilbao, **1**: 7–46.

Health and Safety Commission (2001), *Report on Progress with the Changing Patterns of Employment Programme of Work, Health and Safety Commission Discussion Paper*, London.

Health and Safety Executive (HSE) (2004), *HSG (245)—Investigating Accidents and Incidents*, HSE, UK.

Health Insurance Email Bulletin, 20 August 2008, 'BBS can cut workplace accidents by 85%'.

Health Outcomes International Pty Ltd (2005), *Methods and Systems Used to Measure and Monitor Occupational Disease and Injury in New Zealand: NOHSAC Technical Report 2*, NOHSAC, Wellington.

Hebdon, R. and Hyatt, D. (1998), 'The effects of industrial relations factors on health and safety conflict', *Industrial and Labor Relations Review*, **51**(4): 579–93.

Hee, D., Pickrell, B., Bea, R., Roberts, K. and Williamson, R. (1999), 'Safety measurement assessment system (SMAS): a process for identifying and evaluating human and organizational factors in marine systems operations with field test results', *Reliability Engineering & System Safety*, **65**: 125–40.

Heederik, D. and van Rooy, F. (2008), 'Exposure assessment should be integrated in studies on the prevention and management of occupational asthma', *Occupational and Environmental Medicine*, **65**(3): 149–50.

Heiler, K. (2002), *The Struggle for Time: Background Report*, ACIRRT, University of Sydney. Available at <www.wst.tas.gov.au/__data/assets/pdf_file/0008/76418/sft_overview.pdf>

Heiler, K. (2006), 'Is the Australian mining industry ready for a safety case regime?', *Working Paper 45*, National Research Centre for OHS Regulation, Australian National University.

Heimendinger, J., Thompson, B., Ockene, J., Sorensen, G., Abrams, D., Emmons, K., Varnes, J., Eriksen, M., Probart, C. and Himmelstein, J. (1990), 'Reducing the risk of cancer through worksite intervention', *Occupational Medicine: State of the Art Reviews*, **5**(4): 707–23.

Heinrich, H. (1931), *Industrial Accident Prevention: A Scientific Approach*, McGraw-Hill, New York.

Hemerik, H. and Cena, K. (1993), 'Back injuries among migrant workers in Western Australia', *Journal of Occupational Health and Safety—Australia and New Zealand*, **9**(3): 255–8.

Henderson, M. (1981), 'Occupational psychology, safety and health in Australia: a personal 1980 position paper', in Hatton, M. (ed.) *Work and Health: Proceedings of a National Conference*, Centre for Continuing Education, Australian National University, Canberra.

Hertzman, C., McGrail, K. and Hirtle, B. (1999), 'Overall pattern of health care and social welfare use by injured workers in the British Columbia cohort', *International Journal of Law and Psychiatry*, **22**(5 & 6): 581–601.

Hewitt, J., Hush, J., Martin, M., Herbert, R. and Latimer, J. (2007), 'Clinical prediction rules can be derived and validated for injured Australian workers with persistent musculoskeletal pain: an observational study', *Australian Journal of Physiotherapy*, **53**: 269–76.

Heymans, M., de Vet, H., Knol, D., Bongers, P., Koes, K. and Van Mechelen, W. (2006), 'Workers' beliefs and expectations affect return to work over 12 months', *Journal of Occupational Rehabilitation*, **16**(4): 685–95.

Hickman, J. and Geller, E. (2003a), 'Self-management to increase safe driving among short-haul truck drivers', *Journal of Organisational Behaviour Management*, **23**(4): 1–20.

Hickman, J. and Geller, E. (2003b), 'A safety self-management intervention for mining operations', *Journal of Safety Research*, **34**: 299–308.

Hidden, A. (1989), *Investigation into the Clapham Junction Railway Accident*, HMSO & Department of Transport, London.

Higgs, P.E. and Mackinnon, S.E. (1995), 'Repetitive motion injuries', *Annual Review of Medicine*, **46**: 1–16.

Hignett, W. (2003), 'Intervention strategies to reduce musculoskeletal injuries associated with handling patients: a systematic review', *Occupational and Environmental Medicine*, **60**(9): e6.

Hildebrandt, G. (1980), 'Survey of current concepts relative to rhythms and shift work', in Scheving, L.E. and Halberg, F. (eds) *Chronobiology: Principles and Applications to Shifts in Schedules*, Sijhoff and Noordhoff, Alphen aan den Rijn, Netherlands.

Hildebrandt, G. (1986), 'Individual differences in susceptibility to night-and shift work: introductory remarks', in Haider, M., Koller, M. and Cervinka, R. (eds) *Night and Shift Work: Longterm Effects and their Prevention*, Verlag Peter Lang, Frankfurt Am Main.

Hildebrandt, G. and Stratmann, I. (1979), 'Circadian system response to night work in relation to individual circadian phase position', *International Archives of Occupational and Environmental Health*, **43**: 73–83.

Hiller, W. (2003), 'New tasks of ergonomics with respect to health management systems', in Strasser, H., Kluth K., Rausch, H. and Bubb, H. (eds) *Quality of Work and Products in Enterprises of the Future*, Ergonomica Verlag OHG, Stuttgart: 961–4.

Hills, B. (1989), *Blue Murder*, Sun Books, Melbourne.

Hines, C., Nilsen Hope, N., Deddens, J., Calafat, A., Silva, M., Grotte, A. and Sammons, D. (2009), 'Urinary phthalate metabolite concentrations among workers in selected industries: a pilot biomonitoring study', *Annals of Occupational Hygiene*, **53**(1): 1–17.

Hipple, S. (2001), 'Contingent work in the late-1990s', *Monthly Labor Review*, **124**: 3–27.

Hobbs, M., Woodwards, S., Murphy, B., Musk, A. and Elder, J. (1980), 'The incidence of pneumoconiosis, mesothelioma and other respiratory cancer in men engaged in mining and milling crocidolite in Western Australia', in Wagner, J. (ed.) *Biological Effects of Mineral Fibres*, IARC, Lyon.

Hochschild, A. (1983), *The Managed Heart: Commercialisation of Human Feeling*, University of California Press, Berkeley.

Hocking, B. (1992), 'Cost-benefit analysis of health promotion in industry', *Journal of Occupational Health and Safety—Australia and New Zealand*, **8**(6): 511–15.

Hodson, R. (2002), 'Worker participation and teams: new evidence from analyzing organizational ethnographies', *Economic and Industrial Democracy*, **23**(4): 491–528.

Hoffman, B., Papas, R., Chatkoff, D. and Kerns, R. (2007), *Health Psychology*, **26**(1): 1–9.

Hoffmann, J. and Larison, C. (1998), 'Drugs and the workplace', NORC, Chicago University.

Hoffman, T. and Cantoni, N. (2008), 'Occupational therapy services for adult neurological clients in Queensland and therapists use of telehealth to provide services', *Australian Occupational Therapy Journal*, **55**: 239–48.

Hoivik, D., Baste, V., Brandsdal, E. and Moen, B. (2007), 'Associations between self-reported working conditions and registered health and safety results', *Journal of Occupational and Environmental Medicine*, **49**(2): 139–47.

Holder, M. and O'Brien, T. (2007), 'Protest and survive, the UK construction safety campaign', *International Journal of Occupational and Environmental Health*, **13**(1): 27–31.

Holder, Y., Peden, M., Krug, E., Lund, J., Gururaj, G. and Kobusingye, O. (2001), *Injury Surveillance Guidelines, Health & Development Networks*, Centers for Disease Control and Prevention, the World Health Organization, Atlanta, USA, <whqlibdoc.who.int/publications/2001/9241591331.pdf>

Holland, P., Pyman, A., Cooper, B.K., Teicher, J. (2009), 'The development of alternative voice mechanisms in Australia: the case of joint consultation', *Economic and Industrial Democracy*, **30**: 67–92.

Holland, P., Pyman, A. and Teicher, J. (2005), 'Negotiating the contested terrain of drug testing in the Australian workplace', *The Journal of Industrial Relations*, **47**(3): 326–38.

Hollnagel, E. (2002), 'Time and time again', *Theoretical Issues in Ergonomics Science*, **3**(2): 143–58.

Hollnagel, E. and Woods, D.D. (2006), 'Epilogue: resilience engineering precepts', in Hollnagel, E., Woods, D.D. and Leveson, N.G. (eds) *Resilience Engineering: Concepts and Precepts*, Ashgate Publishing Ltd., Aldershot: 347–58.

Hollway, W. (1991), *Work Psychology and Organisational Behaviour: Managing the Individual at Work*, Sage, London.

Holmgren, K. and Ivanoff, S. (2007), 'Supervisors' views on employer responsibility in the return to work process: a focus group study', *Journal of Occupational Rehabilitation*, **17**(1): 93–106.

Holtslag, H.R., Post, M.W., van der Werken, C. and Linderman, E. (2007), 'Return to work after major trauma', *Clinical Rehabilitation*, **21**(4): 373–83.

Holtzman, N. (1996), 'Medical and ethical issues in genetic screening—an academic view', *Environmental Health Perspectives*, **104**(Supp. 5): 987–90.

Holtzman, W., Evans, R., Kennedy, S. and Iscoe, I. (1987), 'Psychology and health: contributions of psychology to the improvement of health and health care', *Bulletin of the World Health Organization*, **65**: 913–35.

Hondros, J. (1991), 'The application of expert systems in occupational health and safety', *Journal of Occupational Health and Safety—Australia and New Zealand*, **7**(3): 203–8.

Hong, J.H. (2005), 'Problems and suggestions to be considered in updating ICD-10 and revision of ICD-11', *WHO—Family of International Classifications Network Meeting*, Tokyo.

Hooker, R. (2006), *Final Report: Review of Occupational Health and Safety Act 1984*, Government of Western Australia, Perth.

Hooper, B. (2006), 'Epistemological transformation of occupational therapy: educational implications and challenges', *OTJR: Occupation, Participation and Health*, **26**(1): 16–24.

Hopkins, A. (1988), 'Deskilling, job control and safety: why coal miners violate safety regulations', *Labour and Industry*, **1**(2): 322–34.

Hopkins, A. (1989), 'The social construction of repetition strain injury', *Australia and New Zealand Journal of Sociology*, **25**(2): 239–59.

Hopkins, A. (1990), 'The social recognition of repetition strain injuries: an Australian/American comparison', *Social Science and Medicine*, **30**(3): 365–72.

Hopkins, A. (1994a), 'Are workers' compensation statistics a health and safety hazard?', *Australian Journal of Public Administration*, **53**(1): 78–86.

Hopkins, A. (1994b), 'The impact of workers' compensation premium incentives on health and safety', *Journal of Occupational Health and Safety—Australia and New Zealand*, **10**(2): 129–36.

Hopkins, A. (1995), *Making Safety Work: Getting Management Commitment to Occupational Health and Safety*, Allen & Unwin, Sydney.

Hopkins, A. (1999a), *Managing Major Hazards: The Lessons of the Moura Mine Disaster*, Allen and Unwin, Sydney.

Hopkins, A. (1999b), 'For whom does safety pay? The case of major accidents', *Safety Science*, **32**: 143–53.

Hopkins, A. (2000), *Lessons from Longford: the Esso Gas Plant Explosion*, CCH Australia, Sydney.

Hopkins, A. (2002), 'Lessons from Longford: the trial', *Journal of Occupational Health and Safety— Australia and New Zealand*, **18**(6): 3–71.

Hopkins, A. (2006a), 'What are we to make of safe behaviour programs?', *Safety Science*, **44**: 583–97.

Hopkins, A. (2006b), 'Studying organizational cultures and their effects on safety', *Safety Science*, **44**: 875–89.

Hopkins, A. (2008), *Failure to Learn: The Texas City Oil Refinery Disaster*, CCH Australia, Sydney.

Hopkins, A. and Palser, J. (1984), *The Causes of Accidents in New South Wales Coal Mines*, Department of Sociology, Australian National University.

Hopkins, A. and Palser, J. (1987), 'The causes of coal mine accidents', *Industrial Relations Journal*, **18**(1): 26–49.

Horne, J. and Ostberg, D. (1976), 'A self-assessment questionnaire to determine morningness-eveningness in human circadian rhythms', *International Journal of Chronobiology*, **4**: 97–110.

Horsley, R. and Goddard, D. (2007), 'Community occupational medicine in 2007 and beyond', *Journal of Occupational Health and Safety—Australia and New Zealand*, **23**(6): 531–8.

Hoskins, A. (2005), 'Occupational injuries, illnesses and fatalities among women', *Monthly Labor Review*, October: 31–7.

Hou, W., Tsauo, J., Lin, C., Liang, H. and Du, C. (2008), 'Workers' compensation and return-to-work following orthopaedic injury to extremities', *Journal of Rehabilitation Medicine*, **40**(6): 440–5.

Houben, G. (1991), 'Production control and chronic stress in work organisations', *International Journal of Health Services*, **21**(2): 309–27.

Houben, G. and Nijhuis, F. (1996), 'The role of production control in the development of burnout', International Journal of Health Services, **26**(2): 331–53.

House, R., Liss, G. and Wills, M. (1994), 'Periphery sensory neuropathy associated with 1,1,1-trichloroethane', *Archives of Environmental Health*, **49**(3): 196–9.

Houtman, I., Jettinghoff, K. and Cedillo, L. (2007), *Raising Awareness of Stress at Work in Developing Countries: A Modern Hazard in a Traditional Working Environment*, World Health Organization, Geneva.

Hovden, J., Lie, T., Karlsen, J. and Alteren, B. (2008), 'The safety representative under pressure: a study of occupational health and safety management in the Norwegian oil and gas industry', *Safety Science*, **46**: 493–509.

Howe, J. and Landau, I. (2007), 'Light touch labour regulation by state governments', *Melbourne University Law Review*, **31**: 367–99.

Hu, C. and Raymond, D. (2004), 'Lessons learned from hazardous chemical incidents—Louisiana hazardous substances emergency events surveillance (HSEES) system', *Journal of Hazardous Materials*, **115**: 33–8.

Huberman, M. (2004), 'Working hours of the world unite? New international evidence of worktime 1870–1913', *Journal of Economic History*, **64**(4): 964–1001.

Huff, J. (2007a), 'Industry influence on occupational and environmental public health', *International Journal of Occupational and Environmental Health*, **13**(1): 107–16.

Huff, J. (2007b), 'Benzene-induced cancers: abridged history and occupational health impact', *International Journal of Occupational and Environmental Health*, **13**(2): 213–21.

Hughes, E. and Parkes, K. (2007), 'Work hours and wellbeing: the roles of work-time control and work-family interference', *Work & Stress*, **21**(3): 264–78.

Human Resource Executive Online, 9 October 2008.

Human Rights Commission (2008), *Annual Report 2007*, Office of the Human Rights Commission Proceedings, Wellington.

Hunt, L., Boone, J., Fransway, A., Fremstad, C., Jones, R., Swanson, M., McEvoy, M., Miller, L., Majerus, E., Luker, P., Scheppman, D., Webb, M. and Yunginger, J. (1996), 'A medical-centre-wide, multidisciplinary approach to the problem of natural rubber latex allergy', *Journal of Occupational and Environmental Medicine*, **38**(8): 765–70.

Hunt, V. (2008), 'Investigation of the experience of contact centre workers in the PSA: does contact centre employment in the public service represent decent work?', report for Public Service Association, Auckland.

Hunter, C. and LaMontagne, A. (2008), 'Investigating "community" through a history of responses to asbestos-related disease in an Australian industrial region', *Social History of Medicine*, **21**(2): 361–79.

Hurrell, J.J., Nelson, D.L. and Simmons, B.L. (1998), 'Measuring job stressors and strains: where we have been, where we are, and where we need to go', *Journal of Occupational Health Psychology*, **3**(4): 368–89.

Hurst, P. and Palya, W. (2003), 'Selecting an effective BBS process', *Professional Safety*, **48**(9): 39–41.

Husman, K. and Husman, P. (2006), 'Challenges of OHS for changing working life', *International Congress Series*, **1294**: 19–22.

Hutcheson, G., Henderson, M. and Davies, J. (1995), *Alcohol in the Workplace: Costs and Responses*, Research Series No. 59, Department for Education and Employment, UK.

Hyam, S. (2007), Ex-manager Workplace Standards Tasmania, personal communication, 8 February 2007.

Hyatt, A. and Krajl, B. (1995), 'The impact of workers' compensation experience rating on employer appeals activity', *Industrial Relations*, **34**(1): 95–106.

Hyslop, D.R. and Maré, D.C. (2007), *Job Employment Intensity, Matching, and Earnings 1999–2005*, Statistics New Zealand, Wellington.

IAEA (1986), *Summary Report on the Post-Accident Review Meeting on the Chernobyl Accident*, International Safety Advisory Group, Safety Series 75-INSAG-1, Vienna.

ICOH (2002), *International Code of Ethics of Occupational Health Professionals*. Updated 2002, International Commission on Occupational Health, Rome.

Iles, R., Davidson, M. and Taylor, N. (2008), 'Psychosocial predictors of failure to return to work in non-chronic non-specific low back pain: a systematic review', *Occupational and Environmental Medicine*, **65**: 507–17.

Ilmarinen, J. and Rantanen, J. (1999), 'Promotion of work ability during ageing', *American Journal of Industrial Medicine*, (Supp. 2): 21–3.

ILO (2009), *Global Employment Trends January 2009*, International Labour Organisation, Geneva.

Industry Commission (1994), *Workers' Compensation in Australia*, Australian Government Publishing Service, Canberra.

Industry Commission (1995), *Work, Health and Safety: An Inquiry into Occupational Health and Safety*, Report No.47, Two volumes, Australian Government Publishing Service, Canberra.

Industrial Relations Commission of NSW (1996), *Report to the Minister for Industrial Relations and Employment on 'Engineered Standards' in the Warehouse Operations and Distribution Industry Pursuant to s34(5) of the Industrial Relations Act 191, Matter No. IRC 1145 of 1994*, Volume and Appendices, NSW Government Printer, Sydney.

Innstrand, S., Langballe, E., Espnes, G., Falkum, E. and Aasland, O. (2008), 'Positive and negative work-family interaction and burnout', *Work & Stress*, **22**(1): 1–15.

International Agency for Research on Cancer (1997), 'Polychlorinated dibenzo-*para*-dioxins and polychlorinated dibenzofurans', IARC Monogr Eval Carcinog Risks Hum 69, IARC, World Health Organization, Lyon.

International Agency for Research on Cancer (2007), *Attributable Causes of Cancer in France in the Year 2000*, World Health Organization, Lyon.

International Labour Office (1988), *Report V (1): Night Work: Fifth Item of the Agenda, International Labour Conference, 76th Session*, 1989, Geneva.

International Labour Organisation (1991), *Occupational Exposure Limits for Airborne Toxic Substances*, 3rd edition, ILO, Geneva.

Iriat, J., de Oliveira, R., Xavier, S., da Silva Costa, A., de Araujo, G. and Santaner, V. (2008), 'Representations of informal jobs and health risks among housemaids and construction workers', *Ciencia & Saude Coletivia*, **13**(1): 164–74.

Irwin Mitchell and the Centre for Corporate Accountability, (2009), *Migrant Workplace Deaths in Britain*, London.

Iskra-Golec, I., Oginska, H. and Szramel, W. (1987), 'Some psychological aspects of tolerance to shiftwork', in Oginski, A., Pokorski, J. and Rutenfranz, J. (eds) *Contemporary Advances in Shiftwork Research*, Nicolaus Copernicus Medical Academy, Krakow.

Ison, T. (1990), 'Rights to employment under the workers' compensation Acts and other statues', *Osgoode Hall Law Journal*, **24**(4): 839–58.

Iwasaki, K., Takahashi, M. and Nakata, K. (2006), 'Health problems due to long working hours in Japan', *Industrial Health*, **44**(4): 537–40.

Jacobson, M., Yenney, S. and Bisgard, J. (1990), 'An organisational perspective on worksite health promotion', *Occupational Medicine: State of the Art Reviews*, **5**(4): 653–64.

Jacinto, C. and Aspinwall, E. (2003), 'Work accidents investigation technique (WAIT)—part I', *Safety Science Monitor*, **7**(1): 1–16.

Jacinto, C. and Aspinwall, E. (2004), 'WAIT (part II)—results of application in real accidents', *Safety Science Monitor*, **8**(1): 5–18.

Jackson, S., Zedeck, S. and Summers, E. (1985), 'Family life disruptions: effects of job-induced structural and emotional interference', *Academy of Management Journal*, **28**(3): 574–86.

Jacques, P., Moens, G., Van Damme, P., Goubau, P., Vranckx, R., Steeno, J., Muylle, L. and Desmyter, J. (1994), 'Increased risk for hepatitis A among female day nursery workers in Belgium', *Occupational Medicine*, **44**(5): 259–61.

Jamal, M. (2007), 'Short communication: burnout and self-employment: a cross cultural empirical study', *Stress and Health*, **23**: 249–56.

James, C. (1987), 'Occupational injury: accidental or a reflection of conflict between capital and labour?', *Australian and New Zealand Journal of Sociology*, **23**(1): 47–64.

James, C. (1989), 'Social sequelae of occupational injury and illness', unpublished PhD thesis, Griffith University.

James, M. (1993), 'The struggle against silicosis in the Australian mining industry: the role of the Commonwealth Government, 1920–1950', *Labour History*, **65**: 75–95.

James, P. (1992), 'Reforming British health and safety law: a framework for discussion', *Industrial Law Journal*, **21**(2): 83–105.

James, P. (2006), Guest editorial, *Employee Relations*, **28**(3): 1–8.

James, P., Johnstone, R., Quinlan, M. and Walters, D. (2007), 'Regulating supply chains for safety and health', *Industrial Law Journal*, **36**(2): 163–87.

James, P. and Walters, D. (1997), 'Non-union rights of involvement: the case of health and safety at work', *Industrial Law Journal*, **26**(1): 35–50.

James, P. and Walters, D. (2002), 'Worker representation in health and safety: options for regulatory reform', *Industrial Relations Journal*, **33**(2): 141–56.

Jamieson, S. (2005), 'The neoliberal state and the gendered prosecution of work injury', *Health Sociology Review*, **14**(1): 69–76.

Jamieson, S. (2006), 'The long distance trucking industry in New South Wales and the role of the State', *Employment Relations Record*, **6**(2): 21–30.

Janssen, N., van den Heuvel, W., Beurskens, A., Nijhuis, F., Schroer, C. and van Eijk, J. (2003), 'The demand-control model as a predictor of return to work', *International Journal of Rehabilitation Research*, **26**(1): 1–9.

Jeffress, C. (1998a), 'Statement of Assistant Secretary Occupational Safety and Health Administration before the Committee on Education and the Workforce' Subcommittee on Workforce Protections', United States House of Representatives, April 29, Washington.

Jeffress, C. (1998b), 'Occupational exposure to bloodborne pathogens: request for information', *Federal Register*, **63**(174): 48250–2.

Jeffrey, G. (1995), 'The industrial relations context of workplace health and safety', in Slappendel, C. (ed.) *Health and Safety in New Zealand Workplaces*, Dunmore Press, Palmerston North.

Jensen, P. (2002), 'Assessing assessment: the Danish experience of worker participation in risk assessment', *Economic and Industrial Democracy*, **23**(2): 201–27.

Jia, L. and Johns, G. (1995), 'Job scope and stress: can job scope be too high?', *Academy of Management Journal*, **38**(5): 1288.

Jim Pearson Transport and Transport Workers' Union of Australia, Australian Industrial Relations Commission, RE2007/2418 6 July 2007.

Jobb, D. (1994), *Calculated Risk, Greed, Politics and the Westray Tragedy*, Nimbus, Halifax.

Johansson, G. (1989), 'Job demands and stress reactions in repetitive and uneventful monotony at work', *International Journal of Health Services*, **19**(2): 365–77.

Johansson, J. and Abrahamsson, L. (2009), 'The organisation of production and work', in Bohgard, L. et al. (eds) (2009) *Work and Technology on Human Terms*, Prevent, Stockholm: 71–127.

Johnson, C. (2008), 'Ten contentions of corporate manslaughter legislation: public policy and the legal response to workplace accidents', *Safety Science*, **46**: 349–70.

Johnson, J. (1989), 'Structural barriers to change in the workplace', *International Journal of Health Services*, **19**(1): 117–19.

Johnson, J. (2008), 'Globalisation, workers' power and the psychosocial work environment—is the demand-control-support model still useful in the neoliberal era?', *Scandinavian Journal of Work Environment and Health* (Supp. No.6): 15–21.

Johnson, S.E. (2003), 'Behavioral safety theory', *Professional Safety*, **48**(10): 39.

Johnson, W.G. (1980), *MORT Safety Assurance Systems (ed.)* Marcel Dekker Inc, New York, in Katsakiori, P., Sakellaropoulos, G. and Manatakis, E. (2009), 'Towards an evaluation of accident investigation methods in terms of their alignment with accident causation models', *Safety Science*, **47**(7): 1007–15.

Johnston, V., Jimmieson, N., Souvlis, T. and Jull, G. (2007), 'Interaction of psychosocial risk factors explain increased neck problems among female office workers', *Pain*, **129**: 311–20.

Johnstone, R. (1993), 'The legal regulation of pre-employment screening', Quinlan, M. (ed.) *Work and Health: The Origins, Management and Regulation of Occupational Illness*, Macmillan, Melbourne.

Johnstone, R. (1994), *The Court and the Factory: The Legal Construction of Occupational Health and Safety Offences in Victoria*, unpublished PhD thesis, Law School, University of Melbourne.

Johnstone, R. (ed.) (1996), *New Directions in Occupational Health and Safety Prosecutions: The Individual Liability of Corporate Officers and Prosecutions for Industrial Manslaughter and Related Offences*, Centre for Employment and Labour Relations Law Working Paper No. 9, University of Melbourne.

Johnstone, R. (1997), *Occupational Health and Safety Law and Policy: Text and Materials*, LBC Information Services, Sydney.

Johnstone, R. (1999), 'Paradigm crossed? The statutory occupational health and safety obligations of the business undertaking', *Australian Journal of Labour Law*, **12**: 73.

Johnstone, R. (2004), *Occupational Health and Safety Law and Policy*, 2nd edition, Law Book Company, Sydney.

Johnstone, R. and Jones, N. (2006), 'Constitutive regulation of the firm: occupational health and safety, dismissal, discrimination and sexual harassment', in Arup, C., Gahan, P., Howe, J., Johnstone, R., Mitchell, R. and O'Donnell, A. (eds) *Labour Law and Labour Market Regulation: Essays on the Construction, Constitution and Regulation of Labour Markets and Work Relationships*, Federation Press, Sydney.

Johnstone, R. and King, M. (2008), 'A responsive sanction to promote systematic compliance? Enforceable undertakings in occupational health and safety regulation', *Australian Journal of Labour Law*, **21**: 280–315.

Johnstone, R., Mitchell, R. and O'Donnell, A. (eds) (2006), *Labour Law and Labour Market Regulation*, Federation Press, Sydney: 483–502.

Johnstone, R. and Quinlan, M. (2006), 'The OHS regulatory challenges of agency labour: evidence from Australia', *Employee Relations*, **28**(3): 273–89.

Johnstone, R. and Quinlan, M. (2008), 'The shift to process standards in OHS in Australia', presentation to Australia and New Zealand Forum of OHS Inspectors, Melbourne, 26 November.

Johnstone, R., Quinlan, M. and Mayhew, C. (2001), 'Outsourcing risk? The regulation of OHS where contractors are employed', *Comparative Labor Law and Policy Journal*, **22**(2 & 3): 351–93.

Johnstone, R., Quinlan, M. and Walters, D. (2005), 'Statutory occupational health and safety workplace arrangements for the modern labour market', *Journal of Industrial Relations*, **47**(1): 93–116.

Johnstone, R. and Sarre, R. (eds) (2004), 'Regulation: enforcement and compliance', *Research and Public Policy Series*, Number 57, Australian Institute of Criminology, Canberra.

Jones, C., Dorrian, J. and Dawson, D. (2003), 'Legal implications of fatigue in the Australian transport industries', *The Journal of Industrial Relations*, **45**(3): 344–59.

Jones, T., Ram, M. and Edwards, P. (2006), 'Ethnic minority business and the employment of illegal immigrants', *Entrepreneurship & Regional Development*, **18**: 133–50.

Jordan, J.L., Foster, N.E., Holden, M.A. and Mason, E.E.J. (2009), 'Interventions to improve adherence to exercise for chronic musculoskeletal pain in adults (protocol): The Cochrane Collaboration', *The Cochrane Library*, Issue 2.

Judge Saunders, *Masters* v. *Wanaka Tourist Craft Ltd*, Unreported, DC, 28 May 1996, CRN 500200415849.

Kagan, R. (1989), Editor's introduction: 'Understanding regulatory enforcement', *Law and Policy*, **11**(2): 89–119.

Kagan, R.A., Gunningham, N. and Thornton, D. (2003), 'Explaining corporate environmental performance: how does regulation matter?', *Law & Society Review*, **37**(1): 50–90.

Kamp, A. (2009), 'Bridging collective and individual approaches to occupational safety and health: what promises does workplace health promotion hold?', *Policy and Practice in Health and Safety*, **7**(1): 85–102.

Kapoor, S., Shaw, W.S., Pansky, G. and Patterson, W. (2006), 'Initial patient and clinician expectations of return to work after acute onset of work-related low back pain', *Journal of Occupational Environmental Medicine*, **48**(11): 1173–80.

Karasek, R. (1979), 'Job demands, job decision latitude, and mental strain: implications for job re-design', *Administrative Science Quarterly*, **24**: 285–308.

Karasek, R., Baker, D., Marxer, F., Ahlbom, A. and Theorell, T. (1981), 'Job decision latitude, job demands, and cardiovascular disease: a prospective study of Swedish men', *American Journal of Public Health*, **71**: 694–705.

Karasek, R., Theorell, T., Schwartz, J., Pieper, C. and Alfredsson, I. (1982), 'Job, psychological factors and coronary heart disease', *Advances in Cardiology*, **March**: 62–7.

Karasek, R., Theorell, T., Schwartz, J., Schnall, P., Pieper, C. and Michela, J. (1988), 'Job characteristics in relation to the prevalence of myocardial infarction in the US health examination survey (HES) and the health and nutrition examination survey (HANES)', *American Journal of Public Health*, **78**: 910–18.

Karjalainen, K.A., Malmivaara, A., van Tulder, M.W., Roine, R., Jauhiainen, M., Hurri, H. and Koes, B.W. (2009), 'Multidisciplinary rehabilitation for fibromyalgia and musculoskeletal pain in working age adults (review)', in *The Cochrane Library 2009, Issue 2*, John Wiley & Sons, Ltd.

Karsh, B-T. (2006), 'Theories of work-related musculoskeletal disorders: implications for ergonomic interventions', *Theoretical Issues in Ergonomics Science*, **7**(1): 71–88.

Karwowski, W. (2005), Invited plenary paper: 'Ergonomics and human factors: the paradigms for science, engineering, design, technology and management of human-compatible systems', *Ergonomics*, **48**(5): 436–63.

Karwowski, W., Cuevas, H.M., Weaver, J.L., Hettinger, L., Matthews, G., Gielo-Perczak, K. and Hancock, P.A. (2003), 'Considering the importance of individual differences in human factors research: no longer simply confounding noise', *Proceedings of the Human Factors and Ergonomics Society 47th Annual Meeting*: 1082–6.

Katsakiori, P., Sakellaropoulos, G. and Manatakis, E. (2009), 'Towards an evaluation of accident investigation methods in terms of their alignment with accident causation models', *Safety Science*, **47**(7): 1007–15.

Katz, P. and Showstack, J. (1990), 'Is it worth it? Evaluating the economic impact of worksite health promotion', *Occupational Medicine: State of the Art Reviews*, **5**(4): 837–50.

Kawachi, I., Colditz, G.A., Stampfler, M.J., Willett, W.C., Manson, J.E., Speizer, F.E., Hennekens, C.H. (1995), 'Prospective study of shift work and risk of coronary heart disease in women', *Circulation*, **92**(11): 3178–82.

Keegal, T., Ostry, A. and LaMontagne, A. (2009), 'Job strain exposures versus stress-related workers' compensation claims in Victoria, Australia: developing a public health response to job stress', *Journal of Public Health Policy*, **30**(1): 17–39.

Keller, S.D. (2001), 'Quantifying social consequences of occupational injuries and illnesses: state of the art and research agenda', *American Journal of Industrial Medicine*, **40**: 438–51.

Kelloway, E. (2004), 'Labour unions and occupational injury: conflict and cooperation', in Barling, J. and Frone, M. (eds) *The Psychology of Workplace Safety*, American Psychological Association, Washington: 265–98.

Kelloway, E., Teed, M. and Kelley, E. (2008), 'The psychosocial environment: towards an agenda for research', *International Journal of Workplace Health Management*, **1**(1): 50–64.

Kelman, R. (1985), 'Medical examination in the prevention of occupational disease', *The University of New South Wales Occasional Papers*, **10**: 11–13.

Kendall, E., Muenchberger, H. and Clapton, J. (2007), 'Trends in Australian rehabilitation: reviving its humanitarian core', *Disability and Rehabilitation*, **29**(10): 817–23.

Kendall, N. (2006), *Management and Governance of Occupational Health and Safety in Five Countries (United Kingdom, United States, Finland, Canada, Australia)*, National Occupational Health and Safety Advisory Committee: NOHSAC Technical Report 8, Wellington.

Kenny, D. (1994), 'The relationship between workers' compensation and occupational rehabilitation: an historical perspective', *Journal of Occupational Health and Safety—Australia and New Zealand*, **10**(2): 157–64.

Kenny, D.T. (1995a), 'Barriers to occupational rehabilitation: an exploratory study of long-term injured workers', *Journal of Occupational Health and Safety—Australia and New Zealand*, **11**(3): 249–56.

Kenny, D.T. (1995b), 'Common themes, different perspectives: a systemic analysis of employer-employee experiences of occupational rehabilitation', *Rehabilitation Counseling Bulletin*.

Kenny, D. (1996), 'Occupational rehabilitation assessed: the verdict of employers', *Journal of Occupational Health and Safety—Australia and New Zealand*, **12**(2): 145–53.

Kenny, D. (2000), 'Occupational stress: reflections on theory and practice', in Kenny, D.T., Carlson, J.G., McGuigan, F.J. and Sheppard, J.L. (eds) *Stress and Health: Research and Clinical Applications*, Gordon Breach/Harwood Academic Publishers, Amsterdam.

Kerkhof, G. (1985), 'Inter-individual differences in the human circadian system: a review', *Biological Psychology*, **20**: 83–112.

Kerr, C., Morrell, S., Salkeld, G., Corbett, S., Taylor, R. and Webster, F. (1996), *Best Estimate of the Magnitude of Health Effects of Occupational Exposure to Hazardous Substances*, Worksafe Australia Development Grant Final Report, Australian Government Publishing Service, Canberra.

Kerr, L.E. (1981), 'The health of workers', *Journal of Public Health Policy*, **2**(1): 3–7.

Kerr, L.E. (1990), 'Occupational health: a classic example of class conflict', *Journal of Public Health Policy*, **11**(1): 39–48.

Kesselring, R.G. and Pittman, J.R. (2002), 'Drug testing laws and employment injuries', *Journal of Labor Research*, **23**(2): 294–301.

Kessler, S., Spector, P., Chang, C. and Parr, A. (2008), 'Organizational violence and aggression: development of the three-factor violence climate survey', *Work & Stress*, **22**(2): 108–24.

Keyserling, W. (1983), 'Occupational safety and ergonomics', in Levy, B. and Wegmann, D. (eds) *Occupational Health: Recognizing and Preventing Work-Related Disease*, Little, Brown and Co., Boston.

Kiesler, S. and Finholt, T. (1988), 'The mystery of RSI', *American Psychologist*, **43**(12): 1004–15.

Kiesswetter, E. and Seeber, A. (1995), 'Modification of shiftwork effects by chemical workplace exposure', *Work and Stress*, **9**(2 & 3): 351–9.

Kiesswetter, E., Seeber, A., Golka, K. and Sietmann, B. (1997), 'Solvent exposure, shiftwork, and sleep', *International Journal of Occupational and Environmental Health*, **3**(3): S61–66.

Killey, J., Temperley, J. and Fragar, L. (2009), 'In Australia, can a user know whether a pesticide is a hazardous substance?', *Journal of Occupational Health and Safety—Australia and New Zealand*, **25**(2): 123–8.

Kim, D., Ridzon, R., Giles, B., Mireles, T., Garrity, K., Hathcock, A., Crowder, D., Jackson, R. and Taylor, Z. (2003), 'A no-name tuberculosis tracking system', *American Journal of Public Health*, **93**(10): 1637–9.

Kim, I., Kang, Y., Muntaner, C., Chun, Y. and Cho, S. (2008), 'Gender, precarious work and chronic diseases in Korea', *American Journal of Industrial Medicine*, **51**(10): 748–57.

King, E. (1990), 'Occupational hygiene aspects of biological monitoring', *Annals of Occupational Hygiene*, **34**(3): 315–22.

King, J., Hibbert, P., Butt, H. and Schulz, L. (2005), *Methods and Systems Used to Measure and Monitor Occupational Disease and Injury in New Zealand*, NOHSAC, Technical Report 2, Wellington.

Kingston, J., Frei, R., Koornneef, F. and Schallier, P. (2007), *Defining Operational Readiness to Investigate: White Paper 1*, Noordwijk Risk Initiative Foundation, <www.nri.eu.com/WP1.pdf>

Kinnunen, U., Mauno, S. (1998), 'Antecedents and outcomes of work–family conflict among employed women and men in Finland', *Human Relations*, **51**(2): 157–77.

Kinoulty, M. and Williams, N. (2006), 'Occupational health provision and health surveillance in the semiconductor industry', *Occupational Medicine*, **56**: 100–1.

Kirk, A. and Brown, D. (2003), 'Employee assistance programs: a review of the management of stress and wellbeing through workplace counseling and consulting', *Australian Psychologist*, **38**(2): 138–43.

Kitching, J. (2008), 'Rethinking UK small employers' skills policies and the role of workplace learning', *International Journal of Training and Development*, **12**(2): 100–20.

Kivimaki, M., Honkonen, T., Wahlbeck, K., Elovainio, M., Pentti, J., Klaukka, T., Virtanen, M. and Vahtera, J. (2007), 'Organisational downsizing and increased use of psychotropic drugs among employees who remain in employment', *Journal of Epidemiology and Community Health*, **61**: 154–8.

Kivimaki, M., Theorell, T., Westerlund, H., Vahtera, J. and Alfredsson, L. (2008), 'Job strain and ischaemic disease: does the inclusion of older employees in a cohort dilute the association? The WOLF Stockholm study', *Journal of Epidemiology and Community Health*, **62**: 372–4.

Kivisto, S., Verbeek, J., Hirvonen, M. and Varonen, H. (2008), 'Return to work policies in Finnish occupational health services', *Occupational Medicine*, **55**: 88–93.

Kjellén, U., Motet, G. and Hale, A. (2008), 'Resolving multiple criteria in decision-making involving risk of accidental loss', *Safety Science*, **47**: 795–7.

Klatt, R. and Ollman, R. (2007), 'Health risks and prevention strategies in the modern working world', *Diabetes Stoffwechsel Und Herz*, **16**(4): 263–70.

Klen, T. (1989), 'Costs of occupational accidents in forestry', *Journal of Safety Research*, **20**(1): 31–40.

Kletz, T. (1993), 'Accident data—the need for a new look at the sort of data that are collected and analysed', *Safety Science*, **16**: 407–15.

Knauth, P. (1995), 'Speed and direction of shift rotation', *Journal of Sleep Research*, **4**(Supp. 2): 41–6.

Knauth, P., Emde, E., Rutenfranz, J. and Kiesswetter, E. (1981), 'Re-entrainment of body temperature in field studies of shift work', *International Archives of Occupational and Environmental Health*, **49**: 137–49.

Knauth, P. and Kiesswetter, E. (1987), 'A change from weekly to quicker shift rotations: a field study of discontinuous three-shift rosters', *Ergonomics*, **30**(9): 1311–21.

Knauth, P., Landau, K., Droge, C., Schwitteck, M., Wydinski, M. and Rutenfranz, J. (1980), 'Duration of sleep depending on the type of shift work', *International Archives of Occupational and Environmental Health*, **46**: 167–77.

Knauth, P. and Rutenfranz, J. (1981), 'Duration of sleep related to the type of shiftwork', in Reinberg, A., Vieux, N. and Andlauer, P. (eds) *Night and Shift Work: Biological and Social Aspects*, Pergamon Press, Oxford.

Knauth, P., Rutenfranz, J., Herrmann, G. and Popel, S. (1978), 'Re-entrainment of body temperature in experimental shiftwork studies', *Ergonomics*, **21**: 775–83.

Knight, K.W. (2002), 'Developing a risk management standard—the Australian experience', *Safety Science*, **40**: 69–74.

Knutsson, A. (1989), 'Shift work and coronary heart disease', *Scandinavian Journal of Social Medicine*, Supp. 44.

Knutsson, A. (2003), 'Health disorders of shift workers', *Occupational Medicine*, **53**: 103–8.

Knutsson, A., Akerstedt, T., Jonsson, B. and Orth-Gomer, K. (1986), 'Increased risk of ischaemic heart disease in shift workers', *The Lancet*, 12 July 1986: 89–92.

Kobasa, S. (1979), 'Stressful life events, personality, and health: an inquiry into hardiness', *Journal of Personality and Social Psychology*, **37**(1): 1–11.

Kobasa, S. (1984), 'Barriers to work stress, II: the "hardy" personality', in Gentry, W., Benson, H. and de Wolff, C. (eds) *Behavioral Medicine: Work Stress and Health*, Sijthoff and Nordhoff International Publishers, B.V.

Kobasa, S., Maddi, S. and Courington, S. (1981), 'Personality and constitution as mediators in the stress-illness relationship', *Journal of Health and Social Behaviour*, **22**: 368–78.

Kobasa, S. and Puccetti, M. (1983), 'Personality and social resources in stress resistance', *Journal of Personality and Social Psychology*, **45**(4): 839–50.

Kobayashi, Y., Kaneyoshi, A., Yokota, A. and Kawakami, N. (2008), 'Effects of a worker participatory program for improving work environments on job stressors and mental health among workers: a controlled trial', *Journal of Occupational Health*, **50**: 455–70.

Kogi, K. (1981), 'Comparison of resting conditions between various shift rotation systems for industrial workers', in Reinberg, A., Vieux, N. and Andlauer, P. (eds) *Night and Shift Work: Biological and Social Aspects*, Pergamon Press, Oxford.

Kogi, K. (1985), 'Introduction to the problem of shift work', in Folkard, S. and Monk, T. (eds) *Hours of Work: Temporal Factors in Work-Scheduling*, John Wiley, Chichester, UK.

Koh, D. (1995), 'Occupational health and safety promotion: problems and solutions', *Safety Science*, **20**(2 & 3): 323–8.

Koh, D. and Aw, T.C. (2003), 'Surveillance in occupational health', *Occupational and Environmental Medicine*, **60**(9): 705–10.

Koh, D. and Lee, S-M., (2003), Editorial: 'Good medical practice for occupational physicians', *Occupational and Environmental Medicine*, **60**: 1–2.

Kohte, W. (2003), 'Occupational safety and health promotion: competition or cooperation?', *Gersunheitswesen*, **65**(3): 187–9.

Koller, M. (1983), 'Health risks related to shift work', *International Archives of Occupational and Environmental Health*, **53**: 59–75.

Koller, M., Kundi, M., Cervinka, R. and Haider, M. (1984), 'Health risk factors due to sensitisation processes in shift workers', in Wedderburn, A. and Smith, P. (eds) *Psychological Approaches to Night and Shift Work: International Research Papers*, Heriot Watt University, Edinburgh.

Kominski, G., Pourat, N., Roby, D. and Cameron, M. (2008), 'Return to work and degree of recovery among injured workers in California's workers' compensation system', *Journal of Workers' Compensation*, **50**(3): 296–305.

Körvers, P.M.W. and Sonnemans, P.J.M. (2008), 'Accidents: a discrepancy between indicators and facts!', *Safety Science*, **46**(7): 1067–77.

Krantz, D., Grunberg, N. and Baum, A. (1985), 'Health psychology', *Annual Review of Psychology*, **36**: 349–83.

Krause, N., Dasinger, L., Deegan, L., Rudolph, L. and Brand, R. (2001), 'Psychosocial job factors and return-to-work after compensated low back injury: a disability phase-specific analysis', *American Journal of Industrial Medicine*, **40**: 374–92.

Krause, N., Dasinger, L.K. and Neuhauser, F. (1998), 'Modified work and return to work: a review of the literature', *Journal of Occupational Rehabilitation*, **8**(2): 113–39.

Krause, N. and Lund, T. (2004), 'Returning to work after occupational injury', in Barling, J. and Frone, M. (eds) *The Psychology of Workplace Safety*, American Psychological Association, Washington: 249–64.

Krause, N., Ragland, D., Greiner, B., Fisher, J., Holman, B. and Selvin, S. (1997a), 'Physical workload and ergonomic factors associated with prevalence of back and neck pain in urban transit operators', *Spine*, **22**(18): 2117–27.

Krause, N., Ragland, D., Greiner, B., Syme, L. and Fisher, J. (1997b), 'Psychosocial job factors associated with back and neck pain in public transit operators', *Scandinavian Journal of Work Environment and Health*, **23**(3): 179–86.

Krause, T.R. (2001), 'Moving to the 2nd generation in behavior-based safety', *Professional Safety*, **46**(5): 27–32.

Krausz, M., Sagie, A. and Biderman, Y. (2000), 'Actual and preferred work schedules and scheduling control as determinants of job-related attitudes', *Journal of Vocational Behavior*, **56**: 1–11.

Krieger, N. (2008), 'Ladders, pyramids and champagne: the iconography of health inequities', *Journal of Epidemiology and Community Health*, **62**: 1098–104.

Krieger, N., Waterman, P.D., Hartman, C., Bates, L.M., Stoddard, A.M., Quinn, M.M., Sorensen, G. and Barbeau, E.M. (2006), 'Social hazards on the job: workplace abuse, sexual harassment, and racial discrimination—a study of Black, Latino and White low-income women and men workers in the United States', *International Journal of Health Services*, **36**(1): 51–85.

Kristensen, T. (2008), 'Psychosocial intervention studies', keynote address to 3rd ICOH WOPS conference, Quebec City, 2 September.

Kristovskis, A. (1995), *Occupational Health and Safety in the Diving Industry: A Small Industry with Secular Communication*, unpublished case study, School of Industrial Relations and Organisational Behaviour, University of New South Wales.

Kroemer, K. and Grandjean, E. (1997), *Fitting the Task to the Human: A Textbook of Occupational Ergonomics*, 5th edition, Taylor & Francis, London.

Kruger, J., Yore, M., Bauer, D. and Kohl, H. (2007), 'Selected barriers and incentives to worksite health promotion services', *American Journal of Health Promotion*, **21**(5): 439–47.

Kumar, S. (2001), 'Theories of musculoskeletal injury causation', *Ergonomics*, **44**(1): 17–47.

Kundi, M., Koller, M., Cervinka, R. and Haider, M. (1979), 'Consequences of shift work as a function of age and years on shift', *Chronobiologica*, **6**: 123.

Kuoppala, J. and Lamminpaa, A. (2008), 'Rehabilitation and work ability: a systematic literature review', *Journal of Rehabilitation Medicine*, **40**: 796–804.

Kuoppala, J., Lamminpaa, A. and Husman, P. (2008), 'Work health promotion, job well-being and sickness absences—a systematic review and meta-analysis', *Journal of Occupational and Environmental Medicine*, **50**(11): 1216–27.

Kuorinka, I. and Patry, L. (1995), 'Participation as a means of promoting occupational health', *International Journal of Industrial Ergonomics*, **15**(5): 365–70.

Kurtz, J., Robins, T. and Schork, M. (1997), 'An evaluation of peer and professional trainers in a union-based occupational health and safety training program', *Journal of Occupational and Environmental Medicine*, **39**(7): 661–71.

Kusnetz, H. (1986), 'Occupational nursing: a mainstay in industry', *American Journal of Public Health*, **76**(4): 465.

Labbe, E., Moulin, J., Sass, C., Chatain, C. and Gerbaud, L. (2007), 'Relations entre formes particulieres d'emploi, vulnerabilite sociale et sante', *Archives des Maladies Professionnelles et de l'Environnement*, **68**(4): 365–75.

Labonte, R. and Schrecker, T. (2007), 'Globalisation and social determinants of health: the role of the global marketplace', *Globalization and Health*, **3**: 6.

Labor Council of NSW (1995), *Drug and Alcohol Policy*, Sydney.

Lacey, R., Lewis, M. and Sim, J. (2007), 'Piecework, musculoskeletal pain and the impact of workplace psychosocial factors', *Occupational Medicine*, **57**: 430–7.

LaDou, J. (1997), *Occupational and Environmental Medicine*, 2nd edition, Appleton & Lange, Stamford, Connecticut.

LaDou, J. (1998), 'ICOH caught in the act', *Archives of Environmental Health*, **53**(4): 247–8.

LaDou, J. (2002), 'The rise and fall of occupational medicine in the United States', *American Journal of Preventative Medicine*, **22**(4): 285–95.

LaDou, J. (2006), 'Occupational and environmental medicine in the United States: a proposal to abolish workers' compensation and re-establish the public health model', *International Journal of Occupational and Environmental Health*, **12**(2): 154–68.

Lahiri, S., Gold, J. and Levenstein, C. (2005), 'Net-cost model for workplace interventions', *Journal of Safety Research*, **36**: 241–55.

Laing, R. (2002), *Review of the Occupational Safety and Health Act: Final Report*, Western Australia, November.

Lamm, F. (1992), 'Persuasion or coercion—enforcement strategies in occupational safety and health', in Deeks, J. and Perry, N. (eds) *Controlling Interests: Business, the State and Society in New Zealand*, Auckland University Press, Auckland.

Lamm, F. (1997), 'Small business and OHS Advisors', *Safety Science*, **25**(1–3): 153–61.

Lamm, F. (2000), *Occupational Health & Safety in Queensland and New Zealand Small Businesses*, PhD Thesis, University of New South Wales.

Lamm, F. (2002), 'OHS in small businesses', in Lloyd, M. (ed.) *Occupational Health and Safety in New Zealand: Contemporary Social Research*, Dunmore Press, Wellington: 93–118.

Lamm, F. (2008), 'Occupational safety and health', in Rasmussen, E. (ed.) *Employment Relations in New Zealand*, 2nd edition, Prentice Hall, Auckland.

Lamm, F., Massey, C. and Perry, M. (2007) 'Is there a link between workplace health and safety and firm performance and productivity?', *New Zealand Journal of Employment Relations*, **32**(1): 72–86.

Lamm, F. and Pio, E. (2008), *Cultural Diversity, Communication & Workplace Health & Safety*, prepared for the Workplace Group of the Department of Labour, Work & Labour Market Institute, AUT University School of Business, Auckland.

Lamm, F. and Walters, D. (2004), 'OHS in small organisations: some challenges and ways forward', in Buff, L., Gunningham, N. and Johnston, R. (eds) *OHS Regulations for the 21st Century*, Federation Press, Sydney.

LaMontagne, A.D., Barbeau, E., Youngstrom, R.A., Lewiton, M., Stoddard, A.M., McLellan, D., Wallace, L.M. and Sorensen, G. (2004), 'Assessing and intervening on OSH programmes: effectiveness evaluation of the Wellworks-2 intervention in 15 manufacturing worksites', *Occupational and Environmental Medicine*, **61**(8): 651–60.

LaMontagne, A., Keegel, T., Louie, A., Ostry, A. and Landsbergis, P. (2007), 'A systematic review of the job-stress intervention evaluation literature, 1990–2005', *International Journal of Occupational and Environmental Health*, **13**(3): 268–80.

LaMontagne, A., Keegel, T., Vallance, D., Ostry, A. and Wolfe, R. (2008), 'Job strain—attributable depression in a sample of working Australians: assessing the contribution to health inequalities', *BMC Public Health*, **8**: 181–90.

LaMontagne, A., Shaw, A., Ostry, A., Louie, A. and Keegel, T. (2006), *Workplace Stress in Victoria: Developing a Systems Approach*, Victorian Health Promotion Foundation, Melbourne, <www.vichealth.vic.gov.au/workplacestress>

LaMontagne, A., Smith, P., Louie, A., Quinlan, M., Shoveller, J. and Ostry, A. (2009), 'Unwanted sexual advances at work: variations by employment arrangement in a sample of working Australians', *Australian and New Zealand Journal of Public Health*, **33**(2): 173–9.

LaMontagne, A., Stoddard, A., Youngstrom, R., Lewiton, M. and Sorenson, G. (2005), 'Improving the prevention and control of hazardous substance exposures: a randomized controlled trial in manufacturing worksites', *American Journal of Industrial Medicine*, **48**: 282–92.

Landau, K., Meschke, H., Brauchler, R., Kiesel, J. and Knoerzer, J. (2007), 'Ergonomics diagnosis components in rehabilitation: statistical evaluation of an assessment instrument', *Ergonomics*, **50**(11): 1871–96.

Landeweer, J.A., Urling, J.M., de Jong, A.H.J. and Bouter, L.M. (1990), 'Risk-taking tendency among construction workers', *Journal of Occupational Accidents*, **11**: 183–96.

Landsbergis, P.A. (2003), 'The changing organization of work and the safety and health of working people: a commentary', *Journal of Occupational and Environmental Medicine*, **45**: 61–72.

Landsbergis, P. and Cahill, J. (1994), 'Labor union programs to reduce or prevent occupational stress in the United States', *International Journal of Health Services*, **24**(1): 105–29.

Landsbergis, P., Cahill, J. and Schnall, P. (1999), 'The impact of lean production and related new systems of work organisation on health', *Journal of Occupational Health Psychology*, **4**(2): 108–30.

Landstad, B., Wendleborg, C. and Hedlund, M. (2009), 'Factors explaining return to work for long-term sick workers in Norway', *Disability and Rehabilitation*, **31**(15): 1215–26.

Lanfranchi, J.B. and Duveau, A. (2008), 'Explicative models of musculoskeletal disorders (MSD): from biomechanical and psychosocial factors to clinical analysis of ergonomics', *Revue Européenne de Psychologie Appliquée*, **58**: 201–13.

Lanoie, P. and Trottier, L. (1998), 'Costs and benefits of preventing workplace accidents: going from a mechanical to a manual handling system', *Journal of Safety Research*, **29**(2): 65–75.

Lanyon, R.I. and Goodstein, L.D. (2004), 'Validity and reliability of a pre-employment screening test: the Counterproductive Behavior Index (CBI)', *Journal of Business and Psychology*, **18**(4): 533–53.

Larsen, A.I., Johnsen, C.R., Frickmann, J. and Mikkelsen, S. (2007), 'Incidence of respiratory sensitisation and allergy to enzymes among employees in an enzyme producing plant and the relation to exposure and host factors', *Occupational and Environmental Medicine* **64**(11): 763–8.

Larsson, T. and Clayton, A. (eds) (1994), *Insurance and Prevention: Some Thoughts on Social Engineering in Relation to Externally Caused Injury and Disease*, Institute for Human Safety and Accident Research (IPSO), Stockholm.

Latack, J.C. and Havlovic, S.J. (2006), 'Coping with job stress: a conceptual evaluation framework for coping measures', *Journal of Organizational Behavior*, **13**(5): 479–508.

Laurence, D. (2005), 'Safety rules and regulations on mine sites—the problem and a solution', *Journal of Safety Research*, **36**: 39–50.

Lawton, R. and Parker, D. (1998), 'Individual differences in accident liability: a review and integrative approach', *Human Factors*, **40**(4): 655–71.

Lay, B., Nordt, C. and Rössler, W. (2007), 'Mental hospital admission rates of immigrants in Switzerland', *Social Psychiatry and Psychiatric Epidemiology*, **42**(3): 229–36.

Lebailly, P., Bouchart, V., Baldi, I., Lecluse, Y., Heutte, N., Gislard, A. and Malas, J. (2009), 'Exposure to pesticides in open-field farming in France', *Annals of Occupational Hygiene*, **55**(1): 69–81.

Le Blanc, P., Hox, J., Schaufeli, W., Taris, T. and Peeters, M. (2007), 'Take care! The evaluation of a team-based burnout intervention program for oncology care providers', *Journal of Applied Psychology*, **92**(1): 213–27.

Leclercq, S., Thouy, S. and Rossignol, E. (2007), 'Progress in understanding processes underlying occupational accidents on the level based on case studies', *Ergonomics*, **50**(1): 59–79.

Le Coze, J. (2005), 'Are organisations too complex to be integrated in technical risk assessment and current safety auditing?', *Safety Science*, **43**: 613–38.

Le Coze, J. (2008), 'Disasters and organisations: from lessons learnt to theorising', *Safety Science*, **46**: 132–49.

Lee, G. and Wrench, J. (1980), 'Accident prone immigrants: an assumption challenged', *Sociology*, **14**(4): 551–6.

Lee, M. and Quinlan, M. (1994), 'Federal co-ordination of OHS laws in Australia', *Australian Journal of Labour Law*, **7**(1): 33–68.

Lee, P. and Krause, N. (2002), 'The impact of a worker health study on working conditions', *Journal of Public Health Policy*, **23**(2): 268–85.

Legg, S., Harris, L.A., Laird, I., Lamm, F. and Massey, C. (2008), *Technical Report on OHS in Small Businesses*, NOHSAC Technical Report, Wellington.

Leggat, P. (1998), 'Reporting of industrial accident statistics for back injury in Queensland', *Journal of Occupational Health and Safety—Australia and New Zealand*, **14**(3): 267–74.

Leggat, P. and Smith, D. (2006), 'Dermatitis and aircrew', *Contact Dermatitis*, **54**: 1–4.

Legislative Council Standing Committee on Law and Justice, (1998), *Final Report of the Inquiry into Workplace Safety*, 2 vols, Parliament of New South Wales, Sydney.

Leigh, J.P. (1991), 'No evidence of compensating wages for occupational fatalities', *Industrial Relations*, **30**(3): 382–95.

Leigh, J. (1998), 'Workers' compensation and common law: how the civil legal system discourages occupational injury prevention', in Feyer, A. and Williamson, A. (eds) *Occupational Injury: Risk, Prevention and Intervention*, Taylor and Francis, London.

Leigh, J. (2005), 'Long-latency disease: the long-lasting epidemic', in Peterson, C. and Mayhew, C. (eds) *Occupational Health and Safety: International Influences and the 'New' Epidemics*, Baywood, New York: 75–96.

Leigh, J. (2007), 'History of occupational disease recognition and control', *Journal of Occupational Health and Safety—Australia and New Zealand*, **23**(6): 519–30.

Leigh, J., Hendrie, L. and Berry, D. (1998), *The Incidence of Mesothelioma in Australia 1993 to 1995, Australian Mesothelioma Register Report, 1998*, Epidemiology Unit, NOHSC, Sydney.

Leigh, J.P., Markowitz, S., Fahs, M., Shin, C. and Landrigan, P. (1997), 'Occupational injury and illness in the United States: estimates of costs, morbidity and mortality', *Archives of Internal Medicine*, **157**(14): 1557–68.

Leigh, J.P. and Robbins, J. (2004), 'Occupational disease and workers' compensation: coverage, costs, and consequences', *The Milbank Quarterly*, **82**(4): 689–721.

Leighton Kumagai Joint Centre and Construction, Forestry, Mining and Energy Union, AIRC, December 2005.

Le Jeune, G., Belisle, A. and Messing, K. (2008), 'The data gap in Canadian women's occupational health', *Policy and Practice in Health and Safety*, **6**(2): 51–81.

Le Nevez, C. and Strange, L. (1989), 'Delivering workplace solutions in OHS: the workers' health centre model', *Journal of Occupational Health and Safety—Australia and New Zealand*, **5**(1): 45–52.

Lentz, T., Okum, A., Schulte, P. and Stayner, L. (1999), *Identifying High-Risk Small Business Industries: The Basis for Preventing Occupational Injury, Illness, and Fatality*, National Institute for Occupational Safety and Health, US Department of Health and Human Services, Washington.

Leopold, J. and Beaumont, P. (1983), 'Health, safety and industrial relations: a United Kingdom study', *New Zealand Journal of Industrial Relations*, **8**: 135–45.

Leplat, J. (1978), 'Accident analysis and work analysis', *Journal of Occupational Accidents*, **1**: 331–40.

Lerner, M. (1982), 'Stress at the workplace', *Issues in Radical Therapy*, **10**(3): 14–16.

Levenstein, C. (2008), Editorial: 'Some notes on the politics of occupational medicine', *New Solutions*, **18**(3): 283–4.

Lever-Tracy, C. and Quinlan, M. (1988), *A Divided Working Class: Ethnic Segmentation and Industrial Conflict in Australia*, Routledge and Kegan Paul, London.

Leveson, N. (2004), 'New accident model for engineering safer systems', *Safety Science*, **42**: 237–70.

Levin, M., Froom, P., Trajber, I. and Lerman, Y. (1996), 'Health assessment in sewage workers', *Israel Journal of Occupational Health*, **2**(3): 205–10.

Levine, M. and Rennie, W. (2004), 'Pre-employment urine drug testing of hospital employees: future questions and review of current literature', *Occupational and Environmental Medicine*, **61**(4): 318–24.

Levine, S. (2006), 2006 Donald E. Cummings Memorial Award Lecture: 'Industrial hygiene: the founders, the pioneers, and the next generation', *Journal of Occupational and Environmental Hygiene*, **3**: 102–9.

Levy, B. (1984), 'The teaching of occupational health in United States medical schools: five-year follow-up of an initial survey', *American Journal of Public Health*, **75**(1): 79–80.

Levy, B. and Wegman, D. (1988), 'Occupational health in the United States: an overview', in Levy, B. and Wegman, D. (eds) *Occupational Health: Recognising and Preventing Work-Related Disease*, Little, Brown and Co., Boston.

Levy-Leboyer, C. (1988), 'Success and failure in applied psychology', *American Psychologist*, **43**(10): 779–85.

Lewchuk, W., Clarke, M. and de Wolff, A. (2008), 'Working without commitments: precarious employment and health', *Work, Employment & Society*, **22**(3): 387–406.

Lewchuk, W. and Robertson, D. (1996), 'Working conditions under lean production: a worker based benchmarking study', *Asia Pacific Business Review*, **Summer**: 60–81.

Light, D. (2001), 'Cost containment and the backdraft of competition policies', *International Journal of Health Services*, **31**(4): 681–708.

Lin, A. (2009), *Deciphering the Chemical Soup: Using Public Nuisance to Compel Chemical Testing*, School of Law, University of California, <works.bepress.com/albert_lin/3>

Lin, C., Du, C., Chan, C. and Wang, J. (2005), 'Saved by a material safety data sheet', *Occupational Medicine*, **55**: 635–7.

Linacre, S. (2007), *Work-Related Injuries*, Australian Social Trends 2007, Australian Bureau of Statistics, Canberra.

Lingard, H. (2002) 'The effect of first aid training on Australian construction workers' occupational health and safety motivation and risk control behavior', *Journal of Safety Research*, **33**: 209–30.

Lippel, K. (1989), 'Workers' compensation and psychological stress claims in North American law: A microcosmic model of systematic discrimination', *International Journal of Law and Psychiatry*, **12**: 41–70.

Lippel, K. (1999a), 'Workers' compensation and stress: gender and access to compensation', *International Journal of Law and Psychiatry*, **22**(1): 79–89.

Lippel, K. (1999b), 'Therapeutic and anti-therapeutic consequences of workers' compensation', *International Journal of Law and Psychiatry*, **22**(5 & 6): 521–46.

Lippel, K. (2003), 'Compensation for musculoskeletal disorders in Quebec: systematic discrimination against women workers?', *International Journal of Health Services*, **33**(2): 253–81.

Lippel, K. (2005), 'Les enjeux juridiques et sociaux di recours aux enqueteurs prives pour surveiller les victims de lesions professionelles', *Canadian Journal of Criminology and Criminal Justice*, 127–73.

Lippel, K. (2006), 'Precarious employment and occupational health and safety regulation in Quebec', in Vosko, L.F. (ed.) *Precarious Employment*, McGill-Queen's University of Press, Montreal.

Lippel, K. (2007a), 'Research, policy and practice in work and mental health: a multidisciplinary discussion', *International Journal of Law and Psychiatry*, **30**: 269–71.

Lippel, K. (2007b), 'Workers describe the effect of the workers' compensation process on their health: a Quebec study', *International Journal of Law and Psychiatry*, **30**: 427–43.

Lipscomb, H., Dale, A., Kaskutas, V., Sherman-Voellinger, R. and Evanoff, B. (2007), 'Challenges in residential prevention: insight from apprentice carpenters', *American Journal of Industrial Medicine*, DOI 10.1002/ajim.20544.

Lipscomb, H., Kucera, K., Epling, C. and Dement, J. (2008), 'Upper extremity musculoskeletal symptoms and disorders among a cohort of women employed in poultry processing', *American Journal of Industrial Medicine*, **51**: 21–36.

Lipsett, M. and Campleman, S. (1999), 'Occupational exposure to diesel exhaust and lung cancer: a meta-analysis', *American Journal of Public Health*, **89**(7): 1009–17.

Li-Tsang, C.W.P., Li, E.J.Q., Lam, C.S., Hui, K.Y.L. and Chan, C.C.H. (2008), 'The effect of a job placement and support program for workers with musculoskeletal injuries: a randomized control trial (RCT) study', *Journal of Occupational Rehabilitation*, **18**: 299–306.

Liu, Y. and Tanaka, H. (2002), 'Overtime work, insufficient sleep, and risk of non-fatal myocardial infarction in Japanese men', *Occupational & Environmental Medicine*, **59**: 447–51.

Lloyd, C. and James, S. (2008), 'Too much pressure? Retailer power and occupational health and safety in the food processing industry', *Work, Employment & Society*, **22**(4): 713–30.

Lloyd, M. (ed.) (2002), *Occupational Health and Safety in New Zealand: Contemporary Social Research*, Dunmore Press, Wellington.

Lo, K. and Lamm, F. (2005), 'Occupational stress in the hospitality industry: an employment relations perspective', *New Zealand Journal of Employment Relations*, **30**(1): 23–48.

Lofland, J.H., Pizzi, L. and Frick, K.D. (2004), 'A review of health-related workplace productivity loss instruments', *Pharmacoeconomics*, **22**(3): 165–84.

Löfstedt, R.E. (2004), 'The swing of the regulatory pendulum in Europe: from precautionary principle to (regulatory) impact analysis', *The Journal of Risk and Uncertainty*, **28**(3): 237–60.

Loh, K. and Richardson, S. (2004), 'Foreign-born workers: trends in fatal occupational injuries, 1996–2001', *Monthly Labor Review*, **12**(6).

London, L. (2005), 'Dual loyalties and the ethical and human rights obligations of occupational health professionals', *American Journal of Industrial Medicine*, **47**: 322–32.

Lötters, F. and Burdorf, A. (2006), 'Prognostic factors for duration of sickness absence due to musculoskeletal disorders', *Clinical Journal of Pain*, **22**(2): 212–21.

Loudoun, R. and Bohle, P. (1997), 'Work/non-work conflict and health amongst shiftworkers: relationships with family status and social support', *International Journal of Occupational and Environmental Health*, **3**(2) (Supp.): S71–S77.

Louie, A., Ostry, A., Quinlan, M., Keegel, T., Shoveller, J. and LaMontagne, A. (2006), 'Empirical study of employment arrangements and precariousness in Australia', *Relations Industrielles*, **61**(3): 465–86.

Low, I. and Holz, A. (1987), 'Health assessments before job placement', *Journal of Industrial Relations*, **29**(3): 273–80.

Lowe, G., Schellenberg, G. and Shannon, H. (2003), 'Correlates of employees' perceptions of a healthy work environment', *American Journal of Health Promotion*, **17**(6): 390–9.

Lowenson, R. (1991), 'Occupational hazards in the informal sector—a global perspective', paper presented to conference entitled Health Hazards and Challenges in the New Working Life, Stockholm, 11–13 January.

Lucas, J. (1991), 'Sexual harassment, current models of occupational health and safety and women', *Australian Feminist Studies*, **13**: 59–70.

Lucire, Y. (1988a), 'Social iatrogenesis of the Australian disease "RSI"', *Community Health Studies*, **12**(2): 146–50.

Lucire, Y. (1988b), 'A reply to Dr Russell', *Community Health Studies*, **12**(2): 140–3.

Luntz, H. (2004), *The Australian Picture*, The University of Melbourne Faculty of Law, Legal Studies Research Paper No. 78, Melbourne.

Luntz, H. (2008), *A View from Abroad*, University of Melbourne Faculty of Law, Legal Studies Research Paper No. 305, Melbourne.

Luria, G., Zohar, D. and Erev, I. (2008), 'The effect of workers' visibility on effectiveness of intervention programs: supervisory-based safety interventions', *Journal of Safety Research*, **39**(3): 273–80.

Luttmann, A., Jäger, M. and Griefahn, B. (2003), *Preventing Musculoskeletal Disorders in the Workplace*, Protecting Workers' Health Series No. 5, World Health Organization.

Lynch, T. (2009), 'Ageing America: the iceberg dead ahead', *AIIABC Journal*, **45**(1): 37–51.

MacDonald, L., Cohen, A., Baron, S. and Burchfiel, C. (2009), 'Occupation as socioeconomic status or environmental exposure? A survey of practice amongst population-based cardiovascular studies in the United States', *American Journal of Epidemiology*, **169**(12): 1411–21.

Mace, C. (1954), Editorial Introduction, in Brown, J. *The Social Psychology of Industry*, Penguin, Melbourne.

MacEachen, E. (2000), 'The mundane administration of worker bodies: from welfarism to neo-liberalism', *Health, Risk & Society*, **2**(3): 315–27.

MacEachen, E. (2005), 'The demise of repetitive strain injury in skeptical governing rationalities of workplace managers', *Sociology of Health & Illness*, **27**(4): 490–514.

MacEachen, E., Clarke, J., Franche, R. and Irvin, E. (2006), 'Systematic review of the qualitative literature on return to work after injury', *Scandinavian Journal of Work Environment and Health*, **32**(4): 257–69.

Mackay, C. and Cooper, C. (1987), 'Occupational stress and health: some current issues', in Cooper, C. and Robertson, I. (eds) *International Review of Industrial and Organisational Psychology 1987*, John Wiley and Sons, Chichester: 167–99.

MacKenzie, E.J., Morris, Jr, J.A., Jurkovich, G.J., Yasui, Y., Cushing, B.M., Burgess, A.R., DeLateur, B.J., McAndrew, M.P. and Swiontkowski, M.F. (1998), 'Return to work following injury: the role of economic, social, and job-related factors', *American Journal of Public Health*, **88**(11): 1630–7.

MacLeod, D. (1995), *The Ergonomics Edge: Improving Safety, Quality and Productivity*. John Wiley and Sons, New York.

Maconachie, G. (1988), 'The origins, development and effectiveness of health and safety aspects of the Queensland Factories and Shops Act, 1896–1931', unpublished B.Admin (honours) thesis, Griffith University.

Maconachie, G. (1997), 'Blood on the rails: the Cairns–Kuranda railway construction and the Queensland Employers' Liability Act', *Labour History*, **73**: 76–92.

Magnani, C., Terracini, B., Ivaldi, C., Botta, M., Budel, P., Mancini, A. and Zanetti, R. (1993), 'A cohort study of mortality among wives of workers in the asbestos cement industry in Casale Monferrato, Italy', *British Journal of Industrial Medicine*, **50**: 779–84.

Mahdavi, A. and Unzeitig, U. (2005), 'Occupational implications of spatial, indoor-environmental, and organizational features in office spaces', *Building and Environment*, **40**: 113–23.

Maitra, S. and Siddiqui, K. (1999), *Learning Strategies of Resistance: Immigrant Women in Contingent Work in Toronto*, OISE/University of Toronto, Toronto.

Makin, A. and Winder, C. (2008), 'A new conceptual framework to improve the application of occupational health and safety management systems', *Safety Science*, **46**: 935–48.

Malchaire, J., Glass, N. and Vergracht, S. (2001), 'Review of the factors associated with musculoskeletal problems in epidemiological studies', *International Archives of Occupational and Environmental Health*, **74**: 79–90.

Malenfant, R., LaRue, A. and Vezina, M. (2007), 'Intermittent work and well-being: one foot in the door, one foot out', *Current Sociology*, **55**(6): 814–35.

Marchand, A. (2008), 'Alcohol use and misuse: what are the contributions of occupation and work organisation conditions?' *BMC Public Health*, **8**: 333.

Marfleet v Kaptive Pty Ltd [2008], QIC, 6 October 2008.

Marin, A., Grzywacz, J., Arcury, T., Carrillo, L., Coates, M. and Quandt, S. (2008), 'Evidence of organizational injustice in poultry processing plants: possible effects on occupational health and safety among Latino workers in North Carolina', *American Journal of Industrial Medicine*, **52**: 37–48.

Marmot, M. (1998), 'Contribution of psychosocial factors to socioeconomic differences in health', *The Millbank Quarterly*, **76**(3): 403–48.

Marmot, M., Bosma, H., Hemingway, H., Brunner, E. and Stansfeld, S. (1997), 'Contribution of job control and other risk factors to social variations in coronary heart disease', *The Lancet*, **350**: 235–9.

Marr, S. (1991), 'Problems associated with the wearing of safety footwear', *Journal of Occupational Health and Safety—Australia and New Zealand*, **7**(5): 437–9.

Marshall, L., Weir, E., Abelsohn, A. and Sanborn, M. (2002), 'Identifying and managing adverse environmental health impacts: 1. taking an exposure history', *Canadian Medical Association Journal*, **166**(8): 1049–55.

Martin, C. (2008), 'Contribution à la définition d'actions pour la pérennisation de la prevention des risques professionnels dans les PME-PMI', Doctoral Thèses, Docteur de l'Ecole des Mines de Paris, Paris.

Martin, E., Baggaley, K., Buchbinder, R., Johnston, R., Tugwell, P., Maxwell, L. and Santesso, N. (2008), 'Occupational therapists should be more involved in the Cochrane Collaboration: the example of the Australian Cochrane Musculoskeletal Review Group', *Australian Occupational Therapy Journal*, **55**: 207–11.

Marx, D.A. and Slonim, A.D. (2003), 'Assessing patient safety risk before the injury occurs: an introduction to sociotechnical probabilistic risk modelling in health care', *Qual Saf Health Care* **12**(Supp. 1): ii33–ii38.

Massey, C., Lamm, F., and Perry, M. (2006), *Understanding the Link between Workplace Health & Safety and Firm Performance and Productivity: Report for the Department of Labour*, Department of Labour, Wellington.

Mastekaasa, A. (2005), 'Sickness absence in female- and male-dominated occupations and workplaces', *Social Science & Medicine*, **60**(10): 2261–72.

Mastrangelo, G., Ballarin, M., Bellini, E., Bizzotto, R. and Zannol, F. (2008), 'Feasibility of a screening programme for lung cancer in former asbestos workers', *Occupational Medicine* (London), **58**(3): 175–80.

Mathews, J. (1985), *Health and Safety at Work: A Trade Union Safety Representatives Handbook*, Pluto Press, Sydney.

Mathews, J. (1993), *Health and Safety at Work: Australian Trade Union Safety Representatives Handbook*, 2nd edition, Pluto Press, Sydney.

Mathews, L. (2005), 'Work potential of road accident survivors with post-traumatic stress disorder', *Behaviour and Research Therapy*, **43**: 475–83.

Mathews, L. (2006), 'Posttrauma employability of people with symptoms of PTSD and the contribution of work environments', *International Journal of Disability Management Research*, **1**(1): 87–96.

Mathews, L. and Chinnery, D. (2005), 'Prediction of work functioning following accidental injury: the contribution of PTSD symptom severity and other established risk factors', *International Journal of Psychology*, **40**(5): 339–48.

Mathur, C. and Morehouse, W. (2002), 'Twice poisoned Bhopal: notes on the continuing aftermath of the world's worst industrial disaster', *International Labor and Working Class History*, **62**: 69–75.

Matteson, M.T. and Ivancevich, J.M. (1988), 'Health promotion at work', in Cooper, C.L. and Robertson, I.T. (eds) *International Review of Industrial and Organisational Psychology 1988*, John Wiley and Sons, Chichester: 279–306.

Maxwell, C. (2004), *Occupational Health and Safety Act Review: Discussion Paper*, Victorian State Government, Melbourne.

Mayhew, C. (1997a), 'Self-employed builders in Australia and the United Kingdom: a comparison of occupational health and safety outcomes and regulatory compliance', *Journal of Occupational Health and Safety—Australia and New Zealand*, **13**(3): 229–38.

Mayhew, C. (1997b), *Barriers to Implementation of Known Occupational Health and Safety Solutions in Small Business*, Australian Government Publishing Services, Canberra.

Mayhew, C. (1999a), 'Occupational violence: a case study of the taxi industry', in Mayhew, C. and Peterson, C. (eds) *Occupational Health and Safety in Australia*, Allen & Unwin, Sydney.

Mayhew, C. (1999b), 'Identifying patterns of injury in small business: piecing together the data jigsaw', in Mayhew, C. and Peterson, C. (eds) *Occupational Health and Safety in Australia*, Allen & Unwin, Sydney.

Mayhew, C. and Chappell, D. (2007), 'Workplace violence: an overview of patterns of risk and the emotional stress consequences on targets', *International Journal of Law and Psychiatry*, **30**: 327–39.

Mayhew, C., McCarthy, P., Chappell, D., Barker, M., Quinlan, M. and Sheehan, M. (2004), 'Measuring the extent of impact from occupational violence and bullying on traumatized workers', *Employee Responsibilities and Rights Journal*, **16**(3): 117–34.

Mayhew C. and Peterson, C. (eds) (2005), *Occupational Health and Safety: International Influences and the New Epidemics*, Baywood, New York.

Mayhew, C. and Quinlan, M. (1997), 'Subcontracting and OHS in the residential building sector', *Industrial Relations Journal*, **28**(3): 192–205.

Mayhew, C. and Quinlan, M. (1998), *Outsourcing and Occupational Health and Safety: A Comparative Study of Factory-Based and Outworkers in the Australian TCF Industry*, Industrial Relations Research Centre, University of New South Wales, Sydney.

Mayhew, C. and Quinlan, M. (1999), 'The effects of outsourcing on occupational health and safety: a comparative study of factory-based and outworkers in the Australian clothing industry', *International Journal of Health Services*, **29**(1): 83–107.

Mayhew, C. and Quinlan, M. (2000), 'The relationship between precarious employment and patterns of occupational violence: survey evidence from seven occupations', in Isaksson, K., Hogstedt, C., Eriksson, C. and Theorell, T. (eds) *Health Effects of the New Labour Market*, Kluwer/Plenum Publishers, New York: 183–205.

Mayhew, C. and Quinlan, M. (2001), 'Occupational violence in the long distance transport industry: a case study of 300 truck drivers', *Current Issues in Criminal Justice*, **13**(1): 36–46.

Mayhew, C. and Quinlan, M. (2002), 'Fordism in the fast food industry: pervasive management control and occupational health and safety risks for young temporary workers', *Sociology of Health and Illness*, **24**(3): 261–84.

Mayhew, C. and Quinlan, M. (2006), 'Economic pressure, multi-tiered subcontracting and occupational health and safety in the Australian long haul trucking industry', *Employee Relations*, **28**(3): 212–29.

Mayhew, C. and Wyatt, T. (1995), 'Serious occupational injuries: an evaluation of the Queensland legal requirement to report', *Journal of Occupational Health and Safety—Australia and New Zealand*, **11**(1): 59–66.

Mayhew, C., Young, C., Ferris, R. and Hartnett, C. (1997), *An Evaluation of the Impact of Targeted Interventions on the OHS Behaviours of Small Business Building Industry Owners/Managers/Contractors*, Workplace Health & Safety Program (DTIR) and National Occupational Health and Safety Commission, AGPS, Canberra.

Maynard, A. (2006), 'Nanotechnology: the next big thing or much ado about nothing?', *Annals of Occupational Hygiene*, 1–12, doi:10.1093/annhyg/mel071.

Mayo, E. (1933), *The Human Problems of Industrial Civilisation*, Macmillan, New York.

McAteer, D. (2001), *Report to Governor Bob Wise on Mine Safety and Health in West Virginia and Recommendations to Make West Virginia Mines the Safest and Healthiest in the Nation*, State of West Virginia, Charleston.

McBride, D.I., Burns, C., Herbison, P., Humphry, N., Bodner, K. and Collins, J. (2009), 'Mortality in employees at a New Zealand agrochemical manufacturing site', *Occupational Medicine*, forthcoming, doi:10.1093/occmed/kqp030.

McBride, D., Herbison, P., Collins, J., Burns, C. and Humphry, N. (2008) 'New health study eases dioxin concerns', <http://homepage.mac.com/j.monro/090227TheMyth/HealthConcerns EasedDowNPlymouth.html>

McCall, B. and Horwitz, I. (2004), 'Workplace violence in Oregon: an analysis using workers' compensation claims from 1990–1997', *Journal of Occupational and Environmental Medicine*, **46**(4): 357–65.

McCauley, M. and Mirin, E. (1990), 'Employer-sponsored health promotion: why and how to make it a family affair', *Occupational Medicine: State of the Art Reviews*, **5**(4): 771–87.

McCloskey, E. (2008), 'The health and safety at work of young people: a Canadian perspective', *International Journal of Workplace Health Management*, **1**(1): 41–9.

McCulloch, J. (1986), *Asbestos: Its Human Cost*, University of Queensland Press, St Lucia.

McCulloch, J. and Tweedale, G. (2008), *Defending the Indefensible: The Global Asbestos Industry and its Fight for Survival*, Oxford University Press, Oxford.

McCunney, R. (1986), 'Health effects of work at waste water treatment plants: a review of the literature with guidance for medical surveillance', *American Journal of Industrial Medicine*, **9**(3): 271–9.

McCunney, R. (2001), 'Health and productivity: a role for occupational health professionals', *Journal of Occupational & Environmental Medicine*, **43**(1): 30–5.

McCunney, R.J. and Barbanel, C. (1993), 'Auditing workers' compensation claims targets expensive injuries, job tasks', *Occupational Health & Safety*, **62**(10): 75–8.

McDade, J., Brenner, D. and Bozeman, F. (1979), 'Legionnaires' disease bacterium isolated in 1947', *Annals of Internal Medicine*, **90**: 659–61.

McDermott, F. (1986), 'Repetition strain injury: a review of current understanding', *Medical Journal of Australia*, **144**: 196–200.

McDiarmid, M., Marc, O., Ruser, J. and Gucer, P. (2000) 'Male and female rate differences in carpal tunnel syndrome injuries: personal attributes or job tasks?', *Environmental Research*, **83**(1): 23–32.

McDowell, L., Batnitzky, A. and Dyer, S. (2008), 'Internationalization and the spaces of temporary labour: the global assembly of a local workforce', *British Journal of Industrial Relations*, **46**(4): 750–70.

McGrath, J., Kelly, J. and Machatka, D. (1984), 'The social psychology of time: entrainment of behaviour in social and organizational settings', *Applied Social Psychology Annual*, **5**: 21–44.

McGrath, S. and DeFilippis, J. (2009), 'Social reproduction as unregulated work', *Work, Employment and Society*, **23**(1): 66–83.

McIntyre, D. (2005), 'My way or the highway: managerial prerogative, the labour process and workplace health', *Health Sociology Review*, **14**(1): 58–68.

McKay, S., Craw, M. and Chopra, D. (2006), *Migrant Workers in England and Wales: An Assessment of Migrant Worker Health and Safety Risks*, HSE Books, London.

McKenna, F.P. (1983) 'Accident proneness: a conceptual analysis', *Accident Analysis and Prevention*, **15**: 65–71.

McKenzie, L. and Shaw, S. (1979) 'Occupational health and women', *New Doctor*, **13**: 38–43.

McLaren, E., Firkin, P., Spoonley, P., Dupuis, A., de Bruin, A. and Inkson, K. (2004), 'At the margins: contingency, precariousness and non-standard work', *Research Report Series 2004/1*, Massey University, Auckland.

McLaughlin, M.C. (2000), 'Mutually beneficial agreements in the retail sector?', *New Zealand Journal of Industrial Relations*, **25**(1): 1–17.

McLean, D. (2002), 'Mortality and cancer incidence in New Zealand pulp and paper mill workers', *New Zealand Medical Journal*, **26**: 186–90.

McLean, D. (2005), 'Mortality and morbidity studies of former timber treatment workers', in Purnell, H., Slater, T., Eng, A. and Pearce, N. *Dioxin: Exposures, Health Effects and Public Health Policy Proceedings of the Fifth Annual CPHR Symposium in Health Research and Policy*, Wellington.

McLean, D., Boffeta, P., Berry, R. and Pearce, N. (2002), 'Occupational cancer', in Pearce, N., McLean, N. and Berry, R. *Priorities in Occupational Health and Safety Proceedings of the Second Annual CPHR, Symposium in Health Research and Policy*, Wellington.

McLean, D., Eng, A., 't Mannetje, A., Walls, C., Dryson, E., Cheng, S., Wong, K. and Pearce, N. (2008), *Health Outcomes in Former New Zealand Timber Workers Exposed to Pentachlorophenol (PCP)*, Centre for Public Health Research, Massey University, Wellington, <www.dol.govt.nz/PDFs/Final_PCP_Report_Jan_2008.pdf>

McMichael, A. (1989), 'Coronary heart disease: interplay between changing concepts of aetiology, risk distribution and strategies for prevention', *Community Health Studies*, **1**: 5–13.

McQuiston, T. (2000), 'Empowerment evaluation of worker safety and health education programs', *American Journal of Industrial Medicine*, **38**: 584–97.

Mearns, K.J. and Flin, R. (1999), 'Assessing the state of organizational safety—culture or climate?', *Current Psychology*, **18**(1): 5–18.

Mearns, K., Whitaker, S., Flin, R., Gordon, R. and O'Connor, P. (2000), *Benchmarking Human and Organisational Factors in Offshore Safety*, Report No. 2000 036, HSE OTO, London.

Mearns, K., Rundmo, T., Gordon, R. and Fleming, M. (2004), 'Evaluation of psychosocial and organizational factors in offshore safety: a comparative study', *Journal of Risk Research* **7**(5): 545–61.

Mearns, K., Whitaker, S.M. and Flin, R. (2003), 'Safety climate, safety management practice and safety performance in offshore environments', *Safety Science*, **41**(8): 641–80.

Mearns, K.J. and Yule, S. (2009), 'The role of national culture in determining safety performance: challenges for the global oil and gas industry', *Safety Science*, **47**: 777–85.

Meers, A., Maasen, A. and Verhaegen, P. (1978), 'Subjective health after six months and after four years of shift work', *Ergonomics*, **21**: 857–85.

Melamed, S., Luz, J., Najenson, T., Jucha, E. and Green, M. (1989), 'Ergonomic stress levels, personal characteristics, accident occurrence and sickness absence among factory workers', *Ergonomics*, **32**(9): 1101–10.

Mellor, G. and St John, W. (2007) 'Occupational health nurses' perceptions of their current and future roles', *Journal of Advanced Nursing*, **58**(6), 585–93.

Mellor, G. and St John, W. (2009), 'Managers' perceptions of the current and future role of occupational health nurses in Australia', *American Association of Occupational Health Nurses Journal* (AAOHN J), **57**(2): 79–87.

Mellor, G., St John, W. and McVeigh, C. (2006), 'Occupational health nursing practice in Australia: what occupational health nurses say they do and what they actually do', *Collegian*, **13**(3): 18–24.

Menendez, M., Benach, J., Muntaner, C., Amable, M. and O'Campo, P. (2007), 'Is precarious employment more damaging to women's health than men's?', *Social Science & Medicine* **64**: 776–81.

Menendez, M., Benach, J. and Vogel, L. (2007), *The Effectiveness of Safety Representatives in Occupational Health: A European Perspective*, Draft, European Trade Union Technical Bureau for Health and Safety, Brussels.

Meng, R. and Smith, D. (1993), 'Union impacts on the receipt of workers' compensation benefits', *Relations Industrielles*, **8**(3): 503–18.

Meredith, F. (2000), 'South Australian workers compensation disputes: from conciliation to adjudication and back again', *The Journal of Industrial Relations*, **Sept**: 398–416.

Meredith, S. and McDonald, J. (1994), 'Work-related respiratory disease in the United Kingdom, 1989–1992: report on the SWORD project', *Occupational Medicine*, **44**: 183–9.

Messing, K. (1992), 'Research directed to improving women's occupational health', *Women and Health*, **18**(3): 1–9.

Messing, K. (1998), *One-Eyed Science: Occupational Health and Women Workers*, Temple University Press, Philadelphia.

Messing, K. (2002), 'Women's place in workplace health research priorities in Quebec', *Relations Industrielles*, **57**(4): 660–86.

Messing, K., Neis, B. and Dumais, L. (eds) (1995), *Invisible: Issues in Women's Occupational Health*, Gynergy Books, Charlottetown.

Messing, K., Vezina, M., Major, E., Ouellet, S., Tissot, F., Couture, V. and Riel, J. (2008), 'Body maps: an indicator of physical pain for worker-orientated ergonomic interventions', *Policy and Practice in Health and Safety*, **6**(2): 31–49.

Mialon, M. (1990), 'Safety at work in French firms and the effect of the European directives of 1989', *International Journal of Comparative Labour Law and Industrial Relations*, **6**: 129–45.

Michel, E., Amar, A., Josselin, V., Caroly, S., Merceron, G. and de Gaudermaris, R. (2007), 'Evaluation of a multidisciplinary strategy for keeping workers in their jobs and enabling return to work in Grenoble hospital', *Archives des Maladies Professionnelles et de l'Environnement*, **68**(5 & 6): 474–81.

Midford, R., Marsden, A., Phillips, M. and Lake, J. (1997), 'Workforce alcohol consumption patterns at two Pilbara mining-related worksites', *Journal of Occupational Health and Safety—Australia and New Zealand*, **13**(3): 267–74.

Miettinen, O.S. (1985), *Theoretical Epidemiology: Principles of Occurrence Research in Medicine*, John Wiley, New York.

Mikatavage, M. (1992), 'Industrial hygiene and national health objectives for the year 2000', *American Industrial Hygiene Association Journal*, **53**(8): 528–30.

Milgate, N., Innes, E. and O'Loughlin, K. (2002), 'Examining the effectiveness of health and safety committees and representatives: a review', *Work*, **19**(3): 281–90.

Miller, D. and Han, W. (2008), 'Maternal nonstandard work schedules and adolescent overweight', *American Journal of Public Health*, **98**(8): 1495–502.

Miller, G. (chair) (2008), *Hidden Tragedy: Underreporting of Workplace Injuries and Illness*, Committee on Education and Labor, United States House of Representatives, Washington.

Miller, K., Reeves, S., Zwarenstein, M., Beales, J., Kenaszchuk, C. and Conn, L. (2008), 'Nursing emotion work and interprofessional collaboration in general internal medicine wards: a qualitative study', *Journal of Advanced Nursing*, **64**(4): 332–43.

Milles, D. (1985), 'From workmen's diseases to occupational diseases: the impact of experts' concepts on workers' attitudes', in Weindling, P. (ed.) *The Social History of Occupational Health*, Croom Helm, London.

Mills, P., Kessler, R., Cooper, J. and Sullivan, S. (2007), 'Impact of a health promotion program on employee health risks and work productivity', *American Journal of Health Promotion*, **22**(1): 45–53.

Mills, P. and Kwong, S. (no date), 'Cancer incidence in the United Farmworkers of America (UFW), 1987–1997', Cancer Registry of Central California, Fresno.

Ministerial Advisory Panel (2005), *Work Related Gradual Process, Disease or Infection*, report on Section 31 Injury, Prevention, Rehabilitation and Compensation Act 2001, Wellington.

Minors, D. and Waterhouse, J. (1983), 'Circadian rhythm amplitude—is it related to rhythm adjustment and/or worker motivation?', *Ergonomics*, **26**: 229–41.

Minors, D. and Waterhouse, J. (1985a), 'Introduction to Circadian Rhythms', in Folkard, S. and Monk, T. *Hours of Work: Temporal Factors in Work Scheduling*, John Wiley, Chichester, UK.

Minors, D. and Waterhouse, J. (1985b), 'Circadian rhythms in deep body temperature, urinary excretion and alertness in nurses on night work', *Ergonomics*, **28**(11): 1523–30.

Mirsky, J. (2009), 'Mental health implications of migration: a review of mental health community studies on Russian-speaking immigrants in Israel', *Social Psychiatry and Psychiatric Epidemiology*, **44**(3): 179–87.

Mitchell, R. and Mandryk, J. (1998), *The 1995 Australian Workplace Industrial Relations Survey (AWIRS 95): An OHS Perspective*, National Occupational Health and Safety Commission, Sydney.

Mitchell, R. and Williamson, A. (2008), 'Examining the burden of work-related hospitalized injuries: definitional issues', *Injury Prevention*, **14**: 101–5.

Moatt v Mid Western Health Service, (1996) NSW Chief Magistrate's Court Matter No.95/1371, Reasons for Decision, 19 December 1996.

Monk, T.H. (1986), 'Advantages and disadvantages of rapidly rotating shift schedules—a circadian viewpoint', *Human Factors*, **28**(5): 553–7.

Monk, T. (1988), 'Coping with the stress of shiftwork', *Work Stress*, **2**: 169–72.

Monk, T. and Folkard, S. (1985), 'Individual differences in shiftwork adjustment', in Folkard, S. and Monk, T. *Hours of Work: Temporal Factors in Work Scheduling*, John Wiley, Chichester, UK.

Montreuil, S. and Lippel, K. (2003), 'Telework and occupational health: a Quebec empirical study and regulatory implications', *Safety Science*, **41**(4): 339–58.

Moog, R. (1987), 'Optimization of shift work: physiological contributions', *Ergonomics*, **30**(9): 1249–59.

Moog, R. and Hildebrandt, G. (1986), 'Comparison of different causes of masking effects', in Haider, M., Koller, M. and Cervinka, R. (eds) *Night and Shift Work: Longterm Effects and their Prevention*, Verlag Peter Lang, Frankfurt Am Main.

Moore, S., Grunberg, L. and Greenberg, E. (2004), 'Repeated downsizing contact: the effects of similar and dissimilar layoff experiences on work and wellbeing outcomes', *Journal of Occupational Health Psychology*, **9**(3): 247–57.

Moore, S., Sikora, P., Grunberg, L. and Greenberg, E.S. (2007), *Expanding the Tension-Reduction Model of Work Stress and Alcohol Use: Comparison of Managerial and Non-Managerial Men and Women*, Workplace Change Project Working Paper WP-010, National Institute on Alcohol Abuse and Alcoholism (NIAAA), Bethesda.

Moore-Ede, M. and Richardson, G. (1985), 'Medical implications of shift-work', *Annual Review of Medicine*, **36**: 607–17.

Morantz, A.D. and Mas, A. (2008), 'Does post-accident drug testing reduce injuries? Evidence from a large retail chain', *American Law and Economic Review*, **10**(2): 246–302.

Morata, T., Dunn, D. and Sieber, W. (1994), 'Occupational exposure to noise and ototoxic organic solvents', *Archives of Environmental Health*, **49**(5): 359–65.

Morehead, A., Steele, M., Alexander, M., Stephen, K. and Duffin, L. (1997), *Changes at Work: The 1995 Australian Workplace Industrial Relations Survey*, Longman, Melbourne.

Morgan, H.S. (2007), 'Personality traits as risk factors for occupational injury in health care workers', Doctorial Thesis, University of Florida, Tallahassee.

Morris, J. (1998), 'In strictest confidence: the chemical industry's secrets', *Houston Chronicle*, 28 June.

Morris, J.N. (2007), 'Uses of epidemiology', *International Journal of Epidemiology*, **36**(6): 1165–172.

Morrison, D., Wood, G. and McDonald, S. (1995), 'Factors influencing model of claims settlement in workers' compensation cases', *International Journal of Rehabilitation Research*, **18**: 1–18.

Morrison, D., Wood, G., McDonald, S. and Munrowd, D. (1993), 'Duration and cost of workers' compensation claims: an empirical study', *Journal of Occupational Health and Safety—Australia and New Zealand*, **9**(2): 117–30.

Morrissey, M. and Jakubowicz, A. (1980), *Migrants and Occupational Health*, Social Welfare Research Centre, Univeristy of New South Wales, Paper 3.

Morse, T., Dillon, C., Kenta-Bibi, E., Weber, J., Diva, U., Warren, N. and Grey, M. (2005), 'Trends in work-related musculoskeletal disorder reports by year, type, and industrial sector: a capture-recapture analysis', *American Journal of Industrial Medicine*, **48**: 40–9.

Morse, T., Dillon, C., Weber, J., Warren, N., Bruneau, H. and Fu, R. (2004), 'Prevalence and reporting of occupational illness by company size: population trends and regulatory implications', *American Journal of Industrial Medicine*, **45**: 361–70.

Mortelmans, A.K., Donceel, P., Lahaye, D. and Bulterys, S. (2008), 'Work-related sickness absences and mandatory occupational health surveillance', *Occupational Medicine (London)*, **58**(7): 464–7.

Moshe, S., Shilo, M., Yagev, Y., Levy, D., Slodownik, D., Chodick, G. and Levin, M. (2008) 'Comparison of three methods of pre-employment medical evaluations', *Occupational Medicine (London)*, **58**(1): 46–51.

Mossink, J. and De Greef, M. (2002), *Inventory of Socio-Economic Costs of Work Accidents Report*, European Agency for Safety and Health at Work, Office for Official Publications of the European Communities, Luxembourg.

Motor Accidents Authority (2001), *Report of Inquiry into Safety in the Long Haul Trucking Industry*, prepared for MAA by Michael Quinlan, MAA, Sydney.

Mott, P., Mann, F., McLoughlin, Q. and Warwick, D. (1965), *Shiftwork: The Social, Psychological and Physical Consequences*, University of Michigan Press, Ann Arbor.

Mottel, W., Long, J. and Morrison, D. (1995), *Industrial Safety is Good Business: The DuPont Story*, Van Reinhold, New York.

Mourell, M. and Allan, C. (2005), 'The statutory regulation of child labour in Queensland', Published proceedings of the Conference of Association of Industrial Relations Academics of Australia and New Zealand (AIRAANZ): 395–403.

Mtika, M. (2007), 'Political economy, labour migration and the AIDS epidemic in rural Malawi', *Social Science & Medicine*, **64**: 2454–63.

Muchinsky, P.M. (1987), *Psychology Applied to Work: An Introduction to Industrial and Organisational Psychology*, The Dorsey Press, Chicago.

Mukherjee, S., Overman, L., Leviton, L. and Hilyer, B. (2000), 'Evaluation of worker safety and health training', *American Journal of Industrial Medicine*, **38**: 155–63.

Mullaly, J. and Grigg, L. (1988), 'RSI: integrating the major theories', *Australian Journal of Psychology*, **40**(1): 19–33.

Mullen, J. (2004), 'Investigating factors that influence individual safety behavior at work', *Journal of Safety Research*, **35**: 275–85.

Murphy, P., Sorock, G., Courtney, T., Webster, B. and Leamon, T. (1996), 'Injury and illness in the American workplace: a comparison of data sources', *American Journal of Industrial Medicine*, **30**(2): 130–41.

Murry, W.D., Wimbush, J.C. and Dalton, D.R. (2001), 'Genetic screening in the workplace: legislative and ethical implications', *Journal of Business Ethics*, **29**(4): 365–78.

Muscio, B. (1917), *Lectures on Industrial Psychology*, Angus and Robertson, Sydney.

Mustard, C., Cole, D., Shannon, H., Pole, J., Sullivan, T. and Allingham, R. (2003), 'Declining trends in work-related morbidity and disability: a comparison of survey estimates and compensation insurance claims', *American Journal of Public Health*, **93**(8): 1283–6.

Mustard, C. and Hertzman, C. (2001), 'Relationship between health services outcomes and social and economic outcomes in workplace injury and disease: data sources and methods', *American Journal of Industrial Medicine*, **40**: 335–43.

Myers, D., Kriebel, D., Karasek, R., Punnett, L. and Wegman, D. (2007), 'The social distribution of risk at work: acute injuries and physical assaults among healthcare workers working in a long-term care facility', *Social Science & Medicine*, **64**: 794–806.

Nachreiner, F. (1975), 'Role perceptions, job satisfaction and attitudes towards shiftwork of workers in different shift systems as related to situational and personal factors', in Colquhoun, P., Folkard, S., Knauth, P. and Rutenfranz, J. (eds) *Experimental Studies in Shiftwork*, Westdeutsher Verlag, Opladen.

Najman, J., Toloo, G. and Williams, G. (2008), 'Increasing socio-economic inequalities in drug-induced deaths in Australia: 1982–2002', *Drug and Alcohol Review*, **27**: 613–8.

National Institute of Occupational Safety and Health (1999), *Identifying High-Risk Small Business Industries: The Basis for Preventing Occupational Injury, Illness, and Fatality*, NIOSH Special Hazard Review, NIOSH, Cincinnati.

National Occupational Health and Safety Commission (2002), *Changes to Working Agreements and Underreporting of Work Related Injury and Disease in Compensation Systems—An Assessment of Data from Pertinent ABS Household-Based Surveys*, Australian Government, Canberra.

National Occupational Health and Safety Commission (2004), *The Cost of Work-Related Injury and Illness for Employers, Workers and the Community*, Australian Government, Canberra.

National Research Council and Institute of Medicine (2001), *Musculoskeletal Disorders and the Work-place: Low Back and Upper Extremities*, Panel on Musculoskeletal Disorders and the Workplace and Commission on Behavioral and Social Sciences and Education, National Academy Press, Washington, DC.

National Transport Commission (2008), *Safe Payments: Addressing the Underlying Cause of Unsafe Practices in the Road Transport Industry*, based on report prepared for the NTC by Lance Wright and Michael Quinlan, NTC, Melbourne.

Naumanen, P. (2007), 'The expertise of Finnish occupational health nurses', *Nursing and Health Services*, **9**(2): 96–102.

Neary, J. (1998), 'The impact of competitive pricing on occupational health and safety', *Journal of Occupational Health and Safety—Australia and New Zealand*, **14**(5): 511–16.

Nelson, T. (1957), *The Hungry Mile*, Waterside Workers Federation, Sydney.

Netterstrom, B. and Hansen, A. (2000), 'Outsourcing and stress: physiological effects on bus drivers', *Stress Medicine*, **16**: 149–60.

Netterstrom, B. and Laursen, P. (1981), 'Incidence and prevalence of ischaemic heart disease among urban bus drivers in Copenhagen', *Scandinavian Journal of Social Medicine*, **9**: 75–9.

Nevada Commission on Workplace Safety and Community Protection, (1998), *Report on Sierra Chemical Incident*, report to the Governor, State of Nevada, Carson City.

New South Wales Commission for Children and Young People, (2005), *Children at Work*, Government of New South Wales, Sydney.

New South Wales Department of Primary Industries (1997a), *Risk Management Handbook for the Mining Industry: How to Conduct a Risk Assessment of Mine Operations and Equipment and How to Manage Risks*, MDG 1010, Government of New South Wales, Sydney.

New South Wales Department of Primary Industries (1997b), *Guide to Reviewing a Risk Assessment of Mine Equipment and Operations*, MDG 1014, Government of New South Wales, Sydney.

New York Times, various issues.

New Zealand Amalgamated Engineering Printing and Manufacturing Union Incorporated v Air New Zealand, Judgment Number: AC 22/04 File Number: ARC 42/03, Employment Court (2004)).

New Zealand Department of Labour, (2006), *Annual Report*, Wellington.

New Zealand Department of Labour (2007), *Investigation of Causative Factors Associated with Summertime Workplace Fatalities, New Zealand Department of Labour*, <www.dol.govt.nz/PDFs/summer-fatalities-full-report.pdf>

Ng, T., Foo, S. and Yoong, T. (1992), 'Risk of spontaneous abortion in workers exposed to toluene', *British Journal of Industrial Medicine*, **49**(12): 804–8.

Nguyen, T. and Randolph, D. (2007), 'Nonspecific low back pain and return to work', *American Family Physician*, **76**(10): 1497–502.

Nichols, T. (1990), 'Industrial safety in Britain and the 1974 Health and Safety Act: the case of manufacturing', *International Journal of the Sociology of Law*, **18**: 317–42.

Nichols, T. (1997), *The Sociology of Industrial Injury*, Mansell, London.

Nichols, T., Dennis, A. and Guy, W. (1995), 'Size of employment unit and injury rates in British manufacturing: a secondary analysis of WIRS 1990 data', *Industrial Relations Journal*, **26**(1): 45–56.

Nichols, T., Walters, D. and Tasiran, A.C. (2007), 'Trade unions, institutional mediation and industrial safety: evidence from the UK', *Journal of Industrial Relations*, **49**(2): 211–225.

Nicholson, N., Soane, E., Fenton-O'Creevy, M. and Willman, P. (2005) 'Personality and domain-specific risk taking', *Journal of Risk Research*, **8**(2): 157–76.

Nicholson, V., Bunn, T. and Costich, J. (2008), 'Disparities in work-related injuries associated with workers' compensation coverage status', *American Journal of Industrial Medicine*, **51**: 393–8.

Nickless, R. (2005), 'What's to fear from right of entry by authorized union reps?', *Thompson Inside OHS*, **39**: 1–4.

Niedhammer, I., Chastang, J., David, S., Barouhiel, L. and Barrington, G. (2006), 'Job-strain and effort–reward imbalance models in a context of major organisational changes', *International Journal of Occupational and Environmental Health*, **12**(2): 111–19.

NIEHS Working Group, (1998), *Assessment of the Health Effects from Exposure to Power-Line Frequency Electric and Magnetic Fields*, National Institute of Environmental Health Sciences of the National Institutes of Health, US Department of Health and Human Services, Washington.

Nielsen, K., Randall, R. and Albertsen, K. (2008), 'Participants' appraisal of process issues and the effects of stress management interventions', *Journal of Organisational Behaviour*, **28**: 793–810.

Nielsen, M., Skogstad, A., Matthiesen, S., Glaso, L., Aasland, M., Notelaers, G. and Einaren, S. (2009), 'Prevalence of workplace bullying in Norway: comparisons across time and estimation methods', *European Journal of Work and Organizational Psychology*, **18**(1): 81–101.

Nieuwenhuijsen, K., Verbeek, J., de Boer, A., Blonk, R. and van Dijk, F. (2004), 'Supervisory behaviour as a predictor of return to work in employees absent from work due to mental health problems', *Occupational and Environmental Medicine*, **61**: 817–23.

Nile, F. (chair) (2004), *Serious Injury and Death in the Workplace*, Legislative Council General Purposes Standing Committee No.1, Parliament of New South Wales, Sydney.

NIOSH, (1996a), *Criteria for a Recommended Standard Occupational Noise Exposure—Revised Criteria 1996* (draft document), DHHS (NIOSH) Publication No.96-XXX.

NIOSH (1996b), *Report to Congress on Workers' Home Contamination Study Conducted under the Workers' Family Protection Act (29 USC 617A)*, National Institute of Occupational Safety and Health, Washington DC.

NIOSH, (1996c), *Alert: Preventing Asthma and Death from Diisocyanate Exposure*, Publication No. 96–111, Centre for Disease Control /DHHS, Washington.

NIOSH (1999), *Identifying High-Risk Small Business Industries*, US Department of Health and Human Services, Cincinnati.

NIOSH (2002), *The Changing Organization of Work and the Safety and Health of Working People: Knowledge Gaps and Research Directions*, US Department of Health and Human Services, Cincinnati.

NIOSH, (2003), *NIOSH Alert: Preventing Lung Disease in Workers who Use or Make Flavorings*, US Department of Health and Human Services, Cincinnati.

NIOSH (2004), *Worker Health Chartbook, 2004*, US Department of Health and Human Services, Cincinnati.

Noble, C. (1986), *Liberalism at Work: The Rise and Fall of OSHA*, Temple University Press, Philadelphia.

NOHSC, (1986), *Repetition Strain Injury: A Report and Model Code of Practice*, Australian Government Publishing Service, Canberra.

NOHSC, (1998), *Work-Related Traumatic Fatalities in Australia, 1989 to 1992*, Epidemiology Unit, National Occupational Health and Safety Commission, Sydney.

NOHSC (2004), *The Cost of Work-Related Injury and Illness for Australian Employers, Workers and the Community*, National Occupational Health and Safety Commission, Canberra.

NOHSC (2005), *Surveillance Alert: OHS and the Ageing Workforce*, National Occupational Health and Safety Commission, Canberra.

Nolan, M. (2005), *Revolution: The 1913 Great Strike in New Zealand*, Canterbury University Press, Christchurch.

Norman, K., Tornquist, E. and Toomingas, A. (2008), 'Working conditions in a selected sample of call centre companies in Sweden', *International Journal of Occupational Safety and Ergonomics*, **14**(2): 177–94.

Norrefalk, J., Ekholm, K., Linder, J., Borg, K. and Ekholm, J. (2008), 'Evaluation of a multiprofessional rehabilitation programme for persistent musculoskeletal-related pain: economic benefits of return to work', *Journal of Rehabilitation Medicine*, **40**(1): 15–22.

Nossar, I., Johnstone, R. and Quinlan, M. (2001), 'Regulating supply-chains to address the occupational health and safety problems associated with precarious employment: the case of home-based clothing workers in Australia', *Working Paper 21*, National Research Centre for OHS Regulation, Canberra, The Australian National University.

Nossar, I., Johnstone, R. and Quinlan, M. (2004), 'Regulating supply-chains to address the occupational health and safety problems associated with precarious employment: the case of home-based clothing workers in Australia', *Australian Journal of Labour Law*, **17**(2): 1–24.

Nugent, A. (1985), 'Organizing trade unions to combat disease: the Workers' Health Bureau, 1921–1928', *Labor History*, **26**(3): 423–46.

Nurminen, M., Corvalan, C., Leigh, J. and Baker, G. (1992), 'Prediction of silicosis and lung cancer in the Australian labour force exposed to silica', *Scandinavian Journal of Work Environment and Health*, **18**(6): 393–9.

Nyberg, A., Alfredsson, L., Theorell, T., Westerlund, H., Vahtera, J. and Kivimaki, K. (2009), 'Managerial leadership and ischaemic heart disease among employees: the Swedish WOLF study', *Occupational and Environmental Medicine*, **66**: 51–5.

Nytro, K., Saksvik, P., Mikkelsen, A., Bohle, P. and Quinlan, M. (2000), 'An appraisal of key factors in the implementation of occupational stress interventions', *Work and Stress*, **14**: 213–25.

Nytro, K., Saksvik, P. and Torvatn, H. (1998), 'Organisational prerequisites for the implementation of systematic health, environment and safety work in enterprises', *Safety Science*, **30**: 297–307.

NZ Amalgamated Engineering Printing and Manufacturing Union Incorporated v Air New Zealand, Judgment Number: AC 22/04 File Number: ARC 42/03, Employment Court (2004).

O'Brien, G. (1984), 'Group productivity', in Gruneberg, M. and Wall, T. *Social Psychology and Organizational Behaviour*, John Wiley, Chichester, UK.

O'Connor, T., Loomis, D., Runyan, C., Abboud dal Santo, J. and Schulman, M. (2005), 'Adequacy of health and safety training among young Latino construction workers', *Journal of Occupational and Environmental Medicine*, **47**: 272–7.

Office of the Inspector General—Office of Audit (2009a), *Employers with Reported Fatalities were not Always Properly Identified and Inspected under OSHA's Enhanced Enforcement Program*, Report No. 02-09-203-10-105 US Department of Labor, Washington DC.

Office of the Inspector General—Office of Audit (2009b), *Procurement Violations and Irregularities Occurred in OSHA's Oversight of the Blanket Purchase Agreement*, Report No. 03-09-002-10-001 US Department of Labor, Washington DC.

Oh, J-H. and Shin, E.H. (2007), 'Inequalities in nonfatal work injury: the significance of race, human capital, and occupations', *Social Science & Medicine*, **57**: 2173–82.

O'Hara, R. (2002), 'Scoping exercise for research into health and safety of homeworkers', Health and Safety Laboratory, HSL/2002/18, Sheffield.

OHS Alert 21 July 2008.

Oliphant, K. (2004), 'Beyond Woodhouse: devising new principles for determining ACC boundary issues', *Victoria University of Wellington Law Review*, **35**(4): 915–936.

Oliver, B. (1997), '"Lives of misery and melancholy": the rhetoric and reality of industrial reform in post-World War I Western Australia', *Labor History*, **73**: 105–22.

Olmstead, A. and Rhode, P. (2004), 'The "Tuberculosis Cattle Trust": disease contagion in an era of regulatory uncertainty', *Journal of Economic History*, **64**(4): 929–63.

O'Loughlin, K. (2005), 'From industrial citizen to therapeutic client: the 1987 workers' compensation "reforms" in NSW', *Health Sociology Review*, **14**(1): 21–32.

Olson, D., Lohman, W., Brosseau, L., Frederickson, A., McGovern, P., Gerberich, S. and Nachreiner, N. (2005), 'Crosscutting competencies for occupational health and safety professionals', *Journal of Public Health Management Practice*, **11**(3): 235–43.

Olsson, K., Kandolin, I. and Kauppinen-Toropainen, K. (1987), 'Shiftworkers' coping with stress', in Oginski, A., Pokorski, J. and Rutenfranz, J. (eds) *Contemporary Advances in Shiftwork Research: Theoretical and Practical Aspects in the Late Eighties*, Nicholaus Copernicus Medical Academy, Krakow.

Olsson, M. (2008), 'Employment protection and sickness absence', *Labour Economics*, doi:10.1016/j.labeco.2008.08.003.

Omura, T. (2001), 'The situation of nurses in night and shift work', paper presented at the XVth International Symposium on Night and Shift Work, Hayama, Japan, 10–13 September.

O'Neil, W. (1987), *A Century of Psychology in Australia*, Sydney University Press, Sydney.

Oppen, M. (1988), Structural discrimination against foreigners and work-related health risks', *Economic and Industrial Democracy*, **9**(1): 43–64.

Osler, T., Rutledge, R., Deis, J.R.N. and Bedrick, E. (1996), 'International classification of disease-9 based injury severity score', *The Journal of Trauma, Injury, Infection and Critical Care*, **41**(3): 380–8.

Ostberg, O. (1973), 'Interindividual differences in the circadian fatigue patterns of shift workers', *British Journal of Industrial Medicine*, **30**: 341–51.

Ostiguy, C., Soucy, B., Lapointe, G., Woods, C. and Menard, L. (2008), *Health Effects of Nanoparticles*, IRSST Research Report r-589, 2nd edition, Montreal.

Ostry, A., Marion, S., Green, L., Demers, P., Teschke, K., Hershler, R., Kelly, S. and Hertzman, C. (2000a), 'Downsizing and industrial restructuring in relation to changes in psychosocial conditions of work in British Columbia sawmills', *Scandinavian Journal of Work Environment and Health*, **26**(3): 273–7.

Ostry, A., Marion, S., Green, L., Demers, P., Teschke, K., Hershler, R., Kelly, S. and Hertzman, C. (2000b), 'The relationship between unemployment, technological change and psychosocial work conditions in British Columbia sawmills', *Critical Public Health*, **10**(2): 179–92.

Ostry, A., Marion, S., Green, L., Demers, P., Teschke, K., Hershler, R., Kelly, S. and Hertzman, C. (2002), 'Effects of de-industrialisation on working conditions and self-reported health in a sample of manufacturing workers', *Journal of Epidemiology and Community Health*, **56**(7): 506–9.

Osvalder, A. and Ulfvengren, P. (2009), 'Human-technology systems', in Bohgard, L. et al. (eds) *Work and Technology on Human Terms*, Prevent, Stockholm: 339–424.

Otto, R. (1985), 'Health damage through work stress: is "stress management" the answer?', *New Doctor*, **35**(March): 13–15.

Oxenburgh, M. (1991), *Increasing Productivity & Profit through Health & Safety*, CCH, Sydney.

Oxenburgh, M. (1993), 'Quality and productivity through health and safety', *The Quality Magazine*, **April**: 40–2.

Oxenburgh, M. and Marlow, P. (2005), 'The productivity assessment tool: computer-based cost benefit analysis model for the economic assessment of occupational health and safety interventions in the workplace', *Journal of Safety Research*, **36**: 209–14.

Page, S. (2002), *Worker Participation in Health & Safety: A Review of Australian Provisions for Worker Health & Safety Representation*, UK Health and Safety Executive (HSE), London.

Palmer, K., Harris, K. and Coggon, D. (2008), 'Chronic health problems and risk of accidental injury in the workplace: a systematic literature', *Occupational and Environmental Medicine*, **65**: 757–64.

Palmer, K.T., Poole, J., Rawbone, R.G. and Coggon, D. (2004), 'Quantifying the advantages and disadvantages of pre-placement genetic screening', *Occupational and Environmental Medicine*, **61**(5): 448–53.

Pangagos, A., Sable, A.W., Zuhosky, J.P., Irwin, R.W., Sullivan, W.J. and Foye, P.M. (2007), 'Diagnostic testing in industrial and acute musculoskeletal injuries', *Industrial Medicine and Acute Musculoskeletal Rehabilitation*, **88**(Supp. 1): S3-9.

Parker, D., Lawrie, M. and Hudson, P. (2006), 'A framework for understanding the development of organisational safety culture', *Safety Science*, **44**(6): 551–62.

Parrish, M. and Schofield, T. (2005), 'Injured workers' experiences of the workers' compensation claims process: institutional disrespect and the neoliberal state', *Health Sociology Review*, **14**(1): 33–46.

Parry, R. (2008), 'Are interventions to enhance communication performance in allied health professionals effective, and how should they be delivered? Direct and indirect evidence', *Patient Education and Counseling*, **73**: 186–95.

Parsons, J. (2002), 'Liability rules, compensation systems and safety at work in Europe', *The Geneva Papers on Risk and Insurance*, **27**(3): 358–82.

Passel, J. (2007), *Unauthorized Migrants in the United States: Estimates, Methods, and Characteristics*, Organisation for Economic Co-operation and Development, France, Directorate for Employment, Labour and Social Affairs.

Patterson, J. (1997), 'OSHA and EPA sign agreement on investigating chemical accidents', *Job Safety and Health Quarterly*, **8**(2 & 3): 33–6.

Pearce, N. (1996), 'Traditional epidemiology, modern epidemiology, and public health', *Epidemiology and Public Health*, **86**(5): 678–83.

Pearce, N. (2006), 'Introduction' in *Dioxin: Exposures, Health Effects and Public Health Policy: Proceedings of the Fifth Annual CPHR, Symposium in Health Research and Policy*, Centre for Public Health Research, Massey University Wellington Campus, Wellington, <publichealth.massey.ac.nz>

Pearce, N., Checkoway, H. and Kriebel, D. (2007), 'Bias in occupational epidemiology studies', *Occupational and Environmental Medicine*, **64**: 562–8.

Pearce, N., Dryson, E., Feyer, A-M., Gander, P., McCracken, S. and Wagstaffe, M. (2005), *Surveillance of Occupational Disease and Injury: Report to the Minister of Labour*, NOHSAC, Wellington.

Pearce, N., Dryson, E., Gander, P., Langley, J. and Wagstaffe, M. (2007), *National Profile of Occupational Health and Safety in New Zealand: Report to the Minister of Labour*, NOHSAC, Wellington.

Pehkonen, I., Takala, E-P., Ketola, R., Viikari-Juntura, E., Leino-Arjas, P., Hopsu, L., Virtanen, T., Haukka, E., Holtari-Leino, M., Nykyri, E. and Riihimäki, H. (2009), 'Evaluation of a participatory ergonomic intervention process in kitchen work', *Applied Ergonomics*, **40**(1): 115–23.

Pelham, N. (2005), 'Policy analysis of workplace rehabilitation policy within workers' compensation arrangements in NSW coal mines from 1987 to 1997: towards improved occupational health outcomes for injured coal miners', unpublished PhD thesis, University of Wollongong.

Penrose, B. (1997), 'Occupational lead poisoning at Mount Isa Mines', *Labor History*, **73**: 123–41.

Penrose, B. (1998), 'Medical experts and occupational illness: Weil's disease in North Queensland, 1933–36', *Labour History*, **75**: 125–43.

Peppard, W. (2007), *Summary Report—Innovation in Worker Safety Representation Systems: An Examination of Worker Involvement in Britain, Australia and New Zealand, and the Potential Benefits for British Columbia's Construction Workers*, British Columbia & Yukon Territory, Building & Construction Trades Council, Vancouver.

Perneger, T. (2005), 'The Swiss cheese model of safety incidents: are there holes in the metaphor?', *BMC Health Services Research*, **5**: 71 doi:101.1186/1472-6963-5-71.

Perrone, S. (2000), *When Life is Cheap: Governmental Responses to Work-Related Fatalities in Victoria 1987–1990*, unpublished PhD thesis, Department of Criminology, University of Melbourne.

Perrow, C. (1999), *Normal Accidents: Living with High-Risk Technologies*, Basic Books, New York.

Peters, J., Pickvance, S., Wilford, J., MacDonald, E. and Blank, L. (2007), 'Predictors of delayed return to work or job loss with respiratory ill-health: a systematic review', *Journal of Rehabilitation*, **17**(2): 317–26.

Petersen, C. (ed.) (2005), *Work Stress: Studies in the Context, Content and Outcomes of Stress*, Baywood, New York.

Petterson, I., Hertting, A., Hagberg, L. and Theorell, T. (2005), 'Are trends in work and health conditions interrelated? A study of Swedish hospital employees in the 1990s', *Journal of Occupational Health Psychology*, **10**(2): 110–20.

Pettersson-Stromback, A., Liljelind, I., Neely, G. and Jarvholm, B. (2008), 'Workers' interpretation of self-assessment of exposure', *Annals of Occupational Hygiene*, **52**(7): 663–71.

Pezerat, H. (2009), 'Chrysotile biopersistance: the misuse of biased studies', *International Journal of Occupational and Environmental Health*, **15**(1): 102–6.

Pezzullo, L. and Crook, A. (2006), *The Economic and Social Costs of Occupational Disease and Injury in New Zealand*, Access Economics, NOHSAC Technical Report 4, Wellington.

Pheasant, S. and Haslegrave, C. (2006), *Bodyspace: Anthropometry, Ergonomics and the Design of Work*, 3rd edition, Taylor and Francis, London.

Phoon, W. (1988), *Practical Occupational Health*, PG Publishing, Singapore.

Pidd, K. (2004), 'The impact of workplace support and identity on training transfer: a case study of drug and alcohol safety training in Australia', *International Journal of Training and Development*, **8**(4): 254–88.

Pilkington, P., Gray, S. and Golmore, A. (2007), 'Health impacts of exposure to second hand smoke (SHS) amongst a highly exposed workforce: survey of London casino workers', *BMC Public Health*, **7**: 257.

Pinch, D. (2004), 'Supplement to the findings into the deaths of Barry Supple, Timothy Walsh and Anthony Forsyth', *Report of Deputy State Coroner of NSW*, Sydney.

Piotrowski, C. and Armstrong, T. (2006), 'Current recruitment and selection practices: a national survey of Fortune 1000 firms', *North American Journal of Psychology*, **8**(3): 489–96.

Pisarski, A., Bohle, P. and Callan, V. (1998), 'Work/non-work conflict and health in shiftwork: effects of coping strategies and social support', *Scandinavian Journal of Work, Environment and Health*, **24**(Supp. 3): 141–5.

Pisarski, A., Brook, C., Bohle, P., Gallois, C., Watson, B. and Winch, S. (eds) (2006), 'Extending a model of shift-work tolerance', *Chronobiology International*, **23**(6): 1363–77.

Pisarski, A., Lawrence, S. A., Bohle, P. and Brook, C. (2008), 'Organizational influences on the work life conflict and health of shiftworkers', *Applied Ergonomics*, **39**(5): 580–8.

Platman, K. (2003), 'The self-designed career in later life: a study of older portfolio workers in the United Kingdom', *Ageing and Society*, **23**: 281–302.

Platman, K. (2004), 'Portfolio careers' and the search for flexibility in later life', *Work, Employment and Society*, **18**(3): 573–91.

Plouvier, S., Renahy, E., Chastang, J. F., Bonenfant, S. and Leclerc, A. (2008), 'Biomechanical strains and low back disorders: quantifying the effects of the number of years of exposure on various types of pain', *Occupational and Environmental Medicine*, **65**: 268–74.

Plumb, J. and Cowell, J. (1998), 'An overview of workers' compensation', *Occupational Medicine: State of the Art Reviews*, **13**(2): 241–73.

Politi, B., Arena, V., Schwerha, J. and Sussman, N. (2004), 'Occupational medical history taking: how are today's physicians doing? A cross sectional investigation of the frequency of occupational history taking by physicians in a major US teaching centre', *Journal of Occupational and Environmental Medicine*, **46**(6): 550–5.

Popma, J. (2008), 'Does worker participation improve health and safety? Findings from the Netherlands', in *Safety Reps in Europe: A Vital Asset for Preventive Strategies*, A joint Conference of the European Trade Union Confederation and the Health and Safety Department of the ETUI-REHS, Brussels.

Post, M., Krol, B. and Groothoff, J. (2005), 'Work-related determinants of return to work of employees on long-term sickness absence', *Disability and Rehabilitation*, **27**(9): 481–8.

Pragnell, B. (1995), 'Occupational health and safety committees in New South Wales: their scope, operations and role in future policy developments', paper presented at the Health and Safety in the Workplace: Have Self-Regulation and Enterprise Bargaining Failed? Conference, Sydney.

Pransky, G., Benjamin, K. and Savageau, J. (2005), 'Early retirement due to occupational injury: who is at risk?', *American Journal of Industrial Medicine*, **47**: 285–95.

Pransky, G., Benjamin, K., Savageau, J., Currivan, D. and Fletcher, K. (2005c), 'Outcomes in work-related injuries: a comparison of older and younger workers', *American Journal of Industrial Medicine*, **47**(2): 104–12.

Pransky, G., Gatchel, R., Linton, S. and Loisel, P. (2005b), 'Improving return to work research', *Journal of Occupational Rehabilitation*, **15**(4): 453–7.

Premji, S., Messing, K. and Lippel, K. (2008a), 'Broken English, broken bones? Mechanisms linking language proficiency and occupational health in a Montreal garment factory', *International Journal of Health Services*, **38**(1): 1–19.

Premji, S., Messing, K. and Lippel, K. (2008b), 'Would a "one-handed" scientist lack rigor? How scientists discuss work-relatedness of musculoskeletal disorders in formal and informal communications', *American Journal of Industrial Medicine*, **51**: 173–85.

Premji, S., Messing, K. and Lippel, K. (2008c), '"We work by the second!" Piecework remuneration and occupational health and safety from an ethnicity- and gender-sensitive perspective', *Pistes*, **1**(1): 1–22.

Presmanes, G.T. and Eisenberg, S. (2008), 'Hazardous condition: the status of illegal immigrants and their entitlement to workers' compensation benefits', *Tort Trial and Insurance Practice Law Journal*, **43**(2): 247–56.

Prezant, D., Levin, S., Kelly, K. and Aldrich, T. (2008), 'Upper and lower respiratory diseases after occupational and environmental disasters', *Mount Sinai Journal of Medicine*, **75**: 89–100.

Price, R. and Burgard, S. (2006), 'Nonstandard work and health: who is at risk and who benefits', paper presented to Health effects of Non-Health Policy conference, Bethesda, Maryland, 9–10 February.

Pringle, D. (1995), 'Managing occupational health and safety', in Slappendel, C. (ed.) *Health and Safety in New Zealand Workplaces*, Dunmore Press, Palmerston North.

Pritchard, C. and McCarthy, A. (2002), 'Promoting health in the construction industry', *Journal of Occupational and Environmental Medicine*, **44**(6): 540–5.

Prizmic, Z., Vidacek, S., Radosevic-Vidacek, B., Kaliterna, L., Cabrajec-Grbac, S., Lalic, V. and Fornazar-Knezevic, B. (1995), 'Shiftwork tolerance and 24-hr variations in moods', *Work and Stress*, **9**(2 & 3): 227–34.

Probst, T., Brubaker, T. and Barsotti, A. (2008), 'Organizational injury rate underreporting: the moderating effect of organizational safety climate', *Journal of Applied Psychology*, **93**(5): 1147–54.

Productivity Commission (2008), *Chemicals and Plastics Regulation: Research Report*, Australian Government, Canberra.

Productivity Commission (2009), 'Performance benchmarking of Australian business regulation: occupational health & safety', *Issues Paper*, Australian Government, Canberra.

Proust, C. (2006), 'A few fundamental aspects about ignition and flame propagation in dust clouds', *Journal of Loss Prevention in the Process Industries*, **19**: 104–20.

Pukkala, E., Auvinen, A. and Wahlberg, G. (1995), 'Incidence of cancer among Finnish airline cabin attendants 1967–1992', *British Medical Journal*, **311** (7006): 649–52.

Punnett, L. and Wegman, D.H. (2004), 'Work-related musculoskeletal disorders: the epidemiologic evidence and the debate', *Journal of Electromyography and Kinesiology*, **14**: 13–23.

Purnell, N., Slater, T., Eng, A. and Pearce, N. (eds) (2005), *Dioxin: Exposures, Health Effects and Public Health Policy: Proceedings of the Fifth Annual CPHR*, Symposium in Health Research and Policy, Wellington.

Purse, K. (1997), 'Workplace safety and microeconomic reform in Australia', *International Journal of Employment Studies*, **5**(2): 135–53.

Purse, K. (1998a), 'Workers' compensation policy in Australia: best practice or lowest common denominator', *Journal of Industrial Relations*, **40**(2): 179–203.

Purse, K. (1998b), 'Workers' compensation, employment security and the return to work process', *Economics and Labour Relations Review*, **9**(2): 246–61.

Purse, K. (2000), 'The dismissal of injured workers and workers' compensation in Australia', *International Journal of Health Services*, **30**(4): 849–71.

Purse, K. (2005), 'The evolution of workers' compensation policy in Australia', *Health Sociology Review*, **14**(1): 8–20.

Purvis, M. (1996), 'Safety: does the market know best?', *Journal of Occupational Health and Safety— Australia and New Zealand*, **12**(4): 395–7.

Pybus, R. (1996), *Safety Management: Strategy and Practice*, Butterworth-Heinemann, Oxford.

Quandt, S., Grzywacz, J., Marin, A., Carrillo, L., Coates, M., Burke, B. and Arcury, T. (2006a), 'Illnesses and injuries reported by Latino poultry workers in western North Carolina', *American Journal of Industrial Medicine*, **49**: 343–51.

Quandt, S., Hernandez-Valero, M., Grzywacz, J., Hovey, J., Gonzales, M. and Arcury, T. (2006b), 'Workplace, household and personal predictors of pesticide exposure for farmworkers', *Environmental Health Perspectives*, **114**(6): 943–52.

Queensland Department of Employment and Industrial Relations (2006), Workplace health and safety Queensland: Annual Report, Brisbane.

Quick, J. (1999), 'Occupational health psychology: historical routes and future directions', *Health Psychology*, **18**(1): 82–8.

Quinlan, M. (1987), 'Occupational illness, industrial conflict and state regulation: establishing some linkages', in Ford, G., Hearn, J. and Lansbury, R. (eds) *Australian Labour Relations Readings*, 4th edition, Macmillan, Melbourne.

Quinlan, M. (1993), 'The industrial relations of occupational health and safety', in Quinlan, M. (ed.) *Work and Health*, Macmillan, Melbourne: 140–69.

Quinlan, M. (1996), 'Women and OHS: the challenges still waiting to be met', *Journal of Occupational Health and Safety—Australia and New Zealand*, **12**(4): 409–22.

Quinlan, M. (1997), 'The toll from toil does matter: occupational health and labour history', *Labour History*, **73**: 1–29.

Quinlan, M. (1998), 'Labour market restructuring in industrialized societies: an overview', *Economic and Labour Relations Review*, **9**(1): 1–30.

Quinlan, M. (1999), 'The impact of labour market restructuring on occupational health and safety in industrialised societies', *Economic and Industrial Democracy*, **20**(3): 427–60.

Quinlan, M. (2000), 'Forget evidence: the demise of research involvement by NOHSC since 1996', *Journal of Occupational Health and Safety—Australia and New Zealand*, **16**(3): 213–27.

Quinlan, M. (2001), *Inquiry into Safety in the Long Haul Trucking Industry*, Motor Accidents Authority of New South Wales, Sydney.

Quinlan, M. (2002), *Developing Strategies to Address OHS and Workers' Compensation Responsibilities Arising from Changing Employment Relationships*, research report prepared for WorkCover Authority of NSW, Sydney.

Quinlan, M. (2004a), 'Regulatory responses to OHS problems posed by the increasing use of direct-hire temporary workers in Australia', *Journal of Occupational Health and Safety—Australia and New Zealand*, **20**(3): 241–54.

Quinlan, M. (2004b), 'Flexible work and organisational arrangements—regulatory problems and responses', in Bluff, L., Gunningham, N. and Johnstone, R. (eds) *OHS Regulation in the 21st Century*, Federation Press, Sydney: 120–45.

Quinlan, M. (2004c), 'Workers' compensation and the challenges posed by changing patterns of work: evidence from Australia', *Policy and Practice in Health and Safety*, **2**(1): 25–52.

Quinlan, M. (2005), 'The hidden epidemic of injuries and illness associated with the global expansion of precarious employment', in Mayhew, C. and Peterson, C. (eds) *Occupational Health and Safety: International Influences and the New Epidemics*, Baywood, New York: 53–74.

Quinlan, M. (2006), 'The ASCC: heralding a new era in OHS?', *CCH OHS Alert*, January.

Quinlan, M. (2007a) 'Organisational restructuring/downsizing, OHS regulation and worker health and wellbeing', *International Journal of Law and Psychiatry*, **30**: 385–99.

Quinlan, M. (2007b), *Report on OHS Management at the Beaconsfield Joint Venture Gold Mine, Tasmania up to and Including the Time of the Rock Fall Incident at the 925 Level of the Mine that Occurred at around 9.23pm, Resulting in the Death of Larry Paul Knight and the Entrapment of Todd Andrew Russell and Brant George Webb*. Expert report prepared for Greg Melick SC, Independent Investigator appointed by the Tasmanian Government, Hobart.

Quinlan, M. and Bohle, P. (1991), *Managing Occupational Health and Safety in Australia: A Multi-disciplinary Approach*, Macmillan, Melbourne.

Quinlan, M. and Bohle, P. (2004), 'Contingent work and occupational safety', In Barling, J. and Frone, M.R. (eds) *The Psychology of Workplace Safety*, American Psychological Association Books, Washington: 81–106.

Quinlan, M. and Bohle, P. (2008), 'Under pressure, out of control or home alone? Reviewing research and policy debates on the OHS effects of outsourcing and home-based work', *International Journal of Health Services*, **38**(3): 489–525.

Quinlan, M. and Bohle, P. (2009), 'Over-stretched and unreciprocated commitment: reviewing research on the OHS effects of downsizing and job insecurity', *International Journal of Health Services*, **39**(1): 1–44.

Quinlan, M. and Goodwin, M. (2005), 'Combating the tyranny of flexibility: the struggle to regulate shop closing hours in Victoria 1880–1900', *Social History*, **30**(3): 342–65.

Quinlan, M. and Johnstone, R. (2009), 'The implications of de-collectivist industrial relations laws and associated developments for worker health and safety in Australia, 1996–2007', *Industrial Relations Journal*.

Quinlan, M., Johnstone, R. and Mayhew, C. (2006), 'Trucking tragedies: the hidden disaster of mass death in the long haul road transport industry', in Tucker, E. (ed.) *Working Disasters*, Baywood, New York: 19–64.

Quinlan, M., Johnstone, R. and McNamara, M. (2009), 'Australian health and safety inspectors' perceptions and actions in relation to changed work arrangements', *Journal of Industrial Relations*, **51**(4): 557–75.

Quinlan, M. and Mayhew, C. (1999), 'Precarious employment and workers' compensation', *International Journal of Law and Psychiatry*, **22**(5 & 6): 491–520.

Quinlan, M. and Mayhew, C. (2000), 'Precarious employment, work re-organisation and the fracturing of OHS', in Frick, K., Jensen, P.L., Quinlan, M. and Wilthagen, T. (eds) *Systematic Occupational Health and Safety Management: Perspectives on an International Development*, Pergamon, Oxford.

Quinlan, M. and Mayhew, C. (2001), *Evidence versus Ideology: Lifting the Blindfold on OHS in Precarious Employment*, Industrial Relations Working Paper Series 138, <wwwdocs.fce.unsw.edu.au/orgmanagement/WorkingPapers/WP138.pdf>

Quinlan, M., Mayhew, C. and Bohle, P. (2001), 'The global expansion of precarious employment, work disorganisation and occupational health: a review of recent research', *International Journal of Health Services*, **31**(2): 335–414.

Quinlan, M. and Sokas, R. (2009), 'Community campaigns, supply chains and protecting the health and wellbeing of workers: examples from Australia and the USA', *American Journal of Public Health*, 99 (supplement 4): 51–9.

Quinn, M., Sembajwe, G., Stoddard, A., Kriebel, D., Krieger, N., Sorenson, G., Hartman, C., Naishadham, D. and Barbeau, E. (2007), 'Social disparities in the burden of occupational exposures: results of a cross-sectional study', *American Journal of Industrial Medicine*, **50**: 861–75.

Quintner, J. (1991), 'The RSI syndrome in historical perspective', *International Disability Studies*, **13**: 99–104.

Quintner, J. (1995), 'The Australian RSI debate: stereotyping and medicine', *Disability and Rehabilitation* **17**(5): 256–62.

RAAF, (2001), *Chemical Exposure of Airforce Maintenance Workers: Report of the Board of Inquiry into F-111 (Fuel Tank) Deseal/Reseal and Spray Seal Programs*, Royal Australian Airforce, Canberra.

Rae, I. (2008), 'Unfinished business: PC reviews chemicals and plastics regulation', *OHS Alert* (3): 1–3.

Raediker, B., Janssen, D., Schomann, C. and Nachreiner, F. (2006), 'Extended working hours and health', *Chronobiology International*, **23**(6): 1305–16.

Raffle, P. (1975), 'The purpose of occupational medicine', *British Journal of Industrial Medicine*, **32**: 102–9.

Ragland, D., Greiner, B., Krause, N., Holman, B. and Fisher, J. (1995), 'Occupational and non-occupational correlates of alcohol consumption in urban transit operators', *Preventive Medicine*, **24**: 634–45.

Rainnie, A., Barrett, R., Burgess, J. and Connell, J. (2008), 'Introduction: call centres, the networked economy and the value chain', *Journal of Industrial Relations*, **50**(2): 195–208.

Ralph, D. (1983), *Work and Madness: The Rise of Community Psychiatry*, Black Rose Books, Montreal.

Ramazzini, B. (1964 reprint), *Diseases of Workers*, Hafner, New York.

Randall, R., Cox, T. and Griffiths, A. (2007), 'Participants' accounts of a stress management intervention', *Human Relations*, **60**(8): 1181–209.

Randall, R., Neilsen, K. and Tveldt, S. (2009), 'The development of five scales to measure employees' appraisal of organizational-level stress management interventions', *Work & Stress*, **23**(1): 1–23.

Rasmussen, E. and Lamm, F. (2002), *An Introduction to New Zealand Employment Relations*, 2nd edition, Prentice Hall, Auckland.

Rasmussen, J. (1985), *A Framework for Cognitive Task Analysis in Systems Design*, Risø National Laboratory, Denmark.

Rauser, E., Foley, M., Bonauto, D., Edwards, S., Spiedholz, P. and Silverstein, B. (2008), *Preventing Injuries in the Trucking Industry—Focus Report 1997–2005*, Technical Report No. 90-17-2008, Department of Labor & Industries, Washington State, Olympia.

Rawling, M. (2007), 'The regulation of outwork and the federal takeover of labour law', *Australian Journal of Labour Law*, **20** (3): 189–206.

Ray, P., Bishop, P. and Wang, M. (1997), 'Efficacy of the components of a behavioral safety program', *International Journal of Industrial Ergonomics*, **19**: 19–29.

Reason, J. (1990), *Human Error*, University Press, Cambridge.

Reason, J. (1995), 'Understanding adverse events: human factors', *Quality in Health Care*, **4**: 80–9.

Reason, J.T. (1997), *Managing the Risks of Organizational Accidents*, Aldershot, Ashgate, England.

Reason, J.T. (1998), 'Achieving a safe culture: theory and practice', *Work & Stress*, **12**: 293–306.

Reason, J. (2000a), 'Human error: models and management', *British Medical Journal*, **320**: 768–70.

Reason, J. (2000b), 'Safety paradoxes and safety culture', *Injury Control & Safety Promotion*, **7**(1): 3–14.

Reason, J., Parker, D. and Lawton, R. (1998), 'Organizational controls and safety: the varieties of rule-related behaviour', *Journal of Occupational and Organizational Psychology*, **71**(4): 289–304.

Reber, R. and Wallin, J. (1984), 'The effects of training, goal setting, and knowledge of results on safe behaviour: a component analysis', *Academy of Management Journal*, **27**(3): 544–60.

Reilly, B., Paci, P. and Holl, P. (1995), 'Unions, safety committees and workplace injuries', *British Journal of Industrial Relations*, **33**(2): 275–88.

Reinberg, A. (ed.) (1979), 'Chronobiological field studies of oil refinery shift workers', *Chronobiologica*, **6**(Supp. 1): 1–119.

Reinberg, A., Andlauer, P., DePrins, J., Malbecq, W., Viewx, N. and Bourdeleau, P. (1984), 'Desynchronisation of the oral temperature circadian rhythm and intolerance to shift work', *Nature*, **308**: 272–4.

Reinberg, A., Chaumont, A. and Laporte, A. (1975), 'Circadian temporal structure of 20 shift-workers (8-hour shift-weekly rotation): an autometric field study', in Colquhoun, W., Folkard, S., Knauth, P. and Rutenfranz, J. *Experimental Studies of Shiftwork*, Westdeutsher Verlag, Opladen.

Reinberg, A., Smolensky, M., Labrecque, G., Levi, F. and Canbar, J. (1986), 'Biological rhythms and exposure limits to potentially noxious agents', in Haider, M., Koller, M. and Cervinka, R. (eds) *Night and Shift Work: Longterm Effects and their Prevention*, Verlag Peter Lang, Frankfurt Am Main.

Reinberg, A., Vieux, N., Andlauer, P., Guillet, P.H. and Nicolai, A. (1981), 'Tolerance of shiftwork, amplitude of circadian rhythms and aging', in Reinberg, A., Vieux, N. and Andlauer, P. (eds) *Night and Shift Work: Biological and Social Aspects*, Pergamon Press, Oxford.

Reinberg, A., Vieux, N., Andlauer, P. and Smolensky, M. (1983), 'Tolerance to shiftwork: a chronobiological approach', *Advances in Biological Psychiatry*, **11**: 35–47.

Reiner, I. and Chatten-Brown, J. (1989), 'Deterring death in the workplace: the prosecutors' perspective', *Law, Medicine and Health Care*, **17**(1): 23–31.

Reisine, S. and Fifield, J. (1995), 'Family work demands, employment demands and depressive symptoms in women with rheumatoid arthritis', *Women and Health*, **22**(3): 25–45.

Reiso, H., Nygard, J., Jorgensen, G., Holanger, R., Soldal, D. and Bruusgaard, D. (2003), 'Back to work: predictors of return to work among patients with back disorders certified as sick', *Spine*, **28**(13): 1468–74.

Ren, J., Jenkinson, I., Wang, J., Xu, D. and Yang, J. (2008), 'A methodology to model causal relationships on offshore safety assessment focusing on human and organizational factors', *Journal of Safety Research*, **39**: 87–100.

Reniers, G., Ale, B., Dullaert, W. and Soudan, K. (2009), 'Designing continuous safety improvement within chemical industrial areas', *Safety Science*, **47**: 578–90.

Rennie, D. (1995), 'Compensation for work-related injury', in Slapendel, C. (ed.) *Health and Safety in New Zealand Workplaces*, Dunmore Press, Palmerston North.

Rennie, R. (2005), 'The historical origins of an industrial disaster: occupational health and labour relations in the fluorspar mines, St Lawrence, Newfoundland 1933–1945', *Labour/Le Travail*, **55**: 107–42.

Reville, R. T., Bhattacharya, J. and Weinstein, L. R. A. (2001), 'New methods and data sources for measuring economic consequences of workplace injuries', *American Journal of Industrial Medicine*, **40**: 452–63.

Reynolds, S. and Briner, R.B. (1994), 'Stress management at work: with whom, for whom and to what ends?', *British Journal of Guidance and Counselling*, **22**(1): 75–89.

Reynolds, S. and Shapiro, D. (1991). 'Stress reduction in transition: conceptual problems in the design, implementation, and evaluation of worksite stress management interventions', *Human Relations*, **44**(7): 717–33.

Richardson, D. (1995), 'An assessment of risk for recreational dive instructors at work', *The Undersea Journal*, Second Quarter: 14–38.

Richman, J., Rospenda, K., Flaherty, J., Freels, S. and Zlatoper, K. (2004), 'Perceived organizational tolerance for workplace harassment and distress and drinking over time', *Women & Health*, **40**(4): 1–23.

Richman, J., Rospenda, K., Nawyn, S., Flaherty, J., Fendrich, M., Drum, M. and Johnson, T. (1999), 'Sexual harassment and generalized workplace abuse among university employees: prevalence and health correlates', *American Journal of Public Health*, **89**(3): 358–63.

Richman, J., Shinsako, S., Rospenda, K., Flaherty, J. and Freels, S. (2002), 'Workplace harassment/abuse and alcohol-related outcomes: the mediating role of psychological distress', *Journal of Studies on Alcohol*, **63**(4): 412–19.

Rickards, J. (2008), 'The human factor in forest operations: engineering for health and safety', *Forestry Chronicle*, **84**(4): 539–42.

Ridley, A. and Dunford, L. (1997), 'Corporate killing—legislating for unlawful death?', *Industrial Law Journal*, **26**(2): 99–113.

Riedel, J.E., Lynch, W., Baase, C., Itymel, P. and Peterson, K. (2001), 'The effect of disease prevention and health promotion on workplace productivity: a literature review', *The Science of Health Promotion*, **15**(3): 167–91.

Riegen, J. and McAllister, L. (2008), 'Change, cheese and occupational health nursing: what is the connection?', *OHSIG Conference Proceedings: 11–12 September 2008*, Auckland, <www.ohsig.org.nz/c_home.html>

Riley, J. (2007), 'Employing minors in New South Wales: the Industrial Relations (Child Employment) Act 2006 (NSW), *Australian Journal of Labour Law*, **20**(3): 295–301.

Ritter, M. (2004), *Ministerial Inquiry: Occupational Health and Safety Systems and Practice of BHP Billiton Iron Ore and Boodarie Iron Sites in Western Australia and Related Matters*, report to the Minister for State Development, Perth.

Rivara, F.P. and Thompson, D.C. (2000), 'Systematic reviews of injury-prevention strategies for occupational injuries: an overview', *American Journal of Preventive Medicine*, **18**(4, Supl 1): 1–3.

Rivilis, I.D., Van Eerd, D., Cullen, K., Cole, D.C., Irvin, E., Tyson, J. and Mahood, Q. (2008), 'Effectiveness of participatory ergonomic interventions on health outcomes: a systematic review', *Applied Ergonomics*, **39**(3): 342–58.

Rix, B.A. and Lynge, E. (1996), 'Cancer incidence in Danish health care workers', *Scandinavian Journal of Social Medicine*, **24**: 114–20.

Robens, Lord (1972), *Report of the Committee on Safety and Health at Work*, HMSO, London.

Robertson, D. (1927), 'Factory and shop legislation in Australia', *Journal of Industrial Hygiene*, **7**(11): 494–504.

Robinson, A.M. and Smallman, C. (2006), 'The contemporary British workplace: a safer and healthier place?', *Work, Employment and Society*, **20**(1): 87–107.

Robinson, G. and Morely, C. (2007), 'Running the electronic sweatshop: call centre managers' views on call centres', *Journal of Management & Organization*, **13**: 249–63.

Robinson, J. (1991), *Toil and Toxics: Workplace Struggles and Political Strategies for Occupational Health*, University of California Press, Berkeley.

Robroek, S., Bredt, F. and Burdorf, A. (2007), 'The (cost-) effectiveness of an individually tailored long-term worksite health promotion programme on physical activity and nutrition of a pragmatic cluster randomized control trial', *BMC Public Health*, **7**: 259.

Robson, L., Clarke, J., Cullen, K., Bielecky, A., Severin, C., Bigelow, P., Irvin, E., Culyer, A. and Mahood, Q. (2007), 'The effectiveness of occupational health and safety management system interventions: a systematic review', *Safety Science*, **45**(3): 329–53.

Roed-Larsen, S., Valvisto, T., Harms-Ringdahl, L. and Kirchsteiger, C. (2004), 'Accident investigation practices in Europe—main responses from a recent study of accidents in industry and transport', *Journal of Hazardous Materials*, **111**: 7–12.

Roelofs, C., Barbeau, E., Ellenbecker, M. and Moure-Eraso, R. (2003), 'Prevention strategies in industrial hygiene: a critical literature review', *AIHA Journal*, **64**(1): 62–7.

Roethlisberger, G. and Dickson, W. (1939), *Management and the Worker*, Harvard University Press, Cambridge, Mass.

Rogers, E. and Wiatrowski, W.J. (2005), 'Injuries, illnesses, and fatalities among older workers', *Monthly Labor Review*, **October**, 128(10): 24–30.

Ron, P. (2008), 'Relations between work stressors and well-being among nursing assistants in nursing homes', *Aging Clinical and Experimental Research*, **20**(4): 359–67.

Roquelaure, Y. (2008), 'Workplace intervention and musculoskeletal disorders: the need to develop research on implementation strategy', *Occupational and Environmental Medicine*, **65**: 4–5.

Roscoe, R., Deddens, J., Salvan, A. and Schnoor, T. (1995), 'Mortality amongst Najavo uranium miners', *American Journal of Public Health*, **85**: 535–40.

Rose, J. (2006), 'A model of care for managing traumatic psychological injury in a workers' compensation context', *Journal of Traumatic Stress*, **19**(3): 315–26.

Rose, M. (1971), 'The doctor in the industrial revolution', *British Journal of Industrial Medicine*, **28**: 22–6.

Rosekind, M., Smith, R., Miller, D., Co, E., Gregory, K., Webbon, L., Gander, P. and Lebacqz, J. (1995), 'Alertness management: strategic naps in operational settings', *Journal of Sleep Research*, **4**(Supp. 2): 62–6.

Rosen, R. (1998), 'Existing infrastructure for the control of radioactive material in Australia', *Journal of Occupational Health and Safety—Australia and New Zealand*, **14**(4): 395–400.

Rosenberg, J. and Harrison, R.J. (1997), 'Biological monitoring', in LaDou, J. *Occupational and Environmental Medicine*, 2nd edition, Appleton and Lange, Stamford, Connecticut.

Rosenman, K., Gardiner, J., Wang, J., Biddle, J., Hogan, A., Reilly, M., Roberts, K. and Welch, E. (2000), 'Why most workers with occupational repetitive trauma do not file for compensation', *Journal Occupational Environmental Medicine*, **42**(1): 25–34.

Rosenman, K.D., Kalush, A., Reilly, M.J., Gardiner, J.C., Reeves, M. and Luo, Z. (2006), 'How much work-related illness and injury is missed by the national surveillance system?', *Journal of Occupational and Environmental Medicine*, **48**: 357–65.

Rosenstock, L. (1997), 'Foreword', in Bernard, B.P. *Workplace Factors: A Critical Review of Epidemiologic Evidence for Work-Related Musculoskeletal Disorders of the Neck, Upper Extremity and Low Back*, US Department of Health and Human Services, (NIOSH), Publication No. 97-141, National Institute of Occupational Safety and Health, Cincinnati.

Rosenstock, L., Cullen, M. and Fingerhut, M. (2005), 'Advancing worker health and safety in the developing world', *Journal of Occupational and Environmental Medicine*, **47**(2): 132–6.

Rosner, D. and Markowitz, G. (eds) (1989) *Dying for Work: Workers' Health and Safety in Twentieth Century America*, Indiana University Press, Bloomington.

Rosner, D. and Markowitz, G. (1991), *Deadly Dust: Silicosis and the Politics of Occupational Disease in Twentieth Century America*, Princeton University Press, Princeton, New Jersey.

Rospenda, K., Richman, J., Ehmke, J. and Zlatoper, K. (2005), 'Is workplace harassment hazardous to your health?', *Journal of Business and Psychology*, **20**(1): 95–110.

Rospenda, K., Richman, J. and Nawyn, S. (1998), 'Doing power: the confluences of gender, race, and class in contrapower sexual harassment', *Gender and Society*, **12**(1): 40–60.

Rospenda, K., Richman, J. and Shannon, C. (2009), 'Prevalence and mental health correlates of harassment and discrimination in the workplace', *Journal of Interpersonal Violence*, **24**(5): 819–43.

Rossi, K., Heinonen, K. and Heikkinen, M. (2000), 'Factors affecting the work of the occupational health nurse', *Occupational Medicine*, **50**(5): 369–72.

Rouelaure, Y., Ha, C., Gohier, B., Dano, C., Touranchet, A., Leclerc, A., Imbernon, E. and Goldberg, M. (2007), 'Exposure to psychosocial stressors at work in the Pays de la Loire', *Encephale—Revue de Psychiatre Clinique Biologique et Therapeutique*, **33**(2): 160–8.

Roy, R. (1997), *The Cost of Fires: A Review of the Information Available*, The Home Office Publications Unit, London.

Royal Commission into the Building and Construction Industry (RCBC) (2003), 'Final report: summary of findings and recommendations', Vol. 1, Royal Commissioner, The Honourable Terence Rhoderic Hudson Cole RFD QC, Commonwealth of Australia.

Rusch, G. (1993), 'The history and development of emergency response planning', *Journal of Hazardous Materials*, **33**: 193–202.

Rushton, L. and Betts, D. (2000), 'Collection of data for occupational epidemiologic research—results from a survey of European industry', *Scandinavian Journal of Work Environment and Health*, **26**(4): 317–21.

Russell, B. (2008), 'Call centres: a decade of research', *International Journal of Management Reviews*, **10**(3): 195–219.

Russell, C. and Schofield, T. (1989), 'Professional control', in Jagtenberg, T. and D'Alton, P. (eds) *Four Dimensional Social Space: Class, Gender, Ethnicity and Nature*, Harper and Row, Sydney.

Russell, D. (1988), 'Repetition strain injury and psychiatry', *Community Health Studies*, **XII**(2): 134–9.

Russell, G. and Bowman, L. (2000), '*Work and Family: Current Thinking, Research and Practice*', Department of Family and Community Services, Canberra.

Russell, R. (1995), 'The link between environmental and occupational health', *Journal of Occupational Health and Safety—Australia and New Zealand*, **11**(1): 3–4.

Rutenfranz, J., Haider, M. and Koller, M. (1985), 'Occupational health measures for nightworkers and shiftworkers', in Folkard, S. and Monk, T. (eds) *Hours of Work: Temporal Factors in Work Scheduling*, John Wiley, Chichester, UK.

Rutenfranz, J. and Knauth, P. (1986), 'Combined effects: introductory remarks', in Haider, M., Koller, M. and Cervinka, R. (eds) *Night and Shift Work: Longterm Effects and their Prevention*, Verlag Peter Lang, Frankfurt Am Main.

Rutenfranz, J., Knauth, P. and Angersbach, D. (1981), 'Shift work research issues', in Johnson, L., Tepas, D., Colquhoun, W. and Colligan, M. (eds) *Biological Rhythms, Sleep and Shiftwork*, MTP Press, New York.

Ryan, O. and John, A. (2001), 'ABCs for lone workers: a behavior-based study of bus drivers', *Professional Safety*, **46**(11): 20.

Sabino v The Industrial Commission of Arizona and Others, Supreme Court of Arizona, CV-08-0359-PR, 2009.

Sacker, A., Head, J. and Bartley, M. (2008), 'Impact of coronary heart disease on health functioning in an aging population: are there differences according to socioeconomic position?', *Psychosomatic Medicine*, **70**: 133–40.

Safety WA Autumn, 1992: 1–2.

Safe Work Australia (2009a), *Comparison of Workers' Compensation Arrangements in Australia and New Zealand*, Commonwealth of Australia, Barton, ACT.

Safe Work Australia (2009b), *Mesothelioma in Australia: Incidence 1982 to 2005 & Deaths 1997 to 2006*, Commonwealth of Australia, Canberra.

Sager, L. and James, C. (2005), 'Injured workers' perspectives of their rehabilitation process under the New South Wales workers compensation system', *Australian Occupational Therapy Journal*, **52**: 127–35.

Saksvik, P. and Nytro, K. (1996), 'Implementation of internal control (IC) of health, environment and safety (HES) in Norwegian Enterprises', *Safety Science*, **23**(1): 53–61.

Saksvik, P. and Quinlan, M. (2003), 'Regulating systematic occupational health and safety management: comparing the Norwegian and Australian experience', *Relations Industrielles*, **58**(1): 81–107.

Saksvik, P., Torvatn, H. and Nytro, K. (2003), 'Systematic occupational health and safety work in Norway: a decade of implementation', *Safety Science*, **41**: 721–38.

Saksvik, P., Tvedt, S. D., Nytro, K., Andersen, R. G., Andersen, T. K., Buvik, M. P. and Torvatn, H. (2007), 'Developing criteria for healthy organizational change', *Work & Stress*, **21**(3): 243–63.

Salminen, S., Saari, J., Saarela, K. and Rasanen, T. (1993), 'Organisational factors influencing serious occupational accidents', *Scandinavian Journal of Work Environmental and Health*, **19**: 352–7.

Salminen, S. (2004), 'Have young workers more injuries than older ones? An international literature review', *Journal of Safety Research*, **35**: 513–21.

Saltzman, G. and Belzer, M. (2007), *Truck Driver Occupational Safety and Health 2003 Conference Report and Selective Literature Review*, Department of Health and Human Services, Centres for Disease Control and Prevention, National Institute for Occupational Safety and Health.

Sanborn, M., Cole, D., Abelsohn, A. and Weir, E. (2002), 'Identifying and managing adverse environmental health impacts: 4. pesticides', *Canadian Medical Association Journal*, **166**(11): 1431–6.

Sanders, M.S. and McCormick, E.J. (1987), *Human Factors in Engineering & Design*, McGraw-Hill, New York.

Santana, V., Araujo-Filho, J., Silva, M., Albuquerque-Oliveira, P., Barbosa-Branco, A. and da Costa Nobre, L. (2007), 'Mortality, years of life lost, and incidence of occupational accidents in the state of Bahia, Brazil', *Cad Saude Publica*, **23**(11): 2643–52.

Santana, V., Cooper, S., Roberts, R. and Araujo-Filho, J. (2005), 'Adolescent students who work: gender differences in school performances and self-perceived health', *International Journal of Occupational and Environmental Health*, **11**: 294–301.

Santana, V., Loomis, D., Newman, B. and Harlow, S. (1997), 'Informal jobs: another occupational hazard for women's mental health?', *International Journal of Epidemiology*, **26**(6): 1236–42.

Sarkus, D. (2001), 'Safety and psychology', *Professional Safety*, **46**(1): 18–25.

Sasaki, T. and Matsumoto, S. (2005), 'Actual conditions of work, fatigue and sleep in non-employed home-based female information technology workers with pre-school children', *Industrial Health*, **43**(1): 142–50.

Sass, R. (1999), 'The unwritten story of women's role in the birth of occupational health and safety legislation', *International Journal of Health Services*, **29**(1): 109–45.

Saunders, P., Huynh, A. and Goodman-Delahunty, J. (2007), 'Defining workplace bullying behaviour: professional lay definitions of workplace bullying', *International Journal of Law and Psychiatry*, **30**: 340–54.

Sauni, R., Paakkonen, R., Virtema, P., Toppila, E. and Uitti, J. (2009), 'Dose-relationship between exposure to hand-arm vibration and health effects among metalworkers', *Annals of Occupational Hygiene*, **53**(1): 55–62.

Sauter, S.L. and Swanson, N.G. (1996), 'An ecological model of musculoskeletal disorders in office work', in Moon, S.D. and Sauter, S.L. (eds) *Beyond Biomechanics: Psychological Aspects of Musculoskeletal Disorders in Office Work*, Taylor & Francis, Bristol, PA: 3–22.

Schaubroeck, J. and Fink, L. (1998), 'Facilitating and inhibiting effects of job control and social support of stress outcomes and role behaviour: a contingency model', *Journal of Organizational Behaviour*, **19**: 167–95.

Schaubroeck, J. and Merrit, D. (1997), 'Divergent effects of job control on coping with work stressors: the key role of self-efficacy', *Academy of Management Journal*, **40**(3): 738–54.

Schein, E. (1988), *Organisational Psychology*, Prentice Hall, Englewood Cliffs, New Jersey.

Schemm, R. (1994), 'Bridging conflicting ideologies—the origins of American and British occupational therapy', *American Journal of Occupational Therapy*, **48**(11): 1082–8.

Scherrer, J. (1981), 'Man's work and circadian rhythm through the ages', in Reinberg, A., Vieux, N. and Andlauer, P. (eds) *Night and Shift Work: Biological and Social Aspects*, Pergamon Press, Oxford.

Scherzer, T., Rugulies, R. and Krause, N. (2005), 'Work-related pain and injury and barriers to workers' compensation among Las Vegas hotel room cleaners', *American Journal of Public Health*, **95**(3): 483–8.

Schnaul, P., Belkic, K., Landsbergis, P. and Baker, D. (eds) (2000), 'The workplace and cardiovascular disease', *Occupational Medicine: State of the Art Reviews*, **15**(1): 24–40.

Schnaul, P., Pierper, C. and Schwartz, J. (1990), 'The relationship between "job strain", workplace diastolic blood pressure, and left ventricular mass index: results of a case control study', *Journal of the American Medical Association*, **263**: 1929–35.

Schneider, T., Skov, P. and Valbjorn, O. (1999), 'Challenges to indoor environment research in the new office', *Scandinavian Journal of Work Environment & Health*, **25**(6): 574–9.

Schoeff, M. (2007), 'House, Senate address genetic bias in hiring', *Workforce Management*, **86**(3): 11–12.

Schofield, D. and Fletcher, S. (2008), 'The physiotherapy workforce is ageing, becoming more masculinised, and is working longer hours: a demographic study', *Australian Journal of Physiotherapy*, **53**: 121–6.

Schofield, D., Shrestha, R., Passey, M., Earnest, A. and Fletcher, S. (2008), 'Chronic disease and labour force participation among older Australians', *Medical Journal of Australia*, **189**(8): 447–50.

Schofield, T. (2005), 'Introduction: the impact of neoliberal policy on workplace health', *Health Sociology Review*, **14**: 5–7.

Schroeder, E. (1986), 'Legislative and judicial responses to the inadequacy of compensation for occupational disease', *Law and Contemporary Problems*, **49**: 151–82.

Schroer, C., Janssen, M., van Amelsvoort, L., Bosma, H., Swaen, G., Nijhuis, F. and van Eick, J. (2005), *Journal of Occupational Rehabilitation*, **15**(3): 435–45.

Schuler, R. (1980), 'Definition and conceptualisation of stress in organisations', *Organisational Behaviour and Human Decision Processes*, **25**: 184–215.

Schulte, P. (2005), 'Characterizing the burden of occupational injury and disease', *Journal of Occupational and Environmental Medicine*, **47**(6): 607–22.

Schulte, P. (2007), 'The contributions of genetics and genomics to occupational safety and health', *Occupational and Environmental Medicine*, **64**(11): 717–18.

Schulte, P., Wagner, G., Downes, A. and Miller, D. (2008), 'A framework for concurrent consideration of occupational hazards and obesity', *Annals of Occupational Hygiene*, **52**(7): 555–66.

Schulte, P., Wagner, G., Ostry, A., Blanciforti, L., Cutlip, R., Krajnak, K., Luster, M., Munson, A., O'Callaghan, J., Parks, C., Simeonova, P. and Miller, D. (2007), 'Work, obesity, and occupational safety and health', *American Journal of Public Health*, **97**(3): 428–36.

Schultz, A. and Edington, D. (2007), 'Employee health and presenteeism: a systematic review', *Journal of Occupational Rehabilitation*, **17**: 547–79.

Schultz, L., Crook, J., Berkowitz, J., Milner, R. and Meloche, G. (2005), 'Predicting return to work after low back injury using the psychosocial risk for occupational disability instrument: a validation study', *Journal of Occupational Rehabilitation*, **15**(3): 365–76.

Schwartz, G.T. (1989), 'The character of early American tort law', *UCLA Law Review*, **36**: 641–718.

Schweder, P. (2009), *OHS Experiences of Seasonal Direct-Hire Temporary Employees*, PhD thesis, University of New South Wales.

Scott, A., Monk, T. and Brink, L. (1997), 'Shiftwork as a risk factor for depression: a pilot study', *International Journal of Occupational and Environmental Health*, **3**(3) (Supp.): S2–S9.

Scott, D. (2001), *151 Days: The Great Waterfront Lockout and Supporting Strikes*, Reed Publishing, Auckland.

Seago, J. (2004), 'The effect of registered nurses' unions on heart-attack mortality', *Industrial and Labor Relations Review*, **57**(3): 422–42.

Seale, C. (2008), 'Mapping the field of medical sociology: a comparative analysis of journals', *Sociology of Health & Illness*, **30**(5): 677–95.

Secure Employment Test Case [2006] NSWIRComm 38.

Seeber, A. and Iregren, A. (eds) (1992), 'Behavioural effects of contaminated air: applying psychology in neurotoxicology (special issue)', *Applied Psychology: An International Review*, **42**(3)1–.

Seidler, A., Nienhaus, A., Bernhardt T., Elo, A. and Frolich, L. (2004), 'Psychosoical work factors and dementia', *Occupational and Environmental Medicine*, **61**: 962–71.

Seixas, N.S., Blecker, H., Camp, J. and Neitzel, R. (2008), 'Occupational health and safety experience of day laborers in Seattle, WA', *American Journal of Industrial Medicine*, **51**(6): 399–406.

Selby, C. (1925). 'The promotion of industrial health', *American Journal of Public Health*: 209–12.

Selye, H. (1946), 'The general adaptation syndrome and the disease of adaptation', *Journal of Clinical Endocrinology*, **6**: 117.

Seminar on Safety Investigation of Accidents, Petten, Netherlands, May: 170–6, in Katsakiori, P., Sakellaropoulos, G. and Manatakis, E. (2009), 'Towards an evaluation of accident investigation methods in terms of their alignment with accident causation models', *Safety Science*, **47**(7): 1007–15.

Sengupta, I., Reno, V. and Burton, J.F. (2005), *Workers' Compensation: Benefits, Coverage, and Costs, 2003*, The National Academy of Social Insurance, Washington, DC.

Senior Deputy President Watson Supplementary Decision, Australian Building and Construction Commission (RE2007/2719) [2007] AIRC 934.

Sentes, R. (1989), 'Occupational exposure standards in Canada: From ACGIH to?', *American Journal of Industrial Medicine*, **16**: 719–22.

Serra, C., Rodriguez, M., Delclos, G., Plana, M., Gomez-Lopez, L. and Benavides, F. (2007), 'Criteria and methods used for the assessment of fitness for work: a systematic review', *Occupational and Environmental Medicine*, **64**(5): 304–12.

Seward, J. (1997), 'Occupational stress', in LaDou, J. *Occupational and Environmental Medicine*, 2nd edition, Appleton and Lange, Stamford, Connecticut: 585–601.

Shaham, J., Gurvich, R., Goral, A. and Czerniak, A. (2006), 'The risk of breast cancer in relation to health habits and occupational exposures', *American Journal of Industrial Medicine*, **49**: 1021–30.

Shain, M. and Kramer, D.M. (2004) 'Health promotion in the workplace: framing the concept; reviewing the evidence', *Occupational and Environmental Medicine*, **61**: 643–8.

Shannon, C., Rospenda, K. and Richman, J. (2007), 'Workplace harassment patterning, gender, and the utilization of professional services: findings from a US national study', *Social Science & Medicine*, **64**: 1178–91.

Shannon, H., Walters, V., Lewchuk, W., Richardson, J., Moran, L., Haines, E. and Verma, D. (1996), 'Workplace organizational correlates of lost-time accident rates in manufacturing', *American Journal of Industrial Medicine*, **29**: 258–68.

Shariff, A. and Keng, T. (2008), 'On-line at-risk behaviour analysis and improvement system (e-ARBAIS)', *Journal of Loss Prevention*, **21**: 326–35.

Shaw, A. (1994a), *Positive Performance Indicators for OHS: Beyond Lost Time Injuries—Part Two: Practical Approaches*, Commonwealth of Australia, Canberra.

Shaw, A. (1994b), 'Performance indicators for benchmarking report on the literature review conducted as stage 1 of the WorkSafe Australia Project to develop a benchmarking methodology for OHS', in *Beyond Lost Time Injuries: Positive Performance Indicators for OHS*, WorkSafe Australia, Australian Government Publishing Services, Canberra.

Shaw, A. and Blewett, V. (1995a), 'Enterprise bargaining—supporting or hindering OHS best practice?', *Journal of Occupational Health and Safety—Australia and New Zealand*, **11**(2): 139–44.

Shaw, A. and Blewett, V. (1995b), 'Health promotion, handle with care: issues for health promotion in the workplace', *Journal of Occupational Health and Safety—Australia and New Zealand*, **11**(5): 461–5.

Shaw, W., Hong, Q., Pransky, G. and Loisel, P. (2007), 'A literature review describing the role of return-to-work coordinators in trial programs and interventions designed to prevent workplace disability', *Journal of Occupational Rehabilitation*, **18**(1): 2–15.

Sheehy, N. and Chapman, A. (1987), 'Industrial accidents', in Cooper, C. and Robertson, I. (eds) *International Review of Industrial and Organisational Psychology*, John Wiley and Sons, Chichester: 201–27.

Sheldon, W.S. (2003), Editorial: 'Occupational medicine and its moral discontents', *Journal of Occupational and Environmental Medicine*, **45**(12): 1226–33.

Shikdar, A.A. and Sawaqed, N.M. (2003), 'Worker productivity, and occupational health and safety issues in selected industries', *Computers & Industrial Engineering*, **45**(4): 563–72.

Shinn, M., Rosario, M., Morch, H. and Chestnut, D. (1984), 'Coping with job stress and burnout in the human services', *Journal of Personality and Social Psychology*, **46**(4): 864–76.

Shirom, A., Toker, S., Berliner, S. and Shapira, I. (2008), 'The job demand-control-support model and stress related low-grade inflammatory responses amongst healthy employees: a longitudinal study', *Work & Stress*, **22**(2): 138–52.

Shuchman, M. (1998), 'Secrecy in science: the flock worker's lung investigation', *Annals of Internal Medicine*, **129**: 341–4.

SIA Safety Week, various issues.

Siddiqui, K. (2006), 'Immigrant women in contingent work in Toronto: dealing and coping with health related problems in the workplace', *Canadian Association for the Study of Adult Education (CASAE) 2006 National Conference On-Line Proceedings*, York University, Toronto, Ontario.

Siefert, A. and Messing, K. (2006), 'Cleaning up after globalization: an ergonomic analysis of the work activity of hotel cleaners', *Antipode*: 557–78.

Siefert, A., Messing, K., Reil, J. and Chatigny, C. (2007), 'Precarious employment conditions affect work content in education and social work: results for work analyses', *International Journal of Law and Psychiatry*, **30**: 299–310.

Siegrist, J. (1996), 'Adverse health effects of high-effort/low-reward conditions', *Journal of Occupational Health Psychology*, **1**(1): 27–41.

Silverstein, M. (1994), 'An analysis of medical screening and surveillance in 21 OSHA standards—support for a generic medical surveillance standard', *American Journal of Industrial Medicine*, **26**(3): 283–95.

Silverstein, M. (2008), 'Getting home safe and sound: occupational safety and health administration at 38', *American Journal of Public Health*, **98**(3): 416–23.

Sim, M. (2007), 'The need for an occupational disease surveillance system in Australia', *Journal of Occupational Health and Safety—Australia and New Zealand*, **23**(6): 557–62.

Simard, M. and Marchand, A. (1995), 'A multilevel analysis of organisational factors related to taking of safety initiatives by work groups', *Safety Science*, **21**(2): 113–29.

Simpson, C.G. (1990), 'The cost and benefits in occupational ergonomics', *Ergonomics*, **33**: 28–42.

Simpson, R. (2000), 'Presenteeism and the impact of long hours on managers', in Winstanley, D. and Woodall, J. (eds) *Ethical Issues in Contemporary Human Resource Management*, Macmillan Business, Basingstoke: 156–71.

Singh-Manoux, A., Martikainen, P., Ferrie, J., Zins, M., Marmot, M. and Goldberg, M. (2006), 'What does self rated health measure? Results from the British Whitehall II and French Gazel cohort studies', *Journal of Epidemiology and Community Health*, **60**: 364–72.

Skegg, D. (1991), 'Workplace injury and disease recording standard (AS 1885): a critical review', *Journal of Occupational Health and Safety—Australia and New Zealand*, **7**(6): 509–13.

Skillen, D. (1996), 'Towards a social structural understanding of occupational hazards in public health', *International Journal of Health Services*, **26**(1): 111–46.

Skriver, J., Haukenes, H. and Alme, I. (2003), 'Accident investigation at Norwegian State Railways: a socio-technical methodology', paper presented at the *JRC/ESReDA*.

Slappendel, C. (1995a), 'Dominant theories of work-related injury causation', in Slappendel, C. (ed.) *Health and Safety in New Zealand Workplaces*, Dunmore Press, Palmerston North: 181–212.

Slappendel, C. (ed.) (1995b), *Health and Safety in New Zealand Workplaces*, Dunmore Press, Palmerston North, esp. chapters by Cryer and Laird.

Slattery, J., Selvarajan, T. and Anderson, J. (2008), 'The influence of new employee development practices upon role stressors and work-related attitudes of temporary employees', *International Journal of Human Resource Management*, **19**(12): 2268–93.

Sluiter, J. (2006), 'High-demand jobs: age-related diversity in work ability', *Applied Ergonomics*, **37**: 429–40.

Sluiter, J. and Frings-Dresen, M. (2007), 'What do we know about ageing at work? Evidence-based fitness for duty and health in fire fighters', *Ergonomics*, **50**(11): 1897–913.

Smallman, C. and John, G. (2001), 'British directors' perspective on the impact of health and safety on corporate performance', *Safety Science*, **38**(3): 227–39.

Smith, C., Reilly, C. and Midkiff, K. (1989), 'Evaluation of three circadian rhythm questionnaires with suggestions for an approved measure of morningness', *Journal of Applied Psychology*, **74**(5): 728–38.

Smith, D. (2008), 'Menstrual disorders and their adverse symptoms at work: an emerging occupational health issue in the nursing profession', *Nursing and Health Sciences*, **10**: 222–8.

Smith, G., Huang, Y., Ho, M. and Chen, P. (2006), 'The relationship between safety climate and injury rates across industries: the need to adjust for injury hazards', *Accident Analysis and Prevention*, **38**: 556–62.

Smith, J. (2008), 'Under Bush, OSHA mired in inaction', *Washington Post*, 29 December.

Smith, L., Hammond, I., MacDonald, I. and Folkard, S. (1998), '12-hour shifts are popular but are they a solution?', *International Journal of Industrial Ergonomics*, **21**(3 & 4): 307–22.

Smith, P. (1979), 'A study of weekly and rapidly rotating shiftworkers', *International Archives of Occupational and Environmental Health*, **43**: 211–20.

Smith, P. (1983) *Back-Related Injuries in Nurses*, School of Social and Industrial Administration Internship Report, Giffith University.

Smith, P., Brown, D., Di Milia, L. and Wragg, C. (1993), 'The use of the circadian type inventory as a measure of the circadian constructs of vigour and rigidity', *Ergonomics*, **36**(1–3): 169–76.

Smith, P.M. and Mustard, C.A. (2007), 'How many employees receive safety training during their first year of a new job?', *Injury Prevention*, **13**(1): 37–41.

Smith, P.M. and Mustard, C.A. (2009), 'Comparing the risk of work-related injuries between immigrants to Canada and Canadian-born labour market participants', *Occupational and Environmental Medicine*, **66**(6): 361–7.

Smith, T., Davis, M., Reaser, P., Natkin, J., Hart, J., Laden, F., Heff, A. and Garshick, E. (2006), 'Overview of particulate exposures in the US trucking industry', *Journal of Environmental Monitoring*, **8**: 711–20.

Snider, L. (2000), 'The sociology of corporate crime: an obituary', *Theoretical Criminology*, **4**(2): 169–206.

Snyder, W. (1994), 'Hospital downsizing and increased frequency of assaults on staff', *Hospital and Community Psychiatry*, **45**(4): 378–80.

Sokas, R. (2008), 'Environmental justice at work', *Environmental Justice*, **1**(4): 171–6.

Sokas, R. and Sprince, N. (2008) 'Occupational health overview', in *Encyclopedia of Public Health*, Elsevier Press.

Sorenson, O., Hasle, P. and Bach, E. (2007), 'Working in small enterprises—is there a special risk?', *Safety Science*, **45**: 1044–59.

Sorgdrager, B., Hulshof, C.J. and Dijk, F. (2004), 'Evaluation of the effectiveness of pre-employment screening', *International Archives of Occupational and Environmental Health*, **77**(4): 271–6.

South Australian Occupational Safety, Health and Welfare Steering Committee (1984), *The Protection of Workers' Health and Safety*, report to the Ministers of Labour and Health, Vol. 1.

Souza, N., Santana, V., Albuquerque-Oliveira, P. and Barbosa-Branco, A. (2008), 'Work-related diseases and health-related compensation claims', *Revista de Saude Publica*, **42**(4): 630–8.

Sparks, K., Cooper, C., Fried, Y. and Shirom, A. (1997), 'The effects of hours of work on health: a meta-analytic review', *Journal of Occupational and Organizational Psychology*, **70**: 391–408.

Sparks, K., Faragher, B. and Cooper, C.L. (2001), 'Well-being and occupational health in the 21st century workplace', *Journal of Occupational and Organizational Psychology*, **74**(4): 489.

Specht, M., Chevreau, F.R. and Denis-Rémis, C. (2006), 'Dedicating management to cultural processes: toward a human risk management system', *Journal of Risk Research*, **9**(5): 525–42.

Spector, P.E. (2006), 'Method variance in organizational research: truth or urban legend?', *Organizational Research Methods*, **9**(2): 221–32.

Spillane, R. (1984), 'Psychological aspects of occupational stress and workers' compensation', *Journal of Industrial Relations*, **26**(4): 496–503.

Spillane, R. (2008), 'Medicalising work behaviour: the case of repetition strain injury', *Asia Pacific Journal of Human Resources*, **46**(1): 85–98.

Spillane, R. and Deves, L. (1987), 'RSI: pain, pretence of patienthood?', *The Journal of Industrial Relations*, **26**(1): 41–8.

Sprigg, C.A., Smith, P.R. and Jackson, P.R. (2003), *Psychosocial Risk Factors in Call Centres: An Evaluation of Work Design and Well-Being*, HSE Books, Norwich.

Staal, J.B., Hlobil, H., van Tulder, M.W., Waddell, G., Burton, A.K., Koes, B.W. and van Mechelen, W. (2003), 'Occupational health guidelines for the management of low back pain: an international comparison', *Occupational and Environmental Medicine*, **60**(9): 618–26.

Standards Australia/Standards New Zealand (2004), *Handbook Risk Management Guidelines Companion to AS/NZS 4360: 2004*.

Standing Committee on Law and Justice (1997), *Interim Report of the Inquiry into Workplace Safety*, Parliament of New South Wales Legislative Council, Sydney.

Standing Committee on Law and Justice (1998), *Final Report of the Inquiry into Workplace Safety*, two volumes, Parliament of New South Wales Legislative Council, Sydney.

St-Arnaud, L., Bourbonais, R., Saint-Jean, M. and Rheaume, J. (2007), 'Determinants of return-to-work among employees absent due to mental health problems', *Relations Industrielles*, **62**(4): 690–713.

Statistics New Zealand (2008), *Injury Statistics—Work-Related Claims: 2007*, <www.stats.govt.nz> (retrieved January 2009).

Stave, C., Pousette, A. and Torner, M. (2008), 'Risk and safety communication in small enterprises—how to support a lasting change towards work safety priority', *Journal of Risk Research*, **11**(1 & 2): 195–206.

Steenland, K., Burnett, C., Lalich, N., Ward, E. and Hurrell, J. (2003), 'Dying for work: the magnitude of US mortality from selected causes of death associated with occupation', *American Journal of Industrial Medicine*, **43**: 461–82.

Stegenga, J., Bell, E. and Matlow, A. (2002), 'The role of nurse understaffing in nonsocomial viral gastrointestinal infections on a general pediatrics ward', *Infection Control and Hospital Epidemiology*, **23**(3): 133–9.

Stellman, J., Smith, R., Katz, C., Sharma, V., Charney, D., Herbert, R., Moline, J., Luft, B., Markowitz, S., Udasin, I., Harrison, D., Baron, S., Landrigan, P., Levin, S. and Southwick, S. (2008), 'Enduring mental health morbidity and social function impairment in World Trade Center rescue, recovery, and cleanup workers: the psychological dimension of an environmental health disaster', *Environmental Health Perspectives*, **116**(9): 1248–53.

Stellman, J. and Stellman, S. (1996), 'Cancer and the workplace', *CA—A Cancer Journal for Clinicians*, **46**: 70–92.

Stellman, S. (2003), 'Issues of causality in the history of occupational epidemiology', *Soz-Praventivmed*, **48**: 151–60.

Stephenson, A. (1929), 'Industrial accidents', in Myers, C. (ed.) *Industrial Psychology*, Thornton Butterworth, London.

Stern, M. (2003), 'Industrial structure and occupational health: the American pottery industry, 1897–1929', *Business History Review*, **77**(3): 417–45.

Stevens, A. and Coyle, P. (2000), 'Hepatitis C virus: an important occupational hazard?', *Occupational Medicine*, **50**(6): 377–82.

Stevens, G. (1999), *Workplace Injuries in Small and Large Manufacturing Workplaces 1994/5–1995/6*, Health and Safety Executive, London.

Stevenson, M., Segui-Gomez, M., Lescohier, I., Di Scala, C. and McDonald-Smith, G. (2001), 'An overview of the injury severity score and the new injury severity score', *Inj Prev*, **7**(1): 10–13.

Stewart, D. (1991a), *Workers' Compensation and Social Security: Personal and Social Costs*, UNSW Social Policy Research Centre Reports and Proceedings No. 93, University of New South Wales, Sydney.

Stewart, D. (1991b), 'Resourcing community-based occupational health and safety services', *Journal of Occupational Health and Safety—Australia and New Zealand*, **7**(3): 215–19.

Stewart, D. and Doyle, J. (1988), *Workers' Compensation and Social Security Expenditure in Australia: Anti Social Aspects of the Social Wage?*, UNSW Social Welfare Research Centre Discussion Paper No. 7, University of New South Wales, Sydney.

Stichler, J.F. (2009) 'Healthy, healthful, and healing environments: a nursing imperative', *Critical Care Nursing Quarterly*, **32**(3): 176–88.

Storey, E., Thal, S., Johnson, C., Grey, M., Madray, H., Hodgson, M. and Pfeiffer, C. (2001), 'Reinforcing occupational history taking: a success story', *Teaching and Learning in Medicine*, **13**(3): 176–82.

Storey, K. and Shrimpton, M. (1991), 'Long-distance commuting: mining and hydrocarbon industry management issues', in *Long Distance Commuting in the Mining and Hydrocarbon Industries*, proceedings of a national conference of the Australian Mines and Metals Association, Australian Mines and Metals Association, Melbourne.

Straif, K., Baan, R., Grosse, Y., Secretan, B., El Ghissasi, F., Bouvard, V., Altieri, A., Benbrahim-Tallaa, L. and Cogliano, V. (2007), 'Carcinogenicity of shiftwork, painting, and fire-fighting', *Oncology*, **8**: 1065–6.

Strauss, G. (2006), 'Worker participation—some under-considered issues', *Industrial Relations*, **45**(4): 778–803.

Strazdins, L., D'Souza, R., Lim, L., Broom, D. and Rodgers, B. (2004), 'Job strain, job insecurity, and health: rethinking the relationship', *Journal of Occupational Health Psychology*, **9**(4): 296–305.

Stubbs, D. (2000), 'Ergonomics and occupational medicine: future challenges', *Occupational Medicine*, **50**(4): 277–82.

Stump, J. (2008), 'Drug testing common in the workplace', *Charleston Daily Mail*, 31 December.

Sudhakaran, S. and Mirka, G.A. (2005), 'A laboratory investigation of personality type and break-taking behavior', *International Journal of Industrial Ergonomics*, **35**(3): 237–46.

Sullivan, M., Adams, H., Tripp, D. and Stanish, W. (2008), 'Stage of chronicity and treatment response in patients with musculoskeletal injuries and concurrent symptoms of depression', *Pain*, **135**: 151–9.

Sulzer-Azaroff, B. and Austin, J. (2000), 'Does BBS work?', *Professional Safety*, **45**(7): 19–24.

Sundin, L., Hochwalder, J. and Bildt, C. (2008), 'A scale for measuring specific job demands within the healthcare sector: development and psychometric assessment', *International Journal of Nursing Studies*, **45**: 914–23.

Sundstrom-Frisk, C. (1984), 'Behavioural control through piece-rate wages', *Journal of Occupational Accidents*, **6**: 49–59.

Sung, T., Wang, J. and Chen, P. (2008), 'Increased risk of cancer in the offspring of female electronic workers', *Reproductive Toxicology*, **25**: 115–19.

Suruda, A. (1992), 'Work-related deaths in construction painting', *Sacndinavian Journal of Work Environment and Health*, **18**: 30–3.

Sutinen, R., Kivimaki, M., Elovainio, M. and Virtanen, M. (2002), 'Organizational fairness and psychological distress in hospital physicians', *Scandinavian Journal of Public Health*, **30**: 209–15.

Svenson, O. (2001), 'Accident and incident analysis based on the Accident Evolution and Barrier Function (AEB) model', *Cognition, Technology and Work*, **3**: 42–52.

Swuste, P. and Arnoldy, F. (2003), 'The safety adviser/manager as agent of organisational change: a new challenge to expert training', *Safety Science*, **41**(1): 15–27.

Sydney Morning Herald, various issues.

Taimela, S., Malmivaara, A., Justen, S., Laara, E., Sintonen, H., Tiekso, J. and Aro, T. (2008), 'The effectiveness of two occupational health intervention programmes in reducing sickness absence among employees at risk: two randomized control trials', *Occupational and Environmental Medicine*, **65**(4): 236–41.

Takahashi, M., Sawada, S-i. and Araki, S. (2008), 'Work organization and workers' safety and health', *Industrial Health*, **46**: 103–4.

Taksa, L. (2009), 'Intended or unintended consequences? A critical reappraisal of the Safety First Movement and its non-union safety committees', *Economic and Industrial Democracy*, **30**(1): 9–36.

Tappin, D., Moore, D., Bentley, T., Parker, R., Ashby, L., Vitalis, A., Riley, D. and Hide, S. (2007), *Industry Interventions for Addressing Musculoskeletal Disorders (Strains/Sprains) in New Zealand Meat Processing*, Centre for Human Factors and Ergonomics and Massey University, Palmerston North.

Tappin, D.C., Bentley, T.A. and Vitalis, A. (2008a), 'The role of contextual factors for musculoskeletal disorders in the New Zealand meat processing industry', *Ergonomics*, **51**(10): 1576–93.

Tappin, D.C., Bentley, T.A., Vitalis, A. and Macky, K. (2008b), 'An analysis of sprain and strain injury data for the New Zealand meat processing industry from national and industry injury surveillance databases', *Ergonomics*, **51**(11): 1721–34.

Taris, T.W., Peeters, M.C., Le Blanc, P., Schreurs, P. and Schaufeli, W. (2001), 'From inequity to burnout: the role of job stress', *Journal of Occupational Health Psychology*, **6**(4): 303–23.

Task Force Report (1985), *Repetition Strain Injury in the Australian Public Service*, Australian Government Publishing Service, Canberra.

Tasmanian Workplace Health and Safety Regulations, 1998.

Tasto, D., Colligan, M., Skjei, E. and Polly, S. (1978), *Health Consequences of Shift Work*, SRI Project URU-4426, US Department of Health, Education and Welfare, NIOSH, Washington.

Tavares, L. and Plotnikoff, R. (2008), 'Not enough time? Individual and environmental implications for workplace physical activity programming among women with and without young children', *Health Care for Women International*, **29**(3): 244–81.

Taylor, A., Angerer, J., Arnaud, J., Claeys, F., Kristiansen, J., Mazarrasa, O., Menditto, A., Patriarca, M., Pineau, A., Valkonen, S. and Weykamp, C. (2007), 'Differences in national legislation for the implementation of lead regulations included in the European directive for the protection of the health and safety of workers with occupational exposure to chemical agents (98/24/EC)', *International Archives of Occupational and Environmental Health*, **80**(3): 254–64.

Taylor, E., Folkard, S. and Shapiro, D.A. (1997), 'Shiftwork advantages as predictors of health', *International Journal of Occupational and Environmental Health*, **3**(3): S20–S29.

Taylor, F. (1947), 'The principles of scientific management', in Taylor, F. *Scientific Management*, Greenwood Press, Westport, Conn.

Taylor, P. and Pocock, S. (1972), 'Mortality of shift and day workers 1956–1968', *British Journal of Industrial Medicine*, **29**: 201–7.

Taylor, R. (1979), *Medicine Out of Control: The Anatomy of a Malignant Technology*, Sun Books, Melbourne.

Taylor, R. (2007), 'Duty to consult employees', *National Safety*, **78**(6): 34–5.

Taylor, W. (2005), 'Musculoskeletal pain in the adult New Zealand population: prevalence and impact', *Journal of the New Zealand Medical Association*, **118**(1221): 1–15.

Tepas, D. (1982), 'Adaptation of shiftwork: fact or fallacy', *Journal of Human Ergology*, **11**(Supp. 1): 1–12.

Terris, M. (2001), 'The changing relationships of epidemiology and society: the Robert Cruickshank Lecture', *Journal of Public Health Policy*, **22**(4): 441–63.

Thackrah, C. (1832), *The Effects of the Arts, Trades and Professions and of the Civic States and Habits of Living on Health and Longevity with Suggestions for the Removal of Many of the Agents which Produce Disease and Shorten the Duration of Life*, 2nd edition, Longman, Rees, Orme, Brown, Green & Longman, Leeds.

The Age, various issues.

Thebaud-Mony, A. (1999), 'Contracting and subcontracting by the French nuclear power industry', *International Journal of Occupational and Environmental Health*, **5**(4): 296–9.

Thebaud-Mony, A. and Equipe Scop 93, (2005), 'Occupational cancer in a Paris suburb: first results of a proactive research study in Seine Saint-Denis', *International Journal of Occupational and Environmental Health*, **11**(3): 263–75.

Theberge, N., Granzow, K., Cole, D. and Laing, A. (2006), 'Negotiating participation: understanding the "how" in an ergonomic change team', *Applied Ergonomics*, **37**(2): 239–48.

Thelin, A. (1998), 'Working environment conditions in rural areas according to psychosocial indices', *Annals of Agricultural and Environmental Medicine*, **5**, 139–45.

Theorell, T., Hamsten, A., de Faire, U., Orth-Gormer, K. and Perski, A. (1987), 'Psychosocial work conditions before myocardial infarction in young men', *International Journal of Cardiology*, **15**(1): 33–46.

Thierry, H. (1981), 'Compensation for shiftwork: a model and some results', in Johnson, L., Colquhoun, W., Tepas, D. and Colligan, M. (eds) *Biological Rhythms, Sleep and Shift Work*, MTP Press, New York.

Thierry, H. and Jansen, B. (1982), 'Social support for night and shift workers', *Journal of Human Ergology*, **11**(Supp. 1): 483–98.

Thomas, J., Lavender, S., Corcos, D. and Andersson, G. (1999), 'Effect of lifting belts on trunk muscle activation during a sudden applied load', *Human Factors*, **41**(4): 670–6.

Thomas, M. (2001), 'Pesticide usage monitoring in the United Kingdom', *Annals of Occupational Hygiene*, **45**(1001): S87–S93.

Thomas, N. (1988), 'The ergonomics of protection', in Nicholson, A. and Ridd, J. (eds) *Health, Safety and Ergonomics*, Butterworths, London.

Thomas, P. (1990), 'Safety in smaller manufacturing establishments', *Employment Gazette*, January: 20–5.

Thompson, N., Stradling, S., Murphy, M. and O'Neil, P. (1996), 'Stress and organizational culture', *British Journal of Social Work*, **26**: 647–65.

Thompson, A. (2007), 'The consequences of underreporting workers' compensation claims', *Canadian Medical Association Journal*, **176**(3): 343–4.

Thomson, J.A. (2006), 'Issues in safety education interventions', *Injury Prevention*, **12**(3): 138–9.

Thomson Occupational Health News, various issues.

Thun, M.J., Tanaka, S., Smith, A.B., Halperin, W.E., Lee, S.T., Luggen, M.E. and Hess, E.V. (1987), 'Morbidity from repetitive knee trauma in carpet and floorlayers', *British Journal of Industrial Medicine*, **44**: 611–20.

Thylefors, I. (2009), 'Psychosocial work environment', in Bohgard, L. et al. (eds) *Work and Technology on Human Terms*, Prevent, Stockholm: 21–69.

Tilley, A., Wilkinson, R., Warren, P., Watson, B. and Drud, M. (1982), 'The sleep and performance of shift workers', *Human Factors*, **24**: 629–41.

Timmermans, S. and Haas, S. (2008), 'Towards a sociology of disease', *Sociology of Health & Illness*, **30**(5): 659–76.

Tinghög, P., Hemmingsson, T. and Lundberg, I. (2007), 'To what extent may the association between immigrant status and mental illness be explained by socioeconomic factors?', *Social Psychiatry and Psychiatric Epidemiology*, **42**(12): 990–6.

Tischer, M., Bredendiek-Kamper, S., Poppek, U. and Packroff, R. (2009), 'How safe is control banding? Integrated evaluation by comparing OELs with measurement data and using Monte Carlo simulation', *Annals of Occupational Hygiene*, **53**(5): 449–62.

Toh, S. and Quinlan, M. (2009), 'Protecting a new class of guestworker: the occupational health and safety rights and entitlements of s457 visa holders in Australia', *International Journal of Manpower*, 30(5): 453–71.

Tomicic, C. and Droz, P-O. (2008), 'Age differences in biological monitoring of chemical exposure: a tentative description using a toxicokinetic model', *International Archives of Occupational and Environmental Health*, 21 October 2008: 1–8.

Tomlins, C. (1988), 'A mysterious power: industrial accidents and the legal construction of employment relations in Massachusetts, 1800–1850', *Law and History Review*, **6**: 375–438.

Tompa, E., de Oliveira, C., Dolinschi, R. and Irvin, E. (2006), 'A systematic review of disability management interventions with economic evaluations', *Journal of Occupational Rehabilitation*, **18**: 16–26.

Toohey, J., Borthwick, K. and Archer, R. (2005), *OHS in Australia*, Thomson, Melbourne.

Topping, M. (2001), 'Occupational exposure limits for chemicals', *Occupational and Environmental Medicine*, **58**(2): 138–44.

Torp, S. (2008), 'How a health and safety management training program may improve the working environment in small and medium-sized companies', *Journal of Occupational and Environmental Medicine*, **50**(3): 263–71.

Torp, S. and Grøgaard, J.B. (2008), 'The influence of individual and contextual work factors on workers' compliance with health and safety routines', *Applied Ergonomics*, **40**: 185–93.

Torp, S. and Moen, B. (2006), 'The effects of occupational health and safety management on work environment and health: a prospective study', *Applied Ergonomics*, **37**: 775–83.

Torsvall, L. and Akerstedt, T. (1980), 'A diurnal type scale: construction, consistency, and validation in shift work', *Scandinavian Journal of Work, Environment and Health*, **6**: 283–90.

Townsend, K. (2008), 'Do production employees engage in emotional labour?', *Journal of Industrial Relations*, **50**(1): 175–80.

Trägårdh, B. (2008), *The Role of Health and Safety Representatives in Sweden: The Implementation of EEC Directive 89/391*, Working paper in Studies of Organization and Society, School of Business, Economics and Law, University of Gothenburg, Göteborg.

Transport Industry—Mutual Responsibility for Road Safety (State) Award and Contract Determination (No. 2), Re [2006] NSWIRComm 328.

Tranter, M. (1998), 'An assessment of heat stress among laundry workers in Far North Queensland', *Journal of Occupational Health and Safety—Australia and New Zealand*, **14**(1): 61–3.

Triezenberg, H.L. (1996), 'The identification of ethical issues in physical therapy', *Career and Technical Education*, **76**(10): 1097–107.

Trinkoff, A., Le, R., Geiger-Brown, J., Lipscomb, J. and Lang, G. (2006), 'Longitudinal relationship of work hours, mandatory overtime, and on-call to musculoskeletal problems in nurses', *American Journal of Industrial Medicine*, **49**: 964–71.

Trist, E. (1981), 'The socio-technical perspective: the evolution of the socio-technical systems as a conceptual framework and as an action research program', in Van de Ven, A. and Joyce, W. (eds) *Perspectives on Organisational Design and Behaviour*, Wiley, New York.

Tuchsen, F., Hannerz, H. and Burr, H. (2006), 'A 12 year prospective study of circulatory disease amongst Danish shift workers', *Occupational and Environmental Medicine*, **63**(7): 451–5.

Tuchsen, F., Jeppesen, H.J. and Bach, E. (1994), 'Employment status, non-daytime work and gastric ulcer in men', *International Journal of Epidemiology*, **23**(2): 365–70.

Tucker, D. (2002), *'Precarious' Non-Standard Employment—A Review of the Literature*, Wellington, Labour Market Policy Group.

Tucker, E. (1990), *Administering Danger in the Workplace: The Law and Politics of Occupational Health and Safety Regulation in Ontario 1850–1914*, University of Toronto Press, Toronto.

Tucker, E. (1992), 'Worker participation in health and safety regulation: lessons from Sweden', *Studies in Political Economy*, **37**: 95–127.

Tucker, E. (ed.) (2006), *Working Disasters: The Politics of Recognition and Response*, Baywood, New York.

Turner, B. (1978), *Man Made Disasters*, Wykeham, London.

Turner, J. (2006), 'All in a day's work? Statutory and other failures of the workers' compensation scheme as applied to street corner day laborers', *Fordham Law Review*, **74**: 1521–56.

Turtle, A.M. and Orr, M. (1988), *The Psyching of Oz*, The Australian Psychological Society, Melbourne.

Tuskes, P. and Key, M. (1988), 'Potential hazards in small business: a gap in OSHA protection', *Applied Industrial Hygiene Journal*, **3**(2): 55–7.

Tveldt, S., Saksvik, P. and Nytro, K. (2009), 'Does change process healthiness reduce the negative effects of organizational change on the psychosocial work environment?', *Work & Stress*, **23**(1): 80–98.

Tweedale, G. (2007), 'The Rochdale asbestos cancer studies and the politics of epidemiology', *International Journal of Occupational and Environmental Health*, **13**(1): 70–9.

Tyrer, F. and Lee, K. (1979), *A Synopsis of Occupational Medicine*, John Wright and Sons, Bristol.

Underhill, E. (2008), *Double Jeopardy: Occupational Injury and Rehabilitation of Temporary Agency Workers*, unpublished PhD thesis, University of New South Wales.

United States Chemical Safety and Hazard Investigation Board (2007a), 'US Chemical Safety Board concludes "organizational and safety deficiencies at all levels of the BP Corporation" caused March 2005 Texas City disaster that killed 15, injured 180', *CSB News Release*.

United States Chemical Safety Board (2007b), 'CSB Chairwoman Carolyn Merritt tells House Subcommittee of "striking similarities" in causes of BP Texas City tragedy and Prudhoe Bay pipeline disaster', *CSB News Release*.

United States Government Accountability Office (2007), *Employee Misclassification: Improved Outreach Could Help Ensure Proper Worker Classification*, Washington.

United Steelworkers (2007), *Beyond Texas City: The State of Process Safety in the Unionised US Oil Refining Industry*, United Steelworkers Union, Washington.

US National Institute for Occupational Safety and Health (2002), 'The changing organization of work and the safety and health of working people: knowledge gaps and research directions', NIOSH, Cincinnati.

Uttal, B. (1983), 'The corporate culture vultures', *Fortune Magazine*, 17 October.

Vahtera, J., Kivimaki, M., Forma, P., Wikstrom, J., Halmeenaki, T., Linna, A. and Pentti, J. (2005), 'Organisational downsizing as a predictor of disability pension: the 10-town prospective cohort study', *Journal of Epidemiology and Community Health*, **59**: 238–42.

Vahtera, J., Kivimaki, M. and Pentti, J. (1998), 'Effects of organisational downsizing on health of employees', *The Lancet*, **350**: 1124–8.

Vakas, N. (2007), *Interests and the Shaping of an Occupational Health and Safety Controversy: The BAe 146 Case*, unpublished PhD thesis, School of Social Sciences, University of Wollongong.

van den Berg, M., Birnbaum, L.S., Denison, M., De Vito, M., Farland, W., Feeley, M., Heidelore, F., Hakansson, H., Hanberg, A., Haws, L., Rose, M., Safe, S., Schrenk, D., Tohyama, C., Tritscher, A., Tuomisto, J., Tysklind, M., Walker, N. and Peterson, R. (2006), 'The 2005 World Health Organization reevaluation of human and mammalian toxic equivalency factors for dioxins and dioxin-like compounds', *Toxicological Sciences*, **93**(2): 223–41.

Vandenplas, O., Toren, K. and Blanc, P. (2003), 'Health and socioeconomic impact of work-related asthma', *European Respiratory Journal*, **22**: 689–97.

Van Duijin, M., Lotters, F. and Burdoff, A. (2004), 'Interrelationships between pain, disability, general health, and quality of life and associations with work-related and individual factors', *Spine*, **29**(19): 2178–83.

Van Hooff, M., Geurts, S., Taris, T., Kompier, M., Dikkers, J., Houtman, I. and van den Heuvel, F. (2005), 'Disentangling the causal relationships between work-home interference and employee health', *Scandinavian Journal of Work Environment and Health*, **31**(1): 15–29.

Van Wanrooy, B., Oxenbridge, S., Buchanan, J. and Jakubauskas, M. (2007), *Australia at Work: The Benchmark Report*, Workplace Research Centre, University of Sydney.

Vectra Group (2003), *Literature Review on the Perceived Benefits and Disadvantages of UK Safety Case Regimes*, Health and Safety Executive, London.

Vergara, A. (2005), 'The recognition of silicosis: labor unions and physicians in the Chilean copper industry, 1930s–1960s', *Bulletin of the History of Medicine*, **79**(4): 723–48.

Verger, P., Viau, A., Arnaud, S., Cabut, S., Saliba, M., Iarmarcoval, G. and Souville, M. (2008), 'Barriers to physician reporting of workers' compensation cases in France', *International Journal of Occupational and Environmental Health*, **14**(3): 198–205.

Verhaegen, P., Cober, R., De Smedt, M., Dirkx, K., Kerstens, J., Ryvers, D. and Van Daele, P. (1987), 'The adaptation of night nurses to different work schedules', *Ergonomics*, **30**(9): 1301–9.

Verhaegen, P., Dirkx, K., Maasen, A. and Meers, A. (1986), 'Subjective health after twelve years of shift work', in Haider, M., Koller, M. and Cervinka, R. (eds) *Night and Shift Work: Longterm Effects and their Prevention*, Verlag Peter Lang, Frankfurt Am Main.

Verhaegen, P., Maasen, A. and Meers, A. (1981), 'Health problems of shiftworkers', in Johnson, L., Colquhoun, W., Tepas, D. and Colligan, M. (eds) *Biological Rhythms, Sleep and ShiftWork*, MTP Press, New York.

Verhaeghe, R., Vlerick, P., De Backer, G., Van Maele, G. and Gemmel, P. (2008), 'Recurrent changes in the work environment, job resources and distress among nurses: a comparative cross-sectional survey', *International Journal of Nursing Studies*, **45**: 382–92.

Verhagen, A., Karels, C., Bierma-Zeinstra, S., Burdoff, L., Feleus, A., Dahaghin, S., De Vet, H. and Koes, B. (2006), 'Ergonomic and physiotherapeutic interventions for treating work-related complaints of the arm, neck or shoulder in adults', *Cochrane Database of Systematic Reviews*, **3**: CD003471.

Vidacek, S., Kalitena, L. and Radosevic-Vidacek, B. (1987), 'Predictive validity of individual difference measures for health problems in shiftworkers: preliminary results', in Oginski, A., Pokorski, J. and Rutenfranz, J. (eds) *Contemporary Advances in Shiftwork Research*, Nicholaus Copernicus Medical Academy, Krakow.

Vidacek, S., Radosevic-Vidacek, B., Kaliterna, L. and Prizmic, Z. (1993), 'Individual differences in circadian rhythm parameters and short-term tolerance to shiftwork: a follow up study', *Ergonomics*, **36**(1–3): 117–24.

Vincent, J. (1998), 'International occupational exposure standards: a review and commentary', *American Industrial Hygiene Association Journal*, **59**(10): 729–42.

Virtanen, M., Kivimaki, M., Joensuu, M., Virtanen, P., Elovainio, M. and Vahtera, J. (2005), 'Temporary employment and health: a review', *International Journal of Epidemiology*, **34**: 610–22.

Viscusi, W.K. (2004), 'The value of life: estimates with risks by occupation and industry', *Economic Inquiry*, **42**(1): 29–48.

Von Ebers, D. (1986), 'The application of criminal homicide statutes to work-related deaths: mens rea and deterrence', *University of Illinois Law Review*, **3**: 969–99.

Wadsworth, E. and Smith, A. (2009), 'Safety culture, advice and performance', *Policy and Practice in Health and Safety*, **7**(1): 5–32.

Waehrer, G.M., Dong, X.S., Miller, T., Haile, E. and Men, Y. (2007), 'Costs of occupational injuries in construction in the United States', *Accident Analysis and Prevention*, **39**(6): 1258–66.

Waehrer, G., Dong, X., Miller, T., Men, Y. and Haile, E. (2007), 'Occupational injury costs and alternative employment in construction trades', *Journal of Occupational and Environmental Medicine*, **49**(11): 1218–27.

Wagenaar, W.A., Groeneweg, J., Hudson, P.W. and Reason, J.T. (1994), 'Promoting safety in the oil industry', *Ergonomics*, (37): 1999–2013.

Wagenaar, W. and van der Schrier, J. (1997), 'Accident analysis: the goal, and how to get there', *Safety Science*, **26**(1): 25–33.

Waldron, H. (1990), *Lecture Notes on Occupational Medicine*, 4th edition, Blackwell Scientific, Oxford.

Walker, J. (1985), 'Social problems of shiftwork', in Folkard, S. and Monk, T. (eds) *Hours of Work: Temporal Factors in Work Scheduling*, John Wiley, Chichester, UK.

Wall, T. and Martin, R. (1987), 'Job and work design', in Cooper, C. and Robertson, I. (eds) *International Review of Industrial and Organisational Psychology 1987*, John Wiley and Sons, Chichester: 61–91.

Walsh, J.K, Randazzo, A.C., Stone, K.L. and Schweitzer, P.K. (2004), 'Modafinil improves alertness, vigilance, and executive function during simulated nights', *Sleep*, **27**(3): 434–9.

Walsh, L. (2000), 'Safety issues relating to the use of hydrogen peroxide in dentistry', *Australian Dental Journal*, **45**(4): 257–69.

Walter, N., Bourgois, P. and Loinaz, H.M. (2004), 'Masculinity and undocumented labor migration: injured Latino day laborers in San Francisco', *Social Science & Medicine*, **59**: 1159–68.

Walters, D. (1996), 'Trade unions and the effectiveness of worker representation in health and safety in Britain', *International Journal of Health Services*, **26**(4): 625–41.

Walters, D.R. (1997), *The Role of Regional Health and Safety Representatives in Agriculture: An Evaluation of a Trade Union Initiative on Roving Safety Representatives in Agriculture*, Health and Safety Executive Contract Research Reports, No 157/97. ISBN 7176 1475 1.

Walters, D. (2001a), *Health and Safety in Small Enterprises: European Strategies for Managing Improvement*, PIE-Peter Lang, Brussels.

Walters, D. (2001b), *Prescription to Process: Convergence and Divergence in Health and Safety Regulation in Europe*, National Research Centre for OHS Regulation, Seminar Paper 1, <ohs.anu.edu.au>

Walters, D. (2002a) *Regulating Health and Safety Management in the European Union*, Peter Lang, Brussels.

Walters, D. (2002b), *Working Safety in Small Enterprises in Europe*, ETUC, Brussels.

Walters, D. (2004), 'Worker representation and health and safety in small enterprises in Europe', *Industrial Relations Journal*, **35**(2): 169–86.

Walters, D. (2006), 'One step forward, two steps back: worker representation and health and safety in the United Kingdom', *International Journal of Health Services*, **36**(1): 87–111.

Walters, D. (2007), *An International Comparison of Occupational Disease and Injury Compensation Schemes*, report to Industrial Injuries Advisory Council, UK.

Walters, D. and Frick, K. (2000) 'Worker participation and the management of OHS', in Frick, K., Jensen, P., Quinlan, M. and Wilthagen, T. (eds) *Systematic Occupational Health and Safety Management: Perspectives on an International Development*, Pergamon, Amsterdam: 43–65.

Walters, D., Kirby, P. and Daly, F. (2001), *The Impact of Trade Union Education and Training in Health and Safety on the Workplace Activity of Health and Safety Representatives*, Contract Research Report 321/2001 prepared for the Health and Safety Executive, HMSO, Norwich.

Walters, D. and Nichols, T. (2007), *Worker Representation and Workplace Health and Safety*, Palgrave Macmillan, Basingstoke.

Walters, D., Nichols, T., Connor, J., Tasiran, A. and Cam, S. (2005), *The Role and Effectiveness of Safety Representatives in Influencing Workplace Health and Safety*, Research Report 363 to the Health and Safety Executive, HMSO, Norwich.

Walters, V. (1982), 'Company doctor's perceptions of and responses to conflicting pressures from labor and management', *Social Problems*, **30**(1): 1–25.

Walters, V., Beardwood, B., Eyles, J. and French, S. (1995b), 'Paid and unpaid work roles of male and female nurses', in Messing, K., Neis, B. and Dumais, L. (eds) *Invisible: Issues in Women's' Occupational Health*, Gynergy Books, Charlottetown.

Walters, V., Lewchuk, W., Richardson, R., Moran, L., Haines, E. and Verman, D. (1995a), 'Judgements of legitimacy regarding occupational health and safety', in Pearce, F. and Snider, L. (eds) *Corporate Crime*, University of Toronto Press, Toronto.

Wang, J. (2002), 'Offshore safety case approach and formal safety assessment of ships', *Journal of Safety Research*, **33**: 81–115.

Waring, A. (1996), *Safety Management Systems*, Chapman and Hall, London.

Warren-Langford, P., Biggins, D. and Phillips, M. (1993), 'Union participation in occupational health and safety in Western Australia', *Journal of Industrial Relations*, **35**(4): 585–606.

Watterson, A. (1993), 'Chemical hazards and public confidence', *The Lancet*, **342**: 131–2. WCB of BC (1997), *Determining Who is a Worker under the Workers' Compensation Act: A Briefing Paper*, Workers' Compensation Board of British Columbia.

Wearne, S. (2008), 'Organisational lessons from failures', *Proceedings of the Institution of Civil Engineers—Civil Engineering*, **161**: 4–7.

Webb, S. and Webb, B. (1914), *Industrial Democracy*, Longman, Green & Co., New York.

Wedderburn, A. (1987), 'Unintentional falling asleep at work: what can you do about it?', in Oginski, A., Pokorski, J. and Rutenfranz, J. (eds) *Contemporary Advances in Shiftwork Research: Theoretical and Practical Aspects in the Late Eighties*, Nicholaus Copernicus Medical Academy, Krakow.

Wegman, D. and McGee, P. (eds) (2004), *Health and Safety Needs of Older Workers*, National Academic Press, Washington DC.

Wegmann, H. and Klein, K. (1985), 'Jet lag and air crew scheduling', in Folkard, S. and Monk, T. (eds) *Hours of Work: Temporal Factors in Work Scheduling*, John Wiley, Chichester, UK.

Weil, D. (1991), 'Enforcing OSHA: the role of labor unions', *Industrial Relations*, **30**(1): 20–36.

Weil, D. (1992), 'Building safety: the role of construction unions in the enforcement of OSHA', *Journal of Labor Research*, **13**(1): 121–32.

Weil, D. (1999), 'Are mandated health and safety committees substitutes for or supplements to labor unions?', *Industrial & Labor Relations Review*, **52**(3): 339–60.

Weil, D. (2001), 'Valuing the economic consequences of work injury and illness: a comparison of methods and findings', *American Journal of Industrial Medicine*, **40**(4): 418–37.

Weil, D. and Mallo, C. (2007), 'Regulating labour standards via supply chains combining public/ private interventions to improve workplace compliance', *British Journal of Industrial Relations*, **45**(4): 791–814.

Weindling, P. (ed.) (1985), *The Social History of Occupational Health*, Croom Helm, London.

Weisbrod, R., Pirie, P., Bracht, N. and Elstun, P. (1991), 'Worksite health promotion in four midwest cities', *Journal of Community Health*, **16**(3): 169–77.

Weiss, R. (2004), 'Change at CDC draws protest', *The Washington Post*, 31 August, A19.

Welch, L., Dong, L., Carre, F. and Ringen, K. (2007), 'Is the apparent decrease in injury and illness rates in construction the result of changes in reporting?', *International Journal of Occupational and Environmental Health*, **13**(1): 39–45.

Wesseling, C. (1997), *Health Effects from Pesticide Use in Costa Rica—An Epidemiological Approach*, Carolinska Medical Institute, Stockholm.

Westgaard, R.H. and Winkel, J. (1997), 'Ergonomic intervention research for improved musculo-skeletal health: a critical review', *International Journal of Industrial Ergonomics*, **20**: 463–500.

Westmorland, M. and Buys, N. (2002), 'Disability management in a sample of Australian self-insured companies', *Disability and Rehabilitation*, **24**(14): 746–54.

Westmorland, M. and Williams, R. (2002), 'Employers and policy makers can make a difference to the employment of persons with disabilities', *Disability and Rehabilitation*, **24**(15): 802–9.

Westmorland, M., Williams, R., Shannon, H., Rasheed, F. and Amick, B. (2005), 'Disability management practices in Ontario workplaces: employees' perceptions', *Disability and Rehabilitation*, **27**(14): 825–35.

Wever, R. (1979), '*The Circadian System of Man: Results of Experiments under Temporal Isolation*, Springer Verlag, Frankfurt Am Main.

Wever, R. (1985), 'Man in temporal isolation: basic principles of the circadian system', in Folkard, S. and Monk, T. (eds) *Hours of Work: Temporal Factors in Work Scheduling*, John Wiley, New York.

Whitaker, S. and Baranski, B. (2001), *World Health Organization Report: The Role of the Occupational Health Nurse in Workplace Health Management*, WHO Regional Office for Europe, Copenhagen.

White, K. (1993), 'Managerial style and health promotion programs', *Social Science in Medicine*, **36**(3): 227–35.

White v Illawarra Area Health Service (1996), NSW Chief Industrial Magistrate's Court, Reasons for Decision, 19 September.

Whorton, D. and Davis, M. (1978), 'Ethical conduct and the occupational physician', *Bull NY Academy of Medicine*, **54**(8): 733–41.

Wickens, C. and Kramer, A. (1985), 'Engineering psychology', *Annual Review of Psychology*, **36**: 307–48.

Wickizer, T.M., Kopjar, B., Franklin, G. and Joesch, J. (2004), 'Do drug-free workplace programs prevent occupational injuries? Evidence from Washington State', *Health Services Research*, **39**(1): 91–110.

Wickramasekera, P. (2002), 'Asian labour migration: issues and challenges in an era of globalisation', *International Migration Papers*, **57**.

Wieclaw, J., Agerbo, E., Mortensen, P., Burr, H., Tuchsen, F. and Bonde, J. (2008), 'Psychosocial working conditions and the risk of depression and anxiety disorders in the Danish workforce', *BMC Public Health*, **8**: 280 doi:10.1186/1471-2458-8-280.

Wiegand, D. and Geller, E. (2004), 'Connecting positive psychology and organizational behaviour management: achievement motivation and the power of positive reinforcement', *Journal of Organisational Behaviour Management*, **24**(1 & 2): 3–25.

Wigley, R.D., Turner, W.E.D., Blake, B.L., Darby, F.W., McInnes, R. and Harding, P. (1992), *Occupational Overuse Syndrome: Treatment and Rehabilitation—A Practitioner's Guide*, Occupational Safety and Health Service, Department of Labour, Wellington.

Wilkinson, B. (2003), 'The Accident Compensation Scheme: a case study in public policy failure', *Victoria University of Wellington Law Review*, **34**(2): 313–28.

Wilkinson, C. (2008), 'Policy, progress and occupational health', *International Nursing Review*, **55**(3): 305–8.

William, B., Bass, J., Moser, R., Anstadt, G.W., Loeppke, R.R. and Leopold, R. (1997) 'Defining total corporate health and safety costs—significance and impact: review and recommendations', *Journal of Environmental Medicine*, 39(3): 224–31.

Williams, C. (1997), 'Women and occupational health and safety: from narratives of danger to invisibility', *Labour History*, **73**: 30–52.

Williams, C. (2003), 'Sky service: the demands of emotional labour in the airline industry', *Gender, Work and Organisation*, **10**(5): 513–50.

Williams, C. and Quinlan, M. (1988), 'Social science research in occupational health', *Labour and Industry*, **1**(3): 588–94.

Williams, D. (2003), 'The health of men: structured inequalities and opportunities', *American Journal of Public Health*, **93**: 724–31.

Williams, J.M. (1996), 'Stress, coping resources, and injury risk', *International Journal of Stress Management*, **3**(4): 209–21.

Williams, J. and Geller, E. (2000), 'Behaviour-based intervention for occupational safety: critical impact of social comparison feedback', *Journal of Safety Research*, **31**(3): 135–42.

Willliams, P. (1991), 'Planning factors contributing to on-going health promotion programs', *Journal of Occupational Health and Safety—Australia and New Zealand*, **7**(6): 489–94.

Williams, R., Westmorland, M., Shannon, H. and Amick, B. (2007), 'Disability management practices in Ontario health care workplaces', *Journal of Occupational Rehabilitation*, **17**: 153–65.

Williamson, A. (2007), 'Predictors of psychostimulant use by long distance truck drivers', *American Journal of Epidemiology*, **166**(11): 1320–6.

Williamson, A., Friswell, R. and Feyer, A. (2004), *Fatigue and Performance in Heavy Truck Drivers Working Day Shift, Night Shift or Rotating Shifts*, research report, National Transport Commission, Melbourne.

Williamson, A. and Sanderson, J. (1986), 'Changing the speed of shift rotation: a field study', *Ergonomics*, **29**(9): 1085–96.

Willis, E. (1986), 'Commentary: RSI as a social process', *Community Health Studies*, **10**(2): 210–19.

Willis, E. (1989), 'The industrial relations of occupational health and safety: a labour process approach', *Labour and Industry*, **2**(2): 317–33.

Willis, T., O'Connor, D. and Smith, L. (2008), 'Investigating effort–reward imbalance and work–family conflict in relation to morningness–eveningness and shift work', *Work & Stress*, **22**(2): 125–37.

Wilpert, B. (2008), 'Impact of globalization on human work', *Safety Science*, article in press.

Wilsons and Clyde Coal Co v English, 1938 cited in Brooks, 1993: 21.

Wilson, J., Haines, H. and Morris, W. (2005), 'Participatory ergonomics', in Wilson, J. and Corlett, N. *Evaluation of Human Work*, 3rd edition, Chapter 36, Taylor and Francis, Cornwall.

Wilson, S. (1982), 'Occupational disease—the problems of a comprehensive system of coverage', *Industrial Law Journal*, **11**: 141–55.

Wilson, W.M., QC (2000), *Ministerial Inquiry into Tranz Rail Occupational Safety and Health*, report to the Minsters of Labour and Transport, Wellington.

Windau, J. and Meyer, S. (2005), 'Occupational injuries among young workers', *Monthly Labor Review*, October: 11–23.

Winder, C. (1991), 'Trends in occupational cancer in Australia, 1979–1989', *Journal of Occupational Health and Safety—Australia and New Zealand*, **7**(5): 355–63.

Winder, C. (1993), 'Reproduction, development and occupational health', in Stacey, N. (ed.) *Occupational Toxicology*, Taylor and Francis, Basingstoke: 107–21.

Windle, M., Neis, B., Bornstein, S., Binkley, M. and Navarro, P. (2008), 'Fishing occupational health and safety: a comparison of regulatory regimes and safety outcomes in six countries', *Marine Policy*, **32**: 701–10.

Winefield, A., Gillespie, N., Stough, C., Dua, J., Hapuarachchi, J. and Boyd, C. (2003), 'Occupational stress in Australian university staff: results from a national survey', *International Journal of Stress Management*, **10**(1): 51–63.

Winefield, A. and Jarrett, R. (2001), 'Occupational stress in university staff', *International Journal of Stress Management*, **8**(4): 285–98.

Winget, C., Hughes, L. and LaDou, J. (1978), 'Physiological effects of rotational shiftworking: a review', *Journal of Occupational Medicine*, **20**: 204–10.

Winkleby, M., Ragland, D., Fisher, J. and Syme, L. (1988), 'Excess risk of sickness and disease in bus drivers: a review and synthesis of epidemiological studies', *International Journal of Epidemiology*, **17**(2): 255–62.

Wirth, O. and Sigurdsson, S.O. (2008), 'When workplace safety depends on behavior change: topics for behavioral safety research', *Journal of Safety Research*, **39**(6): 589–98.

Witt, J. (1998), 'The transformation of work and the law of workplace accidents, 1842–1910', *The Yale Law Journal*, **107**(5): 1467–502.

Wojcik, S., Kidd, P., Parshall, M. and Struttmann, T. (2003), 'Performance and evaluation of small construction safety training simulations', *Occupational Medicine (London)* **53**(4): 279–86.

Won, J., Ahn, Y., Song, J., Koh, D. and Roh, J. (2007), 'Occupational injuries in Korea: a comparison of blue-collar and white-collar workers' rates and underreporting', *Journal of Occupational Health*, **49**: 53–60.

Wong, S. and Leung, G. (2008), 'Injury Severity Score (ISS) vs. ICD-derived Injury Severity Score (ICISS) in a patient population treated in a designated Hong Kong trauma centre', *McGill Journal of Medicine*, **11**(1): 9–13.

Wood, G., Morrison, D., Harrison, J. and MacDonald, S. (1995), 'The determination of common law awards to injured workers', *The Australian Economic Review*, 4th Quarter.

Woodhouse, Sir Owen (1967) *Compensation for Personal Injury in New Zealand: Report of the Royal Commission of Inquiry*, Parliament, Wellington.

Woods, A., Collier, J., Kendrick, D., Watts, K., Dewey, M. and Illingworth, R. (2004), 'Injury prevention training: a cluster randomised controlled trial assessing its effect on the knowledge, attitudes, and practices of midwives and health visitors', *Injury Prevention*, **10**(2): 83–7.

Woods, D.D. and Hollnagel, E. (2006), 'Prologue: resilience engineering concepts', in Hollnagel, E., Woods, D.D. and Leveson, N.G. (eds). *Resilience Engineering: Concepts and Precepts*, Ashgate Publishing Ltd., Aldershot: 1–6.

Woolfson, C. (1995), *Deregulation: The Politics of Health and Safety*, Computer Publishing Unit of the University of Glasgow, Glasgow.

Woolfson, C. and Calite, D. (2007), 'New European community strategy for health and safety: the elephant in the room', *International Journal of Occupational and Environmental Health*, **13**(3): 342–55.

Woolfson, C. and Calite, D. (2008), 'Working environment in the new EU member state of Lithuania: examining a worst case example', *Policy and Practice in Health and Safety*, **6**(1): 3–30.

Woolfson, C., Foster, J. and Beck, M. (1996), *Paying for the Piper: Capital and Labour in Britain's Offshore Oil Industry*, Mansell, London.

Woolfson, C. and Likic-Brboric, B. (2008), 'Migrants and the unequal burdening of "toxic" risk: towards a new global governance regime', *Journal of Contemporary Central and Eastern Europe*, **16**(3): 291–308.

WorkCover (Inspector Stewart) v the Crown in the Right of the State of NSW Department of Education and Training, Department of Juvenile Justice and TAFE [2002] NSWIRC 259, 3466 of 2001.

Workers' Comp Insider, various issues.

Workplace Industrial Relations Survey (1980–), <www.statistics.gov.uk/STATBASE/Source. asp?vlnk=1328>

Workplace Relations Ministers' Council (2008a), *Comparative Performance Monitoring Report: Comparison of Occupational Health and Safety and Workers' Compensation Schemes in Australia and New Zealand*, 9th edition, Office of Australian Safety and Compensation Council, Canberra.

Workplace Relations Ministers' Council (2008b), *Comparative Performance Monitoring Report: Comparison of Occupational Health and Safety and Workers' Compensation Schemes in Australia and New Zealand*, 10th edition, Office of Australian Safety and Compensation Council, Canberra.

Worksafe Research Update, (1996), 'Health effects from dusts of biological origin (including microbiological agents) in Australian workers—timber industry', Issue No. 96006.

Wran, N. and McClelland, J. (2005), *NSW Mine Safety Review: Report to The Hon Kerry Hickey MP*, Minister for Mineral Resources, Sydney.

Wren, J. (1997a), 'Understanding the process of change in occupational safety and health policy in advanced industrialised countries: an examination of the international literature, and the experience of New Zealand between 1981 and 1992', unpublished PhD thesis, Massey University, Palmerston North.

Wren, J. (1997b), 'Characterising the transformation of New Zealand's OSH legislation and administration from 1981 to 1992: the "Balkanisation of control" to employer management systems', *Journal of Occupational Health and Safety—Australia and New Zealand*, **13**(3): 221–7.

Wren, J. (2002), 'From the "Balkanisation of Control" to employer management systems: OHS policy and politics in New Zealand 1981–1992', in Lloyd, M. (ed.) *Occupational Health and Safety in New Zealand: Contemporary Social Research*, Dunmore Press, Palmerston North.

Wren, J. (2008), 'A contested workplace: situating New Zealand's OHSM regulatory practice within the literature—an introduction to the policy history and regulatory debates', *New Zealand Journal of Employment Relations*, **33**(3): 45–69.

Wright, C. and Lund, J. (1996), 'Best practice Taylorism: "Yankee speed-up" in Australian grocery distribution', *Journal of Industrial Relations*, **38**(2): 196–212.

Wright, C. and Lund, J. (1998), 'Under the clock: trade union responses to computerised control in US and Australian grocery warehousing', *New Technology, Work and Employment*, **13**(1): 3–15.

Wyatt, A. (1987), 'Occupational health and safety committees—three case studies', *Journal of Occupational Health and Safety—Australia and New Zealand*, **3**(3): 216–33.

Wyatt, A. and Sinclair, K. (1998), 'Getting your occupational health and safety committee to work!', *Journal of Occupational Health and Safety—Australia and New Zealand*, **14**(1): 91–6.

Xu, X., Ding, M., Li, B. and Christiani, D. (1994), 'Association of rotating shiftwork with preterm births and low birth weight among never smoking women textile workers in China', *Occupational and Environmental Medicine*, **51**: 470–4.

Yassi, A. (1997), 'Repetitive strain injuries', *The Lancet*, **349**: 943–7.

Yeh, W., Cheng, Y. and Chen, C. (2009), 'Social patterns of pay systems and their associations with psychosocial characteristics and burnout among paid employees in Taiwan', *Social Science & Medicine*, **68**: 1407–15.

Yong, L., Sigudson, J., Ward, E., Waters, M., Whelan, E., Petersen, M., Bhatti, P., Ramsey, M., Ron, E. and Tucker, J. (2009), 'Increased frequency of chromosome translocations in airline pilots with long-term flying experience', *Occupational and Environmental Medicine*, **66**: 56–62.

Zack, J. and Gaffey, W. (1983), 'A mortality study of workers employed at the Monsanto Company plant in Nitro, West Virginia', in Young, A. and Gray, A. (eds) *Human Environmental Risks of Chlorinated Dioxins and Related Compounds*, Plenum Press, New York: 575–91.

Zalk, D. and Nelson, D. (2008), 'History and evolution of control banding: a review', *Journal of Occupational and Environmental Hygiene*, **5**: 330–46.

Zanoni, J., Kauffman, K., McPhaul, K., Nickels, L., Hayden, M., Glassman, M., Vega, L., Sokas, R. and Lipscomb, J. (2006), 'Personal care assistants and blood exposure in the home environment: focus group findings', *Progress in Community Health Partnerships*, **1**(2): 125–31.

Zapf, D. (1999), 'Organisational, work group related and personal causes of mobbing/bullying at work', *International Journal of Manpower*, **20**(1 & 2): 70–85.

Zella, B., Panzica, M., Vogt, M., Sittaro, N., Krettek, C. and Pape, H. (2005), 'Influence of workers' compensation eligibility upon functional recovery 10 to 28 years after polytrauma', *American Journal of Surgery*, **190**(1): 30–6.

Zerbib, J. (1996), 'Asbestos ban in France: too late for many', *TUTB Newsletter*, **4**: 2–5.

Zhang, X., Yu, S., Wheeler, K., Kelleher, K., Stallones, L. and Xiang, H. (2009), 'Work-Related non-fatal injuries among foreign-born and US-born workers: findings from the US National Health Interview Survey, 1997–2005', *American Journal of Industrial Medicine*, **52**: 25–36.

Ziem, G. E. and Castleman, B. I. (1989), 'Threshold limit values: historical perspectives and current practice', *Journal of Occupational Medicine*, **31**(11): 910–18.

Zuckerman, M. (1971), 'Dimensions of sensation seeking', *Journal of Consulting and Clinical Psychology*, **36**(1): 45–52.

Zuhosky, J.P., Irwin, R.W., Sable, A.W., Sullivan, W.J., Panagos, A. and Foye, P.M. (2007), 'Acute industrial musculoskeletal injuries in the aging workforce', *Industrial Medicine and Acute Musculoskeletal Rehabilitation*, **88**(Supp. 1): S34-9.

Name index

Subject index